LANCASTER HIGH SCHO
W9-ASW-557

McDougal Littell

THE LANGUAGE OF LITERATURE

AMERICAN LITERATURE

THE LANGUAGE OF LITERATURE

AMERICAN LITERATURE

Arthur N. Applebee
Andrea B. Bermúdez
Sheridan Blau
Rebekah Caplan
Franchelle Dorn
Peter Elbow
Susan Hynds
Judith A. Langer
James Marshall

Evanston, Illinois ▪ Boston ▪ Dallas

Acknowledgments

Unit One

Harcourt Brace & Company: "A Worn Path," from *A Curtain of Green and Other Stories* by Eudora Welty; Copyright 1941, renewed © 1969 by Eudora Welty. Reprinted by permission of Harcourt Brace & Company.

McGraw-Hill, Inc.: Excerpt from "The World on the Turtle's Back," from *The Great Tree and the Longhouse* by Hazel W. Hertzberg; Copyright © 1966 by the American Anthropological Association. Reprinted with the permission of McGraw-Hill, Inc.

Sunstone Press: "Song of the Sky Loom," from *Songs of the Tewa,* translated by Herbert Joseph Spinden. By permission of Sunstone Press, P.O. Box 2321, Santa Fe, NM 87504-2321

University of Nebraska Press: "Coyote and the Buffalo" and "Fox and Coyote and Whale," from *Coyote Stories* by Mourning Dove. By permission of the University of Nebraska Press.

Wylie, Aitken & Stone: "The Man to Send Rain Clouds" by Leslie Marmon Silko; Copyright © by Leslie Marmon Silko. Reprinted with the permission of Wylie, Aitken & Stone, Inc.

Continued on page 1267

Cover Art

Background photo: San Gabriel Mountains, California, Copyright © Frank Siteman/Omni-Photo Communications. **Painting:** *En Mer* [At Sea], (1898), Max Bohm. Courtesy of Alfred J. Walker Fine Art, Boston. **Chief Joseph:** Courtesy of the National Museum of the American Indian, Smithsonian Institution. **Book:** Photo by Alan Shortall. **Frame:** Photo by Sharon Hoogstraten.

Warning: No part of this work may be reproduced or transmitted in any form or by any means, electronic or mechanical, including photocopying and recording, or by any information storage or retrieval system without prior written permission of McDougal Littell Inc. unless such copying is expressly permitted by federal copyright law. With the exception of not-for-profit transcription in Braille, McDougal Littell Inc. is not authorized to grant permission for further uses of copyrighted selections reprinted in this text without the permission of their owners. Permission must be obtained from the individual copyright owners as identified herein. Address inquiries to Manager, Rights and Permissions, McDougal Littell Inc., P.O. Box 1667, Evanston, IL 60204

ISBN 0-395-73706-0

Copyright © 1997 by McDougal Littell Inc. All rights reserved.
Printed in the United States of America.

2 3 4 5 6 7 8 9 – VJM – 02 01 00 99 98 97

Senior Consultants

The senior consultants guided the conceptual development for *The Language of Literature* series. They participated actively in shaping prototype materials for major components, and they reviewed completed prototypes and/or completed units to ensure consistency with current research and the philosophy of the series.

Arthur N. Applebee Professor of Education, State University of New York at Albany; Director, Center for the Learning and Teaching of Literature; Senior Fellow, Center for Writing and Literacy

Andrea B. Bermúdez Professor of Studies in Language and Culture; Director, Research Center for Language and Culture; Chair, Foundations and Professional Studies, University of Houston-Clear Lake

Sheridan Blau Senior Lecturer in English and Education and former Director of Composition, University of California at Santa Barbara; Director, South Coast Writing Project; Director, Literature Institute for Teachers; Vice President, National Council of Teachers of English

Rebekah Caplan Coordinator, English Language Arts K-12, Oakland Unified School District, Oakland, California; Teacher-Consultant, Bay Area Writing Project, University of California at Berkeley; served on the California State English Assessment Development Team for Language Arts

Franchelle Dorn Professor of Drama, Howard University, Washington, D.C.; Adjunct Professor, Graduate School of Opera, University of Maryland, College Park, Maryland; Co-founder of The Shakespeare Acting Conservatory, Washington, D.C.

Peter Elbow Professor of English, University of Massachusetts at Amherst; Fellow, Bard Center for Writing and Thinking

Susan Hynds Professor and Director of English Education, Syracuse University, Syracuse, New York

Judith A. Langer Professor of Education, State University of New York at Albany; Co-director, Center for the Learning and Teaching of Literature; Senior Fellow, Center for Writing and Literacy

James Marshall Professor of English and English Education, University of Iowa, Iowa City

Contributing Consultants

Tommy Boley Associate Professor of English, University of Texas at El Paso

Jeffrey N. Golub Assistant Professor of English Education, University of South Florida, Tampa

William L. McBride Reading and Curriculum Specialist; former middle and high school English instructor

Multicultural Advisory Board

The multicultural advisors reviewed literature selections for appropriate content and made suggestions for teaching lessons in a multicultural classroom.

Dr. Joyce M. Bell, Chairperson, English Department, Townview Magnet Center, Dallas, Texas

Dr. Eugenia W. Collier, author; lecturer; Chairperson, Department of English and Language Arts; teacher of Creative Writing and American Literature, Morgan State University, Maryland

Kathleen S. Fowler, President, Palm Beach County Council of Teachers of English, Boca Raton Middle School, Boca Raton, Florida

Noreen M. Rodriguez, Trainer for Hillsborough County School District's Staff Development Division, independent consultant, Gaither High School, Tampa, Florida

Michelle Dixon Thompson, Seabreeze High School, Daytona Beach, Florida

Teacher Review Panels

The following educators provided ongoing review during the development of the tables of contents, lesson design, and key components of the program.

FLORIDA

Judi Briant, English Department Chairperson, Armwood High School, Hillsborough County School District

Beth Johnson, Polk County English Supervisor, Polk County School District

Sharon Johnston, Learning Resource Specialist, Evans High School, Orange County School District

Continued on page 1279

Manuscript Reviewers

The following educators reviewed prototype lessons and tables of contents during the development of *The Language of Literature* program.

Carol Alves, English Department Chairperson, Apopka High School, Apopka, Florida

Jacqueline Anderson, James A. Foshay Learning Center, Los Angeles, California

Kathleen M. Anderson-Knight, United Township High School, East Moline, Illinois

Anita Arnold, Thomas Jefferson High School, San Antonio, Texas

Cassandra L. Asberry, Justin F. Kimball High School, Dallas, Texas

Don Baker, English Department Chairperson, Peoria High School, Peoria, Illinois

Continued on page 1281

Student Board

The student board members read and evaluated selections to assess their appeal for eleventh-grade students.

Joanna Cheng, Spanish River High School, Boca Raton, Florida

Sharon Garnett Counts, Lake Worth High School, Lake Worth, Florida

Shericko Davis, Ramsey High School, Birmingham, Alabama

Leigh Ann Gordon, Plantation High School, Plantation, Florida

Jennifer Halbert, Peoria High School, Peoria, Illinois

Denise Harris, Phineas Banning High School, Wilmington, California

Robbie Hay, Butler High School, Louisville, Kentucky

Katie McGuire, Lyons Township High School, LaGrange, Illinois

Michael Scott, Westerville North High School, Westerville, Ohio

Calvin Yu, Ramsey Alternative High School, Birmingham, Alabama

The Language of Literature

CORE COMPONENTS

Student Anthology & **Literature Connections**

A rich mix of classic and contemporary literature

Longer works with related readings

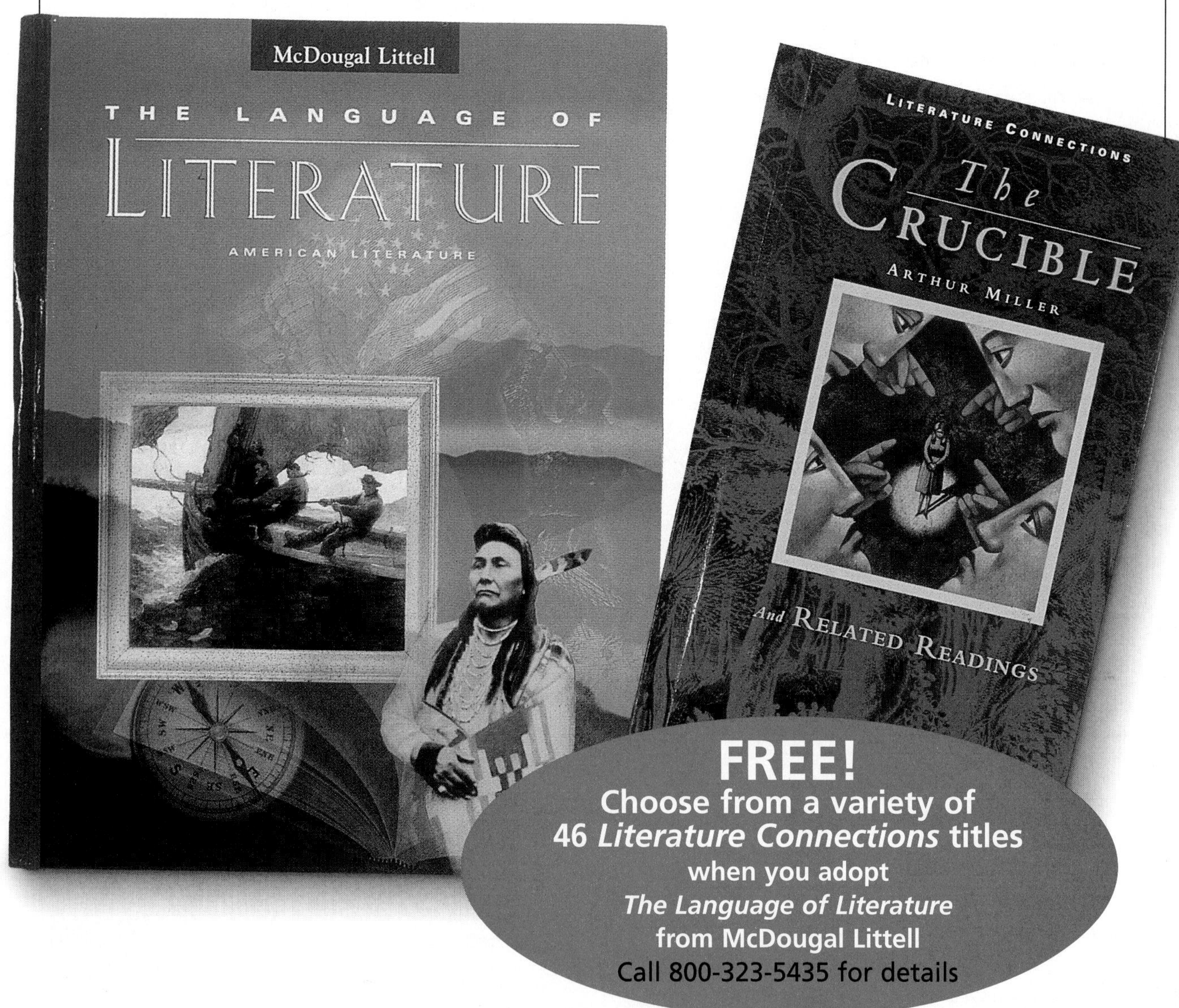

FREE!
Choose from a variety of 46 *Literature Connections* titles when you adopt *The Language of Literature* from McDougal Littell
Call 800-323-5435 for details

Literature Connections

Each hardback volume contains

- **Novel or Play**
- **Related Readings**—poems, stories, plays, and articles that provide new perspectives on the longer works
- **Teacher's SourceBook** filled with background information and activities

The Crucible

by Arthur Miller

and Related Readings

Conversation with an American Writer / POEM
Yevgeny Yevtushenko

Guilt / HISTORICAL ESSAY
Clifford Lindsey Alderman

How to Spot a Witch / ESSAY
Adam Goodheart

Young Goodman Brown / SHORT STORY
Nathaniel Hawthorne

The Great Fear / HISTORICAL ESSAY
J. Ronald Oakley

Justice Denied in Massachusetts / POEM
Edna St. Vincent Millay

The Very Proper Gander / FABLE
James Thurber

A Piece of String / SHORT STORY
Guy de Maupassant

Additional *Literature Connections* such as:

The Adventures of Huckleberry Finn*
Mark Twain

. . . And the Earth Did Not Devour Him*
Tomás Rivera

Animal Farm
George Orwell

The Crucible
Arthur Miller

Ethan Frome
Edith Wharton

Fallen Angels
Walter Dean Myers

The Friends
Rosa Guy

Hamlet
William Shakespeare

Jane Eyre*
Charlotte Brontë

Julius Caesar
William Shakespeare

Macbeth
William Shakespeare

A Midsummer Night's Dream
William Shakespeare

My Ántonia
Willa Cather

Nervous Conditions
Tsitsi Dangarembga

Picture Bride
Yoshiko Uchida

A Place Where the Sea Remembers
Sandra Benítez

Pygmalion
Bernard Shaw

A Raisin in the Sun
Lorraine Hansberry

The Scarlet Letter
Nathaniel Hawthorne

A Tale of Two Cities*
Charles Dickens

Things Fall Apart
Chinua Achebe

To Kill a Mockingbird, the Screenplay
Horton Foote

The Tragedy of Romeo and Juliet*
William Shakespeare

The Underdogs
Mariano Azuela

West with the Night
Beryl Markham

When Rain Clouds Gather
Bessie Head

*A Spanish version is also available.

UNIT ONE *Origins and Encounters*
2000 B.C.–A.D. 1620 14

Part 2 First Encounters: Accounts of Exploration and Exploitation 76

UNIT TWO *From Colony to Country* *1620–1800* 140

Part 1 Between Heaven and Hell: The Puritan Tradition 144

Part 2 The Right to Be Free: Writers in the Time of Revolution 202

UNIT THREE *The Spirit of Individualism* *1800–1850* 264

Part 2 The Dark Side of Individualism: American Gothic 352

UNIT FOUR *Conflict and Expansion* *1850–1900* 438

Part 2 Tricksters and Trailblazers: The Vanishing Frontier 510

UNIT FIVE *The Changing Face of America* *1855–1925* 590

Part 2 The American Dream: Illusion or Reality? 664

UNIT SIX *The Modern Age* *1910–1940* 758

Part 2 Alienation of the Individual: Modernism 816

UNIT SEVEN *Conflict at Home and Abroad 1940–1975* 904

Part 2 Power and Protest: The Sixties

UNIT EIGHT *Issues for Our Time* *1975–present* 1032

Part 1 Where We Are Today: Closer Together or Farther Apart? 1036

Part 2 Future Directions: Which Way Is Tomorrow? 1084

Electronic Library

The Electronic Library is a CD-ROM that contains additional fiction, nonfiction, poetry, and drama for each unit in *The Language of Literature.*

List of Titles, ***Grade 11 Electronic Library***

Unit 1

John Smith	**What Happened Till the First Supply,** *from* **The General History of Virginia**

Unit 2

Edward Taylor	**Upon a Spider Catching a Fly** **Huswifery**
Thomas Jefferson	**The Declaration of Independence**
Benjamin Franklin	**Moral Perfection,** *from* **The Autobiography**
Thomas Paine	*from* **Common Sense** **The Crisis, Number 1**

Unit 3

Henry Wadsworth Longfellow	**The Wreck of the Hesperus** **The Tide Rises, the Tide Falls**
Washington Irving	**Rip Van Winkle**
William Cullen Bryant	**Thanatopsis**
Ralph Waldo Emerson	**Hymn at Concord Monument** **Each and All** **Days**
Henry David Thoreau	**Conclusion,** *from* **Walden** **Civil Disobedience**
Oliver Wendell Holmes	**The Chambered Nautilus**
James Russell Lowell	**Prelude** to **The Vision of Sir Launfal**
Walt Whitman	**Mannahatta** **A Noiseless Patient Spider**
E. B. White	**Walden**
Edgar Allan Poe	**Hop-Frog** **The Fall of the House of Usher**
Nathaniel Hawthorne	**The Minister's Black Veil**
Herman Melville	**Bartleby, the Scrivener**

Note: A complete list of literature available for all grade levels accompanies each CD-ROM.

Unit 4

Negro Spirituals — **Go Down, Moses**
Swing Low, Sweet Chariot

Robert E. Lee — **Letters to His Family: To His Wife, To His Son**
Farewell to His Army

Walt Whitman — **O Captain! My Captain!**

Harriet A. Jacobs — **Childhood,** *from* **Life of a Slave Girl**

Mark Twain — **The Notorious Jumping Frog of Calaveras County**

retold by Julius Lester — **Brer Rabbit and the Tar Baby**
Brer Fox and Brer Rabbit Go Hunting

Bret Harte — **The Outcasts of Poker Flat**

Stephen Crane — **The Open Boat**

Unit 5

Emily Dickinson — **I taste a liquor never brewed**
I heard a Fly buzz—when I died—

Lucy Stone — **Disappointment Is the Lot of Women**

Edith Wharton — **Roman Fever**

Willa Cather — **Paul's Case**

Amy Lowell — **Patterns**

Edwin Arlington Robinson — **Miniver Cheevy**
Mr. Flood's Party

Unit 6

Jean Toomer — **Beehive**
November Cotton Flower

Claude McKay — **The Tropics in New York**

Robert Frost — **The Death of the Hired Man**

Sherwood Anderson — **Sophistication**

Katherine Anne Porter — **He**

Unit 7

Gloria Steinem — **Ruth's Song (Because She Could Not Sing It)**

Betty Friedan — **The Problem That Has No Name,** *from* **The Feminine Mystique**

Selections by Genre, Writing Workshops

Fiction

Nonfiction

Drama

Poetry

Folklore

Writing About Literature

Reading the World: Visual Literacy

Writing from Experience

LEARNING THE LANGUAGE OF LITERATURE

What Do You See Now?

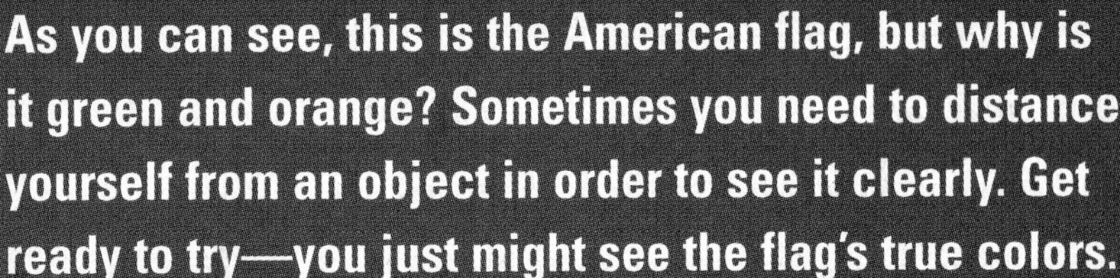

As you can see, this is the American flag, but why is it green and orange? Sometimes you need to distance yourself from an object in order to see it clearly. Get ready to try—you just might see the flag's true colors.

LOOK AGAIN

Try to see the true colors of the flag. Simply follow the steps listed below.

1. Take a piece of plain white paper, and place it beside this book.
2. Hold the book under a bright light, and stare at the center of the flag, roughly at the point where the "green" stripe meets the corner of the orange box.
3. Keep looking straight at the center of the flag—trying not to blink—for at least one minute.
4. After you have looked at the flag for one minute, look at the piece of white paper. If your eyes are tired, you may blink a few times, but try to keep your gaze steady.
5. As you stare at the white paper, what do you see?
6. If you now look at a light-colored wall from a distance, such as across the room, the same after-image will appear, only larger.

CONNECT TO LITERATURE

To see the flag's true colors, you had to look away from it. Literature can reveal itself in a similar way. Sometimes, certain parts of a story or poem, such as characters, images, or bits of dialogue, stay with you and become more meaningful after you have stopped reading. To find out how literature can make an impression on you, turn the page.

Why Does Literature Stay with You?

The country you live in has an impressive literary heritage, as you will see in this book. You will find surprising richness and variety. Some discoveries will have a profound effect on you. Why is literature so unforgettable?

IT ENLIGHTENS YOU

The **literature selections** in this book cover many facets of life in the United States, both past and present. Reading these selections can introduce you to aspects of your country that you may not have known before. For example, ancient forms of Native American storytelling are alive and well even today, as you'll find out in Unit One.

IT SHAPES YOU

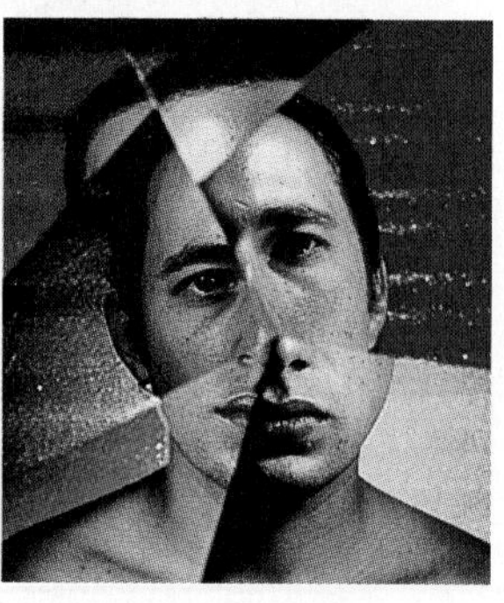

Certain things that you read make a lasting impression on you. Most of the selections begin with a **Previewing** page that taps into your thoughts and feelings about a subject and gives you background information as well. As an example, see page 22 where you learn about the Iroquois before reading an Iroquois myth. The **Responding** pages after a selection help you build on what you learned from the literature. If you would like to see some responding activities, take a look at page 29.

IT CHALLENGES YOU

Literature can challenge you to question every certainty. The **Writing About Literature** workshops guide you as you explore literature and work through ideas. For example, the workshop on page 68 helps you gain understanding of an American culture. You will also find opportunities to connect unit themes to the world you live in. Unit One, for example, shows you how people once used myth and stories to try to understand the complex world around them. In the Unit One **Writing from Experience** workshop on page 130, you will analyze a topic that bewilders or interests you.

IT INTRIGUES YOU

Which way are those birds flying, anyway? Literature, like the world you live in, can make your thoughts whirl. In the **Reading the World** features, the strategies you use to make sense of literature are adapted to help you understand real-world situations. For example, page 74 will show you how to interpret an unfamiliar situation by observing and analyzing differences.

How Can You Play a Role?

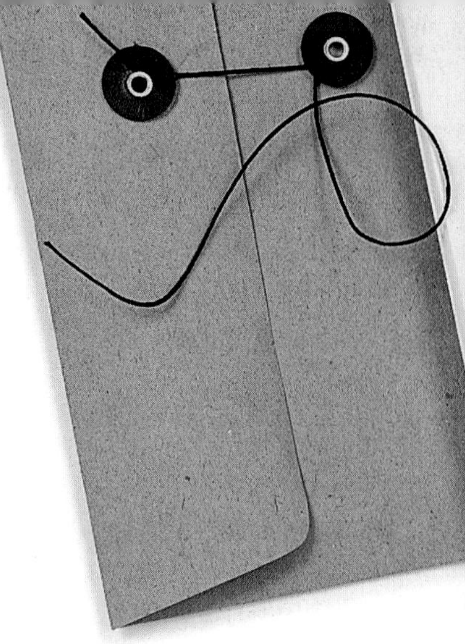

Portfolio

You know that literature can make an impression on you, but what can you do with this? The following techniques can help you develop your ideas and opinions about the literature you read.

MULTIPLE PATHWAYS

Do you learn best working alone or with others? Do your strengths lie mainly in writing, speaking, acting, or art? This book offers you a variety of learning options and allows you to choose the activities that best suit you. You'll be given opportunities to collaborate with classmates to share ideas, improve your writing, and make connections to other subject areas. You may even use technological tools such as the Laserlinks and the Writing Coach software program to further customize your learning.

PORTFOLIO

Many artists, photographers, designers, and writers keep samples of their work in a portfolio that they show to others. Like them, you will be collecting your work—writing samples, records of activities, artwork—in a portfolio throughout the year. You probably won't put all your work in your portfolio, just carefully chosen pieces. Discuss with your teacher portfolio options for this year. Throughout this book, you will find suggestions for how to use your portfolio.

Reading Log

Notebook

She's going to fall down with those unlaced shoes.

"Her eyes were blue with age." I know what that means, because some of my great aunts have bluish eyes now, even though their eyes used to be brown.

Why would her hair smell like copper?

She's got such a vivid imagination. Perhaps she's superstitious or afraid.

miled at her, they ... misju...
with her. I guess we both misjudged ... that—I'm ash...
Today I found out something that—I'm ... discovered that
say—never occurred to me before. I discovered that
beautiful women have feelings too. They're human,
they have a soul.

Susanna, I truly am sorry for what I put you through.
You didn't deserve to be publicly humiliated. I hope you'll
reconsider and stay in town. I'd like you to stay. I know Mr.
Hinkley would like you to stay. What do you say, folks?
Can't we make this beautiful woman feel welcome in this
cold New England town? Can't we make her feel at home?

NOTEBOOK

Choose any type of notebook and dedicate it to your study of literature. Divide the notebook into three sections. Use the first section to jot down ideas and thoughts, describe personal experiences, and take notes before, while, and after you read a selection. Also include any charts, diagrams, and drawings that help you connect your reading to your life. The second section will be for your reading log, described below. Use the third section as a writer's notebook to record ideas and inspirations that you might eventually use in your writing assignments.

READING LOG

Your reading log is for a special kind of response to literature—your direct comments as you read a selection. The reading strategies detailed at the right will help you think through what you read. In your reading log experiment with recording comments as you read. You will find opportunities to use your reading log throughout this book.

"A Worn Path"
by Eudora Welty

Phoenix Jackson was described so vividly I could draw her.

Strategies for Reading

You can play an active role in reading. How? Simply get into the habit of thinking as you read. The strategies below describe the kinds of thinking that active readers do. Using these strategies will help you get the most out of literature.

QUESTION

Question what's happening while you read. Searching for reasons behind events and characters' feelings can help you feel more involved in what you're reading. Note confusing words or statements you don't understand. As you read on, you'll probably begin to see things more clearly.

CONNECT

Connect personally with what you're reading. Think of similarities between the descriptions in the selection and what you have personally experienced, heard about, or read about.

PREDICT

Try to figure out what will happen next and how the selection might end. Then read on to see if you made good guesses.

CLARIFY

Stop occasionally to review what you understand so far, and expect to have your understanding change and develop as you read on. Also, watch for answers to questions you had earlier.

EVALUATE

Form opinions about what you read, both while you're reading and after you've finished. Don't hesitate to judge the characters and develop your own ideas about events.

Now turn the page to see how two student readers put these strategies to work.

Alongside "A Worn Path" are transcripts of the spoken comments made by two 11th-grade students, Robert Lewis and Gesenia Veizaga, while they were reading the story. Their comments provide a glimpse into the minds of readers actively engaged in the process of reading. You'll notice that in the course of their reading, Robert and Gesenia quite naturally used the Strategies for Reading that were introduced on page 5.

To benefit most from this model of active reading, read the story first, jotting down your own responses in your reading log. (Cover up the side comments with a sheet of paper if you're tempted to peek.) Then read Robert's and Gesenia's comments and compare their processes of reading with your own.

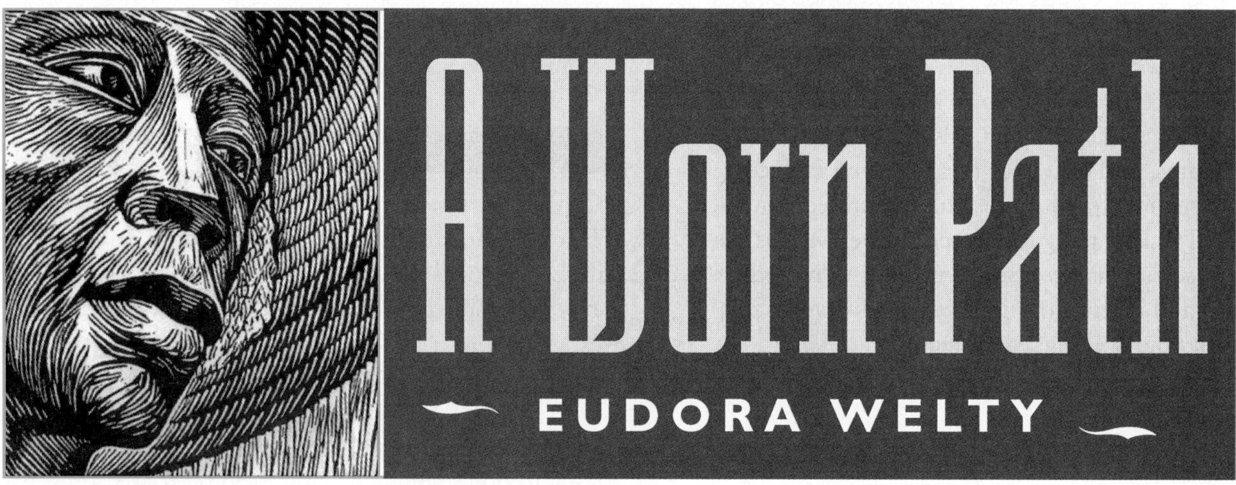

A Worn Path

EUDORA WELTY

Detail of *Sharecropper* (1970), Elizabeth Catlett. Linoleum cut on paper, National Museum of American Art, Smithsonian Institution, Washington D.C./Art Resource, New York.

It was December—a bright frozen day in the early morning. Far out in the country there was an old Negro woman with her head tied in a red rag, coming along a path through the pinewoods. Her name was Phoenix Jackson. She was very old and small and she walked slowly in the dark pine shadows, moving a little from side to side in her steps, with the balanced heaviness and lightness of a pendulum in a grandfather clock. She carried a thin, small cane made from an umbrella, and with this she kept tapping the frozen earth in front of her. This made a grave and persistent noise in the still air, that seemed meditative like the chirping of a solitary little bird.

Robert: *That's a neat image comparing her to a pendulum. I wonder if that means she measures time somehow.*
EVALUATING/QUESTIONING

She wore a dark striped dress reaching down to her shoe tops, and an equally long apron of bleached sugar sacks, with a full pocket: all neat and tidy, but every time she took a step she might have fallen over her shoelaces, which dragged from her unlaced shoes. She looked straight ahead. Her eyes were blue with age. Her skin had a pattern all its own of numberless branching wrinkles and as though a whole

Gesenia: *But she's so tidy. Why would she be sloppy with her shoes?*
QUESTIONING

little tree stood in the middle of her forehead, but a golden color ran underneath, and the two knobs of her cheeks were illumined by a yellow burning under the dark. Under the red rag her hair came down on her neck in the frailest of ringlets, still black, and with an odor like copper.

Gesenia: *You can really picture her skin color from this description.*
EVALUATING

Now and then there was a quivering in the thicket. Old Phoenix said, "Out of my way, all you foxes, owls, beetles, jack rabbits, coons and wild animals! . . . Keep out from under these feet, little bobwhites. . . . Keep the big wild hogs out of my path. Don't let none of those come running my direction. I got a long way." Under her small black-freckled hand her cane, limber as a buggy whip, would switch at the brush as if to rouse up any hiding things.

On she went. The woods were deep and still. The sun made the pine needles almost too bright to look at, up where the wind rocked. The cones dropped as light as feathers. Down in the hollow was the mourning dove—it was not too late for him.

Robert: *Phoenix seems like a down-to-earth person. She just goes about her business.*
EVALUATING

The path ran up a hill. "Seem like there is chains about my feet, time I get this far," she said, in the voice of argument old people keep to use with themselves. "Something always take a hold of me on this hill—pleads I should stay."

Robert: *Phoenix has made this trip before.*
CLARIFYING

After she got to the top she turned and gave a full, severe look behind her where she had come. "Up through pines," she said at length. "Now down through oaks."

Her eyes opened their widest, and she started down gently. But before she got to the bottom of the hill a bush caught her dress.

Her fingers were busy and intent, but her skirts were full and long, so that before she could pull them free in one place they were caught in another. It was not possible to allow the dress to tear. "I in the thorny bush," she said. "Thorns, you doing your appointed work. Never want to let folks pass, no sir. Old eyes thought you was a pretty little *green* bush."

Gesenia: *She's not grumpy like some old people. She sees that the thorns are just doing what they do. It doesn't make her mad.*
EVALUATING/CONNECTING

Finally, trembling all over, she stood free, and after a moment dared to stoop for her cane.

"Sun so high!" she cried, leaning back and looking, while the thick tears went over her eyes. "The time getting all gone here."

At the foot of this hill was a place where a log was laid across the creek.

"Now comes the trial," said Phoenix.

Putting her right foot out, she mounted the log and shut her eyes. Lifting her skirt, leveling her cane fiercely before her, like a festival figure in some parade, she began to march across. Then she opened her eyes and she was safe on the other side.

Gesenia: *Why would she close her eyes? Usually that's for when you do something for the first time, and she's been here before.*
QUESTIONING/CONNECTING

"I wasn't as old as I thought," she said.

But she sat down to rest. She spread her skirts on the bank around her and folded her hands over her knees. Up above her was a tree in a pearly cloud of mistletoe. She did not dare to close her eyes, and when a little boy brought her a plate with a slice of marble-cake on it

Robert: *She seems to be hallucinating, like somebody with Alzheimer's disease.*
CONNECTING

Gesenia: *She's really concerned about tearing her dress. She must be going somewhere important.*
PREDICTING

Robert: *This seems foreboding. Maybe it foreshadows that something bad will happen to her.*
PREDICTING

Gesenia: *Phoenix is kind of like a kid, going around imagining human-like qualities and talking to nature.*
EVALUATING

Gesenia: *Shutting her eyes is like a kid, too, except a kid would probably just run away.*
EVALUATING/ CONNECTING

Robert: *Phoenix just talks to everything. She's ancient, lighthearted, jovial—like Tom Bombadillo in the Hobbit books.*
CONNECTING

she spoke to him. "That would be acceptable," she said. But when she went to take it there was just her own hand in the air.

So she left that tree, and had to go through a barbed-wire fence. There she had to creep and crawl, spreading her knees and stretching her fingers like a baby trying to climb the steps. But she talked loudly to herself: she could not let her dress be torn now, so late in the day, and she could not pay for having her arm or her leg sawed off if she got caught fast where she was.

At last she was safe through the fence and risen up out in the clearing. Big dead trees, like black men with one arm, were standing in the purple stalks of the withered cotton field. There sat a buzzard.

"Who you watching?"

In the furrow she made her way along.

"Glad this not the season for bulls," she said, looking sideways, "and the good Lord made his snakes to curl up and sleep in the winter. A pleasure I don't see no two-headed snake coming around that tree, where it come once. It took a while to get by him, back in the summer."

She passed through the old cotton and went into a field of dead corn. It whispered and shook and was taller than her head. "Through the maze now," she said, for there was no path.

Then there was something tall, black, and skinny there, moving before her.

At first she took it for a man. It could have been a man dancing in the field. But she stood still and listened, and it did not make a sound. It was as silent as a ghost.

"Ghost," she said sharply, "who be you the ghost of? For I have heard of nary death close by."

But there was no answer—only the ragged dancing in the wind.

She shut her eyes, reached out her hand, and touched a sleeve. She found a coat and inside that an emptiness, cold as ice.

"You scarecrow," she said. Her face lighted. "I ought to be shut up for good," she said with laughter. "My senses is gone. I too old. I the oldest people I ever know. Dance, old scarecrow," she said, "while I dancing with you."

She kicked her foot over the furrow, and with mouth drawn down, shook her head once or twice in a little strutting way. Some husks blew down and whirled in streamers about her skirts.

Then she went on, parting her way from side to side with the cane, through the whispering field. At last she came to the end, to a wagon track where the silver grass blew between the red ruts. The quail were walking around like pullets, seeming all dainty and unseen.

"Walk pretty," she said. "This the easy place. This the easy going."

She followed the track, swaying through the quiet bare fields, through the little strings of trees silver in their dead leaves, past cabins silver from weather, with the doors and windows boarded shut, all like old women under a spell sitting there. "I walking in their sleep," she said, nodding her head vigorously.

In a ravine she went where a spring was silently flowing through a hollow log. Old Phoenix bent and drank. "Sweet-gum makes the water sweet," she said, and drank more. "Nobody know who made this well, for it was here when I was born."

***Robert:** Phoenix is a good name for her character—she's old and enduring. But I wonder what ashes she will rise from.*
EVALUATING/QUESTIONING

The track crossed a swampy part where the moss hung as white as lace from every limb. "Sleep on, alligators, and blow your bubbles." Then the track went into the road.

Deep, deep the road went down between the high green-colored banks. Overhead the live-oaks met, and it was as dark as a cave.

A black dog with a lolling tongue came up out of the weeds by the ditch. She was meditating, and not ready, and when he came at her she only hit him a little with her cane. Over she went in the ditch, like a little puff of milkweed.

Down there, her senses drifted away. A dream visited her, and she reached her hand up, but nothing reached down and gave her a pull. So she lay there and presently went to talking. "Old woman," she said to herself, "that black dog come up out of the weeds to stall you off, and now there he sitting on his fine tail, smiling at you."

***Robert:** She's hallucinating again, but she's wishful for help. She's not afraid, not imagining terrible things.*
EVALUATING

A white man finally came along and found her—a hunter, a young man, with his dog on a chain.

"Well, Granny!" he laughed. "What are you doing there?"

"Lying on my back like a June-bug waiting to be turned over, mister," she said, reaching up her hand.

***Gesenia:** She seems to be getting older and more feeble. At first she was just striding along, but now she needs help even to get up.*
CLARIFYING

He lifted her up, gave her a swing in the air, and set her down. "Anything broken, Granny?"

"No sir, them old dead weeds is springy enough," said Phoenix, when she had got her breath. "I thank you for your trouble."

"Where do you live, Granny?" he asked, while the two dogs were growling at each other.

***Robert:** He's so condescending. He's younger but he shows her no respect. His attitude doesn't bother her, though.*
EVALUATING

"Away back yonder, sir, behind the ridge. You can't even see it from here."

"On your way home?"

"No sir, I going to town."

"Why, that's too far! That's as far as I walk when I come out myself, and I get something for my trouble." He patted the stuffed bag he carried, and there hung down a little closed claw. It was one of the bob-whites, with its beak hooked bitterly to show it was dead. "Now you go on home, Granny!"

"I bound to go to town, mister," said Phoenix. "The time come around."

***Gesenia:** Now I don't like this guy. He's being bossy to Phoenix.*
EVALUATING

Georgia Landscape (about 1934–1935), Hale Woodruff. National Museum of American Art, Smithsonian Institution, Washington D.C./Art Resource, New York.

He gave another laugh, filling the whole landscape. "I know you old colored people! Wouldn't miss going to town to see Santa Claus!"

***Robert:** He's a racist, too. What a jerk.*
EVALUATING

But something held old Phoenix very still. The deep lines in her face went into a fierce and different radiation. Without warning, she had seen with her own eyes a flashing nickel fall out of the man's pocket onto the ground.

"How old are you, Granny?" he was saying.

***Gesenia:** The hunter is pretty nosy, asking her so many questions.*
EVALUATING

"There is no telling, mister," she said, "no telling."

Then she gave a little cry and clapped her hands and said, "Git on away from here, dog! Look! Look at that dog!" She laughed as if in admiration. "He ain't scared of nobody. He a big black dog." She whispered, "Sic him!"

"Watch me get rid of that cur," said the man. "Sic him, Pete! Sic him!"

***Gesenia:** It's hard for her to stoop down, even. But she's able to cross all those obstacles.*
CLARIFYING

***Robert:** A nickel is a big deal to her. She must be real poor, or maybe the story happens a long time ago.*
CLARIFYING

Phoenix heard the dogs fighting, and heard the man running and throwing sticks. She even heard a gunshot. But she was slowly bending forward by that time, further and further forward, the lids stretched down over her eyes, as if she were doing this in her sleep. Her chin was lowered almost to her knees. The yellow palm of her hand came out from the fold of her apron. Her fingers slid down and along the ground under the piece of money with the grace and care they would have in lifting an egg from under a setting hen. Then she slowly straightened up, she stood erect, and the nickel was in her apron pocket. A bird flew by. Her lips moved. "God watching me the whole time. I come to stealing."

Robert: She feels bad about taking the coin.
EVALUATING

The man came back, and his own dog panted about them. "Well, I scared him off that time," he said, and then he laughed and lifted his gun and pointed it at Phoenix.

Robert: He seems abnormal. It's cruel to point a gun at her.
EVALUATING

She stood straight and faced him.

"Doesn't the gun scare you?" he said, still pointing it.

"No, sir, I seen plenty go off closer by, in my day, and for less than what I done," she said, holding utterly still.

Gesenia: He's trying to seem bigger and better than she is, like a bully. But it doesn't faze her.
EVALUATING

He smiled, and shouldered the gun. "Well, Granny," he said, "you must be a hundred years old, and scared of nothing. I'd give you a dime if I had any money with me. But you take my advice and stay home, and nothing will happen to you."

Gesenia: That's funny that he's claiming he doesn't have money and she already has it. He's just talking big and being selfish.
EVALUATING

"I bound to go on my way, mister," said Phoenix. She inclined her head in the red rag. Then they went in different directions, but she could hear the gun shooting again and again over the hill.

She walked on. The shadows hung from the oak trees to the road like curtains. Then she smelled wood-smoke, and smelled the river, and she saw a steeple and the cabins on their steep steps. Dozens of little black children whirled around her. There ahead was Natchez shining. Bells were ringing. She walked on.

Robert: Is Natchez the name of a town?
QUESTIONING

Robert: Oh, it must be.
CLARIFYING

In the paved city it was Christmas time. There were red and green electric lights strung and crisscrossed everywhere, and all turned on in the daytime. Old Phoenix would have been lost if she had not distrusted her eyesight and depended on her feet to know where to take her.

She paused quietly on the sidewalk where people were passing by. A lady came along in the crowd, carrying an armful of red-, green- and silver-wrapped presents; she gave off perfume like the red roses in hot summer, and Phoenix stopped her.

"Please, missy, will you lace up my shoe?" She held up her foot.

Robert: The lady is richer and more cultured, but Phoenix asks her for help anyway.
CLARIFYING

"What do you want, Grandma?"

"See my shoe," said Phoenix. "Do all right for out in the country, but wouldn't look right to go in a big building."

"Stand still then, Grandma," said the lady. She put her packages down on the sidewalk beside her and laced and tied both shoes tightly.

"Can't lace 'em with a cane," said Phoenix. "Thank you, missy. I doesn't mind asking a nice lady to tie up my shoe, when I gets out on the street."

Gesenia: So that's why her shoelaces were sloppy—it's too hard for her to bend down.
CLARIFYING

Moving slowly and from side to side, she went into the big building, and into a tower of steps, where she walked up and around and around until her feet knew to stop.

She entered a door, and there she saw nailed up on the wall the

Robert: That's a neat way to say that Phoenix has an image of this place in her mind.
EVALUATING

document that had been stamped with the gold seal and framed in the gold frame, which matched the dream that was hung up in her head.

"Here I be," she said. There was a fixed and ceremonial stiffness over her body.

"A charity case, I suppose," said an attendant who sat at the desk before her.

But Phoenix only looked above her head. There was sweat on her face, the wrinkles in her skin shone like a bright net.

Gesenia: The attendant is so rude.
EVALUATING

Robert: The attendant looks down on Phoenix—treats her like she's not really a person.
EVALUATING

"Speak up, Grandma," the woman said. "What's your name? We must have your history, you know. Have you been here before? What seems to be the trouble with you?"

Old Phoenix only gave a twitch to her face as if a fly were bothering her.

"Are you deaf?" cried the attendant.

But then the nurse came in.

Gesenia: People don't talk about "clockwork" if something happens every week. I'll bet she comes about once a year.
CONNECTING/CLARIFYING

"Oh, that's just old Aunt Phoenix," she said. "She doesn't come for herself—she has a little grandson. She makes these trips just as regular as clockwork. She lives away back off the Old Natchez Trace." She bent down. "Well, Aunt Phoenix, why don't you just take a seat? We won't keep you standing after your long trip." She pointed.

The old woman sat down, bolt upright in the chair.

"Now, how is the boy?" asked the nurse.

Old Phoenix did not speak.

"I said, how is the boy?"

Gesenia: She's changed now. On the way, she talked to everything, but now she's motionless. What's wrong?
QUESTIONING

But Phoenix only waited and stared straight ahead, her face very solemn and withdrawn into rigidity.

"Is his throat any better?" asked the nurse. "Aunt Phoenix, don't you hear me? Is your grandson's throat any better since the last time you came for the medicine?"

Robert: Phoenix definitely has a senility problem or a loss of alertness.
EVALUATING

With her hands on her knees, the old woman waited, silent, erect and motionless, just as if she were in armor.

"You mustn't take up our time this way, Aunt Phoenix," the nurse said. "Tell us quickly about your grandson, and get it over. He isn't dead, is he?"

At last there came a flicker and then a flame of comprehension across her face, and she spoke.

Robert: I like how she's so dignified. My grandparents went through Alzheimer's, and they were both like that—being dignified as they could, knowing they can't help what's happening.
EVALUATING/CONNECTING

"My grandson. It was my memory had left me. There I sat and forgot why I made my long trip."

"Forgot?" The nurse frowned. "After you came so far?"

Then Phoenix was like an old woman begging a dignified forgiveness for waking up frightened in the night. "I never did go to school, I was too old at the Surrender," she said in a soft voice. "I'm an old woman without an education. It was my memory fail me. My little grandson, he is just the same, and I forgot it in the coming."

"Throat never heals, does it?" said the nurse, speaking in a loud, sure voice to old Phoenix. By now she had a card with something written on it, a little list. "Yes. Swallowed lye. When was it?—January—two-three years ago—"

Phoenix spoke unasked now. "No, missy, he not dead, he just the same. Every little while his throat begin to close up again, and he not able to swallow. He not get his breath. He not able to help himself. So the time come around, and I go on another trip for the soothing medicine."

"All right. The doctor said as long as you came to get it, you could have it," said the nurse. "But it's an obstinate case."

"My little grandson, he sit up there in the house all wrapped up, waiting by himself," Phoenix went on. "We is the only two left in the world. He suffer and it don't seem to put him back at all. He got a sweet look. He going to last. He wear a little patch quilt and peep out holding his mouth open like a little bird. I remembers so plain now. I not going to forget him again, no, the whole enduring time. I could tell him from all the others in creation."

"All right." The nurse was trying to hush her now. She brought her a bottle of medicine. "Charity," she said, making a check mark in a book.

Old Phoenix held the bottle close to her eyes, and then carefully put it into her pocket.

"I thank you," she said.

"It's Christmas time, Grandma," said the attendant. "Could I give you a few pennies out of my purse?"

"Five pennies is a nickel," said Phoenix stiffly.

"Here's a nickel," said the attendant.

Phoenix rose carefully and held out her hand. She received the nickel and then fished the other nickel out of her pocket and laid it beside the new one. She stared at her palm closely, with her head on one side.

Then she gave a tap with her cane on the floor.

"This is what come to me to do," she said. "I going to the store and buy my child a little windmill they sells, made out of paper. He going to find it hard to believe there such a thing in the world. I'll march myself back where he waiting, holding it straight up in this hand."

She lifted her free hand, gave a little nod, turned around, and walked out of the doctor's office. Then her slow step began on the stairs, going down.

Gesenia: *She blames her lack of education, but I'm not sure that's why. My great grandmother just sits sometimes when you ask her questions, but then she gets interested and joins in the talk.*
EVALUATING/CONNECTING

Robert: *So that's the important errand.*
CLARIFYING

Gesenia: *The story is getting a serious tone now. The grandson is sick and alone at home, and Phoenix has to go back through all those obstacles.*
CLARIFYING

Robert: *She knows what she wants. She doesn't shy away except with that memory lapse earlier. She's very gutsy.*
EVALUATING

Robert: *She has a hard road ahead. The struggle keeps going, and that fits with the title of the story.*
CLARIFYING

Gesenia: *Is she going to make it back at all? She's so forgetful.*
QUESTIONING/EVALUATING

ORIGINS AND ENCOUNTERS

Pleasant it looked,
this newly created world.
Along the entire length and breadth
of the earth, our grandmother,
extended the green reflection
of her covering
and the escaping odors
were pleasant to inhale.

WINNEBAGO
an Algonkian people

Let us . . . go
to the place that
God will show
us to possess in
peace and plenty,
a land more like
the Garden of
Eden, which the
Lord planted,
than any part else
of all the earth.

REVEREND WILLIAM SYMONDS
Puritan minister

Giovanni da Verrazano becoming the first European to enter New York Bay, 1524. Lithograph done in 1868 by an unknown American artist. The Granger Collection, New York.

TIME LINE

Origins & Encounters

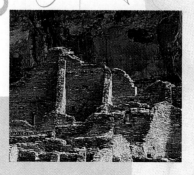

The first Native Americans migrated to the Western Hemisphere from Asia, probably between 2500 and 3500 years ago, during the latest ice age. They came over a land bridge called Beringia. When the ice age ended, Beringia disappeared under the water created by melting ice, leaving the Bering Strait between Asia and what is now the state of Alaska.

2000–1000 B.C.

Native Americans in the Southwest begin to cultivate maize, a forerunner of corn.

A.D. 500

The eastern woodlands is home to various Native American tribes who develop an agricultural economy and widespread trade.

1000–1300

The Anasazi, ancestors of the Pueblo Indians, build elaborate, multistory cliff dwellings in the canyons of the Southwest, many of which still stand.

1492

Christopher Columbus sets foot on a small island in the Bahamas.

1502

Amerigo Vespucci returns from his second exploration of South America and declares it a New World; the Americas are named after him.

1521

Hernán Cortés conquers the Aztecs and claims Mexico for Spain.

1535

Jacques Cartier explores the St. Lawrence River and claims Quebec and Montreal for France.

1540

Horses are first introduced on a large scale in North America by Spanish explorers.

1565

Spain establishes a colony at St. Augustine, Florida; the first missionaries arrive a year later.

1590

When John White returns from England to the Roanoke Island colony he had established in 1587, he finds all the settlers gone. The fate of the "lost colony" remains a mystery to this day.

1607

The first permanent English colony is set up in Jamestown, Virginia. A year later, Captain John Smith assumes leadership and makes peace with the Powhatan Indians, who in turn teach the colonists to plant corn.

Period *Pieces*

> ❦
>
> *Although corn helped to sustain the English colonists, it was tobacco that saved the Jamestown colony. Tobacco use originated among Native Americans and was unknown in Europe until the 16th century when it was introduced by the explorers. It soon became hugely popular. In 1612, John Rolfe became the first European to plant a successful tobacco crop in North America. By 1619, tobacco was the leading export of Virginia, giving Jamestown a steady source of income.*

1614

John Rolfe marries Pocahontas, daughter of the Powhatan chief. She dies three years later of smallpox on a visit to England with her husband.

1616–1617

A smallpox epidemic wipes out entire tribes of Native Americans from Maine to Rhode Island. Survivors join remnants of larger tribes, thus increasing the power of the Narragansett and the Wampanoag.

1618

Virginia governor Samuel Argall declares that all colonists who fail to attend church will be locked in a guardhouse.

1619

The first African slaves arrive in Virginia.

1620

Before landing at Plymouth, Massachusetts, the Pilgrims sign the Mayflower Compact, which establishes a government by will of the majority.

Compass used for navigation in the 15th century

Pilgrim foot warmer

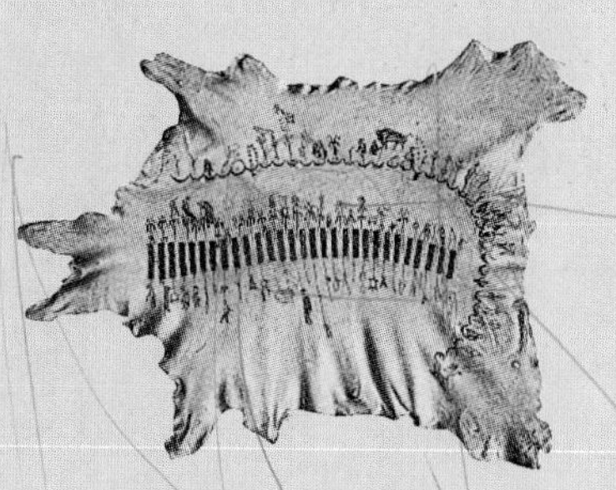

The Anko Calendar from the Kiowa people

PART 1 INTRODUCTION

In Harmony with Nature

Native American Traditions

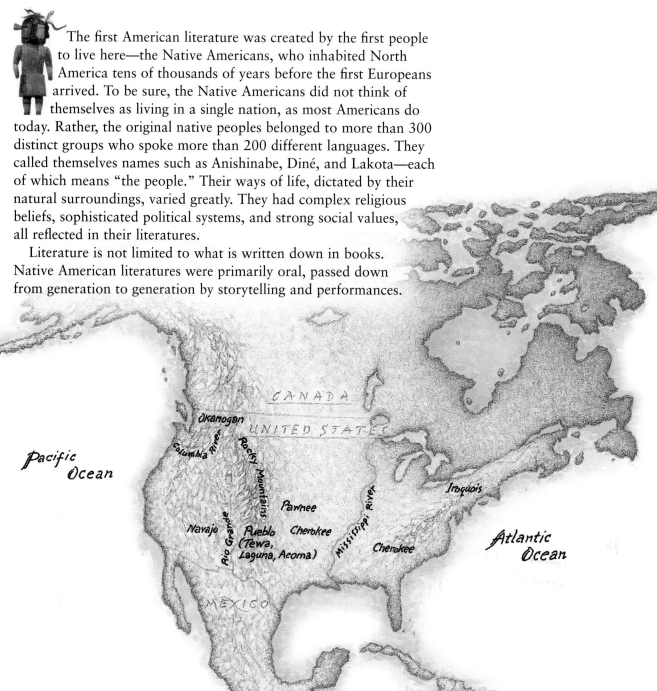

The first American literature was created by the first people to live here—the Native Americans, who inhabited North America tens of thousands of years before the first Europeans arrived. To be sure, the Native Americans did not think of themselves as living in a single nation, as most Americans do today. Rather, the original native peoples belonged to more than 300 distinct groups who spoke more than 200 different languages. They called themselves names such as Anishinabe, Diné, and Lakota—each of which means "the people." Their ways of life, dictated by their natural surroundings, varied greatly. They had complex religious beliefs, sophisticated political systems, and strong social values, all reflected in their literatures.

Literature is not limited to what is written down in books. Native American literatures were primarily oral, passed down from generation to generation by storytelling and performances.

Some widespread types of Native American oral literature are creation myths, which explain the beginning of the world; tales of heroes and tricksters who transformed the world to its present state; and the ritual songs and chants that are part of ceremonies.

This part of Unit One presents a small sampling of works from Native American oral traditions: a creation myth from the Iroquois of the Northeast, two ancient songs from the Tewa and the Navajo of the Southwest, and two trickster tales from the Okanogan of the Pacific Northwest. Preceding these, in Voices from the Times, is a fable from the Pawnee of the central plains.

As readers of a textbook, you will not be experiencing these works as you would if you belonged to the cultures they came from. You will not be hearing them or seeing them performed; you will be reading them on a page, in a language different from the languages in which they were created. These pieces were collected in the early 1900s and translated into English by anthropologists—or in the case of the Okanogan stories, by a bilingual member of the tribe with the help of white editors. Despite the limitations of translations, they remain the best way to expose a wide audience to the beauty, wisdom, and humor of Native American oral literature.

Although traditional Native American literature has many forms and functions, much of it emphasizes the importance of living in harmony with the natural world. In Native American belief, human beings have a kinship with animals, plants, the land, heavenly bodies, and the elements. All of these things are seen as alive and aware, as when singers address Mother Earth and Father Sky in the Tewa "Song of the Sky Loom." Furthermore, the human and the nonhuman are seen as parts of a sacred whole. To Native Americans, human beings do not have dominion over nature; they are part of nature and must act to maintain a right relationship

Voices *from the* Times

The Lesson of the Birds
Pawnee

One day a man whose mind was open to the teaching of the powers wandered on the prairie. As he walked, his eyes upon the ground, he spied a bird's nest hidden in the grass, and arrested his feet just in time to prevent stepping on it. He paused to look at the little nest tucked away so snug and warm, and noted that it held six eggs and that a peeping sound came from some of them. While he watched, one moved and soon a tiny bill pushed through the shell, uttering a shrill cry. At once the parent birds answered and he looked up to see where they were. They were not far off; they were flying about in search of food, chirping the while to each other and now and then calling to the little one in the nest.

The homely scene stirred the heart and the thoughts of the man as he stood there under the clear sky, glancing upward toward the old birds and then down to the helpless young in the nest at his feet. As he looked he thought of his people, who were so often careless and thoughtless of their children's needs, and his mind brooded over the matter. After many days he desired to see the nest again. So he went to the place where he had found it, and there it was as safe as when he left it. But a change had taken place. It was now full to overflowing with little birds, who were stretching their wings, balancing

Voices *from the* TIMES

on their little legs and making ready to fly, while the parents with encouraging calls were coaxing the fledglings to venture forth.

"Ah!" said the man, "if my people would only learn of the birds, and, like them, care for their young and provide for their future, homes would be full and happy, and our tribe be strong and prosperous."

When this man became a priest, he told the story of the bird's nest and sang its song; and so it has come down to us from the days of our fathers.

Translated by Alice C. Fletcher

Senator Ben Nighthorse Campbell at a news conference

Celebration at the Red Earth Festival in Oklahoma City

with the world around them. Notice this perspective as you read the examples of traditional oral literature in this book.

Continuity & Change: Harmonizing Old and New

Native Americans and their traditions have not disappeared from this country. Although some cultures were lost to the diseases and violence of the Europeans, others have survived—changed but not destroyed by forced religious conversion, forced relocation, and forced education. Today, Native Americans live in cities and suburbs as well as on reservations. They are keeping oral traditions alive by singing songs and telling stories, but they are also writing in English.

A new generation of such writers is enjoying unprecedented respect and popularity. They include N. Scott Momaday (whose 1969 novel *House Made of Dawn* won a Pulitzer Prize), Leslie Marmon Silko, Paula Gunn Allen, Simon Ortiz, Louise Erdrich, and Michael Dorris.

Most of these writers display a powerful interest in the problems of harmonizing the old and the new. In many of their works, such as Silko's story "The Man to Send Rain Clouds," characters or speakers are shown reconciling old traditions with new practices. Moreover, the structures of the works themselves are often based on a blend of oral techniques and new literary forms. For example, in Allen's "Deer Woman" a traditional tale is embedded in a contemporary short story, and two contemporary novels by Silko and Momaday are constructed around traditional Native American ceremonies.

That these writers continue to draw on traditional sources for inspiration and have found such wide acclaim demonstrates the enduring value of our country's first literature.

LASERLINKS
• *HISTORICAL LITERARY CONNECTION*

PART 1 **_In Harmony with Nature_**

Native American Traditions

PREVIEWING

MYTH

The World on the Turtle's Back

Iroquois (ĭr′ə-kwoi′)

PERSONAL CONNECTION

In all times and places, people have wondered how the world was created. What different accounts of creation—biblical narratives, scientific theories, or stories from other cultures, for example—have you heard or read? In your notebook, list as many of these accounts as you can and describe each briefly; then share your list with classmates.

CULTURAL CONNECTION

The selection you are about to read is an Iroquois explanation of how the world was created. The term *Iroquois* refers to a league of five separate Native American peoples—the Seneca, Cayuga, Oneida, Onondaga, and Mohawk—who united in a confederation in the 14th century. (In the 18th century, a sixth group, the Tuscarora, joined the Iroquois League, having migrated northward from what is now North Carolina.) The Iroquois lived in the woodlands of what is now New York State, roughly from the Hudson River in the east to the Great Lakes in the west.

The Iroquois groups spoke similar languages, held similar beliefs, and had similar ways of life. They lived in longhouses made of pole frames covered with elm bark, and they built fences around their villages for protection. The women cultivated squash, beans, and corn and gathered berries and nuts. The men hunted, fished, and fought with the neighboring Mahican people. Warfare, an important part of Iroquois culture, gave men power and prestige. The Iroquois League was created primarily to end fighting among the nations that formed the alliance.

READING CONNECTION

Analyzing Creation Myths A myth is a traditional story, passed down through generations, that explains why the world is the way it is. Myths usually present events as resulting from the actions of supernatural beings. This selection is a creation myth that explains how the universe, the earth, and life on earth began. Make a chart like the one started below and, as you read, use it to record the Iroquois explanations of how things in the world came into existence.

Things That Exist in the World	Iroquois Explanation
the earth	created from soil that the muskrat brought up from the ocean floor

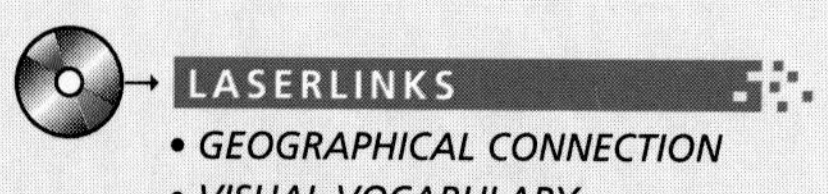

• *GEOGRAPHICAL CONNECTION*
• *VISUAL VOCABULARY*

The World on the Turtle's Back

Iroquois

In the beginning there was no world, no land, no creatures of the kind that are around us now, and there were no men. But there was a great ocean which occupied space as far as anyone could see. Above the ocean was a great void of air. And in the air there lived the birds of the sea; in the ocean lived the fish and the creatures of the deep. Far above this unpeopled world, there was a Sky-World. Here lived gods who were like people—like Iroquois.

In the Sky-World there was a man who had a wife, and the wife was expecting a child. The woman became hungry for all kinds of strange delicacies, as women do when they are with child. She kept her husband busy almost to distraction finding delicious things for her to eat.

In the middle of the Sky-World there grew a Great Tree which was not like any of the trees that we know. It was tremendous; it had grown there forever. It had enormous roots that spread out from the floor of the Sky-World. And on its branches there were many different kinds of leaves and different kinds of fruits and flowers. The tree was not supposed to be marked or mutilated by any of the beings who dwelt in the Sky-World. It was a sacred tree that stood at the center of the universe.

The woman decided that she wanted some bark from one of the roots of the Great Tree—perhaps as a food or as a medicine, we don't know. She told her husband this. He didn't like the idea. He knew it was wrong. But she insisted, and he gave in. So he dug a hole among the roots of this great sky tree, and he bared some of its roots. But the floor of the Sky-World wasn't very thick, and he broke a hole through it. He was terrified, for he had never expected to find empty space underneath the world.

WORDS TO KNOW

void (void) *n.* an empty space

But his wife was filled with curiosity. He wouldn't get any of the roots for her, so she set out to do it herself. She bent over and she looked down, and she saw the ocean far below. She leaned down and stuck her head through the hole and looked all around. No one knows just what happened next. Some say she slipped. Some say that her husband, fed up with all the demands she had made on him, pushed her.

So she fell through the hole. As she fell, she frantically grabbed at its edges, but her hands slipped. However, between her fingers there clung bits of things that were growing on the floor of the Sky-World and bits of the root tips of the Great Tree. And so she began to fall toward the great ocean far below.

To keep the earth growing, the woman walked as the sun goes, moving in the direction that the people still move in the dance rituals.

The birds of the sea saw the woman falling, and they immediately consulted with each other as to what they could do to help her. Flying wingtip to wingtip they made a great feathery raft in the sky to support her, and thus they broke her fall. But of course it was not possible for them to carry the woman very long. Some of the other birds of the sky flew down to the surface of the ocean and called up the ocean creatures to see what they could do to help. The great sea turtle came and agreed to receive her on his back. The birds placed her gently on the shell of the turtle, and now the turtle floated about on the huge ocean with the woman safely on his back.

The beings up in the Sky-World paid no attention to this. They knew what was happening, but they chose to ignore it.

When the woman recovered from her shock and terror, she looked around her. All that she could see were the birds and the sea creatures and the sky and the ocean.

And the woman said to herself that she would die. But the creatures of the sea came to her and said that they would try to help her and asked her what they could do. She told them that if they could find some soil, she could plant the roots stuck between her fingers, and from them plants would grow. The sea animals said perhaps there was dirt at the bottom of the ocean, but no one had ever been down there so they could not be sure.

If there was dirt at the bottom of the ocean, it was far, far below the surface in the cold deeps. But the animals said they would try to get some. One by one the diving birds and animals tried and failed. They went to the limits of their endurance, but they could not get to the bottom of the ocean. Finally, the muskrat said he would try. He dived and disappeared. All the creatures waited, holding their breath, but he did not return. After a long time, his little body floated up to the surface of the ocean, a tiny crumb of earth clutched in his paw. He seemed to be dead. They pulled him up on the turtle's back and they sang and prayed over him and breathed air into his mouth, and finally, he stirred. Thus it was the muskrat, the Earth-Diver, who brought from the bottom of the ocean the soil from which the earth was to grow.

The woman took the tiny clod of dirt and placed it on the middle of the great sea turtle's back. Then the woman began to walk in a circle around it, moving in the direction that the sun goes. The earth began to grow. When the earth was big enough, she planted the roots she had clutched between her fingers when she fell from the Sky-World. Thus the plants grew on the earth.

To keep the earth growing, the woman walked as the sun goes, moving in the direction that the people still move in the dance rituals. She

WORDS TO KNOW

ritual (rĭch'o͞o-əl) *n.* a ceremonial act or a series of such acts

Creation Legend, Tom (Two Arrows) Dorsey. Philbrook Museum of Art, Tulsa, Oklahoma (46.24).

gathered roots and plants to eat and built herself a little hut. After a while, the woman's time came, and she was delivered of a daughter. The woman and her daughter kept walking in a circle around the earth, so that the earth and plants would continue to grow. They lived on the plants and roots they gathered. The girl grew up with her mother, cut off forever from the Sky-World above, knowing only the birds and the creatures of the sea, seeing no other beings like herself.

One day, when the girl had grown to womanhood, a man appeared. No one knows for sure who this man was. He had something to do with the gods above. Perhaps he was the West Wind. As the girl looked at him, she was filled with terror, and amazement, and warmth, and she fainted dead away. As she lay on the ground, the man reached into his quiver, and he took out two arrows, one sharp and one blunt, and he laid them across the body of the girl, and quietly went away.

When the girl awoke from her faint, she and her mother continued to walk around the earth. After a while, they knew that the girl was to bear a child. They did not know it, but the girl was to bear twins.

Within the girl's body, the twins began to argue and quarrel with one another. There could be no peace between them. As the time approached for them to be born, the twins fought about their birth. The right-handed twin wanted to be born in the normal way, as all children are born. But the left-handed twin said no. He said he saw light in another direction, and said he would be born that way. The right-handed twin beseeched him not to, saying that he would kill their mother. But the left-handed twin was stubborn. He went in the direction where he saw light. But he could not be born through his mother's mouth or her nose. He was born through her left armpit, and killed her. And meanwhile, the right-handed twin was born in the normal way, as all children are born.

The twins met in the world outside, and the right-handed twin accused his brother of murdering their mother. But the grandmother told them to stop their quarreling. They buried their mother. And from her grave grew the plants which the people still use. From her head grew the corn, the beans, and the squash—"our supporters, the three sisters." And from her heart grew the sacred tobacco, which the people still use in the ceremonies and by whose upward-floating smoke they send thanks. The women call her "our mother," and they dance and sing in the rituals so that the corn, the beans, and the squash may grow to feed the people.

But the conflict of the twins did not end at the grave of their mother. And, strangely enough, the grandmother favored the left-handed twin.

The right-handed twin was angry, and he grew more angry as he thought how his brother had killed their mother. The right-handed twin was the one who did everything just as he should. He said what he meant, and he meant what he said. He always told the truth, and he always tried to accomplish what seemed to be right and reasonable. The left-handed twin never said what he meant or meant what he said. He always lied, and he always did things backward. You could never tell what he was trying to do because he always made it look as if he were doing the opposite. He was the devious one.

These two brothers, as they grew up, represented two ways of the world which are in

WORDS TO KNOW **devious** (dē'vē-əs) *adj.* shifty; not straightforward all people. The Indians did not call these the right and the wrong. They called them the straight mind and the crooked mind, the upright man and the devious man, the right and the left.

The twins had creative powers. They took clay and modeled it into animals, and they gave these animals life. And in this they contended with one another. The right-handed twin made the deer, and the left-handed twin made the mountain lion which kills the deer. But the right-handed twin knew there would always be more deer than mountain lions. And he made another animal.

The world the twins made was a balanced and orderly world, and this was good.

He made the ground squirrel. The left-handed twin saw that the mountain lion could not get to the ground squirrel, who digs a hole, so he made the weasel. And although the weasel can go into the ground squirrel's hole and kill him, there are lots of ground squirrels and not so many weasels. Next the right-handed twin decided he would make an animal that the weasel could not kill, so he made the porcupine. But the left-handed twin made the bear, who flips the porcupine over on his back and tears out his belly.

And the right-handed twin made berries and fruits of other kinds for his creatures to live on. The left-handed twin made briars and poison ivy, and the poisonous plants like the baneberry and the dogberry, and the suicide root with which people kill themselves when they go out of their minds. And the left-handed twin made medicines, for good and for evil, for doctoring and for witchcraft.

And finally, the right-handed twin made man. The people do not know just how much the left-handed twin had to do with making man. Man was made of clay, like pottery, and baked in the fire. . . .

The world the twins made was a balanced and orderly world, and this was good. The plant-eating animals created by the right-handed twin would eat up all the vegetation if their number was not kept down by the meat-eating animals which the left-handed twin created. But if these carnivorous animals ate too many other animals, then they would starve, for they would run out of meat. So the right- and the left-handed twins built balance into the world.

As the twins became men full grown, they still contested with one another. No one had won, and no one had lost. And they knew that the conflict was becoming sharper and sharper and one of them would have to vanquish the other.

And so they came to the duel. They started with gambling. They took a wooden bowl, and in it they put wild plum pits. One side of the pits was burned black, and by tossing the pits in the bowl, and betting on how these would fall, they gambled against one another, as the people still do in the New Year's rites. All through the morning they gambled at this game, and all through the afternoon, and the sun went down. And when the sun went down, the game was done, and neither one had won.

WORDS TO KNOW

contend (kən-tĕnd') *v.* to compete; vie

So they went on to battle one another at the lacrosse[1] game. And they contested all day, and the sun went down, and the game was done. And neither had won.

And now they battled with clubs, and they fought all day, and the sun went down, and the fight was done. But neither had won.

And they went from one duel to another to see which one would succumb. Each one knew in his deepest mind that there was something, somewhere, that would vanquish the other. But what was it? Where to find it?

Each knew somewhere in his mind what it was that was his own weak point. They talked about this as they contested in these duels, day after day, and somehow the deep mind of each entered into the other. And the deep mind of the right-handed twin lied to his brother, and the deep mind of the left-handed twin told the truth.

On the last day of the duel, as they stood, they at last knew how the right-handed twin was to kill his brother. Each selected his weapon. The left-handed twin chose a mere stick that would do him no good. But the right-handed twin picked out the deer antler, and with one touch he destroyed his brother. And the left-handed twin died, but he died and he didn't die. The right-handed twin picked up the body and cast if off the edge of the earth. And some place below the world, the left-handed twin still lives and reigns.

When the sun rises from the east and travels in a huge arc along the sky dome, which rests like a great upside-down cup on the saucer of the earth, the people are in the daylight realm of the right-handed twin. But when the sun slips down in the west at nightfall and the dome lifts to let it escape at the western rim, the people are again in the domain of the left-handed twin—the fearful realm of night.

Having killed his brother, the right-handed twin returned home to his grandmother. And she met him in anger. She threw the food out of the cabin onto the ground, and said that he was a murderer, for he had killed his brother. He grew angry and told her she had always helped his brother, who had killed their mother. In his anger, he grabbed her by the throat and cut her head off. Her body he threw into the ocean, and her head, into the sky. There "Our Grandmother, the Moon," still keeps watch at night over the realm of her favorite grandson.

The right-handed twin has many names. One of them is Sapling. It means smooth, young, green and fresh and innocent, straightforward, straight-growing, soft and pliable, teachable and trainable. These are the old ways of describing him. But since he has gone away, he has other names. He is called "He Holds Up the Skies," "Master of Life," and "Great Creator."

The left-handed twin also has many names. One of them is Flint. He is called the devious one, the one covered with boils. Old Warty. He is stubborn. He is thought of as being dark in color.

These two beings rule the world and keep an eye on the affairs of men. The right-handed twin, the Master of Life, lives in the Sky-World. He is content with the world he helped to create and with his favorite creatures, the humans. The scent of sacred tobacco rising from the earth comes gloriously to his nostrils.

In the world below lives the left-handed twin. He knows the world of men, and he finds contentment in it. He hears the sounds of warfare and torture, and he finds them good.

In the daytime, the people have rituals which honor the right-handed twin. Through the daytime rituals they thank the Master of Life. In the nighttime, the people dance and sing for the left-handed twin. ❖

1. **lacrosse** (lə-krôs′): a game of Native American origin, played on a field by two teams, in which participants use long-handled sticks with webbed pouches to maneuver a ball into the opposing team's goal.

WORDS TO KNOW

succumb (sə-kŭm′) *v.* to give up or give in; yield

RESPONDING OPTIONS

FROM PERSONAL RESPONSE *TO* CRITICAL ANALYSIS

REFLECT 1. What are your thoughts about this creation myth? Write them in your notebook to share in class later.

RETHINK 2. Look over the chart you made as you read. Of all of the explanations for different features of the world in this myth, which one did you find the most interesting? Explain your choice.

3. What are the most important things you learned about the values and way of life of the Iroquois from reading this myth?
   Consider
   - their attitude toward nature
   - their view of their gods
   - important foods, rituals, and games
   - the roles of men and women

4. Why do you think the Iroquois honor both the left-handed twin and the right-handed twin?
   Consider
   - the characteristics and actions of each twin
   - the characteristics of the world that the twins created

RELATE 5. How would you relate the left-handed and right-handed twins to your own concept of good and evil?

6. How does this Iroquois creation myth compare with other accounts of creation that you know of? Refer to the list you made for the Personal Connection on page 22.

ANOTHER PATHWAY

Cooperative Learning

With a small team of classmates, come up with five questions that are answered in this Iroquois myth. Then form a large circle with all of the other teams. Take turns with the other teams, asking and answering questions until all the questions have been used.

QUICKWRITES

1. Imitating the form of a creation myth, draft a **story** to explain the origin of one feature of the world you live in.
2. This selection states that the twins "represented two ways of the world which are in all people": the "straight mind" and the "crooked mind." Draft a short **reflective essay** in which you agree or disagree with this view of human character. Support your opinion with examples.
3. In a **comparison-and-contrast chart** or the draft of an **essay,** point out similarities and differences between this Iroquois myth and another creation story. If you can, input your prewriting notes on a computer so that they will be easier to organize.

PORTFOLIO *Save your writing. You may want to use it later as a spring-board to a piece for your portfolio.*

LITERARY CONCEPTS

As you recall, a **myth** is a traditional story, passed down through generations, that explains why the world is the way it is. Myths can be viewed as essentially religious, presenting the cosmic views of the cultural groups that create them. According to the scholar Joseph Campbell, myths have four functions: to instill a sense of awe toward the mystery of the universe, to explain the workings of the natural world, to support and validate social customs, and to guide people through the trials of living. Do you think "The World on the Turtle's Back" serves all these functions? Support your answer with examples from the selection.

CRITIC'S CORNER

In everyday speech, calling a story or belief a myth is a way of implying that it is false. Discuss how this common meaning of the word *myth* relates to the literary definition of *myth* given in the Literary Concepts feature.

ALTERNATIVE ACTIVITIES

1. Iroquois traditions, rituals, and history have been passed down orally from generation to generation. Do an **oral interpretation** of part of this Iroquois myth for the class.
2. Native American groups without written languages often used pictographs—pictures that represent objects and ideas—to help them remember important events and stories. For example, the pictograph shown here is from the *Walam Olum,* a record of creation and history made by a Native American people known as the Delaware or Lenni Lenape. It represents the creation of the sun, the moon, and the stars. Create your own **pictographs** to represent significant events in "The World on the Turtle's Back." Display your work in the classroom.

WORDS TO KNOW

EXERCISE A Review the Words to Know in the boxes at the bottom of the selection pages. On your paper, write the vocabulary word that is a synonym of each word below. Then write a sentence containing the vocabulary word.

1. dishonest
2. strive
3. vacuum
4. quit
5. ceremony

EXERCISE B With a partner, make up a story that contains at least three of the Words to Know. Then practice telling the story, partly in words and partly in pantomime. Perform the story for your classmates, and have them try to figure out which vocabulary words it contains.

PREVIEWING

SONGS

Song of the Sky Loom

Tewa (tā'wə)

Hunting Song/Dinni-e Sin

Navajo (năv'ə-hō')

Navajo dwelling in Arizona. The Granger Collection, New York.

PERSONAL CONNECTION

In your notebook, write down the words of a prayer, psalm, vow, hymn, spiritual, or some other form of sacred expression. Then study the words carefully. What, in your opinion, distinguishes sacred language from ordinary language?

CULTURAL CONNECTION

These selections are sacred songs of two Native American groups of the Southwest. The Tewa are a group of Pueblo Indians, so called because they live in pueblos—villages of stone or adobe dwellings. The Tewa live in six pueblos north of Santa Fe, New Mexico: Tesuque, Nambe, Pojoaque, San Ildefonso, Santa Clara, and San Juan. "Song of the Sky Loom" is one of many Tewa songs that are sung in religious rituals by elaborately costumed participants. The translator, Herbert Spinden, states that *sky loom* refers to "small desert rains which resemble a loom hung from the sky."

"Dinni-e Sin" ("Hunting Song" in English translation) is a song of the Navajo. The Navajo were originally hunters and gatherers, but after migrating to the Southwest in the 11th century, they gradually adopted a more settled life of herding and farming. According to the Navajo, "Hunting Song" was given to them by Hastyeyalti, the god of the sunrise and of game animals. Navajo men prepared for the hunt by praying and singing hunting songs, in the belief that if they sang well, they would have success.

READING CONNECTION

Approaching Native American Songs
It is important to remember that the texts you are about to read are not fully representative of these songs. They are lyrics, translated from the original languages, unaccompanied by music and movement, and taken out of the context of the ceremonies they are part of. Still, there is enough left to appreciate. As you read, consider the feelings about nature and the universe created by these sacred songs—both in you and in the singers. Also notice what makes the songs distinctive in style.

LASERLINKS
• *CULTURAL CONNECTION*

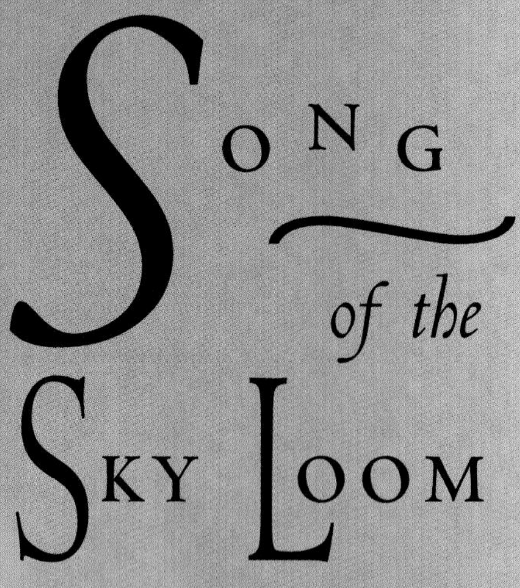

TEWA

Oh our Mother the Earth, oh our Father the Sky,
Your children are we, and with tired backs
We bring you the gifts that you love.
Then weave for us a garment of brightness;
May the warp[1] be the white light of morning,
May the weft[2] be the red light of evening,
May the fringes be the falling rain,
May the border be the standing rainbow.
Thus weave for us a garment of brightness
That we may walk fittingly where birds sing,
That we may walk fittingly where grass is green,
Oh our Mother the Earth, oh our Father the Sky!

1. **warp:** the threads that run lengthwise in a woven fabric.
2. **weft:** the threads interlaced at right angles through the warp threads in a woven fabric.

Copyright © School of American Research Press. Photo by Deborah Flynn.

FROM PERSONAL RESPONSE *TO* CRITICAL ANALYSIS

REFLECT 1. In your notebook, describe the feeling you get from reading this song.

RETHINK 2. The Tewa ask the earth and the sky for a "garment of brightness." What do you think this phrase means? Draw a picture showing how you imagine this garment.

Consider
- the four parts of the garment (lines 5–8)
- why they ask for the garment (lines 10 and 11)

3. How is this sacred song like examples of sacred expression you listed before you read?

Hunting Song

Navajo

Comes the deer to my singing,
Comes the deer to my song,
Comes the deer to my singing.

He, the blackbird, he am I,
Bird beloved of the wild deer,
Comes the deer to my singing.

From the Mountain Black,
From the summit,
Down the trail, coming, coming now,
Comes the deer to my singing.

Through the blossoms,
Through the flowers, coming, coming now,
Comes the deer to my singing.

Through the flower dew-drops,
Coming, coming now,
Comes the deer to my singing.

Through the pollen, flower pollen,
Coming, coming now,
Comes the deer to my singing.

(continued)

Dinni-e Sin

Ye shakaikatal, i-ne-yanga,
Ye shakaikatal, ai-ye-lo,
Ye shakaikatal, i-ne-yanga.

Ka' aiyash-te tilyilc*h*-ye
Shini shlini ko-lo,
Ye shakaikatal, i-ne yanga

Dsic*h*l-tilyilc*h*-iye
Bakashte
Ka' ta-adetin 'shte lo,
Ye shakaikatal, i-ne yanga

Tshilatra hozhoni-ye
Bitra 'shte lo,
Ye shakaikatal, i-ne yanga

Bi datro-iye
Bitra 'shte lo,
Ye shakaikatal, i-ne yanga

Ka' bi tradetin-iye
Bitra 'shte lo,
Ye shakaikatal, i-ne yanga

(continued)

Born Free, Edwin Salomon. Courtesy, Jacques Soussana Graphics, Jerusalem, Israel.

Starting with his left fore-foot,
Stamping, turns the frightened deer,
Comes the deer to my singing.

Quarry mine, blessed am I
In the luck of the chase,
Comes the deer to my singing.

Comes the deer to my singing,
Comes the deer to my song,
Comes the deer to my singing.

Dinnitshe-beka*n*-iye
Bitzil-le deshklashdji-lo
Ye shakaikatal, i-ne yanga

Bisedje
Ka' shinosin-ku lo,
Ye shakaikatal, i-ne-yanga

Ye shakaikatal, i-ne-yanga.
Ye shakaikatal, ai-ye-lo
Ye shakaikatal, i-ne-yanga.

RESPONDING OPTIONS

FROM PERSONAL RESPONSE *TO* CRITICAL ANALYSIS

REFLECT 1. What distinctive features of "Hunting Song" did you notice? Briefly summarize your impressions in your notebook.

RETHINK 2. Describe how you interpret the process of hunting deer as it is portrayed in the song.

Consider
- what attracts the deer
- the hunter's comparison of himself to the bird loved by the deer
- the use of the words "blessed" and "luck"
- the hunter's feelings about the deer

3. In what ways is this song like a prayer? Discuss why the Navajo might consider this song sacred.

RELATE 4. How would you compare "Song of the Sky Loom" and "Hunting Song"?

Consider
- the singers
- the purposes of the songs
- the attitudes toward nature

5. How do the attitudes toward nature expressed in these songs compare with the attitudes toward nature common in American society today?

ANOTHER PATHWAY

Cooperative Learning

With a small group of classmates, prepare oral readings of these two songs and perform them for the class. After the performances, ask the class to vote on which reading they liked best, giving reasons for their choice.

LITERARY LINKS

How does the relationship between humans and animals suggested in "Hunting Song" compare with the relationship between humans and animals suggested in "The World on the Turtle's Back"?

QUICKWRITES

1. In "Song of the Sky Loom," the Tewa express a wish to "walk fittingly." Draft a **definition essay** describing how a person might walk fittingly in today's world.
2. The singer of "Hunting Song" attempts to draw deer to himself. Write notes for an **inspirational speech** in which you discuss how people today can draw to themselves what they desire.
3. Using the style either of "Song of the Sky Loom" or of "Hunting Song," write a **poem** in which you express a personal wish for well-being or success.

PORTFOLIO *Save your writing. You may want to use it later as a springboard to a piece for your portfolio.*

LITERARY CONCEPTS

One feature of these songs you may have noticed is **repetition**—the recurrence of words, phrases, or lines. For example, the first line of "Song of the Sky Loom" is the same as the last line. Sometimes repetition is incremental: the structure of a line or stanza is repeated a certain number of times, with a slight variation in wording each time. The sequence "May the warp be . . . / May the weft be . . . / May the fringes be . . . / May the border be . . ." is an example of incremental repetition. Identify other instances of repetition in these songs.

Scholars of Native American song have proposed that repetition creates a regular rhythm for dancing, reinforces important ideas, makes a song easier to remember, gives power to a song, and has a hypnotic effect on consciousness. Which of these purposes for repetition are apparent in "Song of the Sky Loom" and "Hunting Song"? Is repetition used in any of the examples of sacred speech and song that you noted for the Personal Connection on page 31?

ACROSS THE CURRICULUM

Geography Recall that the term *sky loom* refers to desert rains. Point out images in "Song of the Sky Loom" that relate to rain. Why would rain be important to a farming culture in the Southwest? Research the terrain and climate of New Mexico. Predict what other things might be subjects of Tewa songs.

ALTERNATIVE ACTIVITIES

1. Compose a **song** that expresses your own feelings about some aspect of nature. Perform your song for the class.
2. Both the Tewa and the Navajo sing songs and perform dances during their religious rituals. Create your own **dance** to accompany one of these songs, illustrating the meaning and following the rhythm of the words. If you wish and are able to, incorporate traditional Tewa or Navajo dance movements in your dance.
3. How do the techniques and attitudes of modern hunters compare with those expressed in "Hunting Song"? Give an **oral report** to the class, based on an interview with a hunter or local game warden or on your own experiences.

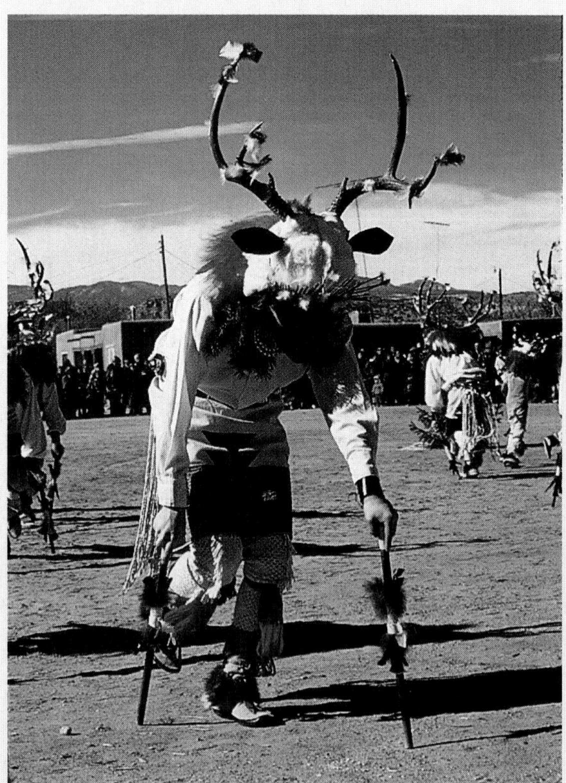

Tewa deer dancer. Copyright © 1974 Roger Sweet.

PREVIEWING

FOLK TALES

Coyote Stories

Okanogan (ō'kə-nŏg'ən)

Retold by Mourning Dove

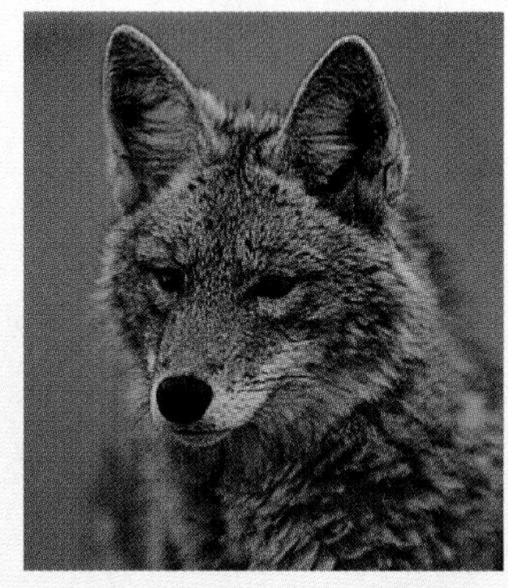

PERSONAL CONNECTION

A coyote is a small, wolflike animal that is native to western North America and found in many other regions of the continent. You might have observed coyotes in the wild or in a zoo, or you might have seen them depicted in Westerns or cartoons. What traits do you associate with coyotes? Record your impressions in a word web, with the word *coyote* in the center of the web.

CULTURAL CONNECTION

The two stories you are about to read have been told for generations by the Okanogan, a Salish-speaking people of north central Washington State and southern British Columbia. Many of the Okanogan now live on the Colville Reservation in Washington. Both stories belong to an oral tradition of the history of the Animal People, a race of supernatural beings believed to have been the first inhabitants of the world. The Animal People had magical powers and could alter their shapes. They usually appeared in animal form but could also take human form. When human beings appeared on earth, the Animal People were changed into different animal species. Coyote, one of the most important Animal People, is a central figure in these stories. He is thought to have made the world habitable for humans by killing monsters and bringing fire and salmon, among other deeds. Coyote tales are told in many Native American cultures across the western United States.

READING CONNECTION

Understanding Folk Tales A folk tale is a story that is handed down, usually by word of mouth, from generation to generation. Folk tales, which include legends, fairy tales, and fables, often involve supernatural beings and events. Magical transformations are common, as are animal characters that act human. Folk tales may serve to teach social values or to explain natural phenomena, and in this way they reflect the unique characteristics of the societies and regions from which they spring.

These two folk tales were originally told by Okanogan storytellers who traveled from village to village. They told the stories in their native language, Salish, and referred to places near the Columbia River, where they lived. As you read Mourning Dove's retellings, pay attention to Salish words and concepts, and notice specific references to geographical features to get an insight into the Okanogan culture. (The Salish words in the tales are spelled in a way that reflects their pronunciation.)

OKANOGAN

COYOTE and the BUFFALO

Retold by Mourning Dove

Buffalo skull. Private collection. Photo by John Oldenkamp.

No buffalo ever lived in the *Swah-netk'-qhu*[1] country. That was Coyote's fault. If he had not been so foolish and greedy, the people beside the *Swah-netk'-qhu* would not have had to cross the Rockies to hunt the *quas-peet-za*[2] (curled-hairs).

This is the way it happened:

COYOTE was traveling over the plains beyond the big mountains. He came to a flat. There he found an old buffalo skull. It was the skull of Buffalo Bull. Coyote always had been afraid of Buffalo Bull. He remembered the many times Bull Buffalo had scared him, and he laughed upon seeing the old skull there on the flat.

"Now I will have some fun," Coyote remarked. "I will have revenge for the times Buffalo made me run."

He picked up the skull and threw it into the air; he kicked it and spat on it; he threw dust in the eye sockets. He did these things many times, until he grew tired. Then he went his way. Soon he heard a rumbling behind him. He thought it was thunder, and he looked at the sky. The sky was clear. Thinking he must have imagined the sound, he walked on, singing. He heard the rumbling again, only much closer and louder. Turning around, he saw Buffalo Bull pounding along after him, chasing him. His old enemy had come to life!

Coyote ran, faster than he thought he could run, but Buffalo gained steadily. Soon Buffalo was right at his heels. Coyote felt his hot breath.

"Oh, *Squas-tenk'*,[3] help me!" Coyote

1. ***Swah-netk'-qhu:*** the Salish name for Kettle Falls on the Columbia River or for the river itself.
2. ***quas-peet-za:*** a Salish word for buffalo.
3. ***Squas-tenk':*** a Salish word that refers to Coyote's power or spirit helper.

begged, and his power answered by putting three trees in front of him. They were there in the wink of an eye. Coyote jumped and caught a branch of the first tree and swung out of Buffalo's way. Buffalo rammed the tree hard, and it shook as if in a strong wind. Then Buffalo chopped at the trunk with his horns, first with one horn and then the other. He chopped fast, and in a little while over went the tree, and with it went Coyote. But he was up and into the second tree before Buffalo Bull could reach him. Buffalo soon laid that tree low, but he was not quick enough to catch Coyote, who scrambled into the third and last tree.

"Buffalo, my friend, let me talk with you," said Coyote, as his enemy hacked away at the tree's trunk. "Let me smoke my pipe. I like the *kinnikinnick*.[4] Let me smoke. Then I can die more content."

"You may have time for one smoke," grunted Bull Buffalo, resting from his chopping.

Coyote spoke to his medicine-power, and a pipe, loaded and lighted, was given to him. He puffed on it once and held out the pipe to Buffalo Bull.

"No, I will not smoke with you," said that one. "You made fun of my bones. I have enough enemies without you. Young Buffalo is one of them. He killed me and stole all my fine herd."

"My uncle,"[5] said Coyote, "you need new horns. Let me make new horns for you. Then you can kill Young Buffalo. Those old horns are dull and worn."

Bull Buffalo was pleased with that talk. He decided he did not want to kill Coyote. He told Coyote to get down out of the tree and make the new horns. Coyote jumped down and called to his power. It scolded him for getting into trouble, but it gave him a flint knife and a stump of pitchwood.[6] From this stump Coyote carved a pair of fine heavy horns with sharp points. He gave them to Buffalo Bull. All buffalo bulls have worn the same kind of horns since.

BUFFALO BULL was very proud of his new horns. He liked their sharpness and weight and their pitch-black color. He tried them out on what was left of the pitchwood stump. He made one toss and the stump flew high in the air, and he forgave Coyote for his mischief. They became good friends right there. Coyote said he would go along with Buffalo Bull to find Young Buffalo.

They soon came upon Young Buffalo and the big herd he had won from Buffalo Bull. Young Buffalo laughed when he saw his old enemy, and he walked out to meet him. He did not know, of course, about the new horns. It was not much of a fight, that fight between Young Buffalo and Buffalo Bull. With the fine new horns, Buffalo Bull killed the other easily, and then he took back his herd, all his former wives and their children. He gave Coyote a young cow, the youngest cow, and he said:

He heard the rumbling again, only much closer and louder. Turning around, he saw Buffalo Bull pounding along after him, chasing him. His old enemy had come to life!

"Never kill her, *Sin-ka-lip'*![7] Take good care of her and she will supply you with meat forever. When you get hungry, just slice off some choice fat with a flint knife. Then rub ashes on the wound and the cut will heal at once."

Coyote promised to remember that, and they parted. Coyote started back to his own country, and the cow followed. For a few suns he ate only the fat when he was hungry. But after awhile he became

4. ***kinnikinnick:*** the Salish word for the bearberry, a shrub that is native to North America and Eurasia. The Okanogan toasted bearberry leaves and then crumbled and mixed them with tobacco for pipe smoking.

5. **my uncle:** Native Americans commonly use terms such as *uncle, cousin, brother,* and *sister* to express affection or respect or to flatter someone. Coyote uses this term of endearment to flatter Buffalo Bull.

6. **pitchwood:** the sap-filled wood of a pine or fir tree.

7. ***Sin-ka-lip':*** the Salish name for Coyote; it means "Imitator."

tired of eating fat, and he began to long for the sweet marrow-bones and the other good parts of the buffalo. He smacked his lips at the thought of having some warm liver.

"Buffalo Bull will never know," Coyote told himself, and he took his young cow down beside a creek and killed her.

VAIN COYOTE!

He was flattered. He believed she spoke her true mind. He stretched out to rest and he fell asleep. In his sleep he had a bad dream.

As he peeled off the hide, crows and magpies came from all directions. They settled on the carcass and picked at the meat. Coyote tried to chase them away, but there were too many of them. While he was chasing some, others returned and ate the meat. It was not long until they had devoured every bit of the meat.

"Well, I can get some good from the bones and marrow-fat," Coyote remarked, and he built a fire to cook the bones. Then he saw an old woman walking toward him. She came up to the fire.

"Sin-ka-lip'," she said, "you are a brave warrior, a great chief. Why should you do woman's work? Let me cook the bones while you rest."

Vain Coyote! He was flattered. He believed she spoke her true mind. He stretched out to rest and he fell asleep. In his sleep he had a bad dream. It awoke him, and he saw the old woman running away with the marrow-fat and the boiled grease. He looked into the cooking-basket. There was not a drop of soup left in it. He chased the old woman. He would punish her! But she could run, too, and she easily kept ahead of him. Every once in awhile she stopped and held up the marrow-fat and shouted: *"Sin-ka-lip',* do you want this?"

Finally Coyote gave up trying to catch her. He went back to get the bones. He thought he would boil them again. He found the bones scattered all around, so he gathered them up and put them into the cooking-basket. Needing some more water to boil them in, he went to the creek for it, and when he got back, there were no bones in the basket! In place of the bones was a little pile of tree limbs!

Coyote thought he might be able to get another cow from Buffalo Bull, so he set out to find him. When he came to the herd, he was astonished to see the cow he had killed. She was there with the others! She refused to go with Coyote again, and Buffalo Bull would not give him another cow. Coyote had to return to his own country without a buffalo.

That is why there never have been any buffalo along the *Swah-netk'-qhu.* ❖

FROM PERSONAL RESPONSE *TO* CRITICAL ANALYSIS

REFLECT 1. What did you find most interesting about the characters in this tale? Jot down your thoughts in your notebook.

RETHINK 2. Folk tales often serve to teach or explain. In your view, what does "Coyote and the Buffalo" teach or explain?

Consider
- what actions are rewarded or punished
- what changes occur in the characters
- the first and last paragraphs of the tale

3. Okanogan storytellers might tell "Coyote and the Buffalo" during a winter night. Why do you think people would want to hear this story over and over again?

OKANOGAN

FOX and COYOTE and WHALE

Retold by Mourning Dove

FOX had a beautiful wife. He was very much in love with her, but she had stopped caring for him. Fox was a great hunter, and every day he brought home food and fine skins for his wife to make into robes and clothing. He did not know that, while he was away hunting, his wife would sit beside the *Swah-netk'-qhu* and sing love songs to the water. Painting her face with bright colors, she would pour out her love thoughts in song.

Coyote came to visit his twin brother, and he soon noticed the strange actions of his sister-in-law. He spoke to Fox. "*Why-ay'-looh,*"[1] he said, "I think your wife is in love with somebody else." But Fox could not believe she loved anyone but him. He was blinded by his love for her. Then, one sun, he and Coyote returned from a hunt and she was not in the lodge. So Fox started to look for her. He walked down toward the river and there he saw his wife. She was sitting on the river bank, singing a love song. She did not see Fox. He watched her.

Nootka wood whale effigy rattle (about 1870). Courtesy, Morning Star Gallery, Santa Fe, New Mexico. Photo by Addison Doty.

As Fox watched, the water began to rise. Slowly it rose, higher and higher, and soon, out of the middle of the river, appeared a big monster of the fish-kind. The monster was *En-hah-et'-qhu,* the Spirit of the Water—Whale. It swam to the shore. As it

1. ***Why-ay'-looh:*** the Salish name for Fox.

touched dry land, it changed into a tall handsome man with long braided hair. This monster-man made love to the wife of Fox.

Sad at heart, Fox turned away. He went to his lodge. He said nothing, but he wondered how he could win back his wife's love. He worried about her as the suns passed. She grew pale and thin. Nothing that Fox could do pleased her. Her thoughts always were with the man who was not a man but a monster. One day when Fox and Coyote came home from hunting, she was gone, and the fire in the lodge was cold. Fox called and called. He got no answer. His heart was heavy.

A few suns later Fox looked up the river and saw an odd-shaped canoe coming. It was only half of a canoe. Two Water Maidens were standing in it, rocking it from side to side. They were singing:

We come for food,
Food for the Chief's stolen wife.
The water-food does not suit her.
That is why we come! We come!

As the Water Maidens approached, Fox and Coyote hid in the tepee. The maidens beached the half-canoe and entered the lodge. They began to pick up dried meat to take to the stolen wife. Coyote and Fox sprang from their hiding places and caught the maidens, and Fox asked about his wife—where she was and how to get to her. The maidens were silent. Then the brothers threatened to kill them unless they answered, and the maidens said:

"To find the person who stole her, you must go over the Big Falls[2] and under the water. His lodge is under the falls, under the water—a dangerous trip for Land People. Every trail is watched. Even if you get there, the mighty Whale chief will kill you. He is bad."

The Water Maidens had told all they knew, so Fox broke their necks. He and Coyote dressed in the maidens' robes and started down the river in the half-canoe. Standing on the sides of the strange craft, they rocked it as they had seen the maidens do, and rode it down the river and over the roaring falls. "Let me do all the talking," Fox warned Coyote. "I know better what to say." Down through the pouring, flashing waters they shot with the half-canoe. The thunder of the falls hurt their ears. And then, suddenly, they were landing at a great encampment of Water People, a strange kind of people to them. All of the people were strange except *Gou-kouh-whay'-na*—Mouse. She was there. She knew them and they knew her. Fox jumped ashore. Coyote, following, tripped and touched the water, and Mouse, the Sly One, laughed. "Ha-ha!" said Mouse, "Coyote nearly fell into the water."

"Do not speak," Fox whispered to Mouse. "Say nothing. I will pay you well."

But some of the Water People had heard. "What, *Gou-kouh-whay'-na,* did you say?" they inquired.

"Nothing," Mouse answered. "Nothing of importance. I was just joking."

"Yes, you did say something," said a Water Person. "You said that Coyote nearly fell into the water. You cannot fool me."

MOUSE insisted that she had not said that, and the other Water People believed her. They knew she was a fickle person and giddy, and they did not think much of her because she went everywhere to steal. She went everywhere, and that is why she understood all the different languages.

Carrying packs of dried meat and berries they had brought with them, Coyote and Fox made their way to the lodge of Whale, the chief. He and the stolen wife sat side by side in the lodge. The wife was glad to get the meat and berries, her kind of food.

---

2. **Big Falls:** Kettle Falls on the Columbia River in northeastern Washington.

FOX AND COYOTE kept their robes over their faces until everyone else was asleep. Then, when everything was quiet, Fox slipped up to Whale and cut off the monster's head with a flint knife. At the same time Coyote picked up the stolen wife and ran for the broken canoe. The noise they made awoke the camp, and the people rushed out of their lodges to see Coyote carrying off Fox's wife and Fox close behind, carrying the head of their chief. The people chased them, but the three got into the broken canoe, and Fox quickly put Coyote and the woman into his *shoo'-mesh*[3] pipe. Then Fox pushed the half-canoe into the water and it shot up to the river's surface below the falls. There Fox landed. He took Coyote and his twice-stolen wife out of the medicine pipe, and the head of the Whale Monster he threw toward the setting sun.

"In the Big Salt Water (ocean) shall Whale Monster stay," said Fox. "No longer shall he live in the smaller waters, in the rivers, where he can make love to the wives of men, where he can lure wives from their husbands."

As Fox and his wife and brother walked up the bank to their tepee, the headless body of Whale Monster turned over and over in the depths of the river, making the Big Falls of the *Swah-netk'-qhu* more fearful and thunderous, the way they are today, spilling with such force over the great rocks.

The wife of Fox became contented and happy again, glad to be back in her husband's lodge. But since that day Whale Monster was vanquished the Land People and the Water People have not loved each other. Fox made it so. ❖

Mask for Coyote Dance. Courtesy, University of Texas at Austin. Photo by Donald Codry.

3. ***shoo'-mesh:*** the Salish word for medicine, or magic power.

RESPONDING OPTIONS

FROM PERSONAL RESPONSE *TO* CRITICAL ANALYSIS

REFLECT 1. In your notebook, describe what was most memorable about "Fox and Coyote and Whale."

RETHINK 2. What did you learn about the Okanogan culture from reading this story?

Consider
- their values, attitudes, and beliefs
- geographical features of their area
- their way of life

3. What might be Okanogan storytellers' purpose for telling this story?

RELATE 4. Compare Coyote in these stories with your previous mental image of a coyote, using the word web you made for the Personal Connection on page 37.

5. Do you view Coyote as admirable? Explain why or why not.

6. What do these Coyote stories have in common with other folk tales you know?

7. Some Native Americans have argued that stories about the Animal People constitute "the first history of America." Do you agree? Explain.

ANOTHER PATHWAY

Prepare a reading of one of these stories for a group of children in kindergarten, and prepare a reading of the other for a group of adults. How similar and how different are your two readings? With the rest of the class, discuss the assumptions and decisions you made in preparing each kind of reading. Read passages aloud to illustrate your remarks.

LITERARY CONCEPTS

A **trickster tale** is a folk tale about an animal or person who engages in trickery, violence, and magic. Neither all good nor all bad, a trickster may be foolish yet clever, greedy yet helpful, immoral yet moral. Although the trickster tales you have read feature Coyote, other tricksters in Native American oral traditions include Raven, Mink, Hare, and Blue Jay. In other trickster tales told around the world, the trickster is a spider, a rabbit, or a fox. According to the folklorist Stith Thompson, a trickster "may appear in any one of three roles: the beneficent culture hero, the clever deceiver, or the numskull." Which of these roles does Coyote play in "Coyote and the Buffalo" and "Fox and Coyote and Whale"? What evidence in the stories supports your conclusions? What roles do tricksters play in other trickster tales with which you are familiar?

QUICKWRITES

1. ***Cooperative Learning*** What tricksters are admired in American society? Brainstorm in a small group to name four, then compare and contrast them with Coyote. Use this group discussion to outline a **magazine article** about one of these tricksters.

2. Some modern American writers have used the figure of Coyote in their own stories and poetry, updating the traditional tales for their own times. Drawing on the characters and plot structures of the Coyote tales you have just read, write your own contemporary **trickster tale.**

PORTFOLIO *Save your writing. You may want to use it later as a springboard to a piece for your portfolio.*

ALTERNATIVE ACTIVITIES

1. It was customary for storytellers to visit different villages and tell stories about the Animal People to children. To dramatize the stories, the storytellers used facial expressions, gestures, and different voices. Choose one of the two Coyote tales and give a **storytelling performance** for your classmates.
2. Draw a **caricature** of Coyote, exaggerating his most prominent features. Then display your drawing in class or use it as the basis for developing a cartoon storyboard, as described below.
3. "Road Runner" cartoons feature a character called Wile E. Coyote. Imagine how either "Coyote and the Buffalo" or "Fox and Coyote and Whale" could be turned into a TV cartoon. Make a **storyboard**—a series of drawings—showing the action of your favorite scene from either story, including dialogue or camera directions to accompany each drawing.

LITERARY LINKS

Compare the twins Coyote and Fox with the right-handed and left-handed twins in the Iroquois creation myth "The World on the Turtle's Back." What role does each set of twins play in creating the present order of the world?

CRITIC'S CORNER

When the Nez Perce anthropologist Archie Phinney recorded his people's animal stories in writing, he felt that their spirit had been lost. He said, "When I read my story mechanically I find only the cold corpse." Do you think that the spirit has been lost in transferring these stories from oral to written form? What would you add to recapture the spirit if you were performing them?

MOURNING DOVE

"Mourning Dove" (1888?–1936) was the pen name of Christine Quintasket, who grew up on the Colville Reservation in north central Washington State. As a child, she listened eagerly to the stories told by her mother, Lucy; her father, Joseph; Broken Nose Abraham; Long Woman; and other storytellers. As she recalls in the preface to *Coyote Stories,* her collection of tribal tales, these storytellers taught her about the *chip-chap-tiqulk,* or Animal People:

> **Vividly I recall old *S'whist-kane* (Lost-Head), also known as Old Narciss, and how, in the course of a narrative, he would jump up and mimic his characters, speaking or singing in a strong or weak voice, just as the Animal Persons were supposed to have done. And he would dance around the fire in the tule-mat covered lodge until the pines rang with the gleeful shouts of the smallest listeners.**

Mourning Dove not only was educated in her people's oral traditions but also had some formal education at government and Catholic mission schools. Determined to be a writer, she learned to write English and later attended secretarial school in Canada to learn how to type. She drafted a novel in 1912 but put it away for several years, until she met Lucullus Virgil McWhorter, an author and Native American–rights activist, who offered to edit it. *Cogewea, the Half-Blood* was published in 1927.

McWhorter encouraged Mourning Dove to record the traditional stories of the Okanogan and the other Colville tribes. Although she was a migrant worker, picking apples ten hours a day, she managed to write at night. *Coyote Stories,* which McWhorter and the journalist Heister Dean Guie helped edit, was published in 1933. By collecting and preserving some of the stories that tell the history of her people, Mourning Dove in her own way carried on the work of the storytellers she had heard as a child.

OTHER WORKS *Mourning Dove: A Salishan Autobiography, Mourning Dove's Stories*

PREVIEWING

FICTION

The Man to Send Rain Clouds

Leslie Marmon Silko

PERSONAL CONNECTION

Certain ceremonies, or prescribed acts, are performed on holidays or at events that mark important passages in life, such as christenings, bar mitzvahs, weddings, and funerals. Blowing out candles at a birthday party is a ceremony, as is passing out diplomas at a graduation. With your classmates, make a list of as many such ceremonies as you can think of.

CULTURAL CONNECTION

This contemporary short story concerns a present-day funeral ceremony held among the Laguna people of western New Mexico. Like the Tewa, the Laguna are a Pueblo group, but they speak a Keresan language. Pueblo groups had settled in the Southwest thousands of years before the first Spanish conquistadors arrived in 1540. The Spanish came to establish a colony and to convert the Pueblos to Catholicism but were driven away in 1680 during the Pueblo Rebellion. The Spanish soon returned, however, completing their reconquest of New Mexico in 1692. The Laguna pueblo was founded in 1699 by emigrants from other pueblos to the north. In the 1700s and 1800s, the Laguna and other Pueblo groups were harassed by Mexican slavers; raiders from the Navajo, Apache, and Ute tribes; and Protestant settlers from the United States.

Despite being influenced by outside cultures, the Laguna have kept many of their values and beliefs. For example, they perform traditional ceremonies when a person dies because they believe that dead persons' spirits will become *Shiwanna*—Cloud People—who bring the precious gift of rain.

READING CONNECTION

Making Inferences An inference is a logical guess or conclusion based on evidence. By using information from what you read and from your own experience, you can make inferences about things left unstated in a work of literature. As you read this story, use a chart like the one started below to record the ceremonies surrounding Teofilo's death. Use the second or third column to indicate which tradition you infer that the ceremony belongs to, Laguna or European.

Ceremony:	Laguna:	European:
painting on face	X	

THE MAN TO SEND RAIN CLOUDS

Leslie Marmon Silko

THEY FOUND HIM UNDER A BIG COTTONWOOD TREE. His Levi jacket and pants were faded light-blue so that he had been easy to find. The big cottonwood tree stood apart from a small grove of winterbare cottonwoods which grew in the wide, sandy arroyo. He had been dead for a day or more, and the sheep had wandered and scattered up and down the arroyo. Leon and his brother-in-law, Ken, gathered the sheep and left them in the pen at the sheep camp before they returned to the cottonwood tree. Leon waited under the tree while Ken drove the truck through the deep sand to the edge of the arroyo. He squinted up at the sun and unzipped his jacket—it sure was hot for this time of year. But high and northwest the blue mountains were still deep in snow. Ken came sliding down the low, crumbling bank about fifty yards down, and he was bringing the red blanket.

Before they wrapped the old man, Leon took a piece of string out of his pocket and tied a small gray feather in the old man's long white hair. Ken gave him the paint. Across the brown wrinkled forehead he drew a streak of white and along the high cheekbones he drew a strip of blue paint. He paused and watched Ken throw pinches of corn meal and pollen into the wind that fluttered the small gray feather. Then Leon painted with yellow under the old man's broad nose, and finally, when he had painted green across the chin, he smiled.

"Send us rain clouds, Grandfather." They laid the bundle in the back of the pickup and covered it with a heavy tarp before they started back to the pueblo.

They turned off the highway onto the sandy pueblo road. Not long after they passed the store and post office they saw Father Paul's car coming toward them. When he recognized their faces he slowed his car and waved for them to stop. The young priest rolled down the car window.

"Did you find old Teofilo?" he asked loudly.

Leon stopped the truck. "Good morning, Father. We were just out to the sheep camp. Everything is O.K. now."

WORDS TO KNOW

arroyo (ə-roi'ō) *n.* a deep gully cut by an intermittent stream; a dry gulch

"Thank God for that. Teofilo is a very old man. You really shouldn't allow him to stay at the sheep camp alone."

"No, he won't do that any more now."

"Well, I'm glad you understand. I hope I'll be seeing you at Mass this week—we missed you last Sunday. See if you can get old Teofilo to come with you." The priest smiled and waved at them as they drove away.

Louise and Teresa were waiting. The table was set for lunch, and the coffee was boiling on the black iron stove. Leon looked at Louise and then at Teresa.

"We found him under a cottonwood tree in the big arroyo near sheep camp. I guess he sat down to rest in the shade and never got up again." Leon walked toward the old man's bed. The red plaid shawl had been shaken and spread carefully over the bed, and a new brown flannel shirt and pair of stiff new Levis were arranged neatly beside the pillow. Louise held the screen door open while Leon and Ken carried in the red blanket. He looked small and shriveled, and after they dressed him in the new shirt and pants he seemed more shrunken.

It was noontime now because the church bells rang the Angelus.[1] They ate the beans with hot bread, and nobody said anything until after Teresa poured the coffee.

Ken stood up and put on his jacket. "I'll see about the gravediggers. Only the top layer of soil is frozen. I think it can be ready before dark."

Leon nodded his head and finished his coffee. After Ken had been gone for a while, the neighbors and clanspeople came quietly to embrace Teofilo's family and to leave food on the table because the gravediggers would come to eat when they were finished.

The sky in the west was full of pale-yellow light. Louise stood outside with her hands in the pockets of Leon's green army jacket that was too big for her. The funeral was over, and the old men had taken their candles and medicine bags[2] and were gone. She waited until the body was laid into the pickup before she said anything to Leon. She touched his arm, and he noticed that her hands were still dusty from the corn meal that she had sprinkled around the old man. When she spoke, Leon could not hear her.

"What did you say? I didn't hear you."

"I said that I had been thinking about something."

"About what?"

"About the priest sprinkling holy water[3] for Grandpa. So he won't be thirsty."

Leon stared at the new moccasins that Teofilo had made for the ceremonial dances in the summer. They were nearly hidden by the red blanket. It was getting colder, and the wind pushed gray dust down the narrow pueblo road. The sun was approaching the long mesa where it disappeared during the winter. Louise stood there shivering and watching his face. Then he zipped up his jacket and opened the truck door. "I'll see if he's there."

Ken stopped the pickup at the church, and Leon got out; and then Ken drove down the hill to the graveyard where people were waiting. Leon knocked at the old carved door with its symbols of the Lamb. While he waited he looked up at the twin bells from the king of Spain with the last sunlight pouring around them in their tower.

The priest opened the door and smiled when he saw who it was. "Come in! What brings you here this evening?"

The priest walked toward the kitchen, and

1. **rang the Angelus** (ăn′jə-ləs)**:** was rung to remind Roman Catholics to recite a prayer in commemoration of the Annunciation, the archangel Gabriel's announcing to the Virgin Mary that she had conceived Jesus, the Son of God.
2. **medicine bags:** pouches containing collections of sacred items believed to possess magical influence.
3. **holy water:** water blessed by a priest and used for religious purposes.

WORDS TO KNOW

mesa (mā′ sə) *n.* a broad, flat-topped hill with clifflike sides

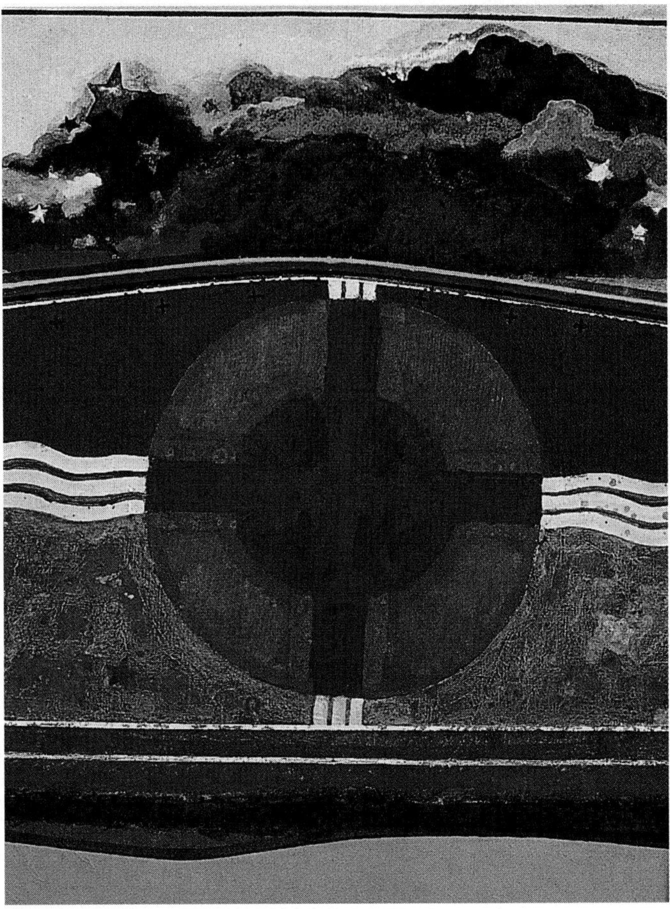

Between Heaven and Earth; Earth and Sky (1976), Frank LaPena. Acrylic on canvas, 24″ × 18″, WINTU-NOMTIPOM.

Leon stood with his cap in his hand, playing with the earflaps and examining the living room—the brown sofa, the green armchair, and the brass lamp that hung down from the ceiling by links of chain. The priest dragged a chair out of the kitchen and offered it to Leon.

"No thank you, Father. I only came to ask you if you would bring your holy water to the graveyard."

The priest turned away from Leon and looked out the window at the patio full of shadows and the dining-room windows of the nuns' cloister across the patio. The curtains were heavy, and the light from within faintly penetrated; it was impossible to see the nuns inside eating supper. "Why didn't you tell me he was dead? I could have brought the Last Rites[4] anyway."

Leon smiled. "It wasn't necessary, Father."

The priest stared down at his scuffed brown loafers and the worn hem of his cassock. "For a Christian burial it was necessary."

His voice was distant, and Leon thought that his blue eyes looked tired.

"It's O.K. Father, we just want him to have plenty of water."

4. **Last Rites:** a sacrament in which a priest anoints a dying person with holy oil and prays for his or her salvation.

WORDS TO KNOW

cloister (kloi′stər) *n.* a place devoted to religious seclusion; a monastery or convent

cassock (kăs′ək) *n.* an ankle-length garment, with close-fitting waist and sleeves, worn by clergymen

He felt good because it was finished, and he was happy about the sprinkling of the holy water; now the old man could send them big thunderclouds for sure.

The priest sank down into the green chair and picked up a glossy missionary magazine. He turned the colored pages full of lepers and pagans without looking at them.

"You know I can't do that, Leon. There should have been the Last Rites and a funeral Mass at the very least."

Leon put on his green cap and pulled the flaps down over his ears. "It's getting late, Father. I've got to go."

When Leon opened the door Father Paul stood up and said, "Wait." He left the room and came back wearing a long brown overcoat. He followed Leon out the door and across the dim churchyard to the adobe steps in front of the church. They both stooped to fit through the low adobe entrance. And when they started down the hill to the graveyard only half of the sun was visible above the mesa.

The priest approached the grave slowly, wondering how they had managed to dig into the frozen ground; and then he remembered that this was New Mexico, and saw the pile of cold loose sand beside the hole. The people stood close to each other with little clouds of steam puffing from their faces. The priest looked at them and saw a pile of jackets, gloves, and scarves in the yellow, dry tumbleweeds that grew in the graveyard. He looked at the red blanket, not sure that Teofilo was so small, wondering if it wasn't some perverse Indian trick—something they did in March to ensure a good harvest—wondering if maybe old Teofilo was actually at sheep camp corralling the sheep for the night. But there he was, facing into a cold dry wind and squinting at the last sunlight, ready to bury a red wool blanket while the faces of his parishioners were in shadow with the last warmth of the sun on their backs. His fingers were stiff, and it took him a long time to twist the lid off the holy water. Drops of water fell on the red blanket and soaked into dark icy spots. He sprinkled the grave and the water disappeared almost before it touched the dim, cold sand; it reminded him of something—he tried to remember what it was, because he thought if he could remember he might understand this. He sprinkled more water; he shook the container until it was empty, and the water fell through the light from sundown like August rain that fell while the sun was still shining, almost evaporating before it touched the wilted squash flowers.

The wind pulled at the priest's brown Franciscan robe[5] and swirled away the corn meal and pollen that had been sprinkled on the blanket. They lowered the bundle into the ground, and they didn't bother to untie the stiff pieces of new rope that were tied around the ends of the blanket. The sun was gone, and over on the highway the eastbound lane was full of headlights. The priest walked away slowly. Leon watched him climb the hill, and when he had disappeared within the tall, thick walls, Leon turned to look up at the high blue mountains in the deep snow that reflected a faint red light from the west. He felt good because it was finished, and he was happy about the sprinkling of the holy water; now the old man could send them big thunderclouds for sure. ❖

5. **Franciscan robe:** the distinctive garment of a Roman Catholic religious order founded by Saint Francis of Assisi in 1209. After Spain established a colony in New Mexico in 1598, Franciscan missionaries began to settle there and build churches in the pueblos.

WORDS TO KNOW

perverse (pər-vûrs′) *adj.* stubbornly opposed to what is right or reasonable; wrong-headed

RESPONDING OPTIONS

FROM PERSONAL RESPONSE *TO* CRITICAL ANALYSIS

REFLECT 1. In your notebook, jot down your impressions of Teofilo's funeral.

RETHINK 2. Of the two kinds of ceremonies surrounding Teofilo's death—Laguna and European—which, if either, do you think is more important to his people? Refer to the chart you made for the Reading Connection on page 46.

3. Louise and Leon want Father Paul to sprinkle holy water on Teofilo's grave. Why do you think this act is so important to them?

4. In your opinion, does Father Paul do the right thing at the end of the story?

Consider
- his attitude toward Laguna ceremonies
- his attitude toward Christian burial
- possible reasons for his decision

RELATE 5. Who or what do you think is "in harmony with nature" in this story?

6. What do you believe is the function of ceremonies? When should a ceremony be changed, if ever?

ANOTHER PATHWAY

If Father Paul were a Laguna who had been raised in the pueblo, how might the conflicts or events in this story be different? With a partner, review the story and discuss this question. Share your speculations in class.

LITERARY CONCEPTS

A **conflict** is a struggle between opposing forces that is the basis of a story's plot. An **external conflict** pits a character against nature, society, or another character. An **internal conflict** is a conflict between opposing forces within a character. In "Coyote and the Buffalo," for example, Coyote's struggle to keep Buffalo Bull from killing him is an external conflict, whereas Coyote's struggle to decide whether to kill and eat the buffalo cow is an internal conflict.

Cooperative Learning In a small group, discuss the conflicts you see in "The Man to Send Rain Clouds," and classify each as external or internal. Are all the conflicts resolved?

QUICKWRITES

1. Assuming the role either of Father Paul's religious superior or of a leader of the Laguna community, write an **evaluation** of Father Paul, assessing his relationship with the community he serves.

2. Go over your list of ceremonies from the Personal Connection activity on page 46. Pick one that is familiar to you, such as a graduation or a wedding, and write a detailed **description** of it for someone who has never seen it before. If you can, explain any symbolic actions, garments, or colors associated with the ceremony.

PORTFOLIO Save your writing. You may want to use it later as a springboard to a piece for your portfolio.

38041

ALTERNATIVE ACTIVITIES

Draw or paint a **scene** from the story, including specific objects and colors mentioned in relation to Teofilo's death. Then display your picture, explaining significant details to the class.

WORDS TO KNOW

Review the Words to Know at the bottom of the selection pages. Then, on your paper, write the vocabulary word or words that belong in each group below. For each group, draw a picture that illustrates the words.

Group A: irrational, obstinate, ____(1)____

Group B: mission, ____(2)____, ____(3)____

Group C: desert, ____(4)____, ____(5)____

ACROSS THE CURRICULUM

Biology The Laguna scatter corn meal and corn pollen in their ceremonies for Teofilo. Find out the function of pollen in plant life. Why might it be appropriate to use pollen at a funeral ceremony? Present your findings and interpretations to the class.

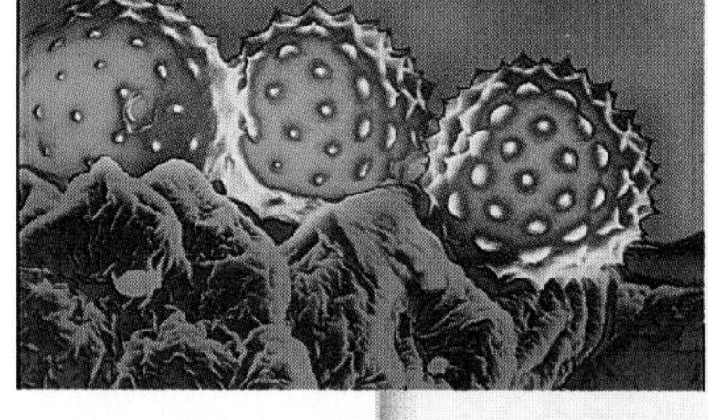

A microscopic view of pollen, with color enhancement. Copyright © Ralph C. Eagle/Science Source/Photo Reseachers Inc.

LESLIE MARMON SILKO

1948–

Leslie Marmon Silko was raised in the Southwest. She grew up in the pueblo of Old Laguna, about 45 miles west of Albuquerque, New Mexico. Although she is of mixed European, Laguna, and Mexican ancestry, Silko derives inspiration for her stories, poems, and novels from the traditional Native American myths and tales she learned as a child. "I grew up at Laguna listening," she has said, "and I hear the ancient stories, I hear them very clearly in the stories we are telling right now. Most important, I feel the power which the stories still have, to bring us together, especially when there is loss and grief."

In *Storyteller,* which was published in 1981 and includes the story "The Man to Send Rain Clouds," Silko pays tribute to Native American storytelling traditions, weaving together poems, photographs, ancient tales, stories about her family, and stories about memorable characters like Father Paul and Leon. As she told an interviewer, "Storytelling for Indians is like a natural resource. Some places have oil, some have a lot of water or timber or gold, but around here, it's the ear that has developed."

Silko, who was educated at the University of New Mexico, considered a law career before becoming a writer and a teacher. She has taught English at the University of Arizona and has won numerous grants and awards for her poetry and fiction, including a prestigious MacArthur Foundation grant in 1983.

OTHER WORKS *Laguna Woman, Ceremony, Almanac of the Dead*

LASERLINKS
• *ART GALLERY*

PREVIEWING

FICTION

Deer Woman

Paula Gunn Allen

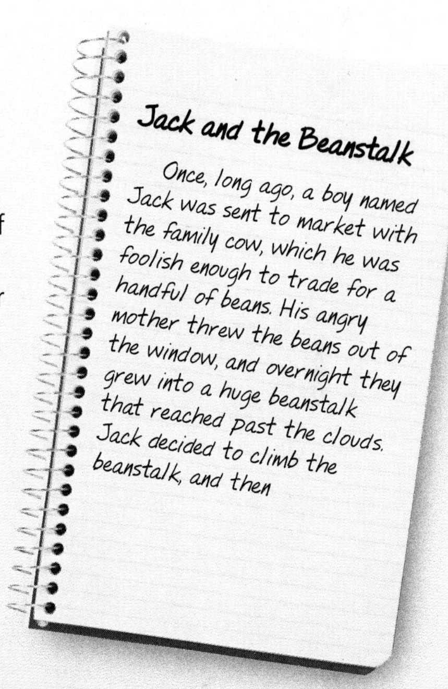

Jack and the Beanstalk
Once, long ago, a boy named Jack was sent to market with the family cow, which he was foolish enough to trade for a handful of beans. His angry mother threw the beans out of the window, and overnight they grew into a huge beanstalk that reached past the clouds. Jack decided to climb the beanstalk, and then

PERSONAL CONNECTION

Think of a traditional story—one that has been passed down from generation to generation—that you know and that you think most of your classmates also know. It might be a well-known local legend, a religious story, or a fairy tale such as "Jack and the Beanstalk." In your notebook, write a summary of this story to share with a small group of classmates. Invite the other members of the group to add details that they remember. Just as your story is familiar to your audience, the story you are about to read is based on a traditional tale that would be familiar to a Native American audience. As you read the story, notice which elements seem traditional and which seem contemporary.

CULTURAL CONNECTION

"Deer Woman" is a contemporary story based on traditional Cherokee tales about a deer who appears in the form of a woman and lures away a hunter. The Cherokee once lived in the Southeast, in what is now Tennessee, Kentucky, North and South Carolina, Virginia, Alabama, and Georgia. They settled near rivers and streams, where they fished and hunted deer and other game. In 1838 and 1839, most of the Cherokee people were forcibly moved to Oklahoma, where this story takes place. Stories about Deer Woman are also told by other Native American groups, such as the Dakota (Sioux) and the Menominee.

READING CONNECTION

Using a Reading Log The reading strategies discussed on page 5 are based on the kinds of connections active readers make when they read. To help you practice some of these strategies, questions have been inserted at various points in "Deer Woman." Record your response to each of the questions in your reading log. Also record other questions, thoughts, and feelings that come to you as you read. After you finish reading, discuss some of your responses with classmates.

LASERLINKS
• *BACKGROUND CONNECTION*

Untitled (1986), Jerry Uelsmann. Copyright © 1986 Jerry Uelsmann.

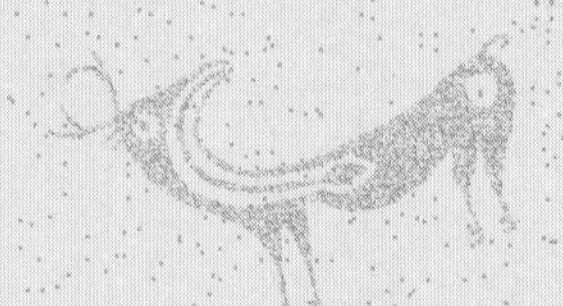

Deer Woman

Paula Gunn Allen

Two young men were out "snagging"—chasing girls—one afternoon. They rode around in their pickup, their Indian Cadillac, cruising up this road and down that one through steamy green countryside, stopping by friends' places here and there to lift a few. The day was sultry as summer days in Oklahoma get, hot as a sweat.

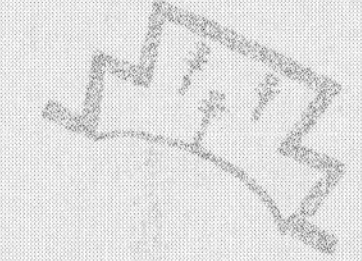

Long after dark, they stopped at a tavern twenty or thirty miles outside of Anadarko,[1] and joined some skins[2] gathered around several tables. After the muggy heat outside, the slowly turning fan inside felt cool. When they'd been there a while, one of the men at their table asked them if they were headed to the stomp dance.[3] "Sure," they said, though truth to tell, they hadn't known there was a stomp dance that night. The three headed out to the pickup.

They drove for some distance along narrow country roads, turning occasionally at unmarked crossings, bumping

1. **Anadarko:** a town in Oklahoma, about 45 miles southwest of Oklahoma City.
2. **skins:** Native Americans.
3. **stomp dance:** a traditional tribal dance of the Cherokee that is held at sacred "stomp grounds." All night long, men and boys sing while male and female dancers dance in a circle around a fire. Women and girls, who wear pebble-filled turtle shells on their legs, create a rhythm when they stamp their feet.

across cattle guards,[4] until at length they saw the light of the bonfire. Several unshaded lights hung from small huts that ringed the danceground, and headlights shone from a couple of parking cars.

They pulled into a spot in the midst of a new Winnebago, a Dodge van, two Toyotas, and a small herd of more battered models, and made their way to the danceground. The dance was going strong, and the sound of turtle shell and aluminum can rattles and singing, mixed with occasional laughter and bits of talk, reached their ears. "Alright!" exclaimed Ray, the taller and heavier of the two, slapping his buddy's raised hand in glee. "Yeah!" his pal Jackie responded, and they grinned at each other in the unsteady light. Slapping the man who'd ridden along with them on the back, the taller one said, "Man, let's go find us some snags!"

They hung out all night, occasionally starting a conversation with one good-looking woman or another, but though the brother who'd accompanied them soon disappeared with a long-legged beauty named Lurine, the two anxious friends didn't score. They were not the sort to feel disheartened, though. They kept up their spirits, dancing well and singing even better. They didn't really care so much about snagging. It simply gave them something to think about while they filled the day and night with interesting activity. They were among their own people, and they were satisfied with their lives and themselves.

Toward morning, though, Ray spotted two strikingly beautiful young women stepping onto the danceground. Their long hair flowed like black rivers down their backs. They were dressed in traditional clothes, and something about them—some elusive something—made Ray shiver with what felt almost like recognition and, at the same time, like dread. "Who are they?" he asked his friend, but the smaller man shrugged silently. Ray could see his eyes shining for a moment as the fire near them flared up suddenly.

At the same moment, they both saw the young women looking at them out of the corners of their eyes as they danced modestly and almost gravely past. Jackie nudged Ray and let out a long slow sigh. "Alright," he said in a low, almost reverent voice. "Alright!"

When the dance was ended, the young women made their way to where the two youths were standing. One of them said, "My friend and I need a ride to Anadarko, and they told us you were coming from there." As she said that, she gestured with her chin over her left shoulder toward a vaguely visible group standing on the other side of the danceground.

"What's your friend's name?" Ray countered.

"Linda," the other woman said. "Hers is Junella."

"My friend's name's Jackie," Ray said, grinning. "When do you want to take off?"

"We'll go whenever you do," Junella answered. She held his eyes with hers. "Where are you parked?"

They made their way to the pickup and got in. It was a tight fit, but nobody seemed to mind. Ray drove, backing the pickup carefully to thread among the haphazardly parked vehicles. As he did, he glanced down for a second, and he thought he saw the feet of both women as deer hooves. "Man," he thought, "I gotta lay off the weed." He didn't remember he'd quit smoking it months before, and he hadn't had even a beer since they'd left the tavern hours before. The women tucked their

4. **cattle guards:** shallow ditches across which rows of parallel metal bars are set, used at fence openings to prevent the passage of cattle while allowing access to vehicles and pedestrians.

WORDS TO KNOW **reverent** (rĕv′ər-ənt) *adj.* expressing awe and respect feet under their bags, and in the darkness he didn't see them anymore. Besides, he had more engaging things on his mind.

They drove companionably for some time, joking around, telling a bit about themselves, their tastes in music, where they'd gone to school, when they'd graduated. Linda kept fiddling with the dial, reaching across Junella to get to the knob. Her taste seemed to run to either hard core country-and-western or what Ray privately thought of as "space" music.

QUESTION

What questions do you have about the characters or their situation?

She and Junella occasionally lapsed into what seemed like a private conversation or joke, Ray couldn't be sure which; then, as though remembering themselves, they'd laugh and engage the men in conversation again.

After they'd traveled for an hour or so, Linda suddenly pointed to a road that intersected the one they were on. "Take a left," she said, and Ray complied. He didn't even think about it or protest that they were on the road to Anadarko already. A few hundred yards further she said, "Take a right." Again he complied, putting the brake on suddenly as he went into the turn, spilling Junella hard against him. He finished shifting quickly and put his arm around her. She leaned into him, saying nothing.

The road they had turned onto soon became gravel, and by the time they'd gone less than a quarter mile turned into hard-packed dirt. Ray could smell water nearby. He saw some trees standing low on the horizon and realized it was coming light.

"Let's go to the water," Linda said. "Junella and I are traditional, and we try to wash in fresh running water every morning."

"Yeah," Junella murmured. "We were raised by our mother's grandmother, and the old lady was real strict about some things. She always made sure we prayed to Long Man[5] every day."

Jackie and Ray climbed out of the truck, the women following. They made their way through the thickest of scrub oak and bushes and clambered down the short bank to the stream, the men leading the way. They stopped at the edge of the water, but the young women stepped right in, though still dressed in their dance clothes. They bent and splashed water on their faces, speaking the old tongue softly as they did so. The men removed their tennis shoes and followed suit, tucking their caps in the hip pockets of their jeans.

After a suitable silence, Junella pointed to the opposite bank with her uplifted chin. "See that path," she asked the men. "I think it goes to our old house. Let's go up there and see."

"Yes," Linda said, "I thought it felt familiar around here. I bet it is our old place." As the women didn't move to cross the shallow river and go up the path, the men took the lead again. Ray briefly wondered at his untypical pliability, but he banished the thought almost as it arose. He raised his head just as he reached the far bank and saw that the small trees and brush were backed by a stone bluff that rose steeply above them. As he tilted his head back to spot the top of the bluff, he had a flashing picture of the small round feet he'd thought he'd seen set against the floorboard of the truck. But as the image flashed into his mind, the sun blazed out over the bluff; the thought faded as quickly as it had come, leaving him with a slightly dazed feeling and a tingling that climbed rapidly up his spine. He put on his cap.

Jackie led the way through the thicket, walking as quickly as the low branches would allow, bending almost double in places. Ray followed him, and the women came after. Shortly they emerged from the trees onto a rocky area

5. **Long Man:** the Cherokee term for a river. Long Man represents water, one of the four principal elemental gods. Important Cherokee ceremonies begin with a traditional dip in Long Man or a prayer to Long Man.

WORDS TO KNOW

pliability (plī'ə-bĭl'ĭ-tē) *n.* the quality of being easily influenced or persuaded that ran along the foot of the bluff like a narrow path. When he reached it, Jackie stopped and waited while the others caught up. "Do you still think this is the old homestead?" he quipped. The women laughed sharply, then fell into animated conversation in the old language.

Neither Ray nor Jackie could speak it, so they stood waiting, admiring the beauty of the morning, feeling the cool dawn air on their cheeks and the water still making their jeans cling to their ankles. At least their feet were dry, and so were the tennies they'd replaced after leaving the river.

After a few animated exchanges, the women started up the path, the men following. "She says it's this way," Linda said over her shoulder. "It can't be far." They trudged along for what seemed a long time, following the line of the bluff that seemed to grow even higher. After a time, Junella turned into a narrow break in the rock and began to trudge up its gradual slope, which soon became a steep rise.

"I bet we're not going to grandma's house," Jackie said in quiet tones to his friend. "I didn't know this bluff was even here," Ray replied. "It's not much farther," Junella said cheerfully. "What's the matter, you dudes out of shape or something?"

"Well, I used to say I'd walk a mile for a Camel," Jackie said wryly, "but I didn't say anything about snags!" He and Ray laughed, perhaps more heartily than the joke warranted.

"This is the only time I've heard of Little Red Riding Hood leading the wolves to grandma's," Ray muttered. "Yah," Linda responded brightly. "And wait'll you see what I'm carrying in my basket of goodies." The women glanced at each other, amused, and Jackie laughed abashedly.

"Here's the little creek I was looking for," Junella said suddenly. "Let's walk in it for a while." Ray looked at Jackie quizzically.

"I don't want to walk in that," Jackie said quickly. "I just got dry from the last dip." The women were already in the water walking upstream. "Not to worry," Junella said. "It's not wet—it's the path to the old house."

"Yeah, right," Ray mumbled, stepping into the water with a sigh. Jackie followed him, falling suddenly silent. As they stepped into what they thought was a fast-running stream, their feet touched down on soft grass. "Hey!" Ray exclaimed. "What's happening?" He stopped abruptly, and Jackie ploughed into him. "Watch it, man," the smaller man said shortly. He brushed past Ray and made after the women, who were disappearing around a sharp turn. Ray stood rooted a moment, then hurried after him. "Wait up," he called. His voice sounded loudly against the cliff and came back to him with a crack.

As he turned the corner, he saw Linda reaching upward along the cliff where a tall rock slab leaned against it. She grasped the edge of the slab and pulled. To the men's astonishment, it swung open, for all the world like an ordinary door. The women stepped through.

Ray and Jackie regarded each other for long moments. Finally Ray shrugged, and Jackie gestured with his outspread arm at the opening in the cliff. They followed the women inside.

PREDICT

What do you think will happen to the men?

Within, they were greeted with an astonishing scene. Scores of people, upward of two hundred, stood or walked about a green land. Houses stood scattered in the near distance, and smoke arose from a few chimneys. There were tables spread under some large trees, sycamore or elm, Ray thought, and upon them food was spread in large quantities and tantalizing variety. Suddenly aware they hadn't eaten since early the day before, the men started forward. But before they'd taken more than a few steps, Linda and Junella took their arms and led them away from

WORDS TO KNOW

wryly (rī'lē) *adv.* humorously; ironically

abashedly (ə-băsh'ĭd-lē) *adv.* in an embarrassed way; uneasily the feast toward the doorway of one of the houses.

There sat a man who seemed ancient to the young men. His age wasn't so much in his hair, though it hung in waist-long white strands. It wasn't even so much in his skin, wrinkled and weathered though his face was beneath the tall crowned hat he wore. It was just that he seemed to be age personified. He seemed to be older than the bluff, than the river, than even the sky.

Next to him lay two large mastiffs,[6] their long, lean bodies relaxed, their heads raised, their eyes alert and full of intelligence. "So," the old one said to the women, "I see you've snagged two strong young men." He shot an amused glance in the young men's direction. "Go, get ready," he directed the women, and at his words they slipped into the house, closing the door softly behind them.

The young men stood uneasily beside the old one, who disregarded them completely, lost in his own thoughts as he gazed steadily at some point directly before him.

After half an hour or more had passed, the old man addressed the young men again. "It was a good thing that you did," he mused, "following my nieces here. I wonder that you didn't give up or get lost along the way." He chuckled quietly as at a private joke. "Maybe you two are intelligent men." He turned his head suddenly and gave them an appraising look. Each of the young men shifted under that knowing gaze uncomfortably. From somewhere, the ground, the sky, they didn't feel sure, they heard thunder rumbling. "I have told everybody that they did well for themselves by bringing you here."

Seeing the surprised look on their faces, he smiled. "Yes, you didn't hear me, I know. I guess we talk different here than you're used to where you come from. Maybe you'll be here long enough to get used to it," he added, "that is, if you like my nieces well enough. We'll feed you soon," he said. "But first there are some games I want you to join in." He pointed with pursed lips and chin in the direction of a low hill that rose just beyond the farthest dwelling. Again the thunder rumbled, louder than before.

A moment later the women appeared. Their long, flowing hair was gone, and their heads shone in the soft light that filled the area, allowing distant features to recede into its haze. The women wore soft clothing that completely covered their bodies, even their hands and feet. The bright, gleaming cloth reflected light at the same intensity as their bald heads. Their dark eyes seemed huge and luminous against skin that gave off a soft radiance. Seeing them, both men were nearly overcome with fear. "They have no hair at all," Ray thought. "Where is this place?" He glanced over at Jackie, whose face mirrored his own unease. Jackie shook his head almost imperceptibly, slowly moving it from side to side in a gesture that seemed mournful and at the same time oddly resigned.

CLARIFY

Who do the women turn out to be?

Linda and Junella moved to the young men, each taking one by the hand and drawing him toward the central area nearby. In a daze, Ray and Jackie allowed themselves to be led into the center of the area ringed by heavily laden tables, barely aware that the old man had risen from his place and with his dogs was following behind them. They were joined by a number of other young men, all wearing caps like the ones Ray and Jackie wore. Two of the men carried bats, several wore gloves, and one was tossing a baseball in the air as he walked. Slowly the throng made their way past the tables and came to an open area where Jackie and Ray saw familiar shapes. They were bases, and the field

6. **mastiffs:** large, strong dogs of a breed used for hunting and as guard dogs.

WORDS TO KNOW

personified (pər-sŏn′ə-fīd′) *adj.* embodied in human form; incarnate **personify** *v.*
imperceptibly (ĭm′pər-sĕp′tə-blē) *adv.* so slightly or gradually as to be unnoticeable
throng (thrông) *n.* a crowd

that the soft light revealed to them was a baseball diamond.

The old man took his place behind home plate, and one of the young men crouched before him as a loud peal of thunder crashed around them. "Play ball!" the old man shouted, and the men took up their places as the women retired to some benches at the edge of the field.

The bewildered young men found their positions, and the game was on. It was a hard-played game, lasting some time. At length it reached a rowdy end, the team Jackie and Ray were on barely edging out the opposition in spite of a couple of questionable calls the old man made against them. Their victory was due in no small measure to the wiry Jackie's superb pitching. He'd pitched two no-hit innings, and that had won them the game.

As they walked with the players back toward the houses, the old man came up to them. Slapping each in turn on the back a couple of times, he told them he thought they were good players. "Maybe that means you'll be ready for tomorrow's games," he said, watching Jackie sharply. "They're not what you're used to, I imagine, but you'll do alright."

They reached the tables and were helped to several large portions of food by people whose faces never seemed to come quite into focus but whose goodwill seemed unquestionable. They ate amid much laughter and good-natured joshing, only belatedly realizing that neither Linda nor Junella was among the revelers. Ray made his way to Jackie and asked him if he'd seen either woman. Replying in the negative, Jackie offered to go look around for them.

They both agreed to make a quick search and to rendezvous at the large tree near the old man's house. But after a fruitless hour, Ray went to the front of the house and waited. His friend didn't come. At last, growing bored, he made his way back to the tables where a group had set up a drum and were singing lustily. A few of the younger people had formed a tight circle around the drummers and were slowly stepping round in it, their arms about each others' waists and shoulders. "Alright!" Ray thought, "49's!"[7] He was cheered at the anticipation of the close social bond dancing, drumming and singing, the joking and relaxation the social signified. He joined the circle between two women he hadn't seen before who easily made way for him and smoothly closed about him, each wrapping an arm around his waist. He forgot all about his friend.

When Ray awoke, the sun was beating down on his head. He sat up and realized he was lying near the river's edge, his legs in the thicket, his head and half-turned face unshielded from the sun. It was about a third of the way up in a clear sky. As he looked groggily around, he discovered Junella sitting quietly a few yards away on a large stone. "Hey," she said, smiling.

"How'd I get here?" Ray asked. He stood and stretched, surreptitiously feeling to see if everything worked. His memory seemed hesitant to return, but he had half-formed impressions of a baseball game and eating and then the '49. He looked around. "Where's Jackie, and, uh—"

"Linda?" Junella supplied as he paused.

"Yeah, Linda," he finished.

"Jackie is staying there," she told him calmly. She reached into her bag and brought out a man's wristwatch. "He said to give you this," she said, holding it out to him.

Ray felt suddenly dizzy. He swayed for a moment while strange images swept through him. Junella with no hair and that eerie light—that pale tan but with spots or a pattern of soft gray dots that sort of fuzzed out at the edges to blend into the tan. The old man.

7. **49's:** Native American dances usually performed by younger people, starting after midnight and ending at dawn.

WORDS TO KNOW

reveler (rĕv′əl-ər) *n.* a person participating in noisy festivities or celebrations
rendezvous (rän′dā-vo͞o′) *v.* to meet at a prearranged time and place

Untitled (1985), Jerry Uelsmann. Copyright © 1985 Jerry Uelsmann.

Deer Woman would come to dances sometimes,

and if you weren't careful

she'd put her spell on you

and take you inside the mountain.

He took a step in her direction. "Hey," he began. "What the hell's—" He broke off. The rock where she sat was empty. On the ground next to it lay Jackie's watch.

◆◆◆◆

QUESTION

Who is the "me" that is speaking to the reader?

When he told me the story, about fifteen months afterward, Ray had heard that Jackie had showed up at his folks' place. They lived out in the country, a mile or so beyond one of the numerous small towns that dot the Oklahoma landscape. The woman who told him about Jackie's return, Jackie's cousin Ruth Ann, said he had come home with a strange woman who was a real fox. At thirteen, Ruth Ann had developed an eye for good looks and thought herself quite a judge of women's appearance. They hadn't stayed long, he'd heard. They packed up some of Jackie's things and visited with his family. Ray had been in Tulsa and hadn't heard Jackie was back. None of their friends had seen him either. There had been a child with them, he said, maybe two or so, Ruth Ann had thought, because she could walk by herself.

"You know," he'd said thoughtfully, turning a Calistoga[8] slowly between his big hands. The gesture made him seem very young and somehow vulnerable. "One of my grandma's brothers, old Jess, used to talk about the little people[9] a lot. He used to tell stories about strange things happening around the countryside here. I never paid much attention. You know how it is, I just thought he was putting me on, or maybe he was pining away for the old days. He said Deer Woman would come to dances sometimes, and if you weren't careful she'd put her spell on you and take you inside the mountain to meet her uncle. He said her uncle was Thunder, one of the old gods or supernaturals, whatever the traditionals call them."

He finished his drink in a couple of swallows, pushing away from the table where we sat. "I dunno," and he gave me a look that I still haven't forgotten, a look somehow wounded and yet with a kind of wild hope mixed in. "Maybe those old guys know something, eh?"

It was a few years before I saw Ray again. Then I ran into him unexpectedly in San Francisco a couple of years ago. We talked for a while, standing on the street near the Mission BART station.[10] He started to leave when my curiosity got the better of my manners. I asked if he'd ever found out what happened to Jackie.

Well, he said that he'd heard that Jackie came home off and on, but the woman—probably Linda, though he wasn't sure—was never with him. Then he'd heard that someone had run into him, or a guy they thought sure was him, up in Seattle. He'd gone alcoholic. They'd heard he'd died. "But the weird thing is that he'd evidently been telling someone all about that time inside the mountain, and that he'd married her, and about some other stuff, stuff I guess he wasn't supposed to tell." Another guy down on his luck, he guessed. "Remember how I was telling you about my crazy uncle, the one who used to tell about Deer Woman? Until I heard about Jackie, I'd forgotten that the old man used to say that the ones who stayed there were never supposed to talk about it. If they did, they died in short order."

After that there didn't seem to be much more to say. Last time I saw Ray, he was heading down the steps to catch BART. He was on his way to a meeting, and he was running late. ❖

8. **Calistoga:** a brand of mineral water.
9. **little people:** three-foot-tall supernatural beings who the Cherokee believe live in rock cliffs and river bluffs.
10. **Mission BART station:** a stop on the Bay Area Rapid Transit system in San Francisco.

WORDS TO KNOW

vulnerable (vŭl'nər-ə-bəl) *adj.* susceptible to injury; easily hurt

INSIGHT

ABOUT DEER WOMAN

PAULA GUNN ALLEN

Like the Pueblos and their cultural descendants the Navajo, the Cherokee tell stories featuring two men—sometimes brothers, sometimes twins, sometimes half-brothers. I have followed that tradition in this account of a contemporary encounter with Deer Woman and another who may be like her. While I can find no explicit comment on the presence of more than one Deer Woman, some old accounts specify that there are two or more such supernatural beings.

While the old stories relate encounters with Deer Woman—one of those ephemeral[1] beings called the little people, Yunwitsansdi—among the Cherokee in regions of the old Cherokee homelands in the southeastern part of the country, now known as Georgia and North Carolina, encounters with them in Oklahoma, where the majority of the Cherokee now reside, are not uncommon. In her notes to the section entitled "The Little People" in *Friends of Thunder* (1964), Anna G. Kilpatrick, the Cherokee folklorist, comments that she and her husband Jack F. Kilpatrick have collected "a sheaf of anecdotes relating to encounters with the Little People either by persons known to the narrator or, in one case, by the narrator herself." She adds, "to the average Cherokee with some degree of traditional upbringing, the existence of the Little People is an indisputable fact." According to Kilpatrick, the Oklahoma Cherokee don't seem to feel that any danger is associated with these encounters except "the danger of becoming fascinated by them and following them off to unpredictable adventures." Nor, it seems, are these encounters confined to Cherokee people. Deer Woman has shown up at dances among Kiowa and Chocktaws, or so some stories I've been told assert. Maybe she and the other Yunwitsansdi moved to Oklahoma (which was to be Indian territory "as long as the grass should grow," so the broken treaties proclaimed) during the great removal period in the early nineteenth century. At that time, almost all the nations and tribes of the American Southeast, along with a number from the Prairies, were compelled to leave their own lands and take up residence hundreds of miles inland. In the latter part of the nineteenth century, many tribes and bands from the West and the Southwest were also forced to move to the region, by then part of eastern Oklahoma.

My rendition of the Deer Woman story is composed from a combination of stories I have read and been told by witnesses or friends of witnesses of encounters with Deer Woman. I have included some details in this account from my own encounters with the shadowy Yunwitsansdi, who are often described as being "three feet tall."

1. **ephemeral** (i-fĕm′ ər-əl): elusive and quick to vanish.

RESPONDING OPTIONS

FROM PERSONAL RESPONSE *TO* CRITICAL ANALYSIS

REFLECT 1. What questions do you still have about this story? Review what you wrote in your reading log, and discuss any unanswered questions in class.

RETHINK 2. What do you think has happened to Jackie? Give reasons for your answer.

3. What are your impressions of life inside the mountain?

   Consider
   - who lives inside the mountain
   - what activities take place there
   - why Jackie and Ray may have been brought there

4. Which elements of the story seem traditional, and which seem contemporary? Does the writer successfully harmonize old and new?

RELATE 5. What does the Insight selection "About Deer Woman" add to your understanding?

6. In your view, what does the story seem to warn against?

7. What other reports of supernatural experiences in the modern world have you heard? What is your reaction to such reports?

ANOTHER PATHWAY

Cooperative Learning

With four classmates, brainstorm ideas for a movie version of "Deer Woman." Divide the responsibilities of the following positions among the members of the group: screenwriter, production designer, cinematographer, music director, casting director. Then write up your ideas as an informal proposal.

LITERARY CONCEPTS

The **narrator** of a story is the character or voice that relates the story's events to the reader. When the narrator is a character in the story who tells everything in his or her own words, the story is said to be told from the **first-person point of view.** A first-person narrator uses pronouns like *I* and *me.* When a story is told by a narrator who stands outside the action and is not one of the characters, the story is said to be told from the **third-person point of view.** A third-person narrator uses pronouns like *he, she,* and *they.*

Which point of view is used at the beginning of "Deer Woman," and which is used at the end? Identify the point at which the narration changes, and discuss the effect of this change.

QUICKWRITES

1. Draft an **article** about Jackie's disappearance for a tabloid newspaper. If you like, include a description of his life inside the mountain, along with a touched-up photograph or an illustration. Share your article with classmates.
2. "Deer Woman" is a contemporary version of a traditional tale. Write an outline for a **story** that updates a traditional story you know, such as the one you summarized for the Personal Connection on page 53.

PORTFOLIO *Save your writing. You may want to use it later as a springboard to a piece for your portfolio.*

CRITIC'S CORNER

Commenting on "Deer Woman," Shericko Davis, a member of our student board, wrote: "What I like least ... is the end, which I guess is from the author after she has told the story. This part of the selection is confusing, and I feel that it should have ended differently." How would you respond to this student?

ART CONNECTION

Look again at the photographs in this selection. How do these photographs and the story "Deer Woman" suggest similar ideas about the world?

Detail of *Untitled* (1986), Jerry Uelsmann.
Copyright © 1986 Jerry Uelsmann.

WORDS TO KNOW

Review the Words to Know at the bottom of the selection pages. Then write the vocabulary word that best replaces the italicized word or phrase in each sentence below.

1. The loud *merrymaker* will probably keep the neighbors awake all night.
2. A *mob* gathered at the stomp dance.
3. Where did you decide to *meet* with your old friend Jackie?
4. Linda and Junella were *respectful* toward the river, praying to it every day.
5. Ray and Jackie showed their *yieldingness* as they followed every suggestion the women made.
6. Although Linda looks like other women at the dance, there is something *very slightly* different about her.
7. With their old-fashioned clothes and ways, the women seemed to be Cherokee tradition *given human shape*.
8. Speaking to Jackie, the old one said *jokingly,* "Wait until tomorrow's games!"
9. Ray *uneasily* told his anxious family about his adventure with the Deer Woman.
10. According to legend, young men are *defenseless* when they meet Deer Woman.

PAULA GUNN ALLEN

Poet, critic, novelist, and short story writer Paula Gunn Allen was born in 1939 on the Cubero land grant in New Mexico, near Laguna pueblo. Because Allen is of mixed Laguna, Sioux, Scottish, and Lebanese ancestry, much of her work reflects the influence of a variety of cultures. As she said in an interview, "My poetry has a haunted sense to it and it has a sorrow and a grievingness in it that comes directly from being split, not in two but in twenty, and never being able to reconcile all the places that I am."

Like her cousin from Laguna pueblo, Leslie Marmon Silko, Allen believes that old stories should not be preserved in a rigid form but should change as they are carried into the future: "Storytellers, in the way of the Pueblo potters, take those storysherds, grind and mix them into new contexts. They shape the fragments of the old into new stories, strong yet part of all that has gone before."

Allen is a professor of English at the University of California, Berkeley.

OTHER WORKS *Spider Woman's Granddaughters* (ed.), *Grandmothers of the Light: A Medicine Woman's Sourcebook, Skins and Bones, The Woman Who Owned the Shadows*

LASERLINKS
• *AUTHOR BACKGROUND*

My Father's Song

SIMON J. ORTIZ

Wanting to say things,
I miss my father tonight.
His voice, the slight catch,
the depth from his thin chest,
the tremble of emotion
in something he has just said
to his son, his song:

We planted corn one Spring at Acu[1]—
we planted several times
but this one particular time
I remember the soft damp sand
in my hand.

My father had stopped at one point
to show me an overturned furrow;[2]
the plowshare[3] had unearthed
the burrow nest of a mouse
in the soft moist sand.

Very gently, he scooped tiny pink animals
into the palm of his hand
and told me to touch them.
We took them to the edge
of the field and put them in the shade
of a sand moist clod.

I remember the very softness
of cool and warm sand and tiny alive mice
and my father saying things.

---

1. **Acu** (ä'ko͞o): the Acoma people's name for the Acoma pueblo.
2. **furrow:** a long, shallow trench made in the ground by a plow.
3. **plowshare:** the cutting blade of a plow.

Copyright © 1991 Greg Spalenka/The Image Bank, Chicago.

Simon J. Ortiz

1941–

Simon J. Ortiz was born in Albuquerque, New Mexico, and raised in the Acoma Pueblo community about 65 miles to the west. He attended Bureau of Indian Affairs and Roman Catholic elementary schools and a public high school, continuing his education at the University of New Mexico and the University of Iowa. Although best known as a poet, he has also written short stories and essays and has edited anthologies of Native American writing.

Ortiz, who has worked as a baker's helper, a clerk, a laborer, a soldier in the U.S. Army, and a university professor, had his first poem published when he was in the fifth grade. In part, he attributes his love of words to his father, who sang and talked to his son as he worked. Ortiz told an interviewer that his father "was a good singer in Acoma, in English, in Spanish, and in other languages like Zuni and some Navajo. He had a beautiful voice. He was an inspiration to me."

Ortiz also traces his love of words to his Native American heritage. He has said, "The voices of the stories, poems, songs are as old as Acu, which is my home. What I do is listen and watch as carefully as I am able and then tell what happens. The source of my writing comes from my community and people."

OTHER WORKS *Going for the Rain, Woven Stone, Fightin', Howbah Indians*

WRITING ABOUT
LITERATURE

AN EYE FOR DETAIL

Did you notice how Leslie Marmon Silko and Paula Gunn Allen use details to make images vivid and explanations clear? In books, movies, TV, even in daily life, it's the details that draw you in. It's the special effects that make a movie vivid and exciting. It's what you put in your locker that makes the locker clearly yours. On the following pages you will

- study how authors use different types of details
- infer ideas about a people's customs and beliefs
- use details to observe and adjust to new situations

The Writer's Style: Adding Details Good writers use details to paint pictures and to elaborate. Some details are sensory; others are more factual. But all details provide information.

Read the Literature

Notice how these writers use sensory details to create a scene.

Literature Models

Can You See It?
Which details appeal to a reader's sense of sight?

They found him under a big cottonwood tree. His Levi jacket and pants were faded light-blue so that he had been easy to find. The big cottonwood tree stood apart from a small grove of winterbare cottonwoods which grew in the wide, sandy arroyo.

Leslie Marmon Silko
from "The Man to Send Rain Clouds"

Can You Hear It?
Which details capture the sounds of this special party?

The dance was going strong, and the sound of turtle shell and aluminum can rattles and singing, mixed with occasional laughter and bits of talk, reached their ears. "Alright!" exclaimed Ray, the taller and heavier of the two, slapping his buddy's raised hand in glee.

Paula Gunn Allen
from "Deer Woman"

Connect to Life

Magazines, newspapers, films, and television use a variety of visual and verbal details. When describing unfamiliar events, objects, or processes, the media use facts, statistics, examples, and quotations to make their explanations clear. What kinds of details does this article use?

Magazine Article

"Rain is life," comments Gary Roybal of San Ildefonso Pueblo, a village alongside the Rio Grande. People have lived in the area around the Rio Grande and its tributaries since at least A.D. 1100, but it is a comparatively dry region; rainfall is approximately 15 inches annually and water is a highly prized and contested commodity.

Ann Marshall
from "Rain"
Native Peoples, Summer 1993

Can You Understand It?
How does this article use statistics and quotations to stress the importance of rain?

Try Your Hand: Adding Details

1. **Add On the Details** Create vivid images by adding at least three details to each of these sentences.
   - She lifted the squash flowers to her nose.
   - Ken tasted the coffee.
   - The two of them stood and watched the clouds.
2. **Sense It** In a small group, ask someone to select an object and to pass it around. Ask each person to come up with a different detail to describe the object. Keep going until the group runs out of new details to describe it.
3. **Describe It** Using details, write a paragraph describing something unique or interesting about your culture. It might be a food you eat, a special event you attend, or a holiday you celebrate. Help the reader experience your culture too.

SkillBuilder

GRAMMAR FROM WRITING

Using Commas with a Series of Adjectives
When you add details, several adjectives often end up together in a sentence. In most cases, punctuating two or more adjectives is like punctuating any other series—you add a comma after each adjective. For example, Silko uses a comma as she describes "the wide, sandy arroyo." However, there are exceptions.

- If a modifier describes another adjective, rather than a noun, no comma is needed (e.g., the clear glass bottle).
- If the adjective describes number, size, shape, color, or age, no comma is needed (e.g., the brown wrinkled forehead).

APPLYING WHAT YOU'VE LEARNED
Copy the following sentences onto a separate sheet of paper. Add commas where needed.

1. He slid down the steep crumbling sandy bank.
2. They dressed him in a new brown flannel shirt.
3. Eight tired relatives all gathered to say goodbye to the tiny wrapped body.
4. Ken drove his uncle's old red pickup truck.

GRAMMAR HANDBOOK

For more information on using commas in a series, see pages 1235–1236 of the Grammar Handbook.

Interpretation

Literature sometimes provides information that helps you infer ideas about other people and appreciate their cultures. If you look closely, the selections in this unit give you a picture of the beliefs, customs, and behavior of several different Native American cultures.

GUIDED ASSIGNMENT

Write an Interpretive Essay Your assignment is to examine the details in one or more of the selections in this unit to gain an understanding of the cultures that are portrayed. Combine your own knowledge with any new information the details provide. Then write your interpretation of what the details mean and what they reveal about the people.

Student's Prewriting Questions

RAIN CLOUDS
Leslie Marmon Silko
Why corn meal?
I've never seen this done before.
Do they really think he can make rain?

1 Prewrite and Explore

Think about the selections you've just read. Which ones contain cultural details that sparked your interest, impressed you, or taught you something? Which do you have the most questions about? Choose one or two selections that present you with the clearest picture of another way of life.

RECORD YOUR REACTIONS

Read through the selection again. As you read, use self-sticking notes to comment on details that describe or explain the people and their culture. Identify any significant details that

- raise questions
- support what you know
- differ from details about your own culture
- cause you to recall an experience you've had
- have an impact on you

Decision Point Look back over your notes. Which significant details will you use to infer ideas about one or more aspects of a culture?

2 Freewrite and Discover

Now it's time to explore the details you have chosen. Open your notebook log and start freewriting. Jot down anything suggested by your notes. You may also want to ask yourself

- What does this detail suggest about the culture?
- What evidence supports my interpretation?

Notice this student's first try at freewriting.

Student's Notebook

Silko mentions the corn meal several times in "The Man to Send Rain Clouds" so it must have some importance. Corn is a staple in some diets. Some southwest cultures use corn meal to make tortillas and other foods. Corn meal could be their bread of life. I remember that Egyptians provided food for the afterlife. Maybe the corn meal provides the old man with food for the next life.

3 Draft and Share

Are you ready to write a more focused draft? Keep in mind that your essay should include

- an introduction that identifies the selection by author and title and briefly describes the story
- a body that describes the details you selected and the inferences you made; each paragraph could deal with a different inference
- a conclusion that explains what you think the details say about the people and their culture

You may want to do some research or find someone knowledgeable about the culture, to confirm or correct your inferences. When you've finished, invite other students to look at your draft. Be open to their suggestions. But realize that there are many different interpretations of a selection—no one interpretation is correct.

PEER RESPONSE

- What parts, if any, of my interpretation are unclear?
- What interpretations do you see that I haven't considered?

SkillBuilder

CRITICAL THINKING

Making Inferences

When you make an inference, you make an educated guess. You start with several details. The details might be remarks someone makes or action someone takes. You think about what those details might mean. Then you use everything you know about the details to draw a conclusion.

For example, in "The Man to Send Rain Clouds," Silko never explains why Ken tied a gray feather in the old man's hair. Knowing that eagle feathers are important to some Native American cultures, you might infer that the feather is used to transport Teofilo to the next world—raising him up on eagle's wings.

Each time you read the selection, you're likely to make new inferences and change some of your old ones.

APPLYING WHAT YOU'VE LEARNED

Discuss the following items in a small group.

- Choose a detail from one of the selections. See how many inferences you can make about that detail.
- Draw a thought web to show the steps and processes you went through to reach your conclusion.

4 Revise and Edit

Consider the Standards for Evaluation at the bottom of this page as you revise and edit your essay. You may also want to review Grammar in Context on the opposite page. Then revise and edit your draft. Can you think of a unique way to publish your essay?

Student's Final Draft

Gray Feathers and Corn Meal

When would a gray feather be used in a funeral? Why would corn meal be sprinkled on a blanket? In "The Man to Send Rain Clouds," both of these customs are used by a group of Native Americans who are burying a loved one. From the tying of a gray feather in the old man's hair to the sprinkling of the corn meal, Leslie Marmon Silko paints a very special picture of this culture.

How does the introduction provide an overview of the essay?

How does the use of details support this interpretation?

When my grandfather died, we dressed him in a blue suit and tie. When Teofilo dies, Ken and Leon tie a gray feather in his hair. Why a feather? Many Native American cultures hold the eagle in high esteem. According to Charlie Knight, a Ute medicine man, an eagle feather will "help you find the right path." If corn meal and pollen are sent as food for the afterlife, it is possible that the feather is sent to help Teofilo find his way to the next world.

How does the quotation add credibility and new information? Are there any personal examples you could use in your own essay?

Standards for Evaluation

An interpretive essay
- identifies the work by title and author in the introduction and briefly describes its contents
- presents a plausible, well-organized interpretation of one or two aspects of the work
- supports the interpretation with evidence and with details and quotations from the selection

Grammar in Context

Misplaced Modifiers When you add details to support your interpretation, you'll probably use phrases and clauses to describe or modify. When a modifier is separated from the word it modifies, it is misplaced. A misplaced modifier can be confusing, or it can change the meaning of the entire sentence.

> ~~Wrapping up the tiny body,~~ Holy water is sprinkled on the red blanket *wrapping up the tiny body*. But why a red blanket? What does the red represent? Was the author thinking *of the color of blood* when she chose red? ~~of the color of blood? Indicating a chance of rain,~~ Was she thinking of brilliant red skies *indicating a chance of rain*? Or was Silko merely thinking of her favorite color!

In the example above, notice how the sentences were changed. The modifiers were moved as close as possible to the words they modify, reducing the chance of confusion.

Try Your Hand: Correcting Misplaced Modifiers

On a separate sheet of paper, rewrite the following sentences so that the modifiers modify the correct word.

1. He bumped into a cottonwood tree thinking about the beauty of the arroyo.
2. Working alone at the sheep camp, a gray feather caught Teofilo's eye.
3. Scattered up and down the arroyo, Leon and Ken gathered the sheep.

SkillBuilder

GRAMMAR FROM WRITING

Using Adverb Phrases
Have you ever used an adverb phrase to add detail? **Adverb phrases** are prepositional phrases that modify a verb, an adjective, or an adverb. Since they act like an adverb, they tell when, where, how, or to what extent. They're a great way to add precision to your writing. Notice how Silko uses adverb phrases to describe when and where.

They turned off the highway onto the sandy pueblo road. Not long after they passed the store and post office they saw Father Paul's car coming toward them.

You don't need to worry about misplacing adverb phrases that modify a verb. They can appear almost anywhere in a sentence.

APPLYING WHAT YOU'VE LEARNED
Complete the following sentences with an adverb phrase.

1. They drove . . . (where?)
2. The rain came . . . (when?)
3. Ken and Leon wrapped him . . . (how?)
4. The wind blew . . . (to what extent?)

GRAMMAR HANDBOOK

For more information about modifiers, see pages 1218–1222 of the Grammar Handbook.

R E A D I N G
THE WORLD

Culture Shock

You've been to cemeteries—maybe you've gone to funerals or you've visited a relative's grave. But nothing prepared you for this funeral in New Orleans. What do you do?

View Look closely at the situation pictured. Focus on the details. What do you see? Are there any clues about how you're expected to behave? Should you join in the funeral procession? Should you talk? Is it okay to smile? Is it okay to cry?

Interpret How does this situation make you feel? Would you feel comfortable at a funeral like this? What details about this situation are appealing to you? What details are unappealing? Is it similar to any other events you've seen?

Discuss In a group, compare the clues you've generated. Did some people notice different things about the situation than you did? Take into consideration the new information. Does it change your ideas about how to behave? Use the SkillBuilder on the right to analyze your information.

SkillBuilder

CRITICAL THINKING

Analyzing Differences

There's an old saying, "When in Rome, do as the Romans do." It's a reminder to be sensitive to the customs of other cultures.

For example, the way other people honor their dead might be new to you. Some Native Americans sprinkle corn meal and pollen on the dead. Some Irish Americans throw a partylike wake. Some Mexican Americans celebrate the Day of the Dead every year.

When you find yourself in a situation that's new and different, learn how to read the details. Look at the expressions on people's faces. Notice what they're doing and how they're doing it. Use this information to make inferences about their beliefs and customs. Also use the information to determine what you should do and how you should act.

APPLYING WHAT YOU'VE LEARNED

Try one or more of the following in a small group.

- Discuss times you've experienced a culturally different way of doing things. How did you adjust?
- Brainstorm a list of coping strategies—ways to adjust when you experience "culture shock."

PART 2 INTRODUCTION

First Encounters

Accounts of Exploration and Exploitation

When Christopher Columbus landed on a tiny Caribbean island in 1492, he called the inhabitants Indians because he thought he was near the East Indies. One of the first men to try to communicate with Columbus inadvertently cut his hand on Columbus's sword because he didn't know what a sword was. Such events—mistaken identity and injury—marked the first recorded encounter between the native people of the Americas and the Europeans who were to come in increasing numbers over the next 500 years.

Although the first explorers' motivations for coming to the Americas were complex, many came for the reason people often seek out dangers and challenges: a desire for fame and adventure. In addition, the early explorers expected to find great riches. European rulers had already sent explorers to India and China to bring back spices, silks, gold, jewelry, and other luxuries. Columbus, of course, was looking for a shortcut to these countries when he unexpectedly bumped into a new world. Once the European monarchs realized that Columbus had led the way to two previously unknown continents, they put their best explorers to work finding out what wealth they could gain from these new lands.

Not all motivations for coming to the Americas were selfish ones, however. Reports of the existence of people in the Americas stirred many to come to spread Christianity. Others, such as the English Puritans, came seeking the religious freedom that they were denied

The Landing of Columbus at San Salvador (Guanahani), October 12, 1492. The Granger Collection.

in their homeland. Nevertheless, for both Catholics and Protestants, Christianity was the only true religion. People who were not Christian had to be converted by persuasion or by force. Those who rejected Christianity were considered enemies of God, suitable only for enslavement or death.

The story of cultural contact, like the story of America itself, would not be complete without the experiences of the Africans who were brought here as slaves. The European trade in African slaves had been started by the Portuguese during the 1400s, and African slaves accompanied most of the Spanish and Portuguese explorers in the Americas. In fact, one of the three men who survived with Cabeza de Vaca on his disastrous journey was an African slave named Estéban.

Africans were first brought in large numbers to the West Indies to provide labor for the vast sugar plantations. At first, the Spanish plantation owners had tried to use Indian labor, but the native peoples proved too susceptible to European diseases and unable to withstand the harsh treatment of their masters. Africans took their place. Before long, English colonists were also participating in the slave trade. In 1619, twelve years after the founding of Jamestown, Virginia—the first permanent English settlement in the Americas—20 African slaves were brought there to be sold. Eighteen years later, the first

Voices from the Times

from *The Log of Christopher Columbus*

Friday, October 12, 1492

No sooner had we concluded the formalities of taking possession of the island than people began to come to the beach, all as naked as their mothers bore them, and the women also, although I did not see more than one very young girl. All those that I saw were young people, none of whom was over 30 years old. They are very well-built people, with handsome bodies and very fine faces, though their appearance is marred somewhat by very broad heads and foreheads, more so than I have ever seen in any other race. Their eyes are large and very pretty, and their skin is the color of Canary Islanders or of sunburned peasants, not at all black, as would be expected because we are on an east-west line with Hierro in the Canaries. These are tall people and their legs, with no exceptions, are quite straight, and none of them has a paunch. They are, in fact, well proportioned. Their hair is not kinky, but straight, and coarse like horsehair. They wear it short over the eyebrows, but they have a long hank in the back that they never cut. Many of the natives paint their faces; others paint their whole bodies; some, only the eyes or nose. Some are painted black, some white, some red; others are of different colors.

The people here called this island *Guanahaní* in their language, and their speech is very fluent, although I do not understand any of it. They are friendly and well-dispositioned people who bear no arms except for small spears, and they have no iron. I showed one my sword, and through ignorance he grabbed it by the blade and cut himself. Their spears are made of wood, to which they attach a fish tooth at one end, or some other sharp thing.

Voices *from the* TIMES

I want the natives to develop a friendly attitude toward us because I know that they are a people who can be made free and converted to our Holy Faith more by love than by force. I therefore gave red caps to some and glass beads to others. They hung the beads around their necks, along with some other things of slight value that I gave them. And they took great pleasure in this and became so friendly that it was a marvel. They traded and gave everything they had with good will, but it seems to me that they have very little and are poor in everything. I warned my men to take nothing from the people without giving something in exchange.

This afternoon the people of San Salvador[1] came swimming to our ships and in boats made from one log. They brought us parrots, balls of cotton thread, spears, and many other things, including a kind of dry leaf[2] that they hold in great esteem. For these items we swapped them little glass beads and hawks' bells.

Many of the men I have seen have scars on their bodies, and when I made signs to them to find out how this happened, they indicated that people from other nearby islands come to San Salvador to capture them; they defend themselves the best they can. I believe that people from the mainland come here to take them as slaves. They ought to make good and skilled servants, for they repeat very quickly whatever we say to them. I think they can easily be made Christians, for they seem to have no religion. If it pleases Our Lord, I will take six of them to Your Highnesses when I depart, in order that they may learn our language.

Translated by Robert H. Fuson

1. San Salvador (săn săl'və-dôr'): the name that Columbus gave the island he first landed on; it means "Holy Savior" in Spanish.
2. dry leaf: tobacco

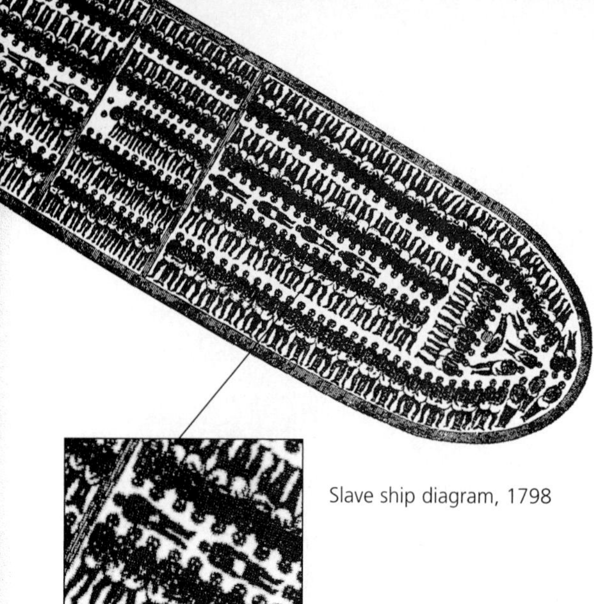

Slave ship diagram, 1798

American-built slave ship, the *Desire,* set sail from Marblehead, Massachusetts.

One of the few firsthand accounts of the perilous two months that African slaves spent packed in ships bound for the Americas is that of Olaudah Equiano. You will read about his experiences in this part of the unit.

Continuity & Change: The New Explorers

The tradition of writing about the exploration of a new place and what is encountered there has continued up to the present day. But what, you might ask, is left to explore in a world of jet propulsion, TV, computers, and fiber optics? In the remaining selections in this part of Unit One, you will read about some contemporary explorations: William Least Heat-Moon's exploration of forgotten areas of his own country; Maya Angelou's journey across the ocean to discover the Africa of her ancestors; and, in an unusual science fiction story, Terry Bisson's "visit" to outer space to eavesdrop on a very interesting conversation.

PART 2 *First Encounters*

Accounts of Exploration and Exploitation

PREVIEWING

NONFICTION

from La Relación

Álvar Núñez Cabeza de Vaca

(äl′vär no͞o′nyĕs kä-bĕ′sä dĕ vä′kä)

Francisco Pizarro

PERSONAL CONNECTION

Think about famous conquistadors you have learned about in school—perhaps Cortés, who defeated the Aztecs, or Pizarro, who conquered the Incas. What image do you have of conquistadors? What did they look like? How did they act? Jot down ideas or draw a picture in your notebook, then share your ideas or drawing with classmates.

HISTORICAL CONNECTION

In 1527, Pánfilo de Narváez, a Spanish conquistador, led a five-ship, 600-man expedition to Florida. His second in command was Álvar Núñez Cabeza de Vaca. The expedition was a disaster from the moment the Spaniards entered the Caribbean. After the loss of two ships in a hurricane and of more than 200 men by drowning and desertion, the Narváez expedition finally made its way to the west coast of Florida. Against the advice of Cabeza de Vaca, Narváez separated 300 of his men from the ships and marched these forces overland. Narváez intended for the ships to meet the land forces at a Spanish settlement on the coast of central Mexico, but he had grossly underestimated the vastness of the territory and the difficulty of crossing it. Eventually, overwhelmed by hunger, disease, and Indian attacks, the land forces decided to build five crude barges to get them to Mexico more quickly. These barges, each carrying about 50 men, soon drifted apart, and the one commanded by Cabeza de Vaca was shipwrecked on Galveston Island, off the coast of what is now Texas.

Ultimately, Cabeza de Vaca and three companions were the only survivors of the Narváez expedition. They wandered for more than eight years before reaching Mexico City, thus becoming the first Europeans to cross North America. After returning to Spain in 1537, Cabeza de Vaca wrote *La Relación,* a report addressed to the king of Spain.

WRITING CONNECTION

Think about a time when you faced a serious challenge. Perhaps you competed in a tournament, an audition, or a hard-fought sporting event. You may have even lived through a natural disaster or a daring rescue. Write about the challenge you faced, and as you read, compare your experience to Cabeza de Vaca's.

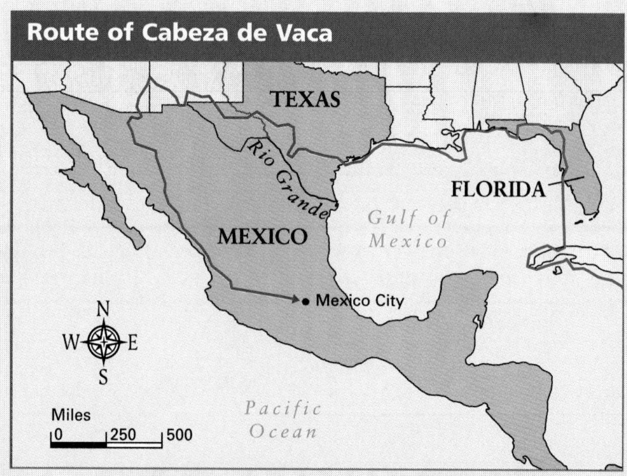

Álvar Núñez Cabeza de Vaca

from

La Relación

At this point in the account, Narvaez's barge has abandoned the rest, and Cabeza de Vaca's barge has joined one commanded by two other officers. The next three chapters describe the crew's shipwreck on Galveston Island and their encounter with the Karankawa Indians who lived there.

A Sinking and a Landing

Our two barges continued in company for four days, each man eating a ration of half a handful of raw corn a day. Then the other barge was lost in a storm. Nothing but God's great mercy kept us from going down, too.

It was winter and bitterly cold, and we had suffered hunger and the heavy beating of the waves for many days. Next day, the men began to collapse. By sunset, all in my barge had fallen over on one another, close to death. Few were any longer conscious. Not five could stand. When night fell, only the navigator and I remained able to tend the barge. Two hours after dark he told me I must take over; he believed he was going to die that night.

So I took the tiller.[1] After midnight I moved over to see if he were dead. He said no, in fact was better, and would steer till daylight. In that hour I would have welcomed death rather than see so many around me in such a condition. When I had returned the helm[2] to the navigator, I lay down to rest—but without much rest, for nothing was farther from my mind than sleep.

Near dawn I seemed to hear breakers[3] resounding; the coast lying low, they roared louder. Surprised at this, I called to the navigator, who said he thought we were coming close to land. We sounded[4] and found ourselves in seven fathoms.[5] The navigator felt we should stay clear of the shore till daylight; so I took an oar and pulled it on the shore side, wheeling the stern to seaward about a league[6] out.

As we drifted into shore, a wave caught us and heaved the barge a horseshoe-throw [about 42 feet] out of the water. The jolt when it hit brought the dead-looking men to. Seeing land at hand, they crawled through the surf to some rocks. Here we made a fire and parched some of our corn. We also found rain water. The men began to regain their senses, their locomotion, and their hope.

This day of our landing was November 6.

What Befell Oviedo with the Indians

After we ate, I ordered Lope de Oviedo, our strongest man, to climb one of the trees not far off and ascertain the lay of the land. He complied and found out from the treetop that we were on

1. **tiller:** a lever used to turn a rudder and steer a boat.
2. **helm:** the steering gear of a boat.
3. **breakers:** waves breaking against a shoreline.
4. **sounded:** measured the depth of the water.
5. **fathoms** (făth′əmz): units used in measuring the depth of water; a fathom is equal to 6 feet (1.83 meters).
6. **league:** a unit of distance; Cabeza de Vaca probably used the Spanish league, equal to 3.1 miles (5 kilometers).

WORDS TO KNOW **comply** (kəm-plī′) *v.* to obey another's command, request, rule, or wish

Indians forced to carry baggage and supplies of the Spanish invaders (1590), Theodor de Bry. Rare Books and Manuscripts Division, The New York Public Library, Astor, Lenox, and Tilden Foundations.

an island. [This was Galveston Island.] He also said that the ground looked as if cattle had trampled it and therefore that this must be a country of Christians.

I sent him back for a closer look, to see if he could find any worn trails, but warned him not to risk going too far. He went and came upon a path which he followed for half a league to some empty huts. The Indians were gone to shoal-flats[7] [to dig roots]. He took an earthen pot, a little dog, and a few mullets[8] and started back.

We had begun to worry what might have happened to him, so I detailed another two men to check. They met him shortly and saw three Indians with bows and arrows following him. The Indians were calling to him and he was gesturing them to keep coming. When he reached us, the Indians held back and sat down on the shore.

Half an hour later a hundred bowmen reinforced the first three individuals. Whatever their stature, they looked like giants to us in our fright. We could not hope to defend ourselves; not half a dozen of us could even stand up.

The Inspector [Solís] and I walked out and greeted them. They advanced, and we did our best to placate and ingratiate. We gave them beads and bells, and each one of them gave us an arrow in pledge of friendship. They told us by signs that they would return at sunrise and bring food, having none then.

The Indians' Hospitality Before and After a New Calamity

As the sun rose next morning, the Indians appeared as they promised, bringing an abundance of fish and of certain roots which taste like nuts, some bigger than walnuts, some smaller, mostly grubbed from the water with great labor.

That evening they came again with more fish and roots and brought their women and children to look at us. They thought themselves rich with the little bells and beads we gave them, and they repeated their visits on other days.

Being provided with what we needed, we thought to embark again. It was a struggle to dig our barge out of the sand it had sunk in, and another struggle to launch her. For the work in the water while launching, we stripped and stowed our clothes in the craft.

---

7. **shoal-flats:** stretches of level ground under shallow water.

8. **mullets** (mŭl'ĭts): a kind of edible fish.

WORDS TO KNOW

placate (plā'kāt') *v.* to soothe another's feelings; appease
ingratiate (ĭn-grā'shē-āt') *v.* to gain another's favor by deliberate effort

Quickly clambering in and grabbing our oars, we had rowed two crossbow shots from shore when a wave inundated us. Being naked and the cold intense, we let our oars go. The next big wave capsized the barge. The Inspector and two others held fast, but that only carried them more certainly underneath, where they drowned.

A single roll of the sea tossed the rest of the men into the rushing surf and back onto shore half-drowned.

We lost only those the barge took down; but the survivors escaped as naked as they were born, with the loss of everything we had. That was not much, but valuable to us in that bitter November cold, our bodies so emaciated we could easily count every bone and looked the very picture of death. I can say for myself that from the month of May I had eaten nothing but corn, and that sometimes raw. I never could bring myself to eat any of the horse-meat at the time our beasts were slaughtered; and fish I did not taste ten times. On top of everything else, a cruel north wind commenced to complete our killing.

The Lord willed that we should find embers while searching the remnants of our former fire. We found more wood and soon had big fires raging. Before them, with flowing tears, we prayed for mercy and pardon, each filled with pity not only for himself but for all his wretched fellows.

At sunset the Indians, not knowing we had gone, came again with food. When they saw us looking so strangely different, they turned back in alarm. I went after them calling, and they returned, though frightened. I explained to them by signs that our barge had sunk and three of our number drowned. They could see at their feet two of the dead men who had washed ashore. They could also see that the rest of us were not far from joining these two.

The Indians, understanding our full plight, sat down and lamented for half an hour so loudly they could have been heard a long way off. It was amazing to see these wild, untaught savages howling like brutes in compassion for us. It intensified my own grief at our calamity and had the same effect on the other victims.

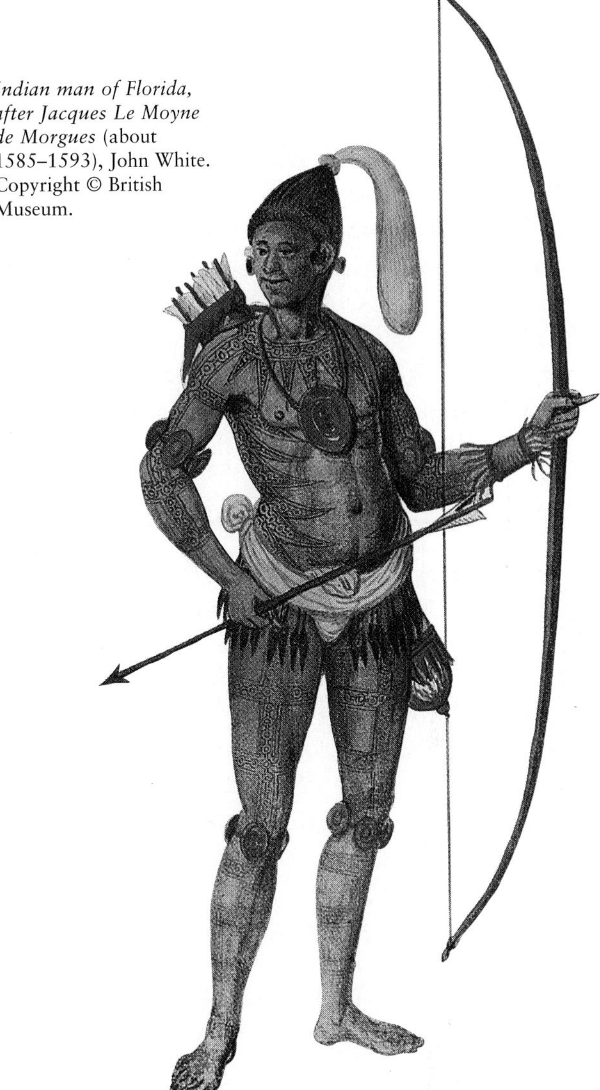

Indian man of Florida, after Jacques Le Moyne de Morgues (about 1585–1593), John White. Copyright © British Museum.

When the cries died down, I conferred with the Christians about asking the Indians to take us to their homes. Some of our number who had been to New Spain warned that the Indians would sacrifice us to their idols.[9] But death being surer and nearer if we stayed where we were, I

9. **New Spain . . . their idols:** New Spain included what is now the southwest United States, Mexico, Central America north of Panama, and some West Indian islands. In Mexico, conquistadors had encountered Aztecs who practiced human sacrifice.

WORDS TO KNOW

inundate (ĭn'ŭn-dāt') *v.* to cover with water; overwhelm

lament (lə-mĕnt') *v.* to grieve; wail

went ahead and beseeched the Indians. They were delighted. They told us to tarry a little while, then they would do as we wished.

Presently thirty of them gathered loads of wood and disappeared to their huts, which were a long walk away; while we waited with the remainder until near nightfall. Then, supporting us under our arms, they hurried us from one to another of the four big fires they had built along the path. At each fire, when we regained a little warmth and strength, they took us on so swiftly our feet hardly touched ground.

Thus we made their village, where we saw they had erected a hut for us with many fires inside. An hour later they began a dance celebration that lasted all night. For us there was no joy, feasting, or sleep, as we waited the hour they should make us victims.

In the morning, when they brought us fish and roots and acted in every way hospitably, we felt reassured and somewhat lost our anxiety of the sacrificial knife.

CABEZA DE VACA learned that men from one of the other barges had also landed on the island, bringing the number of Europeans there to about 90. In a matter of weeks, all but 16 of them died of disease, which spread to the Karankawas and killed half of them as well. Some of the Karankawas wanted to put the remaining Europeans to death but were dissuaded by Cabeza de Vaca's host. Cabeza de Vaca and his men were later forced to act as healers.

How We Became Medicine-Men

The islanders wanted to make physicians of us without examination or a review of diplomas. Their method of cure is to blow on the sick, the breath and the laying-on of hands supposedly casting out the infirmity. They insisted we should do this too and be of some use to them. We scoffed at their cures and at the idea we knew how to heal. But they withheld food from us until we complied. An Indian told me I knew not whereof I spoke in saying their methods had no effect. Stones and other things growing about in the fields, he said, had a virtue whereby passing a pebble along the stomach could take away pain and heal; surely extraordinary men like us embodied such powers over nature. Hunger forced us to obey, but disclaiming any responsibility for our failure or success.

An Indian, falling sick, would send for a medicine-man, who would apply his cure. The patient would then give the medicine-man all he had and seek more from his relatives to give. The medicine-man makes incisions over the point of the pain, sucks the wound, and cauterizes it. This remedy enjoys high repute among the Indians. I have, as a matter of fact, tried it on myself with good results. The medicine-men blow on the spot they have treated, as a finishing touch, and the patient regards himself relieved.

Our method, however, was to bless the sick, breathe upon them, recite a *Pater noster* and *Ave Maria,*[10] and pray earnestly to God our Lord for their recovery. When we concluded with the sign of the cross, He willed that our patients should directly spread the news that they had been restored to health.

In consequence, the Indians treated us kindly. They deprived themselves of food to give to us, and presented us skins and other tokens of gratitude. ❖

Translated by Cyclone Covey

10. ***Pater noster*** (pä′tər-nŏs′tər) **and *Ave Maria*** (ä′vā mə-rē′ə): the Lord's Prayer and the Hail Mary, so called from the prayers' opening words in Latin.

WORDS TO KNOW

beseech (bĭ-sēch′) *v.* to implore; beg
infirmity (ĭn-fûr′mĭ-tē) *n.* a sickness or weakness
scoff (skŏf) *v.* to mock
embody (ĕm-bŏd′ē) *v.* to represent in bodily form
cauterize (kô′tə-rīz′) *v.* to burn or sear to destroy abnormal tissue

RESPONDING OPTIONS

FROM PERSONAL RESPONSE *TO* CRITICAL ANALYSIS

REFLECT 1. What event or idea in Cabeza de Vaca's account struck you most? Write it down in your notebook and share it with classmates.

RETHINK 2. How closely do Cabeza de Vaca and his men fit your image of conquistadors?

3. What can you infer about the feelings of Cabeza de Vaca and his men as they went through their ordeals?

4. How would you say Cabeza de Vaca and his men viewed themselves in relation to the Karankawa Indians in this first encounter?

Consider
- the reason Lope de Oviedo assumed that the island was a country of Christians
- the terms Cabeza de Vaca uses to describe his men, and those he uses to describe the Karankawas
- Cabeza de Vaca's opinion of the Karankawas' method of healing

5. How do you think the Karankawas viewed Cabeza de Vaca and his men?What parts of the report support your interpretation?

RELATE 6. Sixteenth-century conquistadors described, mapped, and claimed territory that was previously unknown to them. They also replaced traditional belief systems with their own. Who are the present-day equivalents of conquistadors, and what do they explore or conquer?

LITERARY LINKS

At the beginning of this part of Unit One, you read an excerpt from the log of Christopher Columbus. Compare Cabeza de Vaca's and Columbus's encounters with the native peoples of America. What similarities and differences do you see in their attitudes toward the Native Americans they met?

ANOTHER PATHWAY

Working with a partner, create a bar graph like the one started below. List five physical or mental challenges that Cabeza de Vaca and his men faced and numbers to indicate degrees of success. Then draw bars to show the degrees to which the men were able to overcome the challenges. Finally, discuss your graph with the class.

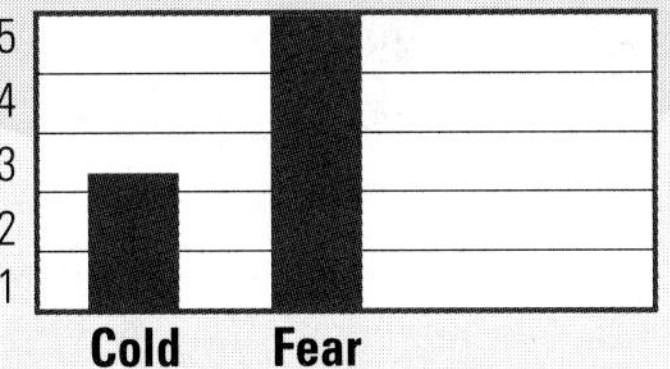

QUICKWRITES

1. Cabeza de Vaca was a devoutly religious man. Try to imagine his feelings, and compose a **prayer** he might have uttered during one of the experiences in the selection.

2. From your reading of this selection, do you think Cabeza de Vaca was a good leader? Draft a short **persuasive essay** that states your opinion and the reasons for it.

3. Visit an unfamiliar place and, in the style of Cabeza de Vaca, begin a detailed **report** about what you encounter there. As an alternative, you might recall a time when you were in a strange place and write about that experience.

PORTFOLIO *Save your writing. You may want to use it later as a spring-board to a piece for your portfolio.*

LITERARY CONCEPTS

La Relación was intended for a specific **audience:** the king of Spain. The form Cabeza de Vaca chose, the level of diction he used, the details he included, and the attitude he expressed toward his subject all were determined by his knowledge of who would read what he wrote. How might his account be different if it had been written for a different audience? Choose any brief passage in this selection and rewrite it as a diary entry of Cabeza de Vaca or as a letter to his wife. Give your rewritten passage to a partner and ask him or her to comment on the differences between the two versions.

THE WRITER'S STYLE

The scholar William T. Pilkington writes, "*La Relación* possesses many of the attributes of a good novel, especially its subtle presentation of character and its dramatic tension." On the basis of the passages you've read, would you agree? Explain why or why not.

ALTERNATIVE ACTIVITIES

1. Imagine that you are planning a television miniseries based on the adventures of Cabeza de Vaca. Prepare a **storyboard**—a series of rough sketches—depicting any scene from this selection. Combine your work with classmates' to make a bulletin-board display.
2. Speaking as one of the Karankawas who met the shipwrecked Spaniards, make an **informal speech** to members of a neighboring clan, giving your impressions of the strangers.
3. ***Cooperative Learning*** With a small group of classmates, have an **informal debate** based on one of two situations: either you are Cabeza de Vaca's men deciding whether to go with the Karankawas, or you are Karankawas deciding whether to take the shipwrecked strangers to your homes. Doubtless there will be varying opinions about what is best to do. Consider the following factors:
   - the weather
   - your food supply
   - your moral values
   - your alternatives

   Afterward, tell your group's decision to the rest of the class, summarizing key points of your discussion.

CRITIC'S CORNER

Cabeza de Vaca reports that he and his men were able to cure ailing Karankawas and other Indians they met during their journey. Readers over time have had differing explanations for these reported cures. Some have believed that Cabeza de Vaca was exaggerating or lying; some have believed that the Indians were lying when they said they were cured. Some have thought that the Indians' symptoms were psychological and disappeared because of the Indians' belief in the Europeans' powers. One commentator has proposed that Cabeza de Vaca's extreme experiences somehow awakened in him the miraculous ability to heal. How do *you* interpret Cabeza de Vaca's accounts of healing?

ACROSS THE CURRICULUM

Health Cabeza de Vaca states that from May until November he ate virtually nothing but corn. What nutrients—fats, protein, vitamins, minerals, carbohydrates, water—does corn provide? What health problems might Cabeza de Vaca have had as a result of his limited diet? Research the answers to these questions and report your findings to the class.

ART CONNECTION

The reports of 16th-century European explorers documented what they saw in America. The art created by Europeans in this land had a documentary purpose as well. Traveling with the first English colony established in America was artist John White, commissioned to make drawings of the native people, plants, and wildlife. White's watercolor of a Florida man appears on page 83. Theodor de Bry was a Flemish printer and artist who made hand-colored engravings based on the work of White and other artists who had been to America. On page 82 is a de Bry engraving of Indians and Spanish invaders. Discuss what these works document—for example, what can you tell about the man depicted in White's painting? What do you learn from de Bry's scene?

Detail of *Indians forced to carry baggage and supplies of the Spanish invaders (1590),* Theodor de Bry.

WORDS TO KNOW

Write the vocabulary word that is closest in meaning to the italicized word or phrase in each sentence.

1. The Indians learned to *burn* a wound to make it stop bleeding.
2. Starvation caused *illness* among many of the conquistadors.
3. Huge waves threatened to *flood* the barges and capsize them.
4. Why did the navigator *beg* Cabeza de Vaca to take control of the barge?
5. Cabeza de Vaca did not expect the Indians to *express sorrow for* the conquistadors' predicament.
6. The conquistadors learned not to *sneer* at the Indians' healing methods.
7. Cabeza de Vaca seems to *personify* many positive qualities.
8. When Cabeza de Vaca gave an order, his men had no choice but to *obey.*
9. How did the conquistadors *calm* the Indians who were carrying bows?
10. The conquistadors gave away bells and beads to *gain favor for* themselves with the Indians.

Álvar Núñez Cabeza de Vaca

1490?–1557?

As a young man, Cabeza de Vaca joined the Spanish army and fought in many battles. His military successes eventually led to his appointment as an officer of the Narváez expedition to Florida. His report of this ill-fated expedition, *La Relación,* describes his adventures as he crossed the North American continent, living with various Native American tribes and trading shells, beads, skins, and other items to survive. He was the first European to describe a Caribbean hurricane, the Mississippi River, and herds of buffalo.

In 1540, Cabeza de Vaca returned to the Americas as governor of the province of Río de la Plata in South America. While there, he led a yearlong expedition 1,000 miles across the continent, becoming the first European to cross both North and South America on foot. As governor, he prohibited the mistreatment of Native Americans by Spaniards. For that reason and others he was thrown out of office by a group of rebels in 1543 and sent back to Spain two years later. In 1551 he was tried and found guilty of the charges that the rebels had brought against him. He was sentenced to an eight-year exile in Africa, stripped of his titles, and ordered to pay damages to his accusers. In 1556 the king of Spain pardoned him and awarded him a small pension, but his last years were marked by illness and poverty.

LASERLINKS
• *ART GALLERY*

PREVIEWING

NONFICTION

from Of Plymouth Plantation

William Bradford

PERSONAL CONNECTION

What do you know about the Pilgrims? How, when, and why did they come to North America? With a small group of classmates, discuss facts and images that come to mind when you think of the Pilgrims. Collect the group's impressions in a cluster diagram. Then read this selection to find out more about the Pilgrims.

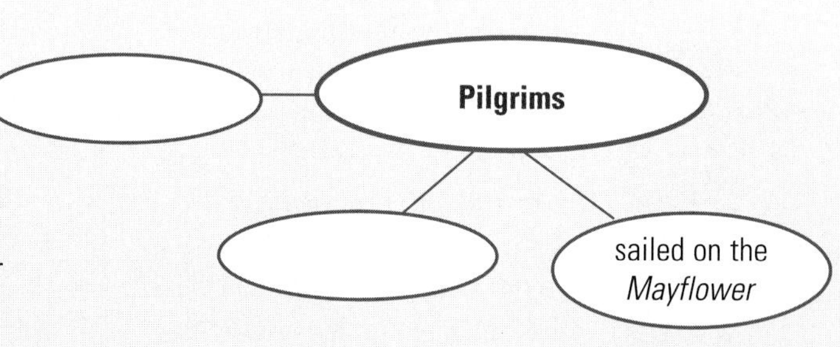

Plymouth Colony

Massachusetts Bay
Atlantic Ocean
Boston
Provincetown
Plymouth
PLYMOUTH COLONY
Cape Cod Bay
Cape Cod
N W E S
Miles
0 10 20

HISTORICAL CONNECTION

During the 1500s and 1600s there was a movement to "purify" the Church of England, led by a group of Protestants called Puritans. One radical group of Puritans, the Separatists, wanted to separate altogether from the established church. Separatist groups were declared illegal, and members faced arrest for practicing their beliefs. In 1608, some Separatists fled to Holland, where they lived for 12 years. However, concerned that their children were becoming too Dutch and forgetting their English heritage, these Separatists eventually sought permission to start a colony near Jamestown, Virginia.

In September 1620, a group of 102 English colonists, including 41 Separatists, sailed across the Atlantic on the *Mayflower.* This group ultimately came to be known as the Pilgrims. Blown off course, the *Mayflower* reached the tip of Cape Cod, in what is now Massachusetts, in early November. While the ship was moored in Provincetown Harbor, some of the group set out in a smaller boat to search for a good place to build a settlement. About a month later, the colonists built their first shelter at Plymouth.

Nearly half of the colonists died during the first brutal winter, but the entire colony might have perished without the aid of the Wampanoag Indians and other tribes. Under Governor William Bradford's leadership, the colony not only survived but grew to about 300 people by 1630. Bradford wrote about the Pilgrims' long journey and their settlement at Plymouth in *Of Plymouth Plantation,* from which the excerpts you are about to read are taken.

READING CONNECTION

Excerpts from Historical Documents

Like the preceding selection, from *La Relación,* this selection consists of excerpts from a historical document. You may find this document more difficult to read than *La Relación,* which is older but has been translated from Spanish into modern English. In this case, you will be reading William Bradford's 17th-century English, with only the spellings modernized. Here are two strategies that may help you:

Previewing As with *La Relación,* it may be useful to preview the selection. Read the section titles, which will tell you what the sections are about. Study the map of Cape Cod and the other illustrations, looking for clues about the places and events the selection will describe.

Summarizing Bradford's sentences tend to be long and complex, and many of his expressions are obsolete. Try to summarize each paragraph as you read. Determine the main idea of the paragraph and state it in one or two sentences. Paraphrase, or restate in your own words, any out-dated expressions.

Bradford is anything but brief here.

But to omit other things (that I may be brief) after long beating at sea they fell with that land which is called Cape Cod; the which being made and certainly known to be it, they were not a little joyful.

"After a long time at sea, they were very happy to land at Cape Cod."

This is how one student paraphrased Bradford's sentence.

Punctuation in Excerpts

As you read these excerpts, you may notice punctuation you do not often see in other selections. **Ellipses** (. . .) are used to indicate that material has been omitted—a word, a phrase, or one or more sentences or paragraphs. **Brackets** ([ ]) are generally used to set off comments, explanations, or corrections.

In this selection, most of the bracketed material has been inserted to clarify pronoun reference.

they [the English] soon got their arms and let fly amongst them [the Indians] and quickly stopped their violence. . . .

The ellipses here indicate omissions that are intended to shorten and focus the selection.

FROM

OF PLYMOUTH PLANTATION

WILLIAM BRADFORD

THEIR SAFE ARRIVAL AT CAPE COD

But to omit other things (that I may be brief) after long beating at sea they[1] fell with that land which is called Cape Cod; the which being made and certainly known to be it, they were not a little joyful. . . .

Being thus arrived in a good harbor, and brought safe to land, they fell upon their knees and blessed the God of Heaven who had brought them over the vast and furious ocean, and delivered them from all the perils and miseries thereof, again to set their feet on the firm and stable earth, their proper element. . . .

But here I cannot but stay and make a pause, and stand half amazed at this

1. **they:** Bradford refers to the Pilgrims in the third person even though he is one of them.

poor people's present condition; and so I think will the reader, too, when he well considers the same. Being thus passed the vast ocean, and a sea of troubles before in their preparation (as may be remembered by that which went before), they had now no friends to welcome them nor inns to entertain or refresh their weatherbeaten bodies; no houses or much less towns to repair to, to seek for succor.[2] It is recorded in Scripture as a mercy to the Apostle and his shipwrecked company, that the barbarians showed them no small kindness in refreshing them,[3] but these savage barbarians, when they met with them (as after will appear) were readier to fill their sides full of arrows than otherwise. And for the season it was winter, and they that know the winters of that country know them to be sharp and violent, and subject to cruel and fierce storms, dangerous to travel to known places, much more to search an unknown coast. Besides, what could they see but a hideous and desolate wilderness, full of wild beasts and wild men—and what multitudes there might be of them they knew not. Neither could they, as it were, go up to the top of Pisgah[4] to view from this wilderness a more goodly country to feed their hopes; for which way soever they turned their eyes (save upward to the heavens) they could have little solace or content in respect of any outward objects. For summer being done, all things stand upon them with a weatherbeaten face, and the whole country, full of woods and thickets, represented a wild and savage hue. If they looked behind them, there was the mighty ocean which they had passed and was now as a main bar and gulf to separate them from all the civil parts of the world. . . .

The First Encounter

Being thus arrived at Cape Cod the 11th of November, and necessity calling them to look out a place for habitation (as well as the master's and mariners' importunity); they having brought a large shallop[5] with them out of England, stowed in quarters in the ship, they now got her out and set their carpenters to work to trim her up; but being much bruised and shattered in the ship with foul weather, they saw she would be long in mending. Whereupon a few of them tendered themselves to go by land and discover those nearest places, whilst the shallop was in mending; . . .

After this, the shallop being got ready, they set out again for the better discovery of this place, and the master of the ship desired to go himself. So there went some thirty men but found it to be no harbor for ships but only for boats. There was also found two of their [the Indians'] houses covered with mats, and sundry of their implements in them, but the people were run away and could not be seen. Also there was found more of their corn and of their beans of various colors; the corn and beans they [the English] brought away, purposing to give them [the Indians] full satisfaction when they should meet with any of them as, about some six months afterward they did, to their good content.[6]

And here is to be noted a special providence of God, and a great mercy to this poor people, that here they got seed to plant them corn the next year, or else they might have starved, for they had none nor any likelihood to get any till

2. **succor** (sŭk'ər): help; relief.
3. **It is . . . refreshing them:** a reference to the biblical account of the courteous reception of Paul and his companions by the inhabitants of Malta (Acts 27:41–28:2).
4. **Pisgah** (pĭz'gə): the mountain from whose peak Moses saw the Promised Land (Deuteronomy 34:1–4).
5. **shallop** (shăl'əp): an open boat usually used in shallow waters.
6. **purposing . . . content:** intending to repay the Nauset Indians whose corn and beans they took, as they in fact did, to the Indians' satisfaction, six months later.

WORDS TO KNOW

desolate (dĕs'ə-lĭt) *adj.* without inhabitants; barren
solace (sŏl'ĭs) *n.* comfort in sorrow or distress
hue (hyo͞o) *n.* appearance; color
providence (prŏv'ĭ-dəns) *n.* an instance of divine care or guidance

View of Plymouth (1627), Cal Sachs. American Heritage Picture Collection, New York.

the season had been past, as the sequel did manifest. Neither is it likely they had had this, if the first voyage had not been made, for the ground was now all covered with snow and hard frozen; but the Lord is never wanting unto His in their greatest needs; let His holy name have all the praise.

The month of November being spent in these affairs, and much foul weather falling in, the 6th of December they sent out their shallop again with ten of their principal men and some seamen, upon further discovery, intending to circulate that deep bay of Cape Cod. The weather was very cold and it froze so hard as the spray of the sea lighting on their coats, they were as if they had been glazed. . . . [The next night they landed and] made them a barricado[7] as usually they did every night, with logs, stakes, and thick pine boughs, the height of a man, leaving it open to leeward,[8] partly to shelter them from the cold and wind (making their fire in the middle and lying round about it) and partly to defend them from any sudden assaults of the savages, if they should surround them; so being very weary, they betook them to rest. But about midnight they heard a hideous and great cry, and their sentinel called "Arm! arm!" So they bestirred them and stood to their arms and

7. **barricado** (băr′ĭ-kā′dō): a barrier for defense.

8. **to leeward** (lē′wərd): on the side sheltered from the wind.

WORDS TO KNOW **sentinel** (sĕn′tə-nəl) *n.* a guard

shot off a couple of muskets, and then the noise ceased. They concluded it was a company of wolves or such like wild beasts, for one of the seamen told them he had often heard such a noise in Newfoundland.

So they rested till about five of the clock in the morning; for the tide, and their purpose to go from thence, made them be stirring betimes. So after prayer they prepared for breakfast, and it being day dawning it was thought best to be carrying things down to the boat. But some said it was not best to carry the arms down, others said they would be the readier, for they had lapped them up in their coats from the dew; but some three or four would not carry theirs till they went themselves. Yet as it fell out, the water being not high enough, they laid them down on the bank side and came up to breakfast.

But presently, all on the sudden, they heard a great and strange cry, which they knew to be the same voices they heard in the night, though they varied their notes; and one of their company being abroad came running in and cried, "Men, Indians! Indians!" And withal, their arrows came flying amongst them. Their men ran with all speed to recover their arms, as by the good providence of God they did. In the meantime, of those that were there ready, two muskets were discharged at them, and two more stood ready in the entrance of their rendezvous[9] but were commanded not to shoot till they could take full aim at them. And the other two charged again with all speed, for there were only four had arms there, and defended the barricado, which was first assaulted. The cry of the Indians was dreadful, especially when they [the Indians] saw their men [the English] run out of the rendezvous toward the shallop to recover their arms, the Indians wheeling about upon them. But some running out with coats of mail on, and cutlasses[10] in their hands, they [the English] soon got their arms and let fly amongst them [the Indians] and quickly stopped their violence. . . .

Thus it pleased God to vanquish their enemies and give them deliverance; and by His special providence so to dispose that not any one of them were either hurt or hit, though their arrows came close by them and on every side [of] them; and sundry of their coats, which hung up in the barricado, were shot through and through. Afterwards they gave God solemn thanks and praise for their deliverance, and gathered up a bundle of their arrows and sent them into England afterward by the master of the ship, and called that place the First Encounter. . . .

The Starving Time

But that which was most sad and lamentable was, that in two or three months' time half of their company died, especially in January and February, being the depth of winter, and wanting houses and other comforts; being infected with the scurvy[11] and other diseases which this long voyage and their inaccommodate condition had brought upon them. So as there died some times two or three of a day in the foresaid time, that of 100 and odd persons, scarce fifty remained. And of these, in the time of most distress, there was but six or seven sound persons who to their great commendations, be it spoken, spared no pains night nor day, but with abundance of toil and hazard of their own health fetched them wood, made them fires, dressed them meat, made their beds, washed their loathsome clothes, clothed and unclothed them. . . . In a word, did all the homely and necessary offices for them which dainty and queasy stomachs cannot endure to hear named; and all this willingly and cheerfully, without any grudging in the least, showing herein their true love unto their friends

9. **rendezvous** (rän′dā-vo͞o′): a gathering place; here used to denote the Pilgrims' encampment.
10. **coats of mail . . . and cutlasses:** armor made of joined metal links, and short curved swords.
11. **scurvy** (skûr′vē): a disease caused by lack of vitamin C.

WORDS TO KNOW
vanquish (văng′kwĭsh) *v.* to defeat in battle

and brethren; a rare example and worthy to be remembered. Two of these seven were Mr. William Brewster, their reverend Elder, and Myles Standish, their Captain and military commander, unto whom myself and many others were much beholden in our low and sick condition. And yet the Lord so upheld these persons as in this general calamity they were not at all infected either with sickness or lameness. . . .

Indian Relations

All this while the Indians came skulking about them, and would sometimes show themselves aloof off, but when any approached near them, they would run away; and once they [the Indians] stole away their [the colonists'] tools where they had been at work and were gone to dinner. But about the 16th of March, a certain Indian came boldly amongst them and spoke to them in broken English, which they could well understand but marveled at it. At length they understood by discourse with him, that he was not of these parts, but belonged to the eastern parts where some English ships came to fish, with whom he was acquainted and could name sundry of them by their names, amongst whom he had got his language. He became profitable to them in acquainting them with many things concerning the state of the country in the east parts where he lived, which was afterwards profitable unto them; as also of the people here, of their names, number and strength, of their situation and distance from this place, and who was chief amongst them. His name was Samoset. He told them also of another Indian whose name was Squanto, a native of this place, who had been in England and could speak better English than himself.

Being, after some time of entertainment and gifts dismissed, a while after he came again, and five more with him, and they brought again all the tools that were stolen away before, and made way for the coming of their great Sachem,[12] called Massasoit. Who, about four or five days after, came with the chief of his friends and other attendance, with the aforesaid Squanto. With whom, after friendly entertainment and some gifts given him, they made a peace with him (which hath now continued this 24 years) in these terms:

1. That neither he nor any of his should injure or do hurt to any of their people.

2. That if any of his did hurt to any of theirs, he should send the offender, that they might punish him.

3. That if anything were taken away from any of theirs, he should cause it to be restored; and they should do the like to his.

4. If any did unjustly war against him, they would aid him; if any did war against them, he should aid them.

5. He should send to his neighbors confederates to certify them of this, that they might not wrong them, but might be likewise comprised in the conditions of peace.[13]

6. That when their men came to them, they should leave their bows and arrows behind them.

After these things he returned to his place called Sowams,[14] some 40 miles from this place, but Squanto continued with them and was their interpreter and was a special instrument sent of God for their good beyond their expectation. He directed them how to set their corn, where to take fish, and to procure other commodities, and was also their pilot to bring them to unknown places for their profit, and never left them till he died.

---

12. **Sachem** (sā′chəm): chief.

13. **He should . . . peace:** Massasoit was to send representatives to inform other tribes of the compact with the Pilgrims so other tribes might also keep peace with them.

14. **Sowams** (sō′ämz): near the site of present-day Barrington, Rhode Island.

WORDS TO KNOW

aloof (ə-lo͞of′) *adj.* distant

procure (prō-kyo͝or′) *v.* to get by special effort; obtain

commodity (kə-mŏd′ĭ-tē) *n.* something useful; an article of commerce

The Bettmann Archive, New York.

First Thanksgiving

They began now to gather in the small harvest they had, and to fit up their houses and dwellings against winter, being all well recovered in health and strength and had all things in good plenty. For as some were thus employed in affairs abroad, others were exercised in fishing, about cod and bass and other fish, of which they took good store, of which every family had their portion. All the summer there was no want; and now began to come in store of fowl, as winter approached, of which this place did abound when they came first (but afterward decreased by degrees). And besides waterfowl there was great store of wild turkeys, of which they took many, besides venison, etc. Besides they had about a peck[15] a meal a week to a person, or now since harvest, Indian corn to that proportion. Which made many afterwards write so largely of their plenty here to their friends in England, which were not feigned but true reports. ❖

15. **peck:** a unit of measurement equal to eight dry quarts.

WORDS TO KNOW

feigned (fānd) *adj.* not real; pretended

INSIGHT

WOMEN AND CHILDREN FIRST:

THE MAYFLOWER PILGRIMS

Alicia Crane Williams

When the ship *Mayflower* sailed from Plymouth, England, in September 1620 on her voyage into history, she carried 102 passengers, of which nearly half were women and children. Eighteen of the passengers were wives accompanying their husbands to the New World; with them they brought thirty-one children ranging in age from a nursing infant to teenagers. In addition, at least three of the women were pregnant during the voyage. . . .

Elizabeth Hopkins gave birth to her son Oceanus at sea while also mothering her two-year-old daughter Damaris and her stepchildren, thirteen-year-old Constance and ten-year-old Giles. Miraculously, all survived the voyage and the first winter, though Oceanus and Damaris did not live to adulthood. Five more children eventually were born to the Hopkinses in this inhospitable new land. . . .

In early December 1620, Susanna White gave birth to her son Peregrine on board the *Mayflower* while it was anchored in the shelter of Cape Cod. Two months later her husband William died, leaving her with the baby and their five-year-old son Resolved. In May, Susanna married Edward Winslow, whose first wife had died during the winter. Susanna and Edward's marriage, the first performed in the new colony, produced five children, though only two survived their childhoods. Resolved and Peregrine lived to adulthood. . . .

Mary Allerton did not fare as well as Elizabeth and Susanna. She made the journey with her husband Isaac and their three young children—eight-year-old Bartholomew, six-year-old Remember, and four-year-old Mary. On December 22, a month after the *Mayflower* reached Cape Cod, Mary gave birth to a stillborn son and in February 1621 followed him to the grave. The other Allertons survived; Isaac remarried twice, was accused of cheating the colonists in business matters, and moved to New Haven. Both Bartholomew and Remember also left the colony; he returned to England, while she moved to Salem. Mary died in 1699, the last survivor of the *Mayflower* passengers (excluding Peregrine White, not yet born during the voyage). . . .

Dorothy Bradford, William's wife, left behind her only child, two-year-old John, when she accompanied her husband to the New World. She fell overboard from the *Mayflower,* anchored near Cape Cod, while William was away searching for a settlement site. Although Bradford and his contemporaries recorded the event as accidental, rumors persist to the present day that Dorothy actually committed suicide.

William and Mary Brewster, who at the time were in their fifties, were the oldest man and woman to survive the "General Sickness" of that first terrible winter. Educated at Cambridge University, William had served as an assistant to one of Queen Elizabeth's secretaries of state before joining with the religious separatists and becoming a lay minister. At one time imprisoned with other members of the church, Brewster became the colonists' spiritual leader when their minister, John Robinson, chose to remain in Holland with the majority of the congregation. The Brewsters brought their two youngest sons, Love, age ten, and Wrestling, age eight, with them to the New World. Like their parents, the two Brewster children lived through the sickness and starvation of the first year. Although Wrestling died unmarried at a young age, Love survived until 1650, leaving four children. Three older Brewster children also arrived from England on later ships.

Forty-one-year-old Elinor Billington and her family numbered among the "Strangers" aboard the *Mayflower.* Bradford called the Billingtons "one of the profanest families among us" and could not imagine how they "shuffled into [our] company." John Billington constantly quarrelled with Bradford and other leaders and kept company with troublemakers. In 1630 he was convicted of murder, gaining the distinction of being the first person executed by hanging in the New World.

The Billingtons' two sons—John, sixteen years old, and Francis, some years younger—apparently terrorized the other passengers throughout the voyage. Francis endangered the ship by firing his father's fowling piece, igniting a fire that almost spread to nearby barrels of gunpowder. And young John got lost in the woods in May 1621, only to be rescued by Indians and returned to a ten-man search party sent from the colony. The troublesome youth died a few years later, but Francis survived to marry and father nine children.

Priscilla Mullins—today probably the best-known of all the *Mayflower* colonists—would have been about sixteen years old when she supposedly attracted the simultaneous attention of friends John Alden, a cooper hired by the company in Southampton, and Myles Standish, a man of military experience who looked after the colony's defense. Priscilla had arrived in New England with her parents, William and Alice, and her brother Joseph, all of whom perished during that first winter. Captain Standish, who was one of only two people not afflicted with the illness that took so many lives, had lost his wife Rose to the epidemic.

Henry Wadsworth Longfellow's poem *The Courtship of Miles Standish* immortalized the legend of how Standish asked Alden to carry his marriage proposal to Priscilla, who replied, "Why don't you speak for yourself, John?" Married soon after, John and Priscilla had ten children, who in turn produced sixty-nine grandchildren and nearly four hundred great-grandchildren. Myles Standish found a bride elsewhere and fathered seven children.

Not all of the children on the *Mayflower* traveled with parents. Four of the youngest, in fact, found themselves virtually given away to the Pilgrim group. Mary, Richard, Jasper, and Ellen More—ages four, six, seven, and eight respectively—had become pawns in a bitter custody battle between their parents, Catherine and Samuel More. At the age of twenty-three, Catherine, an heiress and descendant of English and Scottish kings, married sixteen-year-old Samuel, her third cousin. Catherine subsequently gave birth to four children, but divorce proceedings cast doubt on their paternity. Samuel took the children from their mother and entrusted them to members of the Pilgrim company. In addition to paying for their passage, food, and clothing, Samuel arranged for each child ultimately to receive fifty acres of land in the new settlement. Of the four, only Richard survived to adulthood. It is particularly ironic that these abandoned children were the only *Mayflower* passengers with proved royal ancestry.

RESPONDING OPTIONS

FROM PERSONAL RESPONSE *TO* CRITICAL ANALYSIS

REFLECT **1.** What is your impression of the Pilgrims after reading the excerpts from *Of Plymouth Plantation* and the Insight selection "Women and Children First"? Record your thoughts in your notebook.

RETHINK **2.** Look back at the diagram that you created before reading the selection. What would you change or add as a result of your reading? Why?

3. On the basis of these excerpts, what conclusions can you draw about the Pilgrims' way of looking at the world?
Consider
- their attitude toward nature
- their attitude toward God
- their attitude toward Indians

4. What do you think might have happened if Squanto had not helped the Pilgrims? Explain your opinion.

RELATE **5.** Religious persecution forced the Pilgrims to flee from England to Holland and later to settle in North America. Think of another group of people who faced persecution for their religious or political beliefs. Briefly explain what happened to them, comparing and contrasting them with the Pilgrims.

LITERARY LINKS

Both *Of Plymouth Plantation* and *La Relación* describe Europeans' encounters with Native Americans. Compare the ways in which the Pilgrims and Cabeza de Vaca's men interacted with the Indians they met. What do you think accounts for any similarities or differences?

ANOTHER PATHWAY

Cooperative Learning

Get together with a small group of classmates and decide to act either as lawyers representing the Pilgrims or as lawyers representing the Wampanoag Indians. Reread the treaty on page 94 and discuss whether it is fair to the group you represent. What would you change to help your clients?

QUICKWRITES

1. Imagine that you are Squanto. Write a **diary entry** to explain why you helped the Pilgrims and chose to live with them.
2. How do you think the Indians viewed the arrival and settlement of the Pilgrims? From the Indians' point of view, write a humorous or serious **eyewitness account** of any incident in this selection.
3. If you could speak to one of the Pilgrims or Indians you have read about, what would you ask him or her? Write five **interview questions** that you might ask William Bradford, Samoset, or another person. Then write the answers that the person might give.

PORTFOLIO *Save your writing. You may want to use it later as a spring-board to a piece for your portfolio.*

LITERARY CONCEPTS

Sources of information about a subject can be classified as **primary sources**—those that offer direct, firsthand knowledge—and **secondary sources**—those that offer indirect, secondhand knowledge. *Of Plymouth Plantation* is a primary source of information about the Pilgrims because it was written by a Pilgrim who experienced or witnessed the events described. "Women and Children First" is a secondary source because it was written by a descendant of the Pilgrims more than 350 years after they landed. It summarizes information from primary sources, mainly *Of Plymouth Plantation*. Explore the differences between primary and secondary sources by contrasting these two selections. Consider differences in the writers' purposes (their reasons for writing), points of view (where the writers place themselves in relation to the events and people described), tones (the attitudes expressed toward the events and people), and styles (the ways in which the works are written). Make and fill in a chart like the one shown here to record the differences you find. Set up your chart on a computer, if you have access to one. What do you think are the advantages of reading each type of source?

Source	Purpose	Point of View	Tone	Style
Of Plymouth Plantation				
"Women and Children First"				

ART CONNECTION

Look at the illustration of the Plymouth colony in 1627 on page 92. Notice where the Puritans set up their military fortification. Why do you think they had it so far inland instead of near the sea?

Detail of *View of Plymouth* (1627), Carl Sachs. American Heritage Picture Collection, New York.

ALTERNATIVE ACTIVITIES

1. Design a **memorial**—such as a statue, monument, or historical marker—for the Pilgrims who died either aboard the *Mayflower* or during the first winter at Plymouth. Then work with classmates to display your memorial designs.
2. Think about the mood conveyed by each of the excerpts from *Of Plymouth Plantation*. Then work with a partner to create and record a **musical soundtrack** that evokes these different moods.
3. Create a **time line,** beginning in November 1620 and ending in March 1621, to show important events that happened after the Pilgrims reached Cape Cod.

ACROSS THE CURRICULUM

History Find out the *Mayflower*'s length and width. Then work with classmates, using yardsticks and masking tape or string, to create an outline of the ship's deck on the floor of a gymnasium or on the ground outside. Invite other classes to join you inside the outline. How many Pilgrims could stand on the deck at one time? What do you think the voyage was like for the 102 passengers?

WORDS TO KNOW

EXERCISE A Review the Words to Know in the boxes at the bottom of the selection pages. Then, on your paper, write the vocabulary word that most clearly relates to the situation expressed by each sentence below.

1. The Pilgrims were able to drive the hostile Indians away.
2. The Pilgrims brought with them some necessities, such as flour for baking bread.
3. The Pilgrims felt that God had helped the colony survive through the first harsh winter.
4. At first, the Indians were reluctant to have contact with the Pilgrims and so didn't come near them.
5. When the Pilgrims explored Cape Cod, some of the men kept watch while the others slept.
6. Vast stretches of seemingly uninhabitable wilderness greeted the Pilgrims.
7. In the fall, the leaves on the trees turned scarlet, orange, and golden yellow.
8. Squanto comforted the Pilgrims by befriending them and helping them learn about the new land.
9. Historians generally believe William Bradford's account and do not think he misrepresented anything.
10. Fortunately, after the first winter the Pilgrims were able to get what they needed to survive by hunting and farming.

EXERCISE B With a small group of classmates, play a game of charades, acting out the words *desolate, sentinel, vanquish, aloof,* and *feigned.*

WILLIAM BRADFORD

1590–1657

When the Pilgrims settled at Plymouth, William Bradford was 30 years old and had already endured much hardship. Orphaned as a young child, he ran off to join an outlawed religious group when he was 12. He joined the Separatists at the age of 16 and two years later followed them to Leiden, Holland. Although he was trained to be a farmer, Bradford supported himself by working as a weaver.

After the Separatists received permission to start a colony in North America, Bradford helped direct preparations for their trip across the Atlantic Ocean. When the *Mayflower* finally reached the coast of what is now Massachusetts, Bradford likely helped write the Mayflower Compact, the agreement that set up the government of the colony. He joined the initial expeditions to explore Cape Cod but returned from his exploration to find that his young wife, Dorothy May, had drowned while the *Mayflower* was moored in Provincetown Harbor.

Despite these difficulties, Bradford kept his faith in God and in the struggling colony. In the spring of 1621, he was elected governor, a post he held for 30 years. Bradford turned out to be a good businessman and a skilled diplomat. Under his leadership, the colony grew from a desperate band of survivors into a thriving community.

Largely self-taught, Bradford read widely in English, as well as in Dutch, French, Greek, and Hebrew. He wrote the first ten chapters of his history of the Separatists in 1630, beginning with their persecution in England and concluding with their landing in North America in 1620. He continued to work on *Of Plymouth Plantation* over the next 17 years, but his 500-page manuscript remained unpublished until 1856.

NONFICTION

from The Interesting Narrative of the Life of Olaudah Equiano

Olaudah Equiano (ō-lou′də ĕk′wē-än′ō)

PERSONAL CONNECTION

From the 1500s to the 1800s, millions of Africans were seized from their homelands and brought to the Americas on slave ships. What do you imagine it felt like to be on a slave ship? On what sources—books, movies, magazine articles—do you base your ideas and images of slave ships? Write down your speculations in your notebook.

HISTORICAL CONNECTION

The expansion of European colonies in North and South America led to the growth of the transatlantic slave trade. Large plantations needed great numbers of workers to produce sugar, tobacco, and cotton for sale in Europe. Following a triangular route, traders carried manufactured goods (such as cloth and guns) from Europe to Africa, slaves from Africa to the Americas, and raw materials from the Americas to Europe.

Historians estimate that between 10 million and 20 million Africans were enslaved to work in the Americas. During the Middle Passage, the horrific two-month voyage from Africa to the West Indies, millions of slaves died from the effects of overcrowding, bad food, harsh treatment, disease, and despair. Chained in the dark, airless holds of slave ships, the slaves lay packed side by side. They were allowed on deck only briefly. Olaudah Equiano was one of those who survived the Middle Passage. This book was one of the earliest American **slave narratives,** or autobiographical accounts of slavery. In the following excerpts, he tells what happened when as a child he was shipped to the island of Barbados in the West Indies.

LASERLINKS
- *HISTORICAL CONNECTION*
- *VISUAL VOCABULARY*

READING CONNECTION

Noting Sensory Details Descriptive details in pieces of writing help readers to imagine and understand characters' experiences. In this selection, sensory details—ones that appeal to the five senses—bring to life Olaudah Equiano's first encounter with white men and his ordeal aboard a slave ship. As you read, or after you finish reading, use a chart similar to the one below to note the sensory details of his experience.

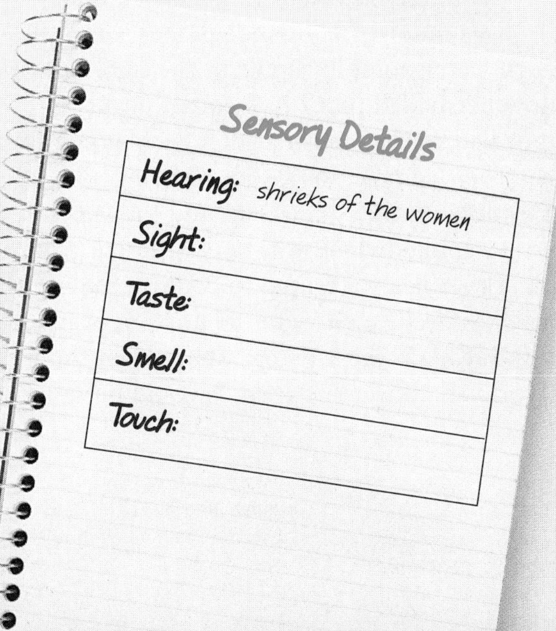

from

The Interesting Narrative *of the* Life of Olaudah Equiano

Olaudah Equiano

When Olaudah Equiano was eleven years old, he and his sister were kidnapped while the adults in his village were working in the fields. After being forced to travel for several days, Equiano and his sister were separated. For the next six or seven months, Equiano was sold to several African masters in different countries. He was eventually taken to the west coast of Africa and carried aboard a slave ship bound for the West Indies.

The first object which saluted my eyes when I arrived on the coast, was the sea, and a slave ship, which was then riding at anchor, and waiting for its cargo. These filled me with astonishment, which was soon converted into terror, when I was carried on board. I was immediately handled, and tossed up to see if I were sound, by some of the crew; and I was now persuaded that I had gotten into a world of bad spirits, and that they were going to kill me. Their complexions, too, differing so much from ours, their long hair, and the language they spoke (which was very different from any I had ever heard), united to confirm me in this belief. Indeed, such were the horrors of my views and fears at the moment, that, if ten thousand worlds had been my own, I would have freely parted with them all to have exchanged my condition with that of the meanest slave in my own country. When I looked round the ship too, and saw a large furnace of copper boiling, and a multitude of black people of every description chained together, every one of their countenances expressing dejection and sorrow, I no longer doubted of my fate; and, quite overpowered with horror and anguish, I fell motionless on the deck and fainted. When I recovered a little, I found some black people about me, who I believed were some of those who had brought me on board, and had been receiving their pay; they talked to me in order to cheer me, but all in vain. I asked them if we were not to be eaten by those white men with horrible looks, red faces, and long hair. They told me I was not, and one of the crew brought me a small portion of spirituous liquor in a wine glass; but, being afraid of him, I would not take it out of his hand. One of the blacks, therefore, took it from him and gave it to me, and I took a little down my palate, which, instead of reviving me, as they thought it would, threw me into the greatest consternation at the strange feeling it produced, having never tasted any such liquor before. Soon after this, the blacks who brought me on board went off, and left me abandoned to despair.

WORDS TO KNOW

anguish (ăng′gwĭsh) *n.* agonizing physical or mental pain
consternation (kŏn′stər-nā′shən) *n.* a state of paralyzing dismay; fear

I now saw myself deprived of all chance of returning to my native country, or even the least glimpse of hope of gaining the shore, which I now considered as friendly; and I even wished for my former slavery in preference to my present situation, which was filled with horrors of every kind, still heightened by my ignorance of what I was to undergo. I was not long suffered to indulge my grief; I was soon put down under the decks, and there I received such a salutation in my nostrils as I had never experienced in my life; so that, with the loathsomeness of the stench, and crying together, I became so sick and low that I was not able to eat, nor had I the least desire to taste anything. I now wished for the last friend, death, to relieve me; but soon, to my grief, two of the white men offered me eatables; and, on my refusing to eat, one of them held me fast by the hands, and laid me across, I think, the windlass,[1] and tied my feet, while the other flogged[2] me severely. I had never experienced anything of this kind before, and, although not being used to the water, I naturally feared that element the first time I saw it, yet, nevertheless, could I have got over the nettings,[3] I would have jumped over the side, but I could not; and besides, the crew used to watch us very closely who were not chained down to the decks, lest we should leap into the water; and I have seen some of these poor African prisoners most severely cut, for attempting to do so, and hourly whipped for not eating. This indeed was often the case with myself. In a little time after, amongst the poor chained men, I found some of my own nation, which in a small degree gave ease to my mind. I inquired of these what was to be done with us? They gave me to understand, we were to be carried to these white people's country to work for them. I then was a little revived, and thought, if it were no worse than working, my situation was not so desperate; but still I feared I should be put to death, the white people looked and acted, as I thought, in so savage a manner; for I had never seen among any people such instances of brutal cruelty; and this not only shown towards us blacks, but also to some of the whites themselves. One white man in particular I saw, when we were permitted to be on deck, flogged so unmercifully with a large rope near the foremast,[4] that he died in consequence of it; and they tossed him over the side as they would have done a brute. This made me fear these people the more; and I expected nothing less than to be treated in the same manner. I could not help expressing my fears and apprehensions to some of my countrymen; I asked them if these people had no country, but lived in this hollow place (the ship)? They told me they did not, but came from a distant one. "Then," said I, "how comes it in all our country we never heard of them?" They told me because they lived so very far off. I then asked where were their women? had they any like themselves? I was told they had. "And why," said I, "do we not see them?" They answered, because they were left behind. I asked how the vessel could go? They told me they could not tell; but that there was cloth put upon the masts by the help of the ropes I saw, and then the vessel went on; and the white men had some spell or magic they put in the water when they liked, in order to stop the vessel. I was exceedingly amazed at this account, and really thought they were spirits. I therefore wished much to be from amongst them, for I expected they would sacrifice me; but my wishes were vain—for we were so quartered that it was impossible for any of us to make our escape. . . .

---

1. **windlass** (wĭnd′ləs): a device for raising and lowering a ship's anchor.
2. **flogged:** beat severely with a whip or rod.
3. **nettings:** networks of small ropes on the sides of a ship used for various purposes, such as to prevent boarding or to stow sails. On slave ships, the nettings helped keep slaves from jumping overboard.
4. **foremast** (fôr′məst): the mast (tall pole that supports sails and rigging) nearest the forward end of a sailing ship.

WORDS TO KNOW

stench (stĕnch) *n.* a strong, foul odor
apprehension (ăp′rĭ-hĕn′shən) *n.* a suspicion of future evil; dread

Detail of *The Slave Ship* (1956), Robert Riggs, N.A. Courtesy of Les Mansfield, Cincinnati, Ohio.

At last, when the ship we were in, had got in all her cargo, they made ready with many fearful noises, and we were all put under deck, so that we could not see how they managed the vessel. But this disappointment was the least of my sorrow. The stench of the hold while we were on the coast was so intolerably loathsome, that it was dangerous to remain there for any time, and some of us had been permitted to stay on the deck for the fresh air; but now that the whole ship's cargo were confined together, it became absolutely pestilential. The closeness of the place, and the heat of the climate, added to the number in the ship, which was so crowded that each had scarcely room to turn himself, almost suffocated us. This produced copious perspirations, so that the air soon became unfit for respiration, from a variety of loathsome smells, and brought on a sickness among the slaves, of which many died. . . . This wretched situation was again aggravated by the galling[5] of the chains. . . . The shrieks of the women, and the groans of the dying, rendered the whole a scene of horror almost inconceivable. Happily perhaps, for myself, I was soon reduced so low here that it was thought necessary to keep me almost always on deck; and from my extreme youth I was not put in fetters.[6] In this situation I expected every hour to share the fate of my companions, some

5. **galling** (gô'lĭng): causing skin sores by rubbing.

6. **fetters:** chains or shackles for the ankles.

WORDS TO KNOW

pestilential (pĕs'tə-lĕn'shəl) *adj.* deadly; poisonous

copious (kō'pē-əs) *adj.* in large amounts; abundant

wretched (rĕch'ĭd) *adj.* miserable

of whom were almost daily brought upon deck at the point of death, which I began to hope would soon put an end to my miseries. . . .

One day they had taken a number of fishes; and when they had killed and satisfied themselves with as many as they thought fit, to our astonishment who were on deck, rather than give any of them to us to eat, as we expected, they tossed the remaining fish into the sea again, although we begged and prayed for some as well as we could, but in vain; and some of my countrymen, being pressed by hunger, took an opportunity, when they thought no one saw them, of trying to get a little privately; but they were discovered, and the attempt procured them some very severe floggings. One day, when we had a smooth sea and moderate wind, two of my wearied countrymen who were chained together (I was near them at the time), preferring death to such a life of misery, somehow made through the nettings and jumped into the sea; immediately, another quite dejected fellow, who, on account of his illness, was suffered to be out of irons, also followed their example; and I believe many more would very soon have done the same, if they had not been prevented by the ship's crew, who were instantly alarmed. . . .

During the rest of his voyage to the West Indies, Equiano continued to endure hardships. After the ship anchored on the coast of Barbados, Equiano and the other slaves were brought ashore and herded together in a slave merchant's yard to be sold.

WE WERE NOT MANY DAYS IN THE MERCHANT'S CUSTODY, BEFORE WE WERE SOLD AFTER THEIR USUAL MANNER, WHICH IS THIS: ON A SIGNAL GIVEN (as the beat of a drum), the buyers rush at once into the yard where the slaves are confined, and make choice of that parcel[7] they like best. The noise and clamor with which this is attended, and the eagerness visible in the countenances of the buyers, serve not a little to increase the apprehension of terrified Africans, who may well be supposed to consider them as the ministers of that destruction to which they think themselves devoted. In this manner, without scruple, are relations and friends separated, most of them never to see each other again. I remember, in the vessel in which I was brought over, in the men's apartment, there were several brothers, who, in the sale, were sold in different lots; and it was very moving on this occasion, to see and hear their cries at parting. O, ye nominal Christians! might not an African ask you—Learned you this from your God, who says unto you, Do unto all men as you would men should do unto you? Is it not enough that we are torn from our country and friends, to toil for your luxury and lust of gain? Must every tender feeling be likewise sacrificed to your avarice? Are the dearest friends and relations now rendered more dear by their separation from their kindred, still to be parted from each other, and thus prevented from cheering the gloom of slavery, with the small comfort of being together, and mingling their sufferings and sorrows? Why are parents to lose their children, brothers their sisters, or husbands their wives? Surely, this is a new refinement in cruelty, which . . . thus aggravates distress, and adds fresh horrors even to the wretchedness of slavery. ❖

7. **parcel:** group of slaves offered for sale.

WORDS TO KNOW
countenance (koun'tə-nəns) *n.* the face, especially as an indicator of emotion
nominal (nŏm'ə-nəl) *adj.* in name but not in reality
avarice (ăv'ə-rĭs) *n.* greed

RESPONDING OPTIONS

FROM PERSONAL RESPONSE TO CRITICAL ANALYSIS

REFLECT 1. What impact did this selection have on you? Describe your responses in your notebook, then share them.

RETHINK 2. Which of the experiences that Equiano describes in his narrative would be hardest for you to endure? Explain why.

3. Why do you think the Africans were treated so brutally?

   Consider
   - how the crew probably viewed them
   - how the number of crew members compared with the number of Africans
   - how the Africans reacted to their situation

4. What did you learn about the slave trade from this selection?

5. Who do you think are the "nominal Christians" that Equiano refers to in the last paragraph? Do you agree with his epithet? Explain.

RELATE 6. Compare the experiences of Africans brought to North America on slave ships with the experiences of some other group who came here from another land. For example, you might recall stories of immigrants in your own family or the experiences of the Pilgrims or Cabeza de Vaca's men.

ANOTHER PATHWAY

Cooperative Learning

In a small group, plan and sketch a museum exhibit designed to show some of the horrors of the Middle Passage that you learned about in this selection. In your sketch, include the pictures, models, and artifacts you would use, and write descriptions of any nonvisual features, such as sound recordings.

LITERARY CONCEPTS

The descriptive words and phrases that a writer uses to re-create sensory experiences are called **imagery.** Examples of imagery are the sensory details you noted as you read. To help you understand the power of images, choose a passage from this selection that contains vivid imagery. Then rewrite the passage, eliminating as much of the imagery as you can. For example, you might substitute "the hold smelled bad" for "the stench of the hold . . . was so intolerably loathsome." Read the original passage and your version aloud to a classmate. Discuss how the effect of your version compares with the effect of the original passage.

CONCEPT REVIEW: Audience Who do you suppose was Equiano's intended audience? Support your opinion.

QUICKWRITES

1. Write a **summary** of this selection for someone who has not read it and wants to know what Equiano's experience was like.
2. Write a **description** of the most horrible place you have ever been. Like Equiano, use vivid imagery to help readers picture this awful place.

PORTFOLIO *Save your writing. You may want to use it later as a springboard to a piece for your portfolio.*

ACROSS THE CURRICULUM

History West Africa, where Equiano was born, was home to several advanced cultures. Find out about African civilizations of the 1700s, such as the kingdom of Benin, and share your findings with the class.

Bronze head of a Benin king

ALTERNATIVE ACTIVITIES

1. Many slaves sang spirituals and other folk songs that expressed their desire for freedom. Find or compose a **song** that might express the feelings of Equiano or one of the other slaves on the ship. After explaining how the song relates to the selection, perform it for the class.
2. Prepare an **oral interpretation** of the last paragraph of the selection. (Practice at home first to polish your presentation.) Then discuss with the class how stylistic elements in the paragraph—such as Equiano's expression of feeling, his use of questions, and his choice of words—combine to give power to his argument.

WORDS TO KNOW

Review the Words to Know in the boxes at the bottom of the selection pages. On your paper, write the vocabulary word that belongs in each group of synonyms below.

1. dread, anxiety, _______
2. odor, _______, stink
3. _______, torment, agony
4. deplorable, terrible, _______
5. _______, plentiful, ample
6. selfishness, _______, greed
7. _______, diseased, polluted
8. alarm, _______, dismay
9. _______, so-called, ostensible
10. expression, visage, _______

OLAUDAH EQUIANO

1745?–1797

Olaudah Equiano grew up in the West African kingdom of Benin in the area that is now eastern Nigeria. His father ruled the village of Essaka, which Equiano himself would have ruled one day had he not been kidnapped by African slave traders and sent first to Barbados, then to colonial Virginia.

After a short time in Virginia, Equiano was sold to a British naval officer, with whom he traveled as far as Nova Scotia, London, and the Mediterranean. In 1763, he was sold again, to a merchant from Philadelphia who allowed him to work as a clerk and captain's assistant on slave and merchant ships. With the extra money that he was able to earn, Equiano bought his freedom in 1766. Working as a barber, sailor, and free servant, he traveled extensively, from England to the Arctic, but never returned to Africa.

During his years of captivity, Equiano had learned to speak and read English. As a free man, he became involved in the antislavery movement, lecturing against British slaveholders. From 1787 to 1788 he worked on his autobiography, *The Interesting Narrative of the Life of Olaudah Equiano, or Gustavus Vassa, the African,* which was first published in London in 1789 and quickly became popular.

PREVIEWING

NONFICTION

from Blue Highways

William Least Heat-Moon

PERSONAL CONNECTION

Culture is everything that makes up the way of life a group of people share. The language you speak, the things you create and use, the customs and traditions you follow, and the beliefs and attitudes you hold are part of your group's culture. In your notebook, describe some important aspects of your culture, then discuss them with classmates. You might consider music, dances, sports and games, fashions, foods, holiday celebrations, religious beliefs, and political beliefs and attitudes.

HISTORICAL CONNECTION

This selection describes some cultural traditions of the Hopi (hō'pē) of northeastern Arizona. For more than four centuries, the Hopi have been pressured to adopt European ways, first by Spanish colonizers and Catholic missionaries, then by settlers from the United States. In response to the Hopi's appeal, the U.S. government made Hopi lands a protected reservation in 1882. However, the government also forced Hopi children to attend government schools, a policy that threatened the Hopi way of life and created a division between traditional and progressive Hopi that still exists today. Despite these pressures, the Hopi have kept alive many of their cultural traditions.

READING CONNECTION

Understanding Details In this selection, the writer William Least Heat-Moon interviews Kendrick Fritz, a Hopi medical student, asking him questions about his culture. As you read, look for details about traditional Hopi culture—what Fritz calls the Hopi Way. For example, notice references to important foods, objects, practices, beliefs, and concepts. Create a cluster diagram like the one started below to organize these details. You will use these details later as you discuss the Hopi Way.

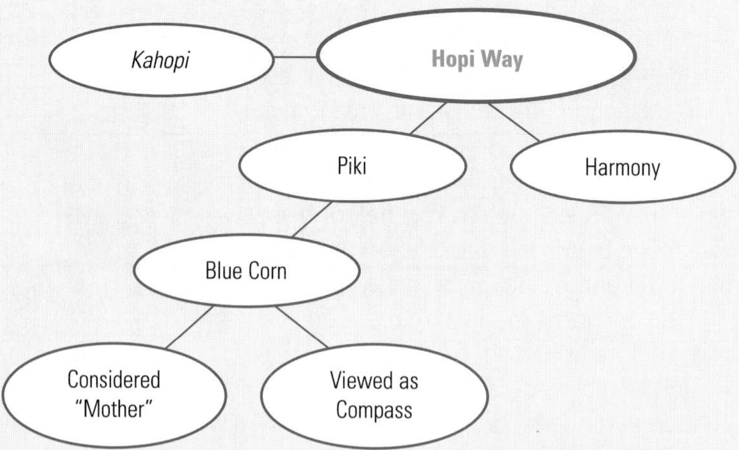

LASERLINKS
• *CULTURAL CONNECTION*

Road Past the View I (1964), Georgia O'Keeffe. Oil on canvas, 24″ × 30″. Copyright © 1996 The Georgia O'Keeffe Foundation/Artists Rights Society (ARS), New York. Photo Copyright © Malcolm Varon.

from

BLUE HIGHWAYS

William Least Heat-Moon

When William Least Heat-Moon set out on a long circular trip around the United States, he drove the back roads—the two-lane highways that were colored blue on old road maps. His goal was to learn about America by seeing the small towns and talking to the people he met there. He was not always successful, however. In Tuba City, Arizona, for instance, he failed to strike up a conversation with several Navajos. This chapter begins a few days later, with Heat-Moon at the top of a snowy mountain pass in Utah. He has slept in his van overnight rather than risk driving down the mountain in the dark.

Dirty and hard, the morning light could have been old concrete. Twenty-nine degrees inside. I tried to figure a way to drive down the mountain without leaving the sleeping bag. I was stiff—not from the cold so much as from having slept coiled like a grub. Creaking open and pinching toes and fingers to check for frostbite, I counted to ten (twice) before shouting and leaping for my clothes. Shouting distracts the agony. Underwear, trousers, and shirt so cold they felt wet.

I went outside to relieve myself. . . . Then to work chipping clear the windows. Somewhere off this mountain, people still lay warm in their blankets and not yet ready to get up to a hot breakfast. So what if they spent the day selling imprinted ballpoint pens? Weren't they down off mountains?

Down. I had to try it. And down it was, Utah 14 a complication of twists and drops descending the west side more precipitately than the east. A good thing I hadn't attempted it in the dark. After a mile, snow on the pavement became slush, then water, and finally at six thousand feet, dry and sunny blacktop.

Cedar City, a tidy Mormon town, lay at the base of the mountains on the edge of the Escalante Desert. Ah, desert! I pulled in for gas, snow still melting off my rig. "See you spent the night in the Breaks," the attendant said. "You people never believe the sign at the bottom."

"I believed, but it said something about winter months. May isn't winter."

"It is up there. You Easterners just don't know what a mountain is."

I didn't say anything, but I knew what a mountain was: a high pile of windy rocks with its own weather.

In the cafeteria of Southern Utah State College, I bought a breakfast of scrambled eggs, pancakes, bacon, oatmeal, grapefruit, orange juice, milk, and a cinnamon roll. A celebration of being alive. I was full of victory.

Across the table sat an Indian student named Kendrick Fritz, who was studying chemistry and wanted to become a physician. He had grown up in Moenkopi, Arizona, just across the highway from Tuba City. I said, "Are you Navajo or Hopi?"

"Hopi. You can tell by my size. Hopis are smaller than Navajos."

His voice was gentle, his words considered, and smile timid. He seemed open to questions. "Fritz doesn't sound like a Hopi name."

"My father took it when he was in the Army in the Second World War. Hopis usually have Anglo[1] first names and long Hopi last names that are hard for other people to pronounce."

I told him of my difficulty in rousing a conversation in Tuba City. He said, "I can't speak for Navajos about prejudice, but I know Hopis who believe we survived Spaniards, missionaries, a thousand years of other Indians, even the BIA.[2] But tourists?" He smiled. "Smallpox would be better."

"Do you—yourself—think most whites are prejudiced against Indians?"

"About fifty-fifty. Half show contempt because they saw a drunk squaw at the Circle K. Another half think we're noble savages—they may be worse because if an Indian makes a mistake they hate him for being human. Who wants to be somebody's ideal myth?"

"My grandfather used to say the Big Vision made the Indian, but the white man invented him."

"Relations are okay here, but I wouldn't call them good, and I'm not one to go around looking for prejudice. I try not to."

"Maybe you're more tolerant of Anglo ways than some others."

1. **Anglo:** European-American.
2. **BIA:** the Bureau of Indian Affairs, established in 1824 by the United States government to supervise Native American reservations; many Native Americans feel that the bureau has interfered too much in their lives.

WORDS TO KNOW
precipitately (prĭ-sĭp'ĭ-tĭt-lē) *adv.* steeply
contempt (kən-tĕmpt') *n.* scorn; disdain

"Could be. I mean, I *am* studying to be a doctor and not a medicine man. But I'm no apple Indian—red outside and white underneath. I lived up in Brigham City, Utah, when I went to the Intermountain School run by the BIA. It was too easy though. Too much time to goof around. So I switched to Box Elder—that's a public school. I learned there. And I lived in Dallas a few months. What I'm saying is that I've lived on Hopi land and I've lived away. I hear Indians talk about being red all the way through criticizing others for acting like Anglos, and all the time they're sitting in a pickup at a drive-in. But don't tell them to trade the truck for a horse."

"The Spanish brought the horse."

He nodded. "To me, being Indian means being responsible to my people. Helping with the best tools. Who invented penicillin doesn't matter."

"What happens after you finish school?"

"I used to want out of Tuba, but since I've been away, I've come to see how our land really is our Sacred Circle—it's our strength. Now, I want to go back and practice general medicine. At the Indian hospital in Tuba where my mother and sister are nurse's aides, there aren't any Indian M.D.'s, and that's no good. I don't respect people who don't help themselves. Hopi land is no place to make big money, but I'm not interested anyway."

"To me, being Indian means being responsible to my people. Helping with the best tools. Who invented penicillin doesn't matter."

Kendrick Fritz in Cedar City, Utah. From *Blue HIghways* by William Least Heat-Moon.

"You don't use the word *reservation.*"

"We don't think of it as a reservation since we were never ordered there. We found it through Hopi prophecies. We're unusual because we've always held onto our original land—most of it anyway. One time my grandfather pointed out the old boundaries to me. We were way up on a mesa. I've forgotten what they are except for the San Francisco Peaks. But in the last eighty years, the government's given a lot of our land to Navajos, and now we're in a hard spot—eight thousand Hopis are surrounded and outnumbered twenty-five to one. I don't begrudge the Navajo anything, but I think Hopis should be in on making the decisions. Maybe you know that Congress didn't even admit Indians to citizenship until about nineteen twenty. Incredible—live someplace a thousand years and then find out you're a foreigner."

"I know an Osage who says, 'Don't Americanize me and I won't Americanize you.' He means everybody in the country came from someplace else."

"Hopi legends are full of migrations."

"Will other Hopis be suspicious of you when you go home as a doctor?"

"Some might be, but not my family. But for a

WORDS TO KNOW

begrudge (bĭ-grŭj') *v.* to resent another person's possession of something lot of Hopis, the worst thing to call a man is *kahopi,* 'not Hopi.' Nowadays, though, we all have to choose either the new ways or the Hopi way, and it's split up whole villages. A lot of us try to find the best in both places. We've always learned from other people. If we hadn't, we'd be extinct like some other tribes."

"Medicine's a pretty good survival technique."

"Sure, but I also like Jethro Tull and the Moody Blues.[3] That's not survival."

"Is the old religion a survival technique?"

"If you live it."

"Do you?"

"Most Hopis follow our religion, at least in some ways, because it reminds us who we are and it's part of the land. I'll tell you, in the rainy season when the desert turns green, it's beautiful there. The land is medicine too."

"If you don't mind telling me, what's the religion like?"

"Like any religion in one way—different clans believe different things."

"There must be something they all share, something common."

"That's hard to say."

"Could you try?"

Human existence is essentially a series of journeys, and the emergence symbol is a kind of map of the wandering soul, an image of a process.

He thought a moment. "Maybe the idea of harmony. And the way a Hopi prays. A good life, a harmonious life, is a prayer. We don't just pray for ourselves, we pray for all things. We're famous for the Snake Dances, but a lot of people don't realize those ceremonies are prayers for rain and crops, prayers for life. We also pray for rain by sitting and thinking about rain. We sit and picture wet things like streams and clouds. It's sitting in pictures."

He picked up his tray to go. "I could give you a taste of the old Hopi Way. But maybe you're too full after that breakfast. You always eat so much?"

"The mountain caused that." I got up. "What do you mean by 'taste'?"

"I'll show you."

We went to his dormitory room. Other than several Kachina dolls[4] he had carved from cottonwood and a picture of a Sioux warrior, it was just another collegiate dorm room—maybe cleaner than most. He pulled a shoebox from under his bed and opened it carefully. I must have been watching a little wide-eyed because he said, "It isn't live rattlesnakes." From the box he took a long cylinder wrapped in waxed paper and held it as if trying not to touch it. "Will you eat this? It's very special." He was smiling. "If you won't, I can't share the old Hopi Way with you."

"Okay, but if it's dried scorpions, I'm going to speak with a forked tongue."

"Open your hands." He unwrapped the cylinder and ever so gently laid across my palms an airy tube the color of a thunderhead. It was about ten inches long and an inch in diameter. "There you go," he said.

"You first."

"I'm not having any right now."

So I bit the end off the blue-gray tube. It was many intricately rolled layers of something with less substance than butterfly wings. The bite crumbled to flakes that stuck to my lips. "Now tell me what I'm eating."

"Do you like it?"

"I think so. Except it disappears like cotton candy just as I get ready to chew. But I think I taste corn and maybe ashes."

"Hopis were eating that before horses came to America. It's piki. Hopi bread you might say. Made from blue-corn flour and ashes from

3. **Jethro Tull . . . Moody Blues:** British rock bands popular from the 1960s to the 1980s.

4. **Kachina** (kə-chē′nə) **dolls:** dolls representing kachinas—spirits of Hopi ancestors that the Hopi believe live in mountains near their lands.

greasewood or sagebrush. Baked on an oiled stone by my mother. She sends piki every so often. It takes time and great skill to make. We call it Hopi cornflakes."

"Unbelievably thin." I laid a piece on a page of his chemistry book. The words showed through.

"We consider corn our mother. The blue variety is what you might call our compass—wherever it grows, we can go. Blue corn directed our migrations. Navajos cultivate a yellow species that's soft and easy to grind, but ours is hard. You plant it much deeper than other corns, and it survives where they would die. It's a genetic variant the Hopi developed."

"Why is it blue? That must be symbolic."

"We like the color blue. Corn's our most important ritual ingredient."

"The piki's good, but it's making me thirsty. Where's a water fountain?"

When I came back from the fountain, Fritz said, "I'll tell you what I think the heart of our religion is—it's the Four Worlds."

Over the next hour, he talked about the Hopi Way, and showed pictures and passages from *Book of the Hopi*. The key seemed to be emergence. Carved in a rock near the village of Shipolovi is the ancient symbol for it:

With variations, the symbol appears among other Indians of the Americas. Its lines represent the course a person follows on his "road of life" as he passes through birth, death, rebirth. Human existence is essentially a series of journeys, and the emergence symbol is a kind of map of the wandering soul, an image of a process; but it is also, like most Hopi symbols and ceremonies, a reminder of cosmic patterns that all human beings move in.

The Hopi believes mankind has evolved through four worlds: the first a shadowy realm of contentment; the second a place so comfortable the people forgot where they had come from and began worshipping material goods. The third world was a pleasant land too, but the people, bewildered by their past and fearful for their future, thought only of their own earthly plans. At last, the Spider Grandmother, who oversees the emergences, told them: "You have forgotten what you should have remembered, and now you have to leave this place. Things will be harder." In the fourth and present world, life is difficult for mankind, and he struggles to remember his source because materialism and selfishness block a greater vision. The newly born infant comes into the fourth world with the door of his mind open (evident in the cranial soft spot[5]), but as he ages, the door closes and he must work at remaining receptive to the great forces. A human being's grandest task is to keep from breaking with things outside himself.

"A Hopi learns that he belongs to two families," Fritz said, "his natural clan and that of all things. As he gets older, he's supposed to move closer to the greater family. In the Hopi Way, each person tries to recognize his part in the whole."

"At breakfast you said you hunted rabbits and pigeons and robins, but I don't see how you can

5. **cranial** (krā′nē-əl) **soft spot:** the soft area on top of an infant's head, a result of the as yet incomplete formation of the bones of the skull (cranium).

WORDS TO KNOW

genetic (jə-nĕt′ĭk) *adj.* relating to genes, the units that determine and transmit hereditary characteristics

variant (vâr′ē-ənt) *n.* something that differs slightly from others of its kind

emergence (ĭ-mûr′jəns) *n.* the process of coming forth or coming into existence

evolve (ĭ-vŏlv′) *v.* to develop gradually

materialism (mə-tîr′ē-ə-lĭz′əm) *n.* a preoccupation with worldly rather than spiritual concerns shoot a bird if you believe in the union of life."

"A Hopi hunter asks the animal to forgive him for killing it. Only life can feed life. The robin knows that."

"How does robin taste, by the way?"

"Tastes good."

"The religion doesn't seem to have much of an ethical code."

"It's there. We watch what the Kachinas say and do. But the Spider Grandmother did give two rules. To all men, not just Hopis. If you look at them, they cover everything. She said, 'Don't go around hurting each other,' and she said, 'Try to understand things.'"

"I like them. I like them very much."

"Our religion keeps reminding us that we aren't just will and thoughts. We're also sand and wind and thunder. Rain. The seasons. All those things. You learn to respect everything because you *are* everything. If you respect yourself, you respect all things. That's why we have so many songs of creation to remind us where we came from. If the fourth world forgets that, we'll disappear in the wilderness like the third world, where people decided they had created themselves."

"Pride's the deadliest of the Seven Deadly Sins in old Christian theology."

"It's *kahopi* to set yourself above things. It causes divisions."

Fritz had to go to class. As we walked across campus, I said, "I guess it's hard to be a Hopi in Cedar City—especially if you're studying biochemistry."

"It's hard to be a Hopi anywhere."

"I mean, difficult to carry your Hopi heritage into a world as technological as medicine is."

"Heritage? My heritage is the Hopi Way, and that's a way of the spirit. Spirit can go anywhere. In fact, it has to go places so it can change and emerge like in the migrations. That's the whole idea." ❖

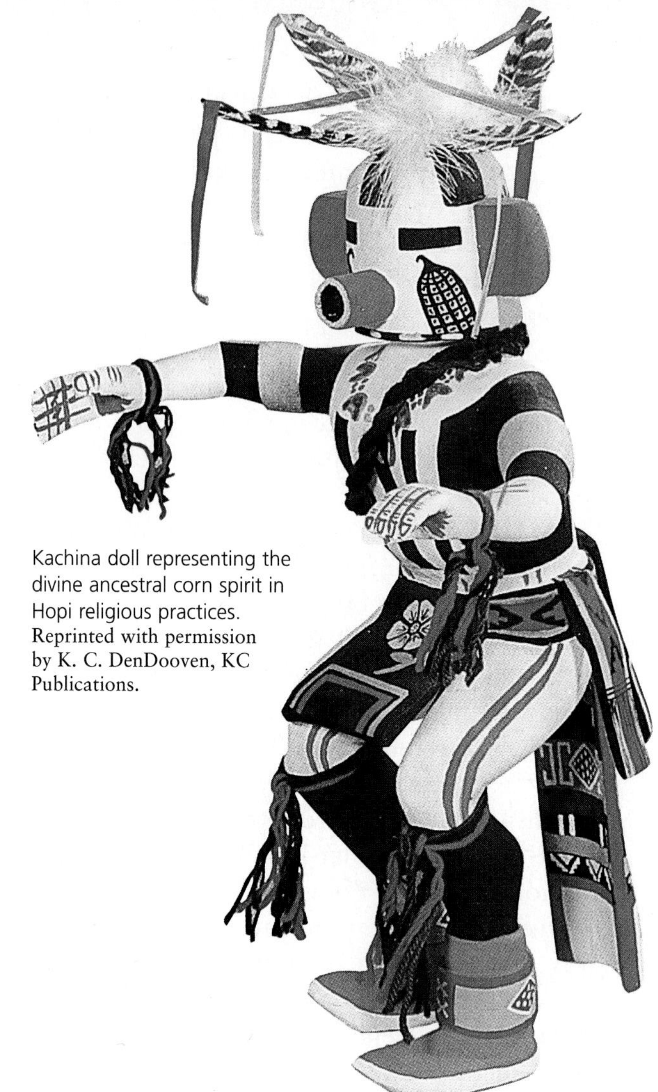

Kachina doll representing the divine ancestral corn spirit in Hopi religious practices. Reprinted with permission by K. C. DenDooven, KC Publications.

"The Spider Grandmother did give two rules. To all men, not just Hopis. If you look at them, they cover everything. She said, 'Don't go around hurting each other,' and she said, 'Try to understand things.'"

WORDS TO KNOW

ethical (ĕth'ĭ-kəl) *adj.* dealing with principles of right and wrong; moral

theology (thē-ŏl'ə-jē) *n.* a system of religious beliefs

RESPONDING OPTIONS

FROM PERSONAL RESPONSE *TO* CRITICAL ANALYSIS

REFLECT 1. What interests you most about Kendrick Fritz? Write your impressions in your notebook.

RETHINK 2. What is your opinion of the Hopi Way? For example, what ways would be easy for you to follow and what ways would be difficult? Refer to the cluster diagram you made as you read.

3. On page 110, Heat-Moon refers to his grandfather's statement that "the Big Vision made the Indian, but the white man invented him." What distinction between making and inventing is implied in this statement?

4. Fritz says, "It's hard to be a Hopi anywhere." What do you think makes it difficult to be a Hopi?

   Consider
   - how most whites view Native Americans
   - how some Native Americans view others for "acting like Anglos"
   - how the Hopi and other Native Americans have historically been treated

RELATE 5. Consider the aspects of your culture that you identified for the Personal Connection. Have you, like Fritz, been influenced by more than one culture? Explain.

ANOTHER PATHWAY

Cooperative Learning

With two classmates, create an imagined dialogue among Kendrick Fritz, an older Hopi with traditional values, and a young Hopi who plans to move away and never return. Assume the roles of these speakers and present your conversation to the rest of the class.

LITERARY CONCEPTS

A writer usually writes for one or more of these **purposes:** to inform, to entertain, to express himself or herself, or to persuade readers to believe or do something. What would you say is Heat-Moon's purpose in writing this selection? Identify one or more purposes and discuss your ideas with a group of classmates. Support your ideas with evidence from the selection.

QUICKWRITES

1. Interview ten people who are not Native Americans to find out about their attitudes toward Native Americans. Present your findings in a **report.** Explain whether the attitudes expressed are similar to those Kendrick Fritz describes on page 110.

2. Write a draft of a **personal essay** about an aspect of Hopi belief described in this selection. You might compare the belief with one of your own beliefs or explain how the belief applies to your own experience.

PORTFOLIO Save your writing. You may want to use it later as a springboard to a piece for your portfolio.

ALTERNATIVE ACTIVITIES

1. Look again at the Hopi emergence symbol on page 113. Create your own **symbol** to represent a person's journey through life. If you have a graphics program on your computer, here's a chance to use it. Explain the symbol to your classmates.
2. According to the Hopi, humankind has evolved through four worlds. Create a **diagram** or **drawing** that illustrates the Hopi concept of the four worlds.

ACROSS THE CURRICULUM

Anthropology Research an aspect of Hopi culture that interests you and report your findings to the class. For example, you might play a recording of Hopi music, prepare a Hopi dish, demonstrate a Hopi dance, draw a sketch of a traditional Hopi building, or show photos of Hopi art.

WORDS TO KNOW

Review the Words to Know in the boxes at the bottom of the selection pages. On your paper, write the letter of the word that does not belong in the group.

1. (a) theology (b) doctrine (c) religion (d) unbelief
2. (a) respect (b) contempt (c) admiration (d) regard
3. (a) immoral (b) improper (c) ethical (d) dishonest
4. (a) materialism (b) spirituality (c) greed (d) consumerism
5. (a) duplicate (b) variant (c) twin (d) replica
6. (a) resent (b) begrudge (c) esteem (d) envy
7. (a) extinction (b) termination (c) emergence (d) disappearance
8. (a) genetic (b) hereditary (c) artificial (d) inheritable
9. (a) precipitately (b) steeply (c) abruptly (d) gradually
10. (a) evolve (b) develop (c) perish (d) unfold

WILLIAM LEAST HEAT-MOON

1939–

"William Least Heat-Moon" is the pen name of William Trogdon, who is of mixed European-American and Native American ancestry. As he explains in *Blue Highways,* "My father calls himself Heat Moon, my elder brother Little Heat Moon. I, coming last, am therefore Least." Heat-Moon says that his father advised him to use his Anglo name for official business, such as paying taxes, and his Native American name for spiritual matters. His choice of pen name therefore indicates the spiritual quality of the journey that he recorded in *Blue Highways.*

It was after being laid off from his job teaching college English and separating from his wife that Heat-Moon decided to tour the small towns and back roads of America. He was inspired by John Steinbeck's *Travels with Charley,* in which Steinbeck describes his three-month exploration of the United States in the company of his dog.

Feeling isolated and tired of the commercialism he saw in mainstream American culture, Heat-Moon traveled in search of "places where change did not mean ruin and where time and men and deeds connected." He made his three-month, 13,000-mile journey in a Ford van that he named Ghost Dancing, a reference to a ceremony of the Plains Indians in which they danced for the return of their old, harmonious way of life. Equipped with a tape recorder, a camera, notebooks, Walt Whitman's *Leaves of Grass,* and John Neihardt's *Black Elk Speaks,* Heat-Moon followed the back roads, interviewing people he met along the way.

After compiling his interviews, Heat-Moon spent the next four years editing his tapes and notebooks to capture "the details of ordinary lives that shape, control, and reveal the nature of an existence." His compelling portrait of rural America, *Blue Highways,* won several awards, became a bestseller, and earned critical acclaim.

OTHER WORKS *PrairyErth*

PREVIEWING

NONFICTION

My Sojourn in the Lands of My Ancestors

Maya Angelou (mī′yə ăn′jə-lō)

PERSONAL CONNECTION

Think about your family heritage. Do you know where your ancestors were living 500 years ago? Where did your great-grandparents, grandparents, and parents come from? How do you think you would feel if you visited your ancestors' homeland? Could you call the place home? Write responses to these questions in your notebook, then share your answers with a small group of classmates.

HISTORICAL/GEOGRAPHICAL CONNECTION

In the 1400s, Europeans began to come to West Africa to trade for pepper, gold, and ivory. Over the years, they built more than 40 massive forts along the African coast to protect their trade and to store goods. As the slave trade grew, these European forts were also used to house enslaved Africans, who were branded, chained, and crowded into hot, dark, bat-infested dungeons for months at a time until they were shipped to colonies in the Americas.

Two such forts are Elmina Castle and Cape Coast Castle in Ghana. Elmina, the older, which could hold 1,000 slaves, was started by the Portuguese in 1481 and captured by the Dutch in 1637. Cape Coast Castle, which could hold 1,500 slaves, was started in 1652 by the Swedes and later taken over by the British. Today, both forts are popular tourist attractions. In this selection, the African-American writer Maya Angelou visits Ghana, the land of her ancestors, and describes what she feels as she passes near the two forts.

READING CONNECTION

Examining Autobiography An autobiography is the story of a person's life, written by that person. Generally written from the first-person point of view, autobiographies vary in style from straightforward chronological accounts to impressionistic narratives. As you read the following autobiographical selection, notice Angelou's feelings as she searches for a place "the heart could call home."

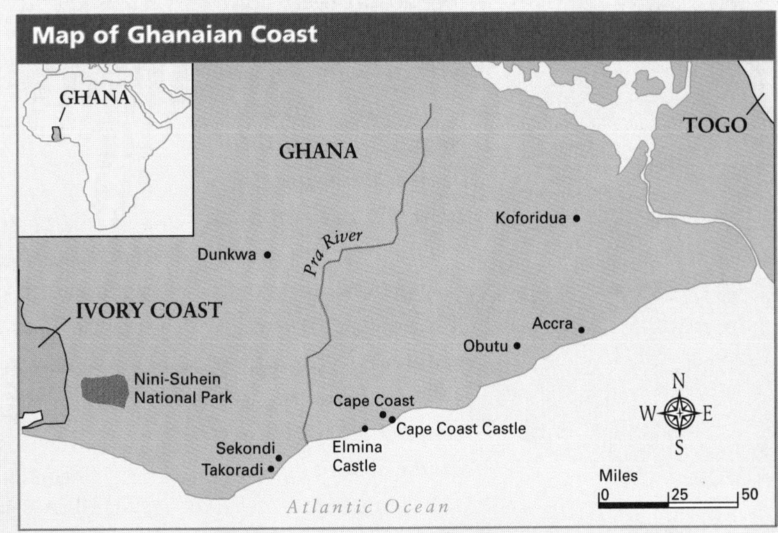

LASERLINKS
• CULTURAL CONNECTION

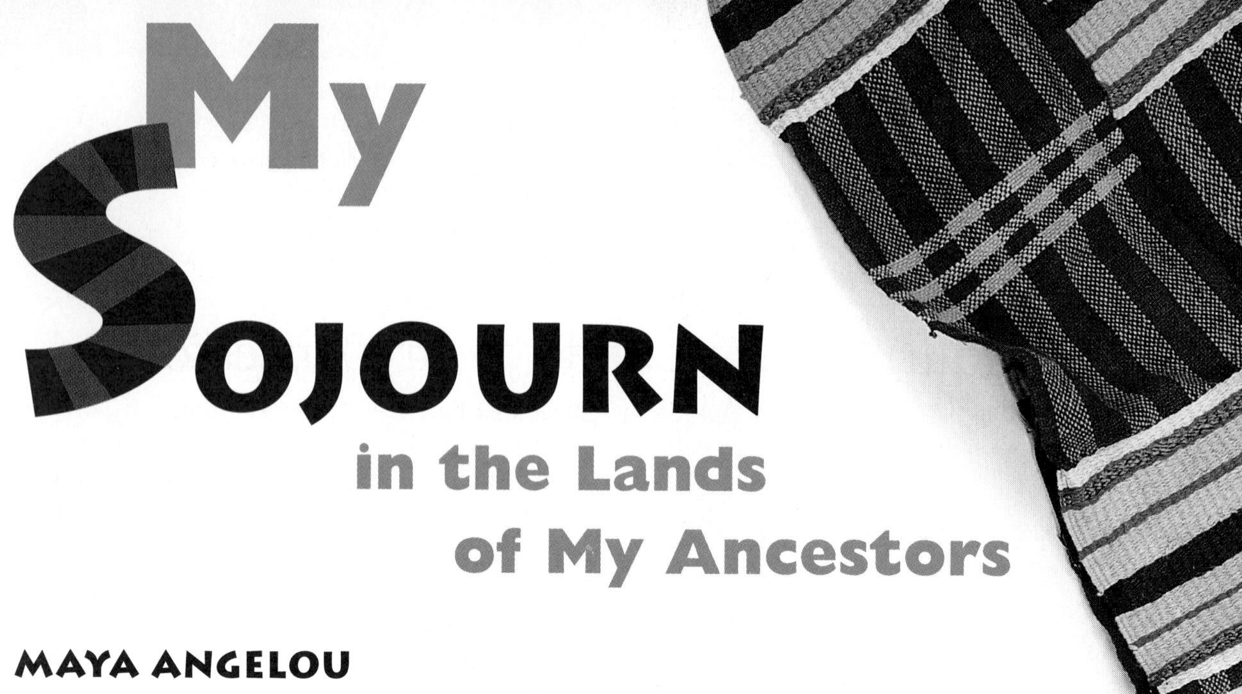

My Sojourn in the Lands of My Ancestors

MAYA ANGELOU

During the early sixties in New York City, I met, fell in love with, and married a South African Freedom Fighter who was petitioning the United Nations over the issue of apartheid.[1] A year later, my 15-year-old son, Guy, and I followed my new husband to North Africa.

I worked as a journalist in Cairo and managed a home that was a haven to Freedom Fighters still trying to rid their countries of colonialism. I was a moderately good mother to a growingly distant teenager and a faithful, if not loving, wife. I watched my romance wane and my marriage end in the shadows of the Great Pyramid.

In 1962, my son and I left Egypt for Ghana, where he was to enter the university and I was to continue to a promised job in Liberia.[2] An automobile accident left Guy with a broken neck and me with the responsibility of securing work and a place for him to recover. Within months I did have a job, a house, and a circle of black American friends who had come to Africa before me. With them I, too, became a hunter for that elusive and much longed-for place the heart could call home.

Despite our sincerity and eagerness, we were often rebuffed. The pain of rejection in Africa caused the spiritual that black slaves sang about their oppressors to come to my mind:

I'm going to tell God
How you treat me
When I get home.

On the delicious and rare occasions when we were accepted, our ecstasy was boundless, and we could have said with our foreparents in the words of another spiritual:

---

1. **apartheid** (ə-pärt′hīt′): an official policy of racial segregation practiced from 1948 to 1991 in South Africa, involving discrimination against nonwhites.
2. **Liberia** (lī-bîr′ē-ə): a West African country; it is on the Atlantic coast to the west of Ghana.

WORDS TO KNOW

wane (wān) *v.* to decrease in size, intensity, or degree
rebuff (rĭ-bŭf′) *v.* to reject bluntly; snub

Afi Negble, Asenema, Ghana, 1964, Paul Strand. Copyright © 1971, Aperture Foundation Inc., Paul Strand Archive.

My soul got happy
When I came out of the wilderness
Came out of the wilderness
Came out of the wilderness.
My soul got happy
When I came out of the wilderness
And up to the welcome table.

I had a long weekend, money in my purse, and working command of Fanti.[3] After a year in Accra,[4] I needed country quiet, so I decided to travel into the bush. I bought roasted plantain stuffed with boiled peanuts, a quart of Club beer, and headed my little car west. The stretch was a highway from Accra to Cape Coast, filled with trucks and private cars passing from lane to lane with abandon. People hung out of windows of the crowded mammie lorries,[5] and I could hear singing and shouting when the drivers careened those antique vehicles up and down hills as if each was a little train out to prove it could.

I stopped in Cape Coast only for gas. Although many black Americans had headed for the town as soon as they touched ground in Ghana, I successfully avoided it for a year. Cape Coast Castle and the nearby Elmina Castle had been holding forts for captured slaves. The captives had been imprisoned in dungeons beneath the massive buildings, and friends of mine who had felt called upon to make the trek reported that they felt the thick stone walls still echoed with old cries.

The palm-tree-lined streets and fine white-stone buildings did not tempt me to remain any longer than necessary. Once out of the town and again onto the tarred roads, I knew I had not made a clean escape. Despite my hurry, history had invaded my little car. Pangs of self-pity and a sorrow for my unknown relatives suffused me. Tears made the highway waver and were salty on my tongue.

What did they think and feel, my grandfathers, caught on those green savannas, under the baobab trees? How long did their families search for them? Did the dungeon wall feel chilly and its slickness strange to my grandmothers, who were used to the rush of air against bamboo huts and the sound of birds rattling their green roofs?

I had to pull off the road. Just passing near Cape Coast Castle had plunged me back into the eternal melodrama.

There would be no purging, I knew, unless I asked all the questions. Only then

3. **Fanti** (făn′tē): the dialect of the Fanti, one of the many ethnic groups who inhabit Ghana.
4. **Accra** (ăk′rə): the capital and largest city of Ghana.
5. **mammie lorries:** small trucks or open-sided buses used for public transportation in West Africa.

WORDS TO KNOW

careen (kə-rēn′) *v.* to swerve, or cause to swerve, from side to side while in motion
suffuse (sə-fyo͞oz′) *v.* to spread through
purging (pûr′jĭng) *n.* getting rid of something unwanted; cleansing **purge** *v.*

would the spirits understand that I was feeding them. It was a crumb, but it was all I had.

I allowed the shapes to come to my imagination; children passed, tied together by ropes and chains, tears abashed, stumbling in a dull exhaustion, then women, hair uncombed, bodies gritted with sand, and sagging in defeat. Men, muscles without memory, minds dimmed, plodding, leaving bloodied footprints in the dirt. The quiet was awful. None of them cried, or yelled, or bellowed. No moans came from them. They lived in a mute territory, dead to feeling and protest. These were the legions, sold by sisters, stolen by brothers, bought by strangers, enslaved by the greedy, and betrayed by history.

For a long time I sat as in an open-air auditorium watching a troupe of tragic players enter and exit the stage.

The visions faded as my tears ceased. Light returned and I started the car, turned off the main road, and headed for the interior. Using rutted track roads, and lanes a little larger than footpaths, I found the River Pra. The black water moving quietly, ringed with the tall trees, seemed enchanted. A fear of snakes kept me in the car, but I parked and watched the bright sun turn the water surface into a rippling cloth of lamé.[6] I passed through villages that were little more than collections of thatch huts, with goats and small children wandering in the lanes. The noise of my car brought smiling adults out to wave at me.

In the late afternoon I reached the thriving town that was my destination. A student whom I had met at Legon (where the University of Ghana is located) had spoken to me often of the gold-mining area, of Dunkwa, his birthplace. His reports had so glowed with the town's virtues, I had chosen that spot for my first journey.

My skin color, features, and the Ghana cloth I wore would make me look like any young Ghanaian woman. I could pass if I didn't talk too much.

As usual, in the towns of Ghana, the streets were filled with vendors selling their wares of tinned pat milk, hot spicy Killi Willis (fried, ripe plantain chips), Pond's cold cream, and antimosquito incense rings. Farmers were returning home, children returning from school. Young boys grinned at mincing girls, and always there were the market women, huge and impervious. I searched for a hotel sign in vain and as the day lengthened, I started to worry. I didn't have enough gas to get to Koforidua, a large town east of Dunkwa, where there would certainly be hotels, and I didn't have the address of my student's family. I parked the car a little out of the town center and stopped a woman carrying a bucket of water on her head and a baby on her back.

"Good day." I spoke in Fanti and she responded. I continued, "I beg you, I am a stranger looking for a place to stay."

She repeated, "Stranger?" and laughed. "You are a stranger? No. No."

To many Africans, only whites could be strangers. All Africans belonged somewhere, to some clan. All Akan[7]-speaking people belong to one of eight blood lines (Abosua) and one of eight spirit lines (Ntoro).

I said, "I am not from here."

For a second, fear darted in her eyes. There was the possibility that I was a witch or some unhappy ghost from the country of the dead. I quickly said, "I am from Accra." She gave me a good smile. "Oh, one Accra. Without a home." She laughed. The Fanti word *Nkran,* for which

6. **lamé** (lă-mā′): a glittering fabric containing metallic threads.

7. **Akan** (ä′kän′): a language spoken in southern Ghana, of which Fanti is a dialect.

WORDS TO KNOW

mincing (mĭn′sĭng) *adj.* acting refined or dainty
impervious (ĭm-pûr′vē-əs) *adj.* incapable of being affected

the capital was named, means the large ant that builds 10-foot-high domes of red clay and lives with millions of other ants.

"Come with me." She turned quickly, steadying the bucket on her head, and led me between two corrugated tin shacks. The baby bounced and slept on her back, secured by the large piece of cloth wrapped around her body. We passed a compound where women were pounding the dinner *foo foo*[8] in wooden bowls.

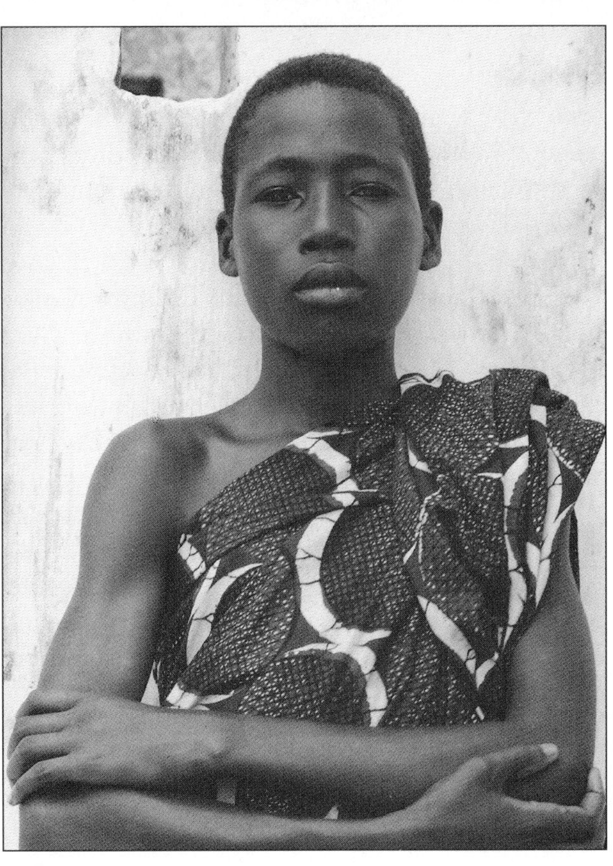

Samuel J. K. Essoun, Shama, Ghana, 1963, Paul Strand. Copyright © 1976, Aperture Foundation Inc., Paul Strand Archive.

The woman shouted, "Look what I have found. One Nkran which has no place to sleep tonight." The women laughed and asked, "One Nkran? I don't believe it."

"Are you taking it to the old man?"

"Of course."

"Sleep well, alone, Nkran, if you can." My guide stopped before a small house. She put the water on the ground and told me to wait while she entered the house. She returned immediately, followed by a man who rubbed his eyes as if he had just been awakened.

He walked close and peered hard at my face. "This is the Nkran?" The woman was adjusting the bucket on her head.

"Yes, Uncle. I have brought her." She looked at me, "Good-bye, Nkran. Sleep in peace. Uncle, I am going." The man said, "Go and come, child," and resumed studying my face. "You are not Ga."[9] He was reading my features.

A few small children had collected around his knees. They could barely hold back their giggles as he interrogated me.

"Aflao?"

I said, "No."

"Brong-ahafo?"

I said, "No. I am . . ." I meant to tell him the truth, but he said, "Don't tell me. I will soon know." He continued staring at me. "Speak more. I will know from your Fanti."

"Well, I have come from Accra and I need to rent a room for the night. I told that woman that I was a stranger . . ."

He laughed. "And you are. Now, I know. You are Bambara from Liberia. It is clear you are Bambara." He laughed again. "I always can tell. I am not easily fooled." He shook my hand. "Yes, we will find you a place for the night. Come." He touched a boy at his right. "Find Patience Aduah and bring her to me."

The children laughed, and all ran away as the man led me into the house. He pointed me to a seat in the neat little parlor and shouted, "Foriwa, we have a guest. Bring beer." A small black woman with an imperial air entered the room. Her knowing face told me that she had witnessed the scene in her front yard.

She spoke to her husband. "And, Kobina, did

8. *foo foo*: a starchy dough made from mashed yams, cassavas, or plantains.

9. **Ga** (gä): like *Aflao, Brong-ahafo,* and *Bambara* in the following sentences, the name of a West African ethnic group.

you find who the stranger was?" She walked to me. I stood and shook her hand. "Welcome, stranger." We both laughed. "Now don't tell me, Kobina, I have ears, also. Sit down, sister, beer is coming. Let me hear you speak."

We sat facing each other while her husband stood over us smiling. "You, Foriwa, you will never get it."

I told her my story, adding a few more words I had recently learned. She laughed grandly. "She is Bambara. I could have told you when Abaa first brought her. See how tall she is? See her head? See her color? Men, huh. They only look at a woman's shape."

Two children brought beer and glasses to the man, who poured and handed the glasses around. "Sister, I am Kobina Artey; this is my wife, Foriwa, and some of my children."

I introduced myself, but because they had taken such relish in detecting my tribal origin I couldn't tell them that they were wrong. Or, less admirably, at the moment I didn't want to remember that I was an American. For the first time since my arrival, I was very nearly home. Not a Ghanaian, but at least accepted for an African. The sensation was worth a lie.

Voices came to the house from the yard.

"Brother Kobina," "Uncle," "Auntie."

Foriwa opened the door to a group of people, who entered, speaking fast and looking at me.

"So this is the Bambara woman? The stranger?" They looked me over and talked with my hosts. I understood some of their conversation. They said that I was nice-looking and old enough to have a little wisdom. They announced that my car was parked a few blocks away. Kobina told them that I would spend the night with the newlyweds, Patience and Kwame Duodu. Yes, they could see clearly that I was a Bambara.

"Give us the keys to your car, sister; someone will bring your bag."

I gave up the keys and all resistance. I was either at home with friends or I would die wishing that to be so.

Later, Patience, her husband, Kwame, and I sat out in the yard around a cooking fire near to their thatched house, which was much smaller than the Artey bungalow. They explained that Kobina Artey was not a chief, but a member of the village council, and all small matters in that area of Dunkwa were taken to him. As Patience stirred the stew in the pot that was balanced over the fire, children and women appeared sporadically out of the darkness carrying covered plates. Each time Patience thanked the bearers and directed them to the house, I felt the distance narrow between my past and present.

In the United States, during segregation, black American travelers, unable to stay in hotels restricted to white patrons, stopped at churches and told the black ministers or

Nana Oparabea, High Priestess, Larteh, Ghana, 1963, Paul Strand. Copyright © 1976, Aperture Foundation Inc., Paul Strand Archive.

deacons of their predicaments. Church officials would select a home and then inform the unexpecting hosts of the decision. There was never a protest, but the new hosts relied on the generosity of their neighbors to help feed and even entertain their guests. After the travelers were settled, surreptitious knocks would sound on the back door.

In Stamps, Arkansas, I heard so often, "Sister Henderson, I know you've got guests. Here's a pan of biscuits."

"Sister Henderson, Mama sent a half a cake for your visitors."

"Sister Henderson, I made a lot of macaroni and cheese. Maybe this will help with your visitors."

My grandmother would whisper her thanks and finally when the family and guests sat down at the table, the offerings were so different and plentiful, it appeared that days had been spent preparing the meal.

Patience invited me inside, and when I saw the table I was confirmed in my earlier impression. Groundnut stew, garden egg stew, hot pepper soup, *kenke, kotomre,* fried plantain, *dukuno,* shrimp, fish cakes, and more, all crowded together on variously patterned plates.

In Arkansas, the guests would never suggest, although they knew better, that the host had not prepared every scrap of food, especially for them.

I said to Patience, "Oh, sister, you went to such trouble."

She laughed. "It is nothing, sister. We don't want our Bambara relative to think herself a stranger anymore. Come let us wash and eat."

After dinner, I followed Patience to the outdoor toilet; then they gave me a cot in a very small room.

In the morning, I wrapped my cloth under my arms, sarong fashion, and walked with Patience to the bathhouse. We joined about 20 women in a walled enclosure which had no ceiling. The greetings were loud and cheerful as we soaped ourselves and poured buckets of water over our shoulders.

Patience introduced me. "This is our Bambara sister."

"She's a tall one, all right. Welcome, sister."

"I like her color."

"How many children, sister?" The woman was looking at my breasts.

I apologized, "I only have one."

"One?"

"One?"

"One!" Shouts reverberated over the splashing water. I said, "One, but I'm trying."

They laughed. "Try hard, sister. Keep trying."

We ate leftovers from the last night feast, and I said a sad good-bye to my hosts. The children walked me back to my car, with the oldest boy carrying my bag. I couldn't offer money to my hosts, Arkansas had taught me that, but I gave change to the children. They bobbed and jumped and grinned.

"Good-bye, Bambara Auntie."

"Go and come, Auntie."

"Go and come."

I drove into Cape Coast before I thought of the gruesome castle and out of its environs before the ghosts of slavery caught me. Perhaps their attempts had been halfhearted. After all, in Dunkwa, although I had let a lie speak for me, I had proved that one of their descendants, at least one, could just briefly return to Africa, and that despite cruel betrayals, bitter ocean voyages, and hurtful centuries, we were still recognizable. ❖

WORDS TO KNOW	
	surreptitious (sûr'əp-tĭsh'əs) *adj.* secret; stealthy
	reverberate (rĭ-vûr'bə-rāt') *v.* to echo
	environs (ĕn-vī'rənz) *n.* a surrounding region

RESPONDING OPTIONS

FROM PERSONAL RESPONSE *TO* CRITICAL ANALYSIS

REFLECT **1.** What thoughts or feelings do you have about Angelou's experiences in Dunkwa? Describe your impressions in your notebook.

RETHINK **2.** Why do you think it matters to Angelou that she "had proved that one of their descendants, at least one, could just briefly return to Africa, and that despite cruel betrayals, bitter ocean voyages, and hurtful centuries, we were still recognizable"?

3. What makes Dunkwa seem like home to Angelou?

4. Do you think Angelou should have revealed that she was an American? Explain your opinion.

Consider
- the reasons she gives for not doing so
- her treatment as a consequence of her not doing so

5. How do you interpret Angelou's strong reaction the first time she passed by Cape Coast Castle?

Consider
- why she avoided the town for a year
- the scenes from the past she imagined
- her references to "purging" and "feeding the spirits"

RELATE **6.** While living in Africa, Angelou explored the lands of her ancestors. If you could visit the home of your ancestors, what would you most like to find out? Why?

LITERARY LINKS

Imagine a conversation between Maya Angelou and Olaudah Equiano, the African who was kidnapped and sent to the Americas on a slave ship (see page 102). What do you think they might say to each other? With a partner, write down some ideas and then dramatize the conversation for the class.

ANOTHER PATHWAY

Cooperative Learning

With a small group of classmates, act out a scene to show the villagers in Dunkwa welcoming Angelou as a fellow African. Or act out another scene to show what might have happened if Angelou had told the villagers that she was an American. Present your dramatization to the class.

QUICKWRITES

1. What makes a place feel like home? Write a **description** of a place (other than your own home) that feels like home to you. Use sensory details—details that appeal to the five senses—to make the place come to life for your readers.
2. Angelou was moved by her journey to her ancestors' lands. Draft a **poem** that captures her feelings about Cape Coast Castle, her visit to Dunkwa, or some other aspect of her experiences. As an alternative, you might draft a poem about your own response to Angelou's journey.

PORTFOLIO *Save your writing. You may want to use it later as a spring-board to a piece for your portfolio.*

LITERARY CONCEPTS

A **flashback** is a scene that interrupts the action of a narrative to describe events that took place at an earlier time. Flashbacks are usually used by writers of fiction and drama, but a writer of an autobiography might include flashbacks to give the background of actions and attitudes presented in the narrative. Consider the flashbacks that Angelou includes in this selection—descriptions of events that happened before her journey from Accra to Dunkwa. Make a time line like the one started to show the order of Angelou's actions on her journey. (Use a computer if you have one to set up your time line.) On this time line, indicate with an X each point at which a flashback occurs. What is the connection between the events of the journey and the events described in the flashbacks? What do the flashbacks illuminate or explain?

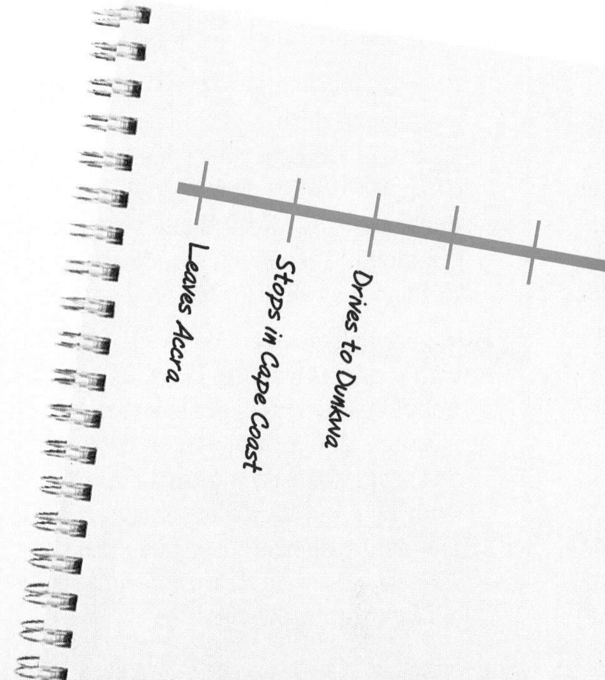

CRITIC'S CORNER

In her 1960 essay "What Is Africa to Me?—A Question of Identity," Pauli Murray writes about "the foreignness" she and other African Americans felt when visiting West Africa: "Finding themselves aliens in Africa is a severe jolt to those who came expecting instant acceptance from their African brothers." Angelou also refers to the pain of being rejected by Africans. Speculate about why some Africans might reject African Americans. Why do you think Angelou was accepted in Dunkwa?

Cape Coast Castle in Ghana. Werner Forman Archive, courtesy of Entwistle Gallery, London/Art Resource, New York.

Nigerian dish. Photo by Dennis Gottlieb.

ACROSS THE CURRICULUM

Home Economics Prepare one of the dishes that Angelou mentions in the selection (or another West African dish) and share it with the class. You might find a recipe in an African or international cookbook or by consulting a person familiar with African cooking. Explain to your classmates what ingredients are used in the dish and how it is prepared.

ALTERNATIVE ACTIVITIES

1. Angelou felt that with her skin color, features, and Ghana cloth, she could pass for a young Ghanaian woman. What does a typical Ghanaian man or woman look like? What does he or she wear? Make an **illustration** of traditional Ghanaian dress, or obtain such clothing and model it for the class.
2. Important events in Ghana are celebrated with music and dancing. Every movement in traditional dances conveys an idea or message, and a combination of movements tells a story. Create a **dance** to illustrate Angelou's journey. Choose your own music and dance steps, or use traditional West African music and dance movements. Perform your dance for the class.

WORDS TO KNOW

Review the Words to Know in the boxes at the bottom of the selection pages. On your paper, write the word that most clearly relates to each phrase below. Then write a sentence containing both the phrase and the vocabulary word.

1. an out-of-control car
2. a map of Accra and its suburbs
3. the light at sunset
4. a stone that is undamaged by harsh weather
5. a slave's secret plan of escape
6. the villagers' loud singing
7. an unwanted offer of money
8. the scent of hot pepper soup
9. sorrow that needs release
10. villagers who try to act sophisticated in front of strangers

MAYA ANGELOU

1928–

Maya Angelou's formal education ended with high school, but she has continued to search for knowledge of herself and the world around her. Her search has taken her from rural Stamps, Arkansas, where as a child she lived with her grandmother, to as far away as Ghana and Egypt. She has said in *Black Women Writers at Work,* "I believe all things are possible for a human being, and I don't think there's anything in the world I can't do." Angelou's life bears witness that she lives by this philosophy.

After high school, Angelou worked days to support herself and her son while she studied dance at night. Her talent led to a scholarship to study dance in New York City, where she eventually worked under the celebrated performer and teacher Martha Graham. She soon made her mark as a dancer, actress, singer, director, and producer, both in the United States and abroad.

Angelou, who began writing in the 1960s, has written poems, plays, songs, short stories, screenplays, articles, and television specials. She has also written five autobiographical works, including *All God's Children Need Traveling Shoes,* the source of this selection. In this book, she writes about the four years she spent in newly independent Ghana in the early 1960s. While living there, Angelou worked as a journalist and an assistant administrator at the University of Ghana and explored her African heritage. "I had not consciously come to Ghana to find the roots of my beginnings," she states in the book, "but I had continually and accidentally tripped over them or fallen upon them in my everyday life."

One of the highlights of Angelou's career was being asked to compose a poem for President Bill Clinton's inauguration. She wrote about 200 pages by hand before finishing the 107-line poem, "On the Pulse of Morning," which she read for the nation in Washington, D.C., on January 20, 1993.

OTHER WORKS *I Know Why the Caged Bird Sings, The Heart of a Woman, The Complete Collected Poems of Maya Angelou*

• *ART GALLERY*

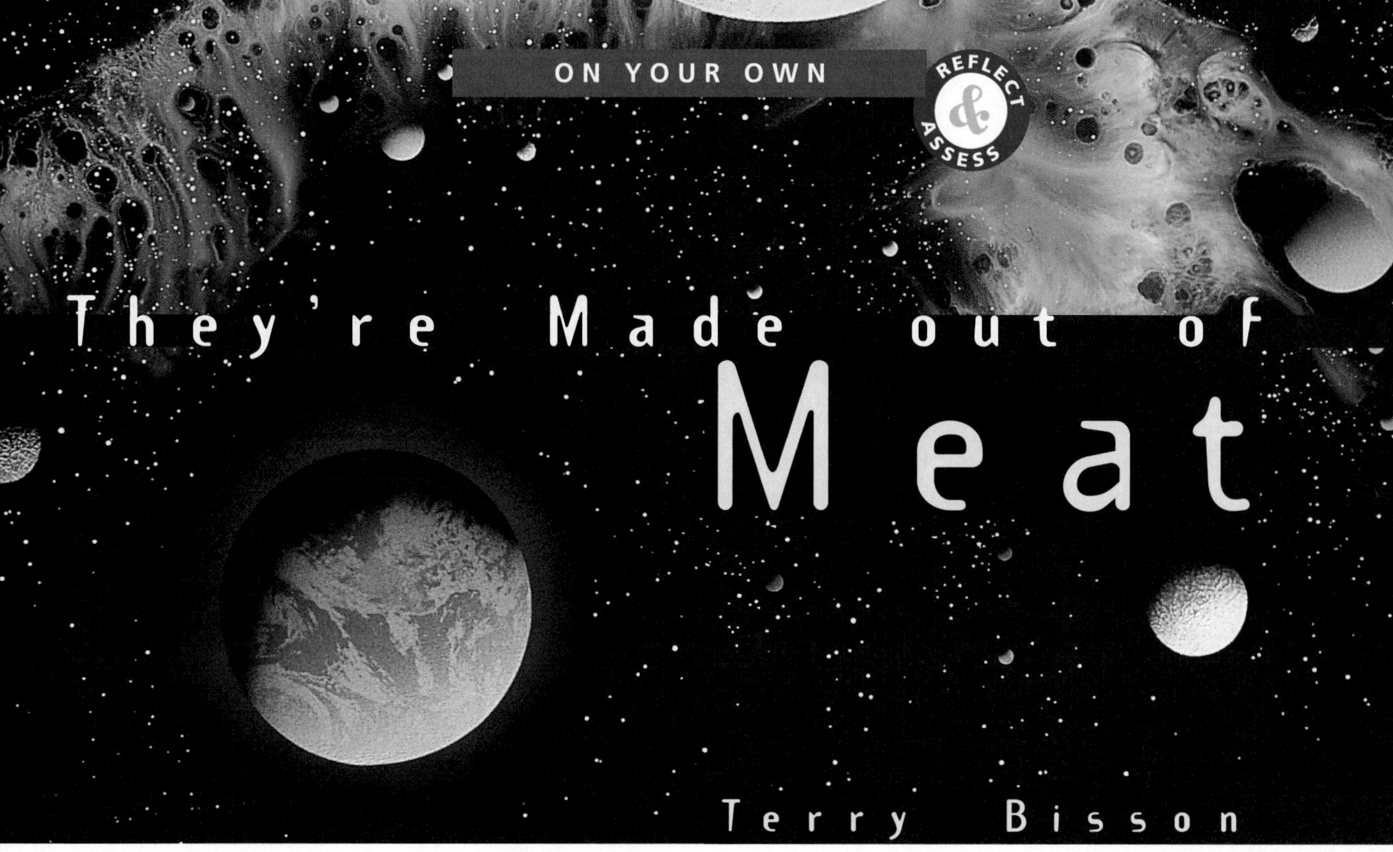

They're Made out of Meat

Terry Bisson

"They're made out of meat."

"Meat?"

"Meat. They're made out of meat."

"Meat?"

"There's no doubt about it. We picked up several from different parts of the planet, took them aboard our recon vessels,[1] and probed them all the way through. They're completely meat."

"That's impossible. What about the radio signals? The messages to the stars?"

"They use the radio waves to talk, but the signals don't come from them. The signals come from machines."

"So who made the machines? That's who we want to contact."

"*They* made the machines. That's what I'm trying to tell you. Meat made the machines."

"That's ridiculous. How can meat make a machine? You're asking me to believe in sentient[2] meat."

"I'm not asking you. I'm telling you. These creatures are the only sentient race in that sector, and they're made out of meat."

"Maybe they're like the orfolei.[3] You know, a carbon-based intelligence that goes through a meat stage."

"Nope. They're born meat and they die meat. We studied them for several of their life spans, which didn't take long. Do you have any idea of the life span of meat?"

"Spare me. Okay, maybe they're only part meat. You know, like the weddilei. A meat head with an electron plasma[4] brain inside."

"Nope. We thought of that, since they do have meat heads, like the weddilei. But I told you, we probed them. They're meat all the way through."

"No brain?"

"Oh, there's a brain all right. It's just that the

---

1. **recon** (rē′kŏn′) **vessels:** vehicles used for exploring and gathering information.
2. **sentient** (sĕn′shənt): capable of feeling or sensation.
3. **orfolei:** like *weddilei* in a following sentence, an invented name for an extraterrestrial race of beings.
4. **electron plasma:** a gaslike material composed of electrons, negatively charged particles that are parts of atoms.

brain is *made out of meat!* That's what I've been trying to tell you."

"So . . . what does the thinking?"

"You're not understanding, are you? You're refusing to deal with what I'm telling you. The brain does the thinking. The meat."

"Thinking meat! You're asking me to believe in thinking meat!"

"Yes, thinking meat! Conscious meat! Loving meat. Dreaming meat. The meat is the whole deal! Are you beginning to get the picture, or do I have to start all over?"

"Omigod. You're serious, then. They're made out of meat."

"Thank you. Finally. Yes. They are indeed made out of meat. And they've been trying to get in touch with us for almost a hundred of their years."

"Omigod. So what does this meat have in mind?"

"First it wants to talk to us. Then I imagine it wants to explore the universe, contact other sentiences, swap ideas and information. The usual."

"We're supposed to talk to meat."

"That's the idea. That's the message they're sending out by radio. 'Hello. Anyone out there? Anybody home?' That sort of thing."

"They actually do talk, then. They use words, ideas, concepts?"

"Oh, yes. Except they do it with meat."

"I thought you just told me they used radio."

"They do, but what do you think is *on* the radio? Meat sounds. You know how when you slap or flap meat, it makes a noise? They talk by flapping their meat at each other. They can even sing by squirting air through their meat."

"Omigod. Singing meat. This is altogether too much. So what do you advise?"

"Officially or unofficially?"

"Both."

"Officially, we are required to contact, welcome, and log in any and all sentient races or multibeings in this quadrant of the universe, without prejudice, fear, or favor. Unofficially, I advise that we erase the records and forget the whole thing."

"I was hoping you would say that."

"It seems harsh, but there is a limit. Do we really want to make contact with meat?"

"I agree one hundred percent. What's there to say? 'Hello, meat. How's it going?' But will this work? How many planets are we dealing with here?"

"Just one. They can travel to other planets in special meat containers, but they can't live on them. And being meat, they can only travel through C space.[5] Which limits them to the speed of light and makes the possibility of their ever making contact pretty slim. Infinitesimal, in fact."

"So we just pretend there's no one home in the universe."

"That's it."

"Cruel. But you said it yourself, who wants to meet meat? And the ones who have been aboard our vessels, the ones you probed? You're sure they won't remember?"

"They'll be considered crackpots if they do. We went into their heads and smoothed out their meat so that we're just a dream to them."

"A dream to meat! How strangely appropriate, that we should be meat's dream."

"And we marked the entire sector *unoccupied.*"

"Good. Agreed, officially and unofficially. Case closed. Any others? Anyone interesting on that side of the galaxy?"

"Yes, a rather shy but sweet hydrogen core cluster intelligence in a class nine star in G445 zone. Was in contact two galactic rotations[6] ago, wants to be friendly again."

"They always come around."

"And why not? Imagine how unbearably, how unutterably cold the universe would be if one were all alone. . . ." ❖

---

5. **C space:** an invented name for the space in which the visible universe exists, where—according to Einstein's special theory of relativity—no material body can travel at a speed equal to or greater than the speed of light (symbolized by the letter *c*).
6. **galactic rotations:** periods defined by the time it takes our galaxy, the Milky Way, to complete a full rotation about its center (about 225 million years).

Officially, we are required to contact, welcome, and log in any and all sentient races or multibeings in this quadrant of the universe, without prejudice, fear, or favor.

Unofficially, I advise that we erase the records and **forget** the whole thing.

Terry Bisson

1942–

Terry Bisson has worked as a magazine comic writer, an auto mechanic, and a book editor, but since 1978 he has focused primarily on writing science fiction, fantasy, and nonfiction. He has won numerous science fiction and fantasy writing awards, including the Nebula Award and the Hugo Award.

Bisson says that he was inspired to write "They're Made out of Meat" by a comment of the contemporary American poet Allen Ginsberg: "Allen Ginsberg once corrected a pompous TV interviewer, who was prating on about their souls communicating, by saying 'We're just meat talking to meat.'" Bisson further explains, "I wrote this story to amuse my family and only afterward realized that . . . I was digging in SF's [science fiction's] richest if most-worked lode, the First Contact tale." This short story, written entirely in dialogue, has also been presented as a dramatization at the West Bank Cafe in New York City.

OTHER WORKS *Wyrldmaker, Talking Man, Voyage to the Red Planet, Bears Discover Fire and Other Stories*

WRITING FROM

EXPERIENCE

WRITING TO EXPLAIN

Unit One, "Origins and Encounters," shows how people once used narrative—myths, stories, and reports—to try to understand their world. Today, we are more likely to use analysis to try to understand something. Analysis can be used to

- solve a problem or mystery
- track changes over time
- explain or understand a situation
- prove a point

GUIDED ASSIGNMENT

Write an Analytical Report What topics have bewildered, intrigued, or disturbed you? Many times in your life—at school or on the job—you may be asked to analyze an event or a situation and present your findings to a group.

1 Indulge Your Curiosity

How does this machine work? What caused this disaster? Why did this event happen? A good analysis starts with your curiosity about a topic. List a few current or historical events, issues, or situations that have fascinated or puzzled you. You might look through encyclopedias, newspapers, magazines, or your personal notebook for ideas. Clip or photocopy articles that interest you.

2 What Would You Like to Know?

The items on these pages are examples of the kinds of materials you may have collected on a particular topic. What information is provided by each source? What questions do the materials raise in your mind? What connections can you make between the materials?

Decision Point Now choose one of your own topics for further exploration. Write your observations and questions in your notebook.

Science Article

What are different types of radioactive waste? How are they being stored?

Wanted: A Garbage Can That Will Last 10,000 Years!

What do you do with something that you can't burn, treat with chemicals, or dump into the ground or ocean? What if it will remain dangerous for several thousand years? Scientists and environmentalists are working on just those problems as they find ways to dispose of radioactive waste from nuclear power plants, uranium mining, and uranium-processing plants.

What makes radioactive waste so dangerous? Even low-level radioactive materials can damage human health if the particles are inhaled or swallowed. High-level waste, such as uranium by-products from mining or processing, can cause skin burns, radiation sickness, and several types of cancer, especially in children.

14 Section 2 Thursday, August 29, 1996

Radioactive Bar

Found in Fi

By Thomas Isaac

Two 11-year

homes f

bar

WRITING COACH

Graph from Textbook

HOW LONG RESERVES WILL LAST

?

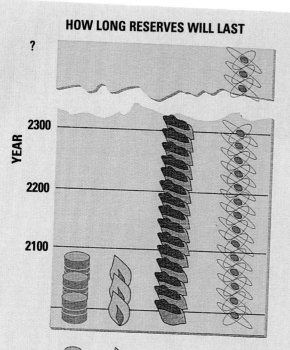

YEAR

2300

2200

2100

OIL GAS COAL URANIUM

What would we use instead of uranium? Oil, gas, and coal supplies are running low!

Uranium is a plentiful source of energy. What information about uranium as an energy source is missing from this graph?

Feature Article

How did this situation develop? Where was federal government all those years?

ENVIRONMENT

The Sequoyah Syndrome

In 1994, the Cherokee Nation won its ten-year battle to shut down the Sequoyah Fuels Company, a uranium-processing plant built on Cherokee land in Gore, Oklahoma. The plant was developed in the 1970s to convert raw uranium ore into uranium fuel rods for nuclear power plants. The company had been dumping radioactive waste into the surrounding land and water for over 20 years.

Federal investigators found that water near the plant contained 35,000 times the level of uranium particles considered safe by federal standards. Now the remaining questions are how to dispose of the radioactive waste and who will pay for the cleanup.

ECOLOGY

PREWRITING

Analyzing Your Topic

Characteristics of Analysis Have you ever taken something apart just to find out how it works? If you have, you've followed the basic steps in analysis:

- Break a subject down into its parts.
- Study the relationship of each part to the whole.
- Draw conclusions from what you learned.

You'll use these same analytical steps whenever you write about a problem or a complex situation.

1 Explore the Topic

Once you have chosen your topic, begin breaking the topic into its parts. These parts might be

- characteristics
- stages
- steps in a process
- issues involved

You can then list the questions you want to investigate and possible sources for each part. The planning chart shows how one student broke a topic into parts, then listed questions and possible resources.

Student's Planning Chart

Radioactive Waste
What It Is–How It's Handled

1. Types of Rad-Waste
Look up what types there are. How long do they stay radioactive? Use encyclopedias, magaz-ines, books, CD-ROM encyclopedia.

2. What are effects of different types?
What kind of damage does each kind do? Talk to science teacher, maybe call EPA, use Internet?

3. How are types stored?
Probably different methods used temporary-permanent?
Use books, check Internet? Might be good sources in government bookstore downtown.

2 Conduct Your Research

Besides using print media, on-line services, and audiovisual resources, you may want to explore these sources:

Museums, Foundations, Local and Federal Agencies These organizations often have a wealth of information available to the public. Your teacher and the reference librarian can help you identify and contact these groups.

Interviews with Experts and Special Interest Groups You may be able to interview an expert on your topic or a member of a special interest group. For example, the writer covering the subject of radioactive waste might interview science teachers, environmental activists, or nuclear power plant officials. Keep in mind that some of these people have biased viewpoints.

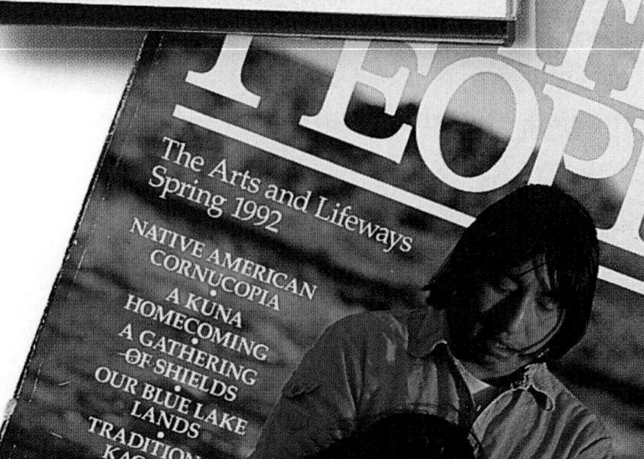

The Arts and Lifeways
Spring 1992
NATIVE AMERICAN CORNUCOPIA
A KUNA HOMECOMING
A GATHERING OF SHIELDS
OUR BLUE LAKE LANDS
TRADITIONAL KACHINA CARVINGS

3 Check with an Expert

After you've done some initial research, you may want to share your thoughts and ideas with one of the people you contacted or someone else who is knowledgeable on the subject.

- Experts can give you feedback on your choice of topic, on your initial analysis, and on the questions you have developed for your research.
- They can also help you evaluate your references and suggest others. See the SkillBuilder for tips on evaluating sources.
- You can talk over any illustrations or charts you might use.

4 Be Open to Change

Your research may change the way you look at your topic or may even cause you to choose a different topic altogether. For example, you may start out analyzing types of radioactive waste and end up describing the Cherokee Nation's dilemma. You may also come up with alternative ways to present your report. (See Share Your Work on page 137 for ideas.)

5 Organize Your Facts

Can you organize your facts using one or more of these formats?

Cause and effect explores the relationship between causes (for example, leaky storage drums) and effects (radioactive materials in our water supply).

Compare and contrast shows the similarities and differences among the parts of a topic (such as looking at how low-level and high-level radioactive wastes are alike and different).

Description examines the characteristics of each part (such as the life span, dangers, and storage of high-level waste) and the part's relationship to the whole.

Problem and solution identifies the problem (what to do with radioactive waste) and various solutions (underground caverns, find a way to recycle it).

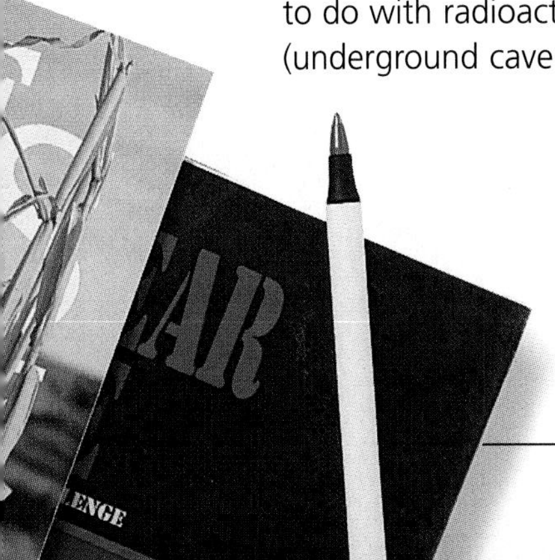

SkillBuilder

CRITICAL THINKING

Evaluating Your Sources
Evaluate the usefulness and reliability of your references by asking:

1. Is the author an expert or a recognized authority on the topic? The book jacket or introduction often gives author credentials.
2. Is the source primary (an eyewitness account or original document) or secondary (an interpretation of primary sources)? Primary sources may be more authentic; secondary sources generally provide more analysis.
3. Does the author seem to have a particular bias (for example, using emotional language or presenting only one side of the story)? A biased viewpoint can make the source less reliable.

APPLYING WHAT YOU'VE LEARNED
As you take notes, crosscheck your facts with at least two sources. You need to verify the accuracy of your information.

THINK & PLAN

Reflecting on Your Topic

1. What do you need to know to do a good analysis? What additional sources do you need to complete your analysis?
2. How can you verify your facts? Which sources seem to offer more reliable details?
3. What preliminary conclusions can you draw from the information you have found?

DRAFTING

Developing Your Ideas

The Heart of the Matter By this point, you have focused on a topic and completed enough research to begin writing. Your first step might be to give some order to the information you've gathered. You can do this with index cards, by using an outline, or just by writing. You might consider using one of the organizing structures on the previous pages.

1 Write a Discovery Draft

Write down your main points and any preliminary conclusions. See the SkillBuilder for tips on classifying and categorizing.

In the draft below, the Writing Coach was used to organize information. How has this topic been broken into parts? What kinds of information are included in each section?

Student's Discovery Draft

Radioactive Trash

My Discovery Draft	My Comments My Discovery Draft
Different types of radioactive waste require their own types of safe, long-term storage. Low-level radiation is only slightly radioactive. Includes things like workers' overalls and gloves. Sealed in steel drums and buried in concrete-lined trenches or underground caverns. This type of radioactivity cannot penetrate the skin but can cause damage if you inhale or swallow it.	Explain what radiation is? How it's produced? Mention natural radiation around us?
Intermediate radiation, by comparison, is more radioactive. It has a half-life of 20 years to become safe, so storage has to be secure, usually encased in concrete. Exposure to this type can cause skin burns and some types of cancer.	Give examples of intermediate and high-level radioactive waste. Better define half-life.
In contrast, high-level radiation (plutonium, uranium waste from mining) can remain radioactive for hundreds or thousands of years. Gamma rays are stopped only by several layers of concrete and steel. Even limited exposure can cause serious illnesses or death within a short time. Must be stored deep underground—maybe inside Western mountains.	Define gamma rays.
Conclusions: Different types of radioactive waste represent different dangers. Each type must be stored securely, some permanently.	Try to get diagrams or pictures of storage containers or sites, maybe from CD-ROM encyclopedia.

② Examine Your First Draft

Are you ready to examine what you have written so far? You might begin by asking yourself the following questions:

- Have I broken down my topic in a logical way?
- How well have I described each part or stage of the subject? (such as low-level, intermediate, high-level waste)
- What definitions of terms or illustrations would make the subject clearer to the reader? (like half-life, gamma rays)
- How reasonable are my preliminary conclusions based on the facts I have? (We know more about disposal now.)

③ Rework Your Draft

The guidelines below can help you develop your draft.

- Be sure your organizing structure still fits your subject.
- Develop a strong introduction that "hooks" the reader. An analysis does not have to be dry, dull reading. You can cite a startling statistic, describe a dramatic moment, ask a question, or stress the importance of your topic.
- Verify your facts and cite your sources. Accuracy is essential when analyzing a subject.
- Create a strong ending that helps summarize the analysis for the readers. Tell them what is important about the analysis and how it might relate to their lives.

PEER RESPONSE

A peer reviewer can point out the strengths and weaknesses of your draft. List questions you might want to ask, such as:

- What is the subject of my analysis? What question or problem was I trying to explain?
- What information could I provide that would make the analysis clearer?
- As you read, please tell me whenever you don't understand the connection between one part and another.
- What points do you find the most, or least, interesting?
- Are the conclusions clear? Why or why not?

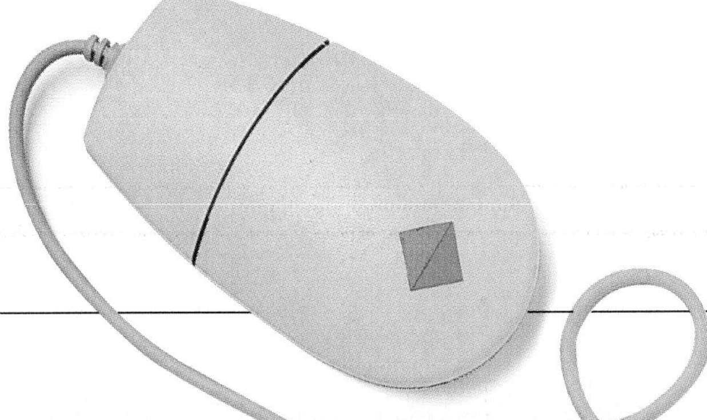

SkillBuilder

CRITICAL THINKING

Classifying/Categorizing

Classification is the process of organizing or grouping items into different categories. You can then analyze each category's features and compare and contrast the similarities and differences within or among categories. Look over the example below.

Radioactive Waste		
low-level	intermediate	high-level
least radioactive	more radioactive	very radioactive
shorter half-life	half-life 20+ years	half-life up to 10,000 years
harmful if inhaled or swallowed	skin burns, cancers	cancers, diseases, death
easier to store	harder to store	hardest to store

APPLYING WHAT YOU'VE LEARNED

Using a graphic organizer can help you to classify your topic into categories and to analyze their features, similarities, and differences.

RETHINK & EVALUATE

Preparing to Revise

1. How can you improve the logical flow of your ideas?
2. Have you covered everything that should be covered?
3. Can you clarify any connections that your peer reviewer didn't understand?

REVISING AND PUBLISHING

Finishing Your Report

The Final Touches Your final step is to make sure your report fulfills your purpose and provides a clear analysis of your topic for the reader. Mistakes in facts or logic, or poor organization, can distract your readers and make them question the accuracy of the rest of your paper. Use peer responses and the tips on these pages to help you identify any remaining weaknesses in your work.

1 Revise and Edit

You can put aside your draft for a day or two, or give it to someone else to read. Then reread it with a fresh eye. Check for the following:

- The topic or issue you are analyzing should be clearly stated in the first paragraph.
- The reader should understand how each part relates to the whole.
- The organizing structure should help the reader follow your points.
- The conclusion should summarize your main ideas.

Look over the Standards for Evaluation and the Editing Checklist on the next page to help you revise your work.

Student's Revised Essay

Taking Out the Radioactive Trash

Imagine this: You take out the trash, only you have to find a place that will store it for a few hundred years without allowing it to leak into the ground, water, or air. That's what has to be done to dispose of radioactive waste from nuclear power plants, nuclear research, and uranium mining. Fortunately, the nuclear industry has learned a lot about how to handle this kind of "trash."

How does the writer catch the reader's attention in the first paragraph? What makes the reader want to know more about the topic?

Disposing of radioactive waste is a lot harder than just "taking out the trash." Low-level, intermediate-level, and high-level waste require different containers and methods of storage to protect the environment. The real challenge is creating storage that will seal the most radioactive material until it decays into a harmless form—which can take from 20 years to several thousand years. Underground caverns in the western mountains may be the answer, which would create a full circle. We take radioactive material out of the ground for fuel; then we return the waste to the earth for safe storage.

What conclusions does the writer draw? What facts are cited to support them?

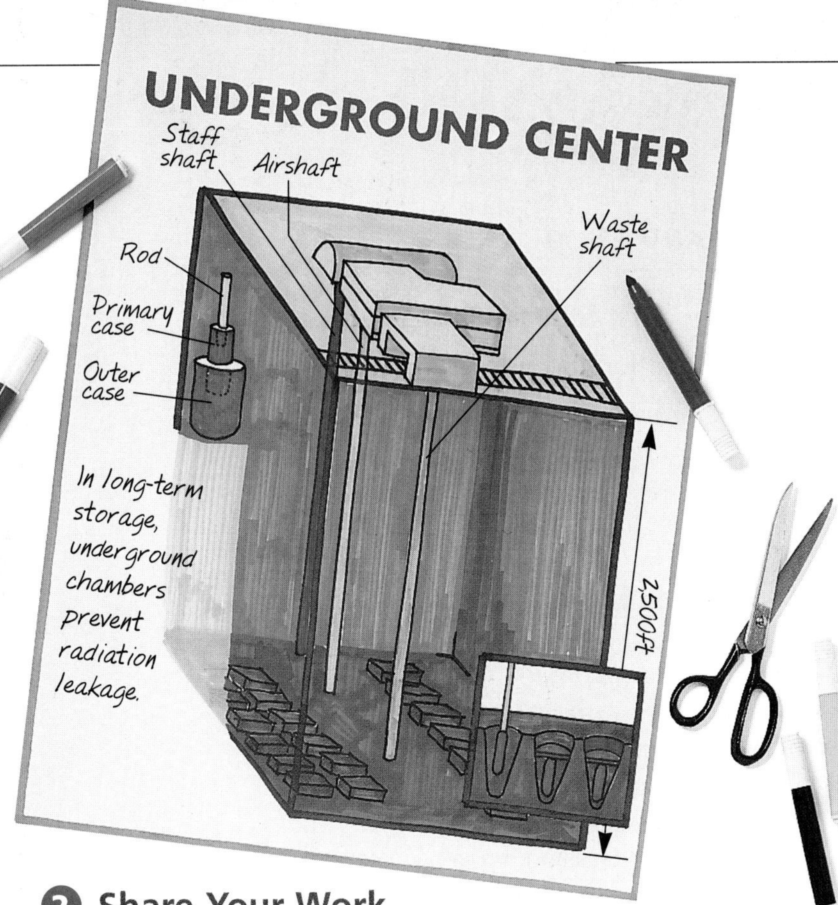

❷ Share Your Work

An analysis might be presented as an illustrated talk or informative booklet. The student writer reporting on radioactive waste might make transparencies or include diagrams in a booklet to show the different types of waste and the containers developed to store them.

Combining visual aids with written material can help your readers understand the individual parts of your analysis as well as the whole.

Standards for Evaluation
An effective analysis • hooks the reader's attention with a strong introduction • clearly states the subject and its individual parts • uses a specific organizing structure to provide a logical flow of information • shows connections among facts and ideas through subordinate clauses and transitional words and phrases • uses appropriate language and details for the audience • ends with a satisfying, effective conclusion

SkillBuilder

Using Subordinate Clauses
Subordinate clauses can help your readers see the connections between facts and ideas more clearly. Compare these examples.

1. Uranium has a long half-life. It can pollute an area for years.
2. *Because uranium has a long half-life*, it can pollute an area for years.

GRAMMAR HANDBOOK

See subordinate clauses, page 1232 in the Grammar Handbook.

Editing Checklist Use these revising and editing tips.

- Are names spelled correctly?
- Have I used subordinate clauses to show logical connections?
- Did I proofread my draft?

REFLECT & ASSESS

Evaluating the Experience

1. What did you enjoy most about writing an analysis? How well did you analyze the relationship of each part to the whole?
2. How did you organize your analysis? How can you use this organizational technique in other situations?

PORTFOLIO List your successes and problems with writing an analytical report. Add your list and finished analysis to your portfolio.

REFLECT & ASSESS

UNIT 1: ORIGINS AND ENCOUNTERS

What did you learn about Native American culture from reading this unit? Did you find out anything new about the first Europeans and Africans to come to this continent? Choose one or more of the options in each of these sections to help you explore how your thinking has developed.

REFLECTING ON THE UNIT

OPTION 1 **Old Beliefs, New Literature** Consider how the ancient Native American selections relate to the more contemporary ones in the first part of this unit. What traditions—such as values, beliefs, and forms of storytelling—do you see continuing into the present? How have these traditions been adapted, or changed, to fit contemporary needs? Write a few paragraphs to explain your ideas.

OPTION 2 **Explorers and Exploiters** Think back over the selections in Part 2 of this unit. What things was each author encountering for the first time? What similarities and differences between the different encounters do you notice? Do any of the selections seem unrelated to the title "First Encounters"? Get together with a partner to discuss these questions, and jot down your conclusions.

OPTION 3 **Different World Views** How do the attitudes expressed in Part 1, "In Harmony with Nature," differ from those expressed in Part 2, "First Encounters"? With a small group of classmates, discuss the differences.

Consider

- ideas about nature
- ideas about good and evil
- ideas about how human beings should behave

REFLECT & ASSESS *Self-Assessment: To explore how your understanding has developed as you read this unit, create a two-column chart. In the first column, list what you knew about Native Americans and explorers before you read the selections. In the second column, list important facts and concepts you discovered.*

REVIEWING LITERARY CONCEPTS

OPTION 1 **Considering Conflict** You know that conflict forms the basis of a plot and that the resolution of the conflict often concludes a story. To help you analyze the conflicts in the stories that you read in this unit, make a chart like the one shown. Then write a few sentences telling why you particularly liked the way one or two of the conflicts were resolved. Write a few more sentences, telling which resolutions, if any, you found unsatisfying and giving reasons for your opinion.

Selection	Conflict	How Conflict Is Resolved
"The World on the Turtle's Back"	Twins struggle to overcome each other.	Straight-minded twin kills his brother, but both continue to have power over different parts of the world.

OPTION 2 **Oral Literature and Historical Records** In this unit you have read not only Native American oral literature—myths, tales, and songs—but also historical documents written by some of the first non-native people in North America. How do these two kinds of literature differ? With a small group of classmates, discuss what each kind of literature contributes to your understanding of early America.

REFLECT & ASSESS *Self-Assessment: Did you understand conflict, oral literature, and historical documents well enough to complete one of the options above? On a sheet of paper, copy the following list of literary terms introduced in this unit. Next to each, rate your understanding of the concept from 1 (none at all) to 5 (absolute mastery).*

myth	*primary and secondary sources*
repetition	*imagery*
trickster tale	*author's purpose*
narrator	*flashback*
audience	

PORTFOLIO BUILDING

- **QuickWrites** Several of the QuickWrites in this unit asked you to relate the ideas presented in selections to your own ideas and experiences. Review your writing for the QuickWrites, and choose two pieces that you feel present particularly insightful or interesting connections. Write a cover note explaining your choices. Then attach your note to the pieces and add them to your portfolio.
- **Writing About Literature** Earlier in this unit, you examined details in a selection to gain a greater understanding of a culture. How has the experience of noting and writing about details influenced what you see when you find yourself in a new environment? Include a note about your thoughts with your writing if you choose to keep it in your portfolio.
- **Writing from Experience** When you wrote an analytical report, you had to take something apart, examine the pieces, and explore their relationships. Did you find this process easy, moderately difficult, or very difficult? Why do you think you found it so?
- **Personal Choice** Look back through your records of the activities in which you interpreted or performed selections in this unit. Also look at the writing you did for assignments and on your own. In which activity or piece of writing do you think you presented your interpretation of a selection most effectively? Choose one and write a note describing why you think your presentation was effective. Attach the note to the piece of writing or activity record and add both to your portfolio.

REFLECT & ASSESS *Self-Assessment: At this point, you may just be beginning your portfolio. Are the pieces you have included so far ones you think you'll keep, or do you think you will replace them as the year goes on?*

SETTING GOALS

As you thought about the selections in this unit, did you want to know more about the original inhabitants of North America and about the Europeans and Africans who came later? Jot down a few questions you would like to investigate on your own.

UNIT TWO

From Colony to Country

A Morning View of Blue Hill Village (1824), Jonathan Fisher. William A Farnsworth Library and Art Museum, Rockland, Maine, museum purchase, 1965 (1465.134).

The Lord will make our name a praise and glory, so that men shall say of succeeding plantations: "The Lord make it like that of New England." For we must consider that we shall be like a City upon a Hill; the eyes of all people are on us.

JOHN WINTHROP
First Governor of the Massachusetts Bay Colony

TIME LINE

From Colony to Country

1630

Under the leadership of John Winthrop, about 900 Puritans from England establish the Massachusetts Bay Colony.

1665

The English mathematician and philosopher Isaac Newton begins his investigations into the laws governing the universe.

Isaac Newton's laws of motion and gravity contributed to the growing belief in the power of reason, a belief that characterized the Age of Reason. The English philosopher John Locke argued that human beings could control their own destiny through the exercise of reason. These new scientific and philosophic ideas greatly influenced the leaders of the American Revolution.

1676

The Puritans' victory in King Philip's War ends Native American resistance in the New England colonies.

The bloodiest conflict of 17th-century New England, King Philip's War was named after the second son of Massasoit, chief of the Wampanoag and a good friend to the early Pilgrims. When Philip (whose Wampanoag name was Metacomet) became chief, he organized the Wampanoag, the Narragansett, and other tribes to fight the increased white settlement of their homeland. Before Philip was killed by the colonists and Indian resistance collapsed, more than 600 colonists and 3,000 Indians had been killed and 12 towns had been destroyed.

1682

Quakers led by William Penn make peace with Native Americans in Pennsylvania, and they live in harmony for about 70 years.

1690

John Locke publishes *Two Treatises on Civil Government,* stating that all people have three natural rights: life, liberty, and property.

1691

A new charter provides for religious tolerance in Massachusetts, weakening the Puritans' control of religious life.

1692

Trials for witchcraft take place in Salem, Massachusetts.

1721

During a smallpox epidemic in New England, Puritan leader Cotton Mather advocates inoculation and incurs the anger of his congregation, which believes that smallpox infection is God's will.

1727

Quakers demand the abolition of slavery.

1763

The British defeat the French in the French and Indian War, claiming virtually all land east of the Mississippi and in Canada.

1765

The British Parliament passes the Stamp Act, which levies a tax on the colonies to help pay off British debts.

1773

To protest a new British tax on tea, enraged colonists stage the Boston Tea Party, dumping huge amounts of tea into Boston Harbor.

1775

The "shot heard round the world" is fired on Lexington Green in Massachusetts, starting the Revolutionary War.

1776

Thomas Paine writes *Common Sense,* convincing many colonists that independence from England is their "destiny."

1781

The British surrender to General George Washington at Yorktown, ending the Revolutionary War.

1789

George Washington is elected the first president of the United States.

Women in America and England had few legal rights. Married women could not own property or make a will. As late as 1770, the British Parliament passed a law forbidding women to use "scents, paints, cosmetics, washes, artificial teeth, false hair, Spanish wool, iron stays, high-heeled shoes, or bolstered hips" to trick men into marriage.

Period *Pieces*

Paul Revere silver tea pot

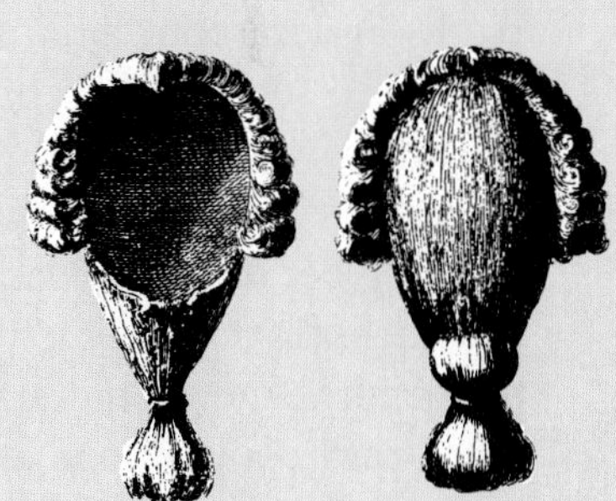

Popular style of wig in the 18th century

Puritan pocket watch

PART 1 INTRODUCTION

Between Heaven and Hell

The Puritan Tradition

Puritans too often have the reputation of being black-clad moralists self-righteously proclaiming the values of thrift and hard work. According to the American writer and humorist H. L. Mencken, a Puritan is one who suspects that "somewhere someone is having a good time." To call someone a puritan is usually not a compliment.

This negative image, however, is based on a stereotype of the 16th-century Puritans that, like most stereotypes, is full of half-truths and misconceptions. True, the Puritans did value hard work and self-sacrifice, but they also honored material success. Wealth was considered to be the reward of a virtuous life. Some Puritans, especially the early Pilgrims, wore severe black clothing because that was all they had. Those who settled the Massachusetts Bay Colony after 1630, however, were better off financially. They could afford decorative and colorful clothing—when they could find it in the colony, that is. These Puritans were even known to drink beer and other alcoholic beverages on occasion.

Puritans also valued family life, community service, art, and literature. They were the first in the colonies to establish a printing press, free public grammar schools, and a college (Harvard).

On the other hand, the Puritans *were* arrogant in their religious faith and completely intolerant of viewpoints different from their own. Puritans who remained in England

Tombstone design from Puritan New England

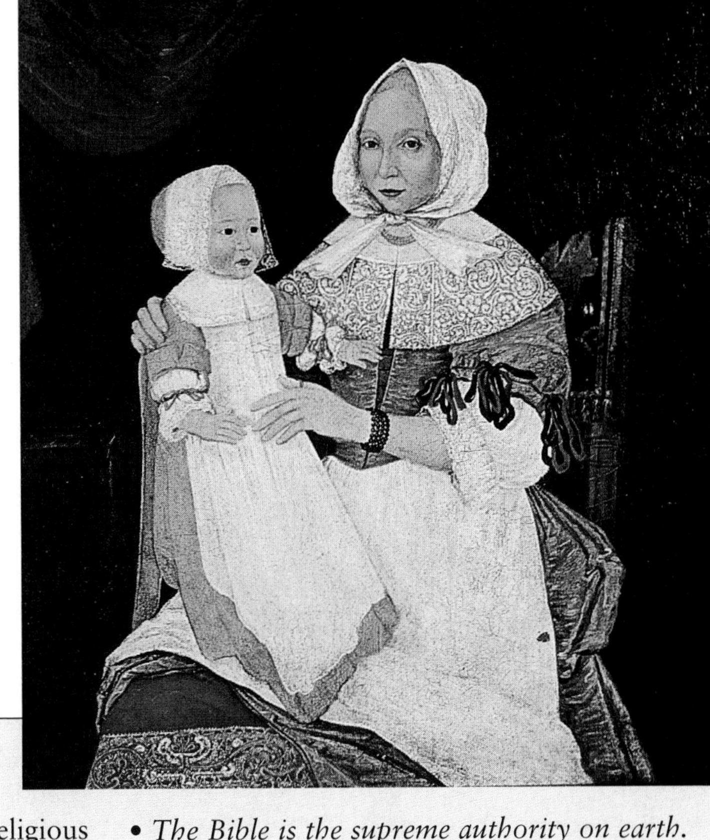

Mrs. Freake and Baby Mary (1674), unknown artist. The Granger Collection, New York.

participated in a revolution that not only toppled the king but had him beheaded as well. Those who had come to North America had even freer rein for their beliefs. With supreme confidence and self-consciousness, they went about setting up their institutions as though not only God but the whole world were watching. "The eyes of all people are on us," proclaimed John Winthrop, the first governor of the Massachusetts Bay

Puritan Beliefs

The key to the Puritan heart and soul is religious belief. What follows is a brief explanation of the Puritans' basic convictions:

- *Human beings are inherently evil and so must struggle to overcome their sinful nature.* This belief in original sin was one of the first things a Puritan child learned. "In Adam's fall / We sinned all" is the rhyme that teaches the letter *A* in *The New England Primer.*
- *Personal salvation depends solely on the grace of God, not on individual effort.* Puritans believed in predestination, the doctrine that only those people who are "elected" by God are saved and go to heaven. The only way an individual could know that he or she was saved was by directly experiencing God's grace in a religious conversion.
- *The Bible is the supreme authority on earth.* Puritans argued that the Bible was the sole guide not only in governing the moral and spiritual life but also in governing the church and society as a whole. One effect of this belief was to make Puritan churches more democratic, organized around their congregations rather than around ruling bishops. On the other hand, it led the Puritans to be more repressive in their political systems and more intolerant of others. For example, they used the Bible to justify their occupation of the land and their use of force against Native Americans: "Whosoever therefore resisteth the power, resisteth the ordinance of God: and they that resist shall receive to themselves damnation" (Romans 13:2). In short, the Puritans saw themselves as God's chosen people, like the "children of Israel" in the Old Testament.

Voices *from the* TIMES

from *The New England Primer*

The New England Primer is a famous American schoolbook that dates from before 1690. The sale of more than 2 million copies of the book during the 18th century is an indication of how widely the primer was used.

A In *Adam's* Fall
We Sinned all.
B Thy Life to Mend
This *Book* Attend.
BIBLE
C The *Cat* doth play
And after slay.
D A *Dog* will bite
A Thief at night.
E An *Eagles* flight
Is out of sight.
F The Idle *Fool*
Is whipt at School.

G As runs the *Glass*
Mans life doth pass.
H My *Book* and *Heart*
Shall never part.
J *Job* feels the Rod
Yet blesses GOD.
K Our *KING* the good
No man of blood.
L The *Lion* bold
The *Lamb* doth hold.
M The *Moon* gives light
In time of night.

N *Nightingales* sing
In Time of Spring.

O The *Royal Oak*
it was the Tree
That sav'd His
Royal Majestie.

P *Peter* denies
His Lord and cries

Q Queen *Esther* comes
in Royal State
To Save the JEWS
from dismal Fate

R *Rachel* doth mourn
For her first born.

S *Samuel* anoints
Whom God appoints

T *Time* cuts down all
Both great and small.
U *Uriah's* beauteous Wife
Made *David* seek his Life.
W *Whales* in the Sea
God's Voice obey.
X *Xerxes* the great did die,
And so must you & I.
Y *Youth* forward slips
Death soonest nips.
Z *Zacheus* he
Did climb the Tree
His Lord to see,

Colony. And so it was that in New England during the 1600s Puritanism gained its fullest and perhaps purest development.

The selections in this part of Unit Two represent the Puritan tradition over a span of approximately 100 years. The poet Anne Bradstreet gives a sense of what ordinary Puritan lives were like. Her voice expresses the view of a heaven ruled by a just God—a goal to which all Puritans aspired. The grace of Bradstreet's voice is followed by the harshness of the judges' voices at the Salem witch trials, an example of the darker aspects of Puritanism. The last Puritan represented is the passionate minister Jonathan Edwards, threatening his congregation with the torments of hell in an excerpt from his famous sermon "Sinners in the Hands of an Angry God."

Continuity & Change: Another Look at the Puritans

Many American writers have been fascinated by the Puritans. Nathaniel Hawthorne, one of whose ancestors had been a presiding judge at the Salem witch trials, set his novel *The Scarlet Letter* and many of his short stories in Puritan times to explore the psychological effects of sin and guilt. More recently, the playwright Arthur Miller dramatized the Salem witch trials in *The Crucible,* which not only personalizes the conflict but warns against similar witch-hunts in our own time.

This part of Unit Two includes two selections showing how 20th-century writers have viewed the Puritan tradition. Like *The Crucible,* Stephen Vincent Benét's essay "We Aren't Superstitious" scrutinizes the Salem witch-hunt from a modern perspective. In the story "Miss Temptation," Kurt Vonnegut, Jr., has fun exploring vestiges of Puritanism in a small New England town during the 1950s.

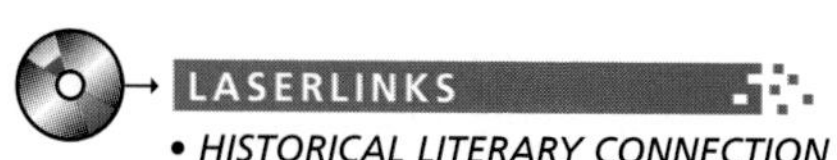

• *HISTORICAL LITERARY CONNECTION*

PART 1

Between Heaven and Hell

The Puritan Tradition

Detail of chair-seat cover (about 1725), embroidered by a member of Anne Bradstreet's family.

PREVIEWING

POETRY

To My Dear and Loving Husband
Upon the Burning of Our House, July 10th, 1666

Anne Bradstreet

PERSONAL CONNECTION

Think about a person or a possession that means a lot to you. What comparison would express the emotions you feel toward this person or thing? In your notebook, complete the following sentence:

_________ *means more to me than* _______________________.

CULTURAL CONNECTION

You may be surprised to learn that Anne Bradstreet was not only the first notable American woman poet—she was essentially the first notable American poet. In the two poems presented here, Bradstreet expresses her intense feelings about her husband and about the loss of her home in a destructive fire. Although Bradstreet's poetic language may seem a bit stiff to you, you'll be able to understand the recognizable emotions of love and sadness she expresses.

Poetry in 17th-century New England was almost exclusively devotional in nature and, as such, was highly recommended reading for the Puritan community. What sets Bradstreet's poems apart from other Puritan verse is their personal subject matter. She focused primarily on the realities of her life—her husband, her children, and her house, for example. However, like any conscientious Puritan, Bradstreet always viewed her life within a spiritual context: every event, no matter how trivial, bore a divine message; every misfortune served to remind her of God's will and the path to salvation. In her poetry, Bradstreet gave us a lasting impression of what it felt like to be a Puritan.

WRITING CONNECTION

Think again about the person or possession you named in the Personal Connection activity. In your notebook, describe how you would feel about the loss of this person or thing. As you read Bradstreet's poems, particularly "Upon the Burning of Our House," notice whether she expresses feelings similar to your own.

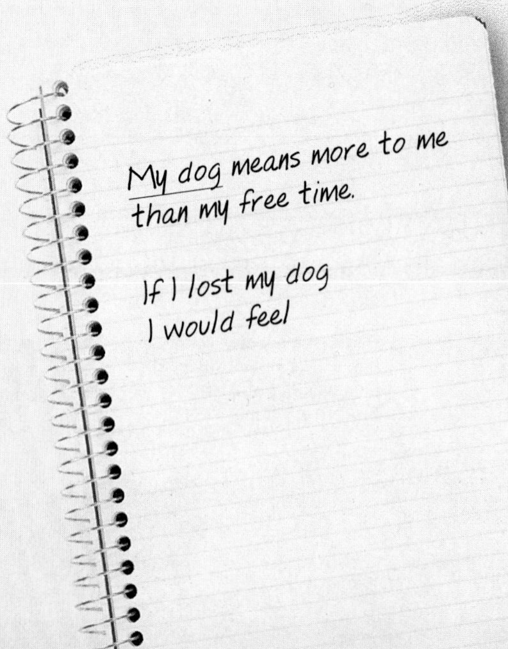

My dog means more to me
than my free time.
If I lost my dog
I would feel

LASERLINKS
• *CULTURAL CONNECTION*

ANNE BRADSTREET

To My Dear and Loving Husband

Chair-seat cover (about 1725), embroidered by a member of the Bradstreet family. Cotton threads, linen warp, wool embroidery, 43 cm × 47 cm. Gift of Samuel Bradstreet, courtesy of Museum of Fine Arts, Boston.

If ever two were one, then surely we.
If ever man were loved by wife, then thee;
If ever wife was happy in a man,
Compare with me, ye women, if you can.
I prize thy love more than whole mines of gold
Or all the riches that the East doth hold.
My love is such that rivers cannot quench,
Nor ought but love from thee, give recompense.
Thy love is such I can no way repay,
The heavens reward thee manifold, I pray.
Then while we live, in love let's so persevere
That when we live no more, we may live ever.

GUIDE FOR READING

8 recompense (rĕk'əm-pĕns'): payment in return for something, such as a service.

9–12 What relationship is seen between earthly love and eternal life?

11 persevere: In Bradstreet's time, *persevere* would have been pronounced pûr-sĕv'ər, which rhymes with *ever.*

FROM PERSONAL RESPONSE *TO* CRITICAL ANALYSIS

REFLECT **1.** Which line or lines in this poem do you like best? Share your choice with your classmates.

RETHINK **2.** What do you think Bradstreet is saying in the last two lines of the poem?

3. What emotions does Bradstreet express toward her husband? Point out the words that make you think so.

RELATE **4.** Do you know of any couples who regard each other as Bradstreet and her husband do? Describe them.

Anne Bradstreet

Upon the Burning of Our House, July 10th, 1666

In silent night when rest I took
For sorrow near I did not look
I wakened was with thund'ring noise
And piteous shrieks of dreadful voice.
That fearful sound of "Fire!" and "Fire!"
Let no man know is my desire.

I, starting up, the light did spy,
And to my God my heart did cry
To strengthen me in my distress
And not to leave me succorless.
Then, coming out, beheld a space
The flame consume my dwelling place.

GUIDE FOR READING

10 succorless (sŭk'ər-lĭs): without help or relief.

And when I could no longer look,
I blest His name that gave and took,
That laid my goods now in the dust:
Yea, so it was, and so 'twas just.
It was His own, it was not mine,
Far be it that I should repine;

He might of all justly bereft,
But yet sufficient for us left.
When by the ruins oft I past,
My sorrowing eyes aside did cast,
And here and there the places spy
Where oft I sat and long did lie:

Here stood that trunk and there that chest,
There lay that store I counted best.
My pleasant things in ashes lie,
And them behold no more shall I.
Under thy roof no guest shall sit,
Nor at thy table eat a bit.

No pleasant tale shall e'er be told,
Nor things recounted done of old.
No candle e'er shall shine in thee,
Nor bridegroom's voice e'er heard shall be.
In silence ever shalt thou lie;
Adieu, Adieu, all's vanity.

Then straight I 'gin my heart to chide,
And did thy wealth on earth abide?
Didst fix thy hope on mold'ring dust?
The arm of flesh didst make thy trust?
Raise up thy thoughts above the sky
That dunghill mists away may fly.

Thou hast an house on high erect,
Framed by that mighty Architect,
With glory richly furnishéd,
Stands permanent though this be fled.
It's purchaséd and paid for too
By Him who hath enough to do.

A price so vast as is unknown
Yet by His gift is made thine own;
There's wealth enough, I need no more,
Farewell, my pelf, farewell my store.
The world no longer let me love,
My hope and treasure lies above.

14 I . . . took: an allusion to Job 1:21—"The Lord gave, and the Lord hath taken away; blessed be the name of the Lord."

13–18 How does Bradstreet view her loss?

18 repine: to complain or fret; to long for something.

21–36 What does Bradstreet miss about her house?

36 all's vanity: an allusion to Ecclesiastes 1:2, "All is vanity," meaning that all is temporary and meaningless.

37 chide: to scold mildly so as to correct or improve.

43–54 What is Bradstreet comparing to a house? What ideas are suggested by this comparison?

52 pelf: wealth or riches, especially when dishonestly acquired.

RESPONDING OPTIONS

FROM PERSONAL RESPONSE *TO* CRITICAL ANALYSIS

REFLECT **1.** After reading "Upon the Burning of Our House," what do you make of Bradstreet's reaction to her loss? Jot down your thoughts in your notebook.

RETHINK **2.** Explain in your own words why Bradstreet feels the way she does at the end of the poem.

Consider
- her attitude toward wealth and material goods
- her religious beliefs and values

3. What different emotions does Bradstreet express at various points in the poem? Point out lines in the poem that support your ideas.

4. If Bradstreet had lost her husband in the fire, how might the poem be different?

RELATE **5.** On the basis of "To My Dear and Loving Husband" and "Upon the Burning of Our House," how would you describe Bradstreet's views of God and heaven?

6. What did you learn about Bradstreet's daily life from reading the two poems?

7. What similarities and differences do you see between the two poems?

THE WRITER'S STYLE

Like other early American poets, Bradstreet often uses inverted syntax, meaning that she reverses the expected order of words. In the first line of "Upon the Burning of Our House," for example, she writes "when rest I took" rather than "when I took rest." Rewrite a stanza of this poem, using normal word order. How does it compare to the original stanza?

ANOTHER PATHWAY

Cooperative Learning

Working with a small group of classmates, create a series of drawings to illustrate the events, emotions, and memories in "Upon the Burning of Our House" or the sentiments in "To My Dear and Loving Husband." Show your drawings to the class, identifying specific lines that you illustrated.

QUICKWRITES

1. Both of Bradstreet's poems are called lyric poems because they are short and express the thoughts and feelings of one speaker. Write a **lyric poem** that expresses your emotions toward the person or possession you described for the Writing Connection on page 148. Imitate Bradstreet's style if you wish.

2. In the last two stanzas of "Upon the Burning of Our House," Bradstreet compares heaven to a house. Develop an **analogy,** an extended comparison of two things that have certain similarities, to explain your personal view of one of the following concepts: heaven, love, God, home, loss, marriage, wealth.

PORTFOLIO *Save your writing. You may want to use it later as a springboard to a piece for your portfolio.*

LITERARY CONCEPTS

If you read these poems aloud, you will hear a distinct rhythm. **Meter** is the repetition of a regular rhythmic unit in a line of poetry. Each unit, known as a foot, has one stressed syllable (indicated by a ′) and either one or two unstressed syllables (indicated by a ˘), as shown on the following chart:

Foot	Syllables	Example
iamb	unstressed, stressed	today (˘ ′)
trochee	stressed, unstressed	later (′ ˘)
anapest	unstressed, unstressed, stressed	interfere (˘ ˘ ′)
dactyl	stressed, unstressed, unstressed	permanent (′ ˘ ˘)

Two words are used to identify the meter of a line. The first word describes the type of metrical foot—iambic, trochaic, anapestic, or dactylic—and the second word describes the number of feet in a line, as follows:

one foot: **monometer**	four feet: **tetrameter**
two feet: **dimeter**	five feet: **pentameter**
three feet: **trimeter**	six feet: **hexameter**

If you were to analyze, or **scan,** line 2 of "To My Dear and Loving Husband," it would look like this:

˘ ′ | ˘ ′ | ˘ ′ | ˘ ′ | ˘ ′
If ev | er man | were loved | by wife | then thee;
1 | 2 | 3 | 4 | 5

"To My Dear and Loving Husband" is an example of iambic pentameter, the most common meter in English poetry. What is the meter of "Upon the Burning of Our House"? Scan the first two lines, count the stressed syllables, and refer to the charts. Then write two lines of poetry that duplicate the meter of either poem.

ANNE BRADSTREET

The first noteworthy poet in the American colonies, Anne Dudley Bradstreet (1612?–1672), was born in England. She grew up in the midst of educated aristocrats because her father, Thomas Dudley, was steward, or manager of affairs, for the Earl of Lincoln. Unlike many women of her day, Bradstreet learned to read, write, and enjoy literature. Her father provided her with tutors and access to the earl's extensive library, and he taught her Greek, Latin, Hebrew, and French.

In 1628, 16-year-old Anne married Simon Bradstreet, who was her father's assistant and a graduate of Cambridge University. Two years later, the young couple sailed for the Massachusetts Bay Colony with Anne's parents and other prominent Puritans. The Bradstreets eventually settled in North Andover, where they raised eight children. Anne's father served as the colony's second governor, and later her husband became governor, after Anne's death.

The life of a colonial woman contrasted sharply with the life of privilege and comfort Bradstreet had known in England. However, despite domestic and religious responsibilities and persistent illnesses, she managed to find time to write. In 1647, Bradstreet's brother-in-law, John Woodbridge, went to England with verses that she had copied for members of her family. Without her knowledge, he had the verses published in London in 1650, in a volume titled *The Tenth Muse Lately Sprung Up in America.* A second edition, published in 1678, contained her corrections and personal poems, including "To My Dear and Loving Husband," which she had not intended for "public view." A third edition, printed in 1867, contained additional poems that had been found in a small notebook, including "Upon the Burning of Our House."

Many critics appreciate Bradstreet's later, more personal poems, such as those you have just read. The contemporary poet Adrienne Rich wrote that these poems respond to "the simple events in a woman's life." Through Bradstreet's eyes, readers today can glimpse what everyday Puritan life in colonial New England was like.

OTHER WORKS *The Complete Works of Anne Bradstreet*

PREVIEWING

NONFICTION

The Examination of Sarah Good

Salem Court Documents, 1692

PERSONAL CONNECTION

Have you ever been accused of doing something that you didn't do, or do you know of someone else who was falsely accused? If so, how did you feel about the accusation? Why do you think it was made? Was it ever disproved? With your classmates, discuss the causes and effects of false accusations.

HISTORICAL CONNECTION

In 1692, the Massachusetts Bay Colony settlement of Salem was gripped by panic after a group of adolescent girls suffered mysterious symptoms such as convulsive fits, hallucinations, loss of appetite, and the temporary loss of hearing, sight, and speech. Diagnosed as being victims of witchcraft, the girls denounced certain townspeople for this crime, including a woman named Sarah Good. The selection you will read consists of excerpts from the court records of Sarah Good's preliminary examination on March 1, 1692, at the Salem meeting house. Good was later jailed, tried in court, and found guilty; she was hanged on July 19, 1692.

Between 1692 and 1693, more than 400 people in Salem and nearby towns were accused of being witches. Ultimately, 19 men and women were found guilty and hanged. When Puritan leaders began to doubt the accusers and their evidence, the Salem witch trials finally ended. Over the next 20 years, most of those falsely accused were pardoned and awarded financial compensation.

READING CONNECTION

Reading Court Documents Court documents are a written record of what is said in a courtroom during a trial. Often these documents are difficult to read, but don't get bogged down in the formal terms they contain—*abovesaid, viz.,* and the like. When reading the summary of Sarah Good's examination, just try to answer this question for each paragraph: Who did what? Then compare the summary with the transcript of the examination, which provides the actual questions and answers, along with some interpretive comments by a court official.

Also, feel free to make inferences. Imagine what tone of voice people spoke in and what the motives for their remarks or actions were. Form your own judgments about the courtroom events.

Richard Mather, Puritan minister.
The Granger Collection, New York.

The Examination of Sarah Good

Salem Court Documents, 1692

Summary

Salem Village, March the 1st, 1691–92.

Sarah Good, the wife of William Good of Salem Village, Laborer. Brought before us by George Locker, Constable in Salem, to Answer, Joseph Hutchinson, Thomas Putnam, etc., of Salem Village, yeomen[1] (Complainants[2] on behalf of their Majesties) against said Sarah Good for Suspicion of witchcraft by her Committed and thereby much Injury done to the Bodies of Elizabeth Parris, Abigail Williams, Ann Putnam, and Elizabeth Hubbard, all of Salem Village aforesaid according to their Complaints as per warrants.

1. **yeomen** (yō′mən): farmers who cultivate their own land.
2. **complainants** (kəm-plā′nənts): people who make a complaint or file a formal charge in court.

Sarah Good upon Examination denieth the matter of fact (viz.) that she ever used any witchcraft or hurt the abovesaid children or any of them.

The above-named Children being all present positively accused her of hurting of them Sundry[3] times with this two months and also that morning.

Sarah Good denied that she had been at their houses in said time or near them, or had done them any hurt. All the abovesaid children then present accused her face to face, upon which they were all dreadfully tortured and tormented for a short space of time, and the affliction and tortures being over, they charged said Sarah Good again that she had then so tortured them, and came to them and did it, although she was personally then kept at a Considerable distance from them.

Sarah Good being Asked if, that she did not then hurt them who did it. And the children being again tortured, she looked upon them And said that it was one of them we brought into the house with us. We Asked her who it was: She then Answered and said it was Sarah Osborne, and Sarah Osborne was then under Custody and not in the house; And the children being quickly after recovered out of their fit said that it was Sarah Good and also Sarah Osborne that then did hurt & torment or afflict them—although both of them at the same time at a distance or Remote from them personally—there were also sundry other Questions put to her and Answers given thereunto by her according as is also given in.

JOHN HATHORNE
JONATHAN CORWIN } ASSISTANTS

3. **sundry** (sŭn′drē): various.

TRANSCRIPT

THE EXAMINATION OF SARAH GOOD BEFORE THE WORSHIPFUL ASSISTANTS JOHN HATHORNE, JONATHAN CORWIN.

Q. Sarah Good, what evil Spirit have you familiarity with?

A. None.

Q. Have you made no contract with the Devil?

Good answered no.

Q. Why do you hurt these children?

A. I do not hurt them. I scorn it.

Q. Who do you employ then to do it?

A. I employ nobody.

Q. What creature do you employ then?

A. No creature, but I am falsely accused.

Q. Why did you go away muttering from Mr. Parris, his house?

A. I did not mutter, but I thanked him for what he gave my child.

Q. Have you made no contract with the devil?

A. No.

H[athorne] desired the children, all of them, to look upon her and see if this were the person that had hurt them, and so they all did look upon her and said this was one of the persons that did torment them—presently they were all tormented.

Q. Sarah Good, do you not see now what you have done? Why do you not tell us the truth? Why do you thus torment these poor children?

A. I do not torment them.

Q. Who do you employ then?

A. I employ nobody. I scorn it.

Q. How came they thus tormented?

A. What do I know? You bring others here and now you charge me with it.

Q. Why, who was it?

A. I do not know, but it was some you brought into the meeting house with you.

Q. We brought you into the meeting house.

A. But you brought in two more.

Q. Who was it then that tormented the children?

A. It was Osborne.

Q. What is it you say when you go muttering away from persons' houses?

A. If I must tell, I will tell.

Q. Do tell us then.

A. If I must tell, I will tell. It is the commandments. I may say my commandments I hope.

Q. What commandment is it?

A. If I must tell, I will tell. It is a psalm.

Q. What psalm?

After a long time she muttered over some part of a psalm.

Q. Who do you serve?

A. I serve God.

Q. What God do you serve?

A. The God that made heaven and earth, though she was not willing to mention the word *God.* Her answers were in a very wicked spiteful manner, reflecting and retorting against the authority with base and abusive words, and many lies she was taken in. It was here said that her husband had said that he was afraid that she either was a witch or would be one very quickly. The worshipful Mr. Hathorne asked him his reason why he said so of her, whether he had ever seen anything by her. He answered no, not in this nature, but it was her bad carriage[4] to him and indeed, said he, I may say with tears that she is an enemy to all good.

SALEM VILLAGE, MARCH THE 1ST, 1691–92
WRITTEN BY EZEKIEL CHEEVER

> **Q.** ***Why do you hurt these children?***
> **A.** ***I do not hurt them. I scorn it.***

4. **carriage:** conduct.

RESPONDING OPTIONS

FROM PERSONAL RESPONSE *TO* CRITICAL ANALYSIS

REFLECT **1.** What is your reaction to Sarah Good's examination? Write your thoughts down in your notebook.

RETHINK **2.** How would you describe the court officials' attitude toward Sarah Good? Support your answer.

Consider

- the questions they ask her
- the comments at the end of the transcript of her examination

3. Why do you think Sarah Good accuses Sarah Osborne of being a witch?

4. Why do you think Sarah Good's husband testifies against her?

5. What explanation can you offer for the apparent torments suffered by the girls who accuse Sarah Good?

RELATE **6.** Do you think that something similar to the Salem witch trials could happen in your community today? Why or why not? Consider the Personal Connection activity in which you discussed false accusations.

ANOTHER PATHWAY

Cooperative Learning

Reenact Sarah Good's examination. Choose students to portray Sarah Good, the court officials, and the afflicted children. Remaining students can act as observers in the courtroom. Repeat the questions and answers from the transcript, and improvise dialogue when necessary.

LITERARY CONCEPTS

Court documents are supposed to be **objective,** meaning free of the writer's personal attitudes, opinions, and speculations. Court documents should be straightforward, factual accounts of what takes place in a courtroom. Which parts of these Salem court documents seem objective, and which do not? If you had been writing up these documents, how could you have made them more objective?

QUICKWRITES

1. Writing as Sarah Good's friend, as a member of her family, or as a resident of Salem, compose a **letter of appeal** asking Judge Hathorne to reconsider his decision to hang Good.
2. Imagine that you are a modern-day reporter observing Sarah Good's preliminary examination. Draft a brief **news report** describing the day's events.
3. Write a **hypothesis** to explain the possible motivations of either the girls who accused Good of witchcraft, the men who pressed charges against Good, or the men who conducted Good's preliminary examination.

PORTFOLIO *Save your writing. You may want to use it later as a springboard to a piece for your portfolio.*

LITERARY LINKS

How does the view of Puritans you get from reading these court documents compare to the view of Puritans you get from reading Anne Bradstreet's poetry?

CRITIC'S CORNER

In the preface to her book on the Salem witch trials, the 20th-century historian Marion L. Starkey writes, "Who in my day has a right to be indignant with people in Salem of 1692?" Why might she have made this comment? Do you agree that it is unfair for people of our time to judge people of earlier times?

ALTERNATIVE ACTIVITIES

1. Assume the duties of a courtroom artist and draw **sketches** of the people and events involved in this examination.
2. ***Cooperative Learning*** With a group of classmates, create a **newscast** in which you report on Sarah Good's examination. At the beginning of the newscast, have a news anchor recap what has happened so far. Then have reporters interview Sarah Good, the examiners, the afflicted girls, and Salem residents. If possible, make a videotape of the interviews.
3. In a **dramatic improvisation,** show what might have happened if Sarah Good had had a modern defense lawyer to represent her. Reenact the examination, with a student assuming the role of a defense attorney who cross-examines witnesses and raises objections.

ART CONNECTION

The engraving on page 155 depicts the examination of an accused witch in Salem. How closely does it match the image of the courtroom you formed as you read about Sarah Good's examination?

ACROSS THE CURRICULUM

Government A basic premise of the U.S. legal system is that a person charged with a crime is presumed innocent until proven guilty. Also, the Bill of Rights in the Constitution provides that a defendant is not required to testify against himself or herself. Why do you think such ideas became so important in our legal system? Use the examination of Sarah Good to illustrate your answer.

History After reading these court documents, you may have additional questions about the Salem witch trials held in 1692. What other girls in the community were afflicted? Who else did they accuse of witchcraft? How many people confessed? How was a person's guilt proven in court? Find out more about the Salem witch trials and present your findings to the class.

PREVIEWING

SERMON

from Sinners in the Hands of an Angry God

Jonathan Edwards

PERSONAL CONNECTION

Think about someone who recently persuaded you to do something—perhaps a parent, friend, teacher, coach, or salesperson. What method of persuasion did this person use? For example, what was emphasized—the benefits of taking the action or the drawbacks of not taking the action? Did this person appeal to your emotions (such as love, fear, or pride)? Or did this person appeal to principles (such as justice, efficiency, or frugality)? In your notebook, write down what you were persuaded to do, and analyze the method of persuasion that worked on you. With your classmates, talk about effective methods of persuasion.

HISTORICAL CONNECTION

One hundred years after a group of Puritans came to colonial America for religious freedom, some Puritans felt that their congregations had grown too complacent, or self-satisfied. To rekindle the fervor that the early settlers had, Jonathan Edwards and other Puritan ministers led the Great Awakening, a religious revival that swept through New England from 1734 to 1750. Edwards's most famous sermon, "Sinners in the Hands of an Angry God," was delivered in Enfield, Connecticut, in 1741. In it he warned his congregation that being church members would not automatically save them from hell. He tried to persuade them that they had to personally experience conversion, a transforming moment in which they felt God's grace.

Rev. George Whitefield preaching in the American colonies in 1739-1741. The Granger Collection, New York.

READING CONNECTION

Analyzing Persuasive Writing Edwards's sermon is an example of persuasive writing, which is intended to convince a reader to adopt a particular opinion or to perform a certain action. As you read pieces like this, analyze the writer's methods of persuasion. Identify what the writer wants you to do and the reasons he or she wants you to do it. If the thread of the argument is not obvious, make an outline. Decide whether you accept the assumptions the argument is based on. Also, monitor how you feel as you read—the writer may use specific words, phrases, or images to arouse certain emotions.

from Sinners in the Hands of an Angry God

JONATHAN EDWARDS

We find it easy to tread on and crush a worm that we see crawling on the earth; so it is easy for us to cut or singe a slender thread that any thing hangs by; thus easy is it for God when he pleases to cast his enemies down to hell. . . .

They[1] are now the objects of that very same *anger* and wrath of God, that is expressed in the torments of hell. And the reason why they do not go down to hell at each moment, is not because God, in whose power they are, is not then very angry with them; as angry as he is with many miserable creatures now tormented in hell, who there feel and bear the fierceness of his wrath. Yea, God is a great deal more angry with great numbers that are now on earth; yea, doubtless, with many that are now in this congregation,[2] who it may be are at ease, than he is with many of those who are now in the flames of hell.

So that it is not because God is unmindful of their wickedness, and does not resent it, that he does not let loose his hand and cut them off. God is not altogether such an one as themselves, though they may imagine him to be so. The wrath of God burns against them, their damnation does not slumber; the pit is prepared, the fire is made ready, the furnace is now hot, ready to receive them; the flames do now rage and glow. The glittering sword is whet,[3] and held over them, and the pit hath opened its mouth under them. . . .

1. **they:** Earlier in the sermon, Edwards refers to all "unconverted men," whom he considers God's enemies. Unconverted men are people who have not been "born again," meaning that they have not accepted Jesus Christ and consequently have not experienced a sense of God's grace and an assurance of salvation.
2. **this congregation:** the Puritans attending the church service at which Edwards spoke.
3. **whet:** sharpened.

WORDS TO KNOW

wrath (răth) *n.* fierce anger, or punishment resulting from such anger

Unconverted men walk over the pit of hell on a rotten covering, and there are innumerable places in this covering so weak that they will not bear their weight, and these places are not seen. The arrows of death fly unseen at noonday; the sharpest sight cannot discern them. God has so many different unsearchable ways of taking wicked men out of the world and sending them to hell, that there is nothing to make it appear, that God had need to be at the expense of a miracle, or go out of the ordinary course of his providence, to destroy any wicked man, at any moment. . . .

So that, thus it is that natural men[4] are held in the hand of God, over the pit of hell; they have deserved the fiery pit, and are already sentenced to it; and God is dreadfully provoked, his anger is as great towards them as to those that are actually suffering the executions of the fierceness of his wrath in hell; and they have done nothing in the least to appease or abate that anger, neither is God in the least bound by any promise to hold them up one moment; the devil is waiting for them, hell is gaping for them, the flames gather and flash about them, and would fain[5] lay hold on them, and swallow them up; the fire pent up in their own hearts is struggling to break out: and they have no interest in any Mediator,[6] there are no means within reach that can be any security to them. In short, they have no refuge, nothing to take hold of. . . .

The bow of God's wrath is bent, and the arrow made ready on the string, and justice bends the arrow at your heart, and strains the bow, and it is nothing but the mere pleasure of God, and that of an angry God, without any promise or obligation at all, that keeps the arrow one moment from being made drunk with your blood. Thus all you that never passed under a great change of heart, by the mighty power of the Spirit of God upon your souls; all you that were never born again, and made new creatures, and raised from being dead in sin, to a state of new, and before altogether unexperienced light and life, are in the hands of an angry God. However you may have reformed your life in many things, and may have had religious affections,[7] and may keep up a form of religion in your families and closets,[8] and in the house of God, it is nothing but his mere pleasure that keeps you from being this moment swallowed up in everlasting destruction. . . .

The God that holds you over the pit of hell, much as one holds a spider, or some loathsome insect over the fire, abhors you, and is dreadfully provoked: his wrath towards you burns like fire; he looks upon you as worthy of nothing else, but to be cast into the fire; he is of purer eyes than to bear to have you in his sight; you are ten thousand times more abominable in his eyes, than the most hateful venomous serpent is in ours. You have offended him infinitely more than ever a stubborn rebel did his prince; and yet it is nothing but his hand that holds you from falling into the fire every moment. It is to be ascribed to nothing else, that you did not go to hell the last night; that you was suffered[9] to awake again in this world, after you closed your eyes to sleep. And there is no other reason to be given, why you have not dropped into hell since you arose in the morning, but that God's hand has held you up. There is no other reason to be given why you

4. **natural men:** people who have not been "born again."
5. **fain:** rather.
6. **Mediator:** Jesus Christ, who mediates, or is the means of bringing about, salvation.
7. **affections:** feelings or emotions.
8. **closets:** private rooms for meditation.
9. **suffered:** permitted.

WORDS TO KNOW

appease (ə-pēz′) *v.* to bring peace, quiet, or calm to; soothe
loathsome (lōth′səm) *adj.* arousing great dislike
abhor (ăb-hôr′) *v.* to regard with disgust
abominable (ə-bŏm′ə-nə-bəl) *adj.* thoroughly detestable
ascribe (ə-skrīb′) *v.* to attribute to a specified cause or source

Un quadro di fuochi preziosi [A painting of precious fires] (1983), Enzo Cucchi. Oil on canvas with neon, 117½" × 153½", private collection, courtesy of Sperone Westwater, New York.

The **pit** is prepared,
the **fire** is made ready,
the **furnace** is now hot,
ready to receive them;
the **flames** do now
rage and **glow**.

have not gone to hell, since you have sat here in the house of God, provoking his pure eyes by your sinful wicked manner of attending his solemn worship. Yea, there is nothing else that is to be given as a reason why you do not this very moment drop down into hell.

O sinner! Consider the fearful danger you are in: it is a great furnace of wrath, a wide and bottomless pit, full of the fire of wrath, that you are held over in the hand of that God, whose wrath is provoked and incensed as much against you, as against many of the damned in hell. You hang by a slender thread, with the flames of divine wrath flashing about it, and ready every moment to singe it, and burn it asunder;[10] and you have no interest in any Mediator, and nothing to lay hold of to save yourself, nothing to keep off the flames of wrath, nothing of your own, nothing that you ever have done, nothing that you can do, to induce God to spare you one moment. . . .

It is *everlasting* wrath. It would be dreadful to suffer this fierceness and wrath of Almighty God one moment; but you must suffer it to all eternity. There will be no end to this exquisite[11] horrible misery. When you look forward, you shall see a long forever, a boundless duration before you, which will swallow up your thoughts, and amaze your soul; and you will absolutely despair of ever having any deliverance, any end, any mitigation, any rest at all. You will know certainly that you must wear out long ages, millions of millions of ages, in wrestling and conflicting with this almighty merciless vengeance; and then when you have so done, when so many ages have actually been spent by you in this manner, you will know that all is but a point to what remains. So that your punishment will indeed be infinite. Oh, who can express what the state of a soul in such circumstances is! All that we can possibly say about it, gives but a very feeble, faint representation of it; it is inexpressible and inconceivable: For "who knows the power of God's anger?"[12]

How dreadful is the state of those that are daily and hourly in the danger of this great wrath and infinite misery! But this is the dismal case of every soul in this congregation that has not been born again, however moral and strict, sober and religious, they may otherwise be. . . .

And now you have an extraordinary opportunity, a day wherein Christ has thrown the door of mercy wide open, and stands in the door calling and crying with a loud voice to poor sinners; a day wherein many are flocking to him, and pressing into the kingdom of God. Many are daily coming[13] from the east, west, north, and south; many that were very lately in the same miserable condition that you are in, are now in a happy state, with their hearts filled with love to him who has loved them, and washed them from their sins in his own blood, and rejoicing in hope of the glory of God. How awful is it to be left behind at such a day! To see so many others feasting, while you are pining and perishing! To see so many rejoicing and singing for joy of heart, while you have cause to mourn for sorrow of heart, and howl for vexation of spirit! How can you rest one moment in such a condition? . . .

Therefore, let every one that is out of Christ, now awake and fly from the wrath to come. . . . ❖

10. **asunder** (ə-sŭn'dər): into separate parts or pieces.
11. **exquisite** (ĕk'skwĭ-zĭt): sharply intense.
12. **"who knows . . . anger?":** an allusion to Psalm 90:11, "Who knoweth the power of thine anger?"
13. **Many . . . coming:** Edwards is referring to the hundreds of people who were being converted during the Great Awakening.

WORDS TO KNOW

incense (ĭn-sĕns') *v.* to cause to be extremely angry
deliverance (dĭ-lĭv'ər-əns) *n.* rescue from danger
mitigation (mĭt'ĭ-gā'shən) *n.* lessening of something that causes suffering
inconceivable (ĭn'kən-sē'və-bəl) *adj.* not able to be understood or imagined

The God that holds you over the pit of **hell,**

much as one holds a **spider,**

or some loathsome insect over the **fire,**

abhors you...

his wrath toward you burns like **fire;**

he looks upon you as worthy of nothing else,

but to be cast into the **fire.**

RESPONDING OPTIONS

FROM PERSONAL RESPONSE *TO* CRITICAL ANALYSIS

REFLECT 1. In your notebook, describe the most vivid image from this sermon and how it made you feel.

RETHINK 2. Would you want to hear another of Edwards's sermons? Explain why or why not.

3. Why do you think people were persuaded to change their lives as a result of Edwards's sermon?

   Consider
   - what he wants his congregation to do and why
   - the emotions he appeals to in the first paragraphs and in the last paragraphs of the excerpt

4. How would you describe the view of human beings and the view of God presented in this sermon?

RELATE 5. Are Edwards's methods of persuasion ones that are likely to work on you? Consider what you wrote for the Personal Connection activity on page 160.

6. Compare Edwards with a contemporary religious or political leader who has inspired great numbers of people.

ANOTHER PATHWAY

Cooperative Learning

Working as a small group, prepare a radio news story about Edwards's sermon. Introduce and follow up a 40-second excerpt from the sermon (roughly 15 lines). Be ready to explain why you chose this passage to repeat.

LITERARY CONCEPTS

Persuasive writing often contains **loaded language**—words with strong **connotations,** or emotional associations. For example, contrast the word *child* with the more loaded words *brat* and *cherub.* A writer would use *brat* to create a negative feeling in the reader and *cherub* to create a positive feeling. Part of what makes Jonathan Edwards's sermon so effective is his choice of loaded words. Choose a passage from the excerpt that you think is especially persuasive, and list words and phrases that arouse strong emotions. Try to weaken the passage by replacing those words and phrases with more neutral ones. Read both passages aloud and discuss differences.

QUICKWRITES

1. Draft a **letter** to Edwards, giving your personal response to the religious views presented in his sermon.
2. Edwards compares a sinful human being to "a spider, or some loathsome insect" held over a fire. Develop a **comparison** to describe your own view of human beings.
3. You are a coach who believes in Jonathan Edwards's methods of persuasion. Write an outline for a **pep talk** that you would give to motivate your players at half-time.

PORTFOLIO *Save your writing. You may want to use it later as a spring-board to a piece for your portfolio.*

ALTERNATIVE ACTIVITIES

1. It is reported that Jonathan Edwards read his sermon in a calm, level voice, with his sermon book in his left hand. Imagine what he would do if he had his own television ministry and were giving the sermon today. Present part of this sermon as an **oral performance,** making it as powerful as you can for a contemporary audience.
2. If you were going to publish "Sinners in the Hands of an Angry God" as a religious tract, how would you illustrate it? Design a **cover** that suggests important ideas in the sermon.

LITERARY LINKS

In your view, is Jonathan Edwards's conception of God consistent with Anne Bradstreet's conception of God? Explain your opinion.

WORDS TO KNOW

Review the Words to Know at the bottom of the selection pages. Then decide if the following pairs of words are synonyms or antonyms. Number your paper from 1 to 10, and write *S* for *synonyms* or *A* for *antonyms.*

1. alleviation—mitigation
2. upset—appease
3. inconceivable—knowable
4. damnation—deliverance
5. pleasant—loathsome
6. blessing—wrath
7. attribute—ascribe
8. adore—abhor
9. agreeable—abominable
10. enrage—incense

JONATHAN EDWARDS

1703–1758

Jonathan Edwards, the only son in a family of 11 children, was born in East Windsor, Connecticut. Intellectually curious as a child, Edwards wrote "Of Insects," a study of the behavior of spiders, when he was 11 years old. Just before turning 13, Edwards entered what is now Yale University. While he was a graduate student there, he had a conversion experience that greatly influenced his religious views.

In 1722, after finishing his education, Edwards launched a career in the ministry, following the path of his father and his maternal grandfather, both of whom were Puritan ministers. Edwards went to assist his grandfather as a minister at the church in Northampton, Massachusetts, in 1726 and became the church's pastor after his grandfather's death in 1729. There, he developed a reputation as a powerful preacher. Following his accounts of some "surprising conversions" in Northampton from 1734 to 1735, Edwards found himself at the center of a religious revival, the Great Awakening.

Throughout his life, Edwards wrote sermons as well as philosophical and religious works. In his most famous sermon, "Sinners in the Hands of an Angry God," Edwards captured the intensity of the Great Awakening. Responding to criticism of his appeal to emotions rather than reason, he said: "I think it is a reasonable thing to fright persons away from hell. They stand upon its brink, and are just ready to fall into it, and are senseless of their danger. Is it not a reasonable thing to fright a person out of a house on fire?"

Although Edwards inspired thousands, he was dismissed from the Northampton church in 1750 because he wanted to limit church membership to those who had undergone conversion, or had been "born again." A year later, Edwards, his wife, and their ten children moved to Stockbridge, where he became a missionary to the Housatonic Indians. In 1757, Edwards accepted an appointment as president of what is now Princeton University, but he died a short time later, as a result of a reaction to a smallpox vaccination.

OTHER WORKS *Images or Shadows of Divine Things, Personal Narrative*

PREVIEWING

NONFICTION

We Aren't Superstitious

Stephen Vincent Benét (bĭ-nā′)

PERSONAL CONNECTION

The following selection is a modern writer's interpretation of the Salem witch trials. In a small group, discuss what you already know about these trials, perhaps based on your reading of the Salem court documents on page 154. List what you know in a chart like the one started here, in the column Prior Knowledge. As you read the Historical/Cultural Connection and the selection, write down new facts in the column New Knowledge. Then compare what you already knew with what is revealed in the essay.

Prior Knowledge	New Knowledge
happened in 1692	
Sarah Good accused	

HISTORICAL/CULTURAL CONNECTION

In the 1600s, people suspected of being witches were persecuted in colonial Massachusetts, Connecticut, and Virginia. To "prove" that someone was a witch, church officials sometimes poked him or her with pins, searching for a so-called devil's mark, a spot where no pain was felt. Another test involved tying together the hands and feet of the accused and throwing him or her into water. Those who floated were declared witches; those who drowned were declared innocent. In the Salem witch trials, spectral evidence—the testimony of a church member who claimed to have seen a person's spirit performing witchcraft—was enough to sentence the accused to death.

Arresting a witch

READING CONNECTION

Understanding Cause and Effect During the Salem witch trials, innocent people were tried and convicted on "evidence" that certain things they did caused children to become sick. This case points to an error people sometimes make in looking at cause and effect: they assume that because two events are related, one causes the other. For example, just because Sarah Good muttered something and children went into hysterics doesn't mean that Sarah Good caused the hysterics. As you read Benét's essay, try to sort out the true causes and effects from the erroneous ones.

Using Your Reading Log Use the reading strategy questions inserted throughout the essay to help you identify causes and effects. Record your responses to the questions in your reading log.

Levant for E. W. R. (1958), Theodoros Stamos. Oil on canvas, 80″ × 70″, Albright-Knox Art Gallery, Buffalo, New York, gift of Seymour H. Knox, 1958.

We Aren't Superstitious

STEPHEN VINCENT BENÉT

Usually, our little superstitious rituals and propitiations[1] don't hurt our daily lives. Usually. And then, on occasion, a superstition—a belief—flares into crowd-madness and kills and kills again before it has run its course. As it did in Salem Village, in 1692.

1. **propitiations** (prō-pĭsh′ē-ā′shənz): offerings meant to appease or gain good will.

That story is worth retelling, as a very typical example of what wild belief and crowd hysteria can do to an average community. For Salem Village, in 1691, was no different in any way from any one of a dozen little New England hamlets.[2] It didn't expect celebrity or notoriety, and its citizens were the average people of their day and age. There was the main road and the parsonage[3] and the meeting house, the block house, the Ingersoll house where travelers put up for the night, the eight or nine other houses that made up the village. Beyond lay the outlying farms with their hard-working farmers—a few miles away lay Salem Town itself—fifteen miles away, the overgrown village that was Boston. King Philip's War[4] had been over for some fourteen years, and the colony was recovered from the shock of it—there were still individual slayings by Indians, but the real power of the Indian was very largely broken. Men might look forward, with hope, to peace and thriving for a time.

And, as for the men and women of Salem Village—they were tough and knotty stock, if you like, not widely lettered,[5] not particularly tolerant, especially in religion—but no different from their neighbors at Andover and Topsfield or in Boston itself. There were sensible men and stupid men among them, model housewives and slatterns,[6] troublemakers and more peaceable folk. The names were the Puritan names that we are accustomed to reverence—Mercy and Abigail and Deborah, Nathaniel and Samuel and John. They lived a life of hard work and long winters, drank rum on occasion, took their religion with that mixture of grimness and enthusiasm that marked the Puritan, and intended, under God's providence, to beat wilderness and Indian, and wax and increase in the land. They were a great deal more human, crotchety and colorful than the schoolbook pictures of dour-faced men in steeple-crowned hats would suggest. In fact, if you want to find out how human they were, you have only to read Judge Sewall's diary. He was one of the judges at the Salem witch trials—and heartily sorry for it later. But his Pepysian[7] account of his own unsuccessful courtship of Madam Winthrop, and how he brought her gloves and sweets, is in the purest vein of unconscious farce.

CONNECT

How do the citizens of Salem compare to the citizens of your community?

And yet, to this ordinary community in the early spring of 1692 came a madness that was to shake all Massachusetts before its fever was burned out. We are wiser, now. We do not believe in witches. But if, say, three cases of Asiatic cholera were discovered in your own hometown and certified as such by the local board of health—and if your local newspaper promptly ran a boxed warning to all citizens on the front page—you would have some faint idea of how the average Salem Villager felt when the "afflicted children" denounced their first victims.

For witchcraft, to almost all the New Englanders of 1692, was as definite, diagnosable, and dangerous an evil as bubonic plague. It had its symptoms, its prognosis, and its appalling results. Belief in it was as firmly fixed in most people's minds as belief in the germ theory of disease is in ours. Cotton Mather was one of the most able and promising young ministers of his

2. **hamlets:** small villages.
3. **parsonage:** the house provided by a church for its minister.
4. **King Philip's War** (1675–1676): the war between the New England colonists and the Indians under Metacomet, chief of the Wampanoags, who was called King Philip by the colonists.
5. **not widely lettered:** not well-educated or well-read.
6. **slatterns:** untidy, dirty women.
7. **Pepysian** (pēp′sē-ən): in the manner of Samuel Pepys (pēps), a famous English diarist who lived from 1633 to 1703.

WORDS TO KNOW
dour (dour) *adj.* gloomy; glum
afflicted (ə-flĭk′tĭd) *adj.* pained or distressed **afflict** *v.*
denounce (dĭ-nouns′) *v.* to accuse publicly

And yet, to this ordinary community in the early spring of 1692 came a madness that was to shake all Massachusetts before its fever was burned out.

day. But when in 1688, in Boston, an eleven-year-old girl named Martha Goodwin accused an unhappy Irish Catholic laundress of bewitching her, Cotton Mather believed the eleven-year-old girl. In fact, he took the precocious brat into his own house to study her symptoms and cure them by fasting and prayer, and wrote and published an elaborate, scientific account of his treatment of the case—which doubtless played its own part in preparing men's minds for the Salem madness.

True, there had been only some twenty witch trials in New England up to the Salem affair—compared to the hundreds and thousands of hangings, burnings, duckings,[8] drownings that had gone on in Europe and the British Isles during the last few centuries. But people believed in witches—why should they not? They were in the Bible—even the Bible itself said, "Thou shalt not suffer a witch to live." They were in every old wives' tale that was whispered about the winter fires. And, in 1692, they were in Salem Village.

Three years before, Salem Village had got a new minister—the Reverend Samuel Parris, ex-merchant in the West Indies. He seems to have been a self-willed, self-important man with a great sense of his own and the church's dignity; and, no sooner were he and his family well settled in the parsonage, than a dispute began as to whether the parsonage property belonged to him or to the congregation. But there was nothing unusual about that—Salem Village was a rather troublesome parish and two, at least, of the three previous ministers had had salary and other difficulties with the good folk of Salem. The quarrel dragged on like the old boundary dispute between Salem and Topsfield, creating faction and hard feeling, a typically New England affair. But there were boundary disputes elsewhere and other congregations divided in mind about their ministers.

But the most important thing about Samuel Parris was neither his self-importance nor his attempt to get hold of the parsonage property. It was the fact that he brought with him to Salem Village two West Indian servants—a man known as John Indian and a woman named Tituba.[9] And when he bought those two or their services in the West Indies, he was buying a rope that was to hang nineteen men and women of New England—so odd are the links in the circumstantial chain.

EVALUATE

Do you agree with Benét's identification of a cause here? Read on before you decide.

Perhaps the nine-year-old Elizabeth Parris, the daughter of the parsonage, boasted to her new friends of the odd stories Tituba told and the queer things she could do. Perhaps Tituba herself let the report of her magic powers be spread about the village. She must have been as odd and imagination-stirring a figure as a parrot or a tame monkey in the small New England town.

8. **duckings:** a form of punishment, practiced in Europe and New England, in which a person was tied in a chair and ducked into water.

9. **Tituba** (tĭch'o͞o-bə).

And the winters were long and white—and any diversion a godsend.

In any case, during the winter of 1691–92, a group of girls and women began to meet nightly at the parsonage, with Tituba and her fortune-telling as the chief attraction. Elizabeth Parris, at nine, was the youngest—then came Abigail Williams, eleven, and Ann Putnam, twelve. The rest were older—Mercy Lewis, Mary Wolcott, and Elizabeth Hubbard were seventeen; Elizabeth Booth and Susan Sheldon, eighteen; and Mary Warren and Sarah Churchill, twenty. Three were servants: Mercy Lewis had been employed by the Reverend George Burroughs—a previous minister of Salem Village—and now worked for the Putnams, Mary Warren was a maid at the John Procters', Sarah Churchill at the George Jacobs'. All, except for Elizabeth Parris, were adolescent or just leaving adolescence.

The elder women included a pair of gossipy, superstitious busybodies—Mrs. Pope and Mrs. Bibber—and young Ann Putnam's mother, Ann Putnam, Senior, who deserves a sentence to herself.

For the Putnams were a powerful family in the neighborhood, and Ann Putnam, married at seventeen and now only thirty, is described as handsome, arrogant, temperamental, and high-strung. She was also one of those people who can cherish a grudge and revenge it.

The circle met—the circle continued to meet—no doubt with the usual giggling, whispering, and gossip. From mere fortune-telling it proceeded to other and more serious matters—table-rapping,[10] perhaps, and a little West Indian voodoo[11]—weird stories told by Tituba and weird things shown, while the wind blew outside and the big shadows flickered on the wall. Adolescent girls, credulous servants, superstitious old women—and the two enigmatic figures of Tituba, the West Indian, and Ann Putnam, Sr.

CLARIFY

Who is Tituba, and what is her relationship to the girls and women?

But soon the members of the circle began to show hysterical symptoms. They crawled under tables and chairs, they made strange sounds, they shook and trembled with nightmare fears. The thing became a village celebrity—and more. Something strange and out of nature was happening—who had ever seen normal young girls behave like these young girls? And no one—certainly not the Reverend Samuel Parris—even suggested that a mixed diet of fortune-telling, ghost stories, and voodoo is hardly the thing for impressionable minds during a long New England winter. Hysteria was possession by an evil spirit; pathological lying, the Devil putting words into one's mouth. No one suggested that even Cotton Mather's remedy of fasting and prayer would be a good deal better for such cases than widespread publicity. Instead, the Reverend Samuel became very busy. Grave ministers were called in to look at the afflicted children. A Dr. Gregg gave his opinion. It was almost too terrible to believe, and yet what else could be believed? Witchcraft!

Meanwhile, one may suppose, the "afflicted children," like most hysterical subjects, enjoyed the awed stares, the horrified looks, the respectful questions that greeted them, with girlish zest. They had been unimportant girls of a little hamlet—now they were, in every sense of the word, spot news. And any reporter knows

10. **table-rapping:** raps or knocking sounds made on a table without a visible cause. Some people believe that these sounds are created by spirits and are a means of communicating with them.

11. **voodoo:** a religion practiced chiefly in Caribbean countries, especially Haiti. Its practitioners believe that spirits communicate with them in dreams, trances, and ritual possessions.

WORDS TO KNOW

diversion (dĭ-vûr'zhən) *n.* distraction
credulous (krĕj'ə-ləs) *adj.* having a tendency to believe too readily
enigmatic (ĕn'ĭg-măt'ĭk) *adj.* puzzling
impressionable (ĭm-prĕsh'ə-nə-bəl) *adj.* easily influenced; suggestible

Dévidoir Enregistreue (1978), Jean Dubuffet. Acrylic and paper collage on canvas, 79″ × 114″, Albright-Knox Art Gallery, Buffalo, New York, George B. and Jenny R. Mathews Fund, 1979.

CLARIFY

What causes the children to behave as they do, according to Benét?

what that does to certain kinds of people. They continued to writhe and demonstrate—and be the center of attention. There was only one catch about it. If they were really bewitched—somebody must be doing the bewitching—

On the 29th of February, 1692, in the midst of an appropriate storm of thunder and lightning, three women, Sarah Good, Sarah Osborne and Tituba, were arrested on the deadly charge of bewitching the children.

The next day, March 1, two Magistrates, Justice Hathorne and Justice Corwin, arrived with appropriate pomp[12] and ceremony. The first hearing was held in the crowded meetinghouse of the Village—and all Salem swarmed to it, as crowds in our time have swarmed to other sleepy little villages, suddenly notorious.

The children—or the children and Tituba—had picked their first victims well. Sarah Good and Sarah Osborne were old women of no particular standing in the community. Sarah Good had been a beggar and a slattern—her husband testified, according to report and with

12. **pomp:** dignified or magnificent display.

WORDS TO KNOW

writhe (rīth) *v.* to move with a twisting or contorted motion a smugness that makes one long to kick him, that she "either was a witch or would be one very quickly," ending "I may say with tears that she is an enemy to all good." As for Sarah Osborne, she had married a redemptioner servant[13] after the death of her former husband and probably lost caste in consequence. Also, she had been bedridden for some time and therefore not as regular in her church attendance as a good Christian should be.

CLARIFY

Why does Benét say that the first victims of the children were well picked?

We can imagine that meetinghouse—and the country crowd within it—on that chill March day. At one end was the majesty of the law—and the "afflicted children" where all might see them and observe. Dressed in their best, very likely, and with solicitous relatives near at hand. Do you see Mercy Lewis? Do you see Ann Putnam?

Red cats and black cats and yellow birds . . . everybody could see that she spoke the truth.

And then the whole crowd turned to one vast, horrified eye. For there was the accused—the old woman—the witch!

The justices—grim Justice Hathorne in particular—had, evidently, arrived with their minds made up. For the first question addressed to Sarah Good was, bluntly:

"What evil spirit have you familiarity with?"

"None," said the piping old voice. But everybody in the village knew worthless Sarah Good. And the eye of the audience went from her to the deadly row of "afflicted children" and back again.

"Have you made no contracts with the devil?" proceeded the Justice.

"No."

The Justice went to the root of the matter at once.

"Why do you hurt these children?"

A rustle must have gone through the meetinghouse at that. Aye, that's it—the Justice speaks shrewdly—hark to the Justice! Aye, but look, too! Look at the children! Poor things, poor things!

"I do not hurt them. I scorn it," said Sarah Good, defiantly. But the Justice had her, now—he was not to be brushed aside.

"Who then do you employ to do it?"

"I employ nobody."

"What creature do you employ then?" For all witches had familiars.[14]

"No creature, but I am falsely accused." But the sweat must have been on the old woman's palms by now.

The Justice considered. There was another point—minor but illuminating.

"Why did you go away muttering from Mr. Parris, his house?"

"I did not mutter, but I thanked him for what he gave my child."

The Justice returned to the main charge, like any prosecuting attorney.

"Have you made no contract with the devil?"

"No."

It was time for Exhibit A. The Justice turned to the children. Was Sarah Good one of the persons who tormented them? Yes, yes!—and a

13. **redemptioner servant:** a colonial emigrant from Europe to America who paid for the voyage by working for a specified time as an unpaid bondservant.

14. **familiars:** attendant spirits, often taking animal form, that assist witches.

WORDS TO KNOW

illuminating (ĭ-lo͞o′mə-nā′tĭng) *adj.* revealing; enlightening **illuminate** *v.*

horrified murmur running through the crowd. And then, before the awestricken eyes of all, they began to be tormented. They writhed, they grew stiff, they contorted, they were stricken moaning or speechless. Yet, when they were brought to Sarah Good and allowed to touch her, they grew quite quiet and calm. For, as everyone knew, a witch's physical body was like an electric conductor—it reabsorbed, on touch, the malefic[15] force discharged by witchcraft into the bodies of the tormented. Everybody could see what happened—and everybody saw. When the meetinghouse was quiet, the Justice spoke again.

"Sarah Good, do you not see now what you have done? Why do you not tell us the truth? Why do you torment these poor children?"

And with these words, Sarah Good was already hanged. For all that she could say was, "I do not torment them." And yet everyone had seen her, with their own eyes.

The questions went on—she fumbled in her answers—muttered a bit of prayer. Why did she mutter? And didn't you see how hard it was for her to pronounce the name of God? Pressed and desperate, she finally said that if anyone tormented the children, it must be Sarah Osborne—she knew herself guiltless. The pitiful fable did not save her. To Boston Jail.

Sarah Osborne's examination followed the same course—the same prosecutor's first question—the same useless denial—the same epileptic feats of the "afflicted children"—the same end. It was also brought out that Sarah Osborne had said that "she was more like to be bewitched than to be a witch"—very dangerous that!—and that she had once had a nightmare about "a thing all black like an Indian that pinched her in the neck."

Then Tituba was examined and gave them their fill of marvels, prodigies,[16] and horrors.

The West Indian woman, a slave in a strange land, was fighting for her life and she did it shrewdly and desperately. She admitted, repentantly, that she had tormented the children. But she had been forced to do so. By whom? By Goody[17] Good and Goody Osborne and two other witches whom she hadn't yet been able to recognize. Her voodoo knowledge aided her—she filled the open ears of Justices and crowds with tales of hairy familiars and black dogs, red cats and black cats and yellow birds, the phantasm[18] of a woman with legs and wings. And everybody could see that she spoke the truth. For, when she was first brought in, the children were tormented at her presence, but as soon as she had confessed and turned King's evidence,[19] she was tormented herself, and fearfully. To Boston Jail with her—but she had saved her neck.

QUESTION

Why do you think Tituba's testimony was so different from Sarah Good's and Sarah Osborne's?

The hearing was over—the men and women of Salem and its outlying farms went broodingly or excitedly back to their homes to discuss the fearful workings of God's providence. Here and there a common-sense voice murmured a doubt or two—Sarah Good and Sarah Osborne were no great losses to the community—but still, to convict two old women of heinous crimes on the testimony of green-sick girls and a West Indian slave! But, on the whole, the villagers of Salem felt relieved. The cause of the plague had been found—it would be stamped out and the afflicted children recover. The Justices, no doubt, congratulated themselves on their

---

15. **malefic** (mə-lĕf'ĭk): evil; malicious.
16. **prodigies** (prŏd'ə-jēz): significant signs or events; omens.
17. **Goody:** short for *goodwife,* a courtesy title used for women not of noble birth.
18. **phantasm** (făn'tăz'əm): something apparently seen but having no physical reality; a phantom or an apparition.
19. **turned King's evidence:** offered to serve as a witness for the prosecution and testify against the other witches.

WORDS TO KNOW

heinous (hā'nəs) *adj.* grossly wicked

prompt and intelligent action. The "afflicted children" slept, after a tiring day—they were not quite so used to such performances as they were to become.

As for the accused women, they went to Boston Jail—to be chained there, while waiting trial and gallows.[20] There is an item of "To chains for Sarah Good and Sarah Osborne, 14 shillings" in the jailor's record. Only, Sarah Osborne was not to go to the gallows—she died in jail instead, some five and a half weeks later, at a recorded expense to the Colony of one pound, three shillings, and five-pence for her keep. And Tituba stayed snugly in prison till the madness collapsed—and was then sold by the Colony to defray the expenses of her imprisonment. One wonders who bought her and whether she ever got back to the West Indies. But, with that, her enigmatic figure disappears from the scene.

Meanwhile, on an outlying farm, Giles Corey, a turbulent, salty old fellow of eighty-one, began to argue the case with his wife, Martha. He believed, fanatically, in the "afflicted children." She did not, and said so—even going so far as to say that the magistrates were blinded and she could open their eyes. It was one of those marital disputes that occur between strong-willed people. And it was to bring Martha Corey to the gallows and Giles Corey to an even stranger doom.

PREDICT

How do you think Martha and Giles Corey get involved in the witch trials? Read on to find out.

Yet now there was a lull, through which people whispered.

As for what went on in the minds of the "afflicted children," during that lull, we may not say. But this much is evident. They had seen and felt their power. The hearing had been the greatest and most exciting event of their narrow lives. And it was so easy to do—they grew more and more ingenious with each rehearsal. You twisted your body and groaned—and grown people were afraid.

Add to this the three girl-servants, with the usual servants' grudges against present or former masters. Add to this that high-strung, dominant woman, Ann Putnam, Sr., who could hold a grudge and remember it. Such a grudge as there might be against the Towne sisters, for instance—they were all married women of the highest standing, particularly Rebecca Nurse. But they'd taken the Topsfield side in that boundary dispute with Salem. So suppose—just suppose—that one of them were found out to be a witch? And hadn't Tituba deposed[21] that there were other women, besides Good and Osborne, who made her torment the children?

On March 19, Martha Corey and Rebecca Nurse were arrested on the charge of witchcraft. On March 21, they were examined and committed. And, with that, the real reign of terror began.

CLARIFY

What, in Benét's view, causes the group members to accuse more people of witchcraft?

For if Martha Corey, notably religious and God-fearing, and Rebecca Nurse, saintly and thoughtful, could be witches, no one in Salem or New England was safe from the charge. The examinations were brutally unfair—the "children" yet bolder and more daring. They would interrupt questions now to shout that "a black man" was whispering in the prisoner's ear—if the accused stood still, they were tormented, if she moved her hands, they suffered even greater agonies. Their self-confidence became monstrous—there was no trick too fantastic for them to try. When Deodat Lawson, a former minister of Salem and a well-educated and intelligent man, came to Ingersoll's on

20. **gallows** (găl′ōz): execution by hanging.

21. **deposed:** testified.

WORDS TO KNOW **turbulent** (tûr′byə-lənt) *adj.* violently agitated or disturbed

For by now, Salem Village, as a community, was no longer sane. . . . All through the summer, the accusations, the arrests, the trials came thick and fast.

March 19, he first saw Mary Wolcott who "as she stood by the door was bitten, so that she cried out of her wrist, and, looking at it, we saw apparently the marks of teeth, both upper and lower set, on each side of her wrist." It would not have deceived a child—but Mary Wolcott was one of the "afflicted children" and her words and self-bitings were as gospel. He then went to the parsonage, where Abigail Williams, another afflicted child, put on a very effective vaudeville-act indeed, throwing firebrands[22] around the house, crying "Whish, whish, whish!" and saying that she was being tormented by Rebecca Nurse who was trying to make her sign the Devil's book.

After that, there was, obviously, nothing for the Reverend Lawson to do but to preach a thunderous sermon on the horrors of witchcraft—interrupted by demonstrations and cries from "the afflicted"—and thus do his little bit toward driving the madness on. For by now, Salem Village, as a community, was no longer sane.

Let us get the rest of it over quickly. The Salem witches ceased to be Salem's affair—they became a matter affecting the whole colony. Sir William Phips, the new governor, appointed a special court of Oyer and Terminer to try the cases. And the hangings began.

On January 1, 1692, no one, except possibly the "Circle children"[23] had heard of Salem witches. On June 10, Bridget Bishop was hanged. She had not been one of the first accused, but she was the first to suffer. She had been married three times, kept a roadhouse on the road to Beverly where people drank rum and played shovelboard, and dressed, distinctively for the period, in a "black cap and black hat and red paragon bodice broidered and looped with diverse colors."[24] But those seem to have been her chief offenses. When questioned, she said "I never saw the Devil in my life."

All through the summer, the accusations, the arrests, the trials came thick and fast till the jails were crowded. Nor were those now accused friendless old beldames[25] like Sarah Good. They included Captain John Alden (son of Miles

---

22. **firebrands:** pieces of burning wood.

23. **"Circle children":** the group of children who had originally met with Tituba.

24. **red paragon bodice** (bŏd′ĭs) **broidered . . . colors:** the upper portion of a woman's dress, which in this case was made of colorfully embroidered red paragon, a type of silk fabric used in the 17th century. Red paragon would stand out among the plain, dark clothing that Puritans usually wore.

25. **beldames** (bĕl′dəmz): old women, especially those who are considered ugly.

There comes a point
when driven
men and women revolt against
blood and horror.

Standish's friend), who saved himself by breaking jail, and the wealthy and prominent Englishes, who saved themselves by flight. The most disgraceful scenes occurred at the trial of the saintly Rebecca Nurse. Thirty-nine citizens of Salem were brave enough to sign a petition for her, and the jury brought in a verdict of "not guilty." The mob in the sweating courtroom immediately began to cry out, and the presiding judge as much as told the jury to reverse their verdict. They did so, to the mob's delight. Then the Governor pardoned her. And "certain gentlemen of Salem"—and perhaps the mob—persuaded him into reversing his pardon. She was hanged on Gallows Hill on July 19 with Sarah Good, Sarah Wilds, Elizabeth How, and Susanna Martin.

QUESTION

Why do you think the crowd insists that Rebecca Nurse be found guilty—and not be pardoned?

Susanna Martin's only witchcraft seems to have been that she was an unusually tidy woman and had once walked a muddy road without getting her dress bedraggled. No, I am quoting from testimony, not inventing. As for Elizabeth How, a neighbor testified, "I have been acquainted with Goodwife How as a naybor for nine or ten years and I never saw any harm in her but found her just in her dealings and faithful to her promises. . . . I never heard her revile any person but she always pitied them and said, 'I pray God forgive them now.'" But the children cried, "I am stuck with a pin. I am pinched," when they saw her—and she hanged.

It took a little more to hang the Reverend George Burroughs. He had been Salem Village's second minister—then gone on to a parish in Maine. And the cloth[26] had great sanctity. But Ann Putnam and Mercy Lewis managed to doom him between them—with the able assistance of the rest of the troupe. Mr. Burroughs was unfortunate enough to be a man of unusual physical strength—anyone who could lift a gun by putting four fingers in its barrel, must do so by magic arts. Also, he had been married three times. So when the ghosts of his first two wives, dressed in winding-sheets, appeared in a sort of magic-lantern show to Ann Putnam and cried out that Mr. Burroughs had murdered them—the cloth could not save him then. Perhaps one of the most pathetic documents connected with the trials is the later petition of his orphaned children. It begins, "We were left a parcel of small children, helpless—"

Here and there, in the records, gleams a flash of frantic common sense. Susanna Martin laughs when Ann Putnam and her daughter go into convulsions at her appearance. When asked why, she says, "Well I may, at such folly. I never hurt this woman or her child in my life." John Procter, the prosperous farmer who employed Mary Warren, said sensibly, before his arrest, "If these girls are left alone, we will all be devils and witches. They ought all to be sent to the whipping-post." He was right enough about it—but his servant helped hang him. White-haired old George Jacobs, leaning on his two sticks, cried out, "You tax[27] me for a wizard, you might as well tax me for a buzzard!" Nevertheless, he hanged. A member of the Nurse family testifies, "Being in court this 29th June, 1692, I saw Goodwife Bibber pull pins out of her clothes and

26. **the cloth:** the clergy.

27. **tax:** to make a charge against; accuse.

WORDS TO KNOW

revile (rĭ-vīl') *v.* to scold; to use abusive language

hold them between her fingers and clasp her hands around her knee and then she cried out and said Goodwife Nurse pinched her." But such depositions did not save Rebecca Nurse or her sister, Mary Easty.

Judge, jury, and colony preferred to believe the writhings of the children, the stammerings of those whose sows had died inexplicably, the testimony of such as Bernard Peach who swore that Susanna Martin had flown in through his window, bent his body into the shape of a "whoope" and sat upon him for an hour and a half.

One hanging on June 10, five on July 19, five on August 19, eight on September 22, including Mary Easty and Martha Corey. And of these the Reverend Noyes remarked, with unction,[28] "What a sad thing it is to see eight firebrands of hell hanging there!" But for stubborn Giles Corey a different fate was reserved.

The old man had begun by believing in the whole hocus-pocus. He had quarreled with his wife about it. He had seen her arrested as a witch, insulted by the magistrates, condemned to die. Two of his sons-in-law had testified against her—he himself had been closely questioned as to her actions and had made the deposition of a badgered and simple man. Yes, she prayed a good deal—sometimes he couldn't hear what she said—that sort of thing. The memory must have risen to haunt him when she was condemned. Now, he himself was in danger.

Well, he could die as his wife would. But there was the property—his goods, his prospering lands. By law, the goods and property of those convicted of witchcraft were confiscated by the State and the name attainted.[29] With a curious, grim heroism, Giles Corey drew up a will leaving that property to the two sons-in-law who had not joined in the prevailing madness. And then at his trial, he said, "I will not plead. If I deny, I am condemned already in courts where ghosts appear as witnesses and swear men's lives away."

A curious, grim heroism? It was so. For those who refused to plead either guilty or not guilty in such a suit were liable to the old English punishment called *peine forte et dure*.[30] It consisted in heaping weights or stones upon the unhappy victim till he accepted a plea—or until his chest was crushed. And exactly that happened to old Giles Corey. They heaped the stones upon him until they killed him—and two days before his wife was hanged, he died. But his property went to the two loyal sons-in-law, without confiscation—and his name was not attainted. So died Giles Corey, New England to the bone.

EVALUATE

Do you agree that Giles Corey is heroic?

And then, suddenly and fantastically as the madness had come, it was gone. . . .

The "afflicted children," at long last, had gone too far. They had accused the governor's lady. They had accused Mrs. Hall, the wife of the minister at Beverly and a woman known throughout the colony for her virtues. And there comes a point when driven men and women revolt against blood and horror. It was that which ended Robespierre's[31] terror—it was that which ended the terror of the "afflicted children." The thing had become a *reductio ad absurdum*.[32] If it went on, logically, no one but

28. **unction** (ŭngk′shən): exaggerated earnestness, especially in use of language.

29. **name attainted:** to have one's name attainted is to be placed in a legal state in which one has no civil rights and cannot inherit or transmit property.

30. ***peine forte et dure*** (pĕn fôrt ā dür) *French:* strong and hard punishment.

31. **Robespierre** (rōbz′pē-âr′): a French revolutionary who, as leader of the Reign of Terror, fanatically tried to wipe out every trace of France's past monarchy and nobility. Robespierre, who lived from 1758 to 1794, was responsible for the deaths of thousands and was himself guillotined after his fellow revolutionaries finally turned on him.

32. ***reductio ad absurdum*** (rĭ-dŭk′tē-ō ăd əb-sûr′dəm) *Latin:* the disproof of a proposition by showing the absurdity of its inevitable conclusion.

WORDS TO KNOW

confiscate (kŏn′fĭ-skāt′) *v.* to seize for the public treasury; to appropriate

But it is not a stranger thing to hang a man for witchcraft than to hang him for the shape of his nose or the color of his skin. We are not superstitious, **no.**

Flight (1954), Karel Appel. Oil on burlap. 43⅜" × 55⅛", Albright-Knox Art Gallery, Buffalo, New York, gift of Seymour H. Knox, 1955.

the "afflicted children" and their protégées would be left alive. . . .

In 1706 Ann Putnam made public confession that she had been deluded by the devil in testifying as she had. She had testified in every case but one. And in 1711 the colony of Massachusetts paid fifty pounds to the heirs of George Burroughs, twenty-one pounds to the heirs of Giles Corey—five hundred and seventy-eight pounds in all to the heirs of various victims. An expensive business for the colony, on the whole.

What happened to the survivors? Well, the Reverend Samuel Parris quit Salem Village to go into business in Boston and died at Sudbury in 1720. And Ann Putnam died in 1716, and from the stock of the Putnams sprang Israel Putnam, the Revolutionary hero. And from the stock of the "Witches," the Nurses and the others, sprang excellent and distinguished people of service to state and nation. And hanging Judge Hathorne's descendant was Nathaniel Hawthorne. . . .[33]

We have no reason to hold Salem up to obloquy.[34] It was a town, like another, and a strange madness took hold of it. But it is not a stranger thing to hang a man for witchcraft than to hang him for the shape of his nose or the color of his skin. We are not superstitious, no. Well, let us be a little sure we are not. For persecution follows superstition and intolerance as fire follows the fuse. And once we light that fire we cannot foresee where it will end or what it will consume—any more than they could in Salem two hundred and forty-five years ago.[35] ❖

CONNECT

What instances of such persecution come to your mind?

33. **Nathaniel Hawthorne:** a well-known American author who lived from 1804 to 1864.

34. **obloquy** (ŏb′lə-kwē): harsh criticism.

35. **two hundred and forty-five years ago:** Benét wrote this essay in 1937.

WORDS TO KNOW

protégée (prō′tə-zhā′) *n.* feminine form of protégé, someone trained or led by an influential person

delude (dĭ-lo͞od′) *v.* to deceive

RESPONDING OPTIONS

FROM PERSONAL RESPONSE *TO* CRITICAL ANALYSIS

REFLECT 1. What was the most surprising new thing you learned about the Salem witch trials from reading this essay? Refer to the chart you were asked to fill out on page 168, and share your choice with the class.

RETHINK 2. Why do you think Benét entitled his essay "We Aren't Superstitious"?

Consider
- who he means by "we"
- what he seems to be referring to in the final paragraph
- whether the essay supports the statement in the title

3. How would you summarize Benét's interpretation of the causes of the Salem witch trials?

Consider
- what he suggests were the motives of the accusers
- why, in his view, the townspeople so readily believed the accusers
- how he portrays the accused witches
- what he suggests was the reason the trials ended so abruptly

4. Do you agree with Benét's interpretation of events? Review what you wrote in your reading log as you read.

5. Why do you think the other accused witches were not able to save themselves as Tituba did?

RELATE 6. Benét says, "But it is not a stranger thing to hang a man for witchcraft than to hang him for the shape of his nose or the color of his skin." The quote suggests that equally tragic "witch hunts" have occurred in modern times. Give an example of a 20th-century witch hunt. Think about instances in which a group of people were irrationally accused of imagined crimes—and tragically punished.

ANOTHER PATHWAY

Cooperative Learning

In a small group, debate who was most responsible for the tragedy of the Salem witch trials as portrayed by Benét—the afflicted girls, Tituba, the complainants (the men who filed the first formal complaints against the witches), the judges, the ministers, or the citizens of Salem.

QUICKWRITES

1. Write a short **diary entry** in the voice of one person named in "We Aren't Superstitious," revealing thoughts and feelings that this person might have had over the course of the trials. You might choose young Ann Putnam, Tituba, Sarah Good, or Giles Corey, for example.
2. Write an outline for an **encyclopedia entry** about the Salem witch trials, including any information you feel is important for the general public to know. You may include what you learned from reading "We Aren't Superstitious," the Salem court documents on pages 155–157, and, if you wish, any other sources.

PORTFOLIO Save your writing. You may want to use it later as a springboard to a piece for your portfolio.

LITERARY CONCEPTS

Irony refers to a contrast between appearance and actuality. One form of irony, **situational irony,** is a contrast between what is expected to happen and what actually happens. That Tituba, who confesses to being a witch, is spared while those who deny being witches are hanged is an example of situational irony. Find at least two other examples of situational irony in this selection. What is an example of situational irony from your own time?

LITERARY LINKS

What comparisons can you make between the Plymouth colonists' view of Indians and the wilderness and the Salem colonists' view of witches? Refer to the excerpt from *Of Plymouth Plantation* (page 88) to refresh your memory. What conclusions about Puritans, if any, would you draw from these comparisons?

THE WRITER'S STYLE

Reread the part of this essay that describes the examination of Sarah Good, beginning on page 174. Tell how Benét's account differs from the accounts given in the Salem court documents on page 156. Discuss the kinds of details Benét includes. What attitudes does he express toward the accusers, the judges, and the defendants? How are his attitudes revealed?

CRITIC'S CORNER

In writing about Stephen Vincent Benét and the body of his work, the critic Joel Roache commented:

> **He saw human history . . . not as merely an endlessly irrational, cyclical burden, but as the richest available source of the knowledge and power that will allow the species, in William Faulkner's famous phrase, not merely to endure, but to prevail.**

In your view, does "We Aren't Superstitious" support or contradict this opinion?

ALTERNATIVE ACTIVITIES

1. Imagine that you are a cartoonist for a Boston newspaper in 1692. Draw a **political cartoon** to express your opinion of the Salem witch trials.
2. Create a **diagram** or a **flowchart** to show the chain of causes and effects that led to the hangings of 19 suspected witches in Salem and, in turn, what effects these hangings had upon the community.

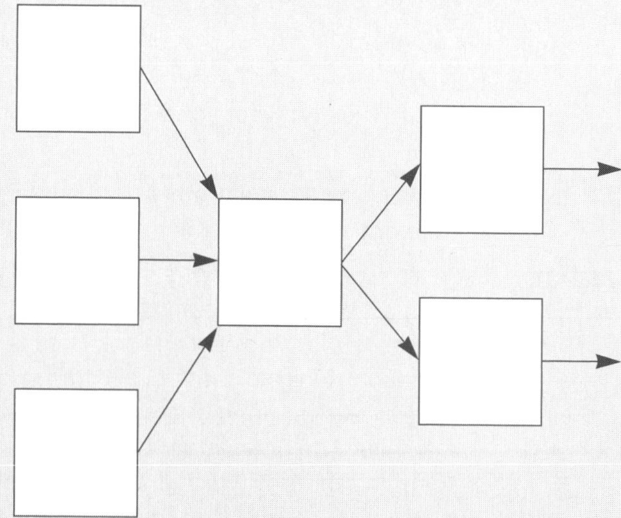

ACROSS THE CURRICULUM

History Research the hearings held by Senator Joseph McCarthy in the early 1950s to investigate suspected Communists in the U.S. government. These hearings often have been described as "witch hunts." Find out what led to the hearings, how they were conducted, and what happened to those who were accused. Report your findings to the class.

Biology In a 1976 article in *Science* magazine, Linda R. Caporael proposed that the strange behavior of the afflicted children in Salem resulted from ergotism, a disease caused by eating contaminated grain, particularly rye. Find out about the ergot fungus—the conditions under which it forms, the symptoms it produces, and the modern drugs derived from it. Share your knowledge in an oral presentation, and state whether Caporael's hypothesis seems valid to you.

WORDS TO KNOW

EXERCISE A Review the Words to Know in the boxes at the bottom of the selection pages. On your paper, write the vocabulary word that best completes each sentence below.

1. The people of Salem blamed witches when their livestock was __________ with mysterious ailments.
2. Witchcraft was thought to be a crime as __________ as murder.
3. A person would have to be __________ to believe accusations made by someone with a grudge.
4. Perhaps some people viewed the trials as a __________ that added excitement to their lives.
5. The events at Salem are __________ in the way they show how hysteria can spread rapidly.

EXERCISE B Play a game of charades using the ten remaining vocabulary words. The class can be divided into opposing teams, and volunteers can act out the meaning of each word for their team to identify. Have your teacher time each attempt and keep score.

STEPHEN VINCENT BENÉT

1898–1943

Stephen Vincent Benét was a poet, short story writer, novelist, essayist, historian, and patriot. The subjects of most of his writings—like the Salem witch trials described in "We Aren't Superstitious"—are the events and people who played a part in American history. Benét's great talent was to capture the truth of the events and to put them in perspective for Americans of his time and ours.

The Benéts were a military family, and Stephen, like many army children, traveled around the country as his father was transferred from post to post. At home, his father read and discussed poetry with Stephen and his brother and sister and instilled in them a love of literature. All three children later became writers.

At age 17, Benét entered Yale University and published his first book of poems, *Five Men and Pompey.* He published a second volume of poetry three years later and graduated with a master's degree from Yale in 1920. Later that year, he went to Paris, where he met the writer Rosemary Carr, whom he later married and with whom he collaborated on several projects. In the 1930s, Benét supported his growing family first by writing scripts in Hollywood and later by writing reviews in New York. During World War II, he worked as a radio and film propagandist.

Because he addressed American themes, Benét gained a wide popular audience for his poems and stories. His best known story, "The Devil and Daniel Webster," has been made into a play, a movie, and an opera. Benét drew on his father's collection of military books to write *John Brown's Body,* a Pulitzer Prize-winning epic poem about the Civil War. Before dying suddenly of a heart attack at age 44, Benét had established himself as one of America's foremost writers. He earned a posthumous Pulitzer Prize for *Western Star,* an unfinished work about the changing American frontier.

OTHER WORKS *A Book of Americans, Thirteen O'Clock*

LASERLINKS
• *HISTORICAL CONNECTION*

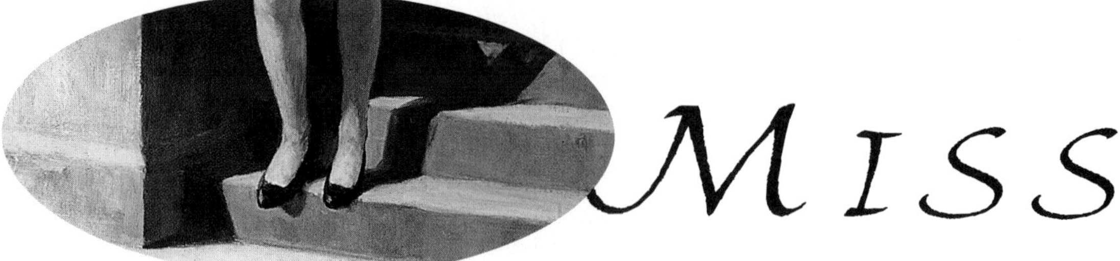

MISS

Puritanism had fallen into such disrepair that not even the oldest spinster thought of putting Susanna in a ducking stool;[1] not even the oldest farmer suspected that Susanna's diabolical beauty had made his cow run dry.

Susanna was a bit-part actress in the summer theater near the village, and she rented a room over the firehouse. She was a part of village life all summer, but the villagers never got used to her. She was forever as startling and desirable as a piece of big-city fire apparatus.

Susanna's feathery hair and saucer eyes were as black as midnight. Her skin was the color of cream. Her hips were like a lyre, and her bosom made men dream of peace and plenty for ever and ever. She wore barbaric golden hoops on her shell-pink ears, and around her ankles were chains with little bells on them.

She went barefoot and slept until noon every day. And, as noon drew near, the villagers on the main street would grow as restless as beagles with a thunderstorm on the way.

At noon, Susanna would appear on the porch outside her room. She would stretch languidly, pour a bowl of milk for her black cat, kiss the cat, fluff her hair, put on her earrings, lock her door, and hide the key in her bosom.

And then, barefoot, she would begin her stately, undulating, titillating, tinkling walk—down the outside stairway, past the liquor store, the insurance agency, the real estate office, the diner, the American Legion post, and the church, to the crowded drugstore. There she would get the New York papers.

She seemed to nod to all the world in a dim, queenly way. But the only person she spoke to during her daily walk was Bearse Hinkley, the seventy-two-year-old pharmacist.

The old man always had her papers ready for her.

"Thank you, Mr. Hinkley. You're an angel," she would say, opening a paper at random. "Now, let's see what's going on back in civilization." While the old man would watch, fuddled by her perfume, Susanna would laugh or gasp or frown at items in the paper—items she never explained.

Then she would take the papers, and return to her nest over the firehouse. She would pause on the porch outside her room, dip her hand into her bosom, bring out the key, unlock the door, pick up the black cat, kiss it again, and disappear inside.

1. **ducking stool:** a device formerly used in Europe and New England for punishment, consisting of a chair in which an offender was tied and ducked into water.

TEMPTATION

Kurt Vonnegut, Jr.

The one-girl pageant had a ritual sameness until one day toward the end of summer, when the air of the drugstore was cut by a cruel, sustained screech from a dry bearing in a revolving soda-fountain stool.

The screech cut right through Susanna's speech about Mr. Hinkley's being an angel. The screech made scalps tingle and teeth ache. Susanna looked indulgently in the direction of the screech, forgiving the screecher. She found that the screecher wasn't a person to be indulged.

The screech had been made by the stool of Cpl. Norman Fuller, who had come home the night before from eighteen bleak months in Korea.[2] They had been eighteen months without war—but eighteen months without cheer, all the same. Fuller had turned on the stool slowly, to look at Susanna with indignation. When the screech died, the drugstore was deathly still.

Fuller had broken the enchantment of summer by the seaside—had reminded all in the drugstore of the black, mysterious passions that were so often the mainsprings of life.

He might have been a brother, come to rescue his idiot sister from the tenderloin;[3] or an irate husband, come to a saloon to horsewhip his wife back to where she belonged, with the baby. The truth was that Corporal Fuller had never seen Susanna before.

He hadn't consciously meant to make a scene. He hadn't known, consciously, that his stool would screech. He had meant to underplay his indignation, to make it a small detail in the background of Susanna's pageant—a detail noticed by only one or two connoisseurs of the human comedy.

But the screech had made his indignation the center of the solar system for all in the drugstore—particularly for Susanna. Time had stopped, and it could not proceed until Fuller had explained the expression on his granite Yankee face.

Fuller felt his skin glowing like hot brass. He was comprehending destiny. Destiny had suddenly given him an audience, and a situation about which he had a bitter lot to say.

Fuller felt his lips move, heard the words come out. "Who do you think you are?" he said to Susanna.

"I beg your pardon?" said Susanna. She drew

2. **eighteen bleak months in Korea:** the Korean War was a conflict between North Korea and South Korea that lasted from 1950 to 1953. In this conflict, South Korea was aided by U.S. troops.

3. **tenderloin:** a city district with a reputation for crime and corruption.

her newspapers about herself protectively.

"I saw you come down the street like you were a circus parade, and I just wondered who you thought you were," said Fuller.

Susanna blushed gloriously. "I—I'm an actress," she said.

"You can say that again," said Fuller. "Greatest actresses in the world, American women."

"You're very nice to say so," said Susanna uneasily.

Fuller's skin glowed brighter and hotter. His mind had become a fountain of apt, intricate phrases. "I'm not talking about theaters with seats in 'em. I'm talking about the stage of life. American women act and dress like they're gonna give you the world. Then, when you stick out your hand, they put an ice cube in it."

"They do?" said Susanna emptily.

"They do," said Fuller, "and it's about time somebody said so." He looked challengingly from spectator to spectator, and found what he took to be dazed encouragement. "It isn't fair," he said.

"What isn't?" said Susanna, lost.

"You come in here with bells on your ankles, so's I'll have to look at your ankles and your pretty pink feet," said Fuller. "You kiss the cat, so's I'll have to think about how it'd be to be that cat," said Fuller. "You call an old man an angel, so's I'll have to think about what it'd be like to be called an angel by you," said Fuller. "You hide your key in front of everybody, so's I'll have to think about where that key is," said Fuller.

He stood. "Miss," he said, his voice full of pain, "you do everything you can to give lonely, ordinary people like me indigestion and the heeby-jeebies, and you wouldn't even hold hands with me to keep me from falling off a cliff."

He strode to the door. All eyes were on him. Hardly anyone noticed that his indictment had reduced Susanna to ashes of what she'd been moments before. Susanna now looked like what she really was—a muddle-headed nineteen-year-old clinging to a tiny corner of sophistication.

Susanna now looked like what she really was—a muddle-headed nineteen-year-old clinging to a tiny corner of sophistication.

"It isn't fair," said Fuller. "There ought to be a law against girls acting and dressing like you do. It makes more people unhappy than it does happy. You know what I say to you, for going around making everybody want to kiss you?"

"No," piped Susanna, every fuse in her nervous system blown.

"I say to you what you'd say to me, if I was to try and kiss you," said Fuller grandly. He swung his arms in an umpire's gesture for "out." "The hell with you," he said. He left, slamming the screen door.

He didn't look back when the door slammed again a moment later, when the patter of running bare feet and the wild tinkling of little bells faded away in the direction of the firehouse.

That evening, Corporal Fuller's widowed mother put a candle on the table, and fed him sirloin steak and strawberry shortcake in honor of his homecoming. Fuller ate the meal as though it were wet blotting paper, and he answered his mother's cheery questions in a voice that was dead.

"Aren't you glad to be home?" said his mother, when they'd finished their coffee.

"Sure," said Fuller.

Summertime (1943), Edward Hopper. Oil on canvas, 29⅛″ × 44″, Delaware Art Museum, gift of Dora Sexton Brown, 1962.

"What did you do today?" she said.

"Walked," he said.

"Seeing all your old friends?" she said.

"Haven't got any friends," said Fuller.

His mother threw up her hands. "No friends?" she said. "You?"

"Times change, ma," said Fuller heavily. "Eighteen months is a long time. People leave town, people get married—"

"Marriage doesn't kill people, does it?" she said.

Fuller didn't smile. "Maybe not," he said. "But it makes it awful hard for 'em to find any place to fit old friends in."

"Dougie isn't married, is he?"

"He's out west, ma—with the Strategic Air Command," said Fuller. The little dining room became as lonely as a bomber in the thin, cold stratosphere.

"Oh," said his mother. "There must be somebody left."

"Nope," said Fuller. "I spent the whole morning on the phone, ma. I might as well have been back in Korea. Nobody home."

"I can't believe it," she said. "Why, you couldn't walk down Main Street without being almost trampled by friends."

"Ma," said Fuller hollowly, "after I ran out of numbers to call, you know what I did? I went down to the drugstore, ma, and just sat there by the soda fountain, waiting for somebody to walk in—somebody I knew maybe just even a little.

Ma," he said in anguish, "all I knew was poor old Bearse Hinkley. I'm not kidding you one bit." He stood, crumpling his napkin into a ball. "Ma, will you please excuse me?"

"Yes. Of course," she said. "Where are you going now?" She beamed. "Out to call on some nice girl, I hope?"

Fuller threw the napkin down. "I'm going to get a cigar!" he said. "I don't know any girls. They're all married too."

His mother paled. "I—I see," she said. "I—I didn't even know you smoked."

"Ma," said Fuller tautly, "can't you get it through your head? I been away for eighteen months, ma—eighteen months!"

"It is a long time, isn't it?" said his mother, humbled by his passion. "Well, you go get your cigar." She touched his arm. "And please don't feel so lonesome. You just wait. Your life will be so full of people again, you won't know which one to turn to. And, before you know it, you'll meet some pretty young girl, and you'll be married too."

"I don't intend to get married for some time, mother," said Fuller stuffily. "Not until I get through divinity school."

"Divinity school!" said his mother. "When did you decide that?"

"This noon," said Fuller.

"What happened this noon?"

"I had kind of a religious experience, ma," he said. "Something just made me speak out."

"About what?" she said, bewildered.

In Fuller's buzzing head there whirled a rhapsody of Susannas. He saw again all the professional temptresses who had tormented him in Korea, who had beckoned from makeshift bedsheet movie screens, from curling pinups on damp tent walls, from ragged magazines in sandbagged pits. The Susannas had made fortunes, beckoning to lonely Corporal Fullers everywhere—beckoning with stunning beauty, beckoning the Fullers to come nowhere for nothing.

The wraith of a Puritan ancestor, stiff-necked, dressed in black, took possession of Fuller's tongue. Fuller spoke with a voice that came across the centuries, the voice of a witch hanger, a voice redolent with frustration, self-righteousness, and doom.

"What did I speak out against?" he said. "Temp-ta-tion."

Fuller's cigar in the night was a beacon warning carefree, frivolous people away. It was plainly a cigar smoked in anger. Even the moths had sense enough to stay away. Like a restless, searching red eye, it went up and down every street in the village, coming to rest at last, a wet, dead butt, before the firehouse.

Bearse Hinkley, the old pharmacist, sat at the wheel of the pumper, his eyes glazed with nostalgia—nostalgia for the days when he had been young enough to drive. And on his face, for all to see, was a dream of one more catastrophe, with all the young men away, when an old man or nobody would drive the pumper to glory one more time. He spent warm evenings there, behind the wheel—and had for years.

"Want a light for that thing?" he said to Corporal Fuller, seeing the dead cigar between Fuller's lips.

"No, thanks, Mr. Hinkley," he said. "All the pleasure's out of it."

"Beats me how anybody finds any pleasure in cigars in the first place," said the old man.

"Matter of taste," said Fuller. "No accounting for tastes."

"One man's meat's another man's poison," said Hinkley. "Live and let live, I always say." He glanced at the ceiling. Above it was the fragrant nest of Susanna and her black cat. "Me? All my pleasures are looking at what used to be pleasures."

Fuller looked at the ceiling, too, meeting the unmentioned issue squarely. "If you were young," he said, "you'd know why I said what I said to her. Beautiful, stuck-up girls give me a big pain."

"Oh, I remember that," said Hinkley. "I'm not so old I don't remember the big pain."

"If I have a daughter, I hope she isn't beautiful," said Fuller. "The beautiful girls at high school—by God, if they didn't think they were something extra-special."

"By God, if I don't think so, too," said Hinkley.

"They wouldn't even look at you if you didn't have a car and an allowance of twenty bucks a week to spend on 'em," said Fuller.

"Why should they?" said the old man cheerfully. "If I was a beautiful girl, I wouldn't." He nodded to himself. "Well—anyway, I guess you came home from the wars and settled that score. I guess you told her."

"Ah-h-h," said Fuller. "You can't make any impression on them."

"I dunno," said Hinkley. "There's a fine old tradition in the theater: The show must go on. You know, even if you got pneumonia or your baby's dying, you still put on the show."

"I'm all right," said Fuller. "Who's complaining? I feel fine."

The old man's white eyebrows went up. "Who's talking about you?" he said. "I'm talking about her."

Fuller reddened, mousetrapped by egoism. "She'll be all right," he said.

"She will?" said Hinkley. "Maybe she will. All I know is, the show's started at the theater. She's supposed to be in it and she's still upstairs."

"She is?" said Fuller, amazed.

"Has been," said Hinkley, "ever since you paddled her and sent her home."

Fuller tried to grin ironically. "Now, isn't that too bad?" he said. His grin felt queasy and weak. "Well, good-night, Mr. Hinkley."

"Good-night, soldier boy," said Hinkley. "Good-night."

As noon drew near on the next day, the villagers along the main street seemed to grow stupid. Yankee shopkeepers made change lackadaisically, as though money didn't matter any more. All thoughts were of the great cuckoo clock the firehouse had become. The question was: Had Corporal Fuller broken it or, at noon, would the little door on top fly open, would Susanna appear?

In the drugstore, old Bearse Hinkley fussed with Susanna's New York papers, rumpling them in his anxiety to make them attractive. They were bait for Susanna.

Moments before noon, Corporal Fuller—the vandal himself—came into the drugstore. On his face was a strange mixture of guilt and sore-headedness. He had spent the better part of the night awake, reviewing his grievances against beautiful women. *All they think about is how beautiful they are,* he'd said to himself at dawn. *They wouldn't even give you the time of day.*

He walked along the row of soda-fountain stools and gave each empty stool a seemingly idle twist. He found the stool that had screeched so loudly the day before. He sat down on it, a monument of righteousness. No one spoke to him.

The fire siren gave its perfunctory wheeze for noon. And then, hearselike, a truck from the express company drove up to the firehouse. Two men got out and climbed the stairs. Susanna's hungry black cat jumped to the porch railing and arched its back as the expressmen disappeared into Susanna's room. The cat spat when they staggered out with Susanna's trunk.

Fuller was shocked. He glanced at Bearse Hinkley, and he saw that the old man's look of anxiety had become the look of double pneumonia—dizzy, blind, drowning.

"Satisfied, corporal?" said the old man.

"I didn't tell her to leave," said Fuller.

"You didn't leave her much choice," said Hinkley.

"What does she care what I think?" said

Fuller. "I didn't know she was such a tender blossom."

The old man touched Fuller's arm lightly. "We all are, corporal—we all are," he said. "I thought that was one of the few good things about sending a boy off to the Army. I thought that was where he could find out for sure he wasn't the only tender blossom on earth. Didn't you find that out?"

"I never thought I was a tender blossom," said Fuller. "I'm sorry it turned out this way, but she asked for it." His head was down. His ears were hot crimson.

"She really scared you stiff, didn't she?" said Hinkley.

Smiles bloomed on the faces of the small audience that had drawn near on one pretext or another. Fuller appraised the smiles, and found that the old man had left him only one weapon—utterly humorless good citizenship.

"Who's afraid?" he said stuffily. "I'm not afraid. I just think it's a problem somebody ought to bring up and discuss."

"It's sure the one subject nobody gets tired of," said Hinkley.

Fuller's gaze, which had become a very shifty thing, passed over the magazine rack. There was tier upon tier of Susannas, a thousand square feet of wet-lipped smiles and sooty eyes and skin like cream. He ransacked his mind for a ringing phrase that would give dignity to his cause.

"I'm thinking about juvenile delinquency!" he said. He pointed to the magazines. "No wonder kids go crazy."

"I know I did," said the old man quietly. "I was as scared as you are."

"I told you, I'm not afraid of her," said Fuller.

"Good!" said Hinkley. "Then you're just the man to take her papers to her. They're paid for." He dumped the papers in Fuller's lap.

Fuller opened his mouth to reply. But he closed it again. His throat had tightened, and he knew that, if he tried to speak, he would quack like a duck.

"If you're really not afraid, corporal," said the old man, "that would be a very nice thing to do—a Christian thing to do."

> *"Did you ever stop to think what it's like to be me?" she said.*

As he mounted the stairway to Susanna's nest, Fuller was almost spastic in his efforts to seem casual.

Susanna's door was unlatched. When Fuller knocked on it, it swung open. In Fuller's imagination, her nest had been dark and still, reeking of incense, a labyrinth of heavy hangings and mirrors, with somewhere a Turkish corner, with somewhere a billowy bed in the form of a swan.

He saw Susanna and her room in truth now. The truth was the cheerless truth of a dirt-cheap Yankee summer rental—bare wood walls, three coat hooks, a linoleum rug. Two gas burners, an iron cot, an icebox. A tiny sink with naked pipes, a plastic drinking glass, two plates, a murky mirror. A frying pan, a saucepan, a can of soap powder.

The only harem touch was a white circle of talcum powder before the murky mirror. In the center of the circle were the prints of two bare feet. The marks of the toes were no bigger than pearls.

Fuller looked from the pearls to the truth of Susanna. Her back was to him. She was packing the last of her things into a suitcase.

She was now dressed for travel—dressed as properly as a missionary's wife.

"Papers," croaked Fuller. "Mr. Hinkley sent 'em."

"How very nice of Mr. Hinkley," said Susanna. She turned. "Tell him—" No more words came. She recognized him. She pursed

Portrait of Orleans (1950), Edward Hopper. Oil on canvas, 26″ × 40″, The Fine Arts Museums of San Francisco, fractional gift of Jerrold and June Kingsley (1991.32).

her lips and her small nose reddened.

"Papers," said Fuller emptily. "From Mr. Hinkley."

"I heard you," she said. "You just said that. Is that all you've got to say?"

Fuller flapped his hands limply at his sides. "I'm—I—I didn't mean to make you leave," he said. "I didn't mean that."

"You suggest I stay?" said Susanna wretchedly. "After I've been denounced in public as a scarlet woman? A tart? A wench?"

"Holy smokes, I never called you those things!" said Fuller.

"Did you ever stop to think what it's like to be me?" she said. She patted her bosom. "There's somebody living inside here, too, you know."

"I know," said Fuller. He hadn't known, up to then.

"I have a soul," she said.

"Sure you do," said Fuller, trembling. He trembled because the room was filled with a profound intimacy. Susanna, the golden girl of a thousand tortured daydreams, was now discussing her soul, passionately, with Fuller the lonely, Fuller the homely, Fuller the bleak.

"I didn't sleep a wink last night because of you," said Susanna.

"Me?" He wished she'd get out of his life again. He wished she were in black and white, a thousandth of an inch thick on a magazine page. He wished he could turn the page and read about baseball or foreign affairs.

"What did you expect?" said Susanna. "I talked to you all night. You know what I said to you?"

"No," said Fuller, backing away. She followed, and seemed to throw off heat like a big iron radiator. She was appallingly human.

"I'm not Yellowstone Park!" she said. "I'm not supported by taxes! I don't belong to everybody! You don't have any right to say anything about the way I look!"

"Good gravy!" said Fuller.

"I'm so tired of dumb toots like you!" said Susanna. She stamped her foot and suddenly looked haggard. "I can't help it if you want to kiss me! Whose fault is that?"

Fuller could now glimpse his side of the question only dimly, like a diver glimpsing the sun from the ocean floor. "All I was trying to say was, you could be a little more conservative," he said.

Susanna opened her arms. "Am I conservative enough now?" she said. "Is this all right with you?"

The appeal of the lovely girl made the marrow of Fuller's bones ache. In his chest was a sigh like the lost chord. "Yes," he said. And then he murmured, "Forget about me."

Susanna tossed her head. "Forget about being run over by a truck," she said. "What makes you so mean?"

"I just say what I think," said Fuller.

"You think such mean things," said Susanna, bewildered. Her eyes widened. "All through high school, people like you would look at me as if they wished I'd drop dead. They'd never dance with me, they'd never talk to me, they'd never even smile back." She shuddered. "They'd just go slinking around like small-town cops. They'd look at me the way you did—like I'd just done something terrible."

The truth of the indictment made Fuller itch all over. "Probably thinking about something else," he said.

"I don't think so," said Susanna. "You sure weren't. All of a sudden, you started yelling at me in the drugstore, and I'd never even seen you before." She burst into tears. "What is the matter with you?"

Fuller looked down at the floor. "Never had a chance with a girl like you— that's all," he said. "That hurts."

Susanna looked at him wonderingly. "You don't know what a chance is," she said.

"A chance is a late-model convertible, a new suit, and twenty bucks," said Fuller.

Susanna turned her back to him and closed her suitcase. "A chance is a girl," she said. "You smile at her, you be friendly, you be glad she's a girl." She turned and opened her arms again. "I'm a girl. Girls are shaped this way," she said. "If men are nice to me and make me happy, I kiss them sometimes. Is that all right with you?"

"Yes," said Fuller humbly. She had rubbed his nose in the sweet reason that governed the universe. He shrugged. "I better be going. Good-by."

"Wait!" she said. "You can't do that—just walk out, leaving me feeling so wicked." She shook her head. "I don't deserve to feel wicked."

"What can I do?" said Fuller helplessly.

"You can take me for a walk down the main street, as though you were proud of me," said Susanna. "You can welcome me back to the human race." She nodded to herself. "You owe that to me."

Cpl. Norman Fuller, who had come home two nights before from eighteen bleak months in Korea, waited on the porch outside Susanna's nest, with all the village watching.

Susanna had ordered him out while she changed, while she changed for her return to the human race. She had also called the express company and told them to bring her trunk back.

Fuller passed the time by stroking Susanna's cat. "Hello, kitty, kitty, kitty, kitty," he said, over and over again. Saying, "Kitty, kitty, kitty, kitty," numbed him like a merciful drug.

He was saying it when Susanna came out of her nest. He couldn't stop saying it, and she had to take the cat away from him, firmly, before she could get him to look at her, to offer his arm.

"So long, kitty, kitty, kitty, kitty, kitty, kitty," said Fuller.

Susanna was barefoot, and she wore barbaric hoop earrings, and ankle bells. Holding Fuller's arm lightly, she led him down the stairs, and began her stately, undulating, titillating, tinkling walk past the liquor store, the insurance agency, the real-estate office, the diner, the American Legion post, and the church, to the crowded drugstore.

"Now, smile and be nice," said Susanna. "Show you're not ashamed of me."

"Mind if I smoke?" said Fuller.

"That's very considerate of you to ask," said Susanna. "No, I don't mind at all."

By steadying his right hand with his left, Corporal Fuller managed to light a cigar. ❖

Kurt Vonnegut, Jr.

1922–

The popular novelist and lecturer Kurt Vonnegut, Jr., was born in Indianapolis, Indiana. His father, a successful architect, insisted that his son learn "something useful," so when Vonnegut entered Cornell University, he studied biology and chemistry. "I was delighted to catch pneumonia during my third year," Vonnegut said, "and upon recovery, to forget everything I ever knew about chemistry, and go to war." Captured by the Germans during World War II and assigned to a work group in Dresden, Germany, Vonnegut was detained in an underground meat locker during the massive Allied firebombing of that city in 1945. When he and his fellow prisoners emerged, "everything was gone but the cellars where 135,000 Hansels and Gretels had been baked like gingerbread men." Vonnegut's wartime experiences became the basis of his 1969 novel, *Slaughterhouse-Five.*

After the war, Vonnegut studied anthropology at the University of Chicago while working as a police reporter. Later, he worked as a publicist at General Electric, but once he began to sell his short stories, he quit his job and moved to Cape Cod to write full time. During the 1950s, he supported his family by holding various jobs and by writing nonfiction and short stories for magazines. Some of these stories, including "Miss Temptation," are collected in *Welcome to the Monkey House.* Vonnegut has said of the stories: "They are sunny because the magazines . . . wanted them to be that way." His novels, on the other hand, express his natural pessimism. In a darkly humorous style, he protests general human folly and such modern horrors as war, genocide, dehumanization, and environmental destruction.

OTHER WORKS *Player Piano, Cat's Cradle, Breakfast of Champions, Galápagos, Hocus Pocus*

WRITING ABOUT LITERATURE

MAKING A POINT

What point was Corporal Fuller making in the drugstore? What was Jonathan Edwards's message in his sermon? Writers and speakers use several effective techniques to get their ideas across. On the following pages you will

- see how writers create emphasis
- write and present a speech, making your own point
- learn how to interpret and use body language

The Writer's Style: Creating Emphasis Skilled writers often say something several times for emphasis. When repetition of a word or phrase or parallelism of a grammatical structure is used well, the effect can be powerful.

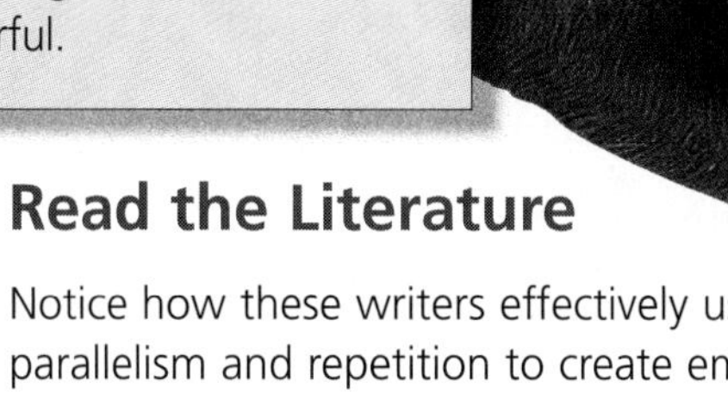

Read the Literature

Notice how these writers effectively use parallelism and repetition to create emphasis.

Literature Models

Emphasis Through Parallelism
What phrases does Fuller repeat? How does this use of parallelism emphasize his anger and frustration?

"You come in here with bells on your ankles, so's I'll have to look at your ankles and your pretty pink feet," said Fuller. "You kiss the cat, so's I'll have to think about how it'd be to be that cat," said Fuller. "You call an old man an angel, so's I'll have to think about what it'd be like to be called an angel by you," said Fuller. "You hide your key in front of everybody, so's I'll have to think about where that key is," said Fuller.

Kurt Vonnegut, Jr., from "Miss Temptation"

Emphasis Through Repetition
How does repeating the word *nothing* build momentum and rhythm? What effect would this have on the listener?

You hang by a slender thread, with the flames of divine wrath flashing about it, and ready every moment to singe it, and burn it asunder; and you have no interest in any Mediator, and nothing to lay hold of to save yourself, nothing to keep off the flames of wrath, nothing of your own, nothing that you ever have done, nothing that you can do, to induce God to spare you one moment. . . .

Jonathan Edwards, from "Sinners in the Hands of an Angry God"

Connect to Politics

People use repetition for emphasis every day. Advertisers use repetition to create name recognition. Politicians use repetition to reinforce the points they are trying to make. Would the speech below be as effective without the repetition and parallelism?

Political Speech

This is not the real spirit of America. I do not believe that it is. This is a time to test the mood and spirit:

To offer in place of doubt—trust.

In place of expediency—right judgment.

In place of ghettos, let us have neighborhoods and communities.

In place of incredibility—integrity.

In place of murmuring, let us have clear speech; let us again hear America singing.

Senator Eugene McCarthy
Speech to Conference of
Concerned Democrats
December 2, 1967

Double Emphasis
How does Eugene McCarthy use both parallelism and repetition to stress replacing the bad with good?

Try Your Hand: Creating Emphasis

1. **Write Without Emphasis** Try rewriting one of the excerpts on these pages to eliminate all repetition. Which version do you like better? Which is more effective? Why?
2. **Customize a Speech** Using the basic format of the excerpt from Senator McCarthy's speech, rewrite the excerpt, changing the words to reflect a different topic or cause.
3. **Compose a Commercial** With a partner, write a radio commercial for a real or imaginary product. Use repetition to help people remember the product.

SkillBuilder

Using Parallelism

Parallelism, or parallel structure, is one of the most powerful ways to create emphasis. In parallelism, ideas are linked together by repeating similar grammatical structures. Notice how Vonnegut uses parallelism in "Miss Temptation."

The screech had been made by the stool of Cpl. Norman Fuller, who had come home the night before from eighteen bleak months in Korea. They had been eighteen months without war—but eighteen months without cheer, all the same.

The parallel structure *eighteen months without* plus a noun appears twice in the second sentence. The secret to effective parallelism is to keep the order of sentence elements the same each time.

APPLYING WHAT YOU'VE LEARNED
Copy the following sentences onto a sheet of paper. Revise the sentences so that the structures are parallel. In the first exercise, combine the two sentences.

1. Each day Susanna would appear on the porch and kiss the cat. She would lock the door and then hide the key.
2. Susanna was barefoot, and she wore barbaric earrings and ankle bells.

WRITING ABOUT LITERATURE

Creative Response

Almost everyone has to speak in front of a group at some time. Ministers, politicians, salespeople, and teachers all give speeches. This activity will help you understand and appreciate some of the great speakers in American history.

GUIDED ASSIGNMENT

Write a Speech Unit Two is full of moving speeches. Now it's your turn to write and give a speech. It might be Jonathan Edwards's "next" sermon, Sarah Good's appeal to the judge, or Patrick Henry's next speech. If these ideas don't appeal to you, then choose any topic you like.

1 Prewrite and Explore

All of the speakers in Unit Two are passionate about their topics. For your speech, explore a topic that you feel strongly about, either from the reading or an idea of your own. What can you picture yourself giving a speech about? Politics? Sports? Music?

EXAMINING SPEAKERS AND TOPICS

For a speech based on a selection, ask yourself:

- Which speaker was I most moved by?
- Which speakers have an easy style to imitate?

For a speech on your own topic, ask yourself:

- What's really been on my mind lately?
- What point would I like to make if I had people in front of me?

DECIDING ON A PURPOSE

Decide what your topic will be. Use a chart to gather your thoughts and ideas. For a speech based on a selection:

- Examine the content and style of the original speech. Jot down ideas and words that your speaker seems to use frequently.
- Begin listing points your speaker might make.

For a speech on your own topic:

- Start listing all the key points you'd like to cover.
- If you need information, research the topic.

Student's Prewriting Notes

2 Prepare a Written Draft

Effective speakers use repetition when they outline and draft.

- *They tell their audience what they're going to say*—opening with a clear, strong, attention-getting statement.
- *They say it*—making their points logically, with supporting data and details.
- *They tell their audience what they just said*—restating their position and calling the audience to action.

Follow the three steps above as you draft your speech. This student decided to write a speech as an apology from Fuller.

Student's Draft

My speech is about Susanna. I've been wrong about her—dead wrong. She doesn't live in a harem. She doesn't sleep in a billowy bed. She's a normal person, just like you and me.

There's got to be a better way to start this speech!

I've lived in this town all my life. We think we know everyone here. But do we? I'm not sure I even know myself. And we sure don't take the time to get to know the strangers in this town.

Would Fuller really have said this?

3 Try It Aloud

Consider the sound of your speech. Read your draft aloud. Are your sentences too long? Will listeners have trouble following the ideas? When you feel your speech is in good shape, invite a few students to critique it. Be open to their suggestions.

PEER RESPONSE

- Where can I add repetition to make my point?
- Was the speech ever hard to follow? When? What section?

SkillBuilder

SPEAKING & LISTENING

Giving a Speech

Giving a speech is different from writing a paper. Your audience can't go back and replay your speech. So what you say has to be clear and understandable the first time. Here are a few secrets to making a speech effective.

- Grab your audience's attention with a question, a story, a joke, or an amazing fact.
- Speak in short sentences; use simpler words.
- Use a conversational tone; use the word *you* to involve your audience.
- Use the imperative mood (*rise* up, *ask* not) to call your audience to action.
- Create emphasis with repetition, hand gestures, and exclamations.

Notice how Patrick Henry uses many of these techniques, such as getting the audience's attention with a series of questions.

Gentlemen may cry, "Peace! peace!"—but there is no peace. The war is actually begun! The next gale that sweeps from the north will bring to our ears the clash of resounding arms! Our brethren are already in the field! Why stand we here idle? What is it that gentlemen wish? What would they have?

APPLYING WHAT YOU'VE LEARNED
Try using the techniques described above as you draft your speech.

4 Revise and Prepare

Have you tried speaking from note cards that outline just the key points of your speech? Many speakers feel that using note cards helps them to make more eye contact with the audience and to sound natural. You could also try tape-recording your speech and playing it back. Where can you make changes to make your speech more interesting? Practice your speech until you feel comfortable.

Student's Final Draft

A Public Apology to Susanna

It's neighborly to smile at people when you pass by. It's neighborly to help them out when they're in trouble. It's neighborly to judge people for what they are, not what they wear. Even though Susanna has only been in town for three months, she has been a good neighbor. I've lived in this town my whole life, and I haven't been too neighborly to anyone lately—especially Susanna.

How does repetition help this speaker make a point and provide an effective introduction?

Student's Speech Notes

✓ It's neighborly to
smile at people
help them out
judge what they are—not what they wear
✓ Susanna
lived here 3 months
good neighbor
✓ Me
whole life
I'm not!

If you were giving this speech, which words on the note card would you underline for emphasis?

When would you use hand gestures?

Standards for Evaluation
An effective speech • has an introduction that states what will be said • supports all opinions with sufficient data and details • is organized in a logical way • uses emphasis effectively • ends with a strong conclusion and a summary

Grammar in Context

Subordinate Clauses Not all parts of a sentence are created equal! Both subordinate and independent clauses contain a subject and a verb, but subordinate clauses do not express a complete thought. Subordinate clauses are therefore less important. Use them to change the emphasis in a sentence.

> I'd like to formally apologize to this woman. Susanna ^who^ is a truly good person, ~~She's~~ ^is^ not a temptress. She didn't deserve to be humiliated in public. ^When^ Susanna walked into the drugstore, She didn't come to tease. She came to buy a newspaper!

Notice how some words become less important when they are part of a subordinate clause. Also see how the independent clause increases in importance. For more information about clauses, see page 1232 of the Grammar Handbook.

Try Your Hand: Using Subordinate Clauses

On a separate sheet of paper, combine the sentences in two different ways. First turn one of the sentences into a subordinate clause. Then turn it around and make the other sentence the subordinate clause. Notice how the emphasis changes.

1. Susanna walks with bells on her ankles. She makes her living as an actress.
2. Bearse Hinkley is a pharmacist. He is one of Susanna's biggest fans.
3. Norman Fuller just got out of the army. He hates all beautiful women.

SkillBuilder

GRAMMAR FROM WRITING

Avoiding Sentence Fragments

Many incomplete sentences are subordinate clauses—they do not express a complete thought. Other incomplete sentences are missing a subject or verb.

People don't always speak in complete sentences. Notice how Jonathan Edwards uses sentence fragments for effect.

How awful is it to be left behind at such a day! To see so many others feasting, while you are pining and perishing! To see so many rejoicing and singing for joy of heart, while you have cause to mourn for sorrow of heart, and howl for vexation of spirit!

APPLYING WHAT YOU'VE LEARNED

On a separate sheet of paper, turn the sentence fragments below into complete sentences—unless you feel a fragment is being used for effect.

O sinner! Consider the fearful danger you are in. It is a great furnace of wrath. A wide and bottomless pit. Full of the fire of wrath.

GRAMMAR HANDBOOK

For more information on sentence fragments, see page 1200 of the Grammar Handbook.

Body Language

In many cases, how you say something is just as important as what you say. Your body language—facial expressions, hand gestures, posture—all deliver a message. Effective public speakers use both verbal and physical language.

View Look at this photo. What is Malcolm X doing? What expression is on his face? What hand gesture is he using? How is he holding his body?

Interpret What does Malcolm X's body language tell you? What is happening at this point in the speech? How do you imagine his voice sounds? Stern? Encouraging?

Discuss Compare your interpretations. Did anyone interpret this speaker's gestures differently? Can body language mean different things to different people? If you were giving a speech and using this hand gesture and facial expression, what might you be saying? Now look at the SkillBuilder on the next page for more tips on interpreting body language.

SkillBuilder

CRITICAL THINKING

Interpreting Body Language

Effective speakers are masters not only at using body language but at reading it. An audience uses body language too. Someone with crossed arms may be indicating resistance to your ideas. Someone who's fidgeting is saying your speech is too long. Someone who doodles is probably bored.

If you watch for signals like these, you can tailor your speech to your audience. For example, if people don't seem receptive to your ideas, address their objections. If several people are fidgeting, cut your speech short or be more energetic. Use your body language and theirs to strengthen your speech.

APPLYING WHAT YOU'VE LEARNED

Try one or both of the following in a small group.

1. Try out hand gestures that you might use to convey the following messages:

- We must . . .
- First of all, . . .
- Eliminate all . . .

2. Watch a video of a speech with the volume turned all the way down. Focusing on the speaker's body language, try to guess when the speaker is making an important point, listing key steps, or calling the audience to action.

PART 2 INTRODUCTION

The Right to Be Free

Writers in the Time of Revolution

"No taxation without representation!" "Give me liberty, or give me death!" "We hold these truths to be self-evident. . . ." "We the people . . ." Many famous phrases have come from the rhetoric of the American Revolution, along with many of our favorite national anecdotes—the Boston Tea Party, "the shot heard round the world," and George Washington at Valley Forge. Behind the rhetoric and the mythologizing of the Revolution, however, lie major philosophical ideas that not only transformed 13 British colonies into a nation but laid the groundwork for democratic institutions throughout the world.

On the surface, the conflict between England and her American colonies was about money—specifically, what the colonists considered unlawful taxation. On a deeper level, what gave the rebellious colonists the mental preparedness and moral strength needed for such a dangerous undertaking as revolution came essentially from two sources: the writings of English philosopher John Locke and the Bible.

Central to John Locke's theory was the notion of "natural rights." In addition to life and liberty, the right to own property was considered a natural right. If any government abridged that right to property—by levying taxes without the consent of the property owners, for example—then the people could organize a new government.

You can see the spirit of Locke reflected in Jefferson's eloquent opening to the Declaration of Independence. Locke's ideas of property rights were echoed in the wording of the U.S. Constitution. The Revolutionary writers in this part of Unit Two—particularly Patrick Henry, Phillis Wheatley, Abigail Adams, and Michel-Guillaume Jean de Crèvecoeur—all appealed to natural rights in their arguments for freedom.

The American Revolution was not solely the enterprise of learned

Statue of John Locke in the classical style

Portrait of Thomas Jefferson

Silhouette of Abigail Adams

men and women of the day, however. Ordinary people were caught up in the struggle and used the Bible to help them make hard decisions about their country and their lives.

From the time of the early Pilgrims, successive generations of Protestant ministers had proclaimed from their pulpits that no man need obey a government that violated the will of God as defined in the Bible. During the Revolution, many preachers recounted Bible stories of unjust rulers who burdened the people with high taxes and unjust laws. While much of the political writing during this time contained lofty philosophical ideas, it also vibrated with the fiery passion of a Puritan minister. In Patrick Henry's famous "Give me liberty, or give me death" speech, you'll hear more references to God and the Bible than to Locke's ideas of natural rights.

The philosophical and religious ideas that spurred the American Revolution also raised other important issues—the most important being slavery. The philosophy of democracy is as much an attack on the institution of slavery as it is on political tyranny. However, the entire plantation economy of the South was dependent on slaves, who were considered the property of plantation owners. As powerful Southern landowners exerted their influence in the new government, reform that might have prohibited slavery was halted.

Another issue for the Founding Fathers was what to do about Native Americans. In the early years of the nation, the policy of the U.S. government was to assimilate Native Americans

We the People of the United Sta
insure domestic Tranquility, provide for the common defence, promote the gen
and our Posterity, do ordain and establish this Constitution for the United Sta
Article. I.
Section. 1. All legislative Powers herein granted shall be vested in a Congr
of Representatives.
Section. 2. The House of Representatives shall be composed of Members cho
in each State shall have the Qualifications requisite for Electors of the most numerous Br
No Person shall be a Representative who shall not have attained to the A
and who shall not, when elected, be an Inhabitant of that State in which he shall be c
Representatives and direct Taxes shall be apportioned among the several Sta

Voices from the TIMES

We hold these truths to be self-evident:— That all men are created equal; that they are endowed by their Creator with certain unalienable rights; that among these are life, liberty, and the pursuit of happiness.

Thomas Jefferson
from the Declaration of Independence

These are the times that try men's souls. The summer soldier and the sunshine patriot will in this crisis, shrink from the service of his country; but he that stands it Now, deserves the love and thanks of man and woman.

Thomas Paine
from Common Sense

Yankee doodle went to town,
A-riding on a pony,
Stuck a feather in his cap
And called it Macaroni.
Yankee Doodle, keep it up,
Yankee Doodle Dandy,
Mind the music and the step
And with the girls be handy.

Anonymous patriotic song

Voices *from the* Times

The United States of America have exhibited, perhaps, the first example of governments erected on the simple principles of nature; and if men are now sufficiently enlightened to disabuse themselves of artifice, imposture, hypocrisy, and superstition, they will consider this event as an era in their history.

John Adams
***from* Defense of the Constitutions of the United States**

When Israel was in Egypt's land,
Let my people go;
Oppressed so hard they could
not stand,
Let my people go.

CHORUS

Go down, Moses, way down
in Egypt's land;
Tell old Pharaoh, to let my people go.

Anonymous Negro spiritual

Benjamin Franklin created this woodcut in 1754 to warn the colonies to unite in their common defense.

into Anglo culture. To this end, government officials worked with existing missions set up by the principal churches of the time to teach Native Americans Christian theology, reading, and writing as well as to train them in agriculture.

Although some Native Americans resisted such efforts—most notably Seneca chief Red Jacket—the U.S. policy worked for a while. However in 1830, U.S. policy toward Native Americans changed. The Indian Removal Act authorized the relocation of tribes from the Southeastern states to land west of the Mississippi River, in order to free up the well-cultivated Indian farmland for white settlers.

Continuity & Change: Demands for Equal Rights

Even though the ideals of equality and natural rights promised by the American Revolution did not fully materialize after the war, the noble words had been written—and they remained to haunt the country. The conflicts also remained for subsequent generations of Americans to resolve—first during the Civil War and later in the civil rights movement of the 20th century. When you read the words of Martin Luther King, Jr., and Malcolm X as they contemplate the meaning of equal rights in their own time, you'll be able to recognize the American tradition of political thought that dates back to the beginnings of our country.

Rodolfo Gonzales in the excerpt from *I Am Joaquín* speaks as eloquently for his people—Chicanos—as Patrick Henry did for his. In the last selection of the unit, Diane Mei Lin Mark argues for the right to define herself as an individual—a right that, centuries before, Crèvecoeur felt every American was entitled to.

LASERLINKS
• *HISTORICAL LITERARY CONNECTION*

PART 2

The Right to Be Free

Writers in the Time of Revolution

Continuity & Change: Demands for Equal Rights

PREVIEWING

NONFICTION

Speech in the Virginia Convention

Patrick Henry

PERSONAL CONNECTION

Think about what patriotism means to you. Then list at least three reasons a patriot might give for fighting in a war. Circle the reason that seems most compelling to you. With a small group of classmates, discuss the reasons that you listed and circled.

HISTORICAL CONNECTION

Until the mid-1700s, American colonists largely had been content to be under British rule. However, tension grew between Great Britain and her American colonies after the end of the French and Indian War in 1763. Although Britain had defeated the French and their Indian allies, thousands of British troops remained quartered in the colonies, which caused resentment among the colonists. Their resentment increased and angry protests ensued when, beginning in 1764, the British Parliament passed a series of harsh laws and taxes.

To discuss the growing crisis, the First Continental Congress, composed of delegates from all 13 colonies except Georgia, met in Philadelphia in 1774. The delegates held out hope that they could restore the colonies' relationship with Great Britain, and they sent formal petitions to King George III and the British people, asking for their rights as British subjects. Six months after this meeting, in March 1775, the Second Virginia Provincial Convention was called to vote on whether Virginia should take up arms to defend against a feared British attack. Patrick Henry, the most famous orator of the American Revolution, delivered a fiery speech to convince delegates of the need for armed resistance. Less than a month after this speech, Massachusetts volunteers fought British troops in the battles at Lexington and Concord. About 15 months after the speech, the Second Continental Congress adopted the Declaration of Independence.

READING CONNECTION

Recognizing Rhetorical Questions A rhetorical question is a question to which no answer is expected because the answer is obvious. Rhetorical questions are often used in persuasive writing to emphasize a point or create an emotional effect. For example, Patrick Henry asks this rhetorical question in his speech: "Is life so dear, or peace so sweet, as to be purchased at the price of chains and slavery?" The obvious answer is no, and the effect of the question is to make listeners feel they should be more brave. As you read Henry's famous speech, look for other rhetorical questions he used to stir the patriotic feelings of the convention delegates.

IN CONGRESS, JULY 4, 1776.

The unanimous Declaration of the thirteen united States of Americ

LASERLINKS
• HISTORICAL CONNECTION

SPEECH *in the* VIRGINIA CONVENTION

PATRICK HENRY

March 23, 1775

Mr. President: No man thinks more highly than I do of the patriotism, as well as abilities, of the very worthy gentlemen who have just addressed the House. But different men often see the same subject in different lights; and, therefore, I hope that it will not be thought disrespectful to those gentlemen, if, entertaining as I do opinions of a character very opposite to theirs, I shall speak forth my sentiments freely and without reserve. This is no time for ceremony. The question before the House is one of awful moment to this country. For my own part I consider it as nothing less than a question of freedom or slavery; and in proportion to the magnitude of the subject ought to be the freedom of the debate. It is only in this way that we can hope to arrive at truth, and fulfill the great responsibility which we hold to God and our country. Should I keep back my opinions at such a time, through fear of giving offense, I should consider myself as guilty of treason towards my country, and of an act of disloyalty towards the majesty of heaven, which I revere above all earthly kings.

Mr. President, it is natural to man to indulge in the illusions of hope. We are apt to shut our eyes against a painful truth, and listen to the song of that siren, till she transforms us into beasts. Is this the part of wise men, engaged in a great and arduous struggle for liberty? Are we disposed to be of the number of those who,

GUIDE FOR READING

1 Mr. President: the president of the Virginia Convention, Peyton Randolph.

5 entertaining: holding in mind.

1–7 Henry states his respect for the previous speakers, a technique called "concession to the opposition." What effect might this have on the audience?

8 The question before the House: Henry proposed resolutions to prepare the Virginia colony for war and gave this speech to support those resolutions.

20 song . . . beasts: an allusion to Homer's *Odyssey.* The sirens' seductive song lured sailors to their deaths. The goddess Circe lured men to her island and then magically transformed them into pigs. Henry compares "the illusions of hope" to these dangerous mythical creatures.

having eyes, see not, and having ears, hear not, the things which so nearly concern their temporal salvation? For my part, whatever anguish of spirit it may cost, I am willing to know the whole truth—to know the worst and to provide for it.

I have but one lamp by which my feet are guided; and that is the lamp of experience. I know of no way of judging of the future but by the past. And judging by the past, I wish to know what there has been in the conduct of the British ministry for the last ten years, to justify those hopes with which gentlemen have been pleased to solace themselves and the House? Is it that insidious smile with which our petition has been lately received? Trust it not, sir; it will prove a snare to your feet. Suffer not yourselves to be betrayed with a kiss.

Ask yourselves how this gracious reception of our petition comports with these warlike preparations which cover our waters and darken our land. Are fleets and armies necessary to a work of love and reconciliation? Have we shown ourselves so unwilling to be reconciled that force must be called in to win back our love? Let us not deceive ourselves, sir. These are the implements of war and subjugation—the last arguments to which kings resort. I ask gentlemen, sir, what means this martial array, if its purpose be not to force us to submission? Can gentlemen assign any other possible motives for it? Has Great Britain any enemy, in this quarter of the world, to call for all this accumulation of navies and armies? No, sir, she has none. They are meant for us; they can be meant for no other. They are sent over to bind and rivet upon us those chains which the British ministry have been so long forging.

And what have we to oppose to them? Shall we try argument? Sir, we have been trying that for the last ten years. Have we anything new to offer on the subject? Nothing. We have held the subject up in every light of which it is capable; but it has been all in vain. Shall we resort to entreaty and humble supplication? What terms shall we find which have not been already exhausted? Let us not, I beseech you, sir, deceive ourselves longer.

Sir, we have done everything that could be done to avert the storm which is now coming on. We have petitioned; we have remonstrated; we have supplicated; we have prostrated ourselves before the throne, and have implored its interposition to arrest the tyrannical hands of the ministry and Parliament. Our petitions have been slighted; our remonstrances have produced additional violence and insult; our supplications have been disregarded; and we have been spurned, with contempt, from the foot of the throne.

23 having eyes . . . hear not: an allusion to Ezekiel 12:2.

24 temporal: worldly.

32 solace (sŏl'ĭs): comfort.

34 snare: trap.

35 betrayed with a kiss: a biblical allusion to the Apostle Judas, who betrayed Jesus. When soldiers came to arrest Jesus, Judas identified him by kissing him.

38–49 What does Henry say is the reason for the British military buildup in America?

50–55 Notice how Henry uses rhetorical questions to anticipate the arguments of his opponents. How effective is this technique?

54 entreaty (ĕn-trē'tē): earnest request; plea; **supplication** (sŭp'lĭ-kā'shən): the act of asking for something humbly or earnestly.

59 remonstrated (rĭ-mŏn'strā-tĭd): objected.

60 interposition: intervention.

WORDS TO KNOW

insidious (ĭn-sĭd'ē-əs) *adj.* treacherous
subjugation (sŭb'jə-gā'shən) *n.* control by conquering
martial (mär'shəl) *adj.* warlike
tyrannical (tĭ-răn'ĭ-kəl) *adj.* harsh; oppressive
spurn (spûrn) *v.* to reject scornfully

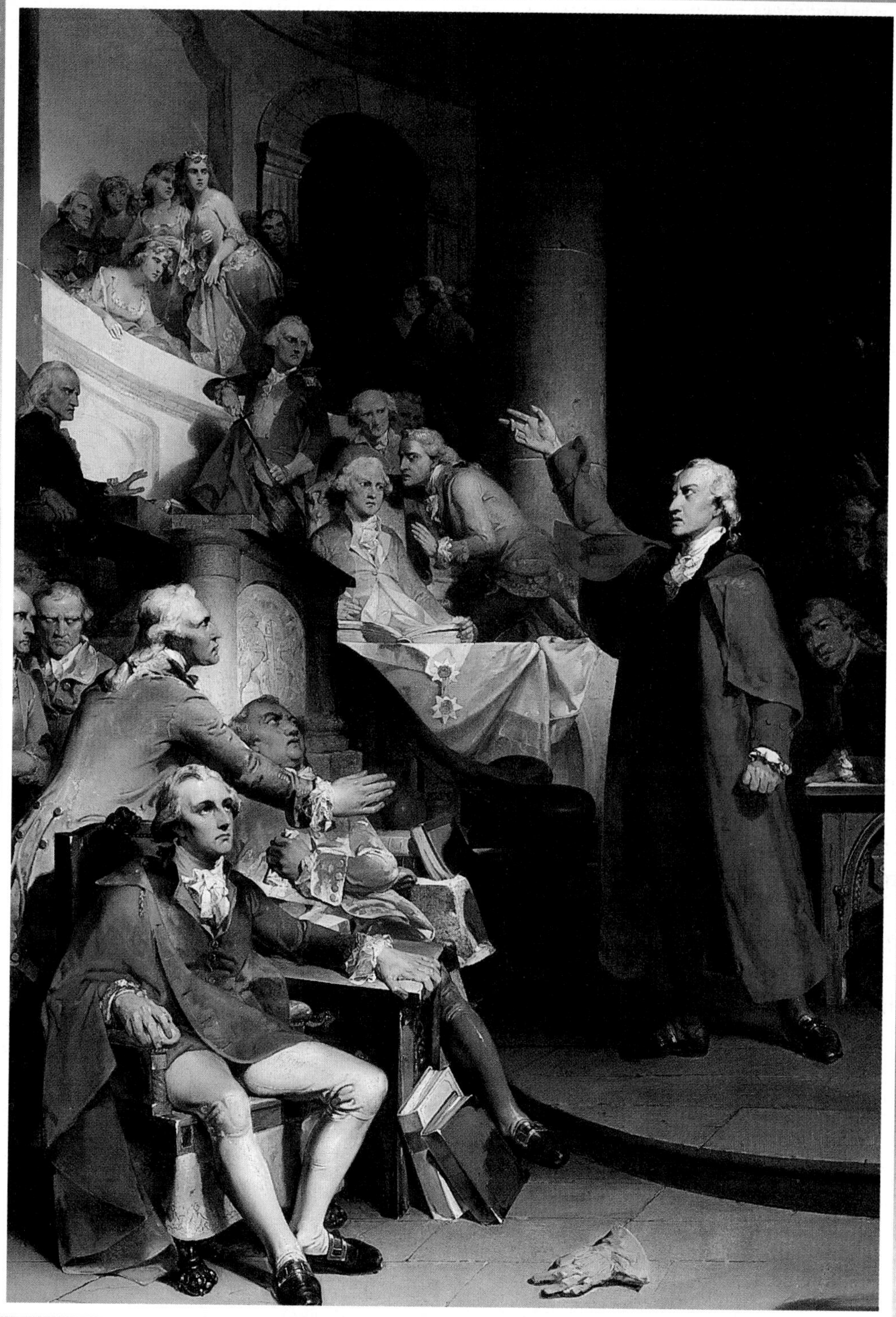

Patrick Henry Before the Virginia House of Burgesses (1851), Peter F. Rothermel. Red Hill, The Patrick Henry National Memorial, Brookneal, Virginia.

In vain, after these things, may we indulge the fond hope of peace and reconciliation. There is no longer any room for hope.

If we wish to be free—if we mean to preserve inviolate those inestimable privileges for which we have been so long contending—if we mean not basely to abandon the noble struggle in which we have been so long engaged, and which we have pledged ourselves never to abandon until the glorious object of our contest shall be obtained, we must fight! I repeat it, sir, we must fight! An appeal to arms and to the God of Hosts is all that is left us!

67 inviolate (ĭn-vī′ə-lĭt): not violated; intact.

68 inestimable (ĭn-ĕs′tə-mə-bəl): extremely valuable.

69 basely (bās′lē): dishonorably.

72–73 Henry has reached the main point of his speech. What is Henry trying to convince his listeners to do?

They tell us, sir, that we are weak—unable to cope with so formidable an adversary. But when shall we be stronger? Will it be the next week, or the next year? Will it be when we are totally disarmed, and when a British guard shall be stationed in every house? Shall we gather strength by irresolution and inaction? Shall we acquire the means of effectual resistance, by lying supinely on our backs, and hugging the delusive phantom of hope, until our enemies shall have bound us hand and foot?

74–94 In these two paragraphs, what reasons does Henry give for taking military action now?

Sir, we are not weak, if we make a proper use of those means which the God of nature hath placed in our power. Three millions of people, armed in the holy cause of liberty, and in such a country as that which we possess, are invincible by any force which our enemy can send against us. Besides, sir, we shall not fight our battles alone. There is a just God who presides over the destinies of nations, and who will raise up friends to fight our battles for us. The battle, sir, is not to the strong alone; it is to the vigilant, the active, the brave. Besides, sir, we have no election. If we were base enough to desire it, it is now too late to retire from the contest. There is no retreat but in submission and slavery! Our chains are forged! Their clanking may be heard on the plains of Boston! The war is inevitable—and let it come! I repeat it, sir, let it come!

89 battle . . . strong alone: an allusion to Ecclesiastes 9:11— "the race is not to the swift, nor the battle to the strong."

90 election: choice.

It is in vain, sir, to extenuate the matter. Gentlemen may cry, "Peace! peace!"—but there is no peace. The war is actually begun! The next gale that sweeps from the north will bring to our ears the clash of resounding arms! Our brethren are already in the field! Why stand we here idle? What is it that gentlemen wish? What would they have? Is life so dear, or peace so sweet, as to be purchased at the price of chains and slavery? Forbid it, Almighty God! I know not what course others may take; but as for me, give me liberty, or give me death! ❖

95 extenuate (ĭk-stĕn′yo͞o-āt′): to lessen the seriousness of, especially by providing partial excuses.

97 the next gale . . . north: Some colonists in Massachusetts had already shown open resistance to the British and were on the brink of war.

102–103 What emotions does Henry appeal to with the last lines of his speech?

WORDS TO KNOW

formidable (fôr′mĭ-də-bəl) *adj.* difficult to defeat
adversary (ăd′vər-sĕr′ē) *n.* an opponent
irresolution (ĭ-rĕz′ə-lo͞o′shən) *n.* uncertainty; indecision
invincible (ĭn-vĭn′sə-bəl) *adj.* unbeatable
vigilant (vĭj′ə-lənt) *adj.* alert; watchful

The Boston Tea Party

Dave Barry

One afternoon some freedom-loving colonists known as the Boston Patriots were sitting around their locker room, trying to think up ways to throw off the yoke of colonial oppression. Suddenly one of them, Bob, had an idea:

"Hey!" he said. "Let's dress up like the locals and throw tea into the harbor!"

Instantly the other Patriots were galvanized. "What was that?" they shouted.

"A galvanic reaction," responded Bob. "Named for the Italian physiologist Luigi Galvani (1737–1798), who conducted experiments wherein he sent electrical currents through the legs of frogs."

But the Boston Patriots were not the only people engaging in inhumane scientific research during the colonial era. Another person doing this was Benjamin Franklin, who, in a famous experiment, sought to prove his theory that if you flew a kite in a rainstorm, a huge chunk of electricity would come shooting down the string and damage your brain. Sure enough, he was right, and he spent the rest of his days making bizarre, useless, and unintelligible statements such as: "A penny saved is a penny earned." Eventually he became so dodderingly pathetic that he had to be placed in charge of the U.S. Postal Service. Also around this time women and minority groups were accomplishing a great many achievements.

But getting back to the Boston Patriots: Later that night, they boldly carried out Bob's bold plan of dressing up as Native Americans and throwing tea into the harbor, but for some reason this did not result in Independence. "Maybe we should also toss in some lemon," somebody suggested. And so they did this, and then they tried some Sweet 'n Low; still no sign of Independence. Also the harbor was starting to look like a toxic-waste dump, which did not go unnoticed by early ancestors of future president George Herbert Walker Piedmont Harrington Armoire Vestibule Bush.

This angered the king, so he ordered Parliament to pass the Stamp Act, under which every time the colonists made a purchase, the cashier would give them some stamps, and they had to paste these into books, which was even more boring than churning butter. When the colonists had acquired a certain number of stamps, they were required to go down to the Royal Stamp Redemption Center and exchange them for cheap cookware (£ 4.5 million) or tacky folding card tables (£ 3 billion). As you can imagine, this was less than popular with the colonists, whose anger was eloquently expressed by Tom Paine in his fiery pamphlet *Common Sense,* which, in its most famous passage, states: "How many fondue sets does any one colonial family *need?*"

This further enraged the king, who, as you have probably gathered by now, had the political savvy of a croissant. He ordered Parliament to pass the Irritation Acts, whose entire purpose was to make life in the colonies even *more* miserable. These included:

1. *The Sneeze Shield Act,* requiring that all colonial salad bars had to have shields suspended over them—allegedly for "sanitary" purposes, but actually intended to make it difficult for short colonists to reach the chickpeas.
2. *The Pill Blockade Act,* requiring that colonial aspirin bottles had to come with wads of cotton stuffed in the top, making the aspirin virtually inaccessible, especially to colonists with hangovers.
3. *The Eternal Container Act,* requiring that colonists who purchased appliances had to save the original packing cartons forever and ever, passing them down through the generations, or else they would void their warranties.

All of these factors caused the tension in the colonies to mount with each passing day, as can be seen from the following chart:

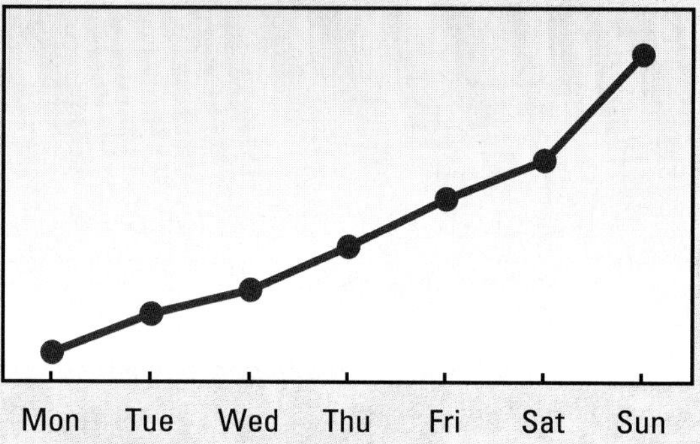

It was amid this climate of rising tension and anger, with a 50 percent chance of lingering afternoon and evening violence, that the First Continental Congress was held. It met in Philadelphia, and its members, realizing that the actions they took in this hour of crisis could very well determine the fate of the New World, voted, after many hours of angry debate, to give themselves a pay raise. There was no turning back now. Clearly, the stage had been set for the Discussion Questions.

Discussion Questions

1. Do you think Unitas should have started for the Colts?
2. What the hell *are* chickpeas, anyway?

RESPONDING OPTIONS

FROM PERSONAL RESPONSE *TO* CRITICAL ANALYSIS

REFLECT 1. After hearing Henry's speech, would you have voted to prepare for war? In your notebook, tell why or why not.

RETHINK 2. In your view, what is the most convincing point Henry makes in his argument?

Consider
- all the main points he makes in the speech
- whether his reason for wanting to fight is the one you circled in the Personal Connection activity as the most compelling reason a patriot might go to war

3. Choose a passage of the speech that you find especially persuasive. Analyze what Henry does to make this passage so persuasive.

Consider
- the effect of rhetorical questions
- the use of loaded language and emotional appeals
- the development of rational arguments
- answers offered to opposing arguments
- other techniques that make his words convincing

4. Think about Henry's famous statement "Give me liberty, or give me death!" Do you agree that liberty is more important than life itself? Explain your answer.

RELATE 5. The Insight selection, "The Boston Tea Party," pokes fun at American patriots and the times in which Patrick Henry delivered his speech. Do you think Dave Barry's spoof of colonial history is funny? Why or why not?

6. Patrick Henry argued that the actions of King George III and the British Parliament posed major threats to the liberty of the American colonists. In your opinion, what threatens liberty today?

ANOTHER PATHWAY

Respond as one of these people might to specific points in Henry's speech: (1) an American-born colonist whose grandparents were British; (2) a Loyalist, or an American colonist who sides with the British; (3) an African enslaved in the Virginia colony; or (4) a Native American.

QUICKWRITES

1. Write the first paragraphs of a **newspaper report** that might have been published in the colonial *Virginia Gazette.* Describe Henry's speech and its probable effect on his audience.
2. Draft a **rebuttal** opposing Henry's point of view. Offer a counter-argument in favor of peaceful compromise with the British.
3. Parody is writing that imitates either the style or the subject matter of a literary work for comic effect. In "The Boston Tea Party," for example, Dave Barry parodies serious historical accounts of the Revolutionary era by adding nonsensical elements from modern times. Write your own **parody** of Patrick Henry's speech.

PORTFOLIO *Save your writing. You may want to use it later as a spring-board to a piece for your portfolio.*

LITERARY CONCEPTS

An **allusion** is an indirect reference to a person, place, event, or literary work with which the author believes the reader will be familiar. Allusions provide the reader or listener with a deeper understanding of the author's main ideas. For example, Patrick Henry warns colonists not to be "betrayed with a kiss." This biblical allusion refers to the Apostle Judas, who betrayed Jesus by kissing him. Henry used this brief, powerful allusion to suggest that there might be something sinister behind Great Britain's friendly gestures. Find other allusions in the speech, and explain how the implied comparisons in them help strengthen Henry's argument.

CONCEPT REVIEW: Repetition Reread the paragraph that begins "Sir, we have done everything . . ." (pages 208–209). What words, phrases, and sentence patterns are repeated in this paragraph? What effect does this repetition have?

ALTERNATIVE ACTIVITIES

1. Plan a **political advertisement** for television that promotes one or more ideas from Henry's speech. Select fitting visual images, music, or slogans to use in the ad. Then share your TV spot with classmates.
2. Which images in Henry's speech do you think are the most powerful? Create a **poster** that conveys Henry's message, using illustrations and quotations that best capture the spirit of his speech. Use a computer to experiment with different type fonts and type sizes for your poster.
3. Prepare and give a **dramatic reading** of Henry's speech, using gestures and tone of voice to make the speech effective.

CRITIC'S CORNER

It has been said that history is written by the winners. Patrick Henry is regarded as a patriot today, but if the British had won the Revolutionary War, how would he be described? Write a brief sketch of him as it might appear in a current British history textbook.

LITERARY LINKS

Cooperative Learning Both Patrick Henry's speech and Jonathan Edwards's sermon (pages 161–164) are examples of effective persuasive writing. In a small group, create a chart to compare these selections, using the following categories: Speaker's Purpose, Audience, Occasion, Appeals to Emotion, Appeals to Reason, Allusions, and Rhetorical Questions. What ideas do you see that you can apply to your own persuasive writing?

ART CONNECTION

Patrick Henry earned fame as an orator long before he made the speech reprinted here. In the painting on page 209, Peter F. Rothermel portrays Henry giving a speech in Virginia's House of Burgesses, which was Virginia's colonial legislature before the Revolution. Look for techniques that make this scene dramatic. Which figure do you think is Henry? What features of the painting focus attention on him? Describe the reactions he seems to be getting from his listeners.

Detail of *Patrick Henry Before the Virginia House of Burgesses (1851)*, Peter F. Rothermel. Red Hill, The Patrick Henry National Memorial, Brookneal, Virginia.

ACROSS THE CURRICULUM

History What events led up to the conflict between Great Britain and the American colonists? What events happened after Patrick Henry called for war on March 23, 1775? Use an encyclopedia or an American history textbook to find out about important events that occurred before and after Henry gave his speech. Then make a time line of these events to share with the class.

Government Name groups of people who have recently fought or are now fighting for independence from another nation. What arguments have they used to support their cause? What do they stand to lose or gain?

WORDS TO KNOW

EXERCISE A On your paper, copy the chart below. Then review the Words to Know at the bottom of the selection pages. Which vocabulary words best fit the American colonists' view of the British? Write these words in the first column of the chart. Which words best fit the colonists' view of themselves? Write them in the second column. Be ready to explain your choices in class.

British	Colonists

EXERCISE B Draft a brief reply to Patrick Henry from a member of the British Parliament, using as many of the Words to Know as you can.

PATRICK HENRY

1736–1799

American patriot Patrick Henry was a self-taught lawyer whose gift of oration helped spark the American Revolution. In acknowledging Henry's gift, fellow Virginian Thomas Jefferson said: "Call it oratory or what you will, but I never heard anything like it. He had more command over the passions than any man I ever knew." An eloquent defender of colonial rights, Henry spent more than 30 years in public life and took part in the creation of a new nation.

In 1765, at the age of 28, Henry joined the House of Burgesses, the lower house of Virginia's colonial legislature. Just nine days after becoming a burgess, Henry introduced the Stamp Act Resolves. He opposed the Stamp Act, which required colonists to buy stamps to put on taxable paper items, on the grounds that only the colonial legislature—not the British Parliament—had the right to tax colonists. Virginia became the first colony to officially protest the Stamp Act.

Ten years later, Henry again proposed resolutions that led toward American independence. At the Second Virginia Provincial Convention, he gave the impassioned speech you have just read. His resolutions to prepare for war passed by five votes, and he was named chairman of a committee to implement the plan to arm Virginia. In 1776, while the American Revolution raged, Henry helped draw up Virginia's first state constitution and was elected Virginia's first governor.

After the Revolution had ended and the U.S. Constitution had been ratified, Henry resumed his law practice. Then, in 1794, he retired to his Virginia estate, Red Hill. Although he was offered a U.S. Senate seat, posts as minister to Spain and to France, and the positions of Secretary of State and Chief Justice, he did not return to politics until George Washington urged him to run for representative in the Virginia state legislature in 1799. Henry won the election, but he died before taking office.

LASERLINKS
• *ART GALLERY*

PREVIEWING

NONFICTION

Letter to the Rev. Samson Occom

Phillis Wheatley

Letter to John Adams

Abigail Adams

PERSONAL CONNECTION

What ideas and phrases come to mind when you think of the words *liberty* and *freedom?* What kinds of liberty and freedom do you believe people should have? Should all people have the same liberties and freedoms? Discuss your thoughts with a small group of classmates, and then write down your ideas in your notebook.

HISTORICAL CONNECTION

The two letters you are about to read are concerned with the issues of liberty and freedom. Both were written at the time of the American Revolution and provide insights into colonial life during the struggle for independence. The first letter is by Phillis Wheatley, a former slave in Boston who was the first African American to have a book of poetry published. It is believed that she was writing to her friend the Reverend Samson Occom, a converted Mohegan Indian minister, in response to his written protest against slave-owning ministers. This letter was dated February 11, 1774, and was published later in the *Connecticut Gazette* and other colonial newspapers.

The second letter is by Abigail Adams, the wife of John Adams, who became the second president of the United States. It was written to her husband shortly before the Declaration of Independence was signed. He had left their Massachusetts home in 1774 to become a delegate to the First Continental Congress in Philadelphia, and they saw each other only rarely in the ten years afterward. During this time, however, they exchanged more than 300 letters, including the one you will read. A grandson saved the letters and first published them in 1840.

READING CONNECTION

Reading Literary Letters Have you ever written a letter to a friend or relative? If so, you probably meant for only that one person to read the letter. A literary letter is a letter that has been published and read by a wider audience because it was written by a well-known public figure or provides information about the period in which it was written. Not only do literary letters reveal a writer's personal concerns, but they may also cast light on public issues of the writer's time—such as the demands for liberty and freedom in Wheatley's and Adams's letters. As you read each letter, fill in a diagram like this one to note the private and public issues that are addressed.

Public

Private

• *HISTORICAL CONNECTION*

Letter to the Rev. Samson Occom

Phillis Wheatley

An engraving of Phillis Wheatley. Reproduced from the collections of the Library of Congress.

Reverend and honored Sir,

"I have this day received your obliging kind epistle,[1] and am greatly satisfied with your reasons respecting the negroes, and think highly reasonable what you offer in vindication of their natural rights: Those that invade them cannot be insensible[2] that the divine light is chasing away the thick darkness which broods over the land of Africa;[3] and the chaos which has reigned so long, is converting into beautiful order, and reveals more and more clearly the glorious

1. **epistle:** letter.
2. **insensible:** unaware.
3. **divine light . . . Africa:** Wheatley is referring to the spread of Christianity to areas of Africa where it had not been practiced.

WORDS TO KNOW

vindication (vĭn′dĭ-kā′shən) *n.* the defense or justification of something, such as one's rights

For in every human breast God has implanted a principle, which we call love of freedom.

dispensation of civil and religious liberty, which are so inseparably united, that there is little or no enjoyment of one without the other: Otherwise, perhaps, the Israelites had been less solicitous for their freedom from Egyptian slavery;[4] I do not say they would have been contented without it, by no means; for in every human breast God has implanted a principle, which we call love of freedom; it is impatient of oppression, and pants for deliverance; and by the leave of our modern Egyptians[5] I will assert, that the same principle lives in us. God grant deliverance in his own way and time, and get him honor upon all those whose avarice impels them to countenance and help forward the calamities of their fellow creatures. This I desire not for their hurt, but to convince them of the strange absurdity of their conduct, whose words and actions are so diametrically opposite. How well the cry for liberty, and the reverse disposition for the exercise of oppressive power over others agree—I humbly think it does not require the penetration[6] of a philosopher to determine."—

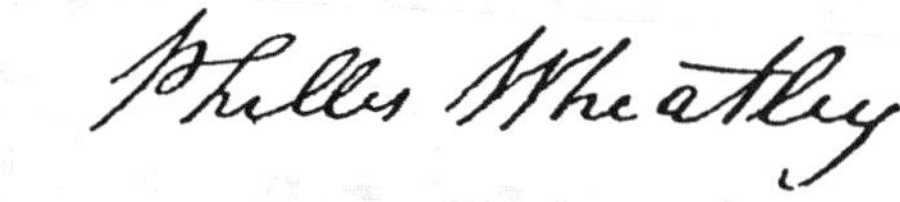

4. **Israelites . . . Egyptian slavery:** a biblical allusion to the enslaved Jews who were led out of Egypt by Moses sometime between 1300 and 1200 B.C.
5. **modern Egyptians:** this comparison refers to the owners of African slaves.
6. **penetration:** understanding; insight.

FROM PERSONAL RESPONSE *TO* CRITICAL ANALYSIS

REFLECT **1.** What single word would you use to describe Wheatley's letter? Share this word with your classmates.

RETHINK **2.** Paraphrase the last sentence of this letter, which begins, "How well the cry. . . ." You could begin such a paraphrase with "It doesn't take a rocket scientist. . . ."

3. In your own words, explain the case that Wheatley makes against slavery.
Consider
- what she says is happening in Africa
- what relationship she sees between civil and religious liberty
- what she claims God has done and what she hopes he will do

WORDS TO KNOW
dispensation (dĭs′pən-sā′shən) *n.* distribution; giving out
solicitous (sə-lĭs′ĭ-təs) *adj.* full of desire; eager
countenance (koun′tə-nəns) *v.* to give or express approval; support

Letter to John Adams

Abigail Adams

This 1775 British cartoon ridicules a group of North Carolina women who, in support of the patriot cause, signed a pledge not to drink tea. Courtesy of the State Department of Cultural Resources, Divison of Archives and History, Raleigh, North Carolina.

Braintree, 7 May, 1776.

How many are the solitary hours I spend, ruminating upon the past, and anticipating the future, whilst you, overwhelmed with the cares of state, have but a few moments you can devote to any individual. All domestic pleasures and enjoyments are absorbed in the great and important duty you owe your country, "for our country is, as it were, a secondary god, and the first and greatest parent. It is to be preferred to parents, wives, children, friends, and all things, the gods only excepted; for, if our country perishes, it is as impossible to save an individual, as to preserve one of the fingers of a mortified[1] hand." Thus do I suppress every wish, and silence every murmur, acquiescing in a painful separation from the companion of my youth, and the friend of my heart.

I believe 't is near ten days since I wrote you a line. I have not felt in a humor to entertain you if I had taken up my pen. Perhaps some unbecoming invective[2] might have fallen from it. The eyes of our rulers have been closed, and a lethargy has seized almost every member. I fear a fatal security has taken possession of them. Whilst the building is in flames, they tremble at the expense of water to quench it. In short, two months have elapsed since the evacuation of

1. **mortified:** decayed; having gangrene.
2. **invective:** abusive language.

WORDS TO KNOW

ruminating (ro͞o'mə-nā-tĭng) *adj.* turning a matter over and over in the mind
ruminate *v.*

acquiescing (ăk'wē-ĕs'ĭng) *adj.* consenting passively or without protest
acquiesce *v.*

lethargy (lĕth'ər-jē) *n.* a state of sluggishness and inactivity

Boston,[3] and very little has been done in that time to secure it, or the harbor, from future invasion. The people are all in a flame, and no one among us, that I have heard of, even mentions expense. They think, universally, that there has been an amazing neglect somewhere. Many have turned out as volunteers to work upon Noddle's Island, and many more would go upon Nantasket, if the business was once set on foot. "'T is a maxim of state,[4] that power and liberty are like heat and moisture. Where they are well mixed, every thing prospers; where they are single, they are destructive."

A government of more stability is much wanted in this colony, and they are ready to receive it from the hands of the Congress. And since I have begun with maxims of state, I will add another, namely, that a people may let a king[5] fall, yet still remain a people; but, if a king let his people slip from him, he is no longer a king. And as this is most certainly our case, why not proclaim to the world, in decisive terms, your own importance?

Shall we not be despised by foreign powers, for hesitating so long at a word?

I cannot say that I think you are very generous to the ladies; for, whilst you are proclaiming peace and good-will to men, emancipating all nations, you insist upon retaining an absolute power over wives. But you must remember, that arbitrary power is like most other things which are very hard, very liable to be broken; and, notwithstanding all your wise laws and maxims, we have it in our power, not only to free ourselves, but to subdue our masters, and, without violence, throw both your natural and legal authority at our feet;—

"Charm by accepting, by submitting sway,
Yet have our humor most when we obey."[6]

I thank you for several letters which I have received since I wrote last; they alleviate a tedious absence, and I long earnestly for a Saturday evening, and experience a similar pleasure to that which I used to find in the return of my friend upon that day after a week's absence. The idea of a year dissolves all my philosophy.

Our little ones, whom you so often recommend to my care and instruction, shall not be deficient in virtue or probity, if the precepts of a mother have their desired effect; but they would be doubly enforced, could they be indulged with the example of a father alternately before them. I often point them to their sire,

"engaged in a corrupted state,
Wrestling with vice and faction."[7]

A. Adams

3. **two months . . . Boston:** British troops under General William Howe and more than a thousand Loyalists evacuated Boston on March 17, 1776.
4. **maxim of state:** rule or short saying related to government.
5. **king:** Adams is referring to the British king George III, who ignored colonists' protests and put Massachusetts under military rule.
6. **"Charm . . . obey":** a couplet taken from Alexander Pope's poem *Moral Essays*.
7. **vice and faction:** corruption and conflict within a nation.

WORDS TO KNOW

emancipate (ĭ-măn'sə-pāt') *v.* to free; liberate
probity (prō'bĭ-tē) *n.* honesty; integrity
precept (prē'sĕpt') *n.* a rule or principle prescribing a particular course of action

RESPONDING OPTIONS

FROM PERSONAL RESPONSE *TO* CRITICAL ANALYSIS

REFLECT 1. What impression of Abigail Adams do you get from her letter? Share your ideas with classmates.

RETHINK 2. How would you describe Adams's attitude toward her husband and his work? Support your answer with evidence from the letter.

3. What can you infer about Adams's views on public issues?

   Consider
   - her description of the local colonial government
   - her maxim about power and liberty
   - her maxim about people and a king
   - her comments about women

RELATE 4. How similar, would you say, are the purposes of Wheatley's letter and Adams's letter? Consider the private and public issues that are addressed in them.

5. This part of Unit Two is subtitled "The Right to Be Free." What ideas do these letters suggest to you about "the right to be free"?

6. Adams and Wheatley did not intend their letters to be published, but many people have read and enjoyed them. Name a contemporary woman whose letters you think might be read 200 years from now, and explain why her letters might be important.

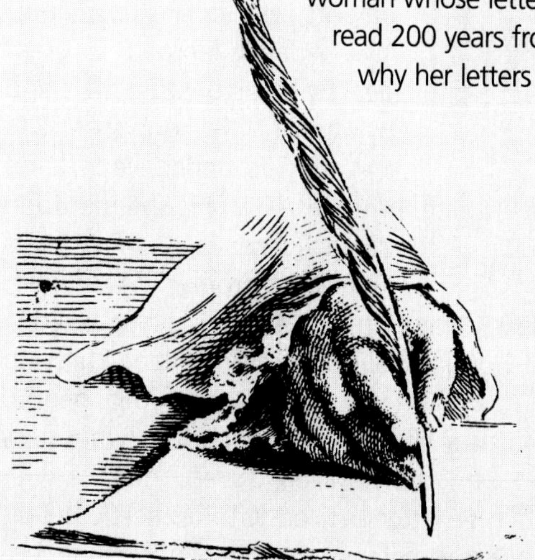

ANOTHER PATHWAY

Cooperative Learning

With other members of your class, stage a colonial talk show with guests Phillis Wheatley and Abigail Adams. The host can introduce the guests and ask a few questions, then open up the questioning to the rest of the audience. To prepare, have small groups coach students playing the characters.

QUICKWRITES

1. Draft a **personal response** to Phillis Wheatley's letter agreeing or disagreeing with her view that civil and religious liberty are inseparable and that one cannot be enjoyed without the other.

2. Write your own **literary letter** addressing the topic of liberty. As a starting point, use the comments you made in the Personal Connection activity (page 216). Publish your letter by displaying it in the classroom or by submitting it to the school newspaper or literary magazine.

PORTFOLIO *Save your writing. You may want to use it later as a spring-board to a piece for your portfolio.*

LITERARY CONCEPTS

Figurative language is language that communicates ideas beyond the literal meaning of words. Two common forms of figurative language—**metaphors** and **similes**—make comparisons between two unlike things that have something in common. A metaphor makes the comparison directly: "Our country is a parent," for example. A simile states the comparison using *like* or *as:* "Our country is like a parent." Metaphors and similes can make descriptions more interesting and also make unfamiliar ideas easier to understand.

Cooperative Learning Working with a small group of classmates, find three or four examples of figurative language in these two letters. Create a chart to classify each example as a simile or a metaphor and to explain what idea the comparison suggests. Share your chart with other groups.

WORDS TO KNOW

Review the Words to Know at the bottom of the selection pages. Then read this fictitious letter by an 18th-century patriot. Rewrite the letter, replacing the underlined word or phrase with the appropriate vocabulary word.

I am eager to learn your views on the burning issue of freedom. While I do not favor violence, I do think there is justification for recent events. It is a fundamental law that those who are attacked must defend themselves if they wish to escape destruction. We must shake off our drowsiness and prepare for war. We should neither be politely consenting to the king's taxes nor blindly trusting his honesty as he says one thing to us and does another. What choice do we have left but to prepare for freeing ourselves from his choking grasp? He will offer no kind gift of freedom, to be sure. While thinking about possible conflict, I pray for God's guidance.

PHILLIS WHEATLEY

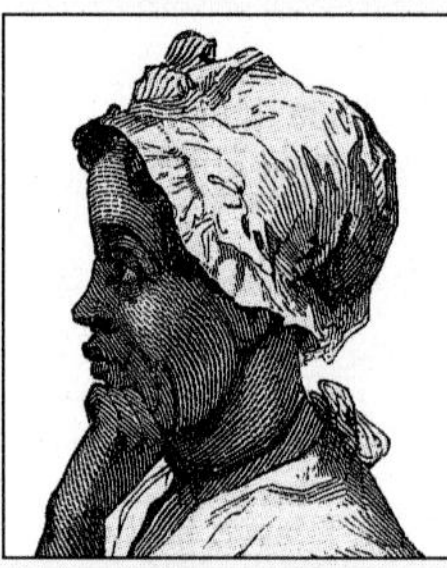

1753?–1784

After being kidnapped by slave traders in 1761, Phillis Wheatley was brought from Africa to Boston on the slave ship *Phillis* and was bought by Susanna Wheatley, the wife of a wealthy merchant. While living at the Wheatleys, she learned English and Latin and studied literature, and she began to write poetry at about age 12. After being examined by a group of prominent Bostonians who attested to the authenticity of her poetry, Wheatley accompanied her master's son to England to seek publication of her poems. Her only book, *Poems on Various Subjects, Religious and Moral,* was published in London in 1773. That same year, she received her freedom, and a short time later she wrote the antislavery letter you have just read.

ABIGAIL ADAMS

1744–1818

Abigail Adams was the wife of President John Adams and the mother of President John Quincy Adams. Educated at home by her parents, grandparents, and future brother-in-law, Adams learned a great deal by reading voraciously and by studying the works of John Milton, Alexander Pope, and William Shakespeare. When she was 15, she met John Adams, a 26-year-old Massachusetts lawyer. Five years later, in 1764, they were married. From 1774 to 1784, John was often away from home, serving first as a delegate to the Continental Congress in Philadelphia and later as a diplomat in Europe. During this period, Abigail raised four children, managed family business matters, and carried on a lively correspondence with her husband. Her letters—filled with domestic details and her strong opinions about colonial independence—today provide us with a vivid portrait of 18th-century life as a new nation was being born.

PREVIEWING

NONFICTION

What Is an American?

Michel-Guillaume Jean de Crèvecoeur (mē-shĕl′ gē-yōm′ zhäɴ də-krĕv-kœr′)

PERSONAL CONNECTION

What words and phrases come to mind when you hear the word *American?* What different traits or qualities do you associate with Americans? Create a word web with "American" in the center space, and fill in the surrounding spaces with words and phrases that describe Americans. As a class, discuss the question, What is an American?

HISTORICAL CONNECTION

During the mid-1700s, many people left Europe for the opportunity and challenge of North America. Some came to escape crowded cities, to own their own land, and to earn a better living. Others came in search of religious freedom, a life with less government interference, and the chance to have a greater voice in government.

Michel-Guillaume Jean de Crèvecoeur was a French immigrant who arrived in New York in 1759. For ten years, he traveled widely throughout the British colonies as a surveyor and a trader, finally settling on a farm he bought in New York. There, he began to write down his impressions of life in America. In 1782, under the name of J. Hector St. John, he published a collection of 12 essays called *Letters from an American Farmer.* These letters were very well received in Europe and were read by many people—some considering the voyage to America and some just curious. The selection you will read is an excerpt from one of the best known of these letters, in which Crèvecoeur offers his definition of an American.

READING CONNECTION

Understanding Contrast In "What Is an American?" Crèvecoeur contrasts America and Americans with Europe and Europeans. To contrast two things is to state or show how they are dissimilar. Some contrasts are stated directly; others are not so obvious. Copy the chart shown in your notebook; then complete it by noting the contrasts Crèvecoeur makes as you read "What Is an American?"

Category	Europe/European	America/American
Government	"despotic prince"	a new government
Work		
Quality of Life		
Ethnic Background		
Religion		

What is an American?

Michel-Guillaume Jean de Crèvecoeur

In this great American asylum,[1] the poor of Europe have by some means met together, and in consequence of various causes; to what purpose should they ask one another, what countrymen they are? Alas, two-thirds of them had no country. Can a wretch who wanders about, who works and starves, whose life is a continual scene of sore affliction or pinching penury[2]—can that man call England or any other kingdom his country? A country that had no bread for him, whose fields procured him no harvest, who met with nothing but the frowns of the rich, the severity of the laws, with jails and punishments, who owned not a single foot of the extensive surface of this planet? No! urged by a variety of motives, here they came. Everything has tended to regenerate them: new laws, a new mode of living, a new social system. Here they are become men; in Europe they were as so many useless plants, wanting vegetative mold[3] and refreshing showers; they withered and were mowed down by want, hunger, and war. But now, by the power of transplantation, like all other plants, they have taken root and flourished! Formerly they were not numbered in any civil list of their country, except in those of the poor; here they rank as citizens. . . .

What attachment can a poor European emigrant have for a country where he had nothing? The knowledge of the language, the love of a few

1. **asylum** (ə-sī′ləm): a shelter.
2. **penury** (pĕn′yə-rē): extreme poverty.
3. **vegetative mold:** loose, crumbly soil that is rich in nutrients and helps plants to grow.

Van Bergen Overmantel (1732–1733), attributed to John Heaten. Oil on wood (fireboard), 15¼″ × 73½″, New York State Historical Association, Cooperstown, New York. Photo Copyright © New York State Historical Association, Cooperstown, New York.

kindred as poor as himself were the only cords that tied him. His country is now that which gives him land, bread, protection, and consequence.[4] *Ubi panis ibi patria* [where my bread is earned, there is my country] is the motto of all emigrants. What then is the American, this new man? He is either a European or the descendant of a European; hence that strange mixture of blood which you will find in no other country. I could point out to you a man whose grandfather was an Englishman, whose wife was Dutch, whose son married a French woman, and whose present four sons have now four wives of different nations. *He* is an American who, leaving behind him all his ancient prejudices and manners, receives new ones from the new mode of life he has embraced, the new government he obeys, and the new rank he holds. He becomes an American by being received in the broad lap of our great alma mater.[5]

Here individuals of all nations are melted into a new race of men, whose labors and posterity will one day cause great change in the world. Americans are the western pilgrims who are carrying along with them that great mass of arts, sciences, vigor, and industry[6] which began long since in the east; they will finish the great circle. The Americans were once scattered all over Europe; here they are incorporated into one of the finest systems of population which has ever appeared, and which will hereafter become distinct by the power of the different climates they inhabit. The American ought, therefore, to love this country much better than that wherein either he or his forefathers were born. Here the rewards of his industry follow with equal steps the progress of his labor; his labor is founded on the basis of nature, self-interest. Can it want a stronger allurement? Wives and children, who before in vain demanded of him a morsel of bread, now, fat and frolicsome, gladly help their father to clear those fields whence exuberant crops are to arise to feed and to clothe them all, without any part being claimed, either by a despotic prince, a rich abbot,[7] or a mighty lord. Here, religion demands but little of him; a small voluntary salary to the minister, and gratitude to God. Can he refuse these?

The American is a new man, who acts upon new principles; he must, therefore, entertain new ideas and form new opinions. From involuntary idleness, servile dependence, penury, and useless labor he has passed to toils of a very different nature, rewarded by ample subsistence. This is an American. ❖

---

4. **consequence:** importance.
5. **alma mater** (ăl′mə mä′tər): A Latin phrase that literally means "nourishing mother."
6. **industry:** energetic devotion to a task or endeavor; diligence.
7. **abbot** (ăb′ət): the head of a monastery.

WORDS TO KNOW

kindred (kĭn′drĭd) *n.* relatives or family
allurement (ə-lo͝or′mənt) *n.* attraction; enticement
despotic (dĭ-spŏt′ĭk) *adj.* like a dictator
servile (sur′vəl) *adj.* humbly submissive; slavish
subsistence (səb-sĭs′təns) *n.* livelihood

LANCASTER HIGH SCHOOL

INSIGHT

from

Poor Richard's Almanack

Benjamin Franklin

He that cannot obey cannot command.

Don't count your chickens
before they are hatched.

A mob's a monster;
heads enough but no
brains.

Well done is better
than well said.

Lost time is never
found again.

Early to bed,
early to rise,
makes a man healthy,
wealthy and wise.

If you would know the worth of money,
go and try to borrow some.

A friend in need is
a friend indeed.

Fish and visitors smell in three days.

Love your neighbor; yet don't pull
down your hedge.

God helps them that help themselves.

If you would keep your secret from
an enemy, tell it not to a friend.

Be slow in choosing a friend,
slower in changing.

Don't throw stones at your neighbors',
if your own windows are glass.

Eat to live and not live to eat.

Love your enemies, for they
tell you your faults.

Better slip with foot
than tongue.

Three may keep a secret,
if two of them are dead.

Never leave that till tomorrow,
which you can do today.

A penny saved is a
penny earned.

A rolling stone
gathers no moss.

Make hay while
the sun shines.

Beware of little expenses;
a small leak will sink a great ship.

He that goes a borrowing
goes a sorrowing.

Honesty is the best policy.

Little strokes fell big oaks.

He that lies down with dogs
shall rise up with fleas.

LANCASTER HIGH SCHOOL

RESPONDING OPTIONS

FROM PERSONAL RESPONSE *TO* CRITICAL ANALYSIS

REFLECT 1. What impressions of America and Americans do you get from Crèvecoeur's letter? In your notebook, write or sketch your impressions.

RETHINK 2. What do you think might make America appealing to Crèvecoeur and other Europeans? Refer to the chart you made for the Reading Connection (page 223).

3. Do you think Crèvecoeur's description of 18th-century America was accurate? Why or why not?

4. Do you think Crèvecoeur's definition of an American describes Americans today? Explain.

Consider
- groups that Crèvecoeur does not mention
- goals and lifestyles of today's Americans
- how you and your classmates defined an American in the Personal Connection activity

RELATE 5. Consider what the proverbs from *Poor Richard's Almanack,* the Insight selection, reveal about the concerns of 18th-century Americans. Is Franklin's picture of Americans consistent with Crèvecoeur's?

6. How similar are the motives of 18th-century immigrants and today's immigrants to the United States? Support your answer.

ANOTHER PATHWAY

Cooperative Learning

With a group of classmates, create a travel brochure encouraging Europeans to come to America in the mid-1700s. Use the excerpt from "What Is an American?" to help you come up with appealing conditions or qualities to emphasize.

QUICKWRITES

1. Write a draft of a **magazine article** comparing and contrasting Crèvecoeur's definition of an American with your own definition.
2. Using the sayings from *Poor Richard's Almanack* as models, write some **proverbs** that capture the spirit of contemporary American life. Then work with your classmates to make a booklet of these sayings.
3. Using "What Is an American?" as a model, write a short **letter** to a friend who lives outside your state, defining what it means to be a resident of your area. You might answer the question "What Is a Texan?" or "What Is a Detroiter?" for example.

PORTFOLIO Save your writing. You may want to use it later as a springboard to a piece for your portfolio.

LITERARY CONCEPTS

The **theme** of a literary work is the central idea the writer wishes to share with the reader. This idea may be a lesson about life or about people and their actions. Some themes are not obvious and must be figured out by the reader, and sometimes different readers discover different themes. Decide what you think is the main idea of "What Is an American?" and write a statement that you think expresses Crèvecoeur's theme. Share your statement with other classmates.

ALTERNATIVE ACTIVITIES

1. Draw an **editorial cartoon** to show the differences between an American and a European, according to Crèvecoeur.
2. As Crèvecoeur, act out or videotape a **television commercial** selling America to the European public.
3. Draw or paint a **landscape** of Crèvecoeur's 18th-century America.

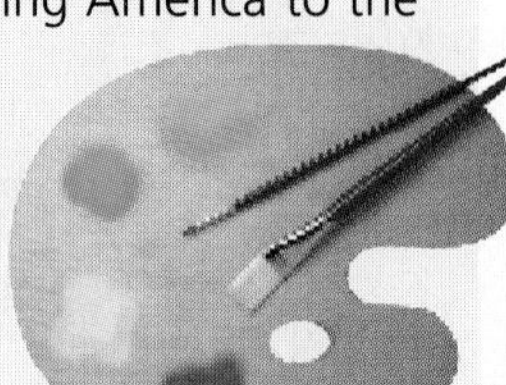

CRITIC'S CORNER

Critics have noted that when Crèvecoeur writes, "Here individuals of all nations are melted into a new race," he anticipates the "melting pot" metaphor commonly used to describe America. Do you think "melting pot" is a good metaphor for this country? Explain why or why not. What other metaphors can you think of to describe America?

WORDS TO KNOW

Review the Words to Know at the bottom of the selection pages and then read the sentences below. On your paper, write the vocabulary word that best completes each sentence.

1. Immigrants found being rewarded fairly for their labor a great ______.
2. Fertile land and good weather offered farmers a good ______.
3. Colonists gladly left behind their ______ existence in Europe.
4. Immigrants often left countries that were ruled by a ______ government.
5. American colonists were frequently separated from their ______ forever.

MICHEL-GUILLAUME JEAN DE CRÈVECOEUR

1735–1813

Born in Caen, France, Michel-Guillaume Jean de Crèvecoeur was educated in a Jesuit school and traveled to England as a young man. In 1755, he left England for Canada, where he enlisted in the French militia. During the French and Indian War, he served as a surveyor and a mapmaker. In 1759, Crèvecoeur came to New York; ten years later, he married an American woman and settled down to farm.

During the period in which Crèvecoeur lived on his farm in New York, he wrote the essays that were published in 1782 in *Letters from an American Farmer.* An immediate success in Europe, Crèvecoeur's book provided an eyewitness account of American life in places ranging from Massachusetts to South Carolina.

During the American Revolution, both the patriots and the British suspected Crèvecoeur's loyalty because he seemed sympathetic to the British side but would not openly state his feelings. He was arrested as a spy and imprisoned by the British army in New York before sailing for Europe with his elder son in 1780. It was not until 1783, after being appointed French consul to New York, New Jersey, and Connecticut, that Crèvecoeur was able to return to America. He found his farm burned, his wife dead, and his two other children housed with strangers in Boston. Reunited with his children in 1784, Crèvecoeur remained in America until 1790. In that year, the "American farmer" returned to France, where he spent the last 23 years of his life.

OTHER WORKS *Sketches of Eighteenth Century America, Eighteenth-Century Travels in Pennsylvania and New York*

LASERLINKS
• *ART GALLERY*

PREVIEWING

NONFICTION

Lecture to a Missionary

Red Jacket

PERSONAL CONNECTION

What do you know about the history of Native American and Anglo relations? How would you describe the relationship between Native Americans and Anglos today? In your notebook, write down your thoughts about Native American–Anglo relations, and then share them with a group of classmates.

HISTORICAL CONNECTION

Relations between Native Americans and Anglos during the first 200 years of the nation were marked by the missionary impulse. Beginning with the French Jesuits and the Puritans in the mid-1600s, missionaries sought to convert Native American tribes to Christianity. In the late 1700s and early 1800s, a number of Protestant missionary societies sent missionaries to establish churches and schools on Iroquois reservations. At the time, the Iroquois consisted of six separate nations: the Seneca, Cayuga, Oneida, Onondaga, Mohawk, and Tuscarora. In the summer of 1805, Reverend Cram of the Boston Missionary Society met with Iroquois chiefs assembled at Buffalo Creek in New York and offered to instruct the Iroquois on "how to worship the Great Spirit agreeably." In the speech you are about to read, Red Jacket, a Seneca chief, responds to this offer.

John Eliot preaching to the Native Americans in the 1600s.
The Granger Collection, New York.

WRITING CONNECTION

In your notebook, write about a time when someone tried to persuade you to do something that you didn't want to do. How did you handle the situation? To get started, copy and complete the following sentences:

______________ tried to persuade me to ______________________.

This was something that I didn't want to do, so I ______________________.

As you read the following speech, compare your experience with Red Jacket's experience.

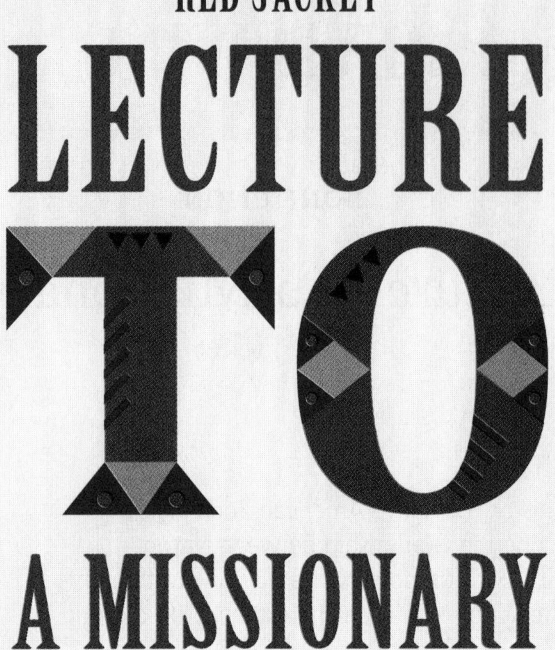

Lecture to a Missionary

RED JACKET

Friend and Brother, it was the will of the Great Spirit that we should meet together this day. He orders all things, and has given us a fine day for our Council. He has taken his garment from before the sun, and caused it to shine with brightness upon us. Our eyes are opened, that we see clearly; our ears are unstopped, that we have been able to hear distinctly the words you have spoken. For all these favors we thank the Great Spirit and Him only.

Brother, this council fire was kindled by you. It was at your request that we came together at this time. We have listened with attention to what you have said. You requested us to speak our minds freely. This gives us great joy; for we now consider that we stand upright before you, and can speak what we think. All have heard your voice, and all speak to you now as one man. Our minds are agreed.

Brother, you say you want an answer to your talk before you leave this place. It is right you should have one; as you are a great distance from home, and we do not wish to detain you. But we will first look back a little, and tell you what our fathers have told us, and what we have heard from the white people.

Brother, listen to what we say. There was a time when our forefathers owned this great island. Their seats extended from the rising to the setting sun. The Great Spirit had made it for the use of Indians. He had created the buffalo, the deer, and other animals for food. He had made the bear and the beaver. Their skins served us for clothing. He had scattered them over the country, and taught us how to take them. He had caused the earth to produce corn for bread. All this He had done for his red children, because he loved them. If we had some disputes about our hunting ground, they were generally settled without the shedding of much blood. But an evil day came upon us. Your forefathers crossed the great water and landed on this island. Their numbers were small. They found friends and not enemies. They told us they had fled from their own country for fear of wicked men, and had come here to enjoy their religion. They asked for a small seat. We took pity on them; granted their request; and they sat down amongst us. We gave them corn and meat; they gave us poison [rum] in return.

The white people, Brother, had now found our country. Tidings were carried back, and more came amongst us. Yet we did not fear them. We took them to be friends. They called us brothers. We believed them and gave them a larger seat. At length their numbers had greatly increased. They wanted more land; they wanted our country. Our eyes were opened, and our minds became uneasy. Wars took place. Indians were hired to fight against Indians, and many of our people were destroyed. They also brought strong liquor amongst us. It was strong and powerful, and has slain thousands.

Brother, our seats were once large and yours were small. You have now become a great people, and we have scarcely a place left to spread our blankets. You have got our country, but are not satisfied; you want to force your religion upon us.

Brother, continue to listen. You say that you are sent to instruct us how to worship the Great Spirit agreeably to his mind, and, if we do not take hold of the religion which you white people teach, we shall be unhappy hereafter. You say that you are right and we are lost. How do we know this to be true? We understand that your religion is written in a book. If it was intended for us as well as you, why has not the Great Spirit given to us, and not only to us, but why did he not give to our forefathers, the knowledge of that book, with the means of understanding it rightly? We only know what you tell us about it. How shall we know when to believe, being so often deceived by the white people?

Brother, you say there is but one way to worship and serve the Great Spirit. If there is but one religion, why do you white people differ so much about it? Why not all agreed, as you can all read the book?

Brother, we do not understand these things. We are told that your religion was given to your forefathers, and has been handed down from father to son. We also have a religion, which was given to our forefathers, and has been handed down to us their children. We worship in that way. It teaches us to be thankful for all the favors we receive; to love each other, and to be united. We never quarrel about religion.

Brother, the Great Spirit has made us all, but He has made a great difference between his white and red children. He has given us different complexions and different customs. To you He has given the arts. To these He has not opened our eyes. We know these things to be true. Since He has made so great a difference between us in other things, why may we not conclude that he has given us a different religion according to our understanding? The Great Spirit does right. He knows what is best for his children; we are satisfied.

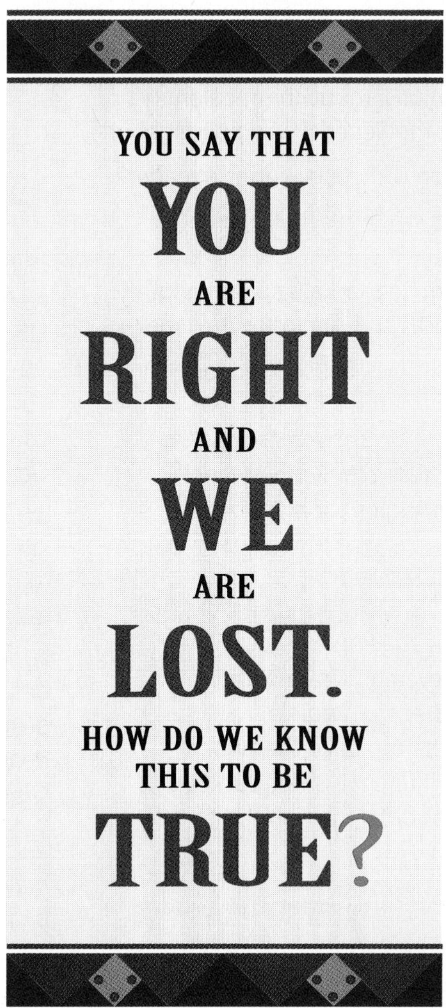
YOU SAY THAT
YOU
ARE
RIGHT
AND
WE
ARE
LOST.
HOW DO WE KNOW
THIS TO BE
TRUE?

Brother, we do not wish to destroy your religion, or take it from you. We only want to enjoy our own.

Brother, you say you have not come to get our land or our money, but to enlighten our minds. I will now tell you that I have been at your meetings, and saw you collect money from the meeting. I cannot tell what this money was intended for, but suppose that it was for your minister, and if we should conform to your way of thinking, perhaps you may want some from us.

Brother, we are told that you have been preaching to the white people in this place. These people are our neighbors. We are acquainted with them. We will wait a little while, and see what effect your preaching has upon them. If we find it does them good, makes them honest and less disposed to cheat Indians, we will then consider again of what you have said.

Brother, you have now heard our answer to your talk, and this is all we have to say at present. As we are going to part, we will come and take you by the hand, and hope the Great Spirit will protect you on your journey, and return you safe to your friends. ❖

RESPONDING OPTIONS

FROM PERSONAL RESPONSE *TO* CRITICAL ANALYSIS

REFLECT 1. What did you think of Red Jacket's lecture? Jot down some comments in your notebook and share them with your classmates.

RETHINK 2. How would you describe Red Jacket's attitude toward Reverend Cram and his proposal?

3. In your own words, explain Red Jacket's reasons for not converting to Reverend Cram's religion. Which of these reasons seems most persuasive to you?

Consider
- the questions Red Jacket asked
- his view of the Great Spirit and his religion
- Red Jacket's observations about the missionary's meetings and about the Senecas' Anglo neighbors

4. What is your impression of Red Jacket as a leader? Cite passages from his speech that support your impression.

5. What can you infer from Red Jacket's speech about relations between Senecas and Anglos at the time?

RELATE 6. Differences in religious views caused friction between the Senecas and the Christian missionaries who sought to convert them. What are some issues that cause conflict between Native Americans and Anglos today?

LITERARY LINKS

Compare Red Jacket's speech to Reverend Cram with Patrick Henry's speech to delegates at the Virginia Convention (page 206). How are the topics of the two speeches alike, and how are they different? Is Red Jacket's attitude toward Anglos similar to or different from Henry's attitude toward the British? Explain.

ANOTHER PATHWAY

Cooperative Learning

With a small group of classmates, list points of conflict between the Senecas and the Christians as revealed in Red Jacket's speech. Then discuss ways that relations between the two groups could be improved. Write a list of recommendations that you would propose.

QUICKWRITES

1. Using Red Jacket's speech as a model, write a **speech** addressed to someone who tried to persuade you to do something that you didn't want to do. You may want to address the person you mentioned in the Writing Connection activity on page 229.
2. After Red Jacket spoke, he and other Senecas walked over to shake hands with Reverend Cram. The missionary refused to shake hands with them, saying there was "no fellowship between the religion of God and the devil." Draft a **personal essay** defending or criticizing Reverend Cram's behavior.

PORTFOLIO Save your writing. You may want to use it later as a springboard to a piece for your portfolio.

LITERARY CONCEPTS

Tone is the attitude a writer takes toward his or her subject and audience. For example, a writer's tone could be ironic, serious, humorous, respectful, or angry. Tone is conveyed by what a writer says about a subject as well as how he or she says it. Different ways that a writer communicates tone are through choice of words, choice of details, and direct statements of his or her position.

How would you describe the tone of Red Jacket's speech? List some examples of specific words, phrases, and details that convey Red Jacket's attitude toward Reverend Cram and his proposal. Then imagine you are Red Jacket's speech-writing consultant. If Red Jacket wanted to use a friendlier tone, what changes would you suggest? If he wanted to use a more defiant tone, what would you suggest?

ALTERNATIVE ACTIVITIES

1. Do a **dramatic reading** of this lecture for your class. Keep in mind Red Jacket's tone and the occasion for his speech as you prepare your reading.
2. Draw a **sketch** that depicts an aspect of the history of the Senecas as recounted by Red Jacket in his speech. Then work with your classmates to design a mural.

ACROSS THE CURRICULUM

History What missionaries or missionary groups other than Jesuits and Puritans aided in the effort to convert Native Americans to Christianity? Do some research, and report your findings to the class.

RED JACKET

1756?–1830

Red Jacket, whose Iroquois name, Sagoyewatha, means "He Keeps Them Awake," was a Seneca chief known for eloquent oratory. Although he did not distinguish himself in battle, he did use his oratorical skills to wage war against the Anglo influence on Iroquois culture. Vehemently opposed to efforts to convert the Iroquois to Christianity, he led the effort to evict a local missionary after the New York legislature passed a law in 1821 forbidding Anglos from living on reservation lands.

During the American Revolution, the Senecas and most other Iroquois nations sided with the British. Sagoyewatha came to be known as Red Jacket after he began wearing the red military coats that British soldiers gave him. After the war, he advocated peace with the Americans. In 1792, he went to Philadelphia with other Iroquois chiefs to meet President George Washington, who gave him a silver medal.

Toward the end of his life, Red Jacket experienced much turmoil. He left his wife for a few months after she became a Christian. As his power waned and his dependence on alcohol grew, he lost his chieftainship in 1827. When he died, Red Jacket, despite his wishes to the contrary, was given a Christian funeral and was buried in a missionary cemetery.

PREVIEWING

NONFICTION

from Stride Toward Freedom

Martin Luther King, Jr.

Necessary to Protect Ourselves

Malcolm X, *Interviewed by* Les Crane

PERSONAL CONNECTION

When, if ever, do you think it is appropriate to use violence? Would it be right to use violence, for example, to protest political or social injustice, to fight a war, to act in self-defense, or to achieve a personal goal? With a group of classmates, discuss times when people use violence and evaluate when, if ever, using violence is justified. You might use a scale like the one on the right to organize your ideas.

Violence Acceptable — **Violence Unacceptable**

self-defense *war* *social protest*

HISTORICAL CONNECTION

Southern states in our country once had segregation laws, that is, laws that imposed social separation of races. African Americans were forced to attend separate schools and to sit in separate parts of buses and trains. Many public facilities, such as restaurants, movie theaters, and hotels, were also segregated. During the civil rights movement that took place in the 1950s and 1960s, African Americans protested in order to gain their civil rights, or rights that are guaranteed to citizens by the Constitution. Through boycotts, sit-ins, and marches, African Americans and their supporters challenged segregation laws, sought better housing and jobs, and fought for voting rights.

In these selections, Martin Luther King, Jr., and Malcolm X—two African-American leaders who fought for racial justice—consider how to overcome injustice. The first selection is an excerpt from *Stride Toward Freedom,* King's 1958 book about the Montgomery, Alabama, bus boycott. The second is a transcript of a television interview with Malcolm X aired on the late-night *Les Crane Show* in 1964. As the selections show, the men disagreed about whether violence should be used in the struggle for justice.

WRITING CONNECTION

Think of a political, social, or religious issue that is important to you. How far would you go to stand up for this issue? In your notebook, briefly describe the issue and what you would do to support it. For example, would you march in a protest demonstration, boycott a business, or break a law? Would you take violent action? How would you respond if the opposition used violence against you? As you read, think about whether you are willing to go as far as Martin Luther King, Jr., or Malcolm X did to stand up for a cause you believe in.

from

stride toward freedom

Martin Luther King, Jr.

Oppressed people deal with their oppression in three characteristic ways. One way is acquiescence: the oppressed resign themselves to their doom. They tacitly adjust themselves to oppression, and thereby become conditioned to it. In every movement toward freedom some of the oppressed prefer to remain oppressed. Almost 2800 years ago Moses set out to lead the children of Israel from the slavery of Egypt to the freedom of the promised land.[1] He soon discovered that slaves do not always welcome their deliverers. They become accustomed to being slaves. They would rather bear those ills they have, as Shakespeare pointed out, than flee to others that they know not of.[2] They prefer the "fleshpots of Egypt" to the ordeals of emancipation.

There is such a thing as the freedom of exhaustion. Some people are so worn down by the yoke of oppression that they give up. A few years ago in the slum areas of Atlanta, a Negro guitarist used to sing almost daily: "Ben down so long that down don't bother me." This is the type of negative freedom and resignation that often engulfs the life of the oppressed.

But this is not the way out. To accept passively an unjust system is to cooperate with that system; thereby the oppressed become as evil as the oppressor. Noncooperation with evil is as much a moral obligation as is cooperation with good. The oppressed must never allow the conscience of the oppressor to slumber. Religion reminds every man that he is his brother's keeper.[3] To accept injustice or segregation passively is to say to the oppressor that his actions are morally right. It is a way of allowing his

1. **promised land:** in general, a longed-for place where complete satisfaction and happiness will be achieved. In the Old Testament of the Bible, the Promised Land is the land of Canaan, promised by the Lord to Abraham's descendants.
2. **bear those ills they have . . . know not of:** an allusion to a line in Act III, Scene I, of *Hamlet* by William Shakespeare.
3. **his brother's keeper:** an allusion to the biblical story of the brothers Cain and Abel. After Cain murdered Abel, God asked him where his brother was. Cain replied, "I know not; am I my brother's keeper?" In general, the saying refers to people's reluctance to accept responsibility for the welfare of others.

WORDS TO KNOW

oppressed (ə-prĕst') *adj.* kept down by severe and unjust use of force or authority **oppress** *v.*

tacitly (tăs'ĭt-lē) *adv.* silently

conscience to fall asleep. At this moment the oppressed fails to be his brother's keeper. So acquiescence—while often the easier way—is not the moral way. It is the way of the coward. The Negro cannot win the respect of his oppressor by acquiescing; he merely increases the oppressor's arrogance and contempt. Acquiescence is interpreted as proof of the Negro's inferiority. The Negro cannot win the respect of the white people of the South or the peoples of the world if he is willing to sell the future of his children for his personal and immediate comfort and safety.

A second way that oppressed people sometimes deal with oppression is to resort to physical violence and corroding hatred. Violence often brings about momentary results. Nations have frequently won their independence in battle. But in spite of temporary victories, violence never brings permanent peace. It solves no social problem; it merely creates new and more complicated ones.

Violence as a way of achieving racial justice is both impractical and immoral. It is impractical because it is a descending spiral ending in destruction for all. The old law of an eye for an eye[4] leaves everybody blind. It is immoral because it seeks to humiliate the opponent rather than win his understanding; it seeks to annihilate rather than to convert. Violence is immoral because it thrives on hatred rather than love. It destroys community and makes brotherhood impossible. It leaves society in monologue rather than dialogue. Violence ends by defeating itself. It creates bitterness in the survivors and brutality in the destroyers. A voice echoes through time saying to every potential Peter, "Put up your sword."[5] History is cluttered with the wreckage of nations that failed to follow this command.

If the American Negro and other victims of oppression succumb to the temptation of using violence in the struggle for freedom, future generations will be the recipients of a desolate night of bitterness, and our chief legacy to them will be an endless reign of meaningless chaos. Violence is not the way.

The third way open to oppressed people in their quest for freedom is the way of nonviolent resistance. Like the synthesis in Hegelian philosophy,[6] the principle of nonviolent resistance seeks to reconcile the truths of two opposites—acquiescence and violence—while avoiding the extremes and immoralities of both. The nonviolent resister agrees with the person who acquiesces that one should not be physically aggressive toward his opponent but he balances the equation by agreeing with the person of violence that evil must be resisted. He avoids the nonresistance of the former and the violent resistance of the latter. With nonviolent resistance, no individual or group need submit to any wrong, nor need anyone resort to violence in order to right a wrong.

It seems to me that this is the method that must guide the actions of the Negro in the present crisis in race relations. Through nonviolent resistance the Negro will be able to rise to the noble height of opposing the unjust system while loving the perpetrators of the system. The Negro must work passionately and unrelentingly for full stature as a citizen, but he must not use inferior methods to gain it. He

4. **an eye for an eye:** an allusion to Exodus 21:23–25—"You shall give life for life, eye for eye, tooth for tooth, hand for hand, foot for foot."

5. **Peter . . . sword:** Peter, one of the 12 disciples of Jesus, drew his sword to protect Jesus from the soldiers who came to arrest him in the Garden of Gethsemane, but Jesus condemned Peter's use of violence.

6. **Hegelian** (hā-gā'lē-ĭn) **philosophy:** Georg Hegel (1770–1831) was a German philosopher who proposed the theory that for each idea or situation there is an opposite and that these two will eventually merge to form a unified whole.

WORDS TO KNOW

corroding (kə-rō'dĭng) *adj.* gradually destructive **corrode** *v.*

legacy (lĕg'ə-sē) *n.* something handed down from an ancestor or a predecessor or from the past

synthesis (sĭn'thĭ-sĭs) *n.* the combining of separate elements or substances to form a coherent whole

"To accept passively an **unjust** system is to cooperate with that system; thereby the oppressed become as **evil** as the oppressor."

Martin Luther King, Jr., on the march from Selma to Montgomery, Alabama, in 1965 to protest voting restrictions on African Americans.
Copyright © Bruce Davidson/Magnum Photos.

must never come to terms with falsehood, malice, hate, or destruction.

Nonviolent resistance makes it possible for the Negro to remain in the South and struggle for his rights. The Negro's problem will not be solved by running away. He cannot listen to the glib suggestion of those who would urge him to migrate en masse[7] to other sections of the country. By grasping his great opportunity in the South he can make a lasting contribution to the moral strength of the nation and set a sublime example of courage for generations yet unborn.

B By nonviolent resistance, the Negro can also enlist all men of good will in his struggle for equality. The problem is not a purely racial one, with Negroes set against whites. In the end, it is not a struggle between people at all, but a tension between justice and injustice. Nonviolent resistance is not aimed against oppressors but against oppression. Under its banner consciences, not racial groups, are enlisted.

If the Negro is to achieve the goal of integration, he must organize himself into a militant and nonviolent mass movement. All three elements are indispensable. The movement for equality and justice can only be a success if it has both a mass and militant character; the barriers to be overcome require both. Nonviolence is an imperative in order to bring about ultimate community.

A mass movement of a militant quality that is not at the same time committed to nonviolence tends to generate conflict, which in turn breeds anarchy. The support of the participants and the sympathy of the uncommitted are both inhibited by the threat that bloodshed will engulf the community. This reaction in turn encourages the opposition to threaten and resort to force. When, however, the mass movement repudiates violence while moving resolutely toward its goal, its opponents are revealed as the instigators and practitioners of violence if it occurs. Then public support is magnetically attracted to the advocates of nonviolence, while those who employ violence are literally disarmed by overwhelming sentiment against their stand. ❖

7. **en masse** (ŏn măs′): in one group or body; all together.

FROM PERSONAL RESPONSE *TO* CRITICAL ANALYSIS

REFLECT 1. In your notebook, write down your immediate response to this selection.

RETHINK 2. In this selection, King describes three responses to oppression. Use a diagram like the one shown to organize King's main ideas and supporting arguments. In the first two boxes, the responses to oppression are named; fill in what King says are the problems with those responses. In the remaining box, fill in the third response and then list what King says are the advantages of that response.

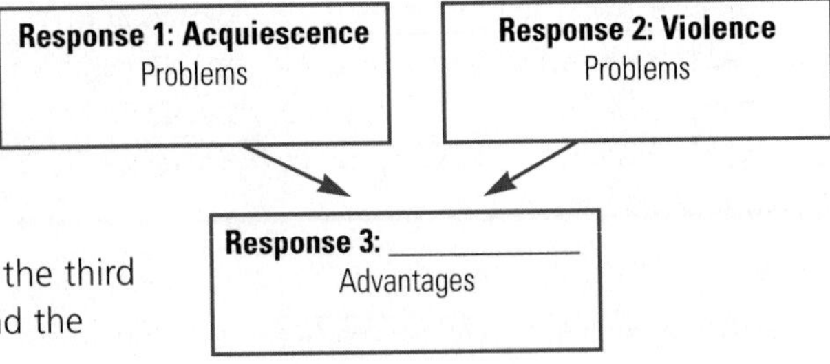

3. Of the arguments King offers in favor of the third response to oppression, which do you find the most persuasive?

WORDS TO KNOW

glib (glĭb) *adj.* showing little thought, preparation, or concern
anarchy (ăn′ər-kē) *n.* absence of any form of political authority
repudiate (rĭ-pyo͞o′dē-āt′) *v.* to reject the validity or authority of

necessary to protect ourselves

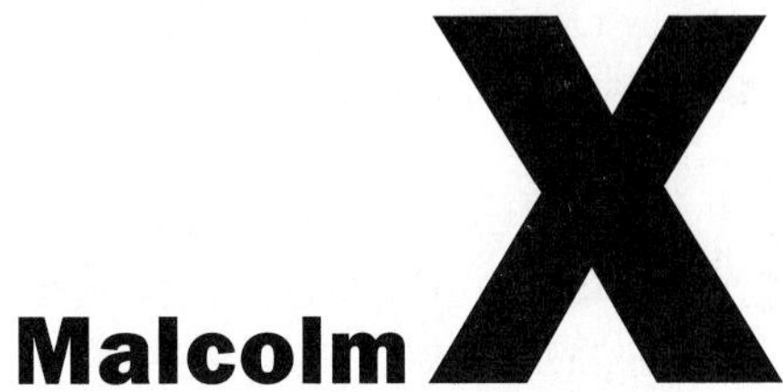

Malcolm X

Interviewed by Les Crane

Crane: You've been a critic of some of the Negro leadership in this country—Martin Luther King, Roy Wilkins, Abernathy,[1] and others—have you changed in your feelings toward them of late?

Malcolm X: I think all of us should be critics of each other. Whenever you can't stand criticism you can never grow. I don't think that it serves any purpose for the leaders of our people to waste their time fighting each other needlessly. I think that we accomplish more when we sit down in private and iron out whatever differences that may exist and try and then do something constructive for the benefit of our people. But on the other hand, I don't think that we should be above criticism. I don't think that anyone should be above criticism.

Crane: Violence or the threat of violence has always surrounded you. Speeches that you've made have been interpreted as being threats. You have made statements reported in the press about how the Negroes should go out and arm themselves, form militias of their own. I read a thing once, a statement I believe you made that every Negro should belong to the National Rifle Association—

Malcolm X: No, I said this: That in areas of this country where the government has proven its—either its inability or its unwillingness to protect the lives and property of our people, then it's only fair to expect us to do whatever is necessary to protect ourselves. And in situations like Mississippi, places like Mississippi where the government actually has proven its inability to protect us—and it has been proven that ofttimes the police officers and sheriffs themselves are involved in the murder that takes place against our people—then I feel, and I say that anywhere, that our people should start doing what is necessary to protect ourselves. This doesn't mean that we should buy rifles and go out and initiate attacks indiscriminately against whites. But it does mean that we should get whatever is necessary to protect ourselves in a country or in an area where the governmental ability to protect us has broken down—

1. **Roy Wilkins, Abernathy:** Roy Wilkins (1901–1981) was executive secretary of the National Association for the Advancement of Colored People (NAACP) from 1955 to 1977. Ralph Abernathy (1926–1990) was a close friend of Martin Luther King, Jr., and helped him found the Southern Christian Leadership Conference to combat racism.

WORDS TO KNOW

indiscriminately (ĭn'dĭ-skrĭm'ə-nĭt-lē) *adv.* randomly

"**My belief in brotherhood would never restrain me in any way from protecting myself in a society from a people whose disrespect for brotherhood makes them feel inclined to put my neck on a tree at the end of a rope.**"

Malcolm X with his daughters Qubilah and Attallah in 1962. Photo by Robert L. Haggins.

Crane: Therefore you do not agree with Dr. King's Gandhian philosophy[2]—

Malcolm X: My belief in brotherhood would never restrain me in any way from protecting myself in a society from a people whose disrespect for brotherhood makes them feel inclined to put my neck on a tree at the end of a rope.[3] *[Applause]*

Crane: Well, it sounds as though you could be preaching a sort of an anarchy—

Malcolm X: No, no. I respect government and respect law. But does the government and the law respect us? If the FBI, which is what people depend upon on a national scale to protect the morale and the property and the lives of the people, can't do so when the property and lives of Negroes and whites who try and help Negroes are concerned, then I think that it's only fair to expect elements to do whatever is necessary to protect themselves.

And this is no departure from normal procedure. Because right here in New York City you have vigilante committees[4] that have been set up by groups who see where their neighborhood community is endangered and the law can't do anything about it. So—and even their lives aren't at stake. So—but the fear, Les, seems to come into existence only when someone says Negroes should form vigilante committees to protect their lives and their property.

I'm not advocating the breaking of any laws. But I say that our people will never be respected as human beings until we react as other normal, intelligent human beings do. And this country came into existence by people who were tired of tyranny and oppression and exploitation and the brutality that was being inflicted upon them by powers higher than they, and I think that it is only fair to expect us, sooner or later, to do likewise. ❖

2. **Gandhian** (gän'dē-ĭn) **philosophy:** Mohandas Gandhi (1869–1948) was an Indian nationalist and spiritual leader who developed the practice of nonviolent civil disobedience that forced Great Britain to grant independence to India in 1947.
3. **put my neck . . . rope:** an allusion to the practice of lynching. Many African Americans were executed by whites without due process of law, especially by hanging.
4. **vigilante** (vĭj'ə-lăn'tē) **committees:** volunteer groups of citizens that without lawful authority assume powers such as pursuing and punishing suspected criminals or offenders.

WORDS TO KNOW

exploitation (ĕk'sploi-tā'shən) *n.* use of another person or group for selfish purposes

RESPONDING OPTIONS

FROM PERSONAL RESPONSE *TO* CRITICAL ANALYSIS

REFLECT **1.** What do you think of the ideas Malcolm X expresses in this interview? Write your first thoughts in your notebook.

RETHINK **2.** Malcolm X compares the oppression of African Americans with that of American colonists under King George III. He believes that "it is only fair to expect" African Americans to react to tyranny as the revolutionaries did. Do you agree?

RELATE **3.** Based on these two selections, which leader do you find more persuasive—King or Malcolm X? Consider the emotional appeals and intellectual arguments they use.

4. Which leader do you think is more revolutionary—King or Malcolm X? Support your opinion, making sure to define what "revolutionary" means to you.

5. Both King and Malcolm X fought for justice for African Americans in the 1960s. Name political, religious, or social causes that people are fighting for in the United States today. What methods do different groups use to promote their causes? Which methods do you think are most effective?

ANOTHER PATHWAY

Cooperative Learning

With your class, debate whether King or Malcolm X has better ideas about resisting oppression. In preparation for the debate, each side should meet to formulate an argument and support it with examples and reasons from the selections.

LITERARY CONCEPTS

A writer's or speaker's choice of words is called **diction.** Diction includes both vocabulary (individual words) and syntax (the order or arrangement of words). Diction can be described in terms such as formal or informal, technical or common, abstract or concrete. In the excerpt from *Stride Toward Freedom,* for example, King's diction is very formal, with difficult words and complex sentences. How do you think King's diction influences your response to his arguments?

In contrast to King, Malcolm X uses diction that is more informal, partly because he is not writing here but speaking in an interview, without preparation. Imagine that you are Les Crane interviewing Martin Luther King, Jr., on your talk show. Create interview questions whose answers can be found in the King selection. Then rewrite several of King's sentences, using the more informal diction that he might use when speaking in a televised interview. If you like, perform your interview with a partner for the class.

QUICKWRITES

1. Write a brief **dramatic scene** in which King and Malcolm X discuss their ideas about how best to help African Americans attain justice.
2. Write notes and organize them for a **persuasive essay** about the use of violence to achieve a goal. Before you start, consider ideas from the selections and Personal Connection and look at the notes you made for the Writing Connection on page 234.

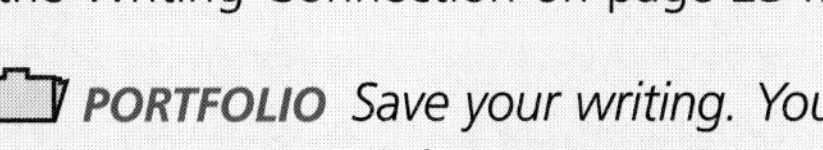

PORTFOLIO *Save your writing. You may want to use it later as a spring-board to a piece for your portfolio.*

ACROSS THE CURRICULUM

World History Research the career of Mohandas Gandhi, a social leader in India whose ideas about nonviolent protest influenced Martin Luther King, Jr. What, exactly, was Gandhi trying to achieve? What particular protests did he lead? Report your findings to the class.

WORDS TO KNOW

For each of the following vocabulary words, write a sentence describing a situation in which the word could be applied.

1. oppressed
2. tacitly
3. corroding
4. legacy
5. synthesis
6. glib
7. anarchy
8. repudiate
9. indiscriminately
10. exploitation

MARTIN LUTHER KING, JR.

1929–1968

The Reverend Dr. Martin Luther King, Jr., was the pastor of a Baptist church in Montgomery, Alabama, in 1955 when a woman named Rosa Parks was arrested for refusing to give up her bus seat to a white passenger as the local segregation law then required. Civil rights activists in Montgomery organized a boycott of buses by African Americans and selected King as their leader. A little over a year after the boycott began, the U.S. Supreme Court determined that segregated seating on public buses in Montgomery violated the Constitution.

The successful Montgomery bus boycott launched King's career in the civil rights movement. He went on to develop a reputation as a powerful leader and a brilliant orator. In his most famous speech, "I Have a Dream," he electrified more than 200,000 demonstrators gathered for the March on Washington in August 1963. The following year, Congress passed the landmark Civil Rights Act of 1964, and King received the Nobel Peace Prize.

For the rest of his life, King continued to work for justice and equality. He was killed by an assassin's bullet on April 4, 1968, in Memphis, Tennessee.

OTHER WORKS "Letter from a Birmingham Jail," *Why We Can't Wait, Where Do We Go from Here*

MALCOLM X

1925–1965

While in prison for burglary from 1946 to 1952, Malcolm Little converted to the faith of the Nation of Islam (popularly known as the Black Muslims), a militant religious and cultural community that believed in black separatism. Like many members of that group, he took the name "X" as a symbol of his lost African name.

Malcolm X was one of the most powerful speakers of his time, and he won many converts to the Black Muslim faith. However, in 1964, after a disagreement with the Black Muslim leader, Elijah Muhammad, Malcolm X left the sect and founded his own organization. On a pilgrimage to Mecca, he saw Muslims of all races joined in common faith and soon embraced the possibility of cooperation among races.

The rivalry between Malcolm X and the Black Muslims grew, resulting in violence and threats against his life. On February 21, 1965, he was shot to death by some Black Muslims as he spoke at a rally in Harlem.

OTHER WORKS *The Autobiography of Malcolm X, Malcolm X: The Last Speeches, Malcolm X Talks to Young People*

LASERLINKS
• *AUTHOR BACKGROUND*

PREVIEWING

POETRY

from I Am Joaquín / Yo Soy Joaquín

Rodolfo Gonzales

PERSONAL CONNECTION

What do you take pride in? Construct a diagram similar to the one modeled here to help you recall things that make you proud. Then circle your three or four strongest points of pride. With a small group of classmates, discuss the ideas that you listed and circled.

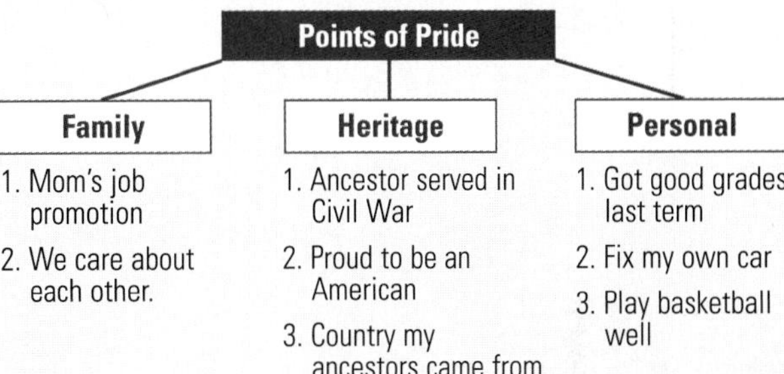

Points of Pride
Family
1. Mom's job promotion
2. We care about each other.
Heritage
1. Ancestor served in Civil War
2. Proud to be an American
3. Country my ancestors came from
Personal
1. Got good grades last term
2. Fix my own car
3. Play basketball well

CULTURAL CONNECTION

During the 1960s, Chicanos—residents of the United States who trace their ancestry to Mexico—demanded economic justice and equal rights. In California, Cesar Chavez organized the United Farm Workers Union and led a successful strike against grape growers. New political groups such as the Alianza in New Mexico, La Raza Unida in Texas, and the Crusade for Justice in Colorado spoke out for the rights of Chicanos. Groups of Chicano students throughout the southwestern states that were once part of Mexico protested unfair treatment and promoted pride in their Chicano heritage.

The Chicano movement inspired much new poetry, prose, and drama. *I Am Joaquín/Yo Soy Joaquín* is one of the earliest and most widely read works associated with the movement. Reprinted here are excerpts from the beginning and the end of this book-length poem by social activist Rodolfo Gonzales. In its entirety the poem describes the modern dilemma of Chicanos in the 1960s, then outlines 2,000 years of Mexican and Mexican-American history, highlighting the different, often opposing strains that make up the Chicano heritage. References are made to such figures as Aztec ruler Nezahualcóyotl, Spanish conquistador Hernán Cortés, Mexican president Benito Juárez, and California bandit Joaquín Murrieta. At the end, the poem returns to the 1960s, offering images of a Chicano revolution.

WRITING CONNECTION

Go back to the diagram you made for the Personal Connection activity, and choose one of the things you take pride in. Write a paragraph or two to explain your reasons for taking pride in that aspect of your life. As you read, compare what you have written with the excerpts from Gonzales's poem asserting Chicano pride.

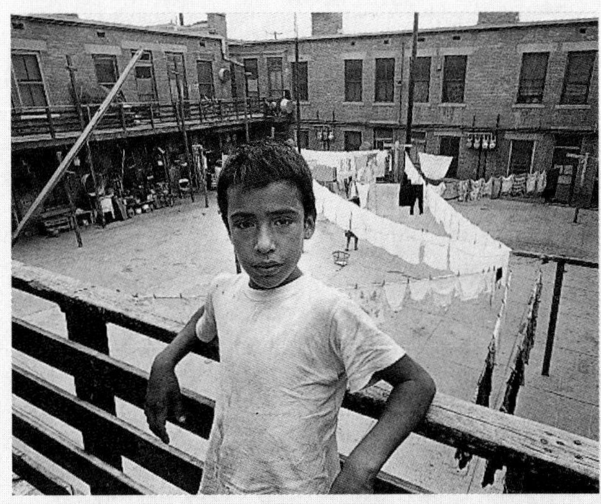

Photo from the book jacket of *I Am Joaquín.* Copyright © 1976 George Ballis/Take Stock, San Rafael, California

I AM JOAQUÍN

Rodolfo Gonzales

from I Am Joaquín

I am Joaquín,
lost in a world of confusion,
caught up in the whirl of a
gringo society,
confused by the rules,
scorned by attitudes,
suppressed by manipulation,
and destroyed by modern society.
My fathers
have lost the economic battle
and won
the struggle of cultural survival.
And now!
I must choose
between
the paradox of
victory of the spirit,
despite physical hunger,
or
to exist in the grasp
of American social neurosis,
sterilization of the soul
and a full stomach. . . .

de Yo Soy Joaquín

Yo soy Joaquín,
perdido en un mundo de confusión,
enganchado en el remolino de una
sociedad gringa,
confundido por las reglas,
despreciado por las actitudes,
sofocado por manipulaciones,
y destrozado por la sociedad moderna.
Mis padres
perdieron la batalla económica
y conquistaron
la lucha de supervivencia cultural.
Y ¡ahora!
yo tengo que escojer
en medio
de la paradoja de
triunfo del espíritu,
a despecho de hambre física,
o
existir en la empuñada
de la neurosis social americana,
esterilización del alma
y un estómago repleto. . . .

Detail of *The Farmworkers of Guadalupe* (1990), Judith F. Baca. From *The Guadalupe Mural*, acrylic on plywood, 8′ × 7′. Copyright © J. Baca, photo by R. Rolle.

I shed the tears of anguish
as I see my children disappear
behind the shroud of mediocrity,
never to look back to remember me.
I am Joaquín.
    I must fight
        and win this struggle
        for my sons, and they
        must know from me
        who I am.

Lloro lágrimas de angustia
cuando veo a mis hijos desaparecer
detrás de la mortaja de mediocridad,
para jamás reflexionar o acordarse de mí.
Yo soy Joaquín.
    Debo pelear
        y ganar la lucha
        para mis hijos, y ellos
        deben saber de mí,
        quien soy yo.

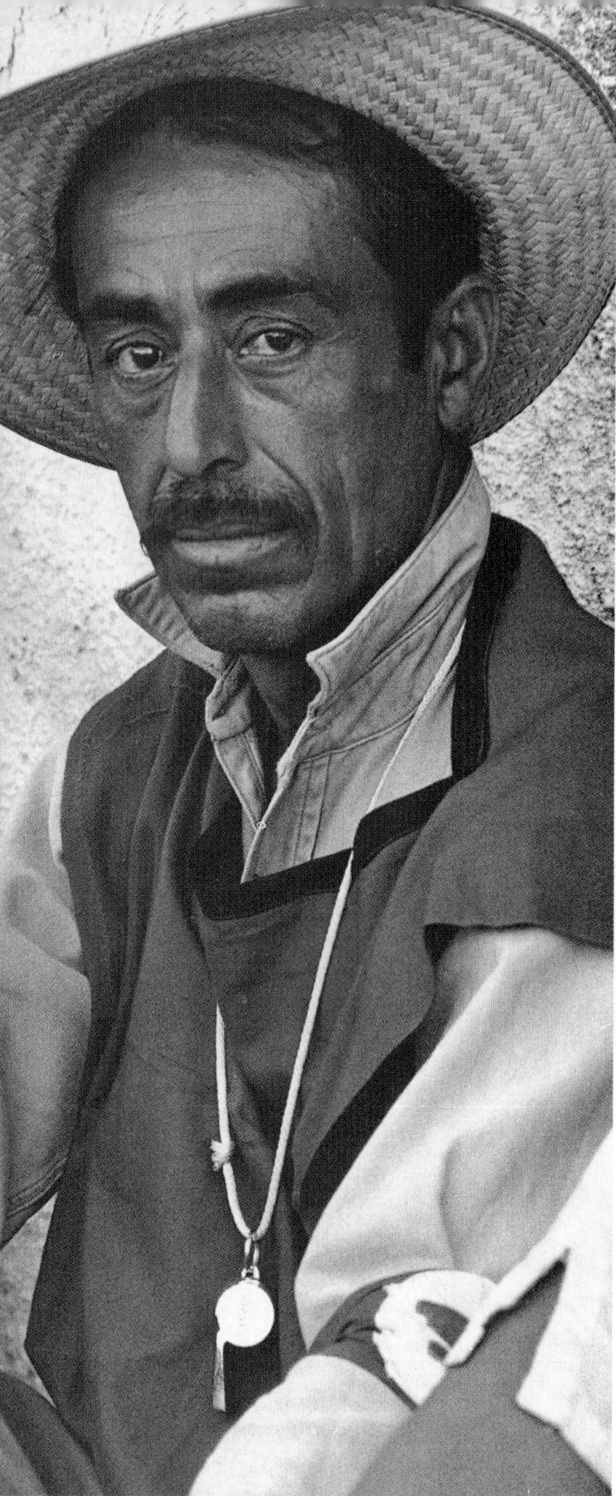

Copyright © 1978 George Ballis/Take Stock, San Rafael, California.

Part of the blood that runs deep in me
could not be vanquished by the Moors.[1]
I defeated them after five hundred years,
and I endured.
Part of the blood that is mine
has labored endlessly four hundred
years under the heel of lustful
Europeans.[2]
I am still here!
I have endured in the rugged mountains
of our country.
I have survived the toils and slavery
of the fields.
I have existed
in the barrios of the city
in the suburbs of bigotry
in the mines of social snobbery
in the prisons of dejection
in the muck of exploitation
and
in the fierce heat of racial hatred.
And now the trumpet sounds,
the music of the people stirs the
revolution.
Like a sleeping giant it slowly
rears its head
to the sound of
tramping feet
clamoring voices
mariachi strains
fiery tequila explosions
the smell of chile verde and
soft brown eyes of expectation for a
better life.

---

1. **Moors** (mo͝orz): followers of the religion of Islam who conquered Spain during the 700s and who lost most of their territory there by the late 1200s.
2. **labored . . . Europeans:** In 1521, Hernán Cortés, a Spanish conquistador, conquered the Aztec empire, located in the area around present-day Mexico City. The speaker suggests that the native population has been dominated by Europeans ever since.

Parte de la sangre que corre hondo en mí
no pudo ser vencida por los moros.
Los derroté después de quinientos años,
y yo perduré.
La parte de sangre que es mía
ha obrado infinitamente cuatrocientos
años debajo el talón de europeos
lujuriosos.
¡Yo todavía estoy aquí!
He perdurado en las montañas escarpadas
de nuestro país.
He sobrevivido los trabajos y esclavitud
de los campos.
Yo he existido
en los barrios de la ciudad
en los suburbios de intolerancia
en las minas de snobismo social
en las prisiones de desaliento
en la porquería de explotación
y
en el calor feroz de odio racial.
Y ahora suena la trompeta,
la música de la gente incita la
revolución.
Como un gigantón soñoliento lentamente
alza su cabeza
al sonido de
patulladas
voces clamorosas
tañido de mariachis
explosiones ardientes de tequila
el aroma de chile verde y
ojos morenos, esperanzosos de una
vida mejor.

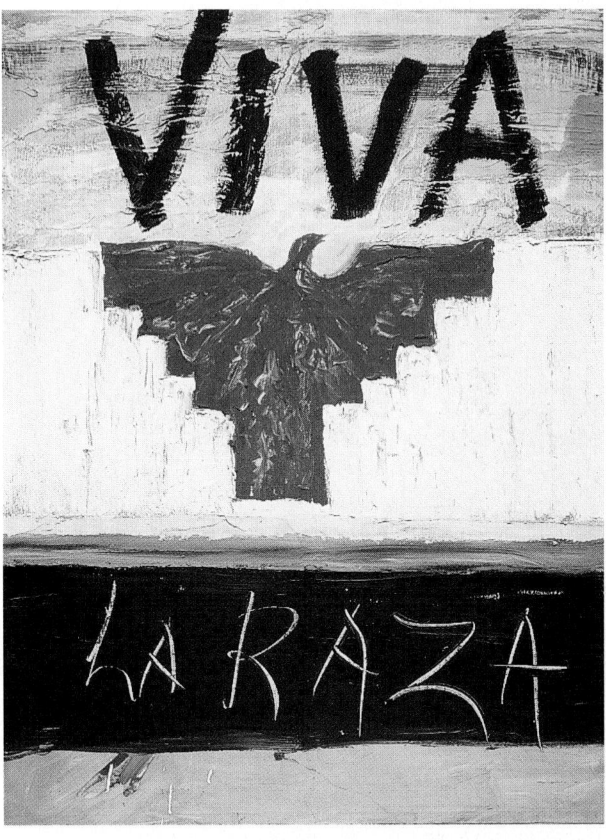

Viva La Raza, Long Live Humanity (1969), Salvador Roberto Torres. Oil on canvas, 35″ × 42″, copyright © 1969.

And in all the fertile farmlands,
the barren plains,
the mountain villages,
smoke-smeared cities,
we start to MOVE.
La Raza![3]
Méjicano!
Español!
Latino!
Hispano!
Chicano!
or whatever I call myself,
I look the same
I feel the same
I cry
and
sing the same.
I am the masses of my people and
I refuse to be absorbed.
I am Joaquín.
The odds are great
but my spirit is strong,
my faith unbreakable,
my blood is pure.
I am Aztec prince and Christian Christ.
I SHALL ENDURE!
I WILL ENDURE!

Farm Workers' Altar (1967), Emanuel Martinez. Acrylic on wood, 37½″ × 53″ × 35½″, UCLA at The Armand Hammer Museum of Art and Cultural Center, Los Angeles.

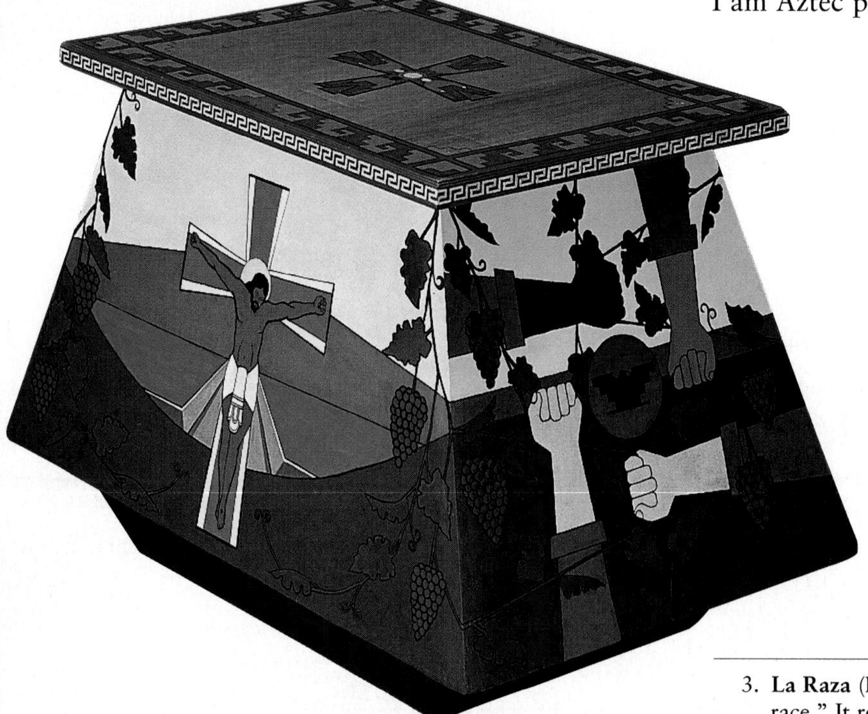

3. **La Raza** (lä rä′sä): literally, the term means "the race." It refers to people who trace their heritage to Mexico.

Y en todos los terrenos fértiles,
los llanos áridos,
los pueblos montañeros,
ciudades ahumadas,
empezamos a AVANZAR.
¡La Raza!
¡Méjicano!
¡Español!
¡Latino!
¡Hispano!
¡Chicano!
o lo que me llame yo,
yo parezco lo mismo
yo siento lo mismo
yo lloro
y
canto lo mismo.
Yo soy el bulto de mi gente y
yo renuncio ser absorbido.
Yo soy Joaquín.
Las desigualdades son grandes
pero mi espíritu es firme,
mi fé impenetrable,
mi sangre pura.
Soy príncipe azteca y Cristo cristiano.
¡YO PERDURARÉ!
¡YO PERDURARÉ!

Copyright © 1978 George Ballis/Take Stock, San Rafael, California.

Copyright © 1978 George Ballis/Take Stock, San Rafael, California.

RESPONDING OPTIONS

FROM PERSONAL RESPONSE *TO* CRITICAL ANALYSIS

REFLECT 1. What immediate thoughts or questions do you have after reading these excerpts? Write them in your notebook.

RETHINK 2. What kind of revolution do you think the speaker is calling for? Explain.

3. Whom or what do you think Joaquín represents?

   Consider
   - who the speaker says he is
   - the references to the past and future

4. In lines 9–23, the speaker suggests that economic success is incompatible with cultural and spiritual survival. What do you think of this idea? Give reasons for your answer.

5. Analyze this poem as an effort to persuade. Who do you believe is the intended audience, and what do you think the poet wants the audience to do, think, or feel?

6. Think about the things that the speaker takes pride in. How do they compare with the points you listed before reading?

RELATE 7. In your opinion, how do the ideas expressed in *I Am Joaquín* relate to people who are not Chicano?

ANOTHER PATHWAY

Cooperative Learning

Many theater groups have performed dramatizations of *I Am Joaquín.* With a group of classmates, plan and present a dramatic reading of these excerpts from the poem. Consider assigning different voices or groups of voices to different phrases or verses.

LITERARY CONCEPTS

I Am Joaquín is subtitled *An Epic Poem.* An **epic poem** is a long narrative poem on a serious subject presented in an elevated or formal style. An epic traces the adventures of a hero whose actions consist of courageous, even superhuman, deeds. Such deeds often represent the ideals and values of a group of people, such as a nation or a race. What aspects of an epic poem do you recognize in the excerpts from *I Am Joaquín* presented here? If you can get a copy of the full text of the poem, read it and look for epic elements.

QUICKWRITES

1. *I Am Joaquín* was first published in 1967. Based on the excerpts you have read, how relevant do you believe the poem is today? Explain your opinion in a **book review.**

2. Create a verse or two of **poetry** that expresses the pride of a group that you feel part of. As an alternative, your verses could deal with a personal moment of pride, such as the topic of your writing on page 243.

***PORTFOLIO** Save your writing. You may want to use it later as a springboard to a piece for your portfolio.*

ALTERNATIVE ACTIVITIES

1. Design a **book jacket** for a new edition of *I Am Joaquín.*
2. Imagine that *I Am Joaquín* is to be distributed as an audio book. Choose or compose pieces of **background music** that you think would be good accompaniment to sections of the poem.

CRITIC'S CORNER

In his introduction to *I Am Joaquín,* Rodolfo Gonzales has written, "Ultimately, there are no revolutions without poets." What do you think he means by this? In what way would *I Am Joaquín* contribute to a revolution?

LITERARY LINKS

Of the other works in this part of the unit, "The Right to Be Free," which do you think is closest in spirit to *I Am Joaquín?* Defend your choice.

ACROSS THE CURRICULUM

History One critical event of the Chicano movement was the farm workers' strike, *La Huelga.* What was it like to be a migrant farm worker before the strike? How are conditions different now? Find out more about the lives of migrant workers at the time of the strike and about their lives today. Present your findings in the form of a chart or an oral report.

Cesar Chavez. AP/Wide World Photos.

Foreign Language Compare the English and Spanish versions of the poem. Do you notice words that are similar in the two languages? Are there similarities in word order? If you know some Spanish, explain to your classmates some basic rules of the Spanish language.

RODOLFO GONZALES

A poet and a leader of the Chicano movement, Rodolfo "Corky" Gonzales (born 1928) has devoted his life to promoting the pride and power of the Chicano people. He founded the Crusade for Justice, an organization based in Denver, Colorado, to promote political action among Chicano youth. During the 1968 Poor People's March, Gonzales presented the "Plan of the Barrio," a declaration demanding rights for Chicanos. Later, the Crusade for Justice proposed "The Spiritual Plan of Aztlán," which identified the Southwestern United States as Aztlán, the mythical place of origin of the Aztecs. By linking Chicano identity to pre-Columbian history, Gonzales connected modern Chicano concerns to the long history of the Chicano people.

Born in Denver to a family of migrant workers, Gonzales began working in the fields in the spring and summer by the time he was ten. During the fall and winter, he went to public school in Denver, graduating from high school at age 16. Gonzales, a skilled boxer, won a Golden Gloves championship and a National Amateur Athletic Union championship, then turned professional. Before he retired from the ring in 1955, he was a contender for the world featherweight championship.

After he left professional boxing, Gonzales became active in politics. He organized the Viva Kennedy presidential campaign in Colorado during the 1960 elections and subsequently served in a variety of government posts. In 1966, however, he left government service to devote himself full time to promoting Chicano issues. Through the Crusade for Justice, he published *El Gallo,* an activist newspaper, and founded Escuela Tlatelolco, a school for Chicano students, from preschool to college, providing formal education in the context of Chicano awareness and pride.

First published in 1967, *I Am Joaquín/Yo Soy Joaquín* grew out of Gonzales's social and political concerns. It is at once an epic poem and a call to action for Chicano people.

SUZIE WONG DOESN'T LIVE HERE

Diane Mei Lin Mark

suzie wong doesn't live here

Illustration Copyright © 1990 Kinuko Y. Craft.

In this poem, Diane Mei Lin Mark contrasts stereotypical images of submissive Asian women with the strong Asian-American women of today. She begins with a reference to the main character in the popular novel The World of Suzie Wong *by Richard Lakin Mason. Suzie Wong is a Chinese prostitute living in Hong Kong who falls in love with and marries an English painter. Mark then mentions the tragic Japanese heroine of Puccini's opera* Madame Butterfly, *who falls in love with an American naval officer and kills herself after he abandons her. The poet also refers to geisha ladies, Japanese women who are trained to entertain and provide company for men.*

Suzie Wong
doesn't live here anymore
yeah, and
Madame Butterfly
and the geisha ladies have all
gone
to
lunch (hey, they might
be gone a very
long
time)

no one here
but
ourselves

stepping on,
without downcast eyes,
without calculating dragon power,
without tight red cheongsams[1]
embroidered with peonies
without the
silence
that you've come to
know so well
and we,
to feel so alien with

seeing each other at last
so little needs to be explained

there is this strength

born female in Asian America,
our dreams stored years
in the backrooms
of our minds

now happening—
like sounds of flowers
bathed in noontime light
reaching righteously skyward!

1. **cheongsams** (chĕ-ong′sam′): high-necked, close-fitting dresses with a side-slit skirt, traditionally worn by women in China and Hong Kong.

Diane Mei Lin Mark

Asian-American poet Diane Mei Lin Mark lives in Hawaii. Her educational background includes a bachelor's degree in English and Asian Studies from Mills College and a master's degree in American Studies from the University of Hawaii. Mark also studied filmmaking at New York University and has worked as a newspaper reporter and an oral history researcher. She served as a writer and an associate producer of PEARLS, a documentary film series about Asian Americans that aired on public television. She co-produced the movie *Picture Bride.* She has written two books on Chinese-American history and has published poetry in *Asian Women, Third World Women, Asian Americans in Hawaii, Impulse, and Breaking Silence: An Anthology of Contemporary Asian American Poets.*

WRITING FROM

EXPERIENCE

Writing to Persuade

In Unit Two, "From Colony to Country," people used sermons, essays, speeches, and letters to argue for or against individual freedom. Their persuasive methods ranged from reasoned statements to fiery rhetoric. Persuasion shows the power of language to stir people's emotions and motivate them to take action in support of a cause or an idea.

GUIDED ASSIGNMENT

Write a Persuasive Piece Throughout your life, you'll find many opportunities to use persuasive writing to take a stand on an issue. You may write a letter to the editor, a proposal, an essay, a leaflet or brochure, or a speech. This lesson helps you explore how to write an effective persuasive piece.

Chart

What reasons might people have to want certain books removed from schools? Why do you think these books were singled out?

1 Explore the Questions

Today, people still argue about individual freedom versus the rights of society. What issues of personal liberty are important to you—human rights? freedom of speech? personal privacy? To generate a list of ideas, look through current magazines and newspapers, brainstorm with your classmates, or review the literature to find an author's opinion about individual freedom.

Buttons

These can reflect your stand on an issue.

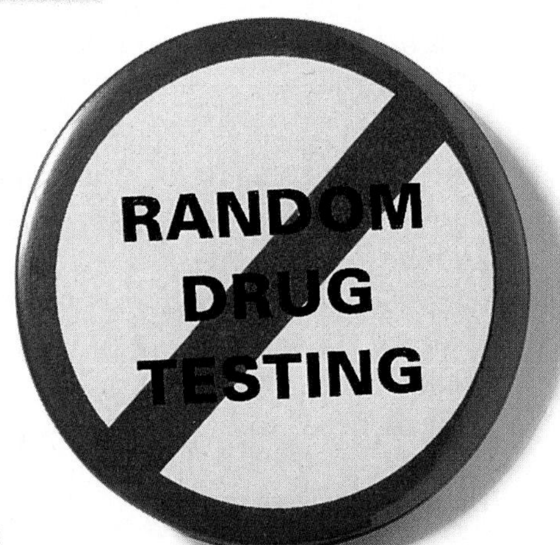

2 Examine the Issues

Each of the issues portrayed in the items on these pages involves personal liberty. Use these or one of the ideas on your list to complete the following activities. You can record your answers in your notebook.

Identify the Issue In a few words, identify the issue raised by each item.

Point Out Bias Do you see any evidence of bias in these items? List the clues that might indicate a biased view.

Evaluate the Data Jot down your questions about each item, as one student did about the censorship articles.

WHAT JOHNNY SHOULDN'T READ?

Most Frequently Challenged Books, 1992–1993
Books that parents most often want removed from public schools.

Scary Stories to Tell in the Dark, Alvin Schwartz
The Bridge to Terabithia, Katherine Paterson
The Catcher in the Rye, J. D. Salinger
The Boy Who Lost His Face, Louis Sachar
Of Mice and Men, John Steinbeck
Halloween ABC, Eve Merriam

What were their reasons? Maybe some articles really were unsuitable.

Newspaper Articles

Student Press Is Hamstrung, Report Says

The Freedom Forum, an international journalism foundation, reports that high school newspapers across the country have lost monetary support while school administrators increasingly censor their stories. According to Judith D. Hines, who helped organize the report, "High school newspapers are dying a slow death." In a survey of 270 high school newspaper advisers, 37 percent said that school principals had rejected newspaper articles or required changes in content.

What does "negative" content mean? What makes a story "too negative"?

Bad News for School Paper

As of Thursday, May 8, Ridley High School no longer has a school newspaper. Administrators cited "too many stories with negative content" as the reason for shutting down the paper. The paper's editor, senior Jenine Hastings, said, "We have real problems in our school and community, and the paper should report them." School officials stated that a 1988 Supreme Court ruling had given them the power to control school newspaper content.

Did court ruling really say this?

❸ What Do *YOU* Think?

Choose one or two topic ideas from your list or from these pages. In your notebook, freewrite your opinions for or against the issues. The topics should be ones you genuinely care about.

LASERLINKS
- *WRITING SPRINGBOARD*

WRITING COACH

PREWRITING

Gathering Information

Building Your Argument Persuasive writing is not simply a statement of your opinion. You are trying to convince the reader to agree with your point of view. To be convincing, you need logic as well as emotion, facts as well as opinions, and a clear knowledge of opposing points of view.

1 Identify the Issue and Your Questions

Choose one topic from your list that appeals to you the most. You can use a graphic organizer to examine your topic. In the word web at the right, the writer is questioning censorship of the student newspaper.

This exercise reveals what you already know and believe about an issue and what more you need to learn. (See the SkillBuilder for a discussion of the difference between fact and opinion.)

Student's Response Web

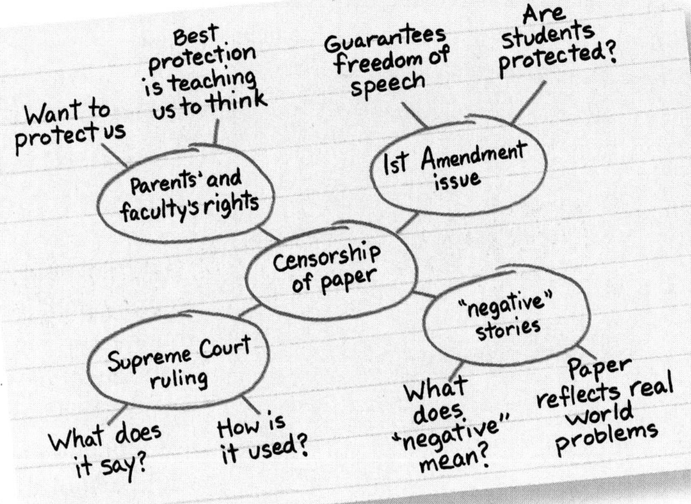

The writer draws on prior knowledge and personal opinions to generate a first response to the issue.

2 Research the Issue

You can conduct research to fill in any gaps in your knowledge of the issue or in your initial logic or arguments. Keep an open mind. As you uncover more facts, you may change your stand on an issue.

Explore Print Media and On-line Databases Look through these resources for articles offering various positions on your issue.

Interview Experts You may be able to talk with teachers, lawyers, activists, and others to learn more about your issue and to discover different viewpoints.

Contact Public Agencies and Private Groups Your teacher or the reference librarian can help you contact organizations such as the Freedom Forum, the American Civil Liberties Union, and law associations. These sources are particularly helpful for topics dealing with personal liberties.

❸ Read and Listen Critically

Keep these tips in mind as you conduct your research.

Don't Assume Anything Commonly accepted "facts" and opinions that "everyone knows" may not be true after all.

Evaluate Your Sources Statistics, facts, and surveys can be used by both sides. Be sure you use a variety of sources, watch out for author bias, and double check your facts.

Role-Play Different Sides For example, in the censorship issue, you and others might role-play the parents' and principal's sides to understand their arguments and viewpoints.

❹ Organize Your Findings

Once you have gathered enough information, you can begin to organize your persuasive arguments. In the example below, the writer uses a chart to list the administration's arguments and her own counterarguments regarding censorship.

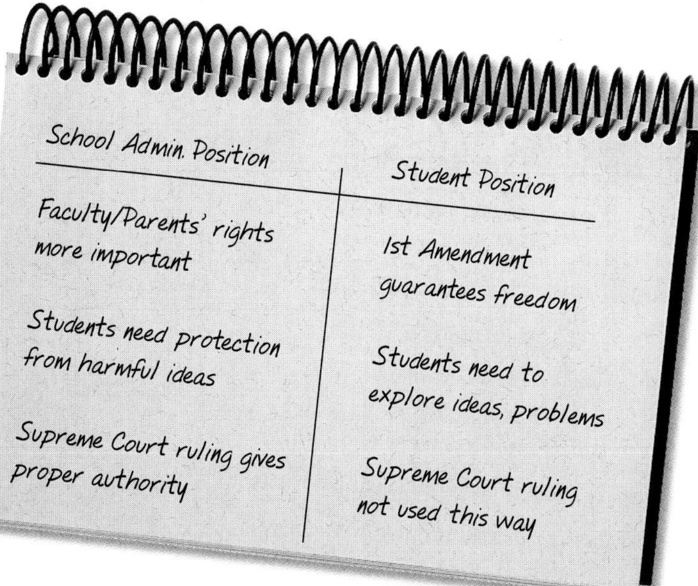

School Admin. Position
Student Position
Faculty/Parents' rights more important
1st Amendment guarantees freedom
Students need protection from harmful ideas
Students need to explore ideas, problems
Supreme Court ruling gives proper authority
Supreme Court ruling not used this way

❺ Formalize Your Opinion

By now you should have an opinion on the issue. Try stating it in a brief sentence. For instance, "Censorship is generally wrong, but the principal may be right about some articles."

SkillBuilder

CRITICAL THINKING

Distinguishing Fact from Opinion

Remember that a fact is a statement that can be proved. An opinion is a statement that cannot be proved. Compare these examples:

Fact	The First Amendment protects individual freedom of speech.
Opinion	Freedom of speech should never be restricted.

You can verify facts by reference to a recognized expert or authoritative written source, such as the Bill of Rights in this case, or by personal observation.

Opinions cannot be proved but can be well supported by facts. In developing opinions, be sure you include all the facts in a case, not just the ones that support your views. You can signal an opinion statement by introducing it with a phrase such as "I feel," "it seems," "in my opinion," or "some experts believe."

THINK & PLAN

Reflecting on Your Topic

1. What do you still need to know to understand your issue?
2. What are the main opposing points of view?
3. Which of your sources presents the most balanced viewpoint?

DRAFTING

Getting Your Ideas Down

Developing a Persuasive Piece To write an effective persuasive piece, you need to clarify your purpose for writing, identify the needs of your audience, and organize your main points.

1 Identify Your Purpose

Do you want people to think or act differently or to take some action? In the student draft shown here, the writer jots down the purpose and audience, then explores how to present the argument to appeal to the readers. This student writer may use a letter or pamphlet form. See Share Your Work, page 261, for other ideas.

Student's Discovery Draft

I want people to write or call the principal so we can publish our paper again. General public may not know about the paper being shut down—have to tell them the facts. I can use alternating arguments to show I understand both sides of the issue.

Make this a pamphlet for our rally! We can hand it out. Watch the tone—keep it positive!

~~1~~ 2. **Principal says:** Too many stories in student newspaper focused on negative content. He says stories should inspire students, not talk about problems all the time. **Students say:** Definition of "negative" is based on personal taste or opinion, not facts. There are problems in school and community students need to explore and learn about.

make this first

~~2~~ 1. Tell how we heard the news through student grapevine that the paper was shut down because stories were too "negative." This violates First Amendment rights and restricts personal liberties.

3. **Principal, parents say:** They have right to monitor what is taught or written in our schools and they want to protect us from harmful ideas and influences. **Students say:** Best protection is teaching us how to think for ourselves, not censoring what we can say or read. We know more than adults give us credit for. Most importantly—censorship goes against First Amendment rights and weakens educational system that principal is supposed to support.

Mention Supreme Court ruling on control of student publications first.

2 Identify Your Audience and Tone

Your persuasive piece must address the attitudes and beliefs of your audience and strike the right tone to persuade them to agree with you. Try asking yourself the following questions:

- What does the audience need to know about the issue?
- What tone—serious, humorous, formal, informal, or some other—will best appeal to this audience? See the SkillBuilder for hints on word choice.
- How strongly will they agree or disagree with what I say? What common ground do we have?
- What do I want them to do?
- Can I use bulleted lists, graphics, or charts to present data?

3 Choose an Organizing Structure

Whether you're writing an essay, a letter, a pamphlet, or something else, try one of the following organizing structures or look in the Writing Handbook (page 1179) for more suggestions.

State One Side First All the arguments of one side are given first, followed by the counterarguments, building from the least to the most important points.

Alternate Arguments Each opposing argument is followed by the counterargument (building from least to most important). The student writer used this format to show her understanding of the issues.

Use Problem-Solution Structure The writer states the problem, analyzes it from various viewpoints, then recommends a solution.

PEER RESPONSE

Peer reviewers can point out the strengths and weaknesses of your draft. Remind them to focus on the paper and not to debate the issue. You might ask them these questions:

- In a few words, what is my position on this issue?
- Which arguments did you find most or least convincing?
- What other viewpoints or arguments should I include?
- Is it clear what I want the reader to do? Why or why not?

SkillBuilder

WRITER'S CRAFT

Choosing Words Carefully: Denotation and Connotation

Denotation refers to the literal or dictionary meaning of a word.

Connotation refers to the feelings and suggested behaviors associated with a word. For example:

*Principal Reed is a **stern** person.*
*Principal Reed is a **harsh** person.*

Although the denotative meanings of *stern* and *harsh* are the same, their connotative meanings differ. ***Harsh*** has many more negative associations, implying the person is excessively severe.

Connotative meanings can make the tone of your writing more positive or negative. However, be careful using this technique. It should be used sparingly and not to manipulate readers.

APPLYING WHAT YOU'VE LEARNED
Be sure your persuasive language adds emphasis without manipulating or alienating the reader.

RETHINK & EVALUATE

Preparing to Revise

1. What organizing structure best fits your topic and purpose?
2. How can you use tone to appeal to your audience?
3. Have you presented a balance of opposing viewpoints?

Finishing Your Work

Polishing Your Writing Before presenting your persuasive piece, make sure you have checked your logic, examined your use of persuasive language, met the needs of your audience, and made corrections based on your peer response. The tips on these pages can help you catch any errors that could weaken or invalidate your persuasive writing.

1 Revise and Edit

Let the draft "cool off" before you reread it. You can use the suggestions below, the Standards for Evaluation, and the Editing Checklist to help you catch mistakes.

- Your organizing structure should help you present your issue and arguments in the strongest light.
- Be sure your tone matches your audience.
- Check your logic to be sure the reader can follow your reasoning point by point.
- Review your facts, opinions, and examples for accuracy, and verify your sources.

What techniques does the writer use to hook the reader's interest? What else does the writer accomplish by using a pamphlet format?

The writer summarizes the main points and tells the reader what to do in response.

Student's Pamphlet

A persuasive piece written as a pamphlet can be part of a more active form of persuasion, as shown on these two pages.

FREEDOM

FREEDOM OF THE PRESS? NOT HERE!

What if someone shut down your daily newspaper because it printed too many "negative" stories?

That's what happened to the student newspaper at Ridley High School.

On May 8, Principal Reed suspended the *Ridley Reporter* for printing too many "negative" stories—including one about students helping the homeless!

Principal Reed says:

- Students need to focus on "good news" not "bad news." Articles should be inspiring, not talk about problems.
- A 1988 Supreme Court ruling gives administrators the right to control content of student publications.
- Faculty and parents are responsible for educating and protecting students.

Ridley Students Say:

- "Bad news" is a matter of opinion, not fact. We need to learn about the problems in our world.
- The ruling said that control of content had to be related to an educational issue, not personal opinion or taste.
- The best protection is teaching us to think for ourselves, not censoring our paper.

We realize not every student article should be printed. But Principal Reed's actions challenge the First Amendment guarantees of freedom of expression.

Please call or write Principal Reed. Urge him to reinstate our paper and restore our freedom of speech!

2 Share Your Work

You can present your persuasive piece in several ways, depending on the topic and your purpose for writing.

- Leaflets, pamphlets, flyers can be used for rallies, meetings, mass mailings; readers can take material with them.
- An article or a letter in the local paper can reach a broad audience and go into more detail about the issues.
- E-mail on Internet to other high schools can reach a wide high school audience but not the general public.

Standards for Evaluation

Persuasive writing
- hooks the reader with a strong introduction and clearly states the issue and writer's position
- presents other points of view and counterarguments
- uses strong evidence to support the writer's position
- summarizes main points or arguments and states any call to action in the conclusion
- uses language and details appropriate for the audience

SkillBuilder

WRITER'S CRAFT

Using Transition Words
Words such as *before, after, first, second, finally, most important,* and *in conclusion* can help guide your reader through your argument point by point. Transition words are used to link ideas within paragraphs and to link one paragraph to another.

HANDBOOKS

See transition words in the Writing Handbook, page 1169.

Editing Checklist Use the following revising and editing tips.

- Have I used transitions and order words to clarify points?
- Have I used persuasive language to add emphasis?
- Did I use correct punctuation?
- Have I proofread my draft?

REFLECT & ASSESS

Learning from Experience

1. Write a brief paragraph on how well you feel you accomplished your goal.
2. What skills did you use in writing this piece that might help you in your other classes? How can you improve the process next time?

PORTFOLIO List what you found easiest and hardest to do in this lesson. Add your list and final work to your portfolio.

REFLECT & ASSESS

UNIT 2: FROM COLONY TO COUNTRY

As a result of reading the selections in this unit, have you gained any new insights into the principles and beliefs of the Puritans and the American revolutionaries? What did you learn about the power of persuasion as you read the examples of persuasive writing? Choose one or more of the options in each of the following sections to explore what you've learned.

REFLECTING ON THE UNIT

OPTION 1 **Strong Beliefs** Many of the selections in this unit express the strong religious and political beliefs held by early Americans. List some of these beliefs, noting the people or groups who supported them. Which of the beliefs do you agree with most? Which do you disagree with? In a few paragraphs, identify your choices and explain why you chose them.

OPTION 2 **The American Way** With a small group of classmates, discuss the principles and values that you believe were the most important in the creation of the United States as a nation. Are those principles and values still important today? Use examples from the selections to support your opinions, but also draw on your previous knowledge.

OPTION 3 **To Form a More Perfect Union** Choose four or more writers from this unit, both historical and contemporary, that have had the greatest influence on your opinions about the values central to American democracy. Using the ideas of these writers as support, write a letter to the President of the United States, commenting on the current government's moral and political policies.

REFLECT & ASSESS *Self-Assessment: To document what you have learned by reading the selections in this unit, make a list of the insights into the development of the nation that you have gained.*

REVIEWING LITERARY CONCEPTS

OPTION 1 **Analyzing Persuasion** Most of the selections in this unit contain persuasive arguments. Make a chart like the one shown here, noting the main points of the writer's argument in each selection you have read. Also note how each writer attempts to persuade the reader—for example, by appeals to reason or emotion, by biblical allusions, by loaded language, or by rhetorical questions. Then write a short paragraph explaining which two or three arguments you found most persuasive and why.

Selection	Points Argued For	Author's Persuasive Tactics
"Speech in the Virginia Convention"	The need to arm and fight the British	Biblical allusions, rhetorical questions, appeals to patriotism, appeals to reason

OPTION 2 **Evaluating Tone** You have learned that tone is the attitude that a writer or speaker takes toward his or her subject. Which selections in this unit have the most serious tone? Which ones have a light or gently ironic tone? With a partner, make a list classifying the tones of the selections. Then discuss how the author's tone can affect the persuasiveness of his or her argument.

Self-Assessment: Look over the following list of literary terms introduced in this unit. Then, on a sheet of paper, list four or five terms that you understand well and four or five that you feel you need to learn more about. Get together with a small group of classmates to help one another learn the terms.

meter	*figurative language*
objectivity	*metaphor*
loaded language	*simile*
connotations	*theme*
situational irony	*diction*
allusion	*epic poem*

PORTFOLIO BUILDING

- **QuickWrites** Several of the QuickWrites in this unit asked for your personal responses to the beliefs and principles presented in the selections. Choose the response that best expresses your opinion about a belief or principle important to you, and explain your choice in a cover note. Attach the note to the response and put them in your portfolio.
- **Writing About Literature** In a recent public-opinion poll, it was found that public speaking was the experience people feared the most. How did you react to preparing and delivering your speech? Do you feel that you have become a better reader, writer, or speaker? Why or why not?
- **Writing from Experience** Now that you have written a persuasive piece about an issue you care about, pretend that you hold an opposing point of view on the same issue. What arguments would you use to persuade someone that your new point of view is the right one? Would your audience be different? If so, how would the difference influence what and how you wrote? Include your thoughts with your writing if you choose to keep it in your portfolio.
- **Personal Choice** Think about the activities and short writing assignments that you have completed for this unit or on your own. Which one taught you the most about the beginnings of this country? Write a note that explains your choice, attach it to the piece of writing or your record of the activity, and add both to your portfolio.

Self-Assessment: Now that you have some pieces of writing in your portfolio, look them over and decide which kinds of writing contain your strongest work. Are you most proud of a personal response? a poem? a letter? a character analysis? What kinds of writing would you like more practice in as the year goes on?

SETTING GOALS

Look back through this unit's selections, your portfolio, and your notebook, identifying the literary genres that you would like to read more examples of or would like to experiment within your writing.

The Spirit of Individualism

If a man does not keep pace
with his companions,
perhaps it is because
he hears a different drummer.
Let him step to the music
which he hears, however measured
or far away.

HENRY DAVID THOREAU

Naturalist and writer

The Wanderer (1818), Caspar David Friedrich. Kunsthalle, Hamburg, Germany, Bridgeman/Art Resource, New York.

TIME LINE

The Spirit of Individualism

The Cherokee were forced to relocate despite a Supreme Court ruling stating that the tribe formed a separate nation independent of state laws. Unlike many Native Americans, the Cherokee had successfully adopted Anglo ways, turning from a hunting to a farming society, establishing schools and manufacturing shops, and creating a written language and newspaper. About 4,000 Cherokee died during their forced relocation from Georgia to the Oklahoma territory on what has since become known as the Trail of Tears.

1803

President Thomas Jefferson doubles the size of the United States by buying the Louisiana territory from Napoleon Bonaparte of France.

1804

Meriwether Lewis and William Clark begin their explorations of the Louisiana territory and beyond to the Pacific coast.

1814

After witnessing a naval battle during the War of 1812, Francis Scott Key composes "The Star-Spangled Banner."

1820

The Missouri Compromise prohibits slavery in western territory north of Missouri's southern border and allows slavery in the Arkansas territory and in Louisiana.

1824

Sequoyah creates the first written Native American language, Cherokee.

1825

The Erie Canal, a 363-mile waterway linking Lake Erie with the Hudson River, is completed.

1827

Freedom's Journal, the first African-American newspaper, is founded.

1830

The Indian Removal Act authorizes the relocation of southeastern Native American tribes—including the Cherokee, Chickasaw, Choctaw, Creek, and Seminole—to the territories west of the Mississippi.

1831

William Lloyd Garrison begins publishing *The Liberator,* a militant antislavery newspaper.

THE LIBERATOR.

1836

The Transcendental Club, which includes Ralph Waldo Emerson, Nathaniel Hawthorne, Henry David Thoreau, and others, meets for the first time.

Period *Pieces*

1837

John Deere produces his first steel-bladed plow, which makes large-scale farming possible in the heavy soil of the Midwest and West.

1844

Samuel F. B. Morse sends the first telegraph message from Washington, D.C., to Baltimore.

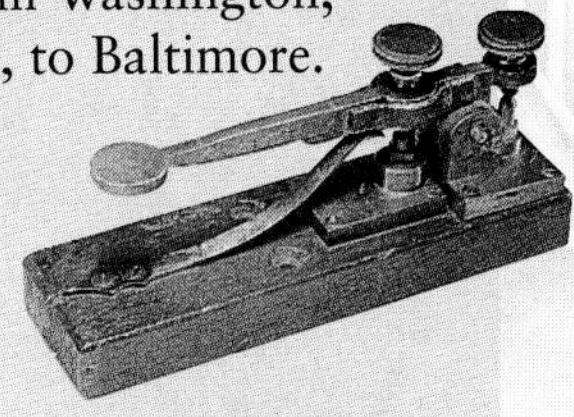

1848

The United States defeats Mexico in the Mexican War and claims land that is now Nevada, California, and part of New Mexico and Arizona.

Henry David Thoreau spent one night in jail for refusing to pay a tax that he felt would be used to support the institution of slavery and to finance the war with Mexico. Legend has it that Ralph Waldo Emerson visited Thoreau in jail and asked, "Why are you here?" Thoreau replied, "Why are you not here?"

1848

Gold discoveries in California lead to the first gold rush.

1850

Congress passes the Fugitive Slave Act, forcing officials in Northern states to return escaped slaves to their owners.

In 1840 a group of American women were denied seats as delegates to the World Antislavery Convention. Lucretia Mott and Elizabeth Cady Stanton decided to organize a women's rights convention to denounce such unfair legal restrictions on women. Eight years later, the first women's rights convention was held in Seneca Falls, New York. The keynote speaker was the well-known abolitionist Frederick Douglass.

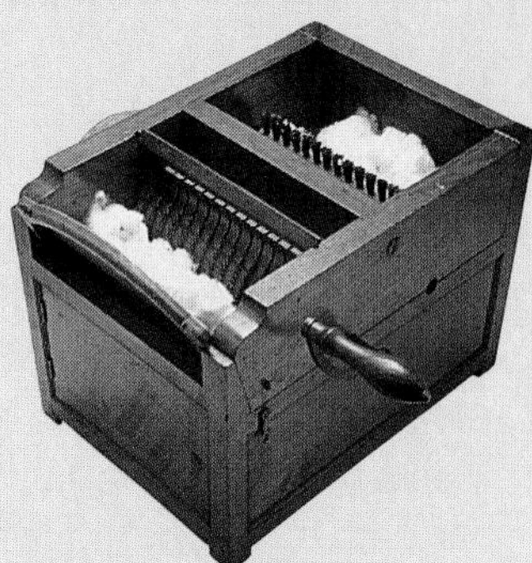

The cotton gin invented by Eli Whitney in 1793

Levi Strauss designed the first blue jeans for prospectors in the 1850's.

Mahogany tall-case clock

PART 1 INTRODUCTION

Celebrations of the Self

Romanticism and Transcendentalism

"Good men must not obey the laws too well," Ralph Waldo Emerson said. His aphorism illustrates a vital key to the American character—after all, if the original colonists *had* obeyed the laws, the American Revolution would never have occurred, and the country might never have existed. This rebelliousness—so much a part of our heritage—reflects an essential aspect of Emerson's philosophy of transcendentalism, a distinctively American offshoot of the romantic movement.

Around the beginning of the 19th century, the movement known as romanticism sprang up in both Europe and America as a reaction to everything that had come before it: the rationalism of the 18th-century

Ralph Waldo Emerson

American Authors of the 19th-century. *Seated from left:* Henry Wadsworth Longfellow, William Cullen Bryant, Washington Irving (at the end of the table), and Margaret Fuller (slightly behind Irving). *Seated in right foreground:* Harriet Beecher Stowe. *Standing from left:* Edgar Allan Poe (in profile facing left) and Nathaniel Hawthorne (in profile facing right). *Standing from right:* James Russell Lowell (with beard facing front) and Ralph Waldo Emerson. The Bettmann Archive.

Age of Reason and, especially in America, the strict doctrines of Puritanism. Romantic artists, philosophers, and writers saw the limitations of reason and celebrated instead the glories of the individual spirit, the emotions, and the imagination as basic elements of human nature. The splendors of nature inspired the romantics more than the fear of God, and some of them felt a fascination with the supernatural.

In the first half of the century, as the U.S. population exploded and the country's borders spread westward, the romantic spirit guided American writers in their efforts to capture the energy and character of the new country. Henry Wadsworth Longfellow and Washington Irving were by far the most popular American writers of the time. Their works exhibit a typical romantic preoccupation with atmosphere, sentiment, and optimism.

Henry Wadsworth Longfellow

Although Washington Irving was the first American writer to achieve international fame, the first really distinctive American literature came from the transcendentalists. The philosophy of transcendentalism, derived in part from German romanticism, was based on a belief that "transcendent forms" of truth exist beyond reason and experience. However, Ralph Waldo Emerson gave this philosophy a peculiarly American spin: he said that every individual is capable of discovering this higher truth on his or her own, through intuition.

Washington Irving

Voices *from the* Times

The groves were God's first temples.
Ere man learned
To hew the shaft, and lay the architrave,
And spread the roof above them—ere
he framed
The lofty vault, to gather and roll back
The sound of anthems; in the darkling
wood,
Amid the cool and silence, he knelt down,
And offered to the Mightiest solemn thanks
And supplication.

William Cullen Bryant
from "A Forest Hymn"

By the shores of Gitche Gumee,
By the shining Big-Sea-Water,
Stood the wigwam of Nokomis,
Daughter of the Moon, Nokomis.
Dark behind it rose the forest,
Rose the black and gloomy pine-trees,
Rose the firs with cones upon them;
Bright before it beat the water,
Beat the clear and sunny water,
Beat the shining Big-Sea-Water.

Henry Wadsworth Longfellow
from *The Song of Hiawatha*

Who goes there? hankering, gross,
mystical, nude;
How is it I extract strength from the
beef I eat?
What is a man anyhow? what am I?
what are you?

Walt Whitman
from "Song of Myself"

Voices *from the* Times

It was a high counsel that I once heard given to a young person, "Always do what you are afraid to do."

Ralph Waldo Emerson

Call me Ishmael. Some years ago—never mind how long precisely—having little or no money in my purse, and nothing particular to interest me on shore, I thought I would sail about a little and see the watery part of the world. It is a way I have of driving off the spleen, and regulating the circulation. Whenever I find myself growing grim about the mouth; whenever it is a damp, drizzly November in my soul; whenever I find myself involuntarily pausing before coffin warehouses, and bringing up the rear of every funeral I meet; and especially whenever my hypos [hypochondria] get such an upper hand of me, that it requires a strong moral principle to prevent me from deliberately stepping into the street, and methodically knocking people's hats off—then, I account it high time to get to sea as soon as I can.

Herman Melville
from *Moby-Dick*

Henry David Thoreau, Emerson's younger friend and colleague, proved a prickly but brilliant embodiment of transcendentalist ideals as, militantly turning his back on material rewards, he devoted his life to the study of nature and his own individual spirit. His *Walden,* an account of the two years he lived alone in a one-room shack in the country (although dining regularly at Emerson's Boston house), remains a genuine American masterwork.

Walt Whitman was championed at the beginning of his career by Emerson for the ideas and style that Emerson believed the new American poetry required. Still, influential as Whitman has been in the 20th century, he waited a long time for his contribution to be recognized by the larger public in his own time. In 1855 he had to print the first collection of his poems, *Leaves of Grass,* himself. Able to sell only a few copies of the book, he gave virtually all of the 795 copies away. Meanwhile the same year of 1855, Longfellow published *The Song of Hiawatha,* which like his earlier books of poetry, sold thousands and became a bestseller.

Continuity & Change: New Expressions of the Self

The celebration of individualism that began with romanticism and flourished with transcendentalism has remained at the core of American literature to the present day. During the first half of the 20th century, the poetry of William Carlos Williams and E. E. Cummings, among others, emphasized the spirit and power of solitary individuals. Contemporary writers, however, tend to temper their celebrations of the individual with more ambiguity. Rosario and Aurora Morales, for instance, try to find a new unity in their separate voices as mother and daughter, and the poet Luis J. Rodriguez makes readers view his eccentric aunt with a mixture of admiration and shock. The down-home voice of Garrison Keillor is shaped by the humorous ironies that are a trademark of our time.

PART 1 # *Celebrations of the Self*

Romanticism and Transcendentalism

Continuity & Change New Expressions of the Self

PREVIEWING

POETRY

A Psalm of Life

Henry Wadsworth Longfellow

PERSONAL CONNECTION

Each of the quotations on this page presents a way of looking at life. Which one comes closest to expressing your own philosophy of life? Copy it down in your notebook and add a few more lines to elaborate its meaning.

The life which is unexamined is not worth living.
Plato

To be what we are, and to become what we are capable of becoming, is the only end of life.
Robert Louis Stevenson

Life is far too important a thing ever to talk seriously about.
Oscar Wilde

Life is like a box of chocolates. You never know what you're going to get.
Forrest Gump

BIOGRAPHICAL CONNECTION

Henry Wadsworth Longfellow was the most popular and famous member of a group of New England romantic writers known as the Fireside Poets—a group that also included Oliver Wendell Holmes, James Russell Lowell, and John Greenleaf Whittier. The name of the group refers to a popular family pastime of the period: reading poetry aloud in front of the fireplace after dinner. Longfellow and his fellow Fireside Poets wrote poems that were morally uplifting and often sentimental.

One summer morning, Longfellow wrote "A Psalm of Life" in the blank spaces of an invitation. After it was published in *Knickerbocker* magazine in October 1838, the poem swept the country and became known around the world. Although widely parodied, even by Longfellow himself, it celebrates an optimistic view of life and reflects the aims of Americans at the time.

READING CONNECTION

Appreciating Rhyme and Rhythm
Much of the poetry written by the Fireside Poets contains obvious patterns of end rhyme (rhyming of words at the end of lines) and regular meter (a repeated sequence of stressed and unstressed syllables). As you read "A Psalm of Life," note its patterns of rhyme and meter. Look for a pattern of end rhymes in each group of four lines. To hear the meter of the poem, read it aloud or tap the rhythm out as you read the poem silently to yourself.

• *BIOGRAPHICAL CONNECTION*

A Psalm of Life

HENRY WADSWORTH LONGFELLOW

En Mer [At sea] (1898), Max Bohm. Courtesy of Alfred J. Walker Fine Art, Boston.

What the Heart of the Young Man Said to the Psalmist[1]

Tell me not, in mournful numbers,[2]
Life is but an empty dream!—
For the soul is dead that slumbers,
And things are not what they seem.

Life is real! Life is earnest!
And the grave is not its goal;
Dust thou art, to dust returnest,
Was not spoken of the soul.

Not enjoyment, and not sorrow,
Is our destined end or way;
But to act, that each tomorrow
Find us farther than today.

Art is long, and Time is fleeting,
And our hearts, though stout and brave,
Still, like muffled drums, are beating
Funeral marches to the grave.

In the world's broad field of battle,
In the bivouac[3] of Life,
Be not like dumb, driven cattle!
Be a hero in the strife!

Trust no Future, howe'er pleasant!
Let the dead Past bury its dead!
Act—act in the living Present!
Heart within, and God o'erhead!

Lives of great men all remind us
We can make our lives sublime,[4]
And, departing, leave behind us
Footprints on the sands of time;

Footprints, that perhaps another,
Sailing o'er life's solemn main,[5]
A forlorn and shipwrecked brother,
Seeing, shall take heart again.

Let us, then, be up and doing,
With a heart for any fate;
Still achieving, still pursuing,
Learn to labor and to wait.

---

1. **Psalmist** (sä′mĭst): the author of the poems in the biblical Book of Psalms, many of which comment on the fleeting nature of life. Traditionally, most of the psalms have been ascribed to King David of Israel.
2. **numbers:** metrical feet or lines; verses.
3. **bivouac** (bĭv′o͞o-ăk′): a temporary encampment of troops.
4. **sublime:** of high spiritual, moral, or intellectual worth.
5. **main:** open ocean.

RESPONDING OPTIONS

FROM PERSONAL RESPONSE *TO* CRITICAL ANALYSIS

REFLECT 1. What are your thoughts about this poem? Record them in your notebook.

RETHINK 2. The psalms in the Bible are actually songs. If "A Psalm of Life" were to be sung, what style of music do you think would fit best with the poem's theme? Explain your choice.

3. How does the speaker's view of life compare with your own view?
Consider
- what the speaker says life is *not*
- his command "Act—act in the living Present!" (line 23)
- the last four lines of the poem
- the thoughts you recorded for the Personal Connection on page 272

4. In your own words, summarize what the speaker says about the value of the lives of great people (lines 25–32). Do you agree with the speaker? Explain.

5. During his lifetime, Longfellow's poetry was extremely popular in America and abroad. On the basis of your reading of "A Psalm of Life," what do you think made Longfellow's poetry so popular?

RELATE 6. Do you think that Americans today share the values expressed in "A Psalm of Life"? Point out lines in the poem that you think contemporary Americans might or might not agree with.

ANOTHER PATHWAY

Cooperative Learning

Work with a small group of classmates to create a bumper sticker that expresses the philosophy of life suggested by the poem. Present your bumper sticker to the class and explain why it is appropriate.

QUICKWRITES

1. How do you think life should be lived? Think about what you wrote for the Personal Connection and how you responded to question 3. In a **personal response** to Longfellow, perhaps in the form of a poem, explain your philosophy of life.

2. "A Psalm of Life" is among the most parodied poems in the English language. Here is an example by Harriet Fleischman:

    Lives of great men all remind us
    As we history's pages turn
    That we often leave behind us
    Letters which we ought to burn.

   Write a stanza or two of **parody** in the style of "A Psalm of Life."

PORTFOLIO Save your writing. You may want to use it later as a springboard to a piece for your portfolio.

LITERARY CONCEPTS

As you probably know, a **stanza** is a group of lines that forms a unit in a poem. "A Psalm of Life" is written in four-line stanzas. A **rhyme scheme** is the pattern of end rhyme in a stanza or a poem. In the first stanza of "A Psalm of Life," which words at the ends of the lines rhyme?

You can chart the rhyme scheme of a stanza or a poem by using letters (beginning with *a*) to designate the lines, assigning the same letter to lines that rhyme. Here is the first stanza of an Anne Bradstreet poem:

In silent night when rest I **took** a
For sorrow near I did not **look** a
I wakened was with thund'ring **noise** b
And piteous shrieks of dreadful **voice.** b
That fearful sound of "Fire!" and **"Fire!"** c
Let no man know is my **desire.** c

Notice that the letters change each time the end rhyme changes. The rhyme scheme of this poem is *aabbcc.*

Identify the rhyme scheme used in "A Psalm of Life" by charting it for the first two stanzas. Then look at the poem as a whole. What words or ideas does the rhyme scheme emphasize?

ALTERNATIVE ACTIVITIES

1. With a partner, present an **interview** of Longfellow by a TV talk-show host. In it, Longfellow might be asked what he meant to convey in this poem or what he thinks about various aspects of modern American life.
2. Find a **photograph** or an **illustration** that suggests an idea or theme in "A Psalm of Life." Combine the images found by the class to create a bulletin-board collage.

LITERARY LINKS

How do you think either Anne Bradstreet (page 148) or Jonathan Edwards (page 160) might have responded to the ideas presented in "A Psalm of Life"?

HENRY WADSWORTH LONGFELLOW

1807–1882

Henry Wadsworth Longfellow, the most famous American poet of the 1800s, had a career that spanned more than 50 years. His first poem was published in a Maine newspaper when he was 13. Two years later, he entered Bowdoin College, where, like his classmate Nathaniel Hawthorne, he decided to become a writer. From college, Longfellow wrote his father, "I most eagerly aspire after further eminence in literature." Although he eventually was to more than fulfill his aspirations, he did not achieve literary eminence for some years.

A brilliant scholar, the 18-year-old Longfellow was offered Bowdoin's first established professorship in modern languages when he graduated in 1825. Since the field was so new, he had to create his own textbooks. Several years later he accepted a similar position at Harvard, where he remained until 1854, when he resigned to write full time.

Longfellow's first book of poetry, *Voices of the Night,* was published when he was 32. As his popularity grew, many of his poems became household favorites. A beloved poet and a scholar able to speak and read ten languages, Longfellow was respected all over the world. He was the first American writer to be honored with a bust in the Poets' Corner of London's Westminster Abbey.

OTHER WORKS *The Courtship of Miles Standish, Evangeline, Paul Revere's Ride, The Song of Hiawatha, Tales of a Wayside Inn*

PREVIEWING

FICTION

The Devil and Tom Walker

Washington Irving

PERSONAL CONNECTION

Should people pursue wealth? Why or why not? How important is wealth to you? What limits, if any, would you put on your own pursuit of wealth? Answer these questions in your notebook, then discuss your answers with a small group of classmates.

HISTORICAL CONNECTION

The first American writer esteemed abroad, Washington Irving is known for his humorous essays and stories. In "The Devil and Tom Walker," Irving adapted the Germanic legend of Johann Faust, a 16th-century magician and alchemist who was said to have sold his soul to the devil in exchange for worldly power and wealth. For his comic retelling, Irving created an American character who strikes the same bargain and faces the same consequences in an American setting. The story takes place in the environs of Boston in the early 1700s, when the Puritans still dominated Massachusetts society.

READING CONNECTION

Interpreting Imagery

Imagery consists of words and phrases that appeal to the five senses, helping the reader to imagine precisely what people and things are like. Think of imagery as a multimedia program in your mind. The pictures, sounds, physical sensations, and sometimes tastes and smells that you imagine as you read can help you interpret what is going on in a story.

For example, imagery can help you understand more about **characters.** Consider the sentences from the second paragraph of "The Devil and Tom Walker" in the box on the right. Notice that the reader is *told* that Tom Walker and his wife are miserly, but the images of the forlorn house, the straggling trees, the starved horse, and the thinly-grown field *show* just how miserly they are. Which form of presentation do you think has a greater impact on you as a reader—the statements or the images? Either way, you learn an important aspect of Tom's character.

> . . . there lived near this place a meager, miserly fellow, of the name of Tom Walker. He had a wife as miserly as himself. . . . They lived in a forlorn-looking house that stood alone and had an air of starvation. A few straggling savin trees, emblems of sterility, grew near it; no smoke ever curled from its chimney; no traveler stopped at its door. A miserable horse, whose ribs were as articulate as the bars of a gridiron, stalked about a field, where a thin carpet of moss . . . tantalized and balked his hunger; and sometimes he would lean his head over the fence, look piteously at the passerby and seem to petition deliverance from this land of famine.

Another important function of imagery is to help create a story's **mood,** or atmosphere. Images can be used to evoke a certain feeling in the reader, such as warmth, hilarity, or suspense. For example, the image of the hungry horse adds to the humor of the passage you just read. Examine the next boxed description from "The Devil and Tom Walker" to see how imagery contributes to its creepy, threatening mood.

Because there is so much description in "The Devil and Tom Walker," an understanding of the story's imagery is crucial to an understanding of the story—and to an enjoyment of its humor. As you read, try to visualize the images. If you like, draw quick sketches in your notebook to help you get their full impact. Notice particular sounds, physical sensations, and smells, and write down your emotional reactions to them. Then, after you finish the story, look back over your notes to help deepen your interpretation. Ask yourself these questions about the images in each passage: Are they related in any way? What ideas do I associate with them? Do they help develop character, mood, plot, or theme? Share your thoughts with your classmates.

On the basis of these images marked in green, what do you visualize "this treacherous forest" to look like? What would it feel like to be there?

> The swamp was thickly grown with great gloomy pines and hemlocks, some of them ninety feet high, which made it dark at noonday, and a retreat for all the owls of the neighborhood. It was full of pits and quagmires, partly covered with weeds and mosses, where the green surface often betrayed the traveler into a gulf of black, smothering mud; there were also dark and stagnant pools, the abodes of the tadpole, the bullfrog, and the water snake; where the trunks of pines and hemlocks lay half-drowned, half-rotting, looking like alligators sleeping in the mire.

What do you feel when you think of these particular creatures marked in purple? What sounds might some of them make?

The Devil and Tom Walker

Washington Irving

A few miles from Boston in Massachusetts, there is a deep inlet, winding several miles into the interior of the country from Charles Bay, and terminating in a thickly wooded swamp or morass. On one side of this inlet is a beautiful dark grove; on the opposite side the land rises abruptly from the water's edge into a high ridge, on which grow a few scattered oaks of great age and immense size. Under one of these gigantic trees, according to old stories, there was a great amount of treasure buried by Kidd the pirate. The inlet allowed a facility to bring the money in a boat secretly and at night to the very foot of the hill; the elevation of the place permitted a good lookout to be kept that no one was at hand; while the remarkable trees formed good landmarks by which the place might easily be found again. The old stories add, moreover, that the devil presided at the hiding of the money and took it under his guardianship; but this, it is well-known, he always does with buried treasure, particularly when it has been ill-gotten. Be that as it may, Kidd never returned to recover his wealth; being shortly after seized at Boston, sent out to England, and there hanged for a pirate.

About the year 1727, just at the time that earthquakes were prevalent in New England, and shook many tall sinners down upon their knees, there lived near this place a meager, miserly fellow, of the name of Tom Walker. He had a wife as miserly as himself: they were so miserly that they even conspired to cheat each other. Whatever the woman could lay hands on, she hid away; a hen could not cackle but she was on the alert to secure the new-laid egg. Her husband was continually prying about to detect her secret hoards, and many and fierce were the conflicts that took place about what ought to have been common property. They lived in a forlorn-looking house that stood alone and had an air of starvation. A few straggling savin trees, emblems of sterility, grew near it; no smoke ever curled from its chimney; no traveler stopped at its door. A miserable horse, whose ribs were as articulate as the bars of a gridiron,[1] stalked about a field, where a thin carpet of moss, scarcely covering the ragged beds of puddingstone,[2] tantalized and balked his hunger; and sometimes he would lean his head over the fence, look piteously at the passerby and seem to petition deliverance from this land of famine.

The house and its inmates had altogether a bad name. Tom's wife was a tall termagant,[3] fierce of temper, loud of tongue, and strong of arm. Her voice was often heard in wordy warfare with her husband; and his face sometimes showed signs that their conflicts were not confined to words. No one ventured, however, to interfere between them. The lonely wayfarer shrunk within himself at the horrid clamor and clapper-clawing;[4] eyed the den of discord askance;[5] and hurried on his way, rejoicing, if a bachelor, in his celibacy.

One day that Tom Walker had been to a distant part of the neighborhood, he took what he considered a shortcut homeward, through the swamp. Like most shortcuts, it was an ill-chosen route. The swamp was thickly grown with great

---

1. **as articulate . . . gridiron:** as clearly separated as the bars of a grill.
2. **puddingstone:** a rock consisting of pebbles and gravel cemented together.
3. **termagant** (tûr′mə-gənt): a quarrelsome, scolding woman.
4. **clapper-clawing:** scratching or clawing with the fingernails.
5. **eyed . . . askance** (ə-skăns′): looked disapprovingly at the house filled with arguing.

gloomy pines and hemlocks, some of them ninety feet high, which made it dark at noonday, and a retreat for all the owls of the neighborhood. It was full of pits and quagmires, partly covered with weeds and mosses, where the green surface often betrayed the traveler into a gulf of black, smothering mud; there were also dark and stagnant pools, the abodes of the tadpole, the bullfrog, and the water snake; where the trunks of pines and hemlocks lay half-drowned, half-rotting, looking like alligators sleeping in the mire.

Tom had long been picking his way cautiously through this treacherous forest; stepping from tuft to tuft of rushes and roots, which afforded precarious footholds among deep sloughs; or pacing carefully, like a cat, along the prostrate trunks of trees; startled now and then by the sudden screaming of the bittern,[6] or the quacking of wild duck rising on the wind from some solitary pool. At length he arrived at a firm piece of ground, which ran out like a peninsula into the deep bosom of the swamp. It had been one of the strongholds of the Indians during their wars with the first colonists. Here they had thrown up a kind of fort, which they had looked upon as almost impregnable, and had used as a place of refuge for their squaws and children. Nothing remained of the old Indian fort but a few embankments, gradually sinking to the level of the surrounding earth, and already overgrown in part by oaks and other forest trees, the foliage of which formed a contrast to the dark pines and hemlocks of the swamp.

It was late in the dusk of evening when Tom Walker reached the old fort, and he paused there awhile to rest himself. Anyone but he would have felt unwilling to linger in this lonely, melancholy place, for the common people had a bad opinion of it, from the stories handed down from the time of the Indian wars, when it was asserted that the savages held incantations[7] here, and made sacrifices to the evil spirit.

Tom Walker, however, was not a man to be troubled with any fears of the kind. He reposed himself for some time on the trunk of a fallen hemlock, listening to the boding cry of the tree toad, and delving with his walking staff into a mound of black mold at his feet. As he turned up the soil unconsciously, his staff struck against something hard. He raked it out of the vegetable mold, and lo! a cloven skull, with an Indian tomahawk buried deep in it, lay before him. The rust on the weapon showed the time that had elapsed since this death-blow had been given. It was a dreary memento of the fierce struggle that had taken place in this last foothold of the Indian warriors.

"Humph!" said Tom Walker, as he gave it a kick to shake the dirt from it.

"Let that skull alone!" said a gruff voice. Tom lifted up his eyes, and beheld a great black man seated directly opposite him, on the stump of a tree. He was exceedingly surprised, having neither heard nor seen anyone approach; and he was still more perplexed on observing, as well as the gathering gloom would permit, that the stranger was neither Negro nor Indian. It is true he was dressed in a rude half-Indian garb, and

6. **bittern:** a wading bird with mottled, brownish plumage and a deep, booming cry.

7. **incantations:** verbal charms or spells recited to produce a magic effect.

WORDS TO KNOW

abode (ə-bōd') *n.* a dwelling place; home
melancholy (mĕl'ən-kŏl'ē) *adj.* gloomy; sad
repose (rĭ-pōz') *v.* to rest or relax

had a red belt or sash swathed round his body; but his face was neither black nor copper-color, but swarthy and dingy, and begrimed with soot, as if he had been accustomed to toil among fires and forges. He had a shock of coarse black hair, that stood out from his head in all directions, and bore an ax on his shoulder.

He scowled for a moment at Tom with a pair of great red eyes.

"What are you doing on my grounds?" said the black man, with a hoarse, growling voice.

"Your grounds!" said Tom, with a sneer, "no more your grounds than mine; they belong to Deacon Peabody."

"Deacon Peabody be d—d," said the stranger, "as I flatter myself he will be, if he does not look more to his own sins and less to those of his neighbors. Look yonder, and see how Deacon Peabody is faring."

Tom looked in the direction that the stranger pointed, and beheld one of the great trees, fair and flourishing without, but rotten at the core, and saw that it had been nearly hewn through, so that the first high wind was likely to blow it down. On the bark of the tree was scored the name of Deacon Peabody, an eminent man, who had waxed wealthy by driving shrewd bargains with the Indians. He now looked around, and found most of the tall trees marked with the name of some great man of the colony, and all more or less scored by the ax. The one on which he had been seated, and which had evidently just been hewn down, bore the name of Crowninshield; and he recollected a mighty rich man of that name, who made a vulgar display of wealth, which it was whispered he had acquired by buccaneering.[8]

"He's just ready for burning!" said the black man, with a growl of triumph. "You see, I am likely to have a good stock of firewood for winter."

"But what right have you," said Tom, "to cut down Deacon Peabody's timber?"

8. **buccaneering:** robbing ships at sea; piracy.

"The right of a prior claim," said the other. "This woodland belonged to me long before one of your white-faced race put foot upon the soil."

"And pray, who are you, if I may be so bold?" said Tom.

"Oh, I go by various names. I am the wild huntsman in some countries; the black miner in others. In this neighborhood I am he to whom the red men consecrated this spot, and in honor of whom they now and then roasted a white man, by way of sweet-smelling sacrifice. Since the red men have been exterminated by you white savages, I amuse myself by presiding at the persecutions of Quakers and Anabaptists;[9] I am the great patron and prompter of slave dealers, and the grand master of the Salem witches."

"The upshot of all which is that, if I mistake not," said Tom, sturdily, "you are he commonly called Old Scratch."[10]

"The upshot of all which is that, if I mistake not," said Tom, sturdily, "you are he commonly called Old Scratch."

"The same, at your service!" replied the black man, with a half-civil nod.

Such was the opening of this interview, according to the old story; though it has almost too familiar an air to be credited. One would think that to meet with such a singular personage, in this wild, lonely place, would have shaken any man's nerves; but Tom was a hard-minded fellow, not easily daunted, and he had lived so long with a termagant wife that he did not even fear the devil.

It is said that after this commencement they had a long and earnest conversation together, as Tom returned homeward. The black man told him of great sums of money buried by Kidd the pirate, under the oak trees on the high ridge, not far from the morass. All these were under his command, and protected by his power, so that none could find them but such as propitiated his favor. These he offered to place within Tom Walker's reach, having conceived an especial kindness for him; but they were to be had only on certain conditions. What these conditions were may be easily surmised, though Tom never disclosed them publicly. They must have been very hard, for he required time to think of them, and he was not a man to stick at trifles when money was in view. When they had reached the edge of the swamp, the stranger paused. "What proof have I that all you have been telling me is true?" said Tom. "There's my signature," said the black man, pressing his finger on Tom's forehead. So saying, he turned off among the thickets of the swamp, and seemed, as Tom said, to go down, down, down, into the earth, until nothing but his head and shoulders could be seen, and so on, until he totally disappeared.

When Tom reached home, he found the black print of a finger burnt, as it were, into his forehead, which nothing could obliterate.

The first news his wife had to tell him was the sudden death of Absalom Crowninshield, the rich buccaneer. It was announced in the papers

---

9. **presiding . . . Anabaptists:** exercising authority over the oppression of Christian groups that the Puritans considered radical.

10. **Old Scratch:** a nickname for the devil.

WORDS TO KNOW

singular (sĭng′gyə-lər) *adj.* unusual or remarkable; unique
daunted (dôn′tĭd) *adj.* intimidated or frightened **daunt** *v.*
surmise (sər-mīz′) *v.* to guess

with the usual flourish that "a great man had fallen in Israel."[11]

Tom recollected the tree which his black friend had just hewn down and which was ready for burning. "Let the freebooter[12] roast," said Tom; "who cares!" He now felt convinced that all he had heard and seen was no illusion.

He was not prone to let his wife into his confidence; but as this was an uneasy secret, he willingly shared it with her. All her avarice was awakened at the mention of hidden gold, and she urged her husband to comply with the black man's terms, and secure what would make them wealthy for life. However Tom might have felt disposed to sell himself to the devil, he was determined not to do so to oblige his wife; so he flatly refused, out of the mere spirit of contradiction. Many and bitter were the quarrels they had on the subject; but the more she talked, the more resolute was Tom not to be damned to please her.

At length she determined to drive the bargain on her own account, and if she succeeded, to keep all the gain to herself. Being of the same fearless temper as her husband, she set off for the old Indian fort toward the close of a summer's day. She was many hours absent. When she came back, she was reserved and sullen in her replies. She spoke something of a black man, whom she met about twilight hewing at the root of a tall tree. He was sulky, however, and would not come to terms; she was to go again with a propitiatory offering, but what it was she forbore to say.

The next evening she set off again for the swamp, with her apron heavily laden. Tom waited and waited for her, but in vain; midnight came, but she did not make her appearance; morning, noon, night returned, but still she did not come. Tom now grew uneasy for her safety, especially as he found she had carried off in her apron the silver teapot and spoons, and every portable article of value. Another night elapsed, another morning came; but no wife. In a word, she was never heard of more.

What was her real fate nobody knows, in consequence of so many pretending to know. It is one of those facts which have become confounded by a variety of historians. Some asserted that she lost her way among the tangled mazes of the swamp, and sank into some pit or slough; others, more uncharitable, hinted that she had eloped with the household booty and made off to some other province; while others surmised that the tempter had decoyed her into a dismal quagmire, on the top of which her hat was found lying. In confirmation of this, it was said a great black man, with an ax on his shoulder, was seen late that very evening coming out of the swamp, carrying a bundle tied in a check apron, with an air of surly triumph.

The most current and probable story, however, observes that Tom Walker grew so anxious about the fate of his wife and his property that he set out at length to seek them both at the Indian fort. During a long summer's afternoon he searched about the gloomy place, but no wife was to be seen. He called her name repeatedly, but she was nowhere to be heard. The bittern alone responded to his voice, as they flew screaming by; or the bullfrog croaked dolefully from a neighboring pool. At length, it is said, just in the brown hour of twilight, when the owls began to hoot, and the bats to flit about, his attention was attracted by the clamor of carrion crows[13] hovering about a cypress tree. He looked up, and beheld a bundle tied in a check apron, and hanging in the branches of the tree, with a great vulture perched hard by, as if

11. **a great man . . . Israel:** a biblical reference—"Know ye not that there is a prince and a great man fallen this day in Israel?" (2 Samuel 3:38)—used, with unconscious irony, by the papers to mean that an important member of God's people on earth has passed away.

12. **freebooter:** pirate.

13. **carrion crows:** crows that feed on dead or decaying flesh.

WORDS TO KNOW

resolute (rĕz′ə-lo͞ot′) *adj.* firm or determined; unwavering

dolefully (dōl′fə-lē) *adv.* mournfully

keeping watch upon it. He leaped with joy; for he recognized his wife's apron and supposed it to contain the household valuables. "Let us get hold of the property," said he consolingly to himself, "and we will endeavor to do without the woman."

As he scrambled up the tree, the vulture spread its wide wings, and sailed off screaming into the deep shadows of the forest. Tom seized the checked apron, but, woeful sight! found nothing but a heart and liver tied up in it!

Such, according to this most authentic old story, was all that was to be found of Tom's wife. She had probably attempted to deal with the black man as she had been accustomed to deal with her husband; but though a female scold is generally considered a match for the devil, yet in this instance she appears to have had the worst of it. She must have died game, however; for it is said Tom noticed many prints of cloven feet stamped upon the tree, and found handfuls of hair that looked as if they had been plucked from the coarse black shock of the woodman. Tom knew his wife's prowess by experience. He shrugged his shoulders, as he looked at the signs of a fierce clapper-clawing. "Egad," said he to himself, "Old Scratch must have had a tough time of it!"

Tom consoled himself for the loss of his property with the loss of his wife, for he was a man of fortitude. He even felt something like gratitude towards the black woodman, who, he considered, had done him a kindness. He sought, therefore, to cultivate a further acquaintance with him, but for some time without success; the old blacklegs played shy, for, whatever people may think, he is not always to be had for calling for: he knows how to play his cards when pretty sure of his game.

At length, it is said, when delay had whetted Tom's eagerness to the quick, and prepared him to agree to anything rather than not gain the promised treasure, he met the black man one evening in his usual woodsman's dress, with his ax on his shoulder, sauntering along the swamp, and humming a tune. He affected to receive Tom's advances with great indifference, made brief replies, and went on humming his tune.

By degrees, however, Tom brought him to business, and they began to haggle about the terms on which the former was to have the pirate's treasure. There was one condition which need not be mentioned, being generally understood in all cases where the devil grants favors; but there were others about which, though of less importance, he was inflexibly obstinate. He insisted that the money found through his means should be employed in his service. He proposed, therefore, that Tom should employ it in the black traffic; that is to say, that he should fit out a slave ship. This, however, Tom resolutely refused: he was bad enough in all conscience; but the devil himself could not tempt him to turn slave trader.

Finding Tom so squeamish on this point, he did not insist upon it, but proposed, instead, that he should turn usurer;[14] the devil being extremely

---

14. **usurer** (yo͞o′zhər-ər): one who lends money, especially at an unusually or unlawfully high rate of interest.

WORDS TO KNOW

prowess (prou′ĭs) *n.* superior strength, courage, or daring, especially in battle anxious for the increase of usurers, looking upon them as his peculiar people.

To this no objections were made, for it was just to Tom's taste.

"You shall open a broker's shop in Boston next month," said the black man.

"I'll do it tomorrow, if you wish," said Tom Walker.

"You shall lend money at two percent a month."

"Egad, I'll charge four!" replied Tom Walker.

"You shall extort bonds, foreclose mortgages, drive the merchants to bankruptcy—"

"I'll drive them to the d——l," cried Tom Walker.

"You are the usurer for my money!" said blacklegs with delight. "When will you want the rhino[15]?"

"This very night."

"Done!" said the devil.

"Done!" said Tom Walker. So they shook hands and struck a bargain.

A few days' time saw Tom Walker seated behind his desk in a countinghouse[16] in Boston.

His reputation for a ready-moneyed man, who would lend money out for a good consideration, soon spread abroad. Everybody remembers the time of Governor Belcher, when money was particularly scarce. It was a time of paper credit. The country had been deluged with government bills; the famous Land Bank[17] had been established; there had been a rage for speculating; the people had run mad with schemes for new settlements; for building cities in the wilderness; land-jobbers[18] went about with maps of grants, and townships, and Eldorados[19] lying nobody knew where, but which everybody was ready to purchase. In a word, the great speculating fever, which breaks out every now and then in the country, had raged to an alarming degree, and everybody was dreaming of making sudden fortunes from nothing. As usual the fever had subsided; the dream had gone off, and the imaginary fortunes with it; the patients were left in doleful plight, and the whole country resounded with the consequent cry of "hard times."

At this propitious time of public distress did Tom Walker set up as usurer in Boston. His door was soon thronged by customers. The needy and adventurous, the gambling speculator, the dreaming land-jobber, the thriftless tradesman, the merchant with cracked credit; in short, everyone driven to raise money by desperate means and desperate sacrifices hurried to Tom Walker.

Thus Tom was the universal friend of the needy and acted like a "friend in need"; that is to say, he always exacted good pay and good security. In proportion to the distress of the applicant was the hardness of his terms. He accumulated bonds and mortgages; gradually squeezed his customers closer and closer; and sent them at length, dry as a sponge, from his door.

In this way he made money hand over hand, became a rich and mighty man, and exalted his cocked hat upon 'Change.[20] He built himself, as usual, a vast house, out of ostentation; but left the greater part of it unfinished and unfurnished,

---

15. **rhino:** a slang term for money.
16. **countinghouse:** an office in which a business firm conducts its bookkeeping, correspondence, and similar activities.
17. **Land Bank:** Boston merchants organized the Land Bank in 1739. Landowners could take out mortgages on their property and then repay the loans with cash or manufactured goods. When the Land Bank was outlawed in 1741, many colonists lost money.
18. **land-jobbers:** people who buy and sell land for profit.
19. **Eldorados:** places of fabulous wealth or great opportunity. Early Spanish explorers sought a legendary country named El Dorado, which was rumored to be rich with gold.
20. **exalted . . . 'Change:** proudly raised himself to a position of importance as a trader on the stock exchange.

WORDS TO KNOW

peculiar (pĭ-kyo͞ol'yər) *adj.* belonging particularly or primarily to one person, group, or kind
propitious (prə-pĭsh'əs) *adj.* helpful or advantageous; favorable
ostentation (ŏs'tĕn-tā'shən) *n.* display meant to impress others; boastful showiness

out of parsimony. He even set up a carriage in the fullness of his vainglory,[21] though he nearly starved the horses which drew it; and as the ungreased wheels groaned and screeched on the axletrees, you would have thought you heard the souls of the poor debtors he was squeezing.

Tom's zeal became as notorious as his riches.

As Tom waxed old, however, he grew thoughtful. Having secured the good things of this world, he began to feel anxious about those of the next. He thought with regret on the bargain he had made with his black friend, and set his wits to work to cheat him out of the conditions. He became, therefore, all of a sudden, a violent churchgoer. He prayed loudly and strenuously, as if heaven were to be taken by force of lungs. Indeed, one might always tell when he had sinned most during the week, by the clamor of his Sunday devotion. The quiet Christians who had been modestly and stead-fastly traveling Zionward[22] were struck with self-reproach at seeing themselves so suddenly outstripped in their career by this new-made convert. Tom was as rigid in religious as in money matters; he was a stern supervisor and censurer of his neighbors, and seemed to think every sin entered up to their account became a credit on his own side of the page. He even talked of the expediency of reviving the persecution of Quakers and Anabaptists. In a word, Tom's zeal became as notorious as his riches.

Still, in spite of all this strenuous attention to forms, Tom had a lurking dread that the devil, after all, would have his due.[23] That he might not be taken unawares, therefore, it is said he always carried a small Bible in his coat pocket. He had also a great folio Bible on his counting-house desk, and would frequently be found reading it when people called on business; on such occasions he would lay his green spectacles in the book, to mark the place, while he turned round to drive some usurious bargain.

Some say that Tom grew a little crackbrained in his old days, and that fancying his end approaching, he had his horse new shod, saddled and bridled, and buried with his feet uppermost; because he supposed that at the last day the world would be turned upside down; in which case he should find his horse standing ready for mounting, and he was determined at the worst to give his old friend a run for it. This, however, is probably a mere old wives' fable. If he really did take such a precaution, it was totally superfluous; at least so says the authentic old legend, which closes his story in the following manner:

One hot summer afternoon in the dog days, just as a terrible black thundergust was coming up, Tom sat in his countinghouse, in his white linen cap and India silk morning gown. He was on the point of foreclosing a mortgage, by which he would complete the ruin of an unlucky land speculator for whom he had professed the greatest friendship. The poor land-jobber begged him to grant a few months' indulgence. Tom had grown testy and irritated, and refused another day.

"My family will be ruined and brought upon the parish," said the land-jobber. "Charity begins at home," replied Tom; "I must take care of myself in these hard times."

"You have made so much money out of me," said the speculator.

21. **vainglory:** boastful, undeserved pride in one's accomplishments or qualities.

22. **Zionward:** toward heaven.

23. **the devil . . . due:** a reference to the proverb "Give the devil his due," used to mean "Give even a disagreeable person the credit he or she deserves." Here, of course, the expression is used literally rather than figuratively.

WORDS TO KNOW

parsimony (pär'sə-mō'nē) *n.* extreme economy; stinginess

censurer (sĕn'shər-ər) *n.* one who expresses strong disapproval or harsh criticism

Tom lost his patience and his piety. "The devil take me," said he, "if I have made a farthing!"[24]

Just then there were three loud knocks at the street door. He stepped out to see who was there. A black man was holding a black horse, which neighed and stamped with impatience.

"Tom, you're come for," said the black fellow, gruffly. Tom shrank back, but too late. He had left his little Bible at the bottom of his coat pocket, and his big Bible on the desk buried under the mortgage he was about to foreclose; never was a sinner taken more unawares. The black man whisked him like a child into the saddle, gave the horse the lash, and away he galloped, with Tom on his back, in the midst of the thunderstorm. The clerks stuck their pens behind their ears, and stared after him from the windows. Away went Tom Walker, dashing down the streets; his white cap bobbing up and down, his morning gown fluttering in the wind, and his steed striking fire out of the pavement at every bound. When the clerks turned to look for the black man, he had disappeared.

Tom Walker never returned to foreclose the mortgage. A countryman, who lived on the border of the swamp, reported that in the height of the thundergust he had heard a great clattering of hoofs and a howling along the road, and running to the window caught sight of a figure, such as I have described, on a horse that galloped like mad across the fields, over the hills, and down into the black hemlock swamp toward the old Indian fort; and that shortly after a thunderbolt falling in that direction seemed to set the whole forest in a blaze.

The good people of Boston shook their heads and shrugged their shoulders, but had been so much accustomed to witches and goblins, and tricks of the devil, in all kinds of shapes, from the first settlement of the colony, that they were not so much horror-struck as might have been expected. Trustees were appointed to take charge of Tom's effects. There was nothing, however, to administer upon. On searching his coffers[25] all his bonds and mortgages were found reduced to cinders. In place of gold and silver, his iron chest was filled with chips and shavings; two skeletons lay in his stable instead of his half-starved horses, and the very next day his great house took fire and burnt to the ground.

Such was the end of Tom Walker and his ill-gotten wealth. Let all griping money brokers lay this story to heart. The truth of it is not to be doubted. The very hole under the oak trees whence he dug Kidd's money is to be seen to this day; and the neighboring swamp and old Indian fort are often haunted in stormy nights by a figure on horseback, in morning gown and white cap, which is doubtless the troubled spirit of the usurer. In fact the story has resolved itself into a proverb so prevalent throughout New England, of "The Devil and Tom Walker." ❖

24. **farthing:** a coin worth one-fourth of a penny, formerly used throughout the British Empire.

25. **coffers:** safes or strongboxes designed to hold money or other valuable items.

WORDS TO KNOW

piety (pī′ĭ-tē) *n.* religious devotion; reverence for God

RESPONDING OPTIONS

FROM PERSONAL RESPONSE *TO* CRITICAL ANALYSIS

REFLECT 1. What is your reaction to what happens to Tom Walker? Write your reaction in your notebook, then share your thoughts with classmates.

RETHINK 2. In your opinion, could Tom Walker have escaped the consequences of his bargain with Old Scratch? Why or why not?

3. What do you think are the features of Tom Walker's character that Irving especially wanted readers to notice? Which of these features are supported or enhanced by imagery?

4. Do you consider Tom Walker better or worse than the other prominent Puritans in Boston?

Consider

- the Puritans' treatment of Native Americans, Quakers, and Anabaptists
- what the marked trees in the swamp suggest about such respected Puritans as Deacon Peabody and Absalom Crowninshield
- why land speculators have "run mad with schemes for new settlements"
- how other Christians react to Tom's religious zeal

5. What do you think was Irving's purpose in writing this story?

RELATE 6. Driven by greed, Tom Walker literally sells his soul to gain wealth. Can you think of a real person or a character in a book or a film who reminds you of Tom Walker? Explain your choice.

ANOTHER PATHWAY

Cooperative Learning

With a small group of classmates, design a board game, a video game, or a computer game based on the major events and characters in "The Devil and Tom Walker." Use the imagery in the story to help you depict specific settings, such as Deacon Peabody's woods. In class, show the game and explain the rules.

QUICKWRITES

1. How might local newspaper headlines describe the events of this story? Write a few **headlines** that sum up what happens to Tom Walker. Share your headlines with the class.
2. Write a set of three **proverbs**—such as "Money is the root of all evil"—that help explain the lesson or moral of "The Devil and Tom Walker."
3. Drawing on your reading of this story and on your notes for the Personal Connection on page 276, draft a **persuasive essay** about the pursuit of wealth.

PORTFOLIO *Save your writing. You may want to use it later as a springboard to a piece for your portfolio.*

LITERARY CONCEPTS

For the Reading Connection on page 277, you were asked to pay close attention to the **imagery** in this story—the words and phrases that appeal to the senses. Identify vivid imagery in the following passages, and discuss its functions. In what ways does the imagery support characterization, mood, plot, or theme?

- the description of the trees marked with the names of men in the colony (page 281)
- the description of Tom's search for his wife in the forest (page 283)
- the description of Tom's house, horses, and carriage (page 279)
- the description of Tom's being carried off by the devil (page 287)

Another interesting element of this story is its **omniscient** (all-knowing) **narrator,** who stands outside the action of the story and reports what different characters are thinking. What seems to be the narrator's attitude toward the events of the story? Talk about what this type of narrator contributes to the story.

CRITIC'S CORNER

It has been noted that Washington Irving received critical acclaim as a writer because in his stories he managed to impart insights about human nature that were amusing without being too moralistic. Do you agree with this statement? Can you point to passages in "The Devil and Tom Walker" where Irving entertains, and to other passages where he enlightens?

THE WRITER'S STYLE

Writers use a variety of elements to create **humor,** including ridiculous characters, absurd situations and images, exaggeration, understatement, and situational irony (a contrast between what is expected to happen and what actually happens). What makes this story humorous? Share your ideas with the class.

ALTERNATIVE ACTIVITIES

1. Create a full-page **newspaper advertisement** for a movie version of "The Devil and Tom Walker." Suggest the theme of the story in your ad, and name the actors playing the major roles. Display your ad in the classroom.
2. Draw an annotated **map** showing the places where the events of this story take place. On your map, indicate the sequence of the events.
3. Create either a **three-dimensional model** or an **illustration** to bring to life one element of this story's setting. You might depict the Walkers' house, Deacon Peabody's woods, or Tom's countinghouse in Boston, for example.

ACROSS THE CURRICULUM

Economics Tom Walker becomes a usurer who lends money to people at a high rate of interest. Call a local bank to find out how to obtain a loan today. Ask about the process involved in getting a loan, the different kinds of loans that are available, the terms of different loans, and the current interest rates. In a chart or a table, record the information you gather. You may want to use a computer to create a spreadsheet display of the information.

Loans Available	Terms	Interest Rate
1.		
2.		
3.		
4.		

WORDS TO KNOW

EXERCISE A Review the Words to Know at the bottom of the selection pages. Then, for each item below, write the letter of the word pair that expresses a relationship similar to that of the capitalized pair.

1. ABODE : COTTAGE ::
   (a) nest : bird (c) vehicle : car
   (b) nail : hammer (d) trumpet : music
2. SINGULAR : ORDINARY ::
   (a) whole : complete (c) warm : hot
   (b) chapter : book (d) flexible : rigid
3. PIETY : NUN ::
   (a) poverty : banker (c) warmth : humidity
   (b) dishonesty : crook (d) simplicity : puzzle
4. DOLEFULLY : GRIEVE ::
   (a) loudly : whisper (c) joyfully : celebrate
   (b) humbly : brag (d) rapidly : stroll
5. OSTENTATION : FLAUNT ::
   (a) cowardice : sneak (c) give : generosity
   (b) love : emotion (d) humility : boast

EXERCISE B Write the vocabulary word, not used in Exercise A, that is suggested by each description below.

1. If you don't give way, give in, or give an inch, and you never say die, this describes you.
2. Facing a vicious dog or having to perform a solo could make a person feel this way.
3. Walking five miles to buy beans at a discount is an example of this.
4. This is someone who finds fault, comes down hard, and rakes people over the coals.
5. This is what sunny skies are for picnic planners, storm clouds are for farmers in need of rain.
6. Clues help a detective to do this about a suspect's guilt.
7. Listening to mournful music on a gray, cloudy day could make you feel this way.
8. Odysseus, Crazy Horse, Davy Crockett, and Hercules all had plenty of this.
9. One could tell workers to do this by saying "Take a break."
10. This could describe an accent, a style of dressing, or a way of celebrating a holiday.

WASHINGTON IRVING

1783–1859

Born at the end of the American Revolution and named after our first president, Washington Irving made many contributions to American literature. He set an example for humorous writing, pioneered the short story as a literary form, influenced important writers—particularly Nathaniel Hawthorne—and put America on the literary map.

While growing up in a large, prosperous New York family, Irving came to know American society intimately. Besides learning to appreciate literature, art, theater, and opera, he loved to explore the countryside along the Hudson River. Gifted with an eye for the pictorial, he considered painting as a career but instead used his talent to write about the American landscapes he knew so well.

Ironically, this first notable American writer spent much of his life abroad. After studying law for 6 years, Irving joined the family exporting business and was sent to work in its British office in 1815. Although the business failed, he stayed in Europe for the next 17 years, traveling extensively and serving as a U.S. diplomat.

Irving captured his European experiences in much of his writing, but American life provided him with some of his richest stories and most memorable characters. In *The Sketch Book of Geoffrey Crayon, Gent.* (1819–1820), he created the first distinctively American tales, such as "Rip Van Winkle" and "The Legend of Sleepy Hollow." Irving spent the last years of his life at his New York estate, Sunnyside, near his beloved Hudson River.

OTHER WORKS *Diedrich Knickerbocker's History of New York, Tales of a Traveller*

• *ART GALLERY*

PREVIEWING

NONFICTION

from Self-Reliance
Ralph Waldo Emerson

PERSONAL CONNECTION

What do you think *self-reliance* means? How self-reliant do you feel you are? What are some advantages and disadvantages of being self-reliant? Answer these questions in your notebook, then discuss your answers with a small group of classmates.

BIOGRAPHICAL CONNECTION

Ralph Waldo Emerson was one of 19th-century America's greatest writers and thinkers. In 1836, Emerson formed the Transcendental Club with a group of friends, including Henry David Thoreau and the feminist writer and critic Margaret Fuller. As the intellectual leader of the transcendentalists, he defined many of his original ideas in lectures, poems, and essays. This excerpt from Emerson's essay "Self-Reliance" is a series of loosely related thoughts and extracts from lectures and journals that Emerson had written in the years between 1832 and 1840. Published in 1841, the essay elaborates Emerson's belief in the importance of the individual.

Emerson and his friends amuse themselves in the summer at this philosopher's camp. Archive Photos.

READING CONNECTION

Summarizing Main Ideas To summarize a piece of writing is to state its main ideas briefly in your own words. After reading this excerpt from "Self-Reliance," try to summarize Emerson's major points. These guidelines might help you.

Guidelines for Summarizing

- As you read each paragraph, identify the one or two most important phrases or statements in it.
- Write a sentence of your own to express the main idea of each statement you identified.
- Try phrasing your sentences as pieces of advice to live by.

FROM

Self-Reliance

RALPH WALDO EMERSON

GUIDE FOR READING

There is a time in every man's education when he arrives at the conviction that envy is ignorance; that imitation is suicide; that he must take himself for better for worse as his portion; that though the wide universe is full of good, no kernel of nourishing corn can come to him but through his toil bestowed on that plot of ground which is given to him to till. . . .

Trust thyself: every heart vibrates to that iron string. Accept the place the divine providence has found for you, the society of your contemporaries, the connection of events. Great men have always done so, and confided themselves childlike to the genius of their age, betraying their perception that the absolutely trustworthy was seated at their heart, working through their hands, predominating in all their being. . . .

Whoso would be a man, must be a nonconformist. He who would gather immortal palms must not be hindered by the name of goodness, but must explore if it be goodness. Nothing is at last sacred but the integrity of your own mind. Absolve you to yourself, and you shall have the suffrage of the world. I remember an answer which when quite young I was prompted to make to a valued adviser who was wont to importune me with the dear old doctrines of the church. On my saying, "What have I to do with the sacredness of traditions, if I live wholly from within?" my friend suggested—"But these impulses may be from below, not from above." I replied, "They do not seem to me to be such; but if I am the Devil's child, I will live then from the Devil." No law can be sacred to me but that of my nature. Good and bad are but names very readily transferable to that or this; the only right is what is after my constitution; the only wrong what is against it. . . .

9 the divine providence: God.

12–13 betraying . . . trustworthy: revealing their awareness that God.

16 immortal palms: everlasting triumph and honor. In ancient times, people carried palm leaves as a symbol of victory, success, or joy.

19 suffrage: approval; support.

21 wont to importune me: accustomed to trouble me.

26–29 What is implied by Emerson's use of the word *sacred?* Why does he believe that one should follow his or her own nature?

29 after my constitution: consistent with my physical and mental nature.

WORDS TO KNOW

bestowed (bĭ-stōd') *adj.* applied; used **bestow** *v.*
predominate (prĭ-dŏm'ə-nāt') *v.* to have controlling power or influence
nonconformist (nŏn'kən-fôr'mĭst) *n.* one who does not follow generally accepted beliefs, customs, or practices
absolve (əb-zŏlv') *v.* to clear of guilt or blame

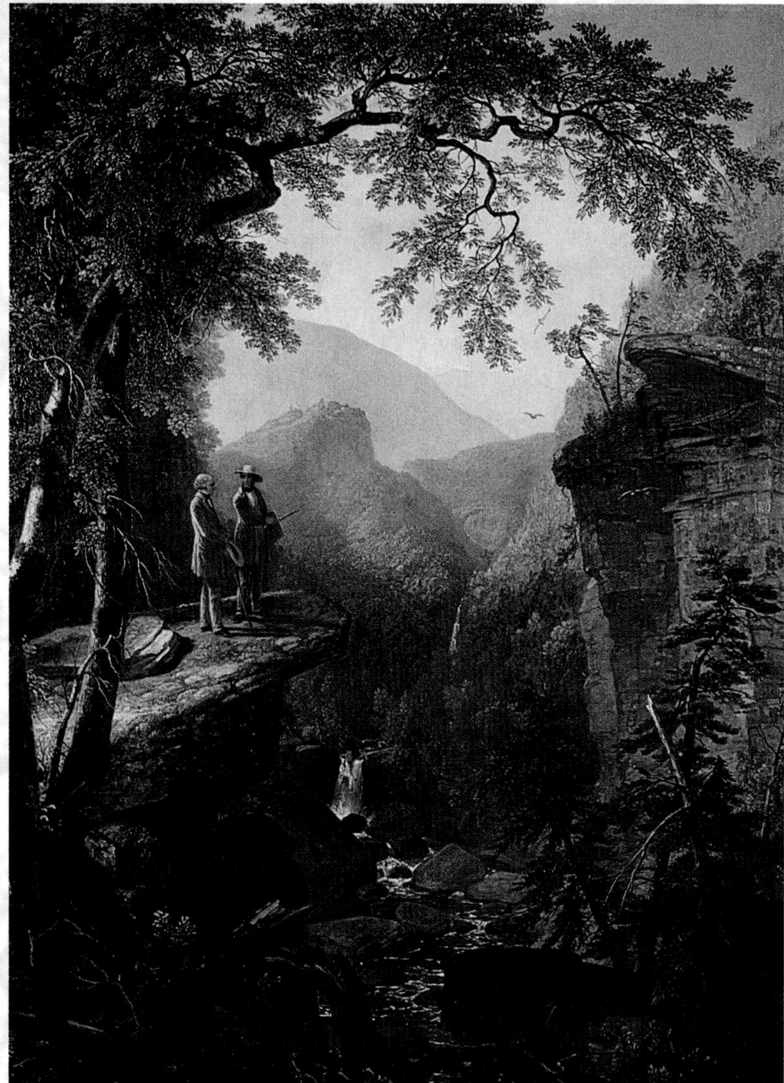

Kindred Spirits (1849), Asher B. Durand. Oil on canvas, collection of The New York Public Library, Astor, Lenox and Tilden Foundations.

What I must do is all that concerns me, not what the people think. This rule, equally arduous in actual and in intellectual life, may serve for the whole distinction between greatness and meanness. It is the harder because you will always find those who think they know what is your duty better than you know it. It is easy in the world to live after the world's opinion; it is easy in solitude to live after our own; but the great man is he who in the midst of the crowd keeps with perfect sweetness the independence of solitude. . . .

33 meanness: the state of being inferior in quality, character, or value.

35–38 What does Emerson say is easy to do? What does he say a great person is able to do?

For nonconformity the world whips you with its displeasure. And therefore a man must know how to estimate a sour face. The by-standers look askance on him in the public street or in the friend's parlor. If this aversion had its origin in contempt and resistance like his own he might well go home with a sad countenance; but the sour faces of the multitude, like their sweet faces, have no deep cause, but are put on and off as the wind blows and a newspaper directs. . . .

The other terror that scares us from self-trust is our consistency; a reverence for our past act or word because the eyes of others have no other data for computing our orbit than our past acts, and we are loth to disappoint them. . . .

A foolish consistency is the hobgoblin of little minds, adored by little statesmen and philosophers and divines. With consistency a great soul has simply nothing to do. He may as well concern himself with his shadow on the wall. Speak what you think now in hard words and to-morrow speak what to-morrow thinks in hard words again, though it contradict every thing you said today.—"Ah, so you shall be sure to be misunderstood."—Is it so bad then to be misunderstood? Pythagoras was misunderstood, and Socrates, and Jesus, and Luther, and Copernicus, and Galileo, and Newton, and every pure and wise spirit that ever took flesh. To be great is to be misunderstood. ❖

39–42 What does Emerson say is one consequence of being a nonconformist?

41 askance (ə-skăns'): with disapproval, suspicion, or distrust.

47–52 Why does consistency scare us from trusting ourselves?

50 loth (lōth): unwilling; reluctant.

51 hobgoblin: a source of fear or dread. Notice that Emerson does not criticize all consistency, only "foolish" consistency that does not allow for change or progress.

52 divines: religious leaders.

58–60 Pythagoras . . . Newton: great thinkers whose radical theories and viewpoints caused controversy.

INSIGHT

from Memoirs

MARGARET FULLER

In the chamber
of death, I prayed
in very early years,
"Give me truth;
cheat me by no illusion."
O, the granting of
this prayer is
sometimes terrible to me!
I walk over the
burning ploughshares,[1]
and they sear[2]
my feet. Yet nothing but
the truth will do.

1. **ploughshares** (plou'shârz'): the cutting blades of plows.
2. **sear:** scorch; burn.

WORDS TO KNOW

aversion (ə-vûr'zhən) *n.* a strong dislike

RESPONDING OPTIONS

FROM PERSONAL RESPONSE *TO* CRITICAL ANALYSIS

REFLECT **1.** Do you think you would like Emerson if you could meet him? Comment in your notebook.

RETHINK **2.** Summarize the main ideas of this selection. Use the sentences you wrote for the Reading Connection on page 291.

3. Tell whether you agree with each of these quotations from "Self-Reliance," and explain why or why not:

- "Envy is ignorance . . . imitation is suicide."
- "Nothing is at last sacred but the integrity of your own mind."
- "What I must do is all that concerns me, not what the people think."

RELATE **4.** Refer to what you wrote about self-reliance for the Personal Connection. How do the ideas in Emerson's essay compare with your own?

5. How do Margaret Fuller's ideas in the Insight poem on page 294 compare with Emerson's ideas in "Self-Reliance"?

6. Do you think the ideas that Emerson expressed in "Self-Reliance" would work for an entire nation?

7. Do you think that nonconformists are accepted today, or do they suffer society's ridicule? Explain.

ANOTHER PATHWAY

Cooperative Learning

Imagine that Emerson has come to you and asked for your help in bringing his message to an audience of contemporary teenagers. Work with a small group of classmates to "translate" each paragraph of the excerpt, stating Emerson's ideas more informally and using up-to-date examples.

LITERARY CONCEPTS

An **aphorism** is a brief statement, usually one sentence long, that expresses a general principle or truth about life. "Self-Reliance" is sprinkled with such memorable aphorisms as "A foolish consistency is the hobgoblin of little minds." Because aphorisms distill complex ideas into easy-to-remember statements, they may help you remember what Emerson is saying in his essay. With a small group of classmates, identify at least three aphorisms in "Self-Reliance" and discuss what they mean. Then compare Emerson's aphorisms with those from Benjamin Franklin's *Poor Richard's Almanack* on page 226.

QUICKWRITES

1. Choose your favorite aphorism from "Self-Reliance," and draft a **personal essay** to explain why it is significant to you. Support your explanation with examples drawn from your life.

2. Write an **aphorism** to summarize one of your own ideas about self-reliance, nonconformity, or greatness. Share your aphorism with the class.

3. Draft a **first-person account** of a time when you were self-reliant, or wished you had been.

PORTFOLIO *Save your writing. You may want to use it later as a spring-board to a piece for your portfolio.*

ALTERNATIVE ACTIVITIES

Ask an adult you know about a time when he or she chose to be a nonconformist, refusing to follow the crowd. What happened as a result? Share with the class the **anecdote** you are told.

ACROSS THE CURRICULUM

History In the last paragraph of the selection, Emerson names several people he considers great men. Choose one to learn more about and report to the class about your choice. After hearing reports on all these people, discuss what qualities make a person "great" in Emerson's opinion.

Galileo Galilei (1852), Samuel Sartain. Mezzotint, The Granger Collection, New York.

WORDS TO KNOW

Review the Words to Know at the bottom of the selection pages, then answer the following questions.

1. Would you be most likely to **bestow** a great deal of thought on a matter that revolted you, one that puzzled you, or one that bored you?
2. What is likely to be most important to a **nonconformist**—tradition, independence, or approval?
3. Is a person who **predominates** in too many situations wimpy, sneaky, or bossy?
4. If you have an **aversion** to a person, are you most likely to avoid the person, ignore the person, or seek the person out?
5. Is a judge most likely to **absolve** an accused criminal if the judge knows that the accused is guilty but sorry, guilty and not sorry, or completely innocent?

RALPH WALDO EMERSON

1803–1882

The distinguished poet, essayist, and lecturer Ralph Waldo Emerson was born in Boston, Massachusetts. As a child, he experienced illness, poverty, and the death of a parent. His father, a Unitarian minister, died when Emerson was 8 years old, and his mother struggled to raise five boys—including a mentally retarded son—alone. With the aid of several grants, however, Emerson was able to enter Harvard College when he was 14. To pay for other expenses, he worked as a tutor, a messenger, and a waiter at the college.

After graduating, Emerson taught for several years at his brother's school for girls. He returned to Harvard to study for the ministry and became a Unitarian minister in 1829. Unfortunately, his brief career as a minister was marred by religious doubt and by his wife's death in 1831. Because he felt that he could no longer perform certain church rituals in good faith, he resigned his ministry in 1832.

After traveling in Great Britain, France, and Italy for a year, Emerson returned to the United States to devote himself to lecturing and writing. In 1835, he remarried and settled in Concord, and a year later he celebrated the birth of his first child as well as the publication of his first book, *Nature.* Emerson soon became the spiritual voice of his generation and a major influence on future generations of writers.

OTHER WORKS *May-Day and Other Poems, Poems, The Conduct of Life*

LASERLINKS
• *HISTORICAL CONNECTION*

PREVIEWING

NONFICTION

from Walden

Henry David Thoreau

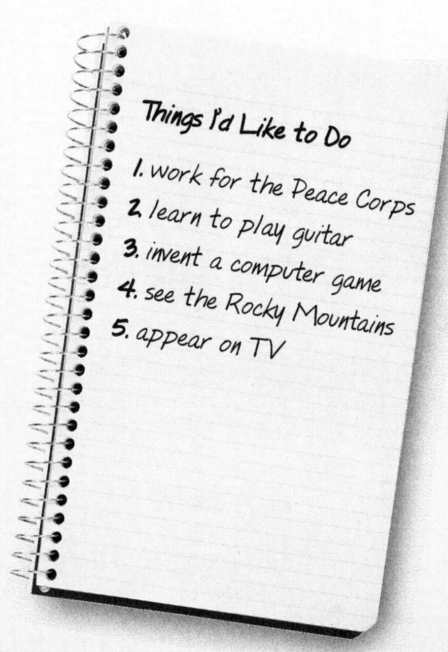

PERSONAL CONNECTION

What do you want to experience in your life? In your notebook, make a list of some experiences you look forward to. Then pick three of the experiences and explain to your classmates why you want to have each one.

BIOGRAPHICAL CONNECTION

Like Ralph Waldo Emerson and other transcendentalists, Thoreau felt a need to confirm his unity with nature. On July 4, 1845, he began his famous experiment in what he thought of as "essential" living—living simply, studying the natural world, and seeking truth within himself. On land owned by Emerson near Concord, Massachusetts, Thoreau built a small cabin by Walden Pond and lived there for more than two years, writing and studying nature. *Walden*—a mixture of philosophy, autobiography, and meditation upon nature—is the record of Thoreau's experiences at the pond.

Thoreau's cabin, 10 by 15 feet, was smaller than a one-car garage of today. The Bettmann Archive.

READING CONNECTION

Appreciating Aphorisms These excerpts from *Walden*, like the preceding excerpt from Emerson's "Self-Reliance," contain a number of aphorisms—brief statements that express general principles or truths about life. As you read the selection, look for some aphorisms that relate to your ideas and experiences. Jot them down in your notebook, and be prepared to share them with classmates.

FROM

Walden

HENRY DAVID THOREAU

FROM

Where I Lived, and What I Lived For

When first I took up my abode in the woods, that is, began to spend my nights as well as days there, which, by accident, was on Independence day, or the fourth of July, 1845, my house was not finished for winter, but was merely a defense against the rain, without plastering or chimney, the walls being of rough weather-stained boards, with wide chinks, which made it cool at night. The upright white hewn studs and freshly planed door and window casings gave it a clean and airy look, especially in the morning, when its timbers were saturated with dew, so that I fancied that by noon some sweet gum would exude from them. . . .

I was seated by the shore of a small pond, about a mile and a half south of the village of Concord and somewhat higher than it, in the midst of an extensive wood between that town and Lincoln, and about two miles south of that our only field known to fame, Concord Battle Ground; but I was so low in the woods that the opposite shore, half a mile off, like the rest, covered with wood, was my most distant horizon. For the first week, whenever I looked out on the pond it impressed me like a tarn high up on the side of a mountain, its bottom far above the surface of other lakes, and, as the sun arose, I saw it throwing off its nightly clothing of mist, and here and there, by degrees, its soft ripples or its smooth reflecting surface was revealed, while the mists, like ghosts, were stealthily withdrawing in every direction into the woods, as at the breaking up of some nocturnal conventicle. The very dew seemed to hang upon the trees later into the day than usual, as on the sides of mountains. . . .

I went to the woods because I wished to live deliberately, to front only the essential facts of life, and see if I could not learn what it had to teach, and not, when I came to die, discover that I had not lived. I did not wish to live what was not life, living is so dear; nor did I wish to practice resignation, unless it was quite necessary. I wanted to live deep and suck out all the marrow of life, to live so sturdily and Spartan-like as to put to rout all that was not life, to cut a broad swath and shave close, to drive life into a corner, and reduce it to its lowest terms, and, if it proved to be mean, why then to get the whole and genuine meanness of it, and publish its meanness to the world; or if it were sublime, to know it by experience, and be able to give a true account of it in my next excursion. For most men, it appears to me, are in a strange uncertainty about it, whether it is of the devil or of God, and have *somewhat hastily* concluded that it is the chief end of man here to "glorify God and enjoy him forever."

Still we live meanly, like ants; though the fable tells us that we were long ago changed into men; like pygmies we fight with cranes; it is error upon error, and clout upon clout, and our best virtue has for its occasion a superfluous and evitable wretchedness. Our life is frittered away by detail. An honest man has hardly need to count more than his ten fingers, or in extreme cases he may add his ten toes, and lump the rest. Simplicity, simplicity, simplicity! I say, let your affairs be as two or three, and not a hundred or a thousand; instead of a million count

GUIDE FOR READING

22 tarn: a small mountain lake or pool.

27–28 nocturnal conventicle (kən-vĕn′tĭ-kəl): a secret religious meeting held at night.

30–42 What are Thoreau's reasons for moving to the woods?

35–36 marrow: the central, most essential part; literally, the soft tissue inside a bone.

36 Spartan-like: in a simple, economical, and disciplined way, like the inhabitants of the ancient Greek city-state of Sparta.

37 cut a broad swath and shave close: gather as much of the essence of life as possible.

45 chief end of man here: most important purpose of human life on earth.

47 the fable: a Greek myth in which Zeus changes ants into men.

48–49 like pygmies . . . cranes: a reference to a legend, mentioned in Homer's *Iliad,* about the continual battles fought by a race of dwarfs against cranes.

50 evitable (ĕv′ĭ-tə-bəl): avoidable.

53–54 What is Thoreau's remedy for our hectic, detail-crowded lives?

WORDS TO KNOW

deliberately (dĭ-lĭb′ər-ĭt-lē) *adv.* in an unhurried and thoughtful manner
resignation (rĕz′ĭg-nā′shən) *n.* an acceptance of something as unavoidable
mean (mēn) *adj.* inferior in quality, value, or importance
sublime (sə-blīm′) *adj.* of high spiritual, moral, or intellectual worth; noble

half a dozen, and keep your accounts on your thumbnail. In the midst of this chopping sea of civilized life, such are the clouds and storms and quicksands and thousand-and-one items to be allowed for, that a man has to live, if he would not founder and go to the bottom and not make his port at all, by dead reckoning, and he must be a great calculator indeed who succeeds. Simplify, simplify. Instead of three meals a day, if it be necessary eat but one; instead of a hundred dishes, five; and reduce other things in proportion. . . .

Why should we live with such hurry and waste of life? We are determined to be starved before we are hungry. Men say that a stitch in time saves nine, and so they take a thousand stitches today to save nine to-morrow. As for *work,* we haven't any of any consequence. We have the Saint Vitus' dance, and cannot possibly keep our heads still. If I should only give a few pulls at the parish bell-rope, as for a fire, that is, without setting the bell, there is hardly a man on his farm in the outskirts of Concord, notwithstanding that press of engagements which was his excuse so many times this morning, nor a boy, nor a woman, I might almost say, but would forsake all and follow that sound, not mainly to save property from the flames, but, if we will confess the truth, much more to see it burn, since burn it must, and we, be it known, did not set it on fire,—or to see it put out, and have a hand in it, if that is done as handsomely; yes, even if it were the parish church itself. Hardly a man takes a half hour's nap after dinner, but when he wakes he holds up his head and asks, "What's the news?" as if the rest of mankind had stood his sentinels. Some give directions to be waked every half hour, doubtless for no other purpose; and then, to pay for it, they tell what they have dreamed. After a night's sleep the news is as indispensable as the breakfast. "Pray tell me any thing new that has happened to a man any where on this globe,"—and he reads it over his coffee and rolls, that a man has had his eyes gouged out this morning on the Wachito River; never dreaming the while that he lives in the dark unfathomed mammoth cave of this world, and has but the rudiment of an eye himself.

For my part, I could easily do without the post-office. I think that there are very few important communications made through it. To speak critically, I never received more than one or two letters in my life—I wrote this some years ago—that were worth the postage. The penny-post is, commonly, an institution through which you seriously offer a man that penny for his

59 founder: to sink like a ship.

60–61 dead reckoning: guesswork. The term, used by sailors, describes a method of estimating a ship's position when the stars cannot be seen.

69 Saint Vitus' (vī'təs) **dance:** a disorder of the nervous system, characterized by rapid, jerky, involuntary movements.

80–92 What situation is Thoreau exaggerating here?

89 Wachito River: a river (now called the Ouachita) in northern Louisiana and southern Arkansas. In Thoreau's time, it was believed that violent men went to that region to escape from the law.

97–99 Thoreau jokingly connects the postage rate (a penny per letter at the time) with the phrase "a penny for your thoughts." What is the point of his joke?

WORDS TO KNOW

rudiment (ro͞o'də-mənt) *n.* an imperfect or undeveloped form

Photo by Ernst Haas. Copyright © 1995 Magnum Photos, Inc.

thoughts which is so often safely offered in jest. And I am sure that I never read any memorable news in a newspaper. If we read of one man robbed, or murdered, or killed by accident, or one house burned, or one vessel wrecked, or one steamboat blown up, or one cow run over on the Western Railroad, or one mad dog killed, or one lot of grasshoppers in the winter,—we never need read of another. One is enough. . . .

Let us spend one day as deliberately as Nature, and not be thrown off the track by every nutshell and mosquito's wing that falls on the rails. Let us rise early and fast, or break fast, gently and without perturbation; let company come and let company go, let the bells ring and the children cry,—determined to make a day of it. . . .

Time is but the stream I go a-fishing in. I drink at it; but while I drink I see the sandy bottom and detect how shallow it

112–126 Thoreau says that we do not have much time on earth. What does he say he wants to spend his time trying to understand? How does he feel that he can find some of the answers he seeks?

WORDS TO KNOW

perturbation (pûr′tər-bā′shən) *n.* a disturbance of the emotions; agitation; uneasiness is. Its thin current slides away, but eternity remains. I would drink deeper; fish in the sky, whose bottom is pebbly with stars. I cannot count one. I know not the first letter of the alphabet. I have always been regretting that I was not as wise as the day I was born. The intellect is a cleaver; it discerns and rifts its way into the secret of things. I do not wish to be any more busy with my hands than is necessary. My head is hands and feet. I feel all my best faculties concentrated in it. My instinct tells me that my head is an organ for burrowing, as some creatures use their snout and fore-paws, and with it I would mine and burrow my way through these hills. I think that the richest vein is somewhere hereabouts; so by the divining rod and thin rising vapors I judge; and here I will begin to mine.

125 divining rod: a forked stick that is believed to indicate the presence of underground water.

FROM *Solitude*

This is a delicious evening, when the whole body is one sense, and imbibes delight through every pore. I go and come with a strange liberty in Nature, a part of herself. As I walk along the stony shore of the pond in my shirt sleeves, though it is cool as well as cloudy and windy, and I see nothing special to attract me, all the elements are unusually congenial to me. The bullfrogs trump to usher in the night, and the note of the whippoorwill is borne on the rippling wind from over the water. Sympathy with the fluttering alder and poplar leaves almost takes away my breath; yet, like the lake, my serenity is rippled but not ruffled. These small waves raised by the evening wind are as remote from storm as the smooth reflecting surface. Though it is now dark, the wind still blows and roars in the wood, the waves still dash, and some creatures lull the rest with their notes. The repose is never complete. The wildest animals do not repose, but seek their prey now; the fox, and skunk, and rabbit, now roam the fields and woods without fear. They are Nature's watchmen,—links which connect the days of animated life. . . .

130–145 What does Thoreau say he is part of, and why does he feel as he does?

WORDS TO KNOW

congenial (kən-gēn′yəl) *adj.* suited to one's needs or nature; agreeable
serenity (sə-rĕn′ĭ-tē) *n.* a mental and spiritual calm; tranquillity

Men frequently say to me, "I should think you would feel lonesome down there, and want to be nearer to folks, rainy and snowy days and nights especially." I am tempted to reply to such,—This whole earth which we inhabit is but a point in space. How far apart, think you, dwell the two most distant inhabitants of yonder star, the breadth of whose disk cannot be appreciated by our instruments? Why should I feel lonely? is not our planet in the Milky Way? This which you put seems to me not to be the most important question. What sort of space is that which separates a man from his fellows and makes him solitary? I have found that no exertion of the legs can bring two minds much nearer to one another. . . .

153–160 Thoreau suggests that because we are all in this life together, the physical distance between us is insignificant.

FROM

The Pond in Winter

Every winter the liquid and trembling surface of the pond, which was so sensitive to every breath, and reflected every light and shadow, becomes solid to the depth of a foot or a foot and a half, so that it will support the heaviest teams, and perchance the snow covers it to an equal depth, and it is not to be distinguished from any level field. Like the marmots in the surrounding hills, it closes its eye-lids and becomes dormant for three months or more. Standing on the snow-covered plain, as if in a pasture amid the hills, I cut my way first through a foot of snow, and then a foot of ice, and open a window under my feet, where, kneeling to drink, I look down into the quiet parlor of the fishes, pervaded by a softened light as through a window of ground glass, with its bright sanded floor the same as in summer; there a perennial waveless serenity reigns as in the amber twilight sky, corresponding to the cool and even temperament of the inhabitants. Heaven is under our feet as well as over our heads. . . .

167 marmots: rodents that hibernate in the winter; groundhogs.

WORDS TO KNOW

perennial (pə-rĕn′ē-əl) *adj.* lasting through the year or through many years; enduring

FROM *Spring*

One attraction in coming to the woods to live was that I should have leisure and opportunity to see the spring come in. The ice in the pond at length begins to be honey-combed, and I can set my heel in it as I walk. Fogs and rains and warmer suns are gradually melting the snow; the days have grown sensibly longer; and I see how I shall get through the winter without adding to my woodpile, for large fires are no longer necessary. I am on the alert for the first signs of spring, to hear the chance note of some arriving bird, or the striped squirrel's chirp, for his stores must be now nearly exhausted, or see the woodchuck venture out of his winter quarters. . . .

191 sensibly: noticeably.

The change from storm and winter to serene and mild weather, from dark and sluggish hours to bright and elastic ones, is a memorable crisis which all things proclaim. It is seemingly instantaneous at last. Suddenly an influx of light filled my house, though the evening was at hand, and the clouds of winter still overhung it, and the eaves were dripping with sleety rain. I looked out the window, and lo! where yesterday was cold gray ice there lay the transparent pond already calm and full of hope as in a summer evening, reflecting a summer evening sky in its bosom, though none was visible overhead, as if it had intelligence with some remote horizon. . . .

200 crisis: turning point.

FROM *Conclusion*

I left the woods for as good a reason as I went there. Perhaps it seemed to me that I had several more lives to live, and could not spare any more time for that one. It is remarkable how easily and insensibly we fall into a particular route, and make a beaten track for ourselves. I had not lived there a week before my feet wore a path from my door to the pond-side; and though it is five or six years since I trod it, it is still quite distinct. It is true, I fear that others may have fallen into it, and so helped to keep it open. The surface of the earth is soft and impressible by the feet of men; and so with the paths which the mind travels. How worn and dusty, then, must be the highways of the world, how deep the ruts of tradition and conformity! I did not wish to take a cabin passage, but rather to go before the mast and on

209–211 Why does Thoreau leave the woods?

220–223 On a sailing ship, passengers stayed in private compartments near the middle of the ship, while the crew shared living quarters at the front ("before the mast"). What is Thoreau comparing here? How does he want to live his life?

Photo by Ernst Haas. Copyright © 1995 Magnum Photos, Inc.

the deck of the world, for there I could best see the moonlight amid the mountains. I do not wish to go below now.

I learned this, at least, by my experiment; that if one advances confidently in the direction of his dreams, and endeavors to live the life which he has imagined, he will meet with a success unexpected in common hours. He will put some things behind, will pass an invisible boundary; new, universal, and more liberal laws will begin to establish themselves around and within him; or the old laws be expanded, and interpreted in his favor in a more liberal sense, and he will live with the license of a higher order of beings. In proportion as he simplifies his life, the laws of the universe will appear less complex, and solitude will not be solitude, nor poverty poverty, nor weakness weakness. If you have built castles in the air, your work need not be lost; that is where they should be. Now put the foundations under them. . . .

Why should we be in such desperate haste to succeed, and in such desperate enterprises? If a man does not keep pace with his companions, perhaps it is because he hears a different drummer. Let him step to the music which he hears, however measured or far away. It is not important that he should mature as soon as an appletree or an oak. Shall he turn his spring into summer? If the condition of things which we were made for is not yet, what were any reality which we can substitute? We will not be shipwrecked on a vain reality. Shall we with pains erect a heaven of blue glass over ourselves, though when it is done we shall be sure to gaze still at the true ethereal heaven far above, as if the former were not? . . .

However mean your life is, meet it and live it; do not shun it and call it hard names. It is not so bad as you are. It looks poorest when you are richest. The fault-finder will find faults even in paradise. Love your life, poor as it is. You may perhaps have some pleasant, thrilling, glorious hours, even in a poorhouse. The setting sun is reflected from the windows of the almshouse as brightly as from the rich man's abode; the snow melts before its door as early in the spring. I do not see but a quiet mind may live as contentedly there, and have as cheering thoughts, as in a palace. The town's poor seem to me often to live the most independent lives of any. May be they are simply great enough to receive without misgiving. Most think that they are above being supported by the town; but it oftener happens that they are not above supporting themselves by dishonest means, which should be more disreputable. Cultivate poverty like a garden herb, like sage. Do not trouble yourself much to get new things, whether clothes or friends. Turn the old; return to them. Things do not change; we change. Sell your clothes and keep your thoughts. God will see that you do not want society. If I were confined to a corner of a garret all my days, like a spider, the world would be just as large to me while I had my thoughts about me. The philosopher said: "From an army of three divisions one can take away its general, and put it in disorder; from the man the most abject and vulgar one cannot take away his thought." Do not seek so anxiously to be developed, to subject yourself to many influences to be played on; it is all dissipation. Humility like darkness reveals the heavenly lights. The shadows of poverty and meanness gather around us, "and lo! creation widens to our view." We are often reminded that if there were bestowed on us

239–242 This is one of the most famous passages in Thoreau's writings. The "different drummer" evolved from one of his journal entries describing an 1839 river voyage when he had fallen asleep to the sound of someone's beating a drum "alone in the silence and the dark." The phrase "marching to the beat of a different drummer" became popular in the nonconformist 1960s. What does it mean to hear a different drummer?

255 almshouse: poorhouse.

255–260 What similarities between poverty and wealth does Thoreau find? What benefits of poverty does Thoreau see?

WORDS TO KNOW

misgiving (mĭs-gĭv'ĭng) *n.* a feeling of doubt, mistrust, or uncertainty
disreputable (dĭs-rĕp'yə-tə-bəl) *adj.* lacking respectability of character or behavior
abject (ăb'jĕkt') *adj.* low; contemptible; wretched
vulgar (vŭl'gər) *adj.* coarse; common
dissipation (dĭs'ə-pā'shən) *n.* a reckless waste of resources; wastefulness

the wealth of Croesus, our aims must still be the same, and our means essentially the same. Moreover, if you are restricted in your range by poverty, if you cannot buy books and newspapers, for instance, you are but confined to the most significant and vital experiences; you are compelled to deal with the material which yields the most sugar and the most starch. It is life near the bone where it is sweetest. You are defended from being a trifler. No man loses ever on a lower level by magnanimity on a higher. Superfluous wealth can buy superfluities only. Money is not required to buy one necessary of the soul. . . .

279 Croesus (krē'səs): a king of Lydia (now part of Turkey) in the sixth century B.C. who became legendary for his great wealth.

The life in us is like the water in the river. It may rise this year higher than man has ever known it, and flood the parched uplands; even this may be the eventful year, which will drown out all our muskrats. It was not always dry land where we dwell. I see far inland the banks which the stream anciently washed, before science began to record its freshets. Every one has heard the story which has gone the rounds of New England, of a strong and beautiful bug which came out of the dry leaf of an old table of apple-tree wood, which had stood in a farmer's kitchen for sixty years, first in Connecticut, and afterward in Massachusetts,—from an egg deposited in the living tree many years earlier still, as appeared by counting the annual layers beyond it; which was heard gnawing out for several weeks, hatched perchance by the heat of an urn. Who does not feel his faith in a resurrection and immortality strengthened by hearing of this? Who knows what beautiful and winged life, whose egg has been buried for ages under many concentric layers of woodenness in the dead dry life of society, deposited at first in the alburnum of the green and living tree, which has been gradually converted into the semblance of its well-seasoned tomb,—heard perchance gnawing out now for years by the astonished family of man, as they sat round the festive board,—may unexpectedly come forth from amidst society's most trivial and handselled furniture, to enjoy its perfect summer life at last!

299–317 What is the message of this famous parable of the "strong and beautiful bug"?

312 alburnum (ăl-bûr'nəm): the part of a tree's trunk through which sap flows.

316 handselled: cheap; discounted; bought from a traveling salesman.

I do not say that John or Jonathan will realize all this; but such is the character of that morrow which mere lapse of time can never make to dawn. The light which puts out our eyes is darkness to us. Only that day dawns to which we are awake. There is more day to dawn. The sun is but a morning star. ❖

318 John or Jonathan: the common man. Thoreau's use of familiar given names here is similar to that in the expression "every Tom, Dick, and Harry."

WORDS TO KNOW

magnanimity (măg'nə-nĭm'ĭ-tē) *n.* generosity

INSIGHT

Thoreau, a Hippie in History

DELBERT L. EARISMAN

Thoreau's major similarity to the hippies [of the 1960s and 1970s] is his attitude towards society (not towards his fellow men, for whom he had some affection, a bit of humorous contempt, and a great deal of pity but no hostility). For while Thoreau's life was in every respect morally irreproachable—that is to say, he was chaste,[1] sober, paid his debts, discharged his obligations, and broke no laws—he was clearly aware that he had dropped out, had set himself apart from the standards of society, and was, indeed, conducting a guerilla warfare primarily for the benefit of his own soul. "The greater part of what my neighbors call good," he wrote, "I believe in my soul to be bad, and if I repent of anything, it is very likely to be my good behavior." He did spend one night in jail because of his refusal to pay taxes to a state that supported and enforced the Fugitive Slave Act. Though his pamphlet, "Civil Disobedience," is his major treatment of that incident, he does mention the episode once in *Walden,* in an attempt to explain his relationship to society: "Wherever a man goes, men will pursue and paw him with their dirty institutions, and, if they can, constrain him to belong to their desperate odd-fellow society. It is true, I might have resisted forcibly with more or less effect, might have run 'amok' against society; but I preferred that society should run 'amok' against me, it being the desperate party." (That last clause is a choice sample of Thoreau's wit, the counterpart among hippies being something like Galahad's[2] offering to paint the walls of the Ninth Precinct the day after he had been arraigned.)

Thoreau's remedy for mankind was that it should learn to live simply and organically, in the way that he himself chose to live, "by truly Indian, botanic, magnetic, and natural means," as he put it, returning to nature not merely by going out to live beside a pond but more radically and spiritually, in something like a kind of natural mysticism. And like the hippies, he not only made a folk-hero out of the American Indian but also quoted again and again in his book from the Indian scriptures.

Thoreau was not, however, like his friend Emerson, a teacher looking for disciples. His ethic, as opposed perhaps to his metaphysic,[3] was precisely the code of the hippies—let each person find his own thing and do it, and don't try to put your thing on anybody else: "I would not have any one adopt *my* mode of living on any account; for, beside that before he has fairly learned it I may have found out another for myself, I desire that there may be as many different persons in the world as possible; but I would have each one be very careful to find out and pursue *his own* way, and not his father's or his mother's or his neighbor's instead."

1. **chaste:** decent and modest.
2. **Galahad:** a hippie who ran a commune in New York City during the 1960s.
3. **metaphysic:** philosophical principles.

RESPONDING OPTIONS

FROM PERSONAL RESPONSE *TO* CRITICAL ANALYSIS

REFLECT 1. Look over the aphorisms of Thoreau's that you jotted down for the Reading Connection on page 297, and share one that you particularly liked.

RETHINK 2. What do you think is the most valuable lesson that Thoreau learned from his experience of living in the woods?

3. In your own words, explain Thoreau's reasons for leaving Walden Pond.
   Consider
   - the meaning of the statement "I had several more lives to live"
   - Thoreau's thoughts about tradition, conformity, and success

4. In this excerpt from *Walden*, Thoreau frequently discusses what is not important. What do you think *was* important to him?

5. To what extent do you agree with the ideas expressed by Thoreau in this selection?
   Consider
   - whether living a simple life is possible or desirable
   - whether beauty and wisdom are to be found in nature
   - whether poverty has benefits
   - other ideas you found thought-provoking

RELATE 6. Look back at the list of desired experiences that you made for the Personal Connection on page 297. How do your desires compare with Thoreau's wish to live simply in the woods?

7. In what ways do you think Thoreau was similar to and different from the hippies of the 1960s and 1970s? Create a comparison chart based on what you learned about Thoreau from *Walden* and what you learned about hippies from the Insight selection "Thoreau, a Hippie in History."

ANOTHER PATHWAY

Cooperative Learning

With a small group of classmates, evaluate Thoreau's experiment of living in the woods. What did he hope to learn? What did he actually learn? Create a brief report that answers these questions, and share it with the rest of the class.

QUICKWRITES

1. Spend some time alone, either observing nature or just thinking. Then draft an **informal essay,** modeled on *Walden*, to describe your thoughts and experiences.

2. Outline a **grant proposal** to an educational foundation, asking for funding so that you can have one of the experiences you listed for the Personal Connection or one of those described by Thoreau. Explain what the experience is, what it will cost, and what benefits you expect to gain.

PORTFOLIO *Save your writing. You may want to use it later as a springboard to a piece for your portfolio.*

LITERARY CONCEPTS

An **essay** is a short work of nonfiction that deals with a single subject. The term comes from the French *essai,* meaning "attempt"—the writer of an essay does not presume to cover a subject completely. Essays are difficult to classify. They are often informal, loosely structured, and highly personal. They can be descriptive, informative, persuasive, narrative, or any combination of these. Frequently, they are meant to improve the human condition; at the same time, most try to be entertaining. What passages from *Walden* illustrate some of these characteristics of essays?

CONCEPT REVIEW: Figurative Language Thoreau was a poet as well as an essayist, and in *Walden* he used striking figurative language to express abstract concepts. Consider the metaphor "Time is but the stream I go a-fishing in." Try to convey the same idea without using figurative language. Find other good examples of figurative language—metaphor, simile, and personification—in these excerpts from *Walden.*

THE WRITER'S STYLE

Thoreau is fond of **paradoxes,** statements that seem to contradict themselves but are nevertheless true. For example, he writes, "I did not wish to live what was not life" (page 299) and "We are determined to be starved before we are hungry" (page 300). Tell what you think he means by each of these statements. What other paradoxes can you find in the selection?

LITERARY LINKS

In Unit One, you read an excerpt from William Bradford's *Of Plymouth Plantation.* Look back at Bradford's description of the "hideous and desolate wilderness" the Pilgrims encountered (page 91). How does Thoreau's attitude toward nature compare with Bradford's attitude?

ACROSS THE CURRICULUM

Biology Walden Pond is now a state reservation where thousands swim, fish, and hike each year. Some people believe that overuse is destroying Walden Pond and that the area should be made into a limited-use nature preserve. Visitors would need permits to enter the area, and swimming would be prohibited. Others say that Walden should remain a public park, freely accessible to everyone. How should Walden Pond be used today? With several classmates, research the current condition of Walden Pond and hold a debate on this issue.

Wood Shop Thoreau built a one-room shingled wood cabin that measured 10 feet by 15 feet, with walls 8 feet high. It had a door, two windows, and a brick chimney. He spent only $28.13 on the materials. Visit a lumber center and find out the current cost of materials needed to build a cabin similar to Thoreau's.

CRITIC'S CORNER

In "Approaching Walden," Richard Conniff makes this statement: "This was the lesson Thoreau meant to teach: not that anyone should make a pilgrimage to Walden Pond, but that we should learn to become pilgrims in our own homes." How does his explanation of Thoreau's lesson fit with your own reading of these excerpts from *Walden*?

Don Henley (center) founded the Walden Woods Project to preserve the area surrounding Walden Pond. AP/Wide World Photos.

WORDS TO KNOW

EXERCISE A For each group of words below, write the letter of the word that is an antonym of the boldfaced vocabulary word.

1. **vulgar:** (a) classy, (b) ordinary, (c) popular
2. **abject:** (a) appropriate, (b) accidental, (c) lofty
3. **disreputable:** (a) honorable, (b) famous, (c) noticeable
4. **mean:** (a) predictable, (b) superior, (c) basic
5. **congenial:** (a) illegal, (b) sophisticated, (c) incompatible
6. **magnanimity:** (a) selfishness, (b) rejection, (c) fragility
7. **sublime:** (a) exciting, (b) average, (c) excessive
8. **rudiment:** (a) completion, (b) estimation, (c) delicacy
9. **serenity:** (a) stupidity, (b) chaos, (c) peace
10. **dissipation:** (a) greed, (b) honesty, (c) thrift

EXERCISE B Write the vocabulary word, not used in Exercise A, that is suggested by each set of familiar expressions.

1. That's the way the cookie crumbles; You can't fight city hall; Like it or lump it.
2. ants in your pants; on pins and needles; climbing the walls
3. Haste makes waste; Look before you leap; Wear your thinking cap.
4. year in, year out; for a month of Sundays; not a flash in the pan
5. smell a rat; think something's fishy; have second thoughts

HENRY DAVID THOREAU

1817–1862

Although some of Henry David Thoreau's neighbors in Concord, Massachusetts, viewed him as a cranky eccentric, he was a careful observer and a deep thinker who tried to record every observation and thought in his journal. Taking to heart the ideas of his friend and mentor Ralph Waldo Emerson, Thoreau constantly tried to live by his own values rather than by society's values, which he considered materialistic.

Thoreau's life was full of examples of his independence. As a Harvard student, he was required to wear a black coat but instead wore a green one. In his first year of teaching, he refused to physically punish his students and resigned. In 1846, during a day trip from Walden Pond to Concord, he was arrested and spent a night in jail for refusing to pay a poll tax. He felt that paying the tax was wrong because it would be used by a government that condoned slavery in the South and was involved in the Mexican War (1846–1848). In his essay "Civil Disobedience," which was inspired by his jail experience, he advocated the use of nonviolent acts of political resistance. This essay influenced such leaders as Mohandas Gandhi and Martin Luther King, Jr.

During his lifetime, Thoreau published only two books, both of which sold poorly. However, his reputation has grown tremendously in the years since his death. His observations about nature and about the simple life have increasing relevance today, as environmental problems multiply and the pace of our lives accelerates.

OTHER WORKS *A Week on the Concord and Merrimack Rivers, The Maine Woods, The Collected Poems of Henry Thoreau,* "A Plea for Captain John Brown"

LASERLINKS
- *CONTEMPORARY CONNECTION*

PREVIEWING

POETRY

Selected Poems

Walt Whitman

PERSONAL CONNECTION

Many of Walt Whitman's poems contain vivid images of America in the mid-1800s. What are your images of America today? Describe or sketch some of them in your notebook.

BIOGRAPHICAL CONNECTION

Walt Whitman's first book of poems, *Leaves of Grass,* was so revolutionary in content and form that publishers would not publish it. After Whitman printed the book himself in 1855, many established poets and critics disparaged it. In 1856, the *Saturday Review* suggested that "if the *Leaves of Grass* should come into anybody's possession, our advice is to throw them instantly behind the fire." Doubtless Whitman was shocked and hurt by such a reception, for he saw himself as capturing the spirit of his country and his times. In the preface to *Leaves of Grass* he wrote, "The United States themselves are essentially the greatest poem." Whitman's images encompass all of American life, including the common and "vulgar." His lines are long and rambling, like the vastly expanding country. His language reflects the vigor and energy of American speech, resounding with new, distinctively American, rhythms. Most of his poems are marked by optimism, vitality, and a love of nature, free expression, and democracy—values often associated with the America of his day.

Portrait of Whitman from title page of *Leaves of Grass.* The Bettmann Archive.

READING CONNECTION

Examining Style The particular way in which you do something is your style. The style of Walt Whitman's poetry differs greatly from the prevalent poetic style of his era—think of Longfellow—and it may also differ from the style of the poetry to which you are accustomed. As you read Whitman's poems, notice these distinctive features of his style.

Features of Whitman's Style

- **Free verse** The lines do not rhyme, nor is there a regular meter.
- **Catalog** There are frequent lists of people, things, and attributes.
- **Repetition** Words or phrases are repeated at the beginning of two or more lines.
- **Parallelism** Related ideas are phrased in similar ways.

• *BIOGRAPHICAL CONNECTION*

I Hear America Singing

WALT WHITMAN

I hear America singing, the varied carols I hear,
Those of mechanics, each one singing his as it should be blithe[1] and
strong,
The carpenter singing his as he measures his plank or beam,
The mason singing his as he makes ready for work, or leaves off work,
The boatman singing what belongs to him in his boat, the deckhand
singing on the steamboat deck,
The shoemaker singing as he sits on his bench, the hatter singing as
he stands,
The wood-cutter's song, the ploughboy's on his way in the morning, or
at noon intermission or at sundown,
The delicious singing of the mother, or of the young wife at work, or
of the girl sewing or washing,
Each singing what belongs to him or her and to none else,
The day what belongs to the day—at night the party of young fellows,
robust, friendly,
Singing with open mouths their strong melodious songs.

1. **blithe** (blīth): carefree and lighthearted.

FROM PERSONAL RESPONSE *TO* CRITICAL ANALYSIS

REFLECT **1.** In your notebook, write down or sketch the images that came to mind as you read this poem.

RETHINK **2.** What do you think singing represents in this poem? Consider who the singers are and what they might be singing about.

3. On the basis of your reading of this poem, how would you describe Whitman's view of America?

Cliff Dwellers (1913), George Bellows. Oil on canvas. $40\,\frac{3}{16}'' \times 42\,\frac{1}{16}''$. Los Angeles County Museum of Art, Los Angeles County Fund. Copyright © 1995 Museum Associates, Los Angeles County Museum of Art, all rights reserved.

I Sit and Look Out

WALT WHITMAN

I sit and look out upon all the sorrows of the world, and upon all oppression and shame,
I hear secret convulsive sobs from young men at anguish with themselves, remorseful after deeds done,
I see in low life the mother misused by her children, dying, neglected, gaunt, desperate,
I see the wife misused by her husband, I see the treacherous seducer of young women,
I mark the ranklings of jealousy and unrequited love attempted to be hid, I see these sights on the earth,
I see the workings of battle, pestilence, tyranny, I see martyrs and prisoners,
I observe a famine at sea, I observe the sailors casting lots who shall be kill'd to preserve the lives of the rest,
I observe the slights and degradations cast by arrogant persons upon laborers, the poor, and upon negroes, and the like;
All these—all the meanness and agony without end I sitting look out upon,
See, hear, and am silent.

GUIDE FOR READING

2 convulsive: intense and uncontrolled.

2–8 Notice how many sorrows the speaker lists in this poem. What effect might this have on a reader?

3 low life: the life of the lower classes.

5 ranklings: bitter feelings or resentments; **unrequited:** not returned.

7 casting lots: deciding by means of a random choice of objects (as in drawing straws).

FROM PERSONAL RESPONSE *TO* CRITICAL ANALYSIS

REFLECT **1.** In your notebook, describe your reaction to the speaker's silence.

RETHINK **2.** Speculate about who the speaker is and why the speaker remains silent.

RELATE **3.** If Whitman were writing this poem today, do you think he would list the same sorrows or different ones? Explain your opinion.

from Song of Myself

WALT WHITMAN

1

I celebrate myself, and sing myself,
And what I assume you shall assume,
For every atom belonging to me as good belongs to you.

I loaf and invite my soul,
I lean and loaf at my ease observing a spear of summer
grass.

My tongue, every atom of my blood, form'd from this soil,
this air,
Born here of parents born here from parents the same, and
their parents the same,
I, now thirty seven years old in perfect health begin,
Hoping to cease not till death.

Creeds and schools in abeyance,
Retiring back a while sufficed at what they are, but never
forgotten,
I harbor for good or bad, I permit to speak at every
hazard,
Nature without check with original energy.

GUIDE FOR READING

1–3 Why do you think the speaker identifies the reader with himself at the very beginning of the poem?

10 in abeyance (ə-bā'əns): temporarily set aside.

11 sufficed at: satisfied with.

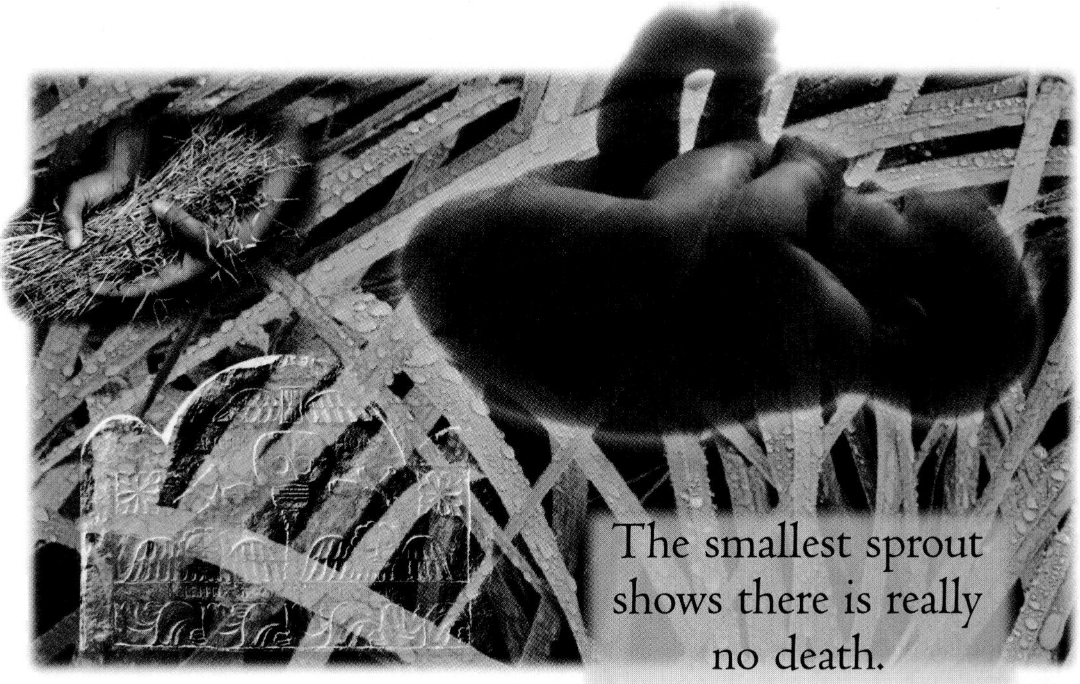
The smallest sprout shows there is really no death.

6

A child said *What is the grass?* fetching it to me with full hands,
How could I answer the child? I do not know what it is any more than he.

I guess it must be the flag of my disposition, out of hopeful green stuff woven.

Or I guess it is the handkerchief of the Lord,
A scented gift and remembrancer designedly dropt,
Bearing the owner's name someway in the corners, that we may see and remark, and say *Whose?*

Or I guess the grass is itself a child, the produced babe of the vegetation.
Or I guess it is a uniform hieroglyphic,
And it means, Sprouting alike in broad zones and narrow zones,
Growing among black folks as among white,
Kanuck, Tuckahoe, Congressman, Cuff, I give them the same, I receive them the same.

16–25 What metaphors does the speaker use to describe what grass means to him?

18 remembrancer designedly dropt: a purposely dropped token of affection.

21 hieroglyphic: a system of symbols that represent meanings or speech sounds.

24 Kanuck, Tuckahoe, . . . Cuff: slang terms for various groups of people. A Kanuck (now spelled Canuck) is a Canadian, especially a French Canadian; a Tuckahoe is someone from the coast of Virginia; and a Cuff is an African American.

And now it seems to me the beautiful uncut hair of graves.

Tenderly will I use you curling grass,
It may be you transpire from the breasts of young men,
It may be if I had known them I would have loved them,
It may be you are from old people, or from offspring taken
soon out of their mothers' laps,
And here you are the mothers' laps.

This grass is very dark to be from the white heads of old
mothers,
Darker than the colorless beards of old men,
Dark to come from under the faint red roofs of mouths.

O I perceive after all so many uttering tongues,
And I perceive they do not come from the roofs of mouths
for nothing.

I wish I could translate the hints about the dead young
men and women,
And the hints about old men and mothers, and the
offspring taken soon out of their laps.

What do you think has become of the young and old men?
And what do you think has become of the women and
children?

They are alive and well somewhere,
The smallest sprout shows there is really no death,
And if ever there was it led forward life, and does not wait
at the end to arrest it,
And ceas'd the moment life appear'd.

All goes onward and outward, nothing collapses,
And to die is different from what any one supposed, and
luckier.

25–33 The speaker presents the grass as "the uncut hair of graves." Who are the dead that he includes in this extended metaphor?

27 transpire: emerge; ooze out.

38–45 What concept of death does the speaker express in these lines?

45 Why does the speaker think that to die is "luckier" than what people suppose?

52

The spotted hawk swoops by and accuses me, he complains of my gab and my loitering.

I too am not a bit tamed, I too am untranslatable,
I sound my barbaric yawp over the roofs of the world.

48 yawp: loud, rough speech.

The last scud of day holds back for me,
It flings my likeness after the rest and true as any on the shadow'd wilds,
It coaxes me to the vapor and the dusk.

49 scud: wind-blown cloud.

I depart as air, I shake my white locks at the runaway sun,
I effuse my flesh in eddies, and drift it in lacy jags.

53 effuse . . . eddies: scatter my flesh in swirling currents.

I bequeath myself to the dirt to grow from the grass I love,
If you want me again look for me under your boot-soles.

54 bequeath: hand over, as if in a will.

You will hardly know who I am or what I mean,
But I shall be good health to you nevertheless,
And filter and fibre your blood.

Failing to fetch me at first keep encouraged,
Missing me one place search another,
I stop somewhere waiting for you.

61 Why do you think the speaker says he's "waiting for you"?

RESPONDING OPTIONS

FROM PERSONAL RESPONSE *TO* CRITICAL ANALYSIS

REFLECT 1. What do you think of the excerpts from "Song of Myself"? Jot down your first reactions in your notebook.

RETHINK 2. What is your impression of the individual celebrated in this poem?

Consider
- the speaker's connection with nature
- the speaker's view of death
- the speaker's view of himself

3. What do you think grass represents in this poem?

Consider
- the different metaphors in which the speaker compares grass to other things
- the connection the speaker makes between grass and the dead

RELATE 4. Do you see consistency or contradiction in the three Whitman poems?

Consider
- the references to singing and silence
- whether they can all be viewed as "celebrations of the self"

LITERARY CONCEPTS

Whitman is often considered the father of **free verse**—poetry that does not have regular patterns of rhyme and meter. Although free verse lacks regular meter, it often does contain devices that create rhythm, such as repetition and parallelism (a repetition of sentence structures). Read several stanzas of "Song of Myself" aloud to appreciate their rhythm. How similar is it to that of normal speech?

Free verse also generally contains other traditional elements of poetry, such as imagery, metaphors, and similes. Find some traditional elements of poetry that Whitman uses in these three poems. Then discuss with a partner why Whitman, in writing poems about America in the 1800s, might have used free verse rather than metrical and rhymed forms.

ANOTHER PATHWAY

Cooperative Learning

With a small group of classmates, create three dictionary entries that define *grass, death,* and *Walt Whitman* the way you think Whitman would, on the basis of your reading of the excerpts from "Song of Myself."

QUICKWRITES

1. Write a short **review** of one of the three Whitman poems. Read or display your review in class.
2. Using Whitman's poetry as a model, write a **free-verse poem** about America today. As a starting point, you might develop one or more of the images you came up with for the Personal Connection. Share your poem with the class.

PORTFOLIO *Save your writing. You may want to use it later as a springboard to a piece for your portfolio.*

ALTERNATIVE ACTIVITIES

1. Using photos, drawings, or other images, create a **collage** that captures the spirit of one of the Whitman poems you have read. If you have a drawing program on your computer and access to a scanner, you can combine images you create with ones scanned from magazines or other sources. You might even include lines from the poem in your collage. Display your work in the classroom.
2. Create and perform a **dance interpretation** of one of Whitman's poems. Let the movements of the dance convey the mood and content of the poem.

LITERARY LINKS

One of Walt Whitman's few early supporters was Ralph Waldo Emerson, who described *Leaves of Grass* as "the most extraordinary piece of wit and wisdom that America has yet contributed." On the basis of what you know of Emerson from reading the excerpt from "Self-Reliance," what do you think he liked about Whitman's poems?

ACROSS THE CURRICULUM

Music Walt Whitman's poems have inspired a number of musical compositions. Find a recording of one of these—such as *I Hear America Singing,* a cantata for mixed voices by George Kleinsinger—and play it for the class. Discuss how well the music fits the poetry and what choices you might make in setting another of Whitman's works to music.

WALT WHITMAN

1819–1892

"I am large. I contain multitudes," says Walt Whitman in "Song of Myself." It is a fitting description of a man whose writing touches on all aspects of life—the unique and the commonplace, the beautiful and the ugly. Whitman knew country life as well as city life, having grown up in rural Long Island and then in crowded Brooklyn. His varied work life included jobs as an office boy, a typesetter and printer, a school teacher, a carpenter, a newspaper editor and journalist, a nurse during the Civil War, and a government clerk in the Bureau of Indian Affairs.

His true life's work, however, was a book of poems called *Leaves of Grass*, which he began to work on in 1848. Whitman quit his job, moved in with his parents, and worked part-time as a carpenter while writing his poems. In 1855, unable to find a firm that would publish his 12-poem book, he had it printed at his own expense. Throughout his lifetime, Whitman rewrote, revised, and expanded *Leaves of Grass*; the ninth and final edition in 1891 contained nearly 400 poems.

Many critics thought the poems in *Leaves of Grass* "barbaric" and "noxious." They were shocked by the poems' radical style and suspicious of the poems' subject matter, particularly the vivid sexual imagery. Other readers, most notably Ralph Waldo Emerson, praised Whitman. Gradually, the literary world recognized the brilliance of the book. By the time the fifth edition was published in 1871, many well-known writers in England and America were traveling to Whitman's home in Camden, New Jersey, to visit him. Today *Leaves of Grass* is often regarded as the greatest, most influential book of poetry in American literature.

OTHER WORKS *Democratic Vistas, Specimen Days*

PREVIEWING

POETRY

Danse Russe

William Carlos Williams

anyone lived in a pretty how town

E. E. Cummings

PERSONAL CONNECTION

Think of a person that you consider a very distinctive individual. How does this person express his or her individuality? Draw a stick figure to represent the person, and include in your drawing anything that distinguishes him or her from others—unique clothing or a unique hairstyle, for example. You might draw the person engaged in a characteristic activity or put a characteristic remark in a speech balloon. If any of your classmates know this person, see if they can guess the person's identity from the drawing.

BIOGRAPHICAL CONNECTION

Both E. E. Cummings and William Carlos Williams were individualistic poets. Each sought to use the American idiom—our characteristic speech—in his poetry. Williams avoided symbolism and figurative language, instead concentrating on the use of specific concrete images to re-create experience. He wrote the poem "Danse Russe" in 1916, after seeing a performance of the Ballets Russes, a famous Russian ballet company that performed in New York that year. The company featured Vaslav Nijinsky, whose emotional expressiveness, perfect body control, and spectacular leaps led audiences to proclaim him a genius.

Cummings turned poetry upside down, inside out, and on its side. He created striking effects by violating rules of punctuation, spelling, grammar, and capitalization. His poem "anyone lived in a pretty how town," first published in the 1940 volume *50 Poems,* tells of the love between two characters—"anyone" and "noone"—and contrasts their experiences with those of their fellow townspeople.

WRITING CONNECTION

How easy do you find it to express your individuality? When you do, how do other people react—with admiration? criticism? bewilderment? Do you express your individuality more often in public or in private? In your notebook, explore what it means to express your individuality, recalling a particular experience, perhaps, or just writing down your general feelings. As you read these two poems, compare your feelings and experiences with those of the people presented in the poems.

danse russe

William Carlos Williams

If I when my wife is sleeping
and the baby and Kathleen[1]
are sleeping
and the sun is a flame-white disc
in silken mists
above shining trees,—
if I in my north room
dance naked, grotesquely
before my mirror
waving my shirt round my head
and singing softly to myself:
"I am lonely, lonely.
I was born to be lonely,
I am best so!"
If I admire my arms, my face,
my shoulders, flanks, buttocks
against the yellow drawn shades,—

Who shall say I am not
the happy genius of my household?

1. **Kathleen:** the nursemaid for the Williamses' children.

FROM PERSONAL RESPONSE *TO* CRITICAL ANALYSIS

REFLECT **1.** What overall feeling do you get from this poem? Describe this feeling in your notebook, then share your response with classmates.

RETHINK **2.** Did the last two lines surprise you? Explain what you think they mean.

3. Why do you think the speaker dances and sings "I am lonely"?

4. How does the poem fit with your own ideas about loneliness?

anyone lived in a pretty how town

E. E. Cummings

anyone lived in a pretty how town
(with up so floating many bells down)
spring summer autumn winter
he sang his didn't he danced his did.

Women and men (both little and small)
cared for anyone not at all
they sowed their isn't they reaped their
   same
sun moon stars rain

children guessed (but only a few
and down they forgot as up they grew
autumn winter spring summer)
that noone loved him more by more

when by now and tree by leaf
she laughed his joy she cried his grief
bird by snow and stir by still
anyone's any was all to her

someones married their everyones
laughed their cryings and did their dance
(sleep wake hope and then) they
said their nevers they slept their dream

stars rain sun moon
(and only the snow can begin to explain
how children are apt to forget to remember
with up so floating many bells down)

one day anyone died i guess
(and noone stooped to kiss his face)
busy folk buried them side by side
little by little and was by was

all by all and deep by deep
and more by more they dream their sleep
noone and anyone earth by april
wish by spirit and if by yes.

Women and men (both dong and ding)
summer autumn winter spring
reaped their sowing and went their came
sun moon stars rain

Icarus (1947), Henri Matisse. Plate VIII from *Jazz,* École des Beaux Arts, Paris/Art Resource, New York. Copyright © 1995 Succession H. Matisse/Artists Rights Society (ARS), New York.

RESPONDING OPTIONS

FROM PERSONAL RESPONSE *TO* CRITICAL ANALYSIS

REFLECT **1.** In your notebook, write down any questions or comments you have about "anyone lived in a pretty how town."

RETHINK **2.** Retell in your own words the story that unfolds in this poem. What, in your view, is the point of the story?

Consider
- how "anyone" compares with the other people who live in the town
- how you would describe the relationship between "anyone" and "noone"

3. Notice the refrains—lines in which the same words are repeated—in this poem. What ideas do they suggest to you?

RELATE **4.** How would you compare the ways in which the main characters in these two poems express their individuality? Are their feelings and experiences similar to those you explored for the Writing Connection on page 322?

ANOTHER PATHWAY

Cooperative Learning

With a small group of classmates, prepare presentations of both of these poems, perhaps combining dramatic readings with pantomime. Then choose one of your performances to present to the class.

LITERARY CONCEPTS

Style is the distinctive way in which a work of literature is written. E. E. Cummings's style is decidedly unconventional, breaking rules of capitalization, punctuation, diction (word choice), and syntax (word order). With a partner, choose about three stanzas of "anyone lived in a pretty how town" to "translate." Rewrite these stanzas, using standard capitalization and punctuation and changing words and phrases, if necessary, to make the stanzas conform to regular English diction and syntax. Have you made the ideas any clearer? Share your translation with the rest of the class and discuss what Cummings's style is able to convey that conventional language cannot.

QUICKWRITES

1. Assume the identity of the speaker of "Danse Russe" and write a **diary entry** about the incident presented in the poem, making sure to explain why you are lonely. For example, your entry might begin, "Today I woke up before my wife, the baby, and Kathleen."
2. In the style of E. E. Cummings, write an **epitaph** for the headstone of "anyone."

PORTFOLIO *Save your writing. You may want to use it later as a springboard to a piece for your portfolio.*

CRITIC'S CORNER

Williams believed that the goal of a poem must be "to refine, to clarify, to intensify that eternal moment in which we alone live." Do you think "Danse Russe" clarifies a particular moment? Do you think Cummings would agree with Williams's description of the goal of poetry? Explain your opinions.

ACROSS THE CURRICULUM

Dance In "Danse Russe," the speaker, Williams himself, dances in his own home after seeing a performance of the Ballets Russes. Find a photograph or a film segment showing the Ballets Russes or its stars, Vaslav Nijinsky and Anna Pavlova. Share your finding with the class, and speculate about why Williams reacted so strongly to the performance he saw.

Ballet costume designed for Vaslav Nijinsky (1912), Léon Bakst. For a production of *The Afternoon of a Faun.* The Granger Collection, New York.

WILLIAM CARLOS WILLIAMS

1883–1963

During the 45 years he practiced medicine, Dr. William Carlos Williams used a typewriter hidden in his desk to write poetry, both between patients' visits and early in the morning or late at night, while his household slept. Convinced that poetry should be grounded in immediate reality, he wrote about the industrialized urban world of northern New Jersey that was familiar to him.

Born in Rutherford, New Jersey, to an English father and a Puerto Rican mother, Williams received his medical degree in 1906 at the University of Pennsylvania, where he met the painter Charles Demuth and the poets H.D. and Ezra Pound. After completing his internship and spending a year in Europe, he established his medical practice in Rutherford in 1910. He wrote when he could, often jotting down ideas on prescription pads. Williams published more than 40 books during his lifetime, including poetry, plays, stories, novels, essays, and an autobiography. In 1963 he was posthumously awarded a Pulitzer Prize.

OTHER WORKS *Paterson, In the American Grain, Spring and All, Pictures from Brueghel*

E. E. CUMMINGS

1894–1962

Edward Estlin Cummings, the son of a well-known Unitarian minister, was born in Cambridge, Massachusetts. Raised in a happy, liberal, intellectually stimulating environment, Cummings developed varied artistic abilities with the encouragement of his family. He began writing when he was six years old and often illustrated his own stories.

During World War I, Cummings went to France to serve as an ambulance driver. After being mistakenly identified as a German sympathizer, he was held for three months in a French prisoner-of-war camp. His surrealistic and savage account of his war experiences, *The Enormous Room,* was published in 1922 and propelled him into the public eye. The next year, his first volume of poetry, *Tulips and Chimneys,* was published.

After the war, Cummings lived in Paris and then in New York's Greenwich Village, where he spent his days painting and writing. By the 1950s, Cummings's playful, innovative style had made him one of the most popular of American poets. His pioneering experiments with innovative forms of language remain a significant influence on the poetry of today.

OTHER WORKS *&, 1 x 1, 95 Poems*

• *AUTHOR BACKGROUND*

PREVIEWING

POETRY

Ending Poem

Aurora Levins Morales
and Rosario Morales

Tía Chucha

Luis J. Rodriguez

PERSONAL CONNECTION

If you had to introduce yourself to a small group of people you didn't know, how would you identify yourself? Would you link yourself to a cultural group? Would you mention unique traits and qualities that you possess? In your notebook, create an identity card for yourself. Include words and phrases that help define who you are. Feel free to draw a self-portrait, or a symbol that represents a part of your identity, in the top left-hand corner.

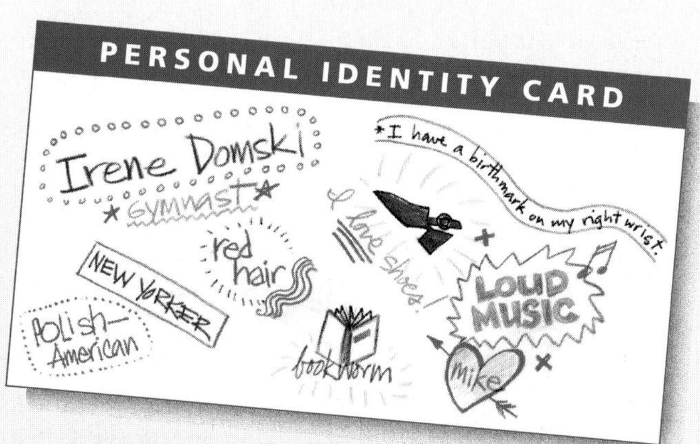

BIOGRAPHICAL CONNECTION

The two poems you are about to read are celebrations of identity. The first, "Ending Poem," was written by Aurora Levins Morales and her mother, Rosario Morales, poets of Puerto Rican ancestry. They created this poem to conclude a reading they did together in San Francisco. Rosario Morales explains: "We used lines from the poems we were performing to create a new whole that reflected . . . our differing yet clearly similar experiences as women, as immigrants and children of immigrants." She adds that the poem also reflects "our connection in spirit and community with the children of other migrations." This poem also appears at the end of a book the Moraleses co-authored, *Getting Home Alive*.

In the second poem, "Tía Chucha," Luis J. Rodriguez celebrates individual identity rather than cultural identity. It is a portrait of the poet's eccentric aunt, who had a great influence on him when he was a child. *Tía* is Spanish for aunt; *Chucha* is a Spanish nickname that may mean either "sweetheart" or "sly and foxy."

READING CONNECTION

Understanding Form The form of a poem involves the way the words, lines, and stanzas are arranged on the page. Before you read "Ending Poem," notice that every other line of the poem is printed in italic type. It is a collaborative poem, with some lines contributed by Aurora and others by Rosario. According to the poets, the alternating typefaces do not signal whose line is whose but instead "blur origins and authorship," making the speaker a "new entity, a collective voice." To get a sense of this collective voice, try reading the poem aloud, alternating lines with a partner.

ending poem

Aurora Levins Morales

and Rosario Morales

I am what I am.
A child of the Americas.
A light-skinned mestiza[1] of the Caribbean.
A child of many diaspora,[2] born into this continent at a crossroads.
I am Puerto Rican. I am U.S. American.
I am New York Manhattan and the Bronx.
A mountain-born, country-bred, homegrown jíbara[3] child,
up from the shtetl,[4] a California Puerto Rican Jew.
A product of the New York ghettos I have never known.
I am an immigrant
and the daughter and granddaughter of immigrants.
We didn't know our forbears'[5] names with a certainty.
They aren't written anywhere.
First names only, or mija, negra, ne,[6] honey, sugar, dear.

I come from the dirt where the cane was grown.
My people didn't go to dinner parties. They weren't invited.
I am caribeña,[7] island grown.
Spanish is in my flesh, ripples from my tongue, lodges in my hips,
the language of garlic and mangoes.
Boricua.[8] As Boricuas come from the isle of Manhattan.
I am of latinoamerica, rooted in the history of my continent.
I speak from that body. Just brown and pink and full of drums inside.

Untitled [The Wedding Quilt] (1981), Rosario Morales.

---

1. **mestiza** (mĕs-tē′sä) *Spanish:* a woman of mixed racial ancestry, especially one of mixed European and Native American ancestry.
2. **diaspora** (dī-ăs′pər-ə): a migration or scattering of a group of people (here used as a plural).
3. **jíbara** (hē′bä-rä) *Spanish:* a girl or woman of rural Puerto Rico; female peasant.
4. **shtetl** (shtĕt′l): one of the small Jewish communities formerly found in Eastern Europe.
5. **forbears:** ancestors (a variant spelling of *forebears*).
6. **mija** (mē′hä), **negra** (nĕ′grä), **ne** (nĕ) *Spanish:* affectionate terms for girls or women.
7. **caribeña** (kä-rē-bĕ′nyä) *Spanish:* a girl or woman of the Caribbean islands.
8. **Boricua** (bô-rē′kwä) *Spanish:* Puerto Rican.

I am not African.
Africa waters the roots of my tree, but I cannot return.

I am not Taína.[9]
I am a late leaf of that ancient tree,
and my roots reach into the soil of two Americas.
Taíno is in me, but there is no way back.

I am not European, though I have dreamt of those cities.
Each plate is different,
wood, clay, papier mâché, metal, basketry, a leaf, a coconut shell.
Europe lives in me but I have no home there.

The table has a cloth woven by one, dyed by another,
embroidered by another still.
I am a child of many mothers.
They have kept it all going
All the civilizations erected on their backs.
All the dinner parties given with their labor.

We are new.
They gave us life, kept us going,
brought us to where we are.
Born at a crossroads.
Come, lay that dishcloth down. Eat, dear, eat.
History made us.
We will not eat ourselves up inside anymore.

And we are whole.

In My Grandmother's Garden (1982), Rosario Morales.

9. **Taína** (tä-ē′nä) *Spanish:* a girl or woman of the Caribbean Taino Indians. The first native people encountered by Columbus, the Taino were wiped out during the Spanish colonization of the 16th century.

FROM PERSONAL RESPONSE *TO* CRITICAL ANALYSIS

REFLECT

1. Pick a line from this poem that you liked or wondered about. Copy it in your notebook to discuss with classmates.

RETHINK

2. In your view, what is the most important thing being said about the identity of the speaker?
3. What do you think the last two lines of the poem mean?
4. Can you think of any reason for the title "Ending Poem" other than the writers' use of the poem to end a poetry reading and a book? Explain your opinion.

Woman with Turban (1985), Gilberto Ruiz. Mixed media on fabric, 36″ × 52″, courtesy of Barbara Gillman Gallery, Miami Beach, Florida.

Luis J. Rodriguez

Every few years
Tía Chucha would visit the family
in a tornado of song
and open us up
as if we were an overripe avocado.
She was a dumpy, black-haired
creature of upheaval,
who often came unannounced
with a bag of presents
including home-made perfumes and colognes
that smelled something like
rotting fish
on a hot day at the tuna cannery.

I didn't learn guitar,
but I learned
something
about her craving
for the new, the unbroken
...so she could break it.

They said she was crazy.
Oh sure, she once ran out naked
to catch the postman
with a letter that didn't belong to us.
I mean, she had this annoying habit
of boarding city buses
and singing at the top of her voice
(one bus driver even refused to go on
until she got off).
But crazy?

To me, she was the wisp
of the wind's freedom,
a music-maker
who once tried to teach me guitar
but ended up singing
and singing,
me listening,
and her singing
until I put the instrument down
and watched the clock
click the lesson time away.

I didn't learn guitar,
but I learned something
about her craving
for the new, the unbroken
. . . so she could break it.
Periodically she banished
herself from the family
and was the better for it.

I secretly admired Tía Chucha.
She was always quick with a story,
another *"Pepito"* joke,
or a hand-written lyric
that she would produce
regardless of the occasion.

She was a despot[1]
of desire;
uncontainable
as a splash of water
on a varnished table.

I wanted to remove
the layers
of unnatural seeing
the way Tía Chucha beheld
the world, with first eyes,
like an infant
who can discern
the elixir[2]
within milk.

I wanted to be
one of the prizes
she stuffed into
her rumpled bag.

1. **despot** (dĕs′pət): a ruler with absolute power.
2. **elixir** (ĭ-lĭk′sər): a medicine believed to have the power to cure all ills.

RESPONDING OPTIONS

FROM PERSONAL RESPONSE *TO* CRITICAL ANALYSIS

REFLECT 1. What are your impressions of Tía Chucha? Write or sketch your impressions in your notebook.

RETHINK 2. Which lines of the poem do you think describe Tía Chucha most effectively?

3. In your own words, explain why the speaker admires Tía Chucha.

   Consider
   - what he learns when she tries to teach him to play the guitar
   - his statement about how she beheld the world

4. Does the speaker succeed in making you admire Tía Chucha? Explain why or why not.

RELATE 5. It is sometimes said that people who are "crazy" see the world more clearly than others. Do you agree or disagree? Explain your opinion, making reference to Tía Chucha or to someone else who reminds you of her.

6. When you defined your identity for the Personal Connection on page 328, did you emphasize what ties you to others (as the poets did in "Ending Poem") or what sets you apart from others (as in the poet's portrait of his aunt in "Tía Chucha")? In general, which do you think is more important?

ANOTHER PATHWAY

Cooperative Learning

With a partner or a small group of classmates, perform a dramatic reading of "Ending Poem" or "Tía Chucha" for the class. Include appropriate gestures or pantomimed scenes in your performance. If necessary, ask a Spanish-speaking classmate to help you with difficult pronunciations.

LITERARY CONCEPTS

The **speaker** of a poem, like the narrator of a story, is the voice that talks to the reader. In "Ending Poem" and "Tía Chucha"—although not in all poetry—the speakers can be identified with the poets themselves. Sometimes the speaker is someone or something other than the poet, such as an invented person, an historical figure, an entire race, or an element of nature. Compare the speakers of "Ending Poem" and "Tía Chucha." What are their **tones,** or attitudes toward their subjects? How intimately does each address the reader?

QUICKWRITES

1. Define your own identity in an **autobiographical sketch** or **poem** titled "I Am What I Am." You might pick up words and phrases from the personal identity card you made for the Personal Connection on page 328. If you like, write a collaborative poem with a partner, modeled on "Ending Poem."
2. Write a brief **testimonial** in verse or prose to pay tribute to a favorite relative or a significant person in your life.

PORTFOLIO Save your writing. You may want to use it later as a springboard to a piece for your portfolio.

LITERARY LINKS

What common characteristics do you see in "Ending Poem," "Song of Myself" (page 328), and "I Am Joaquín" (page 243)?

ALTERNATIVE ACTIVITIES

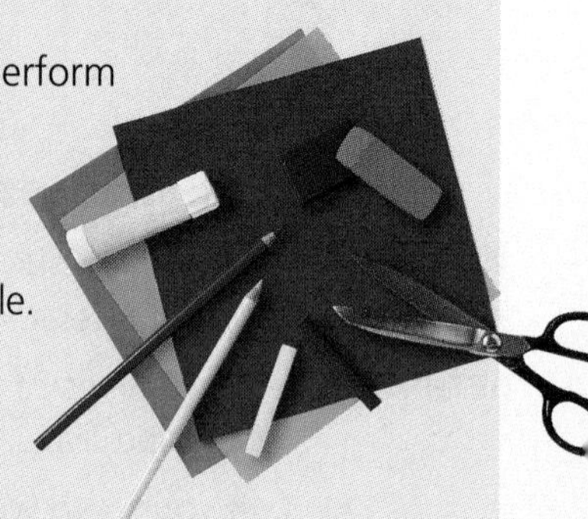

1. Assume the character of Tía Chucha and perform a **monologue** in which you express your feelings about your life and your family.
2. In "Ending Poem" identity and heritage are described in terms of a tree and a dinner table. Create your own **self-representation** — perhaps a drawing or a collage of objects— to show what contributes to your identity.

Aurora Levins Morales, Rosario Morales

1954–, 1930–

Rosario Morales, a child of Puerto Rican immigrants, grew up in New York City. She married Richard Levins, a son of Jewish immigrants, and in 1951 returned to Puerto Rico with him to learn about the island she felt to be "both mine and not mine." In the early 1960s she moved back to the United States with her husband and her young daughter Aurora. Aurora Levins Morales was raised in New York and Chicago. She was influenced by the rich stories of her parents and her Puerto Rican and Jewish grandparents.

Both Rosario and Aurora wrote as young children and were inspired to resume writing by the women's liberation movement of the early 1970s. In *Getting Home Alive,* the book they co-authored in 1986, they explored their cultural, political, generational, and geographical identities. As of 1995, Rosario was living in Cambridge, Massachusetts, and working on her memoirs and a collection of stories; Aurora was working on *Remedios,* a prose-poetry retelling of Puerto Rican and related history through the lives of women.

Luis J. Rodriguez

A son of Mexican immigrants, Luis J. Rodriguez was born in 1954 in El Paso, Texas, and raised in Los Angeles, California. Growing up surrounded by violence, he barely escaped to reach adulthood and explore his creativity as a writer. In the 1960s and 1970s, Rodriguez became involved with Hispanic gangs in Los Angeles. In *Always Running: La Vida Loca—Gang Days in L.A.,* he describes how he eventually left gang life behind through the help of a counselor.

After finishing high school, Rodriguez attended college and at various times worked as a school-bus driver, a truck driver, a factory worker, a carpenter, and a journalist. In addition to writing poetry and his memoirs, he has written articles, reviews, short stories, essays, and screenplays, including one of *Always Running.* Rodriguez told an interviewer, "Despite great odds, today I'm a poet and writer. . . . We all have the capabilities of great art and poetry. It's a matter of tapping into that creative reservoir we contain as human beings. Once tapped, this reservoir is inexhaustible." In 1989, Rodriguez founded Tía Chucha Press, named for his aunt, to publish the first works of emerging young poets.

OTHER WORKS *The Concrete River*

• *ART GALLERY*

gary keillor

Garrison Keillor

When I was sixteen years old, I stood six feet two inches tall and weighed a hundred and forty pounds. I was intense and had the metabolism[1] of a wolverine. I ate two or three lunches a day and three full dinners at night, as my family sat around the kitchen table and observed, and I cleaned off their plates too when they had poor appetites or were finicky. There was no food I disliked except muskmelon, which smelled rotten and loathsome. Everything else I ate. (It was Minnesota so we didn't have seafood, except fish sticks, of course.) I was a remarkable person. I was a junior in high school, Class of 1960. I was smart, so smart that poor grades didn't bother me in the slightest; I considered them no reflection on my intelligence. I read four books a week, and I sometimes walked home from school, all twelve miles, so I could relive favorite chapters out loud, stride along the shoulder of the highway past the potato farms, and say brilliant and outrageous things, and sing in a big throbbing voice great songs like "Til There Was You" and "Love Me Tender."

I had no wish to sing in front of an audience, songs were a private thing with me. I was an intense person, filled with powerful feelings, and I assumed that I would live alone for the rest of my life, perhaps in a monastery, silent, swishing around in a cassock,[2] my heart broken by a tragic love affair with someone like Natalie Wood,[3] my life dedicated to God.

I was a lucky boy. I had learned this two years before on a car trip to Colorado. My Uncle Earl and Aunt Myrna drove there that summer—he had been stationed in Colorado Springs during the war—along with my cousins Gordon and Mel, and I got to go too. I won that trip by dropping over to their house and being extremely nice. I'd say, "Here, let me wash those dishes." I'd say, "Boy, I'm sure in a mood to mow a lawn." And then she'd offer me a glass of nectar and a piece of angel food cake and I'd eat it and say, "Boy, I was looking at *National Geographic* the other night and they had a big article on Colorado. It was so interesting. Just the different rock formations and things. I don't see how people can look at those mountains and not know there's a God." And she'd smile at me, a good boy who mowed lawns and whose faith was pure, and I got to go. Of course my brothers and sisters were fit to be tied. "How come he gets to go? We never get to go. Oh no, we have

1. **metabolism** (mĭ-tăb′ə-lĭz′əm): the set of processes by which food is transformed into energy.
2. **cassock:** an ankle-length garment worn by clergymen.
3. **Natalie Wood:** a glamorous American movie star.

to stay here all summer and work in the garden while he goes riding out to Colorado." They just didn't get it. Trips to Colorado don't fall in your lap. You've got to go out and earn Colorado.

We took off on the trip, and I was a very good passenger. I sat in the favored front seat between my aunt and uncle, looking at the scenery for hours, no stains on my clothes, my face clean, a good strong bladder, never got carsick, and had a subtle sideways technique for picking my nose—you'd never see it even if you looked straight at me. Far off, the mountains appeared, shining on the horizon for almost a whole day, and then we rose up into them—snowcapped peaks, like the last scene in a western in which justice and romance prevail, and when we reached Denver (*EL.5280,* the sign said, exactly a mile), we ate dinner at a Chinese restaurant and my fortune cookie said: "You are enterprising[4]—take advantage of it." Well, there it was in a nutshell.

The mountains were startling in their whiteness and steepness, the valleys dark in the late afternoon, the peaks glittering in pure sunlight, beautiful stands of light gray-green aspen floating like fog, and my aunt took a picture of me with trees and mountains behind me. Just me, tall and intense. You would never guess I was from Minnesota. I thought, "This is my lucky picture. I'll keep it the rest of my life."

My family lived in the country, along the Mississippi River between Minneapolis and Tryon, and I attended New Tryon High School, which was bulging under a tidal wave of children from new subdivisions on the other side of the river, places with names like Riverview Estates and Woodlawn and Forest Hills. Our side, South Tryon Township, along the West River Road, was still rural, truck farms, and scattered houses on big rolling tracts, and we West River Roaders were the cream of the school. The editor of the school paper, *The Beacon,* Elaine Eggert, was one of us; so were the stars of the debate team and the speech team, three of the class officers, and the chairperson of the spring talent show, Dede Petersen, who rode on my bus.

I had been in love with Dede for two years, in an intense and secret way. She had bouncy blonde hair and wore soft sweaters, plaid skirts, penny loafers and knee socks. One winter day I wrote her a fourteen-page letter (single-spaced) saying that she was my ideal of womanhood, a person of pure taste, excellent judgment, stunning beauty, and natural intelligence, a woman to whom I could pledge myself in a spiritual friendship that would last forever no matter what. If the friendship should turn into physical love, good, and if not, fine. We would be friends for the rest of our lives, our souls communing[5] over vast distances.

I did not, after long thought, give her the letter. I guessed that she might laugh at it and also that her boyfriend Bill Swenson might pound me into the ground. He was an intense person too.

One afternoon riding home on the bus, sitting behind her, I heard her complain to her pal Marcy about the miseries of planning the April talent show. Bill Swenson would be in it, lip-synching "All Shook Up," and he was terrific, but there wasn't much other talent around, nothing compared to last year, when all those guys sang "Bali Hai" with the coconuts on their chests,[6] and the skit about school lunch when the kids pretended to vomit and out came green confetti, and of course last year there had been Barbara Lee. Barbara Lee was the most talented person ever to graduate from our school. She danced, she sang, she did the splits, she played

4. **enterprising:** willing to undertake new projects; ambitious.

5. **communing** (kə-myōō′nĭng): talking or meeting in close understanding.

6. **guys sang . . . chests:** In the musical *South Pacific,* sailors stationed on a remote island sing about women while wearing coconut shells (to imitate breasts) and grass skirts; later, a woman sings "Bali Hai," a song about a beautiful, magical island.

Detail of *Play Within a Play* (1963), David Hockney. Oil on canvas and plexiglass, 72″ × 78″. Copyright © David Hockney.

the marimba.[7] She was Broadway bound, no doubt about it.

I leaned forward and said, "Well, I think we have lots of talent." Oh? like who, for example? she said. I said, "Well, I could do something." *You?* she said. "Or I could get together with some other kids and we could do a skit." *Like what?* she said. I said, "Oh, I don't know. Something about the school burning down. It all depends."

"That doesn't sound funny to me," she said. Marcy didn't think it was funny either.

What burned my toast was her saying *"You?"* when I volunteered to be in her talent show. I was only being helpful, I was not claiming to be another Barbara Lee. I had no interest in the stage at all until I heard her incredulity[8] and amusement—*"You?"*—and then I was interested

7. **marimba** (mə-rĭm′bə): a large wooden percussion instrument resembling a xylophone.

8. **incredulity** (ĭn′krĭ-do͞o′lĭ-tē): disbelief.

in being interested. A spiritual friendship with Dede was out of the question, if she thought I was the sort of guy you could say *"You?"* to.

No one in our family sang or performed for entertainment, only for the glory of God and only in groups, never solo. We were Christian people; we did not go in for show. But I was an intense young man. Intensity was my guiding principle. And when I thought about joining that monastery after Natalie Wood rejected me and spending my life in the woodshop making sturdy chairs and tables, I thought that perhaps I ought to get in the talent show at New Tryon High first, get a whiff of show business before I gave my life to God.

"Never give up on beauty," she said. "Never compromise your standards out of fear that someone may not understand." Teachers were full of useless advice like that.

It was one of those ugly and treacherous springs in the Midwest, when winter refuses to quit, like a big surly[9] drunk who heads for home and then staggers back for another round and a few more songs that everyone has heard before. It was cold and wet, and we sat day after day in dim airless classrooms, the fluorescent lights turned on at midday, the murky sky and bare trees filling the big classroom windows, pools of oil-slicked rain in the parking lot, the grass in front dead, the Stars and Stripes hanging limp and wet like laundry. In plane geometry, I was lost in the wilderness, had been lost since Christmas, and in history, we were slogging through World War I, and in English class, we were memorizing poems. "These are treasures you will carry with you forever," said Miss Rasmussen, a big woman in a blue knit suit. In her wanderings around the classroom as she talked about poetry and metaphor, she often stopped in the aisle and stood looming above me, her voice overhead, her hand resting on my desk, her puffy white hand and red knuckles and short ringless fingers. Her stopping there indicated, I knew, her fondness for me. I was the only student of hers who wrote poems. She had even suggested that I memorize and recite one of my own poems. I declined. Part of the memorization assignment was reciting the poem in front of the class. My poems were far too intense and personal to be said out loud in front of people. I was memorizing Whitman's elegy[10] on the death of Abraham Lincoln, "O Captain! My Captain!" I walked home through the rain one cold day crying out, "O Captain! my Captain! our fearful trip is done,/The ship has weather'd every rack,[11] the prize we sought is won."

One day a fuel oil truck backed into our driveway and got stuck in the mud and the driver put it into forward gear and got dug in deeper. He gunned it in reverse and gunned it forward and rocked the truck loose and pulled forward and unwound his hose and started filling our fuel oil tank, but meanwhile he had left deep ruts in my mother's garden and the front yard. She was home alone, washing clothes. She heard the grinding and roaring from down in the laundry room and came outdoors to find her garden dug up and the tulips and irises destroyed, and the driver looked at her and said, "You ought to do something about your driveway." Not a word of apology, acted like it was the driveway's fault. My mother was the quietest, politest person ever, she felt that raising your voice indicated a flawed character, but she put her hands on her hips and said, "Mister, if

9. **surly:** bad-tempered; rude.

10. **elegy** (ĕl′ə-jē): a poem lamenting a person's death.

11. **rack:** buffeting (as by a storm).

you can't figure out how to drive a truck, then they oughta find you a job you'd be able to handle." And she told him to get out and she would be sending the company a bill for the flower garden. And he did. And she did. And the company sent us a check and an apology from the general manager, a Harold L. Bergstrom.

It was the first time in my memory that my mother had fought back and raised her voice to a stranger, a watershed[12] moment for me. I heard the story from our neighbor, Mr. Couture, and I admired her so much for standing up to the jerk and defending our family's honor. Her principles had always told her to be quiet and polite and turn the other cheek and never make trouble, but there comes a time to let go of principle and do the right thing. To me, this seemed to open the door to show business.

And then, about a week before the talent show, suddenly I was in. The real power behind the show wasn't Dede, it was Miss Rasmussen, my teacher, the adviser to the talent show, and the day I stood before the class and recited "O Captain! My Captain!" she told Dede to put me in the show. The next day, Miss Rasmussen had me stand up in class and recite it again. It was one of the finest pieces of oral interpretation she had ever seen, she said. She sat in a back corner of the room, her head bowed, her eyes closed, as I stood in front and with dry mouth launched the Captain's ship again, and she did not see the kids smirking and gagging and retching and pulling long invisible skeins of snot from their nostrils when my Captain died and I got to "O the bleeding drops of red,/Where on the deck my Captain lies,/Fallen cold and dead," they rolled their eyes and clutched at their hearts and died. Then, when she stood up, her eyes moist, and clapped, they all clapped too. "Wasn't that good!" she cried. "You really liked it, didn't you! Oh, I'm glad you did! He's going to recite it in the talent show, too! Won't that be nice!" A couple of boys in front clapped their hands over their mouths and pretended to lose their lunch. They seemed to speak for most of the class.

So I was in the talent show, which I wanted to be, but with an inferior piece of material. I suggested to Miss Rasmussen that "O Captain! My Captain!" might not be right for the talent show audience, that maybe I could find a humorous poem, and she said, "Oh, it'll be just fine," not realizing the gravity[13] of the situation. "Never give up on beauty," she said. "Never compromise your standards out of fear that someone may not understand." Teachers were full of useless advice like that.

I tried not to think about "O Captain." I experimented with combing my hair a new way, with the part on the right. I was handsome at certain angles, I thought, and a right-hand part would emphasize a good angle. I stood at the bathroom mirror, a small mirror in my hand, and experimented holding my head cocked back and aimed up and to the right, a pose favored by seniors in their graduation pictures, which looked good from either side, and reciting "O Captain" with my head at that angle. I had good skin except when it flared up, which it did two days before the show, and it took a long time to repair the damage. There were six children in our family and only one bathroom, but I spent fifteen minutes behind a locked door doing surgery and applying alcohol and cold packs and skin-toned cream. The little kids stood banging on the door, pleading to use the toilet. I said, "Well, how bad do you have to go?" I was the one in show business, after all.

I worked on "O Captain" so that every line was set in my head. I recited it to myself in the mirror ("O Captain! O Captain! the fateful day is done,/Your blemishes have disappeared, the skin you sought is won") and for my mother, who said I was holding my head at an unnatural angle, and then, the Friday night before the

12. **watershed:** marking an important turning point.

13. **gravity:** seriousness or importance.

show, I recited it at a party at Elaine Eggert's house, and there my interpretation of "O Captain! My Captain!" took a sharp turn toward the English stage.

Miss Rasmussen loved a recording of Sir John Gielgud[14] reading "Favourites of English Poetry" and she played it once for our class, a whole hour of it, and from that day, all the boys in the class loved to do English accents. A little lisp, endless dramatic pauses, inflections including shrill birdlike tones of wonderment, and instead of the vowel *o* that delicious English *aaooww,* a bleating sound not found anywhere in American speech. In the cafeteria, when my friend Ralph Moody came to the table where all of us West River Road rats sat, he stood holding his tray, peering down at us and the welter of milk cartons and comic books and ice cream wrappers and uneaten macaroni-cheese lunches, and after a long pause he cried "Aaaaoooowww," with a shudder, a great man forced to sit among savages. So at the party, surrounded by kids from the debate team and the newspaper, the cream of West River Road society, when Elaine had said for the sixth time, "Do the poem you're going to do on Monday," I reached back for Ralph's *Aaooww* and did "O Captain" as Sir John might have done it:

Aoowww Cap-tin, myyyyy Cap-tin,
aower ____________ feeah-fool twip eez
done!
Th' sheep has wethah'd ____________ eviddy
rack!
th' priiiiiiize we sot ____________ eez won!
But ____________ aaaoooooooowwwww
th' bleeeeeeeding drrrops ____________ of
rrred ____________
wheahhhh ____________
on th' deck ____________
myyyy Captin liiiiiiies ____________
fallin ____________
caaaoooowwwld ____________
and ____________ ded!

It was a good party poem. I recited it in the basement, and then everyone upstairs had to come down and hear it, and then Elaine had to call up a friend of hers in the city and I did it on the phone. It got better. "Miss Rasmussen is going to burst a blood vessel," said Elaine. She was a true rebel, despite the editorials she wrote extolling[15] the value of team play and school spirit. I was starting to see some of the virtues in her that I had previously imagined in Dede Petersen.

Bill Swenson had worked for weeks on "All Shook Up," and he looked cool and capable backstage before the curtain went up. His hair was slicked down, he wore heavy eye makeup, and he was dressed in a white suit with gold trim, without a single wrinkle in it. He stood, holding his arms out to the sides, avoiding wrinkling, and practiced moving his lips to "A-wella bless my soul, what'sa wrong with me? I'm itching like a man on a fuzzy tree." Dede knelt, shining his black shoes.

He pretended to be surprised to see me. "What are you doing here? You running the p.a. or what?"

I told him I would be in the show, reciting a poem by Walt Whitman.

"Who? Twitman?" No. Whitman, I said.

"Well, I'm glad I don't have to follow that," he said, with heavy sarcasm. He glanced at my outfit, brown corduroy pants, a green plaid cotton shirt, a charcoal gray sweater vest, and said, "You better change into your stage clothes though."

"These are my stage clothes," I said.

"Oh," he said, his eyebrows raised. "Oh." He smiled. "Well, good luck." He did not know

14. **Sir John Gielgud:** a highly respected British actor and director.

15. **extolling** (ĭk-stō′lĭng): praising highly.

how much luck I had. I had my lucky picture in my pocket, the one of me in the mountains.

Dede brushed his forehead with face powder and poofed up his hair. She gave him a light kiss on the lips. "You're going to be great," she said. He smiled. He had no doubt about that. She had put him high on the program, right after "America the Beautiful," a dramatic choral reading from *Antigone,*[16] a solo trumpet rendition of "Nobody Knows the Trouble I've Seen," and a medley of Rodgers and Hammerstein songs performed on the piano by Cheryl Ann Hansen. Then Bill would electrify the crowd with "All Shook Up," and then I would do "O Captain."

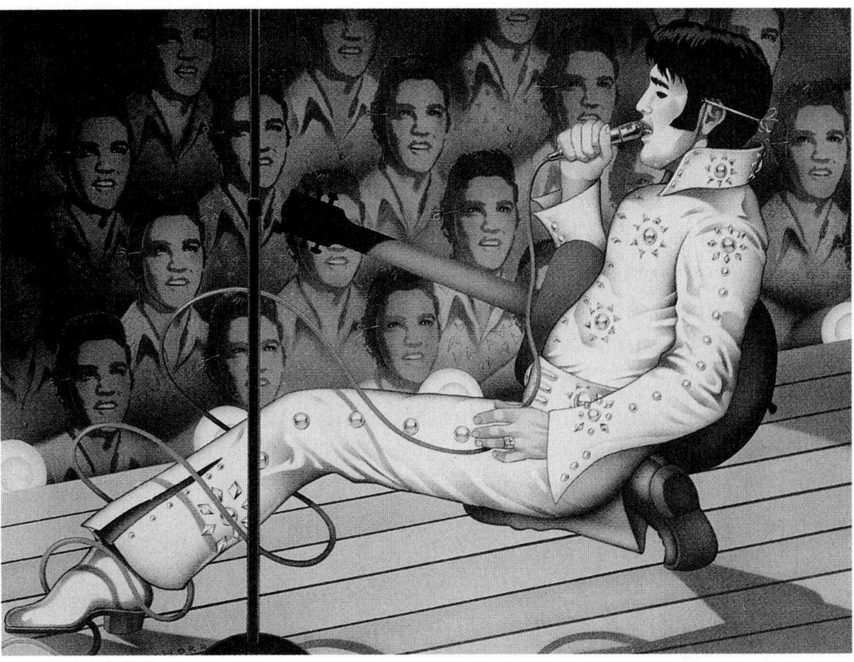

Illustration by Todd Schorr.

He was Mr. Cool. After Cheryl Ann Hansen's interminable[17] medley, which kids clapped and cheered for only because they knew that her mother had recently died of cancer, Bill grinned at Dede and bounced out on stage and yelled, "Hellllll-ooo baby!" in a Big Bopper[18] voice, and the audience clapped and yelled, "Hellllooo baby!" and he yelled, "You knowwwwwwwww what I like!" and he was a big hit in the first five seconds. He said it again, "Helllllllllooo baby!" and the audience yelled back, "Helllllllllooo baby!" And then Dede carefully set the phonograph needle on the record of "All Shook Up" and Elvis's hoody voice blasted out in the auditorium and Bill started shimmying across the stage and tossing his head like a dustmop. "My friends say I'm acting queer as a bug, I'm in love—huh! I'm all shook up," and on the *huh* he stuck both arms in the air and threw his hip to the left, *huh,* and the audience sang along on the "hmm hmm hmm—oh—yeah yeah"—he was the star of the show right there. Dede ran to look out through a hole in the curtain, leaving me standing by the record player. She was so thrilled, she hopped up and down and squealed.

I could see part of him out there, his white suit hanging loose, the red socks flashing, him pulling out the red satin hanky and tossing it into the audience, *hmmm hmmm hmmm oh yeah yeah,* and at the end the whole auditorium stood up and screamed. He came off stage bright with sweat, grinning, and went back out and made three deep bows, and threw his hip, *huh,* and came off and Dede wiped his face with a towel and kissed him, and the audience was still screaming and whistling and yelling, "More! More!" and right then Bill made his fateful decision. He went out and did his other number.

16. ***Antigone*** (ăn-tĭg'ə-nē): an ancient Greek tragedy by Sophocles.

17. **interminable** (ĭn-tûr'mə-nə-bəl): endless.

18. **Big Bopper:** a popular singer of the late 1950s.

It was "Vaya con Dios" by the Conquistadores.[19] Dede put the needle down and the guitars throbbed, and the audience clapped, but Bill hadn't worked as hard on "Vaya con Dios" as on "All Shook Up" and his lips didn't synch very well, but the main problem was that "Vaya con Dios" was "Vaya con Dios," and after "All Shook Up" it seemed like a joke, especially since the Conquistadores were a trio and Bill wasn't. Kids started to laugh, and Bill got mad—perhaps "Vaya con Dios" meant a lot to him personally—and his grim face and his clenched fists made "Vaya con Dios" seem even zanier. Dede ran to the hole in the curtain to see where the hooting and light booing were coming from, and there, standing by the record player, I thought I would help poor Bill out by lightly touching the record with my finger and making the music go flat and sour for a moment.

It was miraculous, the effect this had, like pressing a laugh button. I touched the black vinyl rim and the music warbled, and fifty feet away, people erupted in fits of happiness. I did it again. How wonderful to hear people laugh! and to be able to give them this precious gift of laughter so easily. Then I discovered a speed control that let me slow it down and speed it up. The singers sounded demented,[20] in love one moment, carsick the next. The audience thought this was a stitch. But Bill sort of went to pieces. One prime qualification for a show business career, I would think, is the ability to improvise and go with the audience, but Bill Swenson did not have that ability. Here he was, rescued from his drippy encore, magically transformed into comedy, and he was too rigid to recognize what a hit he was. His lips stopped moving. He shook his fist at someone in the wings, perhaps me, and yelled a common vulgar expression at someone in the crowd, and wheeled around and walked off.

I didn't care to meet him, so I walked fast right past him onto the stage, and coming out of the bright light into the dark, he didn't see me until I was out of reach. There was still some heavy booing when I arrived at the microphone, and I made a deep English-actor type of bow, with princely flourishes and flutters, and they laughed, and then they were mine all the way. I held on to them for dear life for the next two minutes. I sailed into "O Captain," in my ripest accent, with roundhouse[21] gestures, outflung arms, hand clapped to the forehead ___________ I cried:

AOOWWW CAP-TIN, MYYYYY CAP-TIN,
AOWER ___________ FEEAH-FOOL
TWIP EEZ DONE!
TH' SHEEP HAS WETHAH'D
___________ EVIDDY RACK!
TH' PRIIIIIIIZE WE SOT ___________
EEZ WON!
BUT _____ _____
AAAAOOOOOOOWWWWW
TH' BLLEEEEEEEDING DRRROPS
____
OF RRRED ___________
WHEAHH ___________
ON TH' DECK ___________
BEEEL SWEN-SON LIIIIIIIES
____
FALLIN ___________
CAAAOOOOWWWLD
___________ AND ___________
___________ DED!

It wasn't a kind or generous thing to do, but it was successful, especially the "*AAAAAOOOOOOOWWWWW*" and also the part about Bill Swenson, and at the end there was shouting and whistling and pandemonium, and I left the stage with the audience wanting more, but I had witnessed the perils of success, and did not

19. **"Vaya con Dios"** (vī′ä kôn dē′ôs) **by the Conquistadores:** A song (whose title is a Spanish expression of farewell, literally "Go with God") that was the biggest hit for this singing group of the 1950s and 1960s.

20. **demented:** mentally ill; insane.

consider an encore. "Go out and take a bow," said Miss Rasmussen, and out I went, and came back off. Dede and Bill were gone. Dede was not feeling well, said Miss Rasmussen.

I watched the rest of the show standing at the back of the auditorium. The act after me was a girl from the wrong side of the river who did a humorous oral interpretation entitled "Granny on the Phone with Her Minister." The girl had painted big surprise eyebrows and a big red mouth on her so we would know it was comedy, and as the sketch went on, she shrieked to remind us that it was humorous. The joke was that Granny was hard-of-hearing and got the words wrong. Then came an accordionist, a plump young man named David Lee, Barbara's cousin, who was a little overambitious with "Lady of Spain" and should have left out two or three of the variations, and a tap dancer who tapped to a recording of "Nola" and who made the mistake of starting the number all over again after she had made a mistake. I enjoyed watching these dogs, strictly from a professional point of view. And then the choir returned to sing "Climb Every Mountain," and then Miss Rasmussen stood and spoke about the importance of encouraging those with talent and how lucky we should feel to have them in our midst to bring beauty and meaning to our lives. And then the lights came up, and my classmates piled into the aisles and headed for the door and saw me standing in back, modest me, looking off toward the stage. Almost every one of them said how good I was as they trooped past—clapped my shoulder, said, hey, you were great, you should've done more, that was funny—and I stood and patiently endured their attention until the auditorium was empty and then I went home.

"You changed the poem a little," Miss Rasmussen said the next day. "Did you forget the line?" "Yes," I said. "Your voice sounded funny," she said. I told her I was nervous. "Oh well," she said, "they seemed to like it anyway."

"Thank you," I said, "thank you very much." ❖

21. **roundhouse:** wide and sweeping.

Garrison Keillor

1942–

The storyteller, writer, and radio-show host Garrison Keillor (kē′lər) was born in Minnesota. He and his family were members of the Plymouth Brethren, a strict religious sect that frowned on dancing, card playing, and other forms of entertainment. As a child, however, Keillor fell in love with both the written and the spoken word. He enjoyed listening to religious parables and tales told by his relatives and other adults, and he developed a keen appetite for reading and writing: "When I was fourteen, I was happy to read all day every day and into the night." In the eighth grade, he submitted poems to the school paper under the name Garrison instead of his given name, Gary, "to hide behind a name that meant strength."

In addition to reading and writing, Keillor's other childhood passion was listening to the radio. While attending the University of Minnesota, he worked for the campus radio station, and after graduating from college, he became the host of a classical-music show on Minnesota Public Radio. In 1974, Keillor launched the immensely popular radio show *A Prairie Home Companion,* set in the mythical Mid-western town of Lake Wobegon.

In addition to working as the host and writer of *A Prairie Home Companion,* Keillor has written several books. "Gary Keillor" is taken from his 1993 collection of stories, *The Book of Guys.*

OTHER WORKS *Lake Wobegon Days, Happy to Be Here, Leaving Home, We Are Still Married, WLT: A Radio Romance*

WRITING ABOUT
LITERATURE

One Step Beyond

Have you ever been frightened or upset by something you read? If "The Devil and Tom Walker" hasn't unnerved you, "The Masque of the Red Death" will! Writers, advertisers, and speakers all hope to create emotions with their words. The following pages will help you

- see how authors create moods
- interpret the symbolism in one of the selections and explain how it contributes to the mood
- identify the meanings connected to real-world symbols

The Writer's Style: Creating a Mood Joy, fear, anger, suspense—these are just a few of the moods a writer can create. A mood is a feeling or emotional setting created by words and details.

Read the Literature

Notice how these writers skillfully create two very different moods.

Literature Models

Creating a Mood with Words
What mood does Poe create? How does Poe's choice of words create that mood?

But in the western or black chamber the effect of the firelight that streamed upon the dark hangings through the blood-tinted panes, was ghastly in the extreme, and produced so wild a look upon the countenances of those who entered, that there were few of the company bold enough to set foot within its precincts at all.

Edgar Allan Poe, from "The Masque of the Red Death"

Creating a Mood with Details
How do the words and details Thoreau uses differ from Poe's choices?

The bullfrogs trump to usher in the night, and the note of the whippoorwill is borne on the rippling wind from over the water. Sympathy with the fluttering alder and poplar leaves almost takes away my breath; yet, like the lake, my serenity is rippled but not ruffled.

Henry David Thoreau, from *Walden*

Connect to Life

Movies, restaurants, perfume, music, ads—they all create moods. What mood does this speech from a television program create?

Television Script

May I just go and sit in the garden? Just for a little while? Just . . . just to feel the air? J-Just to smell the flowers? Just . . . just to make believe I am normal? If—if I sit out there in the darkness, then the whole world is dark, and I'm more a part of it like that. Not just one grotesque, ugly woman with a bandage on her face, with a special darkness all her own.

Rod Serling
from "The Eye of the Beholder"
The Twilight Zone

Creating a Mood with Words
What mood does Serling create, using words alone?

Try Your Hand: Creating a Mood

1. **Mood Swings** From one of the selections in this unit, choose a passage that creates a strong mood. Then rewrite the passage to change the mood.
2. **Picture This** Draw a picture to illustrate the mood created by one of the excerpts on these two pages. Write a paragraph explaining the colors and shapes you used to create the mood.
3. **Childhood Memories** With a group of classmates, share memories of events and places that created strong moods for you as a child. They might be pleasant memories of celebrations, or they could be frightening memories of places like basements or dusty attics. Select one memory, and brainstorm a list of words that describe the mood it evokes.

WRITER'S CRAFT

Using Vivid Verbs

Verbs can add to the mood of your writing. They can create emotions at least as well as nouns, adverbs, or adjectives. Poe creates a haunting mood in "The Masque of the Red Death" by carefully selecting his verbs. In his story, dreams *writhe*, brows *redden*, and flames *expire*.

Where do you find vivid verbs? A thesaurus is an excellent place to start. Also watch for vivid verbs in your reading. Consider creating a "vivid verb bank" in your notebook. That way you can always refer to the verb bank when you write.

APPLYING WHAT YOU'VE LEARNED

Think of a vivid verb that might be used in place of each of the following verbs. Try to choose verbs that Hawthorne or Poe might use to convey a haunting mood. Then use each verb in an equally haunting sentence.

1. said
2. went
3. suggested
4. smiled

WRITING HANDBOOK

For more information on using precise language, see page 1172 of the Writing Handbook.

INTERPRETATION

Do you ever feel that a story must be deeper than it seems—that a character is more than just a person, a clock more than just a clock? You're reacting to symbolism. A symbol is a word, an object, or an action that suggests something other than itself. Symbols contribute to a story's mood, giving you a richer understanding of the story.

GUIDED ASSIGNMENT

Interpret a Symbol's Meaning In this lesson, you will choose a symbol from a selection and write an interpretive essay that explores the meaning of that symbol.

Student's Reading Log

	"The Masque of the Red Death" Significant Details	
	1st Reading	2nd Reading
pg. 359	big, loud, ugly clock—no one can ignore it	maybe the black color represents evil, or maybe even death???
	eerie mood	significance of 3600 seconds of "Time that flies"?
pg. 360	the chimes are always followed by nervous laughter	makes dreams "stiff—frozen"
		people shy away from the clock and the room it's in
pg. 361	why muffled?	Sound is "solemnly emphatic"
		"heart of life" beats feverishly in the other rooms

1 Prewrite and Explore

Think about the selections anywhere in Unit Three, "The Spirit of Individualism." Note people, objects, and colors that are mentioned often or that seem particularly important. (You might want to start with the forest in "The Devil and Tom Walker" or the grass in "Song of Myself.") Which details seem to suggest meanings beyond the obvious meanings of the words? Choose a selection and one symbol from that selection that you'd like to interpret.

READING AND REREADING

Read through the selection. You might want to use a reading log like the one at the left to organize your thoughts. Note where the symbol appears, what it means to you at that point in the story, what the mood is, and any other significant details. If you have a theory about the meaning of the symbol, write it down.

Now read the selection again. Write down any new ideas you have about the symbol.

Decision Point What do you think the symbol means?

❷ Talking Out Your Draft

Start thinking through your draft. Sometimes it helps to talk about your ideas with someone else. Find a partner and discuss your essay. You may want to answer the following questions together.

PEER RESPONSE

- Does the meaning I've suggested for the symbol make sense? Why or why not?
- Does the symbol work? Would the story be as effective without it?
- How does the symbol contribute to the mood of the story?
- Which supporting details should I be sure to include?

❸ Write Your Draft

Keep in mind that your essay should include the following:

- an introduction that provides an overview of the essay, identifies the title and the author of the selection, and briefly describes the content of the selection
- a thesis statement telling your interpretation of the symbol
- a body that develops your interpretation of the symbol, using supporting examples, details, and quotations from the selection
- a conclusion that summarizes your interpretation

Student's Draft

When I first read "The Masque of the Red Death," I was intrigued by the clock. But I didn't think it was any more than a big, old clock. The more I read the story, the more convinced I became that the clock symbolizes something more than just a timepiece.

Thesis statement: The large, gloomy, noisy clock in Edgar Allan Poe's "The Masque of the Red Death" is actually a symbol of life itself!

Should this go in the intro or the conclusion?

SkillBuilder

WRITER'S CRAFT

Elaborating with Quotations

Have you considered using a line or passage from the selection in your essay? Quotations from the literature can add variety, create emphasis, and support your opinion. Besides using them to illustrate points, you can use quotations to

- introduce new ideas

"The giddiest turned pale." Why would a mere clock have such an effect on people?

- summarize paragraphs

Like the life it symbolizes, the clock also has to die. Poe reports, "The life of the ebony clock went out with that of the last of the gay."

Keep in mind that a quotation should not disrupt the flow of your essay—it should lead right into the next sentence.

APPLYING WHAT YOU'VE LEARNED
Try to find a way to work a quotation or two from the literature into your essay.

WRITING HANDBOOK

For more help with elaboration, see page 1171 of the Writing Handbook.

❹ Revise and Edit

Look over your draft. Have you used the supporting details suggested by your partner? Does your essay have an introduction, a thesis statement, and a conclusion? Review the information on adjective clauses on the opposite page. Revise and edit your draft. Then reread your essay and reflect on the meanings of the symbols in the selection you chose.

Student's Final Draft

The Time That Flies

Edgar Allan Poe's "The Masque of the Red Death" is a haunting tale of a prince who, with a thousand of his closest friends, tries to escape the inevitable "Red Death." The prince and company think that walling themselves up in an abbey will keep them alive. Only the gigantic ebony clock seems to know better.

How does this introduction give you an overview of the story?

BONG! BONG! BONG! BONG! No one can ignore the clock as it announces each hour. Its chimes make even "the giddiest" turn pale. Poe claims that "the heart of life" beats in the other rooms. But the heart of life actually seems to beat in the clock. It ticks away the seconds, the minutes, the hours of life. Why does Poe capitalize the word *Time*? Maybe he is giving the clock human, lifelike qualities.

How are quotations incorporated smoothly into the essay?

Standards for Evaluation

An interpretive essay
- includes an overview in the introduction
- identifies the selection by title and author and briefly describes its contents
- includes a thesis statement that states the interpretation
- presents a sound, well-organized development of the interpretation in the body, supported with examples, details, and quotations
- summarizes the interpretation in the conclusion

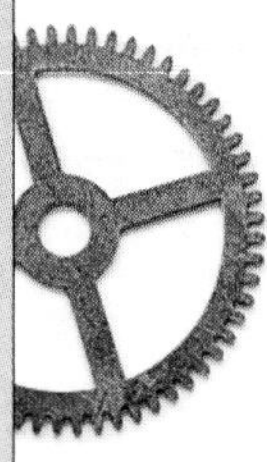

Grammar in Context

Adjective Clauses Adjective clauses are subordinate clauses that modify nouns or pronouns. They often begin with words like *who, whose, that,* or *which*. Adjective clauses can add emotion to your essay by providing mood-creating details.

The clock, *whose ebony case stands out starkly in the red gloom,* has a way of making people stop and think. Its clang forces the merrymakers to reflect on their lives, *which have been darkened by the threat of death*. Even the old and sedate seem to stop and meditate each time the clock chimes. Yet the party, *which defies death with its hideous gaiety,* continues despite the intruding clock.

In the example above, notice how the adjective clauses add to the mood of the paragraph. Also note that the clauses were placed next to the nouns they modify, reducing the chance of confusion. For more information about modifiers, see page 1218 of the Grammar Handbook.

Try Your Hand: Writing Adjective Clauses

On a separate sheet of paper, rewrite the following sentences. Add an adjective clause to each sentence.

1. Prospero lived in a castle.
2. The clock chimed.
3. Someone reported seeing a masked intruder.

SkillBuilder

G→ GRAMMAR FROM WRITING

Punctuating Adjective Clauses

How you punctuate an adjective clause (or any type of clause) depends on whether it is essential to the meaning of the sentence.

If the clause is essential to the meaning of the sentence, do not set it off with commas.

And, anon, there strikes the ebony clock which stands in the hall of velvet.

If the clause is not essential to the meaning of the sentence, set it off with commas. In the example above, if the location of the clock was not needed to identify it, Poe would have added a comma after *clock*.

One way to tell if the clause is essential is to read the sentence without it. If the sentence still has the same meaning, the clause is not essential.

APPLYING WHAT YOU'VE LEARNED

Copy the following sentences onto a sheet of paper, adding commas where needed.

1. The windows whose colors changed to match the chambers were of stained glass.
2. The prince who was a bold and robust man roared loudly.
3. Scarlet stains which were a sure sign of the "Red Death" were scattered across his face.

Check your draft to see if your clauses are punctuated correctly.

READING THE WORLD

More Than a Symbol

Writers aren't the only ones who use symbols. Organizations, corporations, and countries also use symbols to convey ideas and create emotional responses.

View Look closely at these symbols. Which of them have you seen before? Which are new to you?

Interpret Now try to attach a meaning to each symbol on this page. What are organizations, corporations, and countries trying to say with these symbols?

Discuss Compare your interpretations of the symbols with your classmates'. Were any reactions to the symbols negative? Did some people read additional meanings into the symbols? Did anyone have an emotional response to a symbol? Do you think the symbols are effective? See the SkillBuilder for more information on interpreting symbols.

SkillBuilder

CRITICAL THINKING

Making Connections

What do you think of when you see a dove? What about a circle with a slash through it?

When you interpret these symbols, you're making connections. You're linking objects or shapes with ideas or emotions. The connections you make are based on your life experience—they're based on people and places you know and things you've learned.

APPLYING WHAT YOU'VE LEARNED

Try one or more of the following with a partner:

- Look through the ads in a magazine. Focus on the company symbols and logos. Try to figure out the connections companies are trying to suggest with their symbols.
- Brainstorm possible symbols for one of the following causes: working together, gang control, teenagers for peace, creative freedom, safe driving.
- In medieval times, each knight had his own coat of arms with symbols of his family and perhaps his personal qualities. Make a list of your own best qualities. Draw a coat of arms that symbolizes these qualities. See if other students can make the connection between you and your coat of arms.

The Dark Side of Individualism

American Gothic

Set in an ancient castle where strange and terrifying events take place, Horace Walpole's *The Castle of Otranto* (1765) spawned the Gothic tradition in English fiction. Eighteenth-century readers fell in love with the novel's weird setting and macabre plot, and over the next century, Gothic novels of varying literary quality poured from the presses. In them, some of the greatest creatures of all time were born—including the repulsive monster created from human body parts in Mary Shelley's *Frankenstein* (1818) and the dangerously attractive count in Bram Stoker's *Dracula* (1897). Today, Anne Rice's sexy vampire Lestat owes his immortal life to the Gothic tradition.

The spirit and imagery of the Gothic literary tradition came in part from the Gothic architecture of the Middle Ages. Cavernous Gothic cathedrals with their irregularly placed towers and their high stained-glass windows were intended to inspire awe and fear in religious worshipers. Gargoyles—those carvings of small deformed creatures squatting at the corners and crevices of Gothic cathedrals—were supposed to ward off evil spirits, but they often looked more like demonic spirits themselves. Think of a gargoyle—a grotesque creature—as the mascot of Gothic, and you will get a good idea of the kind of imaginative distortion of reality that Gothic represents.

Another force that gave rise to Gothic literature was the romantic movement. As you have already learned, romanticism developed as a reaction against the rationalism of the Age of Reason. Once the romantics freed the imagination from the lordship of reason, they could follow the imagination wherever it might lead them. For some romantic writers, the imagination led to the threshold of the unknown—that shadowy region where the fantastic, the demonic, and the insane reside. This is Gothic territory. Because of this perspective, the Gothic tradition can be called the dark side of individualism. When romantics looked at the individual, they saw hope (think of Longfellow's "A Psalm of Life"); but when Gothic

Gargoyles on the Cathedral of Notre Dame, Paris. Copyright © Van Phillips/Leo de Wys, Inc.

Bodiam Castle in East Sussex, England. Copyright © Penny Tweedie/Tony Stone Images.

writers looked at the individual, they saw potential evil (think of anything you've ever read by Edgar Allan Poe). While romantic writers were extolling the beauties of nature, the Gothic writers were peering into the darkness at the supernatural.

The Gothic tradition was firmly established in Europe before American writers had made names for themselves. By the 19th century, however, Edgar Allan Poe and Nathaniel Hawthorne, and to a lesser extent Washington Irving and Herman Melville, were using Gothic elements in their fiction.

Edgar Allan Poe, of course, was the master of the Gothic form in the United States. In many of his stories, dark medieval castles or decaying ancient estates provide the setting for weird and terrifying events. Many of Poe's male narrators are insane; his female characters, beautiful and dead (or dying). His plots involve extreme situations—not just murder, but live burials, physical and mental torture, and retribution from beyond the grave. For Poe, it was only in such extreme situations that people revealed their true natures. The Gothic dimension of his fictional world offered him a way to explore the human mind in these extreme situations and so arrive at an essential truth.

Hawthorne also used Gothic elements in his fiction to express what he felt were important truths. However, instead of looking at the mind and its functions (or dysfunctions) as Poe did, Hawthorne examined the human heart under various conditions of fear, greed, vanity, mistrust, and betrayal.

Voices *from the* TIMES

The door opened, and a figure glided in. The portmanteau dropped from my arms, and my heart's-blood was chilled. If an apparition of the dead were possible, and that possibility I could not deny, this was such an apparition. A hue, yellowish and livid; bones, uncovered with flesh; eyes, ghastly, hollow, woe-begone, and fixed in an agony of wonder upon me; and locks, matted and negligent, constituted the image which I now beheld.

Charles Brockden Brown
from *Arthur Mervyn*

Imagination is the queen of darkness; night the season of her despotism.

James Kirke Paulding
from *Westward Ho!*

The death . . . of a beautiful woman is, unquestionably, the most poetical topic in the world—and equally is it beyond doubt that the lips best suited for such topic are those of a bereaved lover.

Edgar Allan Poe
from "The Philosophy of Composition"

Voices *from the* TIMES

Moonlight, in a familiar room, falling so white upon the carpet, and showing all its figures so distinctly—making every object so minutely visible, yet so unlike a morning or noontide visibility— . . . [has created] a neutral territory, somewhere between the real world and fairyland, where the Actual and the Imaginary may meet, and each imbue itself with the nature of the other. Ghosts might enter here, without affrighting us.

Nathaniel Hawthorne
from *The Scarlet Letter*

The oldest and strongest emotion of mankind is fear, and the oldest and strongest kind of fear is fear of the unknown.

H. P. Lovecraft
from *Supernatural Horror in Literature*

Continuity & Change: The Revival of Gothic

After the real horrors of the Civil War, the popularity of Gothic writing waned in the United States. Realism replaced romanticism as the preferred American literary style. The Gothic spirit had to wait until the 20th century before it again found fertile ground for its particular brand of truth telling. That ground was the American South.

Modern Southern writers as diverse as William Faulkner, Carson McCullers, Truman Capote, and Flannery O'Connor are sometimes grouped together in the category of Southern Gothic because of the gloom and pessimism of their fiction. For William Faulkner, the crumbling medieval castle of 19th-century Gothic fiction became the decaying plantation, with its fallen aristocratic family isolated in time and place. Instead of ghostly figures stalking noble heroines, Faulkner gave us the ghost of the past hounding his not-so-noble characters to madness and death.

Coming after Faulkner, Flannery O'Connor saw the pressures of modern life making grotesques of us all. Like Hawthorne, O'Connor was interested in the human heart and its potential for evil. In her view, the old moral and religious order was crumbling. Criminals, con men, and fools—rather than ghosts and goblins—were unleashed upon the world.

The contemporary writer Valerie Martin uses many standard Gothic elements in her story "The Consolation of Nature": an unsuspecting heroine, hidden dangers, and violence. The story, however, ends on a more hopeful note than most of the other Gothic selections in the unit.

Although this part of Unit Three focuses on the Gothic, you can see Gothic aspects in the work of writers in other units, such as Ambrose Bierce in Unit Four, Charlotte Perkins Gilman in Unit Five, and Sylvia Plath in Unit Six. Try identifying what's Gothic about the next horror movie you see or the next Stephen King or Anne Rice novel you read.

PART 2

The Dark Side of Individualism

American Gothic

Continuity & Change: The Revival of Gothic

PREVIEWING

FICTION

The Masque of the Red Death

Edgar Allan Poe

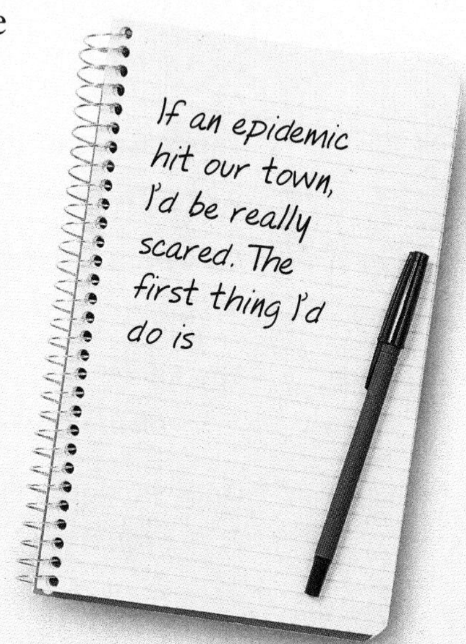
If an epidemic hit our town, I'd be really scared. The first thing I'd do is

PERSONAL CONNECTION

Imagine that your city or town has been struck by an epidemic of an incurable, fatal disease. The disease spreads rapidly but has not reached your particular block. How do you think you and your neighbors would react? What do you think would be the right thing to do? Jot down some ideas in your notebook and then share them with a group of classmates.

HISTORICAL CONNECTION

During the 14th century, an epidemic of bubonic plague—the Black Death—killed approximately 25 million people in Europe, more than a quarter of the total population. Victims of the plague experienced high fever, vomiting, pain, and black swellings that oozed blood. Those whose lungs were infected spit up blood. Death usually came within three to five days. The fictitious plague in this story, the Red Death, is an exaggerated version of this horrible disease. Prince Prospero and his friends react to the epidemic ravaging their country by sealing themselves off in a castle and holding a masque, a formal party at which guests wear masks and elaborate costumes.

Carts full of dead to bury.

During the Great Plague of London, the dead were buried in mass graves. The Granger Collection, New York.

READING CONNECTION

Approaching Difficult Vocabulary Poe uses unusual, archaic vocabulary, partly for Gothic effect and partly to create the impression that his story is set in the distant past. As you read, use the Guide for Reading notes to help you understand this challenging story. These notes define unusual words and contain comments and questions that will lead you through the text. Do not let yourself be slowed down by unfamiliar words. Keep reading and look for the basic story line. You might also make a list of unfamiliar words as you read and then look them up in a dictionary later.

LASERLINKS
• HISTORICAL CONNECTION

EDGAR ALLAN POE

The Masque of the Red Death

Il ridotto [The foyer] (about 1757–1760), Pietro Longhi. Oil on canvas, 62.5 cm × 51 cm, Fondazione Scientifica Querini Stampaglia, Venice, Italy, Erich Lessing/Art Resource, New York.

THE "RED DEATH" HAD LONG DEVASTATED THE COUNTRY. NO PESTILENCE HAD EVER BEEN SO FATAL, OR SO HIDEOUS. BLOOD WAS ITS

GUIDE FOR READING

2 devastated (dĕv'ə-stā'tĭd): laid waste to.

3 pestilence (pĕs'tə-ləns): a very destructive infectious disease.

Avatar and its seal—the redness and horror of blood. There were sharp pains, and sudden dizziness, and then profuse bleeding at the pores, with dissolution. The scarlet stains upon the body, and especially upon the face of the victim, were the pest ban which shut him out from the aid and from the sympathy of his fellow men. And the whole seizure, progress, and termination of the disease were the incidents of half an hour.

But the Prince Prospero was happy and dauntless and sagacious. When his dominions were half depopulated, he summoned to his presence a thousand hale and lighthearted friends from among the knights and dames of his court, and with these retired to the deep seclusion of one of his castellated abbeys. This was an extensive and magnificent structure, the creation of the prince's own eccentric yet august taste. A strong and lofty wall girded it in. This wall had gates of iron. The courtiers, having entered, brought furnaces and massy hammers and welded the bolts. They resolved to leave means neither of ingress or egress to the sudden impulses of despair or of frenzy from within. The abbey was amply provisioned. With such precautions the courtiers might bid defiance to contagion. The external world could take care of itself. In the meantime it was folly to grieve, or to think. The prince had provided all the appliances of pleasure. There were buffoons, there were improvisatori, there were ballet-dancers, there were musicians, there was Beauty, there was wine. All these and security were within. Without was the "Red Death."

It was toward the close of the fifth or sixth month of his seclusion, and while the pestilence raged most furiously abroad, that the Prince Prospero entertained his thousand friends at a masked ball of the most unusual magnificence.

It was a voluptuous scene, that masquerade. But first let me tell of the rooms in which it was held. There were seven—an imperial suite. In many palaces, however, such suites form a long and straight vista, while the folding doors slide back nearly to the walls on either hand, so that the view of the whole extent is scarcely impeded. Here the case was very different; as might have been expected from the duke's love of the *bizarre*. The apartments were so irregularly disposed that the vision embraced but little more than one at a time. There was a sharp turn at every twenty or thirty yards, and at each turn a novel effect. To the right and left, in the middle of each wall, a tall and narrow Gothic window looked out upon a closed corridor which pursued the windings of the suite. These windows were of stained glass whose color

5 Avatar (ăv′ə-tär′): an appearance in physical form of an unseen force.

7 dissolution: death.

8 pest ban: a proclamation announcing that a person is afflicted with the plague.

1–29 How is life outside the abbey different from life inside?

16 castellated abbey (kăs′tə-lā′tĭd ăb′ē): a fortified building formerly used as, or built to resemble, a monastery.

21 ingress (ĭn′grĕs′) **or egress** (ē′grĕs′): entry or exit.

23 provisioned: provided with supplies.

27 improvisatori (ĭm-prŏv′ĭ-zə-tôr′ē): poets who recite verses that they make up as they go along.

34–72 If you are having trouble visualizing the setting, try drawing a floor plan of the abbey's suite of seven rooms and labeling their colors. The arrangement of the rooms will be important later on.

WORDS TO KNOW

dauntless (dônt′lĭs) *adj.* fearless
sagacious (sə-gā′shəs) *adj.* wise
courtier (kôr′tē-ər) *n.* a member of a royal court
contagion (kən-tā′jən) *n.* the spreading of disease

varied in accordance with the prevailing hue of the decorations of the chamber into which it opened. That at the eastern extremity was hung, for example, in blue—and vividly blue were its windows. The second chamber was purple in its ornaments and tapestries, and here the panes were purple. The third was green throughout, and so were the casements. The fourth was furnished and lighted with orange—the fifth with white—the sixth with violet. The seventh apartment was closely shrouded in black velvet tapestries that hung all over the ceiling and down the walls, falling in heavy folds upon a carpet of the same material and hue. But in this chamber only, the color of the windows failed to correspond with the decorations. The panes here were scarlet—a deep blood color. Now in no one of the seven apartments were there any lamp or candelabrum amid the profusion of golden ornaments that lay scattered to and fro or depended from the roof. There was no light of any kind emanating from lamp or candle within the suite of chambers. But in the corridors that followed the suite, there stood, opposite to each window, a heavy tripod, bearing a brazier of fire that projected its rays through the tinted glass and so glaringly illumined the room. And thus were produced a multitude of gaudy and fantastic appearances. But in the western or black chamber the effect of the firelight that streamed upon the dark hangings through the blood-tinted panes, was ghastly in the extreme, and produced so wild a look upon the countenances of those who entered, that there were few of the company bold enough to set foot within its precincts at all.

It was in this apartment, also, that there stood against the western wall a gigantic clock of ebony. Its pendulum swung to and fro with a dull, heavy, monotonous clang; and when the minute hand made the circuit of the face, and the hour was to be stricken, there came from the brazen lungs of the clock a sound which was clear and loud and deep and exceedingly musical, but of so peculiar a note and emphasis that, at each lapse of an hour, the musicians of the orchestra were constrained to pause, momentarily, in their performance, to hearken to the sound; and thus the waltzers perforce ceased their evolutions; and there was a brief disconcert of the whole gay company; and, while the chimes of the clock yet rang, it was observed that the giddiest turned pale, and the more aged and sedate passed their hands over their brows as if in confused reverie or meditation. But when the echoes had fully ceased, a light laughter at once pervaded the assembly; the musicians looked at each other and smiled as if at their own nervousness and folly, and made whispering vows, each to the other, that the

65 brazier (brā′zhər): metal pan for holding a fire.

71 countenances (koun′tə-nən-səz): faces.

74 ebony (ĕb′ə-nē): a hard, very dark wood.

77 brazen: brass.

79–94 How do you explain the effect of the ebony clock's chimes on the assembled guests?

82 evolutions: intricate patterns of movement.

WORDS TO KNOW

pervade (pər-vād′) *v.* to spread throughout

next chiming of the clock should produce in them no similar emotion; and then, after the lapse of sixty minutes (which embrace three thousand and six hundred seconds of the Time that flies), there came yet another chiming of the clock, and then were the same disconcert and tremulousness and meditation as before.

94 disconcert: confusion.

But in spite of these things, it was a gay and magnificent revel. The tastes of the duke were peculiar. He had a fine eye for colors and effects. He disregarded the *decora* of mere fashion. His plans were bold and fiery, and his conceptions glowed with barbaric luster. There are some who would have thought him mad. His followers felt that he was not. It was necessary to hear and see and touch him to be *sure* that he was not.

97 decora: fine things.

He had directed, in great part, the movable embellishments of the seven chambers, upon occasion of this great *fête;* and it was his own guiding taste which had given character to the masqueraders. Be sure they were grotesque. There were much glare and glitter and piquancy and phantasm—much of what has been seen since in *Hernani.* There were arabesque figures with unsuited limbs and appointments. There were delirious fancies such as the madman fashions. There was much of the beautiful, much of the wanton, much of the *bizarre,* something of the terrible, and not a little of that which might have excited disgust. To and fro in the seven chambers there stalked, in fact, a multitude of dreams. And these—the dreams—writhed in and about, taking hue from the rooms, and causing the wild music of the orchestra to seem as the echo of their steps. And, anon, there strikes the ebony clock which stands in the hall of velvet. And then, for a moment, all is still, and all is silent save the voice of the clock. The dreams are stiff-frozen as they stand. But the echoes of the chime die away—they have endured but an instant—and a light, half-subdued laughter floats after them as they depart. And now again the music swells, and the dreams live, and writhe to and fro more merrily than ever, taking hue from the many-tinted windows through which stream the rays of the tripods. But to the chamber which lies most westwardly of the seven, there are now none of the maskers who venture; for the night is waning away; and there flows a ruddier light through the blood-colored panes; and the blackness of the sable drapery appalls; and to him whose foot falls upon the sable carpet, there comes from the near clock of ebony a muffled peal more solemnly emphatic than any which reaches *their* ears who indulge in the more remote gaieties of the other apartments.

102–123 Notice the comparison of the masqueraders to dreams, phantasms, and a madman's fancies. How do such comparisons help you imagine the scene?

107 ***Hernani*** (ĕr'nä-nē): a play by Victor Hugo, first staged in 1830, notable for its use of color and spectacle; **arabesque** (ăr'ə-bĕsk'): characterized by complicated decorations.

124–131 Why do you think none of the revellers venture into the seventh room?

But these other apartments were densely crowded, and in them

WORDS TO KNOW

grotesque (grō-tĕsk') *adj.* having a bizarre, fantastic appearance beat feverishly the heart of life. And the revel went whirlingly on, until at length there commenced the sounding of midnight upon the clock. And then the music ceased, as I have told; and the evolutions of the waltzes were quieted; and there was an uneasy cessation of all things as before. But now there were twelve strokes to be sounded by the bell of the clock; and thus it happened, perhaps, that more of thought crept, with more of time, into the meditations of the thoughtful among those who reveled. And thus, too, it happened, perhaps, that before the last echoes of the last chime had utterly sunk into silence, there were many individuals in the crowd who had found leisure to become aware of the presence of a masked figure which had arrested the attention of no single individual before. And the rumor of this new presence having spread itself whisperingly around, there arose at length from the whole company a buzz, or murmur, expressive of disapprobation and surprise—then, finally of terror, of horror, and of disgust.

In an assembly of phantasms such as I have painted, it may well be supposed that no ordinary appearance could have excited such sensation. In truth the masquerade license of the night was nearly unlimited; but the figure in question had out-Heroded Herod, and gone beyond the bounds of even the prince's indefinite decorum. There are chords in the hearts of the most reckless which cannot be touched without emotion. Even with the utterly lost, to whom life and death are equally jests, there are matters of

144–165 What effect does the strange figure who appears at the stroke of midnight have on the revellers?

Detail of *Adoration of the Magi: Lorenzo il Magnifico as Youngest of Magi* (1459), Benozzo Gozzoli. Palazzo Medici Riccardi, Florence, Italy, Erich Lessing/Art Resource, New York.

171–172 out-Heroded Herod: been more extreme than the biblical king Herod, who ordered the deaths of all male babies up to two years old in an effort to kill the infant Jesus. This expression is used in Shakespeare's *Hamlet.*

WORDS TO KNOW **license** (lī'səns) *n.* a lack of restrictions on behavior; freedom which no jest can be made. The whole company, indeed, seemed now deeply to feel that in the costume and bearing of the stranger neither wit nor propriety existed. The figure was tall and gaunt, and shrouded from head to foot in the habiliments of the grave. The mask which concealed the visage was made so nearly to resemble the countenance of a stiffened corpse that the closest scrutiny must have difficulty in detecting the cheat. And yet all this might have been endured, if not approved, by the mad revellers around. But the mummer had gone so far as to assume the type of the Red Death. His vesture was dabbed in *blood*—and his broad brow, with all the features of the face, was besprinkled with the scarlet horror.

When the eyes of Prince Prospero fell upon this spectral image (which with a slow and solemn movement, as if more fully to sustain its *role,* stalked to and fro among the waltzers), he was seen to be convulsed, in the first moment with a strong shudder either of terror or distaste; but, in the next, his brow reddened with rage.

"Who dares?" he demanded hoarsely of the courtiers who stood near him—"who dares insult us with this blasphemous mockery? Seize him and unmask him—that we may know whom we have to hang at sunrise, from the battlements!"

It was in the eastern or blue chamber in which stood the Prince Prospero as he uttered these words. They rang throughout the seven rooms loudly and clearly—for the prince was a bold and robust man, and the music had become hushed at the waving of his hand.

It was in the blue room where stood the prince, with a group of pale courtiers by his side. At first, as he spoke, there was a slight rushing movement of this group in the direction of the intruder, who at the moment was also near at hand, and now, with deliberate and stately step, made closer approach to the speaker. But from a certain nameless awe with which the mad assumptions of the mummer had inspired the whole party, there were found none who put forth a hand to seize him; so that, unimpeded, he passed within a yard of the prince's person; and, while the vast assembly, as if with one impulse, shrank from the centers of the rooms to the walls, he made his way uninterruptedly, but with the same solemn and measured step which had distinguished him from the first, through the blue chamber to the purple—through the purple to the green—through the green to the orange—through this again to the white—and even thence to the violet, ere a decided movement had been made to arrest him. It was then, however, that the Prince Prospero, maddening with rage and the shame of his own momentary cowardice, rushed hurriedly through the six chambers while none followed him on

179 habiliments (hə-bĭl′ə-mənts): clothing.

180 visage (vĭz′ĭj): face.

184 mummer: a person dressed for a masquerade.

188–196 Why does Prince Prospero get so mad?

207–217 Why do you think the masked figure is allowed to walk the length of the rooms uninterrupted?

account of a deadly terror that had seized upon all. He bore aloft a drawn dagger, and had approached, in rapid impetuosity, to within three or four feet of the retreating figure, when the latter, having attained the extremity of the velvet apartment, turned suddenly and confronted his pursuer. There was a sharp cry—and the dagger dropped gleaming upon the sable carpet, upon which, instantly afterwards, fell prostrate in death the Prince Prospero. Then, summoning the wild courage of despair, a throng of the revellers at once threw themselves into the black apartment, and seizing the mummer, whose tall figure stood erect and motionless within the shadow of the ebony clock, gasped in unutterable horror at finding the grave-cerements and corpselike mask, which they handled with so violent a rudeness, untenanted by any tangible form.

And now was acknowledged the presence of the Red Death. He had come like a thief in the night. And one by one dropped the revellers in the blood-bedewed halls of their revel, and died each in the despairing posture of his fall. And the life of the ebony clock went out with that of the last of the gay. And the flames of the tripods expired. And Darkness and Decay and the Red Death held illimitable dominion over all. ❖

Skull (19th or 20th century), artist unknown. Carved and painted wood, 8⅞″ × 5⅜″ × 6½″, National Museum of American Art, gift of Herbert Waide Hemphill, Jr., and museum purchase made possible by Ralph Cross Johnson, Smithsonian Institution, Washington D.C./Art Resource, New York.

239 cerements (sĕr′ə-mənts): cloth wrappings for the dead.

230–242 Poe's language is hard to understand here. Essentially, he says that when a group of revellers rip off the figure's costume, there is nothing underneath.

253 illimitable dominion (ĭ-lĭm′ĭ-tə-bəl də-mĭn′yən): unlimited power.

WORDS TO KNOW

impetuosity (ĭm-pĕch′o͞o-ŏs′ĭ-tē) *n.* unthinking action

untenanted (ŭn-tĕn′ən-tĭd) *adj.* not occupied

tangible (tăn′jə-bəl) *adj.* able to be touched or felt

from Danse Macabre

STEPHEN KING

I want to say something about imagination purely as a tool in the art and science of scaring people. The idea isn't original with me; I heard it expressed by William F. Nolan at the 1979 World Fantasy Convention. Nothing is so frightening as what's behind the closed door, Nolan said. You approach the door in the old, deserted house, and you hear something scratching at it. The audience holds its breath along with the protagonist as she or he (more often she) approaches that door. The protagonist throws it open, and there is a ten-foot-tall bug. The audience screams, but this particular scream has an oddly relieved sound to it. "A bug ten feet tall is pretty horrible," the audience thinks, "but I can deal with a ten-foot-tall bug. I was afraid it might be a *hundred* feet tall.". . .

Bill Nolan was speaking as a screenwriter when he offered the example of the big bug behind the door, but the point applies to all media. What's behind the door or lurking at the top of the stairs is never as frightening as the door or the staircase itself. And because of this, comes the paradox: the artistic work of horror is almost always a disappointment. It is the classic no-win situation. You can scare people with the unknown for a long, long time (the classic example, as Bill Nolan also pointed out, is the Jacques Tourneur film with Dana Andrews, *Curse of the Demon*), but sooner or later, as in poker, you have to turn your down cards up. You have to open the door and show the audience what's behind it. And if what happens to be behind it is a bug, not ten but a hundred feet tall, the audience heaves a sigh of relief (or utters a scream of relief) and thinks, "A bug a hundred feet tall is pretty horrible, but I can deal with that. I was afraid it might be a *thousand* feet tall." . . .

The danse macabre is a waltz

with death. This is a truth we cannot afford to shy away from. Like the rides in the amusement park which mimic violent death, the tale of horror is a chance to examine what's going on behind doors which we usually keep double-locked. Yet the human imagination is not content with locked doors. Somewhere there is another dancing partner, the imagination whispers in the night—a partner in a rotting ball gown, a partner with empty eyesockets, green mold growing on her elbow-length gloves, maggots squirming in the thin remains of her hair. To hold such a creature in our arms? Who, you ask me, would be so mad?

Well . . . ?

"You will not want to open this door," Bluebeard tells his wife in that most horrible of all horror stories, "because your husband has forbidden it." But this, of course, only makes her all the more curious. . . . and at last, her curiosity is satisfied.

"You may go anywhere you wish in the castle," Count Dracula tells Jonathan Harker, "except where the doors are locked, where of course you will not wish to go." But Harker goes soon enough.

And so do we all. Perhaps we go to the forbidden door or window willingly because we understand that a time comes when we must go whether we want to or not . . . and not just to look, but to be pushed through. Forever.

RESPONDING OPTIONS

FROM PERSONAL RESPONSE *TO* CRITICAL ANALYSIS

REFLECT **1.** In your notebook, describe an image from the story that lingered in your mind.

RETHINK **2.** What feeling do you think Poe wanted readers to have at the end of the story? Explain why you think so.

3. What message, or messages, do you see in this story?

Consider

- what literally happens to the revellers
- what the disease, the Red Death, might symbolize
- any ironies or unexpected contrasts you see

4. What is your opinion of Prince Prospero's efforts to avoid the epidemic? Consider what you wrote earlier about how you and your neighbors might respond to an epidemic.

RELATE **5.** In the Insight selection on page 364, Stephen King discusses the psychology of horror. Think about how you felt as you read "The Masque of the Red Death." Did your feelings bear out King's ideas about what is most frightening in horror movies and stories and why audiences and readers are attracted to horror?

6. Compare the way characters in the story react to the Red Death with the way people today react to the epidemic of AIDS.

ANOTHER PATHWAY

Cooperative Learning

Demonstrate your understanding of this story by dividing your class into two groups and having each group present this story as a pantomime to the other group. See if you can communicate all the important details and the Gothic atmosphere of the story without using costumes or props.

Apparition du Cavalier de la mort [The Horseman Death] from *Trés riches heures du duc de Berry* (about 1415), Limbourg brothers. Musée Condé Chantilly, France. Giraudon/Art Resource, New York.

QUICKWRITES

1. Imagine you are one of the people outside the abbey. Draft a **speech** that you might deliver at a memorial service for Prince Prospero.
2. Tell the story of the destruction of Prospero and his guests in a **ballad** or another type of narrative poem.
3. On the basis of this story, write a brief **critique** of Poe as a horror writer. If you wish, discuss the story in connection with the Insight selection by Stephen King on page 364.

PORTFOLIO *Save your writing. You may want to use it later as a springboard to a piece for your portfolio.*

LITERARY CONCEPTS

This story can be read as an **allegory,** a work of literature in which people, objects, and events stand for abstract qualities. In an allegory, a bird might represent freedom, for example, or a child might represent innocence. Reread the descriptions of Prospero's castle. Then complete a chart, like the one shown, to help you interpret the allegorical meanings of some objects inside the castle. Discuss your ideas with your classmates.

Objects Inside the Castle	Description	Possible Meaning
1. The seventh room in the suite **2.** The fire lighting the suite of rooms **3.** The ebony clock		

LITERARY LINKS

Compare this story with "The Devil and Tom Walker" (page 276). Which story did you find more horrifying? Which do you think presents a darker view of humanity?

THE WRITER'S STYLE

To get a better feeling for Poe's unique style, select a paragraph of the story to read aloud. Then try restating the sentences in simpler language. For example, the first sentence in the story could be restated this way: "The 'Red Death' had been killing people in the land for a long time." How does the effect of the paragraph change when Poe's **diction** is changed?

CRITIC'S CORNER

In addition to being an accomplished writer, Poe was also a critic who helped define the short story form. In a review of Nathaniel Hawthorne's first collection of stories, Poe expressed his opinion that a short story should strive above all to create a single effect or impression. To Poe's mind, a skillful writer does not begin with the incidents of plot; instead, "Having conceived, with deliberate care, a certain unique or single *effect* to be wrought out, he [the writer] then invents such incidents—he then combines such events as may best aid him in establishing this preconceived effect. . . . In the whole composition there should be no word written, of which the tendency, direct or indirect, is not to the one pre-established design." Evaluate the extent to which Poe practices this theory in "The Masque of the Red Death." What single effect might he have been trying to create? Is there anything in the story that does not contribute to that effect?

ALTERNATIVE ACTIVITIES

1. Make an **illustration** based on some aspect of this story. You might do a drawing or a three-dimensional model of the rooms in which the masked ball is held. You could paint a group of revellers or concentrate on the figure of the Red Death. As a starting point, use any sketches you made while reading.
2. Divide this story into three parts, and find appropriate **music** for each part. In a presentation to your class, summarize each part, explain your musical choices, identify the titles and composers, and play the music.

ACROSS THE CURRICULUM

Biology Find out more about the disease known as plague. What causes it? How is it spread? How is it treated? Does it still exist today? Present your findings to the class in an oral report.

History Locate firsthand accounts of life during the time of the Black Death in 14th-century Europe. One such account may be found in the introduction of *The Decameron,* a book of tales by the Italian author Giovanni Boccaccio; others are included in *The Black Death,* a history by Rosemary Horrox. Report to the class on the conditions that people like Prince Prospero and his guests would have wanted to escape.

WORDS TO KNOW

EXERCISE A In the chart below, the Words to Know are grouped under headings based on subjects in the story. Use each group of words to write two or more sentences about the corresponding subject. You may also want to include in your sentences words that you looked up on your own.

EXERCISE B Work in groups to act out some of the sentences you created for Exercise A.

Red Death	Masked Ball	Prince Prospero
contagion pervade untenanted tangible	courtier grotesque license	dauntless sagacious impetuosity

EDGAR ALLAN POE

1809–1849

Tormented throughout his life by painful loss, bitterness, and depression, Edgar Allan Poe found escape in writing stories and poems that portrayed haunted lives even darker than his own. Poe was orphaned at two years of age and was taken in—but never adopted—by a wealthy family in Richmond, Virginia. As a student at the University of Virginia, he showed flashes of brilliance; but when he ran up $2,000 in gambling debts, his foster father removed him from school. Thus began a pattern of achievement, bitter dispute, and loss.

Later, as a cadet at West Point, Poe purposely earned demerits so that he would be expelled. As a magazine editor, he used his abilities to spark immediate improvement in a publication, but invariably a fight with the owner of the publication would result in Poe's being fired. His literary reviews of other writers' work were often so vicious that he was referred to as a hatchet man. His stories and poems gained him recognition but never enough money to raise him from poverty. The one great comfort in his life—his wife, Virginia (a cousin whom he married when she was 13)—died of tuberculosis at the age of 25.

Perhaps because Poe knew suffering so well, he displayed in his writing a brilliant talent for investigating the dark side of the mind and the heart. Revenge, terror, lost love, and insanity were his most frequent subjects. Together with Nathaniel Hawthorne, Poe is credited with shaping and defining the short story form. He is known as the father of the horror story and of the detective tale as well.

OTHER WORKS "The Black Cat," "The Fall of the House of Usher," "Ligeia," "Hop-Frog," "The Murders in the Rue Morgue"

PREVIEWING

POETRY

The Raven

Edgar Allan Poe

PERSONAL CONNECTION

"The Raven," one of the most famous poems in American literature, presents the story of a man grieving over the loss of his beloved, the beautiful Lenore. To understand the speaker's feelings, think about a time when you or someone you know lost a loved one through death or desertion. The loved one does not necessarily have to be a person; it could be a pet. In your notebook, write about the experience of coping with grief.

CULTURAL CONNECTION

While the speaker of this poem is alone in his room one night, trying to forget his grief, a raven flies in and perches on a statue of the Greek goddess Athena. For the ancient Greeks, the raven was a bird of prophecy. In Western culture, ravens have long been associated with mystery, evil omens, and death. A raven's jet-black feathers, threatening stare, and lamenting cry all contribute to the bird's reputation as a prophet of gloom. The raven is also noted for being intelligent, easy to tame, and mischievous. At first, Poe considered using a parrot or an owl as the mysterious visitor in his poem, but because of the cultural associations mentioned, he decided to use the raven.

READING CONNECTION

Appreciating Sound in Poetry "The Raven" is a highly musical poem, with a regular, almost insistent rhythm. It also has a complex rhyme scheme, using both **end rhyme** (rhyme at ends of lines) and **internal rhyme** (rhyme within lines). Consider the rhyming words in the first line of the poem:

"Once upon a midnight **dreary,** while I
pondered, weak and **weary."**

As you read, notice how Poe maintains his rhyme scheme. To better appreciate Poe's use of rhyme and other sound devices, read "The Raven" aloud.

Copyright © 1966 Helen Thurber, from *Thurber & Company,* published by Harper & Row.

Once upon a midnight dreary, while I pondered, weak and weary,
Over many a quaint and curious volume of forgotten lore—
While I nodded, nearly napping, suddenly there came a tapping,
As of someone gently rapping, rapping at my chamber door.
"'Tis some visitor," I muttered, "tapping at my chamber door—
Only this and nothing more."

Ah, distinctly I remember it was in the bleak December;
And each separate dying ember wrought its ghost upon the floor.
Eagerly I wished the morrow;—vainly I had sought to borrow
From my books surcease[1] of sorrow—sorrow for the lost Lenore—
For the rare and radiant maiden whom the angels name Lenore—
Nameless *here* forevermore.

And the silken, sad, uncertain rustling of each purple curtain
Thrilled me—filled me with fantastic terrors never felt before;
So that now, to still the beating of my heart, I stood repeating
"'Tis some visitor entreating entrance at my chamber door;—
Some late visitor entreating entrance at my chamber door;—
That it is and nothing more."

1. **surcease:** an end.

Presently my soul grew stronger; hesitating then no longer,
"Sir," said I, "or Madam, truly your forgiveness I implore;
But the fact is I was napping, and so gently you came rapping,
And so faintly you came tapping, tapping at my chamber door,
That I scarce was sure I heard you"—here I opened wide the door;—
Darkness there and nothing more.

Deep into that darkness peering, long I stood there wondering, fearing,
Doubting, dreaming dreams no mortal ever dared to dream before;
But the silence was unbroken, and the stillness gave no token,
And the only word there spoken was the whispered word, "Lenore!"
This I whispered, and an echo murmured back the word "Lenore!"
Merely this and nothing more.

Back into the chamber turning, all my soul within me burning,
Soon again I heard a tapping somewhat louder than before.
"Surely," said I, "surely that is something at my window lattice;
Let me see, then, what thereat is, and this mystery explore—
Let my heart be still a moment and this mystery explore;—
'Tis the wind and nothing more!"

Open here I flung the shutter, when, with many a flirt and flutter,
In there stepped a stately Raven of the saintly days of yore.[2]
Not the least obeisance[3] made he; not a minute stopped or stayed he;
But, with mien[4] of lord or lady, perched above my chamber door—
Perched upon a bust of Pallas[5] just above my chamber door—
Perched, and sat, and nothing more.

Then this ebony bird beguiling my sad fancy into smiling,
By the grave and stern decorum of the countenance it wore,
"Though thy crest be shorn and shaven, thou," I said, "art sure no craven,[6]
Ghastly grim and ancient Raven wandering from the Nightly shore—
Tell me what thy lordly name is on the Night's Plutonian[7] shore!"
Quoth the Raven, "Nevermore."

---

2. **saintly days of yore:** sacred days of the past.
3. **obeisance** (ō-bā′səns): a polite gesture of respect, such as a bow.
4. **mien** (mēn): a way of carrying oneself; appearance.
5. **bust of Pallas:** statue of the head and shoulders of Athena, the Greek goddess of wisdom.
6. **craven:** cowardly person.
7. **Plutonian:** having to do with Pluto, the Roman god of the dead and ruler of the underworld.

WORDS TO KNOW

implore (ĭm-plôr′) *v.* to beg; earnestly ask for
beguiling (bĭ-gī′lĭng) *adj.* charming or delighting **beguile** *v.*
decorum (dĭ-kôr′əm) *n.* proper and dignified behavior

Much I marveled this ungainly fowl to hear discourse so plainly,
Though its answer little meaning—little relevancy bore;
For we cannot help agreeing that no living human being
Ever yet was blessed with seeing bird above his chamber door—
Bird or beast upon the sculptured bust above his chamber door,
With such name as "Nevermore."

But the Raven, sitting lonely on the placid bust, spoke only
That one word, as if his soul in that one word he did outpour.
Nothing farther then he uttered—not a feather then he fluttered—
Till I scarcely more than muttered "Other friends have flown before—
On the morrow *he* will leave me, as my hopes have flown before."
Then the bird said, "Nevermore."

Startled at the stillness broken by reply so aptly spoken,
"Doubtless," said I, "what it utters is its only stock and store
Caught from some unhappy master whom unmerciful Disaster
Followed fast and followed faster till his songs one burden bore—
Till the dirges of his Hope that melancholy burden bore
Of 'Never—nevermore.'"

But the Raven still beguiling all my fancy into smiling,
Straight I wheeled a cushioned seat in front of bird and bust and door;
Then, upon the velvet sinking, I betook myself to linking
Fancy unto fancy, thinking what this ominous bird of yore—
What this grim, ungainly, ghastly, gaunt, and ominous bird of yore
Meant in croaking, "Nevermore."

This I sat engaged in guessing, but no syllable expressing
To the fowl whose fiery eyes now burned into my bosom's core;
This and more I sat divining, with my head at ease reclining
On the cushion's velvet lining that the lamp-light gloated o'er,
But whose velvet violet lining with the lamp-light gloating o'er,
She shall press, ah, nevermore!

WORDS TO KNOW

- **discourse** (dĭ-skôrs') *v.* to speak
- **placid** (plăs'ĭd) *adj.* undisturbed; calm or quiet
- **dirge** (dûrj) *n.* a slow, mournful piece of music; a funeral hymn
- **ominous** (ŏm'ə-nəs) *adj.* threatening; menacing
- **divining** (dĭ-vī'nĭng) *adj.* finding out through intuition; guessing from incomplete evidence **divine** *v.*

Then, methought, the air grew denser, perfumed from an unseen censer[8]
Swung by Seraphim[9] whose foot-falls tinkled on the tufted floor.
"Wretch," I cried, "thy God hath lent thee—by these angels he hath sent thee
Respite—respite and nepenthe[10] from thy memories of Lenore;
Quaff,[11] oh quaff this kind nepenthe and forget this lost Lenore!"
Quoth the Raven, "Nevermore."

"Prophet!" said I, "thing of evil!—prophet still, if bird or devil!—
Whether Tempter[12] sent, or whether tempest tossed thee here ashore,
Desolate yet all undaunted, on this desert land enchanted—
On this home by Horror haunted—tell me truly, I implore—
Is there—*is* there balm in Gilead?[13]—tell me—tell me, I implore!"
Quoth the Raven, "Nevermore."

"Prophet!" said I, "thing of evil!—prophet still, if bird or devil!
By that Heaven that bends above us—by that God we both adore—
Tell this soul with sorrow laden if, within the distant Aidenn,[14]
It shall clasp a sainted maiden whom the angels name Lenore—
Clasp a rare and radiant maiden whom the angels name Lenore."
Quoth the Raven, "Nevermore."

"Be that word our sign of parting, bird or fiend!" I shrieked, upstarting—
"Get thee back into the tempest and the Night's Plutonian shore!
Leave no black plume as a token of that lie thy soul hath spoken!
Leave my loneliness unbroken!—quit the bust above my door!
Take thy beak from out my heart, and take thy form from off my door!"
Quoth the Raven, "Nevermore."

And the Raven, never flitting, still is sitting, *still* is sitting
On the pallid[15] bust of Pallas just above my chamber door;
And his eyes have all the seeming of a demon's that is dreaming,
And the lamp-light o'er him streaming throws his shadow on the floor;
And my soul from out that shadow that lies floating on the floor
Shall be lifted—nevermore!

---

8. **censer:** a container in which incense is burned, especially during religious services.
9. **Seraphim** (sĕr′ə-fĭm): angels of the highest rank.
10. **nepenthe** (nĭ-pĕn′thē): a drug that eases grief or sorrow by causing forgetfulness.
11. **quaff:** drink deeply.
12. **Tempter:** the Devil.
13. **balm** (bäm) **in Gilead** (gĭl′ē-əd): relief from suffering. The phrase comes from the Bible (Jeremiah 8:22) and refers to a soothing ointment from Gilead, a region of Palestine.
14. **Aidenn** (ād′n): heaven (from the Arabic form of the word *Eden*).
15. **pallid:** pale.

WORDS TO KNOW

respite (rĕs′pĭt) *n.* a brief period of rest or relief from pain or labor
tempest (tĕm′pĭst) *n.* a violent storm

RESPONDING OPTIONS

FROM PERSONAL RESPONSE *TO* CRITICAL ANALYSIS

REFLECT **1.** In your notebook, name the emotions this poem stirs in you.

RETHINK **2.** What is your view of the speaker's mental state?
Consider
- how he has tried to forget his grief
- his thoughts about the raven and the questions he asks it
- his changing moods during the poem
- whether or not he is sane at the end of the poem

3. What meaning or meanings do you think the word *nevermore* has in this poem? Tell what effect the word's repetition has on you.

4. How do you explain the raven and its visit?
Consider
- why the bird comes to the speaker
- whether the bird is real or an illusion

RELATE **5.** Consider what you wrote about coping with grief for the Personal Connection on page 369. Is the speaker's response understandable to you? Do you have any advice for him?

6. In his essay "The Philosophy of Composition," Poe explains that "the human thirst for self-torture" impels the speaker of this poem to ask the questions he does, even though he knows what the raven's reply will be. Do you think such a "thirst" is common in people? Explain.

ANOTHER PATHWAY

On a scale of 1 to 10, with 1 being the least and 10 the most, rate the speaker of "The Raven" in these five areas: sadness, intelligence, sense of humor, devotion, and sanity. Then write a sentence to explain each of your ratings. Organize your thoughts in a chart (or perhaps create a report card), then compare your evaluation with your classmates' evaluations.

LITERARY CONCEPTS

The **rhyme scheme** of "The Raven" is quite unusual. Read the first two stanzas aloud. How many words at the ends of lines rhyme? How many internal rhymes do you see? Notice the interesting pattern of end rhyme and internal rhyme throughout the poem. Do you think this complicated rhyme scheme supports or detracts from the mood and the meaning of the poem? Explain your opinion.

QUICKWRITES

1. Try rewriting part of "The Raven" as a passage of a **short story.** Maintain the tone, imagery, mood, and theme of the poem, adding details to make the speaker come to life and to enhance the plot and setting.

2. Other poets have written humorous parodies of "The Raven." Write one or two stanzas of a **parody** of your own, perhaps using another bird or animal or changing the name of the beloved. Try to imitate Poe's meter and rhyme scheme.

PORTFOLIO *Save your writing. You may want to use it later as a springboard to a piece for your portfolio.*

ALTERNATIVE ACTIVITIES

1. Draw some **sketches** or make a **model** of the set that you would use if this poem were adapted as a play. Display your work in the classroom.
2. ***Cooperative Learning*** With a small group of classmates, do a **dramatic reading** of "The Raven" for the rest of the class. If you like, use sound effects, props, or costumes to communicate important details in the poem.

CRITIC'S CORNER

Alluding to Barnaby Rudge, a character in a Charles Dickens novel who carries a raven on his back, the poet James Russell Lowell wrote this critical couplet: "There comes Poe, with his raven, like Barnaby Rudge, / Three-fifths of him genius and two-fifths sheer fudge." What might have made Lowell view Poe this way? Do you agree with Lowell's view? Explain your opinion, referring to the selections by Poe you have read.

THE WRITER'S STYLE

Poe is famous for the musical quality of his verse, and rhyme is just one of many sound devices he employs in "The Raven." Copy the following line in your notebook and read it aloud:

And the silken, sad, uncertain rustling of each purple curtain

Underline all the repeated consonant sounds at the beginning of words in the line; such repetition is called **alliteration.** Next, draw a box around repeated consonant sounds within words; this kind of repetition is called **consonance.** Then circle all the repeated vowel sounds within words; repetition of this sort is called **assonance.** Compare the words you marked with those your classmates marked. Read several more lines aloud and discuss all the sounds that are repeated. What is the point of all the repetition and rhyme in this poem? Do you think Poe is just showing off, or does he have a larger purpose?

WORDS TO KNOW

EXERCISE A Review the Words to Know at the bottom of the selection pages. Then read each magazine-article title below and write the vocabulary word that you would expect to find in the article.

1. "Wild Weather: Protecting Yourself from the Elements"
2. "How to Ask for Forgiveness . . . and Get It"
3. "Vacation Spots for When You Really Need a Break"
4. "Psychics and Fortunetellers: Help or Hype?"
5. "Modern Manners for Modern Times"
6. "Flee or Fight? What to Do When You're in Danger"
7. "Avoiding the Wrong Music for Your Wedding"
8. "Tossing and Turning? You Too Can Sleep Like a Rock"
9. "How to Hold Up Your End of the Conversation"
10. "Putting That Certain Someone Under Your Spell"

EXERCISE B With a partner, take turns acting out the meanings of the words **implore, decorum, placid, ominous, divine,** and **respite.** (In some cases, you may be able to communicate the meaning with a single gesture.)

LASERLINKS
• *AUTHOR BACKGROUND*

PREVIEWING

FICTION

Dr. Heidegger's Experiment

Nathaniel Hawthorne

PERSONAL CONNECTION

What do you like most about being the age you are right now? What aspects of growing older do you look forward to? What aspects of growing older are undesirable to you? Do you think youth and age should be measured by the years a person has lived or by a person's behavior and outlook? With a small group of classmates, discuss these questions about youth and aging, and record your answers in your notebook.

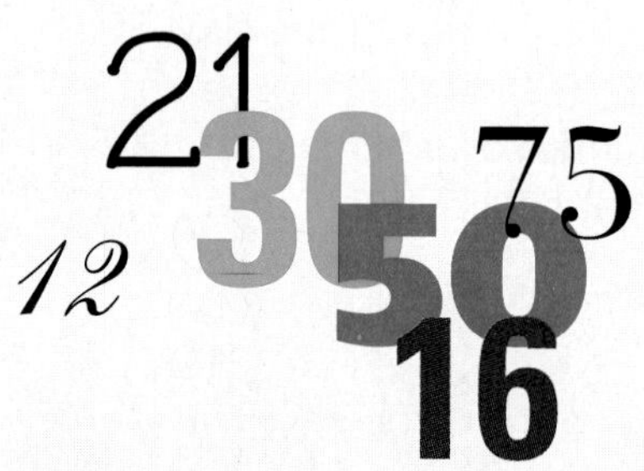

HISTORICAL CONNECTION

You may have heard about the Spanish explorer Ponce de León (pŏns' də lē-ōn') and his travels throughout Florida in search of the Fountain of Youth. People believed that water from this fountain would make old people young again. Although the fountain was a myth, the belief in a magic liquid that could bring the dead to life or that could confer immortality has a long history. During the Middle Ages, alchemists (early chemists who combined science and magic) sought the "elixir of life," a substance they believed would prolong life indefinitely. Nathaniel Hawthorne was fascinated by the concept of immortality, and in several stories—including "Dr. Heidegger's Experiment"—he wrote about men who possessed the secret elixir of life.

READING CONNECTION

Interpreting Allegory As you may recall, an allegory is a work of literature in which people, objects, and events stand for abstract qualities, such as evil, compassion, or greed. Allegories are written not only to entertain but also to teach lessons or moral principles. Draw a chart similar to the one below, and complete it as you read the story or right after you finish reading it. Identify an abstract quality or idea that each of the four guests in the story might represent.

Character	What he or she loses or wastes	What happens when he or she is given a second youth	What he or she might represent
Mr. Medbourne	wealth	schemes to make money again	greed
Col. Killigrew			
Mr. Gascoigne			
Widow Wycherly			

Dr. Heidegger's Experiment

NATHANIEL HAWTHORNE

That very singular man, old Dr. Heidegger, once invited four venerable friends to meet him in his study. There were three white-bearded gentlemen, Mr. Medbourne, Colonel Killigrew, and Mr. Gascoigne, and a withered gentlewoman, whose name was the Widow Wycherly. They were all melancholy old creatures, who had been unfortunate in life, and whose greatest misfortune it was, that they were not long ago in their graves. Mr. Medbourne, in the vigor of his age, had been a prosperous merchant, but had lost his all by a frantic speculation, and was now little better than a mendicant. Colonel Killigrew had wasted his best years, and his health and substance, in the pursuit of sinful pleasures, which had given birth to a brood of pains, such as the gout, and divers other torments of soul and body. Mr. Gascoigne was a ruined politician, a man of evil fame, or at least had been so, till time had buried him from the knowledge of the present generation, and made him obscure instead of infamous. As for the Widow Wycherly, tradition tells us that she was a great beauty in her day; but, for a long while past, she had lived in deep seclusion, on account of certain scandalous stories, which had prejudiced the gentry of the town against her. It is a circumstance worth mentioning, that each of these three old gentlemen, Mr. Medbourne, Colonel Killigrew, and Mr. Gascoigne, were early lovers of the Widow Wycherly, and had once been on the point of cutting each other's throats for her sake. And, before proceeding farther, I will merely hint, that Dr. Heidegger and all his four guests were sometimes thought to be a little beside themselves; as is not unfrequently the case with old people, when worried either by present troubles or woful recollections.

"My dear old friends," said Dr. Heidegger, motioning them to be seated, "I am desirous of your assistance in one of those little experiments with which I amuse myself here in my study."

If all stories were true, Dr. Heidegger's study must have been a very curious place. It was a dim, old-fashioned chamber, festooned with cobwebs, and besprinkled with antique dust. Around the walls stood several oaken book-cases, the lower shelves of which were filled with rows of gigantic folios, and black-letter quartos, and the upper with little parchment covered duodecimos. Over the central book-case was a bronze bust of

GUIDE FOR READING

12–25 What has each of these four characters wasted or lost?

15 mendicant (mĕn'dĭ-kənt): beggar.

17 gout: a painful disease of the joints, once thought to be caused by eating too much rich food.

21 obscure instead of infamous (ĭn'fə-məs): little known rather than well-known for wickedness.

25 gentry: respectable or socially high-ranking people.

25–28 What relationship did the four guests have in their youth?

37–60 Notice the details included in this Gothic description of Dr. Heidegger's study. What mood is established by this description?

39 festooned: decorated in draping curves.

41–43 folios . . . quartos . . . duodecimos: books of different sizes.

WORDS TO KNOW

venerable (vĕn'ər-ə-bəl) *adj.* worthy of respect because of age, dignity, or character

Hippocrates, with which, according to some authorities, Dr. Heidegger was accustomed to hold consultations, in all difficult cases of his practice. In the obscurest corner of the room stood a tall and narrow oaken closet, with its door ajar, within which doubtfully appeared a skeleton. Between two of the book-cases hung a looking-glass, presenting its high and dusty plate within a tarnished gilt frame. Among many wonderful stories related of this mirror, it was fabled that the spirits of all the doctor's deceased patients dwelt within its verge, and would stare him in the face whenever he looked thitherward. The opposite side of the chamber was ornamented with the full length portrait of a young lady, arrayed in the faded magnificence of silk, satin, and brocade, and with a visage as faded as her dress. Above half a century ago, Dr. Heidegger had been on the point of marriage with this young lady; but, being affected with some slight disorder, she had swallowed one of her lover's prescriptions, and died on the bridal evening.

44 Hippocrates (hĭ-pŏk′rə-tēz′): a Greek physician, considered to be the father of medicine.

48–50 This is no ordinary mirror. Watch what it reveals as the story continues.

52 verge: border.

53 thitherward: in that direction.

56 visage (vĭz′ĭj): face.

"I am desirous of your assistance in one of those little experiments with which I amuse myself here in my study."

The greatest curiosity of the study remains to be mentioned: it was a ponderous folio volume, bound in black leather, with massive silver clasps. There were no letters on the back, and nobody could tell the title of the book. But it was well known to be a book of magic; and once, when a chambermaid had lifted it, merely to brush away the dust, the skeleton had rattled in its closet, the picture of the young lady had stepped one foot upon the floor, and several ghastly faces had peeped forth from the mirror; while the brazen head of Hippocrates frowned, and said—"Forbear!"

70 forbear: stop; cease.

Such was Dr. Heidegger's study. On the summer afternoon of our tale, a small round table, as black as ebony, stood in the center of the room, sustaining a cut-glass vase, of beautiful form and elaborate workmanship. The sunshine came through the window, between the heavy festoons of two faded damask curtains, and fell directly across this vase; so that a mild splendor was reflected from it on the ashen visages of the five old people who sat around. Four champagne glasses were also on the table.

"My dear old friends," repeated Dr. Heidegger, "may I reckon on your aid in performing an exceedingly curious experiment?"

Now Dr. Heidegger was a very strange old gentleman, whose eccentricity had become the nucleus for a thousand fantastic stories. Some of these fables, to my shame be it spoken, might possibly be traced back to mine own veracious self; and if any passages of the present tale should startle the reader's faith, I must be content to bear the stigma of a fiction-monger.

83–86 The narrator admits to having told fables about Dr. Heidegger in the past.

84 veracious: truthful.

86 fiction-monger: liar.

When the doctor's four guests heard him talk of his proposed experiment, they anticipated nothing more wonderful than the murder of a mouse in an air-pump, or the examination of a cobweb by the microscope, or some similar nonsense, with which he was constantly in the habit of pestering his intimates. But without waiting for a reply, Dr. Heidegger hobbled across the chamber, and returned with the same ponderous folio, bound in black leather, which common report affirmed to be a book of magic. Undoing the silver clasps, he opened the volume, and took from among its black-letter pages a rose, or what was once a rose, though now the green leaves and crimson petals had assumed one brownish hue, and the ancient flower seemed ready to crumble to dust in the doctor's hands.

"This rose," said Dr. Heidegger, with a sigh, "this same withered and crumbling flower, blossomed five-and-fifty years ago. It was given me by Sylvia Ward, whose portrait hangs yonder; and I meant to wear it in my bosom at our wedding. Five-and-fifty years it has been treasured between the leaves of this old volume. Now, would you deem it possible that this rose of half a century could ever bloom again?"

"Nonsense!" said the Widow Wycherly, with a peevish toss of her head. "You might as well ask whether an old woman's wrinkled face could ever bloom again."

107 peevish: irritable.

"See!" answered Dr. Heidegger.

He uncovered the vase, and threw the faded rose into the water which it contained. At first, it lay lightly on the surface of the fluid, appearing to imbibe none of its moisture. Soon, however, a singular change began to be visible. The crushed and dried petals stirred, and assumed a deepening tinge of crimson, as if the flower were reviving from a death-like slumber; the slender stalk and twigs of foliage became green; and there was the rose of half a century, looking as fresh as when Sylvia Ward had first given it to her lover. It was scarcely full-blown; for some of its delicate

113 imbibe: absorb.

119 full-blown: completely open.

WORDS TO KNOW

stigma (stĭg′mə) *n.* a mark of disgrace

Déjeuner [Luncheon] (1876), Gustave Caillebotte. Oil on canvas, 52 cm × 75 cm, private collection.

The crushed and dried petals stirred, . . . as if the flower were reviving from a death-like slumber.

red leaves curled modestly around its moist bosom, within which two or three dewdrops were sparkling.

"That is certainly a very pretty deception," said the doctor's friends; carelessly, however, for they had witnessed greater miracles at a conjurer's show: "pray how was it effected?"

128 conjurer's: magician's.

"Did you never hear of the 'Fountain of Youth,'" asked Dr. Heidegger, "which Ponce De Leon, the Spanish adventurer, went in search of, two or three centuries ago?"

"But did Ponce De Leon ever find it?" said the Widow Wycherly.

"No," answered Dr. Heidegger, "for he never sought it in the right place. The famous Fountain of Youth, if I am rightly informed, is situated in the southern part of the Floridian peninsula, not far from Lake Macaco. Its source is overshadowed by several gigantic magnolias, which, though numberless centuries old, have been kept as fresh as violets, by the virtues of this wonderful water. An acquaintance of mine, knowing my curiosity in such matters, has sent me what you see in the vase."

"Ahem!" said Colonel Killigrew, who believed not a word of the doctor's story: "and what may be the effect of this fluid on the human frame?"

"You shall judge for yourself, my dear colonel," replied Dr. Heidegger; "and all of you, my respected friends, are welcome to so much of this admirable fluid, as may restore to you the bloom of youth. For my own part, having had much trouble in growing old, I am in no hurry to grow young again. With your permission, therefore, I will merely watch the progress of the experiment."

148–149 What do you think of Dr. Heidegger's reason for not wanting to be young again?

While he spoke, Dr. Heidegger had been filling the four champagne glasses with the water of the Fountain of Youth. It was apparently impregnated with an effervescent gas, for little bubbles were continually ascending from the depths of the glasses, and bursting in silvery spray at the surface. As the liquor diffused a pleasant perfume, the old people doubted not that it possessed cordial and comfortable properties; and, though utter skeptics as to its rejuvenescent power, they were inclined to swallow it at once. But Dr. Heidegger besought them to stay a moment.

152–153 was apparently . . . gas: seemed to have a bubbling gas dissolved in it.

157 cordial (kôr′jəl): stimulating.

158 rejuvenescent (rĭ-jo͞o′və-nĕs′ənt): producing renewed youth.

159 besought them to stay: begged them to wait.

"Before you drink, my respectable old friends," said he, "it would be well that, with the experience of a life-time to direct you, you should draw up a few general rules for your guidance, in passing a second time through the perils of youth. Think what a sin and shame it would be, if, with your peculiar advantages,

160–166 What warning does Dr. Heidegger give his guests?

you should not become patterns of virtue and wisdom to all the young people of the age!"

The doctor's four venerable friends made him no answer, except by a feeble and tremulous laugh; so very ridiculous was the idea, that, knowing how closely repentance treads behind the steps of error, they should ever go astray again.

167–170 Should the guests feel so confident that they will not repeat the errors of the past?

"Drink, then," said the doctor, bowing: "I rejoice that I have so well selected the subjects of my experiment."

171–172 What do you think is the purpose of Dr. Heidegger's experiment?

With palsied hands, they raised the glasses to their lips. The liquor, if it really possessed such virtues as Dr. Heidegger imputed to it, could not have been bestowed on four human beings who needed it more wofully. They looked as if they had never known what youth or pleasure was, but had been the offspring of Nature's dotage, and always the gray, decrepit, sapless, miserable creatures, who now sat stooping round the doctor's table, without life enough in their souls or bodies to be animated even by the prospect of growing young again. They drank off the water, and replaced their glasses on the table.

173 palsied: trembling.

175 imputed: attributed; credited.

178 dotage (dō′tĭj): feebleness due to old age.

Assuredly there was an almost immediate improvement in the aspect of the party, not unlike what might have been produced by a glass of generous wine, together with a sudden glow of cheerful sunshine, brightening over all their visages at once. There was a healthful suffusion on their cheeks, instead of the ashen hue that had made them look so corpselike. They gazed at one another, and fancied that some magic power had really begun to smooth away the deep and sad inscriptions which Father Time had been so long engraving on their brows. The Widow Wycherly adjusted her cap, for she felt almost like a woman again.

184 aspect: appearance.

187 healthful suffusion: rosy glow of health.

"Drink, then," said the doctor, bowing: "I rejoice that I have so well selected the subjects of my experiment."

"Give us more of this wondrous water!" cried they, eagerly. "We are younger—but we are still too old! Quick!—give us more!"

"Patience, patience!" quoth Dr. Heidegger, who sat watching the experiment, with philosophic coolness. "You have been a long

WORDS TO KNOW

tremulous (trĕm′yə-ləs) *adj.* marked by trembling, quivering, or shaking

decrepit (dĭ-krĕp′ĭt) *adj.* weakened, worn out, or broken down by old age or hard use

time growing old. Surely, you might be content to grow young in half an hour! But the water is at your service."

Again he filled their glasses with the liquor of youth, enough of which still remained in the vase to turn half the old people in the city to the age of their own grand-children. While the bubbles were yet sparkling on the brim, the doctor's four guests snatched their glasses from the table, and swallowed the contents at a single gulp. Was it delusion! Even while the draught was passing down their throats, it seemed to have wrought a change on their whole systems. Their eyes grew clear and bright; a dark shade deepened among their silvery locks; they sat around the table, three gentlemen of middle age, and a woman, hardly beyond her buxom prime.

207–215 Is the effect of the water physical or psychological? Watch how the narrator blurs the line between what is real and what is an illusion throughout the story.

"My dear widow, you are charming!" cried Colonel Killigrew, whose eyes had been fixed upon her face, while the shadows of age were flitting from it like darkness from the crimson day-break.

The fair widow knew, of old, that Colonel Killigrew's compliments were not always measured by sober truth; so she started up and ran to the mirror, still dreading that the ugly visage of an old woman would meet her gaze. Meanwhile, the three gentlemen behaved in such a manner, as proved that the water of the Fountain of Youth possessed some intoxicating qualities; unless, indeed, their exhilaration of spirits were merely a lightsome dizziness, caused by the sudden removal of the weight of years. Mr. Gascoigne's mind seemed to run on political topics, but whether relating to the past, present, or future, could not easily be determined, since the same ideas and phrases have been in vogue these fifty years. Now he rattled forth full-throated sentences about patriotism, national glory, and the people's right; now he muttered some perilous stuff or other, in a sly and doubtful whisper, so cautiously that even his own conscience could scarcely catch the secret; and now, again, he spoke in measured accents, and a deeply deferential tone, as if a royal ear were listening to his well-turned periods. Colonel Killigrew all this time had been trolling forth a jolly bottle-song, and ringing his glass in symphony with the chorus, while his eyes wandered towards the buxom figure of the Widow Wycherly. On the other side of the

219–257 How do the guests begin to behave as soon as their youth is restored?

WORDS TO KNOW

exhilaration (ĭg-zĭl'ə-rā'shən) *n.* a lively delight
deferential (dĕf'ə-rĕn'shəl) *adj.* extremely respectful

table, Mr. Medbourne was involved in a calculation of dollars and cents, with which was strangely intermingled a project for supplying the East Indies with ice, by harnessing a team of whales to the polar icebergs.

As for the Widow Wycherly, she stood before the mirror, curtseying and simpering to her own image, and greeting it as the friend whom she loved better than all the world beside. She thrust her face close to the glass, to see whether some long-remembered wrinkle or crow's-foot had indeed vanished. She examined whether the snow had so entirely melted from her hair, that the venerable cap could be safely thrown aside. At last, turning briskly away, she came with a sort of dancing step to the table.

245 simpering: smiling in a silly, self-conscious way.

"My dear old doctor," cried she, "pray favor me with another glass!"

"Certainly, my dear madam, certainly!" replied the complaisant doctor; "See! I have already filled the glasses."

254 complaisant (kəm-plā′sənt): willing to please.

There, in fact, stood the four glasses, brim full of this wonderful water, the delicate spray of which, as it effervesced from the surface, resembled the tremulous glitter of diamonds. It was now so nearly sunset, that the chamber had grown duskier than ever; but a mild and moon-like splendor gleamed from within the vase, and rested alike on the four guests, and on the doctor's venerable figure. He sat in a high-backed, elaborately-carved, oaken armchair, with a gray dignity of aspect that might have well befitted

The doctor's four guests snatched their glasses from the table, and swallowed the contents at a single gulp.

that very Father Time, whose power had never been disputed, save by this fortunate company. Even while quaffing the third draught of the Fountain of Youth, they were almost awed by the expression of his mysterious visage.

265 quaffing (kwŏf′ĭng): drinking heartily.

But, the next moment, the exhilarating gush of young life shot through their veins. They were now in the happy prime of youth. Age, with its miserable train of cares, and sorrows, and diseases, was remembered only as the trouble of a dream, from which they

WORDS TO KNOW

dispute (dĭ-spyo͞ot′) *v.* to question or doubt

had joyously awoke. The fresh gloss of the soul, so early lost, and without which the world's successive scenes had been but a gallery of faded pictures, again threw its enchantment over all their prospects. They felt like new-created beings, in a new-created universe.

"We are young! We are young!" they cried, exultingly.

Youth, like the extremity of age, had effaced the strongly marked characteristics of middle life, and mutually assimilated them all. They were a group of merry youngsters, almost maddened with the exuberant frolicksomeness of their years. The most singular effect of their gayety was an impulse to mock the infirmity and decrepitude of which they had so lately been the victims. They laughed loudly at their old-fashioned attire, the wide-skirted coats and flapped waistcoats of the young men, and the ancient cap and gown of the blooming girl. One limped across the floor, like a gouty grandfather; one set a pair of spectacles astride of his nose, and pretended to pore over the black-letter pages of the book of magic; a third seated himself in an arm-chair, and strove to imitate the venerable dignity of Dr. Heidegger. Then all shouted mirthfully, and leaped about the room. The Widow Wycherly—if so fresh a damsel could be called a widow—tripped up to the doctor's chair, with a mischievous merriment in her rosy face.

"Doctor, you dear old soul," cried she, "get up and dance with me!" And then the four young people laughed louder than ever, to think what a queer figure the poor old doctor would cut.

"Pray excuse me," answered the doctor, quietly. "I am old and rheumatic, and my dancing days were over long ago. But either of these gay young gentlemen will be glad of so pretty a partner."

"Dance with me, Clara!" cried Colonel Killigrew.

"No, no, I will be her partner!" shouted Mr. Gascoigne.

"She promised me her hand, fifty years ago!" exclaimed Mr. Medbourne.

They all gathered round her. One caught both her hands in his passionate grasp—another threw his arm about her waist—the third buried his hand among the glossy curls that clustered beneath the widow's cap. Blushing, panting, struggling, chiding, laughing, her warm breath fanning each of their faces by turns, she strove to disengage herself, yet still remained in their triple embrace. Never was there a livelier picture of youthful rivalship, with bewitching beauty for the prize. Yet, by a strange deception, owing to the duskiness of the chamber, and the antique dresses which they still wore, the tall mirror is said to have reflected the figures of the three old, gray, withered grand-sires, ridiculously contending for the skinny ugliness of a shrivelled grand-dam.

278–280 How does the narrator say youth and old age are alike?

279 assimilated: absorbed.

281–296 Whom or what are the guests mocking, and why?

291 mirthfully: joyfully.

298 rheumatic (ro͞o-măt'ĭk): made stiff by a condition such as arthritis.

309 strove to disengage herself: struggled to free herself.

311–315 The narrator is unclear about whether the reflection is real or an illusion. Why? What does the image in the mirror reveal?

314–315 grand-sires . . . grand-dam: old men . . . old woman.

WORDS TO KNOW

exultingly (ĭg-zŭl'tĭng-lē) *adv.* in a joyful and triumphant way

efface (ĭ-fās') *v.* to rub or wipe out; erase

Age, with its
miserable train
of cares,
and sorrows,
and diseases,
was remembered
only as the trouble
of a dream, from
which they had
joyously awoke.

La danse à la campagne [The country dance] (1883), Pierre Auguste Renoir. Private collection.

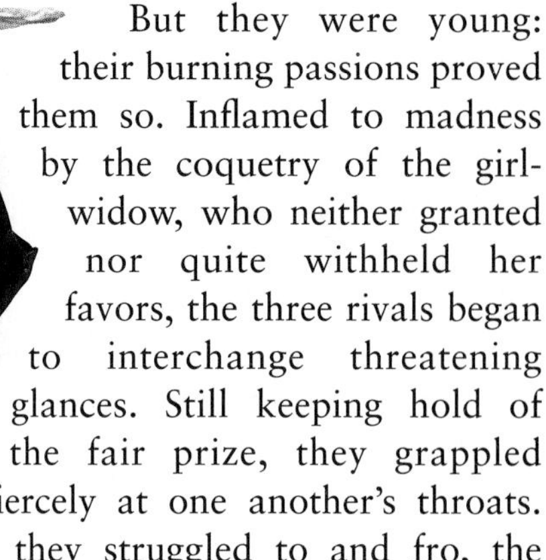

But they were young: their burning passions proved them so. Inflamed to madness by the coquetry of the girl-widow, who neither granted nor quite withheld her favors, the three rivals began to interchange threatening glances. Still keeping hold of the fair prize, they grappled fiercely at one another's throats. As they struggled to and fro, the table was overturned, and the vase dashed into a thousand fragments. The precious Water of Youth flowed in a bright stream across the floor, moistening the wings of a butterfly, which, grown old in the decline of summer, had alighted there to die. The insect fluttered lightly through the chamber, and settled on the snowy head of Dr. Heidegger.

319 coquetry (kō′kĭ-trē): flirtatious behavior.

318–329 How does the characters' behavior in this scene compare with that of their youth?

"Come, come, gentlemen!—come, Madam Wycherly," exclaimed the doctor, "I really most protest against this riot."

They stood still, and shivered; for it seemed as if gray Time were calling them back from their sunny youth, far down into the chill and darksome vale of years. They looked at old Dr. Heidegger, who sat in his carved arm-chair, holding the rose of half a century, which he had rescued from among the fragments of the shattered vase. At the motion of his hand, the four rioters resumed their seats; the more readily, because their violent exertions had wearied them, youthful though they were.

338 vale: valley.

"My poor Sylvia's rose!" ejaculated Dr. Heidegger, holding it in the light of the sunset clouds: "it appears to be fading again."

344 ejaculated: exclaimed.

And so it was. Even while the party were looking at it, the flower continued to shrivel up, till it became as dry and fragile as when the doctor had first thrown it into the vase. He shook off the few drops of moisture which clung to its petals.

"I love it as well thus, as in its dewy freshness," observed he, pressing the withered rose to his withered lips. While he spoke, the butterfly fluttered down from the doctor's snowy head, and fell upon the floor.

350–353 Can you infer how Dr. Heidegger feels about old age from the way he regards the rose?

His guests shivered again. A strange chillness, whether of the body or spirit they could not tell, was creeping gradually over them all. They gazed at one another, and fancied that each fleeting moment snatched away a charm, and left a deepening furrow where none had been before. Was it an illusion? Had the changes of a life-time been crowded into so brief a space, and were they now four aged people, sitting with their old friend, Dr. Heidegger?

"Are we grown old again, so soon!" cried they, dolefully.

In truth, they had. The Water of Youth possessed merely a virtue more transient than that of wine. The delirium which it created had effervesced away. Yes! they were old again. With a shuddering impulse, that showed her a woman still, the widow clasped her skinny hands before her face, and wished that the coffin-lid were over it, since it could be no longer beautiful.

364 delirium: a temporary state of mental confusion and clouded consciousness.

A strange chillness, whether of the body or spirit they could not tell, was creeping gradually over them all.

"Yes, friends, ye are old again," said Dr. Heidegger; "and lo! the Water of Youth is all lavished on the ground. Well—I bemoan it not; for if the fountain gushed at my very doorstep, I would not stoop to bathe my lips in it—no, though its delirium were for years instead of moments. Such is the lesson ye have taught me!"

369-373 What lesson has Dr. Heidegger learned?

But the doctor's four friends had taught no such lesson to themselves. They resolved forthwith to make a pilgrimage to Florida, and quaff at morning, noon, and night, from the Fountain of Youth. ❖

WORDS TO KNOW

transient (trăn′shənt) *adj.* lasting or existing for only a short time

RESPONDING OPTIONS

FROM PERSONAL RESPONSE *TO* CRITICAL ANALYSIS

REFLECT **1.** What are your thoughts about the ending of this story? Comment in your notebook.

RETHINK **2.** What lesson or lessons do you think Hawthorne intended this story to teach?
Consider
- what qualities the characters might represent (refer to the chart you made for the Reading Connection on page 376)
- what Dr. Heidegger is testing
- why Dr. Heidegger says he would not drink from the Fountain of Youth

3. Compare your attitudes toward youth and aging with those expressed by the characters in this story.
Consider
- Dr. Heidegger's comments about the withered rose (page 380)
- the guests' behavior when restored to youth
- the guests' desire to find the Fountain of Youth

4. The narrator is deliberately unclear about whether the guests are actually restored to youth. What do you think? Support your answer.

RELATE **5.** If people could regain their youth, do you think they would make the same mistakes? Explain.

ANOTHER PATHWAY

Cooperative Learning

With a small group, make a list of general rules for people who are going to be restored to youth. Draw on the experience of the characters in the story and on your own ideas. Share your list with the class.

LITERARY CONCEPTS

A writer's use of hints or clues to indicate events that will occur later in a story is called **foreshadowing.** Foreshadowing creates suspense and at the same time prepares the reader for what is to come. For example, the former rivalry for the Widow Wycherly that is mentioned on page 378 foreshadows the rivalry that occurs later in Dr. Heidegger's study (page 386). Look back at the story and identify two other examples of foreshadowing. Does this foreshadowing add to or detract from your enjoyment?

QUICKWRITES

1. Hazardous products carry labels that caution consumers about their use. Write a **warning label** that might appear on a bottle of water from the Fountain of Youth.
2. Write an **abstract,** or summary, of Dr. Heidegger's experiment for a popular scientific or medical journal.
3. If you could be ten years old again, knowing what you know now, would you turn back the clock? Give your answer as the last **paragraphs** of a story about a teenager who chooses to become ten years old again.

PORTFOLIO *Save your writing. You may want to use it later as a springboard to a piece for your portfolio.*

ALTERNATIVE ACTIVITIES

Look for magazine and TV ads promising people that they can look and feel younger. Then, in a **chart,** record the names of the products or services advertised and what they claim to do. How are these products or services similar to or different from the Water of Youth? What advice would you give a consumer who wants to use them?

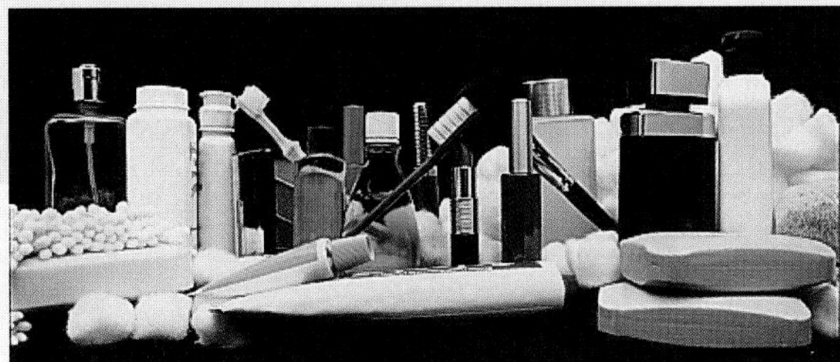

WORDS TO KNOW

For each group of words below, write the letter of the word that is an antonym of the boldfaced word.

1. **efface:** (a) mock, (b) preserve, (c) disguise
2. **stigma:** (a) award, (b) beauty, (c) hero
3. **decrepit:** (a) large, (b) fashionable, (c) sturdy
4. **venerable:** (a) dishonorable, (b) famous, (c) pale
5. **transient:** (a) wealthy, (b) permanent, (c) feeble
6. **deferential:** (a) similar, (b) accepting, (c) contemptuous
7. **exhilaration:** (a) gloom, (b) delay, (c) anticipation
8. **dispute:** (a) accept, (b) challenge, (c) admire
9. **tremulous:** (a) tired, (b) steady, (c) tiny
10. **exultingly:** (a) quietly, (b) arrogantly, (c) sadly

NATHANIEL HAWTHORNE

1804–1864

Nathaniel Hawthorne was born in Salem, Massachusetts. His childhood was not especially happy. His father, a sea captain, died when Hawthorne was four years old, and his grieving mother became reclusive. After graduating from Bowdoin College in Maine, where one of his classmates was Henry Wadsworth Longfellow, Hawthorne secluded himself at his mother's home in Salem for 12 years. He dedicated himself to writing and reading, hoping to develop his craft. Hawthorne, a descendant of a prominent Massachusetts Bay Colony settler and of a Salem witch trial judge, was fascinated by the society of his Puritan ancestors and studied colonial New England history during his long seclusion. Many of Hawthorne's stories are drawn from the darker aspects of his Puritan heritage.

In 1837, Hawthorne published his first collection of short stories, *Twice-Told Tales.* In 1842, he married and settled in Concord, Massachusetts. In 1850, with the publication of *The Scarlet Letter,* Hawthorne gained acclaim as a writer. Despite his success, Hawthorne had a difficult time supporting his family with his pen. To survive, he accepted political appointments—as surveyor in the Salem customhouse and later as U.S. consul in England.

After returning to his Concord home in 1860, Hawthorne became despondent over money, his poor health, and his inability to write. A year before his death at the age of 59, he wrote, "Everything is beautiful in youth—all things are allowed it." Hawthorne died in 1864 while visiting New Hampshire with his old friend the former U.S. president Franklin Pierce. Among the pallbearers at Hawthorne's funeral were Longfellow, Ralph Waldo Emerson, Oliver Wendell Holmes, and James Russell Lowell.

OTHER WORKS *The House of the Seven Gables,* "The Minister's Black Veil," "Rappaccini's Daughter"

LASERLINKS
• *AUTHOR BACKGROUND*

PREVIEWING

FICTION

A Rose for Emily

William Faulkner

PERSONAL CONNECTION

What do you consider your community? How does your community influence your behavior? Discuss these questions with a group of classmates. Talk about how you define your community—whether as a town, a neighborhood, an ethnic group, a student body, or some other entity. Talk about things you may have done—or decided not to do—because of your community. Do you like being part of the community?

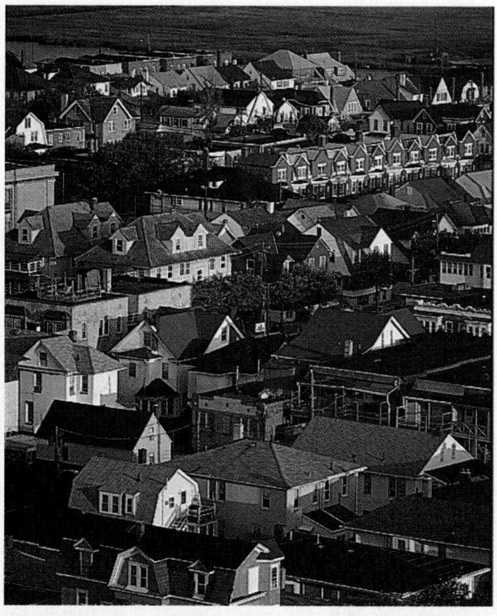

BIOGRAPHICAL CONNECTION

Colonel William C. Falkner

The first-person narrator of "A Rose for Emily" speaks for an entire community—the fictional town of Jefferson, Mississippi. Jefferson is the county seat of William Faulkner's fictional Yoknapatawpha (yŏk′nə-pə-tô′fə) County. Over a span of more than 30 years, Faulkner wrote novels and short stories about the land and the people of Jefferson and Yoknapatawpha County, creating a complete world that was patterned after his own home of Oxford. Many of the inhabitants of Faulkner's fictional world are based on real people. Miss Emily and Homer Barron in "A Rose for Emily," for example, are modeled on Miss Mary Louise Neilson and Captain Jack Hume. Against her family's objections, Neilson married Hume, a Northerner who came to Oxford to oversee the paving of its streets. Faulkner's great-grandfather, Colonel William C. Falkner (who dropped the *u* from the family name) was the inspiration for Colonel Sartoris, a character in this story and in several other Faulkner stories and novels. Faulkner's writing preserves the manners of Southern life at an earlier time; be warned that the narrator refers to African Americans with a term that is offensive to many contemporary readers.

WRITING CONNECTION

Miss Emily, the title character of this story, lives for many years as a recluse, someone who has withdrawn from a community to live in seclusion. You may be familiar with someone in your town or neighborhood who keeps out of the public eye—or perhaps someone in your school who stays isolated from people. In your notebook, briefly describe this person. How do you respond to him or her? How does the community respond? As you read the story, see whether there are any similarities between your community's response and the way the townspeople of Jefferson respond to Miss Emily.

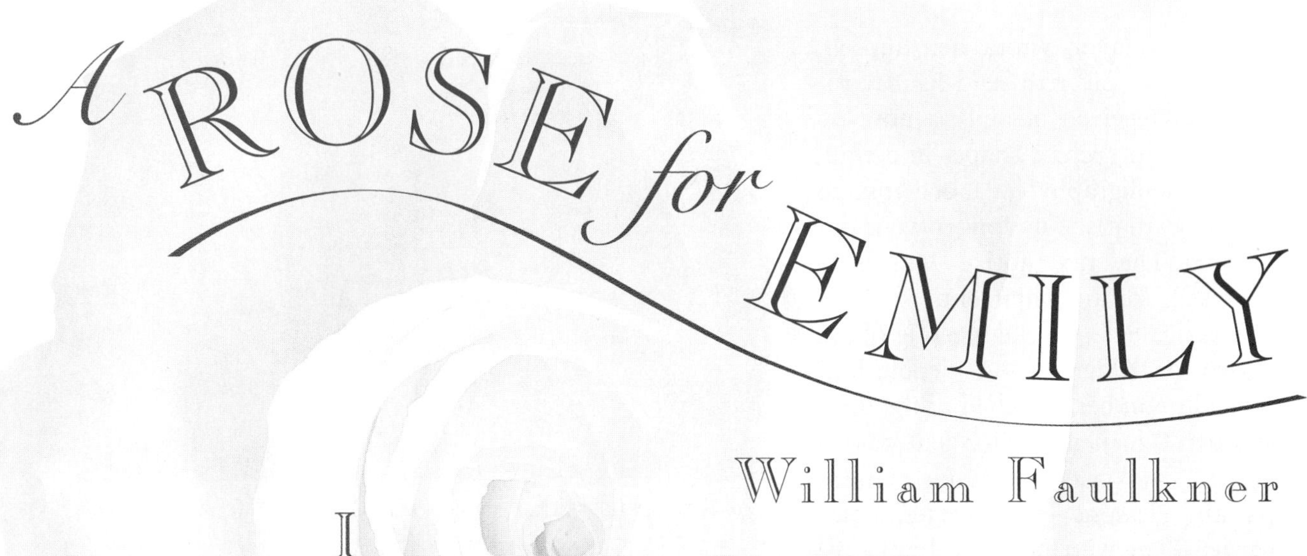

A Rose for Emily

William Faulkner

I

When Miss Emily Grierson died, our whole town went to her funeral: the men through a sort of respectful affection for a fallen monument, the women mostly out of curiosity to see the inside of her house, which no one save an old manservant—a combined gardener and cook—had seen in at least ten years.

It was a big, squarish frame house that had once been white, decorated with cupolas and spires and scrolled balconies in the heavily lightsome style of the seventies,[1] set on what had once been our most select street. But garages and cotton gins had encroached and obliterated even the august names of that neighborhood; only Miss Emily's house was left, lifting its stubborn and coquettish decay above the cotton wagons and the gasoline pumps—an eyesore among eyesores. And now Miss Emily had gone to join the representatives of those august names where they lay in the cedar-bemused[2] cemetery among the ranked and anonymous graves of Union and Confederate soldiers who fell at the battle of Jefferson.

Alive, Miss Emily had been a tradition, a duty, and a care; a sort of hereditary obligation upon the town, dating from that day in 1894 when Colonel Sartoris, the mayor—he who fathered the edict that no Negro woman should appear on the streets without an apron—remitted her taxes, the dispensation dating from the death of her father on into perpetuity.[3] Not that Miss Emily would have accepted charity. Colonel Sartoris invented an involved tale to the effect that Miss Emily's father had loaned money to the town, which the town, as a matter of business, preferred this way of repaying. Only a man of Colonel Sartoris' generation and thought could have invented it, and only a woman could have believed it.

When the next generation, with its more modern ideas, became mayors and aldermen, this arrangement created some little dissatisfaction. On the first of the year they mailed her a tax notice. February came, and there was no reply. They wrote her a formal letter, asking her to call at the sheriff's office at her convenience. A week

1. **the seventies:** the 1870s.
2. **cedar-bemused:** almost lost in cedar trees (literally, confused by cedars).
3. **remitted . . . perpetuity:** released her from paying taxes forever after the time of her father's death.

WORDS TO KNOW

encroach (ĕn-krōch') *v.* to advance beyond original limits; intrude
obliterate (ə-blĭt'ə-rāt') *v.* to wipe out, leaving no trace
coquettish (kō-kĕt'ĭsh) *adj.* flirtatious
edict (ē'dĭkt') *n.* an order put out by a person in authority

later the mayor wrote her himself, offering to call or to send his car for her, and received in reply a note on paper of an archaic shape, in a thin, flowing calligraphy[4] in faded ink, to the effect that she no longer went out at all. The tax notice was also enclosed, without comment.

They called a special meeting of the Board of Aldermen. A deputation[5] waited upon her, knocked at the door through which no visitor had passed since she ceased giving china-painting lessons eight or ten years earlier. They were admitted by the old Negro into a dim hall from which a stairway mounted into still more shadow. It smelled of dust and disuse—a close, dank smell. The Negro led them into the parlor. It was furnished in heavy, leather-covered furniture. When the Negro opened the blinds of one window, they could see that the leather was cracked; and when they sat down, a faint dust rose sluggishly about their thighs, spinning with slow motes[6] in the single sun-ray. On a tarnished gilt easel before the fireplace stood a crayon portrait of Miss Emily's father.

German Teapot (1994), Charles Warren Mundy. Oil on canvas, 14″ × 18″.

They rose when she entered—a small, fat woman in black, with a thin gold chain descending to her waist and vanishing into her belt, leaning on an ebony cane with a tarnished gold head. Her skeleton was small and spare; perhaps that was why what would have been merely plumpness in another was obesity in her. She looked bloated, like a body long submerged in motionless water, and of that pallid hue. Her eyes, lost in the fatty ridges of her face, looked like two small pieces of coal pressed into a lump of dough as they moved from one face to another while the visitors stated their errand.

She did not ask them to sit. She just stood in the door and listened quietly until the spokesman came to a stumbling halt. Then they could hear the invisible watch ticking at the end of the gold chain.

Her voice was dry and cold. "I have no taxes in Jefferson. Colonel Sartoris explained it to me. Perhaps one of you can gain access to the city records and satisfy yourselves."

"But we have. We are the city authorities, Miss Emily. Didn't you get a notice from the sheriff, signed by him?"

"I received a paper, yes," Miss Emily said. "Perhaps he considers himself the sheriff . . . I have no taxes in Jefferson."

"But there is nothing on the books to show that, you see. We must go by the—"

"See Colonel Sartoris. I have no taxes in Jefferson."

"But, Miss Emily—"

"See Colonel Sartoris." (Colonel Sartoris had been dead almost ten years.) "I have no taxes in Jefferson. Tobe!" The Negro appeared. "Show these gentlemen out."

---

4. **calligraphy:** beautiful handwriting.
5. **deputation:** a small group representing a larger one.
6. **motes:** specks.

WORDS TO KNOW

dank (dăngk) *adj.* unpleasantly damp; moist and chilly
pallid (păl′ĭd) *adj.* abnormally pale

II

So she vanquished them, horse and foot, just as she had vanquished their fathers thirty years before about the smell. That was two years after her father's death and a short time after her sweetheart—the one we believed would marry her—had deserted her. After her father's death she went out very little; after her sweetheart went away, people hardly saw her at all. A few of the ladies had the temerity to call, but were not received, and the only sign of life about the place was the Negro man—a young man then—going in and out with a market basket.

"Just as if a man—any man—could keep a kitchen properly," the ladies said; so they were not surprised when the smell developed. It was another link between the gross, teeming world and the high and mighty Griersons.

A neighbor, a woman, complained to the mayor, Judge Stevens, eighty years old.

"But what will you have me do about it, madam?" he said.

"Why, send her word to stop it," the woman said. "Isn't there a law?"

"I'm sure that won't be necessary," Judge Stevens said. "It's probably just a snake or a rat that nigger of hers killed in the yard. I'll speak to him about it."

The next day he received two more complaints, one from a man who came in diffident deprecation.[7] "We really must do something about it, Judge. I'd be the last one in the world to bother Miss Emily, but we've got to do something." That night the Board of Aldermen met—three graybeards and one younger man, a member of the rising generation.

"It's simple enough," he said. "Send her word to have her place cleaned up. Give her a certain time to do it in, and if she don't . . ."

"Dammit, sir," Judge Stevens said, "will you accuse a lady to her face of smelling bad?"

So the next night, after midnight, four men crossed Miss Emily's lawn and slunk about the house like burglars, sniffing along the base of the brickwork and at the cellar openings while one of them performed a regular sowing motion with his hand out of a sack slung from his shoulder. They broke open the cellar door and sprinkled lime there, and in all the outbuildings. As they recrossed the lawn, a window that had been dark was lighted and Miss Emily sat in it, the light behind her, and her upright torso motionless as that of an idol. They crept quietly across the lawn and into the shadow of the locusts that lined the street. After a week or two the smell went away.

"We really must do something about it, Judge. I'd be the last one in the world to bother Miss Emily, but we've got to do something."

That was when people had begun to feel really sorry for her. People in our town, remembering how old lady Wyatt, her great-aunt, had gone completely crazy at last, believed that the Griersons held themselves a little too high for what they really were. None of the young men were quite good enough for Miss Emily and such. We had long thought of them as a tableau,[8] Miss Emily a slender figure in white in the background, her father a spraddled silhouette in

7. **deprecation:** disapproval.

8. **tableau** (tăb′lō′): dramatic scene or picture.

WORDS TO KNOW

temerity (tə-mĕr′ĭ-tē) *n.* foolish boldness
diffident (dĭf′ĭ-dənt) *adj.* shy and timid; lacking self-confidence

the foreground, his back to her and clutching a horsewhip, the two of them framed by the back-flung front door. So when she got to be thirty and was still single, we were not pleased exactly, but vindicated; even with insanity in the family she wouldn't have turned down all of her chances if they had really materialized.

When her father died, it got about that the house was all that was left to her; and in a way, people were glad. At last they could pity Miss Emily. Being left alone, and a pauper, she had become humanized. Now she too would know the old thrill and the old despair of a penny more or less.

The day after his death all the ladies prepared to call at the house and offer condolence and aid, as is our custom. Miss Emily met them at the door, dressed as usual and with no trace of grief on her face. She told them that her father was not dead. She did that for three days, with the ministers calling on her, and the doctors, trying to persuade her to let them dispose of the body. Just as they were about to resort to law and force, she broke down, and they buried her father quickly.

White frame house in Holly Springs, Mississippi

We did not say she was crazy then. We believed she had to do that. We remembered all the young men her father had driven away, and we knew that with nothing left, she would have to cling to that which had robbed her, as people will.

III

She was sick for a long time. When we saw her again, her hair was cut short, making her look like a girl, with a vague resemblance to those angels in colored church windows—sort of tragic and serene.

The town had just let the contracts for paving the sidewalks, and in the summer after her father's death they began the work. The construction company came with niggers and mules and machinery, and a foreman named Homer Barron, a Yankee—a big, dark, ready man, with a big voice and eyes lighter than his face. The little boys would follow in groups to hear him cuss the niggers, and the niggers singing in time to the rise and fall of picks. Pretty soon he knew everybody in town. Whenever you heard a lot of laughing anywhere about the square, Homer Barron would be in the center of the group.

Presently we began to see him and Miss Emily on Sunday afternoons driving in the yellow-wheeled buggy and the matched team of bays from the livery stable.

At first we were glad that Miss Emily would have an interest, because the ladies all said, "Of course a Grierson would not think seriously of a Northerner, a day laborer." But there were still others, older people, who said that even grief could not cause a real lady to forget *noblesse oblige*[9]—without calling it *noblesse oblige*. They just said, "Poor Emily. Her kinsfolk should come to her." She had some kin in Alabama; but years ago her father had fallen out with them over the estate of old lady Wyatt, the crazy woman, and there was no communication between the two families. They had not even been represented at the funeral.

And as soon as the old people said, "Poor Emily," the whispering began. "Do you suppose it's really so?" they said to one another. "Of course it is. What else could . . ." This behind their hands; rustling of craned[10] silk and satin behind jalousies[11] closed upon the sun of Sunday afternoon as the thin, swift clop-clop-clop of the matched team passed: "Poor Emily."

She carried her head high enough—even when we believed that she was fallen. It was as if she demanded more than ever the recognition of her dignity as the last Grierson; as if it had wanted that touch of earthiness to reaffirm her imperviousness. Like when she bought the rat poison, the arsenic. That was over a year after they had begun to say "Poor Emily," and while the two female cousins were visiting her.

"I want some poison," she said to the druggist. She was over thirty then, still a slight woman, though thinner than usual, with cold, haughty black eyes in a face the flesh of which was strained across the temples and about the eye-sockets as you imagine a lighthouse-keeper's face ought to look. "I want some poison," she said.

"Yes, Miss Emily. What kind? For rats and such? I'd recom—"

"I want the best you have. I don't care what kind."

The druggist named several. "They'll kill anything up to an elephant. But what you want is—"

"Arsenic," Miss Emily said. "Is that a good one?"

"Is . . . arsenic? Yes, ma'am. But what you want—"

"I want arsenic."

The druggist looked down at her. She looked back at him, erect, her face like a strained flag. "Why, of course," the druggist said. "If that's what you want. But the law requires you to tell what you are going to use it for."

Miss Emily just stared at him, her head tilted back in order to look him eye for eye, until he looked away and went and got the arsenic and wrapped it up. The Negro delivery boy brought her the package; the druggist didn't come back. When she opened the package at home there was written on the box, under the skull and bones: "For rats."

---

9. ***noblesse oblige*** (nō-blĕs′ ō-blēzh′): the responsibility of people of high social position to behave in a noble fashion.

10. **craned:** stretched.

11. **jalousies** (jăl′ə-sēz): doors or windows containing overlapping slats that can be opened or closed.

IV

So the next day we all said, "She will kill herself"; and we said it would be the best thing. When she had first begun to be seen with Homer Barron, we had said, "She will marry him." Then we said, "She will persuade him yet," because Homer himself had remarked—he liked men, and it was known that he drank with the younger men in the Elks' Club—that he was not a marrying man. Later we said, "Poor Emily" behind the jalousies as they passed on Sunday afternoon in the glittering buggy, Miss Emily with her head high and Homer Barron with his hat cocked and a cigar in his teeth, reins and whip in a yellow glove.

Then some of the ladies began to say that it was a disgrace to the town and a bad example to the young people. The men did not want to interfere, but at last the ladies forced the Baptist minister—Miss Emily's people were Episcopal—to call upon her. He would never divulge what happened during that interview, but he refused to go back again. The next Sunday they again drove about the streets, and the following day the minister's wife wrote to Miss Emily's relations in Alabama.

So she had blood-kin under her roof again and we sat back to watch developments. At first nothing happened. Then we were sure that they were to be married. We learned that Miss Emily had been to the jeweler's and ordered a man's toilet set in silver, with the letters H. B. on each piece. Two days later we learned that she had bought a complete outfit of men's clothing, including a nightshirt, and we said, "They are married." We were really glad. We were glad because the two female cousins were even more Grierson than Miss Emily had ever been.

So we were not surprised when Homer Barron—the streets had been finished some time since—was gone. We were a little disappointed that there was not a public blowing-off,[12] but we believed that he had gone on to prepare for Miss Emily's coming, or to give her a chance to get rid of the cousins. (By that time it was a cabal,[13] and we were all Miss Emily's allies to help circumvent the cousins.) Sure enough, after another week they departed. And, as we had expected all along, within three days Homer Barron was back in town. A neighbor saw the Negro man admit him at the kitchen door at dusk one evening.

We learned that Miss Emily had been to the jeweler's and ordered a man's toilet set in silver, with the letters H. B. on each piece.

And that was the last we saw of Homer Barron. And of Miss Emily for some time. The Negro man went in and out with the market basket, but the front door remained closed. Now and then we would see her at a window for a moment, as the men did that night when they sprinkled the lime, but for almost six months she did not appear on the streets. Then we knew that this was to be expected too; as if that quality of her father which had thwarted her woman's life

12. **blowing-off:** celebration.

13. **cabal** (kə-băl′): a group united in a secret plot.

WORDS TO KNOW

divulge (dĭ-vŭlj′) *v.* to make known something private

circumvent (sûr′kəm-vĕnt′) *v.* to avoid or get around by clever maneuvering

thwart (thwôrt) *v.* to block or hinder; prevent the fulfillment of so many times had been too virulent and too furious to die.

When we next saw Miss Emily, she had grown fat and her hair was turning gray. During the next few years it grew grayer and grayer until it attained an even pepper-and-salt iron-gray, when it ceased turning. Up to the day of her death at seventy-four it was still that vigorous iron-gray, like the hair of an active man.

From that time on her front door remained closed, save for a period of six or seven years, when she was about forty, during which she gave lessons in china-painting. She fitted up a studio in one of the downstairs rooms, where the daughters and granddaughters of Colonel Sartoris' contemporaries were sent to her with the same regularity and in the same spirit that they were sent to church on Sundays with a twenty-five-cent piece for the collection plate. Meanwhile her taxes had been remitted.

Then the newer generation became the backbone and the spirit of the town, and the painting pupils grew up and fell away and did not send their children to her with boxes of color and tedious brushes and pictures cut from the ladies' magazines. The front door closed upon the last one and remained closed for good. When the town got free postal delivery, Miss Emily alone refused to let them fasten the metal numbers above her door and attach a mailbox to it. She would not listen to them.

Daily, monthly, yearly we watched the Negro grow grayer and more stooped, going in and out with the market basket. Each December we sent her a tax notice, which would be returned by the post office a week later, unclaimed. Now and then we would see her in one of the downstairs windows—she had evidently shut up the top floor of the house—like the carven torso of an idol in a niche,[14] looking or not looking at us, we could never tell which. Thus she passed from generation to generation—dear, inescapable, impervious, tranquil, and perverse.

And so she died. Fell ill in the house filled with dust and shadows, with only a doddering Negro man to wait on her. We did not even know she was sick; we had long since given up trying to get any information from the Negro. He talked to no one, probably not even to her, for his voice had grown harsh and rusty, as if from disuse.

She died in one of the downstairs rooms, in a heavy walnut bed with a curtain, her gray head propped on a pillow yellow and moldy with age and lack of sunlight.

V

The Negro met the first of the ladies at the front door and let them in, with their hushed, sibilant[15] voices and their quick, curious glances, and then he disappeared. He walked right through the house and out the back and was not seen again.

The two female cousins came at once. They held the funeral on the second day, with the town coming to look at Miss Emily beneath a mass of bought flowers, with the crayon face of her father musing profoundly above the bier[16] and the ladies sibilant and macabre; and the very old men—some in their brushed Confederate uniforms—on the porch and the lawn, talking of Miss Emily as if she had been a contemporary of theirs, believing that they had danced with her and courted her perhaps, confusing time with its mathematical progression, as the old do, to whom all the past is not a diminishing road but, instead, a huge meadow which no winter ever quite

14. **niche** (nĭch): an indented space in a wall.

15. **sibilant** (sĭb'ə-lənt): making a hissing sound.

16. **bier** (bîr): a platform for a coffin.

WORDS TO KNOW

virulent (vîr'yə-lənt) *adj.* extremely poisonous or harmful

tedious (tē'dē-əs) *adj.* boring because of dullness

profoundly (prə-found'lē) *adv.* deeply; intensely

touches, divided from them now by the narrow bottleneck of the most recent decade of years.

Already we knew that there was one room in that region above stairs which no one had seen in forty years, and which would have to be forced. They waited until Miss Emily was decently in the ground before they opened it.

Woman in Distress (1882), James Ensor. Musée d'Orsay, Paris, Giraudon/Art Resource. Copyright © Estate of James Ensor/VAGA, New York.

The violence of breaking down the door seemed to fill this room with pervading dust. A thin, acrid pall[17] as of the tomb seemed to lie everywhere upon this room decked and furnished as for a bridal:[18] upon the valance curtains of faded rose color, upon the rose-shaded lights, upon the dressing table, upon the delicate array of crystal and the man's toilet things backed with tarnished silver, silver so tarnished that the monogram was obscured. Among them lay a collar and tie, as if they had just been removed, which, lifted, left upon the surface a pale crescent in the dust. Upon a chair hung the suit, carefully folded; beneath it the two mute shoes and the discarded socks.

The man himself lay in the bed.

For a long while we just stood there, looking down at the profound and fleshless grin. The body had apparently once lain in the attitude of an embrace, but now the long sleep that outlasts love, that conquers even the grimace of love, had cuckolded him.[19] What was left of him, rotted beneath what was left of the nightshirt, had become inextricable from the bed in which he lay; and upon him and upon the pillow beside him lay that even coating of the patient and biding dust.

Then we noticed that in the second pillow was the indentation of a head. One of us lifted something from it, and leaning forward, that faint and invisible dust dry and acrid in the nostrils, we saw a long strand of iron-gray hair. ❖

17. **acrid pall** (ăk′rĭd pôl′): bitter-smelling covering.
18. **bridal:** wedding.
19. **cuckolded him:** made his wife or lover unfaithful to him.

WORDS TO KNOW

obscure (ŏb-skyŏŏr′) *v.* to cover over; hide

RESPONDING OPTIONS

FROM PERSONAL RESPONSE *TO* CRITICAL ANALYSIS

REFLECT 1. Using only a facial expression, give your reaction to the ending of this story.

RETHINK 2. What do you think motivates Miss Emily to commit murder?

Consider
- her father's reaction to her previous suitors
- what Homer Barron's intentions toward Miss Emily might have been
- what Miss Emily's deepest feelings and hidden longings might have been
- the appearance of the upstairs room and the bed when discovered

3. How would you judge the way the community responds to Miss Emily throughout her life?

Consider
- the description of her as "a tradition, a duty, and a care; a sort of hereditary obligation upon the town" (page 393)
- the community's attitude toward her romance with Homer Barron
- the outcome of the disputes over her unpaid taxes, the arsenic, and the smell coming from her house
- why girls of the town are sent to her for lessons in china painting

4. How much responsibility, if any, do you think the community bears for Miss Emily's crime?

5. What might the servant, Tobe, say if he were telling the story? Role-play an interview in which he answers questions from a reporter.

RELATE 6. Think about the reclusive person you described for the Writing Connection on page 392. Do you see any similarities in the way your community responds to this person and the way the townspeople respond to Miss Emily? Explain your ideas.

7. How do you think Miss Emily compares with people who have committed shocking crimes in recent years?

ANOTHER PATHWAY

Cooperative Learning

With a small group of classmates, prepare a television news report on the murder of Homer Barron. What angle will you give the story? Was Miss Emily's act a result of parental cruelty? of social pressures? Was it a crime of passion? Look for clues in the story. Present your news report to the class.

QUICKWRITES

1. Drawing on details in the story, write Miss Emily's **obituary** for the *Jefferson Enquirer.* Before you start, look at examples of newspaper obituaries to see how they are written.
2. Suppose that Miss Emily's diary were found in the locked room after her death. Write **entries** that might be found in the diary, describing Miss Emily's feelings about her courtship by Homer Barron, her father's death, her encounter with the aldermen, her decision to buy arsenic, or another incident in her life.

***PORTFOLIO** Save your writing. You may want to use it later as a springboard to a piece for your portfolio.*

LITERARY CONCEPTS

Characterization refers to the techniques a writer uses to develop characters. A writer may reveal a character in one or more of the following ways:

- through physical description of the character
- through the character's actions, words, and feelings
- through a narrator's direct comments about the character's nature
- through the actions, words, and feelings of other characters

Which techniques does Faulkner use to reveal the character of Miss Emily? Find at least three specific examples of characterization that help you learn more about Miss Emily.

CONCEPT REVIEW: Foreshadowing What instances of foreshadowing are there in this story? Find details that give clues about later events.

ALTERNATIVE ACTIVITIES

1. With a partner, rehearse a **dramatic scene** showing what might have happened the night Homer Barron was last seen entering Miss Emily's kitchen. What did Homer say to Miss Emily? What did she say to him? What was the outcome? Perform your scene for classmates.
2. Draw several **panels** for a comic-book version of "A Rose for Emily," showing an episode from the story. Display your work in class.

ART CONNECTION

The house pictured on page 396 is near Faulkner's hometown of Oxford, Mississippi, and exemplifies the kind of house he was familiar with. Is this how, from Faulkner's description, you imagined Miss Emily's house to look? What details of its appearance are not shown in the photo?

THE WRITER'S STYLE

Faulkner often used **flashbacks** in his stories, shuffling the order of events. His unusual use of chronology was based on his notion of the fluidity of time, which he once expressed as follows: "There isn't any time. . . . There is only the present moment, in which I include both the past and the future, and that is eternity." Would the story be hurt or improved by relating events in strict chronological order? Test your ideas by plotting the major events on a time line and then using this time line to retell the story to someone who has not heard it.

CRITIC'S CORNER

The critic Cleanth Brooks stated, "Miss Emily's story constitutes a warning against the sin of pride: heroic isolation pushed too far ends in homicidal madness." Do you agree with his summary? Explain why or why not. What other possible meanings can you draw from Miss Emily's story?

LITERARY LINKS

What, specifically, does this story have in common with other Gothic works you have read in this part of Unit Three? Would you say Faulkner is closer in spirit to Poe or to Hawthorne?

WORDS TO KNOW

EXERCISE A Review the Words to Know at the bottom of the selection pages. Then write the vocabulary word that best completes each sentence.

1. Miss Emily's life held little interest—it consisted merely of one ______ day after another.
2. The mayor had issued a somewhat foolish ______ that Miss Emily would not have to pay taxes.
3. Instead of directly offering financial help to her, he took another route by making up an involved story to ______ the problem.
4. When a new administration tried to make her pay, the obstructions created by her stubbornness made her able to ______ every attempt.
5. When Miss Emily insisted on something, no one in town had the ______ to argue with her.
6. Closed window blinds and inadequate heat gave her house an unpleasantly ______ atmosphere.
7. Miss Emily herself was never exposed to sunlight, and her complexion became unpleasantly ______.
8. Perhaps the judge was normally bold, but he reacted to the foul smell from Miss Emily's house with ______ hesitation.
9. The townspeople thought that sprinkling lime might destroy, or ______ ,the source of the smell.
10. Even in her younger years, Miss Emily had been a no-nonsense kind of woman, not the type to behave in a ______ fashion toward any man.
11. Although the town realized that she kept company with Homer Barron, no one knew just how ______ in love she had been.
12. Only after her death did anyone dare to ______ on the privacy of the upstairs room.
13. Enough tarnish had formed on the silver of the men's toilet things to ______ the monogram.
14. Was it Homer's plans to leave town that made Miss Emily react in such a ______ fashion?
15. Did she know that a clue on the pillow would ______ her closely kept secret?

WILLIAM FAULKNER

1897–1962

William Faulkner, the great-grandson of a colorful Civil War hero, was nurtured on legends of the honor and gallantry of his Mississippi ancestors. As a youth in Oxford, Mississippi, Faulkner was bored by school, preferring hunting, playing football, listening to his grandfather's stories, drawing, and writing. At the end of tenth grade, Faulkner dropped out of high school, but he continued reading and discussing literature with his friends. For years, Faulkner drifted aimlessly. He traveled, did odd jobs, and attended the University of Mississippi for one year as a special student.

By the late 1920s, however, Faulkner had stopped drifting. He was married and had published his first two novels. In 1929, he entered what some have called his great years. In a 13-year period, he published 15 books—novels and collections of short stories—including his masterworks *Light in August* (1932) and *Absalom, Absalom!* (1936).

Following advice to write about what he knew best, Faulkner focused his considerable talents on the land and people of northern Mississippi. His challenging experiments with stream of consciousness and fractured chronology cost him a wide audience, however, so he turned to writing Hollywood film scripts to earn a living. After World War II, his critical reputation and popularity grew, and in 1949 he won the Nobel Prize in literature. By the time he died, Faulkner was widely regarded as one of America's greatest writers.

OTHER WORKS *As I Lay Dying, The Sound and the Fury*

LASERLINKS
• *AUTHOR BACKGROUND*

PREVIEWING

FICTION

The Life You Save May Be Your Own

Flannery O'Connor

PERSONAL CONNECTION

Sometimes people try to get others to do what they want through various methods of manipulation. For example, parents may offer their children rewards for doing better in school, or a salesperson may make false claims to get customers to buy products. Copy the chart shown here, adding to it other methods of manipulation that you can think of. For each method, indicate whether you think it is always, sometimes, or never acceptable.

Methods of Manipulation	Acceptability		
	Always	Sometimes	Never
Pretending friendship			
Offering a bribe			
Making someone feel guilty			

LITERARY CONNECTION

Influenced by Edgar Allan Poe and Nathaniel Hawthorne, Flannery O'Connor wrote stories filled with grotesque characters, violence, and bizarre situations. Drawing on her intense devotion to the Catholic faith and on her sharp comic sense, she constructed a 1940s and 1950s South populated with misfits, fanatics, and manipulative con artists obsessed with innocence and corruption, salvation and damnation. Since her stories are set in her native South and involve freakish characters, O'Connor is often grouped with William Faulkner, Carson McCullers, Truman Capote, and others in a literary tradition known as Southern Gothic.

READING CONNECTION

Evaluating Characters O'Connor never tells the reader directly whether her characters are good or evil; she wants you to make your own judgments, based on the characters' thoughts, words, and actions. As you read this story, notice what methods of manipulation the characters use and decide whether these methods are acceptable to you. O'Connor will guide your judgment about the characters with the names she gives them and the imagery she uses to describe them, so pay attention to these aspects as well.

Using Your Reading Log To help you evaluate the characters, use the reading-strategy questions inserted throughout the selection. Write your responses in your reading log. Also jot down other questions, thoughts, and feelings that come to you as you read. After you finish, discuss your responses with classmates.

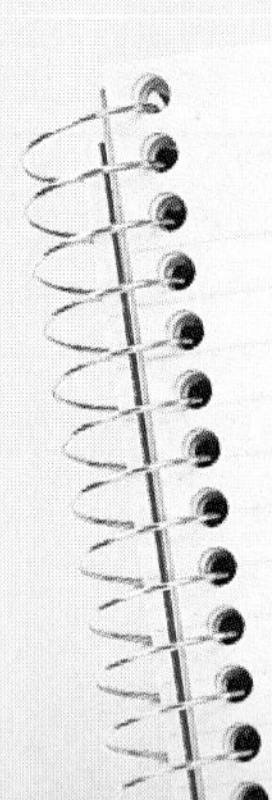

Evaluate
How would you characterize Mr. Shiftlet? Mrs. Crater? her daughter, Lucynell?

The Life You Save May Be Your Own

Flannery O'Connor

The old woman and her daughter were sitting on their porch when Mr. Shiftlet came up their road for the first time. The old woman slid to the edge of her chair and leaned forward, shading her eyes from the piercing sunset with her hand. The daughter could not see far in front of her and continued to play with her fingers. Although the old woman lived in this desolate spot with only her daughter and she had never seen Mr. Shiftlet before, she could tell, even from a distance, that he was a tramp and no one to be afraid of. His left coat sleeve was folded up to show there was only half an arm in it, and his gaunt figure listed slightly to the side as if the breeze were pushing him. He had on a black town suit and a brown felt hat that was turned up in the front and down in the back and he carried a tin toolbox by a handle. He came on, at an amble, up her road, his face turned toward the sun which appeared to be balancing itself on the peak of a small mountain.

The old woman didn't change her position until he was almost into her yard; then she rose with one hand fisted on her hip. The daughter, a large girl in a short blue organdy dress, saw him all at once and jumped up and began to stamp and point and make excited speechless sounds.

Mr. Shiftlet stopped just inside the yard and set his box on the ground and tipped his hat at her as if she were not in the least afflicted; then he turned toward the old woman and swung the hat all the way off. He had long black slick hair that hung flat from a part in the middle to beyond the tips of his ears on either side. His face descended in forehead for more than half its length and ended suddenly with his features just balanced over a jutting steel-trap jaw. He seemed to be a young man but he had a look of composed

WORDS TO KNOW

gaunt (gônt) *adj.* thin and bony
list (lĭst) *v.* to lean or tilt to one side
composed (kəm-pōzd') *adj.* calm; cool and collected

dissatisfaction as if he understood life thoroughly.

"Good evening," the old woman said. She was about the size of a cedar fence post and she had a man's gray hat pulled down low over her head.

The tramp stood looking at her and didn't answer. He turned his back and faced the sunset. He swung both his whole and his short arm up slowly so that they indicated an expanse of sky and his figure formed a crooked cross. The old woman watched him with her arms folded across her chest as if she were the owner of the sun, and the daughter watched, her head thrust forward and her fat helpless hands hanging at the wrists. She had long pink-gold hair and eyes as blue as a peacock's neck.

He held the pose for almost fifty seconds and then he picked up his box and came on to the porch and dropped down on the bottom step. "Lady," he said in a firm nasal voice, "I'd give a fortune to live where I could see me a sun do that every evening."

"Does it every evening," the old woman said and sat back down. The daughter sat down too and watched him with a cautious, sly look as if he were a bird that had come up very close. He leaned to one side, rooting in his pants pocket, and in a second he brought out a package of chewing gum and offered her a piece. She took it and unpeeled it and began to chew without taking her eyes off him. He offered the old woman a piece but she only raised her upper lip to indicate she had no teeth.

Mr. Shiftlet's pale, sharp glance had already passed over everything in the yard—the pump near the corner of the house and the big fig tree that three or four chickens were preparing to roost in—and had moved to a shed where he saw the square rusted back of an automobile. "You ladies drive?" he asked.

"That car ain't run in fifteen year," the old woman said. "The day my husband died, it quit running."

"Nothing is like it used to be, lady," he said. "The world is almost rotten."

"That's right," the old woman said. "You from around here?"

"Name Tom T. Shiftlet," he murmured, looking at the tires.

"I'm pleased to meet you," the old woman said. "Name Lucynell Crater and daughter Lucynell Crater. What you doing around here, Mr. Shiftlet?"

He judged the car to be about a 1928 or '29 Ford. "Lady," he said, and turned and gave her his full attention, "lemme tell you something. There's one of these doctors in Atlanta that's taken a knife and cut the human heart—the human heart," he repeated, leaning forward, "out of a man's chest and held it in his hand," and he held his hand out, palm up, as if it were slightly weighted with the human heart, "and studied it like it was a day-old chicken, and lady," he said, allowing a long significant pause in which his head slid forward and his clay-colored eyes brightened, "he don't know no more about it than you or me."

"That's right," the old woman said.

"Why, if he was to take that knife and cut into every corner of it, he still wouldn't know no more than you or me. What you want to bet?"

"Nothing," the old woman said wisely. "Where you come from, Mr. Shiftlet?"

He didn't answer. He reached into his pocket and brought out a sack of tobacco and a package of cigarette papers and rolled himself a cigarette, expertly with one hand, and attached it in a hanging position to his upper lip. Then he took a box of wooden matches from his pocket and struck one on his shoe. He held the burning match as if he were studying the mystery of flame while it traveled dangerously toward his skin. The daughter began to make loud noises and to point to his hand and shake her finger at him, but when the flame was just before touching him, he leaned down with his hand cupped over it as if he were going to set fire to his nose and lit the cigarette.

He flipped away the dead match and blew a stream of gray into the evening. A sly look came

Mrs. Gamely (1930), George Luks. Oil on canvas, 66″ × 48″, collection of Whitney Museum of American Art, purchase (31.289). Copyright © 1995 Whitney Museum of American Art.

over his face. "Lady," he said, "nowadays, people'll do anything anyways. I can tell you my name is Tom T. Shiftlet and I come from Tarwater, Tennessee, but you never have seen me before: how you know I ain't lying? How you know my name ain't Aaron Sparks, lady, and I come from Singleberry, Georgia, or how you know it's not George Speeds and I come from Lucy, Alabama, or how you know I ain't Thompson Bright from Toolafalls, Mississippi?"

"I don't know nothing about you," the old woman muttered, irked.

"Lady," he said, "people don't care how they lie. Maybe the best I can tell you is, I'm a man; but listen lady," he said and paused and made his tone more ominous still, "what is a man?"

The old woman began to gum a seed. "What you carry in that tin box, Mr. Shiftlet?" she asked.

"Tools," he said, put back. "I'm a carpenter."

"Well, if you come out here to work, I'll be able to feed you and give you a place to sleep but I can't pay. I'll tell you that before you begin," she said.

There was no answer at once and no particular expression on his face. He leaned back against the two-by-four that helped support the porch roof. "Lady," he said slowly, "there's some men that some things mean more to them than money." The old woman rocked without comment and the daughter watched the trigger that moved up and down in his neck. He told the old woman then that all most people were interested in was money, but he asked what a man was made for. He asked her if a man was made for money, or what. He asked her what she thought she was made for but she didn't answer, she only sat rocking and wondered if a one-armed man could put a new roof on her garden house. He asked a lot of questions that she didn't answer. He told her that he was twenty-eight years old and had lived a varied life. He had been a gospel singer, a foreman on the railroad, an assistant in an undertaking parlor, and he come over the radio for three months with Uncle Roy and his Red Creek Wranglers. He said he had fought and bled in the Arm Service of his country and visited every foreign land and that everywhere he had seen people that didn't care if they did a thing one way or another. He said he hadn't been raised thataway.

A fat yellow moon appeared in the branches of the fig tree as if it were going to roost there with the chickens. He said that a man had to escape to the country to see the world whole and that he wished he lived in a desolate place like this where he could see the sun go down every evening like God made it to do.

"Are you married or are you single?" the old woman asked.

There was a long silence. "Lady," he asked finally, "where would you find you an innocent woman today? I wouldn't have any of this trash I could just pick up."

The daughter was leaning very far down, hanging her head almost between her knees watching him through a triangular door she had made in her overturned hair; and she suddenly fell in a heap on the floor and began to whimper. Mr. Shiftlet straightened her out and helped her get back in the chair.

"Is she your baby girl?" he asked.

"My only," the old woman said, "and she's the sweetest girl in the world. I would give her up for nothing on earth. She's smart too. She can sweep the floor, cook, wash, feed the chickens, and hoe. I wouldn't give her up for a casket of jewels."

"No," he said kindly, "don't ever let any man take her away from you."

"Any man come after her," the old woman said, " 'll have to stay around the place."

Mr. Shiftlet's eye in the darkness was focused on a part of the automobile bumper that glittered in the distance. "Lady," he said, jerking his short arm up as if he could point with it to her house and yard and pump, "there ain't a broken thing on this plantation that I couldn't fix for you, one-arm jackleg[1] or not. I'm a

1. **jackleg:** someone who does work he or she has not been trained to do.

man," he said with a sullen dignity, "even if I ain't a whole one. I got," he said, tapping his knuckles on the floor to emphasize the immensity of what he was going to say, "a moral intelligence!" and his face pierced out of the darkness into a shaft of door light and he stared at her as if he were astonished himself at this impossible truth.

EVALUATE

How would you characterize Mr. Shiftlet? Mrs. Crater? her daughter, Lucynell?

The old woman was not impressed with the phrase. "I told you you could hang around and work for food," she said, "if you don't mind sleeping in that car yonder."

"Why listen, lady," he said with a grin of delight, "the monks of old slept in their coffins!"

"They wasn't as advanced as we are," the old woman said.

The next morning he began on the roof of the garden house while Lucynell, the daughter, sat on a rock and watched him work. He had not been around a week before the change he had made in the place was apparent. He had patched the front and back steps, built a new hog pen, restored a fence, and taught Lucynell, who was completely deaf and had never said a word in her life, to say the word bird. The big rosy-faced girl followed him everywhere, saying "Burrttddt ddbirrrttdt," and clapping her hands. The old woman watched from a distance, secretly pleased. She was ravenous for a son-in-law.

Mr. Shiftlet slept on the hard narrow back seat of the car with his feet out the side window. He had his razor and a can of water on a crate that served him as a bedside table and he put up a piece of mirror against the back glass and kept his coat neatly on a hanger that he hung over one of the windows.

In the evenings he sat on the steps and talked while the old woman and Lucynell rocked violently in their chairs on either side of him. The old woman's three mountains were black against the dark blue sky and were visited off and on by various planets and by the moon after it had left the chickens. Mr. Shiftlet pointed out that the reason he had improved this plantation was because he had taken a personal interest in it. He said he was even going to make the automobile run.

He had raised the hood and studied the mechanism, and he said he could tell that the car had been built in the days when cars were really built. You take now, he said, one man puts in one bolt and another man puts in another bolt and another man puts in another bolt so that it's a man for a bolt. That's why you have to pay so much for a car: you're paying all those men. Now if you didn't have to pay but one man, you could get you a cheaper car and one that had had a personal interest taken in it, and it would be a better car. The old woman agreed with him that this was so.

Mr. Shiftlet said that the trouble with the world was that nobody cared, or stopped and took any trouble. He said he never would have been able to teach Lucynell to say a word if he hadn't cared and stopped long enough.

"Teach her to say something else," the old woman said.

"What you want her to say next?" Mr. Shiftlet asked.

The old woman's smile was broad and toothless and suggestive. "Teach her to say 'sugarpie,'" she said.

CLARIFY

What do you think is on the old woman's mind?

Mr. Shiftlet already knew what was on her mind.

The next day he began to tinker with the automobile, and that evening he told her that if she would buy a fan belt, he would be able to make the car run.

The old woman said she would give him the money. "You see that girl yonder?" she asked, pointing to Lucynell who was sitting on the floor a foot away, watching him, her eyes blue even in the dark. "If it was ever a man wanted to take her away, I would say, 'No man on earth is going to take that sweet girl of mine away from me!' but if he was to say, 'Lady, I don't want to take her away, I want her right here,' I would say, 'Mister, I don't blame you none. I wouldn't pass up a chance to live in a permanent place and get the sweetest girl in the world myself. You ain't no fool,' I would say."

"How old is she?" Mr. Shiftlet asked casually.

"Fifteen, sixteen," the old woman said. The girl was nearly thirty but because of her innocence it was impossible to guess.

"It would be a good idea to paint it too," Mr. Shiftlet remarked. "You don't want it to rust out."

"We'll see about that later," the old woman said.

The next day he walked into town and returned with the parts he needed and a can of gasoline. Late in the afternoon, terrible noises issued from the shed and the old woman rushed out of the house, thinking Lucynell was somewhere having a fit. Lucynell was sitting on a chicken crate, stamping her feet and screaming, "Burrddttt! bddurrddtttt!" but her fuss was drowned out by the car. With a volley of blasts it emerged from the shed, moving in a fierce and stately way. Mr. Shiftlet was in the driver's seat, sitting very erect. He had an expression of serious modesty on his face as if he had just raised the dead.

That night, rocking on the porch, the old woman began her business, at once. "You want you an innocent woman, don't you?" she asked sympathetically. "You don't want none of this trash."

"No'm, I don't," Mr. Shiftlet said.

"One that can't talk," she continued, "can't sass you back or use foul language. That's the kind for you to have. Right there," and she pointed to Lucynell sitting cross-legged in her chair, holding both feet in her hands.

"That's right," he admitted. "She wouldn't give me any trouble."

"Saturday," the old woman said, "you and her and me can drive into town and get married."

Mr. Shiftlet eased his position on the steps.

"I can't get married right now," he said. "Everything you want to do takes money and I ain't got any."

"What you need with money?" she asked.

"It takes money," he said. "Some people'll do anything anyhow these days, but the way I think, I wouldn't marry no woman that I couldn't take on a trip like she was somebody. I mean take her to a hotel and treat her. I wouldn't marry the Duchesser Windsor," he said firmly, "unless I could take her to a hotel and giver something good to eat.

"I was raised thataway and there ain't a thing I can do about it. My old mother taught me how to do."

"Lucynell don't even know what a hotel is," the old woman muttered. "Listen here, Mr. Shiftlet," she said, sliding forward in her chair, "you'd be getting a permanent house and a deep well and the most innocent girl in the world. You don't need no money. Lemme tell you something: there ain't any place in the world for a poor, disabled, friendless drifting man."

The ugly words settled in Mr. Shiftlet's head like a group of buzzards in the top of a tree. He didn't answer at once. He rolled himself a cigarette and lit it and then he said in an even voice, "Lady, a man is divided into two parts, body and spirit."

The old woman clamped her gums together.

"A body and a spirit," he repeated. "The body, lady, is like a house: it don't go anywhere; but the spirit, lady, is like a automobile: always on the move, always . . ."

"Listen, Mr. Shiftlet," she said, "my well never goes dry and my house is always warm in the winter and there's no mortgage on a thing about this place. You can go to the courthouse and see for yourself. And yonder under that shed is a fine automobile." She laid the bait carefully. "You can have it painted by Saturday. I'll pay for the paint."

The Interloper (1958), Billy Morrow Jackson. Collection of Mrs. Virginia Penofsky.

"THE SPIRIT IS LIKE A AUTOMOBILE: ALWAYS ON THE MOVE, ALWAYS."

"THE BODY IS LIKE A HOUSE: IT DON'T GO ANYWHERE."

"A MAN IS DIVIDED INTO TWO PARTS, BODY AND SPIRIT."

In the darkness, Mr. Shiftlet's smile stretched like a weary snake waking up by a fire. After a second he recalled himself and said, "I'm only saying a man's spirit means more to him than anything else. I would have to take my wife off for the weekend without no regards at all for cost. I got to follow where my spirit says to go."

"I'll give you fifteen dollars for a weekend trip," the old woman said in a crabbed voice. "That's the best I can do."

"That wouldn't hardly pay for more than the gas and the hotel," he said. "It wouldn't feed her."

"Seventeen-fifty," the old woman said. "That's all I got so it isn't any use you trying to milk me. You can take a lunch."

Mr. Shiftlet was deeply hurt by the word *milk*. He didn't doubt that she had more money sewed up in her mattress, but he had already told her he was not interested in her money. "I'll make that do," he said and rose and walked off without treating[2] with her further.

EVALUATE

What can you conclude about Mr. Shiftlet's intentions from these negotiations?

On Saturday the three of them drove into town in the car that the paint had barely dried on, and Mr. Shiftlet and Lucynell were married in the Ordinary's[3] office while the old woman witnessed. As they came out of the courthouse, Mr. Shiftlet began twisting his neck in his collar. He looked morose and bitter as if he had been insulted while someone held him. "That didn't satisfy me none," he said. "That was just something a woman in an office did, nothing but paperwork and blood tests. What do they know about my blood? If they was to take my heart and cut it out," he said, "they wouldn't know a thing about me. It didn't satisfy me at all."

"It satisfied the law," the old woman said sharply.

"The law," Mr. Shiftlet said and spit. "It's the law that don't satisfy me."

He had painted the car dark green with a yellow band around it just under the windows. The three of them climbed in the front seat and the old woman said, "Don't Lucynell look pretty? Looks like a baby doll." Lucynell was dressed up in a white dress that her mother had uprooted from a trunk and there was a Panama hat on her head with a bunch of red wooden cherries on the brim. Every now and then her placid expression was changed by a sly isolated little thought like a shoot of green in the desert. "You got a prize!" the old woman said.

Mr. Shiftlet didn't even look at her.

They drove back to the house to let the old woman off and pick up the lunch. When they were ready to leave, she stood staring in the window of the car, with her fingers clenched around the glass. Tears began to seep sideways out of her eyes and run along the dirty creases in her face. "I ain't ever been parted with her for two days before," she said.

Mr. Shiftlet started the motor.

"And I wouldn't let no man have her but you because I seen you would do right. Goodbye, Sugarbaby," she said, clutching at the sleeve of the white dress. Lucynell looked straight at her and didn't seem to see her there at all. Mr. Shiftlet eased the car forward so that she had to move her hands.

The early afternoon was clear and open and surrounded by pale blue sky. Although the car would go only thirty miles an hour, Mr. Shiftlet imagined a terrific climb and dip and swerve that went entirely to his head so that he forgot his morning bitterness. He had always wanted an automobile, but he had never been able to afford one before. He drove very fast because he wanted to make Mobile by nightfall.

2. **treating:** discussing terms; negotiating.

3. **Ordinary's:** judge's.

WORDS TO KNOW

morose (mə-rōs') *adj.* gloomy and ill-tempered

Occasionally he stopped his thoughts long enough to look at Lucynell in the seat beside him. She had eaten the lunch as soon as they were out of the yard and now she was pulling the cherries off the hat one by one and throwing them out the window. He became depressed in spite of the car. He had driven about a hundred miles when he decided that she must be hungry again and at the next small town they came to, he stopped in front of an aluminum-painted eating place called The Hot Spot and took her in and ordered her a plate of ham and grits. The ride had made her sleepy and as soon as she got up on the stool, she rested her head on the counter and shut her eyes. There was no one in The Hot Spot but Mr. Shiftlet and the boy behind the counter, a pale youth with a greasy rag hung over his shoulder. Before he could dish up the food, she was snoring gently.

"Give it to her when she wakes up," Mr. Shiftlet said. "I'll pay for it now."

The boy bent over her and stared at the long pink-gold hair and the half-shut sleeping eyes. Then he looked up and stared at Mr. Shiftlet. "She looks like an angel of Gawd," he murmured.

"Hitchhiker," Mr. Shiftlet explained. "I can't wait. I got to make Tuscaloosa."

The boy bent over again and very carefully touched his finger to a strand of the golden hair, and Mr. Shiftlet left.

Road to Rhome (1938), Alexander Hogue. Private collection.

QUESTION

Why do you think Mr. Shiftlet feels "more depressed than ever"?

He was more depressed than ever as he drove on by himself. The late afternoon had grown hot and sultry and the country had flattened out. Deep in the sky a storm was preparing very slowly and without thunder as if it meant to drain every drop of air from the earth before it broke. There were times when Mr. Shiftlet preferred not to be alone. He felt too that a man with a car had a responsibility to others, and he kept his eye out for a hitchhiker. Occasionally he saw a sign that warned: "Drive carefully. The life you save may be your own."

The narrow road dropped off on either side into dry fields, and here and there a shack or a filling station stood in a clearing. The sun began to set directly in front of the automobile. It was a reddening ball that through his windshield was slightly flat on the bottom and top. He saw a boy in overalls and a gray hat standing on the edge of the road and he slowed the car down and stopped in front of him. The boy didn't have his hand raised to thumb the ride, he was only standing there, but he had a small cardboard suitcase and his hat was set on his head in a way to indicate that he had left somewhere for good. "Son," Mr. Shiftlet said, "I see you want a ride."

The boy didn't say he did or he didn't but he opened the door of the car and got in, and Mr. Shiftlet started driving again. The child held the suitcase on his lap and folded his arms on top of it. He turned his head and looked out the window away from Mr. Shiftlet. Mr. Shiftlet felt oppressed. "Son," he said after a minute, "I got the best old mother in the world so I reckon you only got the second best."

The boy gave him a quick dark glance and then turned his face back out the window.

"It's nothing so sweet," Mr. Shiftlet continued, "as a boy's mother. She taught him his first prayers at her knee, she give him love when no other would, she told him what was right and what wasn't, and she seen that he done the right thing. Son," he said, "I never rued a day in my life like the one I rued when I left that old mother of mine."

The boy shifted in his seat but he didn't look at Mr. Shiftlet. He unfolded his arms and put one hand on the door handle.

"My mother was a angel of Gawd," Mr. Shiftlet said in a very strained voice. "He took her from heaven and giver to me and I left her." His eyes were instantly clouded over with a mist of tears. The car was barely moving.

QUESTION

Why do you think Mr. Shiftlet is speaking this way to the hitchhiker?

The boy turned angrily in the seat. "You go to the devil!" he cried. "My old woman is a fleabag and yours is a stinking polecat!" and with that he flung the door open and jumped out with his suitcase into the ditch.

Mr. Shiftlet was so shocked that for about a hundred feet he drove along slowly with the door still open. A cloud, the exact color of the boy's hat and shaped like a turnip, had descended over the sun, and another, worse looking, crouched behind the car. Mr. Shiftlet felt that the rottenness of the world was about to engulf him. He raised his arm and let it fall again to his breast. "Oh Lord!" he prayed. "Break forth and wash the slime from this earth!"

The turnip continued slowly to descend. After a few minutes there was a guffawing peal of thunder from behind and fantastic raindrops, like tin-can tops, crashed over the rear of Mr. Shiftlet's car. Very quickly he stepped on the gas, and with his stump sticking out the window, he raced the galloping shower into Mobile. ❖

WORDS TO KNOW

rue (ro͞o) *v.* to regret

RESPONDING OPTIONS

FROM PERSONAL RESPONSE *TO* CRITICAL ANALYSIS

REFLECT **1.** What is your opinion of Mr. Shiftlet? Jot down your feelings in your notebook, then share them in class.

RETHINK **2.** Do you blame Mrs. Crater for what happens to Lucynell? Why or why not?

3. At what point did you first suspect Mr. Shiftlet of manipulating Mrs. Crater? Why do you think he is successful?

4. If the story ended with Mr. Shiftlet's leaving The Hot Spot and before he meets the hitchhiker, how might your perceptions of him be different?

5. Do you think Lucynell, abandoned at the diner, will be worse off or better off if she never gets back home? Explain your reasoning.

6. How do you interpret the story's title?
Consider
- the road sign Mr. Shiftlet sees
- whose life needs to be saved
- who is a potential savior

RELATE **7.** What punishment does Mr. Shiftlet deserve?

ANOTHER PATHWAY

Cooperative Learning

With a small group of classmates, plan a television play based on this story. Who will you cast in it? Which parts of the story will you choose to include, and which will you omit? What scenery and props will you use to convey the setting? What lighting, music, and sound effects will you use to set the mood? Present your plan in class.

LITERARY CONCEPTS

As you have learned, **irony** is a contrast between what is expected and what actually exists or happens. In literature, **situational irony** is a contrast between what a character expects to happen and what actually happens. For example, at the end of this story, Mr. Shiftlet prays that the world's rottenness—slime—be washed away, and a rain shower soon chases *him.* **Dramatic irony** occurs when readers know more about a situation in a story than the characters do. For example, readers know what the counter boy at The Hot Spot does not—that the "angel of Gawd" will be a major problem when she wakes up. Find other examples of irony in the story. Think especially about how manipulations backfire. What view of the world does O'Connor suggest with these ironies?

QUICKWRITES

1. In 1957, a television adaptation of this story was broadcast. In the TV version, the ending was changed, according to O'Connor, "by having Shiftlet suddenly get a conscience and come back for the girl." Write a **letter** to the network that presented the show, either protesting or supporting this change. Give reasons for your opinion.
2. Extend the story by writing a brief **episode** revealing what happens to Lucynell after Mr. Shiftlet leaves her at The Hot Spot or what Mr. Shiftlet encounters when he reaches Mobile.

PORTFOLIO *Save your writing. You may want to use it later as a springboard to a piece for your portfolio.*

ALTERNATIVE ACTIVITIES

By hand or with the help of a computer, create a **wanted poster** for Mr. Shiftlet. Include comments on his appearance, behavior, and manipulative techniques.

CRITIC'S CORNER

The critic Dorothy Walters notes that "the grotesque, in many of its forms, relies for effect upon a balance between the two contrary impulses of the terrible and the comic." What in O'Connor's story do you see as terrible, and what do you see as comic? Does O'Connor achieve a satisfactory balance to you?

WORDS TO KNOW

Write the letter of the word pair that expresses a relationship similar to that expressed by the capitalized pair.

1. LIST : TOPPLE :: (a) need : want, (b) damage : ruin, (c) laugh : cry, (d) irritate : annoy
2. GAUNT : SKELETON :: (a) tall : giant, (b) timid : lion, (c) bold : villain, (d) mountainous : hill
3. COMPOSED : EXCITED :: (a) proud : arrogant, (b) hesitant : foolish, (c) careful : skillful, (d) cowardly : brave
4. MOROSE : PARTY POOPER :: (a) sassy : smart aleck, (b) clumsy : athlete, (c) rich : hero, (d) lazy : student
5. RUE : SORROW :: (a) admire : scorn, (b) yearn : superiority, (c) trust : confidence, (d) appreciate : adoration

FLANNERY O'CONNOR

1925–1964

Flannery O'Connor lived a short, brilliant life. Born in Savannah, Georgia, O'Connor began drawing cartoons and writing as a young girl. In her high school yearbook, she wrote that her chief hobby was "collecting rejection slips." After high school, O'Connor attended college in Georgia and the Writers' Workshop at the University of Iowa.

In 1950, while completing her first novel, *Wise Blood,* O'Connor learned that she was suffering from lupus, the degenerative disease that had killed her father when she was 15. O'Connor returned to Milledgeville, Georgia, to live with her mother on a farm for the last 14 years of her life. Despite her debilitating illness and the specter of an early death, O'Connor continued to write, producing two acclaimed volumes of short stories and a second novel.

As a writer, O'Connor is noted for her wry comic sense, her intense faith as a Catholic, and her portrayal of violent, grotesque characters. Since she believed that fiction writers often have to distort reality in order to drive a point home to an audience, she used elements of the grotesque to convey a message about the need for spiritual renewal. O'Connor's grim humor is at once her writing's most disturbing feature and its strength, allowing the reader to acknowledge the severe human faults of her characters while at the same time begrudging them sympathy. O'Connor herself commented, "I like [my stories] better than anybody and read them over and over and laugh and laugh."

OTHER WORKS *Everything That Rises Must Converge, A Good Man Is Hard to Find, The Violent Bear It Away, The Habit of Being: Letters*

The Consolation of Nature

VALERIE MARTIN

Putting up Her Hair (1983), Malcolm Liepke. Courtesy of Eleanor Ettinger Gallery, New York.

Lily's hair was her mother's pride. In the afternoons, when she came home from school, she sat at the kitchen table, her head resting on the back of her chair, while her mother dragged the wooden brush through the long strands. Lily told her mother what had happened at school that day, or she talked of her many ambitions. Her mother, preoccupied with her work, holding up a thick lock and pulling out with her fingers a particularly tenacious knot, responded laconically.[1] She looked upon this ritual of her daughter's hair as a solemn duty, like the duties of feeding and clothing.

One afternoon they sat so engaged, conversing softly while outside the rain beat against the house. Lily's mother observed that she couldn't take much more rain, that it would surely rot her small, carefully tended vegetable garden, that it seemed to be rotting her own imagination. Lily agreed. It had rained steadily for three days. Her head rose and

1. **laconically** (lə-kŏn′ĭk-lē): using few words.

fell, like a flower on its stalk, with each stroke of her mother's care, and each time it did she lifted her eyes a bit, taking in a larger section of the tiled floor before her.

Her mother shouted and threw the brush toward the stove. Lily sat up and looked after the brush. She was quick enough to see the disappearing tail and hindquarters of a rat as he scurried beneath the refrigerator. These parts, Lily thought, were unusually large, and this notion was quickly confirmed by her mother's cry as she clung momentarily to the edge of the table. Her mother said, "That's the biggest rat I've ever seen."

Lily drew her legs up under her and watched the spot where the rat had been. Her mother was already on the telephone to her father's secretary. "No," she said, "don't bother him. Just tell him there's a rat as big as a cat in the kitchen and he needs to stop at the K & B on the way home for a trap. Tell him to get the biggest trap they make." When she got off the phone, she suggested that they move to the dining room to finish Lily's hair. "It's the rain," her mother said as she closed the kitchen door carefully behind them. "The river is so high it's driving them out."

"It's the rain," her mother said as she closed the kitchen door carefully behind them. "The river is so high it's driving them out."

Lily sat at the dining table and pulled her long hair up over the back of her chair. Her mother resumed her vigorous brushing. It was strange, Lily thought, to sit at the big dining table in the dull afternoon light. The steady beating of the rain against the windows made her drowsy and her mind wandered. She thought of how the river must look, swollen with brown water, swirling along hurriedly toward the Gulf of Mexico. She had never been to the mouth of the river, though she had gone down as far as Barataria[2] once with her father. It had not been, as she had imagined, a neat little breaking-up of water fingers, the way it looked on the map. Instead, it was a great marsh with a road through it. There were fishing shacks on piers, wood, and other odd debris scattered in the shallow areas. She remembered that trip clearly, though two years had passed and she had been, she thought, only nine at the time. They had stopped to buy shrimp and her father had laughed at her impatience to have hers peeled. That was when she had learned to peel shrimp, and she did it so well that the job now regularly fell to her.

Her mother had not stopped thinking of the rat. "I can't get over his coming out in broad daylight like that," she remarked as she pulled the loose hairs from the brush.

"Who?" Lily asked.

"That rat," her mother replied. "I don't even want to cook dinner with that thing in there."

Lily could think of no response, so she stood up, turning to her mother and fluffing her hair out past her shoulders.

"That looks lovely," her mother said, touching Lily's hair at the temple. Then, as if she were shy of her daughter's beauty, she drew her hand away. "Do you have a lot of homework?" she asked.

"Plenty," Lily said. "I guess I'd better get to it."

When her father arrived that evening at his usual time, it was with chagrin[3] that his wife and daughter learned he hadn't gotten their message and had come home trapless to his family.

"Well, go out and get one now," her mother

2. **Barataria** (bär′ə-tăr′ē-ə): the name of a town and a bay in Louisiana, south of New Orleans.

3. **chagrin** (shə-grĭn′): mental uneasiness caused by disappointment.

complained. "I don't want to spend a night in the house with that thing alive."

"It's pouring down rain," Lily's father protested. "I'll get one tomorrow. He's probably moved on already anyway."

"Give me the keys," she said. "I'll get it myself."

Lily stood in the kitchen doorway during this argument and she stepped aside as her mother came storming past her, the keys clutched in her angry fist. Her father sat down at the kitchen table and smiled after his affronted[4] mate.

"Did you see this giant rat?" he asked Lily.

"Sort of," she said.

"Are you sure he wasn't a mouse?"

"I think it was a rat," Lily speculated. "His back was kind of high, not flat like a mouse."

"When have you ever seen a rat?" her father asked impatiently.

Lily looked away. She had, she realized, never seen a rat, except in pictures, and she knew that if she said "In pictures," her father would consider her to have less authority than she had already. "He was big, Dad," she said at last, turning away.

When her mother pulled the trap from its purple bag, Lily felt a twinge of sympathy for the rat. The board was large, the bar, which snapped closed when it was set, was wide enough to accommodate Lily's hand, the spring was devilishly strong and so tight that her father forced the bar back with difficulty. He tested it with a wooden spoon, and the bar snapped closed, lifting the board well off the floor. Her father baited it with a slice of potato, and the family turned out the lights and settled in their beds. Lily lay with her eyes open, listening for the snap of the bar, but she didn't hear it, and while she was listening she fell asleep.

The next morning the trap was discovered just as it had been left. Lily's father gave her mother a cold skeptical look and sprung the trap again with a spoon. Her mother concentrated on cooking the breakfast, allowing the matter to drop. When he was gone to work she turned to Lily as if to a conspirator and said, "I'll get some poison today and we can try again tonight."

Lily didn't think of the rat again during the day. Her school work was oppressive, but at lunch break, for the first time that week, the students were turned out of doors. The clouds had cleared off, leaving a sky of hectic blue, a sun that beat down on the wet ground with the thoroughness of a shower. Lily and her best friend sat on the breezeway, watching the braver students, who sloshed through the puddles in search of exercise. They discussed their summer plans and confided in each other their mutual fear that they would be separated the following fall.

"If I get that grouch Miss Bambula," Lily's friend said, "I think I'll die. She looks just like a horse."

Lily wondered which would be worse, to be with her friend and have Miss Bambula or to be without her friend and Miss Bambula. One of the boys in the yard hailed the two girls, holding up for their long-distance inspection the squirming green body of a lizard. Lily stood up and went out to him, for she liked lizards, and this one, she saw at once, was of a good size.

That afternoon, when her mother brushed her hair, the rat didn't appear. "Maybe your father's right," her mother said hopefully. Later, after she had practiced piano, Lily rejoined her mother in the kitchen to help with dinner. She sat at the table with a large bowl of green beans, which she proceeded to snap, throwing the ends into a small bowl, the fat centers into another. Her mother stood at the counter, peeling potatoes. They worked without speaking and it was so quiet in the room that they heard the scratching

4. **affronted:** offended.

of the rat's claws against the floor before they saw him. They both turned, looking in shocked silence at the refrigerator. His ugly face appeared first; then he took a few timid steps forward and stood before them. Lily saw that his black lips were drawn back over his teeth and his cheeks pulsated with his nervous breathing. She sucked in her own breath and dropped the bean she was holding. The rat made a sudden dash for the stove, moving so quickly that Lily's mother let out a little cry as she jumped out of his path. "Mama," Lily said softly as they both bolted for the kitchen door. Her mother held the swinging door open and wrapped her arm protectively around her daughter's shoulder as she passed through. In the dining room they stood together and Lily allowed herself, for a moment, the luxury of closing her eyes against her mother's shoulder. "Don't worry, baby," her mother said. "I got the poison this morning; we'll get him tonight."

Lily's father was incredulous when they told him of the intruder's boldness and he smiled in disbelief when Lily, holding up her hands, estimated the creature's true dimensions. "She's not kidding," her mother said angrily. "He's really big. We got a good look at him this time."

"All right," her father said. "We'll put out the trap again. I just wish he'd show his face when I'm here."

Her mother replied, "That's not my fault. If he's still here tomorrow I'll take his picture. Would you believe that?"

"That's not a bad idea," her father said.

That night, before they went to bed, the family gathered in the kitchen and laid out their arsenal.[5] The trap was baited and placed near the wall; the poison, which was inside a plastic box with a hole at one end, was placed near the stove with the hole turned toward the wall.

"Can he get in that little hole?" Lily asked.

"I hope so," her mother replied.

Alone in her bed, Lily slept, then woke, then slept again. Toward morning she opened her eyes abruptly, with the sensation that she had cause to do so. She raised herself on one elbow and looked out into the darkness of her room. She could see nothing, but she heard distinctly a scratching sound, the sound, she knew at once, of claws against wood. She fell back and put her hands over her mouth, as if to hold in a scream, though she made no sound. Her heart pounded so furiously that she could hear it, and she felt in her legs, which were drawn up now beneath the sheet, the sudden ebbing[6] of strength that usually follows a nightmare. The sound continued and it seemed to her that it became louder, closer, as the moments passed. She consoled herself with the thought that the rat would doubtless find little to interest him in her room and would soon opt for the swift or slow death that awaited him in the kitchen. If only she'd put a trap in her room, she thought.

The scratching was very close and then, when it sounded as though the creature was under the bed, abruptly it stopped. Lily breathed uneasily, afraid and unable to move. Then she heard a sound she was never to forget, the metallic protest of the bed springs as they received the weight of the animal's body. Lily's eyes burned into the humid dark air and she opened her mouth, but still no sound came. She had begun to perspire; her gown clung wetly to her narrow chest. Again she heard the squeaking springs and this time she knew exactly where the sound came from. The rat was just behind her head and though she couldn't see him and didn't have the strength even to turn her head so that she might see him, she felt the nervous twitching of his snout, the horrible inhalation of his breath, as he pulled himself up over the headboard of the bed and looked down upon the paralyzed young girl before him.

5. **arsenal:** stock of weapons.

6. **ebbing:** decreasing.

Interior: Mousehole; 8:40 am, Ken Howard. Courtesy of Manya Igel Fine Art.

For a moment the animal contemplated her, and then, as if they were one, both moved. The rat sprang forward, his front legs stretching out before him as his back feet propelled him out into the air. Lily, finding her strength and her voice at once, sat up, throwing her hands over her head and screaming "No!" But it was too late. Her left hand encountered the rat's side and inadvertently she slapped him toward her own back. He landed squarely on the top of her head, and as she swung her legs over the side of the bed and rose to her feet, he slid down her back. His body was enormously heavy and in his panic he clawed at her hair, tangling himself and enraging Lily so that she threw herself against the wall, thinking to crush him. This gave him the leverage he needed to pull free of her hair. He slipped down over her buttocks and dropped to the floor. He was running when he hit the wood, scrambling back toward the bed. Lily was already in the hall. Now, she thought, she could run until she dropped. But she only ran to her parents' door, throwing it open before her with a scream. Her mother was raised up on her elbow looking at her; her father sat on the edge of the bed fumbling for his slippers. It was to her father that she ran, but not for comfort. She caught him by his shoulders, forcing him to fall back across the sheets, and she held him down there, her hair falling wildly about her as she screamed into his astonished face, "You kill him, you kill him now! Go and kill him now!"

Her mother sat up, pulling back Lily's hair, feeling her neck and shoulders frantically. "Did he bite you?" she asked. "Are you cut?" Then Lily turned on her mother, thinking that she would strike her, but when she was folded into the eager, smothering embrace, she gave in and clung to her mother's neck, hugging her close. Her mother glared over the girl's shoulders at the still prostrate form of her husband and repeated to him the injunction his daughter had just given him. "Go and kill him now," she said. "Don't leave this house until that animal is dead."

Lily's father sat up and resumed fumbling for his slippers. Lily and her mother lay locked together and neither watched him as he shuffled off toward the bathroom. They clung to each other, pulling the sheets up and adjusting the pillows so that they could sleep as they had when Lily was a baby, with their arms around each other. Outside, the rain began, softly at first, punctuated with the low rumble of thunder and flashes of heat lightning that radiated like nerves across the sky. Lily's father had turned on the light in the hall and she could hear him in the kitchen, opening the refrigerator, running water in the sink. The rain grew more intense; it beat insistently against the window in her parents' room and she thought of how it must be outdoors, beating the flowers down into the already water-logged soil, beating the leaves back on the trees. She thought especially of the big plantain tree in the side yard, of how it bent down in the rain, its great leaves shiny and smooth, like sheets of brilliantly painted plastic. The rain washed over the house and seemed to carry great waves of sleep with it, impossible to resist.

She had been elevated from the position of hysterical visionary to that of reliable reporter.

In the morning Lily and her mother found her father asleep at the kitchen table, his arms spread out before him, his cheek pressed against the wood, his mouth slack from weariness. He had prepared himself a cup of coffee, which sat on the table near his left hand, but he had not drunk half of it.

Lily's mother woke him impatiently. He lifted his head, rubbed his eyes, and looked sleepily at his wife, then at his daughter. He put out his hand to Lily and drew her toward him. "Are you OK now, baby?" he said. "Are you sure it wasn't a dream?" Then, as she was about to protest, his face changed. He looked across her shoulder and Lily knew, without turning, what he saw. Her mother followed his gaze and changed her expression from aggravation to horror. Lily turned around and saw him. He had come out silently and stood, calm, though as he was always, poised for flight. He moved his ugly head back and forth, watching, sniffing, and Lily could hear again the horrible sound of his breathing. He confronted them and they couldn't look away, for his boldness was as wonderful as his size. Lily's mother reached back suddenly, took the half-full coffee cup, and threw it with all her strength at the animal. He was gone before the cup hit the ground.

For two days and nights the rat was under siege. The animal sensed the change in his situation and responded with the obsessive wiles of the hunted. Traps and poison failed to entice him, though he made frequent appearances in the vicinity of both. The family spent the weekend in an ecstasy of determination, baiting all possible hiding places with poison. Lily's parents moved the stove and refrigerator out from the wall. Lily herself helped to seal off any holes they discovered, along the baseboards, in the window casings, holes Lily thought much too small to be of use to the large creature who had glared at them so balefully.[7] Her father assured her that it was in the power of rats to make themselves fit into small places, that they were like yogis[8] who know the secret of folding themselves down into suitcases. Lily plugged the holes with spoons of wet plaster. Now that her father believed in the creature's existence, he seemed unable to give it enough credence,[9] and she had been elevated from the position of hysterical visionary to that of reliable reporter on the natural scene.

On Monday morning her father called his office to say he wasn't coming in. The sky was black with clouds, and flood predictions were easily come by; he used this as his excuse. Lily's mother called the school and

7. **balefully:** in a way that threatens great harm or evil.

8. **yogis:** those who practice yoga, a Hindu method of training the body and mind.

9. **credence** (krēd′ns): belief.

said that she was ill and needed Lily at home. This easy lie shocked Lily, though she was glad of it. Then the three sat at the kitchen table and discussed their plans. They had sealed the rat in the kitchen; they were sure of this. And when next he appeared, he wouldn't find it easy to escape. The pots and pans sat out on the floor in little groups; all the food was set in boxes in the dining room. The cabinets stood open and empty. If he showed his face again there would be no place left to conceal it.

But though they sat at the table scanning the room for the better part of the morning, he took them by surprise. He appeared inside the cabinet beneath the sink, and none could say where he came from. Lily's father, who had armed himself with a hammer and a small axe, leaped to his feet and raced to the animal. By the time he had crossed the room the rat was gone. He fell on his knees and inspected every inch of the cabinet with his hands. "How the hell does he do it?" he said, and then, "Oh, this is it." Lily and her mother joined him and they all looked with wonder at the hole, which was really a broken flap in the plasterboard at the back of the cabinet. Behind it was another hole, smaller, ragged, and deep. It opened into darkness, and the outside edge of it was lined with a half inch of wood.

"Do you know what it is?" Lily's father asked.

"Why is it so dark?" she said, for it seemed to Lily that such a hole should open into daylight.

"Because it's inside a drawer," her father replied. He seemed immensely pleased with this pronouncement, like a detective who has discovered the long-sought final clue.

"The old dresser?" her mother said.

Her father stood up, gripping his gleaming axe, and started out the back door for the porch. Then Lily understood. On the porch there was a dresser in which, as a baby, she had kept her toys. It backed up against the house, against, she realized, this very cabinet. The rat had disappeared into the dark hole, but the dark hole was the inside of that dresser. Lily and her mother exchanged looks of mild surprise; then they too rushed out onto the porch. Her father stood poised before the dresser. "He's in there," he said. "I can hear him."

"Which drawer?" her mother asked.

"The middle, I think."

"What are you going to do?" Lily cried. She was suddenly desperately frightened.

"I'm going to open the drawer just a little and try to catch him in it." As he said this he squatted down, laying his axe near his feet and pulled the middle drawer open an inch. Lily could hear the scratching of the animal's claws against the wood. Another inch, she thought, and they would see his dreadful face. Her father pulled the drawer out carefully, leaning back a little so that his face wouldn't be near the opening. Now he could see into the drawer. Then, abruptly, he pulled the drawer all the way out and threw it down on the porch. Lily saw her old metal tea set scattered across the bottom, and there was a plastic strainer, which she had once used for sand, that flew out of the drawer when it hit the ground and rolled in a dizzy circle toward the screen. Except for that, the drawer was empty, and the space in the dresser where the drawer had been was empty as well.

"Did he go back in the kitchen?" her mother asked. The hole that had allowed the creature's easy entrance into their lives was now visible, and they stood looking into it as their greatest oversight. They heard a scratching, then a thudding sound that came distinctly from the top drawer. The rat was trapped at last and he was frantic. Lily's father turned toward them. "Get back," he warned. Then he pulled the drawer out slowly, carefully, an inch, then another. Inside the drawer the rat was still, crouched, silent, as light flooded his last dark refuge.

Lily grasped her mother's hand and found it cold but willing to hold her own. Her father leaned over the dresser, placing one hand against the front of the drawer while with the other he began to pound on the top. Still there was no sound, no movement from inside the drawer.

"Is he in there?" Lily's mother asked. Her father turned his head to answer his wife and in that moment the rat made his move. He hit the front of the drawer with such force that her father's hand fell away, leaving the crack opened and unprotected. In the next instant the creature flew up before them, straight up; his legs battled the air like wings, his teeth were bared. He leaped straight at Lily's father, who staggered backward and put out his hands to stop this attack. But the rat caught him at the base of his throat, sinking his sharp teeth into the flesh and clinging to the shirt cloth with his fierce sharp claws.

Her father made a gasping sound and whirled around, clutching the animal at his throat. Lily saw his face—his eyes opened wide in shock, his teeth bared too now—in such a fury as she had never imagined. The rat clung to him as he fell to his knees, dropping one hand for the axe while the other closed over the animal's face. His fingers went inside the rat's mouth, prying the teeth from his flesh, and when he had pulled them free he raised the gray body over his head and dashed it to the floor. Then the rat screamed. It was the only sound he had made in the struggle, and his voice was high, clear, terror-stricken. Lily saw the oily edge of the axe blade as it came down through the air. She remembered how her father had sharpened and oiled it that morning in preparation for this blow.

The edge came down and Lily turned to her mother, who was too stunned by what she saw to look away. There was the soft sound of flesh giving way, of small bones cracking, and it was quiet. When Lily looked back, the rat was in two pieces, his head and forequarters on one side of the axe, his back legs and long tail severed completely and thrown a foot away by the force of the blade. Lily's father stood looking down at the sight, clutching his throat with one hand. He knew that the job was over, but his rage, Lily saw, was not yet under control. Her mother rushed to him, throwing her arms about him with a passion she had never shown him before, and he held her against him tightly. Lily looked away, allowing her eyes their fill of the curiously rewarding sight of the rat's bisected body. His blood oozed out upon the boards from his wounds and from his open mouth, which was already stiffening with death. The wonder of his death afflicted her. A moment before he had threatened everything; now his harmless body lay before her, bereft[10] of horror, only dull, large, gray, mysteriously still. She turned away from them all and went back into the kitchen. Her hands were sticky from fear and she washed them at the sink.

That night Lily slept fitfully. When she woke she could think of nothing but the rat, of how she had lain and listened to him as he came closer and closer. She sat up and looked about the room. Didn't she hear the scratching of his claws against the floor; wasn't that hushing sound caused by his breath? She lay back and turned to face the wall. Her mother had kissed her when she went to bed and

10. **bereft** (bĭ-rĕft′): deprived of; lacking.

her father had held her for a moment with warm confidence. She had touched the bandage on his neck tentatively. The doctor had suggested that the wound would become more painful before it began to heal. A rat bite, he told the family, was no joke, but there was no reason to expect complications. Her father had astounded the doctor with the story, keeping, as he talked, one hand resting protectively on his daughter's shoulder. He had, he was convinced, done what was necessary to set her fears at rest.

But now she was as full with fear as ever and she knew she wouldn't sleep. She got up and turned on the light in her bedroom; then she looked under the bed and in the closet. But not seeing anything didn't give her the rest she sought. At length she decided to go out, to take the plastic bag out of the garbage can, and look again on the remains of her enemy. She slipped on her robe, turned off her light, and went stealthily down the hall, passing her parents' bedroom door without a pause.

She opened the kitchen door, unlatched and opened the screen, and stepped out on the porch. The rain had stopped, and through the swiftly moving clouds the moon cast its desultory[11] beams. Lily accustomed her eyes to the light and to the unexpected beauty of the scene before her. She focused her eyes on the moonflowers, like pools of milk among the dark leaves that covered the fence. The roses nearby raised their thorny branches, holding out papery leaves and flowers, gray and black, toward the sky. Her mother's vegetable garden fairly hummed with life, and, as she stood there, Lily thought of her mother and of how they had worked together one day, preparing the soil for the seeds.

Her mother had turned the soil with a shovel, and Lily, crouched barefoot in the dirt, had come behind her with a garden spade, breaking the big clods down with childish energy. She had stopped, then stood up and stepped forward into the rough dirt her mother had just turned. As her foot came down she noticed that the soil was warm; it invited her to press her toes into it. Lily looked at her feet and smiled, overcome with a delicious sensation. "What's funny?" her mother had asked and when Lily looked up she saw that her mother was smiling on her in the same way she smiled, sometimes, on her roses, with undisguised admiration.

"It's warm," Lily said. "Underneath. You should take off your shoes."

Her mother's smile had deepened and she indicated her shod foot, which rested on the wing of the shovel, with a look that explained her dilemma: she couldn't dig barefoot. Then she bent down and pressed her hand into the dirt near Lily's feet. She dug her fingers down and came up with a handful of the dark soil. She studied it intently for a moment, sifting it through her fingers. She had lectured Lily that morning on this chore and made it clear that the preparation of the soil was the most important work they would do that day. Everything, by which Lily understood her to mean the future of the garden, depended on its being done right. Now it was Lily's turn to smile, for she saw that her mother couldn't take her mind off the importance she attached to doing this work correctly. It was true, her fingers told her, the soil was warm, but her fingers asked a more penetrating question: would it yield?

Lily paused, examining this memory as she stood on the porch in the warm night air, and she shook her head slowly, affectionately, at the thought of her mother's passionate gardening. The fruit of that passion stood before her: tomatoes and eggplants heavy on their vines, lettuce like great balls of pearl, luminous in the darkness, the airy greens of the carrots, rustling continuously with the movement of the air, the black tangle of the green peas, climbing skyward on their tall tubes of screen. The scent of the mint and parsley bed rose to Lily and the sweetness of the air drew her out toward the steps. She looked down at the drawers of the old

---

11. **desultory:** shifting or skipping about.

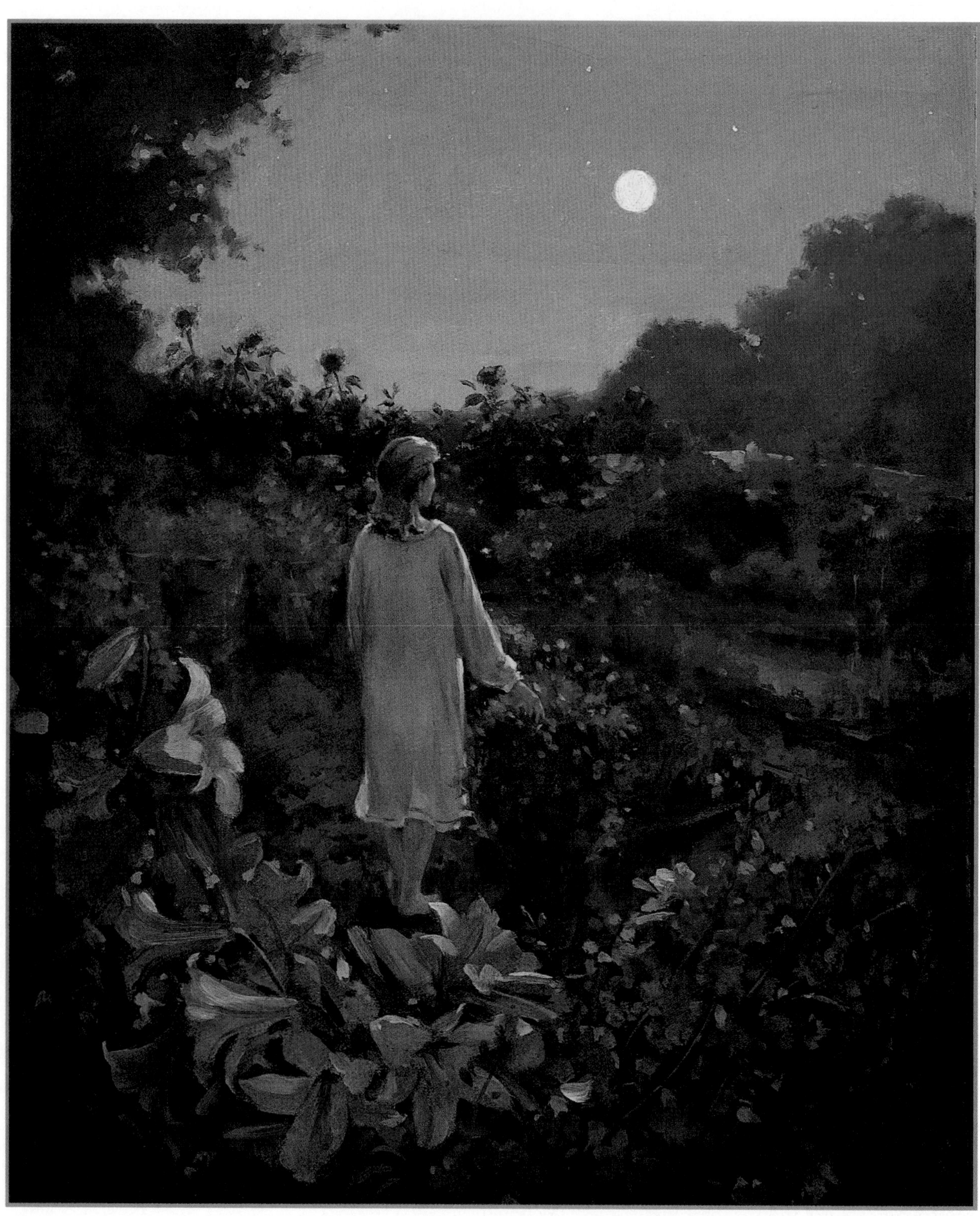

dresser, which lay scattered on the porch. Her mother had washed them furiously, as if to wash away the evidence of a desecration.[12] Then Lily thought of the rat and she looked toward the garbage can with a sensation of dismay. It would be, she thought, foolish and unnecessary trouble to pull out his corpse now. She could consult her memory for a fresh, distinct, and detailed picture of his death; she could see, in her mind's eye, the blood darkening around his mouth, the dullness of his dead eyeballs. She wasn't certain that he wouldn't seek her out again, but, she thought, he would never again seek her in that particular form. His menace had quite gone out of that form; she had seen it with her own eyes. Her father had discarded the pieces of the rat's body without anger; he had even commented on the creature's remarkable size, taking, Lily had observed, some comfort in having defeated so formidable[13] an enemy. Now that he was a danger to no one, the rat possessed the power to be marvelous.

Lily turned away, pushing her hair back from her face. She had told her mother she wanted her hair cut off and, to her surprise, had received no objection. But now this seemed an unnecessary precaution. She returned to her bed, possessed of a strange fearlessness; it was as insistent as her own heartbeat, and as she drifted off to sleep it swelled and billowed within her and she understood, for the first time, that she was safe. ❖

12. **desecration:** a violation of something sacred.

13. **formidable:** difficult to defeat.

Valerie Martin

Born in Missouri in 1948 and raised in New Orleans, Valerie Martin was educated at the University of New Orleans and at the University of Massachusetts. Her first collection of short stories, *Love,* was published in 1977; her first novel, *Set in Motion,* was released a year later. In a review of this novel, Anatole Broyard said of Martin: "She writes as if she felt that, now that we know the worst about ourselves, we might as well sit back and enjoy it." Since then, Martin has continued to explore "the worst" about people—their dark sides.

While most of Martin's stories and novels explore themes of love, passion, and betrayal, she frequently experiments by using different narrative perspectives to examine those themes. In her novel *A Recent Martyr,* for instance, she shifts from first-person to third-person point of view—from the point of view of the woman to that of the man. In *Mary Reilly,* her acclaimed work of historical fiction, Martin retells Robert Louis Stevenson's classic story *The Strange Case of Dr. Jekyll and Mr. Hyde* from the point of view of the doctor's housemaid.

The Consolation of Nature and Other Stories, from which this story was taken, was published in 1988. In reviewing this collection, Michiko Kakutani described it as showing "a preoccupation with the dark underside of life, a taste for disturbing, even macabre imagery, and a tendency to use that imagery to delineate turning points in people's lives—the moment when innocence is replaced by an acute awareness of death and pain." Such characteristics and themes put Martin's story "The Consolation of Nature" in the gloomy company of works by Poe, Hawthorne, and other Gothic writers.

OTHER WORKS *Alexandra, The Great Divorce*

WRITING FROM EXPERIENCE

WRITING A FIRSTHAND NARRATIVE

In Unit Three, "The Spirit of Individualism," people wrote about themselves, human nature, and life's lessons. What have you learned in your life? It may be more than you think. This lesson can help you put your ideas and experiences into words.

GUIDED ASSIGNMENT

Write a Personal Essay A letter to a friend, a magazine article, a class assignment, and a college application are all forms of personal essays you may be called on to write.

CALL FOR ENTRIES

For our fall **TEEN LIFE** issue, we're looking for personal essays on an experience that changed your life. Did you discover a lost relative? Have you survived a close call? Did you realize you were wrong about something? Tell us what you learned, in 700 words or less. See the entry form for essay rules. If you like, attach a photo of yourself to your essay.

I could write about mom's accident— how it changed me.

Call for Entries

❶ Analyze the Prompts

Take a few minutes to study the items on these pages. Discuss with one or two classmates the following questions:

- What types of information is each item asking you to share?
- What form of response, if any, is being requested?

❷ Choose Your Topic

In your notebook, freewrite a paragraph on one or both of the following:

- For an application essay, list the qualities, interests, and achievements you would include.
- For a magazine article, describe two or three experiences that you think were significant or life changing.

Then decide which form of personal essay—an application essay or a submission to a magazine—you want to try writing.

GSU Green State University
Application for Admission

6. PERSONAL STATEMENT/ESSAY

The essay offers you an opportunity to help us get to know you better outside of grades and test scores. The essay will show us your ability to organize your thoughts and to express yourself in a more creative manner. Write an essay of 400–700 words on what you feel are your strongest personal qualities and accomplishments that make you a candidate for the undergraduate program of the film school.

This is the school I want to attend. Mr. Angelo says the film program is great!

Application Form

This is your LIFE!

OUR READERS SAY . . .

This month we're asking "Which life experience has most affected you?" Let us hear from you on any of these topics:

1. The loss of a parent or grandparent
2. An award or achievement you worked hard to earn
3. A personal first—first job, first date, first pet
4. An accident or a bad mistake
5. Getting a new brother or sister

POW!

Magazine Poll

Short articles like this one can stimulate your memories and help you recall your thoughts and feelings about such experiences.

 LASERLINKS
- *WRITING SPRINGBOARD*

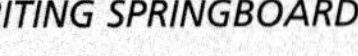

 WRITING COACH

PREWRITING

Exploring Your Experiences

Creating a Picture If your life story could be considered a movie, a personal essay is more like a snapshot or a collage. To write your essay, you will not only describe some of the key events and experiences you have had but also explain their significance. The suggestions on these pages will help you gather the information you need.

1 Fill in the Details

Now that you have selected a specific experience or have decided to try your hand at an application essay, you need to gather more details. The following suggestions can help you recall or obtain key facts to make your snapshot clearer.

Time Line Create a chronology of personal achievements, turning points, and goals. The example below shows how one student used this method to develop his college application essay.

Photo Review Use family albums, yearbooks, slides, or videos to jog your memory and add forgotten details.

Interviews Ask friends, relatives, teachers, and others for their recollections and for words they would use to describe you (for example, determined, inventive, caring).

Personal Journals/Diaries Review what you may have written about the events or experiences you have chosen.

Brian's Time Line for College Application

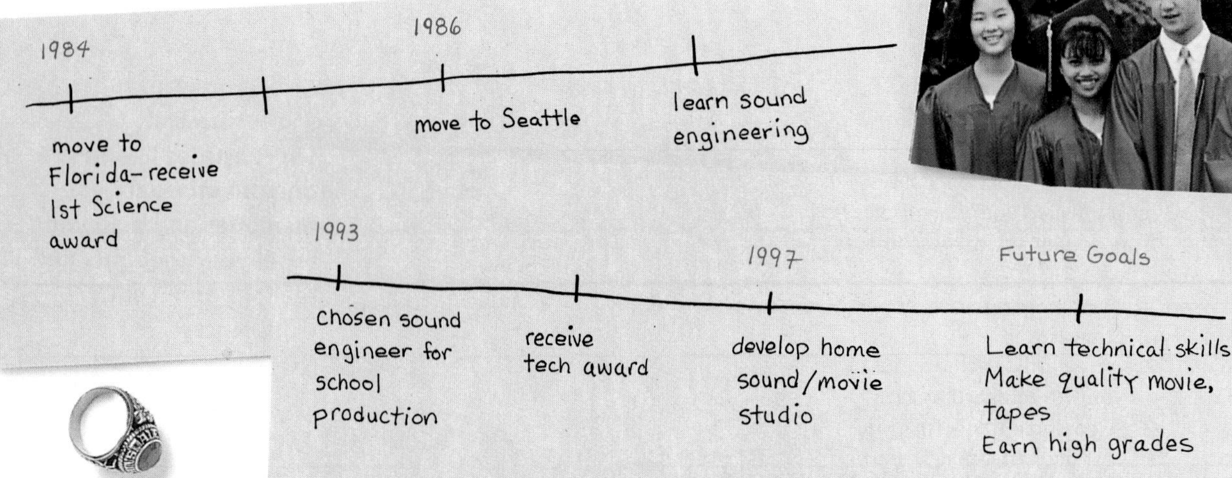

② Match Your Ideas and Purpose

You can use these guidelines to help you identify the needs of your reader and clarify your purpose for writing.

Review the Prompt What information is the prompt asking you to supply—a list of qualifications, a life-changing event, a personal reminiscence? Study the prompts carefully.

Evaluate Your Audience Think about who will read your essay. Does the college you want to apply to expect a creative or traditional essay? Does the magazine you want to write for favor informal or formal writing? You will need to do background research to answer these questions.

Talk It Over You may want to discuss your essay ideas, audience, and selected details with others. They may point out gaps in information or suggest other qualities or details you might wish to include in your essay.

③ Explore What You Find

You can explore the significance of your experience in several ways in order to tell the reader why it was important. For instance, in the example below, another student, Alisha, used a mapping strategy to examine how her attitudes and behavior changed as a result of her mother's accident.

The SkillBuilder provides other techniques to help you understand and interpret your experiences, no matter what type of personal essay you may choose to write.

Alisha's Word Web

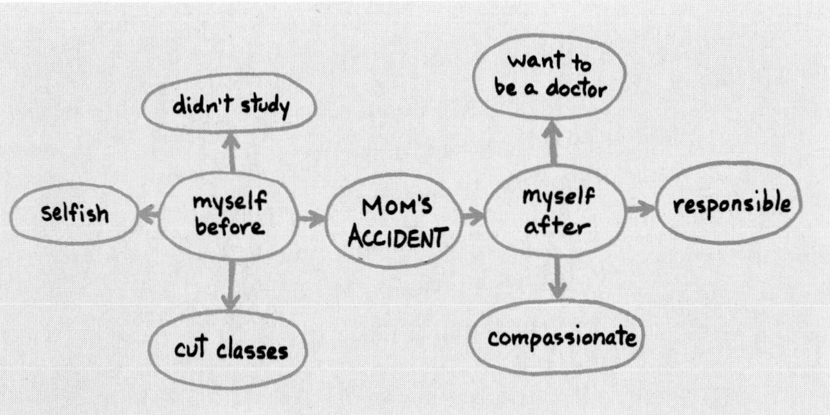

SkillBuilder

CRITICAL THINKING

Interpreting Experiences
These tips can help you interpret and explain your experiences.

1. How did the experience change you? Describe what you believed or how you acted before and after an event.
2. What did you learn about yourself? Divide an experience into its stages or steps. List what you learned at each stage, then summarize the experience. ("It wasn't until I nearly lost my mother that I found myself.")
3. What did you learn about other people, human nature, or life in general? Freewrite a paragraph on each part of this question, describing what you learned.

APPLYING WHAT YOU'VE LEARNED
Choose an incident or a memory from your list and try one or all of the techniques above to help you interpret the experience.

THINK & PLAN

Reflecting on Your Essay

1. What resource or person can give you the most information about an incident or memory?
2. Which qualities and experiences provide the best snapshot of you?
3. How well do you understand the needs of your audience?

DRAFTING

Telling Your Story

Developing Your Snapshot Create a vivid picture of yourself by developing a strong opening, choosing distinctive details, using narrative and dramatic techniques, and ending with a strong summary of your main points. The two examples below show how Brian and Alisha developed their essays to meet their different goals.

1 Try a Discovery Draft

When drafting your personal essay, always keep your audience and purpose in mind. For example, Brian wants the film school to accept him into the undergraduate program, while Alisha wants to have her article accepted by the magazine for publication.

Brian's Discovery Draft

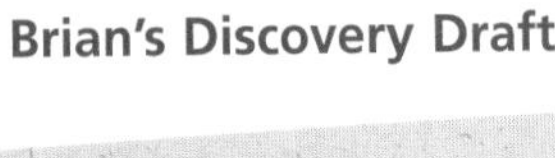

Film School Application: Personal Statement

OK, since this is for film school, and they'll be looking for creativity, I could present my life as a video game! The goal is to graduate the hero, Brian, from the film school prepared to design exciting, creative movies.

Each level of the game describes my science awards, offices held, honors earned. Also leadership skills—peer counseling, counselor at camps, leader in sports, student council offices.

Experience as sound engineer for school productions and my own films shows technical expertise and leadership. Last level could be future goals—my desire to study hard, learn everything I can, and make film school better place for everyone to work.

Outline levels of video games.

Alisha's Discovery Draft

Magazine article: Write about a life-changing experience you had

"Alisha, Mom's been in a car accident!" Those words changed my life forever. What an awful day that was! This event was the worst and best thing that happened to me. What did I learn? Compassion, value of hard work, importance of applying myself and developing my talents for others. I had to run the household and help Mom recover. Before the accident, I was selfish, always rebelling and cutting classes, fighting at home, and not taking responsibility—a real four-star jerk.

This was one of the questions in the call for entries, so I want to be sure to emphasize what I learned.

2 Choose an Organizing Structure

Now it's time to give some structure to your ideas. A writer can choose from several organizing patterns when developing a personal essay.

Chronological Events or achievements are listed in the order in which they occurred. (Brian describes his accomplishments from grade school on up, using game levels.)

Compare-Contrast The writer uses a turning point or significant event to show changes before and after. (Alisha is lazy and self-centered before her mother's accident and becomes responsible and compassionate after.)

Least to Most Important Events, achievements, or ideas are listed in order of importance rather than in order of occurrence.

See Share Your Work on page 435 for ideas on how to present your personal essay.

3 Begin and End with a Bang

You can experiment with ways of beginning and ending your essay to engage and inform the reader and to emphasize your main points.

Opening Paragraph Try to hook the reader without sounding contrived or cute. In the example, Alisha opens with the crisis that radically changed her life. Brian makes himself the main character of a video game.

Concluding Paragraph You can underscore your main points and include details that support your conclusions. Brian shows why he feels he should be admitted to his chosen school, and Alisha reveals how she changed.

PEER RESPONSE

Ask a peer reviewer to point out the strengths and weaknesses of your draft. You may want to ask these questions.

- Pretend you don't know me. How would you describe the person who wrote this essay?
- What details do I need to add or take out to make my snapshot clearer or more appealing?
- How can I make the opening and concluding paragraphs more engaging or informative?
- What narrative or dramatic techniques could I use to improve the essay?

SkillBuilder

Using Personal Voice

Personal voice is the unique way writers express themselves. You reveal your personality through your choice of words, imagery, and sentence structure. Study the two examples below.

Mom's accident was the worst thing that happened in my life. In a sudden, blinding flash, I saw how selfish I had been.

My mother's accident was a very serious event and marked a significant turning point for me. I changed my selfish attitudes and the way I behaved.

The first writer, whose voice is more emotional, uses vivid language to convey how she felt. The second writer is more formal, describing the event and its effects in an objective voice.

APPLYING WHAT YOU'VE LEARNED Experiment with your personal "voice" by writing about the same incident or memory, using different images and word choices.

RETHINK & EVALUATE

Preparing to Revise

1. What changes can make your snapshot clearer?
2. In what ways can you improve your organizational structure?
3. How does your personal voice help convey your story?

Finishing Your Work

Polishing Your Essay You want your snapshot to show you in the best possible light. Review the previous pages to make sure you have selected the best details and organizing structure for your essay. Use the Standards for Evaluation and the Editing Checklist to catch errors in content and grammar.

1 Revise and Edit

After you've put your draft aside for a day or two, look it over again with the following points in mind.

- Make sure you have matched your selected experiences and ideas with your purpose.
- Ask someone to read your opening paragraph and comment on its effectiveness.
- Be sure you have explained the significance of your experiences and incorporated any peer reviewer comments.
- Check your concluding paragraph to make sure it summarizes your main points.

Brian's Revised Essay
How does the writer demonstrate his creativity? How would you describe this person from the details given?

GSU **Green State University**
Application for Admission

6. PERSONAL STATEMENT/ESSAY

Eleven people sit at a large rosewood table in the office of Fantasy Video, Inc. Two engineers explain their new game.

"The goal of this game is to graduate the main character, Brian, from a film program, prepared to design exciting, creative films. We programmed him with a great love of adventure, exploration, and invention and the ability to deal with all types of people.

"The first level of the game is set in Florida, where points are earned by developing creativity and imagination. Brian writes a science fiction series and produces a three-minute animated film."

Alisha's Revised Essay
How do you know what the writer felt about this incident? What techniques does she use to tell her story?

Turning Point

"Alisha, Mom's been in a serious car accident! Meet us at County General." At the hospital, I looked at the doctor's drawn, grayish face and knew he didn't expect Mom to live.

In that moment, my life changed forever. For fifteen years I had thought only about me. I did what I wanted, when I wanted. Although I was considered very bright, I was barely passing most of my classes. But when I almost lost my mother, I learned that growing up involves a lot more than just becoming another year older.

Dramatizing a personal experience can be an effective way to show what you have learned.

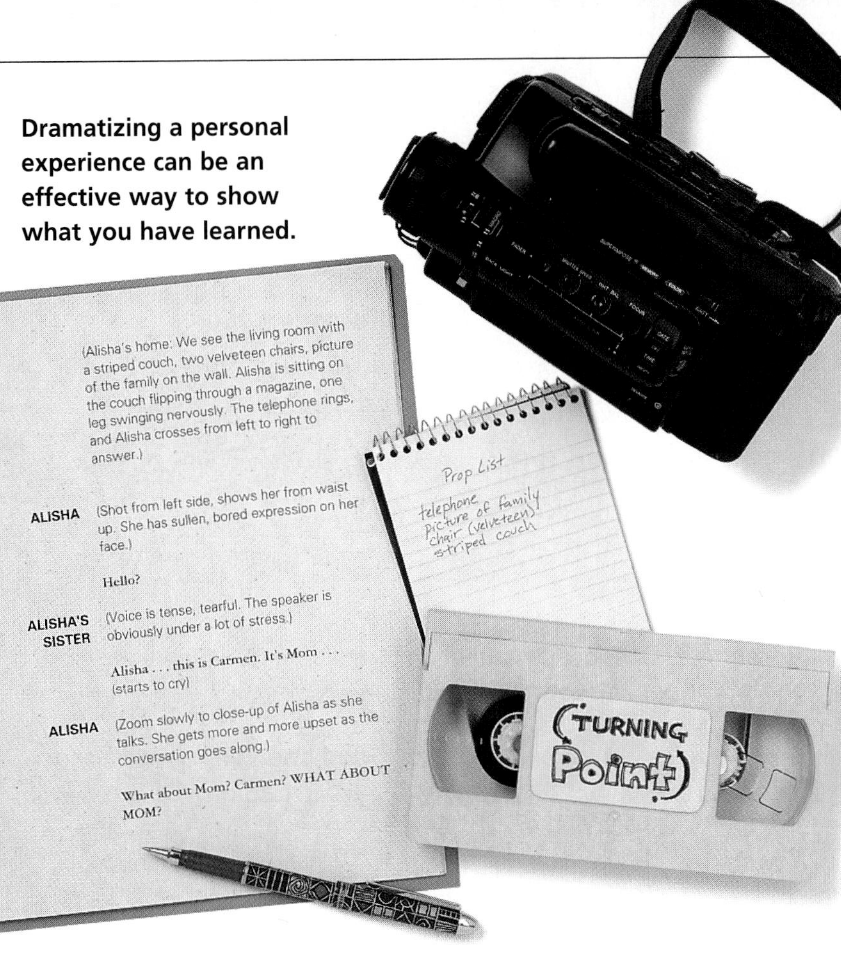

(Alisha's home: We see the living room with a striped couch, two velveteen chairs, picture of the family on the wall. Alisha is sitting on the couch flipping through a magazine, one leg swinging nervously. The telephone rings, and Alisha crosses from left to right to answer.)
ALISHA (Shot from left side, shows her from waist up. She has sullen, bored expression on her face.)
Hello?
ALISHA'S SISTER (Voice is tense, tearful. The speaker is obviously under a lot of stress.)
Alisha . . . this is Carmen. It's Mom . . . (starts to cry)
ALISHA (Zoom slowly to close-up of Alisha as she talks. She gets more and more upset as the conversation goes along.)
What about Mom? Carmen? WHAT ABOUT MOM?
Prop List
telephone
picture of family
chair (velveteen)
striped couch
TURNING Point

❷ Share Your Work

Your personal essay can be the basis for an engaging or dramatic skit or video play. You might ask the speech teacher or drama coach to help you stage your story and present the final work to your class.

Standards for Evaluation
A personal essay • is written for a specific purpose and audience • engages and informs the reader in the opening paragraph • includes only the most important events, qualities, or ideas from the writer's life • clearly states the significance of these events, qualities, and ideas • summarizes and emphasizes the writer's main points in the final paragraph • uses narrative and dramatic techniques and personal voice to tell the story or to convey the message

SkillBuilder

GRAMMAR FROM WRITING

Keeping Referents Clear
The indefinite pronouns *this/these* and *that/those* refer to specific nouns, or referents. For example:

I have been a peer counselor, science club president, and director of stage production. ***These*** *are positions that required me to lead others and to accept responsibility.*

The pronoun *these* refers to the positions listed.

GRAMMAR HANDBOOK

See pages 1213–1214 of the Grammar Handbook for more information on pronoun referents.

Editing Checklist Use these revising and editing tips.

- Is the punctuation correct?
- Do my pronouns refer to specific nouns?
- Have I proofread the draft?

REFLECT & ASSESS

Learning from Experience

1. Describe what you learned about how to interpret your experiences.
2. Write a brief paragraph on what you found easy and difficult about this lesson.

PORTFOLIO List ways you could have taken more risks in your personal essay. Add your essay and list to the portfolio.

REFLECT & ASSESS

UNIT 3: THE SPIRIT OF INDIVIDUALISM

Do you feel you have gained a deeper understanding of the American philosophy of individualism as it developed in the 19th century? Has reading 19th-century literature sharpened your reading skills? To explore what you've learned from the selections in this unit, choose one or more of the options in each of the following sections.

REFLECTING ON THE UNIT

OPTION 1 **The Concept of the Individual** The selections in this unit reflect two different concepts of the individual. To illustrate the difference, create two portraits of individuals—one representing the romantic and transcendentalist view, the other representing the Gothic view. Choose your own medium for the portrait: an illustration, an oral description, a written character sketch, or any combination of these.

OPTION 2 **Roundtable Discussion** Reread the quotation from Thoreau that begins this unit (page 264). Do you think the other writers in this unit—especially the 20th-century writers—would agree with Thoreau? Get together with a group of five classmates, with each student choosing a writer from the unit to role-play. Make sure your group represents writers from both centuries and from both parts of the unit. Then participate in a group discussion about individual freedom, evaluating Thoreau's statement from the point of view of the writer you are playing. During the discussion, pay attention to the writers' different attitudes toward individual freedom.

OPTION 3 **Visions of Good and Evil** Compare and contrast the portrayals of human nature in the two parts of the unit: "Celebrations of the Self" and "The Dark Side of Individualism." What generalizations about the views of romantic and transcendentalist writers can you infer from the selections in Part 1? Compile a list of them, then come up with a similar list for the Gothic writers in Part 2. Write a few paragraphs explaining which vision of human nature you agree with more.

REFLECT & ASSESS *Self-Assessment: To show how your understanding has deepened as you have read this unit, create a cluster diagram or list in which you identify about five key characteristics of American individualism. For each characteristic, indicate which of the writers represented in the unit would consider it admirable.*

REVIEWING LITERARY CONCEPTS

OPTION 1 **Analyzing Imagery** The 19th-century writers represented in this unit used imagery for a variety of purposes:

- to illustrate ideas
- to enhance descriptions of character and setting
- to create moods
- to reflect psychological realities—the inner workings of characters' minds

Selection	Primary Use of Imagery	Example of Imagery
"A Psalm of Life"	to illustrate ideas	"Footprints on the sands of time" (l. 28)
"The Devil and Tom Walker"	to enhance description and to create mood	"The swamp was thickly grown with great gloomy pines and hemlocks . . ." (pp. 279–280)

Go back through the selections in the unit and identify, in a chart like the one shown, which of these purposes each writer's imagery primarily serves. Then put checks next to the titles of the selections whose imagery best helped you understand ideas or visualize things.

OPTION 2 **Evaluating Rhyme and Meter** With a partner, review the unit to identify traditional poems, with regular patterns of rhyme and rhythm, and poems written in free verse. Then draw some conclusions about the strengths and limitations of each type of poetry. What is gained by using one rather than the other? What is lost? What subjects or themes might be more appropriate for one than for the other? Which do you prefer?

REFLECT & ASSESS *Self-Assessment: From the following list of literary terms discussed in this unit, select the ones that you think you need to learn more about. On a sheet of paper, jot down those terms and their definitions. As you read the next unit, concentrate on the literary elements they refer to.*

stanza	*tone*
omniscient narrator	*allegory*
aphorism	*foreshadowing*
essay	*characterization*
free verse	*situational irony*
style	*dramatic irony*
speaker	

PORTFOLIO BUILDING

- **QuickWrites** Many of the QuickWrites in this unit suggest summarizing selections' events or themes in formats different from the original. For example, you were asked to sum up the events of "The Devil and Tom Walker" in a few newspaper headlines. Choose the two responses in which you think you most concisely expressed the themes or plots of selections. Then write a cover note explaining what you think makes a good summary, citing your own responses as examples.
- **Writing About Literature** Reread the essay in which you explored the meaning of a symbol. Then imagine the selection without the symbol. How would its absence affect your response to the selection? Write a letter to the author, recommending the inclusion or omission of the symbol.
- **Writing from Experience** You're going to be famous! Your personal essay has been selected from among thousands to be turned into a movie. The producer has called, asking your opinions about background music, setting, and possible lead actors and actresses. What advice will you give? Include your thoughts with your writing if you choose to keep it in your portfolio.
- **Personal Choice** Think back to the activities and writing assignments you completed for this unit, as well as any you have done on your own. Which one would you like to expand for a larger audience? Write a cover note telling why you want to present the activity or writing to a larger audience and what kind of audience you would like to reach. Attach the note to your record of the activity or to the piece of writing, and include both in your portfolio.

REFLECT & ASSESS *Self-Assessment: Look over the pieces you have added to your portfolio so far. Is there enough variety in the writing and activities you've selected? Make a note of ways to add more diversity as the year goes on.*

SETTING GOALS

Look back through the responses in your notebook to find ideas or issues that interested you. Jot down the ones that you'd like to explore further as you read literature from the second half of the 19th century in the next unit.

CONFLICT *and* EXPANSION

We all declare for liberty; but in using the same word we do not mean the same thing.

Abraham Lincoln
16th president of the United States

If the Indians had tried to make the whites live like them, the whites would have resisted, and it was the same way with many Indians.

Wamditanka
(Big Eagle)
Santee Sioux

Pictorial quilt (1895–1898), Harriet Powers. Pieced and appliquéd cotton embroidered with plain and metallic yarns, 69″ × 105″, bequest of Maxim Karolik, courtesy of Museum of Fine Arts, Boston.

TIME LINE

Conflict & Expansion

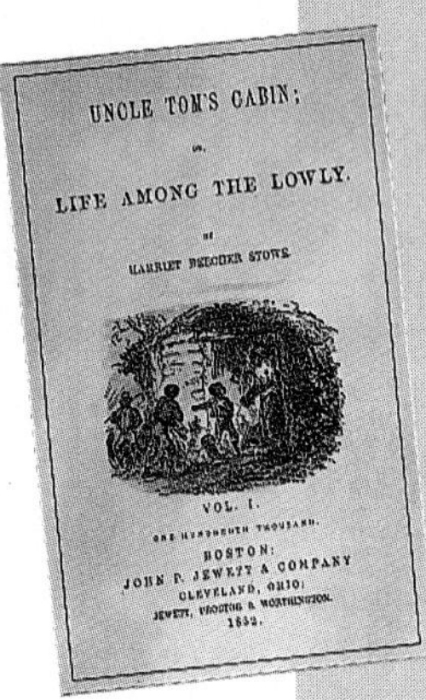
UNCLE TOM'S CABIN;
OR,
LIFE AMONG THE LOWLY.
BY
HARRIET BEECHER STOWE.
VOL. I.
BOSTON:
JOHN P. JEWETT & COMPANY
CLEVELAND, OHIO:
JEWETT, PROCTOR & WORTHINGTON.
1852.

1852

Harriet Beecher Stowe publishes *Uncle Tom's Cabin,* increasing tension between proslavery and antislavery forces.

1857

The Supreme Court's *Dred Scott* decision declares that slaves and former slaves are not U.S. citizens and thus are not entitled to basic rights.

1859

Abolitionist John Brown is hanged for treason after leading a raid on a federal arsenal at Harpers Ferry in an unsuccessful attempt to provoke a slave revolt.

1860

Abraham Lincoln is elected President; in response, South Carolina secedes from the Union, followed eventually by ten other Southern states.

1862

Congress passes the Homestead Act, offering public land to persons willing to settle the West.

The Homestead Act offered 160 acres to any citizen—or person willing to become a citizen—who would settle on public land for five years and pay a nominal fee. About 400,000 families took advantage of the offer.

1863

Lincoln signs the Emancipation Proclamation, freeing slaves in the Confederate states.

1865

The Civil War ends; Lincoln is assassinated; and the 13th Amendment to the Constitution abolishes slavery.

1866

A group of Confederate Army veterans organizes the Ku Klux Klan to oppose the advancement of African Americans.

1868

Congress passes the 14th Amendment to the Constitution, prohibiting discrimination against African Americans.

1869

The first transcontinental railroad is completed when the tracks of the Central Pacific and Union Pacific railroads are joined with a golden spike at Promontory Point, Utah.

1873

Colt's Patent Fire-Arms Manufacturing Company introduces the Peacemaker revolver, the most famous sidearm of the West.

1874

Joseph F. Glidden patents barbed wire, a key development in the settlement of the West.

Period *Pieces*

1876

At the Battle of Little Bighorn, several thousand Sioux and Cheyenne warriors, the largest Native American army ever assembled, defeat and kill about 200 U.S. Army troops under the command of Lieutenant Colonel George Armstrong Custer.

Native Americans of the Great Plains presented a formidable obstacle to white settlers and to the U.S. Army. The incessant fighting lasted from the 1860s through the 1880s. The loss of the buffalo struck a severe blow to the Plains Indians. Not only did the building of the Union Pacific Railroad divide the herd, but buffalo meat provided food for workers building the railroad. By 1886 only 600 buffalo remained out of an estimated 15 million in 1865.

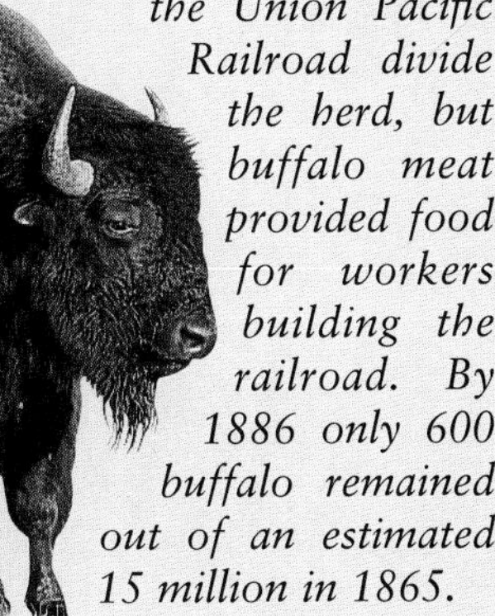

1877

Chief Joseph of the Nez Perce surrenders to the U.S. Army.

1883

"Buffalo Bill" Cody organizes his Wild West show and tours the U.S. and Europe for many years.

1890

At Wounded Knee Creek in South Dakota, U.S. soldiers kill more than 200 Sioux men, women, and children in the last battle of the Indian Wars; the U.S. Bureau of Census published a report declaring the end of the American frontier.

1896

In *Plessy v. Ferguson,* the Supreme Court upholds the separate but equal doctrine of Jim Crow laws, widely used to discriminate against African Americans.

1899

The Spanish-American War results in the United States gaining control of Cuba, Puerto Rico, and the Philippines.

Confederate money

Steam engine

Decorative carriage clock from 1870

PART 1 INTRODUCTION

A House Divided

Slavery and the Civil War

By the time of Abraham Lincoln's inauguration as President in March of 1861, seven states—South Carolina, Mississippi, Florida, Alabama, Georgia, Louisiana, and Texas—had seceded from the Union and formed the Confederate States of America, with Jefferson Davis as President. A month later, Confederate troops opened fire on Northern troops attempting to resupply Fort Sumter, a federal installation in the Charleston, South Carolina, harbor. Three days later, Lincoln ordered additional troops to enforce the law. In response, Virginia, Arkansas, North Carolina, and Tennessee joined the Confederacy. The Civil War had begun.

When the war ended on April 9, 1865, with General Robert E. Lee's surrender to General Ulysses S. Grant at Appomattox Court House, Virginia, more than 620,000 men had been killed—nearly as many as have died in all other wars that the United States has fought—and at least that many more had been wounded. Much of the South lay in ruins, scarred by gutted plantation houses, burned bridges, and uprooted railroad lines. However, the Union had been preserved, and nearly 4 million slaves had gained their freedom.

Ulysses S. Grant

Before the Civil War, *United States* had been a plural noun. People were used to saying, "The United States *are* . . ." with the emphasis on the individual *states* more than the *united* interests of all. However, a strong belief in states' rights ultimately threatened the union itself and allowed the institution of slavery a longer history in the Southern states than in the Northern states and in most of Latin America and Europe as well. "A house divided against itself cannot stand," maintained Abraham Lincoln. "I believe this government cannot endure permanently half slave and half free." After the Civil War, the United States had become irrevocably one country. People began saying, "The United States *is* . . ."

Robert E. Lee

In the years before the war, slavery was a major subject engaging a large number of writers. Public lectures were a forum by which many writers supported themselves. Henry David Thoreau, as active in the political and social world as he was in the literary, lectured on the individual's responsibility to take action against unjust laws. His lecture, published as the essay "Civil Disobedience" in 1849, has since become famous, providing some of the basis for the American tradition of nonviolent protest that took hold about 100 years later during the civil rights movement.

This crucial time period also generated some of the first important literature by African Americans. Frances Ellen Watkins Harper became the first popular African-American poet, as she traveled throughout the North lecturing to substantial audiences in favor of abolition and punctuating her lectures with recitations of her poems. Most eloquent of all, however, was Frederick Douglass, the escaped slave who taught himself to read and write and later became a champion of the abolitionist cause and woman suffrage. Douglass's autobiography remains one of the most moving, authentic

Voices from the TIMES

I know this well, that if one thousand, if one hundred, if ten men whom I could name—if ten *honest* men only—ay, if *one* HONEST man, in this State of Massachusetts, *ceasing to hold slaves*, were actually to withdraw from this copartnership [with government by refusing to pay taxes], and be locked up in the county jail therefor, it would be the abolition of slavery in America. For it matters not how small the beginning may seem to be: what is once well done is done forever.

Henry David Thoreau
from "Civil Disobedience"

The South, in my opinion, has been aggrieved by the acts of the North, as you say. I feel the aggression, and am willing to take every proper step for redress. . . . As an American citizen, I take great pride in my country, her prosperity and institutions, and would defend any State, if her rights were invaded. But I can anticipate no greater calamity for the country than a dissolution of the Union. It would be an accumulation of all the evils we complain of, and I am willing to sacrifice everything but honor for its preservation.

Robert E. Lee
from a letter to his son three months before the war

This Southern Confederacy must be supported now by calm determination and cool brains. We have risked all and we must play our best, for the stake is life or death.

Mary Boykin Chesnut
from her diary

Voices *from the* Times

Both parties deprecated war, but one of them would make war rather than let the nation survive, and the other would accept war rather than let it perish. And the war came.

Abraham Lincoln
from *Second Inaugural Address*

I saw, crowded into one old sunken hotel, lying upon its bare, wet, bloody floors, 500 fainting men hold up their cold, bloodless, dingy hands as I passed, and beg me in Heaven's name for a cracker to keep them from starving (and I had none); or to give them a cup that they might have something to drink water from, if they could get it (and I had no cup and could get none).

Clara Barton
on wounded soldiers awaiting transfer to hospitals

War is hell.

William Tecumseh Sherman

Look down fair moon and bathe this
 scene,
Pour softly down night's nimbus floods
 on faces ghastly, swollen, purple,
On the dead on their backs with arms
 toss'd wide,
Pour down your unstinted nimbus
 sacred moon.

Walt Whitman
"Look Down Fair Moon"

accounts we have of the bitter history of slavery.

As always during periods of great change, it is the experience of individuals caught up in large historical forces that finally gives life to events and makes them real. Walt Whitman worked as an army nurse in New York and Washington and on the front lines during the first three years of the war. Many of his poems written at this time are painfully personal. His famous elegies for Abraham Lincoln, "When Lilacs Last in the Dooryard Bloom'd" and "O Captain! My Captain!" express the grief of a nation still mourning the losses of the Civil War. Ambrose Bierce's story "An Occurrence at Owl Creek Bridge" has its origins in his own experience as a foot soldier in the war. The strange twists of that story, like others he wrote, prefigure his own mysterious disappearance years later in Mexico. The play *The Clod*, by Lewis Beach, depicts the grim circumstances of ordinary people trapped literally between the North and the South.

Continuity & Change: The Civil Rights Movement

Though the horrors of slavery cannot be minimized, its end turned out to be only the first step in a long, arduous struggle for equal rights for African Americans. With publications and speeches by Martin Luther King, Jr., Malcolm X, and others, the civil rights movement of the 1950s and 1960s generated some of the most memorable work. Included in this part of Unit Four is Anne Moody's graphic and vivid account of one of the first sit-ins in Mississippi. Also, in the tradition of James Russell Lowell, Frances Ellen Watkins Harper, and other abolitionist poets, Robert Hayden and Dudley Randall address the struggle in historical as well as personal terms.

PART 1

A House Divided

Slavery and the Civil War

Continuity & Change: The Civil Rights Movement

AM I NOT A WOMAN AND A SISTER?

PREVIEWING

NONFICTION

from Narrative of the Life of Frederick Douglass, an American Slave

Frederick Douglass

PERSONAL CONNECTION

What do you know about slavery in the United States? Get together with a group of classmates and share what you have learned from slave narratives such as the one by Olaudah Equiano (page 101), from movies and TV programs you have seen, or from books you have read. In your notebook, record your group's knowledge about slavery in a diagram like the one started here.

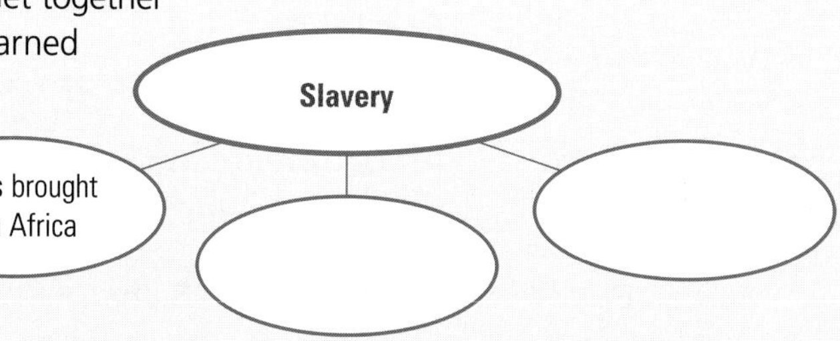

BIOGRAPHICAL CONNECTION

After escaping from slavery in 1838, Frederick Douglass gave public lectures about his experiences. To convince skeptics who doubted that such an eloquent speaker could have ever been a slave, Douglass decided to write his autobiography, *Narrative of the Life of Frederick Douglass.* This book became one of the most famous slave narratives. As a boy, Douglass was a servant in the home of Hugh Auld of Baltimore, where Mrs. Auld taught Douglass the alphabet and some simple spelling. After Mr. Auld commanded his wife to stop educating the boy, Douglass taught himself to read with the help of white playmates. When Douglass was 16, he was sent back to his first home to live with Hugh Auld's brother, Thomas. Thomas Auld believed that Douglass had been too spoiled as a house slave to be useful on a plantation and decided it was necessary to break the young man's spirit. Auld rented Douglass for a year to Edward Covey, who had a reputation as a slave breaker. This excerpt from Douglass's narrative covers the time that Douglass spent with Mr. Covey.

WRITING CONNECTION

In your notebook, describe what you think it might have felt like to be a field slave in the early 19th century. Jot down your ideas about such areas as the following:

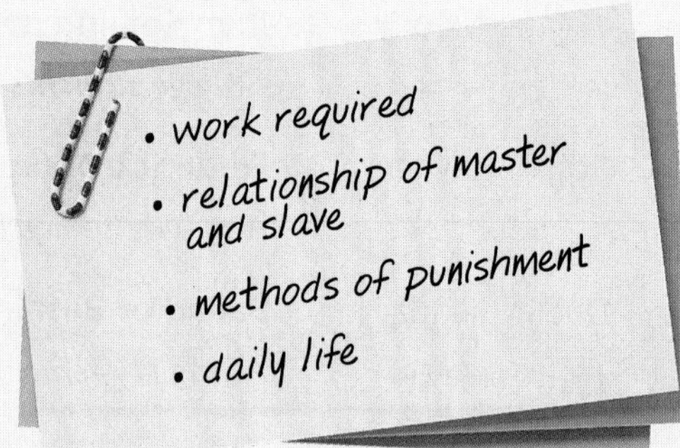

• work required
• relationship of master and slave
• methods of punishment
• daily life

Then as you read this excerpt, compare your own ideas about slavery with Frederick Douglass's firsthand account of his life as a field slave.

from Narrative of the Life of Frederick Douglass

Frederick Douglass

I left Master Thomas's house, and went to live with Mr. Covey, on the 1st of January, 1833. I was now, for the first time in my life, a field hand. In my new employment, I found myself even more awkward than a country boy appeared to be in a large city. I had been at my new home but one week before Mr. Covey gave me a very severe whipping, cutting my back, causing the blood to run, and raising ridges on my flesh as large as my little finger. The details of this affair are as follows: Mr. Covey sent me, very early in the morning of one of our coldest days in the month of January, to the woods, to get a load of wood. He gave me a team of unbroken oxen. He told me which was the in-hand ox, and which the off-hand[1] one. He then tied the end of a large rope around the horns of the in-hand ox, and gave me the other end of it, and told me, if the oxen started to run, that I must hold on upon the rope. I had never driven oxen before, and of course I was very awkward. I, however, succeeded in getting to the edge of the woods with little difficulty; but I had got a very few rods into the woods, when the oxen took fright, and started full tilt, carrying the cart against trees, and over stumps, in the most frightful manner. I expected every moment that my brains would be dashed out against the trees. After running thus for a considerable distance, they finally upset the cart, dashing it with great force against a tree, and threw themselves into a dense thicket. How I escaped death, I do not know. There I was, entirely alone, in a thick wood, in a place new to me. My cart was upset and shattered, my oxen were entangled among the young trees, and there was none to help me. After a long spell of effort, I succeeded in getting my cart righted, my oxen disentangled, and again yoked to the cart. I now proceeded with my team to the place where I had, the day before, been chopping wood, and loaded my cart pretty heavily, thinking in this way to tame my oxen. I then proceeded on my way home. I had now consumed one half of the day. I got out of the woods safely, and now felt out of danger. I stopped my oxen to open the woods gate; and just as I did so, before I could get hold of my ox rope, the oxen again started, rushed through the gate, catching it between the wheel and the body of the cart, tearing it to pieces, and coming within a few inches of crushing me against the gate-post. Thus twice, in one short day, I escaped death by the merest chance. On my return, I told Mr. Covey what had happened, and how it happened. He ordered me to return to the woods again immediately. I did so, and he followed on after me. Just as I got into the

1. **in-hand . . . off-hand:** In a team of animals used for pulling loads, the animal trained to work on the left side is the in-hand one; the animal on the right is the off-hand one.

A Load of Brush (1912), Louis Paul Dessar. Oil on canvas, 28 ¼″ × 36 ¼″, National Museum of American Art, gift of John Gellatly, Smithsonian Institution, Washington, D.C./Art Resource, New York.

woods, he came up and told me to stop my cart, and that he would teach me how to trifle away my time, and break gates. He then went to a large gum-tree, and with his axe cut three large switches, and, after trimming them up neatly with his pocket-knife, he ordered me to take off my clothes. I made him no answer, but stood with my clothes on. He repeated his order. I still made him no answer, nor did I move to strip myself. Upon this he rushed at me with the fierceness of a tiger, tore off my clothes, and lashed me till he had worn out his switches, cutting me so savagely as to leave the marks visible for a long time after. This whipping was the first of a number just like it, and for similar offenses.

I lived with Mr. Covey one year. During the first six months, of that year, scarce a week passed without his whipping me. I was seldom free from a sore back. My awkwardness was almost always his excuse for whipping me. We were worked fully up to the point of endurance. Long before day we were up, our horses fed, and by the first approach of day we were off to the field with our hoes and ploughing teams. Mr. Covey gave us enough to eat, but scarce time to eat it. We were often less than five minutes taking our meals. We were often in the field from the first approach of day till its last lingering ray had left us; and at saving-fodder time, midnight often caught us in the field binding blades.[2]

Covey would be out with us. The way he used to stand it, was this. He would spend the most of his afternoons in bed. He would then come out fresh in the evening, ready to urge us on with his words, example, and frequently with the whip. Mr. Covey was one of the few slaveholders who could and did work with his hands. He was a hard-working man. He knew by himself just what a man or a boy could do. There was no deceiving him. His work went on in his absence almost as well as in his presence; and he had the faculty of making us feel that he was ever present with us. This he did by surprising us. He seldom approached the spot where we were at work openly, if he could do it secretly. He always aimed at taking us by surprise. Such was his cunning, that we used to call him, among ourselves, "the snake." When we were at work in

2. **saving-fodder . . . binding blades:** They are gathering and bundling ("binding") corn-plant leaves ("blades") to use as food for livestock ("fodder").

WORDS TO KNOW **faculty** (făk′əl-tē) *n.* a natural power or ability the cornfield, he would sometimes crawl on his hands and knees to avoid detection, and all at once he would rise nearly in our midst, and scream out, "Ha, ha! Come, come! Dash on, dash on!" This being his mode of attack, it was never safe to stop a single minute. His comings were like a thief in the night. He appeared to us as being ever at hand. He was under every tree, behind every stump, in every bush, and at every window, on the plantation. He would sometimes mount his horse, as if bound to St. Michael's, a distance of seven miles, and in half an hour afterwards you would see him coiled up in the corner of the wood-fence, watching every motion of the slaves. He would, for this purpose, leave his horse tied up in the woods. Again, he would sometimes walk up to us, and give us orders as though he was upon the point of starting on a long journey, turn his back upon us, and make as though he was going to the house to get ready; and, before he would get half way thither, he would turn short and crawl into a fence-corner, or behind some tree, and there watch us till the going down of the sun. . . .

My awkwardness was almost always his excuse for whipping me.

If at any one time of my life more than another, I was made to drink the bitterest dregs of slavery, that time was during the first six months of my stay with Mr. Covey. We were worked in all weathers. It was never too hot or too cold; it could never rain, blow, hail, or snow, too hard for us to work in the field. Work, work, work, was scarcely more the order of the day than of the night. The longest days were too short for him, and the shortest nights too long for him. I was somewhat unmanageable when I first went there, but a few months of this discipline tamed me. Mr. Covey succeeded in breaking me. I was broken in body, soul, and spirit. My natural elasticity was crushed, my intellect languished, the disposition to read departed, the cheerful spark that lingered about my eye died; the dark night of slavery closed in upon me; and behold a man transformed into a brute!

Sunday was my only leisure time. I spent this in a sort of beast-like stupor, between sleep and wake, under some large tree. At times I would rise up, a flash of energetic freedom would dart through my soul, accompanied with a faint beam of hope, that flickered for a moment, and then vanished. I sank down again, mourning over my wretched condition. I was sometimes prompted to take my life, and that of Covey, but was prevented by a combination of hope and fear. My sufferings on this plantation seem now like a dream rather than a stern reality. . . .

I have already intimated that my condition was much worse, during the first six months of my stay at Mr. Covey's, than in the last six. The circumstances leading to the change in Mr. Covey's course toward me form an epoch in my humble history. You have seen how a man was made a slave; you shall see how a slave was made a man. On one of the hottest days of the month of August, 1833, Bill Smith, William Hughes, a slave named Eli, and myself, were engaged in

WORDS TO KNOW

languish (lăng′gwĭsh) *v.* to become weak
intimate (ĭn′tə-māt) *v.* to make known indirectly; hint

fanning wheat.[3] Hughes was clearing the fanned wheat from before the fan. Eli was turning, Smith was feeding, and I was carrying wheat to the fan. The work was simple, requiring strength rather than intellect; yet, to one entirely unused to such work, it came very hard. About three o'clock of that day, I broke down; my strength failed me; I was seized with a violent aching of the head, attended with extreme dizziness; I trembled in every limb. Finding what was coming, I nerved myself up, feeling it would never do to stop work. I stood as long as I could stagger to the hopper[4] with grain. When I could stand no longer, I fell, and felt as if held down by an immense weight. The fan of course stopped; every one had his own work to do; and no one could do the work of the other, and have his own go on at the same time.

Mr. Covey was at the house, about one hundred yards from the treading-yard where we were fanning. On hearing the fan stop, he left immediately, and came to the spot where we were. He hastily inquired what the matter was. Bill answered that I was sick, and there was no one to bring wheat to the fan. I had by this time crawled away under the side of the post and rail-fence by which the yard was enclosed, hoping to find relief by getting out of the sun. He then asked where I was. He was told by one of the hands. He came to the spot, and, after looking at me awhile, asked me what was the matter. I told him as well as I could, for I scarce had strength to speak. He then gave me a savage kick in the side, and told me to get up. I tried to do so, but fell back in the attempt. He gave me another kick, and again told me to rise. I again tried, and succeeded in gaining my feet; but, stooping to get the tub with which I was feeding the fan, I again staggered and fell. While down in this situation, Mr. Covey took up the hickory slat with which Hughes had been striking off the half-bushel measure, and with it gave me a heavy blow upon the head, making a large wound, and the blood ran freely; and with this again told me to get up. I made no effort to comply, having now made up my mind to let him do his worst. In a short time after receiving this blow, my head grew better. Mr. Covey had now left me to my fate. At this moment I resolved, for the first time, to go to my master, enter a complaint, and ask his protection. In order to do this, I must that afternoon walk seven miles; and this, under the circumstances, was truly a severe undertaking. I was exceedingly feeble; made so as much by the kicks and blows which I received, as by the severe fit of sickness to which I had been subjected. I, however, watched my chance, while Covey was looking in an opposite direction, and started for St. Michael's. I succeeded in getting a considerable distance on my way to the woods, when Covey discovered me, and called after me to come back, threatening what he would do if I did not come. I disregarded both his calls and his threats, and made my way to the woods as fast as my feeble state would allow; and thinking I might be overhauled by him if I kept the road, I walked through the woods, keeping far enough from the road to avoid detection, and near enough to prevent losing my way. I had not gone far before my little strength again failed me. I could go no farther. I fell down, and lay for a considerable time. The blood was yet oozing from the wound on my head. For a time I thought I should bleed to death; and think now that I should have done so, but that the blood so matted my hair as to stop the wound. After lying there about three quarters of an hour, I nerved myself up again, and started on my way, through bogs and briers, barefooted and bareheaded, tearing my feet sometimes at nearly every step; and after a journey of about seven miles, occupying some five hours to perform it, I arrived at master's

3. **fanning wheat:** using a machine that blows air to separate grains of wheat from the unusable husks.

4. **hopper:** a funnel-shaped container for storing grain.

Head of a Negro (1777–1778), John Singleton Copley. Paint on canvas, 53.3 cm × 41.3 cm. The Detroit Institute of Arts, Founders Society Purchase, Gibbs-Williams Fund.

store. I then presented an appearance enough to affect any but a heart of iron. From the crown of my head to my feet, I was covered with blood. My hair was all clotted with dust and blood; my shirt was stiff with blood. My legs and feet were torn in sundry places with briers and thorns, and were also covered with blood. I suppose I looked like a man who had escaped a den of wild beasts, and barely escaped them. In this state I appeared before my master, humbly entreating him to interpose his authority for my protection. I told him all the circumstances as well as I could, and it seemed, as I spoke, at times to affect him. He would then walk the floor, and seek to justify Covey by saying he expected I deserved it. He asked me what I wanted. I told him, to let me get a new home; that as sure as I lived with Mr. Covey again, I should live with but to die with him; that Covey would surely kill me; he was in a fair way for it. Master Thomas ridiculed the idea that there was any danger of Mr. Covey's killing me, and said that he knew Mr. Covey; that he was a good man, and that he could not think of taking me from him; that, should he do so, he would lose the whole year's wages; that I belonged to Mr. Covey for one year, and that I must go back to him, come what might; and that I must not trouble him with any more stories, or that he would himself *get hold of me*. After threatening me thus, he gave me a very large dose of salts,[5] telling me that I might remain in St. Michael's that night, (it being quite late,) but that I must be off back to Mr. Covey's early in the morning; and that if I did not, he would *get hold of me*, which meant that he would whip me. I remained all night, and, according to his orders, I started off to Covey's in the morning, (Saturday morning,) wearied in body and broken in spirit. I got no supper that night, or breakfast that morning. I reached Covey's about nine o'clock; and just as I was getting over the fence that divided Mrs. Kemp's fields from ours, out ran Covey with his cowskin, to give me another whipping. Before he could reach me, I succeeded in getting to the cornfield; and as the corn was very high, it afforded me the means of hiding. He seemed very angry, and searched for me a long time. My behavior was altogether unaccountable. He finally gave up the chase, thinking, I suppose, that I must come home for something to eat; he would give himself no further trouble in looking for me. I spent that day mostly in the woods, having the alternative before me,—to go home and be whipped to death, or stay in the woods and be starved to death. That night, I fell in with Sandy Jenkins, a slave with whom I was somewhat acquainted. Sandy had a free wife who lived about four miles from Mr. Covey's; and it being Saturday, he was on his way to see her. I told him my circumstances, and he very kindly invited me to go home with him. I went home with him, and talked this whole matter over, and got his advice as to what course it was best for me to pursue. I found Sandy an old adviser. He told

I resolved to fight; and, suiting my action to the resolution, I seized Covey hard by the throat.

5. **salts:** mineral salts used to relieve faintness and headache or reduce swelling.

WORDS TO KNOW

sundry (sŭn′drē) *adj.* various; miscellaneous
interpose (ĭn′tər-pōz′) *v.* to interfere in order to help; intervene

me, with great solemnity, I must go back to Covey; but that before I went, I must go with him into another part of the woods, where there was a certain *root,* which, if I would take some of it with me, carrying it *always on my right side,* would render it impossible for Mr. Covey, or any other white man, to whip me. He said he had carried it for years; and since he had done so, he had never received a blow, and never expected to while he carried it. I at first rejected the idea, that the simple carrying of a root in my pocket would have any such effect as he had said, and was not disposed to take it; but Sandy impressed the necessity with much earnestness, telling me it could do no harm, if it did no good. To please him, I at length took the root, and, according to his direction, carried it upon my right side. This was Sunday morning. I immediately started for home; and upon entering the yard gate, out came Mr. Covey on his way to meeting.[6] He spoke to me very kindly, bade me drive the pigs from a lot near by, and passed on towards the church. Now, this singular conduct of Mr. Covey really made me begin to think that there was something in the *root* which Sandy had given me; and had it been on any other day than Sunday, I could have attributed the conduct to no other cause than the influence of that root; and as it was, I was half inclined to think the *root* to be something more than I at first had taken it to be. All went well till Monday morning. On this morning, the virtue of the *root* was fully tested. Long before daylight, I was called to go and rub, curry, and feed, the horses. I obeyed, and was glad to obey. But whilst thus engaged, whilst in the act of throwing down some blades from the loft, Mr. Covey entered the stable with a long rope; and just as I was half out of the loft, he caught hold of my legs, and was about tying me. As soon as I found what he was up to, I gave a sudden spring, and as I did so, he holding to my legs, I was brought sprawling on the stable floor. Mr. Covey seemed now to think he had me, and could do what he pleased; but at this moment—from whence came the spirit I don't know—I resolved to fight; and, suiting my action to the resolution, I seized Covey hard by the throat; and as I did so, I rose. He held on to me, and I to him. My resistance was so entirely unexpected, that Covey seemed taken all aback.[7] He trembled like a leaf. This gave me assurance, and I held him uneasy, causing the blood to run where I touched him with the ends of my fingers. Mr. Covey soon called out to Hughes for help. Hughes came, and, while Covey held me, attempted to tie my right hand. While he was in the act of doing so, I watched my chance, and gave him a heavy kick close under the ribs. This kick fairly sickened Hughes, so that he left me in the hands of Mr. Covey. This kick had the effect of not only weakening Hughes, but Covey also. When he saw Hughes bending over with pain, his courage quailed. He asked me if I meant to persist in my resistance. I told him I did, come what might; that he had used me like a brute for six months, and that I was determined to be used so no longer. With that, he strove to drag me to a stick that was lying just out of the stable door. He meant to knock me down. But just as he was leaning over to get the stick, I seized him with both hands by his collar, and brought him by a sudden snatch to the ground. By this time, Bill came. Covey called upon him for assistance. Bill wanted to know what he could do. Covey said, "Take hold of him, take hold of him!" Bill said his master hired him out to work, and not to help to whip me; so he left Covey and myself to fight our own battle out. We were at it for nearly two hours. Covey at length let me go, puffing and blowing at a great rate, saying that if I had not resisted, he would not have whipped me half so much. The truth was, that he had not whipped me at all. I considered him as getting entirely the worst end of the bargain; for he had drawn no

6. **meeting:** church service.

7. **taken all aback:** so surprised as to be unable to move or respond.

blood from me, but I had from him. The whole six months afterwards, that I spent with Mr. Covey, he never laid the weight of his finger upon me in anger. He would occasionally say, he didn't want to get hold of me again. "No," thought I, "you need not; for you will come off worse than you did before."

This battle with Mr. Covey was the turning-point in my career as a slave. It rekindled the few expiring embers of freedom, and revived within me a sense of my own manhood. It recalled the departed self-confidence, and inspired me again with a determination to be free. The gratification afforded by the triumph was a full compensation for whatever else might follow, even death itself. He only can understand the deep satisfaction which I experienced, who has himself repelled by force the bloody arm of slavery. I felt as I never felt before. It was a glorious resurrection, from the tomb of slavery, to the heaven of freedom. My long-crushed spirit rose, cowardice departed, bold defiance took its place; and I now resolved that, however long I might remain a slave in form, the day had passed forever when I could be a slave in fact. I did not hesitate to let it be known of me, that the white man who expected to succeed in whipping, must also succeed in killing me.

From this time I was never again what might be called fairly whipped, though I remained a slave four years afterwards. I had several fights, but was never whipped. ❖

RESPONDING OPTIONS

FROM PERSONAL RESPONSE *TO* CRITICAL ANALYSIS

REFLECT **1.** Write your impression of Frederick Douglass in your notebook to share in class.

RETHINK **2.** Explain what you think Douglass means when he states, "However long I might remain a slave in form, the day had passed forever when I could be a slave in fact" (page 454).

3. What do the choices Douglass makes reveal to you about his character?

Consider
- his resolve to ask Master Thomas for protection
- his agreeing to take the root from Sandy
- his decision to fight Mr. Covey

4. What would you say freedom means to Douglass?

Consider
- how he feels on Sunday, his only day of leisure
- the remark "You have seen how a man was made a slave; you shall see how a slave was made a man" (page 449)
- what he says in the next-to-last paragraph

5. What do the conflicts between Douglass and Mr. Covey reveal about slavery's effects on both slaves and masters?

6. How has reading this excerpt increased your understanding of the life of a plantation slave?

RELATE **7.** In what situations today might a person be inspired by Douglass's story?

LITERARY LINKS

Reread the next-to-last paragraph, in which Douglass describes his feelings of freedom and manhood after resisting Mr. Covey's brutality. Cite specific examples to explain how Douglass's ideas compare with Emerson's philosophy in the excerpt from "Self-Reliance" on page 291.

ANOTHER PATHWAY

Cooperative Learning

Work in a small group to prepare a student who has not done the reading (either in pretense or actuality) for a test on this selection. Each "teacher" has only three minutes to speak to the unprepared student and therefore should coordinate a presentation that covers the main events and ideas.

QUICKWRITES

1. Douglass founded an antislavery newspaper, the *North Star.* Based on your reading of this excerpt, write an outline for an **editorial** about slavery that Douglass might have printed in his newspaper.
2. Douglass's fight with Mr. Covey on page 453 was a turning point for him. Think of an incident from your own life that you would describe as a turning point. Write about this incident in a short **autobiographical sketch,** explaining why it changed your life.

PORTFOLIO *Save your writing. You may want to use it later as a springboard to a piece for your portfolio.*

LITERARY CONCEPTS

An **autobiography** is the story of a person's life written by that person. One of the challenges of writing a good autobiography is to combine **objective** (factual, unprejudiced) description with the expression of **subjective** (personal, emotional) feelings. In this excerpt from Douglass's autobiography, for example, his description of the circumstances of his service with Mr. Covey is told in surprisingly objective, unemotional language that is free of Douglass's personal attitudes, opinions, and speculations. He writes: "We were worked fully up to the point of endurance. Long before day we were up, our horses fed, and by the first approach of day we were off to the field with our hoes and ploughing teams. Mr. Covey gave us enough to eat, but scarce time to eat it."

In contrast, when Douglass relates his own subjective feelings, he uses emotionally charged words and figurative expressions that convey the experience of being a slave. For example, "It was a glorious resurrection, from the tomb of slavery, to the heaven of freedom."

Go back through the selection and select three passages that you think give an especially vivid picture of slavery. Then decide whether you think the most effective passages in this excerpt are primarily objective, subjective, or a combination of both. Share your conclusions.

ART CONNECTION

The 18th-century portrait on page 451 does not depict Frederick Douglass but an unnamed man, perhaps a servant of the artist, John Singleton Copley. Realistic portraits of African Americans were rare during the 18th and 19th centuries. What seems to be this man's state of mind? If you had to pull out a line from the Frederick Douglass selection to go with this painting, which line would you choose, and why?

Detail of *Head of a Negro* (1777–1778), John Singleton Copley.

ALTERNATIVE ACTIVITIES

1. ***Cooperative Learning***
   Collaborate with several classmates on a **picture book** for young readers. Recount this excerpt from Douglass's narrative, simplifying the language and illustrating important scenes. Then share the picture book with younger readers at home or in your school.
2. Retell an episode from this selection in a short **speech** Douglass might have delivered to the Anti-Slavery Society.

THE WRITER'S STYLE

Douglass wrote three versions of his autobiography, expanding his work in 1855 and 1881, as he became more famous and influential. Following is his explanation of the significance of the battle with Covey, from the 1881 version:

> It was a resurrection from the dark and pestiferous tomb of slavery, to the heaven of comparative freedom. I was no longer a servile coward, trembling under the frown of a brother worm of the dust, but my long-cowed spirit was roused to an attitude of independence. I had reached the point at which I was not afraid to die. This spirit made me a freeman in fact, though I still remained a slave in form. When a slave cannot be flogged, he is more than half free. He has a domain as broad as his own manly heart to defend, and he is really "a power on earth."

What differences do you notice between this passage and the corresponding passage from the original 1845 autobiography? Which passage do you think is more powerful? Explain why you think so.

ACROSS THE CURRICULUM

History Find another slave narrative, such as *Incidents in the Life of a Slave Girl,* by Harriet Jacobs, or *The History of Mary Prince, a West Indian Slave.* How does the writer's experience of slavery compare to Frederick Douglass's experience? Make comparisons in an oral presentation to your classmates.

Health In this excerpt, Douglass describes how he becomes ill while fanning wheat on one of the hottest days in August. Research the causes and effects of heat exhaustion and describe how to treat a person who suffers from it. Report your findings to the class.

WORDS TO KNOW

EXERCISE A Review the Words to Know in the boxes at the bottom of the selection pages. Then read each magazine article title below and write the vocabulary word that you would expect to find in that article.

1. "Sibling Rivalry: When to Step In"
2. "Making the Most of Your Natural Talents"
3. "Energy Boosters: Some Perfect Pick-Me-Ups"
4. "How to Get What You Want Without Having to Ask"
5. "Too Much Junk? How to Have a Successful Garage Sale"

EXERCISE B Team up with a partner to write a sentence that uses as many of the Words to Know as possible. Describing a humorous or unlikely situation is fine, as long as the words are used accurately. Then either act out this sentence as someone reads it to the class, or draw an illustration of it to show to your classmates.

FREDERICK DOUGLASS

1817?–1895

After having grown up in slavery in Maryland, Frederick Douglass escaped when he was 21 and went to New York City disguised as a sailor. Three years later, Douglass spoke so eloquently to the Massachusetts Anti-Slavery Society that they hired him to lecture about his experiences as a slave. Soon afterward, he became one of the country's most prominent antislavery speakers, devoting his life to fighting for abolition, suffrage, and civil rights. The publication of his autobiography, *Narrative of the Life of Frederick Douglass, an American Slave* (1845), resulted in widespread publicity and the possibility of recapture by his former owner. To remove himself from this dangerous situation, Douglass embarked on a two-year speaking tour in England, Scotland, Wales, and Ireland.

During Douglass's trip abroad, two friends raised the money to purchase his freedom. After returning to America in 1847 as a free man, Douglass settled in Rochester, New York, and founded an antislavery newspaper called the *North Star.* He continued lecturing against slavery and in 1848 addressed the first Women's Rights Convention in Seneca Falls, New York. As the Civil War began, Douglass was instrumental in recruiting the first African-American troops for the 54th Massachusetts Volunteers, including his own sons. During the war, he advised President Abraham Lincoln. Douglass held several government positions after the war, including the post of Minister to Haiti. Throughout his life, Douglass continued to champion civil rights for African Americans and for women.

OTHER WORKS *My Bondage and My Freedom, The Life and Times of Frederick Douglass,* "What to the Slave Is the Fourth of July?" "The Color Line"

PREVIEWING

POETRY

Stanzas on Freedom
James Russell Lowell

Free Labor
Frances Ellen Watkins Harper

PERSONAL CONNECTION

Name a current social or political situation you think should be protested. How would you attempt to generate public interest in solving this problem? In your notebook, write down ten ways to publicize issues, adding to the list shown here. Then rate the effectiveness of the methods you listed on a scale of 1 to 10, with 10 being the most effective.

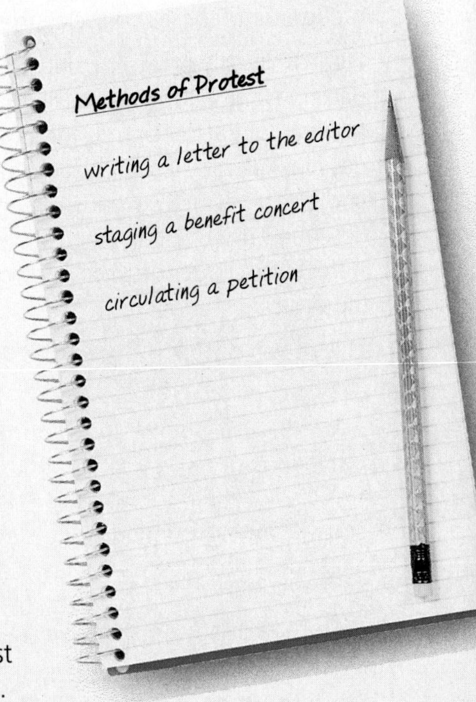

Methods of Protest
writing a letter to the editor
staging a benefit concert
circulating a petition

HISTORICAL CONNECTION

These two poems were written before the Civil War to protest slavery. In the United States, public opposition to slavery began in the 1680s when Quakers criticized slavery on religious grounds. Although the antislavery movement grew steadily in the 1700s, it gained momentum in the decades prior to the Civil War. By 1840, there were more than 2,000 antislavery societies and at least a dozen abolitionist newspapers. At the height of the movement, abolitionists in the North not only gave public lectures that denounced slavery but also published antislavery almanacs, magazines, and pamphlets. These publications often featured antislavery poems. In 1843, poet James Russell Lowell, a lifelong abolitionist, published "Stanzas on Freedom." Frances Ellen Watkins Harper, an antislavery lecturer and the most popular African-American poet of her time, published "Free Labor" in 1857.

Police and rioters break up a Boston abolitionist meeting in 1860 while Frederick Douglass continues his speech. The Granger Collection, New York.

READING CONNECTION

Reading Protest Poetry These works are examples of protest poetry, written primarily not to express personal feelings but to persuade readers to support a certain political cause or take a particular action. You might approach these poems much as you approached the political speeches, letters, and essays in the second part of Unit Two, "The Right to Be Free." On a first reading, get a sense of the general ideas and overall feeling of each poem. Then on a second or third reading, be more analytical. Figure out who the audience is intended to be. Determine what the poet wants this audience to do or feel, and why. Pay attention to your emotional reactions as you read and notice images or devices that trigger them.

• *HISTORICAL CONNECTION*

Stanzas on Freedom

JAMES RUSSELL LOWELL

Men! whose boast it is that ye
Come of fathers brave and free,
If there breathe on earth a slave,
Are ye truly free and brave?
If ye do not feel the chain,
When it works a brother's pain,
Are ye not base[1] slaves indeed,
Slaves unworthy to be freed?

Women! who shall one day bear
Sons to breathe New England air,
If ye hear, without a blush,
Deeds to make the roused blood rush
Like red lava through your veins,
For your sisters now in chains,—
Answer! are ye fit to be
Mothers of the brave and free?

Is true Freedom but to break
Fetters[2] for our own dear sake,
And, with leathern hearts, forget
That we owe mankind a debt?
No! true freedom is to share
All the chains our brothers wear,
And, with heart and hand, to be
Earnest to make others free!

They are slaves who fear to speak
For the fallen and the weak;
They are slaves who will not choose
Hatred, scoffing, and abuse,
Rather than in silence shrink
From the truth they needs must think;
They are slaves who dare not be
In the right with two or three.

1. **base:** having little or no honor, courage, or decency; low or inferior.
2. **fetters:** chains or other bonds.

FROM PERSONAL RESPONSE *TO* CRITICAL ANALYSIS

REFLECT **1.** What feeling were you left with at the end of this poem? Describe this feeling in your notebook.

RETHINK **2.** Judging from this poem, how do you think Lowell would define *freedom* and *slavery?*

Consider

- his view of the "free" men and women he addresses in the first and second stanzas
- his definition of "true freedom" in the third stanza
- whom he describes as slaves in the last stanza

3. What kind of people do you believe Lowell is speaking to in this protest poem—slaveholders, abolitionists, or some other group? Explain what he wants his audience to do.

RELATE **4.** Think again about the way Lowell uses the term *slaves* in the last stanza. Who in present-day America might Lowell view as slaves in this sense?

Free Labor

Frances Ellen Watkins Harper

I wear an easy garment,
O'er it no toiling slave
Wept tears of hopeless anguish,
In his passage to the grave.

And from its ample folds
Shall rise no cry to God,
Upon its warp and woof[1] shall be
No stain of tears and blood.

Oh, lightly shall it press my form,
Unladened[2] with a sigh,
I shall not 'mid its rustling hear,
Some sad despairing cry.

This fabric is too light to bear
The weight of bondsmen's[3] tears,
I shall not in its texture trace
The agony of years.

Too light to bear a smother'd sigh,
From some lorn[4] woman's heart,
Whose only wreath of household love
Is rudely torn apart.

Then lightly shall it press my form,
Unburden'd by a sigh;
And from its seams and folds shall rise,
No voice to pierce the sky,

And witness at the throne of God,
In language deep and strong,
That I have nerv'd[5] Oppression's hand,
For deeds of guilt and wrong.

1. **warp and woof:** In weaving cloth, the lengthwise threads ("warp") pass over and under the crosswise threads ("woof").
2. **unladened:** unburdened.
3. **bondsmen's:** slaves'.
4. **lorn:** forlorn; lonely and unhappy.
5. **nerv'd:** strengthened.

Collection of The New-York Historical Society.

From the collections of the Library of Congress.

RESPONDING OPTIONS

FROM PERSONAL RESPONSE *TO* CRITICAL ANALYSIS

REFLECT **1.** In your notebook, draw the image that the poem "Free Labor" creates in your mind. Share your drawing with classmates.

RETHINK **2.** In your own words, explain how "Free Labor" protests slavery.

Consider
- what the title might mean
- what makes the speaker's garment "easy" and "light"
- what it means to "have nerv'd Oppression's hand"
- what specific action the poet might want her audience to take

3. What kind of person might the speaker in this poem be? What would you guess about the speaker's past?

4. Which do you think are the most effective lines in this poem? Explain your choice.

RELATE **5.** If both "Stanzas on Freedom" and "Free Labor" had been read widely before the Civil War, which one do you think would be more likely to stir people to take a stand against slavery? Why?

6. What examples of art today do you think are comparable to the antislavery poems of the 19th century?

ANOTHER PATHWAY

Cooperative Learning

If Lowell and Harper had been making speeches instead of writing poetry, what would they have said? Work as a small group to paraphrase each of these poems as a short speech. Make sure the speeches state what the audience should do and why. Choose members of your group to deliver the two speeches to the class.

LITERARY CONCEPTS

A **symbol** is a person, a place, or an object that has a concrete meaning in itself and also stands for something beyond itself, such as an idea or a feeling. In "Dr. Heidegger's Experiment," for example, the blooming and fading rose symbolizes human life or life in general. What do you think the chains in "Stanzas on Freedom" might symbolize? What do you think the garment in "Free Labor" might symbolize? Work out possible interpretations with a partner, and share your thoughts in class.

QUICKWRITES

1. The first and second stanzas of "Stanzas on Freedom" begin "Men!" and "Women!" Imagine that the next stanza begins "Youths!" Complete such a **stanza,** writing what you believe would reflect a teenager's situation in those times. Read your stanza to classmates.
2. Write a **protest poem** to influence people to take a stand on some contemporary issue, perhaps the one you named in the Personal Connection activity on page 458. You might model your poem on Lowell's, making it a call to arms, or you might imitate Harper by developing one unusual image.

PORTFOLIO *Save your writing. You may want to use it later as a springboard to a piece for your portfolio.*

ALTERNATIVE ACTIVITIES

1. Create a **poster** to persuade people in the 1850s to take a stand against slavery. As an alternative, create a poster urging people today to take a stand against a modern injustice.
2. Hold an **antislavery rally.** Activities might include dramatic readings of poems by Lowell and Harper and a speech by Frederick Douglass. Display posters, distribute pamphlets, and chant slogans to support the cause.

ACROSS THE CURRICULUM

History Find out some of the methods—besides writing antislavery poems—that enslaved and free people used to protest slavery. Consider what you have already read in the slave narratives by Frederick Douglass (page 447) and Olaudah Equiano (page 101) and in Phillis Wheatley's "Letter to the Rev. Samson Occom" (page 216). Also consult other sources, such as history texts or books about slavery. Make a list of the methods and share it with classmates.

JAMES RUSSELL LOWELL

1819–1891

James Russell Lowell, a member of a prominent Massachusetts family, had achieved fame for his poetry and essays by the time he was 30. A well-known abolitionist, he wrote editorials for the antislavery newspaper the *Pennsylvania Freeman* and also contributed to the *National Anti-Slavery Standard* and other periodicals. In addition to "Stanzas on Freedom," Lowell wrote other antislavery poems, including "On the Capture of Fugitive Slaves Near Washington," and dealt with this subject in The Biglow Papers, a collection of poetic letters attributed to the fictional Hosea Biglow.

While Lowell's literary reputation grew, his life took a tragic turn when his wife and three of his four children died in the period from 1847 to 1853. In 1856 he became professor of modern languages at Harvard, succeeding Henry Wadsworth Longfellow in that post. A year later, he accepted the editorship of the newly founded magazine *Atlantic Monthly,* and he remarried. In 1877 Lowell was appointed U.S. minister to Spain, and he took a similar post in England three years later. After the death of his second wife in 1885, Lowell returned home, where he remained for the rest of his life.

OTHER WORKS *Poems, A Fable for Critics, My Study Windows, Under the Willows*

FRANCES ELLEN WATKINS HARPER

1825–1911

Called the "Bronze Muse," poet, novelist, lecturer, and social reformer Frances Ellen Watkins Harper was born free in the slave city of Baltimore, Maryland. Orphaned at the age of three, she was raised by her aunt and uncle and attended her uncle's private school until she was 13. Harper then began working as a housekeeper. Because the family for whom she worked owned a bookstore, Harper was able to read books in her spare time. When she was 14, she began to write poems and essays.

In 1850, Harper moved to Ohio and became a teacher, but she soon decided to devote herself to the abolitionist cause. She traveled throughout the North and the Midwest, giving lectures on the evils of slavery. Harper, who combined her artistic and political lives by reciting her poems during her speeches, wrote to a friend: "You would be amused to hear some of the remarks which my lectures call forth. 'She is a man,' . . . 'She is not colored, she is white. She is painted.'" After marrying in 1860, Harper settled on a farm in Ohio. After her husband's death in 1864, she began lecturing on the topic of equal rights for the newly freed slaves. Until the end of her life, Harper continued to fight for equality for African Americans and for women.

OTHER WORKS "The Slave Mother," *Poems on Miscellaneous Subjects, Iola Leroy*

PREVIEWING

FICTION

An Occurrence at Owl Creek Bridge

Ambrose Bierce

PERSONAL CONNECTION

This story is about a man who is facing death. It is often said that when people have a close brush with death, their lives flash before their eyes. What do you think might be the last thoughts of someone about to die? Would such a person think about the meaning of life, the loved ones left behind, or the immediate situation? Write your speculations in your notebook.

BIOGRAPHICAL CONNECTION

Ambrose Bierce enlisted in the Union Army at 18 and fought bravely in several major battles of the Civil War. After the war, he moved to San Francisco and began an equally distinguished career as a journalist. In "An Occurrence at Owl Creek Bridge," Bierce fictionalizes a real hanging that took place in 1862 at the time of the bloody battle of Shiloh in Tennessee. Bierce's firsthand knowledge of the Civil War and his training as a reporter can be seen in the opening two paragraphs of this story, in which he objectively describes the setting for a hanging that is about to occur, first in close-up and then from a distance.

READING CONNECTION

Understanding Sequence of Events This story is arranged in three numbered sections. Section I describes the preparations to hang the main character, section II is a flashback that explains how the character came to be in this situation, and section III returns to the moment of the hanging.

Using Your Reading Log To help you follow the sequence of events and clarify what happens in each section, use the reading strategy questions inserted throughout the story. Write down answers to the questions in your reading log. Also, jot down other thoughts and feelings that come to you, especially those that relate to the main character's last thoughts. After you finish reading, discuss some of your responses with classmates.

From the 1962 film *An Occurrence at Owl Creek Bridge*. National Film Archive, London.

AN OCCURRENCE AT OWL CREEK BRIDGE

Ambrose Bierce

I

A man stood upon a railroad bridge in northern Alabama, looking down into the swift water twenty feet below. The man's hands were behind his back, the wrists bound with a cord. A rope closely encircled his neck. It was attached to a stout cross-timber above his head and the slack fell to the level of his knees. Some loose boards laid upon the sleepers[1] supporting the metals of the railway supplied a footing for him and his executioners—two private soldiers of the Federal army, directed by a sergeant who in civil life may have been a deputy sheriff. At a short remove upon the same temporary platform was an officer in the uniform of his rank, armed. He was a captain. A sentinel at each end of the bridge stood with his rifle in the position known as "support," that is to say, vertical in front of the left shoulder, the hammer resting on the forearm thrown straight across the chest—a formal and unnatural position, enforcing an erect carriage of the body. It did not appear to be the duty of these two men to know what was occurring at the center of the bridge; they merely blockaded the two ends of the foot planking that traversed it.

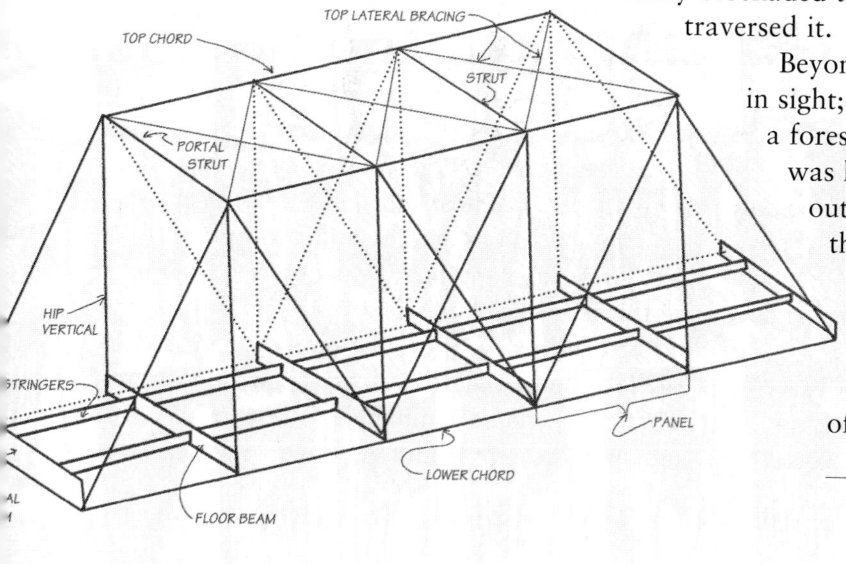

Beyond one of the sentinels nobody was in sight; the railroad ran straight away into a forest for a hundred yards, then, curving, was lost to view. Doubtless there was an outpost farther along. The other bank of the stream was open ground—a gentle acclivity topped with a stockade of vertical tree trunks, loopholed for rifles, with a single embrasure through which protruded the muzzle of a brass cannon commanding the

1. **sleepers:** railroad ties.

Union soldiers. From the collections of the Library of Congress.

bridge. Midway of the slope between bridge and fort were the spectators—a single company of infantry in line, at "parade rest," the butts of the rifles on the ground, the barrels inclining slightly backward against the right shoulder, the hands crossed upon the stock. A lieutenant stood at the right of the line, the point of his sword upon the ground, his left hand resting upon his right. Excepting the group of four at the center of the bridge, not a man moved. The company faced the bridge, staring stonily, motionless. The sentinels, facing the banks of the stream, might have been statues to adorn the bridge. The captain stood with folded arms, silent, observing the work of his subordinates, but making no sign. Death is a dignitary who when he comes announced is to be received with formal manifestations of respect, even by those most familiar with him. In the code of military etiquette silence and fixity are forms of deference.

The man who was engaged in being hanged was apparently about thirty-five years of age. He was a civilian, if one might judge from his habit, which was that of a planter. His features were good—a straight nose, firm mouth, broad forehead, from which his long, dark hair was combed straight back, falling behind his ears to the collar of his well-fitting frock-coat. He wore a mustache and pointed beard, but no whiskers; his eyes were large and dark gray, and had a kindly expression which one would hardly have expected in one whose neck was in the hemp. Evidently this was no vulgar assassin. The liberal military code makes provision for hanging many kinds of persons, and gentlemen are not excluded.

The preparations being complete, the two private soldiers stepped aside and each drew away the plank upon which he had been standing. The sergeant turned to the captain, saluted and placed himself immediately behind that officer, who in turn moved apart one pace. These movements left the condemned man and the sergeant standing on the two ends of the same plank, which spanned three of the cross-ties of the bridge. The end upon which the civilian stood almost, but not quite, reached a fourth. This plank had been held in place by the weight of the captain; it was now held by that of the sergeant. At a signal from the former the latter would step aside, the plank would tilt and the condemned man go down between two ties. The arrangement commended itself to his judgment as simple and effective. His face

WORDS TO KNOW

subordinate (sə-bôr′dn-ĭt) *n.* one who is lower in rank had not been covered nor his eyes bandaged. He looked a moment at his "unsteadfast footing," then let his gaze wander to the swirling water of the stream racing madly beneath his feet. A piece of dancing driftwood caught his attention and his eyes followed it down the current. How slowly it appeared to move! What a sluggish stream!

QUESTION

Whose thoughts and feelings does the narrator begin to tell about?

He closed his eyes in order to fix his last thoughts upon his wife and children. The water, touched to gold by the early sun, the brooding mists under the banks at some distance down the stream, the fort, the soldiers, the piece of drift—all had distracted him. And now he became conscious of a new disturbance. Striking through the thought of his dear ones was a sound which he could neither ignore nor understand, a sharp, distinct, metallic percussion like the stroke of a blacksmith's hammer upon the anvil; it had the same ringing quality. He wondered what it was, and whether immeasurably distant or near by—it seemed both. Its recurrence was regular, but as slow as the tolling of a death knell.[2] He awaited each stroke with impatience and—he knew not why—apprehension. The intervals of silence grew progressively longer; the delays became maddening. With their greater infrequency the sounds increased in strength and sharpness. They hurt his ear like the thrust of a knife; he feared he would shriek. What he heard was the ticking of his watch.

He unclosed his eyes and saw again the water below him. "If I could free my hands," he thought, "I might throw off the noose and spring into the stream. By diving I could evade the bullets and, swimming vigorously, reach the bank, take to the woods and get away home. My home, thank God, is as yet outside their lines; my wife and little ones are still beyond the invader's farthest advance."

As these thoughts, which have here to be set down in words, were flashed into the doomed man's brain rather than evolved from it the captain nodded to the sergeant. The sergeant stepped aside.

CLARIFY

What does the captain's nod mean?

II

Peyton Farquhar was a well-to-do planter, of an old and highly respected Alabama family. Being a slave owner and like other slave owners a politician he was naturally an original secessionist[3] and ardently devoted to the Southern cause. Circumstances of an imperious nature, which it is unnecessary to relate here, had prevented him from taking service with the gallant army that had fought the disastrous campaigns ending with the fall of Corinth,[4] and he chafed under the inglorious restraint, longing for the release of his energies, the larger life of the soldier, the opportunity for distinction. That opportunity, he felt, would come, as it comes to all in war time. Meanwhile he did what he could. No service was too humble for him to perform in aid of the South, no adventure too perilous for him to undertake if consistent with the character of a civilian who was at heart a soldier, and who in good faith and without too much qualification assented to at least a part of the frankly villainous dictum that all is fair in love and war.

One evening while Farquhar and his wife were sitting on a rustic bench near the entrance to his grounds, a gray-clad soldier rode up to the gate and asked for a drink of water. Mrs. Farquhar

2. **tolling of a death knell:** the slow, steady ringing of a bell at a funeral or to indicate death.

3. **secessionist** (sĭ-sĕsh′ə-nĭst): one who supported the withdrawal of Southern states from the Union.

4. **Corinth:** a town in Mississippi that was the site of a Civil War battle in 1862.

WORDS TO KNOW **evade** (ĭ-vād′) *v.* to escape or avoid

was only too happy to serve him with her own white hands. While she was fetching the water her husband approached the dusty horseman and inquired eagerly for news from the front.

"The Yanks are repairing the railroads," said the man, "and are getting ready for another advance. They have reached the Owl Creek bridge, put it in order and built a stockade on the north bank. The commandant has issued an order, which is posted everywhere, declaring that any civilian caught interfering with the railroad, its bridges, tunnels or trains will be summarily hanged. I saw the order."

"How far is it to the Owl Creek bridge?" Farquhar asked.

"About thirty miles."

"Is there no force on this side the creek?"

"Only a picket post[5] half a mile out, on the railroad, and a single sentinel at this end of the bridge."

"Suppose a man—a civilian and student of hanging—should elude the picket post and perhaps get the better of the sentinel," said Farquhar, smiling, "what could he accomplish?"

The soldier reflected. "I was there a month ago," he replied. "I observed that the flood of last winter had lodged a great quantity of driftwood against the wooden pier at this end of the bridge. It is now dry and would burn like tow."[6]

The lady had now brought the water, which the soldier drank. He thanked her ceremoniously, bowed to her husband and rode away. An hour later, after nightfall, he repassed the plantation, going northward in the direction from which he had come. He was a Federal scout.

CLARIFY

How did Farquhar come to be captured by the Union Army?

III

As Peyton Farquhar fell straight downward through the bridge he lost consciousness and was as one already dead. From this state he was awakened—ages later, it seemed to him—by the pain of a sharp pressure upon his throat, followed by a sense of suffocation. Keen, poignant[7] agonies seemed to shoot from his neck downward through every fiber of his body and limbs. These pains appeared to flash along well-defined lines of ramification[8] and to beat with an inconceivably rapid periodicity. They seemed like streams of pulsating fire heating him to an intolerable temperature. As to his head, he was conscious of nothing but a feeling of fullness—of congestion. These sensations were unaccompanied by thought. The intellectual part of his nature was already effaced; he had power only to feel, and feeling

5. **picket post:** the camp of soldiers who are assigned to guard against a surprise attack.
6. **tow:** coarse, dry fiber.
7. **poignant** (poin′yənt): physically painful.
8. **flash . . . ramification:** spread out rapidly along branches from a central point.

WORDS TO KNOW

summarily (sə-mĕr′ə-lē) *adv.* in a way that is quick and bypasses usual procedures was torment. He was conscious of motion. Encompassed in a luminous cloud, of which he was now merely the fiery heart, without material substance, he swung through unthinkable arcs of oscillation, like a vast pendulum. Then all at once, with terrible suddenness, the light about him shot upward with the noise of a loud plash; a frightful roaring was in his ears, and all was cold and dark. The power of thought was restored; he knew that the rope had broken and he had fallen into the stream. There was no additional strangulation; the noose about his neck was already suffocating him and kept the water from his lungs. To die of hanging at the bottom of a river!—the idea seemed to him ludicrous. He opened his eyes in the darkness and saw above him a gleam of light, but how distant, how inaccessible! He was still sinking, for the light became fainter and fainter until it was a mere glimmer. Then it began to grow and brighten, and he knew that he was rising toward the surface—knew it with reluctance, for he was now very comfortable. "To be hanged and drowned," he thought, "that is not so bad; but I do not wish to be shot. No; I will not be shot; that is not fair."

EVALUATE

Would these be the thoughts and sensations of a man on the brink of death?

He was not conscious of an effort, but a sharp pain in his wrist apprised him that he was trying to free his hands. He gave the struggle his attention, as an idler might observe the feat of a juggler, without interest in the outcome. What splendid effort!—what magnificent, what superhuman strength! Ah, that was a fine endeavor! Bravo! The cord fell away; his arms parted and floated upward, the hands dimly seen on each side in the growing light. He watched them with a new interest as first one and then the other pounced upon the noose at his neck. They tore it away and thrust it fiercely aside, its undulations resembling those of a water-snake. "Put it back, put it back!" He thought he shouted these words to his hands, for the undoing of the noose had been succeeded by the direst pang that he had yet experienced. His neck ached horribly; his brain was on fire; his heart, which had been fluttering faintly, gave a great leap, trying to force itself out at his mouth. His whole body was racked and wrenched with an insupportable anguish![9] But his disobedient hands gave no heed to the command. They beat the water vigorously with quick, downward strokes, forcing him to the surface. He felt his head emerge; his eyes were blinded by the sunlight; his chest expanded convulsively, and with a supreme and crowning agony his lungs engulfed a great draught of air, which instantly he expelled in a shriek!

He was now in full possession of his physical senses. They were, indeed, preternaturally keen and alert. Something in the awful disturbance of his organic system had so exalted and refined them that they made record of things never before perceived. He felt the ripples upon his face and heard their separate sounds as they struck. He looked at the forest on the bank of the stream, saw the individual trees, the leaves and the veining of each leaf—saw the very insects upon them: the locusts, the brilliant-bodied flies, the gray spiders stretching their webs from twig to twig. He noted the prismatic colors in all the dewdrops upon a million blades of grass. The humming of the gnats that danced above the eddies of the stream, the beating of the dragon-flies' wings, the strokes of the water-spiders' legs, like oars which had lifted their boat—all these made audible music. A fish slid along beneath his eyes and he heard the rush of its body parting the water.

---

9. **racked . . . anguish:** stretched and twisted with unendurable physical pain.

WORDS TO KNOW

ludicrous (lo͞o'dĭ-krəs) *adj.* laughably absurd; ridiculous
inaccessible (ĭn'ăk-sĕs'ə-bəl) *adj.* not obtained easily, if at all; unreachable
apprise (ə-prīz') *v.* to give notice to; inform
preternaturally (prē'tər-năch'ər-əl-ē) *adv.* more than naturally; extraordinarily

He had come to the surface facing down the stream; in a moment the visible world seemed to wheel slowly round, himself the pivotal point, and he saw the bridge, the fort, the soldiers upon the bridge, the captain, the sergeant, the two privates, his executioners. They were in silhouette against the blue sky. They shouted and gesticulated, pointing at him. The captain had drawn his pistol, but did not fire; the others were unarmed. Their movements were grotesque and horrible, their forms gigantic.

Suddenly he heard a sharp report and something struck the water smartly within a few inches of his head, spattering his face with spray. He heard a second report, and saw one of the sentinels with his rifle at his shoulder, a light cloud of blue smoke rising from the muzzle. The man in the water saw the eye of the man on the bridge gazing into his own through the sights of the rifle. He observed that it was a gray eye and remembered having read that gray eyes were keenest, and that all famous marksmen had them. Nevertheless, this one had missed.

A counter-swirl had caught Farquhar and turned him half round; he was again looking into the forest on the bank opposite the fort. The sound of a clear, high voice in a monotonous singsong now rang out behind him and came across the water with a distinctness that pierced and subdued all other sounds, even the beating of the ripples in his ears. Although no soldier, he had frequented camps enough to know the dread significance of that deliberate, drawling, aspirated chant; the lieutenant on shore was taking a part in the morning's work. How coldly and pitilessly—with what an even, calm intonation, presaging,[10] and enforcing tranquillity in the men—with what accurately measured intervals fell those cruel words:

"Attention, company! . . . Shoulder arms! . . . Ready! . . . Aim! . . . Fire!"

Farquhar dived—dived as deeply as he could. The water roared in his ears like the voice of Niagara, yet he heard the dulled thunder of the volley and, rising again toward the surface, met shining bits of metal, singularly flattened, oscillating slowly downward. Some of them touched him on the face and hands, then fell away, continuing their descent. One lodged between his collar and neck; it was uncomfortably warm and he snatched it out.

As he rose to the surface, gasping for breath, he saw that he had been a long time under water; he was perceptibly farther down stream—nearer to safety. The soldiers had almost finished reloading; the metal ramrods flashed all at once in the sunshine as they were drawn from the barrels, turned in the air, and thrust into their sockets. The two sentinels fired again, independently and ineffectually.

The hunted man saw all this over his shoulder; he was now swimming vigorously with the current. His brain was as energetic as his arms and legs; he thought with the rapidity of lightning.

"The officer," he reasoned, "will not make that martinet's[11] error a second time. It is as easy to dodge a volley as a single shot. He has probably already given the command to fire at will. God help me, I cannot dodge them all!"

An appalling plash within two yards of him was followed by a loud, rushing sound, *diminuendo*,[12] which seemed to travel back through the air to the fort and died in an explosion which stirred the very river to its deeps! A rising sheet of water curved over him, fell down upon him, blinded him, strangled him! The cannon had taken a hand in the game. As he shook his head free from the commotion of the smitten water he heard the deflected shot humming through the air ahead, and in an

10. **presaging** (prĕs′ĭj-ĭng): predicting.

11. **martinet** (mär′tn-ĕt′): strict disciplinarian; one who demands that regulations be followed exactly.

12. ***diminuendo*** (dĭ-mĭn′yo͞o-ĕn′dō) Italian: gradually decreasing in loudness.

WORDS TO KNOW

perceptibly (pər-sĕp′tə-blē) *adv.* in a way that can be perceived by the senses or the mind; noticeably

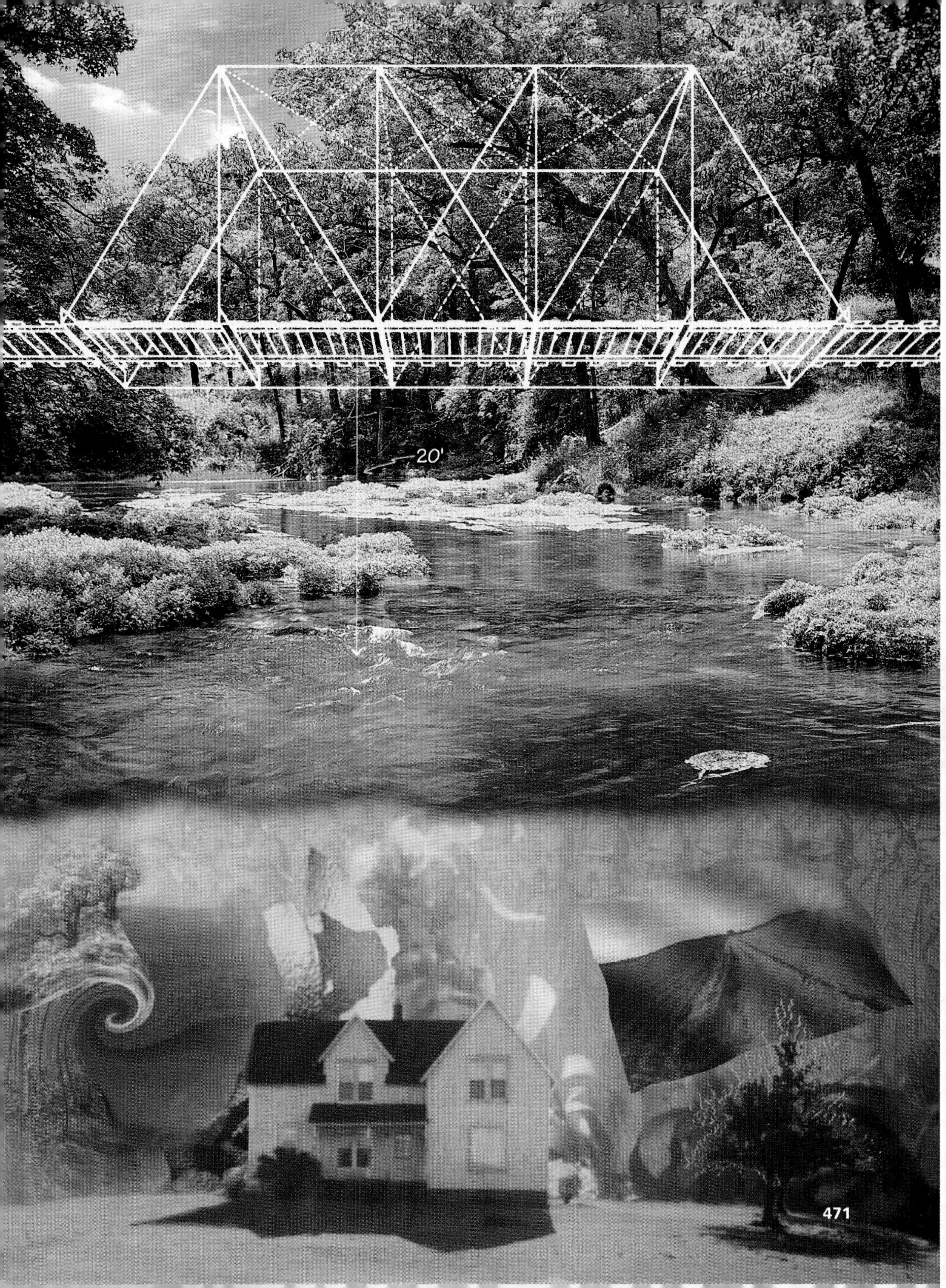
20'

instant it was cracking and smashing the branches in the forest beyond.

"They will not do that again," he thought; "the next time they will use a charge of grape.[13] I must keep my eye upon the gun; the smoke will apprise me—the report arrives too late; it lags behind the missile. That is a good gun."

Suddenly he felt himself whirled round and round—spinning like a top. The water, the banks, the forests, the now distant bridge, fort and men—all were commingled and blurred. Objects were represented by their colors only; circular horizontal streaks of color—that was all he saw. He had been caught in a vortex and was being whirled on with a velocity of advance and gyration that made him giddy and sick. In a few moments he was flung upon the gravel at the foot of the left bank of the stream—the southern bank—and behind a projecting point which concealed him from his enemies. The sudden arrest of his motion, the abrasion of one of his hands on the gravel, restored him, and he wept with delight. He dug his fingers into the sand, threw it over himself in handfuls and audibly blessed it. It looked like diamonds, rubies, emeralds; he could think of nothing beautiful which it did not resemble. The trees upon the bank were giant garden plants; he noted a definite order in their arrangement, inhaled the fragrance of their blooms. A strange, roseate light shone through the spaces among their trunks and the wind made in their branches the music of æolian harps.[14] He had no wish to perfect his escape—was content to remain in that enchanting spot until retaken.

A whiz and rattle of grapeshot among the branches high above his head roused him from his dream. The baffled cannoneer had fired him a random farewell. He sprang to his feet, rushed up the sloping bank, and plunged into the forest.

All that day he traveled, laying his course by the rounding sun. The forest seemed interminable; nowhere did he discover a break in it, not even a woodman's road. He had not known that he lived in so wild a region. There was something uncanny in the revelation.

By night fall he was fatigued, footsore, famishing. The thought of his wife and children urged him on. At last he found a road which led him in what he knew to be the right direction. It was as wide and straight as a city street, yet it seemed untraveled. No fields bordered it, no dwelling anywhere. Not so much as the barking of a dog suggested human habitation. The black bodies of the trees formed a straight wall on both sides, terminating on the horizon in a point, like a diagram in a lesson in perspective. Overhead, as he looked up through this rift in the wood, shone great golden stars looking unfamiliar and grouped in strange constellations. He was sure they were arranged in some order which had a secret and malign[15] significance. The wood on either side was full of singular noises, among which—once, twice, and again, he distinctly heard whispers in an unknown tongue.

EVALUATE

How do you account for the changes in Farquhar's surroundings?

His neck was in pain and lifting his hand to it he found it horribly swollen. He knew that it had a circle of black where the rope had bruised it. His eyes felt congested; he could no longer close them. His tongue was swollen with thirst; he relieved its fever by thrusting it forward from between his teeth into the cold air. How softly the turf had carpeted the untraveled avenue—he could no longer feel the roadway beneath his feet!

Doubtless, despite his suffering, he had fallen asleep while walking, for now he sees another scene—perhaps he has merely recovered from a

13. **grape:** short for *grapeshot,* a cluster of several small iron balls fired in one shot from a cannon.

14. **music of æolian** (ē-ō′lē-ən) **harps:** heavenly, or unearthly, music.

15. **malign** (mə-līn′): evil; harmful; threatening harm or evil.

WORDS TO KNOW

interminable (ĭn-tûr′mə-nə-bəl) *adj.* endless

Copyright © Ed Simpson/Tony Stone Images.

delirium.[16] He stands at the gate of his own home. All is as he left it, and all bright and beautiful in the morning sunshine. He must have traveled the entire night. As he pushes open the gate and passes up the wide white walk, he sees a flutter of female garments; his wife, looking fresh and cool and sweet, steps down from the veranda to meet him. At the bottom of the steps she stands waiting, with a smile of ineffable joy, an attitude of matchless grace and dignity. Ah, how beautiful she is! He springs forward with extended arms. As he is about to clasp her he feels a stunning blow upon the back of the neck; a blinding white light blazes all about him with a sound like the shock of a cannon—then all is darkness and silence!

Peyton Farquhar was dead; his body, with a broken neck, swung gently from side to side beneath the timbers of the Owl Creek bridge. ❖

CLARIFY

What kills Farquhar?

16. **delirium** (dĭ-lîr′ē-əm): a temporary state of extreme mental confusion, marked by hallucinations.

WORDS TO KNOW

ineffable (ĭn-ĕf′ə-bəl) *adj.* unable to be expressed in words

INSIGHT

Letter to Sarah Ballou

SULLIVAN BALLOU

Major Sullivan Ballou of the 2nd Rhode Island regiment wrote the following letter to his wife on July 14, 1861. He was killed about a week later at the first battle of Bull Run.

My very dear Sarah:

The indications are very strong that we shall move in a few days—perhaps tomorrow. Lest I should not be able to write again, I feel impelled to write a few lines that may fall under your eye when I shall be no more. . . .

I have no misgivings about, or lack of confidence in the cause in which I am engaged, and my courage does not halt or falter. I know how strongly American Civilization now leans on the triumph of the Government, and how great a debt we owe to those who went before us through the blood and sufferings of the Revolution. And I am willing—perfectly willing—to lay down all my joys in this life, to help maintain this Government, and to pay that debt. . . .

Sarah my love for you is deathless, it seems to bind me with mighty cables that nothing but Omnipotence could break; and yet my love of Country comes over me like a strong wind and bears me unresistibly on with all these chains to the battle field.

The memories of the blissful moments I have spent with you come creeping over me, and I feel most gratified to God and to you that I have enjoyed them so long. And hard it is for me to give them up and burn to ashes the hopes of future years, when, God willing, we might still have lived and loved together, and seen our sons grown up to honorable manhood, around us. I have, I know, but few and small claims upon Divine Providence, but something whispers to me—perhaps it is the wafted prayer of my little Edgar, that I shall return to my loved ones unharmed. If I do not my dear Sarah, never forget how much I love you, and when my last breath escapes me on the battle field, it will whisper your name. Forgive my many faults, and the many pains I have caused you. How thoughtless and foolish I have often times been! How gladly would I wash out with my tears every little spot upon your happiness. . . .

But, O Sarah! if the dead can come back to this earth and flit unseen around those they loved, I shall always be near you; in the gladdest days and in the darkest nights . . . *always, always,* and if there be a soft breeze upon your cheek, it shall be my breath, as the cool air fans your throbbing temple, it shall be my spirit passing by. Sarah do not mourn me dead; think I am gone and wait for thee, for we shall meet again. . . .

RESPONDING OPTIONS

FROM PERSONAL RESPONSE *TO* CRITICAL ANALYSIS

REFLECT **1.** Share your reaction to the ending of this story.

RETHINK **2.** How did the ending change the way you interpreted events in the story?

3. Why do you think Peyton Farquhar has the last thoughts he does before he dies?

4. Why are the Union soldiers hanging Farquhar? Cite evidence from section II to support your view.

5. Judging from this story, how do you think the author, Ambrose Bierce, views war?

Consider

- the statement about hanging and "the liberal military code" (page 466)
- Farquhar's sentiments about the Southern cause, and the result of these sentiments
- the action of the Federal scout who visits Farquhar

6. How would changing the order of the three numbered sections affect the story?

RELATE **7.** Compare Farquhar's and Sullivan Ballou's last thoughts to the ones you imagined before reading.

ANOTHER PATHWAY

Cooperative Learning

This story was adapted as a film in 1962. What parts are easy to visualize as a movie? What parts are harder to visualize? What scenery, sound effects, and costumes would bring the story to life? Who might play the different characters? Work with a small group of classmates to plan your own film version.

LITERARY LINKS

Ambrose Bierce is thought to have been influenced by Edgar Allan Poe. What similarities and differences do you see in their styles and concerns?

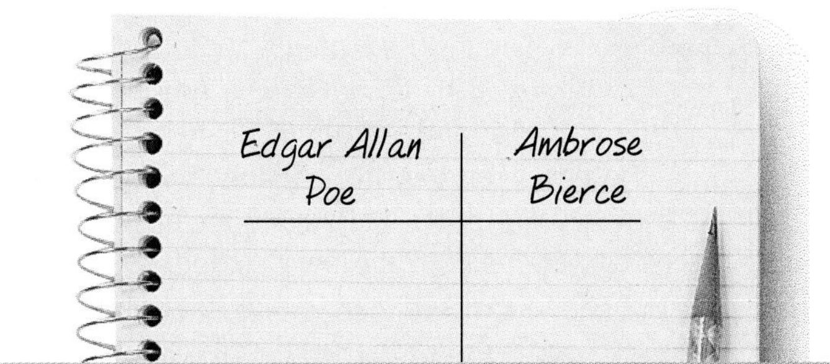

QUICKWRITES

1. Imagine that Peyton Farquhar is allowed to communicate with his wife before being executed. Write a **letter** in which he expresses his last thoughts to her. You may wish to use Sullivan Ballou's letter as a model.
2. Draft an **evaluation** of Ambrose Bierce as a storyteller, based on "An Occurrence at Owl Creek Bridge." Consider how convincing you find his description of Farquhar's last thoughts, how you feel about the ending, and what meaning you draw from the story.

PORTFOLIO *Save your writing. You may want to use it later as a springboard to a piece for your portfolio.*

LITERARY CONCEPTS

Point of view refers to the narrative perspective from which events in a story are told. In the **third-person point of view,** events are related by a voice outside the action, not by one of the characters. Part of the power of Bierce's story comes from his manipulation of third-person point of view. Notice that the first three paragraphs are told from a **third-person omniscient,** or all-knowing, point of view, as though the narrator is an objective observer of the entire scene. Then, in the fourth paragraph, the point of view subtly shifts to focus on Peyton Farquhar's personal thoughts and sensations as he waits to be executed. This focus on one character's thoughts, observations, and feelings is called **third-person limited** point of view. In the last paragraph of section I, the point of view shifts back to show the actions of the captain and the sergeant—actions that "the doomed man," Farquhar, may not be aware of.

Analyze the point of view in sections II and III of the story. Notice where the point of view shifts from omniscient to limited and back again. Do the shifts heighten or decrease the level of suspense?

WORDS TO KNOW

EXERCISE A For each phrase in the first column, write the letter of the synonymous phrase from the second column.

1. dodge the servant	a. apprise the spies
2. favored the ludicrous	b. wager on the major
3. interminable noise	c. evade the maid
4. notify the secret agents	d. preferred the absurd
5. bet on the general's subordinate	e. ceaseless peacelessness

EXERCISE B Draw cartoons that illustrate the meaning of the following vocabulary words: **ineffable, inaccessible, preternaturally, perceptibly, summarily.**

AMBROSE BIERCE

1842–1914?

Ambrose Bierce was born into a large, poor, intensely religious family and spent his early years on an Indiana farm. After a miserable childhood, he left home for good at the age of 15 and landed a job at a newspaper, working as a typesetter. Three years later, he enlisted in the Union Army and served brilliantly, fighting in some of the fiercest battles of the Civil War and receiving numerous citations for bravery.

After the war, Bierce worked as a surveyor in the West. He moved to San Francisco in 1866, where he worked for a newspaper and published some of his short stories. He married in 1872 and lived in London for several years with his wife. He earned the nickname "Bitter Bierce" for his cynical humor and cruel wit. His finest stories, such as "An Occurrence at Owl Creek Bridge" published in *Tales of Soldiers and Civilians* in 1891, concern the ironic futility of war.

During the latter part of his life, Bierce continued to publish short stories, essays, and poems and to work as a journalist, acting as a political reporter and columnist for the San Francisco *Examiner.* At the age of 71, Bierce revisited Civil War battle sites where he had fought and then went to Mexico to report on the Mexican Revolution as an observer with Pancho Villa's rebel army. He never returned to the United States, and all trace of him vanished. Before he left he wrote to a niece, "If you hear of my being stood up against a Mexican stone wall and shot to rags, please know that I think that a pretty good way to depart this life. It beats old age, disease or falling down the cellar stairs."

OTHER WORKS *Black Beetles in Amber, Can Such Things Be?, The Devil's Dictionary*

LASERLINKS
• *HISTORICAL CONNECTION*

PREVIEWING

DRAMA

The Clod

Lewis Beach

PERSONAL CONNECTION

Consider what you know about war from your reading, from news reports, from television shows or movies, or from your own experiences. What do you think it would be like to live in a combat zone during a war? What dangers might you face? Complete a chart like this one, adding your ideas about what it might be like to be a civilian during wartime.

Physical Effects	Emotional Effects	Economic Effects
loss of freedom	anxiety	lack of goods to buy

HISTORICAL CONNECTION

The Clod shows how the Civil War affects an ordinary farm couple, Mary and Thaddeus Trask. Civilians, like the Trasks in this play, paid a high price during the war. Marching through the South, the Union Army waged the world's first "total war," ransacking homes, destroying crops, stealing livestock, and burning towns. Union General W. T. Sherman said, "We are not only fighting hostile armies but a hostile people, and must make old and young, rich and poor, feel the hard hand of war." The Confederate Army, too, made life difficult for civilians. Southern farm families were taxed beyond their means to provide food for Confederate soldiers. The Confederate government's Impressment Act of 1863 allowed agents to seize food, horses, and other needed supplies from civilians. Those who lived in the states where fighting took place faced the loss of their personal belongings, homelessness, severe food shortages, and even death. As you read this drama, notice the Civil War's impact on the characters.

A Southern family displaced by the Civil War. From the Meserve Collection, Library of Congress.

READING CONNECTION

Conventions of Drama

Most dramas follow similar conventions, or rules, in how they are presented on stage and in written form. For example, a play is generally performed by actors in front of an audience; the play is usually written as a script first. As the reader of a script, you do not have the advantage of seeing and hearing a live performance. You are more like actors and directors imagining what the set looks like and interpreting the characters. An understanding of basic dramatic conventions—such as the functions of stage directions and dialogue—can help you gain some of the pleasure an audience feels while at the same time sharing the excitement actors and directors feel at bringing a play to life.

Interpreting Stage Directions At the beginning of a script, there is often a lengthy set of instructions, or stage directions. These usually tell the time and place of the action; for example, *"It is ten o'clock in the evening, September, 1863."* They also describe characters, scenery, props, lighting, costumes, music, or sound effects. When you first start reading a play, take time to study the opening stage directions carefully, and try to visualize what the stage will look like. For example, the stage directions in *The Clod* detail stark visual images that help establish mood and reinforce important themes developed in the play.

The moon shines into the room through the windows, but at no time is the kitchen brightly lighted. The characters appear as silhouettes except when they stand near the candle or the lantern, and then the lights throw huge shadows on the roughly plastered walls.

What kind of mood is created by the high contrast between darkness and light and by the looming shadows on the walls?

Because another important function of stage directions is to explain how characters move and speak, these instructions appear not only at the beginning, but throughout a script. You may have noticed that they are set in different type, usually italic. When interspersed with lines of speech, they are separated by parentheses or brackets.

Analyzing Dialogue In a play, the story is told primarily through dialogue, the words spoken by the characters. To make speech sound realistic, playwrights often use **dialect,** the distinct form of a language as it is spoken in one geographical area or by a particular social or ethnic group. A group's dialect is reflected in its characteristic pronunciations, vocabulary, expressions, and grammatical constructions. When trying to reproduce a given dialect, writers often use unconventional spellings to suggest the way words actually sound. The playwright does this in *The Clod,* so try to hear the words as you read them.

Thaddeus. I'd help if I could, but it ain't my fault if the Lord seed fit t' lay me up so I'm always ailin'. (*rises lazily*) Yuh better try an' take things easy t'morrow.

What do the character's words and way of speaking suggest about him?

The Clod

Lewis Beach

Cast of Characters—

Thaddeus Trask
Mary Trask
A Northern private
A Southern sergeant
Dick, a Southern private

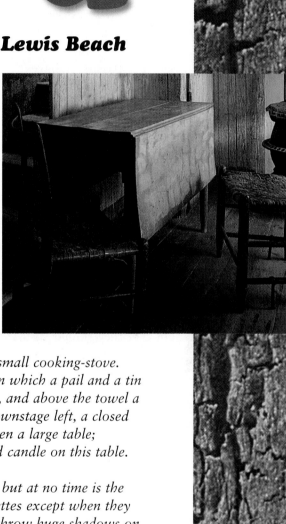

Scene— *The kitchen of a farmhouse on the borderline between the Northern and Southern states. It is ten o'clock in the evening, September, 1863.*

The back wall is broken at stage left by the projection at right angles of a partially enclosed staircase; the four steps leading to the landing cut into the room. Underneath the enclosed part of the stairway, a cubby-hole; in front of it a small table which partially hides the door. To the left of the table a kitchen chair. A door, leading to the yard, is the center of the unbroken wall, back. To the right of the door, a cupboard; to the left, a small cooking-stove. Two windows in the right wall. Between them a bench on which a pail and a tin dipper stand. Above the bench a towel hanging on a nail, and above the towel a double-barreled shotgun suspended on two pegs. Well downstage left, a closed door leading to a second room. In the center of the kitchen a large table; straight-backed chairs to the right and left of it. A lighted candle on this table. ("Right" and "left" are the actors' right and left.)

The moon shines into the room through the windows, but at no time is the kitchen brightly lighted. The characters appear as silhouettes except when they stand near the candle or the lantern, and then the lights throw huge shadows on the roughly plastered walls. When the door, back, is opened one sees a bit of the farmyard, desolate even in the moonlight.

As the curtain rises, Thaddeus Trask, *a man of sixty-odd years, short and thick-set, slow in speech and action, yet in perfect health, sits at the left of the center table. He is pressing tobacco into his corncob pipe. He lights it with the candle. After a moment,* Mary Trask, *a tired, emaciated woman, whose years equal her husband's, enters from the yard carrying a heavy pail of water and a lighted*

WORDS TO KNOW

emaciated (ĭ-mā'shē-ā'tĭd) *adj.* extremely thin, especially as a result of starvation *lantern. She puts the pail on the bench and hangs the lantern above it; then crosses to the stove.*

Mary. Ain't got wood 'nough fer breakfast, Thad.

Thaddeus. I'm too tired t' go out now. Wait 'til mornin'. (*Pause.* Mary *lays the fire in the stove.*) Did I tell yuh that old man Reed saw three Southern troopers pass his house this mornin'?

Mary (*takes coffee-pot from stove, crosses to bench, fills pot with water*). I wish them soldiers would git out o' the neighborhood. Whenever I see 'em passin', I have t' steady myself 'gainst somethin' or I'd fall. I couldn't hardly breathe yesterday when them Southerners came after fodder.[1] I'd died if they'd spoke t' me.

Thaddeus. Yuh needn't be afraid o' Northern soldiers.

Mary (*carries coffee-pot to stove*). I hate 'em all—Union or Southern. I can't make head or tail t' what all this fightin's 'bout. An' I don't care who wins, so long as they git through, an' them soldiers stop stealin' our corn an' potatoes.

Thaddeus. Yuh can't hardly blame 'em if they're hungry, ken yuh?

Mary. It ain't right that they should steal from us poor folk. *(lifts a huge gunny sack of potatoes from the table, and begins setting the table for breakfast, getting knives, forks, spoons, plates, cups and saucers—two of each—from the cupboard)* We have hard 'nough times t' make things meet now. I ain't set down onct today 'cept fer meals. An' when I think o' the work I got t' do t'morrow, I ought t' been in bed hours ago.

Thaddeus. I'd help if I could, but it ain't my fault if the Lord seed fit t' lay me up so I'm always ailin'. (*rises lazily*) Yuh better try an' take things easy t'morrow.

Mary. It's well enough t' say, but them apples is got t' be picked an' the rest o' the potatoes sorted. If I could sleep at night it'd be all right, but with them soldiers 'bout, I can't.

Thaddeus (*crosses right; fondly handles his gun*). Golly, wish I'd see a flock o' birds.

Mary (*nervously*). I'd rather go without than hear yuh fire. I wish yuh didn't keep it loaded.

Thaddeus. Yuh know I ain't got time t' stop an' load when I see the birds. They don't wait fer yuh. (*hangs gun on wall, drops into his chair; dejectedly*) Them pigs has got t' be butchered.

Mary. Wait 'til I git a chance t' go t' sister's. I can't stand it t' hear 'em squeal.

Thaddeus (*pulling off his boots—grunting meanwhile*). Best go soon then, 'cause they's fat as they'll ever be, an' there ain't no use in wastin' feed on 'em. (*pause; rises*) Ain't yuh 'most ready fer bed?

Mary. Go on up. (Thaddeus *takes the candle in one hand, his boots in the other, and climbs the stairs.* Mary *speaks when he reaches the landing.*) An' Thad, try not t' snore t'night.

1. **fodder:** feed for livestock.

You better not lie to me or it'll

Thaddeus. Poke me if I do. (*disappears*)

(Mary *fills the kettle with water and puts it on the stove; closes the door, back; takes the lantern from the wall and tries twice before she succeeds in blowing it out. Puts the lantern on the table before the cubby-hole. Slowly drags herself up the stairs, pausing a moment on the top step for breath before she disappears. There is a silence. Then the door, back, is opened a trifle and a man's hand is seen. Cautiously the door is opened wide and a young Northern private stands silhouetted on the threshold. He wears a dirty uniform, and a bloody bandage is tied about his head. He is wounded, sick, and exhausted. He stands at the door a moment, listening intently; then hastily moves to the center table looking for food. He bumps against a chair and mutters an oath. Finding nothing on the table, he hurries to the cupboard. Suddenly the galloping of horses is heard in the distance. The* Northerner *starts, then rushes to the window nearer the audience. For a moment the sound ceases, then it begins again, growing gradually louder and louder. The* Northerner *hurries into the room at the left. Horses and voices are heard in the yard, and almost immediately heavy, thundering knocks sound on the door, back. The men at the door grow impatient and push the door open. A large, powerfully built Southern* Sergeant, *and a smaller, younger trooper of the same army enter.* Thaddeus *appears on the stairs, carrying a candle.*)

Sergeant (*to* Thaddeus*; not unkindly*). Sorry, my friend, but you were so darn slow 'bout openin' the door that we had to walk in. Has there been a Northern soldier round here today?

Thaddeus (*timidly*). I ain't seed one. (*comes down the stairs*)

Sergeant. Have you been here all day?

Thaddeus. I ain't stirred from the place.

Sergeant. Call the rest of your family down.

go tough with you.

Thaddeus. My wife's all there is. (*goes to foot of stairs, and calls loudly and excitedly*) Mary! Mary! Come down. Right off!

Sergeant. You better not lie to me or it'll go tough with you.

Thaddeus. I swear I ain't seed no one. (Mary *comes downstairs slowly. She is all atremble.*) Say, Mary, you was here—

Sergeant. Keep still, man. I'll do the talkin'. (*to* Mary) You were here at the house all day? (Mary *is very frightened and embarrassed, but after a moment manages to nod her head slowly.*) You didn't take a trip down to the store? (Mary *shakes her head slowly.*) Haven't you got a tongue?

Mary (*with difficulty*). Y-e-s.

Sergeant. Then use it. The Northern soldier who came here a while ago was pretty badly wounded, wasn't he?

Mary. I—I—no one's been here.

Sergeant. Come, come, woman, don't lie. (Mary *shows a slight sign of anger.*) He had a bad cut in his forehead, and you felt sorry for him, and gave him a bite to eat.

Mary (*haltingly*). No one's been near the house t'day.

Sergeant (*trying a different tone*). We're not going to hurt him, woman. He's a friend of ours. We want to find him, and put him in a hospital, don't we, Dick? (*turning to his companion*)

Dick. He's sick and needs to go to bed for a while.

Mary. He ain't here.

Sergeant. What do you want to lie for?

Mary (*quickly*). I ain't lyin'. I ain't seed no soldier. (*She stands rooted to the spot where she stopped when she came downstairs. Her eyes are still fixed on the* Sergeant.)

Sergeant. I reckon you know what'll happen if you are hidin' the spy.

Thaddeus. There ain't no one here. We both been

here all day, an' there couldn't no one come without our knowin' it. What would they want round here anyway?

Sergeant. We'll search the place, Dick.

Mary (*quickly*). Yuh ain't got no—

Sergeant (*sharply*). What's that, woman?

Mary. There ain't no one here, an' yer keepin' us from our sleep.

Sergeant. Your sleep? This is an affair of life and death. Get us a lantern. (Thaddeus *moves to the small table and lights the lantern with the candle which he holds in his hand. He gives the lantern to the* Sergeant. *The* Sergeant *notices the door to the cubby-hole.*) Ha! Tryin' to hide the door, are you, by puttin' a table in front of it? You can't fool me. (*to* Thaddeus) Pull the table away and let's see what's behind the door.

Thaddeus. It's a cubby-hole an' ain't been opened in years.

Sergeant (*sternly and emphatically*). I said to open the door. (Thaddeus *sets the candle on the larger table, moves the smaller table to the right, and opens the door to the cubby-hole.* Mary *is angry. The* Sergeant *takes a long-barreled revolver from his belt and peers into the cubby-hole. Returning his revolver to his belt.*) We're goin' to tear this place to pieces 'til we find him. You might just as well hand him over now.

Mary. There ain't no one here.

Sergeant. All right. Now we'll see. Dick, you stand guard at the door. (Dick *goes to the door, back, and stands gazing out into the night—his back to the audience. To* Thaddeus.) Come along, man. I'll have to look at the upstairs. (*to* Mary) You sit down in that chair. (*points to chair at right of center table, and feels for a sufficiently strong threat.*) Don't you stir or I'll—I'll set fire to your house. (*to* Thaddeus) Go on ahead.

(Thaddeus *and the* Sergeant *go upstairs.* Mary *sinks lifelessly into the chair. She is the picture of fear. She sits facing left. Suddenly she leans forward. She opens her eyes wide, and draws her breath sharply. She opens her mouth as though she would scream, but makes no sound. The* Northerner *has opened the door. He enters slowly and cautiously, his gun pointed at* Mary. Dick *cannot see him because of the jog in the wall.* Mary *only stares in bewilderment at the* Northerner, *as he, with eyes fixed appealingly on her, opens the door to the cubby-hole and crawls inside.*)

Dick. Woman!

Mary (*almost with a cry, thinking that* Dick *has seen the* Northerner). Yes.

Dick. Have you got an apple handy? I'm starved.

(Mary *rises and moves to the cupboard. The* Sergeant *and* Thaddeus *come downstairs. The* Sergeant, *seeing that* Mary *is not where he left her, looks about rapidly and discovers her at the cupboard.*)

Sergeant. Here, what did I tell you I'd do if you moved from that chair?

Mary (*terrified*). Oh, I didn't—I only—he wanted—

Dick. It's all right, Sergeant. I asked her to get me an apple.

Sergeant. Take this lantern and search the barn. (Dick *takes the lantern from the* Sergeant *and goes out, back. To* Thaddeus.) Come in here with me. (*The* Sergeant *picks up the candle. He and* Thaddeus *move toward the door, left. As though in a stupor,* Mary *starts to follow.*) Sit down! (Mary *drops into the chair at the right of the table. The* Sergeant *and* Thaddeus *go into the room, left. They can be heard moving furniture about.* Mary *sees a pin on the floor. She stoops, picks it up, and fastens it in her belt. The* Sergeant *and* Thaddeus *return.*) If I find him now after all the trouble you've given me, you know what'll

WORDS TO KNOW

emphatically (ĕm-făt'ĭk-lē) *adv.* forcefully; strongly
stupor (sto͞o'pər) *n.* a state of mental numbness, as from shock

Confederate soldiers. From the collections of the Library of Congress.

happen. There's likely to be two dead men and a woman, instead of only the Yankee.

Dick (*bounding into the room*). Sergeant!

Sergeant. What is it? (Dick *hurries to the* Sergeant *and says something to him in a low voice. The* Sergeant *smiles.*) Now, my good people, how did that horse get here?

Thaddeus. What horse?

Dick. There's a horse in the barn with a saddle on his back. I swear he's been ridden lately.

Thaddeus (*amazed*). There is?

Sergeant. You know it. (*to* Mary) Come, woman, who drove that horse here?

Mary (*silent for a moment, her eyes on the floor*). I don't know. I didn't hear nothin'.

Thaddeus (*moving toward the door*). Let me go an' see.

Sergeant (*pushing* Thaddeus *back*). No, you don't. You two have done enough to justify the harshest measures. Show us the man's hiding place.

Thaddeus. If there's anybody here, he's come in the night without our knowin' it. I tell yuh I didn't see anybody, an' she didn't, an'—

Sergeant (*has been watching* Mary). Where is he?

(*His tone makes* Thaddeus *jump. There is a pause, during which* Mary *seems trying to compose herself. Then slowly she lifts her eyes and looks at the* Sergeant.)

Mary. There ain't nobody in the house 'cept us two.

Sergeant (*to* Dick). Did you search all the outbuildings?

Dick. Yes. There's not a trace of him except the horse.

Sergeant (*wiping the perspiration from his face; speaks with apparent deliberation at first, but becomes very emphatic*). He didn't have much of a start of us, and I think he was wounded. A farmer down the road said he heard hoof-beats. The man the other side of you heard nothin', *and the horse is in your barn.* (*slowly draws his revolver and points it at* Thaddeus) There are ways of making people confess.

Thaddeus (*covering his face with his hands*). For God's sake, don't. I know that horse looks bad, but, as I live, I ain't heard a sound, or seen anybody. I'd give the man up in a minute if he was here.

Sergeant (*lowering his gun*). Yes, I guess you would. You wouldn't want me to hand you and your wife over to our army to be shot down like dogs. (Mary *shivers.* Sergeant *swings round sharply and points the gun at* Mary.) Your wife knows where he's hid.

Mary (*breaking out in irritating, rasping voice*). I'm sure I wish I did. I'd tell yuh quick an' git yuh out o' here. 'Tain't no fun fer me t' have yuh prowlin' all over my house, trackin' it up with yer dirty boots. Yuh ain't got no right t' torment me like this. Lord knows how I'll git my day's work done, if I can't have my sleep out.

Sergeant (*has been gazing at her in astonishment; lowers his gun*). Good God! Nothing but her own petty existence. (*in different voice to* Mary) I'll have to ask you to get us some breakfast. We're famished. (*With relief but showing some anger,* Mary *turns to the stove. She lights the fire and puts more coffee in the pot.*) Come, Dick, we better give our horses some water. They're all tired out. (*in lower voice*) The man isn't here. If he were he couldn't get away while we're in the yard. (*to* Thaddeus) Get us a pail to give the horses some water in. (*Sees the pails on the bench. Picks one of them up and moves toward the door.*)

Mary. That ain't the horses' pail.

Sergeant (*to* Thaddeus). Come along. You can help.

Mary (*louder*). That's the drinkin' water pail.

Sergeant. That's all right.

(*The* Sergeant, Thaddeus, *and* Dick—*carrying the lantern—go out back.* Mary *needs more wood for the fire, so she follows in a moment. When she has disappeared, the* Northerner *drags himself from the cubby-hole.* Mary *returns with an armful of wood.*)

Mary (*sees the* Northerner; *shows no sympathy for him in this speech nor during the entire scene*). Yuh git back! Them soldiers'll see yuh.

Northerner. Some water. Quick. (*falls into chair at left of table*) It was so hot in there.

Mary (*gives him water in the dipper*). Don't yuh faint here! If them soldiers git yuh, they'll kill me an' Thad. Hustle an' git back in that cubby-hole. (*turns quickly to the stove*)

(*The* Northerner *drinks the water, puts the dipper on the table. Then, summoning all his strength, rises and crosses to* Mary. *He touches her on the sleeve.* Mary *is so startled that she jumps and utters a faint cry.*)

The lives of thirty

Northerner. Be still or they'll hear you. How are you going to get me out of here?

Mary. Yuh git out! Why did yuh come here, a-bringin' me all this extra work, an' maybe death?

Northerner. I couldn't go any farther. My horse and I were ready to drop. Won't you help me?

Mary. No, I won't. I don't know who yuh are or nothin' 'bout yuh, 'cept that them men want t' ketch yuh. (*in a changed tone of curiosity*) Did yuh steal somethin' from 'em?

Northerner. Don't you understand? Those men

belong to the Confederacy, and I'm a Northerner. They've been chasing me all day. (*pulling a bit of crumpled paper from his breast*) They want this paper. If they get it before tomorrow morning it will mean the greatest disaster that's ever come to the Union army.

Mary (*with frank curiosity*). Was it yuh rode by yesterday?

Northerner. Don't you see what you can do? Get me out of here and away from those men, and you'll have done more than any soldier could do for the country—for *your* country.

Mary. I ain't got no country. Me an' Thad's only got this farm. Thad's ailin', an' I do most the work, an'—

Northerner. The lives of thirty thousand men hang by a thread. I must save them. And you must help me!

Mary. I don't know nothin' 'bout yuh, an' I don't know what yer talkin' 'bout.

Northerner. Only help me get away.

Mary (*angrily*). No one ever helped me or Thad. I lift no finger in this business. Why yuh come here in the first place is beyond me—sneakin' in our house, spoilin' our well-earned sleep. If them soldiers ketch yuh, they'll kill me an' Thad. Maybe you didn't know that.

Northerner. What's your life and your husband's compared to thirty thousand? I haven't any money or I'd give it to you.

Mary. I don't want yer money.

Northerner. What do you want?

Mary. I want yuh t' git out. I don't care what happens t' yuh. Only git out o' here.

Northerner. I can't with the Southerners in the yard. They'd shoot me like a dog. Besides, I've got to have my horse.

Mary (*with naive curiosity*). What kind o' lookin' horse is it?

Northerner (*dropping into the chair at left of center table in disgust and despair*). Oh, God! If I'd only turned in at the other farm. I might have found people with red blood. (*pulls out his gun and hopelessly opens the empty chamber*)

Mary (*alarmed*). What yuh goin' t' do with that gun?

Northerner. Don't be afraid.

Mary. I'd call 'em if I wasn't—

Northerner (*leaping to the wall, left, and bracing*

thousand men hang by a thread.

WORDS TO KNOW **naive** (nä-ēv') *adj.* simple and open; unsophisticated

himself against it). Go call them in. Save your poor skin and your husband's if you can. Call them in. You can't save yourself. (*laughs hysterically*) You can't save your miserable skin. 'Cause if they get me, and don't shoot you, *I will.*

Mary (*leaning against the left side of the table for support; in agony*). Oh!

Northerner. You see? You've got to help me whether you want to or not.

Mary (*feeling absolutely caught*). I ain't done nothin'. I don't see why yuh an' them others come here a-threatenin' t' shoot me. I don't want nothin'. I don't want t' do nothin'. I jest want yuh all t' git out o' here an' leave me an' Thad t' go t' sleep. Oh, I don't know what t' do. Yuh got me in a corner where I can't move. (*Passes her hand back along the table. Touches the dipper accidentally, and it falls to the floor. Screams at the sound.*)

Northerner (*leaping toward her*). Now you've done it. They'll be here in a minute. You can't give me up. They'll shoot me if you do. *They'll shoot.* (*hurries up the stairs and disappears*)

(Mary *stands beside the table, trembling terribly. The* Sergeant, Dick, *and* Thaddeus *come running in.*)

Sergeant. What did you yell for? (Mary *does not answer. He seizes her by the arm.*) Answer!

Mary. I knocked the dipper off the table. It scared me.

Sergeant (*dropping wearily into chair at left of center table*). Well, don't drop our breakfast. Put it on the table. We're ready.

Mary (*stands looking at the* Sergeant). It ain't finished.

Sergeant (*worn out by his day's work and* Mary's *stupidity, from now on absolutely brutish*). You've had time to cook a dozen meals. What did you do all the time we were in the yard?

Mary. I didn't do nothin'.

Sergeant. You good-for-nothin'— Get a move on and give us something fit to eat. Don't try to get rid of any left-overs on us. If you do, you'll suffer for it. (Mary *stands looking at him.*) Don't you know anything, you brainless farm-drudge?[2] *Hurry,* I said.

(Mary *picks up the dipper and turns to the stove.* Thaddeus *sits in the chair at left of smaller table.*)

Dick. What a night! My stomach's as hollow as these people's heads. (*takes towel which hangs above the bench, and wipes the barrel of his gun with it*)

Mary. That's one of my best towels.

Dick. Can't help it.

Sergeant. 'Tend to the breakfast. That's enough for you to do at one time. (Dick *puts his gun on the smaller table, and sits at the right of the larger. Then the* Sergeant *speaks, quietly.*) I don't see how he gave us the slip.

Dick. He knew we were after him, drove his horse in here, and went on afoot. Clever scheme, I must admit.

Thaddeus (*endeavoring to get them into conversation*). Have yuh rid far t'night, Misters?

Dick (*shortly*). Far enough.

Thaddeus. Twenty miles or so?

Dick. Perhaps.

Thaddeus. How long yuh been chasin' the critter?

Sergeant. Oh, shut up! Don't you see we don't want to talk to you? Take hold and hurry, woman. My patience's at an end. (Mary *puts a loaf of bread, some fried eggs, and a coffee-pot on the table.*)

Mary. There! I hope yer satisfied.

(Dick *and the* Sergeant *pull up their chairs and begin to eat.*)

Sergeant. Is this all we get? Come, it won't do you any good to be stingy.

Mary. It's all I got.

2. **drudge:** a person who does tiresome, unpleasant work.

Sergeant. It isn't a mouthful for a chickadee! Give us some butter.

Mary. There ain't none.

Sergeant. No butter on a farm? God, the way you lie.

Mary. I—

Sergeant. Shut up!

Dick. Have you got any cider?

Sergeant. Don't ask. She and the man probably drank themselves stupid on it. (*throws fork on floor*) I never struck such a place in my life. Get me another fork. How do you expect me to eat with that bent thing? (Mary *stoops with difficulty and picks up the fork. Gets another from the cupboard and gives it to the* Sergeant.) Now give me some salt. Don't you know that folks eat it on eggs? (Mary *crosses to the cupboard; mistakes the pepper for the salt and puts it on the table.* Sergeant *sprinkles pepper on his food*). I said salt, woman. (*spelling*) *S-a-l-t.* Salt! Salt! (Mary *gets the salt and gives it to the* Sergeant. *Almost ready to drop, she drags herself to the window nearer the back and leans against it, watching the Southerners like a hunted animal.* Thaddeus *is nodding in the corner. The* Sergeant *and* Dick *go on devouring the food. The former pours the coffee, puts his cup to his lips, takes one swallow; then, jumping to his feet and upsetting his chair as he does so, he hurls his cup to the floor. Bellowing and pointing to the fluid trickling on the floor.*) Have you tried to poison us, you damn hag?

(Mary *screams and the faces of the men turn white. It is the cry of an animal goaded beyond endurance.*)

Mary (*screeching*). Break my cup? Call my coffee poison? Call me a hag, will yuh? I'll learn yuh! I'm a woman, but yer drivin' me crazy. (*She has snatched the gun from the wall and pointed it at the* Sergeant. *Fires.*)

(*The* Sergeant *falls to the floor.* Mary *keeps on screeching.* Dick *rushes for his gun.*)

Thaddeus. Mary! Mary!

Mary (*aiming at* Dick *and firing*). I ain't a hag. I'm a woman, but yer killin' me.

(Dick *falls just as he reaches his gun.* Thaddeus *is in the corner with his hands over his ears. The* Northerner *stands on the stairs.* Mary *continues to pull the trigger of the empty gun. The* Northerner *is motionless for a moment; then he goes to* Thaddeus *and shakes him.*)

Northerner. Go get my horse. Quick! (Thaddeus *hurries out. The* Northerner *turns to* Mary *and speaks with great* fervor. *She gazes at him but does not understand a word he says.*) I'm ashamed of what I said. The whole country will hear of this, and you. (*He takes her hand and presses it to his lips; then turns and hurries out of the house.*)

(Mary *still holds the gun in her hand. She pushes a strand of gray hair back from her face, and begins to pick up the fragments of the broken cup.*)

Mary (*in dead, flat tone*). I'll have t' drink out the tin cup now.

(*The hoof-beats of the Northerner's horse are heard.*)

Curtain

WORDS TO KNOW

fervor (fûr'vər) *n.* great warmth and intensity of feeling

RESPONDING OPTIONS

FROM PERSONAL RESPONSE *TO* CRITICAL ANALYSIS

REFLECT **1.** What do you think of Mary at the end of the play? Write your impressions in your notebook.

RETHINK **2.** Is Mary a patriot, a criminal, or neither? Explain how you believe the playwright wants you to view Mary.

Consider

- her line, "I ain't got no country. Me an' Thad's only got this farm."
- why she shoots the Southern soldiers
- what the Northern soldier intends to tell "the whole country" about her

3. Briefly describe what the five characters are like, perhaps by making a large label for each to wear. In your opinion, how realistic are these characters?

4. What is your interpretation of the play's title?

RELATE **5.** How do the Trasks' experiences in this play fit with your own ideas about what life would be like for civilians in wartime? Review the chart you were asked to make on page 477.

6. The Northern soldier says that Mary should risk her life to help save the lives of 30,000 soldiers. Under what circumstances do you think a civilian has a duty to risk his or her own life to aid an army?

ANOTHER PATHWAY

Cooperative Learning

Give a performance of *The Clod* for another class in your school. Use the stage directions to help you visualize what the setting and characters look like and how the characters speak and move. If you are an actor, remember to put appropriate feeling into your lines of dialogue and to speak clearly.

LITERARY LINKS

How would you compare the playwright's view of war to Ambrose Bierce's view of war in "An Occurrence at Owl Creek Bridge"? Consider how the soldiers and civilians are depicted and how military ideals are presented.

Cavalry Soldier (1863), Winslow Homer.

QUICKWRITES

1. Did Mary do the right thing? Why or why not? Write notes for a **persuasive essay** evaluating Mary's actions and her motivations.
2. What are some other possible ways that this play might have concluded? Draft an **alternative ending** to the play and then invite several classmates to help you perform it for the rest of the class. Afterward, discuss whether changing the ending affects the theme of the play.

PORTFOLIO *Save your writing. You may want to use it later as a springboard to a piece for your portfolio.*

LITERARY CONCEPTS

The sequence of actions and events in a literary work is the **plot.** The plot of a traditional drama usually follows five stages that can be illustrated in a diagram like the one shown. The **exposition** provides important background information and introduces the setting, characters, and conflict. The opening stage directions are important in setting up this exposition. During the **rising action,** the conflict becomes more obvious and suspense builds as the main characters struggle to resolve their problem. The **climax** is the turning point in the plot when the outcome of the conflict becomes clear. The climax usually results in a change in the characters or a solution to the conflict. After the climax, the **falling action** occurs and shows the effects of the climax. As the falling action begins, the suspense is over but the results of the decision or action that caused the climax are not yet fully worked out. The **resolution,** which often blends with the falling action, reveals the final outcome of events and ties up loose ends. Try to identify the exposition, rising action, climax, falling action, and resolution in *The Clod,* and discuss your interpretation with your classmates. In your opinion, does the play have a traditional five-part plot structure?

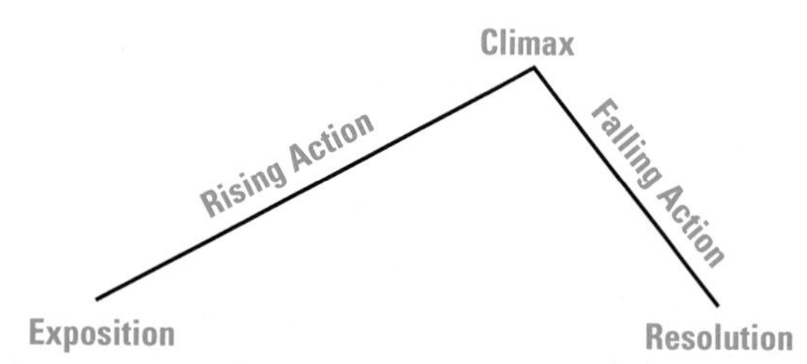

CRITIC'S CORNER

Sharon Counts, a member of our student board, complained that this play "seemed to reach a climax and then dive straight down. No conclusion, just up, up, up, peak, down." Do you agree with her observation about the play's structure? In your opinion, are the conflicts in the play sufficiently resolved?

WORDS TO KNOW

For each boldfaced word, write the letter of the phrase that best suggests its meaning.

1. **naive**
   (a) man about town, (b) babe in the woods, (c) giant of industry
2. **stupor**
   (a) in a fog, (b) in a pickle, (c) in a tailspin
3. **fervor**
   (a) carried away, (b) carried the day, (c) carried the ball
4. **emphatically**
   (a) take five, (b) take for a ride, (c) take off the gloves
5. **emaciated**
   (a) boxing with shadows, (b) in someone's shadow, (c) a shadow of one's former self

LEWIS BEACH

Playwright and novelist Emmett Lewis Beach (1891–1947) was born in Saginaw, Michigan. Educated at the University of Chicago and Harvard University, Beach wrote his first one-act play, *The Clod,* while he was a student at Harvard. *The Clod* was first produced and staged in 1914 by The Harvard Dramatic Club and was later performed by the Washington Square Players at the Bandbox Theatre in New York City. Beach, whose career reached its height in the 1920s, published four one-act plays in 1921. In 1924 Beach's best-known work, his novel *The Goose Hangs High,* was presented as a full-length comedy at the Bijou Theatre by the Dramatists' Theatre, Inc. The play was a success, and *The Goose Hangs High* was later made into a movie.

OTHER WORKS *A Square Peg, Ann Broome*

PREVIEWING

NONFICTION

from Coming of Age in Mississippi

Anne Moody

PERSONAL CONNECTION

The civil rights movement of the 1950s and 1960s succeeded in destroying many of the laws that denied African Americans their full rights as Americans. What do you know about the civil rights movement? What did you learn about this movement when you read the excerpt from *Stride Toward Freedom* by Martin Luther King, Jr., on page 234? In small groups create a concept chart like the one shown, substituting answers for the questions.

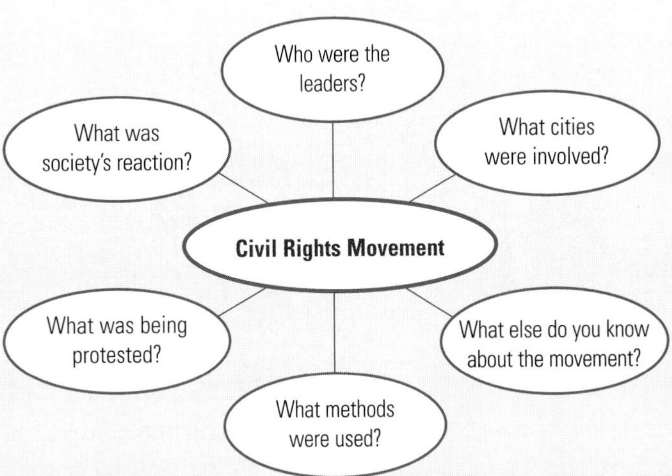

HISTORICAL CONNECTION

Nearly one hundred years after the Civil War and the end of slavery, many states still had laws that denied African Americans the right to vote, the right to attend state universities, even the right to use public facilities like swimming pools and restrooms. During the civil rights movement, volunteers in the South registered African-American voters at risk of their lives; "freedom riders" braved beatings and killings to desegregate interstate buses and bus stations; and protesters took part in sit-ins, like the one you will read about in this selection, to integrate lunch counters, parks, and theaters. The result of the movement was the Civil Rights Act of 1964, the most far-reaching civil rights legislation in American history.

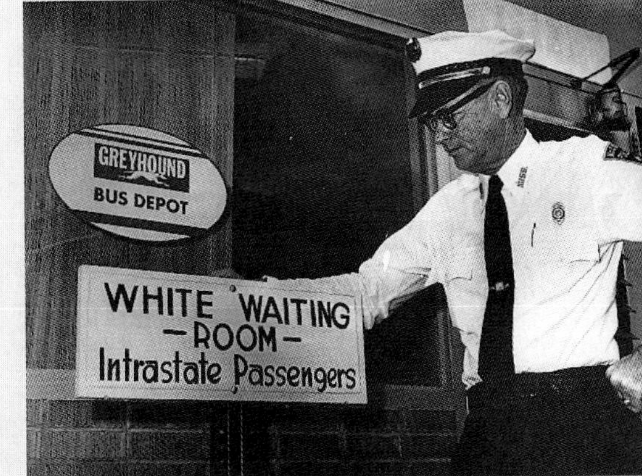

AP/Wide World Photos.

WRITING CONNECTION

In *Coming of Age in Mississippi,* Anne Moody tells the true story of her experiences as a college student in the civil rights movement in Mississippi. Even when she is confronted by anger and violence, Moody is committed to remaining nonviolent. Answer the following questions in your notebook: What cause is worth risking your life for? Why? How difficult do you think taking that risk would be? Read to find out how Anne Moody might answer these questions.

FROM

Coming of Age

I had counted on graduating in the spring of 1963, but as it turned out, I couldn't because some of my credits still had to be cleared with Natchez College. A year before, this would have seemed like a terrible disaster, but now I hardly even felt disappointed. I had a good excuse to stay on campus for the summer and work with the Movement, and this was what I really wanted to do. I couldn't go home again anyway, and I couldn't go to New Orleans—I didn't have money enough for bus fare.

During my senior year at Tougaloo, my family hadn't sent me one penny. I had only the small amount of money I had earned at Maple Hill. I couldn't afford to eat at school or live in the dorms, so I had gotten permission to move off campus. I had to prove that I could finish school, even if I had to go hungry every day. I knew Raymond and Miss Pearl were just waiting to see me drop out. But something happened to me as I got more and more involved in the Movement. It no longer seemed important to prove anything. I had found something outside myself that gave meaning to my life.

I had become very friendly with my social science professor, John Salter, who was in charge of NAACP[1] activities on campus. All during the year, while the NAACP conducted a boycott of the downtown stores in Jackson, I had been one of Salter's most faithful

1. **NAACP:** the National Association for the Advancement of Colored People, an organization that works to end discrimination against African Americans and other minority groups.

in Mississippi

Anne Moody

canvassers[2] and church speakers. During the last week of school, he told me that sit-in demonstrations were about to start in Jackson and that he wanted me to be the spokesman for a team that would sit-in at Woolworth's lunch counter. The two other demonstrators would be classmates of mine, Memphis and Pearlena. Pearlena was a dedicated NAACP worker, but Memphis had not been very involved in the Movement on campus. It seemed that the organization had had a rough time finding students who were in a position to go to jail. I had nothing to lose one way or the other. Around ten o'clock the morning of the demonstrations, NAACP headquarters alerted the news services. As a result, the police department was also informed, but neither the policemen nor the newsmen knew exactly where or when the demonstrations would start. They stationed themselves along Capitol Street and waited.

To divert attention from the sit-in at Woolworth's, the picketing started at J. C. Penney's a good fifteen minutes before. The pickets were allowed to walk up and down in front of the store three or four times before they were arrested. At exactly 11 A.M., Pearlena, Memphis, and I entered Woolworth's from the rear entrance. We separated as soon as we stepped into the store, and made small purchases from various counters. Pearlena had given Memphis her watch. He was to let us know when it was 11:14. At 11:14 we were to join him near the lunch counter and at exactly 11:15 we were to take seats at it.

Seconds before 11:15 we were occupying three seats at the previously segregated Woolworth's lunch counter. In the beginning the waitresses seemed to ignore us, as if they really didn't know what was going on. Our waitress walked past us a couple of times before she noticed we had started to write our own orders down and realized we wanted service. She asked us what we wanted. We began to read to her from our order slips. She told us that we would be served at the back counter, which was for Negroes.

"We would like to be served here," I said.

2. **canvassers:** people who canvass, or go door to door to get support for a cause or gather opinions on an issue.

The waitress started to repeat what she had said, then stopped in the middle of the sentence. She turned the lights out behind the counter, and she and the other waitresses almost ran to the back of the store, deserting all their white customers. I guess they thought that violence would start immediately after the whites at the counter realized what was going on. There were five or six other people at the counter. A couple of them just got up and walked away. A girl sitting next to me finished her banana split before leaving. A middle-aged white woman who had not yet been served rose from her seat and came over to us. "I'd like to stay here with you," she said, "but my husband is waiting."

The newsmen came in just as she was leaving. They must have discovered what was going on shortly after some of the people began to leave the store. One of the newsmen ran behind the woman who spoke to us and asked her to identify herself. She refused to give her name, but said she was a native of Vicksburg and a former resident of California. When asked why she had said what she had said to us, she replied, "I am in sympathy with the Negro movement." By this time a crowd of cameramen and reporters had gathered around us taking pictures and asking questions, such as Where were we from? Why did we sit-in? What organization sponsored it? Were we students? From what school? How were we classified?

I told them that we were all students at Tougaloo College, that we were represented by no particular organization, and that we planned to stay there even after the store closed.

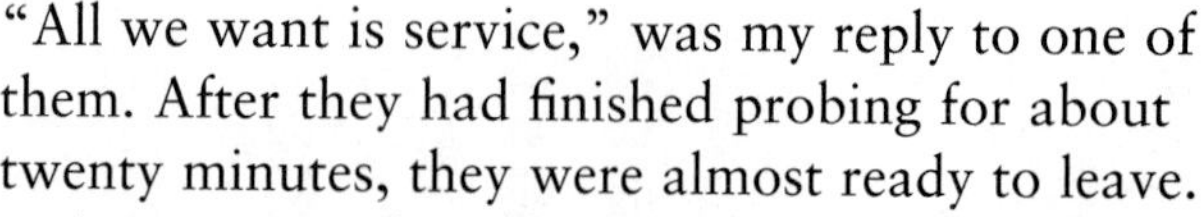

"All we want is service," was my reply to one of them. After they had finished probing for about twenty minutes, they were almost ready to leave.

At noon, students from a nearby white high school started pouring in to Woolworth's. When they first saw us they were sort of surprised. They didn't know how to react. A few started to heckle and the newsmen became interested again. Then the white students started chanting all kinds of anti-Negro slogans. We were called a little bit of everything. The rest of the seats except the three we were occupying had been roped off to prevent others from sitting down. A couple of the boys took one end of the rope and made it into a hangman's noose. Several attempts were made to put it around our necks. The crowds grew as more students and adults came in for lunch.

We kept our eyes straight forward and did not look at the crowd except for occasional glances to see what was going on. All of a sudden I saw a face I remembered—the drunkard from the bus station sit-in. My eyes lingered on him just long enough for us to recognize each other. Today he was drunk too, so I don't think he remembered where he had seen me before. He took out a knife, opened it, put it in his pocket, and then began to pace the floor. At this point, I told Memphis and Pearlena what was going on. Memphis suggested that we pray. We bowed our heads, and all hell broke loose. A man rushed forward, threw Memphis from his seat, and slapped my face. Then another man who worked in the store threw me against an adjoining counter.

Down on my knees on the floor, I saw Memphis lying near the lunch counter with blood running out of the corners of his mouth. As he tried to protect his face, the man who'd thrown him down kept kicking him against the head. If he had worn hard-soled shoes instead of sneakers, the first kick probably would have killed Memphis. Finally a man dressed in plain clothes identified himself as a police officer and arrested Memphis and his attacker.

On May 23, 1963, Anne Moody (right), John R. Salter (left), and Joan Trumpauer (middle) are harassed during a sit-in demonstration at a lunch counter in Jackson, Mississippi. AP/Wide World Photos.

Pearlena had been thrown to the floor. She and I got back on our stools after Memphis was arrested. There were some white Tougaloo teachers in the crowd. They asked Pearlena and me if we wanted to leave. They said that things were getting too rough. We didn't know what to do. While we were trying to make up our minds, we were joined by Joan Trumpauer. Now there were three of us and we were integrated. The crowd began to chant, "Communists, Communists, Communists." Some old man in the crowd ordered the students to take us off the stools.

"Which one should I get first?" a big husky boy said.

"That white nigger," the old man said.

The boy lifted Joan from the counter by her waist and carried her out of the store. Simultaneously, I was snatched from my stool by two high school students. I was dragged about thirty feet toward the door by my hair when someone made them turn me loose. As I was getting up off the floor, I saw Joan coming back inside. We started back to the center of the counter to join Pearlena. Lois Chaffee, a white Tougaloo faculty member, was now sitting next to her. So Joan and I just climbed across the rope at the front end of the counter and sat down. There were now four of us, two whites and two Negroes, all women. The mob started smearing us with ketchup, mustard, sugar, pies, and everything on the counter. Soon Joan and I were joined by John Salter, but the moment he sat down he was hit on the jaw with what appeared to be brass knuckles. Blood gushed from his face and someone threw salt into the open wound. Ed King, Tougaloo's chaplain, rushed to him.

At the other end of the counter, Lois and Pearlena were joined by George Raymond, a CORE[3] field worker and a student from Jackson State College. Then a Negro high school boy sat down next to me. The mob took spray paint from the counter and sprayed it on the new demonstrators. The high school student had on a white shirt; the word "nigger" was written on his back with red spray paint.

We sat there for three hours taking a beating when the manager decided to close the store because the mob had begun to go wild with stuff from other counters. He begged and begged everyone to leave. But even after fifteen minutes of begging, no one budged. They would not leave until we did. Then Dr. Beittel, the president of Tougaloo College, came running in. He said he had just heard what was happening.

About ninety policemen were standing outside the store; they had been watching the whole thing through the windows, but had not come in to stop the mob or do anything. President Beittel went outside and asked Captain Ray to come and escort us out. The captain refused, stating the manager had to invite him in before he could enter the premises, so Dr. Beittel himself brought us out. He had told the police that they had better protect us after we were outside the store. When we got outside, the policemen formed a single line that blocked the mob from us. However, they were allowed to throw at us everything they had collected. Within ten minutes, we were picked up by Reverend King in his station wagon and taken to the NAACP headquarters on Lynch Street.

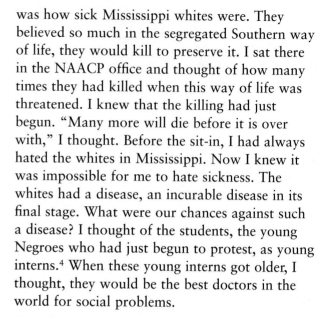

After the sit-in, all I could think of was how sick Mississippi whites were. They believed so much in the segregated Southern way of life, they would kill to preserve it. I sat there in the NAACP office and thought of how many times they had killed when this way of life was threatened. I knew that the killing had just begun. "Many more will die before it is over with," I thought. Before the sit-in, I had always hated the whites in Mississippi. Now I knew it was impossible for me to hate sickness. The whites had a disease, an incurable disease in its final stage. What were our chances against such a disease? I thought of the students, the young Negroes who had just begun to protest, as young interns.[4] When these young interns got older, I thought, they would be the best doctors in the world for social problems.

Before we were taken back to campus, I wanted to get my hair washed. It was stiff with dried mustard, ketchup and sugar. I stopped in at a beauty shop across the street from the NAACP office. I didn't have on any shoes because I had lost them when I was dragged across the floor at Woolworth's. My stockings were sticking to my legs from the mustard that had dried on them. The hairdresser took one look at me and said, "My land, you were in the sit-in, huh?"

"Yes," I answered. "Do you have time to wash my hair and style it?"

"Right away," she said, and she meant right away. There were three other ladies already waiting, but they seemed glad to let me go ahead of them. The hairdresser was real nice. She even took my stockings off and washed my legs while my hair was drying.

There was a mass rally that night at the Pearl Street Church in Jackson, and the place was packed. People were standing two abreast in the aisles. Before the speakers began, all the sit-inners

3. **CORE:** the Congress of Racial Equality, a civil rights organization that coordinated marches and demonstrations in the 1960s.

4. **interns:** students or recent graduates who are undergoing practical training, particularly medical training.

walked out on the stage and were introduced by Medgar Evers.[5] People stood and applauded for what seemed like thirty minutes or more. Medgar told the audience that this was just the beginning of such demonstrations. He asked them to pledge themselves to unite in a massive offensive against segregation in Jackson, and throughout the state. The rally ended with "We Shall Overcome" and sent home hundreds of determined people. It seemed as though Mississippi Negroes were about to get together at last.

Before I demonstrated, I had written Mama. She wrote me back a letter, begging me not to take part in the sit-in. She even sent ten dollars for bus fare to New Orleans. I didn't have one penny, so I kept the money. Mama's letter made me mad. I had to live my life as I saw fit. I had made that decision when I left home. But it hurt to have my family prove to me how scared they were. It hurt me more than anything else—I knew the whites had already started the threats and intimidations. I was the first Negro from my hometown who had openly demonstrated, worked with the NAACP, or anything. When Negroes threatened to do anything in Centreville, they were either shot like Samuel O'Quinn or run out of town, like Reverend Dupree.

I didn't answer Mama's letter. Even if I had written one, she wouldn't have received it before she saw the news on TV or heard it on the radio. I waited to hear from her again. And I waited to hear in the news that someone in Centreville had been murdered. If so, I knew it would be a member of my family. ❖

5. **Medgar Evers:** a civil rights leader and major organizer and supervisor for the NAACP in Mississippi from 1954 until he was killed by a sniper in 1963.

INSIGHT

Frederick Douglass

Robert Hayden

When it is finally ours, this freedom, this liberty, this beautiful
and terrible thing, needful to man as air,
usable as earth; when it belongs at last to all,
when it is truly instinct, brain matter, diastole, systole,[1]
reflex action; when it is finally won; when it is more
than the gaudy mumbo jumbo of politicians:
this man, this Douglass, this former slave, this Negro
beaten to his knees, exiled, visioning a world
where none is lonely, none hunted, alien,
this man, superb in love and logic, this man
shall be remembered. Oh, not with statues' rhetoric,
not with legends and poems and wreaths of bronze alone,
but with the lives grown out of his life, the lives
fleshing his dream of the beautiful, needful thing.

Frederick Douglass (about 1850), unknown photographer. Daguerreotype, 3 1/8" × 2 3/4", National Portrait Gallery, Smithsonian Institution/Art Resource, New York.

1. **diastole** (dī-ăs′tə-lē), **systole** (sĭs′tə-lē): The heart pumps blood in two steps. Diastole refers to the heart's enlargement when it fills with blood; systole refers to the heart's contraction when the blood pumps out.

RESPONDING OPTIONS

FROM PERSONAL RESPONSE *TO* CRITICAL ANALYSIS

REFLECT 1. What is your opinion of Anne Moody's actions? Write your thoughts in your notebook.

RETHINK 2. How would you describe Anne Moody to someone who has not read this selection?

3. How do you explain the behavior of the store manager and the police during the sit-in?

4. Moody describes Mississippi whites' racism as "an incurable disease in its final stage" and the protesters as "interns." Do you think these are good metaphors? Explain your answer.

RELATE 5. Do you think you would have been able to take such a risk as Moody did?

Consider
- the violence she witnesses and endures
- her belief that someone in her family could be murdered
- what you wrote for the Writing Connection on page 491

6. Anne Moody writes about struggling to end segregation in Jackson, Mississippi. In "Frederick Douglass," the Insight selection on page 497, Robert Hayden writes about what will happen when freedom belongs to all. Do you think that the fight against racism in America has been won, or are we still "a house divided"?

ANOTHER PATHWAY

Cooperative Learning

Based on this selection, make a list of Do's and Don'ts for people who are interested in taking part in sit-ins. Include tips on what situations they may encounter, how to deal with violence, and how to respond to hostile people. Combine lists in a handbook, using a computer if available.

LITERARY LINKS

1. In the excerpt from *Stride Toward Freedom* on page 234, you read about nonviolent resistance. Do the events described in this excerpt from *Coming of Age in Mississippi* illustrate the ideas of Martin Luther King, Jr.? Why or why not? Discuss your thoughts with a small group of classmates.
2. Does Robert Hayden's poem capture the Frederick Douglass that you read about in the excerpt from *Narrative of the Life of Frederick Douglass?* Share your ideas in class.

QUICKWRITES

1. Write the **letter** that you think Anne Moody's mother sent to her. Then write the **reply** Anne might have written had she chosen to answer. With a partner, read both letters to the class.
2. Write a **personal essay** about a cause or movement you believe in as passionately as Moody believed in the civil rights movement. As a starting point, use what you wrote for the Writing Connection on page 491.

PORTFOLIO *Save your writing. You may want to use it later as a springboard to a piece for your portfolio.*

ALTERNATIVE ACTIVITIES

1. ***Cooperative Learning*** With several classmates, videotape a **news broadcast** of the sit-in. Be sure to include interviews and analysis. Share your videotape with the rest of the class.
2. The National Civil Rights Museum in Memphis, Tennessee, features exhibits that illustrate key events during the civil rights movement. Plan an **exhibit** based on this selection that might appear in the museum.

ART CONNECTION

The photo on page 495 shows the sit-in that Anne Moody describes in the selection. What does the photo reveal that Moody's description of the scene does not? What does Moody's description reveal that the photo does not?

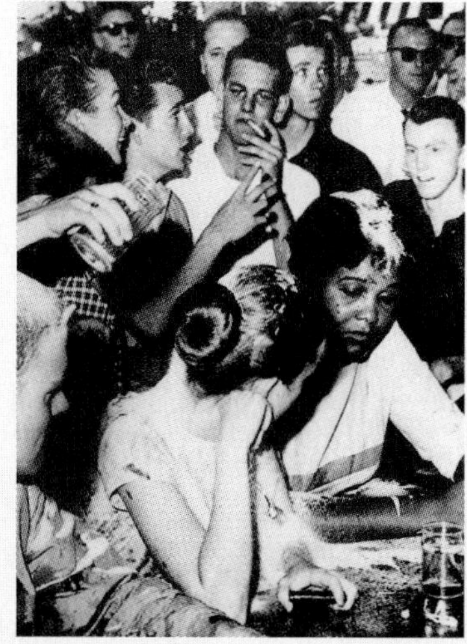

AP/Wide World Photos.

ACROSS THE CURRICULUM

Music Research protest songs from the 1960s civil rights movement, such as "This Little Light of Mine," "We Shall Overcome," "Oh, Wallace," "Ain't Gonna Let Nobody Turn Me Around," and "Birmingham Sunday." You might look for songs sung by some of these performers: Joan Baez; Bob Dylan; Richard Farina; Peter, Paul, and Mary; Odetta; Bernice Johnson Reagon; and Pete Seeger. Prepare a tape of the most stirring songs to share with your classmates.

ANNE MOODY

1940–

When Anne Moody was growing up as the daughter of poor sharecroppers in rural Mississippi, she saw a neighboring family killed when their house was set on fire. The violence was brought about by a white citizens' guild, an organization dedicated to intimidating African Americans who in some way threatened whites' power. Moody's mother advised her, "Just act like you don't know nothing." Moody slowly came to realize that her mother's advice might be the safest course, but it was one that Anne herself could not follow.

In her teens Moody spent summers working in a factory, carefully saving money to make her dream of college a reality. She earned a basketball scholarship to Natchez Junior College but transferred to Tougaloo College, where she became involved with the civil rights movement. She was a volunteer for the Congress of Racial Equality (CORE) and a civil rights coordinator at Cornell University—a position in which she faced constant threats to her life. She worked for voting rights, on literacy projects, and for an end to segregated public facilities. Her experiences in the civil rights movement became the basis for a book that is widely considered to be a masterpiece of the movement, *Coming of Age in Mississippi,* from which this selection is taken.

Although Moody eventually left the civil rights movement, her heart has never deserted the battle for human rights. She explains, "I realized that the universal fight for human rights, dignity, justice, equality, and freedom is . . . the fight of every ethnic and racial minority, every suppressed and exploited person, every one of the millions who daily suffer one or another of the indignities of the powerless and voiceless masses."

OTHER WORKS *Mr. Death: Four Stories*

ON YOUR OWN

Ballad of Birmingham

DUDLEY RANDALL

Birmingham is Alabama's largest city. In the spring of 1963, Dr. Martin Luther King, Jr., led huge demonstrations to protest racial discrimination in Birmingham, which was then considered one of the most segregated cities of the South. Police dogs and fire hoses were used against the peaceful protesters, including children. Later that year, four young African-American girls were killed when the 16th Street Baptist Church was bombed. A white supremacist, Robert Chambliss, was finally convicted of the murders in 1977.

"Mother dear, may I go downtown
instead of out to play,
and march the streets of Birmingham
in a freedom march today?"

"No, baby, no, you may not go,
for the dogs are fierce and wild,
and clubs and hoses, guns and jails
ain't good for a little child."

"But, mother, I won't be alone.
Other children will go with me,
and march the streets of Birmingham
to make our country free."

"No, baby, no, you may not go,
for I fear those guns will fire.
But you may go to church instead,
and sing in the children's choir."

She has combed and brushed her nightdark hair,
and bathed rose petal sweet,
and drawn white gloves on her small brown hands,
and white shoes on her feet.

The mother smiled to know her child
was in the sacred place,
but that smile was the last smile
to come upon her face.

For when she heard the explosion,
her eyes grew wet and wild.
She raced through the streets of Birmingham
calling for her child.

She clawed through bits of glass and brick,
then lifted out a shoe.
"O, here's the shoe my baby wore,
but, baby, where are you?"

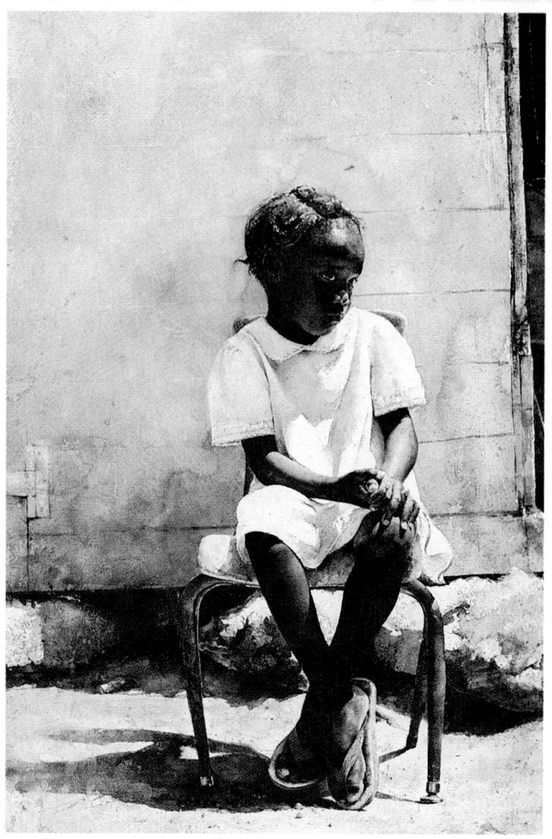

Flip Flops and Lace (1991), Stephen Scott Young. Copyright © Stephen Scott Young. Photo courtesy of John H. Surovek Gallery, Palm Beach, Florida.

Dudley Randall

1914–

Dudley Randall, the first poet laureate of Detroit, Michigan, wrote his earliest poem when he was four years old. His first published poems appeared in the *Detroit Free Press* when he was only 13. Randall, who received his education at Wayne University (now Wayne State University), the University of Michigan, and the University of Ghana, worked for many years at different jobs before becoming a book publisher and an editor. He was employed as a foundry worker for 5 years, a mail carrier for 13 years, and a librarian for 24 years.

"Ballad of Birmingham" was Randall's response to the 1963 church bombing that killed four young girls in that city. This poem eventually led to the birth of Broadside Press, which Randall founded and operated until 1977. As he explains, "Folk singer Jerry Moore of New York had it ["Ballad of Birmingham"] set to music, and I wanted to protect the rights to the poem by getting it copyrighted." After Randall learned that leaflets could be copyrighted, he printed his poem on a single sheet of paper called a broadside. "Ballad of Birmingham" was the first title published by Broadside Press.

As a publisher, Randall provided an important forum for numerous African-American poets. Under Randall's direction, Broadside Press published nearly sixty books by such distinguished writers as Gwendolyn Brooks, Sonia Sanchez, Nikki Giovanni, Haki Madhubuti (Don L. Lee), and Etheridge Knight.

OTHER WORKS *A Litany of Friends: New and Selected Poems, After the Killing, Broadside Memories: Poets I Have Known*

WRITING ABOUT
LITERATURE

The Plot Thickens

Did the endings of "An Occurrence at Owl Creek Bridge" and *The Clod* surprise you? In a good story, play, movie, or television program, the plot may be carefully mapped out, but the result is anything but predictable. On the following pages the plot thickens as you

- see how writers advance the plot
- analyze how plot, setting, character, point of view, language and imagery, and theme work together in a story
- predict the outcome of a real cliffhanger

The Writer's Style: Advancing the Plot Skilled writers weave an intricate story by using three different techniques: dialogue, action, and exposition or explanation.

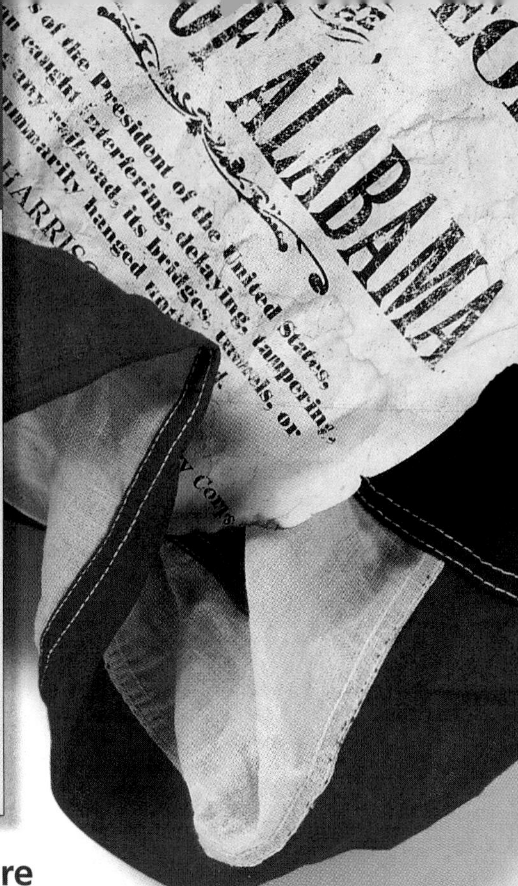

Read the Literature

How did these writers use different techniques to advance the plot?

Literature Models

Advancing the Plot Through Dialogue
What information is provided by this dialogue?

"The Yanks are repairing the railroads," said the man, "and are getting ready for another advance. They have reached the Owl Creek bridge, put it in order and built a stockade on the north bank. The commandant has issued an order, which is posted everywhere, declaring that any civilian caught interfering with the railroad, its bridges, tunnels or trains will be summarily hanged."

Ambrose Bierce
from "An Occurrence at Owl Creek Bridge"

Advancing the Plot Through Action
How does Douglass describe the turning point of this story using action?

Mr. Covey seemed now to think he had me, and could do what he pleased; but at this moment—from whence came the spirit I don't know—I resolved to fight; and, suiting my action to the resolution, I seized Covey hard by the throat; and as I did so, I rose. He held on to me, and I to him. My resistance was so entirely unexpected, that Covey seemed taken all aback. He trembled like a leaf.

Frederick Douglass
from *Narrative of the Life of Frederick Douglass*

Connect to Life

Cartoonists and television, radio, and movie scriptwriters also use dialogue, action, and exposition to advance the plot. Notice the technique that these scriptwriters use to move the plot forward.

Movie Script

Narrator. Then four long years more—alone in his never finished, already decaying, pleasure palace, aloof, seldom visited, never photographed, Charles Foster Kane continued to direct his failing empire . . . vainly attempted to sway, as he once did, the destinies of a nation that had ceased to listen to him . . . ceased to trust him.

Herman J. Mankiewicz and Orson Welles
from the shooting script of *Citizen Kane*

Advancing the Plot Through Exposition
Why do Mankiewicz and Welles use a narrator here, rather than dialogue, to move the plot ahead?

Try Your Hand: Advancing the Plot

1. **Plot Highlights** Find a short story in one of your own magazines. Highlight the dialogue in one color and the action in another. The remainder is exposition. Which plot-advancing technique does the author rely on most?
2. **A Telling Event** Think of something exciting that happened in your school lately. Write a short description of the event using exposition only.
3. **Add Dialogue and Action** Now try rewriting your description, adding dialogue and action to advance the plot. Which version is shorter? Which is more exciting to read?

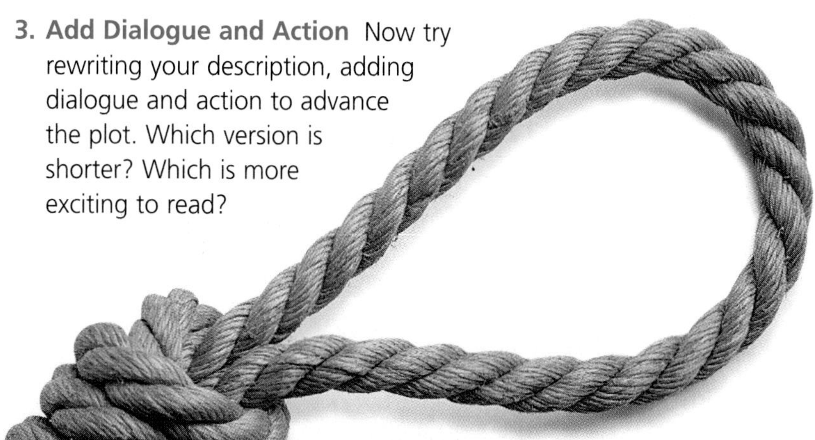

SkillBuilder

WRITER'S CRAFT

Writing Narrative Introductions

A great plot is important. But good writers know that if you don't capture readers' attention in the first sentence or two, you've lost them. Some writers begin a story by shocking their readers; others intrigue them.

When you analyze a story, notice how the writer draws you in. When you write narratives of your own, remember that the introduction can be used to

- set the scene
- describe the main character
- introduce the central conflict
- introduce a major symbol

Bierce describes both the setting and conflict in this introduction:

A man stood upon a railroad bridge in northern Alabama, looking down into the swift water twenty feet below. The man's hands were behind his back, the wrists bound with a cord. A rope closely encircled his neck.

APPLYING WHAT YOU'VE LEARNED

As you work on your analysis, closely examine the introduction. The elements that are revealed in the introduction are often the most important to the story.

WRITING HANDBOOK

For more information on narrative writing, see page 1176 of the Writing Handbook.

Analysis

How do you use analysis? When you analyze, you break a subject into its parts and then examine how all the parts work together. In much the same way that you might take an engine apart to understand how it works, you can analyze a story by breaking it down into its plot, characters, setting, point of view, language and imagery, and theme. What makes a good story good is the way all those elements work together.

GUIDED ASSIGNMENT

Analyzing a Story By writing a literary analysis, you will break a story down into its parts (elements) and then look at how well those elements work as a whole.

1 Prewrite and Explore

Start by choosing one of the selections from Unit Four to analyze. Which story did you really enjoy? Which tale was told in a unique way?

2 Notice What You Notice

What makes this story different from the rest? Which unusual element does the story rely on for its success? You can use this as your "angle" for the analysis. Ask yourself questions like these to find your focus:

- Is there anything unusual about the climax or resolution?
- Which characters change in the course of the story?
- How does the setting create a mood or affect the story?
- How does point of view affect the way the setting or a character is presented?
- Which elements work together to create a certain effect?
- How do these elements drive the meaning of this story?

Now read through the story and look for that unique element. You might want to take notes on color-coded note cards, like the ones on the left for "An Occurrence at Owl Creek Bridge."

Student's Prewriting Cards

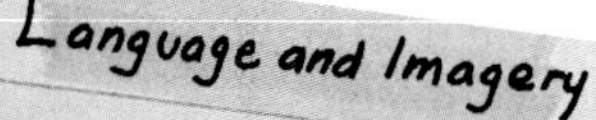

Language and Imagery
nice simile - "The water roared in his ears like the voice of Niagara..."
This could be my angle!
Plot
What a complicated plot!
It looks like this story has 2 turning points!
Character
Condemned man
- 35 years old, married
- planter
- nice features
- well-fitting clothes
- a gentleman
We care about him and want him to escape.

3 Reread and Record

Read through the story again and continue gathering information for your analysis. Add note cards and expand existing cards. Identify aspects of the plot, setting, characters, point of view, language and imagery, and theme that help create the unique effect that you are exploring.

Student's Expanded Notes

Point of View

This might be important!

Beginning - objective, third-person omniscient
"Escape" - gets inside Farquhar's head
Ending - again objective, third-person omniscient

Language and Imagery

nice simile - "The water roared in his ears like the voice of Niagara . . ."

pp. 469–470: The language gets much more descriptive at this point in the story—the author starts to use metaphors and similies.

Could this mean something significant is happening?

4 Talk It Over

Once you have identified your angle and have some supporting information, you may want to talk through your analysis with someone else who is analyzing the same story. Keep in mind that everything in your analysis should relate to your angle.

PEER RESPONSE

- What is the main idea behind my analysis?
- Is there any evidence that contradicts my analysis?
- What pieces of supporting information have I left out?

Once you've worked out your angle, check out the SkillBuilder on organizing your essay for pointers on outlining your draft.

SkillBuilder

WRITER'S CRAFT

Organizing Your Essay

A literary analysis is not just a plot summary. It is an analysis of several story elements. Your analysis should contain the following:

- An introduction that identifies the title and author of the story, briefly describes the story, and introduces the angle
- A body that contains your analysis of the story elements
- A conclusion that summarizes the contribution of the various story elements

But how do you deal with all those story elements in the body of the analysis? One of the easiest ways is to devote a paragraph to each story element. Discuss how that particular element relates or contributes to your angle. Keep in mind that you don't have to deal with all six story elements in your essay. Focus on a few that are the most revealing.

APPLYING WHAT YOU'VE LEARNED
Outline your essay by putting your note cards in a logical order. Don't be afraid to add cards to link ideas together. You may also find that you don't use every note card in your essay. Once you've organized your note cards, it should be easy to write a draft.

5 Revise and Edit

When you revise your draft, you may find you still need to change the sequence of some paragraphs. For example, you might decide to arrange story elements from weakest to strongest. When you're finished, reflect on other ways you can use your analytical skills.

Student's Final Draft

A Strange, Strange Occurrence at Owl Creek Bridge

When is the falling action in a story really the rising action? When is an event both a second turning point and the resolution? Both of these unusual situations occur in "An Occurrence at Owl Creek Bridge," Ambrose Bierce's tale of the hanging of a Confederate sympathizer. The complicated plot drives the entire story. People aren't who you think they are and events don't really happen, as the plot makes unexpected twists and turns.

What technique does this student use to draw in the reader?

What is the angle of this analysis?

As the plot becomes more complicated, so does the language. Bierce goes from straightforward, almost military descriptions at the opening, to much more descriptive metaphors and similes during Peyton's escape. Pains seem "like streams of pulsating fire." Water roars "in his ears like the voice of Niagara." Sand looks like diamonds, rubies, and emeralds. During the escape, Bierce describes everything as though Peyton is seeing it for the first time.

What verb tense does this student use when describing the story?

Standards for Evaluation

A literary analysis
- identifies the story's author and title and your angle
- breaks the story down into its elements
- analyzes how the elements work together in the story
- concludes with a summary of the contribution of each element in the story

Grammar in Context

Verb Tense When you write a literary analysis, use the present tense to summarize the story—the characters, the plot, the author's techniques. Use past tense only to describe something that took place at an earlier time in the story.

> The main character also ~~became~~ *becomes* more complex as the plot ~~twisted and turned~~ *twists and turns*. In the beginning of the story, the condemned man ~~is~~ *was* described in a very superficial way. By the end, Bierce sees inside the man's mind—feeling every pain and emotion.

Notice how the present tense gives the draft a sense of immediacy and moves the analysis forward. For more information on verb tenses, see page 1223 of the Grammar Handbook.

Try Your Hand: Using Verb Tense in Literary Analysis

On a separate sheet of paper, rewrite the following paragraph so that the verb tenses are correct for an analysis.

> Bierce hinted that something unusual was happening to Peyton. Peyton watched his hands, as though they weren't really part of his body. He had almost supernatural powers. He sees an insect yards away. He heard the beating of a dragonfly's wings. Amazingly, Peyton could see that one of the soldiers on shore had gray eyes! Yet, when it came to dodging bullets, his strengths were only human.

SkillBuilder

GRAMMAR FROM WRITING

Using Tense Appropriately
Verb tenses are often the only clues your readers have about when events happen. Notice how Bierce uses past tense to let you know when the events occurred.

The sergeant turned to the captain, saluted and placed himself immediately behind that officer, who in turn moved apart one pace.

Usually the same tense is used for every verb in a sentence or paragraph. However, if events happen at different times, it may be necessary to shift verb tenses. See how Bierce shifts tense.

"The officer," he reasoned, "will not make that martinet's error a second time. It is as easy to dodge a volley as a single shot."

APPLYING WHAT YOU'VE LEARNED
On a separate sheet of paper, use verb tenses appropriately in the following sentences.

1. As he closes his eyes, he remembers the day his family swims in the same river.
2. Peyton Farquhar was a slave owner who is devoted to the Southern cause.
3. He is a well-to-do planter, and he came from a highly respected family.

Double-check your analysis to make sure you are using verb tenses appropriately.

MARVEL COMICS GROUP™

MARVEL WESTERN

19 SEPT 02481

20¢ CC

THE MIGHTY MARVEL WESTERN

featuring

THE RAWHIDE KID

KID COLT

TWO-GUN KID

APPROVED BY THE COMICS CODE AUTHORITY

YOU WON'T TELL *US* WHAT WE WANT TO KNOW, KID!

THEN TALK TO OUR *FRIEND* THERE!

REVENGE ON THE RANGE!

TM & © 1996 Marvel

READING
THE WORLD

CLIFFHANGER!

Cliffhangers—they frustrate us and tease us at the same time. They keep us in suspense. And, as writers of comic strips, continuing dramas, soap operas, and the evening news know, suspense keeps us coming back for more.

View What is happening in this comic panel? Who is this person? Where is he? What does the dialogue tell you about this situation? What does the action tell you?

Interpret Consider what you know about comic books and plot devices and look at the clues in the picture at the left. Do you think this man will escape? If so, how do you think he'll do it? Will he get out of there before the villains return?

Discuss Compare notes with other students. How are your predictions the same? How are they different? Which version is the most exciting? Why? What information did you use to make your predictions? The SkillBuilder at the right can give you more practice in predicting outcomes.

SkillBuilder

CRITICAL THINKING

Predicting Outcomes
Psychics and weather forecasters aren't the only ones who predict the future. You do too—every day. When you predict, you analyze the situation as follows:

- You start by thinking of similar experiences you've had.
- Next, you think about whether the outcomes of any of those situations fit here.
- Then you choose the outcome you feel is most likely to occur.

APPLYING WHAT YOU'VE LEARNED
Try one or more of the following in a small group.

1. Predict the outcome of this comic and create its next panel. Work together on the dialogue and action.
2. As you read a serial comic strip or watch a continuing drama, write down your prediction of what will happen in the next episode and your reason. Tune in next week (or the following day) to see how accurate your predictions are.
3. Friend number one's boyfriend went out with friend number two. Predict what will happen in each of the following cases:
   - Friend number one sees friend number two at the mall with her boyfriend.
   - You tell friend number one what's going on.

PART 2 INTRODUCTION

Tricksters and Trailblazers

The Vanishing Frontier

Before white settlers in large numbers had pushed west of the Mississippi, the vast frontier was populated by many tribes of Native Americans. The Sioux (so͞o), the Cheyenne (shī-ĕn′), the Arapaho (ə-răp′e-hō′), the Kiowa (kī′ə-wô′), and the Comanche (kə-măn′chē) on the Great Plains had developed a way of life that depended almost exclusively on the large herds of buffalo, estimated at 15 million head in 1865. In the Southwest, the Apache had fought against the Spanish for 250 years; but other southwestern tribes, such as the Navajo, had adopted Spanish ways and were raising sheep and goats and cultivating crops. The Nez Perce (nĕz′ pûrs′) of the Pacific Northwest had coexisted peacefully with white traders and trappers since Lewis and Clark first explored their vast territory in 1805.

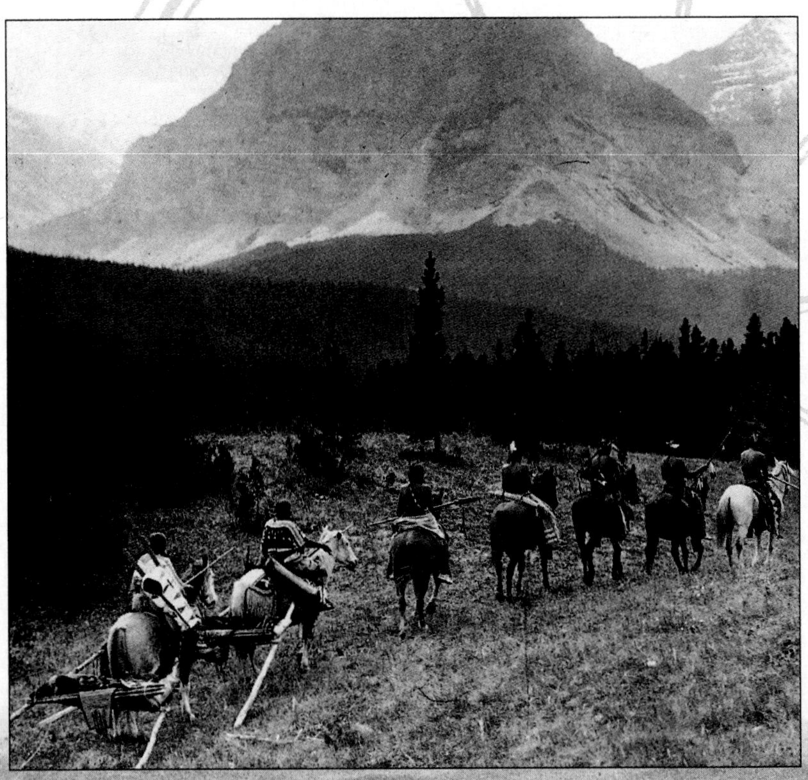

In 1841 the first caravan of covered wagons brought pioneers across the Great Plains, heading for fertile territories in California and Oregon. Within two years, more than 1,000 people had made the journey. During the California gold rush of 1848, the dream of riches lured thousands of miners west. Within 30 years of that first discov-

A 19th-centry artist's rendition of a Native American chief's refusal to allow a wagon train to pass through his country.

ery, gold or silver had been found in every western state and territory.

By the 1860s the plains themselves began to be settled. The free land granted by the Homestead Act of 1862 attracted thousands of settlers west. Newly constructed railroads transported more than 8 million settlers in two decades alone.

This relatively rapid settlement of the West doomed the Native American way of life. White settlers believed that they were bringing civilization to the wilderness, and few considered the Indians as having any legitimate claim to the land. One by one the tribes of the Northwest and of the Great Plains were forced—either through armed conflict or signed treaties—to give up their territories to the U.S. government. The tribes were often relocated onto cramped reservations, on land so poor that no white settlers wanted it.

This part of Unit Four includes a variety of selections to give you an idea of what was lost and gained during this dramatic episode in

Voices *from the* TIMES

No white person or persons shall be permitted to settle upon or occupy any portion of the territory, or without the consent of the Indians to pass through the same.

Treaty of 1868

Our land here is the dearest thing on earth to us. Men take up land and get rich on it, and it is very important for us Indians to keep it.

White Thunder
48th U.S. Congress, 1st session
Senate Report 283

I did not know then how much was ended. When I look back now from this high hill of my old age, I can still see the butchered women and children lying heaped and scattered all along the crooked gulch as plain as when I saw them with eyes still young. And I can see that something else died there in the bloody mud, and was buried in the blizzard. A people's dream died there. It was a beautiful dream.

Black Elk
recalling the Battle of Wounded Knee
in *Black Elk Speaks*

Voices *from the* Times

The dead man lay stretched out on the pool table, right in the middle of the saloon/courtroom. The grizzled old judge walked around the body as if he were measuring it for size. No one knew the dead man's name, so the judge searched his pockets for identification. He found out the man's name was O'Brien. He also found $40 and a six-shooter.

The judge stepped back and thumbed his old dusty law book, the *Revised Statutes of Texas* for 1879. After thinking about the situation for a while, he turned to the coroner's jury and the other men hanging around the saloon.

"Gentlemen," he said, "that man fell from the bridge and that's all there is about it. But there is one thing that is not so plain, and that is what was he doing with that gun? Of course he's dead and can't explain, but that ain't the fault of the law; it's his own misfortune. Justice is justice, and law is law, and as he can't offer no satisfactory explanation of the matter I shall be obliged to fine him forty dollars for carrying a concealed weapon."

Welcome to the court of Judge Roy Bean, the Law West of the Pecos. Not to mention the coroner and the best saloonkeeper. For 20 years, Roy Bean was a legend throughout the Southwest. Texas Rangers, Mexican shepherds, and New York tourists came to his combination courtroom and saloon for justice, whiskey, and entertainment. The justice and whiskey were a little on the shady side, but the entertainment was first rate.

Paul Robert Walker
from *Judge Roy Bean: Law West of the Pecos*

American history. You'll recognize the Native American trickster tradition in the two tales "The Indian and the Hundred Cows" and "High Horse's Courting." You'll also see tricksters in the humorous excerpt from Mark Twain's autobiography. On a more serious note, Willa Cather takes a very unromantic view of life on the plains in her story of hardship and longing, "A Wagner Matinee."

After the Civil War and by the time the West was being settled, American literature was also changing. Realism replaced romanticism as the dominant literary style, in part because people wanted to read more truthful accounts of ordinary life rather than the sentimentality of much romantic fiction. The new regional diversity that sprang up among the mining camps, cattle ranches, farming communities, and frontier towns in the West gave rise to new regional literature called local color realism. Mark Twain, who once lived in a mining camp, was foremost among the local color realists. Later in the century, Willa Cather carried on the spirit of local color realism with increasing sophistication. When you read Twain and Cather, think about the difference between their writing and the writing of Poe, Hawthorne, and Thoreau, who wrote earlier in the century, and you'll understand the direction American literature was going.

Continuity & Change: Writers of the New West

America's unique relationship with the frontier has continued to influence our literature and character, engaging our writers and thinkers to the present day. Although the days of the "Wild West" are gone, its mythic lure of freedom remains a powerful force. Américo Paredes incorporates the trickster tradition into his story "The Legend of Gregorio Cortez," while Pam Houston shows what it's like to be a trailblazer in the 1990s in "A Blizzard Under Blue Sky."

PART 2 # *Tricksters and Trailblazers*

The Vanishing Frontier

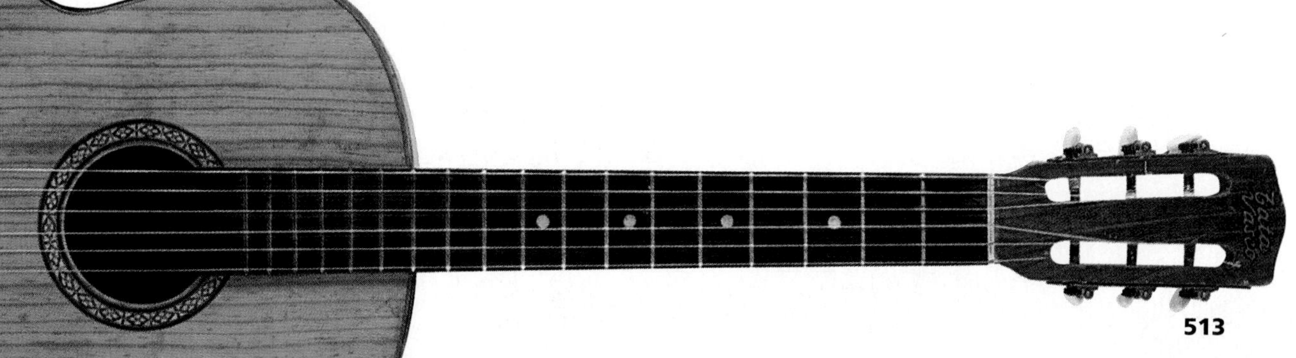

PREVIEWING

FOLK TALE

The Indian and the Hundred Cows / El indito de las cien vacas

Retold by José Griego y Maestas (hô-sĕ′ grē-yĕ′gô ē mä-ĕs′täs)
Translated by Rudolfo A. Anaya (ro͞o-dôl′fô ä-nä′yä)

PERSONAL CONNECTION

Think of a time when you misunderstood or misinterpreted something that someone told you. What do you think caused this breakdown in communication? What was the result of the misunderstanding? Jot down your thoughts about this experience, filling in a diagram like the one shown.

CULTURAL CONNECTION

"The Indian and the Hundred Cows" is a *cuento,* a traditional folk tale that comes from the oral tradition of New Mexico and southern Colorado. First brought to the southwestern part of the United States by Spanish and Mexican settlers, *cuentos* were further shaped and influenced by the landscape and by Native American cultures in this area. Early settlers and their descendants told *cuentos* to entertain, to reinforce cultural values, and to teach traditional customs and beliefs to their children. "The Indian and the Hundred Cows" was published in *Cuentos: Tales from the Hispanic Southwest.* The tales in this collection were selected and adapted in Spanish by the scholar José Griego y Maestas and were translated into English by the novelist Rudolfo A. Anaya. The English version of the tale appears on page 515; the Spanish version, on page 517.

The U. S. Southwest

COLORADO
NEW MEXICO
Miles
0 200 400
N
W E
S

READING CONNECTION

Distinguishing Literal and Figurative Meanings The dictionary definition of a word is its literal meaning. Figurative language is language that communicates ideas beyond the literal meanings of words. For example, the words in figurative expressions such as *He was tickled pink, My name is mud,* and *She has a green thumb* are not literally true; rather, they create images or impressions in the reader's mind. As you read this folk tale, watch for the humorous misunderstanding that results from confusing literal and figurative statements.

The Indian and the Hundred Cows

translated by Rudolfo A. Anaya

In a small pueblo there once lived an Indian who was so devoted to the church he never missed mass on Sunday. One Sunday, during his homily,[1] the priest said:

"Have charity, my children. Give alms[2] to the poor. If you expect God's help it is necessary that you also help the church. You know that when you make a donation to God, He returns it a hundredfold."

The Indian, who was listening carefully, decided to give a cow that he had to the priest. That afternoon he brought his cow to the church and told the priest, "Padre,[3] I have brought you my cow so that God will give me a hundred cows."

"Yes, yes, my son," the priest answered. "Have faith in God and He will repay your gift." Then the priest took the cow and added it to his own herd.

The Indian returned home very satisfied and he began to build a large corral where he could keep his hundred cows when they arrived. When he finished his corral he sat down to wait for the cows. He waited some time and then thought, "Perhaps the cows don't come on their own, maybe I should go for them." So he set out to look for his promised hundred cows. Near the church he came upon a large herd which he drove home and locked securely in his corral.

Later that afternoon the two *vaqueros*[4] who took care of the priest's herd rode to the Indian's home.

"Why do you have these cattle locked up?" they asked gruffly. "Have they done some damage?"

"No, they haven't done any damage," the Indian answered. "I have them locked up because they're mine. I gave the priest a cow and he promised me God would give me a hundred, and here they are!"

"These are the priest's cattle, not yours," the cowboys answered.

"No, these are mine because he promised me a hundred for one!" the Indian insisted.

The cowboys returned to tell the priest what had happened. When he heard the news the

1. **homily** (hŏm′ə-lē): sermon.
2. **alms:** money or goods given as charity to the poor.
3. **Padre** (pä′drĕ) *Spanish:* Father; used as a form of address for a priest.
4. ***vaqueros*** (vä-kĕ′rôs) *Spanish:* cowboys.

Castle Mission, John Runne. Copyright © John Runne, Evergreen Art Company, Evergeen, Colorado.

priest became very angry. He got on his mule and the three rode to the Indian's home. When they arrived at the corral the Indian was sitting by the gate, his bow and quiver of arrows ready.

"Why have you locked up my cattle in your corral!" the priest shouted. "Is this the way you show your gratitude?"

"But these are my cows," the Indian answered.

"And who gave them to you?"

"You did. You said at mass whoever gave one cow would get a hundred in return!"

"That's not what I meant, you thief!" the priest cried angrily. "You are a thief and you must turn my cattle loose." He got down from his mule to open the gate but stopped when he saw the Indian put an arrow to his bow.

"Padre, if you dare touch the lock I will stick this arrow into your heart. Then the devils in hell will give you a hundred more."

The priest backed away. He realized the Indian meant to make him keep the promise he had made in church, and there was nothing he could do. So he got on his mule and quietly rode home, reminding himself to be more careful with what he said in his sermons. ❖

El Indito de las Cien Vacas

interpretado por José Griego y Maestas

Habia un indio del pueblo muy devoto que no faltaba a misa nunca. Y un domingo en el sermón que les echó el padre, les dijo:

"Hagan caridades, hijos. Den limosna. Miren que para que Dios les ayude, es menester que ustedes también le den a la iglesia, porque han de saber que el que le hace una donación a Dios, Dios le devuelve ciento por uno."

El indito, que estaba escuchando, de una vez intentó traerle al padre una vaquita que tenía. En la tarde le trujo la vaquita y le dijo, "Tata padre, aquí te traigo esta vaquita para que Dios me de cien por una vaquita."

"Sí, sí, hijo. Ten fe en que Dios te va a recompensar esta limosna."

El indito se volvió a su casa muy satisfecho y empezó a hacer un corral grande para cuando le vinieran las cien vacas. Acabó su corral y se puso a esperar las vacas. El miraba para todos rumbos a ver por donde venían y viendo que no venían, ya se puso en camino a buscarlas. Pensó, "Quizás las vacas no venir solas. Quizás yo ir por ellas." Pues el primer hatajo de vacas que encontró lo arreó para su corral y lo encerró y atrincó bien la puerta.

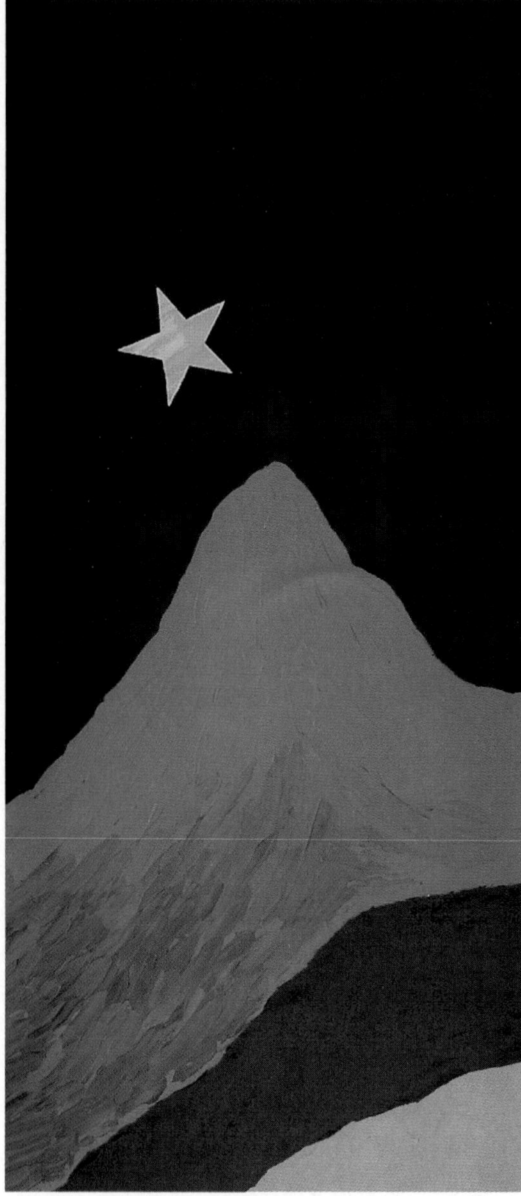

Detail of *Castle Mission,* John Runne.

Más tarde cayeron los que cuidaban las vacas y eran de tata padre las vacas y le dijeron al indio:

"¿Por qué tienes estas vacas encerradas? ¿Qué te hicieron daño?"

"No, no me hicieron daño, pero yo le di a tata padre mi vaquita y él me prometió que Dios me daría cien, y estas son."

"Estas son del padre y no tuyas," le decían los vaqueros.

"No son. Estas son mías porque él me prometió darme el ciento por uno."

Los vaqueros se fueron a avisarle al padre. Luego el padre se enojó, montó en su mula y se fueron los tres junto. Cuando llegaron al corral de las vacas, ya el indito estaba allí en la puerta con su arco y su carcaje.

"Pero, indio grosero, ¿por qué tienes mis vacas encerradas aquí?"

"Porque estas son mías, tata padre."

"¿Quién te las dio?"

"Tú me las distes. Tú decir allá en misa que el que te diera una vaca, tú le dabas cien."

"Pero indio embustero, tú eres un ladrón y estas vacas voy a echarlas." El padre se apeó a abrir la puerta y el indito puso una flecha en su arco.

"Tata padre, si tú mueves una tranca, te ensarto esta flecha en el mero corazón."

"No, no, hijo, con las armas no se juega. Si así quieres, está bien."

Pues le dejó el padre las vacas al indio y se fue el padre muy callado a su casa, recordando que en otra ocasión, valía más descoger sus palabras con cuidado. ❖

RESPONDING OPTIONS

FROM PERSONAL RESPONSE *TO* CRITICAL ANALYSIS

REFLECT 1. Did you enjoy this *cuento*? Jot down your opinion of it in your notebook.

RETHINK 2. What do you think is the moral of this *cuento*?

3. Should the priest have let the Indian keep the hundred cows? Give reasons for your answer.

4. Why do you think the Indian and the priest misunderstand one another?

   Consider
   - what the priest means when he tells the churchgoers that God returns gifts a hundredfold
   - what makes the Indian believe he can take the cows

RELATE 5. At the heart of this *cuento* is a misunderstanding that arises because of differences between cultures. What cultural differences might cause misunderstandings among people who live in your community? Was the misunderstanding you described in the Personal Connection the result of cultural differences?

6. The two Native American Coyote stories you read in Unit One were trickster tales. Would you say that "The Indian and the Hundred Cows" is a trickster tale in the same way that the Coyote stories are? Explain your opinion.

ANOTHER PATHWAY

Cooperative Learning

With four of your classmates, present a storytelling performance of this tale for the rest of the class. One group member will act as the narrator; the others, as the priest, the Indian, and the two cowboys. Remember to speak clearly and slowly, and use appropriate facial expressions and gestures to bring the characters to life.

LITERARY CONCEPTS

As you know, a **folk tale** is a short, simple story that is handed down, usually by word of mouth, from generation to generation. Folk tales, such as this *cuento*, often serve to teach family obligations or societal values. By reading folk tales, you can learn how the inhabitants of a certain region live and what their values are. In reading "The Indian and the Hundred Cows," what did you learn about the frontier Southwest, where the tale originated? What values do you think this tale might teach? What are some folk tales that reveal the ways of living or the values of your community?

QUICKWRITES

1. Imagine that the priest again speaks to churchgoers about the importance of charity when he delivers his next homily, on the Sunday after the incident in the story. Write part of the **sermon** he might give that day.

2. Draft a humorous **folk tale** in which a figurative statement is taken literally. If the misunderstanding you described in the Personal Connection is applicable here, you might use it as the basis for your folk tale.

PORTFOLIO *Save your writing. You may want to use it later as a springboard to a piece for your portfolio.*

ACROSS THE CURRICULUM

Spanish Some words in English are similar to Spanish words. These words—such as Indian and *indio,* deity and *Dios*—often have **common roots** that are based on words with Latin origins.

Choose five words from the Spanish version of "The Indian and the Hundred Cows," and use an English-Spanish dictionary to translate them. Then make a chart showing each Spanish word and its English equivalent. If you can think of any related English words that seem to share a common Latin root with the Spanish word, add them to the chart, as in the example shown.

Spanish Word	English Equivalent	From Common Root
ciento	hundred	cent, century, centennial

LITERARY LINKS

Compare this story with "The Man to Send Rain Clouds" on page 46. Are there similar characters, cultural differences, or conflicts in the two stories? Make a chart showing the similarities and the differences between the two stories.

THE WRITER'S STYLE

Rudolfo A. Anaya, the translator of this tale, wrote: "My English variations of these old, old cuentos are my versions. . . . I started with José Griego's adaptations from the literal transcriptions originally compiled by Juan B. Rael, and I worked from Spanish into English to suit my own rhythm." What do you think might be gained and what might be lost through this process of retelling *cuentos* in written form and then translating them into English? If you know some Spanish, evaluate how Anaya's English version of "The Indian and the Hundred Cows" differs from the Spanish version.

JOSÉ GRIEGO Y MAESTAS

José Griego y Maestas adapted "The Indian and the Hundred Cows" from the original Spanish version gathered by Juan B. Rael from Southwestern storytellers. Griego, who received his master's degree in Spanish literature from the University of New Mexico, has taught at the College of Santa Fe. An expert in the field of bilingual education, he has directed and administered New Mexico's bilingual education program. Griego has also served as the director of the Guadalupe Historic Foundation in Santa Fe.

RUDOLFO A. ANAYA

1937–

Rudolfo A. Anaya, one of the most widely read Mexican-American writers in the United States, was born, raised, and educated in New Mexico. In his novels, short stories, plays, and poetry, he draws on the rich culture and history of his native Southwest and on the myths and legends of the Spanish *cuentos.* As Anaya has observed, "each community has art to offer, and now we've come to a place in American history where we celebrate that." Until his retirement in 1993, Anaya taught creative writing and literature at the University of New Mexico.

OTHER WORKS *Bless Me, Ultima; Heart of Aztlán; Tortuga; Alburquerque*

PREVIEWING

FOLK TALE

High Horse's Courting *from* Black Elk Speaks

Black Elk

Told through John G. Neihardt

PERSONAL CONNECTION

In a small group, share ideas about how important wealth or earning ability is in courtship. Do you believe money should be an important consideration in deciding whom to marry? Do you think some parents would have different ideas than you and your classmates have? Share your group's ideas with the rest of the class.

CULTURAL CONNECTION

Black Elk was an Oglala Sioux medicine man who was born in the 19th century, before his people were driven from their lands in the northern Great Plains onto reservations. "High Horse's Courting" is a story that Black Elk learned from Watanye, an older member of his tribe, and later passed on to Nebraska writer John G. Neihardt, who preserved it in the book *Black Elk Speaks.* The story deals with courtship in the context of traditional Sioux beliefs and customs. Usually, before marrying, a Sioux man had to prove himself in war or hunting. Having many horses increased a man's status, and a man's offer of horses to a woman's family signaled a marriage proposal. If the horses were accepted, the wedding would take place a few days later.

An Indian horse dance. Part 1, Plate 9 from Sioux Indian Painting, notes by H.B. Alexander, courtesy of Department of Library Services, American Museum of Natural History. Copyright © American Museum of Natural History.

WRITING CONNECTION

In your notebook, freewrite about courtship customs within your own circle of friends and family. How do young people arrange a date, make a good impression on someone they are attracted to, or choose a spouse? What role do parents play when their children decide whom to date or to marry? Try to look at these customs with a fresh eye, as you would if you were trying to explain them to someone from another culture. Then, as you read the story, mentally compare the courtship customs of the Sioux with those familiar to you.

HIGH HORSE'S COURTING

Black Elk told through John C. Neihardt

YOU KNOW, IN THE OLD DAYS, IT WAS NOT SO VERY EASY TO GET A GIRL WHEN you wanted to be married. Sometimes it was hard work for a young man and he had to stand a great deal. Say I am a young man and I have seen a young girl who looks so beautiful to me that I feel all sick when I think about her. I cannot just go and tell her about it and then get married if she is willing. I have to be a very sneaky fellow to talk to her at all, and after I have managed to talk to her, that is only the beginning.

Probably for a long time I have been feeling sick about a certain girl because I love her so much, but she will not even look at me, and her parents keep a good watch over her. But I keep feeling worse and worse all the time; so maybe I sneak up to her tepee in the dark and wait until she comes out. Maybe I just wait there all night and don't get any sleep at all and she does not come out. Then I feel sicker than ever about her.

Maybe I hide in the brush by a spring where she sometimes goes to get water, and when she comes by, if nobody is looking, then I jump out and hold her and just make her listen to me. If she likes me too, I can tell that from the way she acts, for she is very bashful and maybe will not say a word or even look at me the first time. So I let her go, and then maybe I sneak around until I can see her father alone, and I tell him how many horses I can give him for his beautiful girl, and by now I am feeling so sick that maybe I would give him all the horses in the world if I had them.

Well, this young man I am telling about was called High Horse, and there was a girl in the village who looked so beautiful to him that he was just sick all over from thinking about her so much and he was getting sicker all the time. The girl was very shy, and her parents thought a great deal of her because they were not young any more and this was the only child they had. So they watched her all day long, and they fixed it so that she would be safe at night too when they were asleep. They thought so much of her that they had made a rawhide bed for her to sleep in, and after they knew that High Horse was sneaking around after her, they took rawhide thongs and tied the girl in bed at night so that nobody could steal her when they were asleep, for they were not sure but that their girl might really want to be stolen.

Wild Horses of Nevada (1927), Maynard Dixon. Oil, 44″ × 50″, courtesy of the William A. Karges Family Trust.

Well, after High Horse had been sneaking around a good while and hiding and waiting for the girl and getting sicker all the time, he finally caught her alone and made her talk to him. Then he found out that she liked him maybe a little. Of course this did not make him feel well. It made him sicker than ever, but now he felt as brave as a bison bull, and so he went right to her father and said he loved the girl so much that he would give two good horses for her—one of them young and the other one not so very old.

But the old man just waved his hand, meaning for High Horse to go away and quit talking foolishness like that.

High Horse was feeling sicker than ever about it; but there was another young fellow who said he would loan High Horse two ponies and when he got some more horses, why, he could just give them back for the ones he had borrowed.

Then High Horse went back to the old man and said he would give four horses for the girl—two of them young and the other two not hardly old at all. But the old man just waved his hand and would not say anything.

So High Horse sneaked around until he could talk to the girl again, and he asked her to run away with him. He told her he thought he would just fall over and die if she did not. But she said she would not do that; she wanted to be bought like a fine woman. You see she thought a great deal of herself too.

That made High Horse feel so very sick that he could not eat a bite, and he went around with his head hanging down as though he might just fall down and die any time.

Red Deer was another young fellow, and he and High Horse were great comrades, always doing things together. Red Deer saw how High Horse was acting, and he said: "Cousin, what is the matter? Are you sick in the belly? You look as though you were going to die."

Then High Horse told Red Deer how it was, and said he thought he could not stay alive much longer if he could not marry the girl pretty quick.

Red Deer thought awhile about it, and then he said: "Cousin, I have a plan, and if you are man enough to do as I tell you, then everything will be all right. She will not run away with you; her old man will not take four horses; and four horses are all you can get. You must steal her and run away with her. Then afterwhile you can come back and the old man cannot do anything because she will be your woman. Probably she wants you to steal her anyway."

SO THEY PLANNED WHAT HIGH HORSE HAD TO DO, AND HE SAID HE loved the girl so much that he was man enough to do anything Red Deer or anybody else could think up.

So this is what they did.

That night late they sneaked up to the girl's tepee and waited until it sounded inside as though the old man and the old woman and the girl were sound asleep. Then High Horse crawled under the tepee with a knife. He had to cut the rawhide thongs first, and then Red Deer, who was pulling up the stakes around that side of the tepee, was going to help drag the girl outside and gag her. After that, High Horse could put her across his pony in front of him and hurry out of there and be happy all the rest of his life.

When High Horse had crawled inside, he felt so nervous that he could hear his heart drumming, and it seemed so loud he felt sure it would 'waken the old folks. But it did not, and afterwhile he began cutting the thongs. Every time he cut one it made a pop and nearly scared him to death. But he was getting along all right and all the thongs were cut down as far as the girl's thighs, when he became so nervous that his knife slipped and stuck the girl. She gave a big, loud yell. Then the old folks jumped up and yelled too. By this time High Horse was outside, and he and Red Deer were running away like antelope. The old man and some other people chased the young men but they got away in the dark and nobody knew who it was.

Well, if you ever wanted a beautiful girl you will know how sick High Horse was now. It was very bad the way he felt, and it looked as though he would starve even if he did not drop over dead sometime.

Red Deer kept thinking about this, and after a few days he went to High Horse and said: "Cousin, take courage! I have another plan, and I am sure, if you are man enough, we can steal her this time." And High Horse said: "I am man enough to do anything anybody can think up, if I can only get that girl."

So this is what they did.

They went away from the village alone, and Red Deer made High Horse strip naked. Then he painted High Horse solid white all over, and after that he painted black stripes all over the white and put black rings around High Horse's eyes. High Horse looked terrible. He looked so terrible that when Red Deer was through painting and took a good look at what he had done, he said it scared even him a little.

"Now," Red Deer said, "if you get caught again, everybody will be so scared they will think you are a bad spirit and will be afraid to chase you."

So when the night was getting old and everybody was sound asleep, they sneaked back to the girl's tepee. High Horse crawled in with his knife, as before, and Red Deer waited outside, ready to drag the girl out and gag her when High Horse had all the thongs cut.

High Horse crept up by the girl's bed and began cutting at the thongs. But he kept thinking, "If they see me they will shoot me because I look so terrible." The girl was restless and kept squirming around in bed, and when a thong was cut, it popped. So High Horse worked very slowly and carefully.

But he must have made some noise, for suddenly the old woman awoke and said to her old man: "Old Man, wake up! There is somebody in this tepee!" But the old man was sleepy and didn't want to be bothered. He said: "Of course there is somebody in this tepee. Go to sleep and don't bother me." Then he snored some more.

But High Horse was so scared by now that he lay very still and as flat to the ground as he could. Now, you see, he had not been sleeping very well for a long time because he was so sick about the girl. And while he was lying there waiting for the old woman to snore, he just forgot everything, even how beautiful the girl was. Red Deer, who was lying outside ready to do his part, wondered and wondered what had happened in there, but he did not dare call out to High Horse.

Afterwhile the day began to break and Red Deer had to leave with the two ponies he had staked there for his comrade and girl, or somebody would see him.

So he left.

Home Is the Hunter (1994), Gary Kapp. Oil, 34″ × 46″.

Now when it was getting light in the tepee, the girl awoke and the first thing she saw was a terrible animal, all white with black stripes on it, lying asleep beside her bed. So she screamed, and then the old woman screamed and the old man yelled. High Horse jumped up, scared almost to death, and he nearly knocked the tepee down getting out of there.

People were coming running from all over the village with guns and bows and axes, and everybody was yelling.

By now High Horse was running so fast that he hardly touched the ground at all, and he looked so terrible that the people fled from him and let him run. Some braves wanted to shoot at him, but the others said he might be some sacred being and it would bring bad trouble to kill him.

Night Horse (1992), C. J. Wells. Oil, 70″ × 60″, courtesy of Joan Marcus Fine Art.

High Horse made for the river that was near, and in among the brush he found a hollow tree and dived into it. Afterwhile some braves came there and he could hear them saying that it was some bad spirit that had come out of the water and gone back in again.

That morning the people were ordered to break camp and move away from there. So they did, while High Horse was hiding in his hollow tree.

Now Red Deer had been watching all this from his own tepee and trying to look as though he were as much surprised and scared as all the others. So when the camp moved, he sneaked back to where he had seen his comrade disappear. When he was down there in the brush, he called, and High Horse answered, because he knew his friend's voice. They washed off the paint from High Horse and sat down on the river bank to talk about their troubles.

High Horse said he never would go back to the village as long as he lived and he did not care what happened to him now. He said he was going to go on the war-path all by himself. Red Deer said: "No, cousin, you are not going on the war-path alone, because I am going with you."

So Red Deer got everything ready, and at night they started out on the war-path all alone. After several days they came to a Crow camp just about sundown, and when it was dark they sneaked up to where the Crow horses were grazing, killed the horse guard, who was not thinking about enemies because he thought all the Lakotas were far away, and drove off about a hundred horses.

They got a big start because all the Crow horses stampeded and it was probably morning before the Crow warriors could catch any horses to ride. Red Deer and High Horse fled with their herd three days and nights before they reached the village of their people. Then they drove the whole herd right into the village and up in front of the girl's tepee. The old man was there, and High Horse called out to him and asked if he thought maybe that would be enough horses for his girl. The old man did not wave him away that time. It was not the horses that he wanted. What he wanted was a son who was a real man and good for something.

So High Horse got his girl after all, and I think he deserved her. ❖

INSIGHT

I Will Fight No More Forever

Chief Joseph

Below is the famous surrender speech made in 1877 by Chief Joseph of the Nez Perce (nĕz′ pûrs′). In that year, Chief Joseph and his people, after being forced from their traditional lands in northeastern Oregon, had won several battles with U.S. Army forces led by General Oliver O. Howard. However, their only recourse lay in retreat. Chief Joseph and his remaining group of 750 traveled more than 1,000 miles and were only 40 miles from the Canadian border when they were surrounded by more U.S. troops. Following a five-day siege in which several chieftains were killed, including his own brother, Chief Joseph handed over his rifle.

Tell General Howard I know his heart. What he told me before I have in my heart. I am tired of fighting. Our chiefs are killed. Looking Glass is dead. Toohoolhoolzote is dead. The old men are all dead. It is the young men who say yes or no. He who led on the young men is dead. It is cold and we have no blankets. The little children are freezing to death. My people, some of them, have run away to the hills, and have no blankets, no food; no one knows where they are—perhaps freezing to death. I want to have time to look for my children and see how many of them I can find. Maybe I shall find them among the dead. Hear me, my chiefs! I am tired; my heart is sick and sad. From where the sun now stands I will fight no more forever.

Chief Joseph. Courtesy of the Heye Foundation, National Museum of the American Indian, Smithsonian Institution (33738).

RESPONDING OPTIONS

FROM PERSONAL RESPONSE *TO* CRITICAL ANALYSIS

REFLECT 1. How entertaining did you find this tale of courtship? Share your reaction with a partner.

RETHINK 2. Do you think High Horse deserved to marry the girl he loved? Give reasons for your answer.

3. How might things have worked out if High Horse had just stolen the girl, as he had first planned to do?

   Consider
   - how he and the girl might have felt about each other afterward
   - how the girl's parents and others might have viewed him

4. "He was always teaching me things," Black Elk said of Watanye, who told him this story. In your opinion, what values does "High Horse's Courting" teach?

RELATE 5. *Black Elk Speaks* was written primarily to record the traditional Sioux way of life that was destroyed with the coming of whites. In one section of the book, Black Elk mourns what was lost when his people were massacred at Wounded Knee (see quotation on page 511), much as Chief Joseph, in the Insight selection, mourns what the Nez Perce lost in their final battle with U.S. Army forces. If you were a spiritual leader of a group, as these men were, how would you help your people survive such a defeat?

ANOTHER PATHWAY

Act out a talk-show interview with High Horse, the girl he loved, the girl's father, and Red Deer. Five students should play the roles of the characters and the talk-show host. The other students should play the studio audience and ask questions about the characters' reasons for acting and feeling as they did at specific points in the tale.

QUICKWRITES

1. Write a **story outline** that adapts this tale to a modern setting. What obstacles might a young person today have to overcome to win his or her love? What would he or she offer instead of horses?
2. Review what you wrote about courtship customs for the Writing Connection on page 521. Then draft a **comparison-and-contrast essay** in which you explore similarities and differences between traditional Sioux courtship customs and the customs of your own culture.

***PORTFOLIO** Save your writing. You may want to use it later as a spring-board to a piece for your portfolio.*

LITERARY CONCEPTS

"High Horse's Courting" is an example of **oral literature,** literature that is passed from one generation to another by performance or word of mouth. Discuss what makes this story sound as if it were being told to someone, not read from a book.

Cooperative Learning Divide this tale among the members of a small group of classmates. Have each group member memorize and then retell his or her portion of the tale, using the gestures and tone of voice that Black Elk might have used.

ACROSS THE CURRICULUM

Economics High Horse offers horses to the father of the girl he wants to marry. Why were horses so important to the Plains Indians? What was the exchange value of a horse? Report your findings to the class.

Anthropology Find out more about traditional Sioux (Lakota) courtship and marriage customs or research any other aspects of Sioux culture that interest you, such as bison hunting or spirituality. Share your knowledge in an oral presentation.

BLACK ELK

1863–1950

At age 9, Black Elk had a vision in which he was given the power to help his fellow Oglala Sioux. He later interpreted his vision to mean that he should help his people survive the coming of white settlers—a belief that grew stronger as he witnessed the defeat of General George Custer's troops at the Battle of Little Bighorn.

In his 20s, Black Elk joined Buffalo Bill's Wild West Show, hoping to learn from the whites something that would benefit his people. In 1889, after touring Europe with the show, he returned home to find that a new treaty had deprived his tribe of half its land. Tensions between the Sioux and the U.S. Army led, in the following year, to the Battle of Wounded Knee, in which soldiers massacred nearly 300 unarmed Sioux men, women, and children.

For the rest of his life, Black Elk lived on the Pine Ridge Reservation in South Dakota, saddened that he had failed to save his people. In 1931 he told the story of his life and visions to John G. Neihardt, who helped him write his life story, *Black Elk Speaks.*

OTHER WORKS *The Sacred Pipe*

JOHN G. NEIHARDT

John G. Neihardt (1881–1973) grew up in the frontier town of Wayne, Nebraska. From 1901 to 1907, he lived near the Omaha Indian Reservation; his experiences with the Omaha and other tribes that lived on the Great Plains influenced his poetry and fiction.

Between 1915 and 1941, Neihardt published a five-part epic poem, *The Cycle of the West,* about the displacement of Native Americans by white settlers in the 1800s. While doing research for the final part of this epic—*The Song of the Messiah*—he met with Black Elk. Black Elk said to him: "There is so much to teach you. What I know was given to me for men and it is true and it is beautiful. Soon I shall be under the grass and it will be lost. You were sent to save it, and you must come back so that I can teach you." The result of their talks was Neihardt's most popular book, *Black Elk Speaks.*

From 1943 to 1948, Neihardt served with the Bureau of Indian Affairs. In earlier years, he had worked as the literary editor of the *Minneapolis Journal* and of the *St. Louis Post-Dispatch.* He also taught poetry at the University of Nebraska and at the University of Missouri. Neihardt was named Nebraska's poet laureate in 1921.

OTHER WORKS *Collected Poems, Indian Tales and Others, When the Tree Flowered*

LASERLINKS
• *CULTURAL CONNECTION*

PREVIEWING

NONFICTION

from The Autobiography of Mark Twain

Mark Twain

PERSONAL CONNECTION

Have you ever pretended to be something that you are not? If you have, why? What did you say or do to convince other people to believe you? How did you feel about misrepresenting yourself to others? Write your thoughts in your notebook, and then share them with a small group of classmates. Alternatively, if you have never misrepresented yourself, explain what has kept you from doing so.

HISTORICAL CONNECTION

It might be hard for you to imagine how Americans entertained themselves before the coming of television, compact disc players, computer games, and movies. In 1850, when the events in the following selection took place, these forms of diversion were, of course, nonexistent. At that time, people who lived in small towns where entertainment was scarce relied on local talent or the periodic visits of traveling shows. These shows passed through towns in wagons pulled by horses or mules—with attached portable stages or "tripes and keisters" (suitcases mounted on tripods). The showmen, who sometimes pretended to be doctors, sorcerers, Indians, or Turks, sold patent medicines they claimed would cure anything from a toothache to love sickness. These showmen drew crowds with demonstrations of magic, ventriloquism, and hypnotism. As you may already know, hypnotism involves placing a person in a highly suggestible, trancelike state during which he or she follows the commands of the hypnotist. In this excerpt from Mark Twain's autobiography, a traveling mesmerizer, or hypnotist, visits Hannibal, Missouri, the town where Twain grew up.

READING CONNECTION

Enjoying Humor Mark Twain has been called "a great American humorist." Many elements make his writing entertaining, such as absurd or ironic situations, trickster characters, colorful dialect, elevated language, exaggeration, and a meandering delivery. As you read about how he once pretended to be something he was not, relax and enjoy the humor of his story. In your notebook, copy sentences or phrases you find particularly amusing, and be prepared to share them in class.

The Quack-Doctor (1889), W. Rogers. The Picture Collection, New York Public Library.

from THE AUTOBIOGRAPHY OF MARK TWAIN

MARK TWAIN

An exciting event in our village was the arrival of the mesmerizer.[1] I think the year was 1850. As to that I am not sure but I know the month—it was May; that detail has survived the wear of fifty years. A pair of connected little incidents of that month have served to keep the memory of it green for me all this time; incidents of no consequence and not worth embalming, yet my memory has preserved them carefully and flung away things of real value to give them space and make them comfortable. The truth is, a person's memory has no more sense than his conscience and no appreciation whatever of values and proportions. However, never mind those trifling incidents; my subject is the mesmerizer now.

He advertised his show and promised marvels. Admission as usual: 25 cents, children half price. The village had heard of mesmerism in a general way but had not encountered it yet. Not many people attended the first night but next day they had so many wonders to tell that everybody's curiosity was fired and after that for a fortnight the magician had prosperous times. I was fourteen or fifteen years old, the age at which a boy is willing to endure all things, suffer all things short of death by fire, if thereby he may be conspicuous and show off before the public; and so, when I saw the "subjects" perform their foolish antics on the platform and make the people laugh and shout and admire I had a burning desire to be a subject myself.

Every night for three nights I sat in the row of candidates on the platform and held the magic disk[2] in the palm of my hand and gazed at it and tried to get sleepy, but it was a failure; I remained wide awake and had to retire defeated, like the majority. Also, I had to sit there and be gnawed with envy of Hicks, our journeyman;[3] I had to sit there and see him scamper and jump when Simmons the enchanter exclaimed, "See the snake! See the snake!" and hear him say, "My, how beautiful!" in response to the suggestion that he was observing a splendid sunset; and so on—the whole insane business. I couldn't laugh, I couldn't applaud; it filled me with bitterness to have others do it and to have people make a hero of Hicks and crowd around him when the show was over and ask him for more and more particulars of the wonders he had seen in his visions and manifest in many ways that they were proud to be acquainted

1. **mesmerizer** (mĕz′mə-rī′zər): hypnotist; from the name of an Austrian physician, Franz Anton Mesmer, who popularized hypnotism in the 1770s.
2. **magic disk:** object used by the mesmerizer to focus a subject's attention, helping him or her to achieve the hypnotic state.
3. **journeyman:** sound and experienced, but not brilliant, craftsman or performer.

with him. Hicks—the idea! I couldn't stand it; I was getting boiled to death in my own bile.[4]

On the fourth night temptation came and I was not strong enough to resist. When I had gazed at the disk a while I pretended to be sleepy and began to nod. Straightway came the professor and made passes over my head and down my body and legs and arms, finishing each pass with a snap of his fingers in the air to discharge the surplus electricity;[5] then he began to "draw" me with the disk, holding it in his fingers and telling me I could not take my eyes off it, try as I might; so I rose slowly, bent and gazing, and followed that disk all over the place, just as I had seen the others do. Then I was put through the other paces. Upon suggestion I fled from snakes, passed buckets at a fire, became excited over hot steamboat-races, made love to imaginary girls and kissed them, fished from the platform and landed mud cats[6] that outweighed me—and so on, all the customary marvels. But not in the customary way. I was cautious at first and watchful, being afraid the professor would discover that I was an impostor and drive me from the platform in disgrace; but as soon as I realized that I was not in danger, I set myself the task of terminating Hicks's usefulness as a subject and of usurping his place.

It was a sufficiently easy task. Hicks was born honest, I without that incumbrance[7]—so some people said. Hicks saw what he saw and reported accordingly, I saw more than was visible and added to it such details as could help. Hicks had no imagination; I had a double supply. He was born calm, I was born excited. No vision could start a rapture in him and he was constipated as to language, anyway; but if I saw a vision I emptied the dictionary onto it and lost the remnant of my mind into the bargain.

At the end of my first half-hour Hicks was a thing of the past, a fallen hero, a broken idol, and I knew it and was glad and said in my heart, "Success to crime!" Hicks could never have been mesmerized to the point where he could kiss an imaginary girl in public or a real one either, but I was competent. Whatever Hicks had failed in, I made it a point to succeed in, let the cost be what it might, physically or morally. He had shown several bad defects and I had made a note of them. For instance, if the magician asked, "What do you see?" and left him to invent a vision for himself, Hicks was dumb and blind, he couldn't see a thing nor say a word, whereas the magician soon found out that when it came to seeing visions of a stunning and marketable sort I could get along better without his help than with it.

Then there was another thing: Hicks wasn't worth a tallow dip[8] on mute mental suggestion. Whenever Simmons stood behind him and gazed at the back of

4. **bile** (bīl): bitterness; ill humor.
5. **discharge . . . electricity:** It was once believed, wrongly, that hypnosis was linked to electricity and magnetism.
6. **mud cats:** catfish.
7. **incumbrance:** burden; obligation.
8. **wasn't worth a tallow dip:** wasn't any good. A tallow dip was an inexpensive candle.

WORDS TO KNOW **usurping** (yo͞o-sûr′pĭng) *n.* taking another's place wrongfully **usurp** *v.*

his skull and tried to drive a mental suggestion into it, Hicks sat with vacant face and never suspected. If he had been noticing he could have seen by the rapt faces of the audience that something was going on behind his back that required a response. Inasmuch as I was an impostor I dreaded to have this test put upon me, for I knew the professor would be "willing" me to do something, and as I couldn't know what it was, I should be exposed and denounced. However, when my time came, I took my chance. I perceived by the tense and expectant faces of the people that Simmons was behind me willing me with all his might. I tried my best to imagine what he wanted but nothing suggested itself. I felt ashamed and miserable then. I believed that the hour of my disgrace was come and that in another moment I should go out of that place disgraced. I ought to be ashamed to confess it but my next thought was not how I could win the compassion of kindly hearts by going out humbly and in sorrow for my misdoings, but how I could go out most sensationally and spectacularly.

There was a rusty and empty old revolver lying on the table among the "properties"[9] employed in the performances. On May Day two or three weeks before there had been a celebration by the schools and I had had a quarrel with a big boy who was the school bully and I had not come out of it with credit.[10] That boy was now seated in the middle of the house, halfway down the main aisle. I crept stealthily and impressively toward the table, with a dark and murderous scowl on my face, copied from a popular romance, seized the revolver suddenly, flourished it, shouted the bully's name, jumped off the platform and made a rush for him and chased him out of the house before the paralyzed people could interfere to save him. There was a storm of applause, and the magician, addressing the house, said, most impressively—

"That you may know how really remarkable this is and how wonderfully developed a subject we have in this boy, I assure you that without a single spoken word to guide him he has carried out what I mentally commanded him to do, to the minutest detail. I could have stopped him at a moment in his vengeful career by a mere exertion of my will, therefore the poor fellow who has escaped was at no time in danger."

> **Hicks had no IMAGINATION; I HAD A DOUBLE SUPPLY. HE WAS BORN CALM, I WAS BORN EXCITED.**

So I was not in disgrace. I returned to the platform a hero and happier than I have ever been in this world since. As regards mental suggestion, my fears of it were gone. I judged that in case I failed to guess what the professor might be willing me to do, I could count on putting up something that would answer just as well. I was right, and exhibitions of unspoken suggestion became a favorite with the public. Whenever I perceived that I was being willed to do something I got up and did something—anything that occurred to me—and the magician, not being a fool, always ratified it.

9. **"properties":** articles, other than costumes and scenery, that are used on the stage during a dramatic performance.

10. **credit:** honor or distinction.

WORDS TO KNOW

rapt (răpt) *adj.* deeply moved, delighted, or absorbed

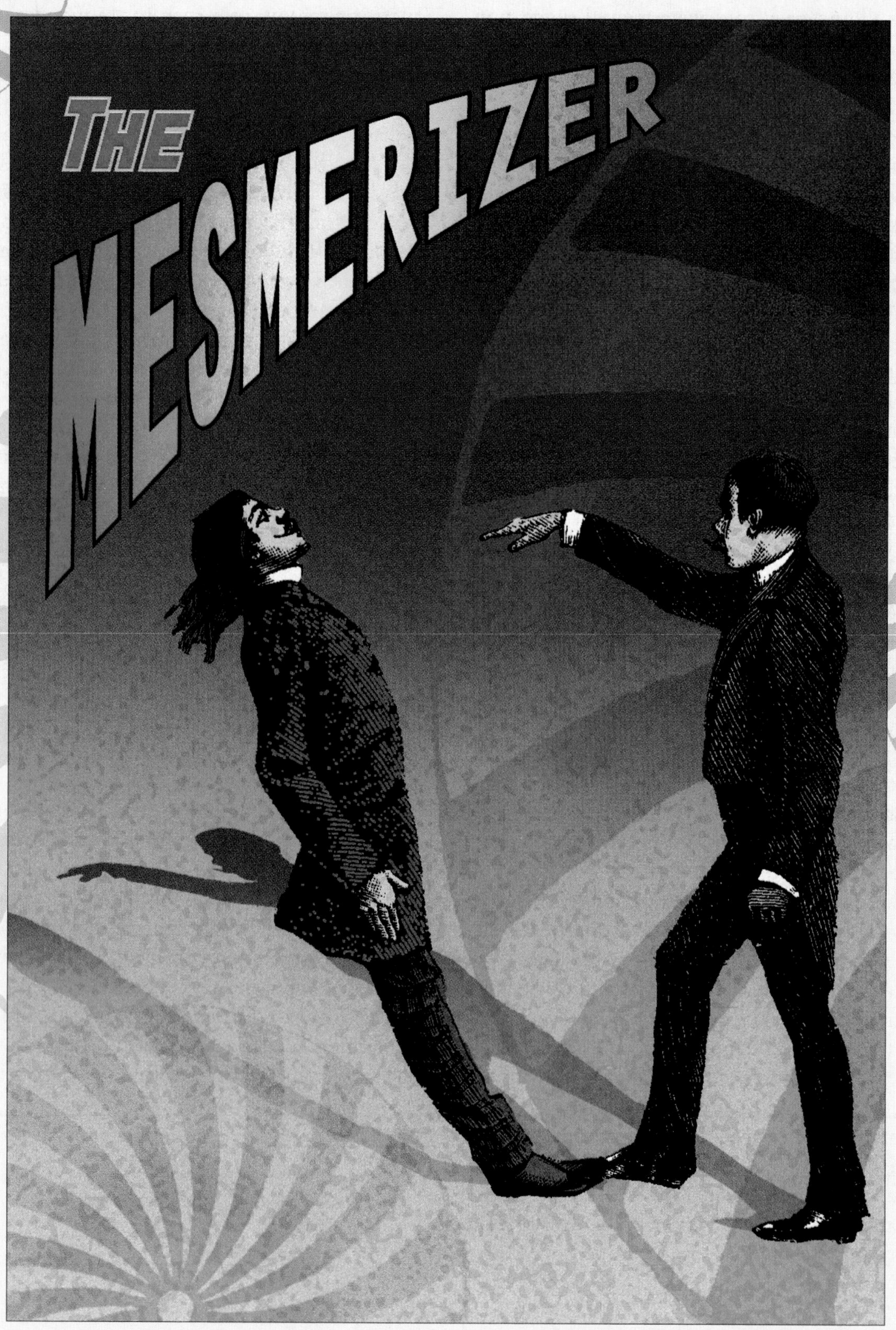
THE
MESMERIZER

When people asked me, "How *can* you tell what he is willing you to do?" I said, "It's just as easy," and they always said admiringly, "Well, it beats *me* how you can do it."

Hicks was weak in another detail. When the professor made passes over him and said "his whole body is without sensation now—come forward and test him, ladies and gentlemen," the ladies and gentlemen always complied eagerly and stuck pins into Hicks, and if they went deep Hicks was sure to wince, then that poor professor would have to explain that Hicks "wasn't sufficiently under the influence." But I didn't wince; I only suffered and shed tears on the inside. The miseries that a conceited boy will endure to keep up his "reputation"! And so will a conceited man; I know it in my own person and have seen it in a hundred thousand others. That professor ought to have protected me and I often hoped he would, when the tests were unusually severe, but he didn't. It may be that he was deceived as well as the others, though I did not believe it nor think it possible. Those were dear good people but they must have carried simplicity and credulity to the limit. They would stick a pin in my arm and bear on it until they drove it a third of its length in, and then be lost in wonder that by a mere exercise of will power the professor could turn my arm to iron and make it insensible to pain. Whereas it was not insensible at all; I was suffering agonies of pain.

After that fourth night, that proud night, that triumphant night, I was the only subject. Simmons invited no more candidates to the platform. I performed alone every night the rest of the fortnight. Up to that time a dozen wise old heads, the intellectual aristocracy of the town, had held out as implacable unbelievers. I was as hurt by this as if I were engaged in some honest occupation. There is nothing surprising about this. Human beings feel dishonor the most, sometimes, when they most deserve it. That handful of overwise old gentlemen kept on shaking their heads all the first week and saying they had seen no marvels there that could not have been produced by collusion; and they were pretty vain of their unbelief too and liked to show it and air it and be superior to the ignorant and the gullible. Particularly old Dr. Peake, who was the ringleader of the irreconcilables and very formidable; for he was an F.F.V.,[11] he was learned, white-haired and venerable, nobly and richly clad in the fashions of an earlier and a courtlier day, he was large and stately, and he not only seemed wise but was what he seemed in that regard. He had great influence and his opinion upon any matter was worth much more than that of any other person in the community. When I conquered him at last, I knew I was undisputed master of the field; and now after more than fifty years I acknowledge with a few dry old tears that I rejoiced without shame.

In 1847 we were living in a large white house on the corner of Hill and Main Streets—a house that still stands but isn't large now although it hasn't lost a plank; I saw it a year ago and noticed that shrinkage. My father died in it in March of the year mentioned but our family did not move out of it until some months afterward. Ours was not the only family in the house; there was another, Dr. Grant's. One day Dr. Grant and Dr. Reyburn argued a matter on the street with sword canes and Grant was brought home

11. **F.F.V.:** First Family of Virginia. Dr. Peake has high social status because his ancestors were among the first settlers of Virginia.

WORDS TO KNOW

credulity (krĭ-do͞o′lĭ-tē) *n.* an inclination to believe too readily
implacable (ĭm-plăk′ə-bəl) *adj.* impossible to satisfy
collusion (kə-lo͞o′zhən) *n.* a secret agreement for a deceitful purpose
gullible (gŭl′ə-bəl) *adj.* easily deceived or tricked

multifariously punctured. Old Dr. Peake caulked the leaks and came every day for a while to look after him.

The Grants were Virginians, like Peake, and one day when Grant was getting well enough to be on his feet and sit around in the parlor and talk, the conversation fell upon Virginia and old times. I was present but the group were probably unconscious of me, I being only a lad and a negligible quantity.[12] Two of the group—Dr. Peake and Mrs. Crawford, Mrs. Grant's mother—had been of the audience when the Richmond theater burned down thirty-six years before, and they talked over the frightful details of that memorable tragedy. These were eye-witnesses, and with their eyes I saw it all with an intolerable vividness: I saw the black smoke rolling and tumbling toward the sky, I saw the flames burst through it and turn red, I heard the shrieks of the despairing, I glimpsed their faces at the windows, caught fitfully through the veiling smoke, I saw them jump to their death or to mutilation worse than death. The picture is before me yet and can never fade.

In due course they talked of the colonial mansion of the Peakes, with its stately columns and its spacious grounds, and by odds and ends I picked up a clearly defined idea of the place. I was strongly interested, for I had not before heard of such palatial things from the lips of people who had seen them with their own eyes. One detail, casually dropped, hit my imagination hard. In the wall by the great front door there was a round hole as big as a saucer—a British cannon ball had made it in the war of the Revolution. It was breathtaking; it made history real; history had never been real to me before.

Very well, three or four years later, as already mentioned, I was king bee and sole "subject" in the mesmeric show; it was the beginning of the second week; the performance was half over; just then the majestic Dr. Peake with his ruffled bosom and wrist-bands and his gold-headed cane entered, and a deferential citizen vacated his seat beside the Grants and made the great chief take it. This happened while I was trying to invent something fresh in the way of vision, in response to the professor's remark—

"Concentrate your powers. Look—look attentively. There—don't you see something? Concentrate—concentrate! Now then—describe it."

THE GLORY WHICH IS BUILT UPON A LIE SOON BECOMES A MOST UNPLEASANT INCUMBRANCE.

Without suspecting it, Dr. Peake, by entering the place, had reminded me of the talk of three years before. He had also furnished me capital and was become my confederate, an accomplice in my frauds. I began on a vision, a vague and dim one (that was part of the game at the beginning of a vision; it isn't best to see it too clearly at first, it might look as if you had come loaded with it). The vision developed by degrees and gathered swing, momentum, energy. It was the Richmond fire. Dr. Peake was cold at first and his fine face had a trace of polite scorn in it; but when he began to recognize that fire, that

12. **negligible quantity:** something insignificant or unimportant; nothing.

WORDS TO KNOW **confederate** (kən-fĕd′ər-ĭt) *n.* one who assists in a plot; associate expression changed and his eyes began to light up. As soon as I saw that, I threw the valves wide open and turned on all the steam and gave those people a supper of fire and horrors that was calculated to last them one while! They couldn't gasp when I got through—they were petrified. Dr. Peake had risen and was standing—and breathing hard. He said, in a great voice:

"My doubts are ended. No collusion could produce that miracle. It was totally impossible for him to know those details, yet he has described them with the clarity of an eyewitness—and with what unassailable truthfulness God knows I know!"

I saved the colonial mansion for the last night and solidified and perpetuated Dr. Peake's conversion with the cannon-ball hole. He explained to the house that I could never have heard of that small detail, which differentiated this mansion from all other Virginian mansions and perfectly identified it, therefore the fact stood proven that I had *seen* it in my vision. Lawks![13]

It is curious. When the magician's engagement closed there was but one person in the village who did not believe in mesmerism and I was the one. All the others were converted but I was to remain an implacable and unpersuadable disbeliever in mesmerism and hypnotism for close upon fifty years. This was because I never would examine them, in after life. I couldn't. The subject revolted me. Perhaps it brought back to me a passage in my life which for pride's sake I wished to forget; though I thought, or persuaded myself I thought, I should never come across a "proof" which wasn't thin and cheap and probably had a fraud like me behind it.

The truth is I did not have to wait long to get tired of my triumphs. Not thirty days, I think. The glory which is built upon a lie soon becomes a most unpleasant incumbrance. No doubt for a while I enjoyed having my exploits told and retold and told again in my presence and wondered over and exclaimed about, but I quite distinctly remember that there presently came a time when the subject was wearisome and odious to me and I could not endure the disgusting discomfort of it. I am well aware that the world-glorified doer of a deed of great and real splendor has just my experience; I know that he deliciously enjoys hearing about it for three or four weeks and that pretty soon after that he begins to dread the mention of it and by and by wishes he had been with the damned before he ever thought of doing that deed. I remember how General Sherman[14] used to rage and swear over "While we were marching through Georgia," which was played at him and sung at him everywhere he went; still, I think I suffered a shade more than the legitimate hero does, he being privileged to soften his misery with the reflection that his glory was at any rate golden and reproachless[15] in its origin, whereas I had no such privilege, there being no possible way to make mine respectable.

How easy it is to make people believe a lie and how hard it is to undo that work again! Thirty-five years after those evil exploits of mine I visited my old mother, whom I had not seen for ten years; and being moved by what seemed to me a rather noble and perhaps heroic impulse, I thought I would humble myself and confess my ancient fault. It cost me a great effort to make up my mind; I dreaded the sorrow that would rise in her face and the shame that would look out of her eyes; but after long and troubled reflection, the sacrifice seemed due and

13. **Lawks!:** an expression of wonder or amusement, shortened from "Lord, have mercy!"

14. **General Sherman:** William Tecumseh Sherman, the Union commander who led a destructive march from Atlanta, Georgia, to the Atlantic Ocean, cutting the Confederacy in two.

15. **reproachless:** so good and upright as to make any criticism impossible.

WORDS TO KNOW

unassailable (ŭn′ə-sā′lə-bəl) *adj.* impossible to dispute or disprove; undeniable

odious (ō′dē-əs) *adj.* arousing, or worthy of, strong dislike right and I gathered my resolution together and made the confession.

To my astonishment there were no sentimentalities, no dramatics, no George Washington effects; she was not moved in the least degree; she simply did not believe me and said so! I was not merely disappointed, I was nettled[16] to have my costly truthfulness flung out of the market in this placid and confident way when I was expecting to get a profit out of it. I asserted and reasserted, with rising heat, my statement that every single thing I had done on those long-vanished nights was a lie and a swindle; and when she shook her head tranquilly and said she knew better, I put up my hand and *swore* to it—adding a triumphant, "*Now* what do you say?"

It did not affect her at all; it did not budge her the fraction of an inch from her position. If this was hard for me to endure, it did not begin with the blister she put upon the raw[17] when she began to put my sworn oath out of court with *arguments* to prove that I was under a delusion and did not know what I was talking about. Arguments! Arguments to show that a person on a man's outside can know better what is on his inside than he does himself. I had cherished some contempt for arguments before, I have not enlarged my respect for them since. She refused to believe that I had invented my visions myself; she said it was folly: that I was only a child at the time and could not have done it. She cited the Richmond fire and the colonial mansion and said they were quite beyond my capacities. Then I saw my chance! I said she was right—I didn't invent those; I got them from Dr. Peake. Even this great shot did not damage. She said Dr. Peake's evidence was better than mine, and he had said in plain words that it was impossible for me to have heard about those things. Dear, dear, what a grotesque and unthinkable situation: a confessed swindler convicted of honesty and condemned to acquittal by circumstantial evidence furnished by the swindled!

I realized with shame and with impotent vexation that I was defeated all along the line. I had but one card left but it was a formidable one. I played it and stood from under. It seemed ignoble to demolish her fortress after she had defended it so valiantly but the defeated know not mercy. I played that master card. It was the pin-sticking. I said solemnly—

"I give you my honor, a pin was never stuck into me without causing me cruel pain."

She only said—

"It is thirty-five years. I believe you do think that now but I was there and I know better. You never winced."

She was so calm! and I was so far from it, so nearly frantic.

"Oh, my goodness!" I said, "let me *show* you that I am speaking the truth. Here is my arm; drive a pin into it—drive it to the head—I shall not wince."

She only shook her gray head and said with simplicity and conviction—

"You are a man now and could dissemble the hurt; but you were only a child then and could not have done it."

And so the lie which I played upon her in my youth remained with her as an unchallengeable truth to the day of her death. Carlyle[18] said "a lie cannot live." It shows that he did not know how to tell them. If I had taken out a life policy on this one the premiums would have bankrupted me ages ago. ❖

---

16. **nettled:** irritated; annoyed.
17. **the blister . . . raw:** a bad thing made even worse.
18. **Carlyle:** Thomas Carlyle, a British historian and essayist.

WORDS TO KNOW **dissemble** (dĭ-sĕm′bəl) *v.* to disguise or conceal behind a false appearance

RESPONDING OPTIONS

FROM PERSONAL RESPONSE *TO* CRITICAL ANALYSIS

REFLECT 1. What did you find humorous about this story? Share some of the lines you copied into your notebook.

RETHINK 2. How vividly does Twain describe the people and incidents in this selection? With other classmates, act out a scene from one of the mesmerizer's shows.

3. Do you think it was wrong for the young Twain to trick people by pretending to be mesmerized? Explain your opinion.

Consider
- why he decides to pretend
- how he feels about pretending
- his later failure to make his mother believe the truth

4. What do you think is Twain's attitude toward himself as a boy and toward the people in his hometown?

5. Do you agree with the pronouncements Twain makes about human nature at various points in the selection?

RELATE 6. Twain wrote that the incidents in his autobiography "must interest the average human being because [these incidents] are of a sort which he is familiar with in his own life." Can you easily relate this selection to your own life? Consider what you wrote for the Personal Connection (page 530).

ANOTHER PATHWAY

Cooperative Learning

Working in a small group, put together tips for an instruction manual called *How to Be a Good Mesmerizer.* Base your tips on the practices of Simmons (the mesmerizer) and his model "subject," the young Mark Twain. Cover topics such as choosing a town to stop in, pleasing a crowd, recognizing good subjects, and persuading skeptics.

QUICKWRITES

1. Pretend that the young Twain goes on the road with the mesmerizer. Create a **flyer** announcing an upcoming engagement of theirs in a new town.
2. Review what you wrote for the Personal Connection on page 530. Then draft an **autobiographical essay** about a time when you pretended to be something you weren't, comparing your experience with that of the young Twain. Read your essay to a classmate.

PORTFOLIO Save your writing. You may want to use it later as a springboard to a piece for your portfolio.

LITERARY CONCEPTS

Local color realism is a style of writing that truthfully imitates ordinary life and brings a particular region alive by portraying the dialects, dress, mannerisms, customs, character types, and landscapes of that region. Local color realists of the 19th century, such as Twain, captured the unique flavor of their particular regions through the use of accurate details. Although the term *local color* is usually applied to short stories and sketches, Twain's autobiography has features of local color writing. What details in this selection establish a specific setting? How attractive is the setting made to seem?

CRITIC'S CORNER

Elmer J. Joseph, a member of our student advisory board, complained about this selection: "Much is left unsaid about what happened to the mesmerizer and whether he knew how much of an impostor the narrator was." What do you think happened to the mesmerizer after his show in Hannibal, Missouri? Do you think he realized that the young Twain was faking? Share your conclusions with other classmates, giving reasons for your views.

ACROSS THE CURRICULUM

Psychology In this selection, Twain recalls how he pretended to be hypnotized when he was a boy. Find out more about hypnosis: What is it? What is it used for today? Does it really work? How is someone hypnotized? What are the dangers of hypnosis? Report your findings to the class.

WORDS TO KNOW

For each group of words below, write the letter of the word that is the best synonym for the boldfaced word.

1. **usurping** (a) seizing, (b) defeating, (c) borrowing
2. **rapt** (a) hidden, (b) casual, (c) spellbound
3. **unassailable** (a) leaky, (b) unquestionable, (c) mistaken
4. **gullible** (a) doubtful, (b) overtrusting, (c) excitable
5. **collusion** (a) conspiracy, (b) mixture, (c) idea
6. **dissemble** (a) feel, (b) disconnect, (c) hide
7. **implacable** (a) quiet, (b) indecisive, (c) unyielding
8. **credulity** (a) payment, (b) trust, (c) respect
9. **odious** (a) disgusting, (b) secretive, (c) humble
10. **confederate** (a) falsity, (b) accomplice, (c) team

MARK TWAIN

1835–1910

The appearance of Halley's comet marked the years of the birth and, 75 years later, the death of one of America's greatest literary stars. Born Samuel Langhorne Clemens in 1835, Mark Twain grew up in Hannibal, Missouri, along the Mississippi River. As a young man, he fulfilled a boyhood ambition and became a steamboat pilot. The experience provided him with insight into "all the different types of human nature" and with his pen name. The term *mark twain,* which is riverboat jargon, denotes water two fathoms deep, or deep enough for safe travel.

When the Civil War broke out, river traffic on the Mississippi came to a halt. Twain served briefly and unhappily in the Confederate army and then headed west with his brother to seek his fortune. After failing as a silver and gold miner, Twain pursued his career as a journalist. By the time Twain left the West in 1866, he had published his first successful short story, "The Notorious Jumping Frog of Calaveras County"; had made his first public lecture tour; and had begun to make a name for himself as a humorist.

In 1870 Twain married. Four years later, he and his family settled in a mansion in Hartford, Connecticut, where he wrote his greatest novels, including *The Adventures of Tom Sawyer* and *The Adventures of Huckleberry Finn.* In later years, however, Twain's personal life was beset by troubles. He declared bankruptcy because of bad investments, and he had to write and lecture at an exhausting pace in order to repay his debts and regain his fortune. The deaths of his wife and two of his daughters left him lonely and weary of the world. Although Twain's later works became increasingly biting and pessimistic, his best works reflect the spirit of America: a love of fun, a commitment to democracy, and a hatred of injustice and self-importance.

OTHER WORKS *The Gilded Age, Life on the Mississippi, Roughing It*

PREVIEWING

FICTION

A Wagner Matinee

Willa Cather

PERSONAL CONNECTION

In this story, the narrator tells us that his aunt Georgiana, a former music teacher, gave up a life of music in Boston, Massachusetts, to move to the Nebraska frontier with her new husband. Recall a time when you had to choose between two things that were very important to you. What were your choices? What factors did you weigh in making your decision? Re-create your decision process by filling out in your notebook a diagram like the one shown. Circle the choice you ended up making. Looking back, do you think you made the right choice?

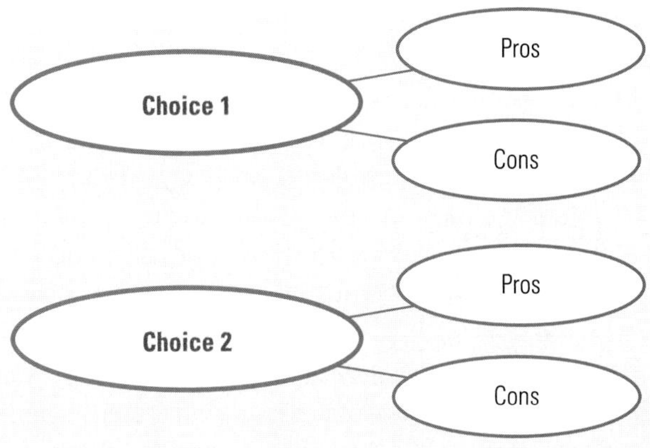

GEOGRAPHICAL/CULTURAL CONNECTION

The years after the Civil War were a time of expansion in the United States. While many people flocked to older cities in the East and the Midwest because of the growth of industry, adventurous pioneers went westward. As a result of the Homestead Act of 1862, hundreds of thousands of homesteaders rushed to settle on the Great Plains.

The story you are about to read is set in Boston around 1900. At that time, many city dwellers were able to enjoy cultural opportunities such as art museums and concerts featuring music by great European composers. In contrast, Easterners who made the choice to go west, like Aunt Georgiana in this story, left such worldly pleasures behind. Instead, these homesteaders faced long hours of strenuous labor and endured natural disasters such as drought, flood, and prairie fires.

This story contains several references to operas by the German composer Richard Wagner (väg′nər). It also mentions other operas and composers as well as musical terms such as *prelude, motive, overture, solo,* and *chorus.* It is not necessary to be familiar with these musical references to understand the story. However, if you do have a knowledge of classical music, you might briefly describe Wagner's operas and explain the musical terms to other students before they read.

LASERLINKS
• *CULTURAL CONNECTION*

READING CONNECTION

Drawing Conclusions About Characters

Meeting a character in a story, particularly in realistic fiction, is often like meeting a real person. You don't always have a mutual friend to explain the person's history, so you have to make guesses about the person from the clues available to you. For example, if you saw someone on a bus crying, you would conclude he or she was sad about something. If you saw someone with worn-out, dirt-caked shoes, carrying a backpack, you would probably conclude that he or she had traveled a long way on foot.

To get the most out of your reading of "A Wagner Matinee," you will have to draw conclusions about the main character, Aunt Georgiana. Because her nephew, the narrator, does not reveal everything there is to know about her, you must draw your own conclusions about what kind of person she is, what kinds of experiences she has had, and what she is feeling at a particular moment.

ONE READER'S RESPONSE

Reprinted below are sections of a paragraph from the exposition of "A Wagner Matinee" that describe Aunt Georgiana from her nephew's point of view. Following each section except the last are conclusions that one reader drew from the passage. After the last passage, you will be asked to draw your own conclusions.

Whatever shock Mrs. Springer [the landlady] experienced at my aunt's appearance, she considerately concealed. As for myself, I saw my aunt's misshapen figure with that feeling of awe and respect with which we behold explorers who have left their ears and fingers north of Franz-Josef-Land, or their health somewhere along the Upper Congo.

Conclusions:
Her body is shockingly misshapen. She is probably old. The narrator's "awe and respect" and his comparison of her to explorers suggest that whatever has injured or changed her is due to something admirable.

My Aunt Georgiana had been a music teacher at the Boston Conservatory, somewhere back in the latter sixties.

Conclusion:
She seems to have a pretty classy background.

One summer, while visiting in the little village among the Green Mountains where her ancestors had dwelt for generations, she had kindled the callow fancy of the most idle and shiftless of all the village lads, and had conceived for this Howard Carpenter one of those extravagant passions which a handsome country boy of twenty-one sometimes inspires in an angular, spectacled woman of thirty.

Conclusions:
She falls for a "shiftless" man 9 years younger, maybe because he's good-looking and she's not. She's "angular" (tall and bony, I imagine) and wears glasses. Since she was 30 years old, I guess she thought this was her last chance for love. But what does he see in her? Maybe he likes her classy background and her "extravagant passion."

When she returned to her duties in Boston, Howard followed her, and the upshot of this inexplicable infatuation was that she eloped with him, eluding the reproaches of her family and the criticisms of her friends by going with him to the Nebraska frontier.

What conclusions would *you* draw about Aunt Georgiana from her sudden elopement? Does it seem very romantic or hopelessly foolish? Do you admire her for it or not? Write down your conclusions in your notebook. As you read, continue to draw conclusions from details about Aunt Georgiana and about the other characters in the story.

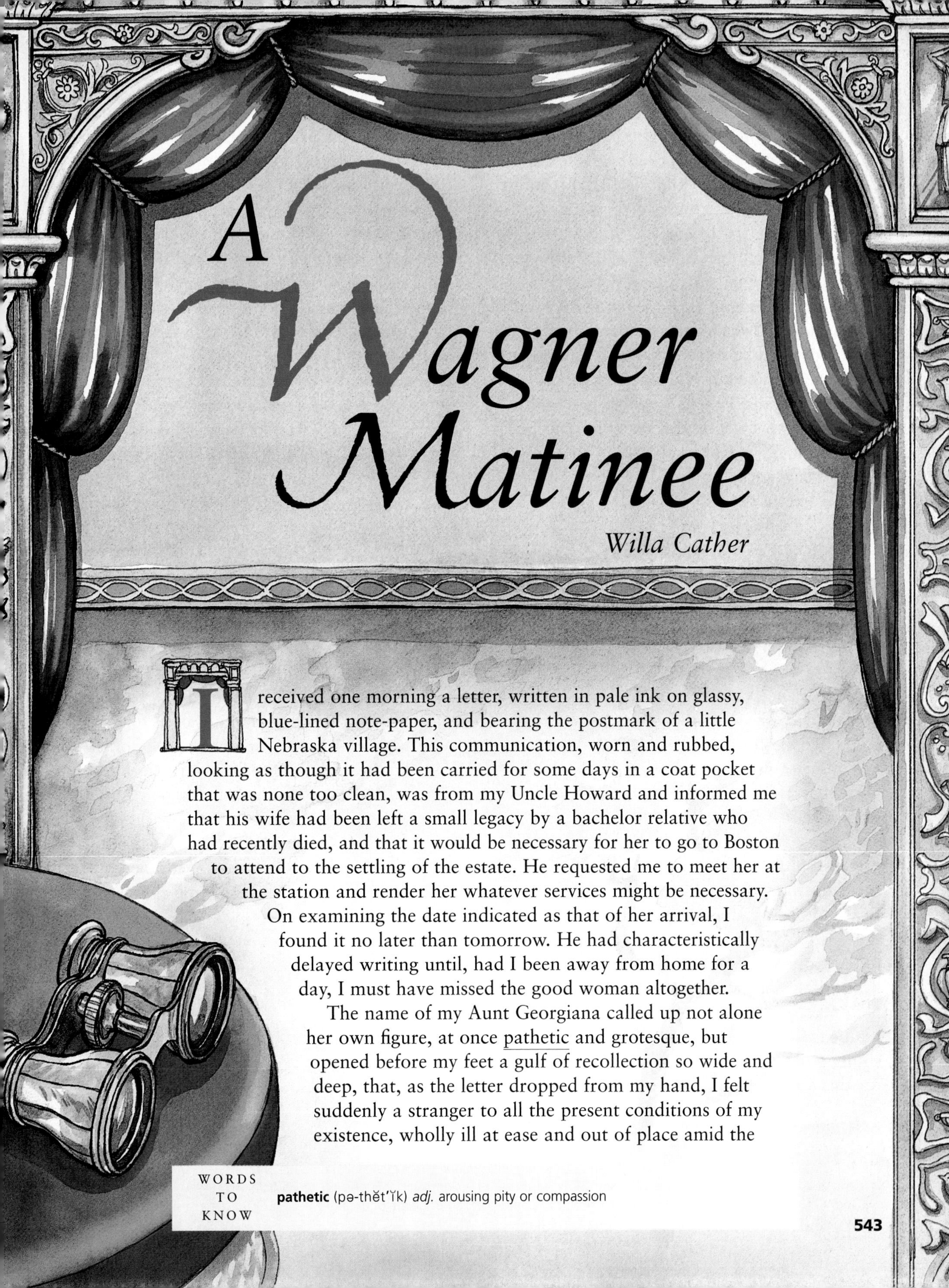

A Wagner Matinee

Willa Cather

I received one morning a letter, written in pale ink on glassy, blue-lined note-paper, and bearing the postmark of a little Nebraska village. This communication, worn and rubbed, looking as though it had been carried for some days in a coat pocket that was none too clean, was from my Uncle Howard and informed me that his wife had been left a small legacy by a bachelor relative who had recently died, and that it would be necessary for her to go to Boston to attend to the settling of the estate. He requested me to meet her at the station and render her whatever services might be necessary. On examining the date indicated as that of her arrival, I found it no later than tomorrow. He had characteristically delayed writing until, had I been away from home for a day, I must have missed the good woman altogether.

The name of my Aunt Georgiana called up not alone her own figure, at once pathetic and grotesque, but opened before my feet a gulf of recollection so wide and deep, that, as the letter dropped from my hand, I felt suddenly a stranger to all the present conditions of my existence, wholly ill at ease and out of place amid the

WORDS TO KNOW **pathetic** (pə-thĕt′ĭk) *adj.* arousing pity or compassion familiar surroundings of my study. I became, in short, the gangling farmer-boy my aunt had known, scourged with chilblains[1] and bashfulness, my hands cracked and sore from the corn husking. I felt the knuckles of my thumb tentatively, as though they were raw again. I sat again before her parlor organ, fumbling the scales with my stiff, red hands, while she, beside me, made canvas mittens for the huskers.[2]

The next morning, after preparing my landlady somewhat, I set out for the station. When the train arrived I had some difficulty in finding my aunt. She was the last of the passengers to alight, and it was not until I got her into the carriage that she seemed really to recognize me. She had come all the way in a day coach; her linen duster had become black with soot and her black bonnet grey with dust during the journey. When we arrived at my boarding-house the landlady put her to bed at once and I did not see her again until the next morning.

Whatever shock Mrs. Springer experienced at my aunt's appearance, she considerately concealed. As for myself, I saw my aunt's misshapen figure with that feeling of awe and respect with which we behold explorers who have left their ears and fingers north of Franz-Josef-Land,[3] or their health somewhere along the Upper Congo.[4] My Aunt Georgiana had been a music teacher at the Boston Conservatory, somewhere back in the latter sixties. One summer, while visiting in the little village among the Green Mountains where her ancestors had dwelt for generations, she had kindled the callow fancy of the most idle and shiftless of all the village lads, and had conceived for this Howard Carpenter one of those extravagant passions which a handsome country boy of twenty-one sometimes inspires in an angular, spectacled woman of thirty. When she returned to her duties in Boston, Howard followed her, and the upshot of this inexplicable infatuation was that she eloped with him, eluding the reproaches of her family and the criticisms of her friends by going with him to the Nebraska frontier. Carpenter, who, of course, had no money, had taken a homestead in Red Willow County, fifty miles from the railroad. There they had measured off their quarter section themselves by driving across the prairie in a wagon, to the wheel of which they had tied a red cotton handkerchief, and counting off its revolutions. They built a dugout in the red hillside, one of those cave dwellings whose inmates so often reverted to primitive conditions. Their water they got from the lagoons where the buffalo drank, and their slender stock of provisions was always at the mercy of bands of roving Indians. For thirty years my aunt had not been further than fifty miles from the homestead.

For thirty years my aunt had not been further than fifty miles from the homestead.

But Mrs. Springer knew nothing of all this, and must have been considerably shocked at what was left of my kinswoman. Beneath the soiled linen duster which, on her arrival, was the most conspicuous

---

1. **chilblains:** painful swelling or sores on the feet or hands, caused by exposure to the cold.
2. **huskers:** farm workers who remove cornhusks by hand.
3. **Franz-Josef-Land:** a group of small, mostly ice-covered islands in the Arctic Ocean north of Russia.
4. **Upper Congo:** river in central Africa, now called the Zaire (zä-îr′) River.

WORDS TO KNOW

callow (kăl′ō) *adj.* lacking adult maturity or experience; immature
inexplicable (ĭn-ĕk′splĭ-kə-bəl) *adj.* difficult or impossible to explain
reproach (rĭ-prōch′) *n.* an expression of blame or disapproval

feature of her costume, she wore a black stuff dress, whose ornamentation showed that she had surrendered herself unquestioningly into the hands of a country dressmaker. My poor aunt's figure, however, would have presented astonishing difficulties to any dressmaker. Originally stooped, her shoulders were now almost bent together over her sunken chest. She wore no stays, and her gown, which trailed unevenly behind, rose in a sort of peak over her abdomen. She wore ill-fitting false teeth, and her skin was as yellow as a Mongolian's from constant exposure to a pitiless wind and to the alkaline water which hardens the most transparent cuticle into a sort of flexible leather.

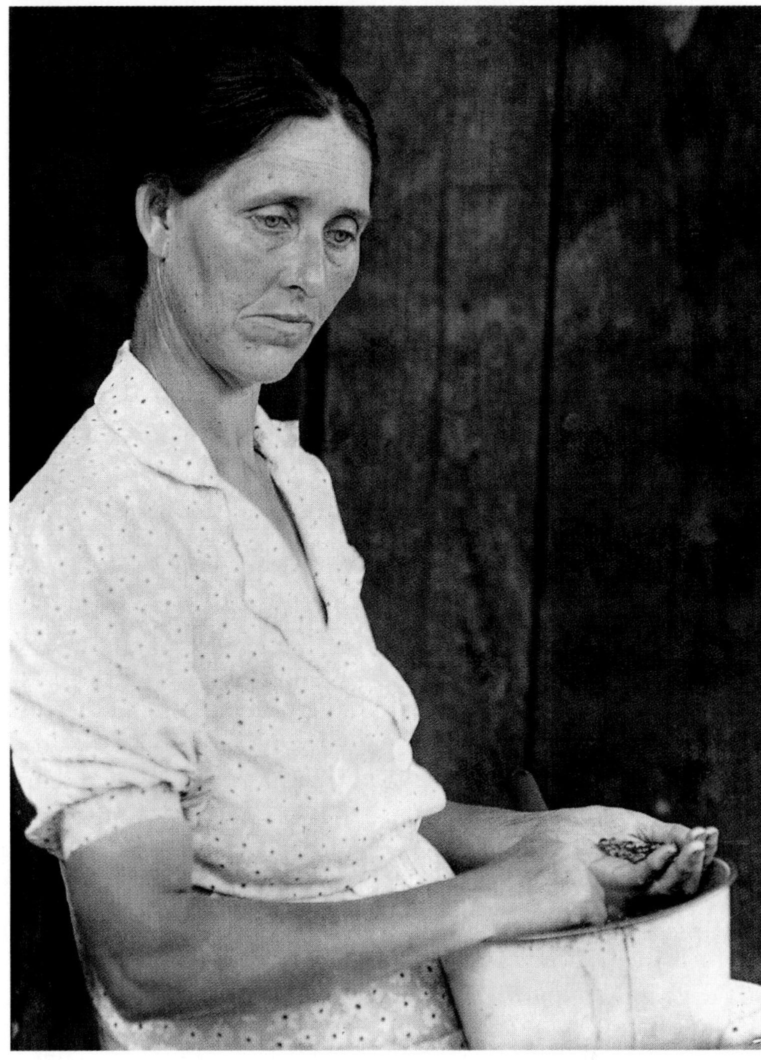

Mrs. Stewart, Housewife and Singer, Brasstown, North Carolina, Doris Ulmann. Doris Ulmann Collection, #635, Special Collections, University of Oregon Library.

I owed to this woman most of the good that ever came my way in my boyhood, and had a reverential affection for her. During the years when I was riding herd for my uncle, my aunt, after cooking the three meals—the first of which was ready at six o'clock in the morning—and putting the six children to bed, would often stand until midnight at her ironing-board with me at the kitchen table beside her, hearing me recite Latin declensions and conjugations, gently shaking me when my drowsy head sank down over a page of irregular verbs. It was to her, at her ironing or mending, that I read my first Shakespeare, and her old text-book on mythology was the first that ever came into my empty hands. She taught me my scales and exercises, too—on the little parlor organ, which her husband had bought her after fifteen years, during which she had not so much as seen any instrument, but an accordion that belonged to one of the Norwegian farmhands. She would sit beside me by the hour, darning and counting while I struggled with the "Joyous Farmer," but she seldom talked to me about music, and I understood why. She was a pious woman; she had the consolations of religion and, to her at least, her martyrdom was not wholly sordid. Once when I had been doggedly beating out some easy passages from an old score of

WORDS TO KNOW

pious (pī'əs) *adj.* having or showing reverence for God
sordid (sôr'dĭd) *adj.* wretched; dirty; morally degraded

Euryanthe[5] I had found among her music books, she came up to me and, putting her hands over my eyes, gently drew my head back upon her shoulder, saying tremulously, "Don't love it so well, Clark, or it may be taken from you. Oh! dear boy, pray that whatever your sacrifice may be, it be not that."

When my aunt appeared on the morning after her arrival, she was still in a semi-somnambulant state. She seemed not to realize that she was in the city where she had spent her youth, the place longed for hungrily half a lifetime. She had been so wretchedly train-sick throughout the journey that she had no recollection of anything but her discomfort, and, to all intents and purposes, there were but a few hours of nightmare between the farm in Red Willow County and my study on Newbury Street. I had planned a little pleasure for her that afternoon, to repay her for some of the glorious moments she had given me when we used to milk together in the straw-thatched cowshed and she, because I was more than usually tired, or because her husband had spoken sharply to me, would tell me of the splendid performance of the *Huguenots*[6] she had seen in Paris, in her youth. At two o'clock the Symphony Orchestra was to give a Wagner program, and I intended to take my aunt; though, as I conversed with her, I grew doubtful about her enjoyment of it. Indeed, for her own sake, I could only wish her taste for such things quite dead, and the long struggle mercifully ended at last. I suggested our visiting the Conservatory and the Common[7] before lunch, but she seemed altogether too timid to wish to venture out. She questioned me absently about various changes in the city, but she was chiefly concerned that she had forgotten to leave instructions about feeding half-skimmed milk to a certain weakling calf, "old Maggie's calf, you know, Clark," she explained, evidently having forgotten how long I had been away. She was further troubled because she had neglected to tell her daughter about the freshly-opened kit of mackerel in the cellar, which would spoil if it were not used directly.

I asked her whether she had ever heard any of the Wagnerian operas,[8] and found that she had not, though she was perfectly familiar with their respective situations, and had once possessed the piano score of *The Flying Dutchman.* I began to think it would have been best to get her back to Red Willow County without waking her, and regretted having suggested the concert.

From the time we entered the concert hall, however, she was a trifle less passive and inert, and for the first time seemed to perceive her surroundings. I had felt some trepidation lest she might become aware of the absurdities of her attire, or might experience some painful embarrassment at stepping suddenly into the world to which she had been dead for a quarter of a century. But, again, I found how superficially I had judged her. She sat looking about her with eyes as impersonal, almost as stony, as those with which the granite Rameses[9] in a museum watches the froth and fret that ebbs and flows[10] about his pedestal—separated from it by the lonely stretch of centuries. I have seen this same aloofness in old miners who drift into the Brown hotel at Denver, their pockets full of bullion,[11] their linen soiled, their haggard faces unshaven; standing in the thronged corridors

---

5. ***Euryanthe*** (yo͞o'rē-ăn'thē): an opera by the German composer Carl Maria von Weber.
6. ***Huguenots*** (hyo͞o'gə-nŏts'): an opera by the German composer Giacomo Meyerbeer.
7. **the Common:** Boston Common, a public park.
8. **Wagnerian operas:** The orchestra will play selections from several operas composed by Wagner, including *The Flying Dutchman, Tannhauser, Tristan and Isolde,* and a cycle of four operas called *The Ring of the Nibelung.*
9. **Rameses** (răm'sēz'): one of the ancient kings of Egypt of that name.
10. **froth . . . flows:** happiness and sadness that comes and goes.
11. **bullion:** gold.

WORDS TO KNOW
trepidation (trĕp'ĭ-dā'shən) *n.* fearful uncertainty or worry
superficially (so͞o'pər-fĭsh'ə-lē) *adv.* in a shallow way; concerned with only what is obvious

The Opera, Paris (about 1924), Raoul Dufy. Watercolor and gouache on paper, 19″ × 25″, The Phillips Collection, Washington, D.C.

as solitary as though they were still in a frozen camp on the Yukon,[12] conscious that certain experiences have isolated them from their fellows by a gulf no haberdasher could bridge.

We sat at the extreme left of the first balcony, facing the arc of our own and the balcony above us, veritable hanging gardens, brilliant as tulip beds. The matinée audience was made up chiefly of women. One lost the contour of faces and figures, indeed any effect of line whatever, and there was only the color of bodices past counting, the shimmer of fabrics soft and firm, silky and sheer; red, mauve, pink, blue, lilac, purple, ecru, rose, yellow, cream, and white, all the colors that an impressionist[13] finds in a sunlit landscape, with here and there the dead shadow of a frock coat. My Aunt Georgiana regarded them as though they had been so many daubs of tube-paint on a palette.

When the musicians came out and took their places, she gave a little stir of anticipation and looked with quickening interest down over the rail at that invariable grouping, perhaps the first

12. **Yukon** (yo͞oʹkŏnʹ): a river in the Yukon Territory, in northwest Canada.

13. **impressionist:** member of a movement in French painting that emphasized the play of light and color.

wholly familiar thing that had greeted her eye since she had left old Maggie and her weakling calf. I could feel how all those details sank into her soul, for I had not forgotten how they had sunk into mine when I came fresh from ploughing forever and forever between green aisles of corn, where, as in a treadmill, one might walk from daybreak to dusk without perceiving a shadow of change. The clean profiles of the musicians, the gloss of their linen, the dull black of their coats, the beloved shapes of the instruments, the patches of yellow light thrown by the green shaded lamps on the smooth, varnished bellies of the 'cellos and the bass viols in the rear, the restless, wind-tossed forest of fiddle necks and bows—I recalled how, in the first orchestra I had ever heard, those long bow strokes seemed to draw the heart out of me, as a conjurer's stick reels out yards of paper ribbon from a hat.

The first number was the *Tannhauser* overture. When the horns drew out the first strain of the Pilgrim's chorus, my Aunt Georgiana clutched my coat sleeve. Then it was I first realized that for her this broke a silence of thirty years; the inconceivable silence of the plains. With the battle between the two motives, with the frenzy of the Venusberg theme and its ripping of strings, there came to me an overwhelming sense of the waste and wear we are so powerless to combat; and I saw again the tall, naked house on the prairie, black and grim as a wooden fortress; the black pond where I had learned to swim, its margin pitted with sun-dried cattle tracks; the rain gullied clay banks about the naked house, the four dwarf ash seedlings where the dish-cloths were always hung to dry before the kitchen door. The world there was the flat world of the ancients; to the east, a cornfield that stretched to daybreak; to the west, a corral that reached to sunset; between, the conquests of peace, dearer bought than those of war.

The overture closed, my aunt released my coat sleeve, but she said nothing. She sat staring at the orchestra through a dullness of thirty years, through the films made little by little by each of the three hundred and sixty-five days in every one of them. What, I wondered, did she get from it? She had been a good pianist in her day I knew, and her musical education had been broader than that of most music teachers of a quarter of a century ago. She had often told me of Mozart's operas and Meyerbeer's, and I could remember hearing her sing, years ago, certain melodies of Verdi's. When I had fallen ill with a fever in her house she used to sit by my cot in the evening—when the cool, night wind blew in through the faded mosquito netting tacked over the window and I lay watching a certain bright star that burned red above the cornfield—and sing "Home to our mountains, O, let us return!" in a way fit to break the heart of a Vermont boy near dead of homesickness already.

She sat staring at the orchestra through a dullness of thirty years.

I watched her closely through the prelude to *Tristan and Isolde,* trying vainly to conjecture what that seething turmoil of strings and winds might mean to her, but she sat mutely staring at the violin bows that drove obliquely downward, like the pelting streaks of rain in a summer shower. Had this music any message for her? Had she enough left to at all comprehend this power which had kindled the world since she

WORDS TO KNOW

conjecture (kən-jĕk′chər) *v.* to make a judgment on the basis of uncertain evidence; guess had left it? I was in a fever of curiosity, but Aunt Georgiana sat silent upon her peak in Darien.[14] She preserved this utter immobility throughout the number from *The Flying Dutchman,* though her fingers worked mechanically upon her black dress, as though, of themselves, they were recalling the piano score they had once played. Poor old hands! They had been stretched and twisted into mere tentacles to hold and lift and knead with; the palms unduly swollen, the fingers bent and knotted—on one of them a thin, worn band that had once been a wedding ring. As I pressed and gently quieted one of those groping hands, I remembered with quivering eyelids their services for me in other days.

Soon after the tenor began the "Prize Song," I heard a quick drawn breath and turned to my aunt. Her eyes were closed, but the tears were glistening on her cheeks, and I think, in a moment more, they were in my eyes as well. It never really died, then—the soul that can suffer so excruciatingly and so interminably; it withers to the outward eye only; like that strange moss which can lie on a dusty shelf half a century and yet, if placed in water, grows green again. She wept so throughout the development and elaboration of the melody.

During the intermission before the second half of the concert, I questioned my aunt and found that the "Prize Song" was not new to her. Some years before there had drifted to the farm in Red Willow County a young German, a tramp cow puncher, who had sung the chorus at Bayreuth,[15] when he was a boy, along with the other peasant boys and girls. Of a Sunday morning he used to sit on his gingham-sheeted bed in the hands' bedroom which opened off the kitchen, cleaning the leather of his boots and saddle, singing the "Prize Song," while my aunt went about her work in the kitchen. She had hovered about him until she had prevailed upon him to join the country church, though his sole fitness for this step, in so far as I could gather, lay in his boyish face and his possession of this divine melody. Shortly afterward he had gone to town on the Fourth of July, been drunk for several days, lost his money at a faro[16] table, ridden a saddled Texas steer on a bet, and disappeared with a fractured collar-bone. All this my aunt told me huskily, wanderingly, as though she were talking in the weak lapses of illness.

"Well, we have come to better things than the old *Trovatore*[17] at any rate, Aunt Georgie?" I queried, with a well meant effort at jocularity.

Her lip quivered and she hastily put her handkerchief up to her mouth. From behind it she murmured, "And you have been hearing this ever since you left me, Clark?" Her question was the gentlest and saddest of reproaches.

The second half of the program consisted of four numbers from the *Ring,* and closed with Siegfried's funeral march. My aunt wept quietly, but almost continuously, as a shallow vessel overflows in a rainstorm. From time to time her dim eyes looked up at the lights which studded the ceiling, burning softly under their dull glass globes; doubtless they were stars in truth to her. I was still perplexed as to what measure of musical comprehension was left to her, she who had heard nothing but the singing of Gospel Hymns at Methodist services in the square frame school-house on Section Thirteen for so many years. I was wholly unable to gauge how much of it had been dissolved in soapsuds, or worked into bread, or milked into the bottom of a pail.

---

14. **peak in Darien** (dâr′ē-ĕn′): an allusion to a poem by the English poet John Keats, in which Keats describes Spanish explorers on a mountain in Darien, a region that is now Panama. The Spaniards stand silent and amazed as they become the first Europeans to view the Pacific Ocean.
15. **Bayreuth** (bī-roit′): the Bayreuth Festival, an annual international music festival in Germany that presents Wagner's operas.
16. **faro:** a gambling game.
17. ***Trovatore*** (trô′vä-tô′rĕ): *Il Trovatore* is an opera by the Italian composer Giuseppe Verdi.

WORDS TO KNOW

excruciatingly (ĭk-skrōō′shē-ā′tĭng-lē) *adv.* in a way that causes great pain or distress

House in Winter (1941), Wright Morris. Photo taken near Lincoln, Nebraska.

The deluge of sound poured on and on; I never knew what she found in the shining current of it; I never knew how far it bore her, or past what happy islands. From the trembling of her face I could well believe that before the last numbers she had been carried out where the myriad graves are, into the grey, nameless burying grounds of the sea; or into some world of death vaster yet, where, from the beginning of the world, hope has lain down with hope and dream with dream and, renouncing,[18] slept.

The concert was over; the people filed out of the hall chattering and laughing, glad to relax and find the living level again, but my kinswoman made no effort to rise. The harpist slipped its green felt cover over his instrument; the flute-players shook the water from their mouthpieces; the men of the orchestra went out one by one, leaving the stage to the chairs and music stands, empty as a winter cornfield.

I spoke to my aunt. She burst into tears and sobbed pleadingly. "I don't want to go, Clark, I don't want to go!"

I understood. For her, just outside the door of the concert hall, lay the black pond with the cattle-tracked bluffs; the tall, unpainted house, with weather-curled boards; naked as a tower, the crook-backed ash seedlings where the dishcloths hung to dry; the gaunt, molting turkeys picking up refuse about the kitchen door. ❖

18. **renouncing:** giving up.

FROM LETTERS of a WOMAN HOMESTEADER

ELINORE PRUITT STEWART

January 23, 1913
Dear Mrs. Coney,—

I am afraid all my friends think I am very forgetful and that you think I am ungrateful as well, but I am going to plead not guilty. Right after Christmas Mr. Stewart came down with *la grippe*[1] and was so miserable that it kept me busy trying to relieve him. Out here where we can get no physician we have to dope ourselves, so that I had to be housekeeper, nurse, doctor, and general overseer. That explains my long silence.

And now I want to thank you for your kind thought in prolonging our Christmas. The magazines were much appreciated. They relieved some weary night-watches, and the box did Jerrine more good than the medicine I was having to give her for *la grippe*. She was content to stay in bed and enjoy the contents of her box.

When I read of the hard times among the Denver poor, I feel like urging them every one to get out and file on land. I am very enthusiastic about women homesteading. It really requires less strength and

Westly Potato Camp, Edison, California, Dorothea Lange (1895–1965). Copyright © 1982 The Dorothea Lange Collection, The Oakland Museum of California, The City of Oakland, gift of Paul S. Taylor.

1. ***la grippe*** (lä-grēp′) *French:* the flu; influenza.

labor to raise plenty to satisfy a large family than it does to go out to wash, with the added satisfaction of knowing that their job will not be lost to them if they care to keep it. Even if improving the place does go slowly, it is that much done to stay done. Whatever is raised is the homesteader's own, and there is no house-rent to pay. This year Jerrine cut and dropped enough potatoes to raise a ton of fine potatoes. She wanted to try, so we let her, and you will remember that she is but six years old. We had a man to break the ground and cover the potatoes for her and the man irrigated them once. That was all that was done until digging time, when they were ploughed out and Jerrine picked them up. Any woman strong enough to go out by the day could have done every bit of the work and put in two or three times that much, and it would have been so much more pleasant than to work so hard in the city and then be on starvation rations in the winter.

To me, homesteading is the solution of all poverty's problems, but I realize that temperament has much to do with success in any undertaking, and persons afraid of coyotes and work and loneliness had better let ranching alone. At the same time, any woman who can stand her own company, can see the beauty of the sunset, loves growing things, and is willing to put in as much time at careful labor as she does over the washtub, will certainly succeed; will have independence, plenty to eat all the time, and a home of her own in the end.

Experimenting need cost the homesteader no more than the work, because by applying to the Department of Agriculture at Washington he can get enough of any seed and as many kinds as he wants to make a thorough trial, and it doesn't even cost postage. Also one can always get bulletins from there and from the Experiment Station of one's own State concerning any problem or as many problems as may come up. I would not, for anything, allow Mr. Stewart to do anything toward improving my place, for I want the fun and the experience myself. And I want to be able to speak from experience when I tell others what they can do. Theories are very beautiful, but facts are what must be had, and what I intend to give some time.

Here I am boring you to death with things that cannot interest you! You'd think I wanted you to homestead, wouldn't you? But I am only thinking of the troops of tired, worried women, sometimes even cold and hungry, scared to death of losing their places to work, who could have plenty to eat, who could have good fires by gathering the wood, and comfortable homes of their own, if they but had the courage and determination to get them.

I must stop right now before you get so tired you will not answer. With much love to you from Jerrine and myself, I am

Yours affectionately,

Elinore Rupert Stewart

RESPONDING OPTIONS

FROM PERSONAL RESPONSE *TO* CRITICAL ANALYSIS

REFLECT **1.** What thoughts do you have about Aunt Georgiana? Write them down in your notebook.

RETHINK **2.** Do you think that Aunt Georgiana will be tempted to stay in Boston and not return to her home in Nebraska? Explain.

Consider
- what she says pleadingly to Clark at the end of the concert
- what she has given up by living on the frontier
- her concern about the farm the morning after she arrives in Boston

3. From the choices that Aunt Georgiana has made in her life, what conclusions can you draw about her character?

Consider
- the circumstances of her elopement with Howard Carpenter
- how she feels about life on the farm
- how she treated Clark as a child in her home
- your own insights into making difficult choices

4. In your opinion, was it a good idea for Clark to take Aunt Georgiana to the concert? Why or why not?

RELATE **5.** The Insight selection on page 551 is a letter from Elinore Stewart (formerly Rupert), a divorced mother in her 30s who homesteaded in Wyoming during the early 1900s. Compare homesteading's effect on her with its effect on Aunt Georgiana. You might use a Venn diagram to show similarities and differences.

LITERARY LINKS

Compare Aunt Georgiana in "A Wagner Matinee" with Mary Trask in the play "The Clod" on page 479. What hardships do each of these female characters face? How has farm life affected them? Discuss the similarities and the differences between these two women.

ANOTHER PATHWAY

With a partner, discuss your conclusions about Aunt Georgiana. Why did she abruptly elope with Howard Carpenter and move to Nebraska? Did she ever regret her choice? What is she feeling and thinking during the concert? What does she mean at the end by saying "I don't want to go!" Compare your interpretation with Clark's and your classmates' interpretations.

QUICKWRITES

1. Draft a short **cause-and-effect analysis** (or make a **diagram**) explaining why Aunt Georgiana chose to marry and move to the Nebraska frontier and what impact this choice had on her life. Input your draft into a computer so that it will be easier to revise later.
2. Aunt Georgiana gave up a life of music that she loved. Ask a friend or family member to reveal to you his or her feelings about something he or she has given up in life. Then write up your **interview** with that person.

PORTFOLIO *Save your writing. You may want to use it later as a springboard to a piece for your portfolio.*

LITERARY CONCEPTS

The **setting** of a story refers to the time and place in which the action occurs. Setting may have a great influence on action; in "A Wagner Matinee," for example, Cather draws sharp contrasts between the Nebraska frontier and the Boston concert hall to call attention to the sacrifices Aunt Georgiana made when she chose to marry. The elegance and vibrancy of the concert hall are set against the barrenness of Red Willow County and the "tall, naked house on the prairie, black and grim as a wooden fortress."

Cooperative Learning Working with two partners, go back through the story and record details describing the Nebraska farm and the Boston concert hall. Then, acting as set designers for a movie, TV program, or play based on the story, sketch the two main locations, or settings, described. Compare your ideas with those of other groups.

CRITIC'S CORNER

1. Michael Scott, a member of our student board, commented, "I was surprised that Willa Cather chose to create a male narrator." What do you think would have been gained or lost if the story had been narrated by Aunt Georgiana herself, or by her niece instead of her nephew?
2. "A Wagner Matinee" created a stir when it appeared in *Everybody's Magazine* in 1904. Cather's family objected to the fictional portrait of her real-life aunt Franc, and friends and neighbors criticized the writer's harsh portrayal of Nebraska. Will Owen Jones, one of these friends, wrote: "The stranger to this state will associate Nebraska with the aunt's wretched figure, her ill-fitting false teeth, her skin yellowed by the weather." Is Cather's portrait of Aunt Georgiana too unflattering? Do you think her portrayal of Nebraska is too harsh? Use details from the story to support your opinions.

ART CONNECTION

On page 550 is a photograph of a Nebraska farmhouse in the winter. What feeling do you get from the picture about life in this setting? What elements of the picture create this feeling? Does the picture correspond to Cather's descriptions of Aunt Georgiana's home? Explain.

Detail of *House in Winter* (1941), Wright Morris. Photo taken near Lincoln, Nebraska.

ALTERNATIVE ACTIVITIES

1. Create a **real estate advertisement** to "sell" the virtues of life on the frontier, using details from your reading of "A Wagner Matinee" and Elinore Pruitt Stewart's letter. As an alternative, you may want to create an ad discouraging people from moving to the frontier.
2. Using music reference books and recordings, research the music of Richard Wagner. Use what you learn to create a **poster** advertising the performance that Clark and Aunt Georgiana attend.

ACROSS THE CURRICULUM

Music Find recordings of operas by Richard Wagner. Then play one or two of the excerpts that Aunt Georgiana hears performed at the concert in Boston, and explain how you think she may have reacted to each piece of music. You may also want to find and play music by some other composers mentioned in the story, such as Mozart and Verdi.

Art In this story, Clark compares the colorful audience at the matinee to an impressionist painting. Research impressionism to find out names of well-known impressionist painters and to discover why Cather chose to make this comparison. Bring art books to class to share examples of your favorite impressionist paintings.

WORDS TO KNOW

EXERCISE A Review the Words to Know in the boxes at the bottom of the selection pages. Then write the vocabulary word that best completes each sentence.

1. If you think of Wagner as the composer of operas featuring large blonds wearing helmets with horns sticking out of them, you might ______ that his music is not relevant to your life.
2. However, bear in mind that it is easy to dismiss or ridicule things that we look at only ______, without considering them in depth.
3. In reacting to opera, to literature, or to art, a person who is scornful of what he or she is unfamiliar with deserves ______.
4. Wagner's music is filled with familiar emotions; one whole opera was composed while he was hopelessly and ______ in love with a woman who could never be his.
5. Brilliant as he was, Wagner was a careless student with childish attitudes who showed many signs of being ______.
6. His continuing financial irresponsibility makes it difficult to pity him and view his money troubles as ______.
7. Puzzled by his music, which was far ahead of its time, many opera lovers at first found his work ______.
8. Financial problems and a lack of quick success may well have filled Wagner with a sense of ______ about the future.
9. Although some musical dramas, called oratorios, involve biblical characters, Wagner's work does not have these ______ connections.
10. Even if the theme of his work is not religiously spiritual, listening to it can lift one out of the petty, mean, and ______ events of the world and provide a glimpse of purity and beauty.

EXERCISE B Try acting out as many of the Words to Know as possible by using only a facial expression and gestures.

WILLA CATHER

1873–1947

Willa Cather believed that "the most basic material a writer works with is acquired before the age of fifteen. . . . Those years determine whether one's work will be poor and thin or rich and fine." Born in Back Creek Valley, Virginia, Cather moved to the prairies of Nebraska when she was nine years old. The land there—and the pioneers who lived on it—gave Cather her distinctive voice. Her acclaimed novels *O Pioneers!* and *My Ántonia* are set on her beloved prairie.

As a child, Cather enjoyed a rich cultural life despite the limitations of growing up in the young frontier town of Red Cloud. She had fine books in her home and excellent teachers at school. Among her Nebraska neighbors were educated European immigrants who introduced her to French and German literature, taught her to read classical Latin and Greek, and taught her the history and appreciation of classical music and opera. The railroad brought traveling stock companies to the opera house in Red Cloud, where Cather saw plays and light operas; she herself wrote, staged, and performed in amateur plays.

After studying journalism at the University of Nebraska, Cather went to Pittsburgh, where she worked as a magazine editor, a critic, and a teacher. From 1906 on, far from the wild Nebraska frontier of her childhood, Cather lived in New York City, supporting herself as a novelist.

OTHER WORKS *Death Comes for the Archbishop, One of Ours, The Song of the Lark*

LASERLINKS
• *MUSIC CONNECTION*

PREVIEWING

FICTION

The Legend of Gregorio Cortez

Américo Paredes

PERSONAL CONNECTION

Think of someone you view as a hero. He or she might be a famous person, a family member, an individual from your neighborhood or school, or a character from a book, a movie, or television. What are his or her qualities or strengths? In your notebook, identify your hero. Then copy the following list of qualities, adding others if you wish. Rate your hero on each of these qualities, on a scale of 1 to 5, with 1 being the lowest and 5 being the highest.

__ honest	__ respectful
__ physically strong	__ intelligent
__ loyal	__ courageous
__ clever	__ hard-working
__ kind	__ wise

HISTORICAL CONNECTION

"The Legend of Gregorio Cortez" is a prose retelling of a *corrido*, a fast-paced ballad that derives from the Mexican oral tradition. Both the original *corrido* and this retelling are based on the life of a real person who was regarded as a hero—Gregorio Cortez, who was born in Mexico in 1875. On June 12, 1901, while Cortez was living in Karnes County, Texas, he shot and killed Sheriff Brack Morris just after the sheriff shot Cortez's brother. In his flight to the border, Cortez walked more than 100 miles and rode another 400 miles. On the way, he killed another sheriff and eluded several posses, some with as many as 300 men. He was finally captured—exhausted, out of ammunition, and on foot—near the border town of Laredo. After a 3-year legal battle, Cortez was acquitted of killing the first sheriff but sentenced to life for killing the second. He spent about 12 years in prison before being pardoned, by the governor of Texas, in 1913. Cortez died 3 years later of unknown causes.

READING CONNECTION

Examining Legends A legend is a story passed down orally from generation to generation and popularly believed to have a historical basis. Like many legends, this retelling of the *corrido* about Gregorio Cortez mixes fact, exaggeration, and fiction, much as a tall tale does, to create an unforgettable hero. As you read, note which events seem factual, which seem exaggerated, and which seem fictitious. Jot down these notes in your notebook.

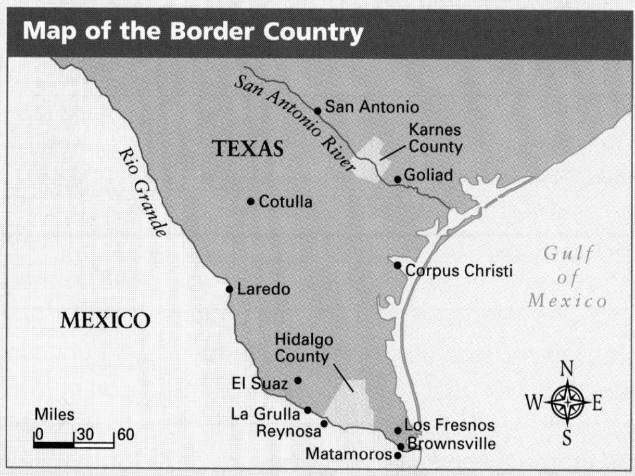

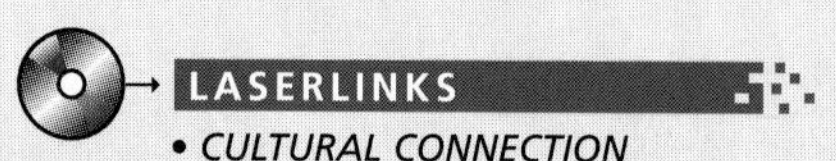

The Legend of Gregorio Cortez

Américo Paredes

THEY still sing of him—in the *cantinas*[1] and the country stores, in the ranches when men gather at night to talk in the cool dark, sitting in a circle, smoking and listening to the old songs and the tales of other days. Then the *guitarreros*[2] sing of the border raids and the skirmishes, of the men who lived by the phrase, "I will break before I bend."

They sing with deadly-serious faces, throwing out the words of the song like a challenge, tearing savagely with their stiff, callused fingers at the strings of the guitars.

And that is how, in the dark quiet of the ranches, in the lighted noise of the saloons, they sing of Gregorio Cortez.

After the song is sung there is a lull. Then the old men, who have lived long and seen almost everything, tell their stories. And when they tell about Gregorio Cortez, the telling goes like this:

---

1. ***cantinas*** (kän-tē′näs) *Spanish:* taverns or bars.
2. ***guitarreros*** (gē-tä-rĕ′rôs) *Spanish:* guitar players.

How Gregorio Cortez Came to Be in the County of El Carmen

That was good singing, and a good song; give the man a drink. Not like these pachucos[3] nowadays, mumbling damn-foolishness into a microphone; it is not done that way. Men should sing with their heads thrown back, with their mouths wide open and their eyes shut. Fill your lungs, so they can hear you at the pasture's farther end. And when you sing, sing songs like *El Corrido de Gregorio Cortez.* There's a song that makes the hackles rise. You can almost see him there—Gregorio Cortez, with his pistol in his hand.

He was a man, a Border man. What did he look like? Well, that is hard to tell. Some say he was short and some say he was tall; some say he was Indian brown and some say he was blond like a newborn cockroach. But I'd say he was not too dark and not too fair, not too thin and not too fat, not too short and not too tall; and he looked just a little bit like me. But does it matter so much what he looked like? He was a man, very much of a man; and he was a Border man. Some say he was born in Matamoros; some say Reynosa; some say Hidalgo county on the other side. And I guess others will say other things. But Matamoros, or Reynosa, or Hidalgo, it's all the same Border; and short or tall, dark or fair, it's the man that counts. And that's what he was, a man.

Not a gunman, no, not a bravo. He never came out of a cantina wanting to drink up the sea at one gulp. Not that kind of man, if you can call that kind a man. No, that wasn't Gregorio Cortez at all. He was a peaceful man, a hard-working man like you and me.

He could shoot. Forty-four and thirty-thirty, they were the same to him. He could put five bullets into a piece of board and not make but one hole, and quicker than you could draw a good deep breath. Yes, he could shoot. But he could also work.

He was a vaquero,[4] and a better one there has not ever been from Laredo to the mouth. He could talk to horses, and they would understand. They would follow him around, like dogs, and no man knew a good horse better then Gregorio Cortez. As for cattle, he could set up school for your best caporal.[5] And if an animal was lost, and nobody could pick up a trail, they would send for Gregorio Cortez. He could always find a trail. There was no better tracker in all the Border country, nor a man who could hide his tracks better if he wanted to. That was Gregorio Cortez, the best vaquero and range man that there ever was.

But that is not all. You farmers, do you think that Gregorio Cortez did not know your business too? You could have told him nothing about cotton or beans or corn. He knew it all. He could look into the sky of a morning and smell it, sniff it the way a dog sniffs, and tell you what kind of weather there was going to be. And he would take a piece of dirt in his hands and rub it back and forth between his fingers—to see if the land had reached its point—and you would say he was looking into it. And perhaps he was, for Gregorio Cortez was the seventh son of a seventh son.[6]

You piddling modern farmers, vain of yourselves when you make a bale! You should have seen the crops raised by Gregorio Cortez. And when harvesting came, he was in there with the rest. Was it shucking corn? All you could see was the shucks fly and the pile grow, until you didn't know there was a man behind the pile. But he was even better at cotton-picking time. He would bend down and never raise his head till he came out the other end, and he would

---

3. **pachucos** (pä-cho͞o′kôs) *Spanish:* young toughs.
4. **vaquero** (vä-kĕ′rō) *Spanish:* cowboy.
5. **caporal** (kä-pô-räl′) *Spanish:* boss of a ranch.
6. **seventh son of a seventh son:** According to the folklore of several cultures, the seventh son of a seventh son is always lucky and may be gifted with certain supernatural powers.

be halfway through another row before the next man was through with his. And don't think the row he went through wasn't clean. No flags, no streamers, nothing left behind, nothing but clean, empty burrs where he had passed. It was the same when clearing land. There were men who went ahead of him, cutting fast along their strip in the early morning, but by noontime the man ahead was always Gregorio Cortez, working at his own pace, talking little and not singing very much, and never acting up.

New Mexico Peon (1945), Ernest L. Blumenschein. Oil on canvas, 40″ × 25″, collection of Kathleen and Gerald Peters, Santa Fe, New Mexico.

FOR Gregorio Cortez was not of your noisy, hell-raising type. That was not his way. He always spoke low, and he was always polite, whoever he was speaking to. And when he spoke to men older than himself he took off his hat and held it over his heart. A man who never raised his voice to parent or elder brother, and never disobeyed. That was Gregorio Cortez, and that was the way men were in this country along the river. That was the way they were before these modern times came, and God went away.

He should have stayed on the Border; he should not have gone up above, into the North. But it was going to be that way, and that was the way it was. Each man has a certain lot in life, and no other thing but that will be his share. People were always coming down from places in the North, from Dallas and San Antonio and Corpus and Foro West. And they would say, "Gregorio Cortez, why don't you go north? There is much money to be made. Stop eating beans and tortillas and that rubbery jerked beef. One of these days you're going to put out one of your eyes, pull and pull with your teeth on that stuff and it suddenly lets go. It's a wonder all you Border people are not one-eyed. Come up above with us, where you can eat white bread and ham."

Román was just like the young men of today,..

But Gregorio Cortez would only smile, because he was a peaceful man and did not take offense. He did not like white bread and ham; it makes people flatulent and dull. And he liked it where he was. So he always said, "I like this country. I will stay here."

But Gregorio Cortez had a brother, a younger brother named Román. Now Román was just like the young men of today, loud-mouthed and discontented. He was never happy where he was, and to make it worse he loved a joke more than any other thing. He would think nothing of playing a joke on a person twice his age. He had no respect for anyone, and that is why he ended like he did. But that is yet to tell.

Román talked to Gregorio and begged him that they should move away from the river and go up above, where there was much money to be made. And he talked and begged so, that finally Gregorio Cortez said he would go with his brother Román, and they saddled their horses and rode north.

Well, they did not grow rich, though things went well with them because they were good workers. Sometimes they picked cotton; sometimes they were vaqueros, and sometimes they cleared land for the Germans. Finally they came to a place called El Carmen, and there they settled down and farmed. And that was how Gregorio Cortez came to be in the county of El Carmen, where the tragedy took place.

Román's Horse Trade and What Came of It

Román owned two horses, two beautiful sorrels[7] that were just alike, the same color, the same markings, and the same size. You could not have told them apart, except that one of them was lame. There was an American who owned a little sorrel mare. This man was dying to get Román's sorrel—the good one—and every time they met he would offer to swap the mare for the horse. But Román did not think much of the mare. He did not like it when the American kept trying to make him trade.

"I wonder what this Gringo[8] thinks," Román said to himself. "He takes me for a fool. But I'm going to make him such a trade that he will remember me forever."

And Román laughed a big-mouthed laugh. He thought it would be a fine joke, besides being a good trade. There were mornings when the American went to town in his buggy along a narrow road. So Román saddled the lame sorrel, led him a little way along the road, and stopped under a big mesquite[9] that bordered on the fence. He fixed it so the spavined[10] side was against the mesquite. Román waited a little while, and soon he heard the buggy coming along the road. Then he got in the saddle and began picking mesquites off the tree and eating them. When the American came around the bend, there was Román on his sorrel horse. The American stopped his buggy beside Román and looked at the horse with much admiration.

7. **sorrels:** horses of a light reddish brown.

8. **gringo** (grēng′gô) *Spanish:* slang term for a foreigner, especially someone from the United States.

9. **mesquite** (mĕ-skēt′): thorny, shrublike tree with sweet seeds.

10. **spavined** (spăv′ĭnd): afflicted with spavin, a disease in which a horse's hind leg joint becomes enlarged, resulting in lameness.

It was a fine animal, exactly like the other one, but the American could not see the spavined leg.

"Changed your mind?" the American said.

Román stopped chewing on a mesquite and said, "Changed my mind about what?"

"About trading that horse for my mare."

"You're dead set on trading your mare for this horse of mine?" Román said.

"You know I am," the American said. "Are you ready to come round?"

"I'm in a trading mood," said Román. "With just a little arguing you might convince me to trade this horse for that worthless mare of yours. But I don't know; you might go back on the deal later on."

"I never go back on my word," the American said. "What do you think I am, a Mexican?"

"We'll see, we'll see," said Román. "How much are you willing to give in hand?"

"Enough to give you the first square meal you've had in your life," the American said.

ROMÁN just laughed, and it was all he could do to keep from guffawing. He knew who was getting the best of things.

So they made the deal, with Román still sitting on his spavined horse under the tree, chewing on mesquites.

"Where's the mare?" Román said.

"She's in my yard," said the American, "hung to a tree. You go get her and leave the horse there for me because I'm in a hurry to get to town."

That was how Román had figured it, so he said, "All right, I'll do it, but when I finish with these mesquites."

"Be sure you do, then," the American said.

"Sure, sure," said Román. "No hurry about it, is there?"

"All right," the American said, "take your time." And he drove off leaving Román still sitting on his horse under the mesquite, and as he drove off the American said, "Now isn't that just like a Mexican. He takes his time."

Román waited until the American was gone, and then he stopped eating mesquites. He got off and led the horse down the road to the American's yard and left him there in place of the little sorrel mare. On the way home Román almost fell off his saddle a couple of times, just laughing and laughing to think of the sort of face the American would pull when he came home that night.

The next morning, when Gregorio Cortez got up he said to his brother Román, "Something is going to happen today."

"Why do you say that?" asked Román.

"I don't know," said Gregorio Cortez. "I just know that something is going to happen today. I feel it. Last night my wife began to sigh for no reason at all. She kept sighing and sighing half the night, and she didn't know why. Her heart was telling her something, and I know some unlucky thing will happen to us today."

But Román just laughed, and Gregorio went inside the house to shave. Román followed him into the house and stood at the door while Gregorio shaved. It was a door made in two sections; the upper part was open and Román was leaning on the lower part, like a man leaning out of a window or over a fence. Román began to tell Gregorio about the horse trade he had made the day before, and he laughed pretty loud about it, because he thought it was a good

...loud-mouthed and discontented.

joke. Gregorio Cortez just shaved, and he didn't say anything.

When what should pull in at the gate but a buggy, and the American got down, and the Major Sheriff of the county of El Carmen got down too. They came into the yard and up to where Román was leaning over the door, looking out.

The American had a very serious face. "I came for the mare you stole yesterday morning," he said.

Román laughed a big-mouthed laugh. "What did I tell you, Gregorio?" he said. "This Gringo . . . has backed down on me." . . .

Just as the word "Gringo . . ." came out of Román's mouth, the sheriff whipped out his pistol and shot Román. He shot Román as he stood there with his head thrown back, laughing at his joke. The sheriff shot him in the face, right in the open mouth, and Román fell away from the door, at the Major Sheriff's feet.

AND then Gregorio Cortez stood at the door, where his brother had stood, with his pistol in his hand. Now he and the Major Sheriff met, each one pistol in hand, as men should meet when they fight for what is right. For it is a pretty thing to see, when two men stand up for their right, with their pistols in their hands, front to front and without fear. And so it was, for the Major Sheriff also was a man.

Yes, the Major Sheriff was a man; he was a gamecock[11] that had won in many pits, but in Gregorio Cortez he met a cockerel[12] that pecked his comb. The Major Sheriff shot first, and he missed; and Gregorio Cortez shot next, and he didn't miss. Three times did they shoot, three times did the Major Sheriff miss, and three times did Gregorio Cortez shoot the sheriff of El Carmen. The Major Sheriff fell dead at the feet of Gregorio Cortez, and it was in this way that Gregorio Cortez killed the first sheriff of many that he was to kill.

When the Major Sheriff fell, Gregorio Cortez looked up, and the other American said, "Don't kill me; I am unarmed."

"I will not kill you," said Gregorio Cortez. "But you'd better go away."

So the American went away. He ran into the brush and kept on running until he came to town and told all the other sheriffs that the Major Sheriff was dead.

Meanwhile, Gregorio Cortez knew that he too must go away. He was not afraid of the law; he knew the law, and he knew that he had the right. But if he stayed, the Rangers[13] would come, and the Rangers have no regard for law. You know what kind of men they are. When the Governor of the State wants a new Ranger, he asks his sheriffs, "Bring all the criminals to me." And from the murderers he chooses the Ranger, because no one can be a Ranger who has not killed a man. So Gregorio Cortez knew that the best thing for him was to go away, and his first thought was of the Border, where he had been born. But first he must take care of his brother, so he put Román in the buggy and drove into town, where his mother lived.

Now there was a lot of excitement in town. All the Americans were saddling up and loading rifles and pistols, because they were going out to kill Cortez. When all of a sudden, what should come rolling into town but the buggy, driven by Gregorio Cortez. They met him on the edge of town, armed to the teeth, on horseback and afoot, and he on the buggy, holding the reins lightly in his hands. Román was in the back, shot in the mouth. He could neither speak nor move, but just lay there like one who is dead.

They asked him, "Who are you?"

And he said to them, "I am Gregorio Cortez."

They all looked at him and were afraid of him, because they were only twenty or twenty-

11. **gamecock:** rooster trained for fighting.

12. **cockerel:** young rooster.

13. **Rangers:** mounted riflemen organized to protect Anglo ranchers and settlers in Texas.

Chama Running Red (1925), John Sloan. Courtesy of The Anschutz Collection. Photo by James O. Milmoe.

five, and they knew that they were not enough. So they stepped aside and let him pass and stood talking among themselves what would be the best thing to do. But Gregorio Cortez just drove ahead, slowly, without seeming to care about the men he left behind. He came to his mother's house, and there he took down his brother and carried him in the house. He stayed there until dawn, and during the night groups of armed men would go by the house and say, "He's in there. He's in there." But none of them ever went in.

At dawn Gregorio Cortez came out of his mother's house. There were armed men outside, but they made no move against him. They just watched as he went down the street, his hands resting on his belt. He went along as if he was taking a walk, and they stood there watching until he reached the brush and he jumped into it and disappeared. And then they started shooting at him with rifles, now that he was out of pistol range.

"I must get me a rifle," said Gregorio Cortez, "a rifle and a horse."

They gathered in a big bunch and started after him in the brush. But they could not catch Gregorio Cortez. No man was ever as good as

They'll never catch me like that,...

him in hiding his own tracks, and he soon had them going around in circles, while he doubled back and headed for home to get himself a rifle and a horse.

How Gregorio Cortez Rode the Little Sorrel Mare All of Five Hundred Miles

He went in and got his thirty-thirty, and then he looked around for the best horse he had. It is a long way from El Carmen to the Border, all of five hundred miles. The first thing he saw in the corral was the little sorrel mare. Gregorio Cortez took a good look at her, and he knew she was no ordinary mare.

"You're worth a dozen horses," said Gregorio Cortez, and he saddled the little mare.

But by then the whole wasp's nest was beginning to buzz. The President of the United States offered a thousand dollars for him, and many men went out to get Gregorio Cortez. The Major Sheriffs of the counties and all their sheriffs were out. There were Rangers from the counties, armed to the teeth, and the King Ranch Rangers from the Capital, the meanest of them all, all armed and looking for Cortez. Every road was blocked and every bridge guarded. There were trackers out with those dogs they call hounds, that can follow a track better than the best tracker. They had railroad cars loaded with guns and ammunition and with men, moving up and down trying to head him off. The women and children stayed in the houses, behind locked doors, such was the fear they all had of Gregorio Cortez. Every town from the Capital to the Border was watching out for him. The brush and the fields were full of men, trying to pick up his trail. And Gregorio Cortez rode out for the Border, through brush and fields and barbed wire fences, on his little sorrel mare.

He rode and rode until he came to a great broad plain, and he started to ride across. But just as he did, one of the sheriffs saw him. The sheriff saw him, but he hid behind a bush, because he was afraid to take him on alone. So he called the other sheriffs together and all the Rangers he could find, and they went off after Gregorio Cortez just as he came out upon the plain.

Gregorio Cortez looked back and saw them coming. There were three hundred of them.

"We'll run them a little race," said Gregorio Cortez.

Away went the mare, as if she had been shot from a gun, and behind her came the sheriffs and the Rangers, all shooting and riding hard. And so they rode across the plain, until one by one their horses foundered and fell to the ground and died. But still the little mare ran on, as fresh as a lettuce leaf, and pretty soon she was running all alone.

"They'll never catch me like that," said Gregorio Cortez, "not even with those dogs called hounds."

Another big bunch of sheriffs rode up, and they chased him to the edge of the plain, and into the brush went Cortez, with the trackers after him, but they did not chase him long. One moment there was a trail to follow, and next moment there was none. And the dogs called hounds sat down and howled, and the men scratched their heads and went about in circles looking for the trail. And Gregorio Cortez went on, leaving no trail, so that people thought he was riding through the air.

There were armed men everywhere, and he could not stop to eat or drink, because wherever he tried to stop armed men were there before him. So he had to ride on and on. Now they saw him, now they lost him, and so the chase went on. Many more horses foundered, but the mare still ran, and Gregorio Cortez rode on and on, pursued by hundreds and fighting hundreds every place he went.

"So many mounted Rangers," said Gregorio Cortez, "to catch just one Mexican."

It was from the big bunches that he ran. Now and again he would run into little ones of ten or a dozen men, and they were so scared of him that they would let him pass. Then, when he was out of range they would shoot at him, and he would shoot back at them once or twice, so they could go back and say, "We met up with Gregorio Cortez, and we traded shots with him." But from the big ones he had to run. And it was the little sorrel mare that took him safe away, over the open spaces and into the brush, and once in the brush, they might as well have been following a star.

So it went for a day, and when night fell Cortez arrived at a place named Los Fresnos and called at a Mexican house. When the man of the house came out, Cortez told him, "I am Gregorio Cortez."

That was all he had to say. He was given to eat and drink, and the man of the house offered Gregorio Cortez his own horse and his rifle and his saddle. But Cortez would not take them. He thanked the man, but he would not give up his little sorrel mare. Cortez was sitting there, drinking a cup of coffee, when the Major Sheriff of Los Fresnos came up with his three hundred men. All the other people ran out of the house and hid, and no one was left in the house, only Gregorio Cortez, with his pistol in his hand.

Then the Major Sheriff called out, in a weepy voice, as the corrido says. He sounded as if he wanted to cry, but it was all done to deceive Gregorio Cortez.

"Cortez," the Major Sheriff said, "hand over your weapons. I did not come to kill you. I am your friend."

"If you come as my friend," said Gregorio Cortez, "why did you bring three hundred men? Why have you made me a corral?"

The Major Sheriff knew that he had been caught in a lie, and the fighting began. He killed the Major Sheriff and the second sheriff under him, and he killed many sheriffs more. Some of the sheriffs got weak in the knees, and many ran away.

"Don't go away," said Gregorio Cortez. "I am the man you are looking for. I am Gregorio Cortez."

They were more than three hundred, but he jumped their corral, and he rode away again, and those three hundred did not chase him any more.

He rode on and on, until he came to a river called the San Antonio. It is not much of a river, but the banks are steep and high, and he could not find a ford. So he rode to a ranch house nearby, where they were holding a baile[14] because the youngest child of the house had been baptized that day, and he asked the man of the house about a ford.

"There are only two fords," the man said. "One is seven miles upstream and the other is seven miles down."

14. **baile** (bäy′lĕ) *Spanish:* dance.

...not even with those dogs called hounds.

"I will take another look at the river," said Gregorio Cortez. He left the baile and rode slowly to the river. It was steep, and far below he could see the water flowing; he could barely see it because it was so dark. He stood there thinking, trying to figure out a way, when he heard the music at the baile stop.

He knew the Rangers were at the baile now. So he leaned over in his saddle and whispered in the mare's ear. He talked to her, and she understood. She came to the edge of the bank, with soft little steps, because she was afraid. But Gregorio Cortez kept talking to her and talking to her, and finally she jumped. She jumped far out and into the dark water below, she and Gregorio Cortez.

The other bank was not so high, but it was just as steep. Gregorio Cortez took out his reata,[15] and he lassoed a stump high on the bank. He climbed up the rope and got a stick, and with the stick he worked on the bank as fast as he could, for he could hear the racket of the dogs. The ground was soft, and he knocked off part of the top, until he made something like a slope. Then he pulled and talked until the mare struggled up the bank to where he was. After that they rested up a bit and waited for the Rangers. Up they came with their dogs, to the spot where the mare had jumped. When they came up to the river's edge, Cortez fired a shot in the air and yelled at them, "I am Gregorio Cortez!"

Then he rode away, leaving them standing there on the other side, because none of them was brave enough to do what Cortez had done.

Cliffs Beyond Abiquiu, Dry Waterfall (1943), Georgia O'Keeffe. Oil on canvas, 76.2 cm × 40.6 cm, The Cleveland (Ohio) Museum of Art, bequest of Georgia O'Keeffe (87.141). Copyright © 1996 The Georgia O'Keeffe Foundation/Artists Rights Society (ARS), New York. Photo Copyright © The Cleveland Museum of Art.

He rode on and on, and sometimes they chased him and sometimes he stood and fought. And every time he fought he would kill them a Ranger or two. They chased him across the Arroyo del Cíbolo and into an oak grove, and there they made him a corral. Then they sent the dogs away and sat down to wait, for they wanted to catch him asleep. Gregorio Cortez thought for a little while what he should do. Then he made his mare lie down on the ground, so she would not be hurt. After that Gregorio Cortez began talking to himself and answering himself in different voices, as if he had many men. This made the Rangers say to one another, "There is a whole army of men with Gregorio Cortez." So they broke up their corral and went away, because they did not think there were enough of them to fight Gregorio Cortez and all the men he had. And Gregorio Cortez rode away, laughing to himself.

He kept riding on and on, by day and by night, and if he slept the mare stood guard and she would wake him up when she heard a noise. He had no food or cigarettes, and his ammunition was running low. He was going along a narrow trail with a high barbed wire fence on one side and a nopal[16] thicket on the other, and right before he hit a turn he heard

15. **reata** (rĕ-ä′tä) *Spanish:* lasso or lariat.

16. **nopal** (nô-päl′) *Spanish:* kind of cactus.

horses ahead. The first man that came around the turn ran into Gregorio Cortez, with his pistol in his hand. There was a whole line of others behind the first, all armed with rifles, but they had to put the rifles away. Then Gregorio Cortez knocked over a tall nopal plant with his stirrup and made just enough room for his mare to back into while the Rangers filed by. He stopped the last one and took away his tobacco, matches, and ammunition. And then he rode away.

He rode on to La Grulla, and he was very thirsty, because he had not had water in a long time, and the mare was thirsty too. Near La Grulla there was a dam where the vaqueros watered their stock. But when Gregorio Cortez got there, he saw twenty armed men resting under the trees that grew close to the water. Gregorio Cortez stopped and thought what he could do. Then he went back into the brush and began rounding up cattle, for this was cattle country and steers were everywhere. Pretty soon he had two hundred head, and he drove them to water and while the cattle drank he and the mare drank too. After he had finished, some of the Rangers that were resting under the trees came over and helped him get the herd together again, and Gregorio Cortez rode off with the herd, laughing to himself.

HE rode on and on, and by now he knew that the Rio Grande was near. He rode till he came to Cotulla, and there he was chased again. The little mare was tired, and now she began to limp. She had cut her leg and it was swelling up. Gregorio Cortez rode her into a thicket, and the Rangers made him a corral. But once in the brush, Gregorio Cortez led the mare to a coma[17] tree and tied her there. He unsaddled her and hung the saddle to the tree, and he patted her and talked to her for a long while. Then he slipped out of the thicket, and the Rangers didn't see him because they were waiting for him to ride out. They waited for three days and finally they crept in and found only the mare and the saddle.

How El Teco Sold Gregorio Cortez for a Morral[18] Full of Silver Dollars

Gregorio Cortez was gone. While all the armed men were guarding the thicket where the mare was tied, he walked into Cotulla itself. He walked into town and mixed with the Mexicans there. He sat on the station platform and listened to other men while they talked of all the things that Gregorio Cortez had done. Then he went to a store and bought himself new clothes and walked out of the town. He went to the river and took a bath and then swam across, because the bridge was guarded. That sort of man was Gregorio Cortez. They don't make them like him any more.

He had only three cartridges left, one for one pistol and two for the other, and he had left his rifle with the mare. But he was very near the Rio Grande, and he expected to cross it soon. Still he needed ammunition, so he walked into El Sauz and tried to buy some, but they did not sell cartridges in that town. Then he thought of trying some of the houses, and chose one in which there was a pretty girl at the door because he knew it would be easier if he talked to a girl. There was not a woman that did not like Gregorio Cortez.

The girl was alone, and she invited him into the house. When he asked for ammunition, she told him she had none.

"My father has taken it all," she said. "He is out looking for a man named Gregorio Cortez."

Gregorio Cortez was embarrassed because he could see that the girl knew who he was. But she did not let on and neither did he. He stayed at the house for a while, and when he left she told him how to get to the Rio Grande by the quickest way.

17. **coma** (kô′mä) *Spanish:* kind of thorn tree.

18. **morral** (mô-räl′) *Spanish:* large bag or pouch.

Now all the people along the river knew that Gregorio Cortez was on the Border, and that he would soon cross, but no one told the sheriffs what they knew. And Gregorio Cortez walked on, in his new clothes, with his pistols in a morral, looking like an ordinary man, but the people he met knew that he was Gregorio Cortez. And he began to talk to people along the way.

SOON he met a man who told him, "You'll be on the other side of the river tonight, Gregorio Cortez."

"I think I will," he said.

"You'll be all right then," said the man.

"I guess so," said Gregorio Cortez.

"But your brother won't," the man said. "He died in the jail last night."

"He was badly wounded," said Gregorio Cortez. "It was his lot to die, but I have avenged his death."

"They beat him before he died," the man said. "The Rangers came to the jail and beat him to make him talk."

This was the first news that Gregorio Cortez had heard, and it made him thoughtful.

He walked on, and he met another man who said, "Your mother is in the jail, Gregorio Cortez."

"Why?" said Gregorio Cortez. "Why should the sheriffs do that to her?"

"Because she is your mother," the man said. "That's why. Your wife is there too, and so are your little sons."

Gregorio Cortez thought this over, and he walked on. Pretty soon he met another man who said, "Gregorio Cortez, your own people are suffering, and all because of you."

"Why should my own people suffer?" said Cortez. "What have I done to them?"

"You have killed many sheriffs, Gregorio Cortez," said the man. "The Rangers cannot catch you, so they take it out on other people like you. Every man that's given you a glass of water has been beaten and thrown in jail. Every man who has fed you has been hanged from a tree branch, up and down, up and down, to make him tell where you went, and some have died rather than tell. Lots of people have been shot and beaten because they were your people. But you will be safe, Gregorio Cortez; you will cross the river tonight."

"I did not know these things," said Gregorio Cortez.

And he decided to turn back, and to give himself up to the Governor of the State so that his own people would not suffer because of him.

He turned and walked back until he came to a place called Goliad, where he met eleven Mexicans, and among them there was one that called himself his friend. This man was a vaquero named El Teco, but Judas should have been his name. Gregorio Cortez was thirsty, and he came up to the eleven Mexicans to ask for water, and when El Teco saw Gregorio Cortez he thought how good it would be if he could get the thousand-dollar reward. So he walked up to Cortez and shook his hand and told the others, "Get some water for my friend Gregorio Cortez."

Then El Teco asked Gregorio Cortez to let him see the pistols he had, and that he would get him some ammunition. Gregorio Cortez smiled, because he knew. But he handed over the guns to El Teco, and El Teco looked at them and put them in his own morral. Then El Teco called the sheriffs to come and get Gregorio Cortez.

Every man that's given you a glass of water...

...has been beaten and thrown in jail.

When Gregorio Cortez saw what El Teco had done, he smiled again and said to him, "Teco, a man can only be what God made him. May you enjoy your reward."

But El Teco did not enjoy the reward, though the sheriffs gave him the money, one thousand dollars in silver, more than a morral could hold. He did not enjoy it because he could not spend it anywhere. If he went to buy a taco at the market place, the taco vender would tell him that tacos were worth two thousand dollars gold that day. People cursed him in the streets and wished that he would be killed or die. So El Teco became very much afraid. He buried the money and never spent it, and he never knew peace until he died.

How Gregorio Cortez Went to Prison, but Not for Killing the Sheriffs

When the sheriffs came to arrest Gregorio Cortez, he spoke to them and said, "I am not your prisoner yet. I will be the prisoner only of the Governor of the State. I was going to the Capital to give myself up, and that is where I'll go."

The sheriffs saw that he was in the right, so they went with him all the way to the Capital, and Cortez surrendered himself to the Governor of the State.

Then they put Cortez in jail, and all the Americans were glad, because they no longer were afraid. They got together, and they tried to lynch him. Three times they tried, but they could not lynch Gregorio Cortez.

And pretty soon all the people began to see that Gregorio Cortez was in the right, and they did not want to lynch him any more. They brought him gifts to the jail, and one day one of the judges came and shook the hand of Gregorio Cortez and said to him, "I would have done the same."

But Gregorio Cortez had many enemies, for he had killed many men, and they wanted to see him hanged. So they brought him to trial for killing the Major Sheriff of the county of El Carmen. The lawyer that was against him got up and told the judges that Cortez should die, because he had killed a man. Then Gregorio Cortez got up, and he spoke to them.

"Self-defense is allowed to any man," said Gregorio Cortez. "It is in your own law, and by your own law do I defend myself. I killed the sheriff, and I am not sorry, for he killed my brother. He spilled my brother's blood, which was also my blood. And he tried to kill me too. I killed the Major Sheriff defending my right."

And Gregorio Cortez talked for a long time to the judges, telling them about their own law. When he finished even the lawyer who was against him at the start was now for him. And all the judges came down from their benches and shook hands with Gregorio Cortez.

The judges said, "We cannot kill this man."

They took Gregorio Cortez all over the State, from town to town, and in each town he was tried before the court for the killing of a man. But in every court it was the same. Gregorio Cortez spoke to the judges, and he told them about the law, and he proved that he had the right. And each time the judges said, "This man was defending his right. Tell the sheriffs to set him free."

Carnival in Huejotzingo (1942), Diego Rivera. Watercolor on paper, 5 7/8″ × 3 3/4″, Courtesy of Sotheby's, New York.

And so it was that Gregorio Cortez was not found guilty of any wrong because of the sheriffs he had killed. And he killed many of them, there is no room for doubt. No man has killed more sheriffs than did Gregorio Cortez, and he always fought alone. For that is the way the real men fight, always on their own. There are young men around here today, who think that they are brave. Dangerous men they call themselves, and it takes five or six of them to jump a fellow and slash him in the arm. Or they hide in the brush and fill him full of buckshot as he goes by. They are not men. But that was not the way with Gregorio Cortez, for he was a real man.

Now the enemies of Gregorio Cortez got together and said to each other, "What are we going to do? This man is going free after killing so many of our friends. Shall we kill him ourselves? But we would have to catch him asleep, or shoot him in the back, because if we meet him face to face there will be few of us left."

Then one of them thought of the little sorrel mare, and there they had a plan to get Gregorio Cortez. They brought him back to court, and the lawyer who was against him asked, "Gregorio Cortez, do you recognize this mare?"

"I do," said Gregorio Cortez. "And a better little mare there never was."

Then the lawyer asked him, "Have you ridden this mare?"

And Gregorio Cortez answered, "She carried me all the way from El Carmen to the Border, a distance of five hundred miles."

THEN the lawyer asked him, "Is this mare yours?"

And Gregorio Cortez saw that they had him, but there was nothing he could do, because he was an honest man and he felt that he must tell the truth. He said no, the mare did not belong to him.

Then the judges asked Gregorio Cortez, "Is this true, Gregorio Cortez? Did you take this mare that did not belong to you?"

And Gregorio Cortez had to say that the thing was true.

So they sentenced Gregorio Cortez, but not for killing the sheriffs, as some fools will tell you even now, when they ought to know better. No, not for killing the sheriffs but for stealing the little sorrel mare. The judge sentenced him to ninety-nine years and a day. And the enemies of Gregorio Cortez were happy then, because they thought Cortez would be in prison for the rest of his life.

How President Lincoln's Daughter Freed Gregorio Cortez, and How He Was Poisoned and Died

But Gregorio Cortez did not stay in prison long. Inside of a year he was free, and this is the way it came about. Every year at Christmastime, a pretty girl can come to the Governor of the State and ask him to give her a prisoner as a Christmas present. And the Governor then has to set the prisoner free and give him to the girl. So it happened to Cortez. One day President Lincoln's daughter visited the prison, and she saw Gregorio Cortez. As soon as she saw him she went up and spoke to him.

"I am in love with you, Gregorio Cortez," President Lincoln's daughter said, "and if you promise to marry me I will go to the Governor next Christmas and tell him to give you to me."

Gregorio Cortez looked at President Lincoln's daughter, and he saw how beautiful she was. It made him thoughtful, and he did not know what to say.

"I have many rich farms," President Lincoln's daughter said. "They are all my own. Marry me and we will farm together."

Gregorio Cortez thought about that. He could see himself already like a German, sitting on the gallery, full of ham and beer, and belching and breaking wind while a half-dozen little blond cockroaches played in the yard. And he was tempted. But then he said to himself, "I can't marry a Gringo girl. We would not make a matching pair."

So he decided that President Lincoln's daughter was not the woman for him, and he told her, "I thank you very much, but I cannot marry you at all."

But President Lincoln's daughter would not take his no. She went to the Governor and said, "I would like to have a prisoner for Christmas."

And the Governor looked at her and saw she was a pretty girl, so he said, "Your wish is granted. What prisoner do you want?"

And President Lincoln's daughter said, "I want Gregorio Cortez."

The Governor thought for a little while and then he said, "That's a man you cannot have. He's the best prisoner I got."

But President Lincoln's daughter shook her head and said, "Don't forget that you gave your word."

"So I did," the Governor said, "and I cannot go back on it."

And that was how Gregorio Cortez got out of prison, where he had been sentenced to ninety-nine years and a day, not for killing the sheriffs, as some fools will tell you, but for stealing the little sorrel mare. Gregorio Cortez kept his word, and he did not marry President Lincoln's daughter, and when at last she lost her hopes she went away to the north.

Still, the enemies of Gregorio Cortez did not give up. When they heard that he was getting out of prison they were scared and angry, and they started thinking of ways to get revenge. They got a lot of money together and gave it to a man who worked in the prison, and this man gave Cortez a slow poison just before Gregorio Cortez got out of jail.

And that was how he came to die, within a year from the day he got out of jail. As soon as he came out and his friends saw him, they said to each other, "This man is sick. This man will not last the year."

And so it was. He did not last the year. He died of the slow poison they gave him just before he was let out, because his enemies did not want to see him free.

AND that was how Gregorio Cortez came to die. He's buried in Laredo some place, or maybe it's Brownsville, or Matamoros, or somewhere up above. To tell the truth, I don't know. I don't know the place where he is buried any more than the place where he was born. But he was born and lived and died, that I do know. And a lot of Rangers could also tell you that.

So does the corrido; it tells about Gregorio Cortez and who he was. They started singing the corrido soon after he went to jail, and there was a time when it was forbidden in all the United States, by order of the President himself. Men sometimes got killed or lost their jobs because they sang *El Corrido de Gregorio Cortez.* But everybody sang it just the same, because it spoke about things that were true.

Now it is all right to sing *El Corrido de Gregorio Cortez,* but not everybody knows it any more. And they don't sing it as it used to be sung. These new singers change all the old songs a lot. But even so, people still remember Gregorio Cortez. And when a good singer sings the song—good and loud and clear—you can feel your neck-feathers rise, and you can see him standing there, with his pistol in his hand. ❖

RESPONDING OPTIONS

FROM PERSONAL RESPONSE *TO* CRITICAL ANALYSIS

REFLECT 1. Did you enjoy this retelling of the *corrido*? Record your opinions in your notebook.

RETHINK 2. Which of Gregorio Cortez's personal qualities do you find most admirable?

3. How does Gregorio Cortez compare with the hero you identified in the Personal Connection (page 556)?
   Consider
   - the occupations in which Cortez excels
   - his skills as a fighter
   - how he handles his legal battles
   - the values that guide his conduct
   - the idea of manhood that he exemplifies

4. Which events in this story seem realistic, and which strike you as exaggerated? Consult the notes you took as you read the story. Then discuss why singers and storytellers might have exaggerated certain events in Cortez's life.

5. What do the comments and attitudes of the speaker in this retelling reveal about cultural conflicts between Anglos and Mexicans in the Texas border area during this time period?
   Consider
   - the portrayal of the sheriffs and the Texas Rangers
   - the number of men required to capture Gregorio Cortez
   - the conversation between Román and the American who owns the mare
   - the treatment Gregorio Cortez receives in U.S. courts

6. Do you think Gregorio Cortez was right to live by the code "I will break before I bend"? Explain your opinion.

RELATE 7. Think of other heroes you have encountered, in movies, TV programs, books, cartoons, or newspaper and magazine articles. Which of them resemble Gregorio Cortez, and in what ways?

ANOTHER PATHWAY

Cooperative Learning

With a small group, report the story of Gregorio Cortez for a national evening news broadcast, a local news program for a U.S. or a Mexican border town, or a tabloid-type newsmagazine show. Include spot interviews to make your report lively. Deliver your news report to the class.

QUICKWRITES

1. Write a **farewell letter** from Gregorio to his young sons in which he explains the reasons for his actions and gives them advice for living their lives.
2. Draft several verses of a **folk ballad,** a song or a poem that tells a story, about the life of Gregorio Cortez. As an alternative, you may want to write a folk ballad about the hero you identified in the Personal Connection. Sing or read your ballad to classmates.

PORTFOLIO *Save your writing. You may want to use it later as a springboard to a piece for your portfolio.*

LITERARY CONCEPTS

A **cultural hero** is a larger-than-life figure who reflects the values of a people. This kind of hero is not the creation of a single writer. Rather, the hero evolves from communal tales—told orally or sung to musical accompaniment—that were passed down from one generation to the next. The role of the cultural hero is to provide a noble image that will inspire and guide the actions of all who share that culture. The qualities of Gregorio Cortez that are celebrated in this story give some clues about the ideals of Mexican Americans of the Texas border region in the early years of the 20th century. For example, Cortez exhibits family loyalty when he shoots the sheriff who shot his brother, Román. Look back through the story and find at least three other cultural values that Cortez might represent.

CRITIC'S CORNER

Some readers argue that because Gregorio Cortez kills many people, he is an inappropriate person to present as a hero. Argue for or against that position, explaining what you think.

ACROSS THE CURRICULUM

Music This story is a prose retelling of a Mexican folk song, "El Corrido de Gregorio Cortez." Find recordings of folk songs about legendary heroes from your own or other cultures and play your favorites for the class. If possible, find and play *corridos* about Cortez or other heroes such as Pancho Villa or José Mosqueda. Use an on-line search service to help you locate recordings in nearby libraries.

Geography Use the map of the Texas border region on page 556 to locate some of the places mentioned in this story. Then trace the escape route followed by Gregorio Cortez as he tried to elude the Texas Rangers and the sheriffs.

AMÉRICO PAREDES

1915–

Américo Paredes, the son of a rancher, grew up near Brownsville, Texas, along the Mexican border. During this time, he absorbed the colorful traditions, songs, and legends of the area. This early experience with these traditions shaped Paredes's lifework. In describing his fascination with Mexican *corridos* and other folk songs, he said, "I started 'collecting' these songs around 1920, when I first became aware of them on the lips of the *guitarreros* and other people of the ranchos and the towns."

After serving in the U.S. Army during World War II, Paredes attended the University of Texas, where he earned his bachelor's, master's, and doctoral degrees. In 1954 he joined the faculty at the university, where he has served as the director of the Center for Intercultural Studies in Folklore and Oral History and of the Mexican-American Studies program.

While a professor of English and anthropology at the University of Texas, Paredes published numerous books documenting Mexican-American folk traditions. Among his best-known works are *"With His Pistol in His Hand": A Border Ballad and Its Hero* (1958), from which "The Legend of Gregorio Cortez" is taken, and *Folktales of Mexico* (1970). Paredes also has been the editor of the Journal of American Folklore and has edited many works on cultural anthropology. For his achievement in preserving the Mexican-American folk tradition, Paredes has received several important awards, among them the Order of the Aztec Eagle, Mexico's highest award to foreigners.

OTHER WORKS *Corridos and Calaveras, Between Two Worlds, The Hammon and the Beans and Other Stories, A Texas-Mexican Cancionero*

ON YOUR OWN

A BLIZZARD UNDER BLUE SKY

Pam Houston

The doctor said I was clinically depressed. It was February, the month in which depression runs rampant in the inversion-cloaked Salt Lake Valley[1] and the city dwellers escape to Park City, where the snow is fresh and the sun is shining and everybody is happy, except me. In truth, my life was on the verge of more spectacular and satisfying discoveries than I had ever imagined, but of course I couldn't see that far ahead. What I saw was work that wasn't getting done, bills that weren't getting paid, and a man I'd given my heart to weekending in the desert with his ex.

The doctor said, "I can give you drugs."

I said, "No way."

She said, "The machine that drives you is broken. You need something to help you get it fixed."

I said, "Winter camping."

She said, "Whatever floats your boat."

One of the things I love the most about the natural world is the way it gives you what's good for you even if you don't know it at the time. I had never been winter camping before, at least not in the high country, and the weekend I chose to try and fix my machine was the same weekend the air mass they called the Alaska Clipper showed up. It was thirty-two degrees below zero in town on the night I spent in my snow cave. I don't know how cold it was out on Beaver Creek. I had listened to the weather forecast, and to the advice of my housemate, Alex, who was an experienced winter camper.

1. **inversion-cloaked . . . Valley:** The valley is frequently filled with haze and pollution because of an unfortunate mix of atmospheric conditions and landforms. In a temperature inversion, a layer of warm air traps cooler air—and pollution—near the surface of the earth, preventing the normal circulation of air.

"I don't know what you think you're going to prove by freezing to death," Alex said, "but if you've got to go, take my bivvy sack;[2] it's warmer than anything you have."

"Thanks," I said.

"If you mix Kool-Aid with your water it won't freeze up," he said, "and don't forget lighting paste for your stove."

"Okay," I said.

"I hope it turns out to be worth it," he said, "because you are going to freeze your butt."

WHEN EVERYTHING IN YOUR LIFE is uncertain, there's nothing quite like the clarity and precision of fresh snow and blue sky. That was the first thought I had on Saturday morning as I stepped away from the warmth of my truck and let my skis slap the snow in front of me. There was no wind and no clouds that morning, just still air and cold sunshine. The hair in my nostrils froze almost immediately. When I took a deep breath, my lungs only filled up halfway.

I opened the tailgate to excited whines and whimpers. I never go skiing without Jackson and Hailey: my two best friends, my yin and yang[3] of dogs. Some of you might know Jackson. He's the oversized sheepdog-and-something-else with the great big nose and the bark that will shatter glass. He gets out and about more than I do. People I've never seen before come by my house daily and call him by name. He's all grace, and he's tireless; he won't go skiing with me unless I let him lead. Hailey is not so graceful, and her body seems in constant indecision when she runs. When we ski she stays behind me, and on the downhills she tries to sneak rides on my skis.

The dogs ran circles in the chest-high snow while I inventoried my backpack one more time to make sure I had everything I needed. My sleeping bag, my Thermarest, my stove, Alex's bivvy sack, matches, lighting paste, flashlight, knife. I brought three pairs of long underwear—tops and bottoms—so I could change once before I went to bed, and once again in the morning, so I wouldn't get chilled by my own sweat. I brought paper and pen, and Kool-Aid to mix with my water. I brought Mountain House chicken stew and some freeze-dried green peas, some peanut butter and honey, lots of dried apricots, coffee and Carnation instant breakfast for morning.

Jackson stood very still while I adjusted his backpack. He carries the dog food and enough water for all of us. He takes himself very seriously when he's got his pack on. He won't step off the trail for any reason, not even to chase rabbits, and he gets nervous and angry if I do. That morning he was impatient with me. "Miles to go, Mom," he said over his shoulder. I snapped my boots into my skis and we were off.

There are not too many good things you can say about temperatures that dip past twenty below zero, except this: They turn the landscape into a crystal palace and they turn your vision into Superman's. In the cold thin morning air the trees and mountains, even the twigs and shadows, seemed to leap out of the background like a 3-D movie, only it was better than 3-D because I could feel the sharpness of the air.

I have a friend in Moab who swears that Utah is the center of the fourth dimension,[4] and although I know he has in mind something much different and more complicated than subzero weather, it was there, on that ice-edged morning, that I felt on the verge of seeing something more than depth perception in the brutal clarity of the morning sun.

As I kicked along the first couple of miles, I noticed the sun crawling higher in the sky and yet the day wasn't really warming, and I wondered if I should have brought another vest,

2. **bivvy sack:** loose, watertight bag used in addition to a sleeping bag for extra protection from the cold and wet. *Bivvy* is short for *bivouac* (a temporary camp).

3. **yin and yang:** In Chinese philosophy, yin is the positive, passive, female force in the universe; yang is the negative, active, male force.

4. **fourth dimension:** time; the first three dimensions are length, width, and depth (or height).

In the cold
thin morning air
the trees and
mountains,
even the twigs
and shadows,
seemed to leap
out of the back-
ground like a 3-D
movie, only it was
better than 3-D.

another layer to put between me and the cold night ahead.

It was utterly quiet out there, and what minimal noise we made intruded on the morning like a brass band: the squeaking of my bindings, the slosh of the water in Jackson's pack, the whoosh of nylon, the jangle of dog tags. It was the bass line and percussion to some primal song, and I kept wanting to sing to it, but I didn't know the words.

Jackson and I crested the top of a hill and stopped to wait for Hailey. The trail stretched out as far as we could see into the meadow below us and beyond, a double track and pole plants carving through softer trails of rabbit and deer.

"Nice place," I said to Jackson, and his tail thumped the snow underneath him without sound.

We stopped for lunch near something that looked like it could be a lake in its other life, or maybe just a womb-shaped meadow. I made peanut butter and honey sandwiches for all of us, and we opened the apricots.

"It's fabulous here," I told the dogs. "But so far it's not working."

There had never been anything wrong with my life that a few good days in the wilderness wouldn't cure, but there I sat in the middle of all those crystal-coated trees, all that diamond-studded sunshine, and I didn't feel any better. Apparently clinical depression was not like having a bad day, it wasn't even like having a lot of bad days, it was more like a house of mirrors, it was like being in a room full of one-way glass.

"Come on, Mom," Jackson said. "Ski harder, go faster, climb higher."

Hailey turned her belly to the sun and groaned.

"He's right," I told her. "It's all we can do."

After lunch the sun had moved behind our backs, throwing a whole different light on the path ahead of us. The snow we moved through stopped being simply white and became translucent, hinting at other colors, reflections of blues and purples and grays. I thought of Moby Dick, you know, the whiteness of the whale, where white is really the absence of all color, and whiteness equals truth, and Ahab's[5] search is finally futile, as he finds nothing but his own reflection.

"Put your mind where your skis are," Jackson said, and we made considerably better time after that.

The sun was getting quite low in the sky when I asked Jackson if he thought we should stop to build the snow cave, and he said he'd look for the next good bank. About one hundred yards down the trail we found it, a gentle slope with eastern exposure that didn't look like it would cave in under any circumstances. Jackson started to dig first.

Let me make one thing clear. I knew only slightly more about building snow caves than Jackson, having never built one, and all my knowledge coming from disaster tales of winter camping fatalities. I knew several things *not* to do when building a snow cave, but I was having a hard time knowing what exactly to do. But Jackson helped, and Hailey supervised, and before too long we had a little cave built, just big enough for three. We ate dinner quite pleased with our accomplishments and set the bivvy sack up inside the cave just as the sun slipped away and dusk came over Beaver Creek.

The temperature, which hadn't exactly soared during the day, dropped twenty degrees in as many minutes, and suddenly it didn't seem like such a great idea to change my long underwear. The original plan was to sleep with the dogs inside the bivvy sack but outside the sleeping bag, which was okay with Jackson the super-metabolizer,[6] but not so with Hailey, the couch potato. She whined and wriggled and managed to stuff her entire fat body down inside my mummy bag, and Jackson stretched out full-length on top.

One of the unfortunate things about winter camping is that it has to happen when the days are so short. Fourteen hours is a long time to lie in a snow cave under the most perfect of circumstances. And when it's thirty-two below, or forty, fourteen hours seems like weeks.

I wish I could tell you I dropped right off to sleep. In truth, fear crept into my spine with the cold and I never closed my eyes. Cuddled there, amid my dogs and water bottles, I spent half of the night chastising myself for thinking I was Wonder Woman, not only risking my own life but the lives of my dogs, and the other half trying to keep the numbness in my feet from crawling up to my knees. When I did doze off, which was actually more like blacking out than dozing off, I'd come back to my senses wondering if I had frozen to death, but the alternating pain and numbness that started in my extremities and

5. **Moby Dick . . . Ahab's:** In *Moby Dick,* a novel by Herman Melville, Moby Dick is the name given to an extraordinary white whale of legendary cunning, and Ahab is the whaling-ship captain who pursues the whale at the cost of his own life.

6. **super-metabolizer:** Metabolism is the process by which the body changes food into energy. The narrator is saying that Jackson's metabolism is so efficient that he has a great deal of energy.

worked its way into my bones convinced me I must still be alive.

It was a clear night, and every now and again I would poke my head out of its nest of down and nylon to watch the progress of the moon across the sky. There is no doubt that it was the longest and most uncomfortable night of my life.

But then the sky began to get gray, and then it began to get pink, and before too long the sun was on my bivvy sack, not warm, exactly, but holding the promise of warmth later in the day. And I ate apricots and drank Kool-Aid-flavored coffee and celebrated the rebirth of my fingers and toes, and the survival of many more important parts of my body. I sang "Rocky Mountain High" and "If I Had a Hammer," and yodeled and whistled, and even danced the two-step with Jackson and let him lick my face. And when Hailey finally emerged from the sleeping bag a full hour after I did, we shared a peanut butter and honey sandwich and she said nothing ever tasted so good.

We broke camp and packed up and kicked in the snow cave with something resembling glee.

I was five miles down the trail before I realized what had happened. Not once in that fourteen-hour night did I think about deadlines, or bills, or the man in the desert. For the first time in many months I was happy to see a day beginning. The morning sunshine was like a present from the gods. What really happened, of course, is that I remembered about joy.

I KNOW THAT ONE NIGHT OUT AT thirty-two below doesn't sound like much to those of you who have climbed Everest or run the Iditarod[7] or kayaked to Antarctica, and I won't try to convince you that my life was like the movies where depression goes away in one weekend, and all of life's problems vanish with a moment's clear sight. The simple truth of the matter is this: On Sunday I had a glimpse outside of the house of mirrors, on Saturday I couldn't have seen my way out of a paper bag. And while I was skiing back toward the truck that morning, a wind came up behind us and swirled the snow around our bodies like a blizzard under blue sky. And I was struck by the simple perfection of the snowflakes, and startled by the hopefulness of sun on frozen trees.

---

7. **Iditarod:** a very strenuous dogsled race run each year in Alaska.

Pam Houston

1962?–

Working as river guide in Alaska and the West in the summer, author Pam Houston has "hauled wild-sheep carcasses on her back across Alaskan mountains, camped in snow caves and defied a river that just a day before had killed a woman. . . ." In her best-selling first book *Cowboys Are My Weakness: Stories,* Houston draws on her own varied outdoor experiences. Most of the twelve stories in the book, including "A Blizzard Under Blue Sky," are narrated by strong outdoorswomen who "discover their own unique relationship to nature, risk and ego."

Besides acting as a river guide, Houston has also worked as a horse trainer and a ski instructor. Her hobbies include white-water rafting, skiing, and rock climbing, and in 1992 she married a former safari guide from South Africa. Houston, who graduated from Denison University and from the University of Utah, has also taught literature and creative writing.

WRITING FROM EXPERIENCE

WRITING TO EXPLAIN

You have seen in Unit Four, "Conflict and Expansion," how people found creative solutions to the problems they faced. Along the way, they met others who offered advice, comfort, and help. Perhaps this unit has given you some ideas about how you, together with other people, can solve problems in your own life or in your community.

GUIDED ASSIGNMENT

Write a Problem-Solution Essay In school, in sports and activity groups, on the job, and in your community, you will encounter a wide range of problems—some mild, some serious. Talking with experts and participants and writing about difficult situations may help you understand, and even solve, many of these problems.

1 Study the Sources

The items on these pages identify problems that concern students and adults. Analyze the sources and record your answers to the following questions in your notebook.

Identify the Problem In a few words, what problem or problems are highlighted in each item?

State the Issues What are the main issues involved in each situation? Might people have differing viewpoints on each problem and on how to solve it?

2 Identify Major Concerns

Do you worry about getting a job? about the ozone layer? about violence in your school? Brainstorm a list of your major concerns.

Now move beyond your personal worries. List some of the problems facing your school, your community, or the world. You can take a poll of your classmates to see what they think are major problems, or you can look through magazines and newspapers for ideas.

Newspaper Article

Mayors Discuss City Problems

Seattle—Some 200 mayors from across the country gathered for their annual meeting of the U.S. Conference of Mayors. Violent crime and industrial pollution headed the list of problems that officials had gathered to discuss. The mayors noted that most of the increase in city crimes has occurred in high-rise urban housing, against the elderly and the homeless, and in inner-city and suburban schools. The major pollution headache concerns companies that dump toxic chemicals into the environment then close their doors and move to another state, making it difficult, if not impossible, to get them to pay for the cleanup.

The mayors sent a message to Congress and the President that U.S. cities lack sufficient funds to fight the rise in violent crime or to clean up polluted sites. All this comes at a time when Congress is trying to cut the budget, which means less money for cities.

Photographs
Vandalism can cost a community thousands of dollars a year.

Hate Crimes on Rise

Over the past decade, law-enforcement and civil rights groups across the country have watched a disturbing rise in hate crimes. The Southern Poverty Law Center, based in Montgomery, Alabama, reports that white supremacist, or "skinhead," groups such as the Aryan Nation are expanding, forming new chapters in the liberal northeastern states. These groups target nonwhites, Jews, and other "enemies" for harassment, vandalism, and injury.

One citizen's answer to hate-group attacks.

But the Federal Bureau of Investigation notes other disturbing trends. For one, hate crimes previously were a strictly white-on-black phenomenon. Now the ranks of both attackers and their victims represent a diverse racial, ethnic, and religious mix.

Second, more hate crimes are being committed by young people, particularly those in the 11- to 20-year-old bracket. Young people who have a history of behavior problems and have been abused or abandoned by their families are particularly susceptible to the appeals of hate groups. Third, the attacks are of a more personal, in-your-face nature, while incidents of vandalism and property destruction have declined somewhat.

In many communities, attempts to counter these trends, such as the sign posted by a storeowner in the picture, are meeting with little success.

We have this problem in our school. What can we do about it?

Can we talk to an expert on hate-group activities?

Magazine Article

3 Choose a Topic

Select two or three of the problems on your list. Freewrite a paragraph on your reactions to the major issues. What solutions can you think of?

Decision Point Select one problem that you would like to explore further in a problem-solution essay. It should be something genuinely important to you.

Exploring the Problem

Problem-Solving Steps If you have ever helped to settle an argument between two friends, you have probably used your problem-solving skills. You found out what the problem was, discovered what the main issues were, and helped brainstorm solutions. The steps on these pages will help you apply these skills to your writing by showing you how to plan your problem-solution essay.

1 Focus the Problem

In a brief sentence or two, describe the problem you will be exploring. Is it something that you face every day, or is it a larger issue that other people are trying to solve?

If you're concerned about a problem that seems too big, such as the worldwide destruction of many forests, don't give up. Think of a way to narrow your focus, such as making people aware of the loss of forests in your own state or community. The student writer of the notes shown here narrowed the topic of hate groups by focusing on the actions of one group in his school.

2 Research the Main Issues

The next step is to find out all you can about the problem. For example, how did it arise? What is at stake? Who is involved? What solutions have been tried in the past?

Besides using print media and on-line databases, you can interview people with special knowledge of your topic. For example, the student writer talked with a civil rights expert. (See the SkillBuilder for tips on asking good questions.)

Student's Prewriting Notes

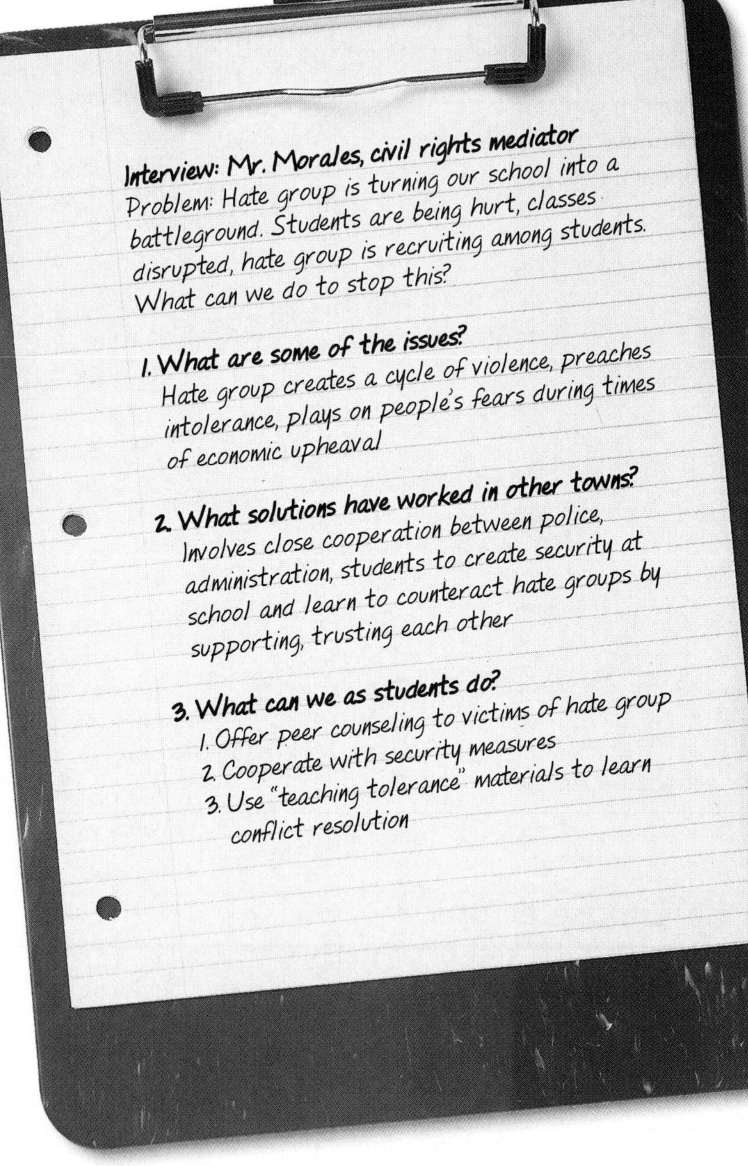

Interview: Mr. Morales, civil rights mediator
Problem: Hate group is turning our school into a battleground. Students are being hurt, classes disrupted, hate group is recruiting among students. What can we do to stop this?
1. What are some of the issues?
Hate group creates a cycle of violence, preaches intolerance, plays on people's fears during times of economic upheaval
2. What solutions have worked in other towns?
Involves close cooperation between police, administration, students to create security at school and learn to counteract hate groups by supporting, trusting each other
3. What can we as students do?
1. Offer peer counseling to victims of hate group
2. Cooperate with security measures
3. Use "teaching tolerance" materials to learn conflict resolution

Local Experts These can include family members, teachers, friends, and other personal acquaintances. Your teacher or reference librarian can help you find experts who work in local government, universities, private businesses, or foundations or associations.

National Experts You may be able to interview national experts on your topic. For example, The Southern Poverty Law Center provides information on hate-group activities.

3 Explore Solutions

After investigating the problem and gathering the facts, you can use these suggestions to help you find the best solutions.

Develop Your Solutions Write down every solution you have uncovered during your investigation and research. Then list the pros and cons of each solution, as shown below.

Talk Them Over Discuss your problem and proposed solutions with classmates, experts, and others to get feedback. Which solutions seem to address the main issues? What are their merits and drawbacks? Which ones are more feasible?

Try Them Out In some cases, you may be able to ask others to role-play your solutions by acting out the parts of those involved in the problem. Role-playing can reveal flaws in your solutions that you may have missed.

Student's Solutions

Solution	Pros	Cons
Peer counseling for victims	We already have peer counseling; way for us to help each other, build trust	Will need skilled supervision to oversee group's efforts
Supporting security measures	Will help protect students, property	Means more inconvenience, less freedom
Teaching tolerance	Materials will teach values; free to school. Worked well in other communities	Will require special class time, teaching

SkillBuilder

SPEAKING & LISTENING

Conducting an Interview
Asking good questions is one key to a successful interview. Keep these points in mind when interviewing others.

- Ask someone to help you brainstorm a list of questions beforehand.
- Ask "what," "how," and "why" questions to elicit more information. For example, "Why do people join hate groups?" will yield more information than "Do many people join these groups?"
- If the person doesn't understand one of your questions, try rephrasing it instead of repeating it word for word.
- Ask if you can contact the person again if you have further questions.

APPLYING WHAT YOU'VE LEARNED
Who might be the best person to interview about your subject? Write down the questions you would like to ask that person.

THINK & PLAN

Reflecting on Your Topic

1. What do you think the reader needs to know to understand the problem and main issues?
2. How realistic are your solutions? Can you think of others?

DRAFTING

Shaping Your Ideas

Strategies for Drafting Now you are ready to pull together facts from your interview and research. In general, a problem-solution draft should contain these four items:

- statement of the problem and its importance to readers
- analysis of the issues and presentation of facts
- discussion of possible solutions
- description of recommended solution

1 Remember Audience and Purpose

Why should people care about your problem? What is the best way to reach them? As you write your draft, keep your audience and purpose in mind. For example, the student writers have asked to address a school assembly where other groups will be discussing the same problem.

Discovery Draft

Coaching Workspace of Prob./Sol.

Coaching Workspace of Problem/Solution	Our Comments on Problem/Solution
Problem: Hate group has turned our school into a battleground. Student members attacking people in school and on the grounds, passing out hate literature, shouting out slogans in class.	
Mr. Morales, expert on hate groups, says that when economic times are hard, as in our town, hate crimes increase. People are more afraid and look for someone to blame. Hate groups create a cycle of violence that divides people and creates suspicion and mistrust. "To defeat this cycle, the police, school administration, parents, and students must all work together to create greater security and a supportive environment that teaches strong values of tolerance and cooperation." Mr. Morales recommended several "teaching tolerance" materials.	In the report, use a graph to show hate-crime statistics Mr. Morales gave us.
Solutions that students can act on: 1. Create peer counseling group to help victims of hate crimes feel that others care about them and support them. 2. Cooperate with security measures, report incidents, look out for each other.	Vivian and I will present our solutions at school assembly.
3. Use "teaching tolerance" materials in classroom to learn more about values of tolerance and cooperation and how to prevent violence in the school and outside.	We can list materials in report—most are free.

2 Review Your Draft

To help you evaluate your draft, ask yourself the following questions.

- Does the opening paragraph clearly explain the problem and the issues? What does the audience need to know?
- Do I state why it's important to solve this problem?
- What additional solutions should I consider?
- How can I use graphics, charts, or illustrations to convey information? See the SkillBuilder for suggestions on integrating statistics into your work.

3 Organize Your Work

There are several organizing strategies you can use within your problem-solution essay. Two of the more common include the following.

Cause and Effect You point out the causes of the problem, explain its effects, and describe the impact your solutions would have if they were implemented.

Narration You use a story, an incident, or an anecdote to gain the reader's or listener's interest, describe the problem, and recommend solutions. For more on organizing strategies, see pages 1176–1185 of the Writing Handbook.

PEER RESPONSE

Ask peer reviewers to evaluate your analysis of the problem and your proposed solutions. You might use these questions as a guide.

- What more do you need to know to understand the problem and the proposed solutions?
- How can I use illustrations or graphics to present the facts?
- What objections might people have to the recommended solutions? How can I overcome these objections?

SkillBuilder

WRITER'S CRAFT

Integrating Statistics

Whenever you include statistics in your work, be sure you tell the reader what they mean. Suppose you are using the graph below.

Hate Crimes in the U.S., 1991–1993

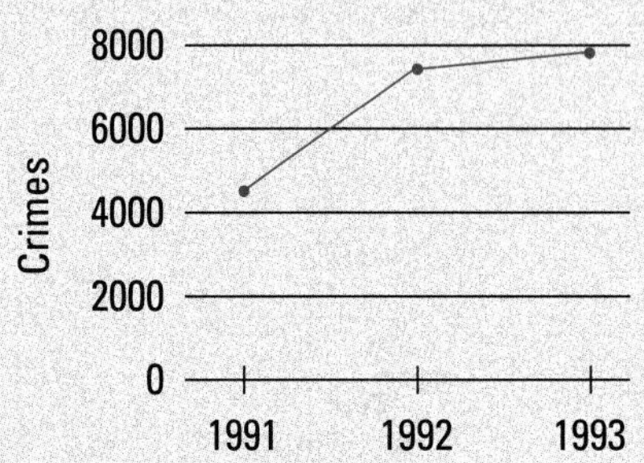

Rather than simply repeat the figures given, explain what they reveal. "The economy declined in the early 1990s. During that time, the number of reported hate crimes rose (see graph). This trend supports the general theory that the less secure people feel, the more willing they are to blame others for their problems."

APPLYING WHAT YOU'VE LEARNED

Check your work to be sure you have interpreted the statistics.

RETHINK & EVALUATE

Preparing to Revise

1. How can you make the problem and issues clearer for the reader?
2. Which organizing structure is best for your essay?
3. How have you resolved any objections to your proposed solutions?

Getting the Word Out

A Final Word Use the questions and suggestions on these pages to help you revise and polish your writing. You want to make sure that your facts are accurate, your analysis reasonable, and your solutions realistic. Revising and checking your work can turn a good paper into a first-rate one.

1 Revise and Edit

Take a break from your work and then read it again. If you are giving a speech based on your essay, practice in front of friends or family members. You can revise your work using peer comments, the Standards for Evaluation, and the Editing Checklist.

- Help your readers understand the problem and why they should care about it.
- Be sure you integrate details from your interviews and research to support your discussion of the issues.
- Make sure your solutions address the main issues and are feasible.

Speech Cards for a School Assembly

1

Pulling Apart—Coming Together

- Over past five months, hate group has turned our school into a battleground—attacking students, disrupting classes, passing out hate literature, trying to recruit members.
- Mr. Edward Morales, expert on hate groups, says
  - Hate groups operate in environment of fear
  - They set up cycle of violence, create mistrust
  - Community must work together to defeat them

3

Solutions that have been tried in other schools:

5

What do the writers describe as the main effects of the problem?

12

Students can help solve the problem in three ways:

1. Volunteer to be on peer counseling groups to help victims of hate-group attacks. Administration could help us find expert advisors for these groups.
2. Support security measures developed by police and school administration. Inconveniences are outweighed by prospect of greater safety for students.
3. Use "teaching tolerance" materials to help us learn how to live together in peace and to prevent violence.

How do the writers' solutions address the main issues?

You can present your problem-solution essay in any of several formats, such as a report or a newspaper article, as shown here.

Tindale Tigers

Tiger Times

How to Say "No" to Hate

By Evan Sutton and Vivian Edwards

How do you fight a hate group that's threatening to tear apart your school? For the past five months that question has been plaguing us at Tindale High School.

To help find some answers, we conducted research on hate groups and talked with Mr. Edward Morales, an expert on the activities of such groups.

Our results have been published in a report, "Pulling Apart—coming Together," which we handed out at the school assembly on Friday evening. Mr. Morales told us that hate groups flourish in an environment of fear. "This is especially true when the economy is weak and people are looking for someone to blame for their troubles." He also mentioned that these groups attract young people who believe they have no future and are looking for some place to vent their anger.

What can students do to fight hate groups? Mr. Morales said that in his experience, students can use peer counseling to help victims of hate attacks. They can support security measures to help Continued on Page 12

SkillBuilder

GRAMMAR FROM WRITING

Avoiding Illogical Comparisons

See if you can spot the mistake in logic in this sentence.

Our school has more problems than other schools.

The sentence literally says that "our school" has more "problems" than it has "other schools." The sentence should read

Our school has more problems than other schools have.

GRAMMAR HANDBOOK

See Illogical Comparisons on page 1219 of the Grammar Handbook.

Editing Checklist

Use the following tips to revise.

- Are direct quotes punctuated?
- Did you use logical comparisons?
- Are all proper names spelled correctly?

❷ Share Your Work

Once you have gathered information and developed your problem-solution essay, you can present it in several ways.

- A newspaper article can reach a wide audience.
- A detailed report can be used as a handout at a meeting.
- A pamphlet or flyer can be used as a handout or mailing.
- A report via the Internet or e-mail can give other schools and communities the benefit of your proposed solutions.

Standards for Evaluation

A problem-solution essay

- identifies the problem and helps the reader understand the issues involved
- analyzes the causes and effects of the problem
- integrates quotes, facts, and statistics into the text
- explores potential solutions to the problem and recommends the best ones
- uses appropriate language, tone, and details to match the audience's needs

REFLECT & ASSESS

Learning from Experience

1. List ways you could improve your interviewing technique.
2. Describe how you tested your solutions. How can these techniques help you evaluate other people's solutions?

PORTFOLIO You can include your answers and your finished essay in your portfolio.

REFLECT & ASSESS

UNIT 4: CONFLICT AND EXPANSION

Did your assumptions about slavery, the Civil War, the civil rights movement, and the development of the West change as you read this unit? As you complete one or more of the options in each of the following sections, think about how your ideas have developed.

REFLECTING ON THE UNIT

OPTION 1 **What is Liberty?** Think about Abraham Lincoln's words on the first page of this unit: "We all declare for liberty; but in using the same word we do not all mean the same thing." How do you think the writers represented in this unit would define *liberty?* Write a series of statements describing what you think liberty means to each author. Then write what liberty means to you.

OPTION 2 **Life in the Wild West** The selections in Part 2 of this unit deal with the ways of life of different peoples in the American West—from Native Americans to Hispanic and Anglo settlers to people facing new conflicts and challenges in the 20th century. What insights into the development of the West have the selections given you? With a small group of classmates, role-play three or four characters from the selections and discuss what was gained and what was lost as the frontier was gradually settled.

OPTION 3 **Irrepressible Conflicts** In the second half of the 19th century, the United States faced wrenching conflicts—over slavery, over preserving the Union, and over the settlement of the West. Some of these conflicts even spilled over into the 20th century. Write a few paragraphs about one of the major conflicts dealt with in this unit's selections, explaining your opinion of the way the conflict was resolved at the time and telling what further progress, if any, needs to be made.

REFLECT & ASSESS *Self-Assessment: Make a list of the selections in this unit that impressed you the most. Briefly explain how and why you were affected by each one. Which ones taught you something you didn't know before?*

REVIEWING LITERARY CONCEPTS

OPTION 1 **Examining Point of View** Work with a partner—one of you listing the selections in this unit that are told from the first-person point of view, the other listing the selections that are told from the third-person point of view. Compare the lists, then discuss the following questions:

- Why do you think the author of each selection chose the point of view that he or she used?
- How would each selection be different if it were told from a different point of view?

OPTION 2 **Evaluating Character** As you read the selections in this unit, what conclusions did you draw about the writers or the main characters? Use a chart like the one shown to record important character traits of each writer and main character, along with statements or events that reveal the traits. With a few classmates, discuss which character you feel is most admirable and why he or she is admirable.

Character/ Writer	Character Traits	Evidence from Selection
Frederick Douglass	strength, bravery, self-respect	asserts his manhood by refusing to let Mr. Covey beat him again

Self-Assessment: In this unit, you have read autobiographies, folk tales, and works of local-color realism. Write down some distinguishing characteristics of each of these kinds of writing, then list a selection from the unit that is a good example of each kind.

PORTFOLIO BUILDING

- **QuickWrites** Several of the QuickWrites in this unit asked you to see things from the points of view of characters in the selections. Review your responses and choose one that you think shows good insight into a character. Write a cover note explaining the character traits and motivations you conveyed. Add the response and the note to your portfolio.
- **Writing About Literature** Reread the essay in which you analyzed a story by exploring how its parts worked together. If you could change one element to make the story stronger, what change would you make? Would you make the main character more complex? the plot less predictable? If you choose to add this essay to your portfolio, write down your ideas in a cover letter and attach it to the essay.
- **Writing from Experience** Review the solution you recommended in your problem-solution essay. Write a letter to someone who you believe could help you implement your solution. Explain why you chose the person, and describe the ways in which he or she could help you. Add the letter and essay to your portfolio.
- **Personal Choice** The activities suggested in this unit included opportunities to create and act out a rally, a newscast, and an interview—even to perform a play. Which of your performances gave you important information about your own preferences and abilities? Write a cover note explaining what you learned about yourself from the activity, attach it to your record of the activity, and add both to your portfolio.

Self-Assessment: At this point your portfolio contains a substantial amount of your work. Review the work it contains and decide which pieces show your thinking and writing abilities best. What other kinds of writing would you like to try as the year goes on?

SETTING GOALS

Look back through your worksheets and notebook to identify writing skills and thinking skills you would like to strengthen. Select three or four skills to improve as you study the next unit.

THE CHANGING FACE OF AMERICA

If we are to achieve a richer culture, rich in contrasting values, we must recognize the whole gamut of human potentialities.

MARGARET MEAD
anthropologist

Mr. and Mrs. Isaac Newton Phelps Stokes (1897), John Singer Sargent. Oil on canvas, 85¼″ × 39¾″, The Metropolitan Museum of Art, bequest of Edith Minturn Phelps Stokes (Mrs. I. N.), 1938. (38.104). Copyright © 1989 The Metropolitan Museum of Art.

TIME LINE

The Changing Face of America

1857

Elizabeth Blackwell establishes the New York Infirmary for Women and Children, the first medical clinic of its kind.

1870

John D. Rockefeller founds the Standard Oil Company.

1872

Susan B. Anthony is arrested and fined for leading a group of women to vote illegally.

1876

Alexander Graham Bell patents the first telephone.

1879

Thomas Edison invents the first practical incandescent light bulb; three years later, the first central electric power plant begins operating in New York City.

1882

Congress passes the Chinese Exclusion Act in response to violent protests against Chinese immigrants. The act prohibits the immigration of Chinese laborers but makes exceptions for others, including family members of immigrants who had become citizens.

Until the 1880s, most immigrants to the U.S. had come from northern, central, and western Europe. After this time, increasing numbers came from southern and eastern Europe and from Asia. These new immigrants were physically and culturally different from the former immigrants and assimilated less quickly and completely.

1883

The first metal-framed skyscraper, ten stories high, is built in Chicago.

1886

The Statue of Liberty is dedicated in New York Harbor; a group of trade unionists organizes the American Federation of Labor (AFL) with about 150,000 members.

1889

Jane Addams and Ellen Gates Starr found Hull House, a settlement house to service the many poor and immigrant families in Chicago.

1892

Ellis Island in New York Harbor becomes the chief U.S. immigration station.

Approximately 16 million people passed through Ellis Island from 1892 to 1924. During the peak years, 1905 to 1907, the facilities were processing 10,000 immigrants a day.

1903

Near Kitty Hawk, North Carolina, Orville and Wilbur Wright make the first flight in an engine-powered airplane.

1907

Japan limits immigration to the U.S. in response to hostility toward Japanese laborers.

1910

Angel Island in San Francisco Bay is set up as an immigration station to process Asian immigrants.

1913

The Ford Motor Company puts the first moving assembly line into place and is soon producing 1,000 Model T automobiles a day; the next year, the company offers a $5-per-day minimum wage, more than doubling its workers' wages.

1915

Margaret Sanger is arrested on obscenity charges for distributing information on birth control.

1920

Congress passes the 19th Amendment, giving women the right to vote.

1924

Ending centuries of relatively open admission, Congress passes the Johnson-Reed Act that limits the number of immigrants from outside the Western Hemisphere and sets quotas for nationalities that would be allowed in. Asians were not allowed to immigrate at all.

The call for restrictions on immigration had been rising for several decades. Some Americans felt that the flood of new immigrants threatened national unity. Others feared increased crime and poverty. Labor leaders such as the AFL's Samuel Gompers (himself an immigrant) complained of the swelling tide of "cheap labor, ignorant labor [that] takes our jobs and cuts our wages."

Period *Pieces*

Charlie Chaplin popularizes silent movies.

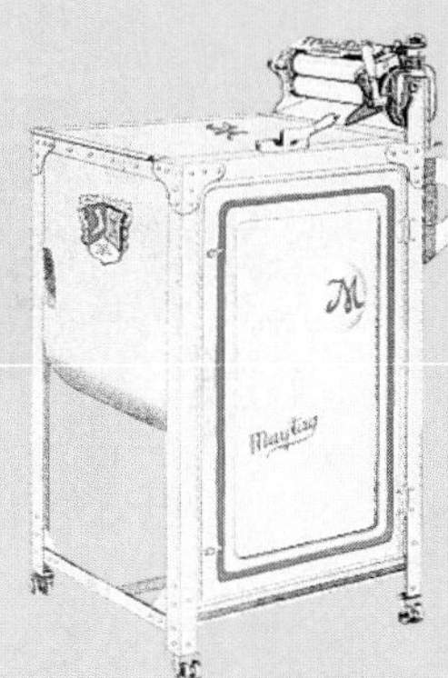

Washing machine from the 1920s

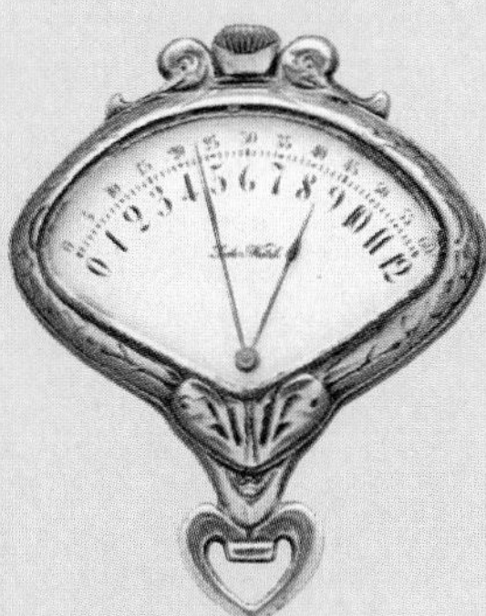

Sector pocket watch circa 1910

Women's Voices, Women's Lives

A New Literature

"The power of a woman is in her refinement, gentleness and elegance; it is she who makes etiquette, and it is she who preserves the order and decency of society. Without women, men soon resume the savage state, and the comfort and the graces of the home are exchanged for the misery of the mining camp." So said a popular book of etiquette in 1880, voicing a widely held notion about women's place in society. At the same time, however, the movement to give women the right to vote was reemerging after a period of inactivity in the years following the Civil War. Both before and after the war, however, the woman's suffrage movement was only the most public aspect of a growing force for women to have a voice in both politics and literature. Sojourner Truth's eloquent speech articulating the realities of women's lives, delivered at one women's rights convention (see Voices from the Times), resonated in the hearts of many 19th-century women.

One important factor in the growth of the women's movement was the spread of university education among women of the era, although popular newspapers of the time trumpeted the dangers: "Are We Destroying Woman's Beauty? The Startling Warning of a Great English Physician Against Higher Education of Women. How Intellectual Work Destroys Beauty" proclaimed a *New York Journal* headline in 1896.

A suffragist struggles with police in 1913 (above) and suffragists argue for the vote before a congressional committee in 1871 (below).

Emily Dickinson

The 1890s also saw the emergence of the poetry of Emily Dickinson—the first major American woman poet—although emergence may not be the right word to apply to a body of work that has become widely known only in the last 40 years. A near contemporary of Walt Whitman, and just as important in the development of a uniquely American literary voice, Dickinson was virtually unknown during her lifetime. Her anonymity was due in large part to the difficulties she would have experienced in trying to overcome prevailing attitudes about women's proper place. When her sister published a collection of her poetry in 1890, after Dickinson's death, most critical reviews were negative, objecting especially to what was considered Dickinson's odd poetic style, with its unusual imagery, untraditional meters, inexact rhymes, and grammatical errors. Nonetheless, a century later, Dickinson looms as one of our most important poets, not only of her time but of any time.

Around the same time, Charlotte Perkins Gilman—related on her father's side to a noted family of writers and social reformers that included Harriet Beecher Stowe, the author of *Uncle Tom's Cabin*—became one of the most noted advocates for women. Fleeing her own repressive marriage, she moved from the East Coast to California, where she wrote and spoke out on behalf of women's rights and against male domination.

Harriet Beecher Stowe

Kate Chopin's fiction articulates the frustrations of generations of women that were confined to a sort of extended childhood by the men in their lives. Her gentle stories depicting some of the most obvious of women's difficulties were extremely popular in the 1890s. Her 1899 novel *The Awakening*, however, stepped over the line in its portrayal of a woman's hidden passion, arousing a public protest so vigorous that Chopin ceased writing completely.

Voices *from the* TIMES

Ain't I a Woman?

Sojourner Truth

This speech was given by the ex-slave Sojourner Truth at a women's rights convention at Akron, Ohio, in 1851. Prior to her speech, male speakers had argued in favor of men's superior rights and privileges on the grounds of their superior intellect and the manhood of Christ. As the convention was heating up, the dignified Sojourner Truth—who was in her 60s at the time—rose slowly from her seat in a corner of the room. Amid shouts of "Don't let her speak!" and hissing, she moved to the front, laid her bonnet down, and began this unprepared speech. A profound hush settled over the crowd as she began to speak.

Well, children, where there is so much racket there must be something out of kilter. I think that 'twixt the Negroes of the South and the women at the North all talking about rights, the white men will be in a fix pretty soon. But what's all this here talking about?

That man over there says that women need to be helped into carriages, and lifted over ditches, and to have the best place everywhere. Nobody ever helps me into carriages, or over mud puddles, or gives me any best place! And ain't I a woman? Look at me! Look at my arm! I have ploughed, and planted, and gathered into barns, and no man could head me. And ain't I a woman? I could work as much and eat as much as a man—when I could get it—and bear the lash as well! And ain't I a woman? I have borne thirteen children, and seen most all sold off to slavery, and when I cried out with my mother's grief, none but Jesus heard me! And ain't I a woman?

Then they talk about this thing in the head; what's this they call it? ["Intellect," someone whispers.] That's it, honey. What's that got to do with women's rights or Negroes' rights? If my cup won't hold but a pint, and yours holds a quart, wouldn't you be mean not to let me have my little half-measure full?

Then that little man in black there, he says women can't have as much rights as men, 'cause Christ wasn't a woman! Where did your Christ come from? From God and a woman! Man had nothing to do with Him.

If the first woman God ever made was strong enough to turn the world upside down all alone, these women together ought to be able to turn it back, and get it right side up again! And now they is asking to do it, the men better let them.

Obliged to you for hearing me, and now old Sojourner hasn't got nothing more to say.

Sojourner Truth

Continuity & Change: A Diversity of Voices

In 1920 the 19th Amendment to the Constitution gave women the right to vote, but suffrage heralded no great revolution. Women did not unite at the polls to gain reforms for themselves; instead, many voted like their fathers or husbands or didn't vote at all. This political failure combined with the cultural changes rocking the 1920s—the rise of advertising, Hollywood glamour, and the flapper image of woman—to further inhibit women's intellectual and literary development. The playwright Lillian Hellman, one of the few American women writing successfully in the 1930s and 1940s, summed up her generation this way: "By the time I grew up, the fight for the emancipation of women, their rights under the law, in the office, in bed, was stale stuff. My generation didn't think much about the place or the problems of women."

Only after the eruption of the feminist movement in the late 1960s were large numbers of women again inspired to examine the quality of their lives and find voices of their own. With the renewed confidence of women came a desire to rediscover female writers of the more recent past. Hence Hisaye Yamamoto's "Seventeen Syllables" and Tillie Olsen's "I Stand Here Ironing"—both stories about women struggling with oppressive conditions—are more popular today than when they were written.

The legacy of 19th-century women writers lives on in the richness and diversity of contemporary women's writing. Women of all ages and ethnic groups are writing today, giving voice to a multitude of experiences and concerns.

LASERLINKS
• *HISTORICAL LITERARY CONNECTION*

PART 1

Women's Voices, Women's Lives

A New Literature

Continuity & Change: A Diversity of Voices

PREVIEWING

POETRY

Selected Poems

Emily Dickinson

PERSONAL CONNECTION

In these four poems, Emily Dickinson makes insightful observations about the concepts of nature, hope, success, and death. Copy this chart in your notebook and use it to record observations of your own about each of these concepts. How would you define each concept? What emotions do you associate with the concept? What persons, animals, objects, or situations does the concept bring to mind? As you read these poems, compare your observations with Dickinson's.

Nature	Hope
Success	Death

LITERARY CONNECTION

Emily Dickinson's observations are as unique and personal as her poetic style. Considered, like Walt Whitman, one of the founders of modern American poetry, Dickinson departed from the poetic traditions of the 19th century in her inventive treatment of rhyme, punctuation, capitalization, and sentence structure. Unlike Whitman's sprawling verse, however, Dickinson's poems are short, usually no longer than 20 lines. She wrote most of her poetry in dense **quatrains** (four-line stanzas) that echo the simple rhythms of the church hymns she knew and loved. However, she added a fresh twist with **slant rhymes,** or words that do not rhyme exactly, and used dashes to highlight important words and help break up the singsong rhythm of her poems. Her **figures of speech** (similes, metaphors, and personifications) are fresh and original and exhibit a playful sense of humor and a love of language.

READING CONNECTION

Enjoying Poetry The following suggestions can help you increase your understanding and enjoyment of Emily Dickinson's poetry:

- Read each poem once for overall impression, then again for meaning, and at least one more time to appreciate Dickinson's unique style and imagery.
- Read the poem aloud, listening for the rhythm.
- Pause when you encounter dashes, just as you do when you come to commas or periods in a poem.
- Ask yourself questions about the meanings of words and metaphors, and be aware of any memories or thoughts that the poem awakes in you.
- Decide whether you agree with Dickinson's ideas and observations.

Emily Dickinson

This is my letter to the World

This is my letter to the World
That never wrote to Me—
The simple News that Nature told—
With tender Majesty

Her Message is committed
To Hands I cannot see—
For love of Her—Sweet—countrymen—
Judge tenderly—of Me

GUIDE FOR READING

1 this: Dickinson's poetry, or this particular poem.

3 What might Nature's "simple News" be?

5 committed: given over; entrusted.

6 Whose might be the "Hands" that the speaker cannot see?

FROM PERSONAL RESPONSE *TO* CRITICAL ANALYSIS

REFLECT **1.** In your notebook, jot down your impressions of the speaker of this poem.

RETHINK **2.** Dickinson's poetry is her "letter to the World." What can you infer about her life from her observation that the world never wrote to her?

3. What connection do you see between the poet's letter to the world and Nature's "simple News"?

4. Most of Dickinson's poems were not published during her lifetime. Do you think she expected that other people would ever read them? What lines in this poem lead you to your conclusion?

Emily Dickinson

"Hope" is the thing with feathers

"Hope" is the thing with feathers—
That perches in the soul—
And sings the tune without the words—
And never stops—at all—

And sweetest—in the Gale—is heard—
And sore must be the storm—
That could abash the little Bird
That kept so many warm—

I've heard it in the chillest land—
And on the strangest Sea—
Yet, never, in Extremity,
It asked a crumb—of Me.

GUIDE FOR READING

1–4 What qualities of hope are suggested by this image?

6 sore: severe.

7 abash: frustrate; baffle.

11 Extremity: greatest need or peril.

FROM PERSONAL RESPONSE *TO* CRITICAL ANALYSIS

REFLECT **1.** In your notebook, sketch the images that came to mind as you read this poem.

RETHINK **2.** Why do you think Dickinson pictures hope as a bird?

Consider

- the qualities of a bird
- the qualities of hope that are similar to those of a bird

3. How do you interpret the last two lines of the poem?

Emily Dickinson

Success is counted sweetest

Success is counted sweetest
By those who ne'er succeed.
To comprehend a nectar
Requires sorest need.

Not one of all the purple Host
Who took the Flag today
Can tell the definition
So clear of Victory

As he defeated—dying—
On whose forbidden ear
The distant strains of triumph
Burst agonized and clear!

GUIDE FOR READING

1–2 Who prizes success most?

2 ne'er: never.

3 comprehend: fully appreciate; **nectar:** a sweet beverage.

5 Host: army.

6 took the Flag: captured the enemy's flag as a token of victory.

5–12 Does the speaker seem to identify more with the winning army or with the defeated army?

FROM PERSONAL RESPONSE *TO* CRITICAL ANALYSIS

REFLECT **1.** Jot down in your notebook what you were thinking as you finished reading this poem.

RETHINK **2.** How do you interpret lines 3 and 4? Explain how they relate to lines 1 and 2.

3. In this poem Dickinson uses the image of a battlefield to make her point. Why might the defeated soldier be better able to define and appreciate victory than the winning soldiers?

4. Do you agree with Dickinson's observations about success in this poem? Support your opinion, citing examples from your own observations and experiences.

Emily Dickinson

Because I could not stop for Death

Because I could not stop for Death—
He kindly stopped for me—
The Carriage held but just Ourselves—
And Immortality.

We slowly drove—He knew no haste
And I had put away
My labor and my leisure too,
For His Civility—

We passed the School, where Children strove
At Recess—in the Ring—
We passed the Fields of Gazing Grain—
We passed the Setting Sun—

Or rather—He passed Us—
The Dews drew quivering and chill—
For only Gossamer, my Gown—
My Tippet—only Tulle—

We paused before a House that seemed
A Swelling of the Ground—
The Roof was scarcely visible—
The Cornice—in the Ground—

Since then—'tis Centuries—and yet
Feels shorter than the Day
I first surmised the Horses' Heads
Were toward Eternity—

GUIDE FOR READING

1–8 How is Death portrayed in these lines?

8 Civility: politeness.

11 Gazing Grain: grain leaning toward the sun.

15 Gossamer: a thin, light cloth.

16 Tippet: shawl; **Tulle:** fine netting.

17–20 What do you think this house represents?

20 Cornice: the molding around the top of a building.

21–24 How does the speaker seem to feel about the length of time that has passed?

RESPONDING OPTIONS

FROM PERSONAL RESPONSE *TO* CRITICAL ANALYSIS

REFLECT 1. What picture of death do you get from "Because I could not stop for Death"? Draw or describe this image in your notebook.

RETHINK 2. Why do you think the speaker could not stop for death? Explain the poem's first two lines.

3. In the third stanza, the carriage passes a school, fields of grain, and the setting sun. What aspects of a person's life might these images symbolize?

4. What does the portrayal of death in the poem say to you about the speaker's attitude toward the subject?

RELATE 5. Give your reaction to the speaker's view of death and the afterlife. How similar is the speaker's view to other views you have encountered?

6. How do Dickinson's observations about nature, hope, success, and death in these four poems compare with the observations you recorded for the Personal Connection on page 598?

7. From these poems, what can you infer about Dickinson's personality, values, and view of the world?

ANOTHER PATHWAY

Cooperative Learning

Working with a small group of classmates, use any or all of the following activities to demonstrate your understanding of the four poems: (1) Make an illustration of a poem. (2) Give a group performance of a poem. (3) List questions that you are prepared to answer about a poem. (4) Paraphrase a poem.

THE WRITER'S STYLE

The Literary Connection on page 598 explains some features of Emily Dickinson's style. How do the poems you have just read illustrate her simple **rhythms, slant rhymes,** and unique **figures of speech?** Name other characteristics of Dickinson's style that you notice. In what ways other than length do her poems differ from Walt Whitman's?

QUICKWRITES

1. After looking back at your Personal Connection chart for ideas, write a short **poem**—using personification if you like—that expresses your views about nature, hope, success, or death. Read your poem to the class.
2. Write a **letter** to Emily Dickinson, telling her what you think of her poetry or her ideas. Use specific examples from her work to support your points.
3. Write a **quatrain** (four-line stanza) on any subject, imitating Dickinson's style. Copy your quatrain onto a page with the opening quatrains of other poems by Dickinson, and see if your classmates or your teacher can pick yours out.

***PORTFOLIO** Save your writing. You may want to use it later as a springboard to a piece for your portfolio.*

LITERARY CONCEPTS

Personification is a figure of speech in which an object, animal, or idea is given human characteristics. Like other types of figurative language, such as simile and metaphor, personification helps writers to communicate ideas and feelings and to create sensory images for the reader. Notice how, in this example from another Dickinson poem, the setting sun comes alive as a personification:

> She sweeps with many-colored Brooms—
> And leaves the shreds behind—
> Oh Housewife in the Evening West—
> Come back, and dust the Pond!

In which of the four poems you have read does Dickinson use personification? What is personified? What qualities of the thing are suggested by the personification? What feelings does the personification lead the reader to have about the thing?

ALTERNATIVE ACTIVITIES

1. Choose **music** that matches the tone and theme of one of Dickinson's poems. Play the music as you read the poem aloud to your class. Alternatively, choose or compose music that matches the rhythm of one of the poems, and sing the lines as lyrics.
2. Choreograph a **dance,** for two or more performers, based on the speaker's carriage ride in "Because I could not stop for Death."

CRITIC'S CORNER

In a letter, Emily Dickinson once defined *poetry* this way: "If I read a book and it makes my whole body so cold no fire can ever warm me, I know *that* is poetry. If I feel physically as if the top of my head were taken off, I know *that* is poetry." What do you think she meant by her definition? In your opinion, do her poems meet the standards expressed in the definition? Explain your ideas.

EMILY DICKINSON

1830–1886

Although Emily Dickinson wrote nearly 1,800 poems, her poetry was virtually unknown during her lifetime. Only 7 of her poems—including "Success is counted sweetest"—were published, anonymously, before her death. The first volume of her poetry was published four years after she died, but her talent was not widely recognized until a complete edition of her poetry was published in 1955.

Dickinson spent all her life in Amherst, Massachusetts, where she lived with her parents and her sister Lavinia, whom she called Vinnie. After one year at Mount Holyoke Female Seminary, she returned home and gradually began to withdraw from the world. Declining a friend's invitation for a visit, she wrote, "I look at my father and mother and Vinnie, and all my friends, and I say no—no, I can't leave them." By the time Dickinson reached middle age, she rarely ventured beyond her house and garden.

The year 1862 marked a turning point in her life. That year the Reverend Charles Wadsworth—an older, married man whom Dickinson admired and reportedly loved—took a position in California. In the same year, Dickinson wrote 366 poems, some revealing great emotional turmoil. She also initiated a lifelong correspondence with Thomas Wentworth Higginson, the literary editor of the *Atlantic Monthly,* by sending him four poems.

Although Dickinson was reclusive, she maintained a prolific correspondence with friends. Yet even those who were closest to her were unaware of the great number of poems that would be found after her death, tied into neat packets and locked in a box. These poems, according to the poet Allen Tate, reveal a life that was "one of the richest and deepest ever lived on this continent."

OTHER WORKS *The Complete Poems of Emily Dickinson, The Letters of Emily Dickinson*

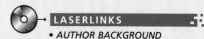

LASERLINKS
• *AUTHOR BACKGROUND*

PREVIEWING

FICTION

The Yellow Wallpaper

Charlotte Perkins Gilman

PERSONAL CONNECTION

What is your mental picture of someone suffering from a "nervous condition"? Would the person be more likely to be male or female? young or old? What symptoms might the person have? What would be the best treatment for the condition? Freewrite in your notebook about the images and thoughts brought to mind by the term *nervous condition.*

HISTORICAL/CULTURAL CONNECTION

This story was written in 1890, when many women—especially nonworking middle-class and upper-class women—suffered from a variety of physical and mental disorders, such as fatigue and depression. If they sought medical treatment and no organic cause could be determined, their ills were often diagnosed as vague, trivial "nervous conditions," curable through isolation and prolonged rest. Although today it is believed that some of these disorders may have been caused by the stress of living within the rigid social roles to which women were confined, doctors in the late 1800s typically felt that the root of many women's illnesses was their gender. They assumed that women, weak and emotionally unstable, were by their very nature predisposed to illness.

READING CONNECTION

Approaching First-Person Narrative The first-person narrator of "The Yellow Wallpaper" is a woman who has been diagnosed with a nervous condition. The story is told in the form of her journal entries. Much of what happens seems distorted or is unexplained; to understand the events, therefore, you must make inferences based on details that the narrator gives you and what you know about life. As you read, allow yourself to perceive things as the narrator does, but stand back from her at times so that you can examine her perceptions and actions with a critical eye.

Using Your Reading Log Use your reading log to record your responses to the questions inserted throughout this story. Also jot down other questions and thoughts that come to you as you read.

LASERLINKS

• *HISTORICAL CONNECTION*

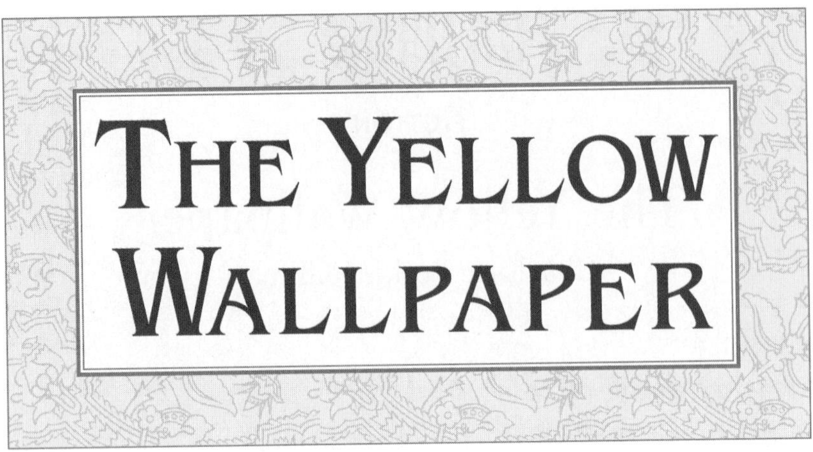

The Yellow Wallpaper

Charlotte Perkins Gilman

It is very seldom that mere ordinary people like John and myself secure ancestral halls for the summer.

A colonial mansion, a hereditary estate, I would say a haunted house, and reach the height of romantic felicity—but that would be asking too much of fate!

Still I will proudly declare that there is something queer about it.

Else, why should it be let so cheaply? And why have stood so long untenanted?

John laughs at me, of course, but one expects that in marriage.

John is practical in the extreme. He has no patience with faith, an intense horror of superstition, and he scoffs openly at any talk of things not to be felt and seen and put down in figures.

John is a physician, and *perhaps*—(I would not say it to a living soul, of course, but this is dead paper and a great relief to my *mind)*—*perhaps* that is one reason I do not get well faster.

You see he does not believe I am sick!

And what can one do?

If a physician of high standing, and one's own husband, assures friends and relatives that there is really nothing the matter with one but temporary nervous depression—a slight hysterical[1] tendency—what is one to do?

My brother is also a physician, and also of high standing, and he says the same thing.

So I take phosphates or phosphites—whichever it is, and tonics, and journeys, and air, and exercise, and am absolutely forbidden to "work" until I am well again.

Personally, I disagree with their ideas.

---

1. **hysterical:** Hysteria is the presence of a physical ailment with no underlying physical cause.

WORDS TO KNOW

felicity (fĭ-lĭs'ĭ-tē) *n.* happiness; bliss

A Woman Sewing in an Interior (about 1900), Vilhelm Hammershøi. Christie's, London, Bridgeman/Art Resource, New York.

Personally, I believe that congenial work, with excitement and change, would do me good.

But what is one to do?

I did write for a while in spite of them; but it *does* exhaust me a good deal—having to be so sly about it, or else meet with heavy opposition.

CLARIFY

Why is the narrator writing in secret?

I sometimes fancy that in my condition if I had less opposition and more society and stimulus—but John says the very worst thing I can do is to think about my condition, and I confess it always makes me feel bad.

So I will let it alone and talk about the house.

The most beautiful place! It is quite alone, standing well back from the road, quite three miles from the village. It makes me think of English places that you read about, for there are hedges and walls and gates that lock, and lots of separate little houses for the gardeners and people.

There is a *delicious* garden! I never saw such a garden—large and shady, full of box-bordered paths, and lined with long grape-covered arbors with seats under them.

There were greenhouses, too, but they are all broken now.

There was some legal trouble, I believe, something about the heirs and coheirs; anyhow, the place has been empty for years.

That spoils my ghostliness, I am afraid, but I don't care—there is something strange about the house—I can feel it.

I even said so to John one moonlight evening, but he said what I felt was a draft, and shut the window.

I get unreasonably angry with John sometimes. I'm sure I never used to be so sensitive. I think it is due to this nervous condition.

But John says if I feel so, I shall neglect proper self-control; so I take pains to control myself—before him, at least, and that makes me very tired.

I don't like our room a bit. I wanted one downstairs that opened on the piazza and had roses all over the window, and such pretty old-fashioned chintz hangings! but John would not hear of it.

He said there was only one window and not room for two beds, and no near room for him if he took another.

He is very careful and loving, and hardly lets me stir without special direction.

I have a schedule prescription for each hour in the day; he takes all care from me, and so I feel basely ungrateful not to value it more.

He said we came here solely on my account, that I was to have perfect rest and all the air I could get. "Your exercise depends on your strength, my dear," said he, "and your food somewhat on your appetite; but air you can absorb all the time." So we took the nursery at the top of the house.

EVALUATE

Describe the relationship between the narrator and her husband.

It is a big, airy room, the whole floor nearly, with windows that look all ways, and air and sunshine galore. It was nursery first and then playroom and gymnasium, I should judge; for the windows are barred for little children, and there are rings and things in the walls.

The paint and paper look as if a boys' school had used it. It is stripped off—the paper—in great patches all around the head of my bed, about as far as I can reach, and in a great place on the other side of the room low down. I never saw a worse paper in my life.

One of those sprawling flamboyant patterns committing every artistic sin.

It is dull enough to confuse the eye in following, pronounced enough to constantly irritate and provoke study, and when you follow the lame uncertain curves for a little distance they suddenly commit suicide—plunge off at outrageous angles, destroy themselves in unheard of contradictions.

WORDS TO KNOW

basely (bās'lē) *adv.* dishonorably; meanly

The color is repellent, almost revolting; a smouldering unclean yellow, strangely faded by the slow-turning sunlight.

It is a dull yet lurid orange in some places, a sickly sulphur tint in others.

No wonder the children hated it! I should hate it myself if I had to live in this room long.

There comes John, and I must put this away,—he hates to have me write a word.

We have been here two weeks, and I haven't felt like writing before, since that first day.

I am sitting by the window now, up in this atrocious nursery, and there is nothing to hinder my writing as much as I please, save lack of strength.

John is away all day, and even some nights when his cases are serious.

I am glad my case is not serious!

But these nervous troubles are dreadfully depressing.

John does not know how much I really suffer. He knows there is no *reason* to suffer, and that satisfies him.

Of course it is only nervousness. It does weigh on me so not to do my duty in any way!

I meant to be such a help to John, such a real rest and comfort, and here I am a comparative burden already!

Nobody would believe what an effort it is to do what little I am able,—to dress and entertain, and order things.

It is fortunate Mary is so good with the baby. Such a dear baby!

And yet I *cannot* be with him, it makes me so nervous.

I suppose John never was nervous in his life. He laughs at me so about this wallpaper!

At first he meant to repaper the room, but afterwards he said that I was letting it get the better of me, and that nothing was worse for a nervous patient than to give way to such fancies.

He said that after the wallpaper was changed it would be the heavy bedstead, and then the barred windows, and then that gate at the head of the stairs, and so on.

CONNECT

What do the details about the room suggest about its function?

"You know the place is doing you good," he said, "and really, dear, I don't care to renovate the house just for a three months' rental."

"Then do let us go downstairs," I said, "there are such pretty rooms there."

Then he took me in his arms and called me a blessed little goose, and said he would go down to the cellar, if I wished, and have it white-washed into the bargain.

But he is right enough about the beds and windows and things.

It is an airy and comfortable room as any one need wish, and, of course, I would not be so silly as to make him uncomfortable just for a whim.

I'm really getting quite fond of the big room, all but that horrid paper.

Out of one window I can see the garden, those mysterious deepshaded arbors, the riotous old-fashioned flowers, and bushes and gnarly trees.

Out of another I get a lovely view of the bay and a little private wharf belonging to the estate. There is a beautiful shaded lane that runs down there from the house. I always fancy I see people walking in these numerous paths and arbors, but John has cautioned me not to give way to fancy in the least. He says that with my imaginative power and habit of story-making, a nervous weakness like mine is sure to lead to all manner of excited fancies, and that I ought to use my will and good sense to check the tendency. So I try.

I think sometimes that if I were only well enough to write a little it would relieve the press of ideas and rest me.

But I find I get pretty tired when I try.

It is so discouraging not to have any advice and companionship about my work. When I get really well, John says we will ask Cousin Henry and

WORDS TO KNOW

atrocious (ə-trō'shəs) *adj.* shockingly bad or lacking in taste; awful

Julia down for a long visit; but he says he would as soon put fireworks in my pillowcase as to let me have those stimulating people about now.

I wish I could get well faster.

But I must not think about that. This paper looks to me as if it knew what a vicious influence it had!

There is a recurrent spot where the pattern lolls like a broken neck and two bulbous eyes stare at you upside down.

I get positively angry with the impertinence of it and the everlastingness. Up and down and sideways they crawl, and those absurd, unblinking eyes are everywhere. There is one place where two breadths didn't match, and the eyes go all up and down the line, one a little higher than the other.

I never saw so much expression in an inanimate thing before, and we all know how much expression they have! I used to lie awake as a child and get more entertainment and terror out of blank walls and plain furniture than most children could find in a toystore.

I remember what a kindly wink the knobs of our big, old bureau used to have, and there was one chair that always seemed like a strong friend.

I used to feel that if any of the other things looked too fierce I could always hop into that chair and be safe.

The furniture in this room is no worse than inharmonious, however, for we had to bring it all from downstairs. I suppose when this was used as a playroom they had to take the nursery things out, and no wonder! I never saw such ravages as the children have made here.

The wallpaper, as I said before, is torn off in spots, and it sticketh closer than a brother—they must have had perseverance as well as hatred.

Then the floor is scratched and gouged and splintered, the plaster itself is dug out here and there, and this great heavy bed which is all we found in the room, looks as if it had been through the wars.

But I don't mind it a bit—only the paper.

There comes John's sister. Such a dear girl as she is, and so careful of me! I must not let her find me writing.

She is a perfect and enthusiastic housekeeper, and hopes for no better profession. I verily believe she thinks it is the writing which made me sick!

But I can write when she is out, and see her a long way off from these windows.

There is one that commands the road, a lovely shaded winding road, and one that just looks off over the country. A lovely country, too, full of great elms and velvet meadows.

This wallpaper has a kind of sub-pattern in a different shade, a particularly irritating one, for you can only see it in certain lights, and not clearly then.

But in the places where it isn't faded and where the sun is just so—I can see a strange, provoking, formless sort of figure, that seems to skulk about behind that silly and conspicuous front design.

CLARIFY

Describe the effect the wallpaper is having on the narrator.

There's sister on the stairs!

Well, the Fourth of July is over! The people are all gone and I am tired out. John thought it might do me good to see a little company, so we just had mother and Nellie and the children down for a week.

Of course I didn't do a thing. Jennie sees to everything now.

But it tired me all the same.

John says if I don't pick up faster he shall send me to Weir Mitchell[2] in the fall.

2. **Weir Mitchell:** Dr. Silas Weir Mitchell, famous for his "rest cure" for nervous diseases, which is no longer considered effective.

WORDS TO KNOW

impertinence (ĭm-pûr'tn-əns) *n.* improper boldness; rudeness
inanimate (ĭn-ăn'ə-mĭt) *adj.* not alive; lifeless
perseverance (pûr'sə-vîr'əns) n. persistence in the face of difficulty; determination

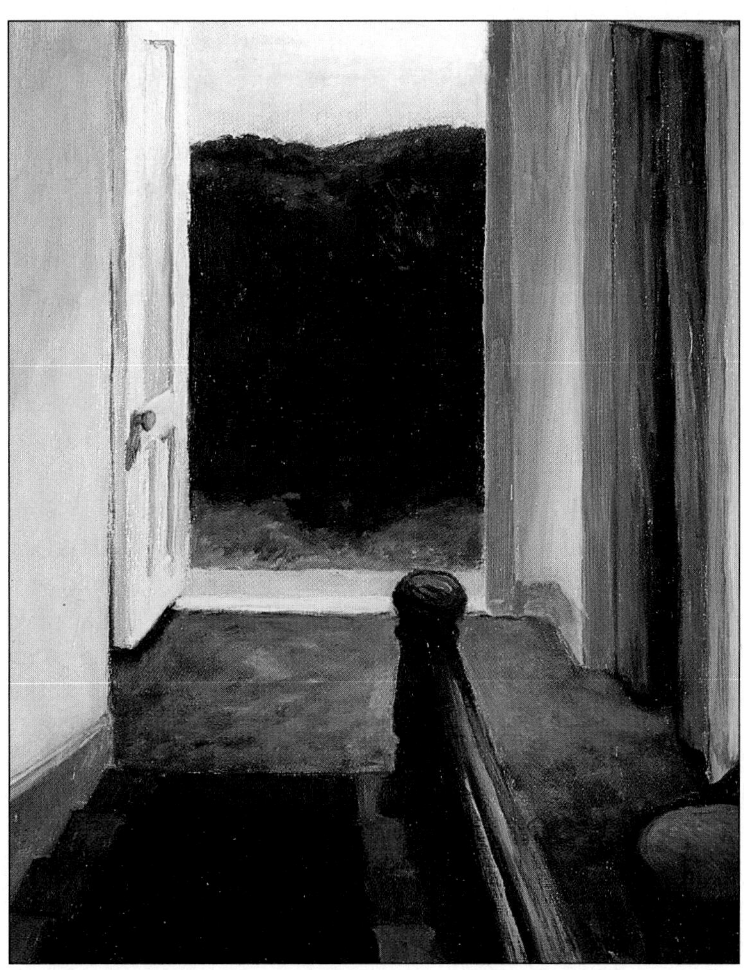

Stairway (1949), Edward Hopper. Oil on wood, 16″ × 11 ⅞″, Collection of Whitney Museum of American Art, New York, Josephine N. Hopper Bequest (70.1265). Copyright © 1995 Whitney Museum of American Art. Photo by Geoffrey Clements.

But I don't want to go there at all. I had a friend who was in his hands once, and she says he is just like John and my brother, only more so!

Besides, it is such an undertaking to go so far.

I don't feel as if it was worth while to turn my hand over for anything, and I'm getting dreadfully fretful and querulous.

I cry at nothing, and cry most of the time.

Of course I don't when John is here, or anybody else, but when I am alone.

And I am alone a good deal just now. John is kept in town very often by serious cases, and Jennie is good and lets me alone when I want her to.

So I walk a little in the garden or down that lovely lane, sit on the porch under the roses, and lie down up here a good deal.

I'm getting really fond of the room in spite of the wallpaper. Perhaps *because* of the wallpaper.

It dwells in my mind so!

I lie here on this great immovable bed—it is nailed down, I believe—and follow that pattern about by the hour. It is as good as gymnastics, I assure you. I start, we'll say, at the bottom, down in the corner over there where it has not been touched, and I determine for the thousandth time that I *will* follow that pointless pattern to some sort of a conclusion.

I know a little of the principle of design, and I know this thing was not arranged on any laws of radiation, or alternation, or repetition, or symmetry, or anything else that I ever heard of.

It is repeated, of course, by the breadths, but not otherwise.

Looked at in one way each breadth stands alone, the bloated curves and flourishes—a kind of "debased Romanesque"[3] with *delirium tremens*[4]—go waddling up and down in isolated columns of fatuity.[5]

But, on the other hand, they connect diagonally, and the sprawling outlines run off in great slanting waves of optic horror, like a lot of wallowing seaweeds in full chase.

The whole thing goes horizontally, too, at least it seems so, and I exhaust myself in trying to distinguish the order of its going in that direction.

They have used a horizontal breadth for a frieze, and that adds wonderfully to the confusion.

There is one end of the room where it is almost intact, and there, when the crosslights fade and the low sun shines directly upon it, I can almost fancy radiation after all,—the interminable grotesques seem to form around a common center and rush off in headlong plunges of equal distraction.

It makes me tired to follow it. I will take a nap I guess.

I don't know why I should write this.

I don't want to.

I don't feel able.

And I know John would think it absurd. But I *must* say what I feel and think in some way—it is such a relief!

But the effort is getting to be greater than the relief.

Half the time now I am awfully lazy, and lie down ever so much.

John says I mustn't lose my strength, and has me take cod liver oil and lots of tonics and things, to say nothing of ale and wine and rare meat.

Dear John! He loves me very dearly, and hates to have me sick. I tried to have a real earnest reasonable talk with him the other day, and tell him how I wish he would let me go and make a visit to Cousin Henry and Julia.

But he said I wasn't able to go, nor able to stand it after I got there; and I did not make out a very good case for myself, for I was crying before I had finished.

It is getting to be a great effort for me to think straight. Just this nervous weakness I suppose.

And dear John gathered me up in his arms, and

3. **Romanesque:** an artistic style characterized by simple ornamentation.

4. ***delirium tremens:*** violent trembling and hallucinations caused by excessive drinking.

5. **fatuity** (fə-to͞o′ĭ-tē): foolishness; smug stupidity.

WORDS TO KNOW **querulous** (kwĕr′ə-ləs) *adj.* given to complaining just carried me upstairs and laid me on the bed, and sat by me and read to me till it tired my head.

He said I was his darling and his comfort and all he had, and that I must take care of myself for his sake, and keep well.

He says no one but myself can help me out of it, that I must use my will and self-control and not let any silly fancies run away with me.

There's one comfort, the baby is well and happy, and does not have to occupy this nursery with the horrid wallpaper.

If we had not used it, that blessed child would have! What a fortunate escape! Why, I wouldn't have a child of mine, an impressionable little thing, live in such a room for worlds.

I never thought of it before, but it is lucky that John kept me here after all, I can stand it so much easier than a baby, you see.

Of course I never mention it to them any more—I am too wise,—but I keep watch of it all the same.

There are things in that paper that nobody knows but me, or ever will.

Behind that outside pattern the dim shapes get clearer every day.

It is always the same shape, only very numerous.

And it is like a woman stooping down and creeping about behind that pattern. I don't like it a bit. I wonder—I begin to think—I wish John would take me away from here!

EVALUATE

How do you explain the figure beginning to appear in the wallpaper?

It is so hard to talk with John about my case, because he is so wise, and because he loves me so.

But I tried it last night.

It was moonlight. The moon shines in all around just as the sun does.

I hate to see it sometimes, it creeps so slowly, and always comes in by one window or another.

John was asleep and I hated to waken him, so I kept still and watched the moonlight on that undulating wallpaper till I felt creepy.

The faint figure behind seemed to shake the pattern, just as if she wanted to get out.

I got up softly and went to feel and see if the paper *did* move, and when I came back John was awake.

"What is it, little girl?" he said. "Don't go walking about like that—you'll get cold."

I thought it was a good time to talk, so I told him that I really was not gaining here, and that I wished he would take me away.

"Why darling!" said he, "our lease will be up in three weeks, and I can't see how to leave before.

"The repairs are not done at home, and I cannot possibly leave town just now. Of course if you were in any danger, I could and would, but you really are better, dear, whether you can see it or not. I am a doctor, dear, and I know. You are gaining flesh and color, your appetite is better, I feel really much easier about you."

"I don't weigh a bit more," said I, "nor as much; and my appetite may be better in the evening when you are here, but it is worse in the morning when you are away!"

"Bless her little heart!" said he with a big hug, "she shall be as sick as she pleases! But now let's improve the shining hours[6] by going to sleep, and talk about it in the morning!"

"And you won't go away?" I asked gloomily.

"Why, how can I, dear? It is only three weeks more and then we will take a nice little trip of a few days while Jennie is getting the house ready. Really dear you are better!"

"Better in body perhaps—" I began, and stopped short, for he sat up straight and looked at me with such a stern, reproachful look that I could not say another word.

6. **improve the shining hours:** make good use of time (an allusion to the poem "Against Idleness and Mischief" by Isaac Watts: "How doth the little busy bee / Improve each shining hour, / And gather honey all the day / From every opening flower!").

WORDS TO KNOW

undulating (ŭn'jə-lā'tĭng) *adj.* moving with a wavelike motion **undulate** *v.*

"My darling," said he, "I beg of you, for my sake and for our child's sake, as well as for your own, that you will never for one instant let that idea enter your mind! There is nothing so dangerous, so fascinating, to a temperament like yours. It is a false and foolish fancy. Can you not trust me as a physician when I tell you so?"

QUESTION

What is the "idea" that John says the narrator should not "let . . . enter your mind"?

So of course I said no more on that score, and we went to sleep before long. He thought I was asleep first, but I wasn't, and lay there for hours trying to decide whether that front pattern and the back pattern really did move together or separately.

On a pattern like this, by daylight, there is a lack of sequence, a defiance of law, that is a constant irritant to a normal mind.

The color is hideous enough, and unreliable enough, and infuriating enough, but the pattern is torturing.

You think you have mastered it, but just as you get well underway in following, it turns a back-somersault and there you are. It slaps you in the face, knocks you down, and tramples upon you. It is like a bad dream.

The outside pattern is a florid arabesque,[7] reminding one of a fungus. If you can imagine a toadstool in joints, an interminable string of toadstools, budding and sprouting in endless convolutions—why, that is something like it.

That is, sometimes!

There is one marked peculiarity about this paper, a thing nobody seems to notice but myself, and that is that it changes as the light changes.

When the sun shoots in through the east window—I always watch for that first long, straight ray—it changes so quickly that I never can quite believe it.

That is why I watch it always.

By moonlight—the moon shines in all night when there is a moon—I wouldn't know it was the same paper.

At night in any kind of light, in twilight, candle light, lamplight, and worst of all by moonlight, it becomes bars! The outside pattern I mean, and the woman behind it is as plain as can be.

I didn't realize for a long time what the thing was that showed behind, that dim sub-pattern, but now I am quite sure it is a woman.

By daylight she is subdued, quiet. I fancy it is the pattern that keeps her so still. It is so puzzling. It keeps me quiet by the hour.

I lie down ever so much now. John says it is good for me, and to sleep all I can.

Indeed he started the habit by making me lie down for an hour after each meal.

It is a very bad habit I am convinced, for you see I don't sleep.

And that cultivates deceit, for I don't tell them I'm awake—O no!

The fact is I am getting a little afraid of John.

He seems very queer sometimes, and even Jennie has an inexplicable look.

It strikes me occasionally, just as a scientific hypothesis,—that perhaps it is the paper!

I have watched John when he did not know I was looking, and come into the room suddenly on the most innocent excuses, and I've caught him several times *looking at the paper!* And Jennie too. I caught Jennie with her hand on it once.

She didn't know I was in the room, and when I asked her in a quiet, a very quiet voice, with the most restrained manner possible, what she was doing with the paper—she turned around as if she had been caught stealing, and looked quite angry—asked me why I should frighten her so!

Then she said that the paper stained everything it touched, that she had found yellow smooches[8] on all my clothes and John's, and she wished we would be more careful!

Did not that sound innocent? But I know she was studying that pattern, and I am determined that nobody shall find it out but myself!

---

7. **florid arabesque:** an elaborate interwoven pattern.

8. **smooches:** dirty marks or spots; smudges.

Life is very much more exciting now than it used to be. You see I have something more to expect, to look forward to, to watch. I really do eat better, and am more quiet than I was.

John is so pleased to see me improve! He laughed a little the other day, and said I seemed to be flourishing in spite of my wallpaper.

I turned it off with a laugh. I had no intention of telling him it was *because* of the wallpaper—he would make fun of me. He might even want to take me away.

PREDICT

The narrator's attitude seems to have changed. Do you think she will get better?

I don't want to leave now until I have found it out. There is a week more, and I think that will be enough.

I'm feeling ever so much better! I don't sleep much at night, for it is so interesting to watch developments; but I sleep a good deal in the daytime.

In the daytime it is tiresome and perplexing.

There are always new shoots on the fungus, and new shades of yellow all over it. I cannot keep count of them, though I have tried conscientiously.

It is the strangest yellow, that wallpaper! It makes me think of all the yellow things I ever saw—not beautiful ones like buttercups, but old foul, bad yellow things.

But there is something else about that paper—the smell! I noticed it the moment we came into the room, but with so much air and sun it was not bad. Now we have had a week of fog and rain, and whether the windows are open or not, the smell is here.

It creeps all over the house.

I find it hovering in the dining room, skulking in the parlor, hiding in the hall, lying in wait for me on the stairs.

It gets into my hair.

Even when I go to ride, if I turn my head suddenly and surprise it—there is that smell!

Such a peculiar odor, too! I have spent hours in trying to analyze it, to find what it smelled like.

It is not bad—at first, and very gentle, but quite the subtlest, most enduring odor I ever met.

In this damp weather it is awful, I wake up in the night and find it hanging over me.

It used to disturb me at first. I thought seriously of burning the house—to reach the smell.

But now I am used to it. The only thing I can think of that it is like is the *color* of the paper! A yellow smell.

There is a very funny mark on this wall, low down, near the mopboard. A streak that runs round the room. It goes behind every piece of furniture, except the bed, a long, straight, even *smooch,* as if it had been rubbed over and over.

I wonder how it was done and who did it, and what they did it for. Round and round and round—round and round and round—it makes me dizzy!

I really have discovered something at last.

Through watching so much at night, when it changes so, I have finally found out.

The front pattern *does* move—and no wonder! The woman behind shakes it!

Sometimes I think there are a great many women behind, and sometimes only one, and she crawls around fast, and her crawling shakes it all over.

Then in the very bright spots she keeps still, and in the very shady spots she just takes hold of the bars and shakes them hard.

And she is all the time trying to climb through. But nobody could climb through that pattern—it strangles so; I think that is why it has so many heads.

They get through, and then the pattern strangles them off and turns them upside down, and makes their eyes white!

If those heads were covered or taken off it would not be half so bad.

I think that woman gets out in the daytime!

And I'll tell you why—privately—I've seen her!

I can see her out of every one of my windows!

It is the same woman, I know, for she is always creeping, and most women do not creep by daylight.

I see her on that long road under the trees, creeping along, and when a carriage comes she hides under the blackberry vines.

I don't blame her a bit. It must be very humiliating to be caught creeping by daylight!

I always lock the door when I creep by daylight. I can't do it at night, for I know John would suspect something at once.

And John is so queer now, that I don't want to irritate him. I wish he would take another room! Besides, I don't want anybody to get that woman out at night but myself.

I often wonder if I could see her out of all the windows at once.

But, turn as fast as I can, I can only see out of one at one time.

EVALUATE

What is the narrator's condition at this point?

And though I always see her, she may be able to creep faster than I can turn!

I have watched her sometimes away off in the open country, creeping as fast as a cloud shadow in a high wind.

If only that top pattern could be gotten off from the under one! I mean to try it, little by little.

I have found out another funny thing, but I shan't tell it this time! It does not do to trust people too much.

There are only two more days to get this paper off, and I believe John is beginning to notice. I don't like the look in his eyes.

And I heard him ask Jennie a lot of professional questions about me. She had a very good report to give.

She said I slept a good deal in the daytime.

John knows I don't sleep very well at night, for all I'm so quiet!

He asked me all sorts of questions, too, and pretended to be very loving and kind.

As if I couldn't see through him!

Still, I don't wonder he acts so, sleeping under this paper for three months.

It only interests me, but I feel sure John and Jennie are secretly affected by it.

Hurrah! This is the last day, but it is enough. John to stay in town over night, and won't be out until this evening.

Jennie wanted to sleep with me—the sly thing! but I told her I should undoubtedly rest better for a night all alone.

That was clever, for really I wasn't alone a bit! As soon as it was moonlight and that poor thing began to crawl and shake the pattern, I got up and ran to help her.

I pulled and she shook, I shook and she pulled, and before morning we had peeled off yards of that paper.

A strip about as high as my head and half around the room.

And then when the sun came and that awful pattern began to laugh at me, I declared I would finish it today!

We go away tomorrow, and they are moving all my furniture down again to leave things as they were before.

Jennie looked at the wall in amazement, but I told her merrily that I did it out of pure spite at the vicious thing.

She laughed and said she wouldn't mind doing it herself, but I must not get tired.

How she betrayed herself that time!

But I am here, and no person touches this paper but me,—not *alive!*

She tried to get me out of the room—it was too patent! But I said it was so quiet and empty and clean now that I believed I would lie down again and sleep all I could; and not to wake me even for dinner—I would call when I woke.

So now she is gone, and the servants are gone, and the things are gone, and there is nothing left but that great bedstead nailed down, with the canvas mattress we found on it.

We shall sleep downstairs tonight, and take the boat home tomorrow.

WORDS TO KNOW

patent (păt'nt) *adj.* obvious; apparent

I quite enjoy the room, now it is bare again.

How those children did tear about here!

This bedstead is fairly gnawed!

But I must get to work.

I have locked the door and thrown the key down into the front path.

I don't want to go out, and I don't want to have anybody come in, till John comes.

I want to astonish him.

I've got a rope up here that even Jennie did not find. If that woman does get out, and tries to get away, I can tie her!

But I forgot I could not reach far without anything to stand on!

This bed will *not* move!

I tried to lift and push it until I was lame, and then I got so angry I bit off a little piece at one corner—but it hurt my teeth.

Then I peeled off all the paper I could reach standing on the floor. It sticks horribly and the pattern just enjoys it! All those strangled heads and bulbous eyes and waddling fungus growths just shriek with derision!

I am getting angry enough to do something desperate. To jump out of the window would be admirable exercise, but the bars are too strong even to try.

Besides I wouldn't do it. Of course not. I know well enough that a step like that is improper and might be misconstrued.

CLARIFY

What does the narrator now believe?

I don't like to *look* out of the windows even—there are so many of those creeping women, and they creep so fast.

I wonder if they all come out of that wallpaper as I did?

But I am securely fastened now by my well-hidden rope—you don't get *me* out in the road there!

I suppose I shall have to get back behind the pattern when it comes night, and that is hard!

It is so pleasant to be out in this great room and creep around as I please!

I don't want to go outside. I won't, even if Jennie asks me to.

For outside you have to creep on the ground, and everything is green instead of yellow.

But here I can creep smoothly on the floor, and my shoulder just fits in that long smooch around the wall, so I cannot lose my way.

Why there's John at the door!

It is no use, young man, you can't open it!

How he does call and pound!

Now he's crying for an axe.

It would be a shame to break down that beautiful door!

"John dear!" said I in the gentlest voice, "the key is down by the front steps, under a plantain leaf!"

That silenced him for a few moments.

Then he said—very quietly indeed, "Open the door, my darling!"

"I can't," said I. "The key is down by the front door under a plantain leaf!"

And then I said it again, several times, very gently and slowly, and said it so often that he had to go and see, and he got it of course, and came in. He stopped short by the door.

"What is the matter?" he cried. "For God's sake, what are you doing!"

I kept on creeping just the same, but I looked at him over my shoulder.

"I've got out at last," said I, "in spite of you and Jane.[9] And I've pulled off most of the paper, so you can't put me back!"

Now why should that man have fainted? But he did, and right across my path by the wall, so that I had to creep over him every time! ❖

9. **in spite of you and Jane:** This reference to a previously unmentioned Jane is a point of debate. It could be an error made by the original printer for the name of the sister-housekeeper Jennie or Cousin Julia. It is also possible, however, that Jane is the narrator, here freeing herself from both her husband and her commonplace, wifely "Jane" self.

WORDS TO KNOW

derision (dĭ-rĭzh'ən) *n.* harsh ridicule or mockery; scorn

INSIGHT

from Complaints and Disorders: The Sexual Politics of Sickness

Barbara Ehrenreich and Deirdre English

In 1900 there were 173 doctors (engaged in primary patient care) per 100,000 population, compared to 50 per 100,000 today. So, it was in the interests of doctors to cultivate the illnesses of their patients with frequent home visits and drawn-out "treatments." A few dozen well-heeled lady customers were all that a doctor needed for a successful urban practice. Women—at least, women whose husbands could pay the bills—became a natural "client caste"[1] to the developing medical profession.

In many ways, the upper-middle-class woman was the ideal patient: her illnesses—and her husband's bank account—seemed almost inexhaustible. Furthermore, she was usually submissive and obedient to the "doctor's orders." The famous Philadelphia doctor S. Weir Mitchell expressed his profession's deep appreciation of the female invalid in 1888:

> With all her weakness, her unstable emotionality, her tendency to morally warp when long nervously ill, she is then far easier to deal with, far more amenable to reason, far more sure to be comfortable as a patient, than the man who is relatively in a like position. The reasons for this are too obvious to delay me here, and physicians accustomed to deal with both sexes as sick people will be apt to justify my position.

In Mitchell's mind women were not only easier to relate to, but sickness was the very key to femininity: "The man who does not know sick women does not know women."

1. **caste** (kăst): a group or class of people.

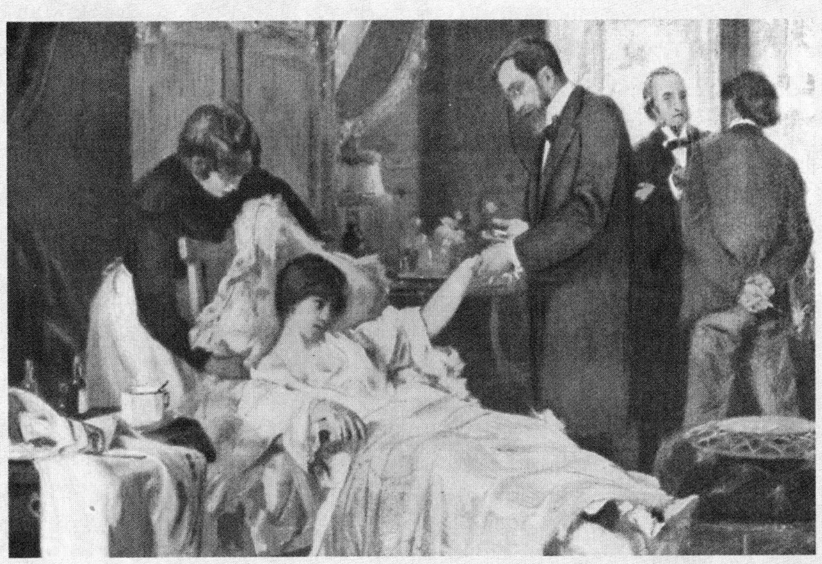

RESPONDING OPTIONS

FROM PERSONAL RESPONSE *TO* CRITICAL ANALYSIS

REFLECT **1.** Go back through your reading log and share any unanswered questions you have about this story.

RETHINK **2.** How do you explain the narrator's behavior at the end of the story?

3. What is your impression of the narrator at the beginning of the story?

Consider
- her first impressions of the house
- her feelings about her husband
- her reactions to the medical treatment that her husband prescribes
- the way she writes

4. Do you agree with the husband's diagnosis and treatment of his wife's condition? Why or why not? Consider what you wrote about nervous conditions for the Personal Connection on page 605.

5. Why do you think the narrator becomes so obsessed with the wallpaper?

6. Over the years, "The Yellow Wallpaper" has been interpreted in different ways: as a Gothic horror tale like those of Edgar Allan Poe, as a semiautobiographical account of a mental breakdown (see the writer's biography on page 622), and as a symbolic presentation of the effects of social and economic oppression on women. What aspects of the story do you think prompted each of these interpretations? State which interpretation you favor, and explain your reasons.

RELATE **7.** From reading the Insight on page 619, do you think Dr. S. Weir Mitchell would have found the narrator of this story to be an ideal patient? Explain.

ANOTHER PATHWAY

With a partner, improvise a dramatic scene in which the narrator and her husband John discuss her illness and treatment. In your scene, have the narrator attempt to explain how she feels and what she needs in order to recover, and have her husband explain to her why *his* treatment is the preferred therapy. When you share your scene with the class, don't forget to stay in character.

QUICKWRITES

1. Write a few sentences of **advertising copy** that you think would intrigue people enough to make them want to read this story.
2. In 1913 Gilman published a brief statement titled "Why I Wrote 'The Yellow Wallpaper.'" One of the reasons she gave for writing the story was "to save people from being driven crazy." Draft a **personal response,** explaining how you think this story might help someone.

PORTFOLIO *Save your writing. You may want to use it later as a springboard to a piece for your portfolio.*

LITERARY LINKS

How do you think Aunt Georgiana in "A Wagner Matinee" (page 541) or the homesteader Elinore Pruitt Stewart (page 551) would view the narrator of this story? What might they have to say to her about marriage, work, motherhood, and sacrifice?

LITERARY CONCEPTS

As this story progresses, the narrator begins to see images in the wallpaper: bars, bulbous eyes, a creeping woman, and more. If the wallpaper is a reflection of the narrator's psychological state, what does this **imagery** suggest to you about her feelings and preoccupations?

Cooperative Learning Working with a small group of classmates, go back through the story and list the images used in describing the wallpaper. Try to interpret each of the images, associating it with some aspect of the narrator's life. (There are no definite answers.) In response to the whole pattern of imagery, what general statement can your group make about the narrator's problem?

CONCEPT REVIEW: First-Person Narrator Why do you think Gilman used a first-person narrator to tell this story? What are the advantages and disadvantages of this point of view, especially in light of the narrator's condition?

THE WRITER'S STYLE

As the story progresses, the narrator's paragraphs become increasingly short, sometimes consisting of just a single sentence or sentence fragment. What reason might Gilman have had for using this curt, choppy style? What effect does the style have on you as a reader?

ACROSS THE CURRICULUM

Psychology A modern clinician might say that after the birth of her child, the narrator of this story experiences a postpartum depression that later develops into postpartum psychosis. Find out more about both of these illnesses. What causes them? What are their symptoms, and which of the symptoms does the narrator exhibit? How are the conditions treated today? What percentage of new mothers experience them? Answer these questions in an oral presentation to the class, and explain whether you think the narrator's condition is in fact produced by these illnesses.

ALTERNATIVE ACTIVITIES

1. Re-create the infamous **yellow wallpaper.** Go back through the story to pinpoint some of its specific characteristics, but also base your work on your psychological impression of what the wallpaper must have looked like to the narrator. Use markers, paints, or crayons—or any combination—on oversized paper or poster board.
2. ***Cooperative Learning*** Work with a small group of classmates to create a three-dimensional **set design** of the nursery as it would have looked at the end of the story. Construct and place the bed, re-create the "smooch" and the sections of torn-away wallpaper, and include figures of the narrator and her husband.

CRITIC'S CORNER

1. Michael Scott, a member of our student advisory board, was critical of this story, commenting, "It constantly referred to male doctors as incompetent fools. There was way too much male bashing." Would you characterize "The Yellow Wallpaper" as a male-bashing story? Support your opinion.
2. When Gilman first tried to get "The Yellow Wallpaper" published, she sent the story to the famous author William Dean Howells, who passed it along to H. E. Scudder, editor of the *Atlantic Monthly*. Scudder wrote the response at right. Do you agree that this story makes readers miserable? Would you recommend it to your friends? Explain why or why not.

Dear Madam,
Mr. Howells has handed me this story. I could not forgive myself if I made others as miserable as I have made myself!
Sincerely yours,
H. E. Scudder

WORDS TO KNOW

EXERCISE A Answer the following questions.

1. Would a child show **impertinence** by being sleepy, by being sassy, or by being shy?
2. Which would most likely be described as **atrocious**—something gross, something elegant, or something amusing?
3. Would a **querulous** person be likely to respond to an unpleasant situation by whining, by suffering in silence, or by making the best of it?
4. Is a **patent** lie one that is unnecessary, one that is highly creative, or one that is evident?
5. Which facial expression communicates **derision**—a grin, a sneer, or a yawn?
6. Does a person who has **perseverance** possess the quality of stick-to-itiveness, of quick-wittedness, or of open-mindedness?
7. Would you see the water in a lake **undulating** as a result of freezing weather, of a jumping fish, or of serious pollution?
8. Which is **inanimate**—a sleeping person, a barking dog, or a shining rock?
9. Would someone experiencing **felicity** be most likely to smile, to glare, or to sob?
10. If you thought someone had behaved **basely,** would you feel critical, jealous, or respectful?

EXERCISE B Working with a partner, act out the meaning of these vocabulary words—*felicity, impertinence, perseverance,* and *derision*—while another pair of students tries to guess them.

CHARLOTTE PERKINS GILMAN

1860–1935

After reading "The Yellow Wallpaper," a doctor wrote to Charlotte Perkins Gilman, praising the story's "detailed account of incipient insanity." Of course, he assumed she had not herself experienced what she had written about. Unfortunately, she had.

After the birth of her daughter in 1885, Gilman suffered from severe depression, a condition known today as postpartum depression. She consulted the noted neurologist Dr. S. Weir Mitchell, who advised her: "Live as domestic a life as possible. Have your child with you all the time. . . . Lie down an hour after each meal. Have but two hours' intellectual life a day. And never touch pen, brush or pencil as long as you live." By following Mitchell's orders, Gilman became even more depressed.

Eventually, Gilman saved herself from a total mental breakdown by ignoring her doctor's advice. In 1894 she divorced her first husband, Charles Stetson, and sent her daughter to live with him and his new wife. An artist and art teacher, she resumed painting and teaching. She gave lectures about women's issues, started a magazine, *The Forerunner,* and began publishing poems and articles. Within a ten-year period, Gilman wrote her best-known work of nonfiction, *Women and Economics* (1898), as well as *Concerning Children* (1900), *The Home: Its Work and Influence* (1903), and *Human Work* (1904).

Gilman wrote "The Yellow Wallpaper" in 1890 to protest doctors' "rest cures" for women. Learning that Dr. Mitchell had changed his treatment after reading her story, Gilman said, "If that is a fact, I have not lived in vain."

At the age of 72, Gilman was diagnosed with incurable cancer. She continued writing for three more years; but when the pain of the disease began to prevent her from working, she committed suicide.

OTHER WORKS *Herland, The Living of Charlotte Perkins Gilman: An Autobiography*

LASERLINKS
• *AUTHOR BACKGROUND*

PREVIEWING

FICTION

The Story of an Hour

Kate Chopin

PERSONAL CONNECTION

"The Story of an Hour" reveals a young woman's private thoughts about her life and marriage. What do you think makes a good marriage? What kind of relationship do you expect to have with a spouse? Make a list like the one shown, with five rules for a good marriage. Then, with a small group of classmates, discuss your thoughts about and expectations of marriage.

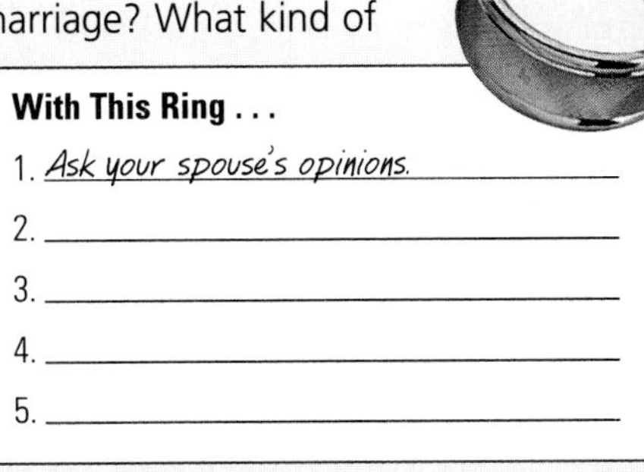

With This Ring . . .

1. *Ask your spouse's opinions.*
2. __________
3. __________
4. __________
5. __________

HISTORICAL CONNECTION

This story takes place about 100 years ago, near the turn of the century, when the status of women was very different from what it is today. Both custom and law severely limited women's actions and their control over their own lives. Because women could not vote, they had almost no political or legal power; and because they could not own property and their educational and employment opportunities were limited, they had little or no financial independence.

Few careers were open to middle-class and upper-class single women, and even fewer to married women—like Mrs. Mallard in this story—who were expected to be supported by their husbands. Those who did work had to turn their wages over to their fathers or their husbands. In most American marriages of the time, the husband was the undisputed head of the household and made all the important decisions.

WRITING CONNECTION

Consider what you have just read about women's role in marriage at the turn of the century. Imagine that a young woman of that time has just learned that her husband is dead. In your notebook, write what you think her reaction to the news would be. Then, as you read this story, see how your ideas compare with the reaction of Mrs. Mallard.

THE STORY OF AN HOUR

Kate Chopin

Knowing that Mrs. Mallard was afflicted with a heart trouble, great care was taken to break to her as gently as possible the news of her husband's death.

It was her sister Josephine who told her, in broken sentences; veiled hints that revealed in half concealing. Her husband's friend Richards was there, too, near her. It was he who had been in the newspaper office when intelligence of the railroad disaster was received, with Brently Mallard's name leading the list of "killed." He had only taken the time to assure himself of its truth by a second telegram, and had hastened to forestall any less careful, less tender friend in bearing the sad message.

> What could love, the unsolved mystery, count for in face of this possession of self-assertion which she suddenly recognized as the strongest impulse of her being!

She did not hear the story as many women have heard the same, with a paralyzed inability to accept its significance. She wept at once, with sudden, wild abandonment, in her sister's arms. When the storm of grief had spent itself she went away to her room alone. She would have no one follow her.

There stood, facing the open window, a comfortable, roomy armchair. Into this she sank, pressed down by a physical exhaustion that haunted her body and seemed to reach into her soul.

She could see in the open square before her house the tops of trees that were all aquiver with the new spring life. The delicious breath of rain was in the air. In the street below a peddler was crying his wares. The notes of a distant song which someone was singing reached her faintly, and countless sparrows were twittering in the eaves.

There were patches of blue sky showing here and there through the clouds that had met and piled one above the other in the west facing her window.

She sat with her head thrown back upon the cushion of the chair, quite motionless, except when a sob came up into her throat and shook her, as a child who has cried itself to sleep continues to sob in its dreams.

She was young, with a fair, calm face, whose lines bespoke repression and even a certain strength. But now there was a dull stare in her eyes, whose gaze was fixed away off yonder on one of those patches of blue sky. It was not a glance of reflection, but rather indicated a suspension of intelligent thought.

There was something coming to her and she was waiting for it, fearfully. What was it? She did not know; it was too subtle and elusive to name. But she felt it, creeping out of the sky, reaching toward her through the sounds, the scents, the color that filled the air.

Now her bosom rose and fell tumultuously. She was beginning to recognize this thing that was approaching to possess her, and she was striving to beat it back with her will—as powerless as her two white slender hands would have been.

When she abandoned herself, a little whispered word escaped her slightly parted lips. She said it over and over under her breath: "free, free, free!" The vacant stare and the look of terror that had followed it went from her eyes. They stayed keen and bright. Her pulses beat fast, and the coursing blood warmed and relaxed every inch of her body.

She did not stop to ask if it were or were not a monstrous joy that held her. A clear and exalted perception enabled her to dismiss the suggestion as trivial.

She knew that she would weep again when she saw the kind, tender hands folded in death; the face that had never looked save with love upon her, fixed and gray and dead. But she saw beyond that bitter moment a long procession of years to come that would belong to her absolutely. And she opened and spread her arms out to them in welcome.

Morning Glories (1873), Winslow Homer. Private Collection.

There would be no one to live for her during those coming years; she would live for herself. There would be no powerful will bending hers in that blind persistence with which men and women believe they have a right to impose a private will upon a fellow creature. A kind intention or a cruel intention made the act seem no less a crime as she looked upon it in that brief moment of illumination.

And yet she had loved him—sometimes. Often she had not. What did it matter! What could love, the unsolved mystery, count for in face of this possession of self-assertion which she suddenly recognized as the strongest impulse of her being!

"Free! Body and soul free!" she kept whispering.

Josephine was kneeling before the closed door with her lips to the keyhole, imploring for admission. "Louise, open the door! I beg; open the door—you will make yourself ill. What are you doing, Louise? For heaven's sake open the door."

"Go away. I am not making myself ill." No; she was drinking in a very elixir of life[1] through that open window.

Her fancy was running riot along those days ahead of her. Spring days, and summer days, and all sorts of days that would be her own. She breathed a quick prayer that life might be long. It was only yesterday she had thought with a shudder that life might be long.

She arose at length and opened the door to her sister's importunities. There was a feverish triumph in her eyes, and she carried herself unwittingly like a goddess of Victory. She clasped her sister's waist, and together they descended the stairs. Richards stood waiting for them at the bottom.

Someone was opening the front door with a latchkey. It was Brently Mallard who entered, a little travel-stained, composedly carrying his grip-sack[2] and umbrella. He had been far from the scene of accident, and did not know there had been one. He stood amazed at Josephine's piercing cry; at Richards's quick motion to screen him from the view of his wife.

But Richards was too late.

When the doctors came they said she had died of heart disease—of joy that kills. ❖

1. **elixir of life:** a medicine that restores vigor or the essence of life.

2. **grip-sack:** a small traveling bag or satchel.

RESPONDING OPTIONS

FROM PERSONAL RESPONSE *TO* CRITICAL ANALYSIS

REFLECT **1.** In your notebook, write the one word that sums up this story for you. Did you accurately predict Mrs. Mallard's reaction to the news of her husband's death?

RETHINK **2.** How would you explain the cause of Mrs. Mallard's death?

3. What is your impression of Mrs. Mallard?
Consider
- how Richards and her sister Josephine treat her
- how she reacts to the news of her husband's death
- why she says under her breath "free, free, free!"
- how she reacts when her husband arrives

4. How would you describe the relationship between Mrs. Mallard and her husband?

5. Mrs. Mallard "breathed a quick prayer that life might be long. It was only yesterday she had thought with a shudder that life might be long." Explain what theme you see expressed by these sentences.

6. What feelings do you think Brently Mallard will have about his wife's sudden death? In your opinion, will his feelings be similar to Mrs. Mallard's feelings about his supposed death? Explain your answer.

RELATE **7.** Think about why Mrs. Mallard finds her marriage unsatisfactory, and consider what you wrote for the Personal Connection on page 623. How can families or couples today make marriage a good experience for themselves and their children?

ANOTHER PATHWAY

This story takes place within the span of an hour. To show what happens to Mrs. Mallard in this all-important hour of her life, draw the outline of a clock as shown. In appropriate parts of the diagram, note the events in the order in which they occur. Also note her feelings about the events. Then discuss your diagram with the class.

1 hour

45 minutes

15 minutes

30 minutes

LITERARY LINKS

Both "The Story of an Hour" and "The Yellow Wallpaper" were written in the 1890s. How would you compare the themes and styles of the two stories? Which story do you prefer, and why?

QUICKWRITES

1. Write an appropriate **epitaph** for Mrs. Mallard, commenting on her life or the circumstances of her death. Remember to draw on your knowledge of her private thoughts.
2. Imagine that Brently Mallard indeed dies in the train wreck. Write a brief summary of an **alternative ending** for the story, and share it with your classmates.

PORTFOLIO *Save your writing. You may want to use it later as a springboard to a piece for your portfolio.*

LITERARY CONCEPTS

"The Story of an Hour" has a **surprise ending**—an unexpected plot twist at its conclusion. With your classmates, discuss your view of the surprise ending. Do you find it clever and fitting? illuminating? unrealistic? a cheap trick? In your opinion, how effective would this story be without the husband's unexpected reappearance or Mrs. Mallard's unexpected death?

CONCEPT REVIEW: Irony Surprise endings, almost by definition, are ironic. Mr. Mallard's return and Mrs. Mallard's death are examples of situational irony. What other examples of situational irony or dramatic irony do you see in this story? Talk about them in class.

THE WRITER'S STYLE

Look again at the fifth and sixth paragraphs of the story, which describe what Mrs. Mallard sees and hears from her open window after learning of her husband's death. What do you think the **imagery** in these paragraphs contributes to the story?

ACROSS THE CURRICULUM

History Find out more about the role of American women around the turn of the century. What rights did they have? What types of work did they do outside the home?

Cooperative Learning Work with a small group of classmates in which each member chooses a particular question about turn-of-the-century women to answer. After researching your question, join your group in a panel discussion to share your findings.

KATE CHOPIN

1851–1904

Kate Chopin was born Catherine O'Flaherty in St. Louis, Missouri. When she was five years old, her father was killed in a railroad disaster similar to the one described in "The Story of an Hour," leaving her mother a 27-year-old widow. As a student at Sacred Heart Academy Chopin exhibited "gifts as a teller of marvelous stories," and as a young woman she was a belle of St. Louis society. In 1870 she married Oscar Chopin, a Creole businessman, and settled with him in New Orleans.

In 1879 financial problems forced the Chopins and their five young sons to move to rural Louisiana, where their sixth child, a daughter, was born. In 1882 Oscar Chopin died of malaria, leaving his family in debt. Before she returned home to St. Louis in 1884, Chopin raised her children alone and managed her husband's business.

In 1889 Chopin's first poem and first story were published. Over the next ten years, she published two novels, over a hundred short stories, and many reviews and poems. According to her son Felix, Chopin would "go weeks and weeks without an idea, then suddenly grab her pencil and old lapboard . . . , and in a couple of hours her story was complete and off to the publisher."

Chopin's local-color stories about the Creoles, Cajuns, African Americans, and Indians whom she had known in Louisiana won her acclaim, but her stories about women seeking to be free often aroused protest. The severe criticism directed at her second novel, *The Awakening* (1899), for its depiction of a woman's adulterous affair brought Chopin's literary career to an end. However, that novel and Chopin's other works dealing with women's issues have since received greater appreciation.

OTHER WORKS *At Fault, Bayou Folk, A Night in Acadie*

PREVIEWING

FICTION

Seventeen Syllables

Hisaye Yamamoto (hē-sä′yĕ yä′mä-mō′tō)

PERSONAL CONNECTION

Rosie, the teenage girl in this story, witnesses a conflict between her parents. Think of a time when you witnessed a major conflict between two people close to you—friends, for example, or family members. In your notebook, describe the conflict and your reaction to it.

HISTORICAL/CULTURAL CONNECTION

Set in California in the 1930s, "Seventeen Syllables" explores conflicts between a Japanese-born husband and wife and between them and their American-born daughter, Rosie. Early Japanese immigrants were mostly single men, who often sought to get married after settling in America. In accordance with Japanese custom, family members arranged marriages for them with Japanese women who then immigrated. While facing the challenges of adjusting to a radically different culture, these Japanese immigrant couples also had to struggle to bridge the cultural differences that separated them from their American-born children.

After coming to the United States, many Japanese immigrants maintained an interest in Japanese literature. Groups were formed to write and study traditional forms of Japanese poetry, and numerous Japanese-language anthologies and magazines were devoted to this literature. In this story, Rosie's mother writes short poems called haiku, each containing 17 syllables.

READING CONNECTION

Recognizing Conflict As you may recall, conflict is a struggle between opposing forces. In an external conflict, a character is pitted against an outside force—another character, a physical obstacle, nature, or society. An internal conflict occurs when a character struggles within himself or herself—for example, when trying to make a decision. As you read this story, note the different conflicts that Rosie, her mother, and her father experience. Organize your observations in a diagram like the one shown. Inside the circles, note the conflicts within the characters; in the boxes between the circles, note the conflicts between the characters. If you notice conflicts arising from other outside forces, add them to your diagram.

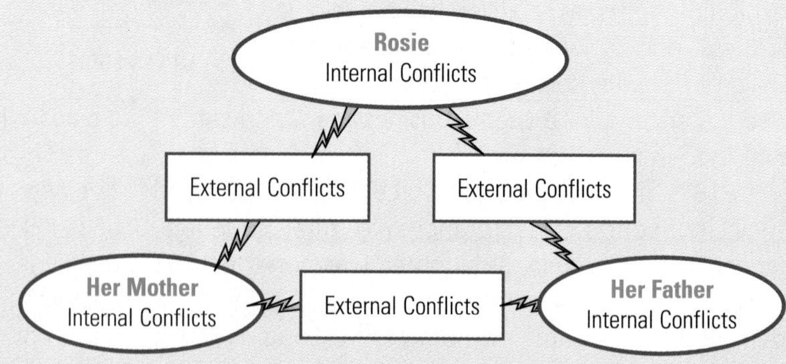

SEVENTEEN SYLLABLES

• Hisaye Yamamoto

Consolation (1961), Ruth Gikow. 30″ × 18″, collection of Dr. Violet Friedman.

The first Rosie knew that her mother had taken to writing poems was one evening when she finished one and read it aloud for her daughter's approval. It was about cats, and Rosie pretended to understand it thoroughly and appreciate it no end, partly because she hesitated to disillusion her mother about the quantity and quality of Japanese she had learned in all the years now that she had been going to Japanese school every Saturday (and Wednesday, too, in the summer). Even so, her mother must have been skeptical about the depth of Rosie's understanding, because she explained afterwards about the kind of poem she was trying to write.

See, Rosie, she said, it was a *haiku*, a poem in which she must pack all her meaning into seventeen syllables only, which were divided into three lines of five, seven, and five syllables. In the one she had just read, she had tried to capture the charm of a kitten, as well as comment on the superstition that owning a cat of three colors meant good luck.

"Yes, yes, I understand. How utterly lovely," Rosie said, and her mother, either satisfied or seeing through the deception and resigned, went back to composing.

• It was a haiku, a poem in which she must pack all her meaning into seventeen syllables only.

The truth was that Rosie was lazy; English lay ready on the tongue but Japanese had to be searched for and examined, and even then put forth tentatively (probably to meet with laughter). It was so much easier to say yes, yes, even when one meant no, no. Besides, this was what was in her mind to say: I was looking through one of your magazines from Japan last night, Mother, and towards the back I found some *haiku* in English that delighted me. There was one that made me giggle off and on until I fell asleep—

It is morning, and lo!
I lie awake, comme il faut,[1]
sighing for some dough.

Now, how to reach her mother, how to communicate the melancholy song? Rosie knew formal Japanese by fits and starts, her mother had even less English, no French. It was much more possible to say yes, yes.

It developed that her mother was writing the *haiku* for a daily newspaper, the *Mainichi Shimbun*,[2] that was published in San Francisco. Los Angeles, to be sure, was closer to the farming community in which the Hayashi[3] family lived and several Japanese vernaculars[4] were printed there, but Rosie's parents said they preferred the tone of the northern paper. Once a week, the *Mainichi* would have a section devoted to *haiku*, and her mother became an extravagant contributor, taking for herself the blossoming pen name, Ume Hanazono.[5]

So Rosie and her father lived for awhile with two women, her mother and Ume Hanazono. Her mother (Tome Hayashi by name) kept house, cooked, washed, and, along with her husband and the Carrascos, the Mexican family hired for the harvest, did her ample share of picking tomatoes out in the sweltering fields and boxing them in tidy strata in the cool packing shed. Ume Hanazono, who came to life after the dinner dishes were done, was an earnest, muttering stranger who often neglected speaking when spoken to and stayed busy at the parlor table as late as midnight scribbling with pencil on scratch paper or

---

1. ***comme il faut*** (kôm′ ēl fō′) *French:* as is proper; as usual.
2. ***Mainichi Shimbun*** (mī-nē′chē shēm′bo͝on).
3. **Hayashi** (hä-yä′shē).
4. **Japanese vernaculars:** newspapers in the Japanese language.
5. **Ume Hanazono** (o͝o′mĕ hä′nä-zō′nō).

carefully copying characters on good paper with her fat, pale green Parker.

The new interest had some repercussions on the household routine. Before, Rosie had been accustomed to her parents and herself taking their hot baths early and going to bed almost immediately afterwards, unless her parents challenged each other to a game of flower cards or unless company dropped in. Now if her father wanted to play cards, he had to resort to solitaire (at which he always cheated fearlessly), and if a group of friends came over, it was bound to contain someone who was also writing *haiku*, and the small assemblage would be split in two, her father entertaining the non-literary members and her mother comparing ecstatic notes with the visiting poet.

If they went out, it was more of the same thing. But Ume Hanazono's life span, even for a poet's, was very brief—perhaps three months at most.

One night they went over to see the Hayano family in the neighboring town to the west, an adventure both painful and attractive to Rosie. It was attractive because there were four Hayano girls, all lovely and each one named after a season of the year (Haru, Natsu, Aki, Fuyu),[6] painful because something had been wrong with Mrs. Hayano ever since the birth of her first child. Rosie would sometimes watch Mrs. Hayano, reputed to have been the belle of her native village, making her way about a room, stooped, slowly shuffling, violently trembling *(always* trembling), and she would be reminded that this woman, in this same condition, had carried and given issue to three babies. She would look wonderingly at Mr. Hayano, handsome, tall, and strong, and she would look at her four pretty friends. But it was not a matter she could come to any decision about.

On this visit, however, Mrs. Hayano sat all evening in the rocker, as motionless and unobtrusive as it was possible for her to be, and Rosie found the greater part of the evening practically anaesthetic.[7] Too, Rosie spent most of it in the girls' room, because Haru, the garrulous[8] one, said almost as soon as the bows and other greetings were over, "Oh, you must see my new coat!"

It was a pale plaid of grey, sand, and blue, with an enormous collar, and Rosie, seeing nothing special in it, said, "Gee, how nice."

"Nice?" said Haru, indignantly. "Is that all you can say about it? It's gorgeous! And so cheap, too. Only seventeen-ninety-eight, because it was a sale. The saleslady said it was twenty-five dollars regular."

"Gee," said Rosie. Natsu, who never said much and when she said anything said it shyly, fingered the coat covetously and Haru pulled it away.

"Mine," she said, putting it on. She minced in the aisle between the two large beds and smiled happily. "Let's see how your mother likes it."

She broke into the front room and the adult conversation and went to stand in front of Rosie's mother, while the rest watched from the door. Rosie's mother was properly envious. "May I inherit it when you're through with it?"

Haru, pleased, giggled and said yes, she could, but Natsu reminded gravely from the door, "You promised me, Haru."

Everyone laughed but Natsu, who shamefacedly retreated into the bedroom. Haru came in laughing, taking off the coat. "We were only kidding, Natsu," she said. "Here, you try it on now."

After Natsu buttoned herself into the coat, inspected herself solemnly in the bureau mirror,

6. **Haru** (hä'ro͞o), **Natsu** (nät'so͞o), **Aki** (ä'kē), **Fuyu** (fo͞o'yo͞o): the Japanese words for spring, summer, autumn, and winter, respectively.

7. **anaesthetic:** causing sleep; boring.

8. **garrulous** (găr'ə-ləs): talkative.

WORDS TO KNOW

repercussion (rē'pər-kŭsh'ən) *n.* a far-reaching effect
unobtrusive (ŭn'əb-tro͞o'sĭv) *adj.* not noticeable; not calling attention to oneself

and reluctantly shed it, Rosie, Aki, and Fuyu got their turns, and Fuyu, who was eight, drowned in it while her sisters and Rosie doubled up in amusement. They all went into the front room later, because Haru's mother quaveringly called to her to fix the tea and rice cakes and open a can of sliced peaches for everybody. Rosie noticed that her mother and Mr. Hayano were talking together at the little table—they were discussing a *haiku* that Mr. Hayano was planning to send to the *Mainichi*, while her father was sitting at one end of the sofa looking through a copy of *Life,* the new picture magazine. Occasionally, her father would comment on a photograph, holding it toward Mrs. Hayano and speaking to her as he always did—loudly, as though he thought someone such as she must surely be at least a trifle deaf also.

The five girls had their refreshments at the kitchen table, and it was while Rosie was showing the sisters her trick of swallowing peach slices without chewing (she chased each slippery crescent down with a swig of tea) that her father brought his empty teacup and untouched saucer to the sink and said, "Come on, Rosie, we're going home now."

"Already?" asked Rosie.

"Work tomorrow," he said.

He sounded irritated, and Rosie, puzzled, gulped one last yellow slice and stood up to go, while the sisters began protesting, as was their wont.

"We have to get up at five-thirty," he told them, going into the front room quickly, so that they did not have their usual chance to hang onto his hands and plead for an extension of time.

Rosie, following, saw that her mother and Mr. Hayano were sipping tea and still talking together, while Mrs. Hayano concentrated, quivering, on raising the handleless Japanese cup to her lips with both her hands and lowering it back to her lap. Her father, saying nothing, went out the door, onto the bright porch, and down the steps. Her mother looked up and asked, "Where is he going?"

"Where is he going?" Rosie said. "He said we were going home now."

"Going home?" Her mother looked with embarrassment at Mr. Hayano and his absorbed wife and then forced a smile. "He must be tired," she said.

Haru was not giving up yet. "May Rosie stay overnight?" she asked, and Natsu, Aki, and Fuyu came to reinforce their sister's plea by helping her make a circle around Rosie's mother. Rosie, for once having no desire to stay, was relieved when her mother, apologizing to the perturbed Mr. and Mrs. Hayano for her father's abruptness at the same time, managed to shake her head no at the quartet, kindly but adamant, so that they broke their circle and let her go.

Rosie's father looked ahead into the windshield as the two joined him. "I'm sorry," her mother said. "You must be tired." Her father, stepping on the starter, said nothing. "You know how I get when it's *haiku*," she continued, "I forget what time it is." He only grunted.

As they rode homeward silently, Rosie, sitting between, felt a rush of hate for both—for her mother for begging, for her father for denying her mother. I wish this old Ford would crash, right now, she thought, then immediately, no, no, I wish my father would laugh, but it was too late: already the vision had passed through her mind of the green pick-up crumpled in the dark against one of the mighty eucalyptus trees they were just riding past, of the three contorted, bleeding bodies, one of them hers.

Rosie ran between two patches of tomatoes, her heart working more rambunctiously than she had ever known it to. How lucky it was that Aunt Taka and Uncle Gimpachi[9] had come tonight, though, how very lucky. Otherwise she

9. **Aunt Taka** (tä′kä) . . . **Uncle Gimpachi** (gēm-pä′chē).

WORDS TO KNOW **adamant** (ăd′ə-mənt) *adj.* stubborn; not giving in

Japanese-American family in the 1930s. Photo by Russell Lee. Underwood Photo Archives, San Francisco.

might not have really kept her half-promise to meet Jesus Carrasco. Jesus was going to be a senior in September at the same school she went to, and his parents were the ones helping with the tomatoes this year. She and Jesus, who hardly remembered seeing each other at Cleveland High where there were so many other people and two whole grades between them, had become great friends this summer—he always had a joke for her when he periodically drove the loaded pick-up up from the fields to the shed where she was usually sorting while her mother and father did the packing, and they laughed a great deal together over infinitesimal repartee[10] during the afternoon break for chilled watermelon or ice cream in the shade of the shed.

What she enjoyed most was racing him to see which could finish picking a double row first. He, who could work faster, would tease her by slowing down until she thought she would surely pass him this time, then speeding up furiously to leave her several sprawling vines behind. Once he had made her screech hideously by crossing over, while her back was turned, to place atop the tomatoes in her green-stained bucket a truly monstrous, pale green worm (it had looked more like an infant snake). And it was when they had finished a contest this morning, after she had

10. **infinitesimal repartee** (ĭn′fĭ-nĭ-tĕs′ə-məl rĕp′ər-tē′): an attempt at witty conversation about trivial matters (a humorous exaggeration of the term *small talk).*

pantingly pointed a green finger at the immature tomatoes evident in the lugs[11] at the end of his row and he had returned the accusation (with justice), that he had startlingly brought up the matter of their possibly meeting outside the range of both their parents' dubious eyes.

"What for?" she had asked.

"I've got a secret I want to tell you," he said.

"Tell me now," she demanded.

"It won't be ready till tonight," he said.

She laughed. "Tell me tomorrow then."

"It'll be gone tomorrow," he threatened.

"Well, for seven hakes,[12] what is it?" she had asked, more than twice, and when he had suggested that the packing shed would be an appropriate place to find out, she had cautiously answered maybe. She had not been certain she was going to keep the appointment until the arrival of mother's sister and her husband. Their coming seemed a sort of signal of permission, of grace, and she had definitely made up her mind to lie and leave as she was bowing them welcome.

So as soon as everyone appeared settled back for the evening, she announced loudly that she was going to the privy outside, "I'm going to the *benjo!*" and slipped out the door. And now that she was actually on her way, her heart pumped in such an undisciplined way that she could hear it with her ears. It's because I'm running, she told herself, slowing to a walk. The shed was up ahead, one more patch away, in the middle of the fields. Its bulk, looming in the dimness, took on a sinisterness that was funny when Rosie reminded herself that it was only a wooden frame with a canvas roof and three canvas walls that made a slapping noise on breezy days.

Jesus was sitting on the narrow plank that was the sorting platform and she went around to the other side and jumped backwards to seat herself on the rim of a packing stand. "Well, tell me," she said without greeting, thinking her voice sounded reassuringly familiar.

"I saw you coming out the door," Jesus said. "I heard you running part of the way, too."

"Uh-huh," Rosie said. "Now tell me the secret."

"I was afraid you wouldn't come," he said.

Rosie delved around on the chicken-wire bottom of the stall for number two tomatoes, ripe, which she was sitting beside, and came up with a left-over that felt edible. She bit into it and began sucking out the pulp and seeds. "I'm here," she pointed out.

"Rosie, are you sorry you came?"

"Sorry? What for?" she said. "You said you were going to tell me something."

- All that remained intact now was

yes

and

no

and

oh,

and even these few sounds would not easily out.

11. **lugs:** shallow boxes in which fruit is shipped.

12. **for seven hakes:** a play on the phrase "for heaven's sake."

WORDS TO KNOW **dubious** (dōō'bē-əs) *adj.* doubtful; suspicious

"I will, I will," Jesus said, but his voice contained disappointment, and Rosie fleetingly felt the older of the two, realizing a brand-new power which vanished without category under her recognition.

"I have to go back in a minute," she said. "My aunt and uncle are here from Wintersburg. I told them I was going to the privy."

Jesus laughed. "You funny thing," he said. "You slay me!"

"Just because you have a bathroom *inside,*" Rosie said. "Come on, tell me."

Chuckling, Jesus came around to lean on the stand facing her. They still could not see each other very clearly, but Rosie noticed that Jesus became very sober again as he took the hollow tomato from her hand and dropped it back into the stall. When he took hold of her empty hand, she could find no words to protest; her vocabulary had become distressingly constricted and she thought desperately that all that remained intact now was yes and no and oh, and even these few sounds would not easily out. Thus, kissed by Jesus, Rosie fell for the first time entirely victim to a helplessness delectable beyond speech. But the terrible, beautiful sensation lasted no more than a second, and the reality of Jesus' lips and tongue and teeth and hands made her pull away with such strength that she nearly tumbled.

Rosie stopped running as she approached the lights from the windows of home. How long since she had left? She could not guess, but gasping yet, she went to the privy in back and locked herself in. Her own breathing deafened her in the dark, close space, and she sat and waited until she could hear at last the nightly calling of the frogs and crickets. Even then, all she could think to say was oh, my, and the pressure of Jesus' face against her face would not leave.

No one had missed her in the parlor, however, and Rosie walked in and through quickly, announcing that she was next going to take a bath. "Your father's in the bathhouse," her mother said, and Rosie, in her room, recalled that she had not seen him when she entered. There had been only Aunt Taka and Uncle Gimpachi with her mother at the table, drinking tea. She got her robe and straw sandals and crossed the parlor again to go outside. Her mother was telling them about the *haiku* competition in the *Mainichi* and the poem she had entered.

Rosie met her father coming out of the bathhouse. "Are you through, Father?" she asked. "I was going to ask you to scrub my back."

"Scrub your own back," he said shortly, going toward the main house.

"What have I done now?" she yelled after him. She suddenly felt like doing a lot of yelling. But he did not answer, and she went into the bathhouse. Turning on the dangling light, she removed her denims and T-shirt and threw them in the big carton for dirty clothes standing next to the washing machine. Her other things she took with her into the bath compartment to wash after her bath. After she had scooped a basin of hot water from the square wooden tub, she sat on the grey cement of the floor and soaped herself at exaggerated leisure, singing "Red Sails in the Sunset" at the top of her voice and using da-da-da where she suspected her words. Then, standing up, still singing, for she was possessed by the notion that any attempt now to analyze would result in spoilage and she believed that the larger her volume the less she would be able to hear herself think, she obtained more hot water and poured it on until she was free of lather. Only then did she allow herself to step into the steaming vat, one leg first, then the remainder of her body inch by inch until the water no longer stung and she could move around at will.

She took a long time soaking, afterwards remembering to go around outside to stoke the embers of the tin-lined fireplace beneath the tub

WORDS TO KNOW

delectable (dĭ-lĕk'tə-bəl) *adj.* highly pleasing; delightful and to throw on a few more sticks so that the water might keep its heat for her mother, and when she finally returned to the parlor, she found her mother still talking *haiku* with her aunt and uncle, the three of them on another round of tea. Her father was nowhere in sight.

At Japanese school the next day (Wednesday, it was), Rosie was grave and giddy by turns. Preoccupied at her desk in the row for students on Book Eight, she made up for it at recess by performing wild mimicry for the benefit of her friend Chizuko.[13] She held her nose and whined a witticism or two in what she considered was the manner of Fred Allen; she assumed intoxication and a British accent to go over the climax of the Rudy Vallee recording of the pub conversation about William Ewart Gladstone; she was the child Shirley Temple piping, "On the Good Ship Lollipop"; she was the gentleman soprano of the Four Inkspots trilling, "If I Didn't Care."[14] And she felt reasonably satisfied when Chizuko wept and gasped, "Oh, Rosie, you ought to be in the movies!"

Her father came after her at noon, bringing her sandwiches of minced ham and two nectarines to eat while she rode, so that she could pitch right into the sorting when they got home. The lugs were piling up, he said, and the ripe tomatoes in them would probably have to be taken to the cannery tomorrow if they were not ready for the produce haulers tonight. "This heat's not doing them any good. And we've got no time for a break today."

It was hot, probably the hottest day of the year, and Rosie's blouse stuck damply to her back even under the protection of the canvas. But she worked as efficiently as a flawless machine and kept the stalls heaped, with one part of her mind listening in to the parental murmuring about the heat and the tomatoes and with another part planning the exact words she would say to Jesus when he drove up with the first load of the afternoon. But when at last she saw that the pick-up was coming, her hands went berserk and the tomatoes started falling in the wrong stalls, and her father said, "Hey, hey! Rosie, watch what you're doing!"

"Well, I have to go to the *benjo,*" she said, hiding panic.

"Go in the weeds over there," he said, only half-joking.

"Oh, Father!" she protested.

"Oh, go on home," her mother said. "We'll make out for awhile."

In the privy Rosie peered through a knothole toward the fields, watching as much as she could of Jesus. Happily she thought she saw him look in the direction of the house from time to time before he finished unloading and went back toward the patch where his mother and father worked. As she was heading for the shed, a very presentable black car purred up the dirt driveway to the house and its driver motioned to her. Was this the Hayashi home, he wanted to know. She nodded. Was she a Hayashi? Yes, she said, thinking that he was a good-looking man. He got out of the car with a huge, flat package and she saw that he warmly wore a business suit. "I have something here for your mother then," he said, in a more elegant Japanese than she was used to.

She told him where her mother was and he came along with her, patting his face with an immaculate white handkerchief and saying something about the coolness of San Francisco. To her surprised mother and father, he bowed and introduced himself as, among other things,

13. **Chizuko** (chē-zo͝o'kō).

14. **Fred Allen . . . "If I Didn't Care":** The comedian Fred Allen had a radio show during the 1930s and 1940s. Rudy Vallee was a singer popular during the 1920s and 1930s, who performed a comedy routine featuring a conversation about Gladstone, a 19th-century British prime minister. Shirley Temple was a famous child star of the 1930s. "If I Didn't Care" was a hit record for the Four Inkspots, a popular African-American singing group, in 1939.

WORDS TO KNOW

preoccupied (prē-ŏk'yə-pīd') *adj.* lost in thought; intensely concerned

Returning Sails to Gyotoku (about 1837–1838) Ichiryusai Hiroshige. From the series *Eight Views of the Edo Suburbs,* woodblock print, 23.5 cm × 36 cm., Edo Period, Japan, The Art Institute of Chicago, Clarence Buckingham Collection (1943.708). Photo Copyright © 1995 The Art Institute of Chicago, all rights reserved.

the *haiku* editor of the *Mainichi Shimbun*, saying that since he had been coming as far as Los Angeles anyway, he had decided to bring her the first prize she had won in the recent contest.

"First prize?" her mother echoed, believing and not believing, pleased and overwhelmed. Handed the package with a bow, she bobbed her head up and down numerous times to express her utter gratitude.

"It is nothing much," he added, "but I hope it will serve as a token of our great appreciation for your contributions and our great admiration of your considerable talent."

"I am not worthy," she said, falling easily into his style. "It is I who should make some sign of my humble thanks for being permitted to contribute."

"No, no, to the contrary," he said, bowing again.

But Rosie's mother insisted, and then saying that she knew she was being unorthodox, she asked if she might open the package because her curiosity was so great. Certainly she might. In fact, he would like her reaction to it, for personally, it was one of his favorite Hiroshiges.[15]

Rosie thought it was a pleasant picture, which looked to have been sketched with delicate quickness. There were pink clouds, containing some graceful calligraphy, and a sea that was a pale blue except at the edges, containing four sampans[16] with indications of people in them.

15. **Hiroshiges** (hē′rō-shē′gĕz): works by Hiroshige, master designer of color prints, considered one of Japan's most important artists. (See art on this page.)

16. **sampans:** small boats, used in Japan, that can be either sailed or rowed.

Pines edged the water and on the far-off beach there was a cluster of thatched huts towered over by pine-dotted mountains of grey and blue. The frame was scalloped and gilt.

After Rosie's mother pronounced it without peer and somewhat prodded her father into nodding agreement, she said Mr. Kuroda[17] must at least have a cup of tea after coming all this way, and although Mr. Kuroda did not want to impose, he soon agreed that a cup of tea would be refreshing and went along with her to the house, carrying the picture for her.

"Ha, your mother's crazy!" Rosie's father said, and Rosie laughed uneasily as she resumed judgment on the tomatoes. She had emptied six lugs when he broke into an imaginary conversation with Jesus to tell her to go and remind her mother of the tomatoes, and she went slowly.

"Tell him I shall only be a minute," her mother said, speaking the language of Mr. Kuroda.

When Rosie carried the reply to her father, he did not seem to hear and she said again, "Mother says she'll be back in a minute."

"All right, all right," he nodded, and they worked again in silence. But suddenly, her father uttered an incredible noise, exactly like the cork of a bottle popping, and the next Rosie knew, he was stalking angrily toward the house, almost running in fact, and she chased after him crying, "Father! Father! What are you going to do?"

He stopped long enough to order her back to the shed. "Never mind!" he shouted. "Get on with the sorting!"

And from the place in the fields where she stood, frightened and vacillating, Rosie saw her father enter the house. Soon Mr. Kuroda came out alone, putting on his coat. Mr. Kuroda got into his car and backed out down the driveway onto the highway. Next her father emerged, also alone, something in his arms (it was the picture, she realized), and, going over to the bathhouse woodpile, he threw the picture on the ground and picked up the axe. Smashing the picture, glass and all (she heard the explosion faintly), he reached over for the kerosene that was used to encourage the bath fire and poured it over the wreckage. I am dreaming, Rosie said to herself, I am dreaming, but her father, having made sure that his act of cremation was irrevocable, was even then returning to the fields.

• *"Do you know why I married your father?"... "No," said Rosie.... Don't tell me now, she wanted to say, tell me tomorrow, tell me next week, don't tell me today.*

Mr. Kuroda was in his shirtsleeves expounding some *haiku* theory as he munched a rice cake, and her mother was rapt. Abashed in the great man's presence, Rosie stood next to her mother's chair until her mother looked up inquiringly, and then she started to whisper the message, but her mother pushed her gently away and reproached, "You are not being very polite to our guest."

"Father says the tomatoes . . ." Rosie said aloud, smiling foolishly.

17. **Kuroda** (ko͝o-rō′dä).

WORDS TO KNOW

vacillating (văs′ə-lā′tĭng) *adj.* swinging from one course of action or opinion to another; indecisive **vacillate** *v.*

irrevocable (ĭ-rĕv′ə-kə-bəl) *adj.* impossible to take back or undo

Rosie ran past him and toward the house. What had become of her mother? She burst into the parlor and found her mother at the back window watching the dying fire. They watched together until there remained only a feeble smoke under the blazing sun. Her mother was very calm.

"Do you know why I married your father?" she said without turning.

"No," said Rosie. It was the most frightening question she had ever been called upon to answer. Don't tell me now, she wanted to say, tell me tomorrow, tell me next week, don't tell me today. But she knew she would be told now, that the telling would combine with the other violence of the hot afternoon to level her life, her world to the very ground.

It was like a story out of the magazines illustrated in sepia,[18] which she had consumed so greedily for a period until the information had somehow reached her that those wretchedly unhappy autobiographies, offered to her as the testimonials of living men and women, were largely inventions: Her mother, at nineteen, had come to America and married her father as an alternative to suicide.

At eighteen she had been in love with the first son of one of the well-to-do families in her village. The two had met whenever and wherever they could, secretly, because it would not have done for his family to see him favor her—her father had no money; he was a drunkard and a gambler besides. She had learned she was with child; an excellent match had already been arranged for her lover. Despised by her family, she had given premature birth to a stillborn son, who would be seventeen now. Her family did not turn her out, but she could no longer project herself in any direction without refreshing in them the memory of her indiscretion. She wrote to Aunt Taka, her favorite sister in America, threatening to kill herself if Aunt Taka would not send for her. Aunt Taka hastily arranged a marriage with a young man of whom she knew, but lately arrived from Japan, a young man of simple mind, it was said, but of kindly heart. The young man was never told why his unseen betrothed was so eager to hasten the day of meeting.

The story was told perfectly, with neither groping for words nor untoward passion. It was as though her mother had memorized it by heart, reciting it to herself so many times over that its nagging vileness had long since gone.

"I had a brother then?" Rosie asked, for this was what seemed to matter now; she would think about the other later, she assured herself, pushing back the illumination which threatened all that darkness that had hitherto been merely mysterious or even glamorous. "A half-brother?"

"Yes."

"I would have liked a brother," she said.

Suddenly, her mother knelt on the floor and took her by the wrists. "Rosie," she said urgently, "promise me you will never marry!" Shocked more by the request than the revelation, Rosie stared at her mother's face. Jesus, Jesus, she called silently, not certain whether she was invoking the help of the son of the Carrascos or of God, until there returned sweetly the memory of Jesus' hand, how it had touched her and where. Still her mother waited for an answer, holding her wrists so tightly that her hands were going numb. She tried to pull free. Promise, her mother whispered fiercely, promise. Yes, yes, I promise, Rosie said. But for an instant she turned away, and her mother, hearing the familiar glib agreement, released her. Oh, you, you, you, her eyes and twisted mouth said, you fool. Rosie, covering her face, began at last to cry, and the embrace and consoling hand came much later than she expected. ❖

18. **sepia** (sē′pē-ə): a dark, reddish-brown color.

WORDS TO KNOW

indiscretion (ĭn′dĭ-skrĕsh′ən) *n.* a lack of good judgment in speech or behavior
untoward (ŭn-tôrd′) *n.* inappropriate

RESPONDING OPTIONS

FROM PERSONAL RESPONSE *TO* CRITICAL ANALYSIS

REFLECT **1.** What character were you most concerned about as you finished reading the story? In your notebook, briefly record your thoughts about that character.

RETHINK **2.** In your opinion, why does Rosie's father react as he does to his wife's writing?

Consider

- the changes in the family's social life
- the intensity of the farm work
- the prize's and Mr. Kuroda's elegance

3. How do you think Rosie has been or will be affected by the conflict between her parents?

4. In your own words, describe the feelings that Rosie struggles with after Jesus kisses her.

5. In your opinion, how does the conversation between Mrs. Hayashi and Rosie after the picture is burned relate to the other conflicts in the story? Refer to your Reading Connection diagram.

RELATE **6.** On the basis of the female characters and authors in this part of Unit Five, what generalizations would you make about women's lives and women's voices in the 19th and 20th centuries?

ANOTHER PATHWAY

Cooperative Learning

With a small group of classmates, discuss the major conflicts between Rosie and her parents. Then work with your group to role-play the conflicts, trying to discover ways of solving them. Keep a record of the conflicts you resolved and the ways you resolved them, as well as of the conflicts you couldn't resolve.

LITERARY CONCEPTS

Plot is the sequence of events and actions in a literary work. Sometimes two or more plots are developed simultaneously in a short story. For example, "Seventeen Syllables" has two main plots: (1) Rosie's developing relationship with Jesus and (2) Mrs. Hayashi's growing interest in writing haiku. Working with a partner, create parallel plot maps to note events that make up the **rising action,** the **climax,** and the **falling action** of each plot. (See the Handbook of Literary Terms for a review.) How do the plots relate to each other? What central idea, or **theme,** is communicated by the interaction of the two plots?

QUICKWRITES

1. Compose a **haiku** that you think Rosie could have written. It might express her feelings about Jesus, the conflict between her parents, or anything else. As a guide to writing the poem, use the details about haiku that are presented in the story. Read your haiku to your classmates.
2. Imagine that a book of haiku by Mrs. Hayashi—under her pen name Ume Hanazono—is soon to be published. Write a **biographical note** about the author that might appear on the book's cover. If you have a desktop-publishing program on your computer, you might create a mockup of the front and back covers, with the biographical note in place.

PORTFOLIO *Save your writing. You may want to use it later as a springboard to a piece for your portfolio.*

ART CONNECTION

Mrs. Hayashi's poetry prize is a Hiroshige print similar, if not identical, to the one shown on page 637. How would you describe the style and mood of this picture? What would make it a fitting prize for a haiku contest?

WORDS TO KNOW

Review the Words to Know at the bottom of the selection pages. Then write the word that best completes each of the following sentences.

1. In the early 1800s, European paintings tended to be quite realistic, showing gorgeous flowers and _____ fruit.
2. Japanese prints were quite detailed but more subtle and _____ than European works.
3. The arrival of some of these prints in Europe had a surprising impact, resulting in many a _____ among European painters.
4. The impressionists abandoned classic Western painting styles, becoming _____ with some of the Japanese techniques.
5. Skeptical critics were _____ about paintings that depicted "impressions" of reality.
6. Still, the course the impressionists took was not a _____ one; it remained focused and steady.
7. Unswayed by criticism, the impressionists were _____ in their desire to convey the effects of light and shadow and capture fleeting moments.
8. One critic who thought Renoir's use of color was decidedly _____ ridiculed him.
9. One would expect such scorn to be directed at a serious _____, not simply a new style of art.
10. The influence of the impressionists and the Japanese printmakers who inspired them proved _____, persisting even today.

LASERLINKS
• *ART GALLERY*

HISAYE YAMAMOTO

1921–

Both personal experiences and historical events shaped Hisaye Yamamoto into a writer who empathizes with people excluded from society's mainstream. The daughter of Japanese immigrants, like her character Rosie, Yamamoto was born in Redondo Beach, California. Along with many other Japanese Americans, she was interned by the U.S. government during World War II. While she was in the detention camp, the interest in writing that she had developed as a teenager led her to write a column for the camp newspaper and to publish a serialized mystery. For three years after the war, she worked as a columnist for the *Los Angeles Tribune,* an African-American weekly. Later, she received a John Hay Whitney Foundation Opportunity Fellowship that allowed her to write fiction full time for a year.

Yamamoto has had a relatively small literary output. She has published only one collection in the United States—*Seventeen Syllables and Other Stories* (1988)—yet she continues to receive critical acclaim. In 1986 she received a lifetime achievement award from the Before Columbus Foundation. Her work, which features Japanese-American protagonists, often focuses on encounters between representatives of different races and cultures. Using irony and realistic detail, Yamamoto shows the oppression caused by racism and sexism.

"Seventeen Syllables," which was first published in 1949, was inspired by the life of Yamamoto's mother, who had published senryu, a traditional form of Japanese poetry, in Japanese-language newspapers. According to Yamamoto, her mother, like most women, did not have a chance to fulfill her potential. "She had us kids to look after, on top of all the housework and working alongside my father in the fields." Sadly, Yamamoto's mother did not live to see her story told.

PREVIEWING

FICTION

I Stand Here Ironing

Tillie Olsen

PERSONAL CONNECTION

What do you think it takes to be a good parent? If you had children, what would you do to help them grow up to be good people? In your notebook, list four or five qualities or attitudes that you think are important in raising children. Then, as you read this story, consider the narrator's thoughts about parenthood.

HISTORICAL CONNECTION

During the Great Depression of the 1930s and World War II and its aftermath in the 1940s, many parents, like the mother in "I Stand Here Ironing," had to struggle to raise their families. After the stock market crashed in 1929 and the American economy collapsed, millions were left without jobs. Work was so scarce that Secretary of Labor Frances Perkins urged women to give up their jobs so that more men could be employed. Working mothers who kept their jobs often relied on government-supported nurseries for child care or on relatives who were better able to provide for the children.

As industry expanded to manufacture the equipment needed to fight World War II, thousands of workers found jobs. Even in the new prosperity, however, families faced problems. With their husbands serving in the armed forces, many women had to care for their children alone. At the same time, the wartime demand for workers brought about 6 million women into the work force. The government built large daycare centers to care for children while their mothers worked. Families now had money to spend, but the war brought shortages of meat, sugar, gasoline, and many other important goods.

READING CONNECTION

Categorizing Events Think about some key experiences in your life—the formative events that have shaped your personality. In this story, a mother relates anecdotes and observations about her daughter Emily's childhood. As you read, look for experiences that have contributed to the shaping of Emily's personality. To help you distinguish the events that, in your opinion, her parents could control from those that you think were beyond her parents' control, make a diagram like the one shown here.

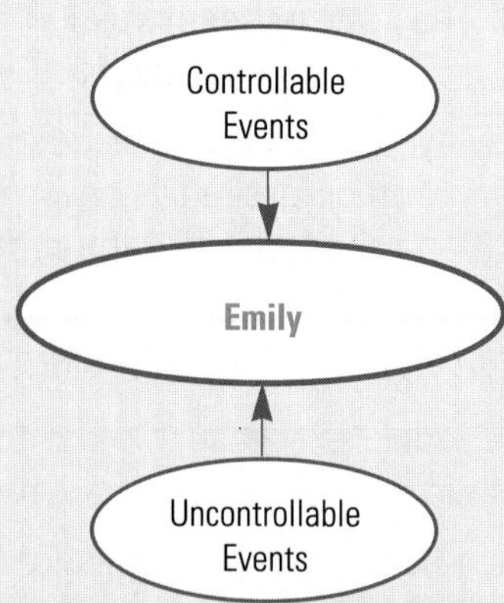

• *HISTORICAL CONNECTION*

I Stand Here Ironing

Tillie Olsen

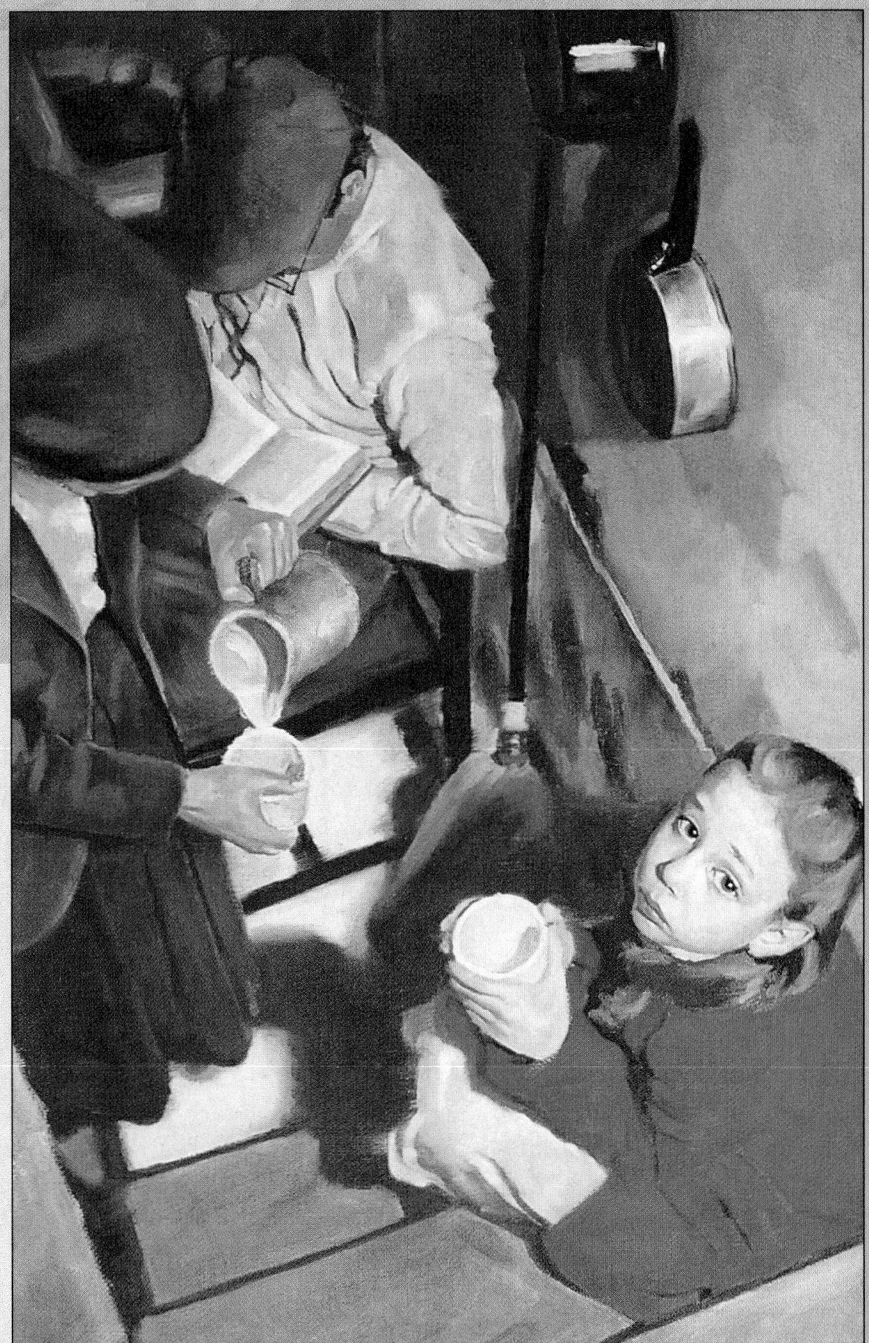

Illustration by Mike Dooling from *Mary McLean and the St. Patrick's Day Parade* by Steven Kroll. Illustration Copyright © 1990 by Mike Dooling, reprinted by permission of Scholastic Inc.

I stand here ironing, and what you asked me moves tormented back and forth with the iron.

"I wish you would manage the time to come in and talk with me about your daughter. I'm sure you can help me understand her. She's a youngster who needs help and whom I'm deeply interested in helping."

"Who needs help." . . . Even if I came, what good would it do? You think because I am her mother I have a key, or that in some way you could use me as a key? She has lived for nineteen years. There is all that life that has happened outside of me, beyond me.

And when is there time to remember, to sift, to weigh, to estimate, to total? I will start and there will be an interruption and I will have to gather it all together again. Or I will become engulfed with all I did or did not do, with what should have been and what cannot be helped.

She was a beautiful baby. The first and only one of our five that was beautiful at birth. You do not guess how new and uneasy her tenancy[1] in her now-loveliness. You did not know her all those years she was thought homely, or see her poring over her baby pictures, making me tell her over and over how beautiful she had been—and would be, I would tell her—and was now, to the seeing eye. But the seeing eyes were few or nonexistent. Including mine.

I nursed her. They feel that's important nowadays. I nursed all the children, but with her, with all the fierce rigidity of first motherhood, I did like the books then said. Though her cries battered me to trembling and my breasts ached with swollenness, I waited till the clock decreed.

Why do I put that first? I do not even know if it matters, or if it explains anything.

She was a beautiful baby. She blew shining bubbles of sound. She loved motion, loved light, loved color and music and textures. She would lie on the floor in her blue overalls patting the surface so hard in ecstasy her hands and feet would blur. She was a miracle to me, but when she was eight months old I had to leave her daytimes with the woman downstairs to whom she was no miracle at all, for I worked or looked for work and for Emily's father, who "could no longer endure" (he wrote in his good-bye note) "sharing want with us."

I was nineteen. It was the pre-relief, pre-WPA[2] world of the depression. I would start running as soon as I got off the streetcar, running up the stairs, the place smelling sour, and awake or asleep to startle awake, when she saw me she would break into a clogged weeping that could not be comforted, a weeping I can hear yet.

After a while I found a job hashing[3] at night so I could be with her days, and it was better. But it came to where I had to bring her to his family and leave her.

It took a long time to raise the money for her fare back. Then she got chicken pox and I had to wait longer. When she finally came, I hardly knew her, walking quick and nervous like her father, looking like her father, thin, and dressed in a shoddy red that yellowed her skin and glared at the pockmarks. All the baby loveliness gone.

She was two. Old enough for nursery school they said, and I did not know then what I know now—the fatigue of the long day, and the lacerations of group life in the kinds of nurseries that are only parking places for children.

Except that it would have made no difference if I had known. It was the only place there was. It was the only way we could be together, the only way I could hold a job.

And even without knowing, I knew. I knew the teacher that was evil because all these years it has curdled into my memory, the little boy hunched in the corner, her rasp, "why aren't you outside, because Alvin hits you? that's no reason, go out, scaredy." I knew Emily hated it even if she did not clutch and implore "don't go Mommy" like the other children, mornings.

---

1. **tenancy** (tĕn′ən-sē): residence.
2. **pre-relief, pre-WPA:** preceding the creation of the welfare and employment programs—such as the Works Progress Administration (WPA)—by which the U.S. government tried to ease the effects of the Great Depression.
3. **hashing:** a slang term for working as a waitress, especially at a diner.

WORDS TO KNOW

laceration (lăs′ə-rā′shən) *n.* a physical, mental, or emotional wound

She always had a reason why we should stay home. Momma, you look sick. Momma, I feel sick. Momma, the teachers aren't there today, they're sick. Momma, we can't go, there was a fire there last night. Momma, it's a holiday today, no school, they told me.

But never a direct protest, never rebellion. I think of our others in their three-, four-year-oldness—the explosions, the tempers, the denunciations, the demands—and I feel suddenly ill. I put the iron down. What in me demanded that goodness in her? And what was the cost, the cost to her of such goodness?

The old man living in the back once said in his gentle way: "You should smile at Emily more when you look at her." What *was* in my face when I looked at her? I loved her. There were all the acts of love.

It was only with the others I remembered what he said, and it was the face of joy, and not of care or tightness or worry I turned to them—too late for Emily. She does not smile easily, let alone almost always as her brothers and sisters do. Her face is closed and somber, but when she wants, how fluid. You must have seen it in her pantomimes, you spoke of her rare gift for comedy on the stage that rouses a laughter out of the audience so dear they applaud and applaud and do not want to let her go.

Where does it come from, that comedy? There was none of it in her when she came back to me that second time, after I had had to send her away again. She had a new daddy now to learn to love, and I think perhaps it was a better time.

Except when we left her alone nights, telling ourselves she was old enough.

"Can't you go some other time, Mommy, like tomorrow?" she would ask. "Will it be just a little while you'll be gone? Do you promise?"

The time we came back, the front door open, the clock on the floor in the hall. She rigid awake. "It wasn't just a little while. I didn't cry. Three times I called you, just three times, and then I ran downstairs to open the door so you could come faster. The clock talked loud. I threw it away, it scared me what it talked."

She said the clock talked loud again that night I went to the hospital to have Susan. She was delirious with the fever that comes before red measles, but she was fully conscious all the week I was gone and the week after we were home when she could not come near the new baby or me.

She did not get well. She stayed skeleton thin, not wanting to eat, and night after night she had nightmares. She would call for me, and I would rouse from exhaustion to sleepily call back: "You're all right, darling, go to sleep, it's just a dream," and if she still called, in a sterner voice, "now go to sleep, Emily, there's nothing to hurt you." Twice, only twice, when I had to get up for Susan anyhow, I went in to sit with her.

Now when it is too late (as if she would let me hold and comfort her like I do the others) I get up and go to her at once at her moan or restless stirring. "Are you awake, Emily? Can I get you something?" And the answer is always the same: "No, I'm all right, go back to sleep, Mother."

They persuaded me at the clinic to send her away to a convalescent home in the country where "she can have the kind of food and care you can't manage for her, and you'll be free to concentrate on the new baby." They still send children to that place. I see pictures on the society page of sleek young women planning affairs to raise money for it, or dancing at the affairs, or decorating Easter eggs or filling Christmas stockings for the children.

They never have a picture of the children so I do not know if the girls still wear those gigantic red bows and the ravaged looks on the every other Sunday when parents can come to visit "unless otherwise notified"—as we were notified the first six weeks.

WORDS TO KNOW

denunciation (dĭ-nŭn′sē-ā′shən) *n.* an act of condemning or accusing another; accusation

ravaged (răv′ĭjd) *adj.* devastated; ruined **ravage** *v.*

Girl Skipping Rope (1943), Ben Shahn. Tempera on board, 15¼" × 23½", gift of the Stephen and Sybil Stone Foundation, Museum of Fine Arts, Boston (1971.702). Copyright © 1996 Estate of Ben Shahn/Licensed by VAGA, New York.

Oh she had physical lightness and brightness... bouncing like a ball up and down up and down over the jump rope... but these were momentary.

Oh it is a handsome place, green lawns and tall trees and fluted flower beds. High up on the balconies of each cottage the children stand, the girls in their red bows and white dresses, the boys in white suits and giant red ties. The parents stand below shrieking up to be heard and the children shriek down to be heard, and between them the invisible wall "Not to Be Contaminated by Parental Germs or Physical Affection."

There was a tiny girl who always stood hand in hand with Emily. Her parents never came. One visit she was gone. "They moved her to Rose Cottage," Emily shouted in explanation. "They don't like you to love anybody here."

She wrote once a week, the labored writing of a seven-year-old. "I am fine. How is the baby. If I write my leter nicly I will have a star. Love."

There never was a star. We wrote every other day, letters she could never hold or keep but only hear read—once. "We simply do not have room for children to keep any personal possessions," they patiently explained when we pieced one Sunday's shrieking together to plead how much it would mean to Emily, who loved so to keep things, to be allowed to keep her letters and cards.

Each visit she looked frailer. "She isn't eating," they told us.

(They had runny eggs for breakfast or mush with lumps, Emily said later, I'd hold it in my mouth and not swallow. Nothing ever tasted good, just when they had chicken.)

It took us eight months to get her released home, and only the fact that she gained back so little of her seven lost pounds convinced the social worker.

I used to try to hold and love her after she came back, but her body would stay stiff, and after a while she'd push away. She ate little. Food sickened her, and I think much of life too. Oh she had physical lightness and brightness, twinkling by on skates, bouncing like a ball up and down up and down over the jump rope, skimming over the hill; but these were momentary.

She fretted about her appearance, thin and dark and foreign-looking at a time when every little girl was supposed to look or thought she should look a chubby blonde replica of Shirley Temple.[4] The doorbell sometimes rang for her, but no one seemed to come and play in the house or be a best friend. Maybe because we moved so much.

There was a boy she loved painfully through two school semesters. Months later she told me how she had taken pennies from my purse to buy him candy. "Licorice was his favorite and I brought him some every day, but he still liked Jennifer better'n me. Why, Mommy?" The kind of question for which there is no answer.

School was a worry to her. She was not glib or quick in a world where glibness and quickness were easily confused with ability to learn. To her overworked and exasperated teachers she was an overconscientious "slow learner" who kept trying to catch up and was absent entirely too often.

I let her be absent, though sometimes the illness was imaginary. How different from my now-strictness about attendance with the others. I wasn't working. We had a new baby, I was home anyhow. Sometimes, after Susan grew old enough, I would keep her home from school, too, to have them all together.

Mostly Emily had asthma, and her breathing, harsh and labored, would fill the house with a curiously tranquil sound. I would bring the two old dresser mirrors and her boxes of collections to her bed. She would select beads and single earrings, bottle tops and shells, dried flowers and pebbles, old postcards and scraps, all sorts of oddments; then she and Susan would play Kingdom, setting up landscapes and furniture, peopling them with action.

Those were the only times of peaceful companionship between her and Susan. I have edged away from it, that poisonous feeling between them, that terrible balancing of hurts and needs I had to do between the two, and did so badly, those earlier years.

Oh there are conflicts between the others too, each one human, needing, demanding, hurting, taking—but only between Emily and Susan, no, Emily toward Susan that corroding resentment. It seems so obvious on the surface, yet it is not obvious. Susan, the second child, Susan, golden- and curly-haired and chubby, quick and articulate and assured, everything in appearance and manner. Emily was not; Susan, not able to resist Emily's precious things, losing or sometimes clumsily breaking them; Susan telling jokes and riddles to company for applause while Emily sat silent (to say to me later: that was *my* riddle, Mother, I told it to Susan); Susan,

4. **Shirley Temple:** a famous child star of the 1930s.

WORDS TO KNOW

articulate (är-tĭk'yə-lĭt) *adj.* clear and effective in speech who for all the five years' difference in age was just a year behind Emily in developing physically.

I am glad for that slow physical development that widened the difference between her and her contemporaries, though she suffered over it. She was too vulnerable for that terrible world of youthful competition, of preening and parading, of constant measuring of yourself against every other, of envy, "If I had that copper hair," "If I had that skin. . . ." She tormented herself enough about not looking like the others, there was enough of the unsureness, the having to be conscious of words before you speak, the constant caring—what are they thinking of me? without having it all magnified by the merciless physical drives.

Ronnie is calling. He is wet and I change him. It is rare there is such a cry now. That time of motherhood is almost behind me when the ear is not one's own but must always be racked and listening for the child cry, the child call. We sit for a while and I hold him, looking out over the city spread in charcoal with its soft aisles of light. *"Shoogily,"* he breathes and curls closer. I carry him back to bed, asleep. *Shoogily.* A funny word, a family word, inherited from Emily, invented by her to say: *comfort.*

In this and other ways she leaves her seal, I say aloud. And startle at my saying it. What do I mean? What did I start to gather together, to try and make coherent? I was at the terrible, growing years. War years. I do not remember them well. I was working, there were four smaller ones now, there was not time for her. She had to help be a mother, and housekeeper, and shopper. She had to set her seal. Mornings of crisis and near hysteria trying to get lunches packed, hair combed, coats and shoes found, everyone to school or Child Care on time, the baby ready for transportation. And always the paper scribbled on by a smaller one, the book looked at by Susan then mislaid, the homework not done. Running out to that huge school where she was one, she was lost, she was a drop; suffering over the unpreparedness, stammering and unsure in her classes.

There was so little time left at night after the kids were bedded down. She would struggle over books, always eating (it was in those years she developed her enormous appetite that is legendary in our family) and I would be ironing, or preparing food for the next day, or writing V-mail[5] to Bill, or tending the baby. Sometimes, to make me laugh, or out of her despair, she would imitate happenings or types at school.

I think I said once: "Why don't you do something like this in the school amateur show?" One morning she phoned me at work, hardly understandable through the weeping: "Mother, I did it. I won, I won; they gave me first prize; they clapped and clapped and wouldn't let me go."

Now suddenly she was Somebody, and as imprisoned in her difference as she had been in anonymity.

She began to be asked to perform at other high schools, even in colleges, then at city and statewide affairs. The first one we went to, I only recognized her that first moment when thin, shy, she almost drowned herself into the curtains. Then: Was this Emily? The control, the command, the convulsing and deadly clowning, the spell, then the roaring, stamping audience, unwilling to let this rare and precious laughter out of their lives.

Afterwards: You ought to do something about her with a gift like that—but without money or knowing how, what does one do? We have left it all to her, and the gift has as often eddied[6] inside,

5. **V-mail:** letters sent to and by soldiers in World War II. The mail was photographed on microfilm to make it easier to transport; enlarged prints were made for reading by the recipients.

6. **eddied:** whirled in circles, without progressing forward.

WORDS TO KNOW

preening (prē′nĭng) *n.* dressing and grooming oneself with excessive care; primping **preen** *v.*

coherent (kō-hîr′ənt) *adj.* understandable; logically consistent

anonymity (ăn′ə-nĭm′ĭ-tē) *n.* a state of being unknown or unrecognized, without special or distinguishing qualities clogged and clotted, as been used and growing.

She is coming. She runs up the stairs two at a time with her light graceful step, and I know she is happy tonight. Whatever it was that occasioned your call did not happen today.

"Aren't you ever going to finish the ironing, Mother? Whistler[7] painted his mother in a rocker. I'd have to paint mine standing over an ironing board." This is one of her communicative nights and she tells me everything and nothing as she fixes herself a plate of food out of the icebox.

She is so lovely. Why did you want me to come in at all? Why were you concerned? She will find her way.

She starts up the stairs to bed. "Don't get me up with the rest in the morning." "But I thought you were having midterms." "Oh, those," she comes back in, kisses me, and says quite lightly, "in a couple of years when we'll all be atom-dead they won't matter a bit."

She has said it before. She *believes* it. But because I have been dredging the past, and all that compounds a human being is so heavy and meaningful in me, I cannot endure it tonight.

I will never total it all. I will never come in to say: She was a child seldom smiled at. Her father left me before she was a year old. I had to work her first six years when there was work, or I sent her home and to his relatives. There were years she had care she hated. She was dark and thin and foreign-looking in a world where the prestige went to blondeness and curly hair and dimples, she was slow where glibness was prized. She was a child of anxious, not proud, love. We were poor and could not afford for her the soil of easy growth. I was a young mother, I was a distracted mother. There were the other children pushing up, demanding. Her younger sister seemed all that she was not. There were years she did not want me to touch her. She kept too much in herself, her life was such she had to keep too much in herself. My wisdom came too late. She has much to her and probably nothing will come of it. She is a child of her age, of depression, of war, of fear.

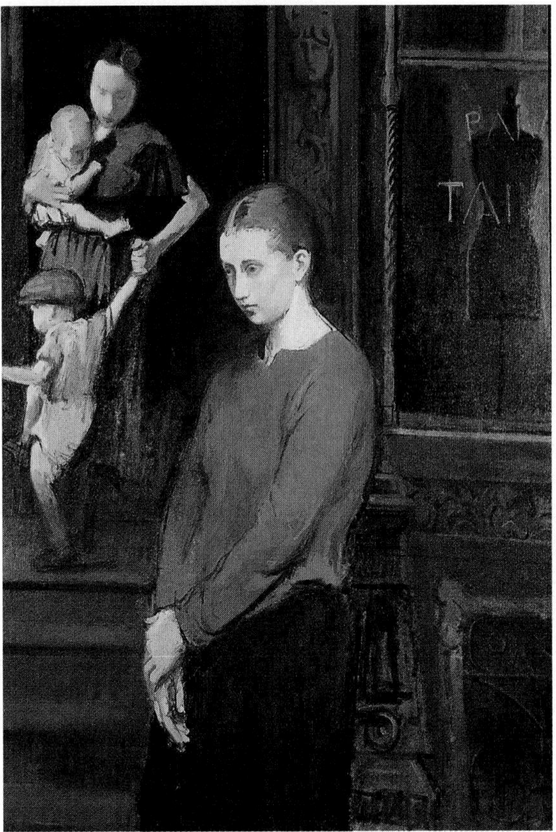

The Brown Sweater (1952), Raphael Soyer. Oil on canvas, 50″ × 34″, Collection of Whitney Museum of American Art, New York, purchase and gift of Gertrude Vanderbilt Whitney by exchange (53.53). Copyright © 1995 Whitney Museum of American Art. Photo by Geoffrey Clements.

Let her be. So all that is in her will not bloom—but in how many does it? There is still enough left to live by. Only help her to know—help make it so there is cause for her to know—that she is more than this dress on the ironing board, helpless before the iron. ❖

7. **Whistler:** James Abbot McNeill Whistler, a 19th-century American painter and etcher. His best-known painting is a portrait of his mother in her chair.

WORDS TO KNOW

dredge (drĕj) *v.* to dig into; unearth

compound (kŏm-pound′) *v.* to form or make up; compose

prestige (prĕ-stēzh′) *n.* honor; admiration

Ironing Their Clothes

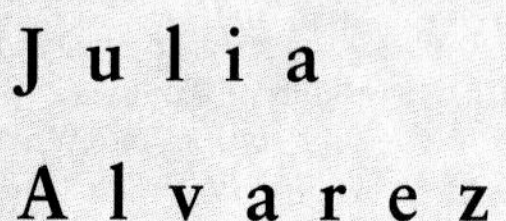

Julia Alvarez

With a hot glide up, then down, his shirts,
I ironed out my father's back, cramped
and worried with work. I stroked the yoke,
the breast pocket, collar and cuffs,
until the rumpled heap relaxed into the shape
of my father's broad chest, the shoulders shrugged off
the world, the collapsed arms spread for a hug.
And if there'd been a face above the buttondown neck,
I would have pressed the forehead out, I would
have made a boy again out of that tired man!

If I clung to her skirt as she sorted the wash
or put out a line, my mother frowned,
a crease down each side of her mouth.
This is no time for love! But here
I could linger over her wrinkled bedjacket,
kiss at the damp puckers of her wrists
with the hot tip. Here I caressed complications
of darts, scallops, ties, pleats which made
her outfits test of the patience of my passion.
Here I could lay my dreaming iron on her lap. . . .

The smell of baked cotton rose from the board
and blew with a breeze out the window
to the family wardrobe drying on the clothesline,
all needing a touch of my iron. Here I could tickle
the underarms of my big sister's petticoat
or secretly pat the backside of her pajamas.
For she too would have warned me not to muss
her fresh blouses, starched jumpers, and smocks,
all that my careful hand had ironed out,
forced to express my excess love on cloth.

RESPONDING OPTIONS

FROM PERSONAL RESPONSE *TO* CRITICAL ANALYSIS

REFLECT 1. What mental picture do you have of the narrator of this story? Imitate her stance, expressions, and manner of movement as she thinks about Emily.

RETHINK 2. Who is the "you" the narrator is addressing, and why is that person asking for her help in understanding Emily? Speculate about what Emily might have said or done to prompt the person's call.

3. What problems do you think Emily might have, and how might her past experiences have contributed to them?

Consider
- her stiffness when her mother would try to hold her
- her resentment toward her younger sister Susan
- her differences from others her age
- the summary in the next-to-last paragraph
- the diagram you made for the Reading Connection on page 642

4. What events in Emily's life might have contributed to her talent for performance?

5. Evaluate Emily's mother as a parent. In your opinion, how responsible is she for the way Emily has turned out?

RELATE 6. Compare the feelings about family members that are expressed in "I Stand Here Ironing" with those expressed in the Insight poem "Ironing Their Clothes." Also, explain what you think ironing represents in each work.

7. Emily is described as "a child of her age." What historical events do you think have shaped your own life, making you a child of *your* age?

ANOTHER PATHWAY

Cooperative Learning

Do you think the narrator of "I Stand Here Ironing" has been a good mother? Get together with a small group of classmates who share your opinion, and jot down evidence to support the opinion. Then join the rest of the class in an informal debate about the narrator's parenting skills.

CRITIC'S CORNER

One critic has pointed out that Olsen writes about people who are victims of harsh social, economic, familial, and political conditions. How well does "I Stand Here Ironing" fit this description? Who are the victims in the story? What conditions have oppressed them?

QUICKWRITES

1. Imagine that Emily has become a star comedienne and that a reporter for a fan magazine has said to her, "Tell me about your mother. How has she influenced your life?" Write Emily's response as part of an **interview.**

2. Drawing on your own knowledge and the experiences of Emily and her mother, draft a **persuasive essay** arguing either (1) that children should not be left in daycare or (2) that children should be provided with better daycare.

PORTFOLIO *Save your writing. You may want to use it later as a springboard to a piece for your portfolio.*

LITERARY CONCEPTS

In a drama, the speech of a character who is alone on stage, voicing his or her thoughts, is known as a soliloquy or a monologue. In a short story or novel, the direct presentation of a character's unspoken thoughts is called an **interior monologue.** An interior monologue may jump back and forth between past and present, displaying thoughts, memories, and impressions just as they might occur to a person's mind. Events follow one another because of the way they fit together in the character's mind, not necessarily because they happened in that order.

"I Stand Here Ironing" is an example of an interior monologue. What is the event that sparks the narrator's interior monologue? What does the interior monologue reveal about the narrator and about her daughter Emily? How do you think the effect of the story would be different if the events were told from the third-person point of view and in chronological order, beginning with Emily's birth?

CONCEPT REVIEW: Metaphor What does the mother mean when she says, in the last sentence of the story, "Only help her [Emily] to know . . . that she is more than this dress on the ironing board, helpless before the iron"? What is being compared to the iron? How appropriate is the comparison?

LITERARY LINKS

1. Compare the mother-daughter relationship in this story with that in "Seventeen Syllables." What do the mothers want for their daughters? How much influence do they believe they have over their daughters' lives?
2. In *Walden,* Henry David Thoreau makes some observations about poverty (page 306, lines 255–256), including that "the setting sun is reflected from the windows of the almshouse as brightly as from the rich man's abode." Imagine a conversation between Thoreau and the narrator of "I Stand Here Ironing." How would their ideas about the effects of poverty differ? What do you think might account for the differences?

ACROSS THE CURRICULUM

Psychology Emily resents her younger sister Susan. Is this a common attitude? Find out what child-development experts say about *sibling rivalry*—conflicts among brothers and sisters. You might search a computer database for current magazine articles on the topic. What contributes to sibling rivalry? What can parents do to lessen it? Report your findings to the class.

History Interview a person who lived through the Great Depression or World War II, asking what family life was like at that time. Were any of the person's experiences similar to Emily's and her mother's? If possible, tape-record the interview and play the tape for the class.

ART CONNECTION

Look again at the paintings shown on pages 643, 646, and 649. What stories do you read into these paintings? Why does the child in the first painting look so sad? What has happened to the red building in the second painting? In the third painting, what is the relationship between the girl in the foreground and the people in the background? Finally, how would you relate these artworks to the story "I Stand Here Ironing"?

Detail of Illustration by Mike Dooling from *Mary McLean and the St. Patrick's Day Parade* by Steven Kroll.

WORDS TO KNOW

Review the Words to Know at the bottom of the selection pages. Then write the word described by each clue below.

1. A whip can cause this; so can a cruel comment.
2. You may do this to buried treasure or to almost-forgotten memories.
3. A mirror isn't required for this activity, but it is helpful.
4. The President has a lot of this; so does a Nobel Prize winner.
5. If a building's design is this, you can probably find your way around in it.
6. Warfare, plague, or famine can cause a nation to be described as this.
7. A secret agent wants and needs this quality; a person seeking fame does not.
8. It is almost impossible to be this if you try to talk with a mouth full of mashed potatoes.
9. One common response to this is "I did not!"; another is "Oh, yeah? Prove it!"
10. Dirt and water do this with respect to mud.

TILLIE OLSEN

1913–

Tillie Olsen began writing as a teenager in the 1930s, during the Great Depression, but stopped to marry and raise a family. A mother of four daughters, she helped support her family by working as a waitress and a secretary, all the time carrying the desire to write "within her" while riding the bus, doing household chores, and working long hours at a job. She has explained, "It is no accident that the first work I considered publishable began: 'I stand here ironing, and what you asked me moves tormented back and forth with the iron.'"

For years hampered in her efforts to write by the struggle to earn a living, Olsen resumed her career only after receiving a fellowship from Stanford University in 1956. She was in her late 40s before she was able to publish *Tell Me a Riddle* (1961), a collection of short stories. Immediately acclaimed, Olsen's book earned her fellowships and university teaching assignments. A high school dropout in the 11th grade, Olsen has nevertheless taught at various schools, including the University of Massachusetts, Stanford University, Amherst College, and the Massachusetts Institute of Technology.

Olsen writes of people who have known economic hardships and whose lives are lived for others. In *Silences* (1978), a book of essays, she explores some of the social, political, and economic conditions that have adversely affected writers—especially women—and the creation of literature throughout history. Through her own personal experiences, Olsen has gained insight into the "thwarting of what struggles to come into being but cannot." Through her writing, she has given voice to those who might otherwise be silent.

OTHER WORKS *Yonnondio: From the Thirties*

LASERLINKS
- *HISTORICAL CONNECTION*
- *AUTHOR BACKGROUND*

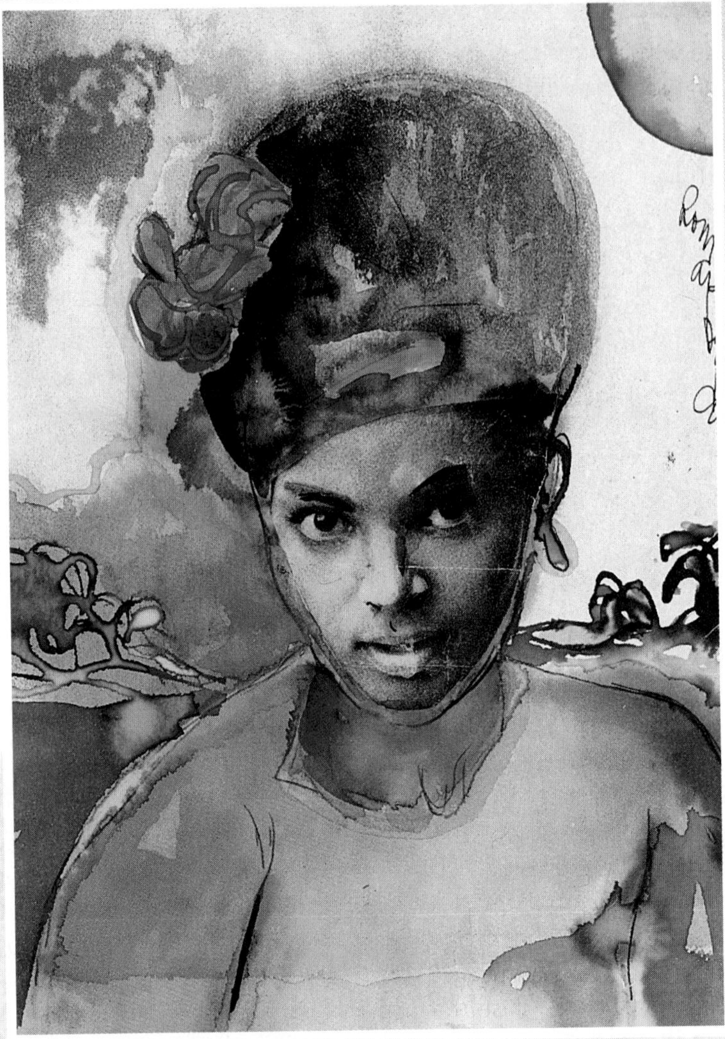

Theresa (1987), Romare Bearden. Watercolor and collage, 8½″ × 11¾″, courtesy of the Estate of Romare Bearden.

ADOLESCENCE—III

RITA DOVE

With Dad gone, Mom and I worked
The dusky rows of tomatoes.
As they glowed orange in sunlight
And rotted in shadow, I too
Grew orange and softer, swelling out
Starched cotton slips.

The texture of twilight made me think of
Lengths of Dotted Swiss.[1] In my room
I wrapped scarred knees in dresses
That once went to big-band dances;
I baptized my earlobes with rosewater.
Along the window-sill, the lipstick stubs
Glittered in their steel shells.

Looking out at the rows of clay
And chicken manure, I dreamed how it would happen:
He would meet me by the blue spruce,
A carnation over his heart, saying,
"I have come for you, Madam;
I have loved you in my dreams."
At his touch, the scabs would fall away.
Over his shoulder, I see my father coming toward us:
He carries his tears in a bowl,
And blood hangs in the pine-soaked air.

1. **Dotted Swiss:** a crisp, sheer cotton fabric decorated with raised dots.

Rita Dove

1952–

Rita Dove has said, "Poetry is language at its most distilled and most powerful. It's like a bouillon cube: You carry it around and then it nourishes you when you need it." In October 1993 Dove became the seventh poet laureate of the United States. She was the youngest person and the first African American to be appointed to that position, which she hoped to use to show that poets are "real people who write about real things" and to cultivate a wider appreciation of poetry, especially among children and teenagers. "Adolescence—III" is the third in a series of three poems she wrote about being young.

Dove grew up in Akron, Ohio, where her father was the first African-American chemist at the Goodyear Tire and Rubber Company. As a child, she wrote plays and stories, created a comic book with her brother, took cello lessons, and listened to music every day with her family. Although her parents restricted the amount of television she could watch, Dove was allowed to visit the library at any time. She would "rush into the local public library with the same eagerness other children reserved for the candy store, thrilled at the prospect of finding many and varied worlds waiting between the covers of all those books."

Educated at Miami University in Ohio and the University of Iowa, Dove also studied drama and poetry in Germany as a Fulbright scholar. She taught English at Arizona State University for eight years and is currently the Commonwealth Professor of English at the University of Virginia. In 1987 Dove won a Pulitzer Prize for *Thomas and Beulah* (1986), a book of poems based on the lives of her maternal grandparents.

OTHER WORKS *Fifth Sunday, Grace Notes, Museum, Through the Ivory Gate, Mother Love*

WRITING ABOUT
LITERATURE

How You Look at It

Can you identify with the teenager Rosie or with the woman imprisoned in a room with hideous wallpaper? A good writer uses point of view to help the reader empathize with some characters, to feel what they're feeling. On the following pages you will

- learn why writers use different points of view
- analyze how point of view shapes a story
- view a scene through someone else's eyes

The Writer's Style: Point of View Point of view is the narrative perspective a writer uses to tell a story. In first person, one of the characters in the story tells the tale, while in third person, an outside observer does so.

Read the Literature

These authors chose specific points of view to tell their stories.

Literature Models

Third-Person Limited Point of View
How much does the narrator see? Which characters' feelings and motivations are described?

And from the place in the fields where she stood, frightened and vacillating, Rosie saw her father enter the house. Soon Mr. Kuroda came out alone, putting on his coat. Mr. Kuroda got into his car and backed out down the driveway onto the highway. Next her father emerged, also alone, something in his arms (it was the picture, she realized), and, going over to the bathhouse woodpile, he threw the picture on the ground and picked up the axe.

Hisaye Yamamoto
from "Seventeen Syllables"

First-Person Point of View
How does the point of view in this paragraph affect the information the reader receives?

John is a physician, and *perhaps*—(I would not say it to a living soul, of course, but this is dead paper and a great relief to my *mind*) —*perhaps* that is one reason I do not get well faster.

You see he does not believe I am sick!

And what can one do?

Charlotte Perkins Gilman
from "The Yellow Wallpaper"

Connect to Life

Writers of both fiction and nonfiction use first- or third-person point of view. Newspapers and magazines generally use an objective third-person point of view in their news articles.

Magazine Article

Today, some folks still think girls are innately weaker in math and science. Others say it's *schools* that are the problem. Recently Myra and David Sadker, two education professors, published a book about this very thing, called *Failing at Fairness*. According to them, because of ingrained, often unconscious, sexism in the way science is taught and tested, girls get turned off.

Margie
from "Three girls and their bunsen burners"
Sassy

Third-Person Point of View
Are several sides of the issue presented?

Try Your Hand: Point of View

1. **A New Point of View** Rewrite the excerpt from "Seventeen Syllables" so it is told from the father's point of view. Use your imagination to fill in missing information.
2. **From Your Eyes Only** Use first-person point of view to briefly describe a situation you've experienced. You might describe a disagreement or difference of opinion you had with someone. Describe only things you saw and felt.
3. **Seeing Things Differently** Now rewrite your description, using a third-person point of view. Compare the differences in the two descriptions. Which version seems more accurate?

SkillBuilder

WRITER'S CRAFT

Recognizing Connotations

Some words have two kinds of meanings. Denotations are their literal dictionary meanings. Connotations are their implied meanings—positive or negative feelings associated with the word.

When Yamamoto describes Rosie's father as having to "resort" to solitaire, *resort* has the negative connotation of "turning to for use as a last available option." Solitaire is a poor substitute for the father's regular card games.

Later, Yamamoto describes an "immaculate" white handkerchief that belongs to Mr. Kuroda. The word *immaculate* has positive connotations that help Yamamoto paint a picture of a meticulous, formal gentleman.

Point of view can influence a writer's choice of words. For example, when using first person, writers often select words for their connotations—words that would signal the attitude held by the narrator.

APPLYING WHAT YOU'VE LEARNED

For each of the following words, find two synonyms. One synonym should have a different connotation, and the other should be more objective.

1. skinny
2. gobbled
3. ecstatic
4. sauntered

Analysis

When you read "Seventeen Syllables," did you want to know how Rosie's father felt about the situation? You were reacting to the third-person limited point of view and its effect on characterization. Point of view can influence how plot and setting are presented too.

GUIDED ASSIGNMENT

Analyzing Point of View In Unit Four, you analyzed all the elements of a story. Here, you will focus on just one element—point of view. You'll look at a story and determine how the point of view affects other story elements.

Student's Prewriting Chart

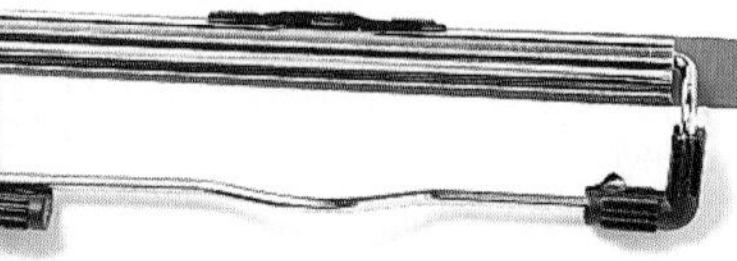

Seventeen Syllables

as Yamamoto tells the story	as the story could have been told
Point of View Third-person limited	**Point of View** First person: Rosie
Plot - Moved by Rosie's action - Do get a feel for what other characters are doing	**Plot** - Still moved by Rosie's actions - However, the story probably would have focused less on haiku-writing and more on Jesus.
Setting - We only see places Rosie sees. - These places are described objectively.	**Setting** - We only see places Rosie sees - These places probably would have been described using words with more connotations.
Characters - We know more about Rosie than anyone else. - But we do learn something about Rosie's mother's and Jesus' feelings.	**Characters** - We would definitely find out more about how Rosie felt. - We wouldn't know how Jesus felt.

1 Prewrite and Explore

Select a story from Unit Five to analyze. Which story has an intriguing point of view? Which characters did you identify with?

IDENTIFY POINT OF VIEW

Read through the story and determine the point of view. Ask yourself

- Who tells this story?
- Is the narrator a participant in the story?
- How much is the narrator able to tell about the characters?

EXAMINE RELATIONSHIPS

Read through the story again. Examine how the point of view influences other story elements. Ask yourself

- Would the plot change if the point of view were different?
- Does the point of view affect which places are shown in the story or how they are viewed?
- Are some characters described more than others? Does the point of view influence how characters are described?
- How would this story be different if told from another point of view?

Use a chart like the one above to organize your thoughts.

Decision Point Look for an angle—the thing that makes the point of view particularly important to the story. Use this as the focus for your analysis.

2 Freewrite

Now it's time to get some ideas down on paper. It might help to freewrite, to start exploring relationships.

Student's Freewriting

When I first read "Seventeen Syllables," I thought it was great the way the author followed Rosie around. Being a teenage girl myself, I felt it is only natural that Rosie should be the focus of the story! But, now that I know more about point of view, I wondered why Yamamoto didn't just write the story in first person. What advantage is there to using third-person limited? Was the author able to get into other people's minds? Did she see things from a more objective point of view?

Advantages of third person might be a good focus for the analysis.

3 Share and Draft

When you're finished, get some feedback from a classmate. Explore answers to the following questions together. Try to select a direction for your analysis.

PEER RESPONSE

- What points am I trying to make in this paper?
- Which aspect of this draft is the strongest?
- Did I analyze all the ways point of view affects the story?
- What other directions should I explore?

With this feedback in mind, revise your draft. Be sure your analysis has an introduction, a body, and a conclusion.

SkillBuilder

WRITER'S CRAFT

Using Formal and Informal Language

The level of language a writer uses is determined by the audience and purpose of the piece. It is also determined, to some extent, by the point of view and who is doing the talking.

Formal Language Formal language is used for formal business or academic purposes, like the analysis you are writing. The tone is serious; contractions, slang, and idioms are avoided. Notice how Yamamoto uses very formal language when Mr. Kuroda talks:

I hope it will serve as a token of our great appreciation for your contributions and our great admiration of your considerable talent.

Informal Language Informal language is used in informal conversation and personal letters. The tone is more casual, the word choice more relaxed. Yamamoto uses contractions, slang (like "gee" and "uh-huh"), and idioms (like "you slay me") when Rosie and her friends talk.

APPLYING WHAT YOU'VE LEARNED
Change the following formal paragraph by Yamamoto to informal English.

I am not worthy. . . . It is I who should make some sign of my humble thanks for being permitted to contribute.

4 Revise, Edit, and Present

As you revise your analysis, try to show as well as tell—use details from the story to make your point. Present your finished analysis to the class, along with other students who analyzed the same story. Discuss the differences in your analyses. Also compare the analyses below. Later, think about which parts of your analysis worked well.

Two Students' Final Drafts

A Point-of-View Haiku!

Told in third person
But longing to be in first
Limited, real, fun!

"Seventeen Syllables" by Hisaye Yamamoto is the story of two Japanese-American women who find new loves. Rosie experiences her first romance; her mother finds happiness through haiku. These loves give them a chance to express themselves and break away from their boring, tomato-farming lives.

Yamamoto effectively uses a third-person limited point of view to tell her tale. This perspective allows the reader to see more than Rosie's limited point of view would. But it also keeps the motivation of others, like Rosie's father, an intriguing mystery.

How does this student briefly describe the story?

Through Rosie's Colored Glasses

Hisaye Yamamoto chose a pointless point of view in "Seventeen Syllables." She uses a third-person limited point of view to tell her story. But instead of getting inside the mind of a really intriguing person like Rosie's father or Jesus, Yamamoto follows Rosie, an inexperienced teenager. So the whole story is told through naive, Rosie-colored glasses!

How does this second student feel about Yamamoto's use of third-person limited?

Standards for Evaluation

A literary analysis
- identifies the author, title, and angle of the story
- breaks the story down into its elements
- analyzes how the elements work together in the story
- summarizes the contribution of each element

Grammar in Context

Pronoun-Antecedent Agreement A pronoun and the noun or pronoun it refers to (its antecedent) should agree in number. In other words, if the antecedent is singular, the pronoun should be too. Pronouns like *another, anyone, anything, each, either, everybody, neither, nobody, one*, and *someone* are singular. *Both, few, many,* and *several* are plural.

> ~~Each~~ *All* of the characters in "Seventeen Syllables"—their emotions and personality—are seen via Rosie. No one is seen unless Rosie sees ~~them~~ *him or her*. For example, readers can tell how Rosie feels about both her parents by the amount of space and dialogue devoted to ~~it~~ *them*.

Notice how the pronouns have been changed so they agree with their antecedents. For more information on pronoun antecedents, see page 1213 of the Grammar Handbook.

Try Your Hand: Making Pronouns and Antecedents Agree

On a separate sheet of paper, rewrite the following sentences so that the pronoun and antecedent agree.

1. Neither of her parents would change their stand on the haiku issue.
2. Another man would have been pleased with their wife's talent and success.
3. Everyone in the family had its own priorities in life.
4. It was either Rosie or Chizuko who turned in their Japanese school lessons.

SkillBuilder

Using First-, Second-, and Third-Person Pronouns

Just as there are first-, second-, and third-person points of view, there are also first-, second-, and third-person pronouns. Nominative case pronouns are used as subjects, objective case as objects.

Person	Nominative	Objective
1st	I	me
2nd	you	you
3rd	he, she, it	him, her, it

Notice how Yamamoto uses third-person pronouns in this narrative:

Her father came after her at noon, bringing her sandwiches of minced ham and two nectarines to eat while she rode, so that she could pitch right into the sorting when they got home.

APPLYING WHAT YOU'VE LEARNED

On a separate sheet of paper, correct the pronouns below. Also identify whether the pronouns are first, second, or third person and nominative or objective case.

1. My best friend and me write poetry too.
2. Mother, should Jesus and I sort these tomatoes?
3. She asked he to stay for tea!

For more information on pronoun forms, see page 1211 of the Grammar Handbook.

R E A D I N G
THE WORLD

THROUGH THEIR EYES

Have you ever seen something clearly, only to find that other people saw that same situation in a completely different way? Detectives, lawyers, and jurors are constantly amazed by the different perspectives people have.

View When you look at this scene, what do you see? Describe the scene on a sheet of paper.

Interpret What do you think happened? Try to describe the situation that led up to this event.

Discuss Compare notes with other students. How many of you described the scene in the same way? Are your descriptions of the situations leading up to the event similar? If not, why not? Have you ever experienced a situation like this? How do you think your mother would describe the situation in this photo? Would her description be different from yours? Check the SkillBuilder at the right for help in understanding other people's perspectives.

SkillBuilder

CRITICAL THINKING

Understanding Other Perspectives

How many times have you been asked to "try and see it from my point of view"? You were being asked to understand someone else's feelings and motives—their perspective.

As you just saw with this photo, not everyone sees a situation in the same way. How you interpret a situation depends on other experiences you've had. Trying to understand why people see things differently is a big step toward understanding how they think and feel.

APPLYING WHAT YOU'VE LEARNED
Try one or more of the following in a small group.

1. Find a controversial photo or quotation in a newspaper or magazine. Survey at least a dozen different people and record their reactions to it. Is there a pattern in how people reacted?
2. Role-play one of the following situations. Halfway through, switch roles. Try to see the situation from the other person's point of view.
   - A parent and teenager disagreeing about curfew
   - Two groups who want to play on the same basketball court
   - Brothers and/or sisters arguing about anything!

PART 2 INTRODUCTION

The American Dream

Illusion or Reality?

In the United States, the closing decades of the 19th century were a time of rapid change and sharp contrasts. Great entrepreneurs—such as Andrew Carnegie, J. P. Morgan, John D. Rockefeller, and Cornelius Vanderbilt—amassed vast fortunes by exploiting cheap labor in the cities and creating giant companies that controlled entire industries. Urban manufacturing centers swelled with the influx of immigrants from Europe and people from rural areas in search of work. Almost half of the U.S. population was crowded in about a dozen cities, and the majority of all U.S. workers were industrial laborers sweating in factories.

As the new century dawned, the belief in America as a unique place where work and merit, rather than social privilege, determined one's fate remained a powerful ideal. Everyone knew of Abraham Lincoln's rise from his early life in a simple log cabin in rural Illinois. Many also knew that the millionaire newspaperman Joseph Pulitzer had come to America as a poor young German-speaking immigrant, recruited to fight in the Civil War. Stories of people who had risen, through their own efforts, from humble beginnings to achieve fabulous success were told and retold.

For many writers, however, the underside of this ideal—the flaws hidden beneath its optimistic simplicity—became a preoccupation. In the novel *Sister Carrie,* Theodore Dreiser challenged the notion of self-improvement by depicting a heroine crushed by forces she cannot control. In *The Jungle,*

Upton Sinclair exposed the appalling working conditions of immigrants in the Chicago stockyards. The poet and folksinger Carl Sandburg presented the seamy side of urban industrialization—the poverty, the crime, the corruption—even as he celebrated the courage and resilience of everyday men and women in the face of these blights.

In their poetry, Edgar Lee Masters and Edwin Arlington Robinson turned their gaze away from the cities to look at the changes surging through rural areas at this time. Each investigated, in a different way, the currents of discontent running beneath the surface stability of small-town life. Paul Laurence Dunbar, the first African American to earn his living solely by his writing, made his own sharp points in America's picturesque veneer by exposing the truth behind popular racial stereotypes of the day.

The American dream of material success was nowhere so minutely explored as in the stories and novels of F. Scott Fitzgerald. Nearly all of his works concern the tension between the very wealthy and those—like him—who were attracted to them. In following the lives of characters whose fates are determined by their responses to wealth and to those who possess it, he gave us intimate insights into the American preoccupation with money.

For the more than 23 million immigrants who came to America in the years 1881–1920, the American dream was not just a compelling ideal

Voices *from the* TIMES

The republic is a dream
Nothing happens unless first a dream.

Carl Sandburg
from "Washington Monument by Night"

The love of wealth is therefore to be traced, as either a principal or accessory motive, at the bottom of all that the Americans do; this gives to all their passions a sort of family likeness. . . . It may be said that it is the vehemence of their desires that makes the Americans so methodical; it perturbs their minds, but it disciplines their lives.

Alexis de Tocqueville
from *Democracy in America*

God gave me my money. I believe the power to make money is a gift from God . . . to be developed and used to the best of our ability for the good of mankind.

John D. Rockefeller

The business of America is business.

Calvin Coolidge

In your rocking chair by your window shall you dream such happiness as you may never feel.

Theodore Dreiser
from *Sister Carrie*

Voices from the Times

Yuh don't belong, get me! Look at me, why don't youse dare? I belong, dat's me! *(pointing to a skyscraper across the street which is in process of construction—with bravado)* See dat building goin' up dere? See de steel work? Steel, dat's me! Youse guys live on it and tink yuh're somep'n. But I'm in it, see! I'm de hoistin' engine dat makes it go up! I'm it—de inside and bottom of it! Sure! I'm steel and steam and smoke and de rest of it! It moves—speed—twenty-five stories up—and me at de top and bottom—movin'! Youse simps don't move. Yuh're on'y dolls I winds up to see 'm spin.

Eugene O'Neill
from *The Hairy Ape*

"Give me your tired, your poor,
Your huddled masses yearning to breathe free,
The wretched refuse of your teeming shore.
Send these, the homeless, tempest-tossed to me:
I lift my lamp beside the golden door!"

Emma Lazarus
from "The New Colossus," inscribed at the base of the Statue of Liberty

America is God's Crucible, the great Melting-Pot where all the races of Europe are melting and re-forming!

Israel Zangwill
from *The Melting Pot*

but a last chance at survival. Many found work building the skyscrapers, the bridges, the subways and trolley lines, the sewers and lighting systems of the growing cities. Anzia Yezierska's moving account of disillusion and persistence in her story "America and I" provides a glimpse of what life was like for immigrants in the sweatshops of New York City's garment district.

Continuity & Change: Dreams Lost and Found

Although the great waves of immigrants from Europe subsided during the 1920s—after the passage of restrictive quota laws—and during the Great Depression of the 1930s, the United States continued to be a "land of opportunity" for those in need. In the 1960s quotas based on nationality were lifted, and another wave of immigration began. This time, however, the immigrants came primarily from Asia and the West Indies rather than from Europe.

These new immigrants came for the same reason as their European predecessors a century before—to make a better life for themselves and their families—but some were also escaping homelands scarred by war and political persecution. A shadow of fear and loss stalks the characters in Lucy Honig's story "English as a Second Language." Gish Jen's delightful story of a Chinese-American family, "In the American Society," injects humor into serious issues of adjustment and assimilation that all immigrants face. And Yvonne Sapia's poem "Defining the Grateful Gesture" addresses the tensions that often exist between immigrant parents and their American-born children.

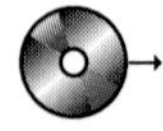

LASERLINKS
• *HISTORICAL LITERARY CONNECTION*

PART 2 *The American Dream*

Illusion or Reality?

Continuity & Change: Dreams Lost and Found

PREVIEWING

POETRY

Chicago
Carl Sandburg

Lucinda Matlock
Edgar Lee Masters

PERSONAL CONNECTION

Where would you prefer to live—the city or the country? Why? Which environment do you think would let you live your life to the fullest? In your notebook, make charts like the ones shown, listing some positive and negative features of city life and of country life. Then, as you read these poems, compare your own ideas with those of the speakers.

City	
Pros	Cons
sports stadiums	smog

Country	
Pros	Cons

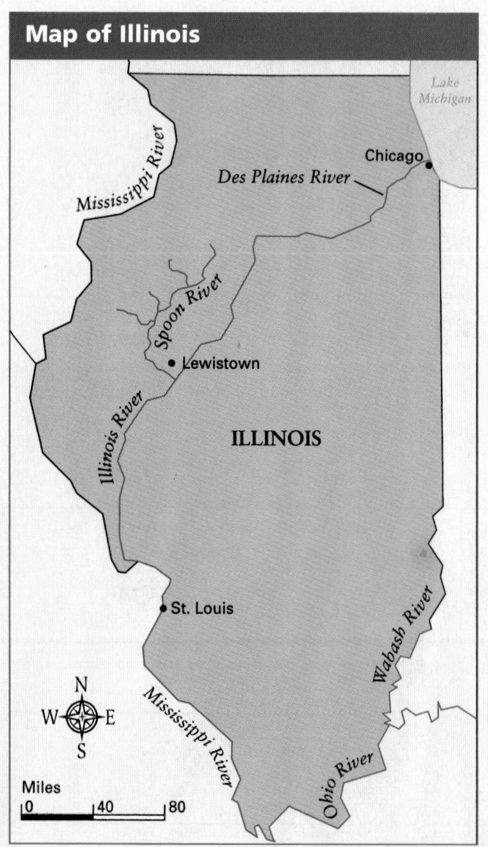

HISTORICAL/BIOGRAPHICAL CONNECTION

Carl Sandburg and Edgar Lee Masters wrote poetry that captured the vitality of America in the early 20th century. What Sandburg found when he moved to Chicago in 1913 was a metropolis of bustling industry and appalling slums, cultural achievements and criminal activity. From the ruins of a devastating 1871 fire, Chicago had risen to become the railroad hub of the nation and a center of meatpacking and manufacturing. At the same time, the city's population had increased explosively as people moved there from small towns in the Midwest and the South to find work. Written in 1914, "Chicago" catalogs both the negative and the positive aspects of the city, reflecting the energy and enthusiasm of its citizens in the early 1900s.

"Lucinda Matlock" is from Masters's *Spoon River Anthology,* a collection of 244 free-verse monologues spoken by deceased inhabitants of the fictional town of Spoon River, who disclose the joys and tragedies of their lives as they speak from the grave. Masters patterned these characters on the people he had observed while growing up in Lewistown, near the Spoon River of central Illinois. His model for Lucinda Matlock was his grandmother Lucinda, who died in 1910 at the age of 96.

LASERLINKS
- *HISTORICAL CONNECTION*

READING CONNECTION

Movies of the Mind

READING STRATEGIES

Reading is an active process of exploration in which your mind is constantly making sense of what you "take in" from the printed page. However, your mind can't take in a piece of writing all at once. You have to read it bit by bit. As your reading proceeds, sometimes the last bits you take in change the meaning of the earlier bits. For example, have you ever started out not liking a character in a story and then found yourself liking the character by the time you finished reading? A surprise ending can even make you rethink your reaction to a whole story.

One way to understand the process of reading is to think of your mind as a video camera with a personality—your personality. In this exercise you are going to turn the video camera down to slow motion so that you can look at what's going on in your mind as you read. What you end up with will be your version of the movie that's playing in your head. Just as athletes can improve their moves by watching videos of themselves in action, you can improve your reading skills by becoming aware of how your mind works when you read a poem.

STEP 1. Turn to the poem "Chicago" on the next page and cover everything after line 8 (the lines beginning "And having answered so . . .") with a sheet of paper. Read lines 1–8, then stop. Take a few minutes to freewrite what was going on in your mind as you were reading the lines and afterward, when you tried to make sense of the words. What does the poem mean to you so far? What ideas, sounds, and pictures stand out in your mind? What did the lines make you feel, think of, or remember?

Sometimes, your mind draws a blank during a first reading. If this happens, read the lines a few more times and then freewrite your response. Write down any words or phrases that stump you, and record any frustration or impatience you feel.

STEP 2. Now uncover and read lines 9–17, still keeping the last lines of the poem covered. Stop and freewrite your response again. What do you think the poem is saying or going to say? Has there been anything that you particularly like in the poem so far? Try to be as specific and as honest as you can. Your goal is to record how your mind is working.

STEP 3. Read the rest of the poem (lines 18–23) and freewrite your response.

STEP 4. Read the poem from start to finish at least two more times. You may have new insights or reversals when you read the poem as a whole, or you may just feel more certain of what you thought before. In any case, be sure to freewrite your response.

Using Your Reading Log Do all your freewriting for this exercise in your reading log so that you can compare your experience of reading poetry with the experiences of reading fiction that you have been recording. Then, as you read the poem "Lucinda Matlock," stop after line 9, after line 15, and at the end to freewrite your responses.

City Building (1930), Thomas Hart Benton. From *America Today,* distemper and egg tempera on gessoed linen with oil glaze, 92″ × 117″. Copyright © The Equitable Life Assurance Society of the United States. Copyright © 1996 T.H. Benton & R.P. Benton Testamentary Trusts/Licensed by VAGA, New York. Photo Copyright © 1988 Dorothy Zeidman.

CHICAGO

Carl Sandburg

Hog Butcher for the World,
Tool Maker, Stacker of Wheat,
Player with Railroads and the Nation's Freight Handler;
Stormy, husky, brawling,
City of the Big Shoulders:

They tell me you are wicked and I believe them, for I have seen your
painted women under the gas lamps luring the farm boys.

And they tell me you are crooked and I answer: Yes, it is true I have
seen the gunman kill and go free to kill again.
And they tell me you are brutal and my reply is: On the faces of
women and children I have seen the marks of wanton hunger.
And having answered so I turn once more to those who sneer at this
my city, and I give them back the sneer and say to them:
Come and show me another city with lifted head singing so proud to
be alive and coarse and strong and cunning.
Flinging magnetic curses amid the toil of piling job on job, here is a
tall bold slugger set vivid against the little soft cities;
Fierce as a dog with tongue lapping for action, cunning as a savage
pitted against the wilderness,
Bareheaded,
Shoveling,
Wrecking,
Planning,
Building, breaking, rebuilding,
Under the smoke, dust all over his mouth, laughing with white teeth,
Under the terrible burden of destiny laughing as a young man laughs,
Laughing even as an ignorant fighter laughs who has never lost a
battle,
Bragging and laughing that under his wrist is the pulse, and under his
ribs the heart of the people,
Laughing!
Laughing the stormy, husky, brawling laughter of Youth, half-naked,
sweating, proud to be Hog Butcher, Tool Maker, Stacker of
Wheat, Player with Railroads and Freight Handler to the Nation.

FROM PERSONAL RESPONSE *TO* CRITICAL ANALYSIS

REFLECT

1. Would you want to live in a city like the one depicted in this poem? Elaborate on your ideas in your notebook.

RETHINK

2. Discuss the "Movies of the Mind" exercise you completed for the Reading Connection on page 669. What did you learn about the poems and about yourself?

3. In your opinion, what are the worst and the best aspects of the Chicago presented in the poem?

4. How well do you think Sandburg's poetic style suits his subject?

Consider

- how the city would seem different if described in formal, rhymed stanzas
- the effectiveness of descriptive names like "Tool Maker" in helping you picture Chicago
- how the repetition in the last three lines affects your final impression of the city

Lucinda Matlock

Edgar Lee Masters

Country Dance (1928), Thomas Hart Benton. Oil on panel, 30″ × 25″, private collection. Copyright © 1996 T.H. Benton & R.P. Benton Testamentary Trusts/Licenses by VAGA, New York.

I went to the dances at Chandlerville,
And played snap-out at Winchester.
One time we changed partners,
Driving home in the moonlight of middle June,
And then I found Davis.
We were married and lived together for seventy years,
Enjoying, working, raising the twelve children,
Eight of whom we lost
Ere I had reached the age of sixty.
I spun, I wove, I kept the house, I nursed the sick,
I made the garden, and for holiday
Rambled over the fields where sang the larks,
And by Spoon River gathering many a shell,
And many a flower and medicinal weed—
Shouting to the wooded hills, singing to the green valleys.
At ninety-six I had lived enough, that is all,
And passed to a sweet repose.
What is this I hear of sorrow and weariness,
Anger, discontent and drooping hopes?
Degenerate sons and daughters,
Life is too strong for you—
It takes life to love Life.

2 snap-out: a game—similar to crack the whip—in which players join hands in a line, then run about trying to shake off those at the end of the line.

17 repose: rest (here the reference is to death, viewed as a quiet, serene sleep).

20 degenerate (dĭ-jĕn′ər-ĭt): showing a decline in vigor or moral strength.

RESPONDING OPTIONS

FROM PERSONAL RESPONSE *TO* CRITICAL ANALYSIS

REFLECT 1. In your notebook, record your opinion of Lucinda Matlock's life.

RETHINK 2. Share with classmates part or all of your "Movies of the Mind" exercise for "Lucinda Matlock." Compare your reading process with those of others.

3. How would you describe Lucinda Matlock's approach to life?

4. Do you think Lucinda is fair in her judgment of the "degenerate sons and daughters"? Explain your opinion.

   Consider
   - the attitudes she attributes to them in lines 18–19
   - what she might mean by her statements in lines 21–22

RELATE 5. How is Lucinda Matlock similar to and different from the people that the speaker of "Chicago" admires? Support your answer.

6. Would you rather live in Sandburg's Chicago or Lucinda Matlock's Spoon River? Consider the positive and negative aspects of country and city life you recorded for the Personal Connection on page 668.

ANOTHER PATHWAY

Cooperative Learning

Get together with a small group of classmates. Imagine that you are a team of anthropologists investigating American life in the early 20th century and that your only two sources of information are "Chicago" and "Lucinda Matlock." Develop a description of the life of the time, based only on the two poems.

LITERARY CONCEPTS

At the beginning and the end of "Chicago," the city is described with a string of **epithets**—descriptive names—such as "Hog Butcher for the World." What do these epithets convey to you about the city? What if Sandburg had instead begun his poem "Here hogs are butchered, / Tools are made, wheat is stacked . . ."? Come up with several epithets that describe your own city or town.

CONCEPT REVIEW: Personification Starting at line 10, Sandburg personifies Chicago as a proud man. What characteristics does the city share with such a man? If you were to personify your own city or town, what kind of person would it be?

QUICKWRITES

1. Write a **poem** about your own city or town or about one you have visited. You might imitate the style of "Chicago," using epithets and personification to depict the town; or you might prefer to present the town indirectly, through a character sketch of a typical resident, as in "Lucinda Matlock." Gather the class's poems into a booklet of poems about communities.

2. Drawing on your charts for the Personal Connection and on your reading of these two poems, draft an **editorial** favoring either city life or country life.

PORTFOLIO Save your writing. You may want to use it later as a springboard to a piece for your portfolio.

ALTERNATIVE ACTIVITIES

1. ***Cooperative Learning*** With a group of classmates, perform a **choral reading** of "Chicago." As you plan the reading, determine the pace, volume, and tones of voice with which the various lines of the poem should be delivered. Also decide which passages will be read by a single voice and which will be read by the whole group.
2. Perform a reading of "Lucinda Matlock" as a **monologue.**

LITERARY LINKS

What similarities do you see between Carl Sandburg's style and Walt Whitman's? After reviewing the lesson on Whitman's poetry (page 312), compare "Chicago" with "I Hear America Singing."

Chicago	I Hear America Singing

CARL SANDBURG

1878–1967

The renowned poet, award-winning historian, and popular folk musician Carl Sandburg was born in Galesburg, Illinois. Forced to leave school when he was 13 in order to find work, he roamed the Midwest as a youth, working at various jobs—including house painting and brick making. Eventually, he turned to journalism. After moving to Chicago in 1913, he became a reporter, editorial writer, and columnist for the Chicago *Daily News.*

The poem "Chicago" was one of Sandburg's earliest literary successes. His verse collections *Chicago Poems*, *Cornhuskers*, and *Smoke and Steel* established his fame as a poet of the people. Because he gave popular public readings around the country, it has been said that no other American writer was so widely read and heard at the same time.

Sandburg won a number of awards and honors, including the 1951 Pulitzer Prize for poetry for *Complete Poems* and the 1939 Pulitzer Prize for history for *Abraham Lincoln: The War Years,* the last four volumes of a six-volume biography.

EDGAR LEE MASTERS

1868?–1950

Edgar Lee Masters had already published 12 books of poetry, essays, and plays before he began writing his masterpiece, *Spoon River Anthology*, which he originally conceived as a work of prose. For the names of the poems' characters, Masters drew on "both the Spoon river and the Sangamon river neighborhoods, combining first names here with surnames there, and taking some also from the constitutions and State papers of Illinois."

The publication of *Spoon River Anthology* in 1915 immediately established Masters as an important American poet. In a review, Carl Sandburg wrote, "The people whose faces look out from the pages of the book are the people of life itself, each trait of them as plain or as mysterious as in the old home valley where the writer came from." In 1920, Masters gave up the Chicago law practice at which he had worked for 30 years and moved to New York City to write full time. He wrote more than 50 books, but none of his later works achieved the critical and popular success of *Spoon River Anthology*.

LASERLINKS
• *AUTHOR BACKGROUND*

PREVIEWING

POETRY

Richard Cory
Edwin Arlington Robinson

We Wear the Mask
Paul Laurence Dunbar

PERSONAL CONNECTION

Have you ever observed people trying to hide their feelings? Why might people sometimes want to conceal their true feelings? What are some situations in which people might have to keep their true feelings secret? Discuss these questions with a small group of classmates. Then as you read these poems, keep in mind why people sometimes hide their feelings.

Illustration by Geoffrey Moss. Copyright © 1977 Washington Post Writer's Group. Reprinted with permission.

HISTORICAL CONNECTION

The first of these poems, Edwin Arlington Robinson's "Richard Cory," is from a famous series of poems depicting the inner lives of people in Tilbury Town, a fictional community modeled on Robinson's hometown of Gardiner, Maine. The second, "We Wear the Mask," is by Paul Laurence Dunbar, one of the first African-American poets to achieve national recognition. This poem was written in the same decade as "Richard Cory"—the 1890s, when a popular form of entertainment was the minstrel show, in which white men with blackened faces performed comedy and variety acts. In an exaggerated mimicry of African-American speech and behavior, blackface minstrels danced and sang sentimental songs while playing banjos, violins, and tambourines. The stereotype of the happy, grinning, dialect-speaking "darky" was the prevailing image of African Americans at the time. In "We Wear the Mask," the speaker reveals the pain such racial stereotyping caused African Americans.

WRITING CONNECTION

Write about a time when you presented a false front to others. Why did you hide your true feelings? In your notebook, copy and complete the following sentences to help you get started.

I can remember hiding my feelings when
I did this because

Richard Cory

Edwin
Arlington
Robinson

Whenever Richard Cory went down town,
We people on the pavement looked at him:
He was a gentleman from sole to crown,
Clean favored, and imperially slim.

And he was always quietly arrayed,
And he was always human when he talked;
But still he fluttered pulses when he said,
"Good-morning," and he glittered when he walked.

And he was rich—yes, richer than a king—
And admirably schooled in every grace:
In fine, we thought that he was everything
To make us wish that we were in his place.

So on we worked, and waited for the light,
And went without the meat, and cursed the bread;
And Richard Cory, one calm summer night,
Went home and put a bullet through his head.

4 clean favored: having a tidy appearance; **imperially:** majestically; royally.

5 arrayed: dressed.

10 schooled in every grace: extremely well-mannered and cultured.

11 In fine: in short

FROM PERSONAL RESPONSE *TO* CRITICAL ANALYSIS

REFLECT **1.** In your notebook, write your reaction to this poem's ending.

RETHINK **2.** Give your impression of Richard Cory, perhaps sketching a picture of him.
Consider
- his physical appearance
- how he speaks to the townspeople
- the feelings he may be hiding and his reasons for hiding them

3. How do the townspeople seem to feel about Richard Cory? Support your ideas with details from the poem.

4. Why do you think Richard Cory kills himself?

5. What would you say is the theme of this poem?

WE WEAR THE MASK

Paul Laurence Dunbar

Detail of *Three Folk Musicians* (1967), Romare Bearden. Collage on canvas on board, 50″ × 60″. Courtesy of the Estate of Romare Bearden.

We wear the mask that grins and lies,
It hides our cheeks and shades our eyes,—
This debt we pay to human guile;
With torn and bleeding hearts we smile,
And mouth with myriad subtleties.

Why should the world be overwise,
In counting all our tears and sighs?
Nay, let them only see us, while
  We wear the mask.

We smile, but, O great Christ, our cries
To Thee from tortured souls arise.
We sing, but oh, the clay is vile
Beneath our feet, and long the mile;
But let the world dream otherwise,
  We wear the mask.

3 guile: slyness and craftiness in dealing with others.

5 myriad subtleties: countless artful statements.

12 vile: disgusting or objectionable.

RESPONDING OPTIONS

FROM PERSONAL RESPONSE *TO* CRITICAL ANALYSIS

REFLECT 1. What lines of "We Wear the Mask" do you have questions about? Share your questions with classmates.

RETHINK 2. In your own words, explain what wearing a mask represents in the poem.
Consider
- the description of wearing the mask as a "debt we pay to human guile"
- who is wearing the mask and why
- the feelings that the mask hides

3. Do you think Dunbar would write this poem if he were living today? Explain your opinion.

4. Is "We Wear the Mask" relevant to people other than African Americans? Why or why not?

RELATE 5. How would you relate "Richard Cory" and "We Wear the Mask" to the idea of the American dream?
Consider
- the life led by Richard Cory
- the lives led by the speakers in each poem

ANOTHER PATHWAY

Both Richard Cory and the speaker of "We Wear the Mask" hide their feelings. To illustrate the contrasts between outer appearances and inner feelings in the poems, complete a diagram like the one shown for each of them. Write descriptive words on the appropriate sides of the diagram.

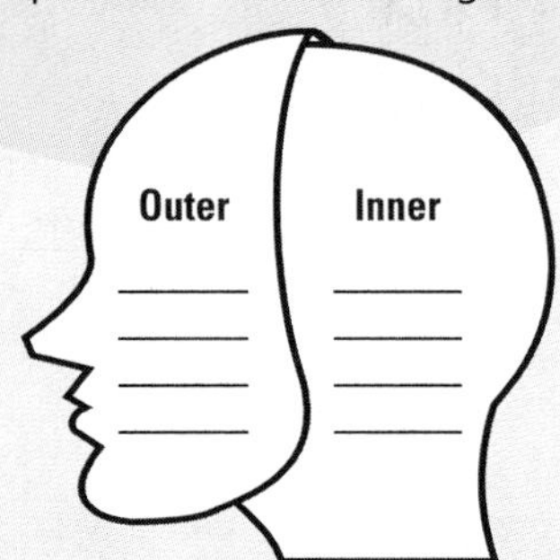

LITERARY CONCEPTS

Both of these poems are traditional in form, with regular patterns of **rhyme** and **meter.** "Richard Cory," for example, consists of four-line stanzas with an *abab* rhyme scheme. Because the poem's meter—iambic pentameter—reflects a rhythm common in English speech, the poem sounds natural, almost conversational. (See the Handbook of Literary Terms to review.) A variation of the meter is used in the next-to-last line—the bunching of stressed syllables in "óne cálm súmmĕr níght" creates a slowing and a tension. This tension is released by the last line, in which the return to the basic meter and the completion of the rhyme scheme with *head* gives the speaker's words a shocking emphasis.

Cooperative Learning With classmates, analyze the rhyme scheme and the meter of "We Wear the Mask." What are the basic patterns? What are the effects of the variant lines?

QUICKWRITES

1. Compose a **note** that Richard Cory might have left, expressing his view of the townspeople and explaining why he took his life.
2. Which poem has more appeal or personal significance for you—"Richard Cory" or "We Wear the Mask"? Write a **personal response** to the poem you choose, telling why you like it or how it relates to your own experiences. You might consider the ideas about hiding true feelings you formulated for the Personal Connection and the Writing Connection on page 675.

PORTFOLIO *Save your writing. You may want to use it later as a springboard to a piece for your portfolio.*

CRITIC'S CORNER

Edwin Arlington Robinson had this to say about "Richard Cory": "There isn't any idealism in it, but there's lots of something else—humanity, may be." What do you think he meant by his comment? Do you agree with his evaluation?

ACROSS THE CURRICULUM

Music Listen to the song "Richard Cory" on Simon and Garfunkel's 1966 album *Sounds of Silence.* Then compare the depiction of Richard Cory in the song with that in Robinson's poem. Which do you prefer? Why?

EDWIN ARLINGTON ROBINSON

1869–1935

A descendant of Anne Bradstreet, New England's first colonial poet, Edwin Arlington Robinson grew up in the river town of Gardiner, Maine. He began writing poetry when he was 11 and had already decided upon a literary career before entering Harvard in 1891. In 1893, after the death of his father, he returned to Gardiner, where he worked as a freelance writer until 1896. He later moved to Greenwich Village in New York City, where he worked at a variety of menial jobs. Although living in poverty and obscurity, Robinson nevertheless continued to pursue his literary ambitions.

Fortunately, Robinson's second volume of poems, the self-published *Children of the Night,* came to the attention of President Theodore Roosevelt, who admired the book so much that he lent the struggling poet a hand by offering him a position as a clerk in the New York Customs House. Robinson gratefully accepted, working there from 1905 until 1909, when he was finally able to begin writing full time. He never married, concentrating instead on his craft, which ultimately rewarded him with a popular following and three Pulitzer Prizes.

OTHER WORKS *Tristram, Merlin, The Selected Poems of Edwin Arlington Robinson*

PAUL LAURENCE DUNBAR

1872–1906

A son of former slaves, Paul Laurence Dunbar was born in Dayton, Ohio, and began to write when he was 12 years old. While in high school, he became editor of the school newspaper and contributed to newspapers published by his friends Orville and Wilbur Wright, later to gain fame as the inventors of the airplane.

After high school, Dunbar took a job as an elevator operator, the only work he could find. His literary career was launched when a former teacher asked him to read a poem before a writers' convention. His first volume of poetry, *Oak and Ivy,* was published in 1893, and the publication of his second volume, *Majors and Minors,* in 1896 attracted the attention of the noted novelist William Dean Howells, whose favorable review helped establish Dunbar's career.

Despite earning critical acclaim, Dunbar felt disappointed that his serious lyric poems, such as "We Wear the Mask," were not as popular as his African-American dialect poems. He told a friend, "I didn't start with dialect, but dialect is what [white] people want. They won't let me do anything else, no matter how much I try. I've got to write dialect if I want them to listen."

By the time Dunbar died from tuberculosis at the age of 33, he had written four novels, four collections of short stories, more than ten volumes of poetry, and several musicals. He unfortunately did not live to see his lyric poems win lasting respect.

OTHER WORKS *Lyrics of Lowly Life, Poems of Cabin and Field, Lyrics of Sunshine and Shadow*

PREVIEWING

FICTION

Winter Dreams

F. Scott Fitzgerald

PERSONAL CONNECTION

This story involves a young man from a small Midwestern town who pursues his dreams. What are your own aspirations? List some of them as labels on a bar graph like the one shown. Then draw bars to indicate, on a rising scale of 1 to 10, the importance you attach to achieving each aspiration.

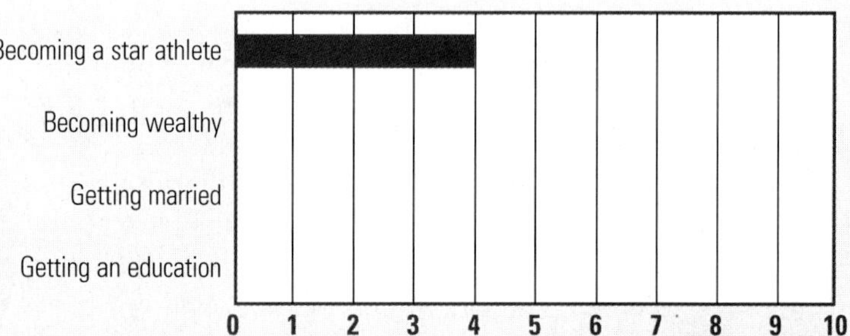

BIOGRAPHICAL CONNECTION

F. Scott Fitzgerald coined the term Jazz Age to convey the glitter and glamour of the 1920s, when many Americans threw themselves into the pursuit of fun, excitement, money, and social status. Fitzgerald and his wife, Zelda, themselves enjoyed the high life, moving among fashionable hotels and resorts in the United States and Europe, giving and attending lavish parties, and engaging in reckless stunts, such as riding on the hoods of taxicabs and jumping into fountains. First published in 1922, "Winter Dreams" provides a glimpse of the wealthy in the United States around the time of World War I. The Minnesota setting is drawn from Fitzgerald's adolescence and early adulthood among the country-club set of St. Paul.

Illustration by Chuck Wilkinson.

READING CONNECTION

Evaluating Characters The characters introduced in the first section of this story are people you will have to make judgments about later. When the story begins, Dexter Green is a teenager and Judy Jones is an 11-year-old girl. As you read, decide what you like and what you dislike about them, and try to figure out why they act as they do. Pay particular attention to the dreams Dexter Green has for his life, forming your own opinions about his aspirations.

Using Your Reading Log Use your reading log to record your responses to the questions inserted throughout the story. Feel free to jot down other thoughts you may have about the story and to make predictions about what will happen to the characters. After you finish reading, share some of your responses with classmates.

• *VISUAL VOCABULARY*

F. Scott Fitzgerald

Winter Dreams

Some of the caddies were poor as sin and lived in one-room houses with a neurasthenic[1] cow in the front yard, but Dexter Green's father owned the second best grocery-store in Black Bear—the best one was "The Hub," patronized by the wealthy people from Sherry Island—and Dexter caddied only for pocket-money.

In the fall when the days became crisp and gray, and the long Minnesota winter shut down like the white lid of a box, Dexter's skis moved over the snow that hid the fairways of the golf course. At these times the country gave him a feeling of profound melancholy—it offended him that the links should lie in enforced fallowness,[2] haunted by ragged sparrows for the long season. It was dreary, too, that on the tees where the gay colors fluttered in summer there were now only the desolate sand-boxes knee-deep in crusted ice. When he crossed the hills the wind blew cold as misery, and if the sun was out he tramped with his eyes squinted up against the hard dimensionless glare.

In April the winter ceased abruptly. The snow ran down into Black Bear Lake scarcely tarrying for the early golfers to brave the season with red and black balls. Without elation, without an interval of moist glory, the cold was gone.

Dexter knew that there was something dismal about this Northern spring, just as he knew there was something gorgeous about the fall. Fall made him clinch his hands and tremble and repeat idiotic sentences to himself, and make brisk abrupt gestures of command to imaginary audiences and armies. October filled him with hope which November raised to a sort of ecstatic triumph, and in this mood the fleeting brilliant impressions of the summer at Sherry Island were ready grist to his mill.[3] He became a golf champion and defeated Mr. T. A. Hedrick in a marvelous match played a hundred times over the fairways of his imagination, a match each detail of which he changed about untiringly—

---

1. **neurasthenic** (no͝or′əs-thĕn′ĭk): weak and lacking in vigor.
2. **fallowness:** disuse.
3. **grist to his mill:** something that he could make good use of.

Illustration Copyright © 1995 Bart Forbes.

Sometimes he won with almost laughable ease, sometimes he came up magnificently from behind.

sometimes he won with almost laughable ease, sometimes he came up magnificently from behind. Again, stepping from a Pierce-Arrow[4] automobile, like Mr. Mortimer Jones, he strolled frigidly into the lounge of the Sherry Island Golf Club—or perhaps, surrounded by an admiring crowd, he gave an exhibition of fancy diving from the spring-board of the club raft. . . . Among those who watched him in open-mouthed wonder was Mr. Mortimer Jones.

And one day it came to pass that Mr. Jones—himself and not his ghost—came up to Dexter with tears in his eyes and said that Dexter was the — — best caddy in the club, and wouldn't he decide not to quit if Mr. Jones made it worth his while, because every other — — caddy in the club lost one ball a hole for him—regularly—

"No, sir," said Dexter decisively, "I don't want to caddy any more." Then, after a pause, "I'm too old."

"You're not more than fourteen. Why the devil did you decide just this morning that you wanted to quit? You promised that next week you'd go over to the State tournament with me."

"I decided I was too old."

Dexter handed in his "A Class" badge, collected what money was due him from the caddy-master, and walked home to Black Bear Village.

"The best — — caddy I ever saw," shouted Mr. Mortimer Jones over a drink that afternoon. "Never lost a ball! Willing! Intelligent! Quiet! Honest! Grateful!"

---

4. **Pierce-Arrow:** a luxury automobile of the day.

The little girl who had done this was eleven—beautifully ugly as little girls are apt to be who are destined after a few years to be inexpressibly lovely and bring no end of misery to a great number of men. The spark, however, was perceptible. There was a general ungodliness in the way her lips twisted down at the corners when she smiled, and in the—Heaven help us!—in the almost passionate quality of her eyes. Vitality is born early in such women. It was utterly in evidence now, shining through her thin frame in a sort of glow.

QUESTION

How does the little girl make Dexter quit?

She had come eagerly out onto the course at nine o'clock with a white linen nurse and five small new golf-clubs in a white canvas bag which the nurse was carrying. When Dexter first saw her she was standing by the caddy house, rather ill at ease and trying to conceal the fact by engaging her nurse in an obviously unnatural conversation graced by startling and irrelevant grimaces from herself.

"Well, it's certainly a nice day, Hilda," Dexter heard her say. She drew down the corners of her mouth, smiled, and glanced furtively around, her eyes in transit falling for an instant on Dexter.

Then to the nurse:

"Well, I guess there aren't very many people out here this morning, are there?"

The smile again—radiant, blatantly artificial—convincing.

"I don't know what we're supposed to do now," said the nurse, looking nowhere in particular.

"Oh, that's all right. I'll fix it up."

Dexter stood perfectly still, his mouth slightly ajar. He knew that if he moved forward a step his stare would be in her line of vision—if he moved backward he would lose his full view of her face. For a moment he had not realized how young she was. Now he remembered having seen her several times the year before—in bloomers.[5]

Suddenly, involuntarily, he laughed, a short abrupt laugh—then, startled by himself, he turned and began to walk quickly away.

"Boy!"

Dexter stopped.

"Boy—"

Beyond question he was addressed. Not only that, but he was treated to that absurd smile, that preposterous smile—the memory of which at least a dozen men were to carry into middle age.

"Boy, do you know where the golf teacher is?"

"He's giving a lesson."

"Well, do you know where the caddy-master is?"

"He isn't here yet this morning."

"Oh." For a moment this baffled her. She stood alternately on her right and left foot.

"We'd like to get a caddy," said the nurse. "Mrs. Mortimer Jones sent us out to play golf, and we don't know how without we get a caddy."

Here she was stopped by an ominous glance from Miss Jones, followed immediately by the smile.

"There aren't any caddies here except me," said Dexter to the nurse, "and I got to stay here in charge until the caddy-master gets here."

"Oh."

Miss Jones and her retinue[6] now withdrew, and at a proper distance from Dexter became involved in a heated conversation, which was concluded by Miss Jones taking one of the clubs and hitting it on the ground with violence. For further emphasis she raised it again and was about to bring it down smartly upon the nurse's bosom, when the nurse seized the club and twisted it from her hands.

---

5. **bloomers:** baggy pants that end just below the knee, formerly worn by young girls.

6. **retinue** (rĕt′n-o͞o′): a group of attendants or followers; entourage.

WORDS TO KNOW

grimace (grĭm′ĭs) *n.* a twisting or distortion of the face
blatantly (blāt′nt-lē) *adv.* in an extremely obvious way; conspicuously

"You damn little mean old *thing!*" cried Miss Jones wildly.

Another argument ensued. Realizing that the elements of comedy were implied in the scene, Dexter several times began to laugh, but each time restrained the laugh before it reached audibility. He could not resist the monstrous conviction that the little girl was justified in beating the nurse.

The situation was resolved by the fortuitous appearance of the caddy-master, who was appealed to immediately by the nurse.

"Miss Jones is to have a little caddy, and this one says he can't go."

"Mr. McKenna said I was to wait here till you came," said Dexter quickly.

"Well, he's here now." Miss Jones smiled cheerfully at the caddy-master. Then she dropped her bag and set off at a haughty mince[7] toward the first tee.

"Well?" The caddy-master turned to Dexter. "What you standing there like a dummy for? Go pick up the young lady's clubs."

"I don't think I'll go out today," said Dexter.

"You don't—"

"I think I'll quit."

The enormity of his decision frightened him. He was a favorite caddy, and the thirty dollars a month he earned through the summer were not to be made elsewhere around the lake. But he had received a strong emotional shock, and his perturbation required a violent and immediate outlet.

CLARIFY

Why does Dexter quit caddying?

It is not so simple as that, either. As so frequently would be the case in the future, Dexter was unconsciously dictated to by his winter dreams.

Now, of course, the quality and the seasonability of these winter dreams varied, but the stuff of them remained. They persuaded Dexter several years later to pass up a business course at the State university—his father, prospering now, would have paid his way—for the precarious advantage of attending an older and more famous university in the East, where he was bothered by his scanty funds. But do not get the impression, because his winter dreams happened to be concerned at first with musings on the rich, that there was anything merely snobbish in the boy. He wanted not association with glittering things and glittering people—he wanted the glittering things themselves. Often he reached out for the best without knowing why he wanted it—and sometimes he ran up against the mysterious denials and prohibitions in which life indulges. It is with one of those denials and not with his career as a whole that this story deals.

He made money. It was rather amazing. After college he went to the city from which Black Bear Lake draws its wealthy patrons. When he was only twenty-three and had been there not quite two years, there were already people who liked to say: "Now *there's* a boy—" All about him rich men's sons were peddling bonds precariously, or investing patrimonies[8] precariously, or plodding through the two dozen volumes of the "George Washington Commercial Course," but Dexter borrowed a thousand dollars on his college degree and his confident mouth, and bought a partnership in a laundry.

It was a small laundry when he went into it but Dexter made a specialty of learning how the

7. **mince:** an artificial, dainty way of walking with short steps.

8. **patrimonies:** estates or money inherited from ancestors.

WORDS TO KNOW **precarious** (prĭ-kâr'ē-əs) *adj.* risky; uncertain

Illustration by Todd Leonardo.

English washed fine woolen golf-stockings without shrinking them, and within a year he was catering to the trade that wore knickerbockers.[9] Men were insisting that their Shetland hose and sweaters go to his laundry just as they had insisted on a caddy who could find golf-balls. A little later he was doing their wives' lingerie as well—and running five branches in different parts of the city. Before he was twenty-seven he owned the largest string of laundries in his section of the country. It was then that he sold out and went to New York. But the part of his story that concerns us goes back to the days when he was making his first big success.

When he was twenty-three Mr. Hart—one of the gray-haired men who liked to say "Now there's a boy"—gave him a guest card to the Sherry Island Golf Club for a weekend. So he signed his name one day on the register, and that afternoon played golf in a foursome with Mr. Hart and Mr. Sandwood and Mr. T. A. Hedrick. He did not consider it necessary to remark that he had once carried Mr. Hart's bag over this same links, and that he knew every trap and gully with his eyes shut—but he found himself glancing at the four caddies who trailed them, trying to catch a gleam or gesture that would remind him of himself, that would lessen the gap which lay between his present and his past.

It was a curious day, slashed abruptly with fleeting, familiar impressions. One minute he had the sense of being a trespasser—in the next he was impressed by the tremendous superiority he felt toward Mr. T. A. Hedrick, who was a bore and not even a good golfer any more.

Then, because of a ball Mr. Hart lost near the fifteenth green, an enormous thing happened. While they were searching the stiff grasses of the rough there was a clear call of "Fore!" from behind a hill in their rear. And as they all turned abruptly from their search a bright new ball sliced abruptly over the hill and caught Mr. T. A. Hedrick in the abdomen.

"By Gad!" cried Mr. T. A. Hedrick, "they ought to put some of these crazy women off the course. It's getting to be outrageous."

A head and a voice came up together over the hill:

"Do you mind if we go through?"

"You hit me in the stomach!" declared Mr. Hedrick wildly.

"Did I?" The girl approached the group of men. "I'm sorry. I yelled 'Fore!'"

Her glance fell casually on each of the men—then scanned the fairway for her ball.

"Did I bounce into the rough?"

It was impossible to determine whether this question was ingenuous or malicious. In a moment, however, she left no doubt, for as her partner came up over the hill she called cheerfully:

"Here I am! I'd have gone on the green except that I hit something."

As she took her stance for a short mashie[10] shot, Dexter looked at her closely. She wore a blue gingham dress, rimmed at throat and shoulders with a white edging that accentuated her tan. The quality of exaggeration, of thinness, which had made her passionate eyes and down-turning mouth absurd at eleven, was gone now. She was arrestingly beautiful. The color in her cheeks was centered like the color in a picture—it was not a "high" color, but a sort of fluctuating and feverish warmth, so shaded that it seemed at any moment it would recede and disappear. This color and the mobility of her mouth gave a continual impression of flux,[11] of intense life, of passionate vitality—balanced only partially by the sad luxury of her eyes.

---

9. **knickerbockers:** loose pants that end in a gathering just below the knee and are worn with long socks—formerly popular as golf wear.

10. **mashie:** an old name for the golf club now known as a five iron.

11. **flux:** change.

WORDS TO KNOW

ingenuous (ĭn-jĕn'yo͞o-əs) *adj.* innocent; naive
malicious (mə-lĭsh'əs) *adj.* wicked; spiteful

She swung her mashie impatiently and without interest, pitching the ball into a sand-pit on the other side of the green. With a quick, insincere smile and a careless "Thank you!" she went on after it.

"That Judy Jones!" remarked Mr. Hedrick on the next tee, as they waited—some moments—for her to play on ahead. "All she needs is to be turned up and spanked for six months and then to be married off to an old-fashioned cavalry captain."

"My God, she's good-looking!" said Mr. Sandwood, who was just over thirty.

"Good-looking!" cried Mr. Hedrick contemptuously, "she always looks as if she wanted to be kissed! Turning those big cow-eyes on every calf in town!"

It was doubtful if Mr. Hedrick intended a reference to the maternal instinct.

"She'd play pretty good golf if she'd try," said Mr. Sandwood.

"She has no form," said Mr. Hedrick solemnly.

"She has a nice figure," said Mr. Sandwood.

"Better thank the Lord she doesn't drive a swifter ball," said Mr. Hart, winking at Dexter.

EVALUATE

What is your opinion of Judy Jones?

Later in the afternoon the sun went down with a riotous swirl of gold and varying blues and scarlets, and left the dry, rustling night of Western summer. Dexter watched from the veranda of the Golf Club, watched the even overlap of the waters in the little wind, silver molasses under the harvest-moon. Then the moon held a finger to her lips and the lake became a clear pool, pale and quiet. Dexter put on his bathing-suit and swam out to the farthest raft, where he stretched dripping on the wet canvas of the springboard.

There was a fish jumping and a star shining and the lights around the lake were gleaming. Over on a dark peninsula a piano was playing the songs of last summer and of summers before that—songs from "Chin-Chin" and "The Count of Luxemburg" and "The Chocolate Soldier"[12]—and because the sound of a piano over a stretch of water had always seemed beautiful to Dexter he lay perfectly quiet and listened.

The tune the piano was playing at that moment had been gay and new five years before when Dexter was a sophomore at college. They had played it at a prom once when he could not afford the luxury of proms, and he had stood outside the gymnasium and listened. The sound of the tune precipitated in him a sort of ecstasy and it was with that ecstasy he viewed what happened to him now. It was a mood of intense appreciation, a sense that, for once, he was magnificently attuned to life and that everything about him was radiating a brightness and a glamour he might never know again.

A low, pale oblong detached itself suddenly from the darkness of the Island, spitting forth the reverberated sound of a racing motor-boat. Two white streamers of cleft water rolled themselves out behind it and almost immediately the boat was beside him, drowning out the hot tinkle of the piano in the drone of its spray. Dexter raising himself on his arms was aware of a figure standing at the wheel, of two dark eyes regarding him over the lengthening space of water—then the boat had gone by and was sweeping in an immense and purposeless circle of spray round and round in the middle of the lake. With equal eccentricity one of the circles flattened out and headed back toward the raft.

"Who's that?" she called, shutting off her motor. She was so near now that Dexter could see her bathing-suit, which consisted apparently of pink rompers.[13]

The nose of the boat bumped the raft, and as the latter tilted rakishly he was precipitated toward her. With different degrees of interest they recognized each other.

---

12. **"Chin-Chin" . . . "The Chocolate Soldier":** three popular Broadway musicals, first performed in 1914, 1912, and 1909 respectively.

13. **rompers:** a loose-fitting one-piece garment with bloomerlike pants.

"Aren't you one of those men we played through this afternoon?" she demanded.

He was.

"Well, do you know how to drive a motorboat? Because if you do I wish you'd drive this one so I can ride on the surf-board behind. My name is Judy Jones"—she favored him with an absurd smirk—rather, what tried to be a smirk, for, twist her mouth as she might, it was not grotesque, it was merely beautiful—"and I live in a house over there on the Island, and in that house there is a man waiting for me. When he drove up at the door I drove out of the dock because he says I'm his ideal."

There was a fish jumping and a star shining and the lights around the lake were gleaming. Dexter sat beside Judy Jones and she explained how her boat was driven. Then she was in the water, swimming to the floating surf-board with a sinuous crawl. Watching her was without effort to the eye, watching a branch waving or a seagull flying. Her arms, burned to butternut, moved sinuously among the dull platinum ripples, elbow appearing first, casting the forearm back with a cadence of falling water, then reaching out and down, stabbing a path ahead.

They moved out into the lake; turning, Dexter saw that she was kneeling on the low rear of the now uptilted surf-board.

"Go faster," she called, "fast as it'll go."

Obediently he jammed the lever forward and the white spray mounted at the bow. When he looked around again the girl was standing up on the rushing board, her arms spread wide, her eyes lifted toward the moon.

"It's awful cold," she shouted. "What's your name?"

He told her.

"Well, why don't you come to dinner tomorrow night?"

His heart turned over like the fly-wheel of the boat, and, for the second time, her casual whim gave a new direction to his life.

3

Next evening while he waited for her to come downstairs, Dexter peopled the soft deep summer room and the sun-porch that opened from it with the men who had already loved Judy Jones. He knew the sort of men they were—the men who when he first went to college had entered from the great prep schools with graceful clothes and the deep tan of healthy summers. He had seen that, in one sense, he was better than these men. He was newer and stronger. Yet in acknowledging to himself that he wished his children to be like them he was admitting that he was but the rough, strong stuff from which they eternally sprang.

When the time had come for him to wear good clothes, he had known who were the best tailors in America, and the best tailors in America had made him the suit he wore this evening. He had acquired that particular reserve peculiar to his university, that set it off from other universities. He recognized the value to him of such a mannerism and he had adopted it; he knew that to be careless in dress and manner required more confidence than to be careful. But carelessness was for his children. His mother's name had been Krimslich. She was a Bohemian of the peasant class and she had talked broken English to the end of her days. Her son must keep to the set patterns.

At a little after seven Judy Jones came downstairs. She wore a blue silk afternoon dress, and he was disappointed at first that she had not put on something more elaborate. This feeling was accentuated when, after a brief greeting, she went to the door of a butler's pantry and pushing it open called: "You can serve dinner, Martha." He had rather expected that a butler would announce dinner, that there would be a cocktail. Then he put these thoughts behind him as they sat down side by side on a lounge and looked at each other.

"Father and mother won't be here," she said thoughtfully.

He remembered the last time he had seen her father, and he was glad the parents were not to be here tonight—they might wonder who he was. He had been born in Keeble, a Minnesota village fifty miles farther north, and he always gave Keeble as his home instead of Black Bear Village. Country towns were well enough to come from if they weren't inconveniently in sight and used as footstools by fashionable lakes.

They talked of his university, which she had visited frequently during the past two years, and of the near-by city which supplied Sherry Island with its patrons, and whither Dexter would return next day to his prospering laundries.

During dinner she slipped into a moody depression which gave Dexter a feeling of uneasiness. Whatever petulance she uttered in her throaty voice worried him. Whatever she smiled at—at him, at a chicken liver, at nothing—it disturbed him that her smile could have no root in mirth, or even in amusement. When the scarlet corners of her lips curved down, it was less a smile than an invitation to a kiss.

Then, after dinner, she led him out on the dark sun-porch and deliberately changed the atmosphere.

"Do you mind if I weep a little?" she said.

"I'm afraid I'm boring you," he responded quickly.

"You're not. I like you. But I've just had a terrible afternoon. There was a man I cared about, and this afternoon he told me out of a clear sky that he was poor as a church-mouse. He'd never even hinted it before. Does this sound horribly mundane?"

"Perhaps he was afraid to tell you."

"Suppose he was," she answered. "He didn't start right. You see, if I'd thought of him as poor—well, I've been mad about loads of poor men, and fully intended to marry them all. But in this case, I hadn't thought of him that way, and my interest in him wasn't strong enough to survive the shock. As if a girl calmly informed her fiancé that she was a widow. He might not object to widows, but—

"Let's start right," she interrupted herself suddenly. "Who are you, anyhow?"

For a moment Dexter hesitated. Then:

"I'm nobody," he announced. "My career is largely a matter of futures."

"Are you poor?"

"No," he said frankly, "I'm probably making more money than any man my age in the Northwest. I know that's an obnoxious remark, but you advised me to start right."

There was a pause. Then she smiled and the corners of her mouth drooped and an almost imperceptible sway brought her closer to him, looking up into his eyes. A lump rose in Dexter's throat, and he waited breathless for the experiment, facing the unpredictable compound that would form mysteriously from the elements of their lips. Then he saw—she communicated her excitement to him, lavishly, deeply, with kisses that were not a promise but a fulfillment. They aroused in him not hunger demanding renewal but surfeit that would demand more surfeit . . . kisses that were like charity, creating want by holding back nothing at all.

It did not take him many hours to decide that he had wanted Judy Jones ever since he was a proud, desirous little boy.

PREDICT

Will Dexter and Judy have a lasting relationship?

WORDS TO KNOW

petulance (pĕch'ə-ləns) *n.* ill temper; annoyance

surfeit (sûr'fĭt) *n.* a fullness beyond the point of satisfaction

4

It began like that—and continued, with varying shades of intensity, on such a note right up to the dénouement.[14] Dexter surrendered a part of himself to the most direct and unprincipled personality with which he had ever come in contact. Whatever Judy wanted, she went after with the full pressure of her charm. There was no divergence of method, no jockeying for position or premeditation of effects—there was a very little mental side to any of her affairs. She simply made men conscious to the highest degree of her physical loveliness. Dexter had no desire to change her. Her deficiencies were knit up with a passionate energy that transcended and justified them.

When, as Judy's head lay against his shoulder that first night, she whispered, "I don't know what's the matter with me. Last night I thought I was in love with a man and tonight I think I'm in love with you—"—it seemed to him a beautiful and romantic thing to say. It was the exquisite excitability that for the moment he controlled and owned. But a week later he was compelled to view this same quality in a different light. She took him in her roadster[15] to a picnic supper, and after supper she disappeared, likewise in her roadster, with another man. Dexter became enormously upset and was scarcely able to be decently civil to the other people present. When she assured him that she had not kissed the other man, he knew she was lying—yet he was glad that she had taken the trouble to lie to him.

He was, as he found before the summer ended, one of a varying dozen who circulated about her. Each of them had at one time been favored above all others—about half of them still basked in the solace of occasional sentimental revivals. Whenever one showed signs of dropping out through long neglect, she granted him a brief honeyed hour, which encouraged him to tag along for a year or so longer. Judy made these forays[16] upon the helpless and defeated without malice, indeed half unconscious that there was anything mischievous in what she did.

When a new man came to town every one dropped out—dates were automatically canceled.

The helpless part of trying to do anything about it was that she did it all herself. She was not a girl who could be "won" in the kinetic[17] sense—she was proof against cleverness, she was proof against charm; if any of these assailed her too strongly she would immediately resolve the affair to a physical basis, and under the magic of her physical splendor the strong as well as the brilliant played her game and not their own. She was entertained only by the gratification of her desires and by the direct exercise of her own charm. Perhaps from so much youthful love, so many youthful lovers, she had come, in self-defense, to nourish herself wholly from within.

Succeeding Dexter's first exhilaration came restlessness and dissatisfaction. The helpless ecstasy of losing himself in her was opiate rather than tonic.[18] It was fortunate for his work during the winter that those moments of ecstasy came infrequently. Early in their acquaintance it had seemed for a while that there was a deep and spontaneous mutual attraction—that first August, for example—three days of long evenings on her dusky veranda, of strange wan[19] kisses through the late afternoon, in shadowy alcoves or behind the protecting trellises of the garden arbors, of mornings when she was fresh as a dream and almost shy at meeting him in the clarity of the rising day. There was all the ecstasy of an engagement about it, sharpened by his realization that there was no engagement. It was

14. **dénouement** (dā′no͞o-mäɴ′): the resolution of the conflicts in a story's plot; a final outcome.
15. **roadster:** a sporty, two-seat open automobile.
16. **forays:** sudden attacks or raids.
17. **kinetic:** involving action.
18. **opiate . . . tonic:** deadening rather than stimulating.
19. **wan** (wŏn): weary or melancholy.

during those three days that, for the first time, he had asked her to marry him. She said "maybe some day," she said "kiss me," she said "I'd like to marry you," she said "I love you"—she said—nothing.

The three days were interrupted by the arrival of a New York man who visited at her house for half September. To Dexter's agony, rumor engaged them. The man was the son of the president of a great trust company. But at the end of a month it was reported that Judy was yawning. At a dance one night she sat all evening in a motor-boat with a local beau, while the New Yorker searched the club for her frantically. She told the local beau that she was bored with her visitor, and two days later he left. She was seen with him at the station, and it was reported that he looked very mournful indeed.

CONNECT

Do you know anyone like Judy? What motivates behavior like hers?

On this note the summer ended. Dexter was twenty-four, and he found himself increasingly in a position to do as he wished. He joined two clubs in the city and lived at one of them. Though he was by no means an integral part of the stag-lines at these clubs, he managed to be on hand at dances where Judy Jones was likely to appear. He could have gone out socially as much as he liked—he was an eligible young man, now, and popular with downtown fathers. His confessed devotion to Judy Jones had rather solidified his position. But he had no social aspirations and rather despised the dancing men who were always on tap for the Thursday or Saturday parties and who filled in at dinners with the younger married set. Already he was playing with the idea of going East to New York. He wanted to take Judy Jones with him. No disillusion as to the world in which she had grown up could cure his illusion as to her desirability.

Remember that—for only in the light of it can what he did for her be understood.

Eighteen months after he first met Judy Jones he became engaged to another girl. Her name was Irene Scheerer, and her father was one of the men who had always believed in Dexter. Irene was light-haired and sweet and honorable, and a little stout, and she had two suitors whom she pleasantly relinquished when Dexter formally asked her to marry him.

Summer, fall, winter, spring, another summer, another fall—so much he had given of his active life to the incorrigible lips of Judy Jones. She had treated him with interest, with encouragement, with malice, with indifference, with contempt. She had inflicted on him the innumerable little slights and indignities possible in such a case—as if in revenge for having ever cared for him at all. She had beckoned him and yawned at him and beckoned him again and he had responded often with bitterness and narrowed eyes. She had brought him ecstatic happiness and intolerable agony of spirit. She had caused him untold inconvenience and not a little trouble. She had insulted him, and she had ridden over him, and she had played his interest in her against his interest in his work—for fun. She had done everything to him except to criticize him—this she had not done—it seemed to him only because it might have sullied the utter indifference she manifested and sincerely felt toward him.

When autumn had come and gone again it occurred to him that he could not have Judy Jones. He had to beat this into his mind but he convinced himself at last. He lay awake at night for a while and argued it over. He told himself the trouble and the pain she had caused him, he enumerated her glaring deficiencies as a wife. Then he said to himself that he loved her, and after a while he fell asleep. For a week, lest he

WORDS TO KNOW

incorrigible (ĭn-kôr′ĭ-jə-bəl) *adj.* impossible to correct or reform; uncontrollable
sully (sŭl′ē) *v.* to spoil; tarnish

imagine her husky voice over the telephone or her eyes opposite him at lunch, he worked hard and late, and at night he went to his office and plotted out his years.

At the end of a week he went to a dance and cut in on her once. For almost the first time since they had met he did not ask her to sit out with him or tell her that she was lovely. It hurt him that she did not miss these things—that was all. He was not jealous when he saw that there was a new man tonight. He had been hardened against jealousy long before.

He stayed late at the dance. He sat for an hour with Irene Scheerer and talked about books and about music. He knew very little about either. But he was beginning to be master of his own time now, and he had a rather priggish[20] notion that he—the young and already fabulously successful Dexter Green—should know more about such things.

That was in October, when he was twenty-five. In January, Dexter and Irene became engaged. It was to be announced in June, and they were to be married three months later.

EVALUATE

Do you approve of Dexter's decision to marry Irene Scheerer?

The Minnesota winter prolonged itself interminably, and it was almost May when the winds came soft and the snow ran down into Black Bear Lake at last. For the first time in over a year Dexter was enjoying a certain tranquillity of spirit. Judy Jones had been in Florida, and afterward in Hot Springs, and somewhere she had been engaged, and somewhere she had broken it off. At first, when Dexter had definitely given her up, it had made him sad that people still linked them together and asked for news of her, but when he began to be placed at dinner next to Irene Scheerer people didn't ask him about her any more—they told him about her. He ceased to be an authority on her.

May at last. Dexter walked the streets at night when the darkness was damp as rain, wondering that so soon, with so little done, so much of ecstasy had gone from him. May one year back had been marked by Judy's poignant, unforgivable, yet forgiven turbulence—it had been one of those rare times when he fancied she had grown to care for him. That old penny's worth of happiness he had spent for this bushel of content. He knew that Irene would be no more than a curtain spread behind him, a hand moving among gleaming tea-cups, a voice calling to children . . . fire and loveliness were gone, the magic of nights and the wonder of the varying hours and seasons . . . slender lips, downturning, dropping to his lips and bearing him up into a heaven of eyes. . . . The thing was deep in him. He was too strong and alive for it to die lightly.

In the middle of May when the weather balanced for a few days on the thin bridge that led to deep summer he turned in one night at Irene's house. Their engagement was to be announced in a week now—no one would be surprised at it. And tonight they would sit together on the lounge at the University Club and look on for an hour at the dancers. It gave him a sense of solidity to go with her—she was so sturdily popular, so intensely "great."

He mounted the steps of the brownstone house and stepped inside.

"Irene," he called.

Mrs. Scheerer came out of the living-room to meet him.

"Dexter," she said, "Irene's gone upstairs with a splitting headache. She wanted to go with you but I made her go to bed."

"Nothing serious, I—"

"Oh, no. She's going to play golf with you in the morning. You can spare her for just one night, can't you, Dexter?"

20. **priggish:** smug; conceited.

WORDS TO KNOW

poignant (poin'yənt) *adj.* emotionally touching or moving

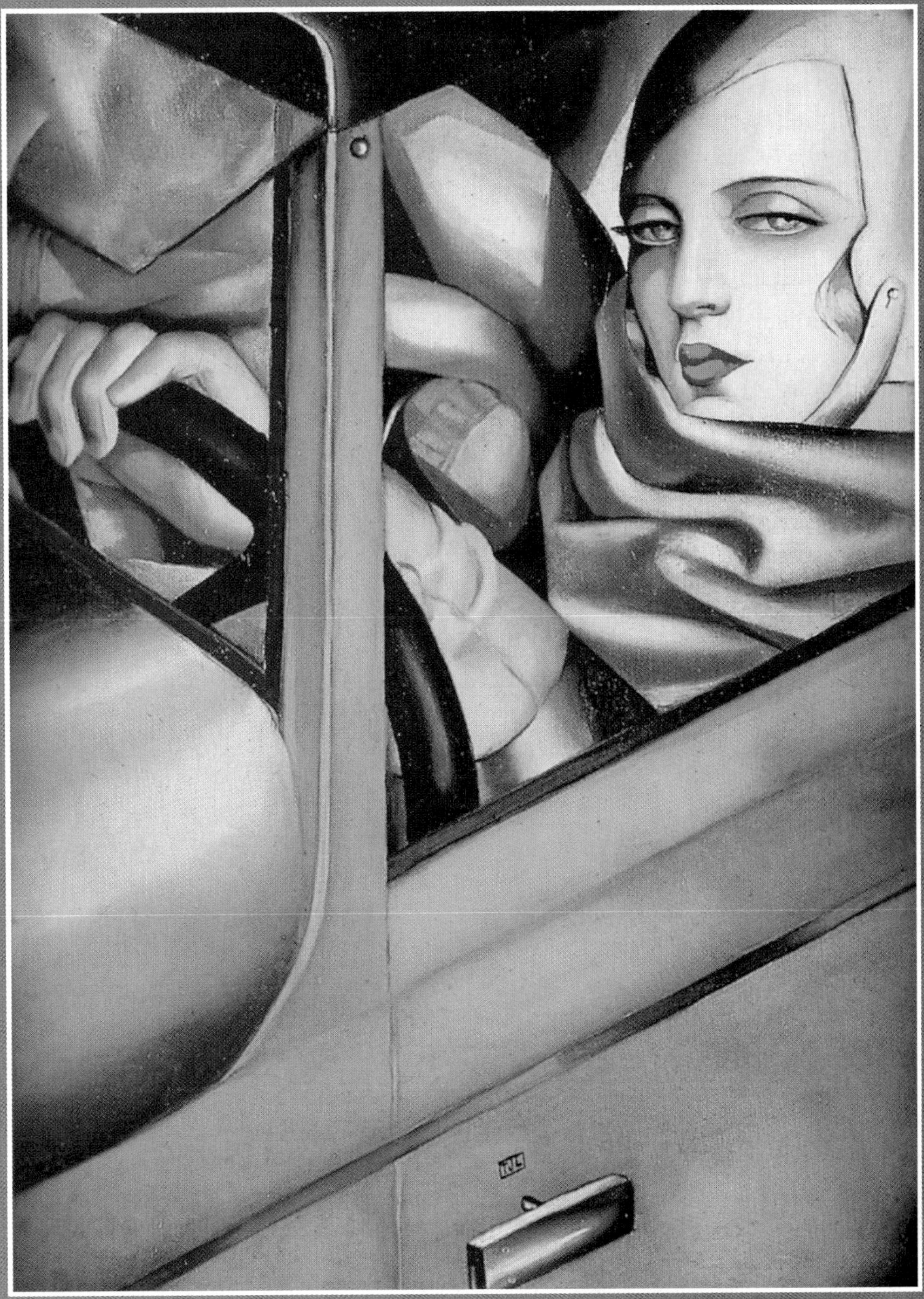

Autoportrait (about 1925), Tamara de Lempicka. Oil on wood, 35 × 26 cm, private collection. Copyright © SPADEM/Kizette de Lempicka Foxhall.

Her smile was kind. She and Dexter liked each other. In the living-room he talked for a moment before he said good night.

Returning to the University Club, where he had rooms, he stood in the doorway for a moment and watched the dancers. He leaned against the door-post, nodded at a man or two—yawned.

"Hello, darling."

The familiar voice at his elbow startled him. Judy Jones had left a man and crossed the room to him—Judy Jones, a slender enameled doll in cloth of gold: gold in a band at her head, gold in two slipper points at her dress's hem. The fragile glow of her face seemed to blossom as she smiled at him. A breeze of warmth and light blew through the room. His hands in the pockets of his dinner-jacket tightened spasmodically. He was filled with a sudden excitement.

"When did you get back?" he asked casually.

"Come here and I'll tell you about it."

She turned and he followed her. She had been away—he could have wept at the wonder of her return. She had passed through enchanted streets, doing things that were like provocative music. All mysterious happenings, all fresh and quickening hopes, had gone away with her, come back with her now.

She turned in the doorway.

"Have you a car here? If you haven't, I have."

"I have a coupé."

In then, with a rustle of golden cloth. He slammed the door. Into so many cars she had stepped—like this—like that—her back against the leather, so—her elbow resting on the door—waiting. She would have been soiled long since had there been anything to soil her—except herself—but this was her own self-outpouring.

With an effort he forced himself to start the car and back into the street. This was nothing, he must remember. She had done this before, and he had put her behind him, as he would have crossed a bad account from his books.

He drove slowly downtown and, affecting abstraction,[21] traversed the deserted streets of the business section, peopled here and there where a movie was giving out its crowd or where consumptive or pugilistic[22] youth lounged in front of pool halls. The clink of glasses and the slap of hands on the bars issued from saloons, cloisters[23] of glazed glass and dirty yellow light.

A perfect wave of emotion washed over him, carrying off with it a sediment of wisdom, of convention, of doubt, of honor.

She was watching him closely and the silence was embarrassing, yet in this crisis he could find no casual word with which to profane the hour. At a convenient turning he began to zigzag back toward the University Club.

"Have you missed me?" she asked suddenly.

"Everybody missed you."

He wondered if she knew of Irene Scheerer. She had been back only a day—her absence had been almost contemporaneous with his engagement.

"What a remark!" Judy laughed sadly—without sadness. She looked at him searchingly. He became absorbed in the dashboard.

---

21. **affecting abstraction:** pretending to be lost in thought.
22. **consumptive or pugilistic** (pyōō′jə-lĭs′tĭk): sickly or aggressive.
23. **cloisters:** places of religious retreat, such as convents and monasteries (here used metaphorically to refer to places of escape from life's problems).

"You're handsomer than you used to be," she said thoughtfully. "Dexter, you have the most rememberable eyes."

He could have laughed at this, but he did not laugh. It was the sort of thing that was said to sophomores. Yet it stabbed at him.

"I'm awfully tired of everything, darling." She called every one darling, endowing the endearment with careless, individual camaraderie. "I wish you'd marry me."

The directness of this confused him. He should have told her now that he was going to marry another girl, but he could not tell her. He could as easily have sworn that he had never loved her.

"I think we'd get along," she continued, on the same note, "unless probably you've forgotten me and fallen in love with another girl."

Her confidence was obviously enormous. She had said, in effect, that she found such a thing impossible to believe, that if it were true he had merely committed a childish indiscretion—and probably to show off. She would forgive him, because it was not a matter of any moment but rather something to be brushed aside lightly.

"Of course you could never love anybody but me," she continued, "I like the way you love me. Oh, Dexter, have you forgotten last year?"

"No, I haven't forgotten."

"Neither have I!"

Was she sincerely moved—or was she carried along by the wave of her own acting?

"I wish we could be like that again," she said, and he forced himself to answer:

"I don't think we can."

"I suppose not. . . . I hear you're giving Irene Scheerer a violent rush."

There was not the faintest emphasis on the name, yet Dexter was suddenly ashamed.

"Oh, take me home," cried Judy suddenly; "I don't want to go back to that idiotic dance—with those children."

Then, as he turned up the street that led to the residence district, Judy began to cry quietly to herself. He had never seen her cry before.

The dark street lightened, the dwellings of the rich loomed up around them, he stopped his coupé in front of the great white bulk of the Mortimer Joneses' house, somnolent, gorgeous, drenched with the splendor of the damp moonlight. Its solidity startled him. The strong walls, the steel of the girders, the breadth and beam and pomp of it were there only to bring out the contrast with the young beauty beside him. It was sturdy to accentuate her slightness—as if to show what a breeze could be generated by a butterfly's wing.

He sat perfectly quiet, his nerves in wild clamor, afraid that if he moved he would find her irresistibly in his arms. Two tears had rolled down her wet face and trembled on her upper lip.

"I'm more beautiful than anybody else," she said brokenly, "why can't I be happy?" Her moist eyes tore at his stability—her mouth turned slowly downward with an exquisite sadness: "I'd like to marry you if you'll have me, Dexter. I suppose you think I'm not worth having, but I'll be so beautiful for you, Dexter."

EVALUATE

How sincere do you believe Judy is?

A million phrases of anger, pride, passion, hatred, tenderness fought on his lips. Then a perfect wave of emotion washed over him, carrying off with it a sediment of wisdom, of convention, of doubt, of honor. This was his girl who was speaking, his own, his beautiful, his pride.

"Won't you come in?" He heard her draw in her breath sharply.

Waiting.

"All right," his voice was trembling, "I'll come in."

5

It was strange that neither when it was over nor a long time afterward did he regret that night. Looking at it from the perspective of ten years, the fact that Judy's flare for him endured just one month seemed of little importance. Nor did it matter that by his yielding he subjected himself to a deeper agony in the end and gave serious hurt to Irene Scheerer and to Irene's parents, who had befriended him. There was nothing sufficiently pictorial about Irene's grief to stamp itself on his mind.

Dexter was at bottom hard-minded. The attitude of the city on his action was of no importance to him, not because he was going to leave the city, but because any outside attitude on the situation seemed superficial. He was completely indifferent to popular opinion. Nor, when he had seen that it was no use, that he did not possess in himself the power to move fundamentally or to hold Judy Jones, did he bear any malice toward her. He loved her, and he would love her until the day he was too old for loving—but he could not have her. So he tasted the deep pain that is reserved only for the strong, just as he had tasted for a little while the deep happiness.

Even the ultimate falsity of the grounds upon which Judy terminated the engagement—that she did not want to "take him away" from Irene—Judy, who had wanted nothing else—did not revolt him. He was beyond any revulsion or any amusement.

EVALUATE

What do you think of Dexter's response to Judy's betrayal?

He went East in February with the intention of selling out his laundries and settling in New York—but the war came to America in March and changed his plans. He returned to the West, handed over the management of the business to his partner, and went into the first officers' training-camp in late April. He was one of those young thousands who greeted the war with a certain amount of relief, welcoming the liberation from webs of tangled emotion.

Illustration by Joseph Lyendecker. Courtesy of Cluett, Peabody & Co., Inc.

He tasted the deep pain

that is reserved

only for the strong,

just as he had tasted

for a little while

the deep happiness.

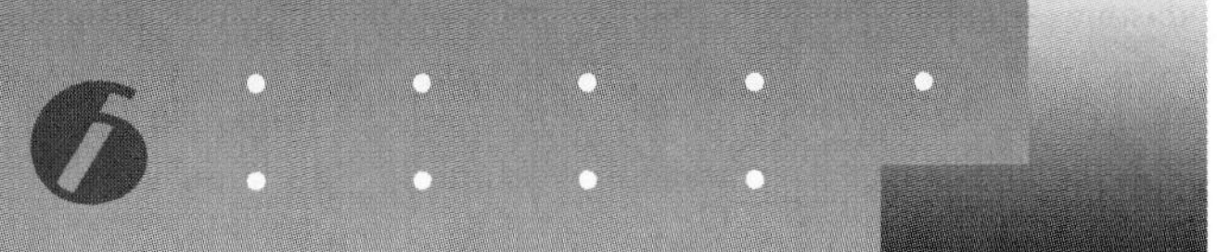

This story is not his biography, remember, although things creep into it which have nothing to do with those dreams he had when he was young. We are almost done with them and with him now. There is only one more incident to be related here, and it happens seven years farther on.

It took place in New York, where he had done well—so well that there were no barriers too high for him. He was thirty-two years old, and, except for one flying trip immediately after the war, he had not been West in seven years. A man named Devlin from Detroit came into his office to see him in a business way, and then and there this incident occurred, and closed out, so to speak, this particular side of his life.

"So you're from the Middle West," said the man Devlin with careless curiosity. "That's funny—I thought men like you were probably born and raised on Wall Street. You know—wife of one of my best friends in Detroit came from your city. I was an usher at the wedding."

Dexter waited with no apprehension of what was coming.

"Judy Simms," said Devlin with no particular interest; "Judy Jones she was once."

"Yes, I knew her." A dull impatience spread over him. He had heard, of course, that she was married—perhaps deliberately he had heard no more.

"Awfully nice girl," brooded Devlin meaninglessly, "I'm sort of sorry for her."

"Why?" Something in Dexter was alert, receptive, at once.

"Oh, Lud Simms has gone to pieces in a way. I don't mean he ill-uses her, but he drinks and runs around—"

"Doesn't she run around?"

"No. Stays at home with her kids."

"Oh."

"She's a little too old for him," said Devlin.

"Too old!" cried Dexter. "Why, man, she's only twenty-seven."

He was possessed with a wild notion of rushing out into the streets and taking a train to Detroit. He rose to his feet spasmodically.

"I guess you're busy," Devlin apologized quickly. "I didn't realize—"

"No, I'm not busy," said Dexter, steadying his voice. "I'm not busy at all. Not busy at all. Did you say she was—twenty-seven? No, I said she was twenty-seven."

"Yes, you did," agreed Devlin dryly.

"Go on, then. Go on."

"What do you mean?"

"About Judy Jones."

Devlin looked at him helplessly.

"Well, that's—I told you all there is to it. He treats her like the devil. Oh, they're not going to get divorced or anything. When he's particularly outrageous she forgives him. In fact, I'm inclined to think she loves him. She was a pretty girl when she first came to Detroit."

A pretty girl! The phrase struck Dexter as ludicrous.

"Isn't she—a pretty girl, any more?"

"Oh, she's all right."

"Look here," said Dexter, sitting down suddenly. "I don't understand. You say she was a 'pretty girl' and now you say she's 'all right.' I don't understand what you mean—Judy Jones wasn't a pretty girl, at all. She was a great beauty. Why, I knew her, I knew her. She was—"

Devlin laughed pleasantly.

"I'm not trying to start a row,[24]" he said. "I think Judy's a nice girl and I like her. I can't understand how a man like Lud Simms could fall madly in love with her, but he did." Then he added: "Most of the women like her."

QUESTION

Why do you think Judy married Lud Simms?

Dexter looked closely at Devlin, thinking wildly that there must be a reason for this, some insensitivity in the man or some private malice.

24. **row** (rou): a noisy argument or dispute.

"Lots of women fade just like *that,*" Devlin snapped his fingers. "You must have seen it happen. Perhaps I've forgotten how pretty she was at her wedding. I've seen her so much since then, you see. She has nice eyes."

A sort of dullness settled down upon Dexter. For the first time in his life he felt like getting very drunk. He knew that he was laughing loudly at something Devlin had said, but he did not know what it was or why it was funny. When, in a few minutes, Devlin went he lay down on his lounge and looked out the window at the New York sky-line into which the sun was sinking in dull lovely shades of pink and gold.

He had thought that having nothing else to lose he was invulnerable at last—but he knew that he had just lost something more, as surely as if he had married Judy Jones and seen her fade away before his eyes.

The dream was gone. Something had been taken from him. In a sort of panic he pushed the palms of his hands into his eyes and tried to bring up a picture of the waters lapping on Sherry Island and the moonlit veranda, and gingham on the golf-links and the dry sun and the gold color of her neck's soft down. And her mouth damp to his kisses and her eyes plaintive with melancholy and her freshness like new fine linen in the morning. Why, these things were no longer in the world! They had existed and they existed no longer.

For the first time in years the tears were streaming down his face. But they were for himself now. He did not care about mouth and eyes and moving hands. He wanted to care, and he could not care. For he had gone away and he could never go back any more. The gates were closed, the sun was gone down, and there was no beauty but the gray beauty of steel that withstands all time. Even the grief he could have borne was left behind in the country of illusion, of youth, of the richness of life, where his winter dreams had flourished.

CLARIFY

What makes Dexter so sad?

"Long ago," he said, "long ago, there was something in me, but now that thing is gone. Now that thing is gone, that thing is gone. I cannot cry. I cannot care. That thing will come back no more." ❖

The gates were closed,

the sun was gone down,

and there was no beauty

but the gray

beauty

of steel

that withstands all time.

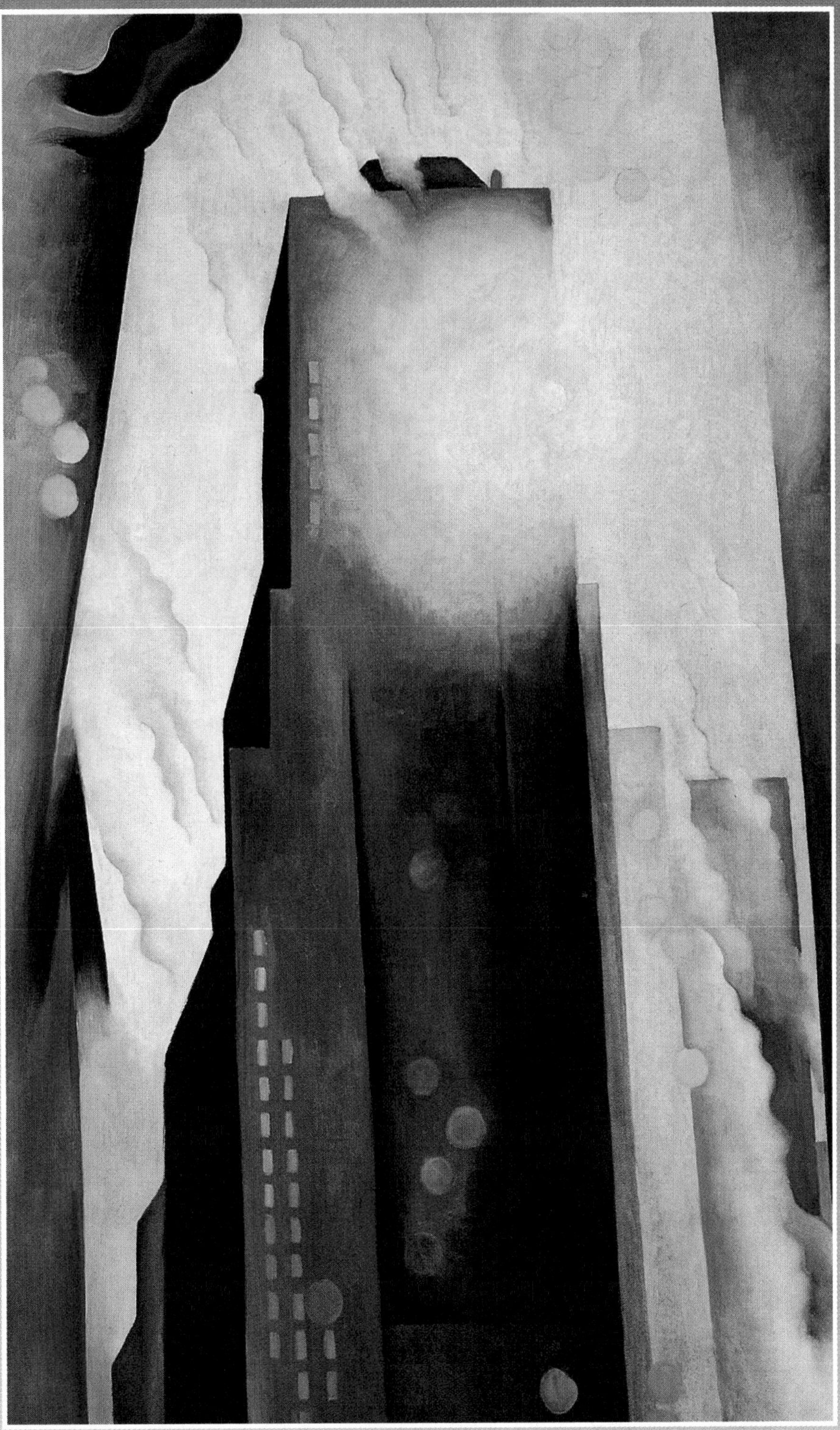

The Shelton with Sunspots (1926), Georgia O'Keeffe. Oil on canvas, 123.1 cm × 76.8 cm, The Art Institute of Chicago, gift of Leigh B. Block (1985.206). Photo Copyright © 1994 The Art Institute of Chicago, all rights reserved.

RESPONDING OPTIONS

FROM PERSONAL RESPONSE *TO* CRITICAL ANALYSIS

REFLECT **1.** In your notebook, describe how you felt about Dexter Green as you finished reading the story.

RETHINK **2.** Are your feelings about what has happened to Judy Jones the same as Dexter's? Explain your answer.

3. How do you account for the attraction between Dexter and Judy?

Consider
- Dexter's awareness of Judy's faults
- how his "winter dreams" relate to her
- her reasons for initially getting involved with Dexter and her reasons for saying she wants to marry him

4. If Dexter and Judy had married, what do you think their life together would have been like?

5. How worthwhile do you find Dexter's "winter dreams"?

Consider
- what the dreams are
- what he gains from the dreams
- what he loses because of the dreams

RELATE **6.** How do the dreams you listed for the Personal Connection on page 680 compare with Dexter Green's "winter dreams"?

ANOTHER PATHWAY

Cooperative Learning

How might Dexter's life look to a psychologist? a businessperson? a feminist? a friend? Get together with three classmates to evaluate Dexter's life, with each member of the group assuming one of these roles. Can your group come to any agreements about Dexter? Share your conclusions with the rest of the class.

QUICKWRITES

1. Pretend that you are a relationship counselor and write a brief **evaluation** of Dexter and Judy's relationship.
2. Write a draft of Dexter Green's **résumé.** Summarize his work experience, beginning with his job as a caddy.
3. If you could offer advice to Dexter at the end of the story, what would you tell him? Outline the **lecture** that you would give to him.

***PORTFOLIO** Save your writing. You may want to use it later as a springboard to a piece for your portfolio.*

LITERARY CONCEPTS

A writer may use the **title** of a work to suggest its **theme,** or main idea. Why is "Winter Dreams" a good title for Fitzgerald's story? Can you come up with alternative titles? Work with a partner to find passages describing Dexter's dreams for the future. Make a two-column chart, listing Dexter's dreams on one side and his actual accomplishments on the other. Study your chart, then consider Dexter's successes and his feeling of loss at the end of the story. Write a brief statement summarizing the story's theme and explaining the title's relevance to the theme.

ALTERNATIVE ACTIVITIES

1. ***Cooperative Learning*** Work with a small group of classmates to create a "Winter Dreams" illustrated **calendar** of the seasons. On the calendar, indicate what feelings Dexter associates with each season and what happens to him during the seasons. Use the calendar to help you investigate Fitzgerald's use of seasonal imagery in the story. What do winter and summer seem to represent?
2. Research fashions of the period just before World War I, then sketch **costume designs** for a movie version of the story and display them in class. Alternatively, put on a fashion show with some of your classmates, modeling clothing of the time with appropriate music playing in the background.

CRITIC'S CORNER

Marius Bewley's critical essay "Scott Fitzgerald: The Apprentice Fiction" contains the sentence "Fitzgerald's ultimate subject is the character of the American Dream in which, in their respective ways, his principal heroes are all trapped." How well do you think this statement applies to "Winter Dreams"? Use examples from the story to support your opinion.

THE WRITER'S STYLE

Fitzgerald is admired for his use of **figurative language**—language (such as metaphors, similes, and personification) that communicates ideas or feelings beyond the literal meaning of the words. In the second paragraph of "Winter Dreams," for example, he writes that "the long Minnesota winter shut down like the white lid of a box." What does this simile suggest about the setting? Find some other examples of figurative language in the story, and explain what ideas or feelings you think each conveys.

ART CONNECTIONS

The self-portrait by the European artist Tamara de Lempicka shown on page 693 is representative of the Art Deco style of the 1920s and 1930s—consciously "modern" with its angularity, streamlined forms, and glorification of machines and technology. The automobile is an important element in this painting, as the punning title *Autoportrait* suggests. Skyscrapers frame the figures in many of Lempicka's other portraits. Such elements are also present in "Winter Dreams"—think of Judy's roadster and motorboat and the concluding images of the New York skyline and the "gray beauty of steel that withstands all time." In what other ways does the artwork remind you of the story?

Detail of *Autoportrait* (about 1925), Tamara de Lempicka. Oil on wood, 35 × 26 cm, private collection. Copyright © SPADEM/Kizette de Lempicka Foxhall.

ACROSS THE CURRICULUM

Sports At the beginning of "Winter Dreams," Dexter Green is working as a caddy at a golf course. Find out more about the sport of golf. What equipment does one need to play? What are the basic rules of the game? What do the terms *tee, trap, rough, fore, green, links,* and *fairway* mean? With your classmates, compile a glossary of all the golf terms you can find in the story.

WORDS TO KNOW

EXERCISE A For each phrase in the first column, write the letter of the synonymous phrase in the second column.

1. a surfeit of change	a. sully the gully
2. mar the ravine	b. poignant oinking
3. fool the ingenuous	c. hopeless soaplessness
4. comically hazardous	d. suspicious and malicious
5. blatantly wishing	e. deceive the naive
6. pathetic pig sounds	f. too many pennies
7. incorrigible filthiness	g. openly hoping
8. grimace during hugs	h. crabbiness and flabbiness
9. wary and evil	i. hilariously precarious
10. petulance and poor muscle tone	j. make faces at embraces

EXERCISE B See how quickly you can communicate some of the vocabulary words to a partner by saying things—other than synonyms—that call the words to mind. For ***poignant,*** for example, you might say "a hungry child; a sad song; Mother's Day cards; tearjerker movies; a puppy's whimper; nostalgic memories . . . ," continuing until the correct word is guessed.

F. SCOTT FITZGERALD

1896–1940

Francis Scott Key Fitzgerald experienced, and depicted in his fiction, the material success and eventual disillusionment that characterized the decade he dubbed the Jazz Age. While in army training in Alabama, he fell in love with Zelda Sayre, the beautiful and high-spirited daughter of an Alabama Supreme Court judge. They had a tumultuous courtship, with Zelda refusing to marry the aspiring writer until he was financially secure. Fortunately, his first novel, *This Side of Paradise* (1920), met with immediate success, and the couple were married within a week of the book's publication.

In the decade that followed, Fitzgerald's career flourished as he published two more novels, three short story collections, and a play. His 1925 novel of overindulgent lives, *The Great Gatsby*—of which "Winter Dreams" is a sort of rough draft—became famous. By 1929 he was selling stories for as much as $3,600 each. Then everything seemed to go wrong.

In 1930, at the onset of the Great Depression, Zelda suffered the first of a number of mental breakdowns that would keep her hospitalized for much of the remainder of her life. At the same time, Fitzgerald was battling alcoholism, which, along with his need to earn money for Zelda's care, caused him to produce poor, hastily written fiction. Readers now rejected his subject matter, the lives of the wealthy, and by 1940 he was no longer a major writer. He died that year in Hollywood, leaving a "comeback" novel—*The Last Tycoon*—unfinished. After World War II, though, prosperity brought nostalgia for the 1920s and new respect for Fitzgerald's work. Today he is considered a major 20th-century writer whose stories make the Jazz Age come alive.

OTHER WORKS *All the Sad Young Men, Tales of the Jazz Age, Tender Is the Night*

- *ART GALLERY*
- *AUTHOR BACKGROUND*

PREVIEWING

FICTION

America and I

Anzia Yezierska (ənz-yä′ yĭ-zyĭr′skə)

PERSONAL CONNECTION

How do you think people who emigrate from their homelands feel? What challenges and opportunities await them in their new countries? Why do you think immigrants come to America? Share your thoughts about immigration with a small group of classmates. Then, as you read this story, compare your group's ideas with those of the narrator.

HISTORICAL/GEOGRAPHICAL CONNECTION

The Jewish narrator of "America and I" emigrates from Russia to the United States in the late 1800s. Between 1880 and 1920, approximately 12 million people flocked to America from Italy, Greece, Russia, and other countries in southern and eastern Europe. Many of these immigrants had left their homelands to escape wars, religious persecution, poverty, and, in some cases, starvation. After arriving in the United States, they had to face the challenges of learning English and finding housing and work. Many settled in ethnic neighborhoods in cities, where they lived in dark, crowded tenements with inadequate sanitation. Those who were uneducated, unskilled, and poor often had to work under dangerous conditions in sweatshops, toiling long hours for low wages.

READING CONNECTION

Appreciating Autobiographical Fiction This selection can be classified as autobiographical fiction; not every detail is true, but the author, Anzia Yezierska, is writing about a character like herself and events like those that happened to her. As you read, try to hear the first-person narrator's voice and form an image of this young immigrant woman. While reading, or immediately after you finish, record your impressions of her in a chart like the one shown here.

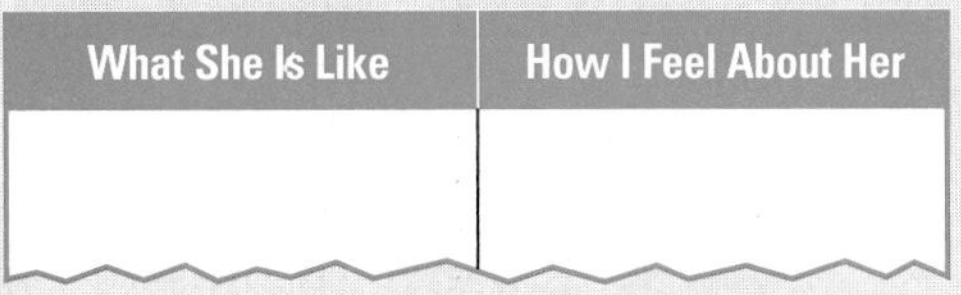

What She Is Like	How I Feel About Her

LASERLINKS
• *HISTORICAL CONNECTION*

AMERICA AND I

I was in America,
among the Americans,
but not of them.

Anzia Yezierska

As one of the dumb, voiceless ones I speak. One of the millions of immigrants beating, beating out their hearts at your gates for a breath of understanding.

Ach! America! From the other end of the earth from where I came, America was a land of living hope, woven of dreams, aflame with longing and desire.

Choked for ages in the airless oppression of Russia, the Promised Land rose up—wings for my stifled spirit—sunlight burning through my darkness—freedom singing to me in my prison—deathless songs tuning prison-bars into strings of a beautiful violin.

I arrived in America. My young, strong body, my heart and soul pregnant with the unlived lives of generations clamoring for expression.

What my mother and father and their mother and father never had a chance to give out in Russia, I would give out in America. The hidden sap of centuries would find release; colors that never saw light—songs that died unvoiced—romance that never had a chance to blossom in the black life of the Old World.

In the golden land of flowing opportunity I was to find my work that was denied me in the sterile village of my forefathers. Here I was to be free from the dead drudgery for bread that held me down in Russia. For the first time in America, I'd cease to be a slave of the belly. I'd be a creator, a giver, a human being! My work would be the living joy of fullest self-expression.

But from my high visions, my golden hopes, I had to put my feet down on earth. I had to have food and shelter. I had to have the money to pay for it.

I was in America, among the Americans, but not of them. No speech, no common language, no way to win a smile of understanding from them, only my young, strong body and my untried faith. Only my eager, empty hands, and my full heart shining from my eyes!

God from the world! Here I was with so much richness in me, but my mind was not wanted without the language. And my body, unskilled, untrained, was not even wanted in the factory. Only one of two chances was left open to me: the kitchen, or minding babies.

My first job was as a servant in an Americanized family. Once, long ago, they came from the same village from where I came. But they were so well-dressed, so well-fed, so successful in America, that they were ashamed to remember their mother tongue.

"What were to be my wages?" I ventured timidly, as I looked up to the well-fed, well-dressed "American" man and woman.

They looked at me with a sudden coldness. What have I said to draw away from me their warmth? Was it so low from me to talk of wages? I shrank back into myself like a low-down bargainer. Maybe they're so high up in well-being they can't any more understand my low thoughts for money.

From his rich height the man preached down to me that I must not be so grabbing for wages. Only just landed from the ship and already thinking about money when I should be thankful to associate with "Americans."

The woman, out of her smooth, smiling fatness assured me that this was my chance for a summer vacation in the country with her two lovely children. My great chance to learn to be a civilized being, to become an American by living with them.

So, made to feel that I was in the hands of American friends, invited to share with them their home, their plenty, their happiness, I pushed out from my head the worry for wages. Here was my first chance to begin my life in the sunshine, after my long darkness. My laugh was all over my face as I said to them: "I'll trust myself to you. What I'm worth you'll give me." And I entered their house like a child by the hand.

The best of me I gave them. Their house cares were my house cares. I got up early. I worked till late. All that my soul hungered to give I put into the passion with which I scrubbed floors, scoured pots, and washed clothes. I was so grateful to mingle with the American people, to hear the music of the American language, that I never knew tiredness.

There was such a freshness in my brains and such a willingness in my heart that I could go on and on—not only with the work of the house, but work with my head—learning new words from the children, the grocer, the butcher, the iceman. I was not even afraid to ask for words from the policeman on the street. And every new word made me see new American things with American eyes. I felt like a Columbus, finding new worlds through every new word.

But words alone were only for the inside of me. The outside of me still branded me for a steerage[1] immigrant. I had to have clothes to forget myself that I'm a stranger yet. And so I had to have money to buy these clothes.

The month was up. I was so happy! Now I'd have money. *My own, earned* money. Money to buy a new shirt on my back—shoes on my feet. Maybe yet an American dress and hat!

Ach! How high rose my dreams! How plainly

1. **steerage:** the section of a passenger ship containing the cheapest accommodations.

I saw all that I would do with my visionary wages shining like a light over my head!

In my imagination I already walked in my new American clothes. How beautiful I looked as I saw myself like a picture before my eyes! I saw how I would throw away my immigrant rags tied up in my immigrant shawl. With money to buy—free money in my hands—I'd show them that I could look like an American in a day.

Like a prisoner in his last night in prison, counting the seconds that will free him from his chains, I trembled breathlessly for the minute I'd get the wages in my hand.

Before dawn I rose.

I shined up the house like a jewel-box.

I prepared breakfast and waited with my heart in my mouth for my lady and gentleman to rise. At last I heard them stirring. My eyes were jumping out of my head to them when I saw them coming in and seating themselves by the table.

Like a hungry cat rubbing up to its boss for meat, so I edged and simpered around them as I passed them the food. Without my will, like a beggar, my hand reached out to them.

The breakfast was over. And no word yet from my wages.

"*Gottuniu!*"[2] I thought to myself. "Maybe they're so busy with their own things they forgot it's the day for my wages. Could they who have everything know what I was to do with my first American dollars? How could they, soaking in plenty, how could they feel the longing and the fierce hunger in me, pressing up through each visionary dollar? How could they know the gnawing ache of my avid fingers for the feel of my own, earned dollars? *My* dollars that I could spend like a free person. *My* dollars that would make me feel with everybody alike!

Breakfast was long past.

Lunch came. Lunch past.

Oi-i weh![3] Not a word yet about my money.

It was near dinner. And not a word yet about my wages.

I began to set the table. But my head—it swam away from me. I broke a glass. The silver dropped from my nervous fingers. I couldn't stand it any longer. I dropped everything and rushed over to my American lady and gentleman.

"*Oi weh!* The money—my money—my wages!" I cried breathlessly.

Four cold eyes turned on me.

"Wages? Money?" The four eyes turned into hard stone as they looked me up and down. "Haven't you a comfortable bed to sleep, and three good meals a day? You're only a month here. Just came to America. And you already think about money. Wait till you're worth any money. What use are you without knowing English? You should be glad we keep you here. It's like a vacation for you. Other girls pay money yet to be in the country."

It went black for my eyes. I was so choked no words came to my lips. Even the tears went dry in my throat.

I left. Not a dollar for all my work.

For a long, long time my heart ached and ached like a sore wound. If murderers would have robbed me and killed me it wouldn't have hurt me so much. I couldn't think through my pain. The minute I'd see before me how they looked at me, the words they said to me—then everything began to bleed in me. And I was helpless.

For a long, long time the thought of ever working in an "American" family made me tremble with fear, like the fear of wild wolves. No—never again would I trust myself to an "American" family, no matter how fine their language and how sweet their smile.

It was blotted out in me all trust in friendship from "Americans." But the life in me still burned to live. The hope in me still craved to hope. In

2. ***Gottuniu!*** (gôt′o͝on-yo͞o) *Yiddish:* Oh, my God!

3. ***Oi-i weh!*** (oi′ vā′) *Yiddish:* Oh, woe! (a common expression of dismay or resignation).

WORDS TO KNOW

simper (sĭm′pər) *v.* to smile in a shy or self-conscious way

avid (ăv′ĭd) *adj.* having an intense desire or craving

"Where is America? Is there an America? What is this wilderness in which I'm lost?"

darkness, in dirt, in hunger and want, but only to live on!

There had been no end to my day—working for the "American" family.

Now rejecting false friendships from higher-ups in America, I turned back to the Ghetto,[4] I worked on a hard bench with my own kind on either side of me. I knew before I began what my wages were to be. I knew what my hours were to be. And I knew the feeling of the end of the day.

From the outside my second job seemed worse than the first. It was in a sweatshop of a Delancey Street basement, kept up by an old, wrinkled woman that looked like a black witch of greed. My work was sewing on buttons. While the morning was still dark I walked into a dark basement. And darkness met me when I turned out of the basement.

Day after day, week after week, all the contact I got with America was handling dead buttons. The money I earned was hardly enough to pay for bread and rent. I didn't have a room to myself. I didn't even have a bed. I slept on a mattress on the floor in a rat-hole of a room occupied by a dozen other immigrants. I was always hungry—oh, so hungry! The scant meals I could afford only sharpened my appetite for real food. But I felt myself better off than working in the "American" family, where I had three good meals a day and a bed to myself. With all the hunger and darkness of the sweatshop, I had at least the evening to myself. And all night was mine. When all were asleep, I used to creep up on the roof of the tenement and talk out my heart in silence to the stars in the sky.

"Who am I? What am I? What do I want with my life? Where is America? Is there an America? What is this wilderness in which I'm lost?"

I'd hurl my questions and then think and think. And I could not tear it out of me, the feeling that America must be somewhere,

4. **Ghetto:** the part of New York City where Jewish immigrants lived and worked.

somehow—only I couldn't find it—*my America,* where I would work for love and not for a living. I was like a thing following blindly after something far off in the dark!

"*Oi weh!*" I'd stretch out my hand up in the air. "My head is so lost in America! What's the use of all my working if I'm not in it? Dead buttons is not me."

Then the busy season started in the shop. The mounds of buttons grew and grew. The long day stretched out longer. I had to begin with the buttons earlier and stay with them till later in the night. The old witch turned into a huge greedy maw for wanting more and more buttons.

For a glass of tea, for a slice of herring over black bread, she would buy us up to stay another and another hour, till there seemed no end to her demands.

One day, the light of self-assertion broke into my cellar darkness.

"I don't want the tea. I don't want your herring," I said with terrible boldness. "I only want to go home. I only want the evening to myself!"

"You fresh mouth, you!" cried the old witch. "You learned already too much in America. I want no clock-watchers in my shop. Out you go!"

I was driven out to cold and hunger. I could no longer pay for my mattress on the floor. I no longer could buy the bite in the mouth. I walked the streets. I knew what it is to be alone in a strange city, among strangers.

But I laughed through my tears. So I learned

I burned to give,
to give something,
to do something,
to be something.

too much already in America because I wanted the whole evening to myself? Well America has yet to teach me still more: how to get not only the whole evening to myself, but a whole day a week like the American workers.

That sweatshop was a bitter memory but a good school. It fitted me for a regular factory. I could walk in boldly and say I could work at something, even if it was only sewing on buttons.

Gradually, I became a trained worker. I worked in a light, airy factory, only eight hours a day. My boss was no longer a sweater and a blood-squeezer. The first freshness of the morning was mine. And the whole evening was mine. All day Sunday was mine.

Now I had better food to eat. I slept on a better bed. Now, I even looked dressed up like the American-born. But inside of me I knew that I was not yet an American. I choked with longing when I met an American-born, and I could say nothing.

Something cried dumb in me. I couldn't help it. I didn't know what it was I wanted. I only knew I wanted. I wanted. Like the hunger in the heart that never gets food.

An English class for foreigners started in our factory. The teacher had such a good, friendly face, her eyes looked so understanding, as if she could see right into my heart. So I went to her one day for an advice:

"I don't know what is with me the matter," I began. "I have no rest in me. I never yet done what I want."

"What is it you want to do, child?" she asked me.

"I want to do something with my head, my feelings. All day long, only with my hands I work."

"First you must learn English." She patted me as if I was not yet grown up. "Put your mind on that, and then we'll see."

So for a time I learned the language. I could almost begin to think with English words in my head. But in my heart the emptiness still hurt. I burned to give, to give something, to do something, to be something. The dead work with my hands was killing me. My work left only hard stones on my heart.

Again I went to our factory teacher and cried out to her: "I know already to read and write the English language, but I can't put it into words what I want. What is it in me so different that can't come out?"

She smiled at me down from her calmness as if I were a little bit out of my head. "What do *you want* to do?"

"I feel. I see. I hear. And I want to think it out. But I'm like dumb in me. I only feel I'm different—different from everybody."

She looked at me close and said nothing for a minute. "You ought to join one of the social clubs of the Women's Association," she advised.

"What's the Women's Association?" I implored greedily.

"A group of American women who are trying to help the working-girl find herself. They have a special department for immigrant girls like you."

I joined the Women's Association. On my first evening there they announced a lecture: "The Happy Worker and His Work," by the Welfare director of the United Mills Corporation.

"Is there such a thing as a happy worker at his work?" I wondered. "Happiness is only by working at what you love. And what poor girl can ever find it to work at what she loves? My old dreams about my America rushed through my mind. Once I thought that in America everybody works for love. Nobody has to worry for a living. Maybe this welfare man came to show me the *real* America that till now I sought in vain.

With a lot of polite words the head lady of the Women's Association introduced a higher-up that looked like the king of kings of business. Never before in my life did I ever see a man with such a sureness in his step, such power in his face, such friendly positiveness in his eye as when he smiled upon us.

"Efficiency is the new religion of business," he began. "In big business houses, even in up-to-date factories, they no longer take the first comer and give him any job that happens to stand empty. Efficiency begins at the employment office. Experts are hired for the one purpose, to find out how best to fit the worker to his work. It's economy for the boss to make the worker happy." And then he talked a lot more on efficiency in educated language that was over my head.

I didn't know exactly what it meant—efficiency—but if it was to make the worker happy at his work, then that's what I had been looking for since I came to America. I only felt from watching him that he was happy by his job. And as I looked on this clean, well-dressed, successful one, who wasn't ashamed to say he rose from an office-boy, it made me feel that I, too, could lift myself up for a person.

He finished his lecture, telling us about the Vocational Guidance Center that the Women's Association started.

The very next evening I was at the Vocational Guidance Center. There I found a young, college-looking woman. Smartness and health shining from her eyes! She, too, looked as if she knew her way in America. I could tell at the first glance: here is a person that is happy by what she does.

"I feel you'll understand me," I said right away.

She leaned over with pleasure in her face: "I hope I can."

"I want to work by what's in me. Only, I don't know what's in me. I only feel I'm different."

She gave me a quick, puzzled look from the corner of her eyes. "What are you doing now?"

"I'm the quickest shirtwaist[5] hand on the floor. But my heart wastes away by such work. I think and think, and my thoughts can't come out."

"Why don't you think out your thoughts in shirtwaists? You could learn to be a designer. Earn more money."

"I don't want to look on waists. If my hands are sick from waists, how could my head learn to put beauty into them?"

"But you must earn your living at what you know, and rise slowly from job to job."

I looked at her office sign: "Vocational Guidance." "What's your vocational guidance?" I asked. "How to rise from job to job—how to earn more money?"

The smile went out from her eyes. But she tried to be kind yet. "What *do* you want?" she asked, with a sigh of last patience.

"I want America to want me."

She fell back in her chair, thunderstruck with my boldness. But yet, in a low voice of educated self-control, she tried to reason with me:

"You have to *show* that you have something special for America before America has need of you."

"But I never had a chance to find out what's in me, because I always had to work for a living. Only, I feel it's efficiency for America to find out what's in me so different, so I could give it out by my work."

Her eyes half closed as they bored through me. Her mouth opened to speak, but no words came from her lips. So I flamed up with all that was choking in me like a house on fire:

"America gives free bread and rent to criminals in prison. They got grand houses with sunshine, fresh air, doctors and teachers, even for the crazy ones. Why don't they have free boarding-schools for immigrants—strong people—willing people? Here you see us burning up with something different, and America turns her head away from us."

Her brows lifted and dropped down. She shrugged her shoulders away from me with the look of pity we give to cripples and hopeless lunatics.

"America is no Utopia.[6] First you must become efficient in earning a living before you can indulge in your poetic dreams."

I went away from the vocational guidance

5. **shirtwaist:** a tailored blouse, usually with a collar and cuffs.

6. **Utopia:** an ideal place of perfect justice and social harmony.

"America is
no Utopia.
First you must
become efficient
in earning a living
before you can
indulge in your
poetic dreams."

office with all the air out of my lungs. All the light out of my eyes. My feet dragged after me like dead wood.

Till now there had always lingered a rosy veil of hope over my emptiness, a hope that a miracle would happen. I would open up my eyes some day and suddenly find the America of my dreams. As a young girl hungry for love sees always before her eyes the picture of lover's arms around her, so I saw always in my heart the vision of Utopian America.

But now I felt that the America of my dreams never was and never could be. Reality had hit me on the head as with a club. I felt that the America that I sought was nothing but a shadow—an echo—a chimera[7] of lunatics and crazy immigrants.

7. **chimera** (kī-mîr′ə): an illusion of the mind; fantasy.

Stripped of all illusion, I looked about me. The long desert of wasting days of drudgery stared me in the face. The drudgery that I had lived through, and the endless drudgery still ahead of me rose over me like a withering wilderness of sand. In vain were all my cryings, in vain were all frantic efforts of my spirit to find the living waters of understanding for my perishing lips. Sand, sand was everywhere. With every seeking, every reaching out I only lost myself deeper and deeper in a vast sea of sand.

I knew now the American language. And I knew now, if I talked to the Americans from morning till night, they could not understand what the Russian soul of me wanted. They could not understand *me* any more than if I talked to them in Chinese. Between my soul and the American soul were worlds of difference that no words could bridge over. What was that difference? What made the Americans so far apart from me?

I began to read the American history. I found from the first pages that America started with a band of Courageous Pilgrims. They had left their native country as I had left mine. They had crossed an unknown ocean and landed in an unknown country, as I.

But the great difference between the first Pilgrims and me was that they expected to make America, build America, create their own world of liberty. I wanted to find it ready made.

I read on. I delved deeper down into the American history. I saw how the Pilgrim Fathers came to a rocky desert country, surrounded by Indian savages on all sides. But undaunted, they pressed on—through danger—through famine, pestilence, and want—they pressed on. They did not ask the Indians for sympathy, for understanding. They made no demands on anybody, but on their own indomitable spirit of persistence.

And I—I was forever begging a crumb of sympathy, a gleam of understanding from strangers who could not sympathize, who could not understand.

I, when I encountered a few savage Indian scalpers, like the old witch of the sweatshop, like my "Americanized" countryman, who cheated me of my wages—I, when I found myself on the lonely, untrodden path through which all seekers of the new world must pass, I lost heart and said: "There is no America!"

Then came a light—a great revelation! I saw America—a big idea—a deathless hope—a world still in the making. I saw that it was the glory of America that it was not yet finished. And I, the last comer, had her share to give, small or great, to the making of America, like those Pilgrims who came in the *Mayflower.*

Fired up by this revealing light, I began to build a bridge of understanding between the American-born and myself. Since their life was shut out from such as me, I began to open up my life and the lives of my people to them. And life draws life. In only writing about the Ghetto I found America.

Great chances have come to me. But in my heart is always a deep sadness. I feel like a man who is sitting down to a secret table of plenty, while his near ones and dear ones are perishing before his eyes. My very joy in doing the work I love hurts me like secret guilt, because all about me I see so many with my longings, my burning eagerness, to do and to be, wasting their days in drudgery they hate, merely to buy bread and pay rent. And America is losing all that richness of the soul.

The Americans of to-morrow, the America that is every day nearer coming to be, will be too wise, too open-hearted, too friendly-handed, to let the least last-comer at their gates knock in vain with his gifts unwanted. ❖

WORDS TO KNOW

delve (dĕlv) *v.* to conduct an investigation; search
pestilence (pĕs′tə-ləns) *n.* any epidemic disease that is usually fatal
indomitable (ĭn-dŏm′ĭ-tə-bəl) *adj.* not easily discouraged or defeated

INSIGHT

from A Nation of Immigrants

Bernard A. Weisberger

After 1865 the United States thundered toward industrial leadership with the speed and power of one of the great locomotives that were the handsomest embodiment of the age of steam. That age peaked somewhere in the 1890s. By 1929 the age of electricity and petroleum was in flower. And the United States was the world's leading producer of steel, oil, coal, automobiles and trucks, electrical equipment, and an infinite variety of consumer goods from old-fashioned overalls to newfangled radios. The majority of Americans lived in supercities, their daily existence made possible by elaborate networks of power and gas lines, telephone wires, highways, bridges, tunnels, and rails.

And the foreign-born were at the center of the whirlwind. Expansion coincided with, depended on, incorporated the greatest wave of migration yet.

All told, some 14,000,000 arrived at the gates between 1860 and 1900; another 18,600,000 followed between 1900 and 1930. Almost all of them came from Europe, a transoceanic transplantation unmatched in history. . . .

Newly arrived immigrants on the dock at Ellis Island. The Granger Collection, New York.

For the most part this was an urban migration. Millions went to the middling-sized red-brick towns dominated by the factory chimney and whistle. More millions went to the big cities, where they grunted and sweated in the creation of the skyscrapers, the bridges, the subways and trolley lines, the sewer and lighting systems—the guts of the metropolis. Or where, if they did not swing a pick or scrub floors, they sold groceries to those of their countrymen who did. . . .

For most, life in the golden land was potentially promising but actually brutal. Wages hung at or below the cost of living and far below the cost of comfort. Some parts of Chicago had three times as many inhabitants as the most crowded sections of Tokyo or Calcutta.[1] A New York survey taker found 1,231 Italians living in 120 rooms. Single toilets and water faucets were shared by dozens of families. Uncollected garbage piled up in alleys. Privacy and health were equally impossible to maintain, and pulmonary diseases[2] raged through the tenement "lung blocks."

Settlement-house workers took up residence in the worst neighborhoods, trying to teach the rudiments of hygiene. The American public school took on a new role. Authorities regarded it as their mission to teach immigrant children not only basic skills but civic responsibility, respect for the flag, and the proper use of the toothbrush. In fact, the schools did produce millions of competent citizens. One alumna, Mary Antin, said that born Americans should be grateful for their role in "the recruiting of your armies of workers, thinkers, and leaders." But the precedent of having schools serve as agents of social policy—in this case of assimilation[3]—would later haunt overburdened teachers and administrators.

The urban center of gravity of the new immigrants made it harder for them to be accepted. Most "native" Americans were encountering the basic problems of the big city—crowding, crime, graft, corruption, disease—for the first time. It was all too easy for them to associate these evils with the immigrants, who seemed always to be at the center of this or that dilemma. Sympathetic men and women like Jane Addams, Emily Balch, Hutchins Hapgood, and Horace M. Kallen did their best to explain immigrant culture to their fellow old-stock Americans and to guide the newcomers in acceptable American ways.

The immigrants themselves did not take on the role of clay awaiting the potter's hand. They organized their own newspapers, theaters, social clubs, night classes, and self-help societies. These, while keeping the old-country languages and folkways alive, steadfastly preached and practiced assimilation and urged members and readers to rush into citizenship and respectability, which the great majority of them did. Single men skimped and struggled to bring over families. Families sacrificed to send children to school. And the children found different paths to Americanization. Some joined political machines and parties; some worked in the union movement; others forged their own steps to success in business. (And some never graduated beyond the streets and dead-end jobs.)

---

1. **Calcutta:** a city in India, known for its crowded living conditions.
2. **pulmonary** (po͝ol′mə-nĕr′ē) **diseases:** diseases of the lungs, such as tuberculosis.
3. **assimilation:** the absorption of a minority group into a prevailing culture.

RESPONDING OPTIONS

FROM PERSONAL RESPONSE TO CRITICAL ANALYSIS

REFLECT 1. Describe the narrator and your attitude toward her, sharing what you wrote for the Reading Connection on page 703.

RETHINK 2. What is your reaction to the narrator's ideas about America?

Consider

- how she hopes immigrants will be treated in the future
- her "revelation" that America is still being made
- her understanding of American history
- what she expects America to provide for her

3. What do you think the narrator learns from her encounters with employers, teachers, and advisers?

4. In your opinion, what is the most important step the narrator takes in learning to live in America?

5. Do you think the American dream is an illusion or a reality for the narrator of this story? Explain.

RELATE 6. What similarities do you see between the narrator's experiences and the immigrants' experiences described in the Insight excerpt from "A Nation of Immigrants"?

ANOTHER PATHWAY

Working with a partner and adopting the role of a social worker, prepare the narrator's case history. Your case history should not only describe the events of the narrator's life but also include your evaluation of her progress in making a satisfying life for herself in America. Share your case history with the class.

LITERARY CONCEPTS

An **analogy** is an extended, point-by-point comparison of two things that have certain similarities. Its purpose is usually to make the less familiar of the two things more comprehensible. For example, the narrator of "America and I" draws an analogy between her experiences in America and those of the Pilgrims. What similarities does she see between herself and the Pilgrims? What conclusion does she reach on the basis of her analogy?

Cooperative Learning With a small group of classmates, look for other analogies in this story. Then create an analogy of your own to clarify the narrator's experience of being an immigrant.

QUICKWRITES

1. Think about the narrator's positive and negative experiences in this story. Write at least five **tips** to help recent immigrants adjust to life in America.
2. Imagine that the narrator receives a letter from a friend back in Russia. Write the narrator's **reply,** answering questions about America, explaining what has happened to her since she arrived, and describing her feelings about her experiences.
3. Compose a passage for a **memoir** you might someday write, describing an experience that was "a bitter memory but a good school" for you. Be sure to tell what you learned from it.

PORTFOLIO *Save your writing. You may want to use it later as a spring-board to a piece for your portfolio.*

ALTERNATIVE ACTIVITIES

Draw on your reading of Yezierska's story and the Insight selection to design a **board game** or **computer game** based on the immigrant experience in America. Players, for example, might strive to avoid dead-end jobs and achieve the American dream. Explain or demonstrate your game to the class.

LITERARY LINKS

1. How does the narrator's account of the Pilgrims compare with William Bradford's account of the Pilgrims' arrival in America (page 90)? Do you think the narrator's analogy between her experience and that of the Pilgrims is a valid one?
2. How do you think the narrator would respond to Crèvecoeur's description of the immigrant experience in "What Is an American?" (page 223)?

WORDS TO KNOW

Review the Words to Know at the bottom of the selection pages. Then write the vocabulary word that best completes each sentence below.

1. Is greed contagious—a _____ like smallpox or the plague?
2. Yezierska wondered this as she tried to _____ into what it meant to be an American.
3. Not content to _____ with pretended gratitude for food and a bed, she pursued her dream, even sacrificing security for independence.
4. Although she was disheartened, her desire for fulfillment remained _____ and could not be crushed.
5. Today, _____ scholars of Yezierska's life and writings labor excitedly to bring her works to wide attention.

ANZIA YEZIERSKA

Born, like the narrator of "America and I," in a village of Russian Poland, Anzia Yezierska (1885?–1970) emigrated with her family to the United States in the late 1800s. The family settled in a tenement in New York City's Lower East Side, where Yezierska briefly attended public school until she was old enough to work to help support her family. She later worked as a cook, a servant, a waitress, and a needleworker, sewing on buttons in a sweatshop.

Although Jewish tradition discouraged the education of women, Yezierska rebelled against her family and went to college. Supporting herself by working at a laundry before and after classes, she began attending Columbia University in 1904. Her studies were designed to make a cooking teacher of her, but she decided to be a writer instead.

In 1920 Yezierska published her first short story collection, *Hungry Hearts.* Paying her $10,000 for the film rights and hiring her to write the script, the Hollywood producer Samuel Goldwyn turned the book into a silent film. Called "the sweatshop Cinderella," Yezierska instantly became famous. She moved to Hollywood, intending to become a screenwriter, but found herself unable to write so far away from the colorful New York neighborhoods that had first inspired her.

Within a year Yezierska returned to New York, and in 1922 she published her first novel, *Salome of the Tenements,* which was followed, over the next 10 years, by three more novels and a second book of short stories. In 1950, after a silence of 18 years, she published the autobiographical novel *Red Ribbon on a White Horse* to critical acclaim. However, it failed to regain for her the fame and success she had experienced in the 1920s, and she spent the last years of her life in obscurity.

OTHER WORKS *Bread Givers, Children of Loneliness*

PREVIEWING

FICTION

In the American Society

Gish Jen

PERSONAL CONNECTION

Get together with a small group of classmates to talk about what it means to fit into a new society. If you can, offer your own observations about immigrants' experiences of adjusting to American society. If you have no such direct knowledge, discuss a comparable experience, such as that of visiting a foreign country or a different region of the United States, that of moving to a new community, or that of transferring from a private to a public school. What misunderstandings can arise when a person is placed in a new setting, and what causes such misunderstandings? What attitude might a person take toward his or her new society?

HISTORICAL CONNECTION

Chinese immigrants have often had difficulty being accepted in American society. In the mid-1800s, large numbers of Chinese men came to California to work in the gold mines and on the Central Pacific railroad. When an economic depression struck in the 1870s, Americans who viewed Chinese workers as unfair, lower-paid competitors for jobs raised such an outcry that in 1882 Congress passed the Chinese Exclusion Act, prohibiting immigration from China to the United States.

The lifting of this ban in 1943 led to a new wave of Chinese immigration after World War II. Many Chinese came to the United States in the late 1940s to escape the bitter civil war between the Communists and the Nationalists in their homeland. After the Communists took over mainland China in 1949, Chinese immigrants—like the character Booker in this story—came mainly from Nationalist China on the island of Taiwan. The family in the story discovers, however, that even though immigration policy has changed, Chinese Americans are still faced with more subtle forms of prejudice.

READING CONNECTION

Recognizing Motivations The forces impelling a character's actions are referred to as the character's motivation. Sometimes a writer will state a character's motivation, but often it must be inferred. You need to look at the psychological and cultural bases of a character's actions, as well as the circumstances in which the character acts, to judge why he or she behaves in a certain way. In this story, the immigrant mother and father have different approaches to fitting into American society. To help you understand what motivations lie behind their actions, make a chart like this one in your notebook and fill it in as you read.

Character	Actions	Motivations
Mr. Chang	1. takes over pancake house 2.	
Mrs. Chang	1. applies to country club 2.	

• *HISTORICAL CONNECTION*

IN THE AMERICAN SOCIETY

GISH JEN

I. HIS OWN SOCIETY

When my father took over the pancake house, it was to send my little sister Mona and me to college. We were only in junior high at the time, but my father believed in getting a jump on things. "Those Americans always saying it," he told us. "Smart guys thinking in advance." My mother elaborated, explaining that businesses took bringing up, like children. They could take years to get going, she said, years.

In this case, though, we got rich right away. At two months we were breaking even, and at four, those same hotcakes that could barely withstand the weight of butter and syrup were supporting our family with ease. My mother bought a station wagon with air conditioning, my father an oversized, red vinyl recliner for the back room; and as time went on and the business continued to thrive, my father started to talk about his grandfather and the village he had reigned over in China—things my father had never talked about when he worked for other people. He told us about the bags of rice his family would give out to the poor at New Year's, and about the people who came to beg, on their hands and knees, for his grandfather to intercede for the more wayward of their relatives. "Like that Godfather in the movie," he would tell us as, his feet up, he distributed paychecks. Sometimes an employee would get two green envelopes instead of one, which meant that Jimmy needed a tooth pulled, say, or that Tiffany's husband was in the clinker again.

"It's nothing, nothing," he would insist, sinking back into his chair. "Who else is going to take care of you people?"

My mother would mostly just sigh about it.

WORDS TO KNOW **intercede** (ĭn'tər-sēd') *v.* to plead on behalf of another or mediate in a dispute

"Your father thinks this is China," she would say, and then she would go back to her mending. Once in a while, though, when my father had given away a particularly large sum, she would exclaim, outraged, "But this here is the U—S—of—A!"—this apparently having been what she used to tell immigrant stock boys when they came in late.

She didn't work at the supermarket anymore; but she had made it to the rank of manager before she left, and this had given her not only new words and phrases, but new ideas about herself, and about America, and about what was what in general. She had opinions, now, on how downtown should be zoned; she could pump her own gas and check her own oil; and for all she used to chide Mona and me for being "copycats," she herself was now interested in espadrilles,[1] and wallpaper, and most recently, the town country club.

"So join already," said Mona, flicking a fly off her knee.

FOR IN MY FATHER'S MIND, A FAMILY OWED ITS HEAD A DEGREE OF LOYALTY THAT LEFT NO ROOM FOR DISSENT. TO EMBRACE WHAT HE EMBRACED WAS TO LOVE; AND TO EMBRACE SOMETHING ELSE WAS TO BETRAY HIM.

My mother enumerated the problems as she sliced up a quarter round of watermelon: There was the cost. There was the waiting list. There was the fact that no one in our family played either tennis or golf.

"So what?" said Mona.

"It would be waste," said my mother.

"Me and Callie can swim in the pool."

"Plus you need that recommendation letter from a member."

"Come *on,*" said Mona. "Annie's mom'd write you a letter in *sec.*"

My mother's knife glinted in the early summer sun. I spread some more newspaper on the picnic table.

"*Plus* you have to eat there twice a month. You know what that means." My mother cut another, enormous slice of fruit.

"No, I *don't* know what that means," said Mona.

"It means Dad would have to wear a jacket, dummy," I said.

"Oh! Oh! Oh!" said Mona, clasping her hand to her breast. "Oh! Oh! Oh! Oh! Oh!"

We all laughed: my father had no use for nice clothes, and would wear only ten-year-old shirts, with grease-spotted pants, to show how little he cared what anyone thought.

"Your father doesn't believe in joining the American society," said my mother. "He wants to have his own society."

"So go to dinner without him." Mona shot her seeds out in long arcs over the lawn. "Who cares what he thinks?"

But of course we all did care, and knew my mother could not simply up and do as she pleased. For in my father's mind, a family owed its head a degree of loyalty that left no room for dissent. To embrace what he embraced was to love; and to embrace something else was to betray him.

1. **espadrilles** (ĕs′pə-drĭlz′): casual shoes with cloth uppers and soles of twisted rope.

He demanded a similar sort of loyalty of his workers, whom he treated more like servants than employees. Not in the beginning, of course. In the beginning all he wanted was for them to keep on doing what they used to do, and to that end he concentrated mostly on leaving them alone. As the months passed, though, he expected more and more of them, with the result that for all his largesse, he began to have trouble keeping help. The cooks and busboys complained that he asked them to fix radiators and trim hedges, not only at the restaurant, but at our house; the waitresses that he sent them on errands and made them chauffeur him around. Our head waitress, Gertrude, claimed that he once even asked her to scratch his back.

"It's not just the blacks don't believe in slavery," she said when she quit.

My father never quite registered her complaint, though, nor those of the others who left. Even after Eleanor quit, then Tiffany, then Gerald, and Jimmy, and even his best cook, Eureka Andy, for whom he had bought new glasses, he remained mostly convinced that the fault lay with them.

"All they understand is that assembly line," he lamented. "Robots, they are. They want to be robots."

There *were* occasions when the clear running truth seemed to eddy,[2] when he would pinch the vinyl of his chair up into little peaks and wonder if he were doing things right. But with time he would always smooth the peaks back down; and when business started to slide in the spring, he kept on like a horse in his ways.

By the summer our dishboy was overwhelmed with scraping. It was no longer just the hash-browns that people were leaving for trash, and the service was as bad as the food. The waitresses served up French pancakes instead of German, apple juice instead of orange, spilt things on laps, on coats. On the Fourth of July some greenhorn[3] sent an entire side of fries slaloming[4] down a lady's *massif centrale*.[5] Meanwhile in the back room, my father labored through articles on the economy.

"What is housing starts?"[6] he puzzled. "What is GNP?"[7]

Mona and I did what we could, filling in as busgirls and bookkeepers and, one afternoon, stuffing the comments box that hung by the cashier's desk. That was Mona's idea. We rustled up a variety of pens and pencils, checked boxes for an hour, smeared the cards up with coffee and grease, and waited. It took a few days for my father to notice that the box was full, and he didn't say anything about it for a few days more. Finally, though, he started to complain of fatigue; and then he began to complain that the staff was not what it could be. We encouraged him in this—pointing out, for instance, how many dishes got chipped—but in the end all that happened was that, for the first time since we took over the restaurant, my father got it into his head to fire someone. Skip, a skinny busboy who was saving up for a sportscar, said nothing as my father mumbled on about the price of dishes. My father's hands shook as he wrote out the severance check;[8] and he spent the rest of the day napping in his chair once it was over.

As it was going on midsummer, Skip wasn't easy to replace. We hung a sign in the window

2. **eddy:** form a whirlpool.
3. **greenhorn:** beginner.
4. **slaloming:** skiing in a zigzag path.
5. ***massif centrale*** (mä-sēf′ sĕn-träl′) *French:* central mass (usually used to refer to the highest group of peaks in a mountain range).
6. **housing starts:** the number of new houses on which construction began during a given period.
7. **GNP:** gross national product—the value of all the goods and services produced in a country during a given period. (As a measure of the strength of the national economy, the U.S. government now uses gross domestic product, or GDP, which is based on a somewhat different set of calculations.)
8. **severance check:** payment given to an employee who is dismissed.

WORDS TO KNOW **largesse** (lär-zhĕs′) *n.* generosity

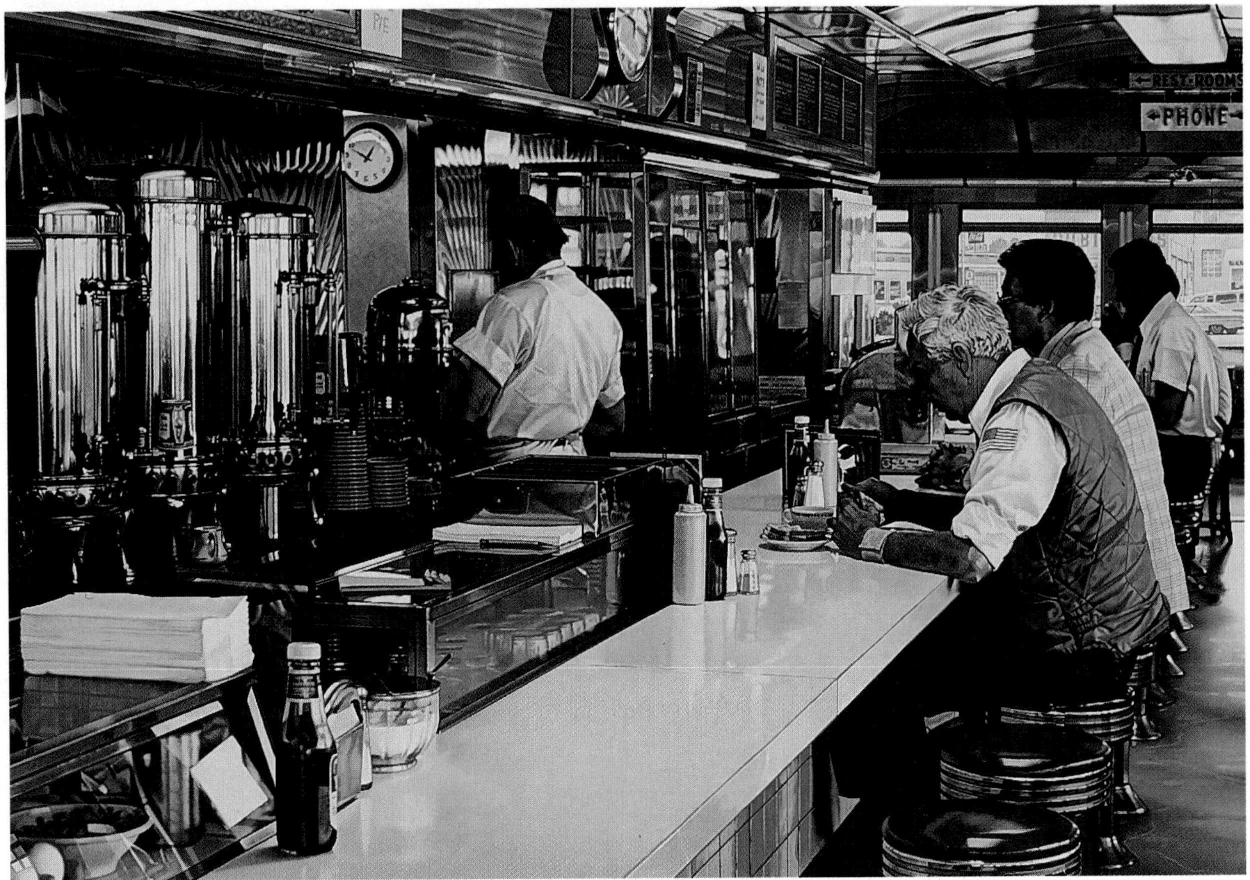

Diner Interior with Coffee Urns (1984), Ralph Goings. Oil on canvas, 44″ × 66″, courtesy of O. K. Harris Works of Art, New York. Photo Copyright © 1985 D. James Dee.

and advertised in the paper, but no one called the first week, and the person who called the second didn't show up for his interview. The third week, my father phoned Skip to see if he would come back, but a friend of his had already sold him a Corvette for cheap.

Finally a Chinese guy named Booker turned up. He couldn't have been more than thirty, and was wearing a lighthearted seersucker suit, but he looked as though life had him pinned: his eyes were bloodshot and his chest sunken, and the muscles of his neck seemed to strain with the effort of holding his head up. In a single dry breath he told us that he had never bussed tables but was willing to learn, and that he was on the lam from the deportation authorities.[9]

"I do not want to lie to you," he kept saying. He had come to the United States on a student visa, had run out of money, and was now in a bind. He was loath[10] to go back to Taiwan, as it happened—he looked up at this point, to be sure my father wasn't pro-KMT[11]—but all he had was a phony social security card and a willingness to absorb all blame, should anything untoward come to pass.

"I do not think, anyway, that it is against law to hire me, only to be me," he said, smiling faintly.

Anyone else would have examined him on

9. **on the lam from the deportation authorities:** running away from immigration officials with the power to send illegal immigrants back to their own countries.

10. **loath:** unwilling.

11. **pro-KMT:** on the side of the Kuomintang, or Nationalist Party, which controls the government of Taiwan.

Illustration Copyright © Darryl Zudeck.

this, but my father conceived of laws as speed bumps rather than curbs. He wiped the counter with his sleeve, and told Booker to report the next morning.

"I will be good worker," said Booker.

"Good," said my father.

"Anything you want me to do, I will do."

My father nodded.

Booker seemed to sink into himself for a moment. "Thank you," he said finally. "I am appreciate your help. I am very, very appreciate for everything." He reached out to shake my father's hand.

My father looked at him. "Did you eat today?" he asked in Mandarin.

Booker pulled at the hem of his jacket.

"Sit down," said my father. "Please, have a seat."

My father didn't tell my mother about Booker, and my mother didn't tell my father about the country club. She would never have applied, except that Mona, while over at Annie's, had let it drop that our mother wanted to join. Mrs. Lardner came by the very next day.

"Why, I'd be honored and delighted to write you people a letter," she said. Her skirt billowed around her.

"Thank you so much," said my mother. "But it's too much trouble for you, and also my husband is . . ."

"Oh, it's no trouble at all, no trouble at all. I tell you." She leaned forward so that her chest freckles showed. "I know just how it is. It's a secret of course, but you know, my natural father was Jewish. Can you see it? Just look at my skin."

"My husband," said my mother.

"I'd be honored and delighted," said Mrs. Lardner with a little wave of her hands. "Just honored and delighted."

Mona was triumphant. "See, Mom," she said, waltzing around the kitchen when Mrs. Lardner left. "What did I tell you? 'I'm just honored and delighted, just honored and delighted.'" She waved her hands in the air.

"You know, the Chinese have a saying," said my mother. "To do nothing is better than to overdo. You mean well, but you tell me now what will happen."

"I'll talk Dad into it," said Mona, still waltzing. "Or I bet Callie can. He'll do anything Callie says."

"I can try, anyway," I said.

"Did you hear what I said?" said my mother. Mona bumped into the broom closet door. "You're not going to talk anything; you've already made enough trouble." She started on the dishes with a clatter.

Mona poked diffidently at a mop.

I sponged off the counter. "Anyway," I ventured. "I bet our name'll never even come up."

"That's if we're lucky," said my mother.

"There's all these people waiting," I said.

"Good," she said. She started on a pot.

I looked over at Mona, who was still cowering in the broom closet. "In fact, there's some black family's been waiting so long, they're going to sue," I said.

My mother turned off the water. "Where'd you hear that?"

"Patty told me."

She turned the water back on, started to wash a dish, then put it back down and shut the faucet.

"I'm sorry," said Mona.

"Forget it," said my mother. "Just forget it."

Booker turned out to be a model worker, whose boundless gratitude translated into a willingness to do anything. As he also learned quickly, he soon knew not only how to bus, but how to cook, and how to wait table, and how to keep the books. He fixed the walk-in door so that it stayed shut, reupholstered the torn seats in the dining room, and devised a system for tracking inventory. The only stone in the rice was that he tended to be sickly; but, reliable even in illness, he would always send a friend to take his place. In this way we got to know Ronald, Lynn, Dirk, and Cedric, all of whom, like Booker, had problems with their legal status and were anxious to please. They weren't all as capable as Booker, though, with the exception of Cedric, whom my father often hired even when Booker was well. A round wag of a man who called Mona and me *shou hou*—skinny monkeys—he was a professed nonsmoker who was nevertheless always begging drags off of other people's cigarettes. This last habit drove our head cook, Fernando, crazy, especially since, when refused a hit, Cedric would occasionally snitch one. Winking impishly at Mona and me, he would steal up to an ashtray, take a quick puff, and then break out laughing so that the smoke came rolling out of his mouth in a great incriminatory cloud. Fernando accused him of stealing fresh cigarettes too, even whole packs.

"Why else do you think he's weaseling around in the back of the store all the time," he said. His face was blotchy with anger. "The man is a thief."

Other members of the staff supported him in this contention and joined in on an "Operation Identification," which involved numbering and initialing their cigarettes—even though what they seemed to fear for wasn't so much their cigarettes as their jobs. Then one of the cooks quit; and rather than promote someone, my father hired Cedric for the position. Rumors flew that he was taking only half the normal salary, that Alex had been pressured to resign, and that my father was looking for a position with which to placate Booker, who had been bypassed because of his health.

The result was that Fernando categorically refused to work with Cedric.

"The only way I'll cook with that piece of slime," he said, shaking his huge tattooed fist, "is if he's frying on the grill."

My father cajoled and cajoled, to no avail, and in the end was simply forced to put them on different schedules.

The next week Fernando got caught stealing a carton of minute steaks. My father would not tell even Mona and me how he knew to be standing by the back door when Fernando was on his way out, but everyone suspected Booker. Everyone but Fernando, that is, who was sure Cedric had been the tip-off. My father held a staff meeting in which he tried to reassure everyone that Alex had left on his own, and that he had no intention of firing anyone. But though he was careful not to mention Fernando, everyone was so amazed that he was being allowed to stay that Fernando was incensed nonetheless.

"Don't you all be putting your bug eyes on me," he said. "*He's* the crook." He grabbed Cedric by the collar.

Cedric raised an eyebrow. "Cook, you mean," he said.

At this Fernando punched Cedric in the mouth; and the words he had just uttered notwithstanding, my father fired him on the spot.

With everything that was happening, Mona and I were ready to be getting out of the restaurant. It was almost time: the days were still stuffy with summer, but our window shade had started flapping in the evening as if gearing up to go out. That year the breezes were full of salt, as they sometimes were when they came in from the East, and they blew anchors and docks through my mind like so many tumbleweeds, filling my dreams with wherries[12] and lobsters and grainy-faced men who squinted, day in and day out, at the sky.

It was time for a change, you could feel it; and yet the pancake house was the same as ever. The day before school started my father came home with bad news.

"Fernando called police," he said, wiping his hand on his pant leg.

My mother naturally wanted to know what police; and so with much coughing and hawing, the long story began, the latest installment of which had the police calling immigration, and immigration sending an investigator. My mother sat stiff as whalebone as my father described how the man summarily refused lunch on the house and how my father had admitted, under pressure, that he knew there were "things" about his workers.

"So now what happens?"

My father didn't know. "Booker and Cedric went with him to the jail," he said. "But me, here I am." He laughed uncomfortably.

The next day my father posted bail for "his boys" and waited apprehensively for something to happen. The day after that he waited again, and the day after that he called our neighbor's law student son, who suggested my father call the immigration department under an alias. My father took his advice; and it was thus that he discovered that Booker was right: it was illegal for aliens to work, but it wasn't to hire them.[13]

In the happy interval that ensued, my father apologized to my mother, who in turn confessed about the country club, for which my father had no choice but to forgive her. Then he turned his attention back to "his boys."

My mother didn't see that there was anything to do.

---

12. **wherries:** light rowboats.

13. **it wasn't to hire them:** Although this statement was true at the time, U.S. law now prohibits the hiring of illegal aliens.

WORDS TO KNOW

cajole (kə-jōl′) *v.* to persuade by pleasant words or flattery; coax

WITH EVERYTHING
THAT WAS HAPPENING,
MONA AND I WERE READY
TO BE GETTING OUT
OF THE RESTAURANT.
IT WAS ALMOST TIME:
THE DAYS WERE STILL
STUFFY WITH SUMMER,
BUT OUR WINDOW SHADE
HAD STARTED FLAPPING
IN THE EVENING AS IF
GEARING UP TO GO OUT.

"I like to talking to the judge," said my father.

"This is not China," said my mother.

"I'm only talking to him. I'm not give him money unless he wants it."

"You're going to land up in jail."

"So what else I should do?" My father threw up his hands. "Those are my boys."

"Your boys!" exploded my mother. "What about your family? What about your wife?"

My father took a long sip of tea. "You know," he said finally. "In the war my father sent our cook to the soldiers to use. He always said it—the province comes before the town, the town comes before the family."

"A restaurant is not a town," said my mother.

My father sipped at his tea again. "You know, when I first come to the United States, I also had to hide-and-seek with those deportation guys. If people did not helping me, I'm not here today."

My mother scrutinized her hem.

After a minute I volunteered that before seeing a judge, he might try a lawyer.

He turned. "Since when did you become so afraid like your mother?"

I started to say that it wasn't a matter of fear, but he cut me off.

"What I need today," he said, "is a son."

My father and I spent the better part of the next day standing in lines at the immigration office. He did not get to speak to a judge, but with much persistence he managed to speak to a judge's clerk, who tried to persuade him that it was not her place to extend him advice. My father, though, shamelessly plied her with compliments and offers of free pancakes until she finally conceded that she personally doubted anything would happen to either Cedric or Booker.

"Especially if they're 'needed workers,'" she said, rubbing at the red marks her glasses left on her nose. She yawned. "Have you thought about sponsoring them to become permanent residents?"

Could he do that? My father was overjoyed. And what if he saw to it right away? Would she perhaps put in a good word with the judge?

She yawned again, her nostrils flaring. "Don't worry," she said. "They'll get a fair hearing."

My father returned jubilant. Booker and Cedric hailed him as their savior, their Buddha incarnate. He was like a father to them, they said; and laughing and clapping, they made him tell the story over and over, sorting over the details like jewels. And how old was the assistant judge? And what did she say?

That evening my father tipped the paperboy a dollar and bought a pot of mums for my mother, who suffered them to be placed on the dining room table. The next night he took us all out to dinner. Then on Saturday, Mona found a letter on my father's chair at the restaurant.

> Dear Mr. Chang,
> You are the grat boss. But, we do not like to trial, so will runing away now. Plese to excus us. People saying the law in America is fears like dragon. Here is only $140. We hope some day we can pay back the rest bale. You will getting intrest, as you diserving, so grat a boss you are. Thank you for every thing. In next life you will be burn in rich family, with no more pancaks.
>
> Yours truley,
> Booker + Cedric

In the weeks that followed my father went to the pancake house for crises, but otherwise hung around our house, fiddling idly with the sump pump and boiler in an effort, he said, to get ready for winter. It was as though he had gone into retirement, except that instead of moving South, he had moved to the basement. He even took to showering my mother with little attentions, and to calling her "old girl," and when we finally heard that the club had entertained all the applications it could for the year, he was so sympathetic that he seemed more disappointed than my mother.

WORDS TO KNOW

scrutinize (skrōōt'n-īz') *v.* to look over carefully; study
jubilant (jōō'bə-lənt) *adj.* joyful and triumphant

Mrs. Lardner tempered the bad news with an invitation to a bon voyage[14] "bash" she was throwing for a friend of hers who was going to Greece for six months.

"Do come," she urged. "You'll meet everyone, and then, you know, if things open up in the spring . . ." She waved her hands.

My mother wondered if it would be appropriate to show up at a party for someone they didn't know, but "the honest truth" was that this was an annual affair. "If it's not Greece, it's Antibes," sighed Mrs. Lardner. "We really just do it because his wife left him and his daughter doesn't speak to him, and poor Jeremy just feels so *unloved.*"

She also invited Mona and me to the goings on, as "*demi*-guests" to keep Annie out of the champagne. I wasn't too keen on the idea, but before I could say anything, she had already thanked us for so generously agreeing to honor her with our presence.

"A pair of little princesses, you are!" she told us. "A pair of princesses!"

The party was that Sunday. On Saturday, my mother took my father out shopping for a suit. As it was the end of September, she insisted that he buy a worsted rather than a seersucker, even though it was only ten, rather than fifty percent off. My father protested that it was as hot out as ever, which was true—a thick Indian summer had cozied murderously up to us—but to no avail. Summer clothes, said my mother, were not properly worn after Labor Day.

The suit was unfortunately as extravagant in length as it was in price, which posed an additional quandary, since the tailor wouldn't be in until Monday. The salesgirl, though, found a way of tacking it up temporarily.

"Maybe this suit not fit me," fretted my father.

"Just don't take your jacket off," said the salesgirl.

He gave her a tip before they left, but when he got home refused to remove the price tag.

"I like to asking the tailor about the size," he insisted.

"You mean you're going to *wear* it and then return it?" Mona rolled her eyes.

"I didn't say I'm return it," said my father stiffly. "I like to asking the tailor, that's all."

The party started off swimmingly, except that most people were wearing bermudas or wrap skirts. Still, my parents carried on, sharing with great feeling the complaints about the heat. Of course my father tried to eat a cracker full of shallots[15] and burnt himself in an attempt to help Mr. Lardner turn the coals of the barbeque; but on the whole he seemed to be doing all right. Not nearly so well as my mother, though, who had accepted an entire cupful of Mrs. Lardner's magic punch, and seemed indeed to be under some spell. As Mona and Annie skirmished over whether some boy in their class inhaled when he smoked, I watched my mother take off her shoes, laughing and laughing as a man with a beard regaled her with navy stories by the pool. Apparently he had been stationed in the Orient and remembered a few words of Chinese, which made my mother laugh still more. My father excused himself to go to the men's room then drifted back and weighed anchor at the hors d'oeuvres table, while my mother sailed on to a group of women, who tinkled at length over the clarity of her complexion. I dug out a book I had brought.

Just when I'd cracked the spine, though, Mrs. Lardner came by to bewail her shortage of servers. Her caterers were criminals, I agreed; and the next thing I knew I was handing out bits of marine life, making the rounds as amicably as I could.

"Here you go, Dad," I said when I got to the hors d'oeuvres table.

14. **bon voyage** (bôɴ′ vwä-yäzh′): a farewell to a traveler.

15. **shallots:** small garliclike onions.

WORDS TO KNOW

amicably (ăm′ĭ-kə-blē) *adv.* in a friendly way

"Everything is fine," he said.

I hesitated to leave him alone; but then the man with the beard zeroed in on him, and though he talked of nothing but my mother, I thought it would be okay to get back to work. Just that moment, though, Jeremy Brothers lurched our way, an empty, albeit corked, wine bottle in hand. He was a slim, well-proportioned man, with a Roman nose and small eyes and a nice manly jaw that he allowed to hang agape.

"Hello," he said drunkenly. "Pleased to meet you."

"Pleased to meeting you," said my father.

"Right," said Jeremy. "Right. Listen. I have this bottle here, this most recalcitrant bottle. You see that it refuses to do my bidding. I bid it open sesame, please, and it does nothing." He pulled the cork out with his teeth, then turned the bottle upside down.

My father nodded.

"Would you have a word with it please?" said Jeremy. The man with the beard excused himself. "Would you please have a damned word with it?"

My father laughed uncomfortably.

"Ah!" Jeremy bowed a little. "Excuse me, excuse me, excuse me. You are not my man, not my man at all." He bowed again and started to leave, but then circled back. "Viticulture[16] is not your forte, yes I can see that, see that plainly. But may I trouble you on another matter? Forget the damned bottle." He threw it into the pool, and winked at the people he splashed. "I have another matter. Do you speak Chinese?"

My father said he did not, but Jeremy pulled out a handkerchief with some characters on it anyway, saying that his daughter had sent it from Hong Kong and that he thought the characters might be some secret message.

"Long life," said my father.

"But you haven't looked at it yet."

"I know what it says without looking." My father winked at me.

"You do?"

"Yes, I do."

"You're making fun of me, aren't you?"

"No, no, no," said my father, winking again.

"Who are you anyway?" said Jeremy.

His smile fading, my father shrugged.

"Who are you?"

My father shrugged again.

Jeremy began to roar. "This is my party, *my party,* and I've never seen you before in my life." My father backed up as Jeremy came toward him. *"Who are you? WHO ARE YOU?"*

Just as my father was going to step back into the pool, Mrs. Lardner came running up. Jeremy informed her that there was a man crashing his party.

"Nonsense," said Mrs. Lardner. "This is Ralph Chang, who I invited extra especially so he could meet you." She straightened the collar of Jeremy's peach-colored polo shirt for him.

"Yes, well we've had a chance to chat," said Jeremy.

She whispered in his ear; he mumbled something; she whispered something more.

"I do apologize," he said finally.

My father didn't say anything.

"I do." Jeremy seemed genuinely contrite. "Doubtless you've seen drunks before, haven't you? You must have them in China."

"Okay," said my father.

As Mrs. Lardner glided off, Jeremy clapped his arm over my father's shoulders. "You know, I really am quite sorry, quite sorry."

My father nodded.

"What can I do, how can I make it up to you?"

"No thank you."

"No, tell me, tell me," wheedled Jeremy. "Tickets to casino night?" My father shook his head. "You don't gamble. Dinner at Bartholomew's?" My father shook his head again.

16. **viticulture:** the growing of grapevines.

WORDS TO KNOW	
	recalcitrant (rĭ-kăl′sĭ-trənt) *adj.* stubborn; hard to deal with
	forte (fôrt) *n.* something in which a person excels
	contrite (kən-trīt) *adj.* sorrowful for one's wrongdoing; repentant

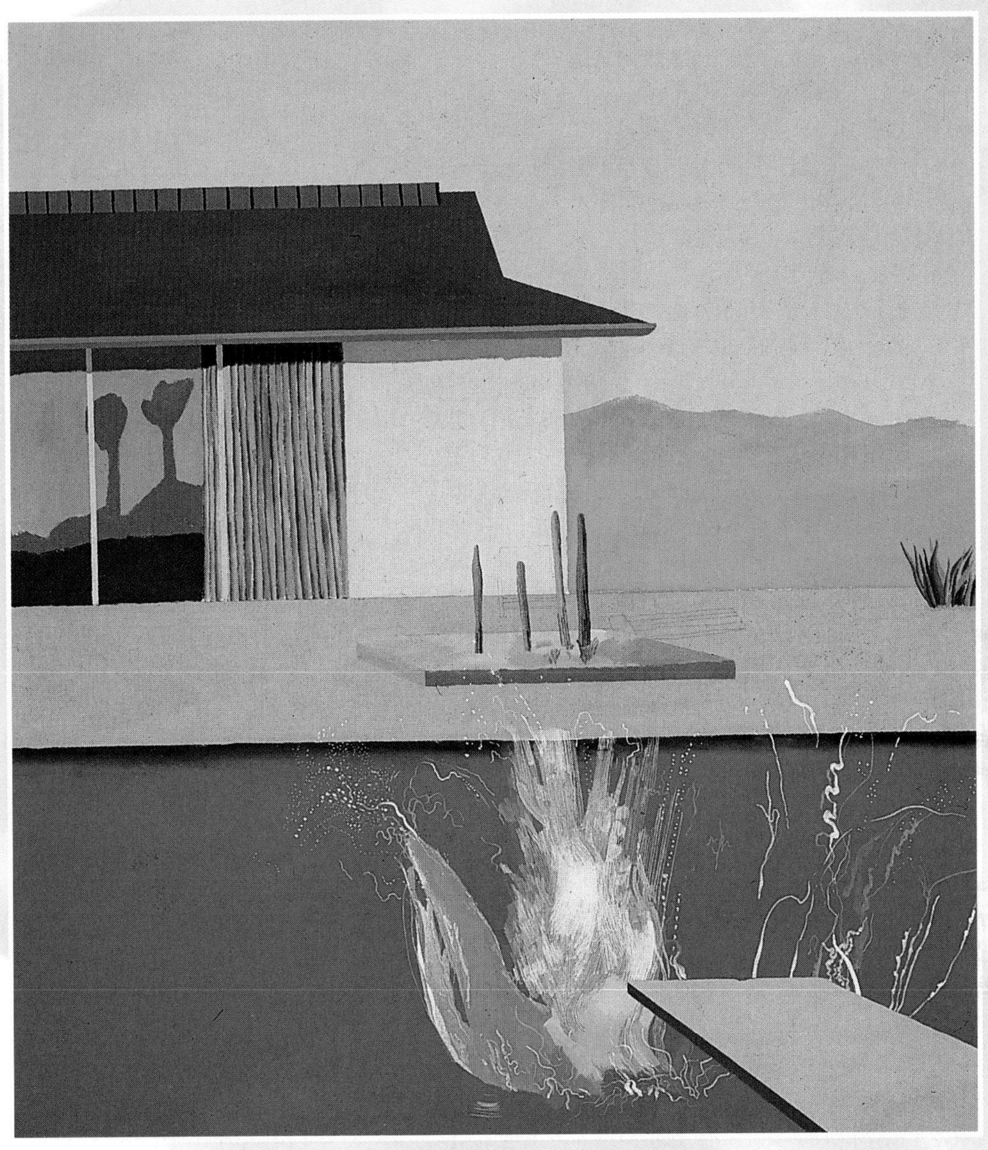

The Splash (1966), David Hockney. Acrylic on canvas, 72″ × 72″.
Copyright © David Hockney.

"WHO ARE YOU?

WHO ARE YOU?"

"You don't eat." Jeremy scratched his chin. "You know, my wife was like you. Old Annabelle could never let me make things up—never, never, never, never, never."

My father wriggled out from under his arm.

"How about sport clothes? You are rather overdressed, you know, excuse me for saying so. But here." He took off his polo shirt and folded it up. "You can have this with my most profound apologies." He ruffled his chest hairs with his free hand.

"No thank you," said my father.

"No, take it, take it. Accept my apologies." He thrust the shirt into my father's arms. "I'm so very sorry, so very sorry. Please, try it on."

Helplessly holding the shirt, my father searched the crowd for my mother.

"Here, I'll help you off with your coat."

My father froze.

Jeremy reached over and took his jacket off. "Milton's, one hundred twenty-five dollars reduced to one hundred twelve-fifty," he read. "What a bargain, what a bargain!"

"Please give it back," pleaded my father. "Please."

"Now for your shirt," ordered Jeremy.

Heads began to turn.

"Take off your shirt."

"I do not take orders like a servant," announced my father.

"Take off your shirt, or I'm going to throw this jacket right into the pool, just right into this little pool here." Jeremy held it over the water.

"Go ahead."

"One hundred twelve-fifty," taunted Jeremy. "One hundred twelve . . ."

My father flung the polo shirt into the water with such force that part of it bounced back up into the air like a fluorescent fountain. Then it settled into a soft heap on top of the water. My mother hurried up.

"You're a sport!" said Jeremy, suddenly breaking into a smile and slapping my father on the back. "You're a sport! I like that. A man with spirit, that's what you are. A man with panache. Allow me to return to you your jacket." He handed it back to my father. "Good value you got on that, good value."

My father hurled the coat into the pool too. "We're leaving," he said grimly. "Leaving!"

"Now, Ralphie," said Mrs. Lardner, bustling up; but my father was already stomping off.

"Get your sister," he told me. To my mother: "Get your shoes."

"That was *great,* Dad," said Mona as we walked down to the car. "You were *stupendous.*"

"Way to show 'em," I said.

"What?" said my father offhandedly.

Although it was only just dusk, we were in a gulch, which made it hard to see anything except the gleam of his white shirt moving up the hill ahead of us.

"It was all my fault," began my mother.

"Forget it," said my father grandly. Then he said, "The only trouble is I left those keys in my jacket pocket."

"Oh *no,*" said Mona.

"Oh no is right," said my mother.

"So we'll walk home," I said.

"But how're we going to get into the *house,*" said Mona.

The noise of the party churned through the silence.

"Someone has to going back," said my father.

"Let's go to the pancake house first," suggested my mother. "We can wait there until the party is finished, and then call Mrs. Lardner."

Having all agreed that that was a good plan, we started walking again.

"God, just think," said Mona. "We're going to have to *dive* for them."

My father stopped a moment. We waited.

"You girls are good swimmers," he said finally. "Not like me."

Then his shirt started moving again, and we trooped up the hill after it, into the dark. ❖

WORDS TO KNOW

panache (pə-năsh′) *n.* a sense of style; flair

RESPONDING OPTIONS

FROM PERSONAL RESPONSE *TO* CRITICAL ANALYSIS

REFLECT 1. As you finished reading this story, what did you think of the Chang family? Respond in your notebook.

RETHINK 2. Look at the motivation chart you made for the Reading Connection on page 717. What does fitting into American society seem to mean to Mr. Chang? to Mrs. Chang?

3. What is your opinion of the way the members of Mr. Chang's family treat him?

4. In your view, is Mr. Chang more effective in his own society (Section I) or in the American society (Section II)?

   Consider
   - the way he treats his employees
   - his efforts to help Booker and Cedric
   - his encounter with Jeremy Brothers

5. How would you describe the American society that the Changs encounter?

RELATE 6. Recall your discussion, for the Personal Connection on page 717, about fitting into a new society. Did the events of the story remind you of any that you had discussed?

ANOTHER PATHWAY

Assume the identity of the narrator, her mother, an original employee of the pancake house, Booker, Cedric, Mrs. Lardner, or Jeremy Brothers. Write a letter to a friend, telling about your experiences with Mr. Chang. Include your ideas about why he acts as he does. Read your letter to the class.

LITERARY CONCEPTS

The **structure** of a work of literature is the way in which it is put together—the arrangement of its parts. Prose writing is most often structured either by idea or by incident. For example, F. Scott Fitzgerald's "Winter Dreams" (page 680) is divided into six sections, each presenting a stage in Dexter Green's relationship with Judy Jones.

Cooperative Learning Work with a small group of classmates to create a chart comparing the two sections of "In the American Society." Note similarities and differences between the settings, the conflicts, the characters, and the events presented in the two sections. What do the sections tell together that neither tells alone?

QUICKWRITES

1. Outline an **argument** for or against assimilation—the process of adapting one's values and expectations in order to fit into the prevailing society. Keep in mind issues such as cultural identity, personal integrity, and economic necessity, and support your argument with reasons and examples drawn from the story, your Personal Connection discussion, and other sources.

2. Did reading this story make you want to read another work by Gish Jen? In a draft of a **critical review,** discuss an aspect of the story—such as tone, characterization, or theme—that you particularly admired or disliked. Quote passages from the story to illustrate your ideas.

PORTFOLIO *Save your writing. You may want to use it later as a springboard to a piece for your portfolio.*

LITERARY LINKS

How are the challenges that the Changs face in America similar to and different from those faced by the narrator of "America and I"? Would they define the American dream in the same way that she does?

ACROSS THE CURRICULUM

Business What does Mr. Chang do wrong in his running of the pancake house? What does he do right? Call or visit a local restaurant owner to find out about the challenges of operating such a business, particularly those involving the managing of employees. Report on your conversation, or invite the restaurant owner to speak to the class.

WORDS TO KNOW

EXERCISE A For each group of words below, write the letter of the word that is a synonym of the boldfaced word.

1. **cajole:** (a) coax, (b) support, (c) control
2. **recalcitrant:** (a) ignorant, (b) unlucky, (c) headstrong
3. **forte:** (a) talent, (b) security, (c) sensitivity
4. **amicably:** (a) intensely, (b) pleasantly, (c) efficiently
5. **contrite:** (a) shallow, (b) clever, (c) apologetic

EXERCISE B Write the vocabulary word, not used in Exercise A, that is suggested by each set of idioms.

1. walking on air, feeling one's heart sing, being A-OK
2. give the shirt off one's back, fork out, shower blessings upon
3. take up the case of, be a go-between, pave the way
4. pore over, dig into, comb through
5. carry it off with style, show a lot of dash, strut one's stuff

GISH JEN

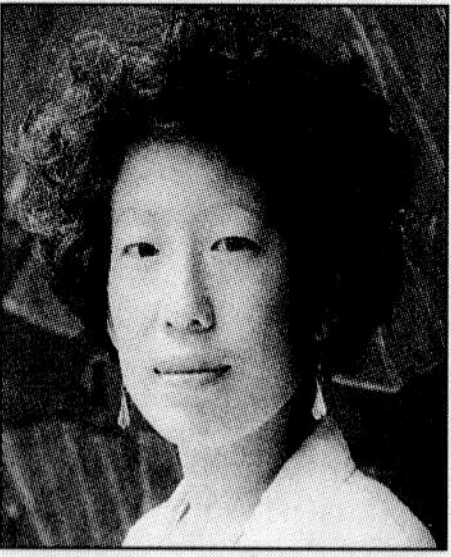

1956?–

Gish Jen, whose real first name is Lillian, began calling herself Gish (from the name of the early motion-picture actress Lillian Gish) when she was in high school. Her parents, who had come to the United States as students, had been forced to stay here when the U.S. government, after China came under Communist rule in 1949, refused to allow Chinese students to return home. She grew up in Scarsdale, New York, where hers was the only Asian family in the neighborhood.

Like Ralph Chang's daughters in "In the American Society," Jen often felt ill at ease growing up in American society: "I'd learn all these manners from my parents . . . and then I found I didn't have the right manners for this society, and so I then had to learn this whole other set of right manners for this place where we were living."

In 1991 Jen published her first novel, *Typical American,* which was nominated for a National Book Critics Circle Award. The novel grew out of several short stories, including "In the American Society," as well as her experiences during a nine-month stay in China, when she taught English to coal-mining engineers. "I realized," she has said, "that there were things in my *thinking,* in my habits of mind, that came from China, and out of many of those realizations rose *Typical American.*"

OTHER WORKS "What Means Switch," "The Water-Faucet Vision"

PREVIEWING

FICTION

English as a Second Language

Lucy Honig

PERSONAL CONNECTION

Do you know someone whose first language is not English? Do you yourself speak or have you tried to learn a language other than English? Have you ever tried to make yourself understood by a person who speaks a different language? Discuss your experiences with the class.

HISTORICAL/GEOGRAPHICAL CONNECTION

Most of the recent immigrants to the United States have come from the Caribbean, Asia, and Latin America. Like the immigrants of the past, many have left their homelands for economic, social, or political reasons and have arrived speaking a language other than English. Maria Perez, the main character in "English as a Second Language," is a Spanish-speaking Guatemalan refugee who came to the United States in the early 1980s. Between 1981 and 1990, nearly 90,000 Guatemalans fled to the United States to escape the recurring warfare between government troops and antigovernment guerrillas in their homeland. Some of these refugees—like Maria—lived in the United States unlawfully until the enactment of a 1986 law allowed them to become legal residents.

READING CONNECTION

Noticing Narrative Technique In "English as a Second Language," events are not narrated in strict chronological order. As you read the story, watch for abrupt shifts in time and place. These shifts are sometimes signaled by spaces between paragraphs or by transitional words such as *now* or *suddenly.* Also look for flashbacks that describe what happened in the past in the characters' home countries.

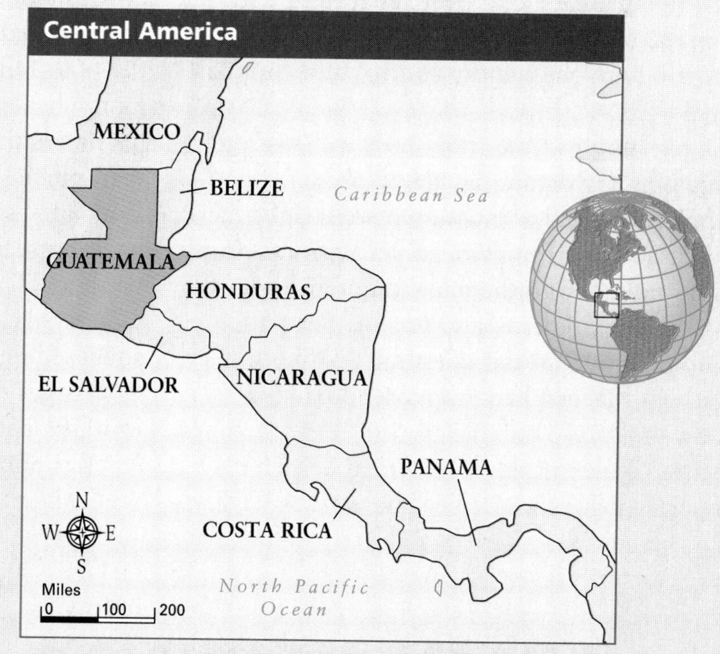

- *HISTORICAL CONNECTION*
- *CULTURAL CONNECTION*

ENGLISH AS A

LUCY HONIG

Inside Room 824, Maria parked the vacuum cleaner, fastened all the locks and the safety chain and kicked off her shoes. Carefully she lay a stack of fluffy towels on the bathroom vanity. She turned the air conditioning up high and the lights down low. Then she hoisted up the skirt of her uniform and settled all the way back on the king-sized bed with her legs straight out in front of her. Her feet and ankles were swollen. She wriggled her toes. She threw her arms out in each direction and still her hands did not come near the edges of the bed. From here she could see, out the picture window, the puffs of green treetops in Central Park, the tiny people circling along the paths below. She tore open a small foil bag of cocktail peanuts and ate them very slowly, turning each one over separately with her tongue until the salt dissolved. She snapped on the TV with the remote control and flipped channels.

The big mouth game show host was kissing and hugging a woman playing on the left-hand team. Her husband and children were right there with her, and *still* he encircled her with his arms. Then he sidled up to the daughter, a girl younger than her own Giuliette, and *hugged* her and kept *holding* her, asking questions. None of his business, if this girl had a boyfriend back in Saginaw!

"Mama, you just don't understand." That's what Jorge always said when she watched TV at home. He and his teenaged friends would sit around in their torn bluejeans dropping potato chips between the cushions of her couch and laughing, writhing with laughter while she sat like a stone.

Now the team on the right were hugging each other, squealing, jumping up and down. They'd just won a whole new kitchen—refrigerator, dishwasher, clothes washer, microwave, *everything!* Maria could win a whole new kitchen too, someday. You just spun a wheel, picked some words. She could do that.

She saw herself on TV with Carmen and Giuliette and Jorge. Her handsome children were so quick to press the buzzers the other team never had a chance to answer first. And they got every single answer right. Her children shrieked and clapped and jumped up and down each time the board lit up. They kissed and hugged that man whenever they won a prize. That man put his hands on her beautiful young daughters. That man pinched and kissed *her,* an old woman, in front of the whole world! Imagine seeing *this* back home! Maria frowned, chewing on the foil wrapper. There was nobody left at home in Guatemala, nobody to care if a strange man squeezed her wrinkled flesh on the TV.

"Forget it, Mama. They don't let poor people on these programs," Jorge said one day.

"But poor people need the money, they can win it here!"

WORDS TO KNOW **sidle** (sīd'l) *v.* to move forward in a shy or sneaky way

Jorge sighed impatiently. "They don't give it away because you *need* it!"

It was true, she had never seen a woman with her kids say on a show: My husband's dead. Jorge knew. They made sure before they invited you that you were the right kind of people and you said the right things. Where would she put a new kitchen in her cramped apartment anyway? No hookups for a washer, no space for a two-door refrigerator . . .

She slid sideways off the bed, carefully smoothed out the quilted spread, and squeezed her feet into her shoes. Back out in the hall she counted the bath towels in her cart to see if there were enough for the next wing. Then she wheeled the cart down the long corridor, silent on the deep blue rug.

Maria pulled the new pink dress on over her head, eased her arms into the sleeves, then let the skirt slide into place. In the mirror she saw a small dark protrusion from a large pink flower. She struggled to zip up in back, then she fixed the neck, attaching the white collar she had crocheted. She pinned the rhinestone brooch on next. Shaking the pantyhose out of the package, she remembered the phrase: the cow before the horse,[1] wasn't that it? She should have put these on first. Well, so what. She rolled down the left leg of the nylons, stuck her big toe in, and drew the sheer fabric around her foot, unrolling it up past her knee. Then she did the right foot, careful not to catch the hose on the small flap of scar.

The right foot bled badly when she ran over the broken glass, over what had been the only window of the house. It had shattered from gunshots across the dirt yard. The chickens dashed around frantically, squawking, trying to fly, spraying brown feathers into the air. When she had seen Pedro's head turn to blood and the two oldest boys dragged away, she swallowed every word, every cry, and ran with the two girls. The fragments of glass stayed in her foot for all the days of hiding. They ran and ran and ran and somehow Jorge caught up and they were found by their own side and smuggled out. And still she was silent, until the nurse at the border went after the glass and drained the mess inside her foot. Then she had sobbed and screamed, "Aaiiiee!"

"Mama, stop thinking and get ready," said Carmen.

"It is too short, your skirt," Maria said in Spanish. "What will they say?"

Carmen laughed. "It's what they all wear, except for you old ladies."

"Not to work! Not to school!"

1. **the cow before the horse:** a mistaken reminiscence of the phrase "putting the cart before the horse," which means doing things in the wrong order.

WORDS TO KNOW

protrusion (prō-trōō'zhən) *n.* something that juts or projects outward

"Yes, to work, to school! And Mama, you are going for an award for your English, for all you've learned, so please speak English!"

Maria squeezed into the pink high heels and held each foot out, one by one, so she could admire the beautiful slim arch of her own instep, like the feet of the American ladies on Fifth Avenue. Carmen laughed when she saw her mother take the first faltering steps, and Maria laughed too. How much she had already practiced in secret, and still it was so hard! She teetered on them back and forth from the kitchen to the bedroom, trying to feel steady, until Carmen finally sighed and said, "Mama, quick now or you'll be late!"

She didn't know if it was a good omen or a bad one, the two Indian women on the subway. They could have been sitting on the dusty ground at the market in San—, selling corn or clay pots, with the bright-colored striped shawls and full skirts, the black hair pulled into two braids down each back, the deeply furrowed square faces set in those impassive expressions, seeing everything, seeing nothing. They were exactly as they must have been back home, but she was seeing them *here,* on the downtown IRT[2] from the Bronx, surrounded by businessmen in suits, kids with big radio boxes, girls in skin-tight jeans and dark purple lipstick. Above them, advertisements for family planning and TWA. They were like stone-age men sitting on the train in loincloths made from animal skins, so out of place, out of time. Yet timeless. Maria thought, they are timeless guardian spirits, here to accompany me to my honors. Did anyone else see them? As strange as they were, nobody looked. Maria's heart pounded faster. The boys with the radios were standing right over them and never saw them. They were invisible to everyone but her: Maria was utterly convinced of it. The spirit world had come back to life, here on the number 4 train! It was a miracle!

"Mama, look, you see the grandmothers?" said Carmen.

"Of course I see them," Maria replied, trying to hide the disappointment in her voice. So Carmen saw them too. They were not invisible. Carmen rolled her eyes and smirked derisively as she nodded in their direction, but before she could put her derision into words, Maria became stern. "Have respect," she said. "They are the same as your father's people." Carmen's face sobered at once.

She panicked when they got to the big school by the river. "Like the United Nations," she said, seeing so much glass and brick, an endless esplanade[3] of concrete.

"It's only a college, Mama. People learn English here, too. And more, like nursing, electronics. This is where Anna's brother came for computers."

"Las Naciones Unidas," Maria repeated, and when the guard stopped them to ask where they were going, she answered in Spanish: to the literacy award ceremony.

"*English,* Mama!" whispered Carmen.

But the guard also spoke in Spanish: take the escalator to the third floor.

"See, he knows," Maria retorted.

"That's not the point," murmured Carmen, taking her mother by the hand.

Every inch of the enormous room was packed with people. She clung to Carmen and stood by the door paralyzed until Cheryl, her teacher, pushed her way to them and greeted Maria with a kiss. Then she led Maria back through the press of people to the small group of award winners from other programs. Maria smiled shakily and nodded hello.

---

2. **IRT:** Interborough Rapid Transit, the oldest of New York City's three subway systems.

3. **esplanade** (ĕs′plə-näd′): a level, open space, especially a public plaza or walkway.

WORDS TO KNOW

retort (rĭ-tôrt′) *v.* to reply; especially, to respond to an argument with a counterargument

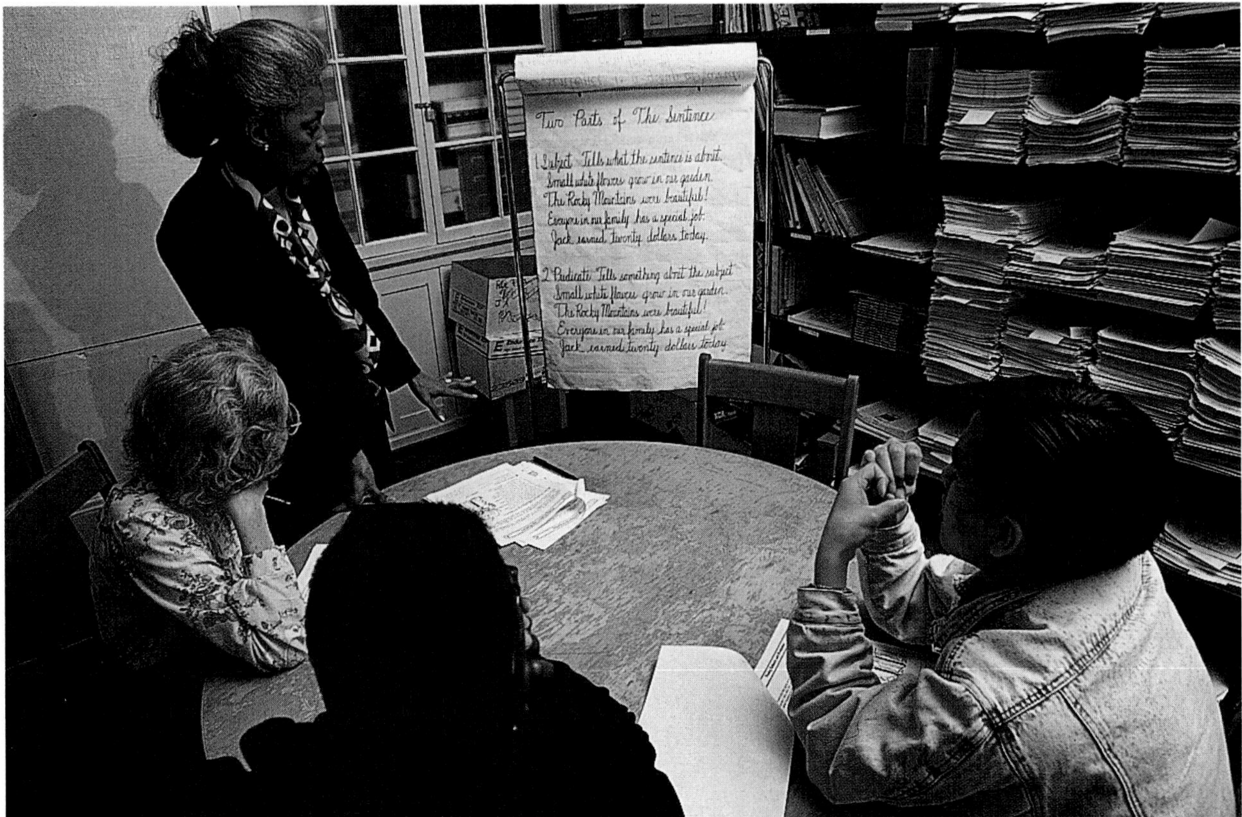

Students learning English as a second language. Copyright © 1987 Lawrence Migdale, all rights reserved.

"They're all here now!" Cheryl called out. A photographer rushed over and began to move the students closer together for a picture.

"Hey Bernie, wait for the Mayor!" someone shouted to him. He spun around, called out some words Maria did not understand, and without even turning back to them, he disappeared. But they stayed there, huddled close, not knowing if they could move. The Chinese man kept smiling, the tall black man stayed slightly crouched, the Vietnamese woman squinted, confused, her glasses still hidden in her fist. Maria saw all the cameras along the sides of the crowd, and the lights, and the people from television with video machines, and more lights. Her stomach began to jump up and down. Would she be on television, in the newspapers? Still smiling, holding his pose, the Chinese man next to her asked, "Are you nervous?"

"Oh yes," she said. She tried to remember the expression Cheryl had taught them. "I have worms in my stomach," she said.

He was a much bigger man than she had imagined from seeing him on TV. His face was bright red as they ushered him into the room and quickly through the crowd, just as it was his turn to take the podium. He said hello to the other speakers and called them by their first names. The crowd drew closer to the little stage, the people standing farthest in the back pushed in. Maria tried hard to listen to the Mayor's words. "Great occasion . . . pride of our city . . . ever since I created the program . . . people who have worked so hard . . . overcoming hardship . . . come so far." Was that them? Was he talking about them already? Why were the people out there all starting to laugh? She strained to understand, but still caught only fragments of his words. "My mother used to say . . . and I said, Look Mama . . ." He was talking about *his* mother now; he called her Mama, just like Maria's kids called *her*. But everyone laughed so hard. At his mother? She forced herself to smile; up front, near the podium, everyone could see her. She should seem to pay attention and understand. Looking out into the crowd she felt dizzy. She tried to find Carmen among all the pretty young women with big eyes and dark hair. There she was! Carmen's eyes met Maria's; Carmen waved. Maria beamed out at her. For a moment she felt like she belonged there, in this crowd. Everyone was smiling, everyone was so happy while the Mayor of New York stood at the podium telling jokes. How happy Maria felt too!

"Maria Perez grew up in the countryside of Guatemala, the oldest daughter in a family of 19 children," read the Mayor as Maria stood quaking by his side. She noticed he made a slight wheezing noise when he breathed between words. She saw the hairs in his nostrils, black and white and wiry. He paused. "Nineteen children!" he exclaimed, looking at the audience. A small gasp was passed along through the crowd. Then the Mayor looked back at the sheet of paper before him. "Maria never had a chance to learn to read and write, and she was already the mother of five children of her own when she fled Guatemala in 1980 and made her way to New York for a new start."

It was her own story, but Maria had a hard time following. She had to stand next to him while he read it, and her feet had started to hurt, crammed into the new shoes. She shifted her weight from one foot to the other.

"At the age of 45, while working as a chambermaid and sending her children through school, Maria herself started school for the first time. In night courses she learned to read and write in her native Spanish. Later, as she was pursuing her G.E.D.[4] in Spanish, she began studying English as a Second Language. This meant Maria was going to school five nights a week! Still she worked as many as 60 hours cleaning rooms at the Plaza Hotel.

"Maria's ESL teacher, Cheryl Sands, says—and I quote—'Maria works harder than any student I have ever had. She is an inspiration to her classmates. Not only has she learned to read and write in her new language, but she initiated an oral history project in which she taped and transcribed interviews with other students, who have told their stories from around the world.' Maria was also one of the first in New York to apply for amnesty under the 1986 Immigration Act. Meanwhile, she has passed her enthusiasm for education to her children: her son is now a junior in high school, her youngest daughter attends the State University, and her oldest daughter, who we are proud to have with us today, is in her second year of law school on a scholarship."

Two older sons were dragged through the dirt, chickens squawking in mad confusion, feathers flying. She heard more gunshots in the distance, screams, chickens squawking. She heard, she ran. Maria looked down at her bleeding feet. Wedged tightly into the pink high heels, they throbbed.

The Mayor turned toward her. "Maria, I think it's wonderful that you have taken the trouble to preserve the folklore of students from so many countries." He paused. Was she supposed to say something? Her heart stopped beating. What was folklore? What was preserved? She smiled up at him, hoping that was all she needed to do.

"Maria, tell us now, if you can, what was one of the stories you collected in your project?"

4. **G.E.D.**: general equivalency diploma—the equivalent of a high school diploma.

WORDS TO KNOW

amnesty (ăm′nĭ-stē) *n.* a general pardon granted by a government, especially for political offenses

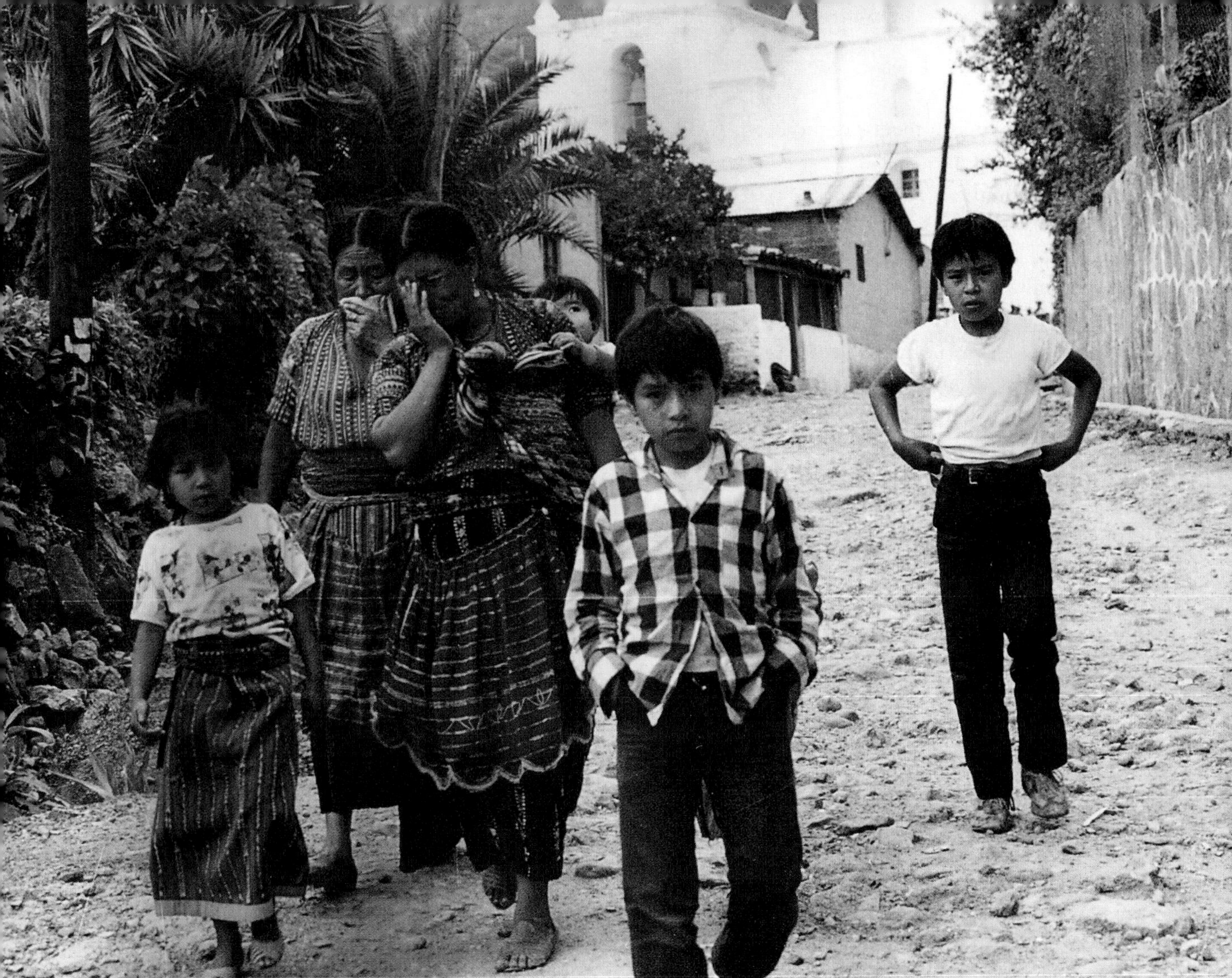

Women and children from the town of Jorge de Laguna in Guatemala. The military had just confiscated the land of the indigenous population and arrested all the men in the town. The men were later released. Copyright © 1983 Sherlyn Bjorkgren/DDB Stock Photo.

This was definitely a question, meant to be answered. Maria tried to smile again. She strained on tiptoes to reach the microphone, pinching her toes even more tightly in her shoes. "Okay," she said, setting off a high-pitched ringing from the microphone.

The Mayor said, "Stand back," and tugged at her collar. She quickly stepped away from the microphone.

"Okay," she said again, and this time there was no shrill sound. "One of my stories, from Guatemala. You want to hear?"

The Mayor put his arm around her shoulder and squeezed hard. Her first impulse was to wriggle away, but he held tight. "Isn't she wonderful?" he asked the audience. There was a low ripple of applause. "Yes, we want to hear!"

She turned and looked up at his face. Perspiration was shining on his forehead and she could see by the bright red bulge of his neck that his collar was too tight. "In my village in Guatemala," she began, "the mayor did not go along—get along—with the government so good."

"Hey, Maria," said the Mayor, "I know exactly how he felt!" The people in the audience laughed. Maria waited until they were quiet again.

"One day our mayor met with the people in

the village. Like you meet people here. A big crowd in the square."

"The people liked him, your mayor?"

"Oh, yes," said Maria. "Very much. He was very good. He tried for more roads, more doctors, new farms. He cared very much about his people."

The Mayor shook his head up and down. "Of course," he said, and again the audience laughed.

Maria said, "The next day after the meeting, the meeting in the square with all the people, soldiers come and shoot him dead."

For a second there was total silence. Maria realized she had not used the past tense and felt a deep, horrible stab of shame for herself, shame for her teacher. She was a disgrace! But she did not have more than a second of this horror before the whole audience began to laugh. What was happening? They couldn't be laughing at her bad verbs? They couldn't be laughing at her dead mayor! They laughed louder and louder and suddenly flashbulbs were going off around her, the TV cameras swung in close, too close, and the Mayor was grabbing her by the shoulders again, holding her tight, posing for one camera after another as the audience burst into wild applause. But she hadn't even finished! Why were they laughing?

"What timing, huh?" said the Mayor over the uproar. "What d'ya think, the Republicans put her here, or maybe the Board of Estimate?[5]" Everyone laughed even louder and he still clung to her and cameras still moved in close, lights kept going off in her face and she could see nothing but the sharp white poof! of light over and over again. She looked for Carmen and Cheryl, but the white poof! poof! poof! blinded her. She closed her eyes and listened to the uproar, now beginning to subside, and in her mind's eye saw chickens trying to fly, chickens fluttering around the yard littered with broken glass.

He squeezed her shoulders again and leaned into the microphone. "There are ways to get rid of mayors, and ways to get rid of mayors, huh Maria?"

The surge of laughter rose once more, reached a crescendo, and then began to subside again. "But wait," said the Mayor. The cameramen stepped back a bit, poising themselves for something new.

"I want to know just one more thing, Maria," said the Mayor, turning to face her directly again. The crowd quieted. He waited a few seconds more, then asked his question. "It says here 19 children. What was it like growing up in a house with 19 children? How many *bathrooms* did you have?"

Her stomach dropped and twisted as the mayor put his hand firmly on the back of her neck and pushed her toward the microphone again. It was absolutely quiet now in the huge room. Everyone was waiting for her to speak. She cleared her throat and made the microphone do the shrill hum. Startled, she jumped back. Then there was silence. She took a big, trembling breath.

"We had no bathrooms there, Mister Mayor," she said. "Only the outdoors."

The clapping started immediately, then the flashbulbs burning up in her face. The Mayor turned to her, put a hand on each of her shoulders, bent lower and kissed her! Kissed her on the cheek!

"Isn't she terrific?" he asked the audience, his hand on the back of her neck again, drawing her closer to him. The audience clapped louder, faster. "Isn't she just the greatest?"

She tried to smile and open her eyes, but the lights were still going off—poof! poof!—and the noise was deafening.

"Mama, look, your eyes were closed *there,* too," chided Jorge, sitting on the floor in front of the television set.

5. **Board of Estimate:** a committee responsible for estimating and managing a city's budget.

WORDS TO KNOW

crescendo (krə-shĕn′dō) *n.* a gradual increase in loudness or intensity

Maria had watched the camera move from the announcer at the studio desk to her own stout form in bright pink, standing by the Mayor.

"In my village in Guatemala," she heard herself say, and the camera showed her wrinkled face close up, eyes open now but looking nowhere. Then the mayor's face filled the screen, his forehead glistening, and then suddenly all the people in the audience, looking ahead, enrapt, took his place. Then there was her wrinkled face again, talking without a smile. ". . . soldiers come and shoot him dead." Maria winced, hearing the wrong tense of her verbs. The camera shifted from her face to the Mayor. In the brief moment of shamed silence after she'd uttered those words, the Mayor drew his finger like a knife across his throat. And the audience began to laugh.

"Turn it off!" she yelled to Jorge. "Off! This minute!"

Late that night she sat alone in the unlighted room, soaking her feet in Epsom salts.[6] The glow of the television threw shadows across the wall, but the sound was off. The man called Johnny[7] was on the screen, talking. The people in the audience and the men in the band and the movie stars sitting on the couch all had their mouths wide open in what she knew were screams of laughter while Johnny wagged his tongue. Maria heard nothing except brakes squealing below on the street and the lonely clanging of garbage cans in the alley.

She thought about her English class and remembered the pretty woman, Ling, who often fell asleep in the middle of a lesson. The other Chinese students all teased her. Everyone knew that she sewed coats in a sweatshop all day. After the night class she took the subway to the Staten Island Ferry, and after the ferry crossing she had to take a bus home. Her parents were old and sick and she did all their cooking and cleaning late at night. She struggled to keep awake in class; it seemed to take all her energy simply to smile and listen. She said very little and the teacher never forced her, but she fell further and further behind. They called her the Quiet One.

One day just before the course came to an end the Quiet One asked to speak. There was no reason, no provocation—they'd been talking informally about their summer plans—but Ling spoke with a sudden urgency. Her English was very slow. Seeing what a terrible effort it was for her, the classmates all tried to help when she searched for words.

"In my China village there was a teacher," Ling began. "Man teacher." She paused. "All children love him. He teach mathematic. He very—" She stopped and looked up toward the ceiling. Then she gestured with her fingers around her face.

"Handsome!" said Charlene, the oldest of the three Haitian sisters in the class.

Ling smiled broadly. "Handsome! Yes, he very handsome. Family very rich before. He have sister go to Hong Kong who have many, many money."

"*Much* money," said Maria.

"Much, much money," repeated Ling thoughtfully. "Teacher live in big house."

"In China? Near you?"

"Yes. Big house with much old picture." She stopped and furrowed her forehead, as if to gather words inside of it.

"Art? Paint? Pictures like that?" asked Xavier.

Ling nodded eagerly. "Yes. In big house. Most big house in village."

"But big house, money, rich like that, bad in China," said Fu Wu. "Those year, Government bad to you. How they let him do?"

"In *my* country," said Carlos, "government bad to you if you got *small* house, *no* money."

"Me too," said Maria.

"Me too," said Charlene.

The Chinese students laughed.

---

6. **Epsom salts:** a white powder that is dissolved in water to make a soothing bath.

7. **Johnny:** Johnny Carson, host of television's *The Tonight Show* from 1962 to 1993.

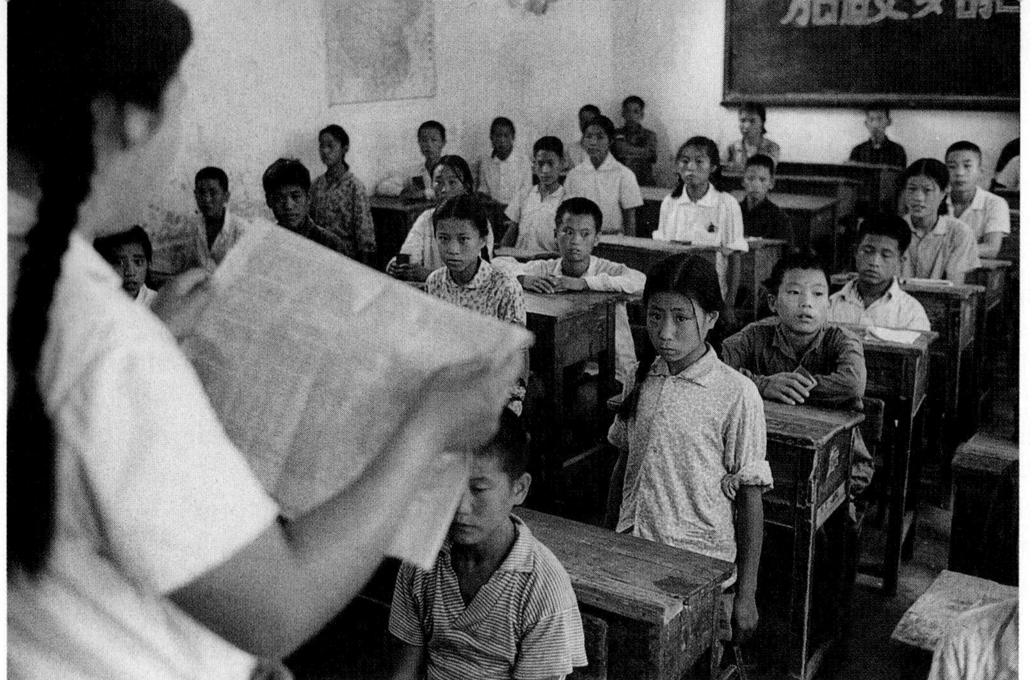

Students at a primary school near Beijing, China.

Ling shrugged and shook her head. "Don't know. He have big house. Money gone, but keep big house. Then I am little girl." She held her hand low to the floor.

"I *was* a little girl," Charlene said gently.

"I *was,*" said Ling. "Was, was." She giggled for a moment, then seemed to spend some time in thought. "We love him. All children love—all children did loved him. He giving tea in house. He was—was—so handsome!" She giggled. All the women in the class giggled. "He very nice. He learn music, he go . . . he went to school far away."

"America?"

Ling shook her head. "Oh no, no. You know, another . . . west."

"Europa!" exclaimed Maria proudly. "Espain!"

"No, no, another."

"France!" said Patricia, Charlene's sister. "He went to school in France?"

"Yes, France," said Ling. Then she stopped again, this time for a whole minute. The others waited patiently. No one said a word. Finally she continued. "But big boys in more old school not like him. He too handsome."

"Oooh!" sang out a chorus of women. "Too handsome!"

"The boys were jealous," said Carlos.

Ling seized the word. "Jealous! Jealous! They very jealous. He handsome, he study France, he very nice to children, he give tea and cake in big house, he show picture on wall." Her torrent of words came to an end and she began to think again, visibly, her brow furrowing. "Big school boys, they . . ." She stopped.

"Jealous!" sang out the others.

"Yes," she said, shaking her head "no." "But more. More bad. Hate. They hate him."

"That's bad," said Patricia.

"Yes, very bad." Ling paused, looking at the floor. "And they heat."

"Hate."

"No, they heat."

All the class looked puzzled. Heat? Heat? They turned to Cheryl.

The teacher spoke for the first time. "Hit? Ling, do you mean hit? They hit him?" Cheryl slapped the air with her hand.

Ling nodded, her face somehow serious and smiling at the same time. "Hit many time. And also so." She scooted her feet back and forth along the floor.

"Oooh," exclaimed Charlene, frowning. "They kicked him with the feet."

"Yes," said Ling. "They kicked him with the feet and hit him with the hands, many many time they hit, they kick."

"Where this happened?" asked Xavier.

"In the school. In classroom like . . ." She gestured to mean their room.

"In the school?" asked Xavier. "But other people were they there? They say stop, no?"

"No. Little children in room. They cry, they . . ." She covered her eyes with her hand, then uncovered them. "Big boys kick and hit. No one stop. No one help."

Everyone in class fell silent. Maria remembered: they could not look at one another then. They could not look at their teacher.

Ling continued. "They break him, very hurt much place." She stopped. They all fixed their stares on Ling, they could bear looking only at her. "Many place," she said. Her face had not changed, it was still half smiling. But now there were drops coming from her eyes, a single tear down each side of her nose. Maria would never forget it. Ling's face did not move or wrinkle or frown. Her body was absolutely still. Her shoulders did not quake. Nothing in the shape or motion of her eyes or mouth changed. None of the things that Maria had always known happen when you cry happened when Ling shed tears. Just two drops rolled slowly down her two pale cheeks as she smiled.

"He very hurt. He *was* very hurt. He blood many place. Boys go away. Children cry. Teacher break and hurt. Later he in hospital. I go there visit him." She stopped, looking thoughtful. "I went there." One continuous line of wetness glistened down each cheek. "My mother, my father say don't go, but I see him. I say, 'You be better?' But he hurt. Doctors no did helped. He alone. No doctor. No nurse. No medicine. No family." She stopped. They all stared in silence for several moments.

Finally Carlos said, "Did he went home?"

Ling shook her head. "He go home but no walk." She stopped. Maria could not help watching those single lines of tears moving down the pale round face. "A year, more, no walk. Then go."

"Go where?"

"End."

Again there was a deep silence. Ling looked down, away from them, her head bent low.

"Oh, no," murmured Charlene. "He died."

Maria felt the catch in her throat, the sudden wetness of tears on her own two cheeks, and when she looked up she saw that all the other students, men and women both, were crying too.

Maria wiped her eyes. Suddenly all her limbs ached, her bones felt stiff and old. She took her feet from the basin and dried them with a towel. Then she turned off the television and went to bed. ❖

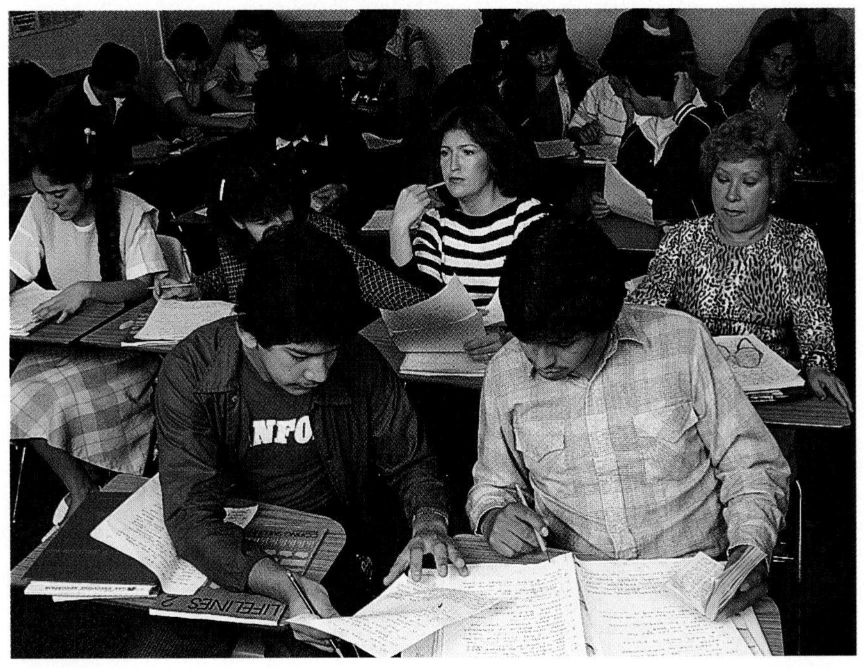

ESL classroom. Copyright © 1991 P. F. Bentley/Black Star.

RESPONDING OPTIONS

FROM PERSONAL RESPONSE *TO* CRITICAL ANALYSIS

REFLECT **1.** In your notebook, write down the thoughts you had as you finished reading this story.

RETHINK **2.** How would you introduce Maria to an audience? Make your introduction in front of the class.

3. In your estimation, how has coming to America changed Maria's life?

4. Give your opinion of the award ceremony. Is it a fitting acknowledgment of the students' achievement?

Consider

- the mayor's speech and introduction of Maria
- the mayor's and the audience's reactions to Maria's story
- Maria's feelings during the event
- her reaction to seeing it on TV

5. What themes do you find in this story? Consider what it reveals about language, American society, and the lives of recent immigrants.

RELATE **6.** Think about Maria's story and the other selections you've read in this part of Unit Five. In what ways can the American dream be an illusion, and in what ways can it be a reality?

ANOTHER PATHWAY

Fill out report cards for Maria, her daughter Carmen, the mayor, and Ling, giving each of them letter grades in the following areas: English fluency, comprehension, effort, compassion, and courage. Include comments to support the grades.

QUICKWRITES

1. In a **story fragment,** try to reproduce the words or thoughts of someone attempting to speak or understand an unfamiliar language. You might flesh out an example from your discussion for the Personal Connection on page 733.
2. Outline a **comparison-contrast essay** in which you examine likenesses and differences between Maria's experiences and those of other immigrants you've read about—the Changs of "In the American Society" or the narrator of "America and I." What conclusions can you draw from your analysis?

PORTFOLIO Save your writing. You may want to use it later as a springboard to a piece for your portfolio.

LITERARY CONCEPTS

A **foil** is a character who provides a striking contrast to another character. A writer might use a foil to emphasize certain traits possessed by a story's main character. In "The Yellow Wallpaper" (page 605), for example, the narrator's sister-in-law, a "perfect and enthusiastic housekeeper," is a foil for the discontented narrator. In this story, what traits of Maria are brought out by contrast with traits of the mayor?

CONCEPT REVIEW: Structure How is the game show like the award ceremony? How is the ceremony unlike the classroom scene in which Ling tells her story?

ALTERNATIVE ACTIVITIES

Cooperative Learning In her English class, Maria initiates an oral history project, taping and transcribing interviews with other ESL students to preserve their stories. If possible, work with your classmates on a similar **oral history project,** with students from an ESL class in your own school. What were their lives like in their former homes? What brought them to your city or town? What were their first impressions of your community? You may want to create a computer database of interview transcripts so that you can add further interviews and access them by students' names or countries of origin.

WORDS TO KNOW

For each boldfaced word, write the letter of the situation that better reflects its meaning.

1. **sidle**
   a. a baseball player's stealing second base
   b. a timid person's approaching someone at a party
2. **crescendo**
   a. the whistling of a teakettle as the water starts to boil
   b. the winding down of a party
3. **amnesty**
   a. the release of political prisoners from jail
   b. a plea of "not guilty" in a murder trial
4. **protrusion**
   a. a shy child's hiding behind his mother
   b. a sassy child's sticking out her tongue
5. **retort**
   a. an argument between two children
   b. an opening statement presented to a jury

LUCY HONIG

As you may have guessed, Lucy Honig is a former teacher of English as a second language. She began teaching ESL classes to adult immigrants in Brooklyn, where she had moved after living in Maine for many years.

According to Honig, "English as a Second Language" grew out of one of her first part-time teaching jobs: "My students had come from all over the third world. In New York they were struggling to live, struggling to be understood, and grasping for insider tips on how to fit in in America. (So was I.) They were not yet saturated with American media hype, and in their very pared-down renderings of their observations, of their lives, they could usually tell the difference between real feeling and baloney." Honig found herself seeing through her students' eyes, finding America "brand new and totally befuddling."

From Brooklyn, Honig moved to upstate New York, where she taught ESL classes and directed a county human rights commission. Recently she began teaching writing in Boston. She published her first novel, *Picking Up,* in 1986, and has published short fiction in a number of journals.

ON YOUR OWN

Defining the Grateful Gesture

Yvonne Sapia

According to our mother,
when she was a child
what was placed before her
for dinner was not a feast,
but she would eat it
to gain back the strength
taken from her by long hot days
of working in her mother's house
and helping her father make
candy in the family kitchen.
No idle passenger
traveling through life was she.

And that's why she resolved
to tell stories about
the appreciation for satisfied hunger.
When we would sit down
for our evening meal
of arroz con pollo[1]
or frijoles negros con plátanos[2]

1. **arroz con pollo** (ä-rôs′ kôn pô′yô) *Spanish:* rice with chicken.
2. **frijoles negros con plátanos** (frē-hô′lĕs nĕ′grôs kôn plä′tä-nôs) *Spanish:* black beans with plantains (banana-like fruits).

Analogía IV (1972)), Victor Grippo. 59 cm × 76 cm × 94.5 cm, collection of Jorge and Marion Helft.

she would expect us
to be reverent to the sources
of our undeserved nourishment,
and to strike a thankful pose
before each lift of the fork
or swirl of the spoon.

For the dishes she prepared
we were ungrateful,
she would say, and repeat
her archetypal[3] tale about the Perez
brothers from her girlhood town of Ponce,[4]
who looked like ripe mangoes,
their cheeks rosed despite poverty.
My mother would then tell us about the day
she saw Mrs. Perez searching
the neighborhood garbage,
picking out with a missionary's care
the edible potato peels, the plantain skins,
the shafts of old celery to take
home to her muchachos[5]
who required more food
than she could afford.

Although my brothers and I never
quite mastered the ritual
of obedience our mother craved,
and as supplicants failed
to feed her with our worthiness,
we'd sit like solemn loaves of bread,
sighing over the white plates
with a sense of realization, or relief,
guilty about possessing appetite.

---

3. **archetypal** (är′kĭ-tī′pəl): serving as an ideal example.
4. **Ponce** (pôn′sā): a seaport city of Puerto Rico.
5. **muchachos** (mo͞o-chä′chôs) *Spanish:* boys.

Yvonne Sapia

Born in 1946 in New York City, the poet and novelist Yvonne Sapia received a bachelor's degree from Florida Atlantic University, a master's degree from the University of Florida, and a doctorate from Florida State University. She has worked as a reporter for the *Village Post* in Miami, taught at Florida state prisons, and conducted poetry workshops for gifted children and the elderly. Since 1976 she has taught English at Lake City Community College in Florida.

Sapia received the Samuel French Morse Poetry Prize for her collection *Valentino's Hair,* which includes "Defining the Grateful Gesture." In 1991 she won the Charles H. and N. Mildred Nilon Excellence in Minority Fiction Award for her first novel, also entitled *Valentino's Hair.* The daughter of a Puerto Rican barber, Sapia was inspired by her father's real-life experience of cutting the hair of Rudolph Valentino, a silent-movie idol of the 1920s.

Sapia has said that her poetry "explores relationships through the reconstruction of memories, dreams, and reflections of each poem's persona. In order to understand what is happening to all of us in a world we have become too busy to observe significantly, I try to convey the intense emotion of illuminating experience with sparse and carefully chosen language."

OTHER WORKS *The Fertile Crescent*

WRITING FROM EXPERIENCE

WRITING TO PERSUADE

As you read the selections in this unit, "The Changing Face of America," you may have had strong reactions or opinions about one or more of them. Could you explain the reasons for your opinions? Which selections would you recommend to others, and why?

GUIDED ASSIGNMENT

Write a Critical Review When you express an opinion about a performance or work of art, you make a critical judgment. By explaining what you liked or didn't like, you can influence people's attitudes toward the piece. This lesson shows you how to present your opinions effectively in a critical review.

Reproductions from Art Exhibit

What feelings do these works of art evoke in you? What would you like to know about them?

Keith Haring

1 Review the Prompts

Look over the items on these pages. Then discuss your answers to the following questions.

- What similar performances, exhibits, or artwork have you seen, either live or on TV? What were your reactions to them?
- Did you read or hear a review of the event before or after seeing it? If so, what points did the reviewer make? How did the review influence your thinking?
- If someone urged you to go see a performance, exhibit, or work of art, what would you want to know about it?

2 You Be the Critic

Now list the names of two or three performances or works of art that you have seen or heard recently (movies, CD's, concerts, TV shows). You might want to include only those you strongly liked or disliked.

Write a paragraph stating your opinion about each one. Would you recommend the event or artwork to your friends? Why or why not?

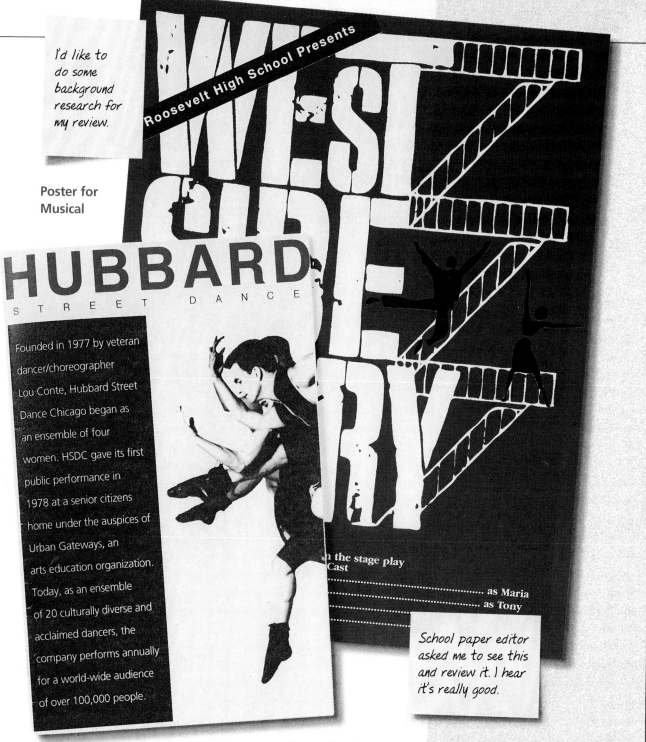

I'd like to do some background research for my review.

Roosevelt High School Presents

n the stage play
Cast

as Maria
as Tony

Poster for Musical

HUBBARD
STREET DANCE

Founded in 1977 by veteran dancer/choreographer Lou Conte, Hubbard Street Dance Chicago began as an ensemble of four women. HSDC gave its first public performance in 1978 at a senior citizens home under the auspices of Urban Gateways, an arts education organization. Today, as an ensemble of 20 culturally diverse and acclaimed dancers, the company performs annually for a world-wide audience of over 100,000 people.

School paper editor asked me to see this and review it. I hear it's really good.

Dance Brochure

❸ Choose Your Review Topic

Select one item as the focus for your critical review. Make sure it's something you have strong positive or negative opinions about.

PREWRITING

Gathering Information

Where to Begin The main purpose of a critical review is to describe the subject, offer a detailed evaluation of it, and recommend whether people should hear or see it. To write a good review, you need to establish objective criteria, learn something about the work of art you are reviewing, and recognize your own biases.

❶ Set Your Criteria

To analyze any performance or work of art, you need to break it down into its various elements or parts. For a musical, for instance, the reviewer might look at the following:

- Acting
- Staging
- Music and singing
- Choreography

Next, you would develop criteria, or standards, for each element. The criteria for a musical performance might look like those shown at the right.

See the SkillBuilder for tips on establishing criteria for other works of art.

Student's Criteria List

REVIEWING A MUSICAL PLAY

ELEMENT	CRITERIA
Acting	Right actors cast for right roles Actors speak clearly, loudly Each actor fits in with rest of cast
Staging	Sets well designed, fit story Lighting sets off action, mood Costumes fit story, characters
Music/Singing	Well performed, doesn't overpower singers Singers' voices match their roles Chorus supports lead singers
Choreography	Fits action and story line Appropriate for dancers' skills

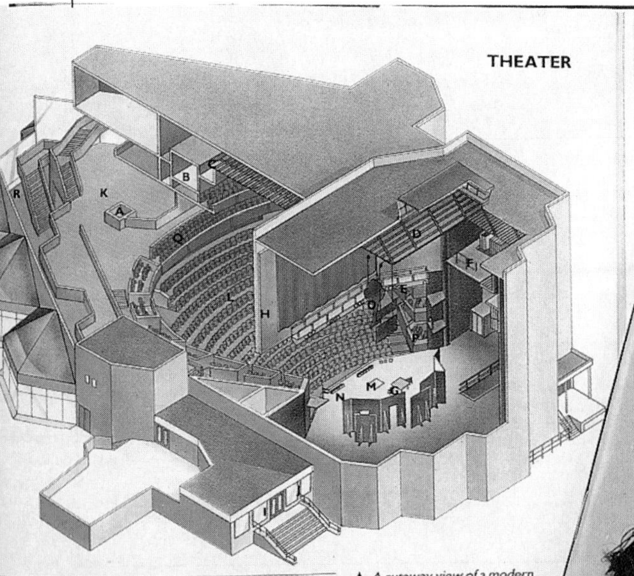
THEATER

▲ A cutaway view of a modern theater, showing:
A Elevator
B Projection room
C Lighting gallery

tcher, Margaret

aret Thatcher (born 1925) became the first
n to head the government of a Western
n. The daughter of a grocer, she went to

Y SOCIAL DRAMA / I AM A MAN
AMERICAN
THEATRE
NOVEMBER 1993

Review Notes West Side Story

Actors:

★★★★ – Gary and Eva perfect for lead roles, voices blend, dance like professionals. Supporting cast very solid as a group.

★★ ½ – Ed and Viv kept losing their Spanish accents.

Staging:

★★★ ½ – Sets and costumes looked realistic, gritty as New York

★ ½ – First act lighting couldn't find lead actors; sound kept fading out; hard to hear dialogue in places.

Student's Review Notes

2 Record Your Impressions

Take Notes It's best to record your reactions and responses while they are fresh, as the student writer did in the example above. For a performance, you may be able to take notes during the show or the intermissions. If not, jot down your opinions and impressions as soon afterward as you can.

Talk It Over You can ask other people for any facts or opinions they might share. In the process, you may discover your own bias for or against a particular form of art. Do you prefer modern art over classical? Do you feel that musicals are the only interesting types of plays? Whatever your personal preferences, be willing to keep an open mind as a reviewer.

3 Do Background Research

Where did Leonard Bernstein get the idea for West Side Story? Who choreographs Janet Jackson's videos? By doing a little background research, either before or after you see the work of art, you can add interest and depth to your review. Resources include print media, on-line databases, and interviews with artists, performers, and experts in the arts.

4 Develop Your Opinions

Now it's time to pull together the ideas you have gathered so far. You can use your notes, background research, and peer comments to begin organizing your first draft.

SkillBuilder

CRITICAL THINKING

Establishing Criteria for Evaluation

You may wish to review other works of art such as sculpture, painting, or musical recordings. These steps can help you establish the criteria for your review.

1. List the key elements of each art form. For painting and sculpture, these are color and materials, technique, design, and composition. For musical recordings, key elements are melody, lyrics, and rhythm; musicians' skill; and elements of sound engineering.
2. Conduct research to learn what standards are used to evaluate these key elements. You might interview teachers, performers, or reviewers in the art field.
3. Use these standards as the basis for your criteria.

APPLYING WHAT YOU'VE LEARNED
List the criteria you are going to use to evaluate your subject.

THINK & PLAN

Reflecting on Your Topic

1. Whom else can you talk with to develop and assess the criteria for your review?
2. What interesting facts or background data will you use?
3. What are your biases, if any, toward your subject?

DRAFTING

Thinking on Paper

Your First Opinions Reviews vary widely in their length, detail, and tone, depending on the intended audience and purpose. Before you begin to write, make sure you clearly understand who your readers are and what the assigned length of your review is.

1 Write a Rough Draft

Get down all your impressions, evaluations, background data, and specific examples. Be sure you give your honest reactions, and consider what the reader needs to know about the subject.

See Share Your Work on page 755 for ideas on publishing your review.

Student's Rough Draft

MOVIE REVIEW

Valeres sc… triumph in H…

However, *Horizons*, which was also done for a budget of under five million, is closer kin to *Brave New World* and *1984* than *Star Wars* or such space operas.

Horizons

The storyline is simple. On a huge planet that is never named, the inhabitants of one side, the Krens, find themselves "invaded" by the inhabitants of the other side, the Trels. The Trels carry, unwittingly, a disease that is fatal to approximately half the Kren population. However, the Trels are fleeing the lethal radiation from a volcano-caused fissure on their side of the planet. The choice faced by the Krens is to allow the Trels to continue to enter their lands, thus ensuring the deaths of half their population, or to refuse, and to doom an entire population.

Turn off your MTV, ~~F~~forget about the movies~~—~~. The Jets and the Sharks are ready to rumble in Bradley Hall, *Roosevelt High's production of* West Side Story combines strong acting and exciting staging and choreography to bring Leonard Bernstein's story vividly alive.

The plot, based on Romeo and Juliet, concerns the *tragic* love between a Puerto Rican girl, Maria, and an Anglo boy, Tony. ~~But~~ Maria's brother, Bernardo, is leader of the Sharks, and Tony is the former leader of a rival gang, the Jets. Tony and Maria try to find their own American dream, ~~but fail to reach it because of~~ *only to be caught up in* gang violence.

Gary Tindle as Tony and Eva de Soto as Maria are perfectly cast in the lead roles. Their singing voices blend beautifully, and they execute their dance scenes ~~well~~ *like professionals*. Supporting actors Ed Hind and Viv Ryan give solid performances. ~~They~~ *but* tend to slip in and out of their Puerto Rican accents.

Mr. Brandon's stage sets and costumes capture *the gritty feel of* New York City's tenements. ¶ The only glitches were the lighting and sound system, which caused problems in the first act. ¶ The fast-paced choreography makes you want to get up and dance, especially for the last fight scene. ¶ Buy your tickets early for this ~~great~~ *powerful* production of West Side Story.

put in comment about Bernstein in last paragraph

say more about problems with lighting, sound system

add details about last fight scene

…ger defines …er of Hope"

❷ Review Your Draft

These questions can help you review your rough draft:

- What tone is appropriate for this review—humorous, negative, enthusiastic?
- How can I catch the reader's attention in the first paragraph?
- Are there more precise words I can use to replace vague adjectives such as *good, great,* and *poor*?
- Have I evaluated all important parts of the subject and supported my opinions with specific examples?
- Is it clear why I make the recommendation I do?

❸ Rework and Share

As you rework your draft, keep in mind that you should always provide a plot summary or description of the work of art you are reviewing. (See the SkillBuilder for tips on summarizing a plot.) You might use one of the organizing strategies listed below for the final draft of your review.

Description In this form, you describe the specific qualities of the subject, provide any background information, and make a final recommendation on whether the reader should see it.

Compare-Contrast You review the subject by comparing and contrasting it with similar subjects, such as different performances of the same play or similar paintings by the same artist or different artists.

Pro-Con Structure You discuss the positive and negative aspects of the subject—either alternating pro-con arguments or giving one side first and then discussing the other side—and end with a final recommendation about its value.

Remind your peer reviewers to focus on the content of your review and not to engage in a debate about your opinions. Here are a few questions you might want to ask them.

- What do you think my overall feeling about the subject is?
- Which parts of the subject need more coverage?
- What details do I need to add to support my opinions?
- Is it clear why I make the recommendation I do?

SkillBuilder

Summarizing a Plot

In a plot summary, you present the main facts of a story and avoid mentioning every character or plot development. You can use these suggestions to write a summary.

1. In two or three sentences, explain what the story is about. (A boy and a girl from rival groups fall in love. They try to run away together but can't escape their violent world.)
2. List the setting, main characters, and any background information that may help the reader understand the story.
3. Freewrite a paragraph combining the facts from steps 1 and 2. Then condense the paragraph to three to five sentences.

APPLYING WHAT YOU'VE LEARNED

Study how the student writer summarized the plot of *West Side Story*. Use the suggestions above to create your own plot summary.

RETHINK & EVALUATE

Preparing to Revise

1. How well do your details support your opinions?
2. Have you used the best organizing structure for your review?
3. How can you make your language more precise?

Informing the Public

The Finishing Touches When your review reaches the final stage, you want to make sure your facts are accurate and your wording reflects your honest evaluation of your subject. Keep in mind that your review not only informs people about the subject but may influence what they think of it.

Student Review

West Side Story: Wow!

Bernstein's classic looks at love, American dream

Darcey Ortiz
Fine Arts Reviewer

Turn off your MTV, forget about the movies! The Jets and the Sharks are ready to "rumble" in Bradley Hall. Roosevelt High's production of *West Side Story* combines strong acting and exciting staging and choreography to bring new life to Leonard Bernstein's musical.

The plot, based on *Romeo and Juliet*, is set in New York City and concerns the tragic love between a Puerto Rican girl, Maria, and an Anglo boy, Tony. Maria's brother, Bernardo, is leader of the Sharks, a Puerto Rican gang, and Tony is the former leader of a rival gang, the Jets. Tony and Maria try to find their own American dream, only to be caught up in gang violence.

Gary Tindle as Tony and Eva de Soto as Maria are perfectly cast in the lead roles. Their singing voices blend beautifully, and they execute their dance scenes like professionals. Supporting actors Ed Hind and Viv Ryan give solid performances but tend to slip in and out of their Puerto Rican accents. Mr. Brandon's stage sets and costumes capture the gritty feel of New York City's tenements.

The only glitch in the performance came from the lighting and sound system. Several times in the first act, the sound faded badly and the spotlights failed to find the lead actors when they walked on stage.

The fast-paced choreography of Ms. Vallenti turned the last fight scene into a real showstopper. The rival gangs rushed down the side aisles and met on stage for the big rumble!

Forty years ago, people doubted that Bernstein's musical would succeed. He's still proving them wrong. Buy your tickets early for this powerful production of *West Side Story*.

1 Revise and Edit

Give your final draft to one or two classmates to read. Use their comments, the Standards for Evaluation, and the Editing Checklist to revise your draft.

- Tell the reader what you are reviewing.
- Be sure all names are the right ones and are spelled correctly.
- Make sure your tone is consistent throughout.
- Cover all the main elements of the subject.
- Add background information for depth.
- Make your final recommendation clear.

How does the writer catch the reader's attention?

What specific details support the writer's opinions? What background facts were included?

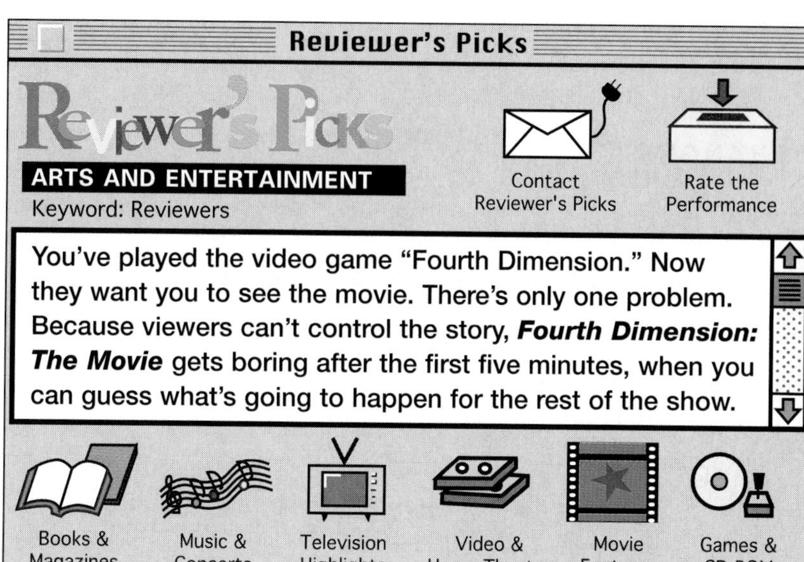
Reviewer's Picks
Reviewer's Picks
ARTS AND ENTERTAINMENT
Keyword: Reviewers
Contact Reviewer's Picks
Rate the Performance
You've played the video game "Fourth Dimension." Now they want you to see the movie. There's only one problem. Because viewers can't control the story, Fourth Dimension: The Movie gets boring after the first five minutes, when you can guess what's going to happen for the rest of the show.
Books & Magazines
Music & Concerts
Television Highlights
Video & Home Theater
Movie Features
Games & CD-ROM

Another student writer put her movie review on the Internet, where it can reach many readers and might provoke a lively discussion of the movie.

2 Share Your Work

Besides being written for a newspaper or magazine, a critical review can be written in the following formats:

- Script for a radio or TV broadcast
- Part of program notes
- E-mail on the Internet or World Wide Web
- Letter to someone interested in the performance (friend, relative, former classmate, pen pal)

Standards for Evaluation

A critical review
- opens with a statement or an opinion
- summarizes the plot or describes the subject
- analyzes the various components of the subject
- uses specific details and facts to support opinions
- provides background information where appropriate
- ends with a recommendation or summary statement

SkillBuilder

GRAMMAR FROM WRITING

Setting Off Titles
The following rules will help you set off titles in your review.

Italics or Underscoring Use these to set off titles of plays, musicals, operas, novels, paintings, sculpture, CD's, albums, and movies. (Newspapers use quotation marks if they have no print for italics or underscoring.)

Quotation Marks Use these to set off titles of songs, individual dance numbers, poems, and short stories.

GRAMMAR HANDBOOK

For more on titles, see page 1230 of the Grammar Handbook.

Editing Checklist Use the following tips for revising:

- Are all names spelled correctly?
- Have you set off titles properly?
- Did you punctuate correctly?

REFLECT & ASSESS

Learning from Experience

1. Discuss with others what you learned about creating a review.
2. What advice would you give someone who wants to review a work of art?

PORTFOLIO List what you enjoyed most about writing a review. You can include your list and final review in your portfolio.

REFLECT & ASSESS

UNIT FIVE: THE CHANGING FACE OF AMERICA

What do you feel you've learned about the social position of American women in the past? What new thoughts do you have about the American dream? Choose one or more of the following options in each section and complete the activities to help determine what knowledge you've gained.

REFLECTING ON THE UNIT

OPTION 1 **A Woman's Proper Place** Many of the selections in the first part of this unit show American women's struggles with social constraints, stereotypes, and inequalities. Review the ways in which the female characters in these selections respond to oppression or limitation. Which character did you find it easiest to identify with? Which character did you find it most difficult to identify with? Jot down a couple of paragraphs explaining your choices.

OPTION 2 **The American Dream** Think about the American dream in relation to the selections in the second part of this unit. Which characters would classify the American dream as an illusion? Which would view it as a reality? Form a group of four or five, with each member role-playing a different character. In a discussion of equality and economic opportunity in the United States, each student should classify the American dream as illusion or reality and defend that position according to the point of view of the character he or she is playing.

REFLECT & ASSESS

Self-Assessment: To illustrate what you've learned about the concerns that native-born and immigrant men and women had at the end of the 19th century, write down their concerns in a diagram like the one shown. Then underline any concerns that do not seem relevant today.

	Women	Men
Native born		
Immigrants		

REVIEWING LITERARY CONCEPTS

OPTION 1 **Understanding Figurative Language** Many of the writers in this unit use figurative language—for example, simile, metaphor, and personification—to communicate ideas, feelings, character qualities, or states of mind. Go back through the unit and select one example of figurative language from at least five different selections. Classify the type of figurative language used in each example and the primary idea or feeling conveyed. Use a chart like the one shown here and use the samples as a guide. After you have finished filling out the chart, circle the example of

Selection	Example of Figurative Language	Type of Figurative Language	Idea, Feeling, or State of Mind Conveyed
"The Yellow Wallpaper"	". . . when you follow the lame uncertain curves for a little distance they suddenly commit suicide—plunge off at outrageous angles, destroy themselves in unheard of contradictions."	personification	suggests narrator's disturbed mental state

figurative language that had the most impact on your understanding of a character, a feeling, or an idea, and explain why.

OPTION 2 **Evaluating Structure** You have learned that the structure of a work is the way in which it is put together—the arrangement of its parts. For example, "Seventeen Syllables" has two overlapping plots, whereas "I Stand Here Ironing" is an interior monologue in which the narrator's thoughts are presented as they occur to her. Which of the prose selections in Unit Five seem most similar in structure, and which seem most dissimilar? You might consider whether incidents are narrated in chronological order, how broad the scope of the story is, or what kind of progression occurs from beginning to end (for example, a movement from hope to disillusionment, or from despair to triumph).

REFLECT & ASSESS

Self-Assessment: Copy the following list of literary terms on a sheet of paper. Place a check next to each item you were able to define. For those you couldn't define, look up the definition in the Handbook of Literary Terms on page 1142.

Personification	*Rhyme*
Imagery	*Meter*
Surprise Ending	*Figurative Language*
Plot	*Analogy*
Interior Monologue	*Structure*
Epithet	*Foil*

PORTFOLIO BUILDING

- **QuickWrites** Many of the QuickWrites in this unit involved persuasive pieces in which you were to respond to the events, themes, or writer's style in a selection. (The rebuttal, critique, and editorial fall into this category.) Choose one response in which you presented especially strong arguments for your opinion. In a cover note, explain why you think those arguments are so convincing.
- **Writing About Literature** Earlier in this unit you analyzed how point of view influences other story elements. Review your analysis and write an entry in your notebook about it. How easy or difficult was your analysis to do? How successful do you think your analysis is? Why? What did you learn from your analysis? You may wish to include a copy of your entry in your portfolio.
- **Writing from Experience** Reread the critical review you wrote earlier in this unit. Imagine you have been asked to review a new production of a play. What do you think is challenging about being a critic? In a note to yourself, write some recommendations for how you might use your skills as a critic in this new situation.
- **Personal Choice** Think about the activities and short writing assignments that you completed in this unit or ones that you may have done on your own. Pick one that you felt was very challenging. In a cover note, explain how the writing or the activity challenged you and what you did to rise to the occasion.

REFLECT & ASSESS

Self-Assessment: By now you should have quite a few pieces in your portfolio. Are you satisfied with the pieces you've chosen so far? If so, why? Or would you like to replace some? If so, which ones, and why?

SETTING GOALS

After completing this unit's reading and writing activities, what topics would you like to continue learning about? Look back through the selections, your portfolio, and your notebook. Jot down one or two topics you would like to read more about.

UNIT SIX

THE MODERN AGE

make it new!

Ezra Pound
poet and critic

Rush Hour, New York (1915), Max Weber. Oil on canvas, 36¼″ × 30¼″. National Gallery of Art, Washington, D.C., gift of the Avalon Foundation (1970.6.1 PA).

TIME LINE

The Modern Age

1909

A group of 60 white and black people found the National Association for the Advancement of Colored People (NAACP) to end discrimination and prevent violence against black people.

The NAACP was originally headed by seven whites and one black, W. E. B. Du Bois. The choice of Du Bois was significant because many black leaders of the time, such as Booker T. Washington, counseled African Americans to focus solely on economic betterment; Du Bois was one of the first to call for full political and civil equality. Du Bois edited the association's influential magazine, The Crisis, *for almost 25 years.*

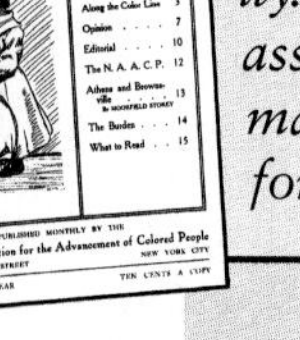
THE CRISIS
A RECORD OF THE DARKER RACES

1912

Harriet Monroe founds the magazine *Poetry,* in which many modernist poets would be introduced.

1913

The Armory Show in New York City exhibits modern art to large crowds and horrified critics.

Now called "a decisive event in the development of American art," the Armory Show introduced the U.S. public to modern European advances in art for the first time. The works of such artists as Marcel Duchamp, Henri Matisse, Constantin Brancusi, and Paul Cézanne were more often reviled than praised, however.

1914

War erupts in Europe, with Germany and Austria-Hungary on one side and Great Britain, France, and Russia on the other.

1917

The United States enters World War I, ensuring an Allied victory a year later.

1919

The 18th Amendment, which prohibits the transportation and sale of alcoholic beverages, is ratified, ushering in the period known as Prohibition.

Prohibition led to widespread crime. Ordinary citizens made their own alcohol, went to illegal speakeasies, and became bootleggers. Criminal gangs, led by the likes of Al Capone, soon gained control of the lucrative liquor trade. The 18th Amendment was repealed in 1933.

1920

For the first time, the U.S. Bureau of the Census reports that the nation's rural population is less than 50 percent of the total.

1921

The first radio coverage of the World Series demonstrates radio's growing popularity.

1922

Louis Armstrong joins King Oliver's Creole Jazz Band in Chicago, heralding the Jazz Age.

1923

A performance of the Charleston in the musical *Runnin' Wild* starts a nationwide dance craze.

1925

John Scopes is found guilty of breaking a Tennessee law that prohibited the teaching of the theory of evolution in public schools.

1927

Charles Lindbergh makes the first solo nonstop flight across the Atlantic, from New York to Paris; Babe Ruth hits a then-record 60 home runs in a season; the first "talking" movie, *The Jazz Singer,* is released.

1929

A stock-market crash on Wall Street plunges the nation into the Great Depression.

The stock-market crash caused banks and businesses to fail, so that many people lost their savings as well as their jobs. Hunger stalked the streets. "When you gits down to your last bean, your backbone and your navel shakes dice to see which gits it," remarked one penniless Southerner with grim humor.

1931

The 102-story Empire State Building, for decades the world's tallest building, is completed.

1932

Franklin Delano Roosevelt is elected president at the height of the Depression; nearly one-third of the work force is unemployed.

1934

Dorothy West founds *Challenge,* a literary magazine for African-American writers.

1938

Congress passes the Fair Labor Standards Act, which establishes a minimum wage and provides for the adoption of a 40-hour workweek.

Period *Pieces*

The fashion of the 1920s

1936 Crosley Radio Corporation's "Majestic"

Art deco wristwatch

PART 1 INTRODUCTION

A New Cultural Identity

The Harlem Renaissance

The Harlem Renaissance was an unprecedented period of literary, musical, and artistic production among African Americans that reached its peak in the 1920s. This movement was centered in the Harlem section of Manhattan in New York City—a magnet for thousands of blacks migrating from the South, the Midwest, and even the West Indies. Southern blacks, in particular, were fleeing poverty and growing racial violence, hoping to find more economic and personal freedom in the North. Politically, the Renaissance years were an extremely difficult time for African Americans. During the "Red Summer" of 1919, there were bloody antiblack riots in 26 cities, including Chicago and Washington, D.C. In the 1920s, membership in the terrorist, white-supremacist Ku Klux Klan rose to more than 4 million nationwide.

Not only a magnet for blacks, Harlem drew whites as well—tourists flocked to nightspots such as the Cotton Club to hear the new jazz music played by Louis Armstrong and Duke Ellington. And white writers, publishers, and patrons of the arts developed a keen interest in Harlem residents and their culture.

For African Americans a new cultural identity crystallized during the Harlem Renaissance; it was the time of "The New Negro," in the words of philosopher Alain Locke, who first defined the movement. "New Negroes" rejected beastlike or sentimental stereotypes, claiming the right to define themselves and defend themselves against attack. "New Negroes" felt a collective identity—they had pride in their race and

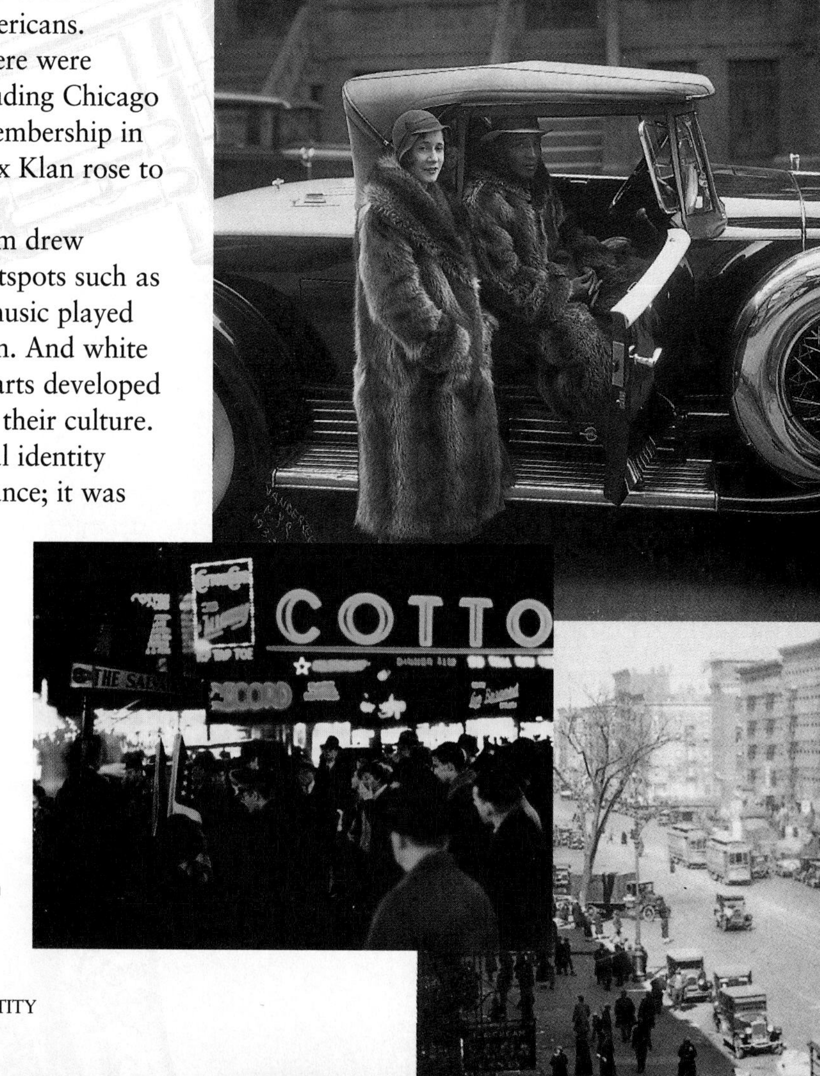

Harlem in the 1920s: a young couple out on the town (top), the Cotton Club (right), and Lenox Avenue (far right)

asserted its contributions to American culture. At the same time, they possessed an international consciousness, recognizing kinship among blacks in the United States, West Indies, and Africa. Such an international outlook was advocated by Marcus Garvey, a Jamaican immigrant whose popular back-to-Africa movement called on African Americans to leave the United States and form their own nation.

The writers of the Harlem Renaissance embodied these "New Negroes." Langston Hughes was one of the most original and important. In 1925, he published his first poetry collection, *The Weary Blues,* following it with dozens of volumes of poetry, fiction, plays, and essays over a career lasting into the 1960s. He praised blackness, embraced common people as subjects, and blended elements of blues and jazz into his work. The exuberant Zora Neale Hurston, raised in a small, all-black Florida town and trained in anthropology at Barnard College, also drew upon African-American folk traditions. Her stories, novels, essays, and folklore collections reflect a love of black language and manners. Hurston was one of the first writers to present African Americans as complete, multifaceted human beings. Other important Renaissance writers were James Weldon Johnson, Claude McKay, Countee Cullen, and Arna Bontemps, all of whom showed mastery of traditional literary forms and poured into them new expressions of individual and collective

Voices from the TIMES

White people began to come to Harlem in droves. For several years they packed the expensive Cotton Club on Lenox Avenue. But I was never there, because the Cotton Club was a Jim Crow club for gangsters and monied whites. They were not cordial to Negro patronage, unless you were a celebrity like Bojangles. So Harlem Negroes did not like the Cotton Club and never appreciated its Jim Crow policy in the very heart of their dark community. Nor did ordinary Negroes like the growing influx of whites toward Harlem after sundown, flooding the little cabarets and bars where formerly only colored people laughed and sang, and where now the strangers were given the best ringside tables to sit and stare at the Negro customers—like amusing animals in a zoo.

The Negroes said: "We can't go downtown and sit and stare at you in your clubs. You won't even let us in your clubs." But they didn't say it out loud—for Negroes are practically never rude to white people. So thousands of whites came to Harlem night after night, thinking the Negroes loved to have them there, and firmly believing that all Harlemites left their houses at sundown to sing and dance in cabarets, because most of the whites saw nothing but the cabarets, not the houses.

Langston Hughes
from "When the Negro Was in Vogue"

Voices from the Times

Here in Manhattan is not merely the largest Negro community in the world, but the first concentration in history of so many diverse elements of Negro life. It has attracted the African, the West Indian, the Negro American; has brought together the Negro of the North and the Negro of the South; the man from the city and the man from the town and village; the peasant, the student, the business man, the professional man, artist, poet, musician, adventurer and worker, preacher and criminal, exploiter and social outcast. Each group has come with its own separate motives and for its own special ends, but their greatest experience has been the finding of one another.

Alain Locke
from *The New Negro*

Man, if you gotta ask you'll never know.

Louis Armstrong
when asked what jazz is

What American literature decidedly needs at the moment is color, music, gusto, the free expression of gay or desperate moods. If the Negroes are not in a position to contribute these items, I do not know what Americans are.

Carl Van Doren
from a speech to young African-American writers

Up you mighty race, you can accomplish what you will.

Marcus Garvey
(a rallying cry for his Universal Negro Improvement Association)

feeling. Yet another significant figure was Jean Toomer, whose experimental *Cane* (1923) blended poetry and prose to evoke the beautiful, terrible South of black experience.

Continuity & Change: Reaffirming Cultural Identity

The Great Depression of the 1930s brought an end to the Harlem Renaissance, causing many of the writers who had gathered in Harlem to scatter and take other jobs to support themselves. But their work planted seeds that continue to generate important writing from the African-American experience.

In 1950, the poet Gwendolyn Brooks became the first African American to win a Pulitzer Prize. Throughout the 1950s and 1960s, James Baldwin, who left the United States and the racism he felt here to live in Paris, gave us some of the most important essays of the period, essays based on his experiences and struggles with racial identity. And in contemporary times, Toni Morrison has become one of the most accomplished American novelists, winning nearly every important literary award, including the Nobel Prize for literature. In her essay in this part of Unit Six, Morrison demonstrates the continuing effort to find and present the essentials of African-American life.

Toni Morrison accepting the 1993 Nobel Prize for literature in Stockholm, Sweden (above) and a close-up of the prize itself (at right)

LASERLINKS
• HISTORICAL LITERARY CONNECTION

PART 1 *A New Cultural Identity*

The Harlem Renaissance

Continuity & Change: Reaffirming Cultural Identity

PREVIEWING

POETRY

I, Too   The Weary Blues

Langston Hughes

PERSONAL CONNECTION

These two poems might be read as reactions to two different kinds of American music. Think about patriotic songs you know, such as "America the Beautiful." What words and images do you associate with such songs? What is their usual mood? Fill out a cluster diagram to record your thoughts. Now think about another kind of music created in the United States—the blues. What subjects, images, and moods do you associate with the blues? Make a second cluster diagram to respond. Keep in mind patriotic songs as you read "I, Too" and blues songs as you read "The Weary Blues."

MUSICAL CONNECTION

The blues is a style of music that African Americans created and developed in the United States in the early 20th century. Blues music is slow and features "blue notes"—flatted third or seventh notes in chords—and breaks in the melody that allow a musician to improvise. Blues lyrics, which typically express feelings of sadness and melancholy, often consist of three-line stanzas in which the second line repeats the first and the third expresses a response to the other two. Langston Hughes said that blues songs are "about being in the midst of trouble, friendless, hungry, disappointed in love right here on earth. . . . The mood of the blues is almost always despondence, but when they are sung people laugh."

READING CONNECTION

"Hearing" Poetry Langston Hughes, inspired by the blues and jazz he heard in Harlem nightclubs, tried to imitate in his poetry the distinctive rhythms of these types of music. Many of his poems were actually set to music. As you read these two poems, try to hear how they would sound spoken aloud or recited over a background of blues or jazz music.

I, Too

LANGSTON HUGHES

I, too, sing America.

I am the darker brother.
They send me to eat in the kitchen
When company comes,
But I laugh,
And eat well,
And grow strong.

Tomorrow,
I'll be at the table
When company comes.
Nobody'll dare
Say to me,
"Eat in the kitchen,"
Then.

Besides,
They'll see how beautiful I am
And be ashamed—

I, too, am America.

Jim, Selma Burke. Art and Artifacts Division, Schomburg Center for Research in Black Culture, The New York Public Library, Astor, Lenox and Tilden Foundations.

FROM PERSONAL RESPONSE *TO* CRITICAL ANALYSIS

REFLECT **1.** Write a response to this poem in your notebook, then share it with a classmate.

RETHINK **2.** What do you believe the poem is saying about America?

Consider

- the first and last lines
- the identities of the speaker and the "they" in lines 3 and 16
- what is meant by "when company comes" in line 4
- how the poem compares with patriotic songs

3. How do you think the speaker expects to move from the "kitchen" to the "table"? How do you view his expectations?

The Weary Blues

LANGSTON HUGHES

Droning a drowsy syncopated[1] tune,
Rocking back and forth to a mellow croon,[2]
I heard a Negro play.
Down on Lenox Avenue the other night
By the pale dull pallor[3] of an old gas light
He did a lazy sway. . . .
He did a lazy sway. . . .
To the tune o' those Weary Blues.
With his ebony hands on each ivory key
He made that poor piano moan with melody.
O Blues!
Swaying to and fro on his rickety stool
He played that sad raggy tune like a musical fool.
Sweet Blues!
Coming from a black man's soul.
O Blues!
In a deep song voice with a melancholy tone
I heard that Negro sing, that old piano moan—
"Ain't got nobody in all this world,
Ain't got nobody but ma self.
I's gwine to quit ma frownin'
And put ma troubles on the shelf."
Thump, thump, thump, went his foot on the floor.
He played a few chords then he sang some more—
"I got the Weary Blues
And I can't be satisfied.
Got the Weary Blues
And can't be satisfied—
I ain't happy no mo'
And I wish that I had died."
And far into the night he crooned that tune.
The stars went out and so did the moon.
The singer stopped playing and went to bed
While the Weary Blues echoed through his head.
He slept like a rock or a man that's dead.

---

1. **syncopated** (sĭng′kə-pā′tĭd): characterized by a shifting of stresses from normally strong to normally weak beats.
2. **croon:** a soft humming or singing.
3. **pallor** (păl′ər): lack of color.

Copyright © John H. Howard/The Newborn Group.

RESPONDING OPTIONS

FROM PERSONAL RESPONSE TO CRITICAL ANALYSIS

REFLECT 1. What vision of the musician did you develop as you read "The Weary Blues"? Draw or act out your image of him.

RETHINK 2. How does the speaker seem to feel about the musician and about blues music? Support your answer with lines from the poem.

3. What, in your opinion, is musical about the style of this poem?

4. What differences do you see between the two blues verses (lines 19–22 and 25–30) and the rest of the poem? How well do you think the two styles work together?

5. Hughes reportedly was dissatisfied with the ending of this poem. What do *you* think of the last three lines?

RELATE 6. "The Weary Blues" and "I, Too" present two different ways of responding to unfair treatment. Which response do you think is better? Give reasons for your answer.

ANOTHER PATHWAY

Cooperative Learning

With a small group of classmates, plan and present oral readings of "I, Too" and "The Weary Blues." Choose appropriate volumes, phrasings, pitches, and gestures. Decide whether the poems should be read by a single voice or by several voices. Explain how your readings help reveal both the meanings and the forms of the poems.

LITERARY CONCEPTS

The **mood** of a piece of literature is the emotional feeling or atmosphere that the writer creates for the reader. Descriptive details, setting, and figurative language contribute to the mood of a work, as do the sound and rhythm of the language used. Describe the mood of "I, Too" and the mood of "The Weary Blues." Then work with a partner to identify elements—images, setting, form, sound, rhythm, and rhyme—that contribute to the mood of each poem. Share your perceptions in class.

QUICKWRITES

1. Do you think blues music is comforting to the singer in "The Weary Blues," or does it make him sadder? Write a brief **answer,** offering evidence to support your conclusion.
2. "The Weary Blues," was the winning entry in a literary contest sponsored by *Opportunity* magazine. Draft a **letter of congratulation** to Hughes, telling him why his poem won first prize.
3. Begin writing a **poem** that in some way suggests a particular style of music you enjoy or dislike. Have a classmate read it and guess what kind of music inspired you.

***PORTFOLIO** Save your writing. You may want to use it later as a springboard to a piece for your portfolio.*

CRITIC'S CORNER

Many African-American critics of the 1920s denounced Hughes's early poetry because they thought that his portrait of African Americans was unflattering. Commenting on Hughes's 1927 book *Fine Clothes to the Jew,* which followed *The Weary Blues,* Eustace Gay wrote: "It does not matter to me whether every poem in the book is true to life. . . . Our aim ought to be to present to the general public, already misinformed both by well-meaning and malicious writers, our higher aims and aspirations, and our better selves." Defending his choice of subjects, Hughes wrote, "I felt that the masses of our people had as much in their lives to put into books as did those more fortunate ones who had been born with some means. . . ." What is your opinion of the way African Americans are portrayed in "I, Too" and "The Weary Blues"?

LITERARY LINKS

Compare "I, Too" with Walt Whitman's poem "I Hear America Singing" (page 312), concentrating on subject, mood, and tone. Which vision of America—Whitman's or Hughes's—is closer to your own vision?

ACROSS THE CURRICULUM

Music Find out more about the blues. What are the roots of blues music? Who are some well-known blues musicians? How has the blues influenced other popular forms of music? Answer these questions in a presentation to the class, accompanied by some recordings of blues music. As an alternative, perform your own interpretation of the "weary blues," adapting or inventing a blues melody and making up additional lyrics.

Bessie Smith
AP/Wide World Photos.

LANGSTON HUGHES

1902–1967

As one of the leading voices of the Harlem Renaissance, Langston Hughes vividly captured the richness of African-American life. Although he traveled widely and lived in half a dozen U.S. cities, Hughes loved Harlem—the "great dark city," as he called it. Many of his early poems, such as those collected in *The Weary Blues* and *Fine Clothes to the Jew,* depict Harlem life in the 1920s.

Although he had never written a poem until his grammar school classmates elected him class poet, Hughes took his duties seriously, composing 16 verses about his teachers and classmates. In high school, he wrote dialect poems in the style of Paul Laurence Dunbar and free-verse poems in the style of Carl Sandburg. By the age of 19, Hughes had found his distinctive poetic voice and had begun publishing in magazines. Although his work was well received by African-American readers, national recognition still eluded him.

Then, by winning a literary contest with "The Weary Blues" in 1925, Hughes won the support of a prominent critic who helped arrange for publication of his early books. He also gained public notice through an encounter with Vachel Lindsay. When the popular poet came to the restaurant where Hughes worked as a busboy, Hughes slipped three poems—including "The Weary Blues"—beside Lindsay's plate. The next morning the newspapers reported that Lindsay had "discovered" an African-American busboy poet. The rest is literary history. Hughes, who became known as the Poet Laureate of Harlem, went on to publish more than 40 books and had an enormous influence on succeeding generations of writers.

OTHER WORKS *The Dream Keeper and Other Poems, Montage of a Dream Deferred, Simple Speaks His Mind, The Big Sea: An Autobiography*

LASERLINKS
• *AUTHOR BACKGROUND*

PREVIEWING

POETRY

My City
James Weldon Johnson

Any Human to Another
Countee Cullen

PERSONAL CONNECTION

Brainstorm with a small group to pool your knowledge about New York City. You might use a cluster diagram like the one shown here to organize your thoughts. What are your attitudes toward the city? Share your ideas with the class.

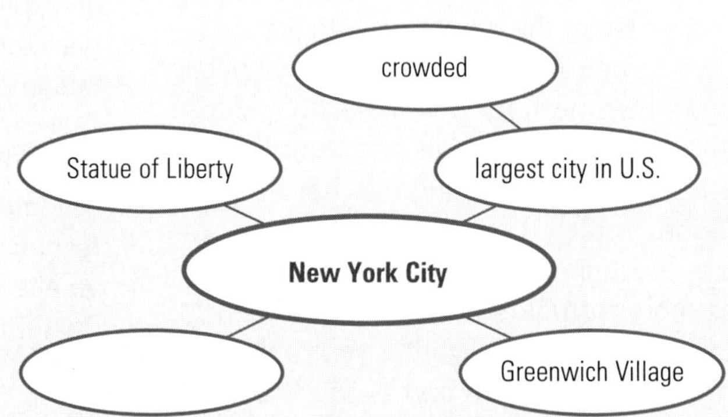

CULTURAL CONNECTION

New York City stirred strong feelings among the African Americans who migrated there in the early 20th century. To some, New York was a place of exciting possibilities, representing freedom and opportunities for self-fulfillment. To others, the harsh realities of urban living—such as overcrowding, prejudice, and unemployment—frustrated the expectations that had originally prompted their migration. In "My City," James Weldon Johnson expresses deep feelings about Manhattan, the New York City borough where Harlem is located.

During the Harlem Renaissance, many African-American writers focused on the racism and injustice that, they felt, robbed them of their humanity. Countee Cullen, however, believed that instead of restricting themselves to matters related to race, African-American writers should more fully explore the *human* condition. In his poem "Any Human to Another," Cullen emphasizes the commonality of the human experience.

Women strolling on Seventh Avenue, Manhattan, 1927. Schomburg Center for Research in Black Culture, New York.

WRITING CONNECTION

Think of a place you would hate never to see again. It might be a city or a town, a solitary place or a busy area, a house, a school, or some other place you feel an attachment for. What makes the place special for you? Write a brief description of your special place and explain why you would miss it. Then, as you read "My City," compare your attitude toward that place with the speaker's feelings about New York City.

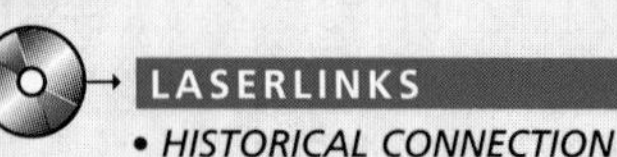

New York Harbor/Paris (about 1925), Jan Matulka. Photo courtesy of Norfolk Southern Corporation.

My City

JAMES WELDON JOHNSON

When I come down to sleep death's endless night,
The threshold of the unknown dark to cross,
What to me then will be the keenest loss,
When this bright world blurs on my fading sight?
Will it be that no more I shall see the trees
Or smell the flowers or hear the singing birds
Or watch the flashing streams or patient herds?
No, I am sure it will be none of these.

But, ah! Manhattan's sights and sounds, her smells,
Her crowds, her throbbing force, the thrill that comes
From being of her a part, her subtle spells,
Her shining towers, her avenues, her slums—
O God! the stark, unutterable pity,
To be dead, and never again behold my city!

FROM PERSONAL RESPONSE *TO* CRITICAL ANALYSIS

REFLECT **1.** In your notebook, describe the impression of New York City that you get from this poem.

RETHINK **2.** Compare the speaker's feelings about New York City with the feelings about a special place you recorded for the Writing Connection on page 772.

3. In your opinion, is the speaker's description of New York City appealing? Is it accurate? Consider your own ideas about New York City.

Any Human to Another

COUNTEE CULLEN

The ills I sorrow at
Not me alone
Like an arrow,
Pierce to the marrow,
Through the fat
And past the bone.

Your grief and mine
Must intertwine
Like sea and river,
Be fused and mingle,
Diverse yet single,
Forever and forever.

Let no man be so proud
And confident,
To think he is allowed
A little tent
Pitched in a meadow
Of sun and shadow
All his little own.

Joy may be shy, unique,
Friendly to a few,
Sorrow never scorned to speak
To any who
Were false or true.

Your every grief
Like a blade
Shining and unsheathed[1]
Must strike me down.
Of bitter aloes[2] wreathed,
My sorrow must be laid
On your head like a crown.

1. **unsheathed:** removed from its protective case.
2. **bitter aloes** (ăl′ōz): a spiny-leaved plant from the juice of which a bad-tasting medicine is made.

Shotgun, Third Ward #1 (1966), John T. Biggers. Oil on canvas, 76.2 × 121.9 cm, National Museum of American Art, Washington, D.C./Art Resource, New York.

RESPONDING OPTIONS

FROM PERSONAL RESPONSE *TO* CRITICAL ANALYSIS

REFLECT 1. In your notebook, write a question you would like to be able to ask Cullen about "Any Human to Another."

RETHINK 2. What do you think is the main theme of the poem?

3. What is your opinion of the speaker's ideas about sorrow and grief?
   Consider
   - "Your grief and mine / Must intertwine . . ." (lines 7–8)
   - "Sorrow never scorned to speak / To any . . ." (lines 22–23)
   - "My sorrow must be laid / On your head like a crown" (lines 30–31)

RELATE 4. Which poem do you think shows greater affection for other people—"My City" or "Any Human to Another"? Support your view.

5. Recall that some critics complained about Langston Hughes's poetry because they thought it presented an unflattering portrait of African Americans (see Critic's Corner, page 771). How do you think those critics would react to "My City" and to "Any Human to Another"?

ANOTHER PATHWAY

Cooperative Learning

Do you agree or disagree with the main ideas in these poems? Get together with a small group of classmates who share your attitude toward the first poem, and write a response. Do likewise for the second poem. Share your responses in class.

Dear Mr. Johnson: I'll take the flowers and birds, thanks. Do you really like grimy concrete?

LITERARY CONCEPTS

A sonnet is a 14-line lyric poem that can have any of several possible rhyme schemes. One type of sonnet is the **Petrarchan** (pĭ-trär′kən) **sonnet** (named for Francesco Petrarch, the Italian poet who perfected the form). It consists of two parts. The first eight lines, called the octave, usually have the rhyme scheme *abbaabba.* In the last six lines, called the sestet, the rhyme scheme may be *cdecde, cdcdcd,* or another variation. Generally, the octave tells a story, introduces a situation, or raises a question, which is then commented on or responded to in the sestet. What characteristics make "My City" a Petrarchan sonnet?

QUICKWRITES

1. The speaker of "My City" has a strong reaction to New York City. Using the poem as a basis, write a **slogan** celebrating the city.
2. The speaker of "Any Human to Another" believes that few people experience joy but many experience sorrow. Write a **persuasive paragraph** explaining why you agree or disagree with the speaker's viewpoint.

PORTFOLIO *Save your writing. You may want to use it later as a springboard to a piece for your portfolio.*

LITERARY LINKS

How does Johnson's portrayal of New York City compare with Carl Sandburg's portrayal of Chicago in "Chicago" (page 668)?

Johnson's New York City	Sandburg's Chicago

ACROSS THE CURRICULUM

Art Find out about artists who were associated with the Harlem Renaissance, such as the sculptors Meta Warrick Fuller and Richmond Barthé, the painters Jacob Lawrence and Palmer C. Hayden, and the illustrator Aaron Douglas. Identify a particular work of art that you think matches "My City" or "Any Human to Another" in mood or images, and share it with the class.

Study for *God's Trombones* (1926), Aaron Douglas. The Evans-Tibbs Collection, Washington, D.C.

JAMES WELDON JOHNSON

1871–1938

James Weldon Johnson was one of the most prominent African-American leaders of his time. Born into a middle-class family in Jacksonville, Florida, Johnson was a precocious child who read the books of Charles Dickens and Sir Walter Scott. After graduating from Atlanta University, he became a school principal, founded a daily newspaper, and became the first African-American lawyer to be admitted to the Florida bar. In 1902, after his newspaper folded and his school burned down, Johnson decided to go to New York, where he and his brother J. Rosamond became successful Broadway songwriters. Their song "Lift Every Voice and Sing" became known as the African-American "national anthem."

During his writing career, Johnson published in all genres of literature. He also wrote *Black Manhattan,* a book about African-American history, and compiled the groundbreaking anthology *The Book of American Negro Poetry* (1922). The first collection of its kind, his anthology provided powerful evidence of African-American contributions to culture.

OTHER WORKS *Autobiography of an Ex-Colored Man, Fifty Years and Other Poems, God's Trombones*

COUNTEE CULLEN

1903–1946

In 1925, while still an undergraduate at New York University, Countee Cullen published his first poetry collection, *Color,* which established his reputation as a poet. A superb student, he also won several poetry prizes. After graduating from college in 1925, Cullen went on to earn a master's degree at Harvard University.

Cullen was influenced by the English romantic poets, especially John Keats. In his introduction to the anthology *Caroling Dusk,* he stated his belief that African-American poets "may have more to gain from the rich background of English and American poetry than from any . . . yearnings towards an African inheritance." This philosophy is apparent throughout the volumes of his own verse.

In the 1930s and 1940s, Cullen wrote a novel, *One Way to Heaven,* as well as children's books, translations, and (in collaboration with Arna Bontemps) a musical. In 1934 he took a job teaching French at Frederick Douglass Junior High School in New York, a position he held until his death.

OTHER WORKS *The Ballad of the Brown Girl, The Black Christ and Other Poems, Copper Sun*

PREVIEWING

POETRY

If We Must Die
Claude McKay

A Black Man Talks of Reaping
Arna Bontemps (bôN-täN′)

PERSONAL CONNECTION

In these poems, Claude McKay and Arna Bontemps speak out against the unfair treatment of African Americans in the early decades of the 20th century. In your notebook, write about a time when you were treated unfairly or you witnessed someone else being treated unfairly. Tell what you think provoked this treatment—was it race, age, gender, religion, income, or some other factor? How did you or the other person respond to the unfair treatment? Was the response, in your opinion, the best possible one? After you finish writing, discuss what you wrote with a group of classmates.

HISTORICAL CONNECTION

Throughout the history of this country, African Americans have endured such unfair treatment as slavery, lynchings, and segregation. While still facing widespread discrimination and violence in the 1920s, writers in Harlem defied convention by writing angrily about the injustices African Americans endured in a predominantly white society. Claude McKay's poem "If We Must Die" was written in response to a wave of violence against African Americans during the so-called Red Summer of 1919, when escalating racial tension resulted in 26 bloody riots across the country. In "A Black Man Talks of Reaping," Arna Bontemps condemns the economic exploitation African Americans suffered even after the end of slavery.

NAACP antilynching march in New York City on July 28, 1917. Special Collections and Archives, University Library, University of Massachusetts Amherst.

READING CONNECTION

Interpreting Extended Metaphors An extended metaphor is a comparison between two things that is developed at some length and in several ways. In both of these poems, extended metaphors are used to describe the unfair treatment experienced by African Americans in the early 20th century. As you read, note important words and try to determine their figurative meanings. You might ask yourself, Who are like hogs? What resembles being hunted and penned? What is comparable to sowing and reaping?

hogs = ?
hunted and penned =?
sowing =?
reaping =?

Copyright © Herbert Tauss.

If We Must Die

Claude McKay

If we must die, let it not be like hogs
Hunted and penned in an inglorious[1] spot,
While round us bark the mad and hungry dogs,
Making their mock at our accursed lot.
If we must die, O let us nobly die,
So that our precious blood may not be shed
In vain; then even the monsters we defy
Shall be constrained[2] to honor us though dead!
O kinsmen! we must meet the common foe!
Though far outnumbered let us show us brave,
And for their thousand blows deal one deathblow!
What though before us lies the open grave?
Like men we'll face the murderous, cowardly pack,
Pressed to the wall, dying, but fighting back!

1. **inglorious:** shameful; disgraceful.
2. **constrained:** forced.

From Personal Response *to* Critical Analysis

REFLECT **1.** If you had just heard this poem read aloud, what would be your first comment?

RETHINK **2.** In your own words, summarize the poem's theme.

3. Do you agree with the speaker's response to unfair treatment? Why or why not?

A Black Man Talks of Reaping

Arna Bontemps

I have sown beside all waters in my day.
I planted deep, within my heart the fear
That wind or fowl would take the grain away.
I planted safe against this stark, lean year.

I scattered seed enough to plant the land
In rows from Canada to Mexico,
But for my reaping only what the hand
Can hold at once is all that I can show.

Yet what I sowed and what the orchard yields
My brother's sons are gathering stalk and root,
Small wonder then my children glean[1] in fields
They have not sown, and feed on bitter fruit.

---

1. **glean:** gather grain left behind by reapers.

Photo by Arthur Rothstein.
From the collections of the
Library of Congress.

RESPONDING OPTIONS

FROM PERSONAL RESPONSE *TO* CRITICAL ANALYSIS

REFLECT 1. In your notebook, write one word to describe the general feeling of "A Black Man Talks of Reaping."

RETHINK 2. How do you interpret this poem?

Consider

- the figurative meanings of "sown," "reaping," "my brother's sons," "glean," and "bitter fruit"
- the difference between reaping and gleaning
- why the speaker has reaped so little

RELATE 3. Compare the wrongs the speakers face in these two poems and the ways they respond to unfair treatment.

4. Which poem do you think has more relevance to the lives of African Americans today?

5. Compare the styles of the two poems. Which do you prefer, and why?

ANOTHER PATHWAY

Cooperative Learning

With a small group of classmates, design two buttons for the speakers of "If We Must Die" and "A Black Man Talks of Reaping" to wear on their lapels. Each button should feature a motto that expresses a goal, principle, or action advocated by the speaker for whom it is designed.

LITERARY CONCEPTS

As you may recall, a **sonnet** is a 14-line lyric poem. The features of a Petrarchan sonnet are described in the Handbook of Literary Terms. A second kind of sonnet, the **Shakespearean sonnet,** is divided into three quatrains (groups of four lines) and a couplet (two rhyming lines). Its rhyme scheme is *abab cdcd efef gg.* The couplet usually expresses a response to the important issue developed in the three quatrains. Explain how "If We Must Die" shows the features of a Shakespearean sonnet. How is its form similar to and different from that of James Weldon Johnson's "My City"? What might have been some of McKay's reasons for using a traditional form to express his ideas?

QUICKWRITES

1. What should a group do when it is made a target of violence or economic exploitation by another group? Write a **prescription,** based on your personal philosophy or your knowledge of history or current world affairs.
2. Try writing a **sonnet** on any subject—perhaps the instance of unfair treatment you wrote about for the Personal Connection on page 777. Use either the Shakespearean or the Petrarchan form, and remember that the end must somehow answer or comment on the beginning. Share a draft of your poem with a partner for comment.

PORTFOLIO *Save your writing. You may want to use it later as a spring-board to a piece for your portfolio.*

LITERARY LINKS

How do you think Martin Luther King, Jr. (page 235), or Malcolm X (page 239) might respond to the ideas expressed by the speaker of "If We Must Die" or "A Black Man Talks of Reaping"? Share your thoughts with a small group of your classmates.

Martin Luther King, Jr., and Malcolm X in 1964. UPI/Bettmann.

CRITIC'S CORNER

When McKay's poem "If We Must Die" was published in 1919, it was read as a protest against white violence and a call for African Americans to resist oppression. After learning that a white American soldier who died in World War II had carried the poem with him, however, McKay said, "I felt assurance that 'If We Must Die' was just what I intended it to be, a universal poem." In your opinion, does this poem have a universal meaning? Why or why not?

CLAUDE MCKAY

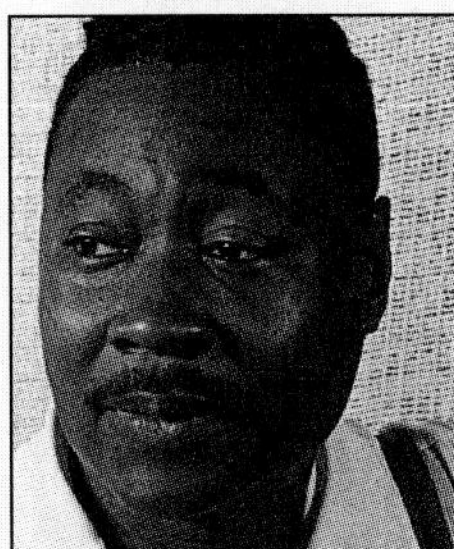

1890?–1948

Born and raised on the island of Jamaica, Claude McKay came to the United States in 1912. After attending Tuskegee Institute in Alabama and Kansas State University, he moved to New York City in 1914. With the publication in 1922 of his major collection of poetry, *Harlem Shadows,* McKay helped launch the Harlem Renaissance.

Called "the poet of rebellion" by James Weldon Johnson, McKay protested racial injustice in both poetry and prose. His powerful sonnet "If We Must Die," first published in *The Liberator* in July 1919, is still one of the best-known African-American poems. The popularity of his novel *Home to Harlem,* about a soldier's life after World War I, made McKay the first best-selling African-American novelist.

Although identified with the Harlem writers of the 1920s, McKay spent most of the decade abroad, living for 12 years in the Soviet Union, France, Spain, and Morocco. Like Countee Cullen, he did not consider himself solely an African-American poet. He said, "I have always felt that my gift of song was something bigger than the narrow confined limits of any one people and its problems."

OTHER WORKS *Banana Bottom, Banjo, Harlem: Negro Metropolis, A Long Way from Home*

ARNA BONTEMPS

1902–1973

Through his poetry, novels, and plays, Arna Bontemps made a significant contribution to the development of African-American identity. Bontemps was born in Alexandria, Louisiana, the son of a teacher and a brick mason. While attending Pacific Union College, he heard the Jamaican social reformer Marcus Garvey speak in Los Angeles and learned about the flourishing Harlem Renaissance.

After graduating from college in 1923, Bontemps moved to Harlem to "see what all the excitement was about." What he discovered was "a foretaste of paradise." While earning a living by teaching, he concentrated as much as possible on his writing and within a year of his arrival in New York City began publishing poems in *Crisis* magazine. His first novel, *God Sends Sunday,* published in 1931, is considered by some to have been the final product of the Harlem Renaissance movement.

During the 1930s and 1940s, Bontemps compiled an anthology of poetry, wrote children's books, and wrote two novels about slave revolts—*Black Thunder* and *Drums at Dusk.* He also collaborated with Countee Cullen on the play *St. Louis Woman* (an adaptation of his first novel) and with Langston Hughes on children's books and two anthologies of African-American literature.

OTHER WORKS *The Old South, Personals*

• *HISTORICAL CONNECTION*

PREVIEWING

NONFICTION

How It Feels to Be Colored Me

Zora Neale Hurston

PERSONAL CONNECTION

In this essay, Zora Neale Hurston presents her feelings about herself as both a unique individual and an African American. What makes you unique or special—an unusual talent or outstanding ability? your personality? your cultural background? your appearance? In your notebook, identify your unique characteristics by drawing a word web like the one shown. Complete the diagram with as many specific characteristics as you can.

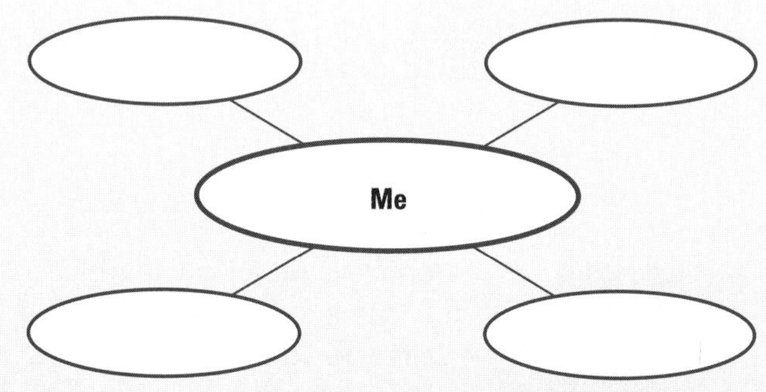

BIOGRAPHICAL CONNECTION

From the time she moved to Harlem in 1925 until her death in 1960, Zora Neale Hurston was the most prolific African-American woman writer. She was also a popular figure on the social scene during the Harlem Renaissance. According to her biographer Robert Hemenway, Hurston "acquired an instant reputation in New York for her high spirits and side-splitting tales of Eatonville," her Florida hometown. Like other writers of the Harlem Renaissance, such as Langston Hughes and Claude McKay, Hurston searched within herself for her identity rather than defining herself according to the racial stereotypes of her day. In this essay, first published in 1928, she uses several unique images to convey her individuality.

Zora Neale Hurston
Courtesy of Edgar B. Hurston.

WRITING CONNECTION

Write about an incident from your past that shows a way in which you are unique. You may want to use words and phrases from the word web you drew for the Personal Connection. Then, as you read the following essay, consider the events that help illustrate Hurston's individuality and notice the images she uses to convey her uniqueness.

How It Feels to Be Colored Me

ZORA NEALE HURSTON

I am colored but I offer nothing in the way of extenuating circumstances except the fact that I am the only Negro in the United States whose grandfather on the mother's side was *not* an Indian chief.

I remember the very day that I became colored. Up to my thirteenth year I lived in the little Negro town of Eatonville, Florida. It is exclusively a colored town. The only white people I knew passed through the town going to or coming from Orlando. The native whites rode dusty horses; the Northern tourists chugged down the sandy village road in automobiles. The town knew the Southerners and never stopped cane chewing when they passed. But the Northerners were something else again. They were peered at cautiously from behind curtains by the timid. The more venturesome would come out on the porch to watch them go past and got just as much pleasure out of the tourists as the tourists got out of the village.

The front porch might seem a daring place for the rest of the town, but it was a gallery seat for me. My favorite place was atop the gatepost. Proscenium box[1] for a born first-nighter.[2] Not only did I enjoy the show, but I didn't mind the actors knowing that I liked it. I usually spoke to them in passing. I'd wave at them and when they returned my salute, I would say something like this: "Howdy-do-well-I-thank-you-where-you-goin'?" Usually the automobile or the horse paused at this, and after a queer exchange of compliments, I would probably "go a piece of the way" with them, as we say in farthest Florida. If one of my family happened to come to the front in time to see me, of course negotiations would be rudely broken off. But even so, it is clear that I was the first "welcome-to-our-state" Floridian, and I hope the Miami Chamber of Commerce will please take notice.

During this period, white people differed from colored to me only in that they rode through town and never lived there. They liked to hear me "speak pieces" and sing and wanted to see me dance the parse-me-la, and gave me generously of their small silver for doing these things,

1. **proscenium** (prō-sē′nē-əm) **box:** a box seat near the stage.
2. **first-nighter:** a person who attends the opening performance of a play, an opera, or a similar show.

WORDS TO KNOW

extenuating (ĭk-stĕn′yo͞o-ā′tĭng) *adj.* lessening a fault by serving as a partial excuse **extenuate** *v.*

Skipping Along, Stephen Scott Young. Copyright © Stephen Scott Young. Photo courtesy of John H. Surovek Gallery, Palm Beach, Flordia.

which seemed strange to me, for I wanted to do them so much that I needed bribing to stop. Only they didn't know it. The colored people gave no dimes. They deplored any joyful tendencies in me, but I was their Zora nevertheless. I belonged to them, to the nearby hotels, to the county—everybody's Zora.

But changes came in the family when I was thirteen, and I was sent to school in Jacksonville. I left Eatonville, the town of the oleanders,[3] as Zora. When I disembarked from the riverboat at Jacksonville, she was no more. It seemed that I had suffered a sea change.[4] I was not Zora of Orange County any more, I was now a little colored girl. I found it out in certain ways. In my heart as well as in the mirror, I became a fast brown—warranted not to rub nor run.

But I am not tragically colored. There is no great sorrow dammed up in my soul, nor lurking behind my eyes. I do not mind at all. I do not belong to the sobbing school of Negrohood who hold that nature somehow has given them a lowdown dirty deal and whose feelings are all hurt about it. Even in the helter-skelter skirmish that is my life, I have seen that the world is to the strong regardless of a little pigmentation[5] more or less. No, I do not weep at the world—I am too busy sharpening my oyster knife.[6]

Someone is always at my elbow reminding me that I am the granddaughter of slaves. It fails to register depression with me. Slavery is sixty years in the past. The operation was successful and the patient is doing well, thank you. The terrible struggle that made me an American out of a potential slave said, "On the line!" The Reconstruction said, "Get set!" and the generation before said, "Go!" I am off to a flying start and I must not halt in the stretch to look behind and weep. Slavery is the price I paid for civilization, and the choice was not with me. It is a bully[7] adventure and worth all that I have paid through my ancestors for it. No one on earth ever had a greater chance for glory. The world to be won and nothing to be lost. It is thrilling to think—to know that for any act of mine, I shall get twice as much praise or twice as much blame. It is quite exciting to hold the center of the national stage, with the spectators not knowing whether to laugh or to weep.

The position of my white neighbor is much more difficult. No brown specter pulls up a chair beside me when I sit down to eat. No dark ghost thrusts its leg against mine in bed. The game of keeping what one has is never so exciting as the game of getting.

3. **oleanders** (ō′lē-ăn′dərz): evergreen shrubs with fragrant flowers.
4. **sea change:** complete transformation.
5. **pigmentation:** darkness of skin coloration.
6. **oyster knife:** a reference to the saying "The world is my oyster," implying that the world contains treasure waiting to be taken, like the pearl in an oyster.
7. **bully:** excellent; splendid.

WORDS TO KNOW

deplore (dĭ-plôr′) *v.* to feel strong disapproval of or deeply regret
specter (spĕk′tər) *n.* a ghostly vision; phantom

I do not always feel colored. Even now I often achieve the unconscious Zora of Eatonville before the Hegira.[8] I feel most colored when I am thrown against a sharp white background.

For instance at Barnard.[9] "Beside the waters of the Hudson"[10] I feel my race. Among the thousand white persons, I am a dark rock surged upon, and overswept, but through it all, I remain myself. When covered by the waters, I am; and the ebb but reveals me again.

Sometimes it is the other way around. A white person is set down in our midst, but the contrast is just as sharp for me. For instance, when I sit in the drafty basement that is The New World Cabaret with a white person, my color comes. We enter chatting about any little nothing that we have in common and are seated by the jazz waiters. In the abrupt way that jazz orchestras have, this one plunges into a number. It loses no time in circumlocutions,[11] but gets right down to business. It constricts the thorax and splits the heart with its tempo and narcotic harmonies. This orchestra grows rambunctious, rears on its hind legs and attacks the tonal veil with primitive fury, rending it, clawing it until it breaks through to the jungle beyond. I follow those heathen—follow them exultingly. I dance wildly inside myself; I yell within, I whoop; I shake my assegai[12] above my head, I hurl it true to the mark *yeeeeooww!* I am in the jungle and living in the jungle way. My face is painted red and yellow and my body is painted blue. My pulse is throbbing like a war drum. I want to slaughter something—give pain, give death to what, I do not know. But the piece ends. The men of the orchestra wipe their lips and rest their fingers. I creep back slowly to the veneer we call civilization with the last tone and find the white friend sitting motionless in his seat, smoking calmly.

"Good music they have here," he remarks, drumming the table with his fingertips.

Music. The great blobs of purple and red emotion have not touched him. He has only heard what I felt. He is far away and I see him but dimly across the ocean and the continent that have fallen between us. He is so pale with his whiteness then and I am *so* colored.

At certain times I have no race. I am *me.* When I set my hat at a certain angle and saunter down Seventh Avenue, Harlem City, feeling as snooty as the lions in front of the Forty-Second Street Library, for instance. So far as my feelings are concerned, Peggy Hopkins Joyce on the Boule Mich with her gorgeous raiment, stately carriage,[13] knees knocking together in a most aristocratic manner, has nothing on me. The cosmic[14] Zora emerges. I belong to no race nor time. I am the eternal feminine with its string of beads.

I have no separate feeling about being an American citizen and colored. I am merely a fragment of the Great Soul that surges within the boundaries. My country, right or wrong.

Sometimes, I feel discriminated against, but it does not make me angry. It merely astonishes

---

8. **Hegira** (hĭ-jī′rə): journey (from the name given to Mohammed's journey from Mecca to Medina in 622).
9. **Barnard:** the college in New York City from which Hurston graduated in 1928.
10. **"Beside the waters of the Hudson":** a reference to the first line of Barnard's school song.
11. **circumlocutions** (sûr′kəm-lō-kyo͞o′shənz): unnecessary elaboration or "beating around the bush."
12. **assegai** (ăs′ə-gī′): a light spear, especially one with a short shaft and long blade, used in southern Africa.
13. **Peggy Hopkins Joyce . . . carriage:** one of the richest women of Hurston's day, walking along the Boulevard Saint-Michel in Paris, dressed in beautiful clothes, carrying herself like a queen.
14. **cosmic:** of or belonging to the universe.

WORDS TO KNOW

rend (rĕnd) *v.* to tear or split apart violently
veneer (və-nîr′) *n.* a thin surface layer that conceals what is below

Bal Jeunesse (about 1927), Palmer Hayden. Watercolor on paper, 14″ × 17″, collection of Meredith and Gail Wright Sirmans.

me. How *can* any deny themselves the pleasure of my company? It's beyond me.

But in the main, I feel like a brown bag of miscellany propped against a wall. Against a wall in company with other bags, white, red, and yellow. Pour out the contents, and there is discovered a jumble of small things priceless and worthless. A first-water[15] diamond, an empty spool, bits of broken glass, lengths of string, a key to a door long since crumbled away, a rusty knife blade, old shoes saved for a road that never was and never will be, a nail bent under the weight of things too heavy for any nail, a dried flower or two still a little fragrant. In your hand is the brown bag. On the ground before you is the jumble it held—so much like the jumble in the bags, could they be emptied, that all might be dumped in a single heap and the bags refilled without altering the content of any greatly. A bit of colored glass more or less would not matter. Perhaps that is how the Great Stuffer of Bags filled them in the first place—who knows? ❖

15. **first-water:** of the highest quality or purity.

INSIGHT

from

Zora Neale Hurston: A Cautionary Tale and a Partisan View

Alice Walker

Novelist Alice Walker was responsible for rediscovering the writings of Zora Neale Hurston in the 1970s and bringing her to the attention of a new generation of readers. In the following excerpt from an essay on Hurston, Walker discusses the impact of Hurston's collection of black folktales, Mules and Men, *first published in 1935.*

. . . When I read *Mules and Men* I was delighted. Here was this perfect book! The "perfection" of which I immediately tested on my relatives, who are such typical black Americans they are useful for every sort of political, cultural, or economic survey. Very regular people from the South, rapidly forgetting their Southern cultural inheritance in the suburbs and ghettos of Boston and New York, they sat around reading the book themselves, listening to me read the book, listening to each other read the book, and a kind of paradise was regained. For what Zora's book did was this: it gave them back all the stories they had forgotten or of which they had grown ashamed (told to us years ago by our parents and grandparents—not one of whom could *not* tell a story to make you weep, or laugh) and showed how marvelous, and, indeed, priceless, they are. This is not exaggerated. No matter how they read the stories Zora had collected, no matter how much distance they tried to maintain between themselves, as new sophisticates, and the lives their parents and grandparents lived, no matter how they tried to remain cool toward all Zora revealed, in the end they could not hold back the smiles, the laughter, the joy over who she was showing them to be: descendants of an inventive, joyous, courageous, and outrageous people; loving drama, appreciating wit, and, most of all, relishing the pleasure of each other's loquacious[1] and *bodacious*[2] company.

This was my first indication of the quality I feel is most characteristic of Zora's work: racial health; a sense of black people as complete, complex, *undiminished* human beings, a sense that is lacking in so much black writing and literature. (In my opinion,

1. **loquacious** (lō-kwā′shəs): very talkative.
2. ***bodacious*** (bō-dā′shəs): a Southern dialect term meaning "remarkable" or "spirited."

only Du Bois[3] showed an equally consistent delight in the beauty and spirit of black people, which is interesting when one considers that the angle of his vision was completely the opposite of Zora's.) Zora's pride in black people was so pronounced in the ersatz[4] black twenties that it made other blacks suspicious and perhaps uncomfortable (after all, *they* were still infatuated[5] with things European). Zora was interested in Africa, Haiti, Jamaica, and—for a little racial diversity (Indians)—Honduras. She also had a confidence in herself as an individual that few people (anyone?), black or white, understood. This was because Zora grew up in a community of black people who had enormous respect for themselves and for their ability to govern themselves. Her own father had written the Eatonville town laws. This community affirmed her right to exist, and loved her as an extension of its self. For how many other black Americans is this true? It certainly isn't true for any that I know. In her easy self-acceptance, Zora was more like an uncolonized African than she was like her contemporary American blacks, most of whom believed, at least during their formative years, that their blackness was something wrong with them.

On the contrary, Zora's early work shows she grew up pitying whites because the ones she saw lacked "light" and soul. It is impossible to imagine Zora envying anyone (except tongue in cheek), and least of all a white person for being white. Which is, after all, if one is black, a clear and present calamity of the mind.

Condemned to a desert island for life, with an allotment of ten books to see me through, I would choose, unhesitatingly, two of Zora's: *Mules and Men,* because I would need to be able to pass on to younger generations the life of American blacks as legend and myth; and *Their Eyes Were Watching God,* because I would want to enjoy myself while identifying with the black heroine, Janie Crawford, as she acted out many roles in a variety of settings, and functioned (with spectacular results!) in romantic and sensual love. *There is no book more important to me than this one. . . .* ❖

---

3. **Du Bois** (do͞o bois′): the U.S. civil rights leader, editor, and author W. E. B. Du Bois (1868–1963).
4. **ersatz** (ĕr′zäts′): artificial; imitation.
5. **infatuated** (ĭn-făch′o͞o-ā′tĭd): carried away by a foolish attraction.

RESPONDING OPTIONS

FROM PERSONAL RESPONSE *TO* CRITICAL ANALYSIS

REFLECT **1.** If you had met Zora Neale Hurston when she was a child or when she was an adult, would you have liked her? Comment in your notebook.

RETHINK **2.** In your opinion, what made Hurston unique?

3. What do you think Hurston's cultural identity meant to her?

Consider

- her statement "I am not tragically colored"
- when she was aware of her color and when she forgot it
- her views of slavery, discrimination, and the United States
- her response to jazz

4. What idea do you think Hurston was trying to communicate in the last paragraph by comparing people to stuffed bags?

RELATE **5.** In the Insight selection, Alice Walker identifies qualities she feels are characteristic of Hurston's writing. Do you detect these qualities in Hurston's essay? Explain.

6. Which of the ideas expressed in Hurston's essay do you think might be controversial today? Give reasons for your answer.

ANOTHER PATHWAY

Cooperative Learning

With a small group of classmates, brainstorm a list of five objects that you think most represent Hurston's individuality. Your list might, for example, include a jazz recording that represents her love of jazz. Share your list with the rest of the class, explaining why you chose each item.

LITERARY CONCEPTS

Tone is the attitude that a writer expresses toward a subject. In "If We Must Die" (page 777), for example, the tone is proud, defiant, and urgent. This tone is conveyed partly through the writer's choice of comparisons (the enemies are "dogs" and "monsters") and through his elevated, poetic diction ("inglorious," "accursed," "foe"). How would you describe Hurston's tone? What attitude is conveyed by her comparisons of life to a "show," a "game," and a "bully adventure"? What else communicates her tone? Compare her attitude toward being African American with the attitudes of the other Harlem Renaissance writers you've read.

QUICKWRITES

1. If Hurston had been born the year you were born, do you think her essay about herself would have been the same? If she were writing today, would she be more optimistic or less optimistic about being African American? Draft a **speculative essay** to answer these questions.
2. Draft an **autobiographical essay,** modeled on Hurston's, in which you explore what makes you unique. Use what you wrote for the Writing Connection on page 782 for ideas.

PORTFOLIO *Save your writing. You may want to use it later as a springboard to a piece for your portfolio.*

CRITIC'S CORNER

Although Alice Walker is one of Zora Neale Hurston's greatest admirers, she had this to say about Hurston's essay:

> "How It Feels to Be Colored Me" is an excellent example of Zora Neale Hurston at her most exasperating. Published in 1928, near the beginning of Hurston's career, this essay presents two stereotypes: the "happy darky" who sings and dances for white folks, for money and for joy; and the educated black person who is, underneath the thin veneer of civilization, still a "heathen." And Hurston actually says, "Slavery is the price I paid for civilization." . . . [I]t makes one's flesh crawl.

Do you agree that Hurston presents herself in a stereotyped way? Why or why not? Why do you think Walker finds Hurston's statement about slavery so disturbing?

WORDS TO KNOW

Answer the following questions.

1. What attraction at an amusement park would probably involve a **specter**—a roller coaster, a ring-toss game, or a haunted house?
2. If you said that someone had a **veneer** of friendliness, would you be suggesting that the person was eager, was hesitant, or was insincere?
3. If you were to **rend** a curtain, would you be closing it, ripping it, or hanging it?
4. Which would be an **extenuating** circumstance for being tardy for school—that you dawdled on the way, that the bus broke down, or that you thought it was Saturday?
5. Is an action that you **deplore** one that you find horrible, one that you find amusing, or one that you find boring?

ZORA NEALE HURSTON

1891?–1960

Born in the all-black town of Eatonville, Florida, Zora Neale Hurston took her mother's advice to "jump at de sun" and overcome poverty and prejudice. She entered Harlem society in 1925, arriving with "$1.50, no job, no friends, and a lot of hope." After she had won two second prizes—one for a short story and one for a play—in a literary contest sponsored by *Opportunity* magazine, Hurston came to the attention of the leaders of the Harlem Renaissance. In the New York City of the 1920s Hurston soon became known for her flamboyant, theatrical personality as well as for her short stories.

In 1928, after graduating from Barnard College, where she had studied with the renowned anthropologist Franz Boas, Hurston returned to her native South to collect African-American folklore. "I had to go back, dress as they did, talk as they did, live their life," she said, "so I could get into my stories the world I knew as a child."

Over the next two decades, Hurston built her reputation as the best African-American woman writer of her time with a steady stream of publications. Among her prominent works were the folklore collection *Mules and Men,* the novel *Their Eyes Were Watching God,* and her autobiography, *Dust Tracks on a Road.*

During the last 20 years of her life, Hurston struggled with financial and health problems. She died in poverty and was buried in an unmarked grave in Fort Pierce, Florida. Many readers have rediscovered Hurston in recent years, however—largely because of the African-American writer Alice Walker's efforts to publicize her life and work.

OTHER WORKS *Jonah's Gourd Vine; Moses, Man of the Mountain; Tell My Horse;* "Sweat"; "The Gilded Six-Bits"

PREVIEWING

NONFICTION

My Dungeon Shook:
Letter to My Nephew on the One Hundredth Anniversary of the Emancipation
James Baldwin

PERSONAL CONNECTION

Think about a difficult political or social problem that teenagers must deal with today. What advice would you give to a younger brother, sister, or friend to help him or her cope with this problem? In your notebook, begin a letter of advice to the person.

HISTORICAL CONNECTION

By the early 1960s, nonviolent protesters led by Martin Luther King, Jr., had begun, through boycotts and sit-ins, to defy Jim Crow segregation laws in the South and to force officials to repeal the laws. Blacks, along with some whites, were marching throughout the country to demand equal treatment for African Americans. However, although discrimination was being challenged on all sides, racist attitudes were so deeply entrenched in U.S. life that change was slow in coming. Many African Americans experienced discrimination as they sought jobs, housing, and community services.

In this essay, written as a letter of advice to his nephew 100 years after Abraham Lincoln's Emancipation Proclamation, Baldwin refers to the harsh social conditions under which African Americans formerly lived, particularly the conditions he himself had witnessed while growing up in Harlem. The center of African-American culture in the 1920s, Harlem later became a bleak ghetto from which residents had little hope of escaping and which they had even less hope of improving. In the 1960s the sense of despair pervading decayed urban neighborhoods like Harlem fueled an atmosphere of violence. From 1964 to 1967, more than 100 race riots erupted in major cities across the United States.

READING CONNECTION

Analyzing Difficult Ideas To convey the complexity of race relations in this country, Baldwin sometimes makes statements that are paradoxical, or seemingly contradictory. For example, he writes, "It is the innocence which constitutes the crime." Since you probably associate innocence with the absence of wrongdoing, you must, in order to understand this sentence, determine what kind of innocence Baldwin means. As you read Baldwin's advice to his nephew, jot down in your notebook any other statements that seem contradictory or that make you think about race relations in a new way.

MY DUNGEON SHOOK

Letter to My Nephew on the One Hundredth Anniversary of the Emancipation

James Baldwin

Dear James:

I have begun this letter five times and torn it up five times. I keep seeing your face, which is also the face of your father and my brother. Like him, you are tough, dark, vulnerable, moody—with a very definite tendency to sound truculent because you want no one to think you are soft. You may be like your grandfather in this, I don't know, but certainly both you and your father resemble him very much physically. Well, he is dead, he never saw you, and he had a terrible life; he was defeated long before he died because, at the bottom of his heart, he really believed what white people said about him. This is one of the reasons that he became so holy.[1] I am sure that your father has told you something about all that. Neither you nor your father exhibit any tendency towards holiness: you really *are* of another era, part of what happened when the Negro left the land and came into what the late E. Franklin Frazier called "the cities of destruction." You can only be destroyed by believing that you really are what the white world calls a *nigger.* I tell you this because I love you, and please don't you ever forget it.

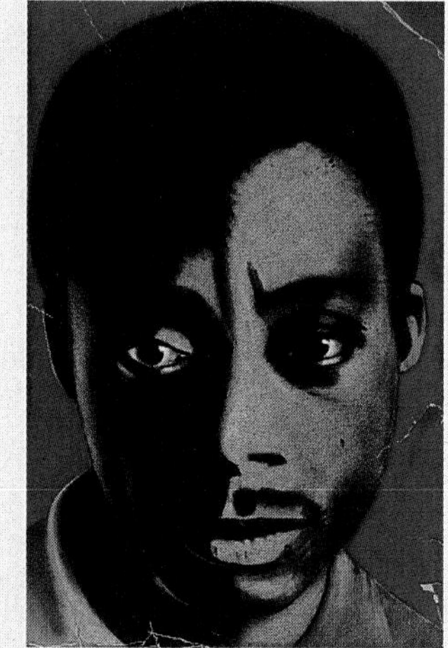

Copyright © Julian Allen.

I have known both of you all your lives, have carried your Daddy in my arms and on my shoulders, kissed and spanked him and watched him learn to walk. I don't know if you've known anybody from that far back; if you've loved anybody that long, first as an infant, then as a child, then as a man, you gain a strange perspective on time and human pain and effort. Other people cannot see what I see whenever I look into your father's face, for behind your father's face as it is today are all those other faces which were his. Let him laugh and I see a cellar your father does not remember and a house he does not remember and I hear in his present laughter his laughter as a child. Let him curse and I remember him falling down the cellar steps, and howling, and I remember, with pain, his tears, which my hand or your grandmother's so easily wiped away. But no one's hand can wipe away those tears he sheds invisibly today, which one hears in his laughter and in his speech and in his songs. I know what the world has done to my brother and how narrowly he has survived it. And I know, which is much worse, and this is the crime of which I accuse my country and my countrymen, and for which neither I nor time nor history will ever

1. **so holy:** Baldwin's stepfather was a minister who raised his children in a strict, conservative, religious atmosphere.

WORDS TO KNOW

truculent (trŭk′yə-lənt) *adj.* eager for a fight; fierce
perspective (pər-spĕk′tĭv) *n.* a mental view or outlook; point of view

forgive them, that they have destroyed and are destroying hundreds of thousands of lives and do not know it and do not want to know it. One can be, indeed one must strive to become, tough and philosophical concerning destruction and death, for this is what most of mankind has been best at since we have heard of man. (But remember: *most* of mankind is not *all* of mankind.) But it is not permissible that the authors of devastation should also be innocent. It is the innocence which constitutes the crime.

Now, my dear namesake, these innocent and well-meaning people, your countrymen, have caused you to be born under conditions not very far removed from those described for us by Charles Dickens in the London of more than a hundred years ago. (I hear the chorus of the innocents screaming, "No! This is not true! How *bitter* you are!"—but I am writing this letter to *you,* to try to tell you something about how to handle *them,* for most of them do not yet really know that you exist. I *know* the conditions under which you were born, for I was there. Your countrymen were *not* there, and haven't made it yet. Your grandmother was also there, and no one has ever accused her of being bitter. I suggest that the innocents check with her. She isn't hard to find. Your countrymen don't know that *she* exists, either, though she has been working for them all their lives.)

It is the innocence which constitutes the crime.

Well, you were born, here you came, something like fifteen years ago; and though your father and mother and grandmother, looking about the streets through which they were carrying you, staring at the walls into which they brought you, had every reason to be heavyhearted, yet they were not. For here you were, Big James, named for me—you were a big baby, I was not—here you were: to be loved. To be loved, baby, hard, at once, and forever, to strengthen you against the loveless world. Remember that: I know how black it looks today, for you. It looked bad that day, too, yes, we were trembling. We have not stopped trembling yet, but if we had not loved each other none of us would have survived. And now you must survive because we love you, and for the sake of your children and your children's children.

This innocent country set you down in a ghetto in which, in fact, it intended that you should perish. Let me spell out precisely what I mean by that, for the heart of the matter is here, and the root of my dispute with my country. You were born where you were born and faced the future that you faced because you were black and *for no other reason.* The limits of your ambition were, thus, expected to be set forever. You were born into a society which spelled out with brutal clarity, and in as many ways as possible, that you were a worthless human being. You were not expected to aspire to excellence: you were expected to make peace with mediocrity. Wherever you have turned, James, in your short time on this earth, you have been told where you could go and what you could do (and *how* you could do it) and where you could live and whom you could marry. I know your countrymen do not agree with me about this, and I hear them saying, "You exaggerate." They do not know Harlem, and I do. So do you. Take no one's word for anything, including mine—but trust your experience.

WORDS TO KNOW

devastation (dĕv′ə-stā′shən) *n.* complete destruction
constitute (kŏn′stĭ-to͞ot′) *v.* to amount to; equal
aspire (ə-spīr′) *v.* to seek to achieve; strive
mediocrity (mē′dē-ŏk′rĭ-tē) *n.* a state of being only average in quality; moderate inferiority

My Brother (1942), John Wilson. Oil on panel, 12″ × 10 ⁵⁄₈″, Smith College Museum of Art, Northampton, Massachusetts, purchased 1943.

Know whence you came. If you know whence you came, there is really no limit to where you can go. The details and symbols of your life have been deliberately constructed to make you believe what white people say about you. Please try to remember that what they believe, as well as what they do and cause you to endure, does not testify to your inferiority but to their inhumanity and fear. Please try to be clear, dear James, through the storm which rages about your youthful head today, about the reality which lies behind the words *acceptance* and *integration.* There is no reason for you to try to become like white people and there is no basis whatever for their impertinent assumption that *they* must accept *you.* The really terrible thing, old buddy, is that *you* must accept *them.* And I mean that very seriously. You must accept them and accept them with love. For these innocent people have no other hope. They are, in effect, still trapped in a history which they do not understand; and until they understand it, they cannot be released from it. They have had to believe for many years, and for innumerable reasons, that black men are inferior to white men. Many of them, indeed, know better, but, as you will discover, people find it very difficult to act on what they know. To act is to be committed, and to be committed is to be in danger. In this case, the danger, in the minds of most white Americans, is the loss of their identity. Try to imagine how you would feel if you woke up one morning to find the sun shining and all the stars aflame. You would be frightened because it is out of the order of nature. Any upheaval in the universe is terrifying because it so profoundly attacks one's sense of one's own reality. Well, the black man has functioned in the white man's world as a fixed star, as an immovable pillar: and as he moves out of his place, heaven and earth are shaken to their foundations. You, don't be afraid. I said that it was intended that you should perish in the ghetto, perish by never being allowed to go behind the white man's definitions, by never being allowed to spell your proper name. You have, and many of us have, defeated this intention; and, by a terrible law, a terrible paradox, those innocents who believed that your imprisonment made them safe are losing their grasp of reality. But these men are your brothers —your lost, younger brothers. And if the word *integration* means anything, this is what it means: that we, with love, shall force our brothers to see themselves as they are, to cease fleeing from reality and begin to change it. For this is your home, my friend, do not be driven from it; great men have done great things here, and will again, and we can make America what America must become. It will be hard, James, but you come from sturdy, peasant stock, men who picked cotton and dammed rivers and built railroads, and, in the teeth of the most terrifying odds, achieved an unassailable and monumental dignity. You come from a long line of great poets, some of the greatest poets since Homer. One of them said, *The very time I thought I was lost, My dungeon shook and my chains fell off.*[2]

You know, and I know, that the country is celebrating one hundred years of freedom one hundred years too soon. We cannot be free until they are free. God bless you, James, and Godspeed.

Your uncle,
James

---

2. ***The very time . . . fell off:*** a quotation from the traditional spiritual "My Dungeon Shook." It contains an allusion to the biblical story of Paul and Silas (Acts 16), who were freed from an unjust imprisonment by an earthquake that broke their chains and opened the prison doors.

WORDS TO KNOW

whence (hwĕns) *adv.* from where
impertinent (ĭm-pûr′ tn ənt) *adj.* rude, ill-mannered
paradox (păr′ə-dŏks′) *n.* a seemingly contradictory statement that may nevertheless be true
monumental (mŏn′yə-mĕn′tl) *adj.* great and lasting

RESPONDING OPTIONS

FROM PERSONAL RESPONSE *TO* CRITICAL ANALYSIS

REFLECT

1. If you were Baldwin's nephew, how would you feel about receiving this letter? Record your thoughts in your notebook.

RETHINK

2. What do you think Baldwin hoped his nephew would gain from the advice in the letter?
3. Do you believe that Baldwin was bitter, as he says his countrymen would claim?
4. Explain what you think Baldwin meant by "It is the innocence which constitutes the crime." Interpret one of the other paradoxical or thought-provoking statements you jotted down as you read.
5. What ideas about cultural identity do you get from Baldwin's letter?

   Consider
   - what he claims can destroy his nephew
   - what he attributes his family's survival to
   - what he says is the root of his dispute with his country
   - what he says white Americans fear and why he thinks they have those fears
   - what he says *integration* means
   - how he describes young James's ancestors

RELATE

6. How do you think Baldwin would view racial attitudes in American society today?

LITERARY LINKS

Cooperative Learning Imagine that you are the host of a radio show featuring a panel discussion with Zora Neale Hurston and James Baldwin. With two other students, write some questions about race relations in the United States, as well as the comments that each writer might make in response. Re-create the panel discussion for the class.

ANOTHER PATHWAY

Cooperative Learning

With a small group of classmates, brainstorm responses that young James might have to his uncle's advice and ideas. Then draft a letter of response in young James's voice and share it with the class.

QUICKWRITES

1. Write a **personal response** to Baldwin's letter, reacting to one or more of his paradoxical or thought-provoking statements.
2. Complete the **letter of advice** to a younger person that you began for the Personal Connection on page 791. You might model the format or tone of your letter on Baldwin's.
3. How do you think the social conditions described in Baldwin's letter compare with the conditions under which African Americans live today? Using specific examples from the news and from your own observation, draft a **comparison-contrast essay** to answer this question.

PORTFOLIO Save your writing. You may want to use it later as a springboard to a piece for your portfolio.

LITERARY CONCEPTS

"My Dungeon Shook" is an **open letter,** addressed to a specific person but published for a wider readership. What in the letter lets you know that Baldwin expected others besides young James to read it? Who do you think his intended audience was? How do you think he wanted them to respond?

CONCEPT REVIEW: Analogy Baldwin draws an analogy between his nephew's probable reaction to seeing the stars shining while the sun is out and whites' reaction to blacks moving out of their fixed places. How does this analogy help you understand Baldwin's ideas about racism better? With a classmate, write your own analogy to illustrate your ideas about a social or political issue that is important to you.

ALTERNATIVE ACTIVITIES

1. Turn some of the ideas expressed by Baldwin in this letter into a **commencement address** that he might deliver at a high school graduation. Present the speech to the class.
2. Research **photographs** of Harlem in the 1960s. Choose several that you think best illustrate Baldwin's letter to his nephew, and show them to the class.
3. In a small-group **discussion,** talk about a time when others' beliefs about you—either positive or negative—influenced your behavior or self-perception. Would you say that Baldwin's warning not to listen to negative messages from society applies more to young African-American men than to others? If you have a computer, extend the discussion through electronic mail, asking for opinions from friends or user groups you belong to.

ART CONNECTION

An interesting aspect of John Wilson's painting *My Brother* (page 794) is that the face is painted in detail, whereas the background is barely sketched in. What do you think the artist achieves by this contrast? What is your impression of his brother?

My Brother (1942), John Wilson. Oil on panel, 12" × 10⅝", Smith College Museum of Art, Northampton, Massachusetts, purchased 1943.

CRITIC'S CORNER

In *Soul on Ice* (1968), the African-American activist Eldridge Cleaver wrote, "There is in James Baldwin's work the most grueling, agonizing, total hatred of the blacks, particularly of himself, and the most shameful, fanatical, fawning, sycophantic love of the whites that one can find in the writing of any black American writer of note in our time." On the basis of your reading of this essay, do you agree or disagree with Cleaver? What evidence do you find to support or refute his opinion?

ACROSS THE CURRICULUM

Music Spirituals, such as the one Baldwin quotes at the end of his letter, express the pain caused by the oppression of slavery, as well as a hope for freedom. Find a recording of "My Dungeon Shook," the spiritual quoted by Baldwin, and play it for the class; or perform the song yourself, alone or with a group. Why do you think Baldwin alluded to the song in his title?

WORDS TO KNOW

EXERCISE A Review the Words to Know at the bottom of the selection pages. Then write the vocabulary word that best completes each sentence.

1. Abraham Lincoln has been praised by some and condemned by others, but virtually no one has accused him of _____.
2. The Emancipation Proclamation he issued in 1863 had a _____ effect on the North's ability to win the Civil War.
3. Many Northerners thought that the nation should _____ to become a true "land of the free."
4. The South, fearing the _____ of its way of life, had seceded from the Union rather than risk losing the power to decide about slavery.
5. Lincoln thought slavery was wrong, but it was his _____ on the war—not on slavery—that caused him to issue the Emancipation Proclamation.
6. He knew that the border states, which were not fighting against the Union, could change their attitude toward the North to a _____ one if he declared that all slaves were free.
7. This concern resulted in the _____ that slaves were freed by the Union only in the areas *outside* any Union control.
8. To achieve freedom, then, a slave who reached Union lines would have to declare _____ he or she had come.
9. Lincoln's belief was that freeing Southern slaves and allowing them to enlist with Union forces could _____ a significant advantage for the North.
10. Does it show an _____ disrespect for Lincoln to suggest that his proclamation was too limited?

EXERCISE B Work with a partner to come up with an appropriate phrase for each vocabulary word—for example, "**aspire** to a goal." Then have another pair of students compete with each other by guessing letters (as in the game hangman or the TV game show *Wheel of Fortune*). The first to guess the phrase wins.

JAMES BALDWIN

1924–1987

Born and raised in Harlem, James Baldwin had to endure not only terrible poverty but harsh treatment by his stepfather and the burden of taking care of eight younger siblings while his mother worked. Baldwin realized later that "my teachers somehow made me believe that I could learn. And when I could scarcely see for myself any future at all, my teachers told me that the future was mine . . . everything was up to me."

When he was 14, Baldwin became a successful preacher, but he had quit preaching by the time he graduated from high school. Determined to become a writer, he moved to Greenwich Village in 1944.

In 1948, tormented by the racial discrimination he saw around him, Baldwin moved to Paris, where he remained for most of the rest of his life. "Once I found myself on the other side of the ocean," he said, "I could see where I came from very clearly, and I could see that I carried myself, which is my home, with me. You can never escape that. I am the grandson of a slave, and I am a writer. I must deal with both."

Although Baldwin's fiction, especially the novel *Go Tell It on the Mountain,* was well received, it was his eloquent nonfiction—such as *Notes of a Native Son* and *The Fire Next Time*—that made him famous. In many of his essays, he took the role of "disturber of the peace," urging whites to face their racism and the damage it did. Baldwin never stopped challenging the country he loved to live up to its democratic ideals.

OTHER WORKS *Nobody Knows My Name, The Price of the Ticket, The Amen Corner,* "Sonny's Blues"

LASERLINKS
• *AUTHOR BACKGROUND*

PREVIEWING

POETRY

Life for My Child Is Simple   Primer for Blacks

Gwendolyn Brooks

PERSONAL CONNECTION

How would you explain the concept of high self-esteem? What are signs of high self-esteem in a person? What encourages its development? What discourages it? Do you think it is important to have? Why or why not? Discuss these questions with a small group of classmates, keeping notes of your discussion.

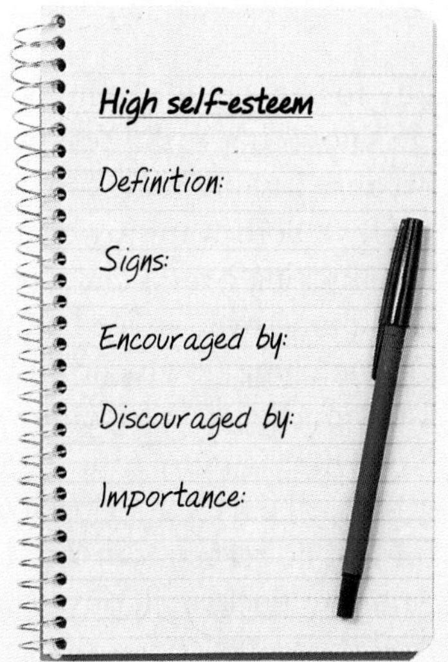

High self-esteem
Definition:
Signs:
Encouraged by:
Discouraged by:
Importance:

LITERARY/BIOGRAPHICAL CONNECTION

At the start of her career, Gwendolyn Brooks often wrote about the effects of racism and poverty on individuals' self-esteem. "Life for My Child Is Simple," from her Pulitzer Prize-winning collection *Annie Allen,* is one of a series of poems that trace the life of a fictitious African-American woman from infancy through motherhood and maturity. Although the speaker is Annie Allen, Brooks drew on her own experiences of raising her son, Henry, in writing this poem.

From 1967 on, Brooks became increasingly committed to political and social issues. Shifting her focus from the individual to African Americans in general, Brooks began to address, in poems such as "Primer for Blacks" and "To Those of My Sisters Who Kept Their Naturals," the lack of black unity and self-esteem that she perceived.

Gwendolyn Brooks with her husband, Henry, and young son, Henry, Jr. Used by permission of Broadside Press.

READING CONNECTION

Understanding Capitalization As you probably know, the names of different races, peoples, nationalities, and ethnic groups, such as *Asians* and *African Americans,* are capitalized. However, the terms *blacks* and *whites* are not usually capitalized. As you read "Primer for Blacks," notice Brooks's capitalization of *Blacks.* She has said that she adopted this style to give African Americans "capitalizations for their *essence*" and to emphasize African-American solidarity and pride. "The capitalized names *Black* and *Blacks,*" according to Brooks, "were appointed to comprise an open, wide-stretching, unifying, empowering umbrella." Also notice, as you read the poem, other words Brooks capitalizes for emphasis.

Life for My Child Is Simple

GWENDOLYN BROOKS

Life for my child is simple, and is good.
He knows his wish. Yes, but that is not all.
Because I know mine too.
And we both want joy of undeep and unabiding[1] things,
Like kicking over a chair or throwing blocks out of a window
Or tipping over an ice box pan
Or snatching down curtains or fingering an electric outlet
Or a journey or a friend or an illegal kiss.
No. There is more to it than that.
It is that he has never been afraid.
Rather, he reaches out and lo the chair falls with a beautiful crash,
And the blocks fall, down on the people's heads,
And the water comes slooshing sloppily out across the floor.
And so forth.
Not that success, for him, is sure, infallible.[2]
But never has he been afraid to reach.
His lesions are legion.[3]
But reaching is his rule.

---

1. **unabiding:** not lasting; continually changing.
2. **infallible** (ĭn-făl′ə-bəl): foolproof.
3. **His lesions are legion:** His injuries are many.

FROM PERSONAL RESPONSE *TO* CRITICAL ANALYSIS

REFLECT **1.** In your notebook, record your impressions of the child described in this poem and of his level of self-esteem.

RETHINK **2.** Why do you think the speaker's son is not "afraid to reach"?

3. What do you think "reaching" means to the speaker of this poem?

4. How would you describe the speaker's feelings for her child? Cite lines to support your answer.

Primer for Blacks

GWENDOLYN BROOKS

110th Street, Romare Bearden (1914–1988), Collage on paper, 14″ × 22″, courtesy of the Estate of Romare Bearden.

Blackness
is a title,
is a preoccupation,
is a commitment Blacks
are to comprehend—
and in which you are
to perceive your Glory.

The conscious shout
of all that is white is
"It's Great to be white."
The conscious shout
of the slack in Black is
"It's Great to be white."
Thus all that is white
has white strength and yours.

The word Black
has geographic power,
pulls everybody in:
Blacks here—
Blacks there—
Blacks wherever they may be.
And remember, you Blacks, what they told you—
remember your Education:
"one Drop—one Drop
maketh a brand new Black."

3 preoccupation: something that takes one's full attention.

12 slack: lack of force.

24 one Drop: Historically in the United States, a person has been considered black if he or she "has only one drop of African blood."

Oh mighty Drop.
And because they have given us kindly
so many more of our people
Blackness
stretches over the land.
Blackness—
the Black of it,
the rust-red of it,
the milk and cream of it,
the tan and yellow-tan of it,
the deep-brown middle-brown high-brown of it,
the "olive" and ochre of it—
Blackness
marches on.

The huge, the pungent object of our prime out-ride
is to Comprehend,
to salute and to Love the fact that we are Black,
which *is* our "ultimate Reality,"
which is the lone ground
from which our meaningful metamorphosis,
from which our prosperous staccato,
group or individual, can rise.

Self-shriveled Blacks.
Begin with gaunt and marvelous concession:
YOU are our costume and our fundamental bone.

All of you—
you COLORED ones,
you NEGRO ones,
those of you who proudly cry
"I'm half INDian"—
those of you who proudly screech
"I'VE got the blood of George WASHington in MY veins—
ALL of you—
you proper Blacks,
you half-Blacks,
you wish-I-weren't Blacks,
Niggeroes and Niggerenes.

You.

37 ochre (ō'kər): brownish orange-yellow.

40 pungent (pŭn'jənt): sharp and intense, like a powerful odor; **prime out-ride:** literally "principal riding out," perhaps here meaning "main effort."

43 "ultimate Reality": Here Brooks is quoting the activist Ron Karenga.

46 staccato (stə-kä'tō): the playing of musical notes in a crisp, disconnected way.

RESPONDING OPTIONS

FROM PERSONAL RESPONSE *TO* CRITICAL ANALYSIS

REFLECT **1.** What is your emotional reaction to "Primer for Blacks"? Jot down your feelings in your notebook.

RETHINK **2.** Whom do you think the speaker is addressing at the end of the poem, and how do you think they are meant to feel?

3. What points about "Blackness" do you think are made in this poem?

Consider

- the definitions in the first stanza
- the comparison with whiteness in the second stanza
- what "geographic power" might mean (line 17)
- the different colors mentioned in lines 32–39
- what can rise from "the fact that we are Black" (lines 42–47)
- what the "concession" asked for in line 49 might be

4. Do you agree with Brooks's ideas about blackness?

RELATE **5.** In your opinion, do "Life for My Child Is Simple" and "Primer for Blacks" suggest similar ways or different ways of approaching life? Explain your response.

6. How do these two poems relate to your discussion of self-esteem for the Personal Connection on page 799?

7. Of the other writers represented in this part of Unit Six, whose ideas about African-American cultural identity are closest to Brooks's? Whose are farthest from hers? Support your views.

ANOTHER PATHWAY

Cooperative Learning

With a small group of classmates, act out an image of the child described in "Life for My Child Is Simple." Then act out an image of the people the speaker addresses in "Primer for Blacks" and an image of the kind of people the speaker wants them to become. Share your interpretations with the rest of the class.

LITERARY CONCEPTS

Anaphora (ə-năf′ər-ə) is a repetition of a word or words at the beginning of successive lines, clauses, or sentences. Gwendolyn Brooks frequently uses this device. In "Primer for Blacks," for example, notice the anaphora in lines 2–4: "is a title / is a preoccupation / is a commitment . . ." This repetition gives equal weight to each definition of "Blackness" and leads the reader to try to reconcile the definitions. Find other examples of anaphora in these two poems. What ideas are balanced in each instance?

QUICKWRITES

1. What do you think the young boy described in "Life for My Child Is Simple" will be like as he grows older? Write a **summary** that you think might appear with his high school yearbook picture.
2. Brooks calls "Primer for Blacks" a "preachment"—a statement intended to teach and to inspire to action. Write an **abstract** of the poem, summarizing the main points of the lesson that Brooks teaches.

PORTFOLIO *Save your writing. You may want to use it later as a springboard to a piece for your portfolio.*

ALTERNATIVE ACTIVITIES

1. Design a **T-shirt** to illustrate the theme of "Life for My Child Is Simple" or "Primer for Blacks." If possible, actually make the T-shirt and wear it to class.
2. Prepare a **sermon** based on "Primer for Blacks" and deliver it to the class. Try to duplicate the speaker's tone in your delivery, and try to make each member of your audience feel as if you were speaking directly to him or her.

THE WRITER'S STYLE

On the basis of these two poems, in what ways would you say Brooks's style changed in the 30 years between "Life for My Child Is Simple" and "Primer for Blacks"? In what ways did it remain the same? Work as a class to answer these questions, perhaps by making a chart. Consider the forms of the poems; the use of capitalization and punctuation; the use of sound devices such as repetition, rhyme, and alliteration; the choices of speaker, subject, diction, and tone; and other poetic elements. You might want to find additional early and later poems by Brooks to see if your theories are correct.

GWENDOLYN BROOKS

1917–

Gwendolyn Brooks was born in Topeka, Kansas, but was taken as an infant to Chicago, which became her permanent home and a frequent setting for her poems. In her family's creative household, her early interest in writing poetry was nurtured by her mother, who told her that she would be the "lady Paul Laurence Dunbar" and took her to meet the Harlem Renaissance writers James Weldon Johnson and Langston Hughes. Her first published poem appeared in a children's magazine when she was 13.

After graduating from junior college, Brooks continued to write. In the early 1940s, she attended a poetry workshop taught by Inez Cunningham Stark, a socialite who was a reader for *Poetry* magazine, where Brooks was introduced to the work of such modernist poets as T. S. Eliot. She published her first poetry collection, *A Street in Bronzeville,* in 1945, and with her second book, *Annie Allen,* she became the first African-American author to win a Pulitzer Prize.

A pivotal point in Brooks's career came in 1967, when she attended the Second Black Writers' Conference at Fisk University. After meeting younger, more militant African-American poets there, Brooks began responding in her poems to the social upheavals of the time, dealing with such subjects as Malcolm X, urban riots, and street-gang warfare. She has said, "Until 1967 my own blackness did not confront me with a shrill spelling of itself."

Among the honors Brooks has received are appointments as poet laureate of Illinois in 1968 and as poetry consultant to the Library of Congress in 1985. She has also received more than 50 honorary doctorates and in 1980 read her poetry at the White House.

OTHER WORKS *Maud Martha, The Bean Eaters, To Disembark, The Near-Johannesburg Boy and Other Poems*

ON YOUR OWN

Thoughts on the African-American Novel

Toni Morrison

The label "novel" is useful in technical terms because I write prose that is longer than a short story. My sense of the novel is that it has always functioned for the class or the group that wrote it. The history of the novel as a form began when there was a new class, a middle class, to read it; it was an art form that they needed. The lower classes didn't need novels at that time because they had an art form already: they had songs, and dances, and ceremony, and gossip, and celebrations. The aristocracy didn't need it because they had the art that they had patronized[1], they had their own pictures painted, their own houses built, and they made sure their art separated them from the rest of the world. But when the industrial revolution began, there emerged a new class of people who were neither peasants nor aristocrats. In large measure they had no art form to tell them how to behave in this new situation. So they produced an art form: we call it the novel of manners, an art form designed to tell people something they didn't know. That is, how to behave in this new world, how to distinguish between the good guys and the bad guys. How to get married. What a good living was. What would happen if you strayed from the fold. So that early works such as *Pamela,* by Samuel Richardson, and the Jane Austen material provided social rules and explained behavior, identified outlaws, identified the people, habits, and customs that one should approve of. They were didactic[2] in that sense. That, I think, is probably why the novel was not missed among the so-called peasant cultures. They didn't need it, because they were clear about what their responsibilities were and who and where was evil, and where was good.

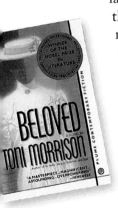

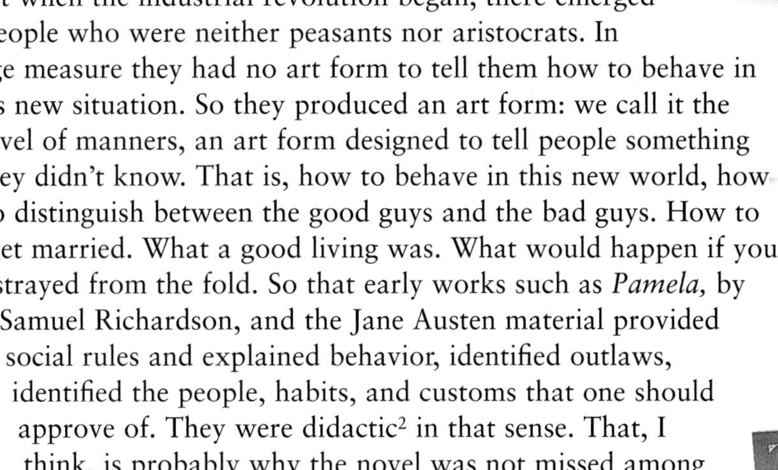

But when the peasant class, or lower class, or what have you, confronts the middle class, the city, or the upper classes, they are thrown a little bit into disarray[3]. For a long time, the art form that was healing for Black

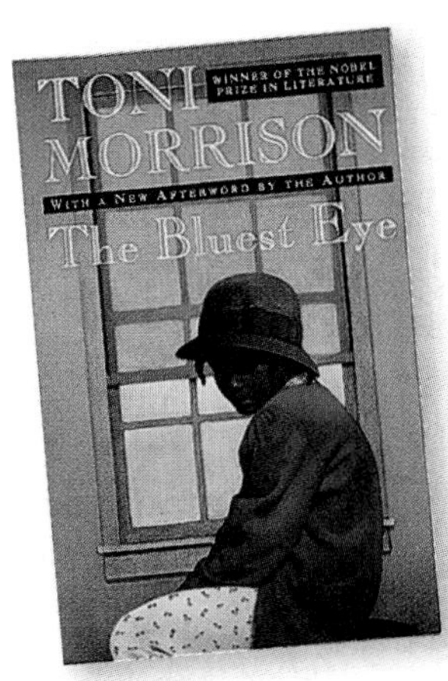

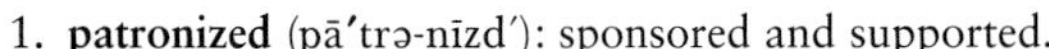

1. **patronized** (pā′trə-nīzd′): sponsored and supported.
2. **didactic** (dī-dăk′tĭk): intended to instruct.
3. **disarray** (dĭs′ə-rā′): disorder; confusion.

people was music. That music is no longer *exclusively* ours, we don't have exclusive rights to it. Other people sing it and play it; it is the mode of contemporary music everywhere. So another form has to take that place, and it seems to me that the novel is needed by African-Americans now in a way that it was not needed before—and it is following along the lines of the function of novels everywhere. We don't live in places where we can hear those stories anymore; parents don't sit around and tell their children those classical, mythological archetypal[4] stories that we heard years ago. But new information has got to get out, and there are several ways to do it. One is in the novel. I regard it as a way to accomplish certain very strong functions—one being the one I just described.

The novel is needed by African-Americans now in a way that it was not needed before.

It should be beautiful, and powerful, but it should also *work*. It should have something in it that enlightens; something in it that opens the door and points the way. Something in it that suggests what the conflicts are, what the problems are. But it need not solve those problems because it is not a case study, it is not a recipe. There are things that I try to incorporate into my fiction that are directly and deliberately related to what I regard as the major characteristics of Black art, wherever it is. One of which is the ability to be both print and oral literature: to combine those two aspects so that the stories can be read in silence, of course, but one should be able to hear them as well. It should try deliberately to make you stand up and make you feel something profoundly in the same way that a Black preacher requires his congregation to speak, to join him in the sermon, to behave in a certain way, to stand up and to weep and to cry and to accede[5] or to change and to modify—to expand on the sermon that is being delivered. In the same way that a musician's music is enhanced when there is a response from the audience. Now in a book, which closes, after all—it's of some importance to me to try to make that connection—to try to make that happen also. And, having at my disposal only the letters of the alphabet and some punctuation, I have to provide the places and spaces so that the reader can participate. Because it is the affective[6] and participatory relationship between the artist or the speaker and the audience that is of primary importance, as it is in these other art forms that I have described.

To make the story appear oral, meandering, effortless, spoken—to have the reader *feel* the narrator without *identifying* that narrator, or hearing him or her knock about, and to have the reader work *with* the author in the construction of the book—is what's important. What is left out is as important as what is there. To describe sexual scenes in such a way that they are not clinical, not even explicit[7]—so that the reader brings his own sexuality to the scene and thereby participates in it in a very personal way. And owns it. To construct the dialogue so that it is heard. So that there are no adverbs attached to them: "loudly," "softly," "he said menacingly." The menace should be in the sentence. To use, even formally, a chorus. The real presence of a chorus. Meaning the community or the reader at large, commenting on the action as it goes ahead.

In the books that I have written, the chorus has changed but there has always been a choral note, whether it is the "I" narrator of *Bluest Eye,* or the town functioning as a character in

4. **archetypal** (är′kĭ-tī′pəl): serving as a pattern for later examples.

5. **accede** (ăk-sēd′): agree.

6. **affective:** emotional.

7. **not clinical, not even explicit:** not coldly impersonal or even clearly detailed.

Sula, or the neighborhood and the community that responds in the two parts of town in *Solomon.* Or, as extreme as I've gotten, all of nature thinking and feeling and watching and responding to the action going on in *Tar Baby,* so that they are in the story: the trees hurt, fish are afraid, clouds report, and the bees are alarmed. Those are the ways in which I try to incorporate, into that traditional genre the novel, unorthodox novelistic characteristics—so that it is, in my view, Black, because it uses the characteristics of Black art. I am not suggesting that some of these devices have not been used before and elsewhere—only the reason why I do. I employ them as well as I can. And those are just some; I wish there were ways in which such things could be talked about in the criticism. My general disappointment in some of the criticism that my work has received has nothing to do with approval. It has something to do with the vocabulary used in order to describe these things. I don't like to find my books condemned as bad or praised as good, when that condemnation or that praise is based on criteria from other paradigms[8]. I would much prefer that they were dismissed or embraced based on the success of their accomplishment within the culture out of which I write.

I don't regard Black literature as simply books written *by* Black people, or simply as literature written *about* Black people, or simply as literature that uses a certain mode of language in which you just sort of drop *g*'s. There is something very special and very identifiable about it and it is my struggle to *find* that elusive but identifiable style in the books. My joy is when I think that I have approached it; my misery is when I think I can't get there. ❖

8. **paradigms** (păr′ə-dīmz′): theoretical frameworks.

Toni Morrison

© Layle Silbert

1931–

Drawing on her childhood in the small town of Lorain, Ohio, Toni Morrison vividly re-creates the African-American experience in her acclaimed fiction. Much of her writing is set in fictional Midwestern African-American communities at various times in history. She has described the influence of her community on her work thus: "I'm completely informed by that community, by my extended family, the language particularly. Not just the survival, but the way they spoke . . . this incredible merging of new language and Biblical language and sermonic language and street language and standard that created a third thing for me."

After receiving a bachelor's degree from Howard University and a master's degree from Cornell University, Morrison taught college English for nine years. Then she worked for 20 years as an editor at Random House in New York City, where she helped publish such African-American writers as Toni Cade Bambara. Since 1989 she has been the Robert F. Goheen Professor in the Council of the Humanities at Princeton University.

Morrison has won numerous awards and honors. In 1977 she won the prestigious National Book Critics Circle Award for her third novel, *Song of Solomon,* and she was awarded the 1988 Pulitzer Prize for *Beloved.* In 1993 she became the first African American to win the Nobel Prize in literature.

OTHER WORKS *The Bluest Eye, Sula, Tar Baby, Jazz, Dreaming Emmett*

WRITING ABOUT LITERATURE

POETIC JUSTICE

Did you feel the beat of Harlem in "The Weary Blues" or "My City"? Words have a musical quality all their own. Poets, playwrights, songwriters, and speakers use that quality to enhance the story they are telling or the mood they are creating. On the following pages, you will

- learn how poets create music with their words
- compare the authors' styles in two poems
- identify rhythms and patterns in your own life

The Writer's Style: Sound Devices Poets create musical language by using rhyme, alliteration (repeating an initial sound), and rhythm. When these devices are chosen well, the result is often lyrical—and always moving.

Read the Literature

How do these writers create music with their words?

Literature Models

Rhyme
Which lines in this poem rhyme? Which lines in Johnson's poem rhyme? What effect do these rhymes have?

Droning a drowsy syncopated tune,
Rocking back and forth to a mellow croon,
    I heard a Negro play.
Down on Lenox Avenue the other night
By the pale dull pallor of an old gas light
    He did a lazy sway. . . .
    He did a lazy sway. . . .

Langston Hughes
from "The Weary Blues"

Alliteration
Which words in this poem repeat the same initial sounds? What impact does this have on you?

But, ah! Manhattan's sights and sounds, her smells,
Her crowds, her throbbing force, the thrill that comes
From being of her a part, her subtle spells,
Her shining towers, her avenues, her slums—

James Weldon Johnson
from "My City"

Connect to Life

A person who writes advertising jingles, song lyrics, or speeches relies on sound devices like repetition and rhythm to make them memorable. Notice the rhythm in this speech.

Speech

That man over there says that women need to be helped into carriages, and lifted over ditches, and to have the best place everywhere. Nobody ever helps me get into carriages, or over mud puddles, or gives me any best place! And ain't I a woman? Look at me! Look at my arm! I have ploughed, and planted, and gathered into barns, and no man could head me. And ain't I a woman? I could work as much and eat as much as a man—when I could get it—and bear the lash as well! And ain't I a woman?

Sojourner Truth
from "Ain't I a Woman?"
speech to women's rights convention, 1851

Repetition
What is the effect of repeating phrases? Read the excerpt aloud. Can you feel the beat?

Try Your Hand: Using Sound Devices

1. **I've Got Rhythm** Read one of your QuickWrites aloud. Rewrite it so that it has more rhythm. Shorten lines, repeat phrases, or substitute words until you create a strong rhythm.
2. **A Single Jingle** Create a jingle (a short, catchy tune) to help sell a real or an imaginary product. Make sure the jingle has a strong beat or a clever rhyme so people will remember it.
3. **Similar Sounds** Write a sentence describing a favorite place. Include alliteration in your description.

SkillBuilder

WRITER'S CRAFT

Using Imagery

Sound devices such as rhyme, rhythm, and alliteration help you hear the words. Imagery helps you see, feel, smell, and taste them as well. Vivid, concrete, sensory images can enrich your stories and poems. Notice how Langston Hughes uses imagery to paint rich pictures in your mind:

Sound: *In a deep song voice with a melancholy tone / I heard that Negro sing, that old piano moan—*

Sight: *By the pale dull pallor of an old gas light*

Touch: *With his ebony hands on each ivory key / He made that poor piano moan with melody.*

APPLYING WHAT YOU'VE LEARNED
On a separate sheet of paper, rewrite the following sentences, adding sensory images.

1. As the night wore on, the streets of Harlem became noisier. (sound)
2. Around midnight, Lenox Avenue was crowded. (touch)
3. The smell of home cooking came out of the kitchen. (smell)
4. The piano man stopped for a bite. (taste)
5. The piano man wore a suit. (sight)

Criticism

What do you consider when you compare brands of jeans? Fit? Price? Comfort? Style? You can compare poems in a similar way—considering sound devices, imagery, and other poetic elements. Comparing poems can help you appreciate each poem's strengths and grasp its weaknesses.

GUIDED ASSIGNMENT

Compare Poets' Styles Your assignment is to evaluate the authors' styles in two poems. You'll look at what the poets do well—and what they don't. Then you'll compare the poems and recommend which one others should read. This is your chance to express an opinion about the literature.

Student's Prewriting Chart

Poem	"The Weary Blues"	"My City"
Rhyme	AAB CCBB unique pattern	ABBA CDDC EFEFGG
Alliteration	a little	fair amount
Rhythm	almost a jazz or blues beat—strong but varying	hardly noticed it—most lines have the same unvarying beat
Imagery	hear sounds, feel crowd	smell flowers, see trees in the country, but few real images of the city

1 Prewrite and Explore

Comparisons can be used to explain something unfamiliar or clarify a point. They can also be used to help you make a decision. When you compare, you identify similarities and differences or strengths and weaknesses.

CHOOSE TWO POEMS

Your first task is to select two poems. Read through all the poetry in Unit Six, "The Modern Age." Select poems that you have strong feelings about. You may want to compare poems about similar topics or poems by the same writer.

EVALUATE EACH POEM'S STYLE

Begin by evaluating each poem separately. Look at how well the poem does each of the following:

Rhyme If the poem rhymes, is the result pleasing or too obvious? If it doesn't rhyme, does it still seem like a poem?

Alliteration Are any initial sounds repeated? Is the result interesting or annoying?

Rhythm Do you feel the poem has a strong beat? Or is the rhythm lost or unimportant to the poem?

Imagery Does the poet use sensory details that put images in your mind? Are the images effective?

Take notes on how the poet deals with each of these elements. You may want to use a compare-and-contrast chart, like the one on the left, to organize your notes.

❷ Compare the Poems

Review your notes and then read through the poems again. Use questions like the following to compare the two poems.

- Which poem uses rhyme most effectively?
- Is the alliteration more effective in one of the poems?
- In which poem is the rhythm more striking?
- Is the use of imagery more successful in one of the poems?

On your compare-and-contrast chart, note the strengths and weaknesses of the poems. If the poems do something equally well, note that too.

Decision Point It's time to decide how you feel about each of these poems.

❸ Write a Draft

As you draft your comparison, keep in mind that it should include the following components:

- An introduction that briefly describes the two poems and gives your overall opinion of their styles
- A body that evaluates and compares the poets' styles by using examples and quotations to support your opinion. (See the SkillBuilder for tips on organizing the body of your essay.)
- A conclusion that summarizes your comparison of the styles of the two poems and recommends a poem to read

Student's Draft

I really could feel the rhythm in Langston Hughes's "The Weary Blues." The beat is so strong, I can imagine someone putting the poem to music. I read that Hughes used the varying rhythm of jazz and the blues in some of his poems. This must be one of them.

I had a hard time feeling the rhythm in James Weldon Johnson's "My City." Most lines have the same unvarying beat, so I hardly noticed it. I think I like the changing rhythm in "The Weary Blues" better.

Be sure to use that fact about Hughes using blues rhythms.

SkillBuilder

Organizing a Compare-and-Contrast Essay

With so much to cover in your essay, it's often difficult to know exactly how to organize your draft. But there are two easy ways to outline this compare-and-contrast essay:

One Poem at a Time In the first half of the essay, evaluate all the elements of one poet's style. Look at how that poet uses rhyme, rhythm, and other poetic elements. In the second half of the essay, evaluate the other poem in the same way—comparing points with the points you made about the first poem.

One Element at a Time Devote one paragraph to each poetic element. For example, one paragraph might compare the rhyme in the two poems. The next paragraph might compare the imagery in the poems.

Once you choose a method of organization, it's important to follow it throughout your essay.

APPLYING WHAT YOU'VE LEARNED
Try both of these organizational methods. See which one works best for your essay.

WRITING HANDBOOK

For more information on writing compare-and-contrast essays, see page 1179 of the Writing Handbook.

 Revise and Edit

Exchange essays with another student. As you review your partner's essay, consider the following questions.

PEER RESPONSE

- How well is this essay organized? Would discussing one poem at a time (or one element at a time) work better?
- Which points of comparison are the strongest?

Examine your partner's suggestions as you revise your draft. When you're finished, think about how you can use comparison again.

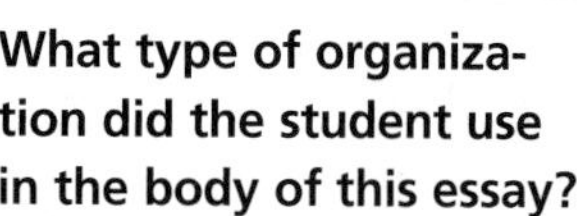

Student's Final Draft

Both Langston Hughes and James Weldon Johnson wrote poems about Harlem—but that's where the similarity ends. In "The Weary Blues," I can feel the crowd swaying, I can hear the "old piano moan with melody"—I'm there on Lenox Avenue! Hughes draws me in with his effective use of imagery. On the other hand, "My City" leaves me out in the cold. Johnson mentions how much he loves "Manhattan's sights and sounds, her smells," but he never says what they are. For some unknown reason, he's much more descriptive when he talks about the country than when he is describing his beloved city.

What type of organization did the student use in the body of this essay?

How is the imagery in these poems compared?

Comparing the two poems, I would have to recommend "The Weary Blues." Langston Hughes's use of rhyme and rhythm is musical. His use of sensory images is magical. Yet his poem seems gritty and down-to-earth. No wonder he was the "Poet Laureate of Harlem"!

What recommendation did this student make in the conclusion?

Standards for Evaluation

A comparison
- identifies the selections and their authors in the introduction
- identifies similarities and differences between the selections
- supports the comparison with examples, quotations, and other specifics
- maintains a consistent organization throughout the essay
- concludes with a recommendation

Grammar in Context

Gerund Phrases Gerunds are verb forms that end in *-ing*. They act as nouns. If you add a modifier or an object to the gerund, it becomes a gerund phrase. Phrases like these can add variety to your essay.

> Generally, I don't like poems that rhyme, but both Hughes and Johnson use rhyme effectively. ~~Rhyme~~ *Rhyming sequential lines* creates an interesting pattern in "The Weary Blues." ~~Repetition~~ *Repeating a refrain* adds music to the poem. As a result, "The Weary Blues" drones anything but a "drowsy" tune.

Notice the cases in which a noun was replaced with a gerund phrase. Gerund phrases can appear anywhere in a sentence. They work especially well describing a process, because they involve action.

Try Your Hand: Using Gerund Phrases

On a separate sheet of paper, write the gerund phrase in each of the following sentences.

1. Writing poetry is Hughes's claim to fame.
2. Living in Harlem in the 1920s inspired his writing.
3. Most people loved hearing the "mellow croon" of the jazz musicians.
4. Hughes enjoyed capturing the rhythm of the blues in his poetry.
5. Following the form of a sonnet makes "My City" a much more traditional poem.

SkillBuilder

GRAMMAR FROM WRITING

Using Verbal Phrases
Gerund phrases are verbal phrases. So are participial and infinitive phrases. All three use verb forms in an unusual way.

Participles Participles are similar to gerunds—an *-ing* is added to the end of a verb form. However, participles act as adjectives rather than nouns. When a modifier is added to a participle, it becomes a participial phrase. See how Zora Neale Hurston uses a participial phrase in this sentence:

The only white people I knew passed through the town going to or coming from Orlando.

Infinitives Infinitives are made from the word *to* plus a verb. They act as nouns, adverbs, or adjectives. Notice how Hurston uses infinitive phrases:

It is quite exciting to hold the center of the national stage, with the spectators not knowing whether to laugh or to weep.

APPLYING WHAT YOU'VE LEARNED
Write these sentences by Hurston on a sheet of paper. Circle the participial or infinitive phrase.

1. The more venturesome would come out on the porch to watch them go past.
2. "Good music they have here," he remarks, drumming the table with his fingertips.

READING

THE WORLD

IT'S BACK!

Traditional poetry has a set pattern of rhyme and rhythm. Life also has its own patterns or rhythms. The moon goes through a cycle, and so does television programming. The way men wear their hair goes through a cycle too.

View Notice the hairstyle in each photo. How long is the hair? Is the style natural or contrived? Are any hairstyles similar?

Interpret Were you surprised by the changes in hairstyles? The similarities? Why do some styles come back and others don't? Is there any pattern to when styles return?

Discuss As a group, discuss how mens' hairstyles have changed. Why do these changes happen? How do you think men will wear their hair in five years? Which styles will come back? For tips on identifying patterns, check the SkillBuilder.

early 1960s

late 1960s

early 1970s

early 1970s

early 1980s

late 1980s

late 1980s

early 1960s

late 1960s

late 1970s

early 1980s

early 1990s

early 1990s

SkillBuilder

CRITICAL THINKING

Identifying Patterns

Patterns add a certain amount of organization to life. They can also be used to predict what's going to happen next.

To identify a pattern, start by making comparisons. Look for similarities. After you've compared these yearbook photos, you could use labels to indicate similar hairstyles. Look at length, sideburns, natural versus contrived, and so on. Next, compare the length of time between similar styles. Do hairstyles seem to reappear on a predictable schedule?

APPLYING WHAT YOU'VE LEARNED

Try one or more of the following in a small group.

- Compare photos in your own high school yearbook with these photos. (You may want to look at your parents' yearbooks too.) See if any patterns change with the addition of these new photos.
- Look through a U.S. history book. Determine when the United States was at war. Chart these dates on a time line. Look at the interval between wars. Is there a pattern? Can you predict when the United States might get involved in another war?

PART 2 INTRODUCTION

Alienation of the Individual

Modernism

World War I remade the map of Europe, but that was only the most visible sign of a monumental change in the lives of nations and individuals. The four-year conflict, involving a total of 32 nations, devastated Europe. It was the first large-scale modern war, utilizing the savage new weapons of modern technology—poison gas, submarines, armored tanks, airplanes, and machine guns. By the time the war ended in 1918, nearly 10 million soldiers and almost as many civilians had been killed. Even though the United States did not enter the war until 1917, Americans shared the sense that civilization, as they had known it, was being destroyed. Uncertainty about what was to result from this political breakdown became a distinguishing characteristic of the age.

Weeping Woman (1937), Pablo Picasso. Tate Gallery, London/Art Resource, New York. Copyright © 1996 Artists Rights Society, (ARS), New York/SPADEM, Paris.

The end of the war signaled an end of idealism and ushered in an era marked by economic growth, technological advancement, and new ways to have fun. During the Roaring Twenties, as the decade of the 1920s is called, people had more money and more things to buy. An increasing number of radios carried the new strains of jazz into American homes. The availability of cars gave people more mobility and freedom. More people went out to nightclubs and to speakeasies, where illegal alcohol was plentiful. Movies became a popular form of entertainment. At the same time, political corruption was rampant; gangsters flourished with the

profits from the sale of illegal alcohol; and Americans, in general, grew distrustful of foreigners and intolerant of political dissent.

The literary movement known as modernism was a direct response to these social and cultural changes. Disillusioned by the war and appalled by the materialism of the age, the new generation of writers searched for different literary forms to express what they understood as the modern consciousness. "Make it new!" was the rallying cry that the poet and critic Ezra Pound inspired in these writers. And they did.

Although the writers in this part of the unit have their own individual styles, they share certain characteristics that have come to be identified with modernism. First of all, they felt that individuals, especially artists, were becoming increasingly threatened by and isolated amid the mass society that was developing at the time. Characters in modernist works are almost always alienated—withdrawn, unresponsive, hurt by unnamed forces.

A second characteristic shared by these modernist writers is experimentation. The playwright Thornton Wilder experimented with theatrical conventions by stripping the stage of props and by trying out different ways of sequencing events in time. In order to reflect the fragmentation of their experience, fiction writers such as Ernest Hemingway, Dorothy Parker, and Richard Wright composed short, fragmentary stories that didn't have traditional beginnings and endings. Poets such as Ezra Pound and T. S. Eliot created verse out of the fragments of modern experience—pieces of dreams, feelings, dialogue, images, and literary allusions. The great modern artists of the 20th century—Picasso, Matisse, and Duchamp, for example—visually captured this fragmentary nature of modern experience in their cubist designs, cutouts, and collages.

Finally, modernist writers are as notable for what they leave out of their writing as for what they put in. There is no narrative voice guiding the reader with explanations or details. The reader is left alone to figure out what is going on in a

Voices from the Times

The apparition of these faces in the crowd;
Petals on a wet, black bough.

Ezra Pound
"In a Station of the Metro"

Poets in our civilization, as it exists at present, must be *difficult*. . . . The poet must become more and more comprehensive, more allusive, more indirect, in order to force, to dislocate if necessary, language into its meaning.

T. S. Eliot
from "The Metaphysical Poets"

Every compulsion is put upon writers to become safe, polite, obedient, and sterile. In protest, I declined election to the National Institute of Arts and Letters some years ago, and now I must decline the Pulitzer Prize.

Sinclair Lewis
from his letter declining the Pulitzer Prize

My candle burns at both ends;
It will not last the night;
But, ah, my foes, and, oh, my friends—
It gives a lovely light.

Edna St. Vincent Millay
"First Fig"

Edna St. Vincent Millay

Voices from the Times

Four be the things I am wiser to know:
Idleness, sorrow, a friend, and a foe.
Four be the things I'd been better without:
Love, curiosity, freckles, and doubt.

Dorothy Parker
from "Inventory"

Which of us has known his brother? Which of us has looked into his father's heart? Which of us has not remained forever prison-pent? Which of us is not forever a stranger and alone?

Thomas Wolfe
from *Look Homeward, Angel*

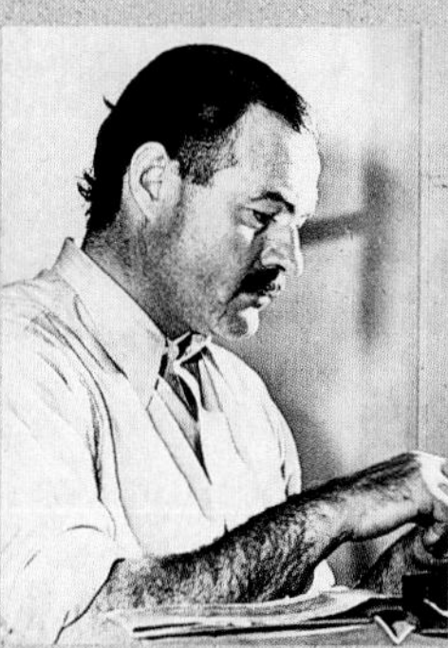

Ernest Hemingway

The further you go in writing the more alone you are.

Ernest Hemingway
from an interview

You are all a lost generation.

Gertrude Stein
spoken to Ernest Hemingway

There are people who eat the earth and eat all the people on it like in the Bible with the locusts. And other people who stand around and watch them eat it.

Lillian Hellman
from *The Little Foxes*

story or a poem and what a character or speaker is feeling or thinking. These omissions place more demands on the reader to put together the pieces of the characters' experience.

Continuity & Change: The Lonely Self

Modernism has dominated the arts and literature throughout the 20th century. The generation that came of age around World War II faced alienation similar to that experienced by the early modernists. Some of the great plays of Tennessee Williams and Arthur Miller feature characters—most notably, Blanche DuBois in *A Streetcar Named Desire* and Willy Loman in *Death of a Salesman*—who are trapped by their own inadequacies and pushed aside by stronger, more brutal forces in society. In the poems of Sylvia Plath and Anne Sexton in this part of the unit, you can see a hostile reaction to the pressures placed on women to conform to established roles during the 1950s and early 1960s.

"Homework" by Peter Cameron is a contemporary story in the modernist vein. You'll be able to recognize the teenage character's feelings of numbness and withdrawal, which today is called angst but in another age was felt as alienation.

A scene from the play *A Streetcar Named Desire,* starring Marlon Brando and Jessica Tandy. Copyright © Eileen Darby.

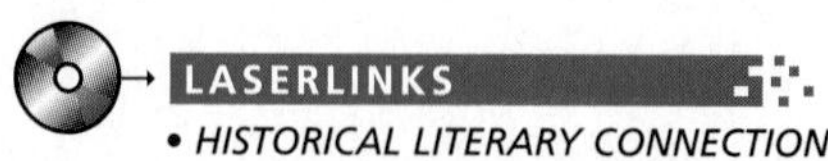

• *HISTORICAL LITERARY CONNECTION*

PART 2 Alienation of the Individual

Modernism

Continuity & Change: The Lonely Self

PREVIEWING

POETRY

Selected Poems

Robert Frost

PERSONAL CONNECTION

In each of these three poems, a person is either alone or separated from others. Think about times when you want to be with other people and times when you choose to be alone. What kinds of feelings and circumstances affect your desire for companionship? In your notebook, complete the sentences shown.

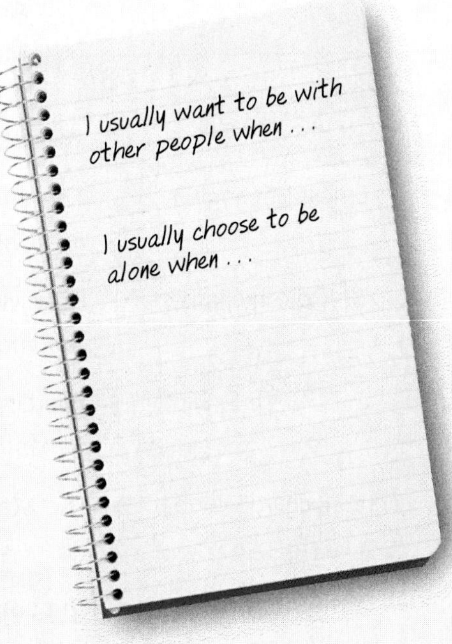

I usually want to be with other people when . . .
I usually choose to be alone when . . .

LITERARY CONNECTION

Without a doubt, Robert Frost is a major American poet—perhaps the most widely read and best-loved poet this country has known. However, in many ways, he is also a transitional figure between the 19th and 20th centuries. Like the transcendentalists before him, Frost loved nature and wrote about the lone individual deliberately making choices about how to live. Like the modernists who were his contemporaries, Frost portrayed the forces in modern society that serve to isolate people. Many of his poems portray tensions in relationships and the advantages and disadvantages of being alone.

READING CONNECTION

Identifying Mood Mood is the emotional feeling, or atmosphere, created in a work of literature. In a poem, the setting, figurative language, images, the sound and rhythm of the language, and descriptive details all contribute to the mood. As you read the following poems, be aware of the different moods that Frost creates. Also notice how the mood in each poem is related to the poem's ideas of being alone or being separated from others.

Photo by Algimantas Kezys.

Acquainted with the Night

ROBERT FROST

I have been one acquainted with the night.
I have walked out in rain—and back in rain.
I have outwalked the furthest city light.

I have looked down the saddest city lane.
I have passed by the watchman on his beat
And dropped my eyes, unwilling to explain.

I have stood still and stopped the sound of feet
When far away an interrupted cry
Came over houses from another street,

But not to call me back or say good-by;
And further still at an unearthly height
One luminary[1] clock against the sky

Proclaimed the time was neither wrong nor right.
I have been one acquainted with the night.

1. **luminary:** giving off light.

Illustration © Litjiun Wong.

FROM PERSONAL RESPONSE *TO* CRITICAL ANALYSIS

REFLECT **1.** What adjectives would you use to describe the speaker of this poem? Write these adjectives in your notebook.

RETHINK **2.** Do you feel sorry for the speaker? Explain why or why not.

3. How do you think the speaker feels about his experience of being alone at night? Cite phrases or lines from the poem that suggest his feelings.

4. Describe the mood of the poem. Cite words, phrases, and images that contribute to the mood.

Mending Wall

ROBERT FROST

Something there is that doesn't love a wall,
That sends the frozen-ground-swell under it
And spills the upper boulders in the sun,
And makes gaps even two can pass abreast.
The work of hunters is another thing:
I have come after them and made repair
Where they have left not one stone on a stone,
But they would have the rabbit out of hiding,
To please the yelping dogs. The gaps I mean,
No one has seen them made or heard them made,
But at spring mending-time we find them there.
I let my neighbor know beyond the hill;
And on a day we meet to walk the line
And set the wall between us once again.
We keep the wall between us as we go.
To each the boulders that have fallen to each.
And some are loaves and some so nearly balls
We have to use a spell to make them balance:

GUIDE FOR READING

1–4 In some parts of New England, the farms are separated by low walls made of stones that are simply piled up, not mortared together. During the winter, moisture in the ground freezes and makes the earth expand, causing portions of the wall to topple.

12–14 Notice that it is the speaker who lets the neighbor know it is time to mend the wall.

"Stay where you are until our backs are turned!"
We wear our fingers rough with handling them.
Oh, just another kind of outdoor game,
One on a side. It comes to little more:
There where it is we do not need the wall:
He is all pine and I am apple orchard.
My apple trees will never get across
And eat the cones under his pines, I tell him.
He only says, "Good fences make good neighbors."
Spring is the mischief in me, and I wonder
If I could put a notion in his head:
"*Why* do they make good neighbors? Isn't it
Where there are cows? But here there are no cows.
Before I built a wall I'd ask to know
What I was walling in or walling out,
And to whom I was like to give offense.
Something there is that doesn't love a wall,
That wants it down." I could say "Elves" to him,
But it's not elves exactly, and I'd rather
He said it for himself. I see him there,
Bringing a stone grasped firmly by the top
In each hand, like an old-stone savage armed.
He moves in darkness as it seems to me,
Not of woods only and the shade of trees.
He will not go behind his father's saying,
And he likes having thought of it so well
He says again, "Good fences make good neighbors."

23–26 According to the speaker, why is there no practical need for the wall?

27 What need does the neighbor see for the wall?

36–38 Notice the speaker's playful, teasing tone here.

38–42 What is the speaker's opinion of his neighbor?

FROM PERSONAL RESPONSE *TO* CRITICAL ANALYSIS

REFLECT 1. Which man in "Mending Wall" would you prefer as a neighbor, and why?

RETHINK 2. How do the speaker of the poem and the neighbor differ?

Consider
- their feelings about the wall and the job of rebuilding it
- the image the speaker has of his neighbor, as expressed in lines 38–42

3. Explain what you think the wall represents in each of the following lines:
- "Something there is that doesn't love a wall,"
- "We keep the wall between us as we go."
- "Before I built a wall I'd ask to know/What I was walling in or walling out."
- "He says again, 'Good fences make good neighbors.'"

4. Does the wall separate the neighbors or bring them closer together? Explain.

"Out, Out—"

Robert Frost

The buzz saw snarled and rattled in the yard
And made dust and dropped stove-length sticks of wood,
Sweet-scented stuff when the breeze drew across it.
And from there those that lifted eyes could count
Five mountain ranges one behind the other
Under the sunset far into Vermont.
And the saw snarled and rattled, snarled and rattled,
As it ran light, or had to bear a load.
And nothing happened: day was all but done.
Call it a day, I wish they might have said
To please the boy by giving him the half hour
That a boy counts so much when saved from work.
His sister stood beside them in her apron
To tell them 'Supper.' At the word, the saw,
As if to prove saws knew what supper meant,
Leaped out at the boy's hand, or seemed to leap—
He must have given the hand. However it was,
Neither refused the meeting. But the hand!
The boy's first outcry was a rueful[1] laugh,
As he swung toward them holding up the hand
Half in appeal, but half as if to keep
The life from spilling. Then the boy saw all—
Since he was old enough to know, big boy
Doing a man's work, though a child at heart—
He saw all spoiled. 'Don't let him cut my hand off—
The doctor, when he comes. Don't let him, sister!'
So. But the hand was gone already.
The doctor put him in the dark of ether.
He lay and puffed his lips out with his breath.
And then—the watcher at his pulse took fright.
No one believed. They listened at his heart.
Little—less—nothing!—and that ended it.
No more to build on there. And they, since they
Were not the one dead, turned to their affairs.

---

1. **rueful** (ro͞o′fəl): expressing sorrow or regret.

RESPONDING OPTIONS

FROM PERSONAL RESPONSE *TO* CRITICAL ANALYSIS

REFLECT

1. What are your impressions of "'Out, Out—'"? Write your response in your notebook.

RETHINK

2. Why do you think the boy dies, even though his injury is not life threatening? Consider his thoughts and feelings described in lines 19–25.
3. How does the speaker of the poem seem to feel about the boy's death?
   Consider
   - the speaker's expressions of personal feelings, as in lines 10–12
   - how the speaker describes the saw in lines 14–18
   - the speaker's comment in the last three lines
4. The title of this poem is an allusion to some lines in William Shakespeare's tragic play *Macbeth* (Act Five, Scene 5):

   Out, out, brief candle!
   Life's but a walking shadow, a poor player
   That struts and frets his hour upon the stage
   And then is heard no more.

   How do you think this quotation relates to the poem?

RELATE

5. Who do you think seems most alone—the speaker in "Acquainted with the Night," the speaker or his neighbor in "Mending Wall," or the boy in "'Out, Out—'"? Support your opinion with references from the poems.
6. Based on your reading of these poems, explain whether you think Frost viewed being alone as a positive or a negative experience. Use details from each poem to explain your answer. Then compare Frost's views with what you wrote for the Personal Connection activity on page 820.
7. Compare the different moods created by these three poems. How is the mood of each poem related to the subject matter?

ANOTHER PATHWAY

Cooperative Learning

With a small group of classmates, plan a short film that presents your interpretation of one of Frost's poems. Make a storyboard outlining your ideas regarding characters, scenes, and action. Add dialogue and description to accompany the appropriate storyboard panels. Share your storyboard with the rest of the class.

QUICKWRITES

1. Imagine that you are the night watchman who walks by the speaker of "Acquainted with the Night." Write a **report** recording your observations of this man who walks alone at night. Include the time and place of your observations and suggest possible reasons for the behavior.
2. Do good fences make good neighbors? Write a **persuasive paragraph** explaining your views.
3. If you could have spoken with the boy in "'Out, Out—'" before he died, what would you have said to encourage him? Draft an **inspirational speech** intended to fortify his will to live after the loss of his hand.

PORTFOLIO *Save your writing. You may want to use it later as a springboard to a piece for your portfolio.*

LITERARY CONCEPTS

A poem written in **blank verse** consists of unrhymed lines of iambic pentameter. In other words, each line of blank verse has five pairs of syllables. In each pair, an unstressed syllable ( ) is followed by a stressed syllable ( ). Here is an example from "Mending Wall":

I let my neighbor know beyond the hill;
And on a day we meet to walk the line.
And set the wall between us once again.

The rhythm in this passage is regular, but other lines vary the pattern. Some lines convey a more conversational tone:

"*Why* do they make good neighbors? Isn't it
Where there are cows? But here there are no cows."

Now look at "'Out, Out—.'" It also is written in blank verse, but Frost varies the rhythm considerably by altering the pattern. Copy any three lines of "'Out, Out—'" and scan the stressed and unstressed syllables. Read several lines aloud. How does the variety in the rhythmic pattern fit the subject matter and theme of the poem?

ALTERNATIVE ACTIVITIES

1. Take **photographs** of a dark and rainy city street or of various kinds of walls and fences in your town. Then compose a photo essay, mounting your photos on poster board. Use quotations from "Acquainted with the Night" or "Mending Wall" as captions for your photos.
2. Create an **illustration** to accompany "Acquainted with the Night," "Mending Wall," or "'Out, Out—.'" Convey the mood of the poem in your illustration by the colors, lines, and shapes you use.

Robert Frost

1874–1963

The man who many consider America's most popular poet did not publish a book of poems until he was 39 years old, and he had to go to another country to do it. Robert Frost made "a late start to market," as he states in one of his poems, but he more than made up for this slow beginning.

Although his poems reflect the attitudes and images of New England, Frost spent his early years in San Francisco. At age 11, he moved to Massachusetts with his widowed mother. Over the next 25 years, he attended Dartmouth College and Harvard University, married and raised a family, and worked as a farmer, a newspaper reporter, and a schoolteacher. He and his family settled on a New Hampshire farm bought for him by his grandfather. There Frost began to write some of his best poetry.

Discouraged by his inability to get his poems published, Frost sold the farm and in 1912 moved his family to England. After interesting a London publisher in his work, his first two books of poems came out—*A Boy's Will,* in 1913, and *North of Boston,* in 1914. Frost's poetry was so well received in England that he soon had offers from American publishers.

After the outbreak of World War I, Frost moved his family back to the United States. While living on farms in New Hampshire and Vermont and teaching and lecturing at various colleges and universities, he produced a steady stream of work that received great acclaim. He won four Pulitzer Prizes for poetry, and Congress voted him a medal "in recognition of his poetry, which . . . enriched the culture of the United States and the philosophy of the world." In 1961 he read a poem at the inauguration of President John F. Kennedy.

OTHER WORKS *A Further Range, In the Clearing, New Hampshire, West-Running Brook*

PREVIEWING

FICTION

The End of Something

Ernest Hemingway

PERSONAL CONNECTION

This story depicts a young couple whose relationship is ending. Their troubles raise the question, Why do people fall out of love? In a small group, discuss various answers to this question and come up with a list of possible reasons. Share your list with those of other groups. Then, as you read the story, try to find out why the couple breaks up.

BIOGRAPHICAL CONNECTION

"The End of Something" is one of a series of Hemingway stories about the character Nick Adams. The stories, which are semiautobiographical, trace the life of this character through his youth in northern Michigan, his adolescence on the road, his days as a soldier in World War I, his postwar return to Michigan, and his married years in Europe. In this story, Nick is a young war veteran struggling to make sense of his life and the end of his love for a young woman. The story is set in Hortons Bay, a resort town on Lake Michigan, where Hemingway himself spent his childhood summers. Like Nick, Hemingway returned to the Hortons Bay area during the summer of 1919 to recover from his war wounds. Although the events of the story are fictional, Nick's pain, loneliness, and disillusionment with the world of adulthood were problems that Hemingway and other young men confronted upon returning from the war.

Hortons Bay at sunset.

READING CONNECTION

Approaching Modernist Literature

The writers included in this part of Unit Six—with the possible exception of Robert Frost—represent a new generation of writers who created new ways of writing to respond directly to the new realities they saw emerging in the wake of World War I. The loss of stability and order that was felt so strongly between 1914 and 1945—the years spanning and including two world wars—was reflected in the very structure of their literature.

For example, look at the way Willa Cather helps the reader understand the character of Aunt Georgiana in this passage from "A Wagner Matinee":

> When my aunt appeared on the morning after her arrival, she was still in a semi-somnambulant state. She seemed not to realize that she was in the city where she had spent her youth, the place longed for hungrily half a lifetime.

The narrator gives the reader details and overt statements—"the place longed for hungrily half a lifetime"—to explain his aunt's feelings.

In contrast, compare Hemingway's spare introduction of his characters in "The End of Something":

> Ten years later there was nothing of the mill left except the broken white limestone of its foundations showing through the swampy second growth as Nick and Marjorie rowed along the shore.

The only thing the reader seems to learn about Nick and Marjorie in this passage is that they are rowing. Hemingway gives little direct information about their feelings or their thoughts.

The reason why the modernists omitted explanations and connections in their writing was probably best expressed by Hemingway himself: "I always try to write on the principle of the iceberg. There is seven-eighths of it under water for every part that shows."

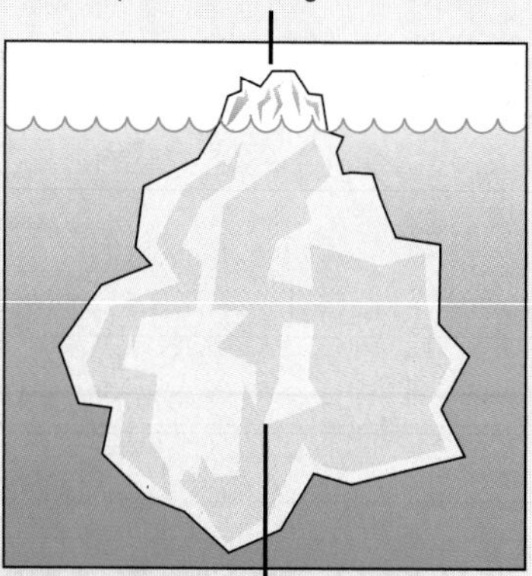

Look again at the passage introducing Nick and Marjorie—the tip of the iceberg. One way to infer the larger meaning is to pay attention to the concrete details in the passage—those describing the mill—and make the connections yourself. In this case, you'll find out as you read further that the crumbling old mill mirrors the broken relationship between Nick and Marjorie.

While reading Hemingway's story and the other modernist works in this part of the unit, keep in mind the following characteristics of modernism:

- the use of understatement and irony
- the use of symbols and images that suggest meanings rather than statements that explain meanings
- characters who are alienated and who have difficulty communicating
- the omission of clear transitions, explanations, and connections
- radical shifts in tone and voice (especially in T. S. Eliot)

Illustration Copyright © D.J. McKay.

The End of Something

Ernest Hemingway

In the old days Hortons Bay was a lumbering town. No one who lived in it was out of sound of the big saws in the mill by the lake. Then one year there were no more logs to make lumber. The lumber schooners came into the bay and were loaded with the cut of the mill that stood stacked in the yard. All the piles of lumber were carried away. The big mill building had all its machinery that was removable taken out and hoisted on board one of the schooners by the men who had worked in the mill. The schooner moved out of the bay toward the open lake carrying the two great saws, the travelling carriage that hurled the logs against the revolving, circular saws and all the rollers, wheels, belts, and iron piled on a hull-deep load of lumber. Its open hold covered with canvas and lashed tight, the sails of the schooner filled and it moved out into the open lake, carrying with it everything that had made the mill a mill and Hortons Bay a town.

The one-story bunk houses, the eating-house, the company store, the mill offices, and the big mill itself stood deserted in the acres of sawdust that covered the swampy meadow by the shore of the bay.

Ten years later there was nothing of the mill left except the broken white limestone of its foundations showing through the

Canoe (1957), David Park. Oil on canvas, 36″ × 48″, Thomas C. Woods Memorial Collection, Sheldon Memorial Art Gallery, University of Nebraska-Lincoln.

swampy second growth as Nick and Marjorie rowed along the shore. They were trolling[1] along the edge of the channel-bank where the bottom dropped off suddenly from sandy shallows to twelve feet of dark water. They were trolling on their way to the point to set night lines for rainbow trout.

"There's our old ruin, Nick," Marjorie said.

Nick, rowing, looked at the white stone in the green trees.

"There it is," he said.

"Can you remember when it was a mill?" Marjorie asked.

"I can just remember," Nick said.

"It seems more like a castle," Marjorie said.

Nick said nothing. They rowed on out of sight of the mill, following the shore line. Then Nick cut across the bay.

"They aren't striking," he said.

"No," Marjorie said. She was intent on the rod all the time they trolled, even when she talked. She loved to fish. She loved to fish with Nick.

Close beside the boat a big trout broke the surface of the water. Nick pulled hard on one oar so the boat would turn and the bait spinning far behind would pass where the trout was feeding. As the trout's back came up out of the water the minnows jumped wildly. They sprinkled the surface like a handful of shot thrown into the water. Another trout broke water, feeding on the other side of the boat.

"They're feeding," Marjorie said.

"But they won't strike," Nick said.

He rowed the boat around to troll past both the feeding fish, then headed it for the point. Marjorie did not reel in until the boat touched the shore.

They pulled the boat up the beach and Nick lifted out a pail of live perch. The perch swam in the water in the pail. Nick caught three of them with his hands and cut their heads off and skinned them while Marjorie chased with her hands in the bucket, finally caught a perch, cut its head off and skinned it. Nick looked at her fish.

"You don't want to take the ventral fin[2] out," he said. "It'll be all right for bait but it's better with the ventral fin in."

He hooked each of the skinned perch through the tail. There were two hooks attached to a leader[3] on each rod. Then Marjorie rowed the boat out over the channel-bank, holding the line in her teeth, and looking toward Nick, who stood on the shore holding the rod and letting the line run out from the reel.

"That's about right," he called.

"Should I let it drop?" Marjorie called back, holding the line in her hand.

"Sure. Let it go." Marjorie dropped the line overboard and watched the baits go down through the water.

She came in with the boat and ran the second line out the same way. Each time Nick set a heavy slab of driftwood across the butt of the rod to hold it solid and propped it up at an angle with a small slab. He reeled in the slack line so the line ran taut out to where the bait rested on the sandy floor of the channel and set the click on the reel. When a trout, feeding on the bottom, took the bait it would run with it, taking line out of the reel in a rush and making the reel sing with the click on.

Marjorie rowed up the point a little way so she would not disturb the line. She pulled hard on the oars and the boat went way up the beach. Little waves came in with it. Marjorie stepped out of the boat and Nick pulled the boat high up the beach.

"What's the matter, Nick?" Marjorie asked.

"I don't know," Nick said, getting wood for a fire.

They made a fire with driftwood. Marjorie went to the boat and brought a blanket. The

1. **trolling:** a method of fishing in which a line and baited hook trail along behind a slow-moving boat.
2. **ventral fin:** fin on the underside of a fish.
3. **leader:** short length of line by which a hook is fastened to a fishing line.

evening breeze blew the smoke toward the point, so Marjorie spread the blanket out between the fire and the lake.

Marjorie sat on the blanket with her back to the fire and waited for Nick. He came over and sat down beside her on the blanket. In back of them was the close second-growth timber[4] of the point and in front was the bay with the mouth of Hortons Creek. It was not quite dark. The fire-light went as far as the water. They could both see the two steel rods at an angle over the dark water. The fire glinted on the reels.

Marjorie unpacked the basket of supper.

"I don't feel like eating," said Nick.

"Come on and eat, Nick."

"All right."

They ate without talking, and watched the two rods and the fire-light in the water.

"There's going to be a moon tonight," said Nick. He looked across the bay to the hills that were beginning to sharpen against the sky. Beyond the hills he knew the moon was coming up.

"I know it," Marjorie said happily.

"You know everything," Nick said.

"Oh, Nick, please cut it out! Please, please don't be that way!"

"I can't help it," Nick said. "You do. You know everything. That's the trouble. You know you do."

Marjorie did not say anything.

"I've taught you everything. You know you do. What don't you know, anyway?"

"Oh, shut up," Marjorie said. "There comes the moon."

They sat on the blanket without touching each other and watched the moon rise.

"You don't have to talk silly," Marjorie said. "What's really the matter?"

"I don't know."

"Of course you know."

"No I don't."

"Go on and say it."

Nick looked on at the moon, coming up over the hills.

"It isn't fun any more."

He was afraid to look at Marjorie. Then he looked at her. She sat there with her back toward him. He looked at her back. "It isn't fun any more. Not any of it."

She didn't say anything. He went on. "I feel as though everything was gone to hell inside of me. I don't know, Marge. I don't know what to say."

He looked on at her back.

"Isn't love any fun?" Marjorie said.

"No," Nick said. Marjorie stood up. Nick sat there his head in his hands.

"I'm going to take the boat," Marjorie called to him. "You can walk back around the point."

"All right," Nick said. "I'll push the boat off for you."

"You don't need to," she said. She was afloat in the boat on the water with the moonlight on it. Nick went back and lay down with his face in the blanket by the fire. He could hear Marjorie rowing on the water.

He lay there for a long time. He lay there while he heard Bill come into the clearing walking around through the woods. He felt Bill coming up to the fire. Bill didn't touch him, either.

"Did she go all right?" Bill said.

"Yes," Nick said, lying, his face on the blanket.

"Have a scene?"

"No, there wasn't any scene."

"How do you feel?"

"Oh, go away, Bill! Go away for a while."

Bill selected a sandwich from the lunch basket and walked over to have a look at the rods. ❖

4. **second-growth timber:** trees that cover an area after the original, "old growth" trees have been cut or burned.

RESPONDING OPTIONS

FROM PERSONAL RESPONSE *TO* CRITICAL ANALYSIS

REFLECT 1. Which character do you feel the most sympathy for? Why? Write your thoughts in your notebook.

RETHINK 2. How do you think Nick feels at the end of the story?
Consider
- his actions after Marjorie leaves
- his remark "Oh, go away, Bill! Go away for a while."

3. Why do you think Nick wants to break up with Marjorie?
Consider
- his remark to Marjorie, "You know everything."
- his answer, "I don't know," to her question, "What's the matter, Nick?"
- his subsequent explanation, "It isn't fun any more. Not any of it."
- your thoughts—those you listed for the Personal Connection activity—about why people fall out of love

4. What details—the tip of the iceberg—in the first half of the story suggest that the relationship between Marjorie and Nick is strained?
Consider
- what they say to each other
- what they do not say to each other
- what the Hortons Bay setting might symbolize

RELATE 5. How does this ending of a relationship compare with breakups you have witnessed or experienced?

CRITIC'S CORNER

In an article published in the *Kenyon Review,* critic George Hemphill wrote that Hemingway's story fails "because no necessary connection (other than biographical, perhaps) between the end of the boy and girl affair between Nick and Marjorie and the end of the old lumbering days in Michigan is suggested." What is your response to Hemphill's criticism? Do you think a connection between the Hortons Bay setting and Nick and Marjorie's relationship is implied or not? Discuss your ideas with your classmates.

ANOTHER PATHWAY

Cooperative Learning

Imagine that you and a small group of your classmates are head writers for a TV soap opera called *Hortons Bay.* Write the script for an episode based on this story, and then perform the episode for the class. After all the groups in your class have performed, discuss what you learned about Marjorie and Nick's relationship and why it ended.

QUICKWRITES

1. What do you think happens to Nick and Marjorie after the end of their relationship? Write a **personal ad** that either Marjorie or Nick might send to a local newspaper, describing the kind of person she or he would like to meet. Read your ad aloud to the class.
2. Write a **letter** from Marjorie to Dear Abby, asking for advice about how to deal with Nick and their crumbling relationship. Then write Dear Abby's **response** to Marjorie.

PORTFOLIO Save your writing. You may want to use it later as a springboard to a piece for your portfolio.

LITERARY CONCEPTS

Point of view refers to the narrative perspective from which events in a story are told. "The End of Something" is related from Nick's perspective—the reader sees and hears what he does—and so the point of view is technically called **third-person limited**. However, notice how Hemingway varies this traditional form of narration: the narrator doesn't tell you what Nick is thinking or feeling, only what he does, says, or observes. This kind of narration marks Hemingway's distinctive style.

Cooperative Learning In a small group, rewrite a passage of the story and include Nick's feelings and thoughts. Share your rewrite with the class, and discuss differences between Hemingway's style and that of your rewrite.

ALTERNATIVE ACTIVITIES

1. Imagine that you have been asked to illustrate "The End of Something" for a collection of Hemingway's stories. Choose one **scene** from the story, and draw or paint it.
2. What is the best way to end a relationship? Conduct an informal **survey** of ten males and ten females in your school or neighborhood. Record their responses, and report your findings to the class.

ERNEST HEMINGWAY

1899–1961

War punctuated Ernest Hemingway's life and career, from the World War I passages of *In Our Time*, his first book of short stories, to his journalistic accounts of chasing German U-boats with his yacht in the Caribbean during World War II. Hemingway found war the ultimate theater, where an artist could observe human nature and what he called "grace under pressure."

At the age of 18, with the onset of World War I, Hemingway volunteered as a Red Cross ambulance driver, serving on the front lines. After three weeks, he was severely wounded. He had a lengthy recovery in an Italian hospital and a love affair with an American nurse. What he experienced during that momentous year—the closeness of death, courage, physical and emotional pain, and romantic love—informs many of his novels and short stories.

Other events of Hemingway's adventurous life also found their way into his fiction. In his highly acclaimed novel *The Sun Also Rises,* he depicted the members of what Gertrude Stein had dubbed the "lost generation"—young people, like himself, who were disillusioned by World War I and living a rather aimless life abroad in the 1920s. His desire for action led him to serve as a war correspondent during the Spanish civil war of the 1930s and during World War II. Out of these war experiences came a highly successful novel, *For Whom the Bell Tolls,* and a much criticized one, *Across the River and Into the Trees.* An avid sports enthusiast, Hemingway also wrote about bullfighting in Spain, big-game hunting in Africa, and deep-sea fishing in Florida.

In 1953 Hemingway won the Pulitzer Prize for *The Old Man and the Sea,* and in 1954 he received the Nobel Prize in literature. However, the final years of his life were not happy. Suffering from the effects of alcoholism, injuries sustained in two plane crashes, and an emotional breakdown, he committed suicide in 1961.

OTHER WORKS *The Nick Adams Stories, A Farewell to Arms, Death in the Afternoon, Men Without Women, To Have and Have Not, A Moveable Feast*

PREVIEWING

FICTION

Here We Are

Dorothy Parker

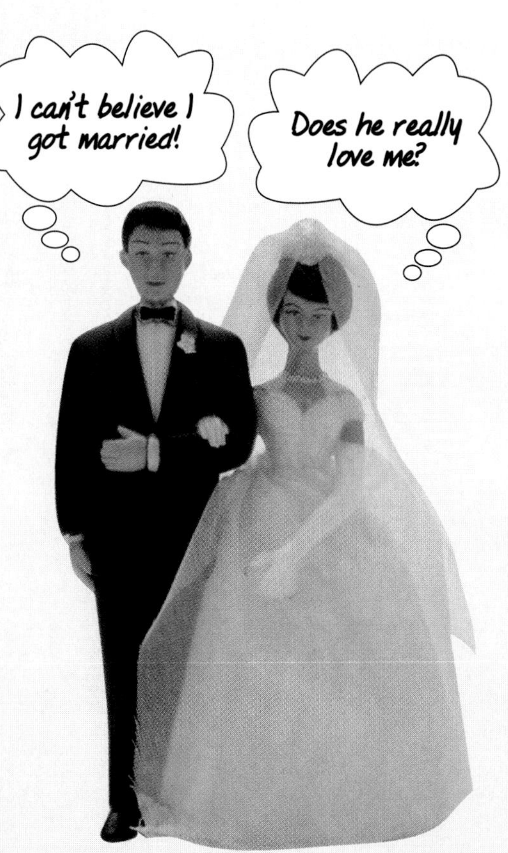

PERSONAL CONNECTION

The couple in this story are newlyweds embarking on their honeymoon. Put yourself in their place. If you had just gotten married, what might you be feeling and thinking? Working with a partner, brainstorm some hopes and fears that a newlywed couple might have, and write them down in your notebook. Then share your ideas with the rest of the class.

LITERARY CONNECTION

Dorothy Parker was known for her sharp wit and keen insight into human behavior. Like others of her generation, such as Hemingway and Fitzgerald, Parker was somewhat cynical about romantic relationships. Her characters are usually unsuccessful in love and full of longing, and they are often confused or depressed. Nevertheless, it is Dorothy Parker's abiding humor that saves her characters from the gloom that surrounds so many other modernist creations.

READING CONNECTION

Interpreting Characters Through Dialogue "Here We Are" is told almost exclusively through dialogue. A brief description occurs at the beginning of the story, as the young man struggles with the luggage in the train compartment and the young woman stares out the window. As you read this story, you have to infer the characters' feelings and motivations from what they say. Fortunately, unlike the characters in "The End of Something," the newlyweds in this story have a lot to say. As you read, analyze their dialogue to discover their underlying hopes and fears about what awaits them at the end of their train ride.

Here We Are

DOROTHY PARKER

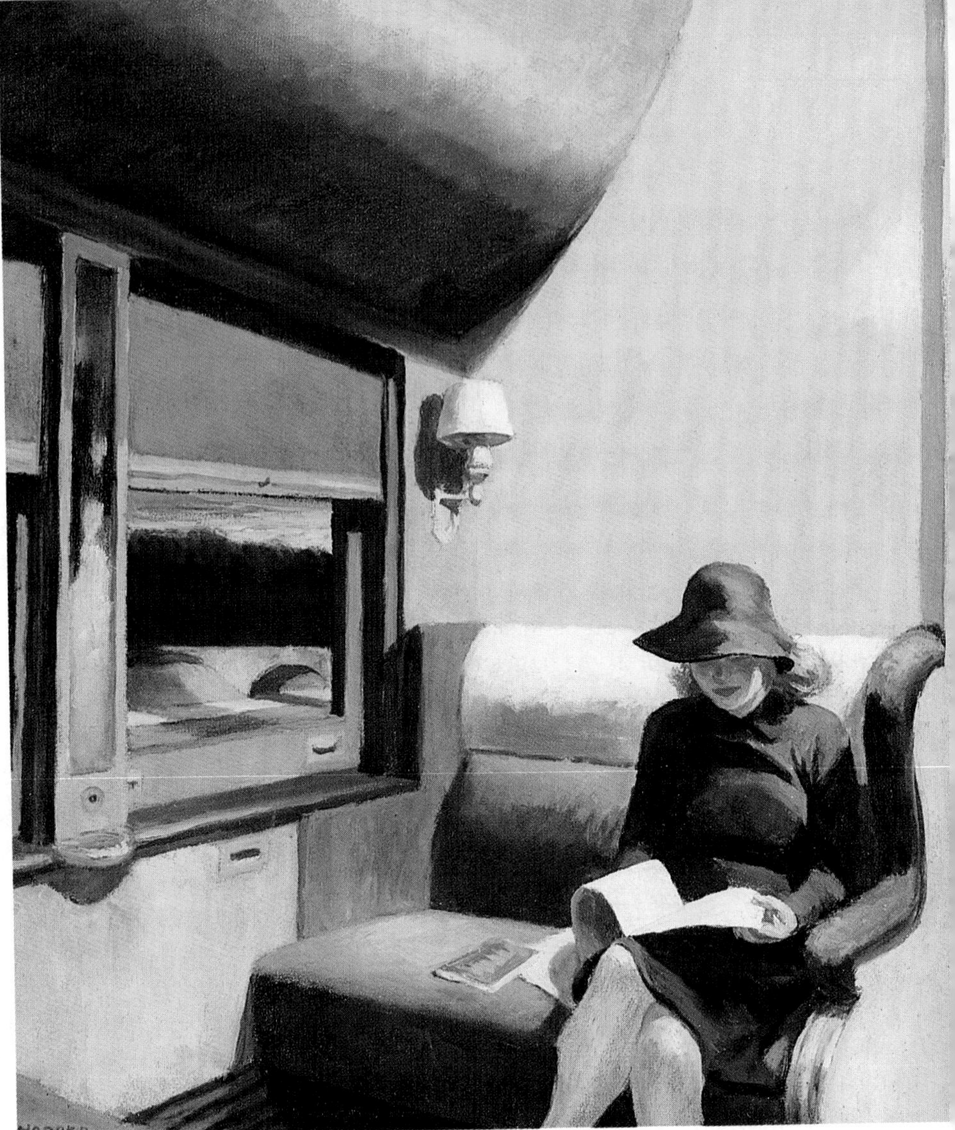

Compartment C, Car 293 (1938), Edward Hopper. Oil on canvas, 20″ × 18″, collection of IBM Corporation, Armonk, New York.

The young man in the new blue suit finished arranging the glistening luggage in tight corners of the Pullman compartment[1]. The train had leaped at curves and bounced along straightaways, rendering balance a praiseworthy achievement and a sporadic[2] one; and the young man had pushed and hoisted and tucked and shifted the bags with concentrated care.

Nevertheless, eight minutes for the settling of two suitcases and a hatbox is a long time.

He sat down, leaning back against bristled green plush, in the seat opposite the girl in beige. She looked as new as a peeled egg. Her hat, her fur, her frock, her gloves were glossy and stiff with novelty. On the arc of the thin, slippery sole of one beige shoe was gummed a tiny oblong of white paper, printed with the price set and paid

1. **Pullman compartment:** a small private room in a railroad car built by the Pullman Company.
2. **sporadic** (spə-răd′ĭk): occurring at irregular intervals; occasional.

for that slipper and its fellow, and the name of the shop that had dispensed them.

She had been staring raptly out of the window, drinking in the big weathered signboards that extolled[3] the phenomena of codfish without bones and screens no rust could corrupt. As the young man sat down, she turned politely from the pane, met his eyes, started a smile and got it about half done, and rested her gaze just above his right shoulder.

"Well!" the young man said.

"Well!" she said.

"Well, here we are," he said.

"Here we are," she said. "Aren't we?"

"I should say we were," he said. "Eeyop. Here we are."

"Well!" she said.

"Well!" he said. "Well. How does it feel to be an old married lady?"

"Oh, it's too soon to ask me that," she said. "At least—I mean. Well, I mean, goodness, we've only been married about three hours, haven't we?"

The young man studied his wristwatch as if he were just acquiring the knack of reading time.

"We have been married," he said, "exactly two hours and twenty-six minutes."

"My," she said. "It seems like longer."

"No," he said. "It isn't hardly half-past six yet."

"It seems like later," she said. "I guess it's because it starts getting dark so early."

"It does, at that," he said. "The nights are going to be pretty long from now on. I mean. I mean—well, it starts getting dark early."

"I didn't have any idea what time it was," she said. "Everything was so mixed up, I sort of don't know where I am, or what it's all about. Getting back from the church, and then all those people, and then changing all my clothes, and then everybody throwing things, and all. Goodness, I don't see how people do it every day."

"Do what?" he said.

"Get married," she said. "When you think of all the people, all over the world, getting married just as if it was nothing. Chinese people and everybody. Just as if it wasn't anything."

"Well, let's not worry about people all over the world," he said. "Let's don't think about a lot of Chinese. We've got something better to think about. I mean. I mean—well, what do we care about them?"

"I know," she said. "But I just sort of got to thinking of them, all of them, all over everywhere, doing it all the time. At least, I mean—getting married, you know. And it's—well, it's sort of such a big thing to do, it makes you feel queer. You think of them, all of them, all doing it just like it wasn't anything. And how does anybody know what's going to happen next?"

"*Let them worry,*" he said. "We don't have to. We know darn well what's going to happen next. I mean. I mean—well, we know it's going to be great. Well, we know we're going to be happy. Don't we?"

"Oh, of course," she said. "Only you think of all the people, and you have to sort of keep thinking. It makes you feel funny. An awful lot of people that get married, it doesn't turn out so well. And I guess they all must have thought it was going to be great."

"Come on, now," he said. "This is no way to start a honeymoon, with all this thinking going on. Look at us—all married and everything done. I mean. The wedding all done and all."

"Ah, it was nice, wasn't it?" she said. "Did you really like my veil?"

"You looked great," he said. "Just great."

"Oh, I'm terribly glad," she said. "Ellie and Louise looked lovely, didn't they? I'm terribly glad they did finally decide on pink. They looked perfectly lovely."

"Listen," he said. "I want to tell you something. When I was standing up there in that old church waiting for you to come up, and I saw

3. **extolled:** praised highly; glorified.

those two bridesmaids, I thought to myself, I thought, 'Well, I never knew Louise could look like that!' Why, she'd have knocked anybody's eye out."

"Oh, really?" she said. "Funny. Of course, everybody thought her dress and hat were lovely, but a lot of people seemed to think she looked sort of tired. People have been saying that a lot, lately. I tell them I think it's awfully mean of them to go around saying that about her. I tell them they've got to remember that Louise isn't so terribly young anymore, and they've got to expect her to look like that. Louise can say she's twenty-three all she wants to, but she's a good deal nearer twenty-seven."

"Well, she was certainly a knockout at the wedding," he said. "Boy!"

"I'm terribly glad you thought so," she said. "I'm glad someone did. How did you think Ellie looked?"

"Why, I honestly didn't get a look at her," he said.

"Oh, really?" she said. "Well, I certainly think that's too bad. I don't suppose I ought to say it about my own sister, but I never saw anybody look as beautiful as Ellie looked today. And always so sweet and unselfish, too. And you didn't even notice her. But you never pay attention to Ellie, anyway. Don't think I haven't noticed it. It makes me feel just terrible. It makes me feel just awful, that you don't like my own sister."

"I do like her!" he said. "I'm crazy for Ellie. I think she's a great kid."

"Don't think it makes any difference to Ellie!" she said. "Ellie's got enough people crazy about her. It isn't anything to her whether you like her or not. Don't flatter yourself she cares! Only, the only thing is, it makes it awfully hard for me you don't like her, that's the only thing. I keep thinking, when we come back and get in that apartment and everything, it's going to be awfully hard for me that you won't want my own sister to come and see me. It's going to make it awfully hard for me that you won't ever want my family around. I know how you feel about my family. Don't think I haven't seen it. Only, if you don't ever want to see them, that's your loss. Not theirs. Don't flatter yourself!"

"Oh, now, come on!" he said. "What's all this talk about not wanting your family around? Why, you know how I feel about your family. I think your old lady—I think your mother's swell. And Ellie. And your father. What's all this talk?"

"Well, I've seen it," she said. "Don't think I haven't. Lots of people they get married, and they think it's going to be great and everything, and then it all goes to pieces because people don't like people's families, or something like that. Don't tell me! I've seen it happen."

"Honey," he said, "what is all this? What are you getting all angry about? Hey, look, this is our honeymoon. What are you trying to start a fight for? Ah, I guess you're just feeling sort of nervous."

"Me?" she said. "What have I got to be nervous about? I mean. I mean, goodness, I'm not nervous."

"You know, lots of times," he said, "they say that girls get kind of nervous and yippy on account of thinking about—I mean. I mean—well, it's like you said, things are all so sort of mixed up and everything, right now. But afterwards, it'll be all right. I mean. I mean—well, look, honey, you don't look any too comfortable. Don't you want to take your hat off? And let's don't ever fight, ever. Will we?"

"Ah, I'm sorry I was cross," she said. "I guess I did feel a little bit funny. All mixed up, and then thinking of all those people all over everywhere, and then being sort of 'way off here, all alone with you. It's so sort of different. It's sort of such a big thing. You can't blame a person for thinking, can you? Yes, don't let's ever, ever fight. We won't be like a whole lot of them. We won't fight or be nasty or anything. Will we?"

"You bet your life we won't," he said.

"I guess I will take this darned old hat off," she said. "It kind of presses. Just put it up on the rack, will you, dear? Do you like it, sweetheart?"

"Looks good on you," he said.

"No, but I mean," she said, "do you really like it?"

"Well, I'll tell you," he said. "I know this is the new style and everything like that, and it's probably great. I don't know anything about things like that. Only I like the kind of a hat like that blue hat you had. Gee, I liked that hat."

"Oh, really?" she said. "Well, that's nice. That's lovely. The first thing you say to me, as soon as you get me off on a train away from my family and everything, is that you don't like my hat. The first thing you say to your wife is you think she has terrible taste in hats. That's nice, isn't it?"

"Now, honey," he said, "I never said anything like that. I only said—"

"What you don't seem to realize," she said, "is this hat cost twenty-two dollars. Twenty-two dollars. And that horrible old blue thing you think you're so crazy about, that cost three ninety-five."

"I don't give a darn what they cost," he said. "I only said—I said I liked that blue hat. I don't know anything about hats. I'll be crazy about this one as soon as I get used to it. Only it's kind of not like your other hats. I don't know about the new styles. What do I know about women's hats?"

"It's too bad," she said, "you didn't marry somebody that would get the kind of hats you'd like. Hats that cost three ninety-five. Why didn't you marry Louise? You always think she looks so beautiful. You'd love her taste in hats. Why didn't you marry her?"

"Ah, now, honey," he said. "For heaven's sakes!"

"Why didn't you marry her?" she said. "All you've done, ever since we got on this train, is talk about her. Here I've sat and sat, and just listened to you saying how wonderful Louise is. I suppose that's nice, getting me all off here alone with you, and then raving about Louise right in front of my face. Why didn't you ask her to marry you? I'm sure she would have jumped at the chance. There aren't so many people asking her to marry them. It's too bad you didn't marry her. I'm sure you'd have been much happier."

"Listen, baby," he said, "while you're talking about things like that, why didn't you marry Joe Brooks? I suppose he could have given you all the twenty-two-dollar hats you wanted, I suppose!"

"Well, I'm not so sure I'm not sorry I didn't," she said. "There! Joe Brooks wouldn't have waited until he got me all off alone and then sneered at my taste in clothes. Joe Brooks wouldn't ever hurt my feelings. Joe Brooks has always been fond of me. There!"

"Yeah," he said. "He's fond of you. He was so fond of you he didn't even send a wedding present. That's how fond of you he was."

"I happen to know for a fact," she said, "that he was away on business, and as soon as he comes back he's going to give me anything I want, for the apartment."

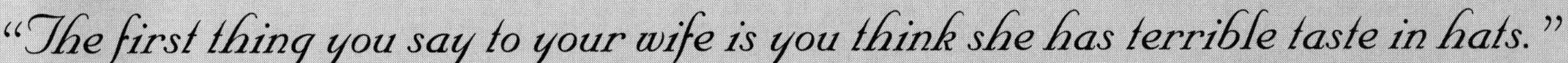
"The first thing you say to your wife is you think she has terrible taste in hats."

"Listen," he said. "I don't want anything he gives you in our apartment. Anything he gives you, I'll throw right out the window. That's what I think of your friend Joe Brooks. And how do you know where he is and what he's going to do, anyway? Has he been writing to you?"

"I suppose my friends can correspond with me," she said. "I didn't hear there was any law against that."

"Well, I suppose they can't!" he said. "And what do you think of that? I'm not going to have my wife getting a lot of letters from cheap traveling salesmen!"

"Joe Brooks is not a cheap traveling salesman!" she said. "He is not! He gets a wonderful salary."

"Oh yeah?" he said. "Where did you hear that?"

"He told me so himself," she said.

"Oh, he told you so himself," he said. "I see. He told you so himself."

"You've got a lot of right to talk about Joe Brooks," she said. "You and your friend Louise. All you ever talk about is Louise."

"Oh, for heaven's sakes!" he said. "What do I care about Louise? I just thought she was a friend of yours, that's all. That's why I ever even noticed her."

"Well, you certainly took an awful lot of notice of her today," she said. "On our wedding day! You said yourself when you were standing there in the church you just kept thinking of her. Right up at the altar. Oh, right in the presence of God! And all you thought about was Louise."

"Listen, honey," he said, "I never should have said that. How does anybody know what kind of crazy things come into their heads when they're standing there waiting to get married? I was just telling you that because it was so kind of crazy. I thought it would make you laugh."

"I know," she said. "I've been all sort of mixed up today, too. I told you that. Everything so strange and everything. And me all the time thinking about all those people all over the world, and now us here all alone, and everything. I know you get all mixed up. Only I did think, when you kept talking about how beautiful Louise looked, you did it with malice and forethought."[4]

"I never did anything with malice and forethought!" he said. "I just told you that about Louise because I thought it would make you laugh."

"Well, it didn't," she said.

"No, I know it didn't," he said. "It certainly did not. Ah, baby, and we ought to be laughing, too. Hell, honey lamb, this is our honeymoon. What's the matter?"

"I don't know," she said. "We used to squabble a lot when we were going together and then engaged and everything, but I thought everything would be so different as soon as you were married. And now I feel so sort of strange

4. **malice and forethought:** a variation of a legal phrase that refers to a wrongful act (especially murder) done intentionally without just cause or excuse.

"Everything so strange and everything. And me all the time thinking about

and everything. I feel so sort of alone."

"Well, you see, sweetheart," he said, "we're not really married yet. I mean. I mean—well, things will be different afterwards. Oh, hell. I mean, we haven't been married very long."

"No," she said.

"Well, we haven't got much longer to wait now," he said. "I mean—well, we'll be in New York in about twenty minutes. Then we can have dinner, and sort of see what we feel like doing. Or I mean. Is there anything special you want to do tonight?"

"What?" she said.

"What I mean to say," he said, "would you like to go to a show or something?"

"Why, whatever you like," she said. "I sort of didn't think people went to theaters and things on their—I mean, I've got a couple of letters I simply must write. Don't let me forget."

"Oh," he said. "You're going to write letters tonight?"

"Well, you see," she said. "I've been perfectly terrible. What with all the excitement and everything. I never did thank poor old Mrs. Sprague for her berry spoon, and I never did a thing about those bookends the McMasters sent. It's just too awful of me. I've got to write them this very night."

"And when you've finished writing your letters," he said, "maybe I could get you a magazine or a bag of peanuts."

"What?" she said.

"I mean," he said, "I wouldn't want you to be bored."

"As if I could be bored with you!" she said. "Silly! Aren't we married? Bored!"

"What I thought," he said, "I thought when we got in, we could go right up to the Biltmore and anyway leave our bags, and maybe have a little dinner in the room, kind of quiet, and then do whatever we wanted. I mean. I mean—well, let's go right up there from the station."

"Oh, yes, let's," she said. "I'm so glad we're going to the Biltmore. I just love it. The twice I've stayed in New York we've always stayed there, Papa and Mamma and Ellie and I, and I was crazy about it. I always sleep so well there. I go right off to sleep the minute I put my head on the pillow."

"Oh, you do?" he said.

"At least, I mean," she said. "Way up high it's so quiet."

"We might go to some show or other tomorrow night instead of tonight," he said. "Don't you think that would be better?"

"Yes, I think it might," she said.

He rose, balanced a moment, crossed over and sat down beside her.

"Do you really have to write those letters tonight?" he said.

"Well," she said, "I don't suppose they'd get there any quicker than if I wrote them tomorrow."

There was a silence with things going on in it.

"And we won't ever fight anymore, will we?" he said.

all those people all over the world, and now us here all alone, and everything."

Railroad Train (1908), Edward Hopper. Oil on canvas, 24″ × 29″, Addison Gallery of American Art, Phillips Academy, Andover, Massachusetts, gift of Fred T. Murphy, Esq. Copyright © Addison Gallery of American Art, Phillips Academy, Andover, Massachusetts. All rights reserved.

"Oh, no," she said. "Not ever! I don't know what made me do like that. It all got so sort of funny, sort of like a nightmare, the way I got thinking of all those people getting married all the time; and so many of them, everything spoils on account of fighting and everything. I got all mixed up thinking about them. Oh, I don't want to be like them. But we won't be, will we?"

"Sure we won't," he said.

"We won't go all to pieces," she said. "We won't fight. It'll all be different, now we're married. It'll all be lovely. Reach me down my hat, will you, sweetheart? It's time I was putting it on. Thanks. Ah, I'm so sorry you don't like it."

"I do so like it!" he said.

"You said you didn't," she said. "You said you thought it was perfectly terrible."

"I never said any such thing," he said. "You're crazy."

"All right, I may be crazy," she said. "Thank you very much. But that's what you said. Not that it matters—it's just a little thing. But it makes you feel pretty funny to think you've gone and married somebody that says you have perfectly terrible taste in hats. And then goes and says you're crazy, beside."

"Now, listen here," he said. "Nobody said any such thing. Why, I love that hat. The more I look at it the better I like it. I think it's great."

"That isn't what you said before," she said.

"Honey," he said. "Stop it, will you? What do you want to start all this for? I love the damned hat. I mean, I love your hat. I love anything you wear. What more do you want me to say?"

"Well, I don't want you to say it like that," she said.

"I said I think it's great," he said. "That's all I said."

"Do you really?" she said. "Do you honestly? Ah, I'm so glad. I'd hate you not to like my hat. It would be—I don't know, it would be sort of such a bad start."

"Well, I'm crazy for it," he said. "Now we've got that settled, for heaven's sakes. Ah, baby. Baby lamb. We're not going to have any bad starts. Look at us—we're on our honeymoon. Pretty soon we'll be regular old married people. I mean. I mean, in a few minutes we'll be getting in to New York, and then we'll be going to the hotel, and then everything will be all right. I mean—well, look at us! Here we are married! Here we are!"

"Yes, here we are," she said. "Aren't we?" ❖

RESPONDING OPTIONS

FROM PERSONAL RESPONSE *TO* CRITICAL ANALYSIS

REFLECT 1. What are your impressions of the man and the woman in this story? Record these impressions in your notebook.

RETHINK 2. What hopes and fears about their marriage do the newlyweds reveal through their dialogue?

Consider

- why the man feels that everything will be all right once they get to the hotel
- what the woman is so nervous about
- why the woman starts fights about her bridesmaid Louise, her family, and her hat
- why the man gets so angry about Joe Brooks

3. Think about the expectations that the newlyweds have for each other. Do you think that they will have a successful marriage? Explain your opinion.

4. Look back at what you wrote for the Personal Connection on page 835. How did your ideas about the hopes and fears of newlyweds compare with the concerns of the characters in this story?

RELATE 5. Would you consider these characters alienated? Are they in touch with their feelings and able to communicate effectively? Support your opinion with evidence from the story.

6. Compare the man and the woman in this story with newly married couples you know or have read about. How are these couples similar? How do they differ?

ANOTHER PATHWAY

Cooperative Learning

Work with a group of classmates to prepare a script for a one-act play based on "Here We Are." Choose dialogue from the story, and add your ideas about what the actors' actions and gestures should be. Then cast two group members to play the man and the woman, rehearse the play, and perform it for the class.

LITERARY LINKS

Compare the couple in "Here We Are" with Nick and Marjorie in "The End of Something." What similarities and differences do you see in the two relationships? Do you think the newlyweds' relationship will suffer the same fate as Nick and Marjorie's? Why or why not?

QUICKWRITES

1. Using what you have learned about newlywed jitters from this story, write notes for a **lecture** that you might deliver to a group of engaged couples.
2. Imagine that you are a marriage counselor and that the couple in this story have come to you for help. Write a brief **analysis** diagnosing the couple's problems and advising them how to solve them.
3. What do you think will happen to the couple in this story? Assume they are celebrating their first wedding anniversary. Write a **dialogue** that reveals what their relationship is like one year after their marriage.

PORTFOLIO Save your writing. You may want to use it later as a springboard to a piece for your portfolio.

LITERARY CONCEPTS

In order to understand how skillfully Parker reveals character, you need to take a close look at her characters' **dialogue.** Working with a partner, choose a passage of dialogue to analyze. First read the dialogue aloud—perhaps several times. Then write down what might be the thoughts and feelings that motivate the characters' statements. For example, early in the story, the woman says:

> It makes you feel funny. An awful lot of people that get married, it doesn't turn out so well. And I guess they all must have thought it was going to be great.

As she says this, she might be thinking,

> I wonder if our marriage has a chance.

For the class, perform a reading of the passage of dialogue with your partner, adding the thoughts and feelings you imagined for the characters.

CRITIC'S CORNER

Members of our student advisory board had lively comments about this story. Most enjoyed the humor. Michael Scott could relate to the story personally: "It reminded me of all the fights I had with past girlfriends." Although Katie McGuire had trouble understanding the characters at first, she said, "I grew to like them as I read on." However, Joanna Cheng was emphatic: "I hated the female protagonist for being so paranoid and whiny . . . she drove me crazy!" On the other hand, Shericko Davis was critical of "how the husband compliments Louise so much." What is your opinion of the characters? Do you like them—or do they drive you crazy?

DOROTHY PARKER

1893–1967

A reporter for *Time* magazine said of Dorothy Parker that "hers was the tongue heard round the world." By the time she was 34, Parker had gained renown for her biting wit. What she said was quoted by columnists in New York City and then repeated throughout the country. Parker was a founder and leader of the famed group of intellectuals known as the Algonquin Round Table, a group that met regularly at the Algonquin Hotel in New York City. About this group and herself Parker observed: "It was the twenties, and we *had* to be smarty. I *wanted* to be cute. That's the terrible thing. I should have had more sense. A smartcracker, they called me. I was the toast of two continents: Greenland and Australia."

To support herself after her father died, Dorothy Rothschild took a job at *Vogue* magazine, writing captions for fashion pictures. In 1917 she married Edwin Parker and joined the staff at *Vanity Fair,* where she met her lifelong friend Robert Benchley. After being fired from *Vanity Fair* in 1920 for writing unfavorable drama reviews, she continued to earn a living as a writer. With her second husband, Alan Campbell, Parker spent more than 20 years in Hollywood working as a successful screenwriter. This work came to a halt, however, after Parker was blacklisted during the McCarthy era of the 1950s for her earlier involvement in radical politics.

Parker's first published prose, "Why I Haven't Married," appeared in *Vanity Fair* in 1915. Her first book of poetry, *Enough Rope,* was a bestseller. In the 1930s, she published two short story collections, *Laments for the Living* and *After Such Pleasures.* Although she did not publish widely, fellow Round Table member Alexander Woollcott commented that "most of it [her work] has been pure gold and the five winnowed volumes of her shelf . . . are so potent a distillation of nectar and wormwood, of ambrosia and deadly nightshade, as might suggest to the rest of us that we all write far too much."

OTHER WORKS *Death and Taxes, Sunset Gun*

LASERLINKS
• *AUTHOR BACKGROUND*

PREVIEWING

POETRY

The Love Song of J. Alfred Prufrock

T. S. Eliot

PERSONAL CONNECTION

In this poem, J. Alfred Prufrock, on his way to a party, is trying to decide what to say to a woman who will be there. Imagine that you are at a party and see someone you would like to get better acquainted with. You do not know how this person feels about you. Would you reach out to this person by starting a conversation, or would you hold back? In your notebook, capture the thoughts you might have as you try to decide what to do. You can record your ideas on a chart like the one shown.

Reach Out	Don't Reach Out
• She's alone now. Go on over.	• What'll I say? I'm not ready.
• She looked at me. Go ahead.	• I better go check my hair first.

LITERARY CONNECTION

In 1914 the poet Ezra Pound read "The Love Song of J. Alfred Prufrock" for the first time and enthusiastically wrote to Harriet Monroe, editor of *Poetry* magazine: "Eliot . . . has sent in the best poem I have yet had or seen from an American. . . . He has actually trained himself *and* modernized himself *on his own.*" Modernist poets like Eliot and Pound sought to make a clear break with the poetic traditions of the past, especially 19th-century romanticism. Whereas romantic poets celebrated the individual and nature, Eliot portrayed the loneliness and alienation of the individual living in a dingy modern city. While romantic poets believed that poems should be written in everyday language for common people, Eliot used elevated diction and classical allusions to separate himself from the masses.

A street in Boston about the time Eliot lived there. Southworth and Hawes.

READING CONNECTION

Understanding Stream of Consciousness Stream of consciousness is a technique that was developed by the modernists to present the chronological flow of the seemingly unconnected thoughts, responses, and sensations of a character. Eliot used this technique to reveal the jumble of ideas, feelings, and daydreams that flow through Prufrock's mind. As the poem begins, Prufrock addresses a silent listener who accompanies him to the party. Pretend you are this listener, and as you read, pay attention to Prufrock's different thoughts and feelings about the decision he is trying to make.

The Love Song of J. Alfred Prufrock

T. S. ELIOT

S'io credessi che mia risposta fosse
a persona che mai tornasse al mondo,
questa fiamma staria senza più scosse.
Ma per ciò che giammai di questo fondo
non tornò vivo alcun, s'i'odo il vero,
senza tema d'infamia ti rispondo.

Let us go then, you and I,
When the evening is spread out against the sky
Like a patient etherized upon a table;
Let us go, through certain half-deserted streets,
The muttering retreats
Of restless nights in one-night cheap hotels
And sawdust restaurants with oyster-shells:
Streets that follow like a tedious argument
Of insidious intent
To lead you to an overwhelming question . . .
Oh, do not ask, "What is it?"
Let us go and make our visit.

In the room the women come and go
Talking of Michelangelo.

The yellow fog that rubs its back upon the window-panes,
The yellow smoke that rubs its muzzle on the window-panes,
Licked its tongue into the corners of the evening,
Lingered upon the pools that stand in drains,
Let fall upon its back the soot that falls from chimneys,
Slipped by the terrace, made a sudden leap,
And seeing that it was a soft October night,
Curled once about the house, and fell asleep.

GUIDE FOR READING

This is a quotation in Italian from Dante's *Inferno*. Speaking to a visitor in hell, one of the damned says that he will describe his torment only because the visitor cannot return alive to the world to repeat it.

2–3 Ether was used to make a patient unconscious during an operation. How can an evening be like an etherized patient?

4–7 What do these lines suggest to you about this section of the city?

9 insidious (ĭn-sĭd'ē-əs): more dangerous than it seems.

10–12 Prufrock appears reluctant to say what his "overwhelming question" is.

13–14 The women mentioned in these lines may be those at the party Prufrock is going to attend, or they may be women at other parties Prufrock has attended. Is Prufrock suggesting that their "talking of Michelangelo" at a party involves a serious or a trivial discussion of this great Renaissance artist?

And indeed there will be time
For the yellow smoke that slides along the street
Rubbing its back upon the window-panes;
There will be time, there will be time
To prepare a face to meet the faces that you meet;
There will be time to murder and create,
And time for all the works and days of hands
That lift and drop a question on your plate;
Time for you and time for me,
And time yet for a hundred indecisions,
And for a hundred visions and revisions,
Before the taking of a toast and tea.

23–34 This stanza reveals part of Prufrock's problem. Look for clues as you read.

26–27 What is Prufrock's idea of how people behave at parties or, perhaps, at any time?

In the room the women come and go
Talking of Michelangelo.

And indeed there will be time
To wonder, "Do I dare?" and, "Do I dare?"
Time to turn back and descend the stair,
With a bald spot in the middle of my hair—
(They will say: "How his hair is growing thin!")
My morning coat, my collar mounting firmly to the chin,
My necktie rich and modest, but asserted by a simple pin—
(They will say: "But how his arms and legs are thin!")
Do I dare
Disturb the universe?
In a minute there is time
For decisions and revisions which a minute will reverse.

37–48 In this stanza, Prufrock seems to grow increasingly insecure. The repeated question "Do I dare?" suggests that he wants to do something extraordinary at the party. What do you think he wants to do?

For I have known them all already, known them all—
Have known the evenings, mornings, afternoons,
I have measured out my life with coffee spoons;
I know the voices dying with a dying fall
Beneath the music from a farther room.
   So how should I presume?

And I have known the eyes already, known them all—
The eyes that fix you in a formulated phrase,
And when I am formulated, sprawling on a pin,
When I am pinned and wriggling on the wall,
Then how should I begin
To spit out all the butt-ends of my days and ways?
   And how should I presume?

55–58 Prufrock recalls being scrutinized by women at other parties. The image of himself is one of a live insect that has been classified, labeled, and mounted for display.

56 formulated: reduced to a formula or prepared according to a formula.

WORDS TO KNOW

presume (prĭ-zo͞om') *v.* to act overconfidently; go beyond the proper limits; dare

And I have known the arms already, known them all—
Arms that are braceleted and white and bare
(But in the lamplight, downed with light brown hair!)
Is it perfume from a dress
That makes me so digress?
Arms that lie along a table, or wrap about a shawl.
   And should I then presume?
   And how should I begin?

• • • • •

Shall I say, I have gone at dusk through narrow streets
And watched the smoke that rises from the pipes
Of lonely men in shirt-sleeves, leaning out of windows? . . .

I should have been a pair of ragged claws
Scuttling across the floors of silent seas.

• • • • •

And the afternoon, the evening, sleeps so peacefully!
Smoothed by long fingers,
Asleep . . . tired . . . or it malingers,
Stretched on the floor, here beside you and me.
Should I, after tea and cakes and ices,
Have the strength to force the moment to its crisis?
But though I have wept and fasted, wept and prayed,
Though I have seen my head (grown slightly bald) brought in
   upon a platter,
I am no prophet—and here's no great matter;
I have seen the moment of my greatness flicker,
And I have seen the eternal Footman hold my coat, and snicker,
And in short, I was afraid.

And would it have been worth it, after all,
After the cups, the marmalade, the tea,
Among the porcelain, among some talk of you and me,
Would it have been worth while,
To have bitten off the matter with a smile,
To have squeezed the universe into a ball
To roll it towards some overwhelming question,
To say: "I am Lazarus, come from the dead,
Come back to tell you all, I shall tell you all"—
If one, settling a pillow by her head,
   Should say: "That is not what I meant at all.
   That is not it, at all."

62–67 How would you describe Prufrock's attitude toward the women at the party? Notice that he wants to say something but doesn't know how.

70–72 Why do you think Prufrock wants to talk about "lonely men"?

73–74 Prufrock has presented an image of himself as an insect (lines 57–58) and, here, as a crab or lobster. What do these images suggest about Prufrock's self-esteem?

81–83 These lines allude to the biblical story of John the Baptist, who is imprisoned by King Herod (Matthew 14; Mark 6). To gratify his stepdaughter Salome, Herod orders the Baptist's head cut off and brought to him on a platter.

85 Who or what do you think is "the eternal Footman"?

86 Who or what do you think Prufrock was afraid of?

87–110 In these two stanzas, Prufrock rationalizes his failure to ask the "overwhelming question."

94 **Lazarus:** In the biblical story (John 11:17–44), Lazarus lay dead in his tomb for four days before Jesus brought him back to life. Why do you think Prufrock compares himself to a character who returns from the dead?

WORDS TO KNOW

digress (dī-grĕs') *v.* to wander away from the main subject in a conversation or in writing; ramble

malinger (mə-lĭng'gər) *v.* to pretend illness in order to avoid duty or work

And would it have been worth it, after all,
Would it have been worth while,
After the sunsets and the dooryards and the sprinkled streets,
After the novels, after the teacups, after the skirts that trail along
   the floor—
And this, and so much more?—
It is impossible to say just what I mean!
But as if a magic lantern threw the nerves in patterns on a
   screen:
Would it have been worth while
If one, settling a pillow or throwing off a shawl,
And turning toward the window, should say:
   "That is not it at all,
   That is not what I meant, at all."

No! I am not Prince Hamlet, nor was meant to be;
Am an attendant lord, one that will do
To swell a progress, start a scene or two,
Advise the prince; no doubt, an easy tool,
Deferential, glad to be of use,
Politic, cautious, and meticulous;
Full of high sentence, but a bit obtuse;
At times, indeed, almost ridiculous—
Almost, at times, the Fool.

I grow old . . . I grow old . . .
I shall wear the bottoms of my trousers rolled.

Shall I part my hair behind? Do I dare to eat a peach?
I shall wear white flannel trousers, and walk upon the beach.
I have heard the mermaids singing, each to each.

I do not think that they will sing to me.

I have seen them riding seaward on the waves
Combing the white hair of the waves blown back
When the wind blows the water white and black.

We have lingered in the chambers of the sea
By sea-girls wreathed with seaweed red and brown
Till human voices wake us, and we drown.

105 The magic lantern was a forerunner of the slide projector. In this image, the "nerves" may be Prufrock's inner self exposed for all to see.

111–119 Notice that Prufrock resigns himself to playing a supporting role rather than a starring one in life.

115 deferential (dĕf′ə-rĕn′shəl): yielding to someone else's opinion.

116 politic (pŏl′ĭ-tĭk): skillful in dealing with others; diplomatic.

124–128 In mythology, mermaids attract mortal men by their beauty and their singing, sometimes allowing men to live with them in the sea. What might the mermaids represent to Prufrock?

129–131 Whom do you think "we" refers to? What does the metaphor of waking and drowning suggest?

WORDS TO KNOW

meticulous (mĭ-tĭk′yə-ləs) *adj.* extremely careful and precise about details
obtuse (ŏb-to͞os′) *adj.* slow to understand; dull

RESPONDING OPTIONS

FROM PERSONAL RESPONSE *TO* CRITICAL ANALYSIS

REFLECT 1. What are your impressions of Prufrock? In your notebook, jot down words and phrases that describe your impressions or draw a quick sketch of him.

RETHINK 2. How do you think Prufrock feels at the end of the poem?

Consider
- how he imagines the rest of his life to be
- his dream image of the mermaids and what they are doing
- his thoughts about waking and drowning

3. Consider what you wrote for the Personal Connection on page 845. Do you think Prufrock makes the right decision in not asking the "overwhelming question"? Support your opinion by citing evidence from the poem.

4. What do you think Prufrock's "overwhelming question" is?

Consider
- what, in lines 1–10, leads him to think about this question
- to whom the question might be directed
- why the question might "disturb the universe"
- what the question might have to do with the "lonely men in shirt-sleeves" in line 72
- the response he anticipates in lines 97–98 and 109–110

5. How would you judge the women at the tea party Prufrock attends?

Consider
- what they do and what they talk about
- why Prufrock must "prepare a face to meet the faces" (line 27)
- how the women judge others, as suggested in lines 41, 44, and 55–58

RELATE 6. Do you think Prufrock is similar to or different from most people?

7. Why do you think this poem is called a love song? How does it compare with love songs you know?

ANOTHER PATHWAY

Imagine that you run a radio show on the arts and that T. S. Eliot will appear as your guest to publicize his new book, *Prufrock and Other Observations.* What questions would you ask him in order to help your listeners understand "The Love Song of J. Alfred Prufrock," and what might he answer? With a partner, prepare the interview and perform it for the class.

QUICKWRITES

1. If you were the person addressed in the poem, what advice would you give Prufrock? Put that advice in a **personal letter** to him.
2. Imagine you are a woman who has been watching Prufrock at the tea party. Draft a brief stream-of-consciousness **narrative** that presents the images, thoughts, and feelings that flow through your mind as you watch him. Using a computer might make it easier to express your ideas in a stream-of-consciousness style.

PORTFOLIO *Save your writing. You may want to use it later as a springboard to a piece for your portfolio.*

LITERARY CONCEPTS

Imagery consists of words and phrases that appeal to any of the five senses and that help the reader imagine precisely what the writer is describing. In keeping with other modernists, Eliot uses powerful images to convey complex ideas and emotions. For example, the image of the evening as "a patient etherized upon a table" is richly suggestive of the general ill health and languor in Prufrock's world. The yellow fog as an aimless alley cat is another striking image. What does it communicate to you about Prufrock's city?

Most of the images in the poem are associated with Prufrock himself and reveal his fears, his self-consciousness, and his sustaining dreams. Get together with a partner to study these images. Create a two-column chart like the one shown. In the first column, list images that Prufrock associates with himself, such as that of a man growing bald and skinny (lines 40–44). In the other column, list images that Prufrock uses in contrast to himself, such as the image of the prophet John the Baptist (lines 81–83). After you have charted several images of Prufrock, analyze what they tell you about him. Write a character sketch of him, or draw a series of portraits showing how he views himself.

Images that Describe Prufrock	Images that Contrast with Prufrock
1. A face to meet other faces (line 27)	1. John the Baptist (lines 81–83)
2.	2.
3.	3.

ALTERNATIVE ACTIVITIES

1. With a partner, improvise a **scene** between Prufrock and the woman he wants to speak with. Add material of your own, but keep it consistent with Prufrock's character and the kind of woman he says will attend the party.
2. A caricature is a drawing of a person that exaggerates features to satirize that person or to highlight some aspect of his or her character. Draw a **caricature** of Prufrock based on details in the poem. Display your drawing for the class.
3. ***Cooperative Learning*** With a small group of classmates, create a short **music video** based on "The Love Song of J. Alfred Prufrock." Videotape a series of scenes inspired by the poem, and set these visual images to music. Show your video to the class, and be prepared to answer questions about your choice of music and scenes.

THE WRITER'S STYLE

Eliot's modernist style in "The Love Song of J. Alfred Prufrock" is to create a verbal collage by weaving together fragments of modern life. What impression do you get from the fragmentary images of the city, the tea party, and the beach in the poem? From the nature of these images, how do you think Eliot feels about the times he lives in?

LITERARY LINKS

Both Nick in "The End of Something" (page 827) and Prufrock seem to have difficulty expressing themselves, especially to women. In your opinion, who seems more alienated—Prufrock or Nick? Explain why you think so.

CRITIC'S CORNER

Although now considered a classic modernist poem, "The Love Song of J. Alfred Prufrock" was not an immediate success. Several well-known American and British literary critics described the poem as dreadful and unpoetic. One critic categorized the poem as "unmetrical, incoherent banalities," while another admitted that he "was unable to make head or tail" of it. How would you respond to these critics? Do you find anything poetic or profound in the poem? Point out particular lines and images to support your argument.

ACROSS THE CURRICULUM

Art In "The Love Song of J. Alfred Prufrock," Eliot repeats the lines "In the room the women come and go / Talking of Michelangelo." Research Michelangelo's life and work. Then present your findings in a written report illustrated with pictures of some of Michelangelo's most important paintings and sculptures. Why do you think Eliot alludes to this great artist in his poem?

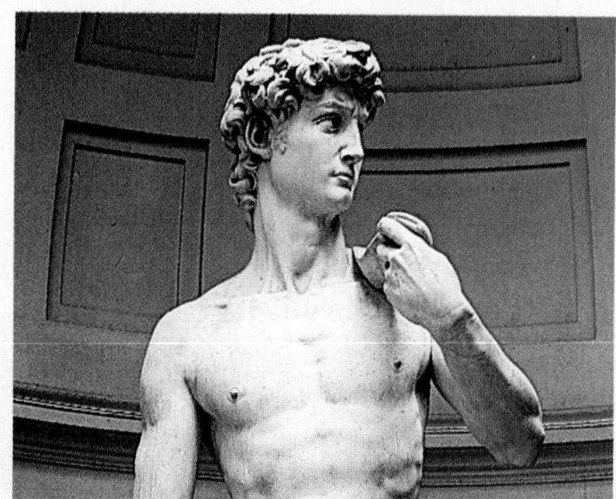

Michelangelo's *David*

WORDS TO KNOW

EXERCISE A
For each phrase in the first column, write the letter of the synonymous phrase from the second column.

1. meticulous yard work
2. to venture to eat
3. to scheme to malinger
4. as dull-witted as a fowl
5. to get way off track

A. as obtuse as a goose
B. to digress to excess
C. painstaking raking
D. to presume to consume
E. to plan faking some aching

EXERCISE B ***Cooperative Learning*** Work with four other classmates to develop a short dramatic scene using five characters. Your scene can deal with any situation; the important thing is to portray each character in such a way that by the end of the scene, he or she has become associated with one of the five vocabulary words *without anyone's having used that word in the scene.* An association with the word can be developed through each character's actions and dialogue as well as through other characters' actions toward, or dialogue about, him or her. Perform your dramatic scene for the rest of your classmates, and have them guess which vocabulary word is associated with each character.

T. S. ELIOT

1888–1965

An American who transformed himself into an Englishman, Thomas Stearns Eliot was born in St. Louis, Missouri, and died in London, England, where he had become a British subject in 1927. Eliot's whole career shows a movement back and forth between what the United States and England each represented to him—the modern and the traditional, the popular and the elite, the secular and the religious, democracy and monarchy. Even his poetry is both learned and colloquial, highly sophisticated yet laced with slang.

Eliot's early poems, such as "The Love Song of J. Alfred Prufrock" and *The Waste Land,* were original, inventive, and irreverent depictions of the decay of civilization. Although Eliot proclaimed a firm belief in tradition, his poems helped create a break with tradition and establish a new modernist poetic voice.

While his poems, plays, and critical essays were critically acclaimed, Eliot did not make enough money from his writing to live on. He worked in England as a teacher, a bank clerk, and an editor for a British publisher. As the founder and editor of *The Criterion,* a literary magazine, he was able to help younger writers, such as Marcel Proust, get a start in their careers.

Eliot won the Nobel Prize in literature in 1948. In the last decades of his life, he lectured widely in the United States. Two years after his death, Eliot was honored by a memorial tablet placed in the Poets' Corner of Westminster Abbey.

OTHER WORKS "The Hollow Men," *Murder in the Cathedral, Old Possum's Book of Practical Cats*

LASERLINKS
• *AUTHOR BACKGROUND*

PREVIEWING

FICTION

The Man Who Was Almost a Man

Richard Wright

PERSONAL CONNECTION

The main character in this story, 17-year-old Dave Saunders, is on the threshold of adulthood. Think about the adults in your family, your school, or your community. What do you think it takes to be an adult? How do people display maturity in their attitudes and actions? In your notebook, jot down your thoughts about what it means to be an adult.

HISTORICAL/BIOGRAPHICAL CONNECTION

Although the institution of slavery was abolished in the South after the Civil War, the economic oppression of African Americans there did not come to an end. Landowners divided large plantations into smaller farms, which they rented to both white and black laborers who worked for a share of the earnings from the crop. Under the brutal systems of tenant farming and sharecropping, many African-American families—like the Saunders family in this story—endured a life of grinding poverty. Neither tenants nor sharecroppers earned enough money to escape a cycle of debt or to buy their own land and become economically independent. Richard Wright's father was a cotton sharecropper in Mississippi in the early 1900s, about the time "The Man Who Was Almost a Man" takes place. In the story, young Dave works in the fields during the summer for his white employer, Mr. Hawkins, and earns a meager wage.

A sharecropper family in Arkansas during the 1930s. AP/Wide World Photos.

READING CONNECTION

Making Judgments About Characters As the story opens, Dave is grumbling to himself about an earlier incident that occurred between him and the other black field hands on the Hawkins plantation. Unlike some modernist stories, this story includes Dave's thoughts and feelings, so it will be easier for you to know him. However, Wright makes no judgments about his character—that is for the reader to decide. As you read the story, jot down in your notebook your judgments about Dave. Which of his decisions do you think are good? Which decisions do you think are mistakes? How well do you think Dave grows into adulthood during the story?

LASERLINKS
• *HISTORICAL CONNECTION*

The Man Who Was

Dave struck out across the fields, looking homeward through paling light. Whut's the use talkin wid em niggers in the field? Anyhow, his mother was putting supper on the table. Them niggers can't understan nothing. One of these days he was going to get a gun and practice shooting, then they couldn't talk to him as though he were a little boy. He slowed, looking at the ground. Shucks, Ah ain scareda them even ef they are biggern me! Aw, Ah know whut Ahma do. Ahm going by ol Joe's sto n git that Sears Roebuck catlog n look at them guns. Mebbe Ma will lemme buy one when she gits mah pay from ol man Hawkins. Ahma beg her t gimme some money. Ahm ol ernough to hava gun. Ahm seventeen. Almost a man. He strode, feeling his long loose-jointed limbs. Shucks, a man oughta hava little gun aftah he done worked hard all day.

He came in sight of Joe's store. A yellow lantern glowed on the front porch. He mounted steps and went through the screen door, hearing it bang behind him. There was a strong smell of coal oil and mackerel fish. He felt very confident until he saw fat Joe walk in through the rear door, then his courage began to ooze.

"Howdy, Dave! Whutcha want?"

"How yuh, Mistah Joe? Aw, Ah don wanna buy nothing. Ah jus wanted t see ef yuhd lemme look at tha catlog erwhile."

"Sure! You wanna see it here?"

"Nawsuh. Ah wans t take it home wid me. Ah'll bring it back termorrow when Ah come in from the fiels."

"You plannin on buying something?"

"Yessuh."

"Your ma lettin you have your own money now?"

"Shucks. Mistah Joe, Ahm gittin t be a man like anybody else!"

Joe laughed and wiped his greasy white face with a red bandanna.

"Whut you plannin on buyin?"

Dave looked at the floor, scratched his head, scratched his thigh, and smiled. Then he looked up shyly.

"Ah'll tell yuh, Mistah Joe, ef yuh promise yuh won't tell."

"I promise."

"Waal, Ahma buy a gun."

"A gun? Whut you want with a gun?"

"Ah wanna keep it."

"You ain't nothing but a boy. You don't need a gun."

"Aw, lemme have the catlog, Mistah Joe.

ALMOST A MAN RICHARD WRIGHT

Ah'll bring it back."

Joe walked through the rear door. Dave was elated[1]. He looked around at barrels of sugar and flour. He heard Joe coming back. He craned his neck to see if he were bringing the book. Yeah, he's got it. Gawddog, he's got it!

"Here, but be sure you bring it back. It's the only one I got."

"Sho, Mistah Joe."

"Say, if you wanna buy a gun, why don't you buy one from me? I gotta gun to sell."

"Will it shoot?"

"Sure it'll shoot."

"Whut kind is it?"

"Oh, it's kinda old . . . a left-hand Wheeler. A pistol. A big one."

"Is it got bullets in it?"

"It's loaded."

"Kin Ah see it?"

"Where's your money?"

"Whut yuh wan fer it?"

"I'll let you have it for two dollars."

"Just two dollahs? Shucks, Ah could buy tha when Ah git mah pay."

"I'll have it here when you want it."

"Awright, suh. Ah be in fer it."

He went through the door, hearing it slam again behind him. Ahma git some money from Ma n buy me a gun! Only two dollahs! He tucked the thick catalogue under his arm and hurried.

"Where yuh been, boy?" His mother held a steaming dish of black-eyed peas.

"Aw, Ma, Ah jus stopped down the road t talk wid the boys."

"Yuh know bettah t keep suppah waitin."

He sat down, resting the catalogue on the edge of the table.

"Yuh git up from there and git to the well n wash yosef! Ah ain feedin no hogs in mah house!"

She grabbed his shoulder and pushed him. He stumbled out of the room, then came back to get the catalogue.

"Whut this?"

"Aw, Ma, it's jusa catlog."

"Who yuh git it from?"

"From Joe, down at the sto."

"Waal, thas good. We kin use it in the outhouse."

"Naw, Ma." He grabbed for it. "Gimme ma catlog, Ma."

She held onto it and glared at him.

1. **elated:** proud and joyful.

"Quit hollerin at me! Whut's wrong wid yuh? Yuh crazy?"

"But Ma, please. It ain mine! It's Joe's! He tol me t bring it back t im termorrow."

She gave up the book. He stumbled down the back steps, hugging the thick book under his arm. When he had splashed water on his face and hands, he groped back to the kitchen and fumbled in a corner for the towel. He bumped into a chair; it clattered to the floor. The catalogue sprawled at his feet. When he had dried his eyes he snatched up the book and held it again under his arm. His mother stood watching him.

"Now, ef yuh gonna act a fool over that ol book, Ah'll take it n burn it up."

"Naw, Ma, please."

"Waal, set down n be still!"

He sat down and drew the oil lamp close. He thumbed page after page, unaware of the food his mother set on the table. His father came in. Then his small brother.

"Whutcha got there, Dave?" his father asked.

"Jusa catlog," he answered, not looking up.

"Yeah, here they is!" His eyes glowed at blue-and-black revolvers. He glanced up, feeling sudden guilt. His father was watching him. He eased the book under the table and rested it on his knees. After the blessing was asked, he ate. He scooped up peas and swallowed fat meat without chewing. Buttermilk helped to wash it down. He did not want to mention money before his father. He would do much better by cornering his mother when she was alone. He looked at his father uneasily out of the edge of his eye.

"Boy, how come yuh don quit foolin wid tha book n eat yo suppah?"

"Yessuh."

"How you n ol man Hawkins gitten erlong?"

"Suh?"

"Can't yuh hear? Why don yuh lissen? Ah ast yu how wuz yuh n ol man Hawkins gittin erlong?"

"Oh, swell, Pa. Ah plows mo lan than anybody over there."

"Waal, yuh oughta keep yo mind on whut yuh doin."

"Yessuh."

He poured his plate full of molasses and sopped it up slowly with a chunk of cornbread. When his father and brother had left the kitchen, he still sat and looked again at the guns in the catalogue, longing to muster courage enough to present his case to his mother. Lawd, ef Ah only had tha pretty one! He could almost feel the slickness of the weapon with his fingers. If he had a gun like that he would polish it and keep it shining so it would never rust. N Ah'd keep it loaded, by Gawd!

"Ma?" His voice was hesitant.

"Hunh?"

"Ol man Hawkins give yuh mah money yit?"

"Yeah, but ain no usa yuh thinking bout throwin nona it erway. Ahm keepin tha money sos yuh kin have cloes t go to school this winter."

He rose and went to her side with the open catalogue in his palms. She was washing dishes, her head bent low over a pan. Shyly he raised the book. When he spoke, his voice was husky, faint.

"Ma, Gawd knows Ah wans one of these."

"One of whut?" she asked, not raising her eyes.

"One of these," he said again, not daring even to point. She glanced up at the page, then at him with wide eyes.

"Nigger, is yuh gone plumb crazy?"

"Aw, Ma—"

"Git outta here! Don yuh talk t me bout no gun! Yuh a fool!"

"Ma, Ah kin buy one fer two dollahs."

"Not ef Ah knows it, yuh ain!"

"But yuh promised me one—"

"Ah don care whut Ah promised! Yuh ain nothing but a boy yit!"

"Ma, ef yuh lemme buy one Ah'll *never* ast yuh fer nothing no mo."

"Ah tol yuh t git outta here! Yuh ain gonna toucha penny of tha money fer no gun! Thas how come Ah has Mistah Hawkins t pay yo wages t me, cause Ah knows yuh ain got no sense."

"But, Ma, we needa gun. Pa ain got no gun. We needa gun in the house. Yuh kin never tell whut might happen."

"Now don yuh try to maka fool outta me, boy! Ef we did hava gun, yuh wouldn't have it!"

He laid the catalogue down and slipped his arm around her waist.

"Aw, Ma, Ah done worked hard alla summer n ain ast yuh fer nothin, is Ah, now?"

"Thas whut yuh spose t do!"

"But Ma, Ah wans a gun. Yuh kin lemme have two dollahs outta mah money. Please, Ma. I kin give it to Pa . . . Please, Ma! Ah loves yuh, Ma."

When she spoke her voice came soft and low.

"Whut yu wan wida gun, Dave? Yuh don need no gun. Yuh'll git in trouble. N ef yo pa jus thought Ah let yuh have money t buy a gun he'd hava fit."

"Ah'll hide it, Ma. It ain but two dollahs."

"Lawd, chil, whut's wrong wid yuh?"

"Ain nothin wrong, Ma. Ahm almos a man now. Ah wans a gun."

"Who gonna sell yuh a gun?"

"Ol Joe at the sto."

"N it don cos but two dollahs?"

"Thas all, Ma. Jus two dollahs. Please, Ma."

She was stacking the plates away; her hands moved slowly, reflectively. Dave kept an anxious silence. Finally, she turned to him.

"Ah'll let yuh git tha gun ef yuh promise me one thing."

"Whut's tha, Ma?"

"Yuh bring it straight back t me, yuh hear? It be fer Pa."

"Yessum! Lemme go now, Ma."

She stooped, turned slightly to one side, raised the hem of her dress, rolled down the top of her stocking, and came up with a slender wad of bills.

"Here," she said. "Lawd knows yuh don need no gun. But yer pa does. Yuh bring it right back t me, yuh hear? Ahma put it up. Now ef yuh don, Ahma have yuh pa lick yuh so hard yuh won fergit it."

"Yessum."

He took the money, ran down the steps, and across the yard.

"Dave! Yuuuuuh Daaaaave!"

He heard, but he was not going to stop now. "Naw, Lawd!"

The first movement he made the following morning was to reach under his pillow for the gun. In the gray light of dawn he held it loosely, feeling a sense of power. Could kill a man with a gun like this. Kill anybody, black or white. And if he were holding his gun in his hand, nobody could run over him; they would have to respect him. It was a big gun, with a long barrel and a heavy handle. He raised and lowered it in his hand, marveling at its weight.

He had not come straight home with it as his mother had asked; instead he had stayed out in the fields, holding the weapon in his hand, aiming it now and then at some imaginary foe. But he had not fired it; he had been afraid that his father might hear. Also he was not sure he knew how to fire it.

To avoid surrendering the pistol he had not come into the house until he knew that they were all asleep. When his mother had tiptoed to his bedside late that night and demanded the gun, he had first played possum; then he had told her that the gun was hidden outdoors, that he would bring it to her in the morning. Now he lay turning it slowly in his hands. He broke it,[2] took out the cartridges, felt them, and then put them back.

He slid out of bed, got a long strip of old flannel from a trunk, wrapped the gun in it, and

2. **broke it:** opened the cartridge chamber.

tied it to his naked thigh while it was still loaded. He did not go in to breakfast. Even though it was not yet daylight, he started for Jim Hawkins' plantation. Just as the sun was rising he reached the barns where the mules and plows were kept.

"Hey! That you, Dave?"

He turned. Jim Hawkins stood eying him suspiciously.

"What're yuh doing here so early?"

"Ah didn't know Ah wuz gittin up so early, Mistah Hawkins. Ah wuz fixin t hitch up ol Jenny n take her t the fiels."

"Good. Since you're so early, how about plowing that stretch down by the woods?"

"Suits me, Mistah Hawkins."

"O.K. Go to it!"

He hitched Jenny to a plow and started across the fields. Hot dog! This was just what he wanted. If he could get down by the woods, he could shoot his gun and nobody would hear. He walked behind the plow, hearing the traces[3] creaking, feeling the gun tied tight to his thigh.

When he reached the woods, he plowed two whole rows before he decided to take out the gun. Finally, he stopped, looked in all directions, then untied the gun and held it in his hand. He turned to the mule and smiled.

"Know whut this is, Jenny? Naw, yuh wouldn know! Yuhs jusa ol mule! Anyhow, this is a gun, n it kin shoot, by Gawd!"

He held the gun at arm's length. Whut t hell, Ahma shoot this thing! He looked at Jenny again.

"Lissen here, Jenny! When Ah pull this ol trigger, Ah don wan yuh t run n acka fool now!"

Jenny stood with head down, her short ears pricked straight. Dave walked off about twenty feet, held the gun far out from him at arm's length, and turned his head. Hell, he told himself, Ah ain afraid. The gun felt loose in his fingers; he waved it wildly for a moment. Then he shut his eyes and tightened his forefinger. Bloom! A report half deafened him and he thought his right hand was torn from his arm. He heard Jenny whinnying and galloping over the field, and he found himself on his knees, squeezing his fingers hard between his legs. His hand was numb; he jammed it into his mouth, trying to warm it, trying to stop the pain. The gun lay at his feet. He did not quite know what had happened. He stood up and stared at the gun as though it were a living thing. He gritted his teeth and kicked the gun. Yuh almos broke mah arm! He turned to look for Jenny; she was far over the fields, tossing her head and kicking wildly.

"Hol on there, ol mule!"

When he caught up with her she stood trembling, walling[4] her big white eyes at him. The plow was far away; the traces had broken. Then Dave stopped short, looking, not believing. Jenny was bleeding. Her left side was red and wet with blood. He went closer. Lawd, have mercy! Wondah did Ah shoot this mule? He grabbed for Jenny's mane. She flinched, snorted, whirled, tossing her head.

"Hol on now! Hol on."

Then he saw the hole in Jenny's side, right between the ribs. It was round, wet, red. A crimson stream streaked down the front leg, flowing fast. Good Gawd! Ah wuzn't shootin at tha mule. He felt panic. He knew he had to stop that blood, or Jenny would bleed to death. He had never seen so much blood in all his life. He chased the mule for half a mile, trying to catch her. Finally she stopped, breathing hard, stumpy tail half arched. He caught her mane and led her back to where the plow and gun lay. Then he stooped and grabbed handfuls of damp black earth and tried to plug the bullet hole. Jenny shuddered, whinnied, and broke from him.

"Hol on! Hol on now!"

He tried to plug it again, but blood came anyhow. His fingers were hot and sticky. He rubbed dirt into his palms, trying to dry them. Then again he attempted to plug the bullet hole, but Jenny shied away, kicking her heels high. He stood helpless. He had to do something. He ran

3. **traces:** side straps or chains connecting the mule to the plow.

4. **walling:** rolling.

Roy Stryker Collection, Photographic Archives, University of Louisville, Kentucky, Negative 78.9.534.

at Jenny; she dodged him. He watched a red stream of blood flow down Jenny's leg and form a bright pool at her feet.

"Jenny . . . Jenny," he called weakly.

His lips trembled. She's bleeding t death! He looked in the direction of home, wanting to go back, wanting to get help. But he saw the pistol lying in the damp black clay. He had a queer feeling that if he only did something, this would not be; Jenny would not be there bleeding to death.

When he went to her this time, she did not move. She stood with sleepy, dreamy eyes; and when he touched her she gave a low-pitched whinny and knelt to the ground, her front knees slopping in blood.

"Jenny . . . Jenny . . ." he whispered.

For a long time she held her neck erect; then her head sank, slowly. Her ribs swelled with a mighty heave and she went over.

Dave's stomach felt empty, very empty. He picked up the gun and held it gingerly between his thumb and forefinger. He buried it at the foot of a tree. He took a stick and tried to cover the pool of blood with dirt—but what was the use? There was Jenny lying with her mouth open and her eyes walled and glassy. He could not tell Jim Hawkins he had shot his mule. But he had to tell something. Yeah, Ah'll tell em Jenny started gittin wil n fell on the point of the plow. . . . But that would hardly happen to a mule. He walked across the field slowly, head down.

It was sunset. Two of Jim Hawkins' men were over near the edge of the woods digging a hole in which to bury Jenny. Dave was surrounded by a knot of people, all of whom were looking down at the dead mule.

"I don't see how in the world it happened," said Jim Hawkins for the tenth time.

The crowd parted and Dave's mother, father, and small brother pushed into the center.

"Where Dave?" his mother called.

"There he is," said Jim Hawkins.

His mother grabbed him.

"Whut happened, Dave? Whut yuh done?"

"Nothin."

"C mon, boy, talk," his father said.

Dave took a deep breath and told the story he knew nobody believed.

"Waal," he drawled. "Ah brung ol Jenny down here sos Ah could do mah plowin. Ah plowed bout two rows, just like yuh see." He stopped and pointed at the long rows of upturned earth. "Then somethin musta been wrong wid ol Jenny. She wouldn ack right a-tall. She started snortin n kickin her heels. Ah tried t hol her, but she pulled erway, rearin n goin in. Then when the point of the plow was stickin up in the air, she swung erroun n twisted herself back on it . . . She stuck herself n started t bleed. N fo Ah could do anything, she wuz dead."

"Did you ever hear of anything like that in all your life?" asked Jim Hawkins.

There were white and black standing in the crowd. They murmured. Dave's mother came close to him and looked hard into his face. "Tell the truth, Dave," she said.

"Looks like a bullet hole to me," said one man.

"Dave, whut yuh do wid the gun?" his mother asked.

The crowd surged in, looking at him. He jammed his hands into his pockets, shook his head slowly from left to right, and backed away. His eyes were wide and painful.

"Did he hava gun?" asked Jim Hawkins.

"By Gawd, Ah tol yuh tha wuz a gun wound," said a man, slapping his thigh.

His father caught his shoulders and shook him till his teeth rattled.

"Tell whut happened, yuh rascal! Tell whut . . ."

Dave looked at Jenny's stiff legs and began to cry.

"Whut yuh do wid tha gun?" his mother asked.

"Whut wuz he doin wida gun?" his father asked.

"Come on and tell the truth," said Hawkins. "Ain't nobody going to hurt you . . ."

His mother crowded close to him.

"Did yuh shoot tha mule, Dave?"

Roy Stryker Collection, Photographic Archives, University of Louisville, Kentucky, Negative 78.9.225.

Dave cried, seeing blurred white and black faces.

"Ahh ddinn gggo tt sshooot hher . . . Ah ssswear ffo Gawd Ahh ddin. . . . Ah wuz a-tryin t sssee ef the old gggun would sshoot—"

"Where yuh git the gun from?" his father asked.

"Ah got it from Joe, at the sto."

"Where yuh git the money?"

"Ma give it t me."

"He kept worryin me, Bob. Ah had t. Ah tol im t bring the gun right back t me . . . It was fer yuh, the gun."

"But how yuh happen to shoot that mule?" asked Jim Hawkins.

"Ah wuzn shootin at the mule, Mistah Hawkins. The gun jumped when Ah pulled the trigger . . . N fo Ah knowed anythin Jenny was there a-bleedin."

Somebody in the crowd laughed. Jim Hawkins walked close to Dave and looked into his face.

"Well, looks like you have bought you a mule, Dave."

"Ah swear fo Gawd, Ah didn go t kill the mule, Mistah Hawkins!"

"But you killed her!"

All the crowd was laughing now. They stood on tiptoe and poked heads over one another's shoulders.

"Well, boy, looks like yuh done bought a dead mule! Hahaha!"

"Ain tha ershame."

"Hohohohoho."

Dave stood, head down, twisting his feet in the dirt.

"Well, you needn't worry about it, Bob," said Jim Hawkins to Dave's father. "Just let the boy keep on working and pay me two dollars a month."

"Whut yuh wan fer yo mule, Mistah Hawkins?"

Jim Hawkins screwed up his eyes.

"Fifty dollars."

"Whut yuh do wid tha gun?" Dave's father demanded.

Dave said nothing.

"Yuh wan me t take a tree n beat yuh till yuh talk!"

"Nawsuh!"

"Whut yuh do wid it?"

"Ah throwed it erway."

"Where?"

"Ah . . . Ah throwed it in the creek."

"Waal, c mon home. N firs thing in the mawnin git to tha creek n fin tha gun."

"Yessuh."

"What yuh pay fer it?"

"Two dollahs."

"Take tha gun n git yo money back n carry it t Mistah Hawkins, yuh hear? N don fergit Ahma lam you black bottom good fer this! Now march yosef on home, suh!"

Dave turned and walked slowly. He heard people laughing. Dave glared, his eyes welling with tears. Hot anger bubbled in him. Then he swallowed and stumbled on.

That night Dave did not sleep. He was glad that he had gotten out of killing the mule so easily, but he was hurt. Something hot seemed to turn over inside him each time he remembered how they had laughed. He tossed on his bed, feeling his hard pillow. N Pa says he's gonna beat me . . . He remembered other beatings, and his back quivered. Naw, naw, Ah sho don wan im t beat me tha way no mo. Dam em all! Nobody ever gave him anything. All he did was work. They treat me like a mule, n then they beat me. He gritted his teeth. N Ma had t tell on me.

Well, if he had to, he would take old man Hawkins that two dollars. But that meant selling the gun. And he wanted to keep that gun. Fifty dollars for a dead mule.

He turned over, thinking how he had fired the gun. He had an itch to fire it again. Ef other men kin shoota gun, by Gawd, Ah kin! He was still, listening. Mebbe they all sleepin now. The house was still. He heard the soft breathing of his brother. Yes, now! He would go down and get that gun and see if he could fire it! He eased out of bed and slipped into overalls.

The moon was bright. He ran almost all the way to the edge of the woods. He stumbled over the ground, looking for the spot where he had buried the gun. Yeah, here it is. Like a hungry dog scratching for a bone, he pawed it up. He puffed his black cheeks and blew dirt from the trigger and barrel. He broke it and found four cartridges unshot. He looked around; the fields were filled with silence and moonlight. He clutched the gun stiff and hard in his fingers. But, as soon as he wanted to pull the trigger, he shut his eyes and turned his head. Naw, Ah can't shoot wid mah eyes closed n mah head turned. With effort he held his eyes open; then he squeezed. *Blooooom!* He was stiff, not breathing. The gun was still in his hands. Dammit, he'd done it. He fired again. *Blooooom!* He smiled. *Blooooom! Blooooom! Click, click.* There! It was empty. If anybody could shoot a gun, he could. He put the gun into his hip pocket and started across the fields.

When he reached the top of a ridge he stood straight and proud in the moonlight, looking at Jim Hawkins' big white house, feeling the gun sagging in his pocket. Lawd, ef Ah had just one mo bullet Ah'd taka shot at tha house. Ah'd like t scare ol man Hawkins jusa little . . . Jusa enough t let im know Dave Saunders is a man.

To his left the road curved, running to the tracks of the Illinois Central. He jerked his head, listening. From far off came a faint *hoooof-hoooof; hoooof-hoooof; hoooof-hoooof.* . . . He stood rigid. Two dollahs a mont. Les see now . . . Tha means it'll take bout two years. Shucks! Ah'll be dam!

He started down the road, toward the tracks. Yeah, here she comes! He stood beside the track and held himself stiffly. Here she comes, erroun the ben . . . C mon, yuh slow poke! C mon! He had his hand on his gun; something quivered in his stomach. Then the train thundered past, the gray and brown box cars rumbling and clinking. He gripped the gun tightly; then he jerked his hand out of his pocket. Ah betcha Bill wouldn't do it! Ah betcha . . . The cars slid past, steel grinding upon steel. Ahm ridin yuh ternight, so hep me Gawd! He was hot all over. He hesitated just a moment; then he grabbed, pulled atop of a car, and lay flat. He felt his pocket; the gun was still there. Ahead the long rails were glinting in the moonlight, stretching away, away to somewhere, somewhere where he could be a man . . . .❖

RESPONDING OPTIONS

FROM PERSONAL RESPONSE *TO* CRITICAL ANALYSIS

REFLECT 1. What do you think about the ending of this story? Write your ideas in your notebook.

RETHINK 2. How do you judge the decisions that Dave makes during the story? Consult the notes you made as you read.

3. Consider the thoughts about adulthood that you wrote down for the Personal Connection. Does Dave behave like an adult at any time during this story? Support your opinion with evidence from the story.

4. Does owning a gun give Dave what he wants? Explain why you think so.

   Consider
   - why Dave wants to own a gun
   - how he handles the responsibility of owning a gun
   - how others treat him after he buys a gun
   - how he deals with the consequences of his actions

5. Do you feel sorry for Dave? Explain why or why not. How do you think Richard Wright feels about him?

RELATE 6. What do you predict might happen to Dave after the end of the story?

7. Do you think any teenagers today feel, like Dave, that owning a gun will make them more grown-up? Why is this attitude a problem?

LITERARY LINKS

Think about James Baldwin's advice to his nephew in "My Dungeon Shook: Letter to My Nephew" on page 791. What advice do you think Baldwin might have for Dave Saunders?

ANOTHER PATHWAY

Cooperative Learning

Do you think Dave is merely a victim of circumstances, or is he primarily responsible for what happens to him? Work with a small group and fill out a chart to analyze what causes the main events in the story. Share your ideas with the class.

Causes	Events
Dave wants to be treated like an adult.	He buys a gun.

QUICKWRITES

1. What does it mean to be an adult? Write a **definition** of adulthood based on your reading of this story and on your own observations and experiences. Share your definition with the class.

2. At the end of the story, Dave hops on a train to go "somewhere where he could be a man." Write the **letter** that Dave might eventually send to his family.

3. Write a short **cause-and-effect analysis** in which you examine the decisions that Dave makes in this story and the effects, or consequences, of those decisions.

PORTFOLIO Save your writing. You may want to use it later as a springboard to a piece for your portfolio.

LITERARY CONCEPTS

Irony is the modernist's tool for revealing the truth in a fictional work, and Wright's story drips with irony, from the title to the last sentence. In **verbal irony,** someone states one thing and means another. For example, if you say "Man, I'm doing really *great* today!" after fumbling the ball several times, you're speaking ironically. Analyze the verbal irony in the title of this story. What two meanings of the word *man* does Wright use to underscore the irony of the phrase?

CONCEPT REVIEW: Situational Irony Discuss the many instances of situational irony in this story. For example, look at the ways in which owning a gun backfires, so to speak, on Dave. What opportunities for proving his manhood exist in the story? Which of those opportunities are lost? Why?

CRITIC'S CORNER

In his autobiography *Black Boy,* Wright says he began to realize the power of the printed word when he read *A Book of Prefaces* by H. L. Mencken. Referring to Mencken, Wright explained: "Yes, this man was fighting, fighting with words. He was using words as a weapon, using them as one would use a club. Could words be weapons? Well, yes, for here they were. Then, maybe, perhaps, I could use them as a weapon?" Do you think Wright uses words as weapons in this story? If so, what do you think he is fighting for or against? Cite examples from the story to support your opinions.

THE WRITER'S STYLE

In this story, Wright uses **third-person limited point of view,** a narrative perspective used by many modernist fiction writers. He also uses **dialect** to capture the way his characters speak. Reread the first paragraph of the story, and notice the way Wright weaves dialect into his narration. Point out where the narration stops and Dave's thoughts begin. With a partner, read the first paragraph aloud, with one of you reading the narration and the other reading Dave's thoughts. What effect does Wright achieve by setting up his story this way? What if Dave's thoughts were not written in dialect? What if Dave's thoughts were not included in the story at all? Discuss these questions with your classmates.

ALTERNATIVE ACTIVITIES

1. Wright uses dialect to bring the characters in his story to life. To appreciate the full effect of this use of dialect, work with a small group of classmates to plan and present a **dramatic reading** of this story.
2. This story was first published in *Harper's Bazaar* under the title "Almos' a Man." Imagine you are an artist who has been asked to illustrate the story for the magazine. Create a simple **pen-and-ink drawing** that captures the mood or the theme of the story. Post your artwork on a classroom bulletin board.

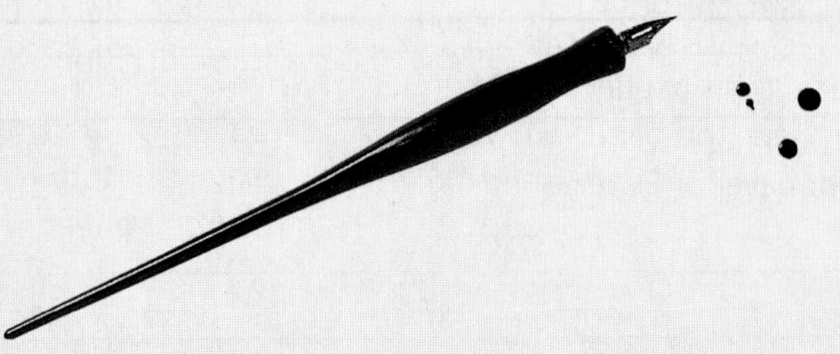

ACROSS THE CURRICULUM

Economics Look back at the story to find out how much Dave is paid each month to work in Mr. Hawkins's fields. If Dave were a teenager today, how long would he have to work to buy the following items: a pair of sneakers, a CD or tape, a meal at a fast-food restaurant, a concert ticket? Record your findings in a chart or a graph.

Item	Cost
Pair of sneakers	
CD or Tape	
Fast Food	
Concert Ticket	

RICHARD WRIGHT

1908–1960

Richard Wright, the son of a poor sharecropper, was born in Mississippi. He endured a childhood marked by gnawing hunger, physical beatings, and an intense internal struggle against the religious and racial restrictions imposed on him by his family and his culture. To escape the poverty of the rural South, his father moved the family to Memphis, Tennessee. Unable to find work, however, Wright's frustrated father abandoned the family, and Wright was raised by his ailing mother and later by his stern grandmother. Often left alone while his relatives worked, Wright encountered the violence of the ghetto streets at age 6. He wrote later that it was only through books that he managed to stay alive, books that he obtained by borrowing a white man's library card. (Black people were not allowed to own library cards at the time.)

Escaping to Chicago at age 19, Wright held a series of odd jobs until he joined the Depression-era Federal Writers' Project to write a guidebook about Illinois. While he was living in Chicago, he joined the Communist Party, and he remained a member until 1944. After Wright moved to New York City in 1937, he became the Harlem editor of the Communist *Daily Worker.* He eventually settled in Paris, where he lived from 1947 until his death.

Wright's first story was published in an African-American newspaper when he was 15. After winning first prize in a contest sponsored by *Story* magazine, he published his first collection of stories, *Uncle Tom's Children*. Two years later, in 1940, Wright gained international fame for his novel *Native Son.* His fiction and his autobiographies, *Black Boy* and *American Hunger,* expose the brutal racism in American life.

OTHER WORKS *Lawd Today; The Outsider; White Man, Listen!*

LASERLINKS
• *ART GALLERY*

PREVIEWING

DRAMA

The Long Christmas Dinner

Thornton Wilder

PERSONAL CONNECTION

In this play, Thornton Wilder depicts the Christmas dinners of the Bayard family over the course of 90 years. Think about the family gathering or holiday that you enjoy most. What family traditions and people do you associate with this celebration? Describe this family gathering in your notebook.

LITERARY CONNECTION

During the late 19th and early 20th centuries, realism was the predominant dramatic style. By means of realistic sets, costumes, and dialogue, playwrights attempted to create the illusion that what was happening on the stage was an exact replica of real life. Thornton Wilder, like other modernists, rejected such traditions in favor of something new. In *The Long Christmas Dinner,* written in 1930, he calls for few props, no curtain, and minimal scenery and costumes. Moreover, he compresses 90 years of family gatherings into one short, continuous act in which events flow into one another. By abandoning the conventions of realistic drama, Wilder demanded that those in his audience use their imagination to provide the setting and fill in the time gaps. In this way, he hoped to visibly represent on stage the drama of "pure existing," as he called it, free from unnecessary details.

READING CONNECTION

Analyzing Sequence of Events In this play what happens to succeeding generations of the Bayard family is represented in accelerated motion, without any delineation between the different time periods. To keep track of the sequence of events mentioned during the family gatherings, make a time line like the one shown and fill it out as you read. Pay particular attention to how the members of the family deal with the changes in their lives.

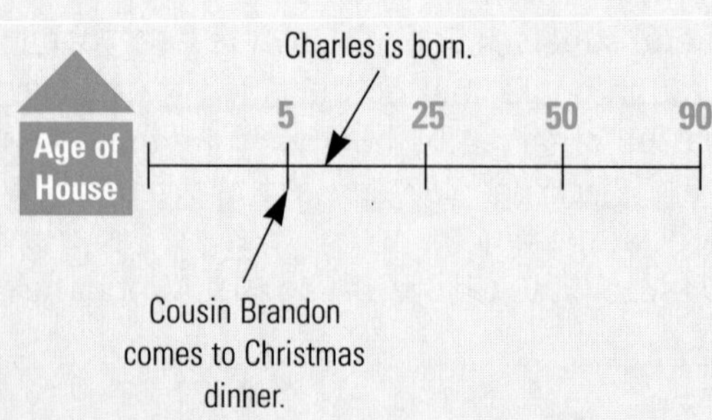

The Long Christmas Dinner

Thornton Wilder

CAST OF CHARACTERS

Mother Bayard
Roderick, her son
Lucia
Cousin Brandon
Charles, Roderick and Lucia's son
Genevieve, Roderick and Lucia's daughter
Leonora Banning
Sam, Charles and Leonora's older son
Lucia, Charles and Leonora's daughter
Roderick, Charles and Leonora's younger son
Cousin Ermengarde

Setting: The dining room of the Bayard home. Close to the footlights a long dining table is handsomely spread for Christmas dinner. The carver's place with a great turkey before it is at the spectator's right.

A door, left back, leads into the hall.

At the extreme left, by the proscenium pillar, is a strange portal trimmed with garlands of fruits and flowers. Directly opposite is another edged and hung with black velvet. The portals denote birth and death.

Ninety years are to be traversed in this play which represents in accelerated motion ninety Christmas dinners in the Bayard household. The actors are dressed in inconspicuous clothes and must indicate their gradual increase in years through their acting. Most of them carry wigs of white hair which they adjust upon their heads at the indicated moment, simply and without comment. The ladies may have shawls concealed beneath the table that they gradually draw up about their shoulders as they grow older.

Throughout the play the characters continue eating imaginary food with imaginary knives and forks.

There is no curtain. The audience arriving at the theatre sees the stage set and the table laid, though still in partial darkness. Gradually the lights in the auditorium become dim and the stage brightens until sparkling winter sunlight streams through the dining room windows.

WORDS TO KNOW **traverse** (trə-vûrs') *v.* to pass over or through

Enter Lucia. *She inspects the table, touching here a knife and there a fork. She talks to a servant girl who is invisible to us.*

Lucia. I reckon we're ready now, Gertrude. We won't ring the chimes today. I'll just call them myself. (*She goes into the hall and calls*) Roderick. Mother Bayard. We're all ready. Come to dinner.

(*Enter* Roderick *pushing* Mother Bayard *in a wheelchair.*)

Mother Bayard. . . . and a new horse, too, Roderick. I used to think that only the wicked owned two horses. A new horse and a new house and a new wife!

Roderick. Well, Mother, how do you like it? Our first Christmas dinner in the new house, hey?

Mother Bayard. Tz-Tz-Tz! I don't know what your father would say!

Lucia. Here, Mother Bayard, you sit between us.

(Roderick *says grace.*)

Mother Bayard. My dear Lucia, I can remember when there were still Indians on this very ground, and I wasn't a young girl either. I can remember when we had to cross the Mississippi on a new-made raft. I can remember when St. Louis and Kansas City were full of Indians.

Lucia (*tying a napkin around* Mother Bayard's *neck*). Imagine that! There!—What a wonderful day for our first Christmas dinner: a beautiful sunny morning, snow, a splendid sermon. Dr. McCarthy preaches a splendid sermon. I cried and cried.

Roderick (*extending an imaginary carving fork*). Come now, what'll you have, Mother? A little sliver of white?

Lucia. Every least twig is wrapped around with ice. You almost never see that. Can I cut it up for you, dear? (*over her shoulder*) Gertrude, I forgot the jelly. You know,—on the top shelf.—Mother Bayard, I found your mother's gravy boat while we were moving. What was her name, dear? What were all your names? You were . . . a . . . Genevieve Wainright. Now your mother—

Mother Bayard. Yes, you must write it down somewhere. I was Genevieve Wainright. My mother was Faith Morrison. She was the daughter of a farmer in New Hampshire who was something of a blacksmith too. And she married young John Wainright—

Lucia (*memorizing on her fingers*). Genevieve Wainright. Faith Morrison.

Roderick. It's all down in a book somewhere upstairs. We have it all. All that kind of thing is very interesting. Come, Lucia, just a little wine. Mother, a little red wine for Christmas day. Full of iron. "Take a little wine for thy stomach's sake."

Lucia. Really, I can't get used to wine! What would my father say? But I suppose it's all right.

(*Enter* Cousin Brandon *from the hall. He takes his place by* Lucia.)

Cousin Brandon (*rubbing his hands*). Well, well, I smell turkey. My dear cousins, I can't tell you how pleasant it is to be having Christmas dinner with you all. I've lived out there in Alaska so long without relatives. Let me see, how long have you had this new house, Roderick?

Roderick. Why, it must be . . .

Mother Bayard. Five years. It's five years, children. You should keep a diary. This is your sixth Christmas dinner here.

Lucia. Think of that, Roderick. We feel as though we had lived here twenty years.

Cousin Brandon. At all events it still looks as good as new.

Roderick (*over his carving*). What'll you have, Brandon, light or dark?—Frieda, fill up Cousin Brandon's glass.

Lucia. Oh, dear, I can't get used to these wines. I don't know what my father'd say, I'm sure. What'll you have Mother Bayard?

(*During the following speeches* Mother Bayard's *chair, without any visible propulsion, starts to draw away from the table, turns toward the right, and slowly goes toward the dark portal.*)

Mother Bayard. Yes, I can remember when there were Indians on this very land.

Lucia (*softly*). Mother Bayard hasn't been very well lately, Roderick.

Mother Bayard. My mother was a Faith Morrison. And in New Hampshire she married a young John Wainright, who was a Congregational minister. He saw her in his congregation one day . . .

Lucia. Mother Bayard, hadn't you better lie down, dear?

Mother Bayard. . . . and right in the middle of his sermon he said to himself: "I'll marry that girl." And he did, and I'm their daughter.

Lucia (*half rising and looking after her with anxiety*). Just a little nap, dear?

Mother Bayard. I'm all right. Just go on with your dinner. I was ten, and I said to my brother—

(*She goes out. A very slight pause.*)

Cousin Brandon. It's too bad it's such a cold dark day today. We almost need the lamps. I spoke to Major Lewis for a moment after church. His sciatica[1] troubles him, but he does pretty well.

Lucia (*dabbing her eyes*). I know Mother Bayard wouldn't want us to grieve for her on Christmas day, but I can't forget her sitting in her wheelchair right beside us, only a year ago. And she would be so glad to know our good news.

Roderick (*patting her hand*). Now, now. It's Christmas. (*Formally*) Cousin Brandon, a glass of wine with you, sir.

Cousin Brandon (*half rising, lifting his glass gallantly*). A glass of wine with you, sir.

Lucia. Does the Major's sciatica cause him much pain?

Cousin Brandon. Some, perhaps. But you know his way. He says it'll be all the same in a hundred years.

Lucia. Yes, he's a great philosopher.

Roderick. His wife sends you a thousand thanks for her Christmas present.

Lucia. I forget what I gave her.—Oh, yes, the workbasket!

(*Through the entrance of birth comes a nurse wheeling a perambulator*[2] *trimmed with blue ribbons.* Lucia *rushes toward it, the men following.*)

O my wonderful new baby, my darling baby! Who ever saw such a child! Quick, nurse, a boy or a girl? A boy! Roderick, what shall we call him? Really, nurse, you've never seen such a child!

Roderick. We'll call him Charles after your father and grandfather.

Lucia. But there are no Charleses in the Bible, Roderick.

Roderick. Of course, there are. Surely there are.

Lucia. Roderick!—Very well, but he will always be Samuel to me.—What miraculous hands he has! Really, they are the most beautiful hands in the world. All right, nurse. Have a good nap, my darling child.

Roderick. Don't drop him, nurse. Brandon and I need him in our firm.

(*Exit nurse and perambulator into the hall. The others return to their chairs,* Lucia *taking the place left vacant by* Mother Bayard *and* Cousin Brandon *moving up beside her.* Cousin Brandon *puts on his white hair.*)

Lucia, a little white meat? Some stuffing? Cranberry sauce, anybody?

Lucia (*over her shoulder*). Margaret, the stuffing is very good today.—Just a little, thank you.

Roderick. Now something to wash it down. (*half rising*) Cousin Brandon, a glass of wine with you, sir. To the ladies, God bless them.

Lucia. Thank you, kind sirs.

Cousin Brandon. Pity it's such an overcast day today. And no snow.

Lucia. But the sermon was lovely. I cried and cried. Dr. Spaulding does preach such a splendid sermon.

---

1. **sciatica** (sī-ăt′ĭ-kə): pain in the hip, thigh, and leg.
2. **perambulator** (pə-răm′byə-lā′tər): a baby carriage.

Roderick. I saw Major Lewis for a moment after church. He says his rheumatism comes and goes. His wife says she has something for Charles and will bring it over this afternoon.

(*Enter nurse again with perambulator. Pink ribbons. Same rush toward the left.*)

Lucia. O my lovely new baby! Really, it never occurred to me that it might be a girl. Why, nurse, she's perfect.

Roderick. Now call her what you choose. It's your turn.

Lucia. Looloolooloo. Aië. Aië. Yes, this time I shall have my way. She shall be called Genevieve after your mother. Have a good nap, my treasure. (*She looks after it as the nurse wheels the perambulator into the hall.*) Imagine! Sometime she'll be grown up and say "Good morning, Mother. Good morning, Father." Really, Cousin Brandon, you don't find a baby like that every day.

Cousin Brandon. *And* the new factory.

Lucia. A new factory? Really? Roderick, I shall be very uncomfortable if we're going to turn out to be rich. I've been afraid of that for years.—However, we mustn't talk about such things on Christmas day. I'll just take a little piece of white meat, thank you. Roderick, Charles is destined for the ministry. I'm sure of it.

Roderick. Woman, he's only twelve. Let him have a free mind. *We* want him in the firm, I don't mind saying. Anyway, no time passes as slowly as this when you're waiting for your urchins to grow up and settle down to business.

Lucia. I don't want time to go any faster, thank you. I love the children just as they are.—Really, Roderick, you know what the doctor said: One glass a meal. (*putting her hand over his glass*) No, Margaret, that will be all.

(Roderick *rises, glass in hand. With a look of dismay on his face he takes a few steps toward the dark portal.*)

Roderick. Now I wonder what's the matter with me.

Lucia. Roderick, do be reasonable.

Roderick (*tottering, but with gallant irony*). But, my dear, statistics show that we steady, moderate drinkers . . .

Lucia (*rises, gazing at him in anguish*). Roderick! My dear! What . . . ?

Roderick (*returns to his seat with a frightened look of relief*). Well, it's fine to be back at table with you again. How many good Christmas dinners have I had to miss upstairs? And to be back at a fine bright one, too.

Lucia. O my dear, you gave us a very alarming time! Here's your glass of milk.—Josephine, bring Mr. Bayard his medicine from the cupboard in the library.

Roderick. At all events, now that I'm better I'm going to start doing something about the house.

Lucia. Roderick! You're not going to change the house?

Roderick. Only touch it up here and there. It looks a hundred years old.

(Charles *enters casually from the hall. He kisses his mother's hair and sits down.*)

Lucia. Charles, you carve the turkey, dear. Your father's not well.—You always said you hated carving, though you *are* so clever at it.

(*Father and son exchange places.*)

Charles. It's a great blowy morning, Mother. The wind comes over the hill like a lot of cannon.

Lucia. And such a good sermon. I cried and cried. Mother Bayard loved a good sermon so. And she used to sing the Christmas hymns all around the year. Oh, dear, oh, dear, I've been thinking of her all morning!

Roderick. Sh, Mother. It's Christmas day. You mustn't think of such things.—You mustn't be depressed.

Lucia. But sad things aren't the same as depressing things. I must be getting old: I like them.

Charles. Uncle Brandon, you haven't anything to

eat. Pass his plate, Hilda . . . and some cranberry sauce . . .

(*Enter* Genevieve. *She kisses her father's temple and sits down.*)

Genevieve. It's glorious. Every least twig is wrapped around with ice. You almost never see that.

Lucia. Did you have time to deliver those presents after church, Genevieve?

Genevieve. Yes, Mama. Old Mrs. Lewis sends you a thousand thanks for hers. It was just what she wanted, she said. Give me lots, Charles, lots.

Roderick (*rising and starting toward the dark portal*). Statistics, ladies and gentlemen, show that we steady, moderate . . .

Charles. How about a little skating this afternoon, Father?

Roderick. I'll live till I'm ninety.

Lucia. I really don't think he ought to go skating.

Roderick (*at the very portal, suddenly astonished*). Yes, but . . . but . . . not yet!

(*He goes out.*)

Lucia (*dabbing her eyes*). He was so young and so clever, Cousin Brandon. (*raising her voice for* Cousin Brandon's *deafness*) I say he was so young and so clever.—Never forget your father, children. He was a good man.—Well, he wouldn't want us to grieve for him today.

Charles. White or dark, Genevieve? Just another sliver, Mother?

Lucia (*putting on her white hair*). I can remember our first Christmas dinner in this house, Genevieve. Twenty-five years ago today. Mother Bayard was sitting here in her wheelchair. She could remember when Indians lived on this very spot and when she had to cross the river on a new-made raft.

Charles and **Genevieve.** She couldn't have, Mother. That can't be true.

Lucia. It certainly was true—even I can remember when there was only one paved street. We were very happy to walk on boards. (*Louder, to* Cousin Brandon) We can remember when there were no sidewalks, can't we, Cousin Brandon?

Cousin Brandon (*delighted*). Oh, yes! And those were the days.

Charles and **Genevieve** (*Sotto voce.*[3] *This is a family refrain.*) Those were the days.

Lucia. . . . and the ball last night, Genevieve? Did you have a nice time? I hope you didn't *waltz,* dear. I think a girl in your position ought to set an example. Did Charles keep an eye on you?

Genevieve. He had none left. They were all on Leonora Banning. He can't conceal it any longer, Mother. I think he's engaged to marry Leonora Banning.

Charles. I'm not engaged to marry anyone.

Lucia. Well, she's very pretty.

Genevieve. I shall never marry, Mother—I shall sit in this house beside you forever, as though life were one long, happy Christmas dinner.

Lucia. O my child, you mustn't say such things!

Genevieve (*playfully*). You don't want me? You don't want me? (Lucia *bursts into tears.*) Why, Mother, how silly you are! There's nothing sad about that—what could possibly be sad about that.

Lucia (*drying her eyes*). Forgive me. I'm just unpredictable, that's all.

(Charles *goes to the door and leads in* Leonora Banning.)

Leonora (*kissing* Lucia's *temple*). Good morning, Mother Bayard. Good morning, everybody. It's really a splendid Christmas day today.

Charles. Little white meat? Genevieve, Mother, Leonora?

Leonora. Every least twig is encircled with ice.—You never see that.

Charles (*shouting*). Uncle Brandon, another?—Rogers, fill my uncle's glass.

Lucia (*to* Charles). Do what your father used to

3. *sotto voce* (sŏt′ō vō′chē): in a low tone; privately.

do. It would please Cousin Brandon so. You know—(*pretending to raise a glass*)—"Uncle Brandon, a glass of wine—"

Charles (*rising*). Uncle Brandon, a glass of wine with you, sir.

Brandon. A glass of wine with you, sir. To the ladies, God bless them every one.

The Ladies. Thank you, kind sirs.

Genevieve. And if I go to Germany for my music I promise to be back for Christmas. I wouldn't miss that.

Lucia. I hate to think of you over there all alone in those strange pensions.[4]

Genevieve. But, darling, the time will pass so fast that you'll hardly know I'm gone. I'll be back in the twinkling of an eye.

(*Enter Left, the nurse and perambulator. Green ribbons.*)

Leonora. Oh, what an angel! The darlingest baby in the world. Do let me hold it, nurse.

(*But the nurse resolutely wheels the perambulator across the stage and out the dark door.*)

Oh, I did love it so!

(Lucia *goes to her, puts her arm around* Leonora's *shoulders, and they encircle the room whispering*—Lucia *then hands her over to* Charles *who conducts her on the same circuit.*)

Genevieve (*as her mother sits down, softly*). Isn't there anything I can do?

Lucia (*raises her eyebrows, ruefully*). No, dear. Only time, only the passing of time can help in these things.

(Charles *and* Leonora *return to the table.*)

Don't you think we could ask Cousin Ermengarde to come and live with us here? There's plenty for everyone and there's no reason why she should go on teaching the first grade for ever and ever. She wouldn't be in the way, would she, Charles?

Charles. No, I think it would be fine.—A little more potato and gravy, anybody? A little more turkey, Mother?

(Brandon *rises and starts slowly toward the dark portal.* Lucia *rises and stands for a moment with her face in her hands.*)

Cousin Brandon (*muttering*). It was great to be in Alaska in those days . . .

Genevieve (*half rising, and gazing at her mother in fear*). Mother, what is . . . ?

Lucia (*hurriedly*). Hush, my dear. It will pass.—Hold fast to your music, you know. (*as* Genevieve *starts toward her*) No, no. I want to be alone for a few minutes.

(*She turns and starts after* Cousin Brandon *toward the Right.*)

Charles. If the Republicans collected all their votes instead of going off into cliques among themselves, they might prevent his getting a second term.

Genevieve. Charles, Mother doesn't tell us, but she hasn't been very well these days.

4. **pensions** (päɴ-syônz′): boarding houses in Europe.

Charles. Come, Mother, we'll go to Florida for a few weeks.

(*Exit* Brandon.)

Lucia (*smiling at* Genevieve *and waving her hand*). Don't be foolish. Don't grieve.

(*She clasps her hands under her chin; her lips move, whispering; she walks* serenely *into the portal.* Genevieve *stares after her, frozen. At the same moment the nurse and perambulator enter from the Left. Pale yellow ribbons.* Leonora *rushes to it.*)

Leonora. O my darlings . . . twins . . . Charles, aren't they glorious! Look at them. Look at them.

Genevieve (*sinks down on the table, her face buried in her arms*). But what will I do? What's left for me to do?

Charles (*bending over the basket*). Which is which?

Leonora. I feel as though I were the first mother who ever had twins.—Look at them now!—But why wasn't Mother Bayard allowed to stay and see them!

Genevieve (*rising suddenly distraught, loudly*). I don't want to go on. I can't bear it.

Charles (*Goes to her quickly. They sit down. He whispers to her earnestly, taking both her hands*). But Genevieve, Genevieve! How frightfully Mother would feel to think that . . . Genevieve!

Genevieve (*shaking her head wildly*). I never told her how wonderful she was. We all treated her as though she were just a friend in the house. I thought she'd be here forever.

Leonora (*timidly*). Genevieve darling, do come one minute and hold my babies' hands. We shall call the girl Lucia after her grandmother,—will that please you? Do just see what adorable little hands they have.

WORDS TO KNOW **serenely** (sə-rēn′lē) *adv.* peacefully; calmly

(Genevieve *collects herself and goes over to the perambulator. She smiles brokenly into the basket.*)

Genevieve. They are wonderful, Leonora.

Leonora. Give him your finger, darling. Just let him hold it.

Charles. And we'll call the boy Samuel.—Well, now everybody come and finish your dinners. Don't drop them, nurse; at least don't drop the boy. We need him in the firm.

Leonora (*stands looking after them as the nurse wheels them into the hall*). Someday they'll be big. Imagine! They'll come in and say "Hello, Mother!" (*She makes clucking noises of rapturous consternation.*)[5]

Charles. Come, a little wine, Leonora, Genevieve? Full of iron. Eduardo, fill the ladies' glasses. It certainly is a keen, cold morning. I used to go skating with Father on mornings like this and Mother would come back from church saying—

Genevieve (*dreamily*). I know: saying "Such a splendid sermon. I cried and cried."

Leonora. Why did she cry, dear?

Genevieve. That generation all cried at sermons. It was their way.

Leonora. Really, Genevieve?

Genevieve. They had had to go since they were children and I suppose sermons reminded them of their fathers and mothers, just as Christmas dinners do us. Especially in an old house like this.

Leonora. It really is pretty old, Charles. And so ugly, with all that ironwork filigree[6] and that dreadful cupola.[7]

Genevieve. Charles! You aren't going to change the house!

Charles. No, no. I won't give up the house, but great heavens! It's fifty years old. This Spring we'll remove the cupola and build a new wing toward the tennis courts.

(*From now on* Genevieve *is seen to change. She sits up more straightly. The corners of her mouth become fixed. She becomes a forthright and slightly disillusioned spinster.* Charles *becomes the plain businessman and a little pompous.*)[8]

Leonora. And then couldn't we ask your dear old Cousin Ermengarde to come and live with us? She's really the self-effacing kind.

Charles. Ask her now. Take her out of the first grade.

Genevieve. We only seem to think of it on Christmas day with her Christmas card staring us in the face.

(*Enter Left, nurse and perambulator. Blue ribbons.*)

Leonora. Another boy! Another boy! Here's a Roderick for you at last.

Charles. Roderick Brandon Bayard. A regular little fighter.

Leonora. Goodbye, darling. Don't grow up too fast. Yes, yes. Aië, aië, aië—stay just as you are.—Thank you, nurse.

Genevieve (*who has not left the table, repeats dryly*). Stay just as you are.

(*Exit nurse and perambulator. The others return to their places.*)

Leonora. Now I have three children. One, two, three. Two boys and a girl. I'm collecting them. It's very exciting. (*over her shoulder*) What, Hilda? Oh, Cousin Ermengarde's come! Come in, Cousin.

(*She goes to the hall and welcomes* Cousin Ermengarde *who already wears her white hair.*)

Ermengarde (*shyly*). It's such a pleasure to be with you all.

Charles (*pulling out her chair for her*). The twins

5. **rapturous consternation** (răp′chər-əs kŏn′stər-nā′shən): joyous anxiety.
6. **filigree:** delicate, lacelike ornamental work.
7. **cupola** (kyo͞o′pə-lə): a small dome or tower on a roof.
8. **pompous** (pŏm′pəs): characterized by excessive self-esteem or exaggerated dignity.

WORDS TO KNOW **self-effacing** (sĕlf′ĭ-fā′sĭng) *adj.* keeping oneself modestly in the background have taken a great fancy to you already, Cousin.

Leonora. The baby went to her at once.

Charles. Exactly how are we related, Cousin Ermengarde?—There, Genevieve, that's your specialty.—First a little more turkey and stuffing, Mother? Cranberry sauce, anybody?

Genevieve. I can work it out: Grandmother Bayard was your . . .

Ermengarde. Your Grandmother Bayard was a second cousin of my Grandmother Haskins through the Wainrights.

Charles. Well, it's all in a book somewhere upstairs. All that kind of thing is awfully interesting.

Genevieve. Nonsense. There are no such books. I collect my notes off gravestones, and you have to scrape a good deal of moss—let me tell you—to find one great-grandparent.

Charles. There's a story that my Grandmother Bayard crossed the Mississippi on a raft before there were any bridges or ferryboats. She died before Genevieve or I were born. Time certainly goes very fast in a great new country like this. Have some more cranberry sauce, Cousin Ermengarde.

Ermengarde (*timidly*). Well, time must be passing very slowly in Europe with this dreadful, dreadful war going on.

Charles. Perhaps an occasional war isn't so bad after all. It clears up a lot of poisons that collect in nations. It's like a boil.

Ermengarde. Oh, dear, oh, dear!

Charles (*with relish*). Yes, it's like a boil.—Ho! ho! Here are your twins.

(*The twins appear at the door into the hall.* Sam *is wearing the uniform of an ensign*[9]. Lucia *is fussing over some detail on it.*)

Lucia. Isn't he wonderful in it, Mother?

Charles. Let's get a look at you.

Sam. Mother, don't let Roderick fool with my stamp album while I'm gone.

Leonora. Now, Sam, do write a letter once in a while. Do be a good boy about that, mind.

Sam. You might send some of those cakes of yours once in a while, Cousin Ermengarde.

Ermengarde (*in a flutter*). I certainly will, my dear boy.

Charles. If you need any money, we have agents in Paris and London, remember.

Sam. Well, goodbye . . .

(Sam *goes briskly out through the dark portal, tossing his unneeded white hair through the door before him.* Lucia *sits down at the table with lowered eyes.*)

Ermengarde (*after a slight pause, in a low, constrained voice, making conversation*). I spoke to Mrs. Fairchild for a moment coming out of church. Her rheumatism's a little better, she says. She sends you her warmest thanks for the Christmas present. The workbasket, wasn't it?—It was an admirable sermon. And our stained-glass window looked so beautiful, Leonora, so beautiful. Everybody spoke of it and so affectionately of Sammy. (Leonora's *hand goes to her mouth.*) Forgive me, Leonora, but it's better to speak of him than not to speak of him when we're all thinking of him so hard.

Leonora (*rising, in anguish*). He was a mere boy. He was a mere boy, Charles.

Charles. My dear, my dear.

Leonora. I want to tell him how wonderful he was. We let him go so casually. I want to tell him how we all feel about him.—Forgive me, let me walk about a minute.—Yes, of course, Ermengarde—it's best to speak of him.

Lucia (*in a low voice to* Genevieve). Isn't there anything I can do?

9. **ensign** (ĕn′sən): the lowest commissioned officer in the U.S. Navy.

WORDS TO KNOW **constrained** (kən-strānd′) *adj.* stiff and unnatural; forced **constrain** *v.*

Genevieve. No, no. Only time, only the passing of time can help in these things.

(Leonora, *straying about the room, finds herself near the door to the hall at the moment that her son* Roderick *enters. He links his arm with hers and leads her back to the table.*)

Roderick. What's the matter, anyway? What are you all so glum about? The skating was fine today.

Charles. Sit down, young man. I have something to say to you.

Roderick. Everybody was there. Lucia skated in the corners with Dan Creighton the whole time. When'll it be, Lucia, when'll it be?

Lucia. I don't know what you mean.

Roderick. Lucia's leaving us soon, Mother. Dan Creighton, of all people.

Charles (*ominously*). Roderick, I have something to say to you.

Roderick. Yes, Father.

Charles. Is it true, Roderick, that you made yourself conspicuous last night at the Country Club—at a Christmas Eve dance, too?

Leonora. Not now, Charles. I beg of you. This is Christmas dinner.

Roderick (*loudly*). No, I didn't.

Lucia. Really, Father, he didn't. It was that dreadful Johnny Lewis.

Charles. I don't want to hear about Johnny Lewis. I want to know whether a son of mine . . .

Leonora. Charles, I beg of you . . .

Charles. The first family of this city!

Roderick (*rising*). I hate this town and everything about it. I always did.

Charles. You behaved like a spoiled puppy, sir, an ill-bred spoiled puppy.

Roderick. What did I do? What did I do that was wrong?

Charles. You were drunk and you were rude to the daughters of my best friends.

Genevieve (*striking the table*). Nothing in the world deserves an ugly scene like this. Charles, I'm ashamed of you.

Roderick. Great God, you gotta get drunk in this town to forget how dull it is. Time passes so slowly here that it stands still, that's what's the trouble.

Charles. Well, young man, we can employ your time. You will leave the university and you will come into the Bayard factory on January second.

Roderick (*at the door into the hall*). I have better things to do than to go into your old factory. I'm going somewhere where time passes, my God! (*He goes out into the hall.*)

Leonora (*rising*). Roderick, Roderick, come here just a moment.—Charles, where can he go?

Lucia (*rising*). Sh, Mother. He'll come back. Now I have to go upstairs and pack my trunk.

Leonora. I won't have any children left!

Lucia. Sh, Mother. He'll come back. He's only gone to California or somewhere.—Cousin Ermengarde has done most of my packing—thanks a thousand times, Cousin Ermengarde. (*She kisses her mother.*) I won't be long. (*She runs out into the hall.*)

(Genevieve *and* Leonora *put on their white hair.*)

Ermengarde. It's a very beautiful day. On the way home from church I stopped and saw Mrs. Foster a moment. Her arthritis comes and goes.

Leonora. Is she actually in pain, dear?

Ermengarde. Oh, she says it'll all be the same in a hundred years!

Leonora. Yes, she's a brave little stoic.

Charles. Come now, a little white meat, Mother?—Mary, pass my cousin's plate.

Leonora. What is it, Mary?—Oh, here's a telegram from them in Paris! "Love and Christmas greetings to all." I told them we'd be eating some of their wedding cake and thinking about them today. It seems to be all decided that they will settle down in the East, Ermengarde. I can't even have my daughter for a neighbor. They hope to build before long somewhere on the shore north of New York.

Genevieve. There is no shore north of New York.

Leonora. Well, east or west or whatever it is.

(*Pause.*)

Charles. My, what a dark day. (*He puts on his white hair. Pause.*) How slowly time passes without any young people in the house.

Leonora. I have three children somewhere.

Charles (*blunderingly offering comfort*). Well, one of them gave his life for his country.

Leonora (*sadly*). And one of them is selling aluminum in China.

Genevieve (*slowly working herself to a hysterical crisis*). I can stand everything but this terrible soot everywhere. We should have moved long ago. We're surrounded by factories. We have to change the window curtains every week.

Leonora. Why, Genevieve!

Genevieve. I can't stand it. I can't stand it any more. I'm going abroad. It's not only the soot that comes through the very walls of this house; it's the *thoughts,* it's the thought of what has been and what might have been here. And the feeling about this house of the years *grinding away.* My mother died yesterday—not twenty-five years ago. Oh, I'm going to live and die abroad! Yes, I'm going to be the American old maid living and dying in a pension in Munich or Florence.

Ermengarde. Genevieve, you're tired.

Charles. Come, Genevieve, take a good drink of cold water. Mary, open the window a minute.

WORDS TO KNOW

stoic (stō′ĭk) *n.* a person who remains calm and unemotional, especially while in pain

Genevieve. I'm sorry. I'm sorry. (*She hurries tearfully out into the hall.*)

Ermengarde. Dear Genevieve will come back to us, I think. (*She rises and starts toward the dark portal.*) You should have been out today, Leonora. It was one of those days when everything was encircled with ice. Very pretty, indeed.

(Charles *rises and starts after her.*)

Charles. Leonora, I used to go skating with Father on mornings like this.—I wish I felt a little better.

Leonora. What! Have I got two invalids on my hands at once? Now, Cousin Ermengarde, you must get better and help me nurse Charles.

Ermengarde. I'll do my best. (*She turns at the very portal and comes back to the table.*)

Charles. Well, Leonora, I'll do what you ask. I'll write the puppy a letter of forgiveness and apology. It's Christmas day. I'll cable it. That's what I'll do. (*He goes out the dark door.*)

Leonora (*drying her eyes*). Ermengarde, it's such a comfort having you here with me. Mary, I really can't eat anything. Well, perhaps, a sliver of white meat.

Ermengarde (*very old*). I spoke to Mrs. Keene for a moment coming out of church. She asked after the young people.—At church I felt very proud sitting under our windows, Leonora, and our brass tablets. The Bayard aisle,—it's a regular Bayard aisle and I love it.

Leonora. Ermengarde, would you be very angry with me if I went and stayed with the young people a little this Spring?

Ermengarde. Why, no. I know how badly they want you and need you. Especially now that they're about to build a new house.

Leonora. You wouldn't be angry? This house is yours as long as you want it, remember.

Ermengarde. I don't see why the rest of you dislike it. I like it more than I can say.

Leonora. I won't be long. I'll be back in no time and we can have some more of our readings-aloud in the evening.

(*She kisses her and goes into the hall.* Ermengarde *left alone, eats slowly and talks to* Mary.)

Ermengarde. Really, Mary, I'll change my mind. If you'll ask Bertha to be good enough to make me a little eggnog. A dear little eggnog.—Such a nice letter this morning from Mrs. Bayard, Mary. Such a nice letter. They're having their first Christmas dinner in the new house. They must be very happy. They call her Mother Bayard, she says, as though she were an old lady. And she says she finds it more comfortable to come and go in a wheelchair.—Such a dear letter . . . And Mary, I can tell you a secret. It's still a great secret, mind! They're expecting a grandchild. Isn't that good news! Now I'll read a little.

(*She props a book up before her, still dipping a spoon into a custard from time to time. She grows from very old to immensely old. She sighs. The book falls down. She finds a cane beside her, and soon totters into the dark portal, murmuring:*)

Dear little Roderick and little Lucia.

THE END

RESPONDING OPTIONS

FROM PERSONAL RESPONSE *TO* CRITICAL ANALYSIS

REFLECT 1. What did you think about the family in this play? Write your thoughts in your notebook, and share them in class.

RETHINK 2. Describe the Bayard family. What family traits emerge and are sustained over time?

Consider
- the importance of the traditional Christmas dinner
- how family members feel about one another
- how they deal with losses and disappointments
- what they regret

3. Look back at the time line that you completed for the Reading Connection. Of all the changes that the family goes through over 90 years, which ones do you think are the hardest for them to deal with? Explain your choices.

4. Do you think this play is generally sad or happy? Support your opinion with evidence from the play.

RELATE 5. How are the traditional Christmas dinners of the Bayard family like your own family gatherings? Refer to what you wrote for the Personal Connection.

LITERARY CONCEPTS

You have studied how **repetition** is used in poetry and prose for emphasis and unity. In *The Long Christmas Dinner,* repetition of the same or similar lines of dialogue is used to support the **theme** of the play. For example, characters from different generations of the Bayard family mention that "Every least twig is wrapped around with ice." Go back through the play to find additional examples of repetition. What does Wilder's use of repetition convey to you about the passage of time? What does it suggest about the Bayard family in particular and about human life in general?

ANOTHER PATHWAY

Cooperative Learning

With a small group of classmates, prepare a Readers Theater of *The Long Christmas Dinner.* Decide what kind of person each character is and how to convey this to the audience. Use the stage directions to determine how the characters act and speak. Rehearse your reading, and then present a portion of it to the class.

QUICKWRITES

1. To mark the changes that take place in the Bayard family during the 90-year period, write **birth announcements** for those characters who are born and **obituaries** for those who die.
2. Imagine that you are directing a performance of *The Long Christmas Dinner.* Reread Wilder's stage directions, and decide how you want this play to look and sound in a live performance. Then write **director's notes** describing your ideas about lighting, sets, props, sound effects, costumes, and so on.
3. Draft a **personal essay** in which you describe a family gathering that you particularly enjoy.

PORTFOLIO *Save your writing. You may want to use it later as a springboard to a piece for your portfolio.*

CRITIC'S CORNER

Thornton Wilder once wrote: "The unencumbered stage encourages the truth operative in everyone. The less seen, the more heard. The eye is the enemy of the ear in real drama. All the masters knew this. Plays of all great ages were performed on a stage with a minimum of scenery and with the public on three sides. . . . The box set, the curtain, the practical door and the window were all mistakes of the nineteenth century, carried on by us in the twentieth." Do you agree with Wilder's thoughts about realistic theater? In your opinion, do sets, costumes, and other conventions of the theater enhance your experience of a play or detract from it?

ALTERNATIVE ACTIVITIES

1. A playbill is a poster that announces a theatrical production. Create a **playbill** to announce a performance of *The Long Christmas Dinner.*
2. Create a **family tree,** or genealogical diagram, of the Bayard family.

WORDS TO KNOW

Identify each pair of words by writing *Synonyms* or *Antonyms.*

1. stoic—crybaby
2. traverse—cross
3. serenely—excitedly
4. constrained—relaxed
5. self-effacing—humble

THORNTON WILDER

1897–1975

The novelist and playwright Thornton Wilder was born in Madison, Wisconsin. His father became U.S. Consul General to Hong Kong when Wilder was nine, and thereafter Wilder was educated alternately in China and California. He attended Oberlin College in Ohio for two years, where he wrote numerous short plays and became a regular contributor to the school's literary magazine. He graduated from Yale University in 1920 and then studied archaeology at the American Academy in Rome. After returning to the United States, Wilder began to teach, and in 1926 he received a master's degree from Princeton University.

Bowing to his father's wishes, Wilder had abandoned his plans to become a full-time writer and instead worked on his first novel in his free time. His second novel, *The Bridge of San Luis Rey,* earned him immediate public recognition and a Pulitzer Prize in 1928.

After winning acclaim as a novelist, Wilder left his teaching job and traveled extensively in Europe. After visiting theaters in Austria and Germany, he returned to writing plays.

In 1938, Wilder won his second Pulitzer Prize, this one for *Our Town,* a play that examines the meaning of life in the face of death. The original production brought Wilder an experience shared by few other playwrights: for two weeks in September of 1938, he replaced the actor playing the character of the Stage Manager, thus starring on Broadway in his own smash hit. Unfortunately, his next play, *The Merchant of Yonkers,* was a dismal failure. However, it was later revised and then adapted as the musical comedy *Hello, Dolly!* which became a huge popular success. In 1943, Wilder won his third Pulitzer, for *The Skin of Our Teeth,* a play inspired by Irish writer James Joyce's modernist masterpiece *Finnegans Wake.*

OTHER WORKS *Heaven's My Destination, The Eighth Day, A Life in the Sun*

PREVIEWING

POETRY

Mirror
Sylvia Plath

Self in 1958
Anne Sexton

PERSONAL CONNECTION

The search for truth and reality is an important aspect of both of these poems. Think about your reality and what it consists of. For example, your school is probably a big part of your reality, as are your home, your family, your friends, your pets, and your activities. Create a cluster diagram and brainstorm parts of your reality. Be as specific as you can. Then discuss the parts of your reality with your classmates.

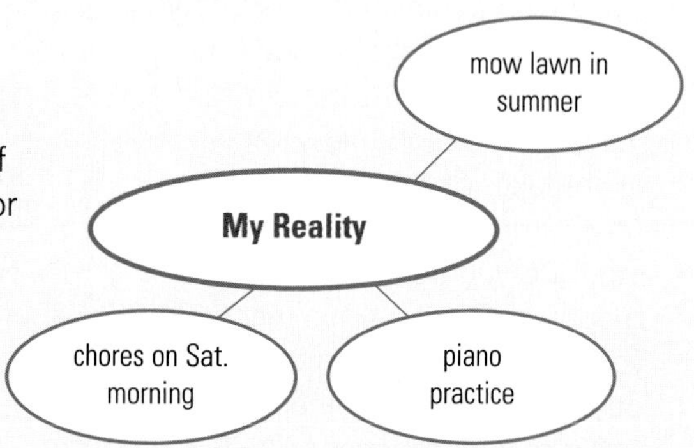

BIOGRAPHICAL CONNECTION

Both Sylvia Plath and Anne Sexton broke new ground by writing openly and honestly about the reality of their lives in the 1950s and early 1960s. Like Charlotte Perkins Gilman and, to some extent, Kate Chopin before them, Plath and Sexton expressed turbulent and often violent emotions. Their poems read like confessions in which they expose their troubled lives in startling images that some readers still find shocking. "Mirror" begins very much like a riddle, asking the reader to figure out who is speaking, and then explores a woman's feelings about aging. Plath wrote the poem just four days before her 29th birthday and a few months before the birth of her second child. In "Self in 1958," Sexton expresses her feelings about her life two years after a suicide attempt and the first of several hospitalizations for psychiatric problems.

The image of the happy housewife from the 1950s.

WRITING CONNECTION

Recall what you filled out in the cluster diagram of your reality. Do you think your reality is the same as someone else's—say, that of one of your parents or another adult? For example, do you worry about getting old in the same way that adults do? Do you worry about taxes or paying bills? Do they worry about their friends as much as you do? Choose one other person to compare yourself with, someone who's different from you, such as an older sibling, a parent, or a neighbor. Write about how this person's reality compares with yours. Then, as you read, be aware of the reality that is depicted in each of these poems.

MIRROR

Sylvia Plath

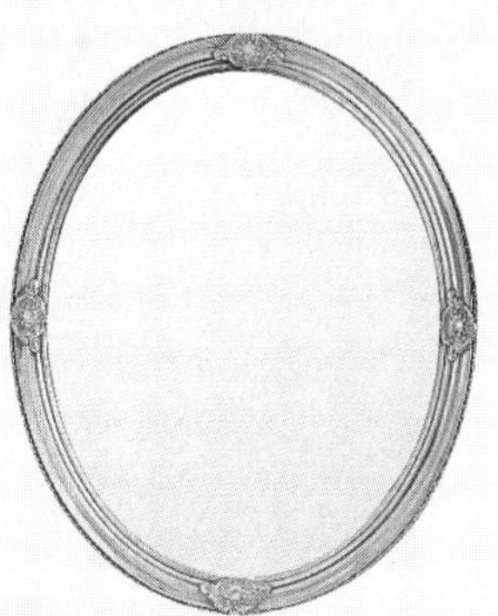

I am silver and exact. I have no preconceptions.[1]
Whatever I see I swallow immediately
Just as it is, unmisted by love or dislike.
I am not cruel, only truthful—
The eye of a little god, four-cornered.
Most of the time I meditate on the opposite wall.
It is pink, with speckles. I have looked at it so long
I think it is a part of my heart. But it flickers.
Faces and darkness separate us over and over.

Now I am a lake. A woman bends over me,
Searching my reaches for what she really is.
Then she turns to those liars, the candles or the moon.
I see her back, and reflect it faithfully.
She rewards me with tears and an agitation of hands.
I am important to her. She comes and goes.
Each morning it is her face that replaces the darkness.
In me she has drowned a young girl, and in me an old woman
Rises toward her day after day, like a terrible fish.

---

1. **preconceptions:** opinions formed before adequate knowledge or understanding is achieved.

Mirror in Corner, New York, 1972, Eva Rubinstein. Copyright © 1972 Eva Rubinstein, all rights reserved.

FROM PERSONAL RESPONSE *TO* CRITICAL ANALYSIS

REFLECT

1. What thoughts did you have after reading this poem? Briefly describe your response in your notebook.

RETHINK

2. Why do you think the mirror is so important to the woman?

3. In your opinion, is the mirror "not cruel, only truthful"?

Consider

- the reality it reflects
- what feelings it has
- how it interprets the woman's reflection

4. What is the mirror's attitude toward the woman?

What is reality?
I am a plaster doll; I pose
with eyes that cut open without landfall or nightfall
upon some shellacked and grinning person,
eyes that open, blue, steel, and close.
Am I approximately an I. Magnin transplant?
I have hair, black angel,
black-angel-stuffing to comb,
nylon legs, luminous arms
and some advertised clothes.

GUIDE FOR READING

6 I. Magnin: a department store that sells expensive clothing.

1–10 What image of the speaker do you form from these first ten lines of the poem? How would you describe her self-image?

I live in a doll's house
with four chairs,
a counterfeit table, a flat roof
and a big front door.
Many have come to such a small crossroad.
There is an iron bed,
(Life enlarges, life takes aim)
a cardboard floor,
windows that flash open on someone's city,
and little more.

Someone plays with me,
plants me in the all-electric kitchen,
Is this what Mrs. Rombauer said?
Someone pretends with me—
I am walled in solid by their noise—
or puts me upon their straight bed.
They think I am me!
Their warmth? Their warmth is not a friend!
They pry my mouth for their cups of gin
and their stale bread.

What is reality
to this synthetic doll
who should smile, who should shift gears,
should spring the doors open in a wholesome disorder,
and have no evidence of ruin or fears?
But I would cry,
rooted into the wall that
was once my mother,
if I could remember how
and if I had the tears.

15 *Crossroad* can refer to an intersection or to a crucial point. What is the crossroad referred to here?

11–20 How does the speaker seem to feel about her home?

23 Mrs. Rombauer: Irma Rombauer, author of *The Joy of Cooking,* a classic cookbook containing advice and instruction as well as recipes.

21–30 Who do you think is the "someone" (and the "they") that plays with and walls in the speaker?

RESPONDING OPTIONS

FROM PERSONAL RESPONSE *TO* CRITICAL ANALYSIS

REFLECT 1. What do you think of the speaker's description of herself in "Self in 1958"? Jot down your thoughts in your notebook.

RETHINK 2. Why do you think the speaker describes herself as a doll? Why can't she be herself?

Consider

- how the speaker looks and acts
- the limitations of her existence in her house
- the expectations that others have of her
- the feelings she has but cannot express

3. Why do you think the speaker has lost the ability to cry?

4. The speaker questions the reality of her existence because she feels so "synthetic," or fake. What might make her life more authentic, or real? Look back at what you wrote for the Previewing activities (page 882) for ideas that might help her.

RELATE 5. Who do you think is more unhappy—the woman in "Mirror" or the speaker in "Self in 1958"? Explain your opinion.

ANOTHER PATHWAY

Cooperative Learning

Working with a group of classmates, create plans for a three-dimensional art display for either "Mirror" or "Self in 1958" to bring to life the situation described in the poem. Be prepared to explain to the class how your display fits the poem.

QUICKWRITES

1. If the speaker of "Mirror" were the woman and not the mirror, how might the poem be different? Rewrite the **poem** so that the woman, rather than the mirror, is the speaker.
2. Keeping Plath's technique in "Mirror" in mind, write a **television advertisement** in the voice of an inanimate object.
3. What if Sexton had painted a picture of herself as we see her in "Self in 1958" instead of writing a poem? Write an **entry** for a museum guide in which you describe such a self-portrait.

PORTFOLIO *Save your writing. You may want to use it later as a springboard to a piece for your portfolio.*

LITERARY CONCEPTS

Tone is a writer's attitude toward a subject. Many modernist works have an **ironic tone,** one that highlights the unexpected twists that life sometimes takes. For example, the story "Here We Are" has a tone that is both ironic and comic. It's ironic that a newlywed couple should have so many fights just after getting married, and Parker herself seems to be laughing at them. "Mirror" also has an ironic tone—the woman both needs and is hurt by the mirror—but the negative images in the last two lines suggest bitterness rather than comedy. How would you describe the tone of "Self in 1958"? What attitude is expressed toward the speaker's existence? Do you see any irony?

ALTERNATIVE ACTIVITIES

1. With a partner, act out a **conversation** between the woman in "Mirror" and the speaker of "Self in 1958."
2. Sketch a **portrait** of the speaker of "Self in 1958" based on details in the poem. Share your artwork with the class.

ACROSS THE CURRICULUM

Sociology Both of these poems touch upon the reality of women's lives in the 1950s and early 1960s. Do research and interview women in your family or community to find out about women's roles at that time. Share your findings with the class, and discuss ways in which women's roles have changed and ways in which they have not.

SYLVIA PLATH

1932–1963

Sylvia Plath was described by the poet Robert Lowell, one of her teachers, as having an "air of maddening docility." Beneath that obedient surface, however, simmered the rage and rebellion that was to inform her best work—and that also led to severe depression and several suicide attempts.

When she was a junior at Smith College, Plath won *Mademoiselle's* fiction contest and was given a month's apprenticeship at the magazine's New York editorial offices. Shortly after her apprenticeship, she became seriously depressed and attempted suicide—an experience detailed in her only novel, *The Bell Jar.* After psychiatric treatment, Plath eventually returned to Smith and graduated with high honors.

After graduation, Plath studied at Cambridge University in England, where she met and married the British poet Ted Hughes. Unfortunately, the marriage deteriorated, and in 1962 Plath left Hughes and took her two children to live in a London flat. As a result of the stress, Plath's buried anger rose to the surface, and she expressed her intense feelings in a frenzy of writing.

In February 1963, Plath again experienced acute depression, and this time she killed herself. Her last poems, considered her best work, were published in *Ariel* after her death. Plath was posthumously awarded a Pulitzer Prize for *Collected Poems.*

OTHER WORKS *The Colossus, Crossing the Water, Winter Trees*

ANNE SEXTON

1928–1974

Anne Sexton graduated from junior college, worked as a fashion model, married at 19, settled in a Boston suburb, and had two daughters. Despite the seeming normality of her life, Sexton suffered repeated mental breakdowns and was haunted by thoughts of suicide. "Until I was twenty-eight," she said, "I had a kind of buried self who didn't know she could do anything but make white sauce and diaper babies. I didn't know I had any creative depths. I was a victim of the American Dream, the bourgeois, middle-class dream. All I wanted was a little piece of life, to be married, to have children. I thought the nightmares, the visions, the demons would go away if there was enough love to put them down. . . . But one can't build little white picket fences to keep nightmares out."

At the suggestion of her psychiatrist, Sexton began writing poetry in her late 20s. In 1958 she attended Robert Lowell's poetry workshop at Boston University, where she and Sylvia Plath became friends. Sexton's first volume of poetry, *To Bedlam and Part Way Back,* details her initial mental breakdown, subsequent hospital stay, and attempt to reconcile with her family upon her return home. Struggling with depression all her life, Sexton still managed to publish ten books of poetry before her death from suicide just shy of her 45th birthday.

OTHER WORKS *All My Pretty Ones, The Awful Rowing Toward God, The Book of Folly*

HOMEWORK

PETER CAMERON

My dog, Keds, was sitting outside of the A & P last Thursday when he got smashed by some kid pushing a shopping cart. At first we thought he just had a broken leg, but later we found out he was bleeding inside. Every time he opened his mouth, blood would seep out like dull red words in a bad silent dream.

Every night before my sister goes to her job she washes her hair in the kitchen sink with beer and mayonnaise and eggs. Sometimes I sit at the table and watch the mixture dribble down her white back. She boils a pot of water on the stove at the same time; when she is finished with her hair, she steams her face. She wants so badly to be beautiful.

I am trying to solve complicated algebraic problems I have set for myself. Since I started cutting school last Friday, the one thing I miss is homework. Find the value for *n*. Will it be a whole number? It is never a whole number. It is always a fraction.

"Will you get me a towel?" my sister asks. She turns her face toward me and clutches her hair to the top of her head. The sprayer hose slithers into its hole next to the faucet.

I hand her a dish towel. "No," she says. "A bath towel. Don't be stupid."

In the bathroom, my mother is watering her plants. She has arranged them in the tub and turned the shower on. She sits on the toilet lid and watches. It smells like outdoors in the bathroom.

I hand my sister the towel and watch her wrap it around her head. She takes the cover off the pot of boiling water and drops lemon slices in. Then she lowers her face into the steam.

This is the problem I have set for myself:

$$\frac{245(n + 17)}{34} = 396(n - 45)$$

$$n =$$

Wednesday, I stand outside the high-school gym doors. Inside students are lined up doing calisthenics. It's snowing, and prematurely dark, and I can watch without being seen.

"Well," my father says when I get home. He is standing in the garage testing the automatic door. Every time a plane flies overhead, the door opens or closes, so my father is trying to fix it. "Have you changed your mind about school?" he asks me.

I lock my bicycle to a pole. This infuriates my father, who doesn't believe in locking things up in his own house. He pretends not to notice. I wipe the thin stripes of snow off the fenders with my middle finger. It is hard to ride a bike in the snow. This afternoon on my way home from the high school I fell off, and lay in the snowy road with my bike on top of me. It felt warm.

"We're going to get another dog," my father says.

"It's not that," I say. I wish everyone would stop talking about dogs. I can't tell how sad I really am about Keds versus how sad I am in general. If I don't keep these things separate, I feel as if I'm betraying Keds.

"Then what is it?" my father says.

"It's nothing," I say.

My father nods. He is very good about bringing things up and then letting them drop. A lot gets dropped. He presses the button on the automatic control. The door slides down its oiled tracks and falls shut. It's dark in the garage. My father presses the button again and the door opens, and we both look outside at the snow falling in the driveway, as if in those few seconds the world might have changed.

My mother has forgotten to call me for dinner, and when I confront her with this she tells me that she did but that I was sleeping. She is loading the dishwasher. My sister is standing at the counter, listening, and separating eggs for her shampoo.

"What can I get you?" my mother asks. "Would you like a meat-loaf sandwich?"

"No," I say. I open the refrigerator and survey its illuminated contents. "Could I have some eggs?"

"O.K.," my mother says. She comes and stands beside me and puts her hand on top of mine on the door handle. There are no eggs in the refrigerator. "Oh," my mother says; then, "Julie?"

"What?" my sister asks.

"Did you take the last eggs?"

"I guess so," my sister says. "I don't know."

"Forget it," I say. "I won't have eggs."

"No," my mother says. "Julie doesn't need them in her shampoo. That's not what I bought them for."

"I do," my sister says. "It's a formula. It doesn't work without the eggs. I need the protein."

"I don't want eggs," I say. "I don't want anything." I go into my bedroom.

My mother comes in and stands looking out the window. The snow has turned to rain. "You're not the only one who is unhappy about this," she says.

"About what?" I say. I am sitting on my unmade bed. If I pick up my room, my mother will make my bed: that's the deal. I didn't pick up my room this morning.

"About Keds," she says. "I'm unhappy, too. But it doesn't stop me from going to school."

"You don't go to school," I say.

"You know what I mean," my mother says. She turns around and looks at my room, and begins to pick things off the floor.

"Don't do that," I say. "Stop."

My mother drops the dirty clothes in an exaggerated gesture of defeat. She almost—almost—throws them on the floor. The way she holds her hands accentuates[1] their emptiness. "If you're not going to go to school," she says, "the least you can do is clean your room."

In algebra word problems, a boat sails down a river while a jeep drives along the bank. Which will reach the capital first? If a plane flies at a certain speed from Boulder to Oklahoma City and then at a different speed from Oklahoma City to Detroit, how many cups of coffee can the stewardess serve, assuming she is unable to serve during the first and last ten minutes of each flight? How many times can a man ride the elevator to the top of the Empire State Building while his wife climbs the stairs, given that the woman travels one stair slower each flight? And if the man jumps up while the elevator is going down, which is moving—the man, the woman, the elevator, or the snow falling outside?

The next Monday I get up and make preparations for going to school. I can tell at the breakfast table that my mother is afraid to acknowledge them for fear it won't be true. I haven't gotten up before ten o'clock in a week. My mother makes me French toast. I sit at the table and write the note excusing me for my absence. I am eighteen, an adult, and thus able to excuse myself from school. This is what my note says:

> Dear Mr. Kelly [my homeroom teacher]:
>
> Please excuse my absence February 17–24. I was unhappy and did not feel able to attend school.
>
> Sincerely,
> MICHAEL PECHETTI

This is the exact format my mother used when she

1. **accentuates:** emphasizes or intensifies.

Ada and Vincent in the Car (1972), Alex Katz. Oil on canvas, 72″ × 96¼″, Hirshhorn Museum and Sculpture Garden, Smithsonian Institution, Washington, D.C., The Joseph H. Hirshhorn Bequest, 1981.786544. Photo by Lee Stalsworth. Copyright © 1996 Alex Katz/Licensed by VAGA, New York.

wrote my notes, only she always said, "Michael was home with a sore throat," or "Michael was home with a bad cold." The colds that prevented me from going to school were always bad colds.

My mother watches me write the note but doesn't ask to see it. I leave it on the kitchen table when I go to the bathroom, and when I come back to get it I know she has read it. She is washing the bowl she dipped the French toast into. Before, she would let Keds lick it clean. He liked eggs.

In Spanish class we are seeing a film on flamenco[2] dancers. The screen wouldn't pull down, so it is being projected on the blackboard, which is green and cloudy with erased chalk. It looks a little like the women are sick, and dancing in Heaven. Suddenly the little phone on the wall buzzes.

Mrs. Smitts, the teacher, gets up to answer it, and then walks over to me. She puts her hand on my shoulder and leans her face close to mine. It is dark in the room. "Miguel," Mrs. Smitts whispers, "*tienes que ir a la oficina de*[3] guidance."

"What?" I say.

She leans closer, and her hair blocks the dancers. Despite the clicking castanets and the roomful of students, there is something intimate about this moment. "*Tienes que ir a la oficina de* guidance," she repeats slowly. Then, "You must go to the guidance office. Now. *Vaya.*"

My guidance counselor, Mrs. Dietrich, used to be a history teacher, but she couldn't take it anymore, so she was moved into guidance. On her immaculate desk is a calendar blotter with "LUNCH" written across the middle of every box, including Saturday and Sunday. The only other things on her desk are an empty photo cube and my letter to Mr. Kelly. I sit down, and she shows me the letter as if I haven't yet read it. I reread it.

"Did you write this?" she asks.

I nod affirmatively. I can tell Mrs. Dietrich is especially nervous about this interview. Our

2. **flamenco:** a dance style characterized by forceful rhythms, which are emphasized by the dancers' playing of castanets—a pair of shell-like instruments that are clapped together with the fingers.

3. **Miguel** (mē-gĕl′) . . . ***tienes que ir a la oficina de*** (tyĕn′ĕs kĕ ēr ä lä ô-fē-sē′nä dĕ).

meetings are always charged with tension. At the last one, when I was selecting my second-semester courses, she started to laugh hysterically when I said I wanted to take Boys' Home Ec. Now every time I see her in the halls she stops me and asks how I'm doing in Boys' Home Ec. It's the only course of mine she remembers.

I hand the note back to her and say, "I wrote it this morning," as if this clarifies things.

"This morning?"

"At breakfast," I say.

"Do you think this is an acceptable excuse?" Mrs. Dietrich asks. "For missing more than a week of school?"

"I'm sure it isn't," I say.

"Then why did you write it?"

Because it is the truth, I start to say. It is. But somehow I know that saying this will make me more unhappy. It might make me cry. "I've been doing homework," I say.

"That's fine," Mrs. Dietrich says, "but it's not the point. The point is, to graduate you have to attend school for a hundred and eighty days, or have legitimate excuses for the days you've missed. That's the point. Do you want to graduate?"

"Yes," I say.

"Of course you do," Mrs. Dietrich says.

She crumples my note and tries to throw it into the wastepaper basket but misses. We both look for a second at the note lying on the floor, and then I get up and throw it away. The only other thing in her wastepaper basket is a banana peel. I can picture her eating a banana in her tiny office. This, too, makes me sad.

"Sit down," Mrs. Dietrich says.

I sit down.

"I understand your dog died. Do you want to talk about that?"

"No," I say.

"Is that what you're so unhappy about?" she says. "Or is it something else?"

I almost mention the banana peel in her wastebasket, but I don't. "No," I say. "It's just my dog."

Mrs. Dietrich thinks for a moment. I can tell she is embarrassed to be talking about a dead dog. She would be more comfortable if it were a parent or a sibling.

"I don't want to talk about it," I repeat.

She opens her desk drawer and takes out a pad of hall passes. She begins to write one out for me. She has beautiful handwriting. I think of her learning to write beautifully as a child and then growing up to be a guidance counselor, and this makes me unhappy.

"Mr. Neuman is willing to overlook this matter," she says. Mr. Neuman is the principal. "Of course, you will have to make up all the work you've missed. Can you do that?"

"Yes," I say.

Mrs. Dietrich tears the pass from the pad and hands it to me. Our hands touch. "You'll get over this," she says. "Believe me, you will."

My sister works until midnight at the Photo-Matica. It's a tiny booth in the middle of the A & P parking lot. People drive up and leave their film and come back the next day for the pictures. My sister wears a uniform that makes her look like a counterperson in a fast-food restaurant. Sometimes at night when I'm sick of being at home I walk downtown and sit in the booth with her.

There's a machine in the booth that looks like a printing press, only snapshots ride down a conveyor belt and fall into a bin and then disappear. The machine gives the illusion that your photographs are being developed on the spot. It's a fake. The same fifty photographs roll through over and over, and my sister says nobody notices, because everyone in town is taking the same pictures. She opens up the envelopes and looks at them.

Before I go into the booth, I buy

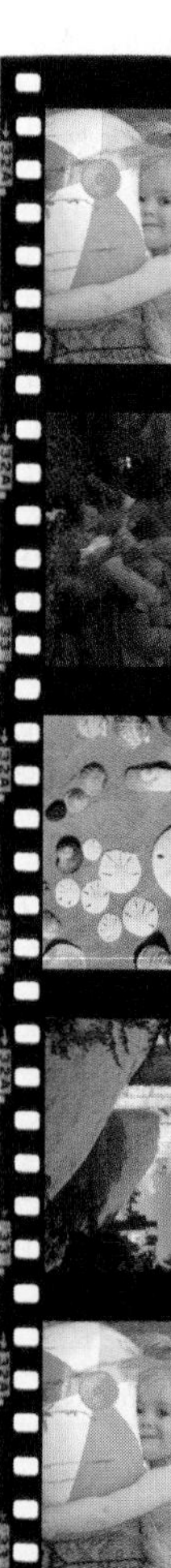

cigarettes in the A & P. It is open twenty-four hours a day, and I love it late at night. It is big and bright and empty. The checkout girl sits on her counter swinging her legs. The Muzak plays "If Ever I Would Leave You."[4] Before I buy the cigarettes, I walk up and down the aisles. Everything looks good to eat, and the things that aren't edible look good in their own way. The detergent aisle is colorful and clean-smelling.

My sister is listening to the radio and polishing her nails when I get to the booth. It is almost time to close.

"I hear you went to school today," she says.

"Yeah."

"How was it?" she asks. She looks at her fingernails, which are so long it's frightening.

"It was O.K.," I say. "We made chili dogs in Home Ec."

"So are you over it all?"

I look at the pictures riding down the conveyor belt. I know the order practically by heart: graduation, graduation, birthday, mountains, baby, baby, new car, bride, bride and groom, house. . . . "I guess so," I say.

"Good," says my sister. "It was getting to be a little much." She puts her tiny brush back in the bottle, capping it. She shows me her nails. They're an odd brown shade. "Cinnamon," she says. "It's an earth color." She looks out into the parking lot. A boy is collecting the abandoned shopping carts, forming a long silver train, which he noses back toward the store. I can tell he is singing by the way his mouth moves.

"That's where we found Keds," my sister says, pointing to the Salvation Army bin.

When I went out to buy cigarettes, Keds would follow me. I hung out down here at night before he died. I was unhappy then, too. That's what no one understands. I named him Keds because he was all white with big black feet and it looked as if he had high-top sneakers on. My mother wanted to name him Bootie. Bootie is a cat's name. It's a dumb name for a dog.

"It's a good thing you weren't here when we found him," my sister says. "You would have gone crazy."

I'm not really listening. It's all nonsense. I'm working on a new problem: Find the value for *n* such that *n* plus everything else in your life makes you feel all right. What would *n* equal? Solve for *n*. ❖

4. **"If Ever I Would Leave You"**: a song of undying love, from the musical *Camelot*.

Peter Cameron

1959–

Peter Cameron's "Homework" was first published in *The New Yorker* and later appeared in his first collection of short stories, *One Way or Another.* Like Michael Pechetti, the narrator in "Homework," many of Cameron's characters are ordinary young people who feel alienated when they face crises in everyday life. Critic Alice H. G. Phillips has observed that Cameron's characters are typically "wrapped up in their own problems, surprised that other people can feel pain."

Cameron's novels and short stories are characterized by objective narration, in which his characters' emotions and inner conflicts are seldom revealed, and by the limited use of descriptive detail. His minimalist style has been compared to that of Ernest Hemingway, Raymond Carver, and Ann Beattie. According to critic Marcia Tager, "Cameron gives us a sharp, almost photographic picture of each character's external features and inner reality simultaneously."

Born in Pompton Plains, New Jersey, Cameron graduated from Hamilton College in 1982. He has taught at Oberlin College and has worked for the Trust for Public Land in New York City. In 1987 Cameron received a National Endowment for the Arts Grant fellowship. Both "Homework" and another of his stories, "Excerpts from Swanlake," have won O. Henry awards.

WRITING FROM EXPERIENCE

WRITING TO EXPRESS

Have you ever been strongly affected by something and wished you had the words to say what you felt? Poetry, with its musical, vivid use of language and rhythm, is a powerful way to express your thoughts and feelings. As you have seen in Unit Six, "The Modern Age," poets write about everything from ordinary objects to complex ideas to express their feelings and thoughts about living in this modern world.

GUIDED ASSIGNMENT

Write a Poem In this lesson, you have an opportunity to write a poem that expresses your feelings about an idea, event, or experience that made a strong impression on you.

Memorabilia Box

What emotions might be associated with each object?

1 Connect to Life

People get ideas for poems from their own experiences and from the world around them. Look over the items on these pages, then discuss how each one might serve as an inspiration for a poem. What feelings, memories, or ideas does each one call to mind? If you had to give a title to each item, what words or phrases could you think of?

2 Find Your Own Inspiration

Now try listing a few ideas of your own for a poem. If you can't think of anything right away, look over the following sources for inspiration.

Using Your Five Senses Things you hear, see, touch, taste, or smell can call up an image or idea you can explore for a poem. Pay close attention to your surroundings at school, at home, or in nature. Keep in mind that even ordinary objects, like Sylvia Plath's mirror, can be good subjects for poems.

Recalling Memories Sometimes a person, a place, a dream, or an experience can leave you with a powerful feeling—grief, joy, anger, fear, wonder.

Tapping People's Experiences These can include books, songs, news items, stories told by family or friends, snatches of conversation you've heard, or even advertisements.

Personal Journal

The difference between the almost right word and the right word is really a large matter—'tis the difference between the lightning-bug and the lightning. —Mark Twain

Overheard a guy on the bus: "I got my first car! It has a rebuilt engine and twin fuel exhausts—you got to see it!"

I could write a poem about when I got my first car last year.

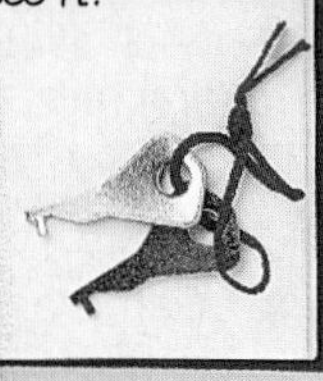

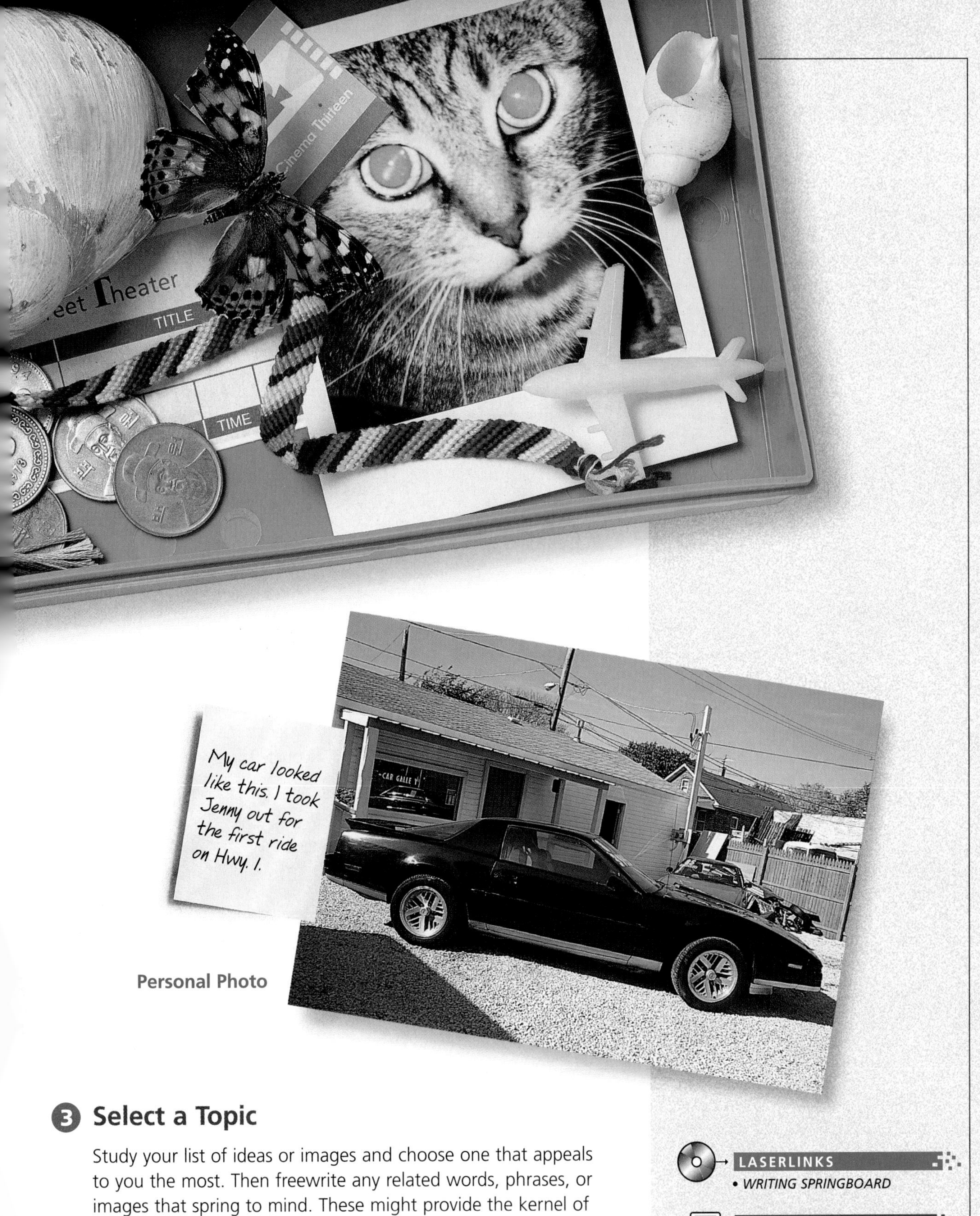
Cinema Thirteen
Theater
TITLE
TIME
My car looked like this. I took Jenny out for the first ride on Hwy. 1.

Personal Photo

❸ Select a Topic

Study your list of ideas or images and choose one that appeals to you the most. Then freewrite any related words, phrases, or images that spring to mind. These might provide the kernel of your poem.

LASERLINKS
• *WRITING SPRINGBOARD*

WRITING COACH

Developing Your Ideas

The First Steps Poets use words as musicians use notes, sculptors use tools, and painters use colors. All of them discover the shape and form of their work as they go along. You can begin by using the suggestions on these pages to discover what you want to say and how you want to say it in your poem.

1 Imagine and Explore

Try to picture as clearly as you can the image or experience that first inspired you. What emotions does it evoke? What do your five senses tell you? You can also use pictures, maps, or objects to help you remember details. The student writer used several items to help him recall the day he got his first car.

2 Sketch Out Your Poem

Write down everything you think of as you explore your topic. Try to identify the main feeling you want to express—sadness, joy, grief, happiness. Then jot down phrases, sentences, titles, images, descriptions, or anything else that comes to mind.

At this point, you don't have to worry about putting things in order or making sense. Just let yourself freewrite.

Student's Freewrite

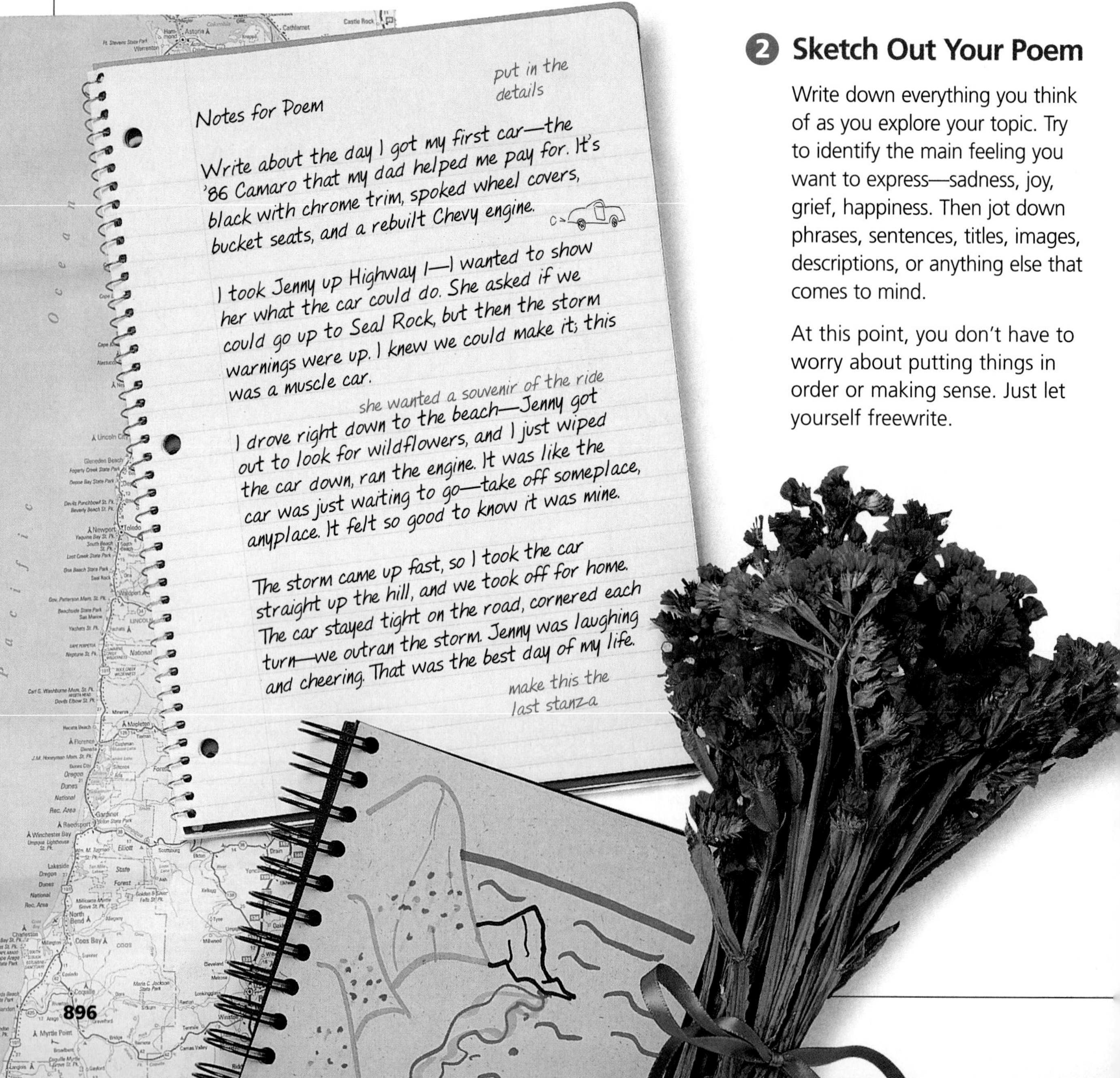

put in the details
Notes for Poem
Write about the day I got my first car—the '86 Camaro that my dad helped me pay for. It's black with chrome trim, spoked wheel covers, bucket seats, and a rebuilt Chevy engine.
I took Jenny up Highway 1—I wanted to show her what the car could do. She asked if we could go up to Seal Rock, but then the storm warnings were up. I knew we could make it; this was a muscle car.
she wanted a souvenir of the ride
I drove right down to the beach—Jenny got out to look for wildflowers, and I just wiped the car down, ran the engine. It was like the car was just waiting to go—take off someplace, anyplace. It felt so good to know it was mine.
The storm came up fast, so I took the car straight up the hill, and we took off for home. The car stayed tight on the road, cornered each turn—we outran the storm. Jenny was laughing and cheering. That was the best day of my life.
make this the last stanza
Pacific Ocean

3 Bring It All Together

You can use these suggestions to help you shape your work.

Mark the Best Words and Lines Highlight words, phrases, or sentences that you really like and that seem to express what you want to say. Cross out what you don't like or what clearly doesn't fit.

Search for Patterns Look for images that fit together, phrases that seem to follow one another, or a sequence of events.

Find the Key Elements Look for a central image, first or last lines, titles, or anything else that can help you write the first draft of your poem.

The SkillBuilder offers hints on establishing tone in your poem.

4 Consider Form and Shape

Your poem can be written in any of many different styles and forms. In this unit, you can find examples of poems with regular patterns of line lengths, rhythms, and rhymes. Others are written in free verse, with varied line lengths, unusual rhythm, and often no rhyme.

In the drafting stage, you might want to experiment with different shapes and forms until you find the one that fits what you are trying to say. In the example below, the student writer discovers that unrhymed free verse is the best choice for him.

Student's Free Verse

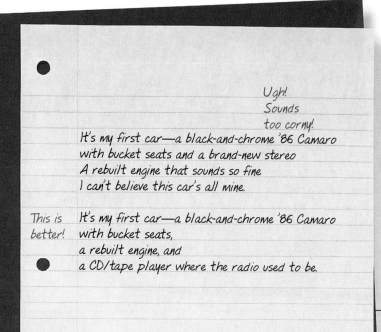

Ugh! Sounds too corny!

It's my first car—a black-and-chrome '86 Camaro
with bucket seats and a brand-new stereo
A rebuilt engine that sounds so fine
I can't believe this car's all mine.

This is better!

It's my first car—a black-and-chrome '86 Camaro
with bucket seats,
a rebuilt engine, and
a CD/tape player where the radio used to be.

SkillBuilder

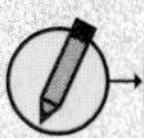

WRITER'S CRAFT

Establishing Tone in Poetry

Tone is a writer's attitude toward a subject—for example, detached, serious, ironic, humorous, angry, critical, or joyful. Tone influences the choice of words and images a writer uses.

The images in Claude McKay's "If We Must Die," for example, reflect an angry tone as the poet urges his readers to "face the murderous, cowardly pack" and fight back, even if it means dying.

On the other hand, the language of Sylvia Plath's "The Mirror" conveys a cool, detached tone: "I am silver and exact. I have no preconceptions." The mirror simply reflects what is there; it does not judge or analyze.

APPLYING WHAT YOU LEARNED

Look over your notes and try to identify your tone, or attitude, toward your subject. What words or images can you use to reflect this tone in your poem?

THINK & PLAN

Reflecting on Your Topic

1. What is the dominant feeling you have about your subject?
2. What images or details seem to capture best what you want to say?
3. Will your poem be like a song, with rhyme, or more like free verse?

DRAFTING

Drafting Your Poem

How to Shape Your Poem The real art of writing a poem is finding just the right words, sounds, and form for what you want to say. You may have to revise or even rewrite your draft several times before you are satisfied. Don't be discouraged. Even skilled poets like Langston Hughes, Robert Frost, and Anne Sexton revised their work many times before the final poems emerged.

1 Write Your Draft

By now you should have a good idea of what you want your poem to convey and its general shape and form. The next step is to write the first draft. You may want to try using different shapes or forms throughout the drafting process. You can revise anything or everything later. In fact, your final poem may end up looking quite different from the first draft.

Student's Rough Draft

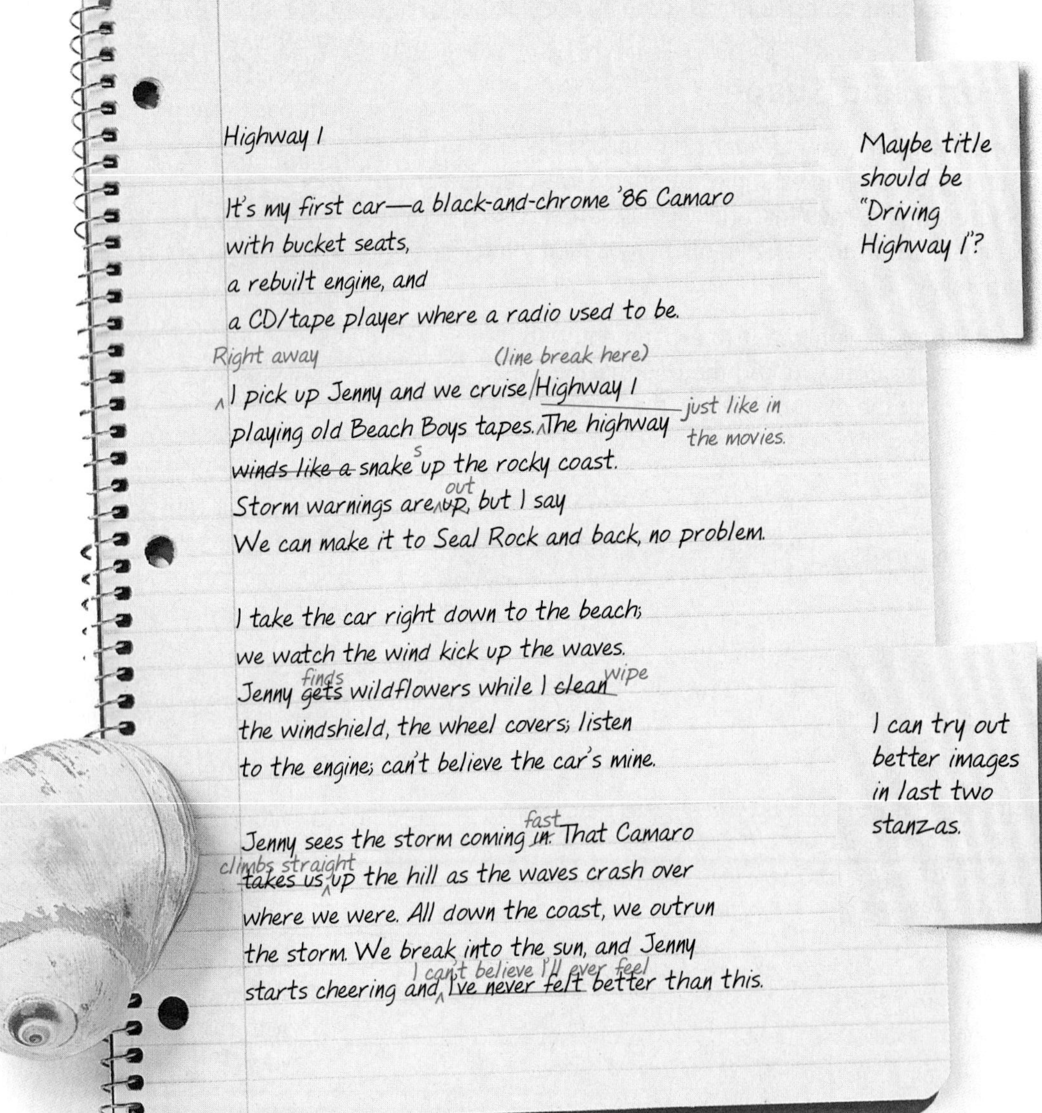

Highway 1

It's my first car—a black-and-chrome '86 Camaro
with bucket seats,
a rebuilt engine, and
a CD/tape player where a radio used to be.
Right away
(line break here)
I pick up Jenny and we cruise Highway 1
just like in the movies.
playing old Beach Boys tapes. The highway
winds like a snake up the rocky coast.
out
Storm warnings are up, but I say
We can make it to Seal Rock and back, no problem.

I take the car right down to the beach;
we watch the wind kick up the waves.
finds
wipe
Jenny gets wildflowers while I clean
the windshield, the wheel covers; listen
to the engine; can't believe the car's mine.

fast
Jenny sees the storm coming in. That Camaro
climbs straight
takes us up the hill as the waves crash over
where we were. All down the coast, we outrun
the storm. We break into the sun, and Jenny
I can't believe I'll ever feel
starts cheering and I've never felt better than this.

Maybe title should be "Driving Highway 1"?

I can try out better images in last two stanzas.

2 Shape Your Draft

Review your drafts and choose one you like best. Then read it with the following questions in mind.

- Which images support the tone and mood you want to portray?
- Can you think of better word choices to say what you mean?
- Which ideas or lines should be discarded? What excess words or details can you eliminate?
- Does a favorite line or image no longer fit into the poem?
- What form seems to suit your poem best?

3 Revise and Share

As you work on your draft, consider how you can use some of these poetic devices that give poetry its special qualities.

Figures of Speech Similes, metaphors, analogies, and personification create images that bring your ideas and descriptions to life. For example, T. S. Eliot personifies fog when he says it "rubs its back upon the window-panes." How can you use these techniques in your poem?

Sound Devices The music of poetry lies in the way words work together. Think about how you can use repetition, assonance, alliteration, onomatopoeia, and rhyme to strengthen the mood and rhythm of your poem. (The SkillBuilder offers tips on using assonance and consonance.)

Line Length and Line Breaks Line length and line breaks establish rhythm and emphasize certain words and sounds. Try experimenting with different line lengths and line breaks until you find the right ones for your poem.

PEER RESPONSE

Let others read your draft, and ask them questions like these.

- How did the poem as a whole affect you?
- Which images, words, lines, or phrases did you like? Which ones seemed inappropriate or out of place?
- What was the main mood and tone of the poem?
- What title do you think fits the draft?
- What didn't you understand about the poem?

SkillBuilder

WRITER'S CRAFT

Using Assonance and Consonance

Assonance is the repetition of vowel sounds (the long e in *leaves* and *streams*). **Consonance** is the repetition of consonant sounds (the *r* in *roaring* and *rumbling*). These sound devices can be used to intensify feeling, rhythm, and meaning in a poem. Compare these two sentences:

Jenny gets wildflowers while
I clean the windshield.

Jenny finds wildflowers while
I wipe the windshield.

In the second example, the repetition of long *i* sounds and *f* and *w* consonants adds a musical quality and creates a stronger connection between the two actions.

APPLYING WHAT YOU LEARNED
Try experimenting with patterns of vowel and consonant sounds to heighten the rhythm and feeling in your poem.

RETHINK & EVALUATE

Preparing to Revise

1. What ideas, images, or lines can you add? Which don't belong?
2. What poetic devices can enhance rhythm and meaning?
3. Where can you make better word choices?

Completing Your Poem

The Last Word Many poets say they reach a point where a poem "feels finished"—that is, they have said what they want to say to the best of their abilities. Give yourself one final chance to put your feelings into the best words by setting aside your poem for a while, then going over it again.

❶ Revise and Edit

Read your poem aloud, listening to the rhythm and music of the words. Use these suggestions, along with the Standards for Evaluation and Editing Checklist, to complete your final draft.

- Be sure every word, image, rhyme, and rhythm is appropriate to the subject.
- Use figures of speech to bring images and details to life.
- Use line lengths and line breaks to enhance mood and rhythm.
- Add music and emphasis with sound devices.

Which words convey the narrator's mood to the reader?

What sound devices are used to enhance rhythm and meaning?

Student's Final Poem

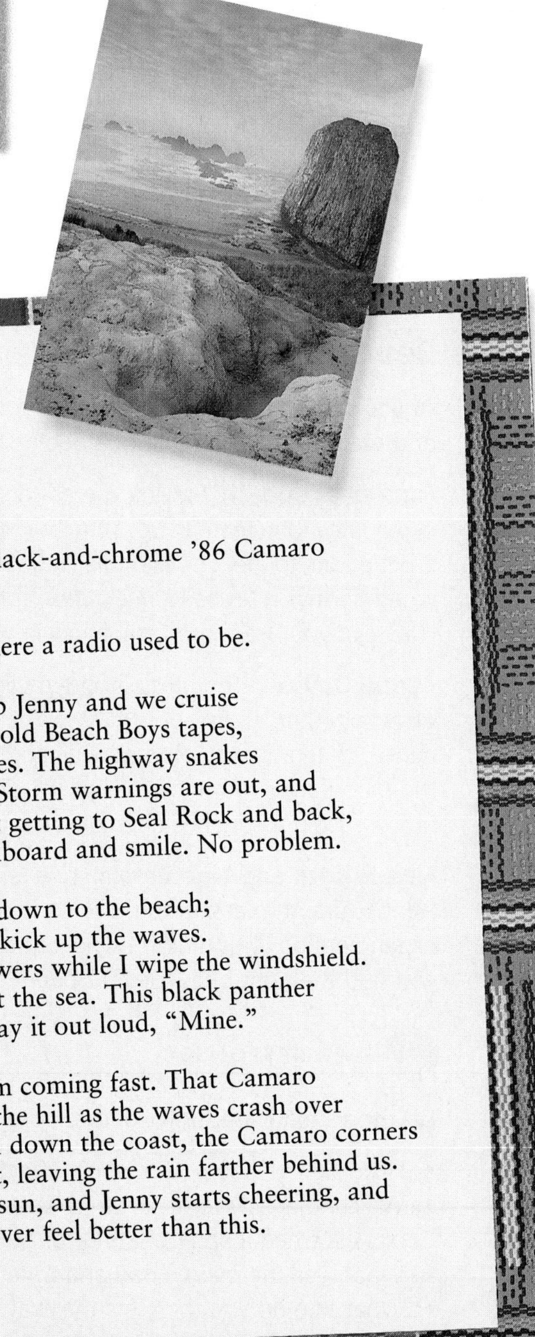

Driving Highway 1

by Robert Lenski

It's my first car—a black-and-chrome '86 Camaro
with bucket seats,
a rebuilt engine, and
a CD/tape player where a radio used to be.

Right away I pick up Jenny and we cruise
Highway 1, playing old Beach Boys tapes,
just like in the movies. The highway snakes
up the rocky coast. Storm warnings are out, and
Jenny worries about getting to Seal Rock and back,
but I touch the dashboard and smile. No problem.

I take the car right down to the beach;
we watch the wind kick up the waves.
Jenny finds wildflowers while I wipe the windshield.
The engine snarls at the sea. This black panther
of a car is mine. I say it out loud, "Mine."

Jenny sees the storm coming fast. That Camaro
climbs straight up the hill as the waves crash over
where we were. All down the coast, the Camaro corners
each turn like a cat, leaving the rain farther behind us.
We break into the sun, and Jenny starts cheering, and
I can't believe I'll ever feel better than this.

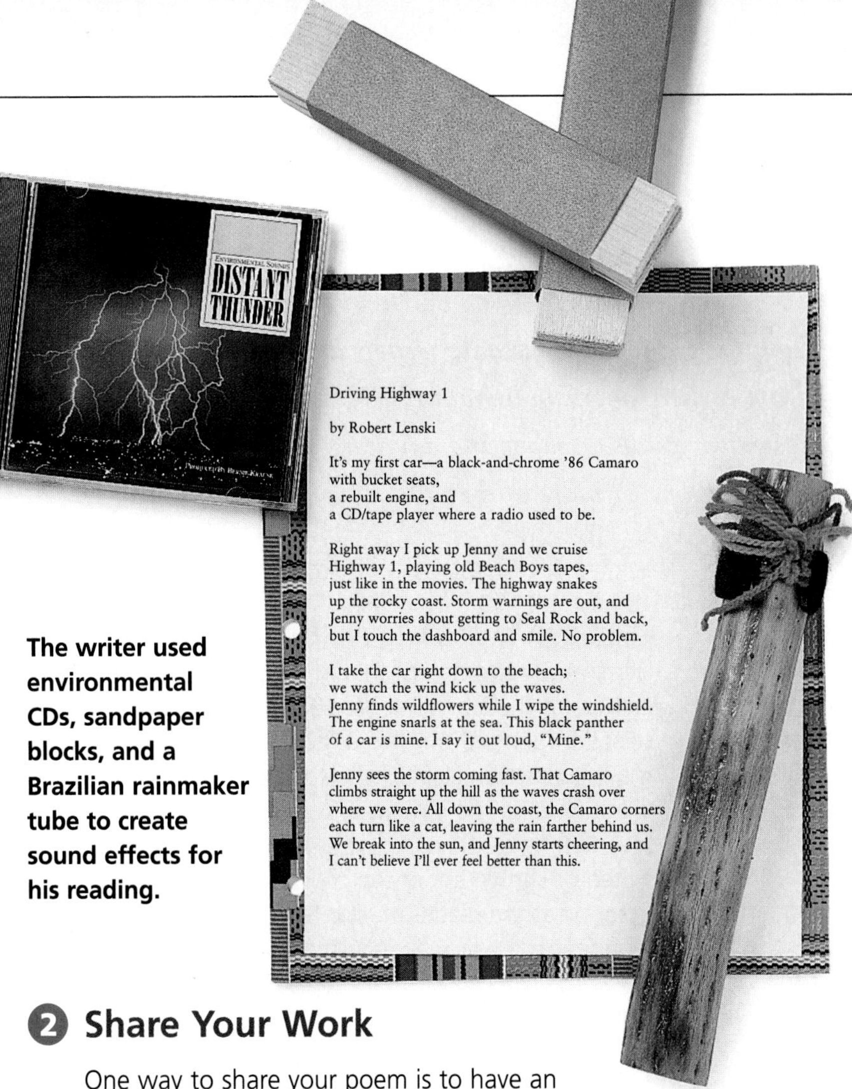

Driving Highway 1

by Robert Lenski

It's my first car—a black-and-chrome '86 Camaro
with bucket seats,
a rebuilt engine, and
a CD/tape player where a radio used to be.

Right away I pick up Jenny and we cruise
Highway 1, playing old Beach Boys tapes,
just like in the movies. The highway snakes
up the rocky coast. Storm warnings are out, and
Jenny worries about getting to Seal Rock and back,
but I touch the dashboard and smile. No problem.

I take the car right down to the beach;
we watch the wind kick up the waves.
Jenny finds wildflowers while I wipe the windshield.
The engine snarls at the sea. This black panther
of a car is mine. I say it out loud, "Mine."

Jenny sees the storm coming fast. That Camaro
climbs straight up the hill as the waves crash over
where we were. All down the coast, the Camaro corners
each turn like a cat, leaving the rain farther behind us.
We break into the sun, and Jenny starts cheering, and
I can't believe I'll ever feel better than this.

The writer used environmental CDs, sandpaper blocks, and a Brazilian rainmaker tube to create sound effects for his reading.

2 Share Your Work

One way to share your poem is to have an "open mike" session in class or after school where you and others read your work. You can create sound effects to go with the reading. Other ideas for sharing your work include

- publishing the poem in the school newspaper
- setting it to music as a song
- sending it to a poetry chatroom on the Internet

Standards for Evaluation

A poem
- usually focuses on one experience or event
- uses fresh, original images that support the meaning
- uses concise, appropriate language, with no unnecessary words
- creates a specific mood that fits the subject
- uses poetic devices to support the meaning and to create specific effects

SkillBuilder

GRAMMAR FROM WRITING

Using Punctuation in Poetry

Punctuation in poetry, as in prose, can be used to emphasize certain words or lines. For example, the student writer used a dash after "It's my first car" to set off the rest of the sentence. Although many poets use punctuation in unconventional ways, for now, follow the same rules as for prose.

GRAMMAR HANDBOOK

For more on punctuation, see page 1231 of the Grammar Handbook.

Editing Checklist

Use the following tips for revising.

- Did you use punctuation correctly, as you would in prose?
- Did you capitalize the first word of each line that starts a sentence?

REFLECT & ASSESS

Learning from Experience

1. Describe what you found easiest and hardest about writing a poem.
2. How could you use poetic devices to improve your prose writing?

   PORTFOLIO List what you would do differently to make writing your next poem easier. You can add the list and your poem to your portfolio.

REFLECT & ASSESS

UNIT SIX: THE MODERN AGE

How does the literature from the Harlem Renaissance writers and other modern writers differ from earlier American literature? What new challenges did this unit present to you as a reader and a writer? Explore these questions by completing one or more of the options below.

REFLECTING ON THE UNIT

OPTION 1 **Ways to Respond to Prejudice** Review the selections in Part 1, "A New Cultural Identity." What possible responses to prejudice and mistreatment do they suggest? Think about the range of responses to prejudice shown in the selections. Then, with a small group of classmates, discuss which responses to prejudice you think are the most effective.

OPTION 2 **What's New?** Recall the opening quotation of this unit: "Make it new!" What do you think the writers in this unit have done to make their writing different from earlier American literature? Jot down your ideas about each selection, and then, in a paragraph, explain which selection seems most innovative to you.

Consider

- the use of rhyme and other techniques in the poetry selections
- the subject matter of all the selections
- the attitudes expressed
- the writers' styles

OPTION 3 **The Iceberg Principle** Recall Ernest Hemingway's comment that in his writing, seven-eighths of the story is concealed. Is that true for other selections in Part 2 of this unit? Working with a small group, create an iceberg chart for each selection, with a line dividing the iceberg into one-eighth above and seven-eighths below. Above the line, write what is stated or shown about the characters. Below the line, write what the reader must infer. Which selections require readers to make the most inferences?

REFLECT & ASSESS *Self-Assessment: To explore how your understanding of modern literature has developed over the course of the unit, jot down words and phrases that you associate with this literature. Then circle at least three words and phrases that you think describe modern literature most accurately. Pair up with a classmate and compare your list with your partner's, explaining your choices.*

REVIEWING LITERARY CONCEPTS

OPTION 1 **The Modern Outlook** What defines a modernist character? Create a chart like the one shown, listing each character from Part 2 in the first column and the modernist qualities of that character in the second. Review your chart, highlighting the features that you think are particularly modern. Write a paragraph describing the main qualities of a modernist character.

Character	Modernist Traits
Speaker of "Acquainted with the Night"	Alone; doesn't want to talk; uncertain—time isn't wrong or right

OPTION 2 **Ironic Views of Life** What examples of irony do you see in the selections in this unit? Brainstorm with a small group of classmates to identify examples of situational irony, dramatic irony, and verbal irony in various selections. Discuss which selections make the most interesting use of irony.

REFLECT & ASSESS *Self-Assessment: Can you explain the difference between the sonnet form and blank verse? Do you recall how mood is different from tone? How does anaphora relate to repetition? Thinking back through the literary concepts discussed in this unit, look for connections and distinctions between them.*

PORTFOLIO BUILDING

- **QuickWrites** Many of the QuickWrites in this unit offered you opportunities to relate a piece of literature to your own ideas about life. Review your QuickWrites for this unit and choose one in which your life experience provided an interesting insight into the selection. Write a cover note to further explain your insight.
- **Writing About Literature** The rhythm and rhyme of poetry is often compared to music. Reread the essay in which you compared two poets' styles. What kind of music would be a good match for each poem? jazz? classical? country? rock and roll? some other kind? In a brief note, describe your choice of music for each poem and explain your recommendations.
- **Writing from Experience** In some ways a poem is never finished. Reread the poem you wrote about something that made a strong impression on you. Which images and words capture your ideas the best? If you were to revise your poem now, which words or images would you change? If you like, attach your notes to your poem and put them in your portfolio.
- **Personal Choice** Look back through the writing assignments and the records and evaluations of the activities you completed for this unit. Which was the most difficult to make the way you wanted it? Choose one activity or writing assignment and write a note describing one frustrating aspect of completing it. Add to your portfolio your note and the writing assignment or activity record that it describes.

REFLECT & ASSESS *Self-Assessment: At this point your portfolio probably has a considerable variety of your work. Think about what abilities you have developed since the beginning of the year and what kinds of writing or activities you would like to experiment with before the end of the year.*

SETTING GOALS

As you read the selections in this unit, you might have wondered how economic, social, or historical events affected the way the literature was written. How can you use the knowledge you have gained from other subjects to broaden your understanding of the first four decades of the 20th century? Think of a few questions you would like to have answered, and then figure out how to answer these questions yourself. You might work with a few other students who share your interests.

Conflict AT HOME AND

Ominous Omen (1987), Rupert Garcia. Chalk, linseed oil, oil paint on canvas, 47″ × 130″, courtesy of Rupert Garcia; Rena Bransten Gallery, San Francisco; and Galerie Claude Samuel, Paris. Copyright © Rupert Garcia.

ABROAD

War is a poor chisel to carve out tomorrows.

MARTIN LUTHER KING, JR.
MINISTER AND CIVIL RIGHTS LEADER

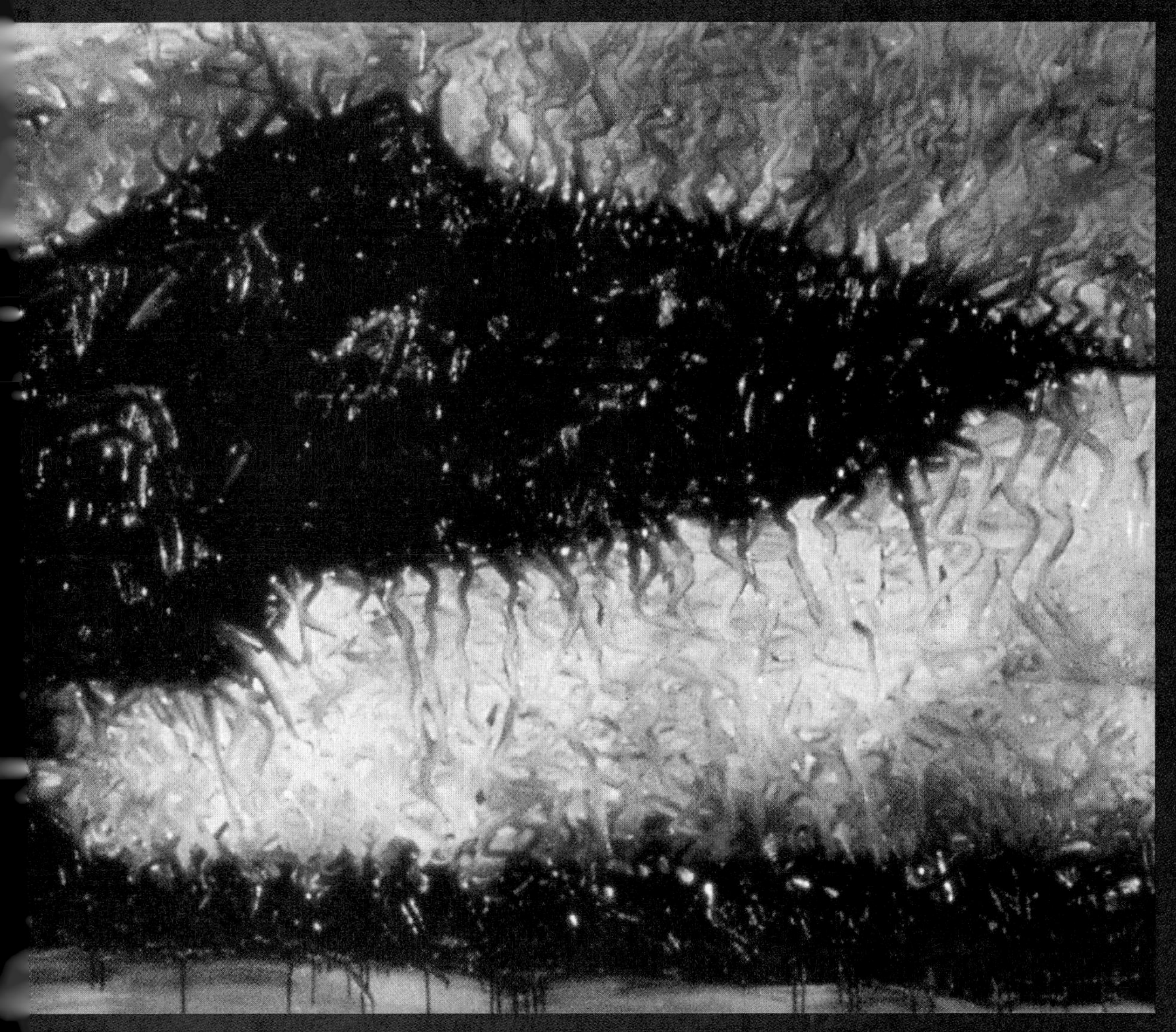

TIME LINE

Conflict at Home and Abroad

The dropping of atomic bombs on Hiroshima and Nagasaki brought World War II to a dramatic end. Soon, however, the growing distrust between the United States and the Soviet Union, aggravated by the awesome power of nuclear weapons, led to the prolonged tensions known as the cold war. These tensions fueled the U.S. and Soviet space programs, the Korean War, the Cuban missile crisis, and the Vietnam War.

1940

German forces conquer Denmark, Norway, Belgium, Luxembourg, the Netherlands, and France; British troops retreat across the English Channel.

1941

The Japanese bomb Pearl Harbor, bringing the United States into World War II.

1945

Germany surrenders to the Allies; the United States drops two atomic bombs on Japan, ending the war in the Pacific.

1950

Senator Joseph McCarthy claims that Communist spies run the U.S. State Department and have infiltrated other government bureaus; in subsequent public hearings, thousands of innocent people are falsely accused of treasonous acts.

1953

The Korean War ends after three years of fighting between Communist troops and an international force sponsored by the United Nations. The United States suffers more than 150,000 casualties.

1954

Ruling in *Brown v. Board of Education,* the Supreme Court declares that segregated schools are unconstitutional.

1962

U.S. ships blockade Cuba during the Cuban missile crisis, forcing the Soviet Union to remove nuclear-missile launchers aimed at the United States.

1963

Betty Friedan's *The Feminine Mystique* questions traditional female roles and launches the modern women's movement.

Although it was not the first feminist book, The Feminine Mystique *has certainly been among the most influential. Friedan argued that since World War II, women had become victimized by the notion that happiness depended on their roles as housewives and mothers. According to her, advertisers, women's magazines, psychiatrists, and politicians, among others, manipulated women into believing in this "feminine mystique," thus imprisoning them in the "comfortable concentration camp" of home life.*

Period *Pieces*

1963

President John F. Kennedy is assassinated in Dallas.

1964

Congress passes the Civil Rights Act of 1964, prohibiting racial discrimination in public accommodations and employment; President Lyndon Johnson outlines his Great Society program, calling for an increase in the number and scope of social-welfare programs.

1965

The first U.S. combat forces land in Vietnam; Malcolm X is assassinated; the National Farm Workers Association (NFWA) begins a strike against California grape growers.

Led by the Mexican-American organizer Cesar Chavez, the NFWA was only three years old when its strike against the $170-million grape-growing industry began. The strike and an accompanying boycott lasted five years, ending when the union signed labor contracts with almost 300 companies.

1968

The assassination of Martin Luther King, Jr., in Memphis is followed by widespread rioting in major U.S. cities; the presidential candidate Robert Kennedy is assassinated in Los Angeles; violence erupts between police and antiwar protesters at the Democratic National Convention in Chicago.

1973

In its *Roe v. Wade* decision, the Supreme Court removes most legal restrictions on abortion; the last U.S. troops leave Vietnam.

1974

President Richard M. Nixon resigns to avoid impeachment over the Watergate scandal.

1975

South Vietnam surrenders as North Vietnamese troops occupy Saigon.

Console TV from 1948

The look of the 1960s

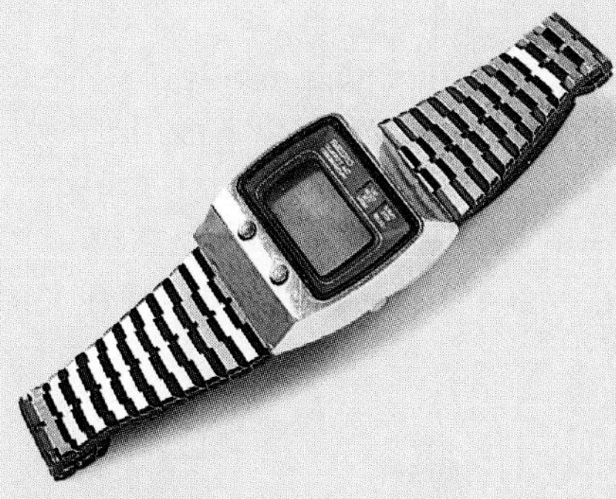

Early digital watch

PART 1 INTRODUCTION

Remembering the Wars

World War II

World War II was a catastrophe of epic dimensions. Never before had so many soldiers fought. Never before had such wholesale slaughter occurred. When the war finally ended in 1945, more than 78 million people had been killed or wounded. For the first time in history, more civilians than soldiers had died in a war.

Adolf Hitler and the National Socialist German Workers' party, commonly called the Nazis, came to power in 1933, at the height of the Great Depression. Full of passionate intensity, Hitler set out to avenge Germany's defeat in World War I and to create a new German state called the Third Reich. He told his followers, "Close your eyes to pity! Act brutally!" Like a tidal wave, the German army overran Europe. By June 1940, British troops had retreated from Dunkirk across the English Channel.

As the Nazis surged across Europe, Hitler targeted certain groups for extermination—political dissenters, homosexuals, mental patients, Gypsies, Poles, Slavs, and especially Jews. Sometimes Jews were confined in squalid ghettoes, but most of the time they were herded into cattle cars for removal to concentration camps. By late 1942, the Nazis had set up six death camps in Poland, where thousands of Jews were gassed each day. In all, approximately 6 million Jews were systematically murdered in what became known as the Holocaust.

Included in this part of the unit is Bernard Malamud's chilling story "Armistice." Set in New York City while the war

KEEP
THESE
HANDS
OFF!
BUY the New VICTORY BONDS

Images from World War II: U.S. troops roll through Europe (top right); a U.S. war propaganda poster (above); the yellow patch that European Jews were forced to wear (left); and the bombing of Pearl Harbor (below).

rages in Europe, the story reveals the roots of the kind of racial hatred that fueled the Holocaust. The armistice, or truce, between the two American characters at the end of the story seems unsatisfactory and temporary, just like the armistice signed by Germany and the allied European and U.S. forces at the end of World War I.

On December 7, 1941, Japanese bombers struck the American naval base at Pearl Harbor, Hawaii, killing approximately 2,000 sailors. This tragedy, which brought the United States into the war, is the occasion of Joan Didion's "Letter from Paradise." Didion describes her feelings as she visits Pearl Harbor a quarter of a century later, views the still-submerged battleships, and recalls the young men who died in the Sunday-morning sneak attack. Dwight Okita's poem "In Response to Executive Order 9066" recalls the unfortunate reaction of the U.S. government to the fear engendered by Japanese aggression: the rounding up and banishing to internment camps of thousands of Japanese Americans.

The U.S. entry into the war turned the tide in favor of the Allies, but it was a long, hard fight. Two selections in this part of the unit deal with the experience of ordinary combat soldiers. Randall Jarrell's jolting poem "The Death of the Ball Turret Gunner" recalls the terror of aerial warfare, in which combatants felt painfully vulnerable under the fire of a faceless enemy. The prize-winning novelist John Steinbeck, whose work always speaks with sympathy for the common people, also reflects the point of view of the fighting soldier in his essay "Why Soldiers Won't Talk."

Voices from the Times

from ***"The Good War": An Oral History of World War Two***
by Studs Terkel

We were on our way to the movies on Sunday afternoon. I was twelve at the time. My dad loved Abbott and Costello. We were going to a matinee. We saw them all. On the way to the theater, the car radio was on. "Oh, my God!" my father said, "Pearl Harbor!" I said, "What's a Pearl Harbor?"

"We can't go to the movies," he said. He turned around right away. There was an outcry from the back seat: "We wanna see Abbott and Costello!" My two sisters were eight and six.

Jean Bartlett

On the morning of December 16, we were suddenly under a fantastic barrage. Every tank in Europe came over the hill, all the panzers in the world. We had no tanks at all. The weather was such that we had no air support. They went over our rifles like they weren't even there. We were completely cut off and surrounded. We ran through the hills, firing at anything. . . .

So there I am wandering around with the whole German army shooting at me, and all I've got is a .45 automatic. There were ample opportunities, however, because every place you went there were bodies and soldiers laying around. Mostly Americans. At one time or another, I think I had in my hands every weapon the United States Army manufactured. You'd run out of ammunition with that one, you'd throw it away and try to find something else. One time I had a submachine gun, first experience I ever had with one.

Richard M. "Red" Prendergast
remembering the Battle of the Bulge

Voices *from the* Times

The only thing that kept you going was your faith in your buddies. It wasn't just a case of friendship. I never heard of self-inflicted wounds out there. Fellows from other services said they saw this in Europe. Oh, there were plenty of times when I wished I had a million-dollar wound. [Laughs softly.] Like maybe shootin' a toe off. What was worse than death was the indignation of your buddies. You couldn't let 'em down. It was stronger than flag and country.

With the Japanese, the battle was all night long. Infiltratin' the lines, slippin' up and throwin' in grenades. Or runnin' in with a bayonet or saber. They were active all night. Your buddy would try to get a little catnap and you'd stay on watch. Then you'd switch off. It went on, day in and day out. A matter of simple survival. The only way you could get it over with was to kill them off before they killed you. The war I knew was totally savage.

E. B. "Sledgehammer" Sledge
remembering the war in the Pacific

I first became aware of it when I was twelve or thirteen. It was one of the most important experiences of my life. In the school library, I was looking at photographs of the Holocaust. They were oversized books. I can still see the bindings and the mottled green cloth. It wasn't an assignment. Why was I doing this? It was a new library, new furniture, clean floors. The sun was coming through on the Appalachian hills. In contrast to the photographs, which were grainy, fuzzy. Parents wouldn't want their children to see these photographs.

In those grainy photos, you first think it's cords of wood piled up. You look again, it shows you human beings. You never get the picture out of your eye.

Nora Watson

A U.S. soldier in Vietnam

Continuity & Change: War in Vietnam

Most Americans supported U.S. participation in World War II. Twenty years later, however, the Vietnam War split the American people into so-called hawks and doves—supporters and opponents of the war.

The United States intervened in South Vietnam to help that republic resist the Viet Cong—South Vietnamese Communist rebels—and the North Vietnamese army. The U.S. government wanted to stop the spread of communism in Southeast Asia, whereas the Vietnamese soldiers fighting U.S. troops wanted an independent nation free of foreign interference.

The war in Vietnam bred a degree of domestic conflict unseen since the Civil War. As the war dragged on and more U.S. soldiers died—approximately 58,000 in all—many Americans at home began to doubt the wisdom of continuing the U.S. presence in Vietnam. Indignant students, pacifists, and some returning Vietnam War veterans marched in the streets, calling for an end to the war. The literature of the time reflects the conflicts within the country, as well as within the ranks of the U.S. military. From Estela Portillo Trambley's "Village," a moving portrait of a small Vietnamese village targeted for destruction, to Tim O'Brien's "Ambush," with its painful memory of an encounter with the enemy, these selections introduce the troublesome issues plaguing the people who were involved in the longest war in American history.

• HISTORICAL LITERARY CONNECTION

PART 1 *Remembering the Wars*

World War II

Continuity & Change: War in Vietnam

PREVIEWING

FICTION

Armistice

Bernard Malamud

PERSONAL CONNECTION

Prejudice is the suspicion, dislike, or hatred of a particular group of people based on preconceived ideas about them. Think about a person you know who is prejudiced, however slightly, against a certain group. What is the group? Why do you think this person is prejudiced against this group? How does he or she demonstrate this prejudice? When is he or she most likely to show this prejudice? Answer these questions in your notebook by filling out a diagram like the one shown.

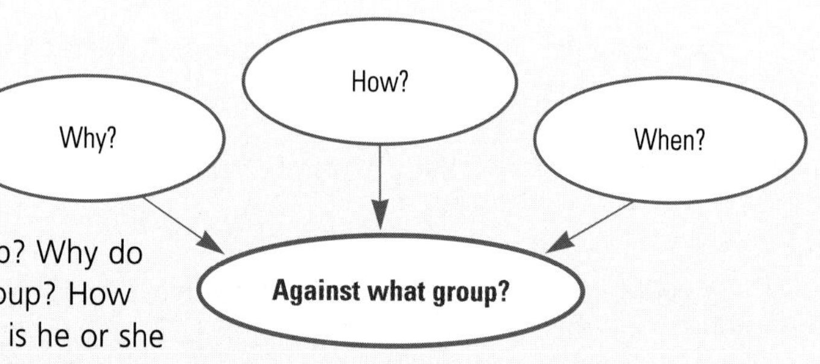

HISTORICAL CONNECTION

Anti-Semitism, prejudice against Jews, plays a major role in "Armistice," a story set during World War II before the United States entered the conflict. When Hitler came to power in Germany in 1933, he made anti-Semitism an official policy of the Nazi government, and during World War II, he instituted a program to exterminate all European Jews. As the Nazis conquered territories, as they did France in 1940, they rounded up the Jews of the area and sent them to concentration camps. Hitler carried anti-Semitism to a terrifying extreme, but the roots of anti-Semitism extend much further back in European history than the 1940s. Since ancient times both Christian and Muslim nations have persecuted and expelled Jews. Originally, Jews were persecuted for not following the dominant religion, but later they were also blamed for society's ills whenever economic or social conditions deteriorated.

Children at a Nazi concentration camp.
The Bettmann Archive

READING CONNECTION

Understanding Motivations As you may recall, motivation refers to the forces impelling a character's actions. There are two main characters in this story, one of Russian Jewish descent and the other of German descent. It is important to try to understand why the two characters act as they do, particularly toward each other. As you read, look at their memories, dreams, and imaginings for clues to their motivation.

Armistice

Bernard Malamud

When he was a boy, Morris Lieberman saw a burly Russian peasant seize a wagon wheel that was lying against the side of a blacksmith's shop, swing it around, and hurl it at a fleeing Jewish sexton.[1] The wheel caught the Jew in the back, crushing his spine. In speechless terror, he lay on the ground before his burning house, waiting to die.

Thirty years later Morris, a widower who owned a small grocery and delicatessen store in a Scandinavian neighborhood in Brooklyn, could recall the scene of the pogrom[2] with the twisting fright that he had felt at fifteen. He often experienced the same fear since the Nazis had come to power.

The reports of their persecution of the Jews that he heard over the radio filled him with dread, but he never stopped listening to them. His fourteen-year-old son, Leonard, a thin, studious boy, saw how overwrought his father became and tried to shut off the radio, but the grocer would not allow him to. He listened, and at night did not sleep, because in listening he shared the woes inflicted upon his race.

When the war began, Morris placed his hope for the salvation of the Jews in his trust of the French army. He lived close to his radio, listening to the bulletins and praying for a French victory in the conflict which he called "this righteous war."

On the May day in 1940 when the Germans ripped open the French lines at Sedan, his long-growing anxiety became intolerable. Between waiting on customers, or when he was preparing salads in the kitchen at the rear of the store, he switched on the radio and heard, with increasing dismay, the flood of reports which never seemed to contain any good news. The Belgians surrendered. The British retreated at Dunkerque,[3] and in mid-June, the Nazis, speeding toward Paris in their lorries,[4] were passing large herds of conquered Frenchmen resting in the fields.

Day after day, as the battle progressed, Morris sat on the edge of the cot in the kitchen listening to the additions to his sorrow, nodding his head the way the Jews do in mourning, then rousing himself to hope for the miracle that would save the French as it had saved the Jews in the wilderness. At three o'clock, he shut off the radio, because Leonard came home from school

1. **sexton:** caretaker of a synagogue or church.
2. **pogrom** (pə-grŏm′): organized persecution or massacre of a minority group, especially one conducted against Jews.
3. **Dunkerque** (dœN-kĕrk′): also spelled *Dunkirk;* a seaport in northern France. In 1940, more than 330,000 Allied troops, under enemy fire, were forced to evacuate the beaches there.
4. **lorries:** a British term for motor trucks.

WORDS TO KNOW

overwrought (ō′vər-rôt′) *adj.* excessively nervous or excited
inflict (ĭn-flĭkt′) *v.* to cause to have or suffer; impose

A butcher at a deli in New York City. Photo by Victor Laredo.

about then. The boy, seeing the harmful effect of the war on his father's health, had begun to plead with him not to listen to so many news broadcasts, and Morris pacified him by pretending that he no longer thought of the war. Each afternoon Leonard remained behind the counter while his father slept on the cot. From the dream-filled, raw sleep of these afternoons, the grocer managed to derive enough strength to endure the long day and his own bitter thoughts.

The salesmen from the wholesale grocery houses and the drivers who served Morris were amazed at the way he suffered. They told him that the war had nothing to do with America and that he was taking it too seriously. Some of the others made him the object of their ridicule outside the store. One of them, Gus Wagner, who delivered the delicatessen meats and provisions, was not afraid to laugh at Morris to his face.

Gus was a heavy man, with a strong, full head and a fleshy face. Although born in America, and a member of the AEF[5] in 1918, his imagination was fired by the Nazi conquests and he believed that they had the strength and power to conquer the world. He kept a scrapbook filled with clippings and pictures of the German army. He was deeply impressed by the Panzer divisions,[6] and when he read accounts of battles in which they tore through the enemy's lines, his mind glowed with excitement. He did not reveal his feelings directly because he considered his business first. As it was, he poked fun at the grocer for wanting the French to win.

Each afternoon, with his basket of liverwursts and bolognas on his arm, Gus strode into the store and swung the basket onto the table in the kitchen. The grocer as usual was sitting on the cot, listening to the radio.

5. **AEF:** American Expeditionary Forces; the 2 million U.S. soldiers sent overseas during World War I.

6. **Panzer divisions:** German armored forces, consisting largely of tanks.

WORDS TO KNOW **derive** (dĭ-rīv') *v.* to obtain; get; receive

"Hello, Morris," Gus said, pretending surprise. "What does it say on the radio?" He sat down heavily and laughed.

When things were going especially well for the Germans, Gus dropped his attitude of pretense and said openly, "You better get used to it, Morris. The Germans will wipe out the Frenchmen."

Morris disliked these remarks, but he said nothing. He allowed Gus to talk as he did because he had known the meat man for nine years. Once they had nearly been friends. After the death of Morris's wife four years ago, Gus stayed longer than usual and joined Morris in a cup of coffee. Occasionally he repaired a hole in the screen door or fixed the plug for the electric slicing machine.

Leonard had driven them apart. The boy disliked the meat man and always tried to avoid him. He was nauseated by Gus's laughter, which he called a cackle, and he would not allow his father to do business with Gus in the kitchen when he was having his milk and crackers after school.

Gus knew how the boy felt about him and he was deeply annoyed. He was angered too when the boy added up the figures on the meat bills and found errors. Gus was careless in arithmetic, which often caused trouble. Once Morris mentioned a five-dollar prize that Leonard had won in mathematics and Gus said, "You better watch out, Morris. He's a skinny kid. If he studies too much, he'll get consumption."[7]

Morris was frightened. He felt that Gus was wishing harm upon Leonard. Their relations became cooler, and after that Gus spoke more freely about politics and the war, often expressing his contempt for the French.

The Germans took Paris and pushed on toward the west and south. Morris, drained of his energy, prayed that the ordeal would soon be over. Then the Reynaud cabinet fell. Marshal Pétain[8] addressed a request to the Germans for "peace with honor." In the dark Compiègne forest, Hitler sat in Marshal Foch's railroad car, listening to his terms being read to the French delegation.[9]

That night, after closing his store, Morris disconnected the radio and carried it upstairs. In his bedroom, the door shut tightly so Leonard would not be awakened, he tuned in softly to the midnight broadcast and learned that the French had accepted Hitler's terms and would sign the armistice tomorrow. Morris shut off the radio. An age-old weariness filled him. He wanted to sleep but he knew that he could not.

...the Germans ripped open the French lines at Sedan...

Morris turned out the lights, removed his shirt and shoes in the dark, and sat smoking in the large bedroom that had once belonged to him and his wife.

The door opened softly, and Leonard looked into the room. By the light of the street lamp which shone through the window, the boy could

7. **consumption:** tuberculosis.

8. **Reynaud** (rā-nō′) . . . **Marshal Pétain** (pā-tăN′): Reynaud was the premier of France at the time of its surrender to Germany in June 1940. After the Germans had occupied most of France, Pétain became premier of the unoccupied southern third of the nation. (Marshal is the highest rank in the French army.)

9. **In the dark Compiègne** (kôN-pyĕn′yə) **forest . . . delegation:** This meeting represents a cruel turnabout of Germany's surrender at the end of World War I. In 1918 a German delegation had heard the Allies' peace terms in a railroad car in this same forest. Leading the Allied delegation at that time was France's Marshal Ferdinand Foch (fôsh).

WORDS TO KNOW

pretense (prē′tĕns′) *n.* the act of pretending; a false appearance or action intended to deceive see his father in the chair. It made him think of the time when his mother was in the hospital and his father sat in the chair all night.

Leonard entered the bedroom in his bare feet. "Pa," he said, putting his arm around his father's shoulders, "go to sleep."

"I can't sleep, Leonard."

"Pa, you got to. You work sixteen hours."

"Oh, my son," cried Morris, with sudden emotion, putting his arms around Leonard, "what will become of us?"

The boy became afraid.

"Pa," he said, "go to sleep. Please, you got to."

"All right, I'll go," said Morris. He crushed his cigarette in the ashtray and got into bed. The boy watched him until he turned over on his right side, which was the side he slept on; then he returned to his room.

Later Morris rose and sat by the window, looking into the street. The night was cool. The breeze swayed the street lamp, which creaked and moved the circle of light that fell upon the street.

"What will become of us?" he muttered to himself. His mind went back to the days when he was a boy studying Jewish history. The Jews lived in an interminable exodus.[10] Long lines trudged forever with their bundles on their shoulders.

He dozed and dreamed that he had fled from Germany into France. The Nazis had found out where he lived in Paris. He sat in a chair in a dark room waiting for them to come. His hair had grown grayer. The moonlight fell on his sloping shoulders, then moved into the darkness. He rose and climbed out onto a ledge overlooking the lighted city of Paris. He fell. Something clumped to the sidewalk. Morris groaned and awoke. He heard the purring of a truck's motor and he knew that the driver was dropping the bundles of morning newspapers in front of the stationery store on the corner.

The dark was soft with gray. Morris crawled into bed and began to dream again. It was Sunday at suppertime. The store was crowded with customers. Suddenly Gus was there. He waved a copy of *Social Justice* and cried out, "The Protocols of Zion![11] The Protocols of Zion!" The customers began to leave. "Gus," Morris pleaded, "the customers, the customers—"

He awoke shivering and lay awake until the alarm rang.

After he had dragged in the bread and milk boxes and had waited on the deaf man who always came early, Morris went to the corner for a paper. The armistice was signed. Morris looked around to see if the street had changed, but everything was the same, though he could hardly understand why. Leonard came down for his coffee and roll. He took fifty cents from the till and left for school.

The day was warm and Morris was tired. He grew uneasy when he thought of Gus. He knew that today he would have difficulty controlling himself if Gus made some of his remarks.

At three o'clock, when Morris was slicing small potatoes for potato salad, Gus strode into the store and swung his basket onto the table.

"Well, Morris"—he laughed—"why don't you turn the radio on? Let's hear the news."

Morris tried to control himself, but his bitterness overcame him. "I see you're happy today, Gus. What great cause has died?"

The meat man laughed, but he did not like that remark.

"Come on, Morris," he said, "let's do business before your skinny kid comes home and wants the bill signed by a certified public accountant."

"He looks out for my interests," answered Morris. "He's a good mathematics student," he added.

"That's the sixth time I heard that," said Gus.

---

10. **exodus:** a departure or emigration, usually of a large number of people.

11. **The Protocols of Zion:** anti-Jewish writings concerning an alleged conspiracy to establish a world government ruled by Jews (a notion that has been shown to be completely false). Zion is a name for Israel or the people of Israel, and *protocols,* here, means "agreements or treaties."

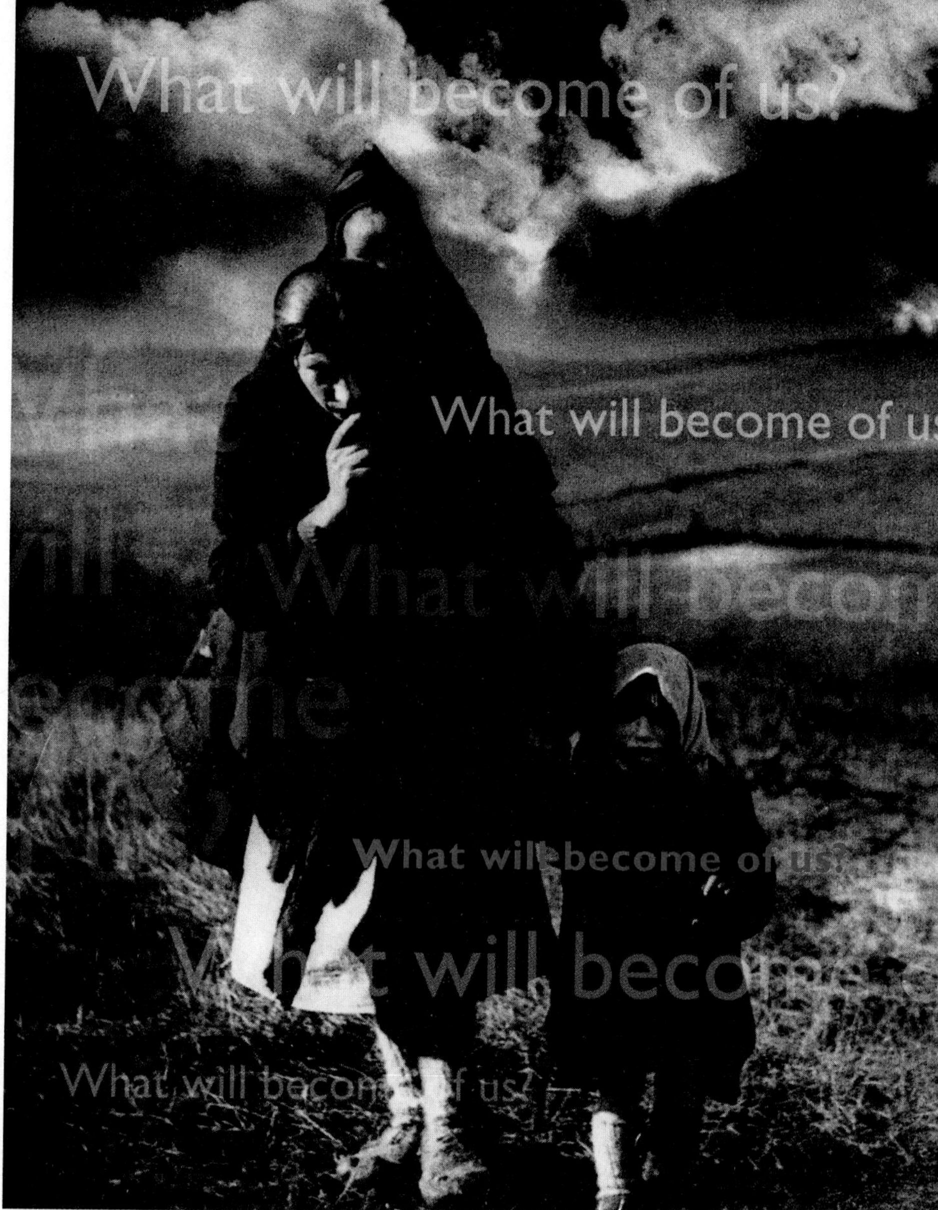

A mother and her children in Yugoslavia in 1943, three of the 10 million Europeans displaced by the war. Photo by George Skrigin.

"You'll never hear it about your children."

Gus lost his temper. "What the hell's the matter with you Jews?" he asked. "Do you think you own all the brains in the world?"

"Gus," Morris cried, "you talk like a Nazi."

"I'm a hundred percent American. I fought in the war," answered Gus.

Leonard came into the store and heard the loud voices. He ran into the kitchen and saw the two men arguing. A feeling of shame and nausea overcame him.

"Pa," he begged, "don't fight."

Morris was still angry. "If you're not a Nazi," he said to Gus, "why are you so glad the French lost?"

"Who's glad?" asked Gus. Suddenly he felt proud and he said, "They deserved to lose, the way they starved the German people. Why the hell do you want them to win?"

"Pa," said Leonard again.

"I want them to win because they are fighting for democracy."

"Like hell," said Gus. "You want them to win because they're protecting the Jews—like that lousy Léon Blum."[12]

"You Nazi, you," Morris shouted angrily, coming from behind the table. "You Nazi! You don't deserve to live in America!"

"Papa," cried Leonard, holding him, "don't fight, please, please."

"Mind your own business, you little . . . ," said Gus, pushing Leonard away.

A sob broke from Leonard's throat. He began to cry.

Gus paused, seeing that he had gone too far.

Morris Lieberman's face was white. He put his

12. **Léon Blum** (bl͞oom): the first Socialist and the first Jew to become, in 1936, premier of France. His social reforms and opposition to the Nazis before and during the war led his enemies to adopt the slogan "Better Hitler than Blum."

arm around the boy and kissed him again and again.

"No, no. No more, Leonard. Don't cry. I'm sorry. I give you my word. No more."

Gus looked on without speaking. His face was still red with anger, but he was afraid that he would lose Morris's business. He pulled two liverwursts and a bologna from his basket.

"The meat's on the table," he said. "Pay me tomorrow."

Gus glanced contemptuously at the grocer comforting his son, who was quiet now, and he walked out of the store. He threw the basket into his truck, got in, and drove off.

As he rode amid the cars on the avenue, he thought of the boy crying and his father holding him. It was always like that with the Jews. Tears and people holding each other. Why feel sorry for them?

Gus sat up straight at the wheel, his face grim. He thought of the armistice and imagined that he was in Paris. His truck was a massive tank rumbling with the others through the wide boulevards. The French, on the sidewalks, were overpowered with fear.

He drove tensely, his eyes unsmiling. He knew that if he relaxed the picture would fade. ❖

Hitler and his advisors parade in Paris ten days after Nazi troops took the city. UPI/Bettmann.

WORDS TO KNOW

contemptuously (kən-tĕmp′cho͞o-əs-lē) *adv.* in a way that shows disdain or disgust; scornfully

RESPONDING OPTIONS

FROM PERSONAL RESPONSE *TO* CRITICAL ANALYSIS

REFLECT **1.** What was your reaction to Gus's daydream at the end of the story? After writing your thoughts in your notebook, share them with classmates.

RETHINK **2.** Why do you think Gus treats Morris and his son, Leonard, the way he does?

3. Why do you think news of the war affects Morris as it does?

Consider
- his memories of the pogrom in Russia
- the two dreams he has

4. In your view, should Morris be as involved in the war as he is?

Consider
- how his health is affected
- what he might mean when he cries "What will become of us?"

5. What connections do you see between the conflict in Europe and the conflict between Gus and Morris?

RELATE **6.** For the Personal Connection, you examined the prejudice of a person you know. How would you compare this person with Gus? Discuss whether the ideas about prejudice that the story presents are borne out by your own experiences.

7. How much anti-Semitism do you think exists in the United States today? Support your answer.

ANOTHER PATHWAY

Cooperative Learning

Gather in groups of three and take on the roles of Gus, Morris, and Leonard in this story. Speaking as the character you've chosen, explain how you see the other two characters. If you are Gus or Morris, recount the fight from your point of view. If you are Leonard, tell how the fight makes you feel.

LITERARY LINKS

Compare Morris Lieberman with Maria from "English as a Second Language" (page 733). Maria, too, fled persecution in her native land. What do you think accounts for the differences between the two characters?

QUICKWRITES

1. Write a **dream interpretation** analyzing the meaning of Morris's two dreams the night before his fight with Gus. Be sure to explain what you think certain actions symbolize and what the dreams reveal about Morris's state of mind.
2. Put yourself in Morris's place. Draft a **letter to the editor** of a newspaper explaining why you consider World War II a "righteous war."
3. Write a **paragraph** about another event abroad that affected how people perceived each other in the United States, perhaps by inflaming prejudices. Read your paragraph in class.

PORTFOLIO *Save your writing. You may want to use it later as a spring-board to a piece for your portfolio.*

LITERARY CONCEPTS

Theme, as you know, refers to the central idea that a writer wishes to share with a reader of a literary work. This idea may be a lesson about life or about people and their actions. Some themes are not obvious and must be figured out by the reader, and sometimes different readers discover different themes. One detail that can suggest the theme of a story is the story's **title**. Think about how the armistice in Europe affects Gus and Morris in Malamud's story. Also think about whether they themselves agree to an armistice at the end of the story. What central idea do you think is suggested by the story's title? What other themes do you see in the story? Write out statements to express these themes, then share them with other students.

CONCEPT REVIEW: Point of View Malamud frequently uses the third-person omniscient point of view, in which the narrator reveals the thoughts of different characters. What do you think would have been lost if "Armistice" had been narrated only from Morris's viewpoint?

CRITIC'S CORNER

Many critics have noted the focus on moral concerns in Bernard Malamud's writing. Evelyn Gross Avery writes in *Rebels and Victims: The Fiction of Richard Wright and Bernard Malamud:* "Malamud defines Jewishness as a willingness to honor the Covenant by sacrificing and suffering for freedom and justice. A good Jew assumes responsibility for all the needy, but has a special obligation to his people. A good Jew awakens others to iniquities." How does Avery's comment affect your understanding of Morris Lieberman?

ALTERNATIVE ACTIVITIES

1. Practice and present a **Readers Theater** performance of this story, with readers taking the parts of Morris, Gus, Leonard, and the narrator. You might use a few items of classroom furniture or some simple props to suggest the setting.
2. Create an **illustration,** perhaps a painting or a collage, to depict Morris's memories of Jewish persecution and his fears for the future.

ART CONNECTION

The photo on page 917 shows a refugee family fleeing during World War II. The photo on page 918 depicts Hitler and his entourage marching through Paris. What emotions and ideas do these pictures call to mind for you? How would you contrast the two processions in the photos?

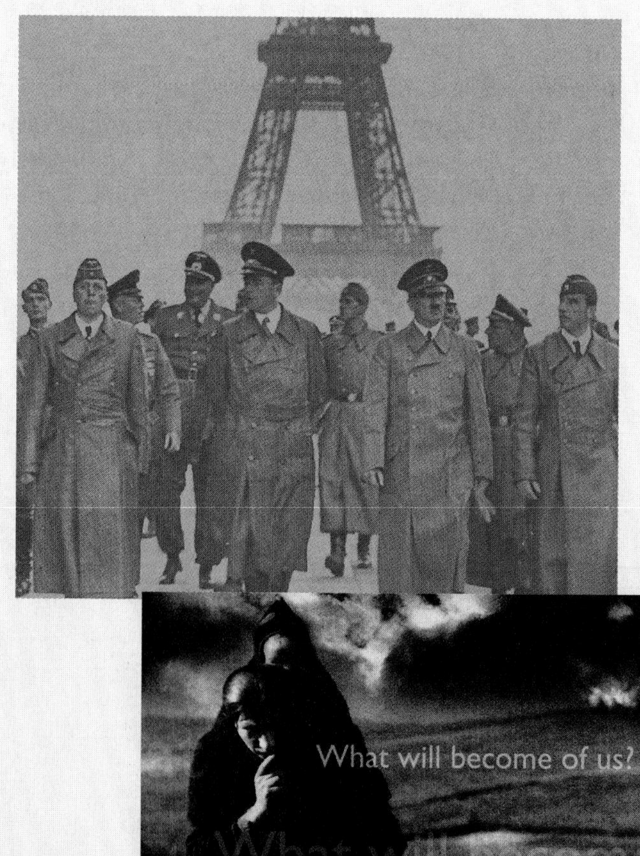
What will become of us?
What will become

ACROSS THE CURRICULUM

History Since ancient times, and in many countries, prejudice against Jews has resulted in discrimination and persecution. Investigate the history of anti-Semitism in Germany, Russia, France, Spain, or some other country, or research details about the Holocaust during World War II. In an oral report, share your knowledge with your classmates.

History Find out more about the German victory over France during World War II, including how it was achieved and what resulted from it. Report your findings in class.

WORDS TO KNOW

EXERCISE A Review the Words to Know in the boxes at the bottom of the selection pages. Then use a vocabulary word to complete each sentence.

1. We Americans can become _____ upon hearing about the tragic results of ethnic discrimination around the world while at the same time failing to recognize our own guilt in this area.
2. During World War II, Americans responded with horror to the Nazis' eagerness to _____ terrible misery on Jews and other minorities.
3. In the novel *Gentleman's Agreement,* published soon after World War II, a journalist uses the _____ that he is Jewish to explore how Jews are treated in the United States.
4. Used to being respected in his dealings with other people, the journalist is dismayed by how _____ he is often treated when he is thought to be Jewish.
5. The conclusions he is able to _____ from his experiment are that anti-Semitism is unfair, destructive, and shockingly widespread in the United States.

EXERCISE B Tell a "round robin" story in which one person begins a story and must keep talking until he or she has used one of the vocabulary words. Another person continues the story until he or she uses another word, and so on, until all the words are used.

LASERLINKS
• *HISTORICAL CONNECTION*

BERNARD MALAMUD

1914–1986

Bernard Malamud grew up in a non-Jewish neighborhood in Brooklyn, New York, where his Russian Jewish immigrant parents owned a grocery store. Many of his stories clearly reflect his early family experience. Like Morris Lieberman in "Armistice," Malamud's father worked long hours just to make a meager living. Noting the close connection between his experience and his writing, Malamud said in an interview published in the *New York Times:* "People say I write so much about misery, but you write about what you write best. As you are grooved, so you are grieved. And the grieving is that no matter how much happiness or success you collect, you cannot obliterate your early experience."

After gaining a master's degree from Columbia University, Malamud taught evening classes at high schools in Brooklyn and Harlem. When he was in his 30s, he moved to Oregon to teach English composition at Oregon State College. During his 12 years at Oregon State, where he taught three days a week and wrote the other four, Malamud produced three novels and a collection of short stories. His first novel, *The Natural,* about a baseball player, was later made into a movie by the same name. In 1961 Malamud began teaching at Bennington College in Vermont. By 1967, when his novel *The Fixer* won both the Pulitzer Prize and the National Book Award, Malamud had become, according to one critic, "one of the foremost writers of moral fiction in America." Throughout his career, he wrote about the need for love, understanding, and responsibility and about the destructiveness of ignorance and hatred. Malamud wrote: "Literature, since it values man by describing him, tends toward morality."

OTHER WORKS *The Assistant, The Magic Barrel, A New Life, Pictures of Fidelman: An Exhibition, The Tenants, Dubin's Lives, God's Grace*

PREVIEWING

POETRY / NONFICTION

The Death of the Ball Turret Gunner
Randall Jarrell

Why Soldiers Won't Talk
John Steinbeck

PERSONAL CONNECTION

The following selections bring to life the old cliché "War is hell." Imagine for a moment, as best you can, what the experience of combat must be like. Visualize yourself as a soldier, suddenly thrust into the nightmare of battle. Then hypothesize an answer to the question John Steinbeck asks: Why do soldiers avoid talking about their combat experience? Jot down your hypothesis in your notebook.

BIOGRAPHICAL CONNECTION

Both Randall Jarrell and John Steinbeck had war-related experiences during World War II. Jarrell served in the U.S. Army Air Force, teaching flight navigation in Arizona. He thus gained firsthand experience with fighter planes and gunners. A ball turret, mentioned in the title of his poem, was a Plexiglas bubble on the underside of certain planes. From it, a machine gunner fired at the enemy during combat. John Steinbeck gained combat experience while working as a news correspondent during World War II. To gather information for his dispatches, he spent time with a Flying Fortress unit in England, reported from North Africa, and accompanied frontline troops during the Allied invasion of Italy.

READING CONNECTION

Analyzing Metaphors and Cause and Effect In "The Death of the Ball Turret Gunner," a combat soldier describes his life and death in a string of metaphors. As you read this poem, try to determine the figurative meaning of important words and phrases, such as "my mother's sleep." In "Why Soldiers Won't Talk," Steinbeck explains the physical experience of combat as a series of causes and effects. As you read the essay, analyze the causes and effects; after reading, list them in a diagram like the one shown. Remember that some events have multiple causes or effects.

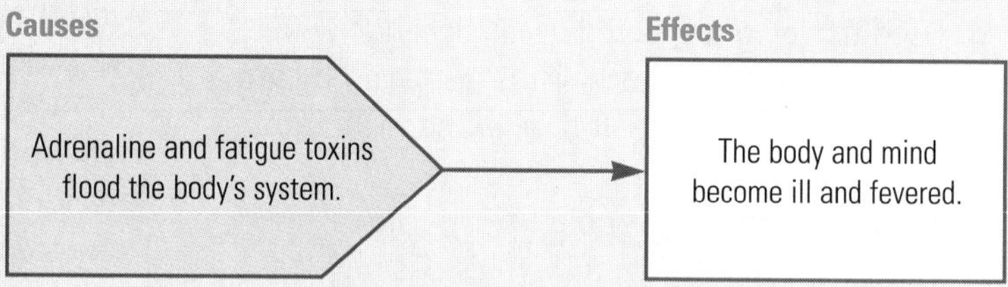
Causes
Effects
Adrenaline and fatigue toxins flood the body's system.
The body and mind become ill and fevered.

LASERLINKS
• PERSONAL CONNECTION

THE DEATH OF THE BALL TURRET GUNNER

RANDALL JARRELL

From my mother's sleep I fell into the State,
And I hunched in its belly till my wet fur froze.
Six miles from earth, loosed from its dream of life,
I woke to black flak[1] and the nightmare fighters.
When I died they washed me out of the turret with a hose.

1. **flak:** the fire of antiaircraft guns.

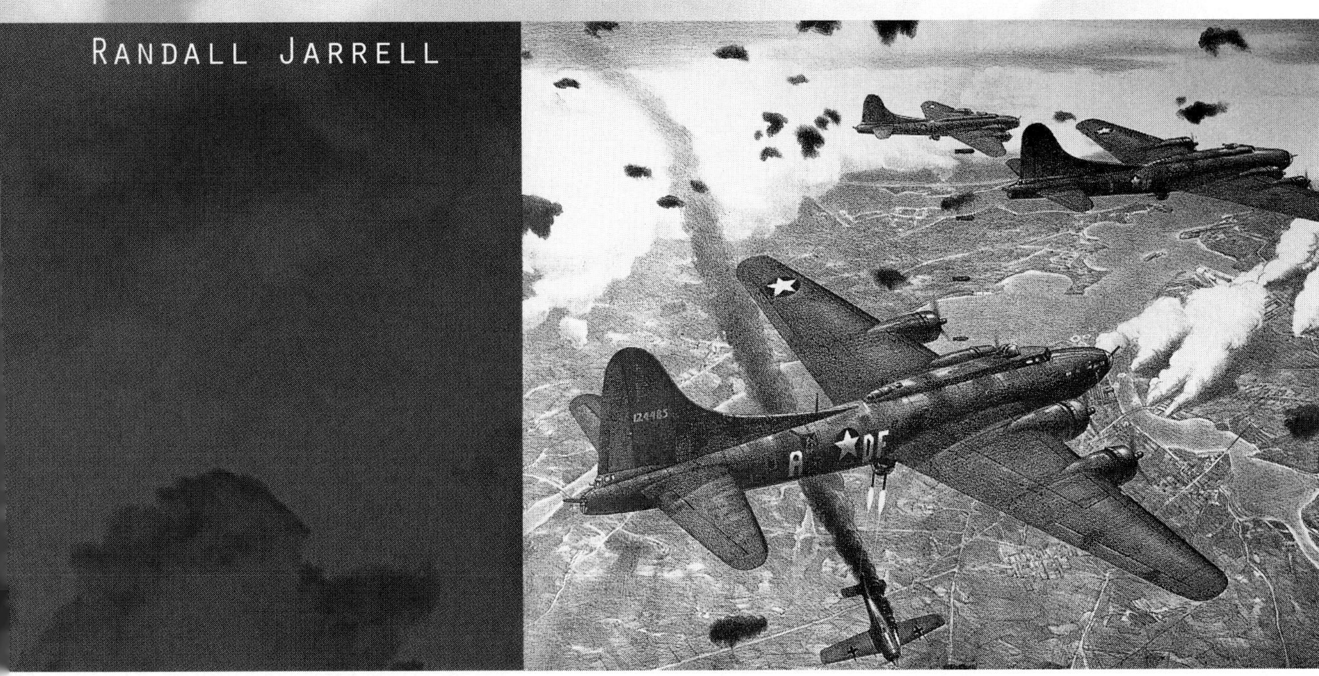

A.F.T.A.D.–"Memphis Belle" B-17 (1943), Stow Wengenroth, by permission of the Estate of Stow Wengenroth.

FROM PERSONAL RESPONSE *TO* CRITICAL ANALYSIS

REFLECT **1.** What is your reaction to the last line of this poem? Share your reaction with your classmates.

RETHINK **2.** In reference to this poem, Randall Jarrell wrote that the gunner, who sat hunched up and revolved with the turret, looked like a fetus in the womb. With this image in mind, try to interpret the first four lines of the poem.

Consider
- what the phrase "fell into the State" might refer to
- what sleeping, dreaming, and waking might mean

3. How would you describe the speaker's attitude toward his death?

4. What does this poem say to you about war and combat?

WHY SOLDIERS WON'T TALK

John Steinbeck

During the years between the last war and this one, I was always puzzled by the reticence[1] of ex-soldiers about their experiences in battle. If they had been reticent men it would have been different, but some of them were talkers and some were even boasters. They would discuss their experiences right up to the time of battle and then suddenly they wouldn't talk any more. This was considered heroic in them. It was thought that what they had seen or done was so horrible that they didn't want to bring it back to haunt them or their listeners. But many of these men had no such consideration in any other field.

Only recently have I found what seems to be a reasonable explanation, and the answer is simple. They did not and do not remember—and the worse the battle was, the less they remember.

In all kinds of combat the whole body is battered by emotion. The ductless glands pour their fluids into the system to make it able to stand up to the great demand on it. Fear and ferocity are products of the same fluid. Fatigue toxins[2] poison the system. Hunger followed by wolfed food distorts the metabolic pattern already distorted by the adrenaline[3] and fatigue. The body and the mind so disturbed are really ill and fevered. But in addition to these ills, which come from the inside of a man and are given him so that he can temporarily withstand pressures beyond his ordinary ability, there is the further stress of explosion.

Under extended bombardment or bombing the nerve ends are literally beaten. The eardrums are tortured by blast and the eyes ache from the constant hammering.

This is how you feel after a few days of constant firing. Your skin feels thick and insensitive. There is a salty taste in your mouth. A hard, painful knot is in your stomach where

1. **reticence:** the tendency to be silent or say little.
2. **toxins:** poisons produced by the body that are capable of causing disease. Fatigue may be a symptom of a toxic infection.
3. **adrenaline** (ə-drĕn′ə-lĭn): a substance, also called epinephrine, secreted by the adrenal gland in response to stress. It speeds up the heartbeat and thereby increases bodily energy and resistance to fatigue.

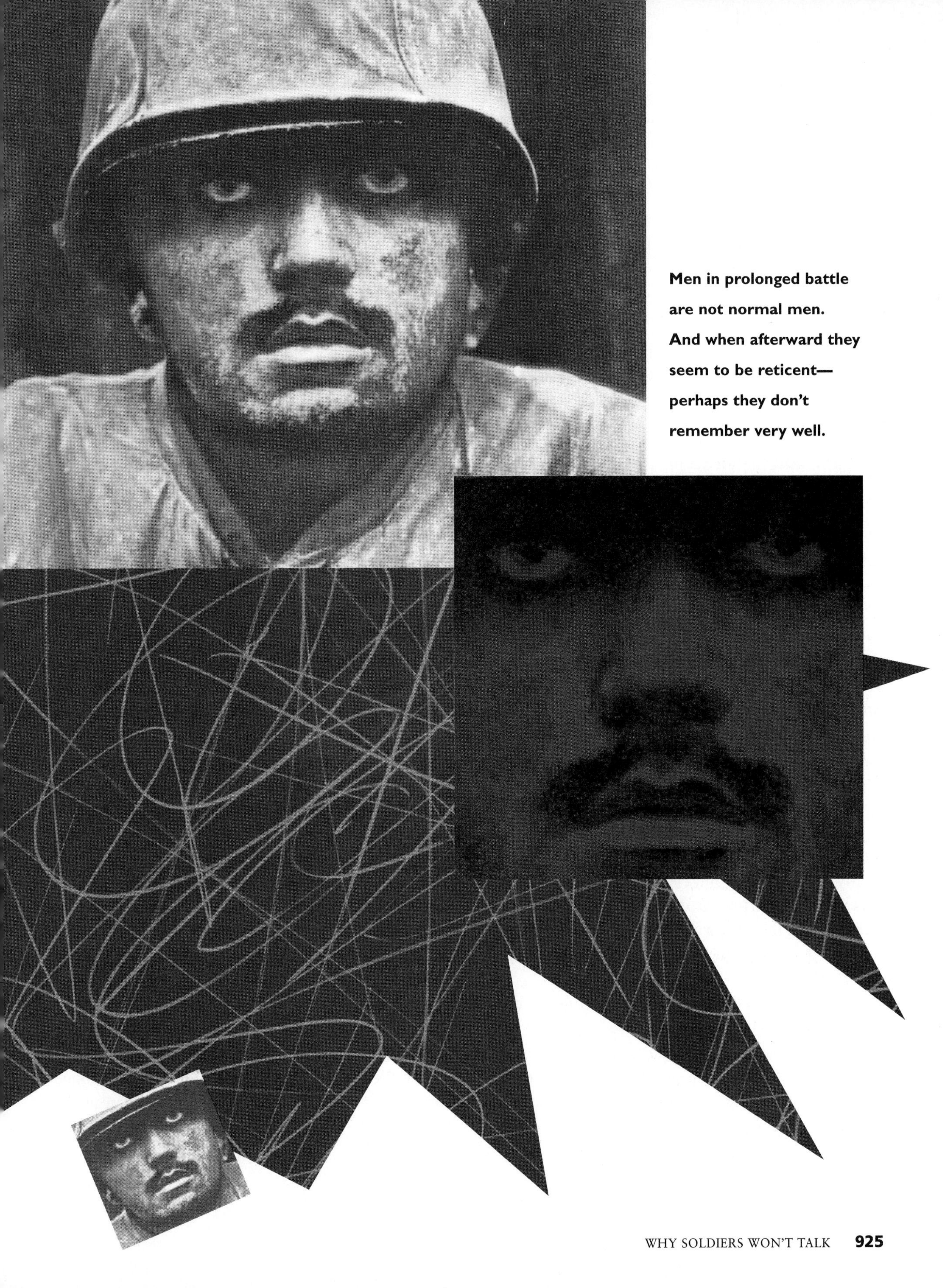

Men in prolonged battle are not normal men. And when afterward they seem to be reticent—perhaps they don't remember very well.

the food is undigested. Your eyes do not pick up much detail and the sharp outlines of objects are slightly blurred. Everything looks a little unreal. When you walk, your feet hardly seem to touch the ground and there is a floaty feeling all over your body. Even the time sense seems to be changed. Men who are really moving at a normal pace seem to take forever to pass a given point. And when you move it seems to you that you are very much slowed down, although actually you are probably moving more quickly than you normally do.

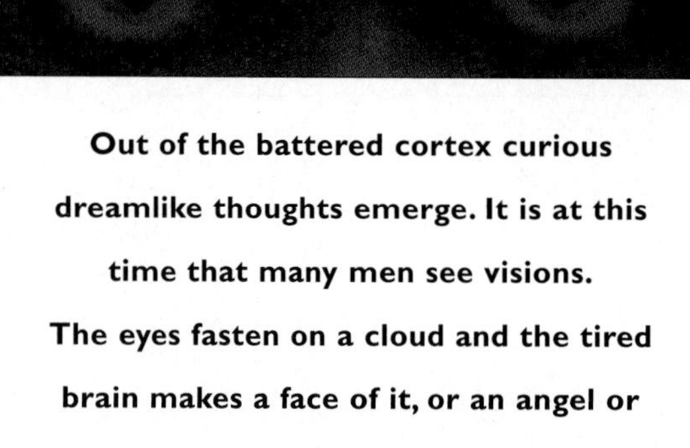

Out of the battered cortex curious dreamlike thoughts emerge. It is at this time that many men see visions. The eyes fasten on a cloud and the tired brain makes a face of it, or an angel or a demon.

Under the blast your eyeballs are so beaten that the earth and the air seem to shudder. At first your ears hurt, but then they become dull and all your other senses become dull, too. There are exceptions, of course. Some men cannot protect themselves this way and they break, and they are probably the ones we call shell-shock cases.

In the dullness all kinds of emphases change. Even the instinct for self-preservation is dulled so that a man may do things which are called heroic when actually his whole fabric of reaction is changed. The whole world becomes unreal. You laugh at things which are not ordinarily funny and you become enraged at trifles. During this time a kind man is capable of great cruelties and a timid man of great bravery, and nearly all men have resistance to stresses beyond their ordinary ability.

Then sleep can come without warning and like a drug. Gradually your whole body seems to be packed in cotton. All the main nerve trunks are deadened, and out of the battered cortex curious dreamlike thoughts emerge. It is at this time that many men see visions. The eyes fasten on a cloud and the tired brain makes a face of it, or an angel or a demon. And out of the hammered brain strange memories are jolted loose, scenes and words and people forgotten, but stored in the back of the brain. These may not be important things, but they come back with startling clarity into the awareness that is turning away from reality. And these memories are almost visions.

And then it is over. You can't hear, but there is a rushing sound in your ears. And you want sleep more than anything, but when you do sleep you are dream-ridden, your mind is uneasy and crowded with figures. The anesthesia your body has given you to protect you is beginning to wear off, and, as with most anesthesia, it is a little painful.

And when you wake up and think back to the things that happened they are already becoming dreamlike. Then it is not unusual that you are frightened and ill. You try to remember what it was like, and you can't quite manage it. The outlines in your memory are vague. The next day the memory slips farther, until very little is left at all. A woman is said to feel the same way when she tries to remember what childbirth was like. And fever leaves this same kind of vagueness on the mind. Perhaps all experience which is beyond bearing is that way. The system provides the shield and then removes the memory, so that a woman can have another child and a man can go into combat again.

It slips away so fast. Unless you made notes on the spot you could not remember how you felt or the way things looked. Men in prolonged battle are not normal men. And when afterward they seem to be reticent—perhaps they don't remember very well. ❖

RESPONDING
OPTIONS

FROM PERSONAL RESPONSE *TO* CRITICAL ANALYSIS

REFLECT 1. For the Personal Connection, you made a hypothesis about why soldiers don't talk about their combat experiences. Were you surprised at the answer proposed in "Why Soldiers Won't Talk"? Write your comments in your notebook.

RETHINK 2. What do you think are the most vivid sensory images Steinbeck uses to make his point?

3. How are you affected by Steinbeck's use of the second-person "you" in his recounting of the physical effects of combat?

4. Does Steinbeck's explanation seem plausible to you?
   Consider
   - the causes and effects he cites
   - your own physical reactions to stress
   - your own memory of stressful events
   - other possible reasons why soldiers might not talk

RELATE 5. Do you think that Jarrell and Steinbeck offer consistent or conflicting accounts of what combat feels like? Explain your answer.

ANOTHER PATHWAY

Cooperative Learning

In a small group, use your Reading Connection diagrams of causes and effects in "Why Soldiers Won't Talk" to create an annotated diagram of the human body, listing physical reactions to the stress of combat. If you have access to a computer, you might use a graphics program to generate the diagram. Share your diagram with the rest of the class.

LITERARY CONCEPTS

As you may recall, **tone** is the attitude a writer takes toward a subject. Tone is communicated partly through **imagery,** words and phrases that appeal to the senses. In "The Death of the Ball Turret Gunner," what mental picture of a soldier is created by the images "hunched in its belly" and "my wet fur froze"? From these images, what would you say is Jarrell's attitude toward the soldier? In "Why Soldiers Won't Talk," Steinbeck uses imagery to convey his attitude toward soldiers. Describe this attitude and show how it is communicated by Steinbeck's imagery. Do Jarrell and Steinbeck seem to have the same attitude toward war as a whole? Explain.

QUICKWRITES

1. Write two **epitaphs**—brief inscriptions on a tombstone—for the ball turret gunner. Write one that an official of "the State" might compose for him and one that the gunner might write for himself if he could.
2. Coin a medical term for the condition that Steinbeck describes in "Why Soldiers Won't Talk." Then write an **encyclopedia entry** giving a definition of the term and detailing the symptoms of the condition.
3. Write a **personal narrative** describing a situation in which you experienced extreme fear or stress. Focus on the physical reactions you had to the stress.

PORTFOLIO *Save your writing. You may want to use it later as a springboard to a piece for your portfolio.*

ALTERNATIVE ACTIVITIES

1. Set up an **interview** with a combat veteran of Vietnam, Desert Storm, or any other world conflict. Does the veteran avoid talking in detail about actual battle experience? If permitted, tape-record your interview and share it with the class.
2. Study the photograph of the B-17 on page 923, or any photograph of a B-17 or B-24 with a ball turret. Create a **model** of the plane with a gunner inside. Show your model to the class, sharing your own thoughts about what it would feel like to be inside such a plane.

ACROSS THE CURRICULUM

Psychology Investigate the condition known as *shell shock,* which is also called *battle fatigue* or *combat fatigue.* In an oral report, describe the symptoms of this condition to your classmates.

RANDALL JARRELL

1914–1965

Randall Jarrell has been called "America's foremost poet of World War II." He drew upon his four years of army service and upon news dispatches from the war front in writing *Little Friend, Little Friend,* the collection in which some of his best-known poems appear. In praise of the collection, critic Suzanne Ferguson wrote, "The motif of the soldier as a child who barely learns the meaning of his life before he loses it, who lives and dies in a dream, . . . is developed in one striking poem after another."

Born into a working-class family in Nashville, Tennessee, Jarrell spent much of his childhood in Long Beach, California. He earned a master's degree from Vanderbilt University in 1939 and went on to become a professor of creative writing and literature and a highly respected literary critic. A man who enjoyed playing tennis and driving sports cars, Jarrell died at the age of 51 after being struck by a car.

OTHER WORKS *Losses, Pictures from an Institution, The Woman at the Washington Zoo, Complete Poems*

JOHN STEINBECK

1902–1968

In 1962 John Steinbeck became the sixth American to win the Nobel Prize in literature. In his acceptance speech, he said: "Literature is as old as speech. It grew out of human need for it, and it has not changed except to become more needed. . . . The ancient commission of the writer has not changed. He is charged with exposing our many grievous faults and failures, with dredging up to the light our dark and dangerous dreams, for the purpose of improvement." In the classic novel that brought him the most acclaim, *The Grapes of Wrath,* Steinbeck brought to light the suffering and exploitation of Depression-era migrant laborers.

Steinbeck's life spanned both world wars, the Korean War, and the Vietnam War, in which one of his sons served. A husky, six-foot-tall man, Steinbeck cherished his privacy and avoided publicity, preferring to live simply and casually. As a young man, he held jobs as a ranch hand, a factory worker, and a construction worker. An avid outdoorsman, Steinbeck developed an early interest in biology, and with his close friend, marine biologist Edward Ricketts, he wrote about sea life in *Sea of Cortez.*

OTHER WORKS *Tortilla Flat, In Dubious Battle, Of Mice and Men, Cannery Row, East of Eden, The Winter of Our Discontent, Travels with Charley*

PREVIEWING

NONFICTION/POETRY

Letter from Paradise
Joan Didion

In Response to Executive Order 9066
Dwight Okita

PERSONAL CONNECTION

"Yesterday, December 7, 1941—a date which will live in infamy—the United States of America was suddenly and deliberately attacked by naval and air forces of the Empire of Japan." With those words, President Franklin D. Roosevelt, in response to the Japanese bombing of the U.S. naval base at Pearl Harbor in Oahu, Hawaii, began his request to Congress to declare war against Japan. What do you know about the attack on Pearl Harbor? What do you know about the later internment, or confinement, of Japanese Americans living on the West Coast of the United States? Brainstorm with a small group of classmates in order to share your knowledge.

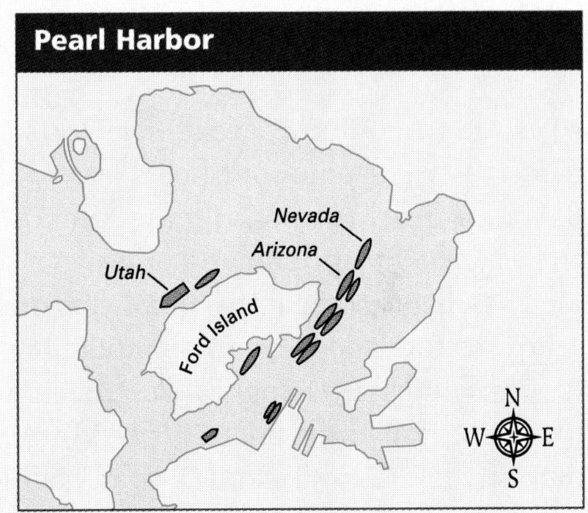

HISTORICAL CONNECTION

When the first Japanese bombs struck Pearl Harbor shortly before eight in the morning, the American forces were utterly unprepared. Anchored ships, such as the *Nevada,* the *Utah,* and the *Arizona,* provided easy targets for bombs and torpedoes. Most American airplanes, parked in orderly rows, were destroyed on the ground. In the attack, 18 ships were sunk or damaged, nearly 200 planes were destroyed, and thousands of people were killed.

The attack spawned American hatred and fear of Japan—and of Japanese Americans. Fearing that Japanese Americans would cooperate with the enemy, people on the West Coast of the United States sought to have all persons of Japanese ancestry—citizens and noncitizens alike—removed from coastal areas. Such a removal was authorized by President Roosevelt in Executive Order 9066. During 1942 more than 110,000 Japanese Americans living along the West Coast were forcibly removed from their homes and sent to internment camps called "relocation centers."

Read Joan Didion's essay, which describes her visit to Pearl Harbor 25 years after the attack, and Dwight Okita's poem, which gives a Japanese-American girl's response to the relocation order, to gauge the repercussions of that "day of infamy" in 1941.

WRITING CONNECTION

Imagine that the United States is suddenly attacked today by a foreign country. How do you suppose Americans would react? Would they support an immediate declaration of war? How would they treat citizens who had originally come from the attacking country, or whose relatives lived there? In your notebook, invent a scenario in which the United States is attacked and then write your prediction of the U.S. government's response.

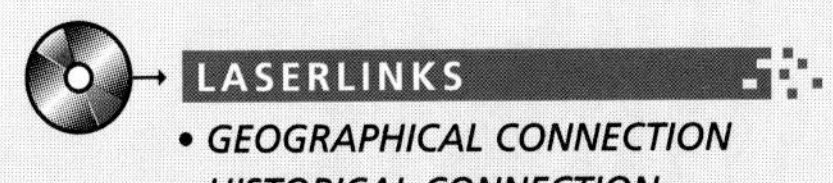

- *GEOGRAPHICAL CONNECTION*
- *HISTORICAL CONNECTION*

Letter from Paradise, 21° 19′ N., 157° 52′ W

Joan Didion

Every afternoon now, twenty-five years after the fact, the bright pink tour boats leave Kewalo Basin for Pearl Harbor. It has a kind of sleazy[1] festivity, the prospect of an outing on a fine day, the passengers comparing complaints about their tour directors and their accommodations and the food at Canlis' Charcoal Broiler, the boys diving for coins around the boats; "Hey Mister Big," they scream. "How's about a coin." Sometimes a woman will throw a bill, and then be outraged when the insolent brown bodies pluck it from the air and jeer at her expectations. As the boat leaves the basin the boys swim back, their cheeks stuffed with money, and the children pout that they would rather be at the beach, and the women in their new Liberty House[2] shifts and leftover leis[3] sip papaya juice and study a booklet billed as *An Ideal Gift—Picture Story of December 7.*

It is, after all, a familiar story that we have come to hear—familiar even to the children, for of course they have seen John Wayne and John Garfield at Pearl Harbor, have spent countless rainy afternoons watching Kirk Douglas and Spencer Tracy and Van Johnson[4] wonder out loud why Hickam[5] does not answer this morning —and no one listens very closely to the guide. Sugar cane now blows where the *Nevada* went aground. An idle figure practices putting on Ford Island.[6] The concessionaire breaks out more papaya juice. It is hard to remember what we came to remember.

And then something happens. I took that bright pink boat to Pearl Harbor on two afternoons, but I still do not know what I went to find out, which is how other people respond a quarter of a century later. I do not know because there is a point at which I began to cry, and to notice no one else. I began to cry at the place where the *Utah* lies in fifty feet of water, water neither turquoise nor bright blue here but the grey of harbor waters everywhere, and I did not stop until after the pink boat had left the *Arizona,* or what is visible of the *Arizona:* the rusted after-gun turret[7] breaking the grey water, the flag at full mast because the Navy considers the *Arizona* still in commission, a full crew aboard, 1,102 men from forty-nine states. All I know about how other people respond is what I am told: that everyone is quiet at the *Arizona.*

---

1. **sleazy:** shabby; cheap; shoddy.
2. **Liberty House:** a major department store in Hawaii.
3. **leis** (lāz): wreaths made of large colorful flowers and worn around the neck.
4. **John Wayne . . . Van Johnson:** Hollywood actors who starred in films dramatizing the attack on Pearl Harbor.
5. **Hickam:** Hickam Air Force Base, near Pearl Harbor. It also was attacked on December 7.
6. **Ford Island:** an island within Pearl Harbor.
7. **after-gun turret:** a low, revolving gun mount located in the "aft," or rear part, of a ship.

A few days ago someone just four years younger than I am told me that he did not see why a sunken ship should affect me so, that John Kennedy's assassination, not Pearl Harbor, was the single most indelible event of what he kept calling "our generation." I could tell him only that we belonged to different generations, and I did not tell him what I want to tell you, about a place in Honolulu that is quieter still than the *Arizona:* the National Memorial Cemetery of the Pacific. They all seem to be twenty years old, the boys buried up there in the crater of an extinct volcano named Punchbowl, twenty and nineteen and eighteen and sometimes not that old.

Copyright © 1991 P.J. Griffiths/Magnum Photos Inc.

"SAMUEL FOSTER HARMON," one stone reads. "PENNSYLVANIA. PVT 27 REPL DRAFT 5 MARINE DIV. WORLD WAR II. APRIL 10 1928—MARCH 25 1945." Samuel Foster Harmon died, at Iwo Jima,[8] fifteen days short of his seventeenth birthday. Some of them died on 7 December, and some of them died after the *Enola Gay* had

---

8. **Iwo Jima** (ē′wə jē′mə): Iwo Jima and Okinawa (ō′kĭ-nä′wə), mentioned later, are islands that lie several hundred miles south of Japan. They were the sites of the last two major World War II battles in the Pacific. In 1942 a battle on the island of Guadalcanal (gwŏd′l-ka-năl′), east of New Guinea, raged for six months. Together, the three battles produced more than 80,000 casualties.

The battleship *Arizona,* sunk in the Pearl Harbor attack. From the white platform (seen from the side in the photo above), observers look down at the submerged wreck. Copyright © 1991 H.K. Owen/Black Star.

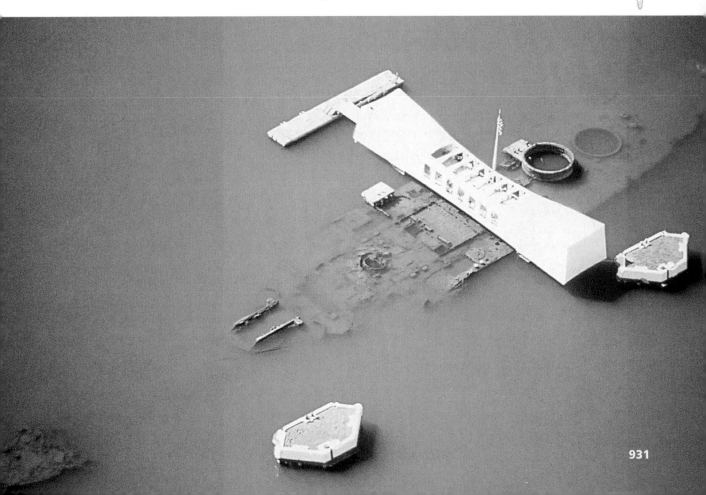

already bombed Hiroshima, and some of them died on the dates of the landings at Okinawa and Iwo Jima and Guadalcanal, and one whole long row of them, I am told, died on the beach of an island we no longer remember. There are 19,000 graves in the vast sunken crater above Honolulu.

I would go up there quite a bit. If I walked to the rim of the crater, I could see the city, look down over Waikiki[9] and the harbor and the jammed arterials,[10] but up there it was quiet, and high enough into the rain forest so that a soft mist falls most of the day. One afternoon a couple came and left three plumeria[11] leis on the grave of a California boy who had been killed, at nineteen, in 1945. The leis were already wilting by the time the woman finally placed them on the grave, because for a long time she only stood there and twisted them in her hands. On the whole I am able to take a very long view of death, but I think a great deal about what there is to remember, twenty-one years later, of a boy who died at nineteen. I saw no one else there but the men who cut the grass and the men who dig new graves, for they are bringing in bodies now from Vietnam. The graves filled last week and the week before that and even last month do not yet have stones, only plastic identification cards, streaked by the mist and splattered with mud. The earth is raw and trampled in that part of the crater, but the grass grows fast, up there in the rain cloud. ❖

---

9. **Waikiki** (wī′kĭ-kē′): a beach and resort district near Honolulu, on the Hawaiian island of Oahu.
10. **arterials:** major streets and highways.
11. **plumeria** (plo͞o-mîr′ē-ə): a tropical tree bearing large fragrant, colorful flowers.

FROM PERSONAL RESPONSE *TO* CRITICAL ANALYSIS

REFLECT

1. What images from this essay stay with you? Record them in your notebook.

RETHINK

2. How do you explain Didion's reaction to visiting Pearl Harbor?
3. Didion first describes Pearl Harbor, then the National Memorial Cemetery of the Pacific. What links do you see between the two places?
4. Do you think the title of this essay is a good one? Offer reasons why Didion might have chosen it.
5. What point do you think Didion is making in this essay?
   Consider
   - the last lines of the selection
   - any ironies you see in the details she includes

RELATE

6. If you have ever visited a war memorial, or any other memorial to the dead, how did your reaction compare with Didion's in this essay?

In Response to Executive Order 9066: ALL AMERICANS OF JAPANESE DESCENT MUST REPORT TO RELOCATION CENTERS

Dwight Okita

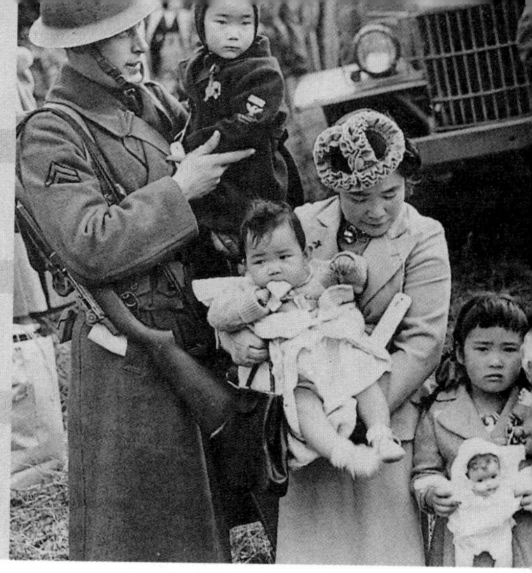

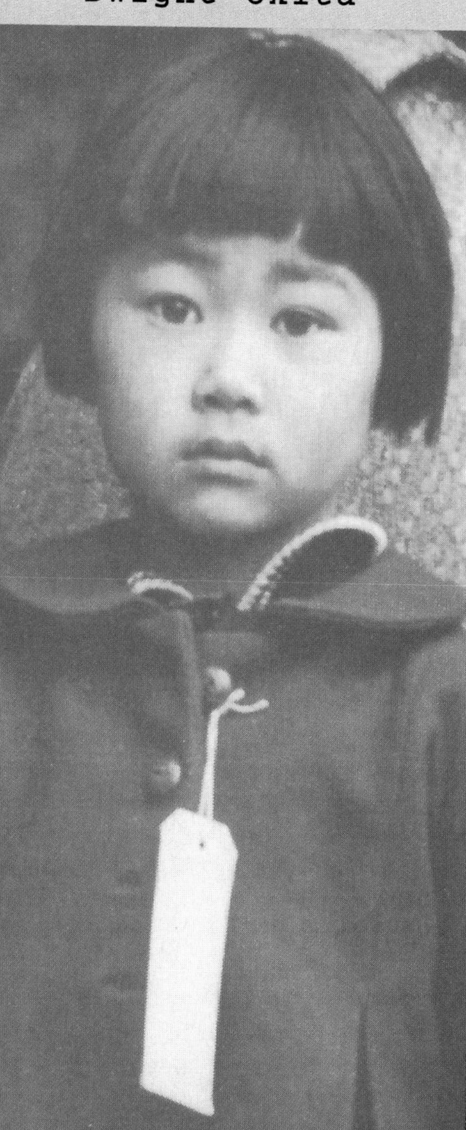

Dear Sirs:
Of course I'll come. I've packed my galoshes
and three packets of tomato seeds. Denise calls them
love apples. My father says where we're going
they won't grow.

I am a fourteen-year-old girl with bad spelling
and a messy room. If it helps any, I will tell you
I have always felt funny using chopsticks
and my favorite food is hot dogs.
My best friend is a white girl named Denise—
we look at boys together. She sat in front of me
all through grade school because of our names:
O'Connor, Ozawa. I know the back of Denise's head very
well.

Clockwise from top: a woman and her children arriving at the relocation center in Manzanar, California; men in Manzanar; a young girl on evacuation day

I tell her she's going bald. She tells me I copy on tests.
We're best friends.

I saw Denise today in Geography class.
She was sitting on the other side of the room.
"You're trying to start a war," she said, "giving secrets
away to the Enemy, Why can't you keep your big
mouth shut?"

I didn't know what to say.
I gave her a packet of tomato seeds
and asked her to plant them for me, told her
when the first tomato ripened
she'd miss me.

Clockwise from top: a car carrying a family to Manzanar; schoolgirls reciting the Pledge of Allegiance a few weeks before evacuation; a sign posted on the boundary of a relocation center; barracks at Manzanar

RESPONDING OPTIONS

FROM PERSONAL RESPONSE *TO* CRITICAL ANALYSIS

REFLECT 1. What thoughts and feelings do you have about the speaker in Okita's poem? Write them in your notebook.

RETHINK 2. What do the details that the speaker mentions communicate to you about her?

3. If you had been in the speaker's situation, would your attitude toward the executive order have been similar to hers? Explain.

4. How do you interpret what the speaker's friend Denise says to her?

5. What do you think the tomato seeds might represent in the poem?
   Consider
   - what Denise calls them
   - where they will not grow
   - what the speaker says Denise will do when they ripen

RELATE 6. Judging from the photos on pages 933 and 934, what do you think the internment experience was like for Japanese Americans?

7. When read together, what do Didion's essay and Okita's poem say to you about the effects of the attack on Pearl Harbor?

LITERARY CONCEPTS

As you know, **mood** is the feeling or atmosphere that the writer creates for the reader. Imagery, setting, dialogue, and figurative language all contribute to the mood of a work, as do the sound and the rhythm of the language used. How would you describe the mood Didion creates in the first paragraph of her essay with such images as bright pink tour boats and boys diving for coins? When does the mood change, and what changes it? Does it change again, or does it stay the same throughout the rest of the selection? Compare the mood of Didion's essay with that of Okita's poem, noting phrases that contribute to the mood of the poem.

ANOTHER PATHWAY

Make two cartoon sketches of the speaker in "In Response to Executive Order 9066." The first should depict her as she views herself, and the second should show her as she is perceived by other Americans after the attack on Pearl Harbor. Base your images on details and dialogue from the poem. Present your sketches to the class.

QUICKWRITES

1. In her essay, Didion says, "I think a great deal about what there is to remember, twenty-one years later, of a boy who died at nineteen." In your mind, re-create this 19-year-old boy, giving him a name as well as physical and personal characteristics. Then write a short **memoir** detailing what a parent or a sister might remember most about him.

2. Draft a **commentary** on the internment of Japanese Americans during World War II. Tell whether you think it was justified and whether you think something like it could ever happen in the future. To prompt your thinking, you might consider the scenario you imagined for the Writing Connection on page 929.

PORTFOLIO *Save your writing. You may want to use it later as a springboard to a piece for your portfolio.*

ALTERNATIVE ACTIVITIES

Cooperative Learning In a small group, discuss what these two selections have to say about the price that young soldiers, their families, and Japanese Americans paid during World War II. Work together to design a **memorial** that commemorates the young lives affected by the war. For example, you might design a plaque that pays tribute in words and symbols to those who suffered.

THE WRITER'S STYLE

Both Didion and Okita write in an understated style, not boldly offering their opinions but instead carefully piling up **descriptive details.** Which do you think are the most telling details included in each piece? Consider ones that are particularly informative or ironic. Explain your choice of details, telling what important ideas you believe the writer is suggesting with them.

JOAN DIDION

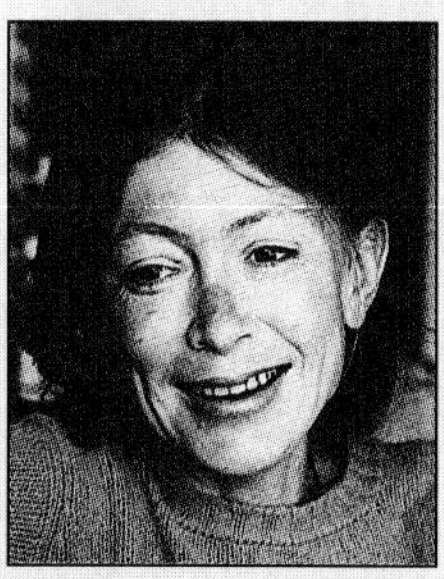

1934–

Joan Didion has received as much acclaim for her essays as she has for her best-selling novels. Critic Robert Towers describes her distinctive talent as "an instinct for details that continue to emit pulsations in the reader's memory and a style that is spare, subtly musical in its phrasing and exact." Like "Letter from Paradise, 21° 19′ N., 157° 52′ W.," her other essays tend to have a personal, confessional tone. In her collections of essays *Slouching Towards Bethlehem* and *The White Album,* as well as in her best-selling novels *Play It as It Lays* and *A Book of Common Prayer,* Didion deals with the themes of personal and cultural loss, disorder, and anxiety.

A screenwriter as well as a journalist and novelist, Didion was born and raised in California, where she has lived most of her life. She is married to the writer John Gregory Dunne, with whom she sometimes collaborates on screenplays. Of her writing, Didion says, "I write entirely to find out what I'm thinking, what I'm looking at, what I see and what it means. What I want and what I fear."

OTHER WORKS *Run River, Salvador, After Henry, Miami*

DWIGHT OKITA

1958–

A Japanese American and a native Chicagoan, Dwight Okita has been writing poetry since first grade. When given writing assignments in school, he had difficulty creating "linear compositions," and so he would add rhymed poems at the end of his assignments. His teachers started grading both his assigned compositions and his poems—giving him poor grades for the compositions but good grades for his poems. In high school, Okita took an interest in writing, acting, and music. Today, he combines these interests by giving dramatic readings of his poetry, which he often sets to music. Besides being a poet, Okita also writes plays and musicals.

In writing "In Response to Executive Order 9066," Okita adopted the voice of his mother, who, as a youngster during World War II, was sent to an internment camp. He imagined how she might have said goodbye to her classmates before being taken away. Okita says that he gives all his poems a test: "I pick it up the next day and if it still moves me, I know it's good." This poem, which has appeared in numerous anthologies, passed the test. Okita's play *Letters I Never Wrote* began as a spinoff of the poem.

OTHER WORKS *Crossing with the Light, The Rainy Season, Salad Bowl Dance, Richard Speck*

PREVIEWING

FICTION

Village

Estela Portillo Trambley

PERSONAL CONNECTION

You've probably heard the saying "All's fair in love and war." The following story investigates the truth of that statement. Imagine yourself in a combat situation. Do the concepts of right and wrong apply? If so, which actions would you consider right, and which ones wrong? To explore these questions, copy in your notebook the chart shown here and evaluate each action listed by marking the "Right" or "Wrong" column. When you are finished, join a small group of classmates to discuss whether it is possible to be a soldier and follow your conscience.

Action	Right	Wrong
Following orders		
Disobeying an officer because you disagree with an order		
Killing an enemy soldier		
Harming civilians		
Harming civilians when following orders		

HISTORICAL CONNECTION

For many reasons, American soldiers in the Vietnam War found it difficult to distinguish between right and wrong. One reason was that soldiers could not always differentiate between enemies and peaceful civilians. Some farming families who lived in villages and worked in rice paddies during the day aided the Viet Cong, the enemy, during the night. On occasion, when U.S. soldiers destroyed villages that were believed to be shelters for the Viet Cong, they injured and killed Vietnamese women and children.

READING CONNECTION

Inferring Author's Purpose Sometimes an author is quite clear in stating his or her specific reason for writing something. At other times, however, the reader must infer the author's purpose. As you read "Village," pay attention to the behavior, thoughts, and feelings of the main character, Rico. Notice what the author seems to present as right and what she seems to present as wrong. Also notice what you are moved to feel or do at the end of the story. Use this information to guess the author's purpose for writing.

Girls help a woman plant new rice in the paddies near their small Vietnamese village during the Vietnam War. UPI/Bettmann.

• *HISTORICAL CONNECTION*

Estela Portillo Trambley

Village

Rico stood on top of a bluff overlooking Mai Cao.[1] The whole of the wide horizon was immersed in a rosy haze. His platoon was returning from an all-night patrol. They had scoured the area in a radius of thirty-two miles, following the length of the canal system along the Delta, furtively on the lookout for an enemy attack. On their way back, they had stopped to rest, smoke, drink warm beer after parking the carry-alls[2] along the edge of the climb leading to the top of the bluff. The hill was good cover, seemingly safe.

Harry was behind him on the rocky slope. Then, the sound of thunder overhead. It wasn't thunder, but a squadron of their own helicopters on the usual run. Rico and Harry sat down to watch the planes go by. After that, a stillness, a special kind of silence. Rico knew it well, the same kind of stillness that was a part of him back home, the kind of stillness that makes a man part of his world—river, clearing, sun, wind. The stillness of a village early in the morning—barrio[3] stillness, the first stirrings of life that come with dawn. Harry was looking down at the village of Mai Cao.

"Makes me homesick . . ." Harry lighted a cigarette.

Rico was surprised. He thought Harry was a city dude. Chicago, no less. "I don't see no freeway or neon lights."

"I'm just sick of doing nothing in this damned war."

No action yet. But who wanted action? Rico had been transformed into a soldier, but he knew he was no soldier. He had been trained to kill the enemy in Vietnam. He watched the first curl of smoke coming out of one of the chimneys. They were the enemy down there. Rico didn't believe it. He would never believe it. Perhaps because there had been no confrontation with Viet Cong[4] soldiers or village people. Harry flicked away his cigarette and started down the slope. He turned, waiting for Rico to follow him. "Coming?"

"I'll be down after a while."

"Suit yourself." Harry walked swiftly down the bluff, his feet carrying with them the dirt yieldings in a flurry of small pebbles and loose earth. Rico was relieved. He needed some time by himself, to think things out. But Harry was right. To come across an ocean just to do routine checks, to patrol ground where there was no real danger . . . it could get pretty bad. The enemy was hundreds of miles away.

The enemy! He remembered the combat bible—kill or be killed. Down a man—the lethal lick: a

1. **Mai Cao** (mī'kou').
2. **carry-alls:** enclosed trucks with lengthwise seats or benches facing each other.
3. **barrio** (bä'rē-ō'): in the United States, a neighborhood inhabited chiefly by Hispanics.
4. **Viet Cong:** Communist rebels who fought to overthrow the South Vietnamese government and against whom U.S. soldiers fought; also called VC.

WORDS TO KNOW
immerse (ĭ-mûrs') *v.* to cover completely in, or as if in, a liquid; submerge
furtively (fûr'tĭv-lē) *adv.* in a secret or hidden manner
lethal (lē'thəl) *adj.* causing death; deadly

garrotte strangling[5] is neater and more quiet than the slitting of a throat; grind your heel against a face to mash the brains. Stomp the ribcage to carve the heart with bone splinters. Kill . . .

Hey, who was kidding who? They almost made him believe it back at boot camp in the States. In fact, only a short while ago, only that morning he had crouched down along the growth following a mangrove[6] swamp, fearing an unseen enemy, ready to kill. Only that morning. But now, looking down at the peaceful village with its small rice field, its scattered huts, something had struck deep, something beyond the logic of war and enemy, something deep in his guts.

He had been cautioned. The rows of thatched

5. **garrotte** (gə-rŏt′) **strangling:** a method of strangulation using a cord or wire.

6. **mangrove:** tropical tree or shrub that grows primarily in coastal swamps.

Looking down
at the peaceful village
with its small rice field,
its scattered huts,

something had struck deep,

something beyond the logic
of war and enemy,

something deep in his guts.

Marble Mountain Patrol (1966), Sherman Loudermilk. Watercolor, courtesy of U.S. Marine Corps Museum Art Collection.

huts were not really peoples' homes, but "hootches," makeshift temporary stays built by the makeshift enemy. But then they were real enemies. There were too many dead Americans to prove it. The "hootches" didn't matter. The people didn't matter. These people knew how to pick up their sticks and go. Go where? Then how many of these villages had been bulldozed? Flattened by gunfire? Good pyre[7] for napalm,[8] these Vietnamese villages. A new kind of battleground.

Rico looked down and saw huts that were homes, clustered in an intimacy that he knew well. The village of Mai Cao was no different than Valverde,[9] the barrio where he had grown up. A woman came out of a hut, walking straight and with a certain grace, a child on her shoulder. She was walking toward a stream east of the slope. She stopped along the path and looked up to say something to the child. It struck him again, the feeling—a bond—people all the same everywhere.

The same scent from the earth, the same warmth from the sun, a woman walking with a child—his mother, Trini. His little mother who had left Tarahumara[10] country and crossed the Barranca del Cobre, taking with her seeds from the hills of Batopilas,[11] withstanding suffering, danger—for what? A dream—a piece of ground in the land of plenty, the United States of America. She had waded across the Rio Grande from Juárez,[12] Mexico, to El Paso, Texas, when she felt the birth pangs of his coming. He had been born a citizen because his mother had had a dream. She had made the dream come true—an acre of riverland in Valverde on the edge of the border. His mother, like the earth and sun, mattered. The woman with the child on her shoulder mattered. Every human life in the village mattered. He knew this not only with the mind but with the heart.

Rico remembered a warning from combat training, from the weary, wounded soldiers who had fought and killed and survived, soldiers sent to Saigon,[13] waiting to go home. His company had been flown to Saigon before being sent to the front. And this was the front, villages like Mai Cao. He felt relieved knowing that the fighting was hundreds of miles away from the people in Mai Cao—but the warning was still there:

Watch out for pregnant women with machine guns. Toothless old women are experts with the knife between the shoulders. Begging children with hidden grenades, the unseen VC hiding in the hootches—village people were not people; they were the enemy. The woman who knew the child on her shoulder, who knew the path to her door, who knew the coming of the sun—she was the enemy.

It was a discord not to be believed by instinct or intuition. And Rico was an Indian, the son of a Tarahumara chieftain. Theirs was a world of instinct and intuitive decisions. Suddenly he heard the sounds of motors. He looked to the other side of the slope, down to the road where the carryalls had started queuing[14] their way back to the post. Rico ran down the hill to join his company.

In his dream, Sergeant Keever was shouting, "Heller, heller . . ." Rico woke with a start. It wasn't a dream. The men around him were scrambling out of the pup tent. Outside most of the men were lining up in uneven formation.

---

7. **pyre** (pīr): pile or heap of material that ignites and burns readily.
8. **napalm** (nā′päm′): jellied gasoline used in some kinds of firebombs and flame-throwers.
9. **Valverde** (väl-vĕr′dĕ).
10. **Tarahumara** (tär′ə-ho͞o-mär′ə): a Native American people of north-central Mexico.
11. **Barranca del Cobre** (bä-räng′kä dĕl kô′brĕ) . . . **Batopilas** (bä-tô-pē′läs).
12. **Juárez** (hwä′rĕs).
13. **Saigon** (sī-gŏn′): formerly the capital of South Vietnam; now called Ho Chi Minh City.
14. **queuing** (kyo͞o′ĭng): moving in a long line.

WORDS TO KNOW

discord (dĭs′kôrd′) *n.* lack of agreement among persons or things
intuition (ĭn′to͞o-ĭsh′ən) *n.* the act or condition of knowing something without consciously learning it

His mother,
like the earth and sun,
mattered.

The woman
with the child on her shoulder
mattered.

Every human life in the village
mattered.

He knew this
not only with the mind
but with the heart.

Madre y niño [Mother and child] (1942), Oswaldo Guayasamin. Courtesy of Christie's, New York.

Rico saw a communiqué[15] in the sergeant's hand. Next to Keever was a lieutenant from communications headquarters. Keever was reading the communiqué:

"Special mission 72 . . . for Company C, platoon 2, assigned at 22 hours. Move into the village of Mai Cao, field manual description—hill 72. Destroy the village."

No! It was crazy. Why? Just words on a piece of paper. Keever had to tell him why. There had to be a reason. Had the enemy come this far? It was impossible. Only that morning he had stood on the slope. He caught up with Keever, blurting out, "Why? I mean—why must we destroy it?"

Sergeant Keever stopped in his tracks and turned steel-blue eyes at Rico. "What you say?"

"Why?"

"You just follow orders, savvy?"[16]

"Are the Viet Cong . . ."

"Did you hear me? You want trouble, private?"

"There's people . . ."

"I don't believe you, soldier. But OK. Tell you as much as I know. We gotta erase the village in case the Viet Cong come this way. That way they won't use it as a stronghold. Now move."

Keever walked away from him, his lips tight in some kind of disgust. Rico did not follow this time. He went to get his gear and join the men in one of the carry-alls. Three carry-alls for the assault—three carry-alls moving up the same road. Rico felt the weight and hardness of his carbine.[17] Now it had a strange, hideous meaning. The machine guns were some kind of nightmare. The mission was to kill and burn and erase all memories. Rico swallowed a guilt that rose from the marrow—with it, all kinds of fear. He had to do something, something to stop it, but he didn't know what. And with all these feelings, a certain reluctance to do anything but follow orders. In the darkness, his lips formed words from the

15. **communiqué** (kə-myo͞o′nĭ-kā′): official communication.

16. **savvy?**: slang for "Do you understand?"

17. **carbine** (kär′bēn′): light automatic or semiautomatic rifle of relatively great power but short range.

The village of Mai Cao was no different than Valverde, the barrio where he had grown up.... It struck him again, the feeling—a bond—people all the same everywhere.

View of Miacatlan, Morelos (1931), René d' Harnoncourt. Painted screen, collection of Anne d' Harnoncourt.

anthem, "My country, 'tis of thee . . ."

They came to the point where the treelines straggled between two hills that rose darkly against the moon. Rico wondered if all the men were of one mind—one mind to kill . . . Was he a coward? No! It was not killing the enemy that his whole being was rejecting, but firing machine guns into a village of sleeping people . . . people. Rico remembered only the week before, returning from their usual patrol, the men from the company had stopped at the stream, mingling with the children, old men, and women of the village. There had been an innocence about the whole thing. His voice broke the silence in the carry-all, a voice harsh and feverish. "We can get the people out of there. Help them evacuate . . ."

"Shut up." Harry's voice was tight, impatient.

The carry-alls traveled through tall, undulant[18] grass following the dirt road that led to the edge of the bluff. It was not all tall grass. Once in a while trees appeared again, clumped around scrub bushes. Ten miles out the carry-alls stopped. It was still a mile's walk to the bluff in the darkness, but they had to avoid detection. Sergeant Keever was leading the party. Rico, almost at the rear, knew he had to catch up to

18. **undulant** (ŭn′jə-lənt): moving with a wavelike motion.

him. He had to stop him. Harry was ahead of him, a silent black bundle walking stealthily through rutted ground to discharge his duty. For a second, Rico hesitated. That was the easy thing to do—to carry out his duty—to die a hero, to do his duty blindly and survive. Hell, why not? He knew what happened to men who backed down in battle. But he wasn't backing down. Hell, what else was it? How often had he heard it among the gringos[19] in his company.

"You Mexican? Hey, you Mexicans are real fighters. I mean, everybody knows Mexicans have guts . . ."

A myth perhaps. But no. He thought of the old guys who had fought in World War II. Many of them were on welfare back in the barrio. But, man! did they have medals! He had never seen so many purple hearts.[20] He remembered old Toque,[21] the wino, who had tried to pawn his medals to buy a bottle. No way, man. They weren't worth a nickel.

He quickly edged past Harry, pushing the men ahead of him to reach the sergeant. He was running, tall grass brushing his shoulder, tall grass that had swayed peacefully like wheat. The figure of Sergeant Keever was in front of him now. There was a sudden impulse to reach out and hold him back. But the sergeant had stopped. Rico did not touch him, but whispered hoarsely, desperately in the dark. "Let's get the people out—evacuate . . ."

"What the hell . . ." Keever's voice was ice. He recognized Rico, and hissed, "Get back to your position soldier or I'll shoot you myself."

Rico did as he was told, almost unaware of the men around him. But at a distance he heard something splashing in the water of the canal, in his nostrils the smell of sweet burnt wood. He looked toward the clearing and saw the cluster of huts bathed in moonlight. In the same moonlight, he saw Keever giving signals. In the gloom he saw the figures of the men carrying machine guns. They looked like dancing grasshoppers as they ran ahead to position themselves on the bluff. He felt like yelling, "For Christ's sake! Where is the enemy?"

The taste of blood in his mouth—he suddenly realized he had bitten his quivering lower lip. As soon as Sergeant Keever gave the signal, all sixteen men would open fire on the huts—machine guns, carbines—everything would be erased. No more Mai Cao—the execution of duty without question, without alternative. They were positioned on the south slope, Sergeant Keever up ahead, squatting on his heels, looking at his watch. He raised himself, after a quick glance at the men. As Sergeant Keever raised his hand to give the signal for attack, Rico felt the cold metallic deadness of his rifle. His hands began to tremble as he released the safety catch. Sergeant Keever was on the rise just above him. Rico stared at the sergeant's arm, raised, ready to fall—the signal to fire. The crossfire was inside Rico, a heavy-dosed tumult—destroy the village, erase all memory. There was ash in his mouth. Once the arm came down, there was no turning back.

In a split second, Rico turned his rifle at a forty-degree angle and fired at the sergeant's arm. Keever half-turned with the impact of the bullet, then fell to his knees. In a whooping whisper the old-time soldier blew out the words, "That . . . —get him." He got up and signaled the platoon back to the carry-alls, as two men grabbed Rico, one hitting him on the side of the head with the butt of his rifle. Rico felt the sting of the blow, as they pinned his arm back and forced him to walk the path back to the carry-all. He did not resist. There was a lump in his throat, and he blinked back tears, tears of relief. The memory of the village would not be erased. Someone shouted in the dark, "They're on to us. There's an old man with a lantern and others coming out of the hootches . . ."

---

19. **gringos** (grĭng′gōs) *Spanish:* a slang term for non-Hispanics, especially white people.

20. **purple hearts:** medals awarded for wounds received in action against an enemy.

21. **Toque** (tō′kĕ).

WORDS TO KNOW

stealthily (stĕl′thə-lē) *adv.* in a quiet, secret, and cautious manner, so as to avoid notice

"People—just people . . ." Rico whispered, wanting to shout it, wanting to tell them that he had done the right thing. But the heaviness that filled his senses was the weight of the truth. He was a traitor—a maniac. He had shot his superior in a battle crisis. He was being carried almost bodily back to the truck. He glanced at the thick brush along the road, thinking that somewhere beyond it was a rice field, and beyond that a mangrove swamp. There was a madman inside his soul that made him think of rice fields and mangrove swamps instead of what he had done. Not once did he look up. Everyone around him was strangely quiet and remote. Only the sound of trudging feet.

In the carry-all, the faces of the men sitting around Rico were indiscernible in the dark, but he imagined their eyes, wide, confused, peering through the dark at him with a wakefulness that questioned what he had done. Did they know his reason? Did they care? The truck suddenly lurched. Deep in the gut, Rico felt a growing fear. He choked back a hysteria rising from the diaphragm. The incessant bumping of the carry-alls as they moved unevenly on the dirt road accused him too. He looked up into a night sky and watched the moon eerily weave in and out of tree branches. The darkness was like his fear. It had no solutions.

Back on the post, Sergeant Keever and a medic passed by Rico, already handcuffed, without any sign of recognition. Sergeant Keever had already erased him from existence. The wheels of justice would take their course. Rico had been placed under arrest, temporarily shackled to a cot in one of the tents. Three days later he was moved to a makeshift bamboo hut, with a guard in front of the hut at all times. His buddies brought in food like strangers, awkward in their silence, anxious to leave him alone. He felt like some kind of poisonous bug. Only Harry came by to see him after a week.

"You dumb jerk, were you on locoweed?" Harry asked in disgust.

"I didn't want people killed, that's all."

"Hell, that's no reason, those chinks[22] aren't even—even . . ."

"Even what?" Rico demanded. He almost screamed it a second time. "Even what?"

"Take it easy, will you? You better go for a Section eight."[23] Harry was putting him aside like everyone else. "They're sending you back to the States next week. You'll have to face Keever sometime this afternoon. I thought I'd better let you know."

"Thanks." Rico knew the hopelessness of it all. There was still that nagging question he had to ask. "Listen, nobody tells me anything. Did you all go back to Mai Cao? I mean, is it still there?"

"Still there. Orders from headquarters to forget it. The enemy were spotted taking an opposite direction. But nobody's going to call you a hero, you understand? What you did was crud. You're no soldier. You'll never be a soldier."

Rico said nothing to defend himself. He began to scratch the area around the steel rings on his ankles. Harry was scowling at him. He said it again, almost shouting, "I said, you'll never be a soldier."

"So?" There was soft disdain in Rico's voice.

"You blew it, man. You'll be locked up for a long, long time."

"Maybe . . ." Rico's voice was without concern.

"Don't you care?"

"I'm free inside, Harry." Rico laughed in relief. "Free . . ."

Harry shrugged, peering at Rico unbelievingly, then turned and walked out of the hut. ❖

---

22. **chinks:** a negative slang term for Chinese or other Asian people.

23. **Section eight:** a discharge from the army based on unfitness for military service or on character traits considered undesirable.

WORDS TO KNOW

indiscernible (ĭn-dĭ-sûr'nə-bəl) *adj.* not seen clearly; not distinguishable
incessant (ĭn-sĕs'ənt) *adj.* never ceasing; constant
eerily (îr'ə-lē) *adv.* in a weird and possibly frightening way
disdain (dĭs-dān') *n.* scorn; contempt

from Dear America: Letters Home from Vietnam

George Olsen

Sept. 17, '69

Red,

Thanks for the letter, but now you've made me self-conscious about my writing. You used some words that rather jolted me: Morbid,[1] Chaplain, and a few others. [They] belong to another world about which I've forgotten an amazing amount as it's irrelevant to anything going on now. I've just about forgotten what college was all about, though there are a few memories that stick in the back of my mind.

Yesterday we took to the bush to recon[2] a river crossing on one of Charlie's[3] major supply routes coming in from Laos. . . . It was an uneventful patrol, but I committed the mortal sin of small-unit patrolling: I broke contact with the man in front of me and split the patrol into two elements, something that could easily prove fatal in the event of contact with the enemy. We'd just crossed the river at a ford to join the team reconning the other bank and were going through fairly green stuff when the man in front of me dropped his lighter. I bent to pick it up and by the time I straightened up he was out of sight and hearing. Had we been hit then, it would have been a bad situation made worse by my stupidity. I've picked up most of the patrolling tricks—taping metal parts to prevent their making noise during movement, wearing bandoliers so the magazines[4] are on your chest and stomach and form makeshift body armor, and other tricks that stretch the odds a little more in your favor and give you a little more of an edge in combat—but I'm still new and yesterday I really loused up. . . .

The fact of the matter is that I was afraid—which I am most of the time over here—but I allowed my fear to interfere with the job at hand, and when that happens to someone, he ceases to be a good soldier. It's all right to be afraid, but you can't allow that fear to interfere with the job because other people are depending on you and you've got responsibility to them and for them. From now on I'll be keeping that in mind and I won't louse up so badly again. Had that happened under fire, people might have died unnecessarily due to me.

One other impression from that patrol is that anyone over here who walks more than 50 feet through elephant grass should automatically get a Purple Heart. Try to imagine grass 8 to 15 feet high so thick as to cut visibility to one yard, possessing razor-sharp edges. Then try to imagine walking through it while all around you are men possessing the latest automatic weapons who desperately want to kill you. You'd be amazed at how such a man can age on one patrol.

---

1. **morbid:** psychologically unhealthy; not wholesome; horrible and gruesome.
2. **recon** (rē′kŏn′): short for *reconnoiter;* to inspect an area in order to gain information, especially military information.
3. **Charlie's:** a slang term referring to the Viet Cong.
4. **bandoliers . . . magazines:** Bandoliers are broad belts with small pockets or loops for carrying ammunition, worn over the shoulder and across the chest. Magazines are small cartridge containers.

U.S. soldiers on patrol in Vietnam in November 1965. Copyright © 1995 Co Rentmeester.

sense precludes[6] giving too many details before the operation. We're going to raid one of Charlie's POW[7] camps and attempt to free some GIs, but that's about all I'll say till we pull it off, if we do.

I may have played up my unit here a bit too much, but I'm proud to be in it and might be inclined to brag. We're not supermen or anything like that, and we're not about to walk into bars, where the music automatically stops at our entrance, and proceed to demolish anybody and everybody in the place. But as far as being soldiers, we're proud of our outfit and its history, and are definitely among the best troops over here. . . . Men have gone on operations here with broken ankles in order not to let their buddies down. So you see, we take our business seriously.

We're supposed to go on a very hard sortie[5] soon which, unless it's canceled, virtually guarantees some hard fighting. I'm not trying to be mysterious or anything, but common

I'm going out now for a run in the sand to toughen my feet up. So I'll be signing out. . . .

George

5. **sortie** (sôr′tē): quick raid.

6. **precludes:** prevents; makes impossible.

7. **POW:** prisoner of war.

George Olsen served seven months in Vietnam as part of an elite reconnaissance patrol. He was killed in action on March 3, 1970.

RESPONDING OPTIONS

FROM PERSONAL RESPONSE *TO* CRITICAL ANALYSIS

REFLECT 1. What comments do you have about Rico's decision to shoot his commander? Write them in your notebook.

RETHINK 2. What do you think Rico means when he tells Harry "I'm free inside"?

3. In your own words, explain Rico's reasons for wanting to save the village. Which of these reasons seems most persuasive to you?

Consider

- Rico's feelings about the Vietnamese landscape, village, and villagers
- his feelings about military training and duty
- his ideas about human life
- his Mexican and Native American heritage
- the reasons Keever gives him for destroying the village

4. Would your impression of Rico's stand change if you learned that Mai Cao had sheltered Viet Cong soldiers all along? Explain your reasoning.

5. What do you think was the author's purpose in writing this story?

RELATE 6. Compare the character Rico with George Olsen, who wrote the Insight letter on page 945. How do you think they would view each other?

7. Look over the chart you completed for the Personal Connection on page 937. Has reading "Village" and the Insight letter changed your ideas about judging right and wrong in a combat situation? Explain why or why not.

ANOTHER PATHWAY

Cooperative Learning

Prepare and stage Rico's trial before a military tribunal. Have individuals take the parts of Rico and the witnesses, with small groups acting as the defense team, the prosecution team, and the tribunal, which serves as both judge and jury. Remaining classmates can act as journalists and write up their observations of the trial.

LITERARY CONCEPTS

As you recall, an **external conflict** is a struggle between a character and an outside force, such as another character, society, or nature. An **internal conflict** is a struggle within a character. What are the external and internal conflicts you see in this story? Which conflicts are resolved, and how are they resolved? Propose other ways in which these conflicts could have been resolved. Are your proposals as satisfying as the author's resolution?

QUICKWRITES

1. Compose your own **definition** of "a good soldier," using examples from "Village" and George Olsen's letter to illustrate your ideas.

2. Write a brief **autobiographical account** of an incident in which you found it hard to distinguish between right and wrong or in which you followed your conscience at a great sacrifice, like Rico.

PORTFOLIO *Save your writing. You may want to use it later as a springboard to a piece for your portfolio.*

ART CONNECTION

The painting on page 939 was done early in the Vietnam War by Sherman Loudermilk, a U.S. soldier. Marble Mountain is a few miles from the city of Da Nang, on the northern coast of the former South Vietnam. The style of the painting shows the influence of traditional Asian watercolors. From the painting, what feelings do you get about the Vietnamese landscape and the people in the landscape? How would you compare this landscape with the Mexican landscape in the three-part painting on page 942?

Detail of *Marble Mountain Patrol* (1966), Sherman Loudermilk. Watercolor, courtesy of U.S. Marine Corps Museum art collection.

CRITIC'S CORNER

Critics Vernon E. Lattin and Patricia Hopkins analyzed Rico's action in this way: "With his respect for the oneness of humankind and the sanctity of life, Rico naturally cannot participate in destroying the village. When he refuses to follow orders, injures his sergeant, and prevents the destruction, he becomes a savior; like other saviors, however, he is not understood. The story leaves him under arrest, . . . externally imprisoned but internally free." Do you view Rico as a misunderstood savior? Explain why or why not.

WORDS TO KNOW

For each group of words below, write the letter of the word that is the best antonym for the boldfaced word.

1. **indiscernible** (a) classy, (b) apparent, (c) difficult
2. **furtively** (a) openly, (b) tightly, (c) courageously
3. **immerse** (a) withdraw, (b) erase, (c) notice
4. **eerily** (a) oddly, (b) dishonestly, (c) normally
5. **lethal** (a) significant, (b) harmless, (c) criminal
6. **disdain** (a) respect, (b) anger, (c) joy
7. **intuition** (a) caution, (b) logic, (c) clumsiness
8. **incessant** (a) sophisticated, (b) resentful, (c) occasional
9. **stealthily** (a) bravely, (b) cheerfully, (c) obviously
10. **discord** (a) harmony, (b) sincerity, (c) preservation

ESTELA PORTILLO TRAMBLEY

1936–

Estela Portillo Trambley is a fiction writer, poet, playwright, and essayist noted for being the first Chicana to publish a book of fiction and the first to write a musical comedy. Born in El Paso, Texas, she was raised by her grandparents until the age of 12, when she returned to live with her parents. She earned a bachelor's and a master's degree in English from the University of Texas at El Paso and has held a variety of jobs, including high school English teacher, drama instructor, and television talk show host. In 1972 she won the annual Quinto Sol Prize for literature.

Portillo Trambley's writings are known for their optimism. Having grown up in barrios, Portillo Trambley has focused her work not on the negative aspects of barrio life but on the joy and spiritual awakening that Chicanos find there. In an interview, she said: "When I was a child, poverty was a common suffering for everybody around me. A common suffering is a richness in itself." Many of her stories, like "Village," portray the importance of family love and the quest for internal freedom.

OTHER WORKS *Rain of Scorpions and Other Stories, The Day of the Swallows, Sun Images, Sor Juana and Other Plays, Trini*

PREVIEWING

POETRY

Camouflaging the Chimera

Yusef Komunyakaa (yo͞o′sĕf kō′mo͞on-yä′kä)

Deciding

Wendy Wilder Larsen and Tran Thi Nga (drän thē nyä)

PERSONAL CONNECTION

These poems present strong personal images of the Vietnam War from two perspectives—that of an American combat soldier and that of a Vietnamese civilian. Think about the mental images you have of the Vietnam War, images acquired from television, movies, newspapers, magazines, books, and/or the experiences of relatives or family friends. In your notebook, create a cluster diagram in which you explore the many images you have of the war.

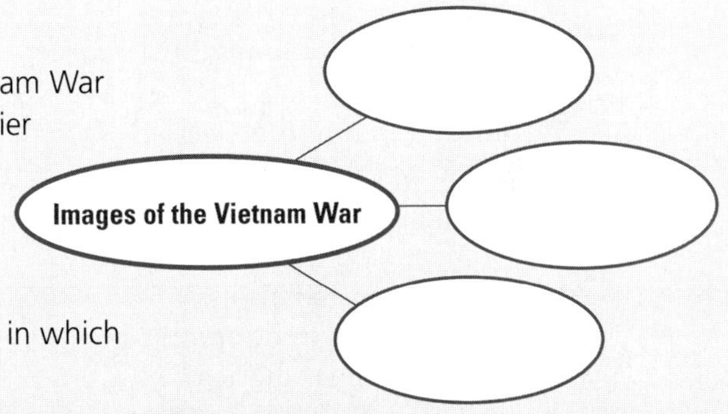

LITERARY/HISTORICAL CONNECTION

The word *chimera* in the title of the first poem has several meanings. It is the name of a mythical fire-breathing monster, a composite of a lion, a goat, and a serpent. The word also refers to a plant created from a mixture of cells of different species. In addition, *chimera* can mean a fantastic or terrible creation of the imagination.

The title of the second poem, "Deciding," refers to the difficult situation the speaker of the poem finds herself in. The speaker is a Vietnamese worker in an American office in Saigon who must decide whether to stay or flee after the United States has withdrawn its troops and the fall of South Vietnam appears imminent. She fears how she will be treated by the Communist victors from North Vietnam.

Bronze statue of a Chimera (about 550 B.C.) Arezzo Etruscan bronze, Archeological Museum, Florence, Italy, Scala/Art Resource, New York.

READING CONNECTION

Appreciating Imagery The power of these two poems comes from their strong visual and tactile images. Read over the images in each poem slowly and more than once. The structure of the poems encourages such a close reading: In "Camouflaging the Chimera," a single image is often developed across a number of short lines, sometimes even across stanzas. In "Deciding," images are often condensed into a single line. These images are fragmentary and concrete, unlike the images in "Camouflaging," which tend to be more evocative and thus perhaps more difficult to grasp—"a way station of shadows," for example. Try to visualize or feel what words in the poems suggest, even if it gives you some difficulty.

Camouflaging the Chimera

Yusef Komunyakaa

We tied branches to our helmets.
We painted our faces & rifles
with mud from a riverbank,

blades of grass hung from the pockets
of our tiger suits. We wove
ourselves into the terrain,
content to be a hummingbird's target.

We hugged bamboo & leaned
against a breeze off the river,
slow-dragging with ghosts

from Saigon to Bangkok,
with women left in doorways
reaching in from America.
We aimed at dark-hearted songbirds.

In our way station of shadows
rock apes tried to blow our cover,
throwing stones at the sunset. Chameleons

crawled our spines, changing from day
to night: green to gold,
gold to black. But we waited
till the moon touched metal,

till something almost broke
inside us. VC struggled
with the hillside, like black silk

wrestling iron through grass.
We weren't there. The river ran
through our bones. Small animals took refuge
against our bodies; we held our breath,

ready to spring the L-shaped
ambush, as a world revolved
under each man's eyelid.

GUIDE FOR READING

1–6 How do you visualize the soldiers from this description?

5 tiger suits: camouflage uniforms with black and green stripes.

7 What might it mean to be "a hummingbird's target"?

10–14 What is revealed about the soldiers' state of mind from their slow-dragging, or dancing, with ghosts and their aiming at songbirds?

11 Saigon (sī-gŏn'): formerly the capital of South Vietnam. **Bangkok** (băng'kŏk'): the capital of Thailand.

15 way station: a station between main stations, as on a railroad line. In what sense is the soldiers' position a "way station"?

16 rock apes: mountain-dwelling monkeys.

16–21 Notice how the passage of time is suggested through these images of nature. In what ways are the soldiers like the chameleons?

23–24 VC . . . silk: The Viet Cong, Communist rebels who fought U.S. soldiers, typically wore black for camouflage during nighttime operations in the jungle.

20–25 How were the American soldiers able to spot the VC?

26–28 How well were the soldiers camouflaged?

Members of a long-range reconnaissance patrol unit. Photo by John Olson for *Life* Magazine.
Copyright © Time Inc.

FROM PERSONAL RESPONSE *TO* CRITICAL ANALYSIS

REFLECT

1. In your notebook, write down what you thought or felt as you visualized the images of the Vietnam War presented in this poem.

RETHINK

2. How do you interpret the last image in the poem?
3. What do you imagine the soldiers thought and felt as they waited in ambush? Support your answer with lines from the poem.
4. In line 26, how do you interpret the statement "We weren't there"?
5. Offer your explanation of the title "Camouflaging the Chimera."

   Consider
   - which definition of *chimera* seems to best fit the poem (see page 949)
   - the visual image brought to your mind by the title

Deciding

Wendy Wilder Larsen and Tran Thi Nga

We went to the office every day.
Though the situation was critical,
people at work said nothing.
Province Chiefs were running.
We told the Big Boss our country would be lost.
We told him we would blow ourselves up
if we could not leave.

I sat at my desk doing the financial report.
My thoughts went round and round.

Should I leave?
Should I go alone?
Should I take my mother?
She did not want to go.
She feared they wouldn't let her chew the betel.
Should I leave my children?
How would I make a living?
What would happen when the communists came?

When I made up my mind,
pictures of my childhood floated to the surface
as clear and strong as dreams.

Our old house in Hadong.
The bamboo in the backyard.
We ate the shoots.
The soldiers made a fence from the stalks.
My sister and I painted the fence
first white, then blue, then her favorite yellow.
The small antigonon vine we planted
with its pink blossoms in spring.

GUIDE FOR READING

1–9 Who are "we"? What state of mind are these people in?

12–14 Who are "they"? What are other reasons the mother might not want to leave?

14 betel (bēt'l): Many Asians chew nuts from the betel palm tree as a mild stimulant.

18–20 Can you tell what the speaker has decided?

21 Hadong (hä'dông'): a town in North Vietnam.

21–34 What can you tell about the speaker's childhood from these images?

27 antigonon (ăn-tĭ'gə-nän').

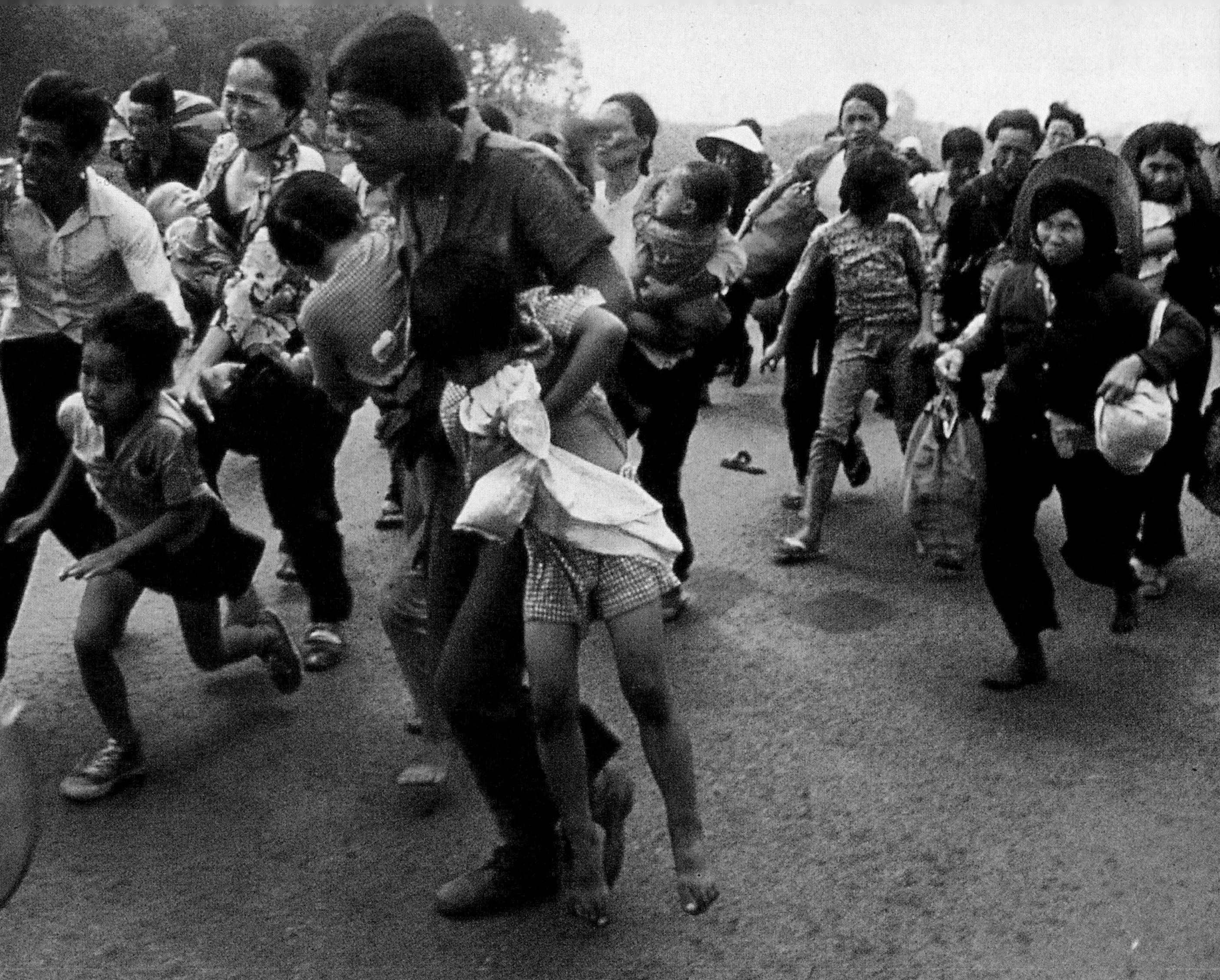

People running for a U.S. helicopter during the fall of Saigon in April 1975. Copyright © 1975 Nik Wheeler/Black Star.

Our ponds.
The many steps down
to the small bridge
where we'd sit hour after hour
letting our hands dip into the water
trying to catch the silver-brown fish.

Airplanes bombing
running from our house
people dying, people calling from outside the walls
don't take me. I'm not dead yet.
The family hiding together in our house in Cholon
sunlight coming through the bullet holes.

39 Cholon (chō-lŏn′): the Chinese section of Saigon, in South Vietnam.

35–40 What mood is created by these images?

RESPONDING OPTIONS

FROM PERSONAL RESPONSE *TO* CRITICAL ANALYSIS

REFLECT

1. If you had been the speaker in "Deciding," would you have stayed or fled? Write your comments in your notebook.

RETHINK

2. How do you think the speaker's childhood memories influenced her decision?
3. What message do you draw from the final image of sunlight shining through bullet holes?

RELATE

4. Look back at the diagram of images you made for the Personal Connection. After reading these poems, what new images of the war would you add?
5. Judging only from these poems, whose experience of war do you think was worse, the American soldiers' or the Vietnamese civilians'?

   Consider
   - the soldiers' feelings as they wait in ambush and what you imagine the attack will be like
   - the memories of the speaker in "Deciding" and the decision she is forced to make
6. What generalizations can you make about the ways people suffer during wartime, based on the selections you've read in this part of Unit Seven?

LITERARY CONCEPTS

Rhythm, as you know, refers to the arrangement of stressed and unstressed syllables in a poem. Poets use rhythm to heighten the power of language, to emphasize ideas, and to create **mood,** or a general atmosphere. The short, staccato rhythm in the third stanza of "Deciding," for example, creates suspense and a mood of urgency and tension. Read several stanzas of each poem aloud to appreciate the various rhythms, and discuss what impact those rhythms have on the mood of the poem.

CONCEPT REVIEW: Imagery How does imagery affect mood in each poem?

ANOTHER PATHWAY

Cooperative Learning

In a small group, prepare a mock television interview with the speakers in the two poems you have just read. Write an opening statement, questions for the interviewer to ask, and answers for the interviewees to give, based on information from the poems. Present your broadcast to the class.

QUICKWRITES

1. Draft a **critical analysis** of either of these poems. State what you think the poet was trying to communicate to you, and evaluate whether he or she was successful. You might identify and interpret the most important lines, point out particularly effective (or ineffective) images, or comment on the structure of the poem.
2. Imagine that you are faced with the necessity of fleeing your country, possibly never to return. In a page of **freewriting,** describe the images of your life that would flood your mind.

PORTFOLIO Save your writing. You may want to use it later as a spring-board to a piece for your portfolio.

ACROSS THE CURRICULUM

Environmental Science Both of these poems give a sense of Vietnam's unique physical environment. Investigate the effects of the war on the natural environment in Vietnam. Create an illustrated and annotated map of the country, detailing the environmental damage wrought.

WENDY WILDER LARSEN

1940–

Born in Boston, Wendy Wilder Larsen lived in Saigon from 1970 to 1971 with her husband, who was head of the local bureau of *Time* magazine. While in Saigon, she taught English literature at the School of Pedagogy and met Tran Thi Nga, a Vietnamese bookkeeper in the *Time* office. In 1975 Larsen encountered Nga again, in New York, after Nga had fled from Saigon with three of her four children and a grandchild. Over lunch, Larsen began to learn about Nga's amazing life.

YUSEF KOMUNYAKAA

1947–

Born in Bogalusa, Louisiana, Yusef Komunyakaa entered the army at age 18, immediately after graduating from high school. After returning from Vietnam, where he earned a Bronze Star, Komunyakaa attended college in Colorado and eventually earned a master of fine arts degree in creative writing from the University of California at Irvine. He has lived in a number of countries for short periods, including Australia, Puerto Rico, and Japan. He is currently professor of English at Indiana University in Bloomington and travels across the United States and abroad to read his poetry. "Camouflaging the Chimera" is the first poem in his collection *Dien Cai Dau,* the title of which is Vietnamese slang for crazy. Komunyakaa won the 1994 Pulitzer Prize for Poetry for his book *Neon Vernacular: New and Selected Poems.*

OTHER WORKS *Lost in the Bonewheel Factory, Copacetic, I Apologize for the Eyes in My Head*

TRAN THI NGA

1927–

Nga was born in China, where her Vietnamese father had been sent to teach. Her family returned to North Vietnam to live when she was still very young. During the Chinese occupation of North Vietnam, 18-year-old Nga married a Chinese general in order to save her father's life. Her husband died in battle, and Nga became the second wife of her sister's husband, who was the man she had originally loved. In 1954, when Vietnam was divided into North and South, Nga's family moved to Saigon. In 1975, as South Vietnam fell, Nga narrowly escaped with her family; they eventually settled in Connecticut.

Larsen and Nga decided to work together to write Nga's story, to be combined with the story of Larsen's experiences in Saigon. The result was a book in verse, *Shallow Graves: Two Women and Vietnam,* from which "Deciding" comes.

LASERLINKS
• *CULTURAL CONNECTION*

AMBUSH

TIM O'BRIEN

When she was nine, my daughter Kathleen asked if I had ever killed anyone. She knew about the war; she knew I'd been a soldier. "You keep writing these war stories," she said, "so I guess you must've killed somebody." It was a difficult moment, but I did what seemed right, which was to say, "Of course not," and then to take her onto my lap and hold her for a while. Someday, I hope, she'll ask again. But here I want to pretend she's a grown-up. I want to tell her exactly what happened, or what I remember happening, and then I want to say to her that as a little girl she was absolutely right. This is why I keep writing war stories:

> "YOU KEEP WRITING THESE WAR STORIES SO I GUESS YOU MUST'VE KILLED SOMEBODY."

He was a short, slender young man of about twenty. I was afraid of him—afraid of something—and as he passed me on the trail I threw a grenade that exploded at his feet and killed him.

Or to go back:

Shortly after midnight we moved into the ambush site outside My Khe.[1] The whole platoon was there, spread out in the dense brush along the trail, and for five hours nothing at all happened. We were working in two-man teams —one man on guard while the other slept, switching off every two hours —and I remember it was still dark when Kiowa shook me awake for the final watch. The night was foggy and hot. For the first few moments I felt lost, not sure about directions, groping for my helmet and weapon. I reached out and found three grenades and lined them up in front of me; the pins had already been straightened for quick throwing. And then for maybe half an hour I kneeled there and waited. Very gradually, in tiny slivers, dawn began to break through the fog, and from my position in the brush I could see ten or fifteen meters up the trail. The mosquitoes were fierce. I remember slapping at them, wondering if I should wake up Kiowa and ask for some repellent, then thinking it was a bad idea, then looking up and seeing the young man come out of the fog. He wore black clothing and rubber sandals and a gray ammunition belt. His shoulders were slightly stooped, his head cocked to the side as if listening for something. He seemed at ease. He

1. **My Khe** (mī′kĕ′).

Fenixes (1984), Rupert Garcia. Pastel on paper, 40″ × 78¾″, courtesy of Rupert Garcia; Rena Bransten Gallery, San Francisco; and Galerie Claude Samuel, Paris. Copyright © Rupert Garcia.

THERE WERE NO THOUGHTS ABOUT KILLING. THE GRENADE WAS TO MAKE HIM GO AWAY—JUST EVAPORATE—AND I LEANED BACK AND FELT MY MIND GO EMPTY AND THEN FELT IT FILL UP AGAIN.

EVEN NOW I HAVEN'T FINISHED SORTING IT OUT. SOMETIMES I FORGIVE MYSELF, OTHER TIMES I DON'T.

carried his weapon in one hand, muzzle down, moving without any hurry up the center of the trail. There was no sound at all—none that I can remember. In a way, it seemed, he was part of the morning fog, or my own imagination, but there was also the reality of what was happening in my stomach. I had already pulled the pin on a grenade. I had come up to a crouch. It was entirely automatic. I did not hate the young man; I did not see him as the enemy; I did not ponder issues of morality or politics or military duty. I crouched and kept my head low. I tried to swallow whatever was rising from my stomach, which tasted like lemonade, something fruity and sour. I was terrified. There were no thoughts about killing. The grenade was to make him go away—just evaporate—and I leaned back and felt my mind go empty and then felt it fill up again. I had already thrown the grenade before telling myself to throw it. The brush was thick and I had to lob it high, not aiming, and I remember the grenade seeming to freeze above me for an instant, as if a camera had clicked, and I remember ducking down and holding my breath and seeing little wisps of fog rise from the earth. The grenade bounced once and rolled across the trail. I did not hear it, but there must've been a sound, because the young man dropped his weapon and began to run, just two or three quick steps, then he hesitated, swiveling to his right, and he glanced down at the grenade and tried to cover his head but never did. It occurred to me then that he was about to die. I wanted to warn him. The grenade made a popping noise—not soft but not loud either—not what I'd expected—and there was a puff of dust and smoke—a small white puff—and the young man seemed to jerk upward as if pulled by invisible wires. He fell on his back. His rubber sandals had been blown off. There was no wind. He lay at the center of the trail, his right leg bent beneath him, his one eye shut, his other eye a huge star-shaped hole.

It was not a matter of live or die. There was no real peril. Almost certainly the young man would have passed by. And it will always be that way.

Later, I remember, Kiowa tried to tell me that the man would've died anyway. He told me that it was a good kill, that I was a soldier and this was a war, that I should shape up and stop staring and ask myself what the dead man would've done if things were reversed.

None of it mattered. The words seemed far too complicated. All I could do was gape at the fact of the young man's body.

Even now I haven't finished sorting it out. Sometimes I forgive myself, other times I don't. In the ordinary hours of life I try not to dwell on it, but now and then, when I'm reading a newspaper or just sitting alone in a room, I'll look up and see the young man coming out of the morning fog. I'll watch him walk toward me, his shoulders slightly stooped, his head cocked to the side, and he'll pass within a few yards of me and suddenly smile at some secret thought and then continue up the trail to where it bends back into the fog. ❖

Tim O'Brien

1946–

In 1968, immediately after graduating from college with a bachelor's degree in political science, Tim O'Brien was drafted into the army. He was wounded in Vietnam, earning a Purple Heart. Discharged from the army as a sergeant, he accepted a full scholarship to Harvard University as a graduate student in government. While studying at Harvard, O'Brien wrote *If I Die in a Combat Zone, Box Me Up and Ship Me Home,* a book of memoirs about his combat experiences. He subsequently left Harvard to pursue writing as a full-time career.

O'Brien's third book, *Going After Cacciato,* won the National Book Award in 1979. Inspired by O'Brien's own struggle with the choice of whether to go to Vietnam or flee the country, the novel tells about a soldier who decides to escape from Vietnam and the army.

Although he writes about war, O'Brien does not consider himself a war novelist. The true concern of his writing, he says, is "the exploration of substantive, important human values." Regarding his most acclaimed novel, O'Brien said in an interview, "It's not really Vietnam that I was concerned about when I wrote *Cacciato;* rather, it was to have readers care about what's right and wrong and about the difficulty of doing right, the difficulty of saying no to a war."

Born and raised in Minnesota, O'Brien studied magic as a young boy, and he sees a connection between magic and writing—a common concern with mystery. He defines a writer as "someone entranced by the power of language . . . to shine light into the darkness of the great human mysteries."

OTHER WORKS *Northern Lights, The Nuclear Age, The Things They Carried, In the Lake of the Woods*

WRITING ABOUT LITERATURE

In Their Own Style

If someone covered up the authors' names, do you think you could tell a story by Estela Portillo Trambley from one by Joan Didion? Writing styles are individual and unique—as unique as your voice or your handwriting. In this lesson, you will

- learn the components of a writer's personal style
- write a story or poem in an author's style
- identify the attributes of your own personal style

The Writer's Style: Developing a Personal Style
An author's writing style is very personal. Writers combine figurative language, sentence structure, punctuation, tone, and word choice in a way that's uniquely their own.

Read the Literature

What makes each of these writers' styles unique? Is it their choice of words or how they put a sentence together?

Literature Models

Figurative Language and Sentence Structure
What metaphor does Trambley use? Does she seem to prefer simple, compound, or complex sentences?

Keever walked away from him, his lips tight in some kind of disgust. Rico did not follow this time. He went to get his gear and join the men in one of the carry-alls. Three carry-alls for the assault—three carry-alls moving up the same road. Rico felt the weight and hardness of his carbine. Now it had a strange, hideous meaning. The machine guns were some kind of nightmare. The mission was to kill and burn and erase all memories.

Estela Portillo Trambley, from "Village"

Sentence Length and Punctuation
Compare Didion's sentence with Trambley's sentences. What do you notice? What is striking about Didion's use of punctuation?

I began to cry at the place where the *Utah* lies in fifty feet of water, water neither turquoise nor bright blue here but the grey of harbor waters everywhere, and I did not stop until after the pink boat had left the *Arizona*, or what is visible of the *Arizona*: the rusted after-gun turret breaking the grey water, the flag at full mast because the Navy considers the *Arizona* still in commission, a full crew aboard, 1,102 men from forty-nine states.

Joan Didion, from "Letter from Paradise, 21° 19′ N., 157° 52′ W."

Connect to Life

Every writer has his or her own style. Many newspaper and magazine columnists are known for their styles. Some are wordy, others are terse. Some are compassionate, others are irreverent. Notice this columnist's unique style.

Newspaper Column

This suicide pact with domesticity continued for a couple more generations until one day I informed my son I had tried to clean his room and was cut on the arm when a spear fell off the wall, had double vision for six hours after the bunk bed top fell on me, and was overcome by the fumes from the dead fish floating in the aquarium.

He said, "Then don't go in there."

Erma Bombeck, from "Cleaning house can be dangerous to your health"
Kokomo Tribune

Tone and Word Choice
How does Bombeck's tone set her apart from other writers? Does she use formal or informal language?

Try Your Hand: Developing a Style

1. **In Didion's Style** Describe a place, imitating Didion's style in the excerpt on page 960.
2. **In Trambley's Style** Describe that same place, using Trambley's style. Model her use of figurative language and sentence structure.
3. **In Bombeck's Style** Rewrite the description again, this time as if Bombeck were writing it. Try to capture her humorous tone and use of exaggeration.
4. **In Your Style** Now describe that same place in your own words. Notice the kinds of changes you make. What makes your writing style unique?

SkillBuilder

WRITER'S CRAFT

Using Figurative Language How an author uses figurative language is part of his or her own personal writing style.

Metaphor See how Trambley and Komunyakaa make unique comparisons:

The machine guns were some kind of nightmare.

. . . a world revolved under each man's eyelid.

Simile Notice how Trambley uses *like* and Tim O'Brien uses *as* in these comparisons:

They looked like dancing grasshoppers as they ran ahead to position themselves on the bluff.

. . . the young man seemed to jerk upward as if pulled by invisible wires.

Using Imagery Vivid imagery can also be an important part of a writer's style. Notice how Steinbeck appeals to your sense of sight and touch with this image:

Under the blast your eyeballs are so beaten that the earth and the air seem to shudder.

APPLYING WHAT YOU'VE LEARNED Describe each of the following, using figurative language or vivid imagery.

1. the sunrise
2. tall grass
3. a harbor
4. a helicopter ride

Creative Response

Did you ever wish that you could write like a famous author? Would you like to be able to put a story together in the style of John Steinbeck or Ernest Hemingway or write a poem as magical as one by Gwendolyn Brooks? In this lesson you'll have a chance to write in an author's style. Learning what makes an author's style unique can help you develop your own personal style.

GUIDED ASSIGNMENT

Writing in the Author's Style Working alone or in a small group, write a story or poem in an author's style. Try to mimic his or her use of figurative language, sentence structure, punctuation, tone, and word choice.

1 Prewrite and Explore

Look over the stories and poems in Unit Seven, "Conflict at Home and Abroad." Which authors have a particularly effective style? Which would be interesting to imitate?

Group's Spider Map

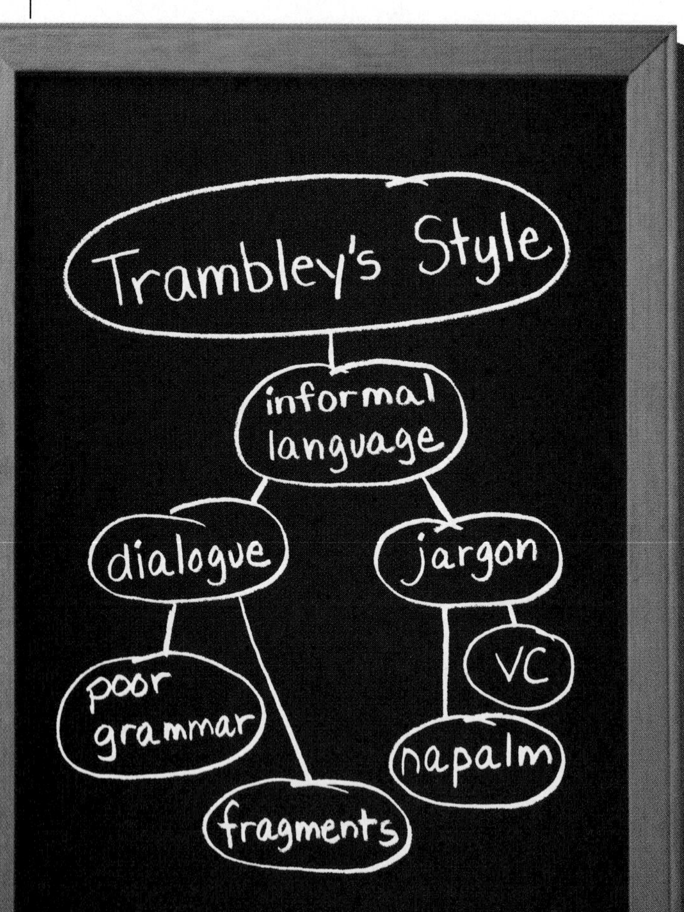

Decision Point Decide which author's style you will try to imitate.

ANALYZE THE AUTHOR'S STYLE

Find other students who selected the same author. Work together to analyze the author's style, looking at the following:

- Does the writer use imagery and figurative language, or does the writer prefer straightforward, objective description?
- What kinds of words does the writer use (abstract words, concrete words, formal words, jargon)?
- How long are the writer's sentences?
- How does the writer structure sentences (simple, compound, complex, or compound-complex)?
- Does the writer show a preference for a specific type of punctuation (such as dashes, colons, or ellipses)?
- What tone or attitude does the writer have toward the subject?

You may want to collect your group's findings on a spider map, like the one a group has just started on the left.

❷ Play with Ideas

Now it's time to get some ideas down on paper. Choose an idea or a theme that your author would be comfortable writing about. It might be a sequel to the story or poem, or it could be about a completely new topic. You can write on your own or with a group. In a group, each student could write a paragraph or stanza and then pass it on, or you might decide to freewrite the entire story or poem together. At this stage, don't worry about mimicking the author's style.

Group's Draft

Thang looked down and saw adobe homes huddled together. Valverde was no different from the village he grew up in. A woman opened the door of her adobe to get the morning paper. The same old news, the same hot sun, the same people. A feeling struck Thang—an overwhelming need to sing "It's a Small World After All."

Thang remembered a warning from basic training. Watch out for teenagers with switchblades in their combs. Little old ladies with handguns under their mattresses. Smiling children with mustard in their supersoakers. These aren't people; they're the enemy!

This is too close to Trambley's story.

❸ Draft and Review

Read your story or poem. Decide where it needs work. Decide whether it's even going in the right direction. Then write your draft. Keep the author's style in mind, but—for now—focus on ideas. When your group's draft is done, evaluate it. Discuss how to add elements of the author's style.

 PEER RESPONSE

- Where is the word choice particularly strong or weak?
- Which sentences seem most like those the author would use?
- Where might imagery be added?

SkillBuilder

 WRITER'S CRAFT

Using Punctuation in the Author's Style

Some authors show a preference for certain types of punctuation. They use such marks as dashes, commas, colons, or ellipses in large quantities or in unusual ways.

Dashes Trambley seems to like dashes. She uses them in place of commas or to represent missing words. Note how Trambley uses a dash to highlight parallel items:

Rico wondered if all the men were of one mind—one mind to kill . . .

Commas Didion likes to combine a multitude of images to create an effect. She uses plenty of commas to string her images together.

It has a kind of sleazy festivity, the prospect of an outing on a fine day, the passengers comparing complaints about their tour directors and their accommodations and the food at Canlis' Charcoal Broiler, the boys diving for coins around the boats; "Hey Mister Big," they scream.

APPLYING WHAT YOU'VE LEARNED

As you write in an author's style, focus on how the author uses punctuation.

 GRAMMAR HANDBOOK

For more information about punctuation, see pages 1231–1239 of the Grammar Handbook.

4 Revise and Edit

As you revise your draft, use your group's suggestions to capture the author's style. When all the stories and poems are finished, see if others can identify the author by the writing style. Have you learned any techniques that you'd like to use in your own style?

Group's Final Draft

Therapy

"They're people—just people!" Rico sat up startled, sweating.

"Don't worry, Mr. Juarez. Just another flashback." Dr. Hroncich leaned back in his chair. "Tell me again, how long have you been having this dream?"

"Almost six years now—ever since Nam."

"Let's go over it one more time. Maybe something new will come up."

Rico lay back on the couch. "It always starts out the same. I see a man standing on a hill overlooking a sleepy town. The big, wide Texas landscape is washed in a yellow glow. He feels the dry desert air and hears the river lapping on the shore. The man looks down at the adobes huddled together. He thinks, This barrio is no different from the village I grew up in. Same cold earth, same rising sun, same people. About this time, I always realize that it's my barrio he's looking at—my Valverde."

How does this dialogue resemble the dialogue in "Village"?

What kind of sentence structure did the group use?

How did this group mimic Trambley's use of punctuation?

Standards for Evaluation

A creative response in the author's style
- mimics the author's use of figurative language
- uses the same sentence structure as the author
- mimics the author's word choice and punctuation
- is similar in tone to the author's tone

Grammar in Context

Combining Sentences Didion and Malamud prefer to use long, complicated compound, complex, or compound-complex sentences. Even Trambley uses them occasionally. If you find your draft sentences are too short or simple for your author's style, combine sentences. Notice how complex sentences are created by turning some simple sentences into clauses; compound sentences are created by combining two simple sentences.

After the

~~The~~ squad struggled across the sandy desert~~. They~~, they followed a well-worn path up to the top of the hill. Some men crouched down, rifles in position~~. Others~~; others positioned themselves behind scattered trees.

Combining sentences can help show or clarify the relationship between ideas. Combining sentences can also eliminate the choppy feeling caused by too many short sentences in a row. For information on punctuating compound and complex sentences, see page 1231 of the Grammar Handbook.

Try Your Hand: Combining Sentences

On a separate sheet of paper, combine each set of two sentences into one compound or complex sentence.

1. Rico, Harry, and the rest of the platoon returned from their patrol. They stopped at the village by the edge of a stream.
2. Four noisy carry-alls traveled through tall, undulant grass. They followed the dirt road to the edge of the bluff.
3. Harry, his best friend for the last six months, walked ahead of him. He was a silent figure walking through rutted ground.
4. Rico quickly edged past Harry, Washington, Ziefel, and Nakagawa. He had to talk to Sergeant Keever before something awful happened.

SkillBuilder

G→ GRAMMAR FROM WRITING

Using Simple and Complex Sentences

The way authors put sentences together is part of their style.

Simple Trambley generally writes in simple sentences. Even her longer sentences are still simple sentences, with just one independent clause and no subordinate clauses. Notice how Trambley's sentences get shorter and simpler— often becoming sentence fragments— when the action is stressful.

No! It was crazy. Why? Just words on a piece of paper. Keever had to tell him why. There had to be a reason. Had the enemy come this far? It was impossible.

Complex In contrast to Trambley's use of simple sentences, Bernard Malamud relies on complex sentences in "Armistice." Notice how he links a subordinate clause to an independent clause:

On the May day in 1940 when the Germans ripped open the French lines at Sedan, his long-growing anxiety became intolerable.

APPLYING WHAT YOU'VE LEARNED

Use the information from the clauses below to create two simple and two complex sentences.

- When the platoon returned from an all-night patrol
- Which had scoured an area 32 miles in radius
- Who were on the lookout for an enemy attack

READING THE WORLD

Express Yourself

Just as authors have their own writing styles, you have your own personal style. Your style makes a statement about who you are and how you want to be treated. You express that style in the way you walk, the way you talk, the way you dress—even in the way you decorate a room.

View Look at these two rooms. Make a list of elements that are unique, different, or distinguishing about each room.

Interpret What are the homeowners trying to say about themselves through their rooms? How would you describe their styles? What does your room say about you?

Discuss In a group, compare your reactions to these two rooms. Did everyone describe the styles in the same way? How would you behave if you met the people who live in these houses? See the SkillBuilder at the right for more tips on identifying a person's style.

SkillBuilder

 CRITICAL THINKING

Identifying Personal Style
You can begin to "read" people if you can identify and analyze their personal styles. One key to identifying a style is knowing how to interpret details.

For example, when you look at each room, what's your first impression? Does the choice of colors say anything about the owner's personality? Do the objects sitting around reveal anything about his or her interests? Each detail provides information about the person living there. Can you tell how old the person who occupies each room is? What do you think he or she is like?

APPLYING WHAT YOU'VE LEARNED
Try one or both of the following:

1. Working alone, look closely at the clothes you wear, the room you sleep in, the objects in your locker, the doodles on your notebook. Make a list of all the characteristics that could be used to describe you. When you're finished, put the lists of several students together. See if you can identify the person described by each list.
2. Writers go to a lot of effort to make sure each of their characters has a unique personal style. Watch a movie or television program. Create a chart to help you identify the personal style of each character.

PART 2 INTRODUCTION

Power and Protest

The Sixties

"The time has come to put our bodies on the machine and stop it!" cried Mario Savio, a student at the University of California, Berkeley, in the fall of 1963. As the civil rights movement gained momentum and the Vietnam War heated up, a number of college students—many of whom were affected by one or both—began to work together for social and political changes. Savio led a protest against a new university regulation that prohibited off-campus organizations from recruiting students for civil rights activities and other political causes. He and about 800 others occupied the administration building and refused to leave until the regulation was repealed. In response, the university called in police to seize and remove the demonstrators. Thus, the Free Speech Movement was born, and "student power" became a force to be reckoned with.

The Free Speech Movement at Berkeley set the tone for a decade in which students, antiwar activists, civil rights workers, feminists, Vietnam veterans, Chicano farm workers, writers, musicians, artists, and ordinary citizens began to join together in ever larger protests against laws and policies they felt were unjust. In the summer of 1963, more than 200,000 demonstrators joined Martin Luther King, Jr., in a march on Washington, D.C., to pressure Congress to pass civil rights legislation. Two "moratoriums" in the fall of 1969 attracted hundreds of thousands of protesters to rally in major U.S. cities for an end to the war in Vietnam.

Like previous national protest movements, the protests of the sixties found support in many writers of the time. In 1967, the poet Robert Bly turned down the prestigious National Book Award to protest U.S. policy in Vietnam. The poet Denise Levertov, who is represented in this part of the unit, wrote about her antiwar

Martin Luther King, Jr. addressing demonstrators in 1963 (right) and the tragedy at Kent State University in 1970 (next page)

activities. Lanford Wilson's play *Wandering* captures the sense of confusion that many young people felt. Pressured by parents to conform and drafted by the government to fight in a foreign war, Wilson's young protagonist just wants to be left alone to live his life. Other writers that exploded on the scene during the decade—such as Allen Ginsberg (the Walt Whitman of the sixties), William Burroughs, Ken Kesey, Tom Wolfe, Norman Mailer, Edward Albee, and Amiri Baraka—used too much profanity and too many references to sexuality and drug use for their works to be included in a high school textbook.

As the decade drew to a close, efforts to achieve peace and justice were often marred by violence. In 1968, the assassinations of Martin Luther King, Jr., and the presidential candidate Robert Kennedy dealt a shattering blow to the ideals of the sixties. After King's death, race riots erupted in Newark, Detroit, Chicago, Cleveland, and Los Angeles. The civil rights movement gave way to the more militant "black power" movement. On college campuses, student protests frequently turned bloody, and charges of police brutality increased. In May 1970, four students were killed and nine wounded when members of the National Guard opened fire on antiwar demonstrators at Kent State University in Ohio.

In different ways, Nikki Giovanni's poem "Revolutionary Dreams" and Gloria Steinem's essay "Sisterhood" reflect the end of the sixties—when the focus shifted from mass, sometimes violent, demonstrations to a search for more personal, inner change.

Voices *from the* TIMES

When I think of 1966, I see pink and orange stripes and wild purple Paisleys and black and white vibrating to make the head ache. We were too young for drugs (they hadn't reached the junior high yet) but we didn't need them. Our world was psychedelic, our clothes and our make-up and our jewelry and our hairstyles were trips in themselves. It was the year of the gimmick, and what mattered was being noticed, which meant being wild and bright and having the shortest skirt and the whitest Yardley Slicker lips and the dangliest earrings. . . .

[B]ack then we tried to look like spacemen, distorting natural forms. Nature wasn't a vanishing treasure to us yet—it was a barrier to be overcome. The highest compliment, the ultimate adjective, was *unreal.*

Joyce Maynard
from *Looking Back: A Chronicle of Growing Up Old in the Sixties*

Hope I die before I get old.
This is my generation.

Peter Townshend
from "My Generation"

Looks like everybody in this whole
round world
Is down on me.

Janis Joplin
from "Down on Me"

Say it loud: "I'm black and I'm proud."

James Brown
from the song so titled

Voices *from the* Times

Come mothers and fathers
Throughout the land,
And don't criticize
What you can't understand.
Your sons and your daughters
Are beyond your command.
Your old road is rapidly agin'.
Please get out of the new one
If you can't lend your hand,
For the times they are a-changin'.

Bob Dylan
from "The Times They Are A-Changin'"

You're either part of the solution or part of the problem.

Eldridge Cleaver
from a speech

We are stardust,
We are golden,
And we've got to get ourselves
Back to the garden.

Joni Mitchell
from "Woodstock"

I live in Woodstock Nation. . . . It is a nation of alienated young people. We carry it around with us as a state of mind in the same way the Sioux Indians carried the Sioux nation around with them. It is a nation dedicated to cooperation versus competition, to the idea that people should have better means of exchange than property or money, that there should be some other basis for human interaction.

Abbie Hoffman
testifying at the Chicago Conspiracy Trial

Continuity & Change: The Legacy of the Sixties

The 1960s were so steeped in controversy that it is difficult to find consensus on the decade's long-term benefits. Certainly, it produced some significant political, social, and cultural changes. New laws and policies have guaranteed more civil rights to minorities and women than ever before. Americans today are less willing to commit U.S. troops to a foreign war. Rock 'n' roll seems here to stay, as does the American fascination with youth culture.

On the other hand, the drug use and violence unleashed during the sixties have continued to tear at the fabric of our society. The American family, in particular, has been strained by the breakdown of traditional values and the emphasis on rights over responsibilities. Anne Tyler's "Teenage Wasteland" and Nash Candelaria's "El Patrón" both examine the new pressures placed on families at a time when the old solutions no longer work.

The Rock and Roll Hall of Fame in Cleveland (top) and protesters against the Persian Gulf War in 1991

Finally, the struggle against racism—a struggle at least as old as the country itself—has still to be won. Although the most overt forms of racism have been significantly reduced, more subtle forms still persist. In the last selection of this unit, Diane Burns voices the frustrations that many minorities feel when confronted with racial ignorance and insensitivity.

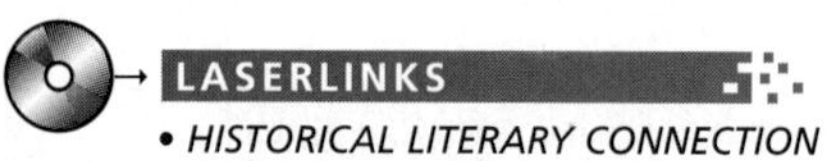
LASERLINKS
• *HISTORICAL LITERARY CONNECTION*

PART 2 *Power and Protest*

The Sixties

Continuity & Change: The Legacy of the Sixties

PREVIEWING

DRAMA

Wandering

Lanford Wilson

PERSONAL CONNECTION

How would you present a person's life story in less than five minutes? Brainstorm with a small group to think of ways you could do this. Consider what events would be important to include and how you would show the passage of time. After your discussion, share your ideas with other groups.

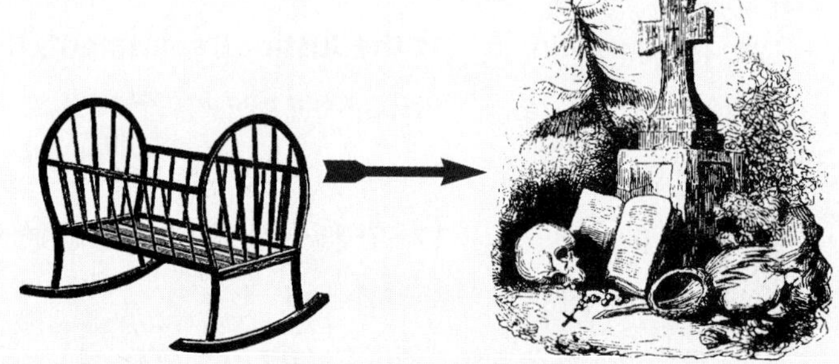

CULTURAL CONNECTION

Wandering is a very brief play sketching the life story of a man who questions the roles society expects him to assume. In the 1960s many young Americans began to reject long-accepted codes of behavior and values that they felt unnecessarily restricted people. For example, some young men wondered why they should register for the draft, become soldiers, and enter professions—duties that were expected of men in the United States. For a variety of reasons, some refused to register for the draft or tried to make themselves ineligible. Some declined to compete for job promotions or declined to take jobs altogether, because they did not want to be forced down conventional career paths. Young people of the time often expressed a wish to live freely, according to their own values and desires rather than those of others. The main character in *Wandering* (called only Him) is such a person. Evaluate his life as you read.

Alternative lifestyles. UPI/Bettmann.

READING CONNECTION

Visualizing Staging Staging refers to the way a play is presented on stage. The arrangement of furniture and properties, the movement and position of actors, the set design, and the lighting are all aspects of the staging of a play.

Carefully read the brief stage directions at the beginning of *Wandering.* Almost no other stage directions are given, so as you continue to read, you must work hard to visualize how the play would look in performance. Think like a director to imagine how the change of scene and the passage of a long period of time can be conveyed with only three actors and a nearly bare stage.

Wandering

Lanford Wilson

He, She, and *Him are all about twenty-five. The stage, which can be very small, should have a bench to be used as chair, bed, couch, bench, whatever.* He *and* She *are standing at attention, side by side.* Him *enters and sits. The actors should retire to the attention position when not speaking. Actions and props should be pantomimed, and the play should be done very rapidly, without pause except toward the end, as indicated. The play runs through* Him's *life—a span of about forty years with several recaps*[1] *at the end. Actions and characterizations should be very simple.*

She. Where have you been?

Him. Wandering around.

She. Wandering around. I don't know why you can't be a man; you just wait till the army gets ahold of you, young man.

He. They'll make a man out of you.

She. Straighten you out.

He. A little regimentation.

She. Regulation.

He. Specification.

She. Indoctrination.

He. Boredom.

She. You'll get up and go to bed.

He. Drill, march.

She. Take orders.

He. Fight.

She. Do what they tell you.

He. Keep in step.

She. Do your part.

He. Kill a man.

She. You'll be a better person to live with, believe me. As a matter of fact your father and I are getting damn tired of having you around.

He. Looking after you.

She. Making your bed.

He. Keeping you out of trouble.

She. How old are you, anyway?

Him. Sixteen.

He. Sixteen, well, my God.

She. Shouldn't you be drafted before long?

Him. Two years.

She. You just better toe the mark.

He. How long at your present address?

Him. Six months.

He. Any previous experience as an apprentice?

Him. No sir.

He. Where did you live before that?

Him. I was just wandering around.

1. **recaps:** short for *recapitulations,* repetitions of the main point or points.

WORDS TO KNOW

regimentation (rĕj′ə-mən-tā′shən) *n.* the process of using discipline and control to organize into a rigid system

indoctrination (ĭn-dŏk′trə-nā′shən) *n.* the process of being taught fundamentals, especially of military customs and discipline

He. Not good; draft status?

Him. Well, I haven't been called but—

He. We like fighters on our team, fellow.

Him. Well, actually I'm a conscientious[2]—

She. Sit down. Roll up your sleeve. Take off your shirt. Stick out your tongue. Bend over, open your mouth, make a fist, read the top line. Cough. (*The boy coughs.*) Very good.

Him. Thank you.

She. Perfect specimen.

Him. I do a considerable amount of walking.

He. I don't follow you.

Him. I don't believe in war.

He. There's no danger of war. Our country is never an aggressor.

Him. But armies, see, I don't believe in it.

He. Do you love your country?

Him. No more than any other, the ones I've seen.

He. That's treason.

Him. I'm sorry.

He. Quite all right; we'll take you.

Him. I won't go.

He. Service is compulsory.

Him. It's my right.

He. You'll learn.

Him. I don't believe in killing people.

He. For freedom?

Him. No.

He. For love?

Him. No.

He. For money?

Him. No.

He. We'll teach you.

Him. I know, but I won't.

He. You'll learn.

Him. I won't!

He. You're going.

Him. I'm not.

He. You'll see.

Him. I'm sure.

He. You'll see.

Him. I'm flat-footed.

He. You'll do.

Him. I'm queer.

He. Get lost.

She. I'm lost.

Him. I'm sorry.

She. Aren't you lost?

Him. I wasn't going anyplace in particular.

She. That's unnatural.

Him. I was just wandering.

She. What will become of you?

Him. I hadn't thought of it.

She. You don't believe in anything.

Him. But you see, I do.

He. I see.

Him. It's just that no one else seems to believe—not really.

He. I see.

Him. Like this pride in country.

He. I see.

Him. And this pride in blood.

He. I see.

Him. It just seems that pride is such a pointless thing; I can't believe in killing someone for it.

She. Oh, my God, honey, it isn't killing, it's merely nudging out of the way . . .

---

2. **conscientious— :** The young man is interrupted in the middle of saying "conscientious objector." This is a person whose conscience does not permit taking an active part in any effort associated with the conduct of war.

WORDS TO KNOW

specimen (spĕs′ə-mən) *n.* an example of a group.
aggressor (ə-grĕs′ər) *n.* one that begins an attack or a quarrel
compulsory (kəm-pŭl′sə-rē) *adj.* required without exception; mandatory

A little regimentation.

Regulation.

Specification.

Indoctrination.

Boredom.

New recruit trying on a garrison hat during the Vietnam War. Photo by Bob Gemel for *Life* Magazine. Copyright © Time Inc.

Him. But we don't need it.

She. Think of our position, think of me, think of the children.

Him. I am.

She. You're shiftless, is what it is.

Him. I'm really quite happy; I don't know why.

She. Well, how do you think I feel?

Him. Not too well really.

She. Where does it hurt?

Him. Nothing to worry about.

She. Yes sir.

Him. Thank you.

She. And that's all for the morning; Mr. Trader is on line six.

Him. Thank you; send Wheeler in.

He. How are you, old boy?

Him. Not well, I'm afraid.

She. Don't be, it isn't serious.

He. Just been working too hard.

She. Why don't you lie down?

He. Best thing for you.

She. I know, but he was quite handsome; a gentle man.

He. Bit of a radical though; not good for the family.

She. I know.

He. You're better off.

She. I have a life of my own.	**He.** You have a life of your own.

She. He was such a lost lamb.

He. Never agreed with anyone.

She. Arguments everywhere we went.

He. What kind of disposition is that?

She. I don't know what I ever saw in him.

He. You need someone who knows his way around.

She. I do.

He. I do.

(*A pause*)

She. I don't know why you can't be a man.

He. Keep in step.

She. Toe the mark.

He. Draft status?

She. Stick out your tongue.

He. You'll learn.

She. What'll become of you?

He. I see.

She. Think of the children.

He. Best thing for you.

She. I do.

(*A pause*)

He. I see.

Him. I mean, that can't be the way people want to spend their lives.

She. Trader on line six.

Him. Thank you.

He. Just been working too hard.

She. I do.

(*Pauses*)

She. Where?

Him. Wandering.

He. I see.

Him. They'll believe anything anyone tells them.

He. I see.

Him. I mean, that can't be the way people want to spend their lives.

She. That's all for the morning.

Him. Quite happy.

He. Best thing for you.

She. I do.

He. I do.

(*A pause*)

She. Where have you been?

(*A pause*)

Him. Can it?

Blackout

RESPONDING OPTIONS

FROM PERSONAL RESPONSE *TO* CRITICAL ANALYSIS

REFLECT **1.** What questions do you want to ask about the characters and events in this play? Write them in your notebook, and then share them in class.

RETHINK **2.** What different people do He and She portray in the course of the play? In general, how would you say they perceive Him? (You might choose one of He's or She's lines to read, and then identify who you are and how you feel about Him at that moment.)

3. How would you evaluate Him's life?

Consider

- what he believes and what he does not believe
- why he says, "I'm really quite happy"
- how his life ends
- his final question, "That can't be the way people want to spend their lives. . . . Can it?"

4. What does the title of the play mean to you?

RELATE **5.** In what ways does Him remind you of anyone you know or have heard about?

6. Could Him represent most young people of your generation, or is he strictly a child of the sixties? Support your opinion.

ANOTHER PATHWAY

Cooperative Learning

In a group of four (three actors and a director), prepare to perform a scene from *Wandering* for your class. To do this, you must interpret which lines cover a scene, where the scene takes place, exactly who the characters are, and how your line readings and gestures will convey what is going on.

LITERARY CONCEPTS

Dialogue—written conversation between two or more characters—makes up most of the script of a play. The dialogue in *Wandering* does not mimic ordinary conversation. It strings together clichéd, stock phrases in a highly rhythmic way. The lines are fragmentary and elliptical, forcing the audience to "fill in the blanks." Certain phrases are repeated, particularly in the recaps at the end. Listen for these qualities as three students read the entire play—rapidly, according to the writer's directions. How does the style of dialogue relate to the theme of the play?

QUICKWRITES

1. In a **review** of *Wandering,* tell whether you like the play, what it would be like when performed on stage, and what meaning you think it was intended to have.
2. Write an **outline** of a play presenting the life story of a person, male or female, from your own generation. What title would you give it? What key events would you include? What important phrases might you repeat?

***PORTFOLIO** Save your writing. You may want to use it later as a springboard to a piece for your portfolio.*

ALTERNATIVE ACTIVITIES

1. With one or more classmates, improvise an additional **scene** from Him's life, perhaps with his children or a good friend.
2. Incidental music usually sets an appropriate mood or picks up a theme in the play; a play about new motherhood, for instance, might use Brahms's "Lullaby." Choose **incidental music** to be played before *Wandering* begins or just after it ends. Explain your choice of music.

LITERARY LINKS

How does *The Long Christmas Dinner* (page 866) compare with *Wandering* in its method of showing the passing of years during the course of the play?

WORDS TO KNOW

Review the Words to Know in the boxes at the bottom of the selection pages. Then write the vocabulary word that best completes each sentence.

1. During the 1960s, many people rebelled against what they considered unnecessary _____ in life in the United States.
2. They felt that short hair and a starched shirt made a man a _____ of conformity.
3. Some believed that in the Vietnam War, the United States was not the victim but the _____.
4. During this war, some men burned their draft cards to protest _____ military service.
5. Some who were drafted fled the country rather than undergo the _____ involved in basic training and the betrayal of their own beliefs.

LANFORD WILSON

1937–

Lanford Wilson grew up in rural Missouri. His parents divorced when he was 5. At the age of 18, he went to California to reunite with his father and attended San Diego State University. Feeling excluded from his father's new family, he moved to Chicago the next year. He never completed his degree. He began writing his first play during the lunch hour at the advertising agency where he was a graphic designer. He describes stumbling upon his vocation: "I was always very excited by theater. Growing up, I had no idea plays were written, for some reason. I started out writing stories, and then suddenly I realized something I was writing was a play. I thought, I don't know how to write a play. I don't even know what a play is."

In 1962 he moved to New York, where he lived in a rundown hotel. To gather material for his plays, he eavesdropped on conversations in all-night coffee shops. He produced his first play in 1963 at a coffeehouse theater that welcomed experimental works. To pay the rent he worked as a complaint-department clerk, a hotel clerk, a dishwasher, and a waiter (he was fired after serving one meal). In 1966, when asked to contribute a two-minute play for a benefit evening, Wilson contributed a sketch he had written earlier. After the benefit he felt "deprived of the challenge to write a two-minute play for a specific event." So he wrote *Wandering*.

In 1969 he cofounded the Circle Repertory Company, where he is still playwright-in-residence. More than 40 of his plays have been produced, and many enjoy frequent revivals. His plays depict real-life issues, yet they incorporate experimental presentational techniques, like dialogue that spans several shifts in setting. Wilson is known for poetically rendering everyday speech and portraying with great empathy wistful idealists who diverge from the mainstream. His awards include a Pulitzer Prize, two New York Drama Critics' Circle Awards, an Emmy award nomination, and three Tony award nominations.

OTHER WORKS *Lemon Sky, The Hot l Baltimore, Fifth of July, Talley's Folly, Burn This, Redwood Curtain, Balm in Gilead*

PREVIEWING

POETRY

At the Justice Department, November 15, 1969

Denise Levertov

Revolutionary Dreams

Nikki Giovanni

PERSONAL CONNECTION

The decade of the sixties brought increasingly vocal, sometimes violent protests against racial injustice, unequal treatment of women, the Vietnam War, and other perceived social ills. If you had been a young person during the sixties, do you think you would have taken part in any of these protests? Why or why not? Explain your views in a small-group discussion with classmates.

HISTORICAL CONNECTION

The next two poems are by poets associated with 1960s protest movements. Denise Levertov was an antiwar activist, and Nikki Giovanni was committed to black revolution. Levertov's poem was written in response to a specific protest march. The New Mobilization to End the War in Vietnam, a coalition committee of antiwar groups, organized two major demonstrations called moratoriums in the fall of 1969. One of the moratoriums took place in Washington, D.C., on November 13–15. The protests were, for the most part, peaceful. On a Thursday, a single file of protesters formed a procession from Arlington National Cemetery, each carrying a candle and a poster with the name of an American killed in Vietnam or the name of a Vietnamese village destroyed by U.S. troops. Each paused at the White House to call out the name on his or her poster, then went on to the Capitol to deposit the poster in a coffin. Two days later, the largest group of protesters ever to gather in the nation's capital—crowd estimates varied from 200,000 to 800,000—assembled peacefully at the Washington Monument to demonstrate their opposition to the war. That evening, a group of a few thousand militants tried to raise the Viet Cong flag in front of the Justice Department. When the demonstration became violent, police used tear gas against the crowd.

WRITING CONNECTION

What do you think it would have been like to be at the November moratorium, particularly on the last day? What might you have seen? heard? smelled? felt? tasted? What emotions might you have had? Write your speculations in your notebook. As you read the poem by Levertov, who was there, see how your images compare to the ones in her poem.

LASERLINKS
• HISTORICAL CONNECTION

At the Justice Department, November 15, 1969

Denise Levertov

Brown gas-fog, white
beneath the street lamps.
Cut off on three sides, all space filled
with our bodies.
    Bodies that stumble
in brown airlessness, whitened
in light, a mildew glare,
    that stumble
hand in hand, blinded, retching.
Wanting it, wanting
to be here, the body believing it's
dying in its nausea, my head
clear in its despair, a kind of joy,
knowing this is by no means death,
is trivial, an incident, a
fragile instant. Wanting it, wanting
    with all my hunger this anguish,
    this knowing in the body
the grim odds we're
up against, wanting it real.
Up that bank where gas
curled in the ivy, dragging each other
up, strangers, brothers
and sisters. Nothing
will do but
to taste the bitter
taste. No life
other, apart from.

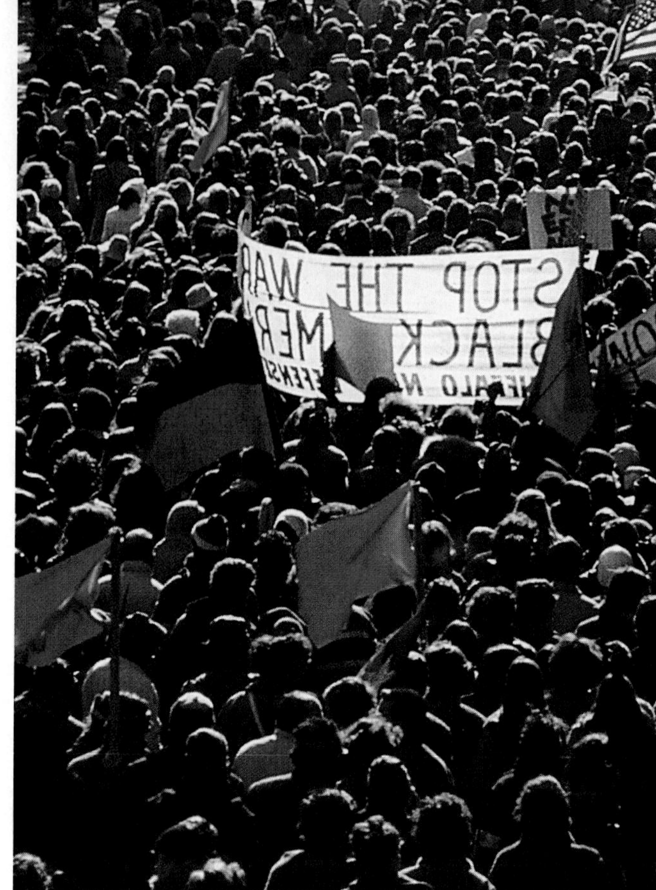

Antiwar demonstrators march to the Washington Monument on Nov. 15, 1969. Photo by John Olson for *Life* Magazine. Copyright © Time Inc.

FROM PERSONAL RESPONSE *TO* CRITICAL ANALYSIS

REFLECT **1.** How do the images in the poem compare with the ones you wrote down before reading?

RETHINK **2.** Describe the speaker's response to being tear-gassed. How do you explain her response?

Consider
- what she says she wants
- what she calls the protesters

3. How do you interpret the last words: "No life other, apart from."

4. How would you connect the style of the poem to its subject?

RELATE **5.** If you were ever in a protest march, were your feelings about participating similar to the speaker's? Elaborate.

Revolutionary Dreams

Nikki Giovanni

i used to dream militant
dreams of taking
over america to show
these white folks how it should be
done
i used to dream radical dreams
of blowing everyone away with my perceptive powers
of correct analysis
i even used to think i'd be the one
to stop the riot and negotiate the peace
then i awoke and dug
that if i dreamed natural
dreams of being a natural
woman doing what a woman
does when she's natural
i would have a revolution

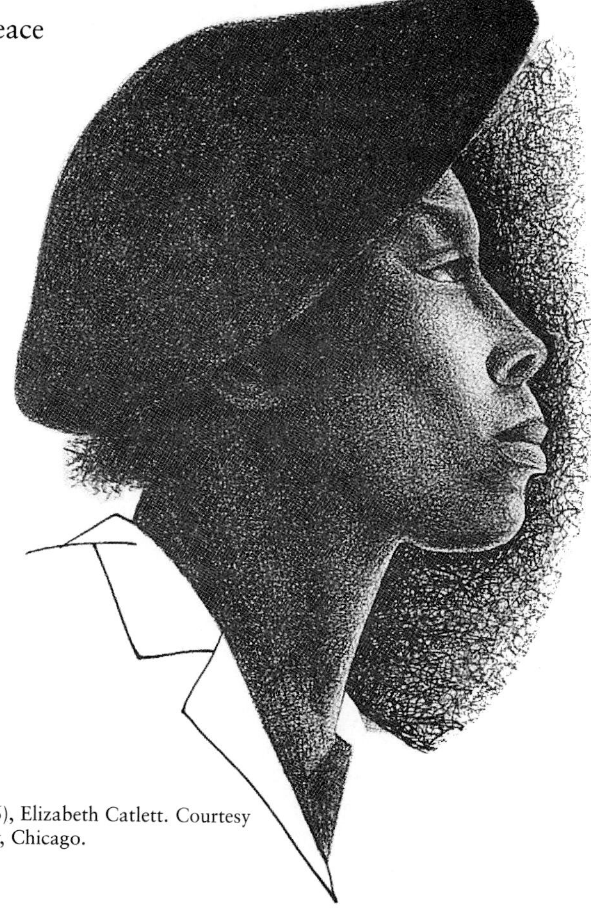

On the Subway (1986), Elizabeth Catlett. Courtesy of Isobel Neal Gallery, Chicago.

RESPONDING OPTIONS

FROM PERSONAL RESPONSE *TO* CRITICAL ANALYSIS

REFLECT **1.** What is your opinion of the speaker in "Revolutionary Dreams"?

RETHINK **2.** How do you think the speaker would define *natural*?

3. What do you think might be revolutionary about being natural?

4. What might have led the speaker to stop dreaming "militant dreams" and "radical dreams"?

Consider
- the content of these dreams
- how they might differ from "natural dreams"

RELATE **5.** How do you think Levertov and Giovanni would react to each other's poems?

6. Which of these two poems is closer to your idea of how a revolution happens?

ANOTHER PATHWAY

Cooperative Learning

Imagine that the speakers of these two poems will appear on a talk show to discuss how to make a revolution. With a small group of classmates, brainstorm questions the host might ask and answers the speakers might give. Choose group members to play the speakers and the host in your presentation to the class.

LITERARY CONCEPTS

Poets use **repetition** to emphasize ideas, to connect ideas, and to create rhythmic effects, among other purposes. For example, in "Revolutionary Dreams," the phrase "i used to dream . . . ," repeated in lines 1 and 6, suggests that the ideas following the phrase connect to each other. The repetition of *natural* at the end of lines 12, 13, and 15 emphasizes the importance of that idea in the poem and at the same time creates an insistent pattern of sound. What words or phrases are repeated in "At the Justice Department, November 15, 1969"? In what ways do you think the repetition functions in the poem?

QUICKWRITES

1. Sketch out the script for a **TV news report** about the incident described in "At the Justice Department, November 15, 1969."
2. As the speaker of "Revolutionary Dreams," write a **journal entry** more fully explaining your ideas about revolution.
3. Write a draft of a **poem** describing an intense or dangerous experience you have had. Include vivid sensory images, as Levertov did, to help your readers share your experience.

PORTFOLIO *Save your writing. You may want to use it later as a springboard to a piece for your portfolio.*

THE WRITER'S STYLE

Compare the ways that capitalization and punctuation are used in these two poems. How do the poems depart from conventional written English? Try adding or deleting capitalization and punctuation, and see how your changes affect the poems.

ACROSS THE CURRICULUM

History Find out more about specific protest demonstrations during the 1960s and early 1970s, particularly antiwar demonstrations. Besides looking at books on the subject, you might look for newspaper and magazine articles of the time to find out what people thought about the protests at the time they were happening. Share your discoveries with your class.

Photo by Bernie Boston.

DENISE LEVERTOV

Denise Levertov (born 1923) grew up in England, where she had an unusual home life. Her father, a Russian Jew who became an Anglican priest, trained Denise in religious philosophy and filled the house with theologians, booksellers, priests, and opera singers. Her mother, the daughter of a Welsh mystic, imparted to her a love of nature and spirituality.

Although Levertov received no formal education, she never lacked the nerve or eloquence to speak out. Her poetic career began at age 5, when she declared she would become a poet. At age 12, she sent some poems to T. S. Eliot, who responded with two pages of criticism and encouragement.

Never a passive observer, Levertov combines poetry and political activism to speak against social injustices. Some critics call her poetry preachy, while she herself has criticized others for "mealy-mouthed" apathy in the face of social ills. In 1965, she cofounded the Writers and Artists Protest against the War in Vietnam. She participated in antiwar demonstrations in the 1960s and was jailed for protesting. In the 1980s she protested against U.S. involvement in civil wars in El Salvador, Honduras, and Nicaragua and spoke against nuclear armament. She also objects to abuse of the environment and decries the growing ignorance of history and language among young people. While these issues haunt her conscience, they also provide her inspiration.

OTHER WORKS *The Jacob's Ladder, O Taste and See, The Sorrow Dance, Relearning the Alphabet, Breathing the Water, Evening Train*

NIKKI GIOVANNI

1943–

Nikki Giovanni is a writer famed for her steadfast outspokenness. She grew up in Ohio, where her close-knit family encouraged her to write. Her happy childhood is a frequent theme in her poetry. Ahead of her class, she entered Fisk University at 16. Already challenging rules, she was suspended for leaving campus without permission. She returned to school three years later and graduated with honors in 1967. During college she became interested in the black power movement, protested, and advocated revolution. Her poetry from this period is angry, calling for black pride, solidarity, and rebellion. After graduating, Giovanni published these poems in two books, *Black Feeling, Black Talk* and *Black Judgement.* They were very successful, especially among her own generation, but their militancy alienated many readers.

After having a child in 1968, Giovanni's outlook mellowed and her poetry became subdued. Her later poetry still advocates change, but it views revolution as a personal rather than a collective movement. According to Giovanni, "the fight in the world today is the fight to be an individual."

Giovanni's poetry, known for its powerful language and musicality, has won many awards. She has published more than twenty books, taught at several universities, made many television and stage appearances, and recorded six albums of poetry readings.

OTHER WORKS *Ego-Tripping and Other Poems for Young People, Cotton Candy on a Rainy Day, Sacred Cows . . . and Other Edibles, Racism 101*

PREVIEWING

NONFICTION

Sisterhood

Gloria Steinem

PERSONAL CONNECTION

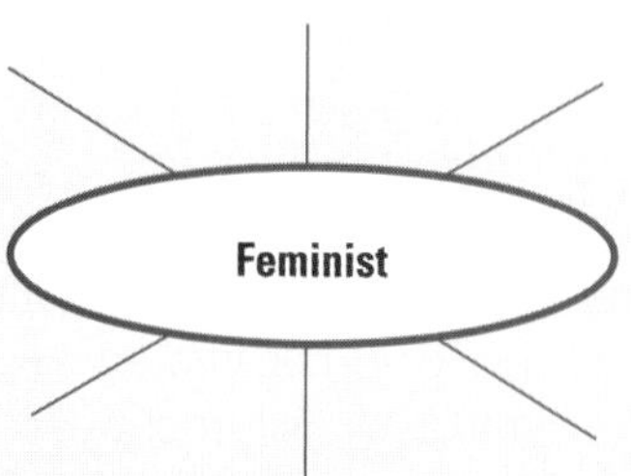

What do you think when you hear the word *feminist?* Do you have a positive or negative reaction? What mental image does the word evoke? Fill out a word web of your associations with the word, and then discuss your reaction with your classmates.

HISTORICAL CONNECTION

Possibly more than any other political term in recent years, the word *feminist* still causes arguments to flare and tempers to rise. One reason for the continuing controversy is that the concept of feminism crosses racial, religious, and political lines and cuts deep into an understanding of who we are as males and females.

The Bettmann Archive.

Feminists have always caused controversy—among women as well as men—for questioning the traditional roles of women solely as wives and mothers. These roles, feminists argue, restrict women to second-class status in society, dependent on men for their rights and for their identity. Just as men can be more than husbands and fathers, so too should women be able to exercise their full human potential.

The majority of women in the 19th-century suffragist movement were not feminists. Believing that women's proper place was in the home, they felt they could influence political decision-making by voting in better men to do the job. The 19th-century feminists, such as Susan B. Anthony, Elizabeth Cady Stanton, and Charlotte Perkins Gilman, comprised a minority within a minority.

It wasn't until the resurgence of feminism in the 1960s that the issue of woman's role resurfaced. This time, there were more discontented women to join the ranks of the minority.

Primarily consisting of college-educated, middle-class women, the women's movement of the early 1960s was inspired by the gains of the civil rights movement and spurred by passage of the Equal Pay Act in 1963 and by the establishment of the Equal Employment Opportunity Commission, in 1964. Two years later, the National Organization for Women (NOW) was founded. Dubbed the NAACP of the women's movement, NOW had a political agenda to work for equal opportunity and equal rights.

In the late 1960s, the women's liberation movement became increasingly militant, as the emphasis expanded from changing laws to changing attitudes. Women from the peace movement, the student movement, and the civil rights movement joined together to make their presence and their feminist views known.

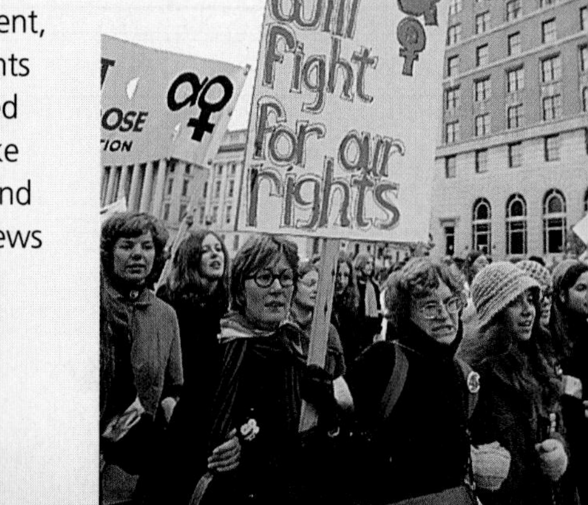

Copyright © Dennis Brack/Black Star.

READING CONNECTION

Feminist Perspectives

When Gloria Steinem wrote the essay "Sisterhood," she was articulating the feminist agenda of the time. One tactic was to raise awareness among women and create a new feeling of solidarity—a feeling of sisterhood. In addition, self-esteem was considered essential to liberation. Feminists set up "consciousness-raising" groups to counteract women's feelings of inferiority to men. Women were encouraged to share their experiences with each other and to discuss common problems and goals. Instead of looking to men for meaning and value in their lives, women were reoriented to look within themselves and to each other.

Another feminist issue addressed in Steinem's essay is the question of female identity. If a woman is more than just a wife and mother, then who or what is she? If a woman is not defined in relation to a man, then how is she defined? In the late 1960s and early 1970s, many women were asking these questions for the first time and searching among themselves for answers.

At the end of the 1960s, many women as well as men believed that men were the superior sex. One study at the time asked women college students to read sets of articles of similar quality with fictitious authors' names attached to them and to choose the best ones. The women overwhelmingly picked the articles with the male names on them. According to the author of the study, "Women seem to think that men are better at everything."

This shift in focus from men to women distinguishes the feminist perspective from traditional perspectives. It is the perspective of Gilman's "The Yellow Wallpaper," Kate Chopin's "The Story of an Hour," Tillie Olsen's "I Stand Here Ironing," and the thousands of books, stories, and poems by and about women that have proliferated since the early 1970s. This perspective was considered radical at the time. Some people today still consider it radical; others say it's common sense.

Following Steinem's essay is an essay by former *New York Times* columnist and editor Anna Quindlen explaining her reasons for quitting her job. Quindlen speaks for many women in the 1980s and 1990s who found that "having it all"—full-time career and family—was just too overwhelming.

To help clarify the issues of feminism addressed in Steinem's essay fill out a chart like the one shown as you read. Then form your own opinion.

Traditional Perspectives	Feminist Perspectives
1. Family comes before a woman's work.	1.
2.	

- In 1910, 20% of all women worked outside the home. That figure rose to 43% in 1970 and to 57% in 1990.
- In 1910, 9% of U.S. doctors were women. In 1970, the figure had dropped to 7%, but in 1990 it rose to 17%.
- In 1920, a woman earned, on average, 56% of what a man earned. In 1970, a woman earned 59% of a man's earnings. In 1990, that percentage had risen to 72%.

Gloria Steinem

S I S T E

A very, very long time ago (about three or four years), I took a certain secure and righteous pleasure in saying the things that women are supposed to say. I remember with pain—

"My work won't interfere with marriage. After all, I can always keep my typewriter at home." Or:

"I don't want to write about women's stuff. I want to write about foreign policy." Or:

Women marching down Fifth Avenue in New York City to celebrate the 50th anniversary of the passage of the 19th Amendment. Photo by John Olson for *Life* Magazine. Copyright © Time Inc.

R H O O D

"Black families were forced into matriarchy,[1] so I see why black women have to step back and let their men get ahead." Or:

"I know we're helping Chicano groups that are tough on women, but *that's their culture.*" Or:

"Who would want to join a women's group? I've never been a joiner, have you?" Or (when bragging):

"He says I write like a man."

I suppose it's obvious from the kinds of statements I chose that I was secretly nonconforming. I wasn't married. I was earning a living at a profession I cared about. I had basically—if

1. **matriarchy** (mā′trē-är′kē): a form of social organization in which the mother is the head of a family or tribe.

quietly—opted out of the "feminine" role. But that made it all the more necessary to repeat the conventional wisdom, even to look as conventional as I could manage, if I was to avoid some of the punishments reserved by society for women who don't do as society says. I therefore learned to Uncle Tom with subtlety, logic, and humor. Sometimes, I even believed it myself.

If it weren't for the women's movement, I might still be dissembling[2] away. But the ideas of this great sea-change in women's view of ourselves are contagious and irresistible. They hit women like a revelation, as if we had left a dark room and walked into the sun.

"Men think we're whatever it is we do for men."

At first my discoveries seemed personal. In fact, they were the same ones so many millions of women have made and are continuing to make. Greatly simplified, they go like this: Women are human beings first, with minor differences from men that apply largely to the single act of reproduction. We share the dreams, capabilities, and weaknesses of all human beings, but our occasional pregnancies and other visible differences have been used—even more pervasively, if less brutally, than racial differences have been used—to create an "inferior" group and an elaborate division of labor. The division is continued for a clear if often unconscious reason: the economic and social profit of males as a group.

Once this feminist realization dawned, I reacted in what turned out to be predictable ways. First, I was amazed at the simplicity and obviousness of a realization that made sense, at last, of my life experience. I couldn't figure out why I hadn't seen it before. Second, I realized how far that new vision of life was from the system around us, and how tough it would be to explain this feminist realization at all, much less to get people (especially, though not only, men) to accept so drastic a change.

But I tried to explain. God knows that women try. We make analogies with other groups that have been marked for subservient roles in order to assist blocked imaginations. We supply endless facts and statistics of injustice, reeling them off until we feel like human information-retrieval machines. We lean heavily on the device of reversal. (If there is a male reader to whom all my *pre*realization statements seem perfectly logical, for instance, let him read each sentence with "men" substituted for "women"—or himself for me—and see how he feels: "My work won't interfere with marriage. . . ."; ". . . Chicana groups that are tough on men. . . ." You get the idea.)

We even use logic. If a woman spends a year bearing and nursing a child, for instance, she is supposed to have the primary responsibility for raising that child to adulthood. That's logic by the male definition, but it often makes women feel children are their only function, keeps them from doing any other kind of work, or discourages them from being mothers at all. Wouldn't it be just as logical to say that the child has two parents, therefore both are equally responsible for child rearing, and the father should compensate for that extra year by spending *more* than half the time caring for the child? Logic is in the eye of the logician.

Occasionally, these efforts at explaining actually succeed. More often, I get the feeling that most women are speaking Urdu and most men are speaking Pali.[3]

---

2. **dissembling** (dĭ-sĕm′blĭng): concealing one's real motives under a false pretense or appearance.

3. **Urdu . . . Pali:** Urdu is a language spoken by Moslems in India and Pakistan, and Pali is an ancient language spoken by Buddhists in parts of southeast Asia.

WORDS TO KNOW

opt (ŏpt) *v.* to make a choice; choose or favor
pervasively (pər-vā′sĭv-lē) *adv.* in a way that spreads throughout; widely
subservient (səb-sûr′vē-ənt) *adj.* slavishly polite and obedient; tamely submissive
compensate (kŏm′pən-sāt′) *v.* to make up for; make amends

Whether joyful or painful, both kinds of reaction to our discovery have a great reward. They give birth to sisterhood.

First, we share the exhilaration of growth and self-discovery, the sensation of having the scales fall from our eyes. Whether we are giving other women this new knowledge or receiving it from them, the pleasure for all concerned is enormous. And very moving.

In the second stage, when we're exhausted from dredging up facts and arguments for the men whom we had previously thought advanced and intelligent, we make another simple discovery: women understand. We may share experiences, make jokes, paint pictures, and describe humiliations that mean little to men, but *women understand.*

The odd thing about these deep and personal connections among women is that they often leap barriers of age, economics, worldly experience, race, culture—all the barriers that, in male or mixed society, seem so impossible to cross.

I remember meeting with a group of women in Missouri who, because they had come in equal numbers from the small town and from its near-by campus, seemed to be split between wives with white gloves welded to their wrists and students with boots who used words like "imperialism" and "oppression." Planning for a child-care center had brought them together, but the meeting seemed hopeless until three of the booted young women began to argue among themselves about a young male professor. The leader of the radicals on campus, he accused all women unwilling to run mimeograph machines[4] of not being sufficiently devoted to the cause. As for child-care centers, he felt their effect of allowing women to compete with men for jobs was part of a dreaded "feminization" of the American male and American culture.

"He sounds just like my husband," said one of the white-gloved women. "He wants me to have bake sales and collect door-to-door for his Republican party."

The young women had sense enough to take it from there. What difference did boots or white gloves make if they were all getting treated like servants and children? Before they broke up, they were discussing some subjects that affected them all and planning to meet every week. "Men think we're whatever it is we do for men," explained one of the housewives. "It's only by getting together with other women that we'll ever find out who we are."

Even racial barriers become a little less formidable once we discover this mutuality[5] of our life experiences as women. At a meeting run by black women domestics who had formed a job cooperative in Alabama, a white housewife asked me about the consciousness-raising sessions or "rap groups" that are often an organic path to feminism. I explained that while men, even minority men, usually had someplace—a neighborhood, a bar, a street corner, something—where they could get together and be themselves, women were isolated in their houses and families; isolated from other females. We had no street corners, no bars, no offices, no territory that was recognized as ours. Rap groups were an effort to create something of our own, a free place—an occasional chance for total honesty and support from our sisters.

As I talked about isolation, about the feeling that there must be something wrong with us if we aren't content to be housekeepers and mothers, tears began to stream down the cheeks of this dignified woman—clearly as much of a surprise to her as to us. For the black women, some distance was bridged by seeing this white woman cry.

"He does it to us both, honey," said the black woman next to her, putting an arm around her shoulders. "If it's your own kitchen or somebody else's, you still don't get treated like people. Women's work just doesn't count."

---

4. **mimeograph** (mĭm′ē-ə-grăf′) **machines:** machines for making copies of written or typed materials by means of stencils.

5. **mutuality** (myo͞o′cho͞o-ăl′ĭ-tē): the quality or condition of belonging equally to all.

The meeting ended with the housewife organizing a support group of white women who would extract from their husbands a living wage for domestic workers and help them fight the local authorities who opposed any pay raises; a support group without which the domestic workers felt their small and brave cooperative could not survive.

As for the "matriarchal" argument that I swallowed in prefeminist days, I now understand why many black women resent it and feel that it's the white sociologists' way of encouraging the black community to imitate a white suburban life-style. "If I end up cooking grits for revolutionaries," explained a black woman poet from Chicago, "it isn't my revolution. Black men and women need to work together: you can't have liberation for half a race." In fact, some black women wonder if criticism of the strength they were forced to develop isn't a way to keep half the black community working at lowered capacity and lowered pay, as well as to attribute some of black men's sufferings to black women, instead of to their real source—white racism. I wonder with them.

Looking back at all those male-approved things I used to say, the basic hang-up seems clear—a lack of esteem for women, whatever our race, and for myself.

This is the most tragic punishment that society inflicts on any second-class group. Ultimately the brainwashing works, and we ourselves come to believe our group is inferior. Even if we achieve a little success in the world and think of ourselves as "different," we don't want to associate with our group. We want to identify up, not down (clearly my problem in not wanting to join women's groups). We want to be the only woman in the office, or the only black family on the block, or the only Jew in the club.

The pain of looking back at wasted, imitative years is enormous. Trying to write like men. Valuing myself and other women according to the degree of our acceptance by men—socially, in politics, and in our professions. It's as painful as it is now to hear two grown-up female human beings competing with each other on the basis of their husband's status, like servants whose identity rests on the wealth or accomplishments of their employers.

And this lack of esteem that makes us put each other down is still the major enemy of sisterhood. Women who are conforming to society's expectations view the nonconformists with justifiable alarm. *Those noisy, unfeminine women,* they say to themselves. *They will only make trouble for us all.* Women who are quietly nonconforming, hoping nobody will notice, are even more alarmed because they have more to lose. And that makes sense, too.

The status quo[6] protects itself by punishing all challengers, especially women whose rebellion strikes at the most fundamental social organization: the sex roles that convince half the population that its identity depends on being first in work or in war, and the other half that it must serve as docile, unpaid, or underpaid labor.

In fact, there seems to be no punishment inside the white male club that quite equals the ridicule and personal viciousness reserved for women who rebel. Attractive or young women who act forcefully are assumed to be either unnatural or male-controlled. If they succeed, it could only have been sexually, through men. Old women or women considered unattractive by male standards are accused of acting out of bitterness, because they could not get a man. Any woman who chooses to behave like a full human being should be warned that the armies of the status quo will treat her as something of a dirty joke. That's their natural and first weapon. She will *need* sisterhood.

All of that is meant to be a warning but not a discouragement. There are more rewards than punishments.

6. **status quo:** the way things are; the existing state of affairs.

WORDS TO KNOW

docile (dŏs′əl) *adj.* easily managed; obedient

For myself, I can now admit anger and use it constructively, where once I would have submerged it and let it fester into guilt or collect for some destructive explosion.

I have met brave women who are exploring the outer edge of human possibility, with no history to guide them, and with a courage to make themselves vulnerable that I find moving beyond the words to express it.

I no longer think that I do not exist, which was my version of that lack of self-esteem afflicting many women. (If male standards weren't natural to me, and they were the only standards, how could I exist?) This means that I am less likely to need male values and approval and am less vulnerable to classic arguments. ("If you don't like me, you're not a real woman"—said by a man who is coming on. "If you don't like me, you can't relate to other people, you're not a real person"—said by anyone who understands blackmail as an art.)

I can sometimes deal with men as equals and therefore can afford to like them for the first time.

I have discovered politics that are not intellectual or superimposed.[7] They are organic. I finally understand why for years I inexplicably identified with "out" groups: I belong to one, too. And I know it will take a coalition of such groups to achieve a society in which, at a minimum, no one is born into a second-class role because of visible difference, because of race or of sex.

I have met brave women who are exploring the outer edge of human possibility, with no history to guide them, and with a courage to make themselves vulnerable that I find moving beyond the words to express it.

I no longer feel strange by myself or with a group of women in public. I feel just fine.

I am continually moved to discover I have sisters.

I am beginning, just beginning, to find out who I am. ❖

7. **superimposed:** having one thing laid or placed on top of another.

INSIGHT

MOTHER'S CHOICE

Anna Quindlen

I am a mom. It's not all I am, but it's the identity that seems to cling to me most persistently right now, like ivy on the walls of an old stone house. Perhaps this is because, just over two years ago, I ditched a perfectly good full-time job in the office for two perfectly good part-time jobs at home, one writing, the other making Tollhouse cookies with assistants who always get eggshell in the batter and praising people who manage to go in the toilet one time out of three. It's a terrific life, but that's not how it's perceived by the outside world. When I quit the job that did not include eggshells and toilet training there was a kind of solemn attitude toward what I was doing, not unlike the feeling people have about Carmelite nuns. People thought I was Doing the Noble Thing. They also thought I was nuts.

There are valid and complicated reasons why they were wrong, but they haven't been ventilated enough. There has always been a feeling on the part of moms that the Women's Movement has not taken them seriously, has in fact denigrated[1] what they do, unless they do it in a Third World country or do it while running a Fortune 500[2] company and the New York marathon.

I once felt the same way about moms. Like almost everything else, this feeling had to do with the past. When I was growing up, motherhood was a kind of cage. The moms I knew had more children than they probably would have chosen, spaced closer together than they probably would have liked. Smart, dumb, rich, poor—as soon as you started throwing up in the powder room at parties and walking around in those horrible little pup-tent dresses your life was over. Your husband still went out every day, talked to other adults about adult things, whether it was the Red Sox bullpen or the price of steel. And you stayed home and felt your mind turn to the stuff that you put in little bowls and tried to spoon into little mouths and eventually would end up wiping off of little floors.

By the time I was a grown-up, the answer, if you were strong and smart and wanted to be somebody, was not to be a mom. I certainly didn't want to be one. I wanted my blouses to stay clean. I wanted my plants to have leaves. And I wanted to climb unencumbered[3] up to the top of whatever career ladder I managed to cling to. The Women's Movement was talking about new choices. Being a mom was an old one, and one that reeked of reliance on a man and loss of identity. What kind of choice was that? So I exchanged one sort of enforced role for another, exchanging poor downtrodden mom, with Pablum in her hair, for tough lonely career woman, eating take-out Chinese from the cardboard container. I was neither imaginative nor secure enough to start from scratch. So my choice wasn't about choice at all, only about changing archetypes.[4]

---

1. **denigrated** (dĕn′ĭ-grāt-ĭd): attacked or belittled.
2. **Fortune 500:** a list published by *Fortune* magazine of the top U.S. corporations in terms of sales volume.
3. **unencumbered:** not burdened.
4. **archetypes** (är′kĭ-tīps′): perfect examples of a type or group.

Thailand: Spirit House (about 1975), Betty La Duke. Acrylic on canvas, 32″ × 48″, collection of the artist. From *Multicultural Celebrations: The Paintings of Betty La Duke 1972–1992,* by Gloria Orenstein, Pomegranate Publications, 1993.

I love my work. Always have. But I have another job now and it's just as good. I don't need anyone to validate[5] me anymore, with a byline or a bonus, which is a good thing, because this job still doesn't get much validation, at least until it's over and you've helped raise someone who isn't a cheat or a con man. I don't need validation. I'm having fun instead.

That's why I did what I did. I didn't do it for the kids. I did it for me. Isn't that what we feminists were supposed to be supporting, a little healthy selfishness? I didn't feel guilty about being away all day at work. I just knew I was missing the best time of my life. Like today. Two guys asked me to have pizza and watch *Sleeping Beauty* with them. Do you remember how terrific *Sleeping Beauty* is, with those three fat little fairies named Flora, Fauna, and Merryweather? I could have been at the office, but instead I Did the Noble Thing: two slices with extra cheese and a long discussion of the difference between enchanted sleep and death.

I suppose I only really learned about choice when I chose to devote more of my time to a life I had previously misunderstood and undervalued: that is, when I became a mom. I was finally strong and smart enough to do something that left me vulnerable but made me feel terrific, too. I should say that it's challenging and invigorating, that the future of the next generation is in my hands. But that doesn't have much to do with my real life. About half of being a mom is just like being a mom was for my mother. It's exhausting and grungy and chaotic and there's an enormous amount of sopping things up with paper towels and yelling things like "Don't you ever stick something like that in his ear again or I will throw you out the window!" It has nothing to do with Doing the Noble Thing. . . .

5. **validate:** to make better or of importance; approve as true or sound.

RESPONDING OPTIONS

FROM PERSONAL RESPONSE *TO* CRITICAL ANALYSIS

REFLECT **1.** What is your impression of Gloria Steinem from this essay? Write or draw your impression in your notebook and share with your classmates.

RETHINK **2.** What is your opinion of the feminist issues addressed in Steinem's essay? Consult the chart you filled out as you read.

Consider

- why the statements "that women are supposed to say" (page 986) are not valid for a feminist
- whether women's roles in child rearing and homemaking create an unfair division of labor among men and women
- whether women play a subservient role in men's work
- whether women lack self-esteem

3. Explain what you think Steinem means by "sisterhood."

4. Consider the word web you completed for the Personal Connection on page 984. Did your ideas change after reading Steinem's essay? Explain why or why not.

RELATE **5.** Do you think that Gloria Steinem would agree with Anna Quindlen that full-time motherhood is a valid option for a feminist? Explain your opinion with support from Steinem's essay.

ANOTHER PATHWAY

Cooperative Learning

Join your classmates in a debate of the feminist issues raised in Steinem's essay. Structure your debate on the following points: the validity of the opening statements; whether women are expected to be subservient to men; whether women feel inferior. Plan for the debate in small groups, preparing arguments on each of these points.

CRITIC'S CORNER

When asked what she liked best about Steinem's essay, Jennifer Halbert of our student review board said, "The date of the essay is very effective. It shows how far we've come in 20-plus years." Do you agree that women's position in society has improved over the past 25 years? If so, how? What issues do you think have stayed the same? What new women's issues have arisen?

QUICKWRITES

1. Write a **letter** to Gloria Steinem or to Anna Quindlen responding to her ideas. Feel free to express your true feelings by commenting on specific points in the essay you choose.
2. Draft an **editorial** on feminism for your school newspaper based on Steinem's essay and your own ideas.
3. Draft a **review** of Steinem's essay for the publisher of this textbook, explaining why this selection should or should not be included in the next edition.

PORTFOLIO *Save your writing. You may want to use it later as a springboard to a piece for your portfolio.*

LITERARY CONCEPTS

The **theme** of an essay is the main idea the writer wishes to share with the reader. The following suggestions will help you to discover theme.

- Review what happened to the writer. Did her ideas change or develop during the selection? What did she learn about life?
- Skim the selection for key phrases or sentences that say something important about life or people.
- Think about the title of the selection. Does it have a special meaning that could lead you to the main idea of the piece?

Write a few sentences or a short paragraph explaining the themes of "Sisterhood" and of "Mother's Choice." Do you think the two themes contradict each other? Which theme do you agree with more?

ALTERNATIVE ACTIVITIES

1. Interview your classmates about what they liked and disliked about "Sisterhood." Organize their responses on a **chart,** and if possible, use a computer to display your results.
2. Create a piece of **art** inspired by Steinem's essay or the women's movement in general.

WORDS TO KNOW

For each group of words below, write the letter of the word that is the best synonym for the boldfaced word.

1. **opt** (a) prefer, (b) react, (c) cancel
2. **docile** (a) frightened, (b) graceful, (c) gentle
3. **subservient** (a) sneaky, (b) humble, (c) ashamed
4. **compensate** (a) correspond, (b) balance, (c) collect
5. **pervasively** (a) corruptly, (b) aggressively, (c) extensively

GLORIA STEINEM

1934–

Labeled a "bluejeaned Joan of Arc" for her leadership role in the women's movement, Gloria Steinem had a humble and difficult childhood in the Toledo, Ohio, area. Her parents divorced when she was ten, and she was left alone to care for her mentally ill mother in a rundown, rat-infested farmhouse. When she was 17, the farmhouse was sold, and the money from the sale paid Steinem's tuition at Smith College.

After graduation, Steinem studied for a year in India, where she got her start in social activism by working to reform the caste system. When she returned to the United States, she supported herself by writing magazine articles on celebrities and fashion. However, she also did volunteer work for the civil rights movement and the farm workers struggle.

In 1968, she cofounded *New York* magazine. A year later, she began writing about women's issues for the magazine and received criticism, especially from male colleagues, for taking on controversial issues. Nevertheless, her articles cultivated a large feminist following. She recalls that spreading the feminist word in the 1970s "was like lighting a match to a haystack."

In 1972 Steinem cofounded *Ms.,* a magazine run by women to provide an open forum for women's issues. She operated *Ms.* until 1987, when she sold it due to financial difficulties. Although Steinem was disappointed at having to sell the magazine, she has been able to refocus her energies on her own writing.

As editor, writer, and activist, Steinem's charisma and intelligence have made her influential in politics and popular with the media. She continues to work for the women's movement and denies that feminism is dead. Instead, she claims that the feminist mind-set has become so pervasive in society that it no longer seems revolutionary. She explains: "I can't think of anything that has influenced American life as much as the women's movement."

OTHER WORKS *Outrageous Acts and Everyday Rebellions, Revolution from Within, Moving Beyond Words*

PREVIEWING

FICTION

Teenage Wasteland

Anne Tyler

PERSONAL CONNECTION

In this story, Daisy and Matt learn that their teenage son, Donny, is having trouble in school. What advice would you give to parents in this situation? In your notebook make a list of things you would do or rules you might enforce to help a teenager improve in school.

HISTORICAL CONNECTION

In keeping with other changes during the 1960s and 1970s, experimental theories of education were being tested in several U.S. schools and universities. Believing that teachers should act as assistants or helpers rather than as authority figures, supporters of "alternative schools" and "the open classroom" wanted to do away with traditional teaching methods. They wanted students to be free to discover their own learning styles, guide their own curriculum, and progress at their own pace. While quite successful in some schools, this academic reform movement met resistance from some educators and parents who felt that students, if left to themselves, would not be taught the basic skills of reading, writing, and arithmetic. In the story you are about to read, Daisy and Matt, like many parents at the time, find themselves caught in the middle of this continuing debate. They receive conflicting advice from educators about how to help their son.

READING CONNECTION

Noting Important Details To help you track the different kinds of advice that Daisy and Matt receive, keep a list in your notebook. As you read, write down what the principal, the teachers, and the tutor say about how to help Donny. Put a check mark or a star beside each piece of advice that Daisy and Matt follow.

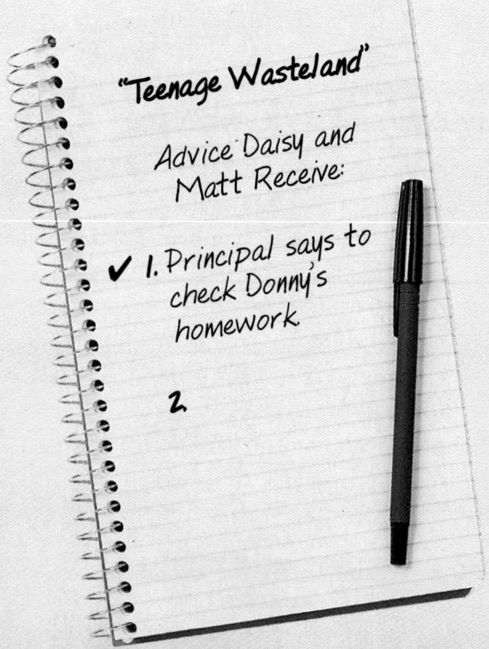

Teenage Waste

He used to have very blond hair—almost white—cut shorter than other children's so that on his crown a little cowlick always stood up to catch the light. But this was when he was small. As he grew older, his hair grew darker, and he wore it longer —past his collar even. It hung in lank, taffy-colored ropes around his face, which was still an endearing face, fine-featured, the eyes an unusual aqua blue. But his cheeks, of course, were no longer round, and a sharp new Adam's apple jogged in his throat when he talked.

In October, they called from the private school he attended to request a conference with his parents. Daisy went alone; her husband was at work. Clutching her purse, she sat on the principal's couch and learned that Donny was noisy, lazy, and disruptive; always fooling around with his friends, and he wouldn't respond in class.

In the past, before her children were born, Daisy had been a fourth-grade teacher. It shamed her now to sit before this principal as a parent, a delinquent parent, a parent who struck Mr. Lanham, no doubt, as unseeing or uncaring. "It isn't that we're not concerned," she said. "Both of us are. And we've done what we could, whatever we could think of. We don't let him watch TV

Table with Fruit (1951–1952), David Park. Oil on canvas, 46″ × 35¾″ collection of Mr. and Mrs. R. Crosby Kemper. Photo by Edward B. Bigelow.

on school nights. We don't let him talk on the phone till he's finished his homework. But he tells us he doesn't *have* any homework or he did it all in study hall. How are we to know what to believe?"

From early October through November, at Mr. Lanham's suggestion, Daisy checked Donny's assignments every day. She sat next to him as he worked, trying to be encouraging, sagging inwardly as she saw the poor quality of everything he did—the sloppy mistakes in math, the illogical leaps in his English themes, the history questions left blank if they required any research.

Daisy was often late starting supper, and she couldn't give as much attention to Donny's younger sister. "You'll never guess what happened at . . ." Amanda would begin, and Daisy would have to tell her, "Not now, honey."

By the time her husband, Matt, came home, she'd be snappish. She would recite the day's hardships—the fuzzy instructions in English, the botched history map, the morass of unsolvable algebra equations. Matt would look surprised and confused, and Daisy would gradually wind down. There was no way, really, to convey how exhausting all this was.

In December, the school called again. This time, they wanted Matt to come as well. She and Matt had to sit on Mr. Lanham's couch like two bad children and listen to the news: Donny had improved only slightly, raising a D in history to a C, and a C in algebra to a B-minus. What was worse, he had developed new problems. He had cut classes on at least three occasions. Smoked in the furnace room. Helped Sonny Barnett break into a freshman's locker. And last week, during athletics, he and three friends had been seen off the school grounds; when they returned, the coach had smelled beer on their breath.

Daisy and Matt sat silent, shocked. Matt rubbed his forehead with his fingertips. Imagine, Daisy thought, how they must look to Mr. Lanham: an overweight housewife in a cotton dress and a too-tall, too-thin insurance agent in a baggy, frayed suit. Failures, both of them—the kind of people who are always hurrying to catch up, missing the point of things that everyone else grasps at once. She wished she'd worn nylons instead of knee socks.

It was arranged that Donny would visit a psychologist for testing. Mr. Lanham knew just the person. He would set this boy straight, he said.

When they stood to leave, Daisy held her stomach in and gave Mr. Lanham a firm, responsible handshake.

Donny said the psychologist was a jackass and the tests were really dumb; but he kept all three of his appointments, and when it was time for the follow-up conference with the psychologist and both parents, Donny combed his hair and seemed unusually sober and subdued. The psychologist said Donny had no serious emotional problems. He was merely going through a difficult period in his life. He required some academic help and a better sense of self-worth. For this reason, he was suggesting a man named Calvin Beadle, a tutor with considerable psychological training.

In the car going home, Donny said he'd be damned if he'd let them drag him to some stupid tutor. His father told him to watch his language in front of his mother.

That night, Daisy lay awake pondering the term "self-worth." She had always been free with her praise. She had always told Donny he had talent, was smart, was good with his hands. She had made a big to-do over every little gift he gave her. In fact, maybe she had gone too far, although, Lord knows, she had meant every word. Was that his trouble?

She remembered when Amanda was born. Donny had acted lost and bewildered. Daisy had been alert to that, of course, but still, a new baby keeps you so busy. Had she really done all she could have? She longed—she ached—for a time machine. Given one more chance, she'd do

WORDS TO KNOW

morass (mə-răs') *n.* a difficult, confused, or entangled state of affairs; puzzling mess

subdued (səb-do͞od') *adj.* made submissive; reduced in intensity; toned down
subdue *v.*

Girl Looking at Landscape (1957), Richard Diebenkorn. Oil on canvas, 59″ × 60 3/8″, collection of Whitney Museum of American Art, New York, gift of Mr. and Mrs. Alan H. Temple (61.49). Photo by Geoffrey Clements, New York. Photo Copyright © 1995 Whitney Museum of American Art.

She longed—
she ached—
for a time machine.
Given one more chance,
she'd do it perfectly—
hug him more,
praise him more,
or perhaps
praise him less.
Oh, who can say . . .

it perfectly—hug him more, praise him more, or perhaps praise him less. Oh, who can say . . .

The tutor told Donny to call him Cal. All his kids did, he said. Daisy thought for a second that he meant his own children, then realized her mistake. He seemed too young, anyhow, to be a family man. He wore a heavy brown handlebar mustache. His hair was as long and stringy as Donny's, and his jeans as faded. Wire-rimmed spectacles slid down his nose. He lounged in a canvas director's chair with his fingers laced across his chest, and he casually, amiably questioned Donny, who sat upright and glaring in an armchair.

"So they're getting on your back at school," said Cal. "Making a big deal about anything you do wrong."

"Right," said Donny.

"Any idea why that would be?"

"Oh, well, you know, stuff like homework and all," Donny said.

"You don't do your homework?"

"Oh, well, I might do it sometimes but not just exactly like they want it." Donny sat forward and said, "It's like a prison there, you know? You've got to go to every class, you can never step off the school grounds."

"You cut classes sometimes?"

"Sometimes," Donny said, with a glance at his parents.

Cal didn't seem perturbed. "Well," he said, "I'll tell you what. Let's you and me try working together three nights a week. Think you could handle that? We'll see if we can show that school of yours a thing or two. Give it a month; then if you don't like it, we'll stop. If *I* don't like it, we'll stop. I mean, sometimes people just don't get along, right? What do you say to that?"

"Okay," Donny said. He seemed pleased.

"Make it seven o'clock till eight, Monday, Wednesday, and Friday," Cal told Matt and Daisy. They nodded. Cal shambled to his feet, gave them a little salute, and showed them to the door.

This was where he lived as well as worked, evidently. The interview had taken place in the dining room, which had been transformed into a kind of office. Passing the living room, Daisy winced at the rock music she had been hearing, without registering it, ever since she had entered the house. She looked in and saw a boy about Donny's age lying on a sofa with a book. Another boy and a girl were playing Ping-Pong in front of the fireplace. "You have several here together?" Daisy asked Cal.

"Oh, sometimes they stay on after their sessions, just to rap. They're a pretty sociable group, all in all. Plenty of goof-offs like young Donny here."

He cuffed Donny's shoulder playfully. Donny flushed and grinned.

Climbing into the car, Daisy asked Donny, "Well? What did you think?"

But Donny had returned to his old evasive self. He jerked his chin toward the garage. "Look," he said. "He's got a basketball net."

Now on Mondays, Wednesdays, and Fridays, they had supper early—the instant Matt came home. Sometimes, they had to leave before they were really finished. Amanda would still be eating her dessert. "Bye, honey. Sorry," Daisy would tell her.

Cal's first bill sent a flutter of panic through Daisy's chest, but it was worth it, of course. Just look at Donny's face when they picked him up: alight and full of interest. The principal telephoned Daisy to tell her how Donny had improved. "Of course, it hasn't shown up in his grades yet, but several of the teachers have noticed how his attitude's changed. Yes, sir, I think we're onto something here."

At home, Donny didn't act much different. He still seemed to have a low opinion of his parents. But Daisy supposed that was unavoidable—part of being fifteen. He said his parents were too "controlling"—a word that made Daisy give him a sudden look. He said they acted like wardens.

WORDS TO KNOW

amiably (ā′mē-ə-blē) *adv.* in a pleasant and friendly manner; good-naturedly
shamble (shăm′bəl) *v.* to walk or move awkwardly or clumsily

On weekends, they enforced a curfew. And any time he went to a party, they always telephoned first to see if adults would be supervising. "For God's sake!" he said. "Don't you trust me?"

"It isn't a matter of trust, honey . . . " But there was no explaining to him.

His tutor called one afternoon. "I get the sense," he said, "that this kid's feeling . . . underestimated, you know? Like you folks expect the worst of him. I'm thinking we ought to give him more rope."

"But see, he's still so suggestible," Daisy said. "When his friends suggest some mischief—smoking or drinking or such—why, he just finds it hard not to go along with them."

"Mrs. Coble," the tutor said, "I think this kid is hurting. You know? Here's a serious, sensitive kid, telling you he'd like to take on some grown-up challenges, and you're giving him the message that he can't be trusted. Don't you understand how that hurts?"

"Oh," said Daisy.

"It undermines his self-esteem—don't you realize that?"

"Well, I guess you're right," said Daisy. She saw Donny suddenly from a whole new angle: his pathetically poor posture, that slouch so forlorn that his shoulders seemed about to meet his chin . . . oh, wasn't it awful being young? She'd had a miserable adolescence herself and had always sworn no child of hers would ever be that unhappy.

She'd had a miserable adolescence herself and had always sworn no child of hers would ever be that unhappy.

They let Donny stay out later, they didn't call ahead to see if the parties were supervised, and they were careful not to grill him about his evening. The tutor had set down so many rules! They were not allowed any questions at all about any aspect of school, nor were they to speak with his teachers. If a teacher had some complaint, she should phone Cal. Only one teacher disobeyed—the history teacher, Miss Evans. She called one morning in February. "I'm a little concerned about Donny, Mrs. Coble."

"Oh, I'm sorry, Miss Evans, but Donny's tutor handles these things now . . ."

"I always deal directly with the parents. You are the parent," Miss Evans said, speaking very slowly and distinctly. "Now, here is the problem. Back when you were helping Donny with his homework, his grades rose from a D to a C, but now they've slipped back, and they're closer to an F."

"They are?"

"I think you should start overseeing his homework again."

"But Donny's tutor says . . ."

"It's nice that Donny has a tutor, but you should still be in charge of his homework. With you, he learned it. Then he passed his tests. With the tutor, well, it seems the tutor is more of a crutch. 'Donny,' I say, 'a quiz is coming up on Friday. Hadn't you better be listening instead of talking?' 'That's okay, Miss Evans,' he says. 'I have a tutor now.' Like a talisman![1] I really think you ought to take over, Mrs. Coble."

"I see," said Daisy. "Well, I'll think about that. Thank you for calling."

Hanging up, she felt a rush of anger at Donny. A talisman! For a talisman, she'd given up all luxuries, all that time with her daughter, her evenings at home!

She dialed Cal's number. He sounded muzzy. "I'm sorry if I woke you," she told him, "but Donny's history teacher just called. She says he isn't doing well."

"She should have dealt with me."

"She wants me to start supervising his homework again. His grades are slipping."

"Yes," said the tutor, "but you and I both

---

1. **talisman** (tăl′ĭs-mən): a thing believed to possess magic power or to bring good luck.

WORDS TO KNOW

forlorn (fər-lôrn′) *adj.* appearing sad or lonely

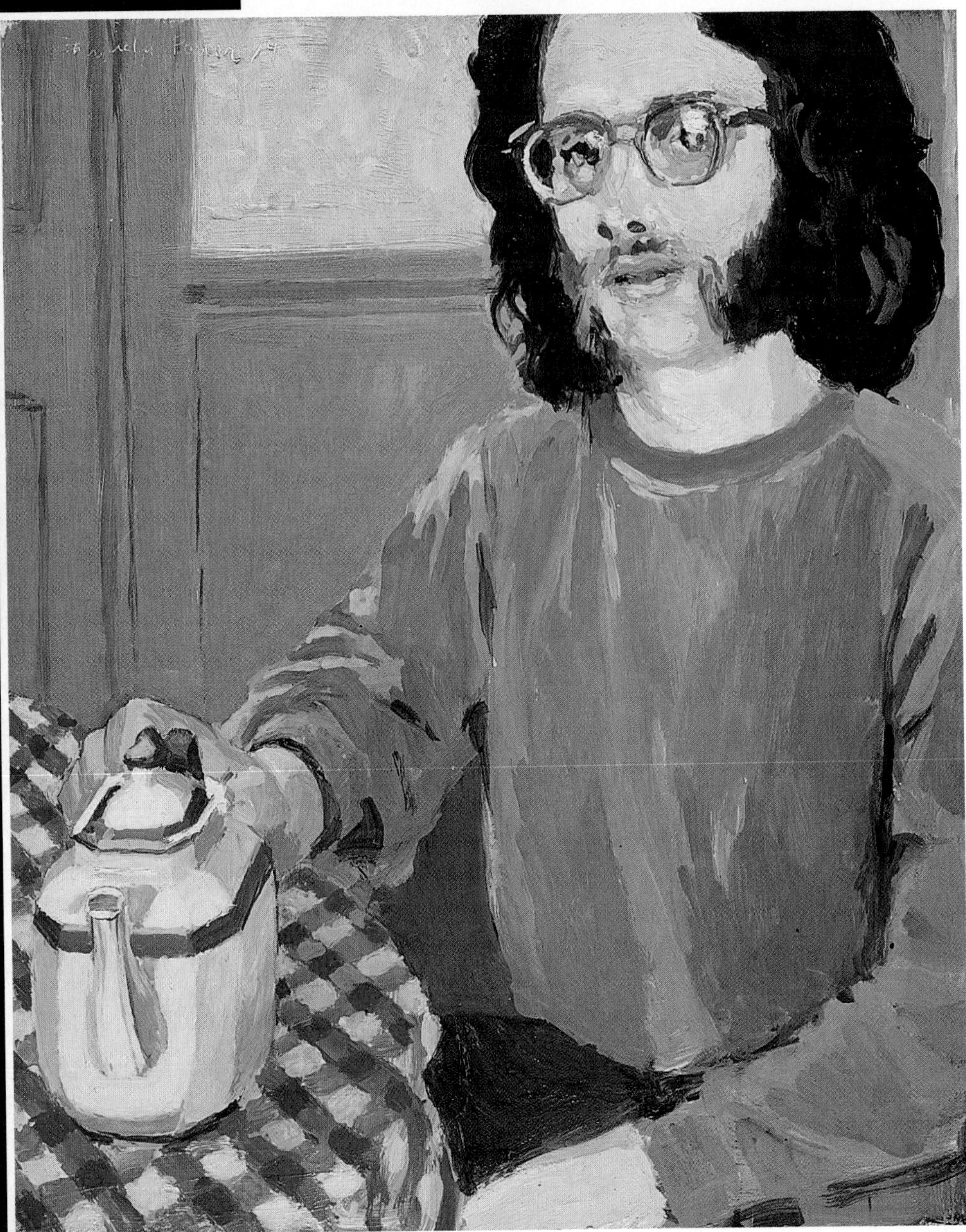

Portrait of Richard Freeman (1974), Fairfield Porter. Oil on panel, Bowdoin College Museum of Art, Brunswick, Maine, anonymous gift (1986,74.1).

"I care about

the *whole* child—

his happiness,

his self-esteem.

The grades will come.

Just give them time."

know there's more to it than mere grades, don't we? I care about the *whole* child—his happiness, his self-esteem. The grades will come. Just give them time."

When she hung up, it was Miss Evans she was angry at. What a narrow woman!

It was Cal this, Cal that, Cal says this, Cal and I did that. Cal lent Donny an album by the Who.[2] He took Donny and two other pupils to a rock concert. In March, when Donny began to talk endlessly on the phone with a girl named Miriam, Cal even let Miriam come to one of the tutoring sessions. Daisy was touched that Cal would grow so involved in Donny's life, but she was also a little hurt, because she had offered to have Miriam to dinner and Donny had refused. Now he asked them to drive her to Cal's house without a qualm.

This Miriam was an unappealing girl with blurry lipstick and masses of rough red hair. She wore a short, bulky jacket that would not have been out of place on a motorcycle. During the trip to Cal's she was silent, but coming back, she was more talkative. "What a neat guy, and what a house! All those kids hanging out, like a club. And the stereo playing rock . . . gosh, he's not like grown-up at all! Married and divorced and everything, but you'd think he was our own age."

"Mr. Beadle was married?" Daisy asked.

"Yeah, to this really controlling lady. She didn't understand him a bit."

"No, I guess not," Daisy said.

Spring came, and the students who hung around at Cal's drifted out to the basketball net above the garage. Sometimes, when Daisy and Matt arrived to pick up Donny, they'd find him there with the others—spiky and excited, jittering on his toes beneath the backboard. It was staying light much longer now, and the neighboring fence cast narrow bars across the bright grass. Loud music would be spilling from Cal's windows. Once it was the Who, which Daisy recognized from the time that Donny had borrowed the album. "Teenage Wasteland,"[3] she said aloud, identifying the song, and Matt gave a short, dry laugh. "It certainly is," he said. He'd misunderstood; he thought she was commenting on the scene spread before them. In fact, she might have been. The players looked like hoodlums, even her son. Why, one of Cal's students had recently been knifed in a tavern. One had been shipped off to boarding school in midterm; two had been withdrawn by their parents. On the other hand, Donny had mentioned someone who'd been studying with Cal for five years. "Five years!" said Daisy. "Doesn't anyone ever stop needing him?"

Donny looked at her. Lately, whatever she said about Cal was read as criticism. "You're just feeling competitive," he said. "And controlling."

She bit her lip and said no more.

In April, the principal called to tell her that Donny had been expelled. There had been a locker check, and in Donny's locker they found five cans of beer and half a pack of cigarettes. With Donny's previous record, this offense meant expulsion.

Daisy gripped the receiver tightly and said, "Well, where is he now?"

"We've sent him home," said Mr. Lanham. "He's packed up all his belongings, and he's coming home on foot."

Daisy wondered what she would say to him. She felt him looming closer and closer, bringing this brand-new situation that no one had prepared her to handle. What other place would take him? Could they enter him in public school? What were the rules? She stood at the living room window, waiting for him to show up. Gradually, she realized that he was taking too long. She checked the clock. She stared up the street again.

2. **the Who:** a British rock group formed in the early 1960s.

3. **"Teenage Wasteland":** The song is actually titled "Baba O'Riley" and can be found on the album *Who's Next* (1971).

WORDS TO KNOW

qualm (kwäm) *n.* a disturbing uneasiness or doubt

looming (lo͞o′mĭng) *adj.* appearing to the mind in a large and threatening form **loom** *v.*

When an hour had passed, she phoned the school. Mr. Lanham's secretary answered and told her in a grave, sympathetic voice that yes, Donny Coble had most definitely gone home. Daisy called her husband. He was out of the office. She went back to the window and thought awhile, and then she called Donny's tutor.

"Donny's been expelled from school," she said, "and now I don't know where he's gone. I wonder if you've heard from him?"

There was a long silence. "Donny's with me, Mrs. Coble," he finally said.

"With you? How'd he get there?"

"He hailed a cab, and I paid the driver."

"Could I speak to him, please?"

There was another silence. "Maybe it'd be better if we had a conference," Cal said.

"I don't *want* a conference. I've been standing at the window picturing him dead or kidnapped or something, and now you tell me you want a—"

"Donny is very, very upset. Understandably so," said Cal. "Believe me, Mrs. Coble, this is not what it seems. Have you asked Donny's side of the story?"

"Well, of course not, how could I? He went running off to you instead."

"Because he didn't feel he'd be listened to."

"But I haven't even—"

"Why don't you come out and talk? The three of us," said Cal, "will try to get this thing in perspective."

"Well, all right," Daisy said. But she wasn't as reluctant as she sounded. Already, she felt soothed by the calm way Cal was taking this.

Cal answered the doorbell at once. He said, "Hi, there," and led her into the dining room.

> **He did his assignments, and he earned average grades, but he gathered no friends, joined no clubs. There was something exhausted and defeated about him.**

Donny sat slumped in a chair, chewing the knuckle of one thumb. "Hello, Donny," Daisy said. He flicked his eyes in her direction.

"Sit here, Mrs. Coble," said Cal, placing her opposite Donny. He himself remained standing, restlessly pacing. "So," he said.

Daisy stole a look at Donny. His lips were swollen, as if he'd been crying.

"You know," Cal told Daisy, "I kind of expected something like this. That's a very punitive school you've got him in—you realize that. And any half-decent lawyer will tell you they've violated his civil rights. Locker checks! Where's their search warrant?"

"But if the rule is—" Daisy said.

"Well, anyhow, let him tell you his side."

She looked at Donny. He said, "It wasn't my fault. I promise."

"They said your locker was full of beer."

"It was a put-up job! See, there's this guy that doesn't like me. He put all these beers in my locker and started a rumor going, so Mr. Lanham ordered a locker check."

"What was the boy's *name*?" Daisy asked.

"Huh?"

"Mrs. Coble, take my word, the situation is not so unusual," Cal said. "You can't imagine how vindictive kids can be sometimes."

"What was the boy's name," said Daisy, "so that I can ask Mr. Lanham if that's who suggested he run a locker check."

"You don't believe me," Donny said.

"And how'd this boy get your combination in the first place?"

"Frankly," said Cal, "I wouldn't be surprised to learn the school was in on it. Any kid that

WORDS TO KNOW

punitive (pyo͞o'nĭ-tĭv) *adj.* punishing or having to do with punishment
vindictive (vĭn-dĭk'tĭv) *adj.* wanting revenge; bearing a grudge

marches to a different drummer,[4] why, they'd just love an excuse to get rid of him. The school is where I lay the blame."

"Doesn't *Donny* ever get blamed?"

"Now, Mrs. Coble, you heard what he—"

"Forget it," Donny told Cal. "You can see she doesn't trust me."

Daisy drew in a breath to say that of course she trusted him—a reflex. But she knew that bold-faced, wide-eyed look of Donny's. He had worn that look when he was small, denying some petty misdeed with the evidence plain as day all around him. Still, it was hard for her to accuse him outright. She temporized and said, "The only thing I'm sure of is that they've kicked you out of school, and now I don't know what we're going to do."

"We'll fight it," said Cal.

"We can't. Even you must see we can't."

"I could apply to Brantly," Donny said.

Cal stopped his pacing to beam down at him. "Brantly! Yes. They're really onto where a kid is coming from, at Brantly. Why, *I* could get you into Brantly. I work with a lot of their students."

Daisy had never heard of Brantly, but already she didn't like it. And she didn't like Cal's smile, which struck her now as feverish and avid—a smile of hunger.

On the fifteenth of April, they entered Donny in a public school, and they stopped his tutoring sessions. Donny fought both decisions bitterly. Cal, surprisingly enough, did not object. He admitted he'd made no headway with Donny and said it was because Donny was emotionally disturbed.

Donny went to his new school every morning, plodding off alone with his head down. He did his assignments, and he earned average grades, but he gathered no friends, joined no clubs. There was something exhausted and defeated about him.

The first week in June, during final exams, Donny vanished. He simply didn't come home one afternoon, and no one at school remembered seeing him. The police were reassuring, and for the first few days, they worked hard. They combed Donny's sad, messy room for clues; they visited Miriam and Cal. But then they started talking about the number of kids who ran away every year. Hundreds, just in this city. "He'll show up, if he wants to," they said. "If he doesn't, he won't."

Evidently, Donny didn't want to.

It's been three months now and still no word. Matt and Daisy still look for him in every crowd of awkward, heartbreaking teenage boys. Every time the phone rings, they imagine it might be Donny. Both parents have aged. Donny's sister seems to be staying away from home as much as possible.

At night, Daisy lies awake and goes over Donny's life. She is trying to figure out what went wrong, where they made their first mistake. Often, she finds herself blaming Cal, although she knows he didn't begin it. Then at other times she excuses him, for without him, Donny might have left earlier. Who really knows? In the end, she can only sigh and search for a cooler spot on the pillow. As she falls asleep, she occasionally glimpses something in the corner of her vision. It's something fleet[5] and round, a ball—a basketball. It flies up, it sinks through the hoop, descends, lands in a yard littered with last year's leaves and striped with bars of sunlight as white as bones, bleached and parched and cleanly picked. ❖

---

4. **marches to a different drummer:** thinks and acts independently; a reference to Henry David Thoreau's famous quotation (page 306).

5. **fleet:** swiftly moving; fast.

WORDS TO KNOW

temporize (tĕm′pə-rīz′) *v.* to avoid immediate action or making a decision in order to gain time

RESPONDING OPTIONS

FROM PERSONAL RESPONSE *TO* CRITICAL ANALYSIS

REFLECT 1. How did you react to Donny's running away? Describe your reaction in your notebook and share it with your classmates.

RETHINK 2. What do you think will happen to Donny?

3. Who or what do you think is most responsible for Donny's running away?

   Consider
   - how Daisy tries to help him
   - what Cal says and does
   - Daisy's question, "Doesn't *Donny* ever get blamed?" (page 1005)

4. Whom do you feel the most sorry for in this story? Explain why.

5. From the tone of this story, do you think Anne Tyler takes sides in the academic reform debate? Which side, if any, do you think she's on? Find specific examples to support your opinion.

RELATE 6. Look back at your record of the conflicting advice that Daisy and Matt receive and follow, as well as your suggestions of what they should do, from the Previewing activities on page 996. Do you think that Daisy and Matt could have handled the situation better if they had done something differently? Explain your opinion with evidence from the story and from your own experience.

ANOTHER PATHWAY

Cooperative Learning

With a small group, act out one of the scenes from this story or imagine a related scene. For example, you might choose to show the first conversation between Daisy and the principal or Cal's interaction with his students. Stage your scene for your classmates and discuss how your dramatization added to their understanding.

LITERARY CONCEPTS

The **protagonist** is the central character in a short story, novel, or play. The **antagonist** is the character or force that the protagonist is pitted against. Both of these characters are involved in a story's central conflict, and after the climax, the protagonist often has a change in feelings, personality, or outlook. Who do you think are the protagonist and the antagonist in "Teenage Wasteland"? Give specific reasons for your answers. Do you think the protagonist changes by the end of the story? If so, how? Share your opinions with a partner.

QUICKWRITES

1. Write the **police report** that might be filed on Donny after the officer has interviewed his parents.
2. Draft a **persuasive speech** that could be delivered to the PTA, explaining how much control parents should exert over their teenage children. Use examples from the story and from your own experience as support.

***PORTFOLIO** Save your writing. You may want to use it later as a springboard to a piece for your portfolio.*

ALTERNATIVE ACTIVITIES

1. Survey at least 20 teenagers, asking them who exerts the most influence in their lives: parents, teachers, friends, religious leaders, or other people. Convert your findings into percentages and illustrate them on a **pie graph.** If possible, create your pie graph on your computer and bring the printout to class.
2. Locate the Who song "Baba O'Riley" from the album *Who's Next.* In an **oral presentation,** play the song for the class and explain how you think it relates to the story.
3. Research clothing styles of the late 1970s. **Sketch** costumes that the characters might wear in a film version of the story. Display your sketches in class.

John Travolta in *Saturday Night Fever* (1977). Photofest.

LITERARY LINKS

Compare "Teenage Wasteland" to another story of childhood troubles and parental guilt, "I Stand Here Ironing" (page 642). Which one do you think is sadder? Which mother do you think faces the greater difficulty in finding the right way to raise her child? How did times change for mothers from the 1930s and 1940s to the 1970s and early 1980s? Imagine what these two mothers would say to each other if they got the chance.

CRITIC'S CORNER

Anne Tyler has said that she uses the family unit to show "how people manage to endure together—how they grate against each other, adjust, intrude, and protect themselves from intrusions, give up, and start all over again in the morning." How effectively do you think Tyler has portrayed the family in "Teenage Wasteland"? Comment on specific details from the story and from what you know based on your own experience.

ART CONNECTION

David Park's painting *Table with Fruit* on page 997 shows a recognizable domestic scene: people seated around a table. Yet, it is a rather flat painting, with little depth, perspective, or fine detail. What feeling do you have about the people in the painting? What is the effect of the empty chair? How does your sense of the people in the painting compare to your understanding of the family in "Teenage Wasteland"?

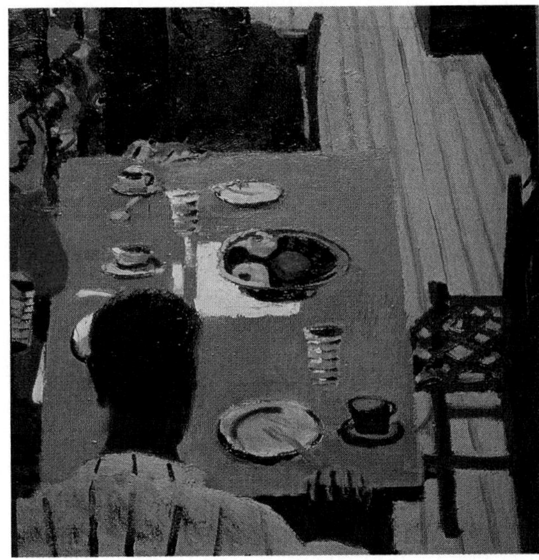

Detail of *Table with Fruit* (1951–1952), David Park. Oil on canvas, 46″ × 35¾″, collection of Mr. and Mrs. R. Crosby Kemper. Photo by Edward B. Bigelow.

ACROSS THE CURRICULUM

Sociology Research teenage runaway rates in the United States. How many young people run away from home each year? Why do they run away? Where do they go? Where can they find shelter? What usually happens to them? Report your findings to the class.

WORDS TO KNOW

EXERCISE A Identify each pair of words by writing Synonyms or Antonyms.

1. temporize–delay
2. punitive–forgiving
3. shamble–stride
4. forlorn–sad
5. qualm–confidence
6. morass–predicament
7. subdued–excited
8. amiably–agreeably
9. looming–menacing
10. vindictive–spiteful

EXERCISE B Working with a partner, act out the meaning of one of the vocabulary words while another pair of students guesses the word. Then switch so that you and your partner guess which word the other pair of students is acting out. Continue the exercise until all the words are used.

ANNE TYLER

1941–

Shy, quiet, and keenly observant, Anne Tyler is the oldest of four children of Quaker parents. On a quest for the ideal community, her family moved frequently, living in several different Quaker communes throughout the Midwest and South. As Tyler later explained, this experience taught her to "look at the normal world with a certain amount of distance and surprise." This unusual point of view continues to influence her fiction.

Tyler began writing while she was a student at Duke University, where she studied under the novelist Reynolds Price. In 1963 she married, and a few years later began both a family and a serious writing career. She did not receive national recognition until the publication of her sixth novel, *Searching for Caleb*, in 1976. Tyler first hit the bestseller list in 1982 with *Dinner at the Homesick Restaurant.* In 1988 another best-selling novel, *The Accidental Tourist,* was made into a movie, and a year later Tyler won a Pulitzer Prize for *Breathing Lessons.*

In her more than 14 novels and 40 short stories, Tyler looks at the loneliness and isolation of middle-class family life. Many of her characters are comical and quirky—like the character who shelves her groceries in alphabetical order in *The Accidental Tourist.* Tyler portrays these characters with sympathy and gentle irony. She has said that the real heroes of her books are "first the ones who manage to endure and second the ones who are somehow able to grant other people the privacy of the space around them and yet still produce some warmth."

Tyler currently lives in Baltimore, Maryland, with her husband and two daughters. She avoids giving interviews and appearing on talk shows, preferring a quiet life with her family and her writing.

OTHER WORKS *Celestial Navigation, Earthly Possessions, Saint Maybe, Ladder of Years*

PREVIEWING

FICTION

El Patrón

Nash Candelaria

PERSONAL CONNECTION

Part of living in a family is learning to deal with disagreements among family members. Think of a time when you disagreed with another member of your family. What caused the disagreement? How did you resolve it? Did other family members contribute to the solution? With a small group, discuss the kinds of conflicts within a family and the ways people resolve these conflicts.

HISTORICAL CONNECTION

In June of 1980, Congress adopted a law requiring all 18-year-old males to register for the draft. The Soviet Union had recently invaded Afghanistan, and President Carter argued that draft registration was necessary in order to prepare for military emergencies and to demonstrate the United States' "resolve as a nation." The government did not plan to draft people to serve in the armed forces; the law required only that young men register their names and addresses with the draft authorities. The U.S. military had not drafted anyone since the end of 1972, and it expected to continue as an all-volunteer force. Even so, the requirement to register for the draft aroused widespread opposition. Local antidraft groups sprang up all over the country. Thousands of people marched in protest rallies. Although nearly 12 million young men registered as the law required, an estimated 500,000 refused. In a Congressional hearing a witness described the refusal to register as "one of the most massive demonstrations of civil disobedience in our nation's history." As "El Patrón" suggests, feelings about the draft and the military led to conflicts in communities and families across the United States.

WRITING CONNECTION

In your notebook, write about an experience you've had with conflict resolution. The conflict could be between yourself and someone else, such as a family member or a friend, or between two other people. Then, generalize from your experience: What is so difficult about resolving conflicts? What are some key ingredients of conflict resolution? As you read "El Patrón," compare your experience with conflict resolution with the experience of the family in the story.

At an army recruitment office.
H. Armstrong Roberts.

LASERLINKS
• *HISTORICAL CONNECTION*

El Patrón

Nash Candelaria

My father-in-law's hierarchy is, in descending order, Dios, El Papa, y el patrón. It is to these that mere mortals bow, as in turn el patrón bows to El Papa, and El Papa bows to Dios.

God and the Pope are understandable enough. It's this el patrón, the boss, who causes most of our trouble. Whether it's the one who gives you work and for it pay, the lifeblood of hard-working little people—or others: Our parents (fathers affectionately known as jefe,[1] mothers known merely as mama, military commanders el capitán), or any of the big shots in the government (el alcalde, el gobernador, el presidente and never forget la policía).[2]

It was about some such el patrón trouble that Señor Martínez boarded the bus in San Diego and headed north toward L.A.—and us.

Since I was lecturing to a midafternoon summer school class at Southwestern U., my wife, Lola, picked up her father at the station. When I arrived home, they were sitting politely in the living room talking banalities: "Yes, it does look like rain. But if it doesn't rain, it might be sunny. If only the clouds would blow away."

Lola had that dangerous look on her face that usually made me start talking too fast and too long in hope of shifting her focus. It never worked. She'd sit there with a face like a brown-skinned kewpie doll[3] whose expression was slowly turning into that of an angry maniac. When she could no longer stand it, she'd give her father a blast: "You never talk to me about

1. **jefe** (hĕ′fĕ) *Spanish:* chief.
2. **el alcalde, el gobernador, el presidente . . . la policía** (ĕl äl-käl′dĕ, ĕl gô-bĕr-nä-dôr′, ĕl prĕ-sē-dĕn′tĕ, lä pô-lē-sē′ä) *Spanish:* the mayor, the governor, the president, the police.
3. **kewpie doll** (kyo͞o′pē): a small, wide-eyed doll with a curl of hair on top of the head.

WORDS TO KNOW

hierarchy (hī′ə-rär′kē) *n.* an organization of persons or things arranged into higher and lower ranks

banality (bə-năl′ĭ-tē) *n.* something that is obvious, predictable, overused, or uninteresting anything important, you macho,[4] chauvinist[5] jumping bean!" Then it would escalate to nastiness from there.

But tonight it didn't get that far. As I entered, Señor Martínez rose, dressed neatly in his one suit as for a wedding or a funeral, and politely shook my hand. Without so much as a glance at Lola, he said, "Why don't you go to the kitchen with the other women."

"There are no other women," Lola said coldly. She stood and belligerently received my kiss on the cheek before leaving.

Señor Martínez was oblivious to her reaction, sensing only the absence of "woman," at which he visibly relaxed and sat down.

"Rosca," he said, referring to me as he always did by my last name. "Tito is in trouble with the law."

His face struggled between anger and sadness, tinged with a cross-current of confusion. Tito was his pride and joy. His only son after four daughters. A twilight gift born to his wife at a time when he despaired of ever having a son, when their youngest daughter, Lola, was already ten years old and their oldest daughter twenty.

"He just finished his examinations at the state university. He was working this summer to save money for his second year when this terrible thing happened."

I could not in my wildest fantasies imagine young Vicente getting into any kind of trouble. He had always impressed me as a bright, polite young man who would inspire pride in any father. Even when he and old Vicente had quarreled about Tito going to college instead of working full-time, the old man had grudgingly come around to seeing the wisdom of it. But now. The law! I was stunned.

"Where is he?" I asked, imagining the nineteen-year-old in some filthy cell in the San Diego jail.

"I don't know." Then he looked over his shoulder toward the kitchen, as if to be certain no one was eavesdropping. "I think he went underground."

Underground! I had visions of drug-crazed revolutionary zealots. Bombs exploding in federal buildings. God knows what kind of madness.

"They're probably after him," he went on. Then he paused and stared at me as if trying to understand. "Tito always looked up to you and Lola. Of all the family it would be you he would try to contact. I want you to help me." Not help *Tito*, I thought, but help *me*.

It's this el patrón, THE BOSS, who causes most of our trouble.

I went to the cabinet for the bottle that I keep there for emergencies. I took a swallow to give me enough courage to ask the question. "What . . . did . . . he do?"

Señor Martínez stared limply at the glass in his hand. "You know," he said, "my father fought with Pancho Villa."[6]

Jesus! I thought. If everyone who told me his father had fought with Pancho Villa was telling the truth, that army would have been big enough to conquer the world. Besides—what did this have to do with Tito?

"When my turn came," he continued, "I enlisted in the Marines at Camp Pendleton.

4. **macho** (mä′chō): having or showing a strong manliness, especially stressing aggressiveness and domination of women.

5. **chauvinist** (shō′və-nĭst): excessively enthusiastic about one's own sex, race, or group; most likely used here to mean "male chauvinist"—one who behaves as if women were inferior to men.

6. **Pancho Villa** (pän′chô vē′ə): Mexican revolutionary leader who, in 1914–1915, tried to overthrow the president of Mexico.

WORDS TO KNOW

escalate (ĕs′kə-lāt′) *v.* to increase by stages; expand
belligerently (bə-lĭj′ər-ənt-lē) *adv.* in a hostile or unfriendly manner; aggressively
oblivious (ə-blĭv′ē-əs) *adj.* not paying attention; unaware
zealot (zĕl′ət) *n.* a person who is intensely devoted, usually to a cause, and enthusiastically supportive

Fought los Japonés[7] in the Pacific." Finally he took a swallow of his drink and sat up stiffly as if at attention. "The men in our family have never shirked their duty!" He barked like the Marine corporal he had once been.

It slowly dawned on me what this was all about. It had been *the* topic all during summer school at Southwestern U. Registration for the draft. "No blood for Mideast oil!" the picket signs around the campus post office had shouted. "Boycott the Exxon army!"

"Yes, PAPÁ. So we could come back, if we survived, to our jobs as busboys and ditch diggers; *that's* why I have to go to college. I don't want to go to the Middle East and fight and die for some oil company when you can't even afford to own a car."

"I should never have let him go to college," Señor Martínez said. "That's where he gets such crazy radical ideas. From those rich college boys whose parents can buy them out of all kinds of trouble."

"So he didn't register," I said.

"The FBI is probably after him right now. It's a federal crime you know. And the Canadians don't want draft dodgers either."

He took a deep swallow and polished off the rest of his drink in one gulp, putting the empty glass on the coffee table. There, his gesture seemed to say, now you know the worst.

Calmer now, he went on to tell me more. About the American Civil War; a greater percentage of Spanish-speaking men of New Mexico had joined the Union Army than the men from any other group in any other state in the Union. About the Rough Riders,[8] including young Mexican-Americans, born on horseback, riding roughest of all over the Spanish in Cuba. About the War-to-End-All-Wars,[9] where tough, skinny, brown-faced doughboys[10] from farms in Texas, New Mexico, Arizona, Colorado, and California gave their all "Over There." About World War II, from the New Mexico National Guard captured at Bataan[11] to the tough little Marines whom he was proud to fight alongside; man for man there were more decorations for bravery among Mexican-Americans than among any other group in this war. Then Korea, where his younger brother toughed it out in the infantry. Finally Vietnam, where kids like his nephew, Pablo, got it in some silent, dark jungle trying to save a small country from the Communists.

By now he had lost his calm. There were tears in his eyes, partly from the pride he felt in this tradition of valor in war. But partly for something else, I thought. I could almost hear his son's reply to his impassioned call to duty: "Yes, papá. So we could come back, if we survived, to our jobs as busboys and ditch diggers; *that's* why I have to go to college. I don't want to go to the Middle East and fight and die for some oil company when you can't even afford to own a

7. **los Japonés** (lôs hä-pô-nĕs′) *Spanish:* the Japanese.
8. **Rough Riders:** a volunteer cavalry regiment organized by Theodore Roosevelt during the Spanish-American War (1898), which developed from Cuba's war for independence from Spain.
9. **War-to-End-All-Wars:** World War I (1914-1918).
10. **doughboys:** U.S. infantry soldiers during World War I.
11. **Bataan** (bə-tăn′): a World War II battle in the Philippines in which U.S. troops surrendered to the Japanese.

WORDS TO KNOW

shirk (shûrk) *v.* to neglect or avoid doing something
valor (văl′ər) *n.* courage; bravery
impassioned (ĭm-păsh′ənd) *adj.* full of strong feeling; stirring; emotional

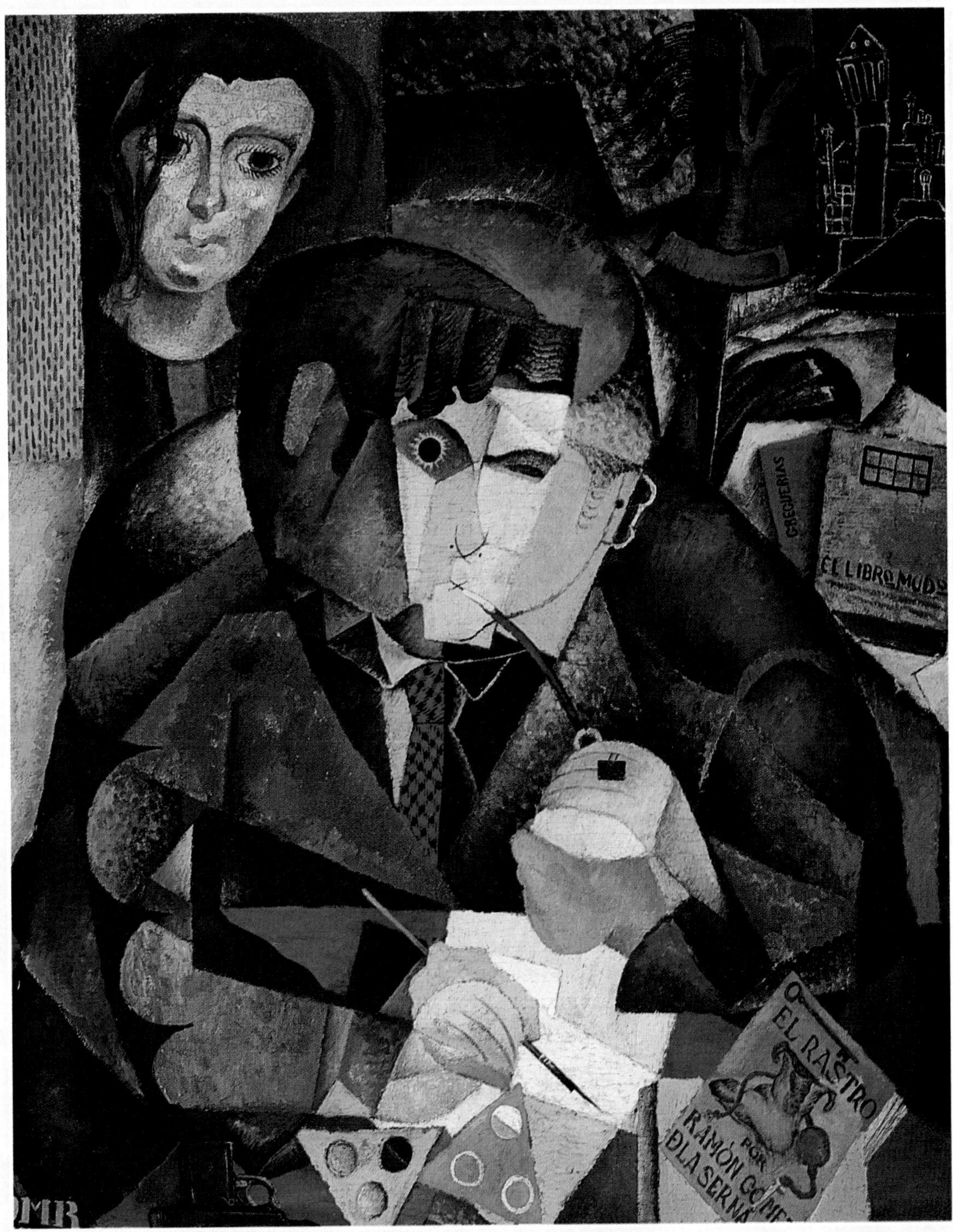

Portrait of Ramón Gómez de la Serna (1915), Diego Rivera. Private collection. Photo courtesy of The Detroit Institute of Arts. Photo Copyright © Dirk Bakker.

car. If the Russians invaded our country, I would defend it. If a robber broke into our house, I would fight him. If someone attacked you, I would save you. But this? No, papá."

But now Tito was gone. God knows where. None of his three sisters in San Diego had seen him. Nor any of his friends in the neighborhood or school or work.

I could hear preparations for dinner from the kitchen. Señor Martínez and I had another tragito[12] while Lolita and Junior ate their dinner early, the sounds of their childish voices piercing through the banging of pots and pans.

When Lola called me Emiliano instead of my nickname, Pata, I knew we were in for a lousy meal. Everything her father disliked must have been served. It had taken some kind of perverse gourmet expending a tremendous amount of energy to fix such rotten food. There was that nothing white bread that presses together into a doughy flat mass instead of the tortillas papá thrived on. There was a funny little salad with chopped garbage in it covered by a blob of imitation goo. There was no meat. No meat! Just all those sliced vegetables in a big bowl. Not ordinary vegetables like beans and potatoes and carrots, but funny, wiggly long things like wild grass . . . or worms. And quivering cubes of what must have been whale blubber.

Halfway through the meal, as Señor Martínez shuffled the food around on his plate like one of our kids resisting what was good for them, the doorbell rang.

"You'd better get that, Emiliano," Lola said, daring me to refuse by her tone of voice and dagger-throwing glance.

Who needs a fight? In a sense I was the lucky one because I could leave the table and that pot of mess-age.[13] When I opened the door, a scraggly young man beamed a weak smile at me. "I hitchhiked from San Diego," Tito said.

Before I could move onto the steps and close the door behind me, he stumbled past me into the house. Tired as he was, he reacted instantly to seeing his father at the table. "You!" he shouted, then turned and bolted out the door.

"PAPÁ, how old were you when you left Mexico for the U.S.? . . . And what did your father say?"

She knew she had him, and he knew it too.

Even tired he could run faster than I, so I hopped into the car and drove after him while Lola and Señor Martínez stood on the steps shouting words at me that I couldn't hear.

Two blocks later Tito finally climbed into the car after I bribed him with a promise of dinner at a fast-food restaurant. While his mouth was full I tried to talk some sense into him, but to no avail. He was just as stubborn as his father and sister. Finally, I drove him to the International House on campus where the housing manager, who owed me a favor, found him an empty bed.

"You should have *made* him come back with you," Lola nagged at me that night.

"He doesn't want to be under the same roof with his father." From her thoughtful silence I knew that she understood and probably felt the same way herself. When I explained to her what it was all about—her father had said nothing to her—it looked for a moment as if she would get out of bed, stomp to the guest room, and heave Señor Martínez out into the street.

The next day seemed like an endless two-way

12. **tragito** (trä-hē'tô) *Spanish:* small drink; swig.

13. **pot of mess-age:** a wordplay on "mess of pottage," which, figuratively, is a bad deal—a thing of value exchanged for one of little or no value. In the biblical story of Jacob and Esau (Genesis 25), Esau sells his birthright to his brother Jacob in exchange for pottage, a dish of cooked vegetables.

shuttle between our house and the I House. First me. Then Lola. If Señor Martínez had had a car and could drive, he would have followed each of us.

Our shuttle diplomacy finally wore them down. I could at last discern cracks in father's and son's immovable positions.

"Yes. Yes. I love my son."

"I love my father."

"I know. I know. Adults should be able to sit down and air their differences, no matter how wrong he is."

"Maybe tomorrow. Give me a break. But definitely not at mealtime. I can't eat while my stomach is churning."

The difficulty for me, as always, was in keeping my opinions to myself. Lola didn't have that problem. After all, they were her brother and father, so she felt free to say whatever she pleased.

"The plan is to get them to talk," I said to her. "If they can talk they can reach some kind of understanding."

"Papá has to be set straight," she said. "As usual, he's wrong, but he always insists it's someone else who messed things up."

"He doesn't want Tito to go to jail."

"That's Tito's choice!" Of course she was right; they were both right.

The summit meeting was set for the next afternoon. Since I had only one late morning lecture, I would pick up Tito, feed him a hamburger or two, then bring him to the house. Lola would fix Señor Martínez some nice tortillas and chili, making up for that abominable dinner of the night before last. Well fed, with two chaperones mediating, we thought they could work something out.

When Tito and I walked into the house, my hope started to tremble and develop goose bumps. It was deathly silent and formal. Lola had that dangerous look on her face again. The macho, chauvinist jumping bean sat stiffly in his suit that looked like it had just been pressed—all shiny and sharply creased, unapproachable and potentially cutting, an inanimate warning of what lay behind Señor Martínez's stone face.

Tito and I sat across from the sofa and faced them. Or rather I faced them. Both Tito and Señor Martínez were looking off at an angle from each other, not daring to touch glances. I smiled, but no one acknowledged it so I gave it up. Then Lola broke the silence.

"What this needs is a woman's point-of-view," she began.

That's all Señor Martínez needed. The blast his eyes shot at her left her open-mouthed and silent as he interrupted. "I don't want you to go to jail!" He was looking at Lola, but he meant Tito.

Tito's response was barely audible, and I detected a trembling in his voice. "You'd rather I got killed on some Arabian desert," he said.

The stone face cracked. For a moment it looked as if Señor Martínez would burst into tears. He turned his puzzled face from Lola toward his son. "No," he said. "Is that what you think?" Then, when Tito did not answer, he said, "You're my only son, and damn it! Sons are supposed to obey their fathers!"

"El patrón, El Papa, and Dios," Tito said with a trace of bitterness.

But Lola could be denied no longer. "Papá, how old were you when you left Mexico for the U.S.?" She didn't expect an answer, so didn't give him time to reply. "Sixteen, wasn't it? And what did your father say?"

Thank God that smart-ass smile of hers was turned away from her father. She knew she had him, and he knew it too, but he didn't need her smirk to remind him of it.

He sighed. The look on his face showed that sometimes memories were best forgotten. When he shook his head but did not speak, Lola went on. She too had seen her father's reaction, and her voice lost its hard edge and became more sympathetic.

WORDS TO KNOW

discern (dĭ-sûrn′) *v.* to see clearly; perceive; recognize

"He disowned you, didn't he? Grandpa disowned you. Called you a traitor to your own country. A deserter when things got tough."

"I did not intend to stay in Mexico and starve," he said. He looked around at us one by one as if he had to justify himself. "He eventually came to Los Estados Unidos[14] himself. He and Mamá died in that house in San Diego."

"What did you think when Grandpa did that to you?"

No answer was necessary. "Can't you see, Papá?" Lola pleaded, meaning him and Tito. He could see.

Meanwhile Tito had been watching his father as if he had never seen him before. I guess only the older children had heard Papá's story of how he left Mexico.

"I don't intend to go to jail, Papá," Tito said. "I just have to take a stand along with thousands of others. In the past old men started wars in which young men died in order to preserve old men's comforts. It just has to stop. There's never been a war without a draft. Never a draft without registration. And this one is nothing but craziness by el patrón in Washington, D.C. If enough of us protest, maybe he'll get the message."

PAPÁ still believed in el patrón, El Papa, and Dios. What I hoped they now saw was that Tito did too.

"They almost declared it unconstitutional," I said. "They may yet."

"Because they aren't signing women," Papá said in disgust. But from the look on Lola's face, I'd pick her over him in any war.

"If they come after me, I'll register," Tito said. "But in the meantime I have to take this stand."

There. It was out. They had had their talk in spite of their disagreements.

"He's nineteen," Lola said. "Old enough to run his own life."

Señor Martínez was all talked out. He slumped against the back of the sofa. Even the creases in his trousers seemed to have sagged. Tito looked at his sister, and his face brightened.

"Papá," Tito said. "I . . . I'd like to come home, if you want me to."

On Papá's puzzled face I imagined I could read the words: "My father fought with Pancho Villa." But it was no longer an accusation, only a simple statement of fact. Who knows what takes more courage—to fight or not to fight?

"There's a bus at four o'clock," Señor Martínez said.

Later I drove them in silence to the station. Though it felt awkward, it wasn't a bad silence. There are more important ways to speak than with words, and I could feel that sitting shoulder to shoulder beside me, father and son had reached some accord.

Papá still believed in el patrón, El Papa, and Dios. What I hoped they now saw was that Tito did too. Only in his case, conscience overrode el patrón, maybe even El Papa. In times past, popes too declared holy wars that violated conscience. For Tito, conscience was the same as Dios. And I saw in their uneasy truce that love overrode their differences.

I shook their hands as they boarded the bus, and watched the two similar faces, one old, one young, smile sadly at me through the window as the Greyhound pulled away.

When I got back home, Junior and Lolita were squabbling over what channel to watch on TV. I rolled my eyes in exasperation, ready to holler at them, but Lola spoke up first.

"I'm glad Papá got straightened out. The hardest thing for parents with their children is to let go."

Yeah, I started to say, but she stuck her head into the other room and told Junior and Lolita to stop quarreling or they were going to get it. ❖

---

14. **los Estados Unidos** (lôs ĕs-tä′dôs o͞o-nē′dôs) *Spanish:* the United States.

Portrait of J. R. with Roses (1954), Pablo Picasso. Private collection. Copyright © 1996 Artists Rights Society (ARS), New York/SPADEM, Paris.

RESPONDING OPTIONS

FROM PERSONAL RESPONSE *TO* CRITICAL ANALYSIS

REFLECT 1. What do you think about the resolution of the conflict between Tito and his father? Record your reaction in your notebook.

RETHINK 2. Why do you think Tito and his father were able to resolve their differences? Compare their experience with what you discussed and wrote about conflict resolution for the Previewing activities on page 1009.

3. Analyze the conflict between Lola and her father. How do you think their conflict can be resolved?

Consider

- their different views of a woman's role
- Señor Martínez's stubbornness and Lola's resentment
- Lola's helping solve the conflict between her brother and her father

4. The narrator says at the end that both Señor Martínez and Tito believe in *Dios, El Papa,* and *el patrón*—except that, for Tito, "conscience was the same as Dios." Do you think Lola and the narrator believe in this hierarchy? Support your opinion.

RELATE 5. What hierarchy, if any, do you believe in?

6. What issues from the 1960s and 1970s do you see present in this story? In terms of the Martínez family, do you consider this legacy as positive or negative? Explain your opinion.

ANOTHER PATHWAY

Cooperative Learning

Using the conflict resolution in this story and others you know about as models, stage a "summit meeting" between Lola and Señor Martínez that Tito and the narrator might arrange. In a small group, decide the best way to approach the conflict and then act out the meeting for the class, showing how the conflict can be resolved, if at all.

LITERARY CONCEPTS

The **narrator** is the character or voice from whose point of view events are told. Events in "El Patrón" are told by a first-person narrator, who is a character in the story. However, because he is not part of the major conflicts of the story, the narrator seems to relate events objectively—that is, his attitude toward the other characters does not seem to color his description of events. How do you think the story would change if another character told the story? Write a brief summary of the story as Lola, Tito, or Señor Martínez might have narrated it.

QUICKWRITES

1. Based on what you have learned from this story, write an **instruction manual** for conflict resolution.
2. Is it possible for family members to have different opinions and still live peacefully? Draft a **personal essay** on this issue, using examples from "El Patrón" and from your own experience.

PORTFOLIO *Save your writing. You may want to use it later as a springboard to a piece for your portfolio.*

LITERARY LINKS

Compare the family in "El Patrón" with the one in "Teenage Wasteland." What are the sources of conflict in each? What do you think the Martínez family would say to Daisy and Matt?

ACROSS THE CURRICULUM

History Investigate the history of Mexican Americans in the armed forces of the United States. Is Señor Martínez's account accurate? If you prefer, investigate the military record of another group of your choice.

WORDS TO KNOW

Answer the following questions.

1. Is a **zealot** someone whose enthusiasm is brief, misguided, or extreme?
2. Is an **impassioned** essay one that is long, dull, or moving?
3. Which is a good example of a **hierarchy**—a telephone book, the army, or a jury?
4. Are people most likely to speak in **banalities** if they are conceited, unimaginative, or hostile?
5. Which would help a person **discern** bacteria—antibiotics, a microscope, or warm, moist conditions?
6. Would people who are reacting **belligerently** be most likely to raise their fists, their eyebrows, or a white flag?
7. Which person is known for his or her **valor**—Albert Einstein, Benedict Arnold, or Joan of Arc?
8. If arguments **escalate,** is the most likely result a fight, a grudging compromise, or a satisfying peace?
9. Which quality is most likely to make a person **shirk** his or her work—laziness, cleverness, or honesty?
10. If a woman were **oblivious** to what was going on, would she be in a bad mood, in a fog, or in over her head?

NASH CANDELARIA

Nash Candelaria (born 1928) grew up in Anglo neighborhoods in Los Angeles but spent his summers in Los Candelarias, a section of Albuquerque bearing his family name. He traces his ancestry to some of the earliest European settlers in New Mexico: two Candelaria brothers were among the founders of Albuquerque in 1706, and another ancestor, Juan Candelaria, wrote a history of New Mexico in 1776. Despite his California roots, Candelaria identifies with the New Mexican experience and often focuses on it in his writing.

Candelaria attended UCLA, where he majored in chemistry. After college he worked as a chemist for a pharmaceutical firm. About this time he began to write seriously, taking night classes in writing. When the Korean conflict began, he enlisted in the air force as a second lieutenant and wrote his first novel while in the service. After the war he held a series of positions in technical writing, advertising, and marketing, while writing fiction on the side. He wrote eight novels before he self-published one in 1977.

Much of Candelaria's fiction centers on the breaking down of tradition and the struggle to preserve it within the family. He views culture as continuously evolving and in his writing rejects "that there is a fixed Chicano culture that we can go back to, like Eden, when in reality it is changing all the time." Instead, he accepts change and assimilation as inevitable: "we will all evolve into a common culture, an American culture, in this country, or perhaps a world culture on this planet."

Candelaria is regarded by many critics as one of the top ten Chicano novelists today. He has published a collection of short stories and four novels, the most recent in 1992. He has lectured at Rutgers University and resides in Palo Alto, California.

OTHER WORKS *Memories of the Alhambra, Not by the Sword, Inheritance of Strangers, Leonor Park*

Sure You Can Ask Me a PERSONAL Question

Diane Burns

How do you do?
    No, I am not Chinese.
No, not Spanish.
    No, I am American Indi–uh, Native American.
No, not from India.
    No, not Apache.
No, not Navajo.
    No, not Sioux.
No, we are not extinct.
    Yes, Indian.
Oh?
    So that's where you got those high cheekbones.
Your great grandmother, huh?
    An Indian Princess, huh?
Hair down to there?
    Let me guess. Cherokee?
Oh, so you've had an Indian friend?
    That close?
Oh, so you've had an Indian lover?
    That tight?
Oh, so you've had an Indian servant?
    That much?
Yeah, it was awful what you guys did to us.

Flemmie (1978), Milton L. Sherrill. Bronze, 18½", Copyright © Milton L. Sherrill, all rights reserved.

It's real decent of you to apologize.
No, I don't know where you can get peyote.[1]
No, I don't know where you can get Navajo rugs real cheap.
No, I didn't make this. I bought it at Bloomingdales.
Thank you. I like your hair too.
I don't know if anyone knows whether or not Cher is really Indian.
No, I didn't make it rain tonight.
Yeah. Uh-huh. Spirituality.
Uh-huh. Yeah. Spirituality. Uh-huh. Mother
Earth. Yeah. Uh'huh. Uh-huh. Spirituality.
No, I didn't major in archery.
Yeah, a lot of us drink too much.
Some of us can't drink enough.
This ain't no stoic look.
This is my face.

1. **peyote** (pă-ō′tē): a drug that produces hallucinations and that is traditionally used by some Native American peoples of the Southwest.

Diane Burns

Diane Burns is of Chemehuevi (Southern Paiute) and Anishinabe (Chippewa) heritage. Her poems address the Native American experience within urban American culture, the experience of "belonging and not belonging because, as American Indians, you always have the feeling of not belonging but you also have this feeling of belonging." Burns draws ideas from New York mainstream culture and from her grandfather's and uncles' Anishinabe stories and songs. She explains, "The words of our ancestors, the great chiefs and warriors, especially my own family, have shaped my voice . . . they teach me the ways people have faced difficulties and evil in the outside world." Her poetry mixes New York City slang with Chemehuevi and Anishinabe terms, and the rhythms of contemporary music with those of traditional Native American songs.

Burns's career as a poet began soon after she graduated from Barnard College in 1978, when the American Indian Community House contacted her on behalf of a feminist group that was sponsoring a women's poetry reading. They needed a Native American woman poet to perform at the reading and would pay $50 for the job. Burns accepted their proposal, wrote some poetry, recited it at the reading, and got her first book offer that night. That book, *Riding the One-Eyed Ford,* established Burns as one of the most important Native American poets of the 1980s.

WRITING FROM EXPERIENCE

WRITING A REPORT

To understand the selections in Unit Seven, "Conflict at Home and Abroad," it helps to know something about their historical background. For example, how did the civil rights movement get started? What was an infantry soldier's life like in Vietnam? The more you know about the past, the more you can judge how authentically a writer has captured a particular period in history.

GUIDED ASSIGNMENT

Write a Research Paper In this lesson, you will research and write a report that gives historical background for a piece of literature.

1 What Was It Like?

Imagine yourself twenty years from now. Discuss in class how you would explain to your children events that took place when you were younger. If they read a poem about the fall of apartheid in South Africa, for example, what would they need to know to understand the poem?

2 Study the Sources

The following activities will help you understand how research can enhance your appreciation of a piece of literature and the experiences of the person who wrote it.

Reading for Information Look over the sources on these pages. What point of view is adopted by the author of the literature selection excerpted on the next page? How does the author feel about the historical event he describes? What do the other sources tell you about this period in history?

Newspaper Article

Far West Finishes Moving Japanese

By Lawrence E. Davies

San Francisco, Oct. 31, 1942—This week-end the last step in the West Coast's evacuation program, dictated by "military necessity," is being completed. Sixteen temporary assembly [relocation] centers, each of which was home to from 250 to 19,000 persons, were used until permanent centers in the interior could be prepared for use. Now, except for a few thousand residents who migrated to the Middle West and East when voluntary evacuation was permitted, all the West Coast's Japanese population is living at ten carefully selected agricultural sites, designed for occupancy, for the duration of the war.

—from *The New York Times*

Identifying the Unfamiliar What items mentioned in the literature selection are unfamiliar to you? Make a list. Next to each item, jot down resources that could help you fill in these gaps in your knowledge.

LASERLINKS
• *WRITING SPRINGBOARD*

WRITING COACH

3 Choose a Topic

What works of literature have you read that tell about life during a certain period in history? Which selection or time would you like to understand better? Choose one work to be the topic for your report.

Identification Tag
Why do you think the government required every Japanese American to wear an ID tag, similar to the one shown at right?

Poem and Historical Photos

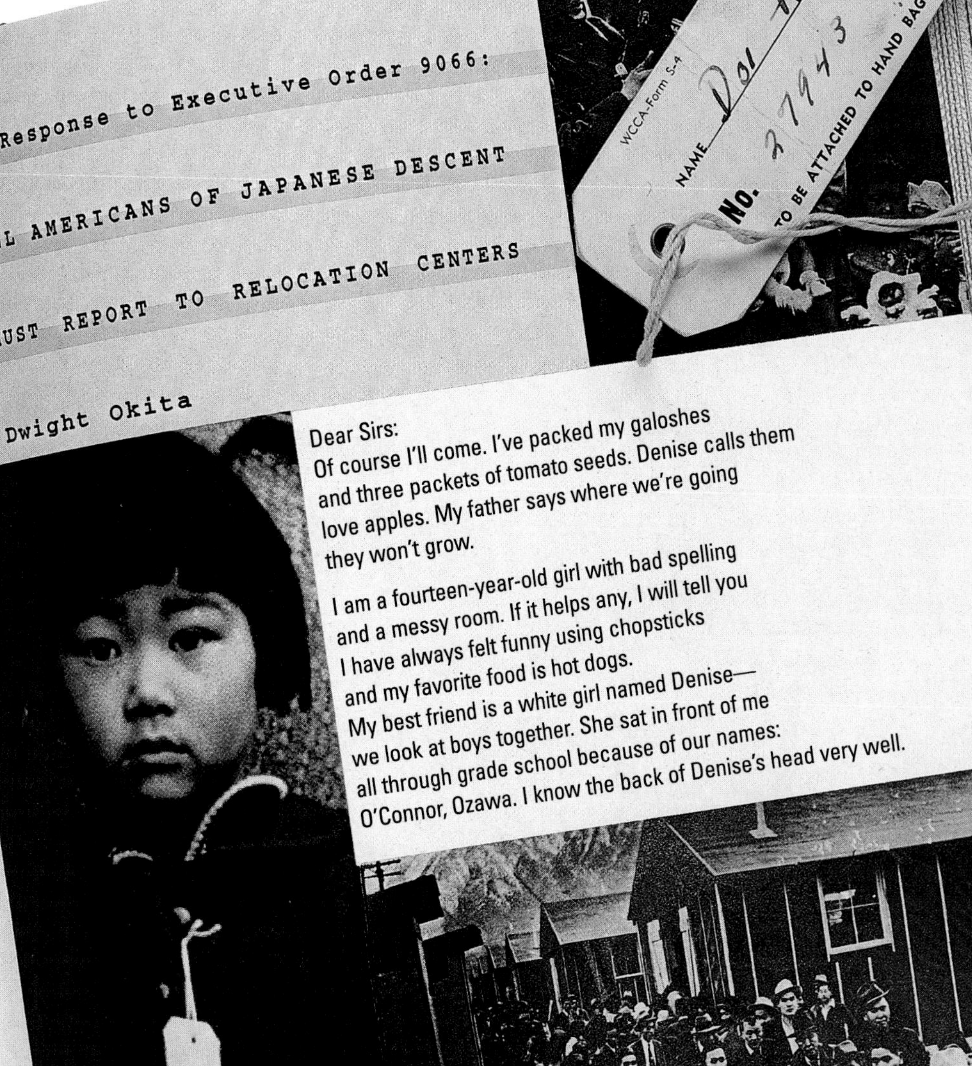

In Response to Executive Order 9066:
ALL AMERICANS OF JAPANESE DESCENT
MUST REPORT TO RELOCATION CENTERS
Dwight Okita
Dear Sirs:
Of course I'll come. I've packed my galoshes
and three packets of tomato seeds. Denise calls them
love apples. My father says where we're going
they won't grow.
I am a fourteen-year-old girl with bad spelling
and a messy room. If it helps any, I will tell you
I have always felt funny using chopsticks
and my favorite food is hot dogs.
My best friend is a white girl named Denise—
we look at boys together. She sat in front of me
all through grade school because of our names:
O'Connor, Ozawa. I know the back of Denise's head very well.
WCCA-Form S-4
NAME Doi Haruye
NO. 27943
TO BE ATTACHED TO HAND BAGGAGE CARRIED BY PE
What was Exec Order 9066? Why was it considered necessary?
Did Japanese Americans fight the relocation? What happened to their homes and property?

Researching the Era

Research Strategies Your report will explain and expand on ideas and events in the literature, using historical data from the same period. To begin, you need to narrow your topic, draw up a research plan, and gather information.

1 Focus Your Topic

To narrow your topic, particularly for a book or long story, focus on key events, main characters, or specific circumstances mentioned in the work.

Statement of Controlling Purpose After you choose a focus, write a statement of controlling purpose that explains what your report will be about. For example, "I want to know how accurately the author captured the events and emotions of the time." Or you might want to understand the events better or compare two versions of the same story. The statement of purpose will help guide your research.

2 Plan Your Research

These suggestions can help you gather data.

Set Up a Research Strategy Start with general references such as encyclopedias and move on to books, periodicals, and on-line databases. The SkillBuilder offers research tips.

Evaluate Your Sources As you gather sources, ask yourself the following questions.

- Is the source up-to-date?
- Is the author an expert in the field?
- Does the source describe events from different points of view?

If a source doesn't meet these requirements, it may be unreliable.

Create Source Cards Fill out a card for every source and number each card. See page 1186 of the Writing Handbook if you need help.

Source Cards
for Encyclopedia (left), Newspaper (right), Book (middle)

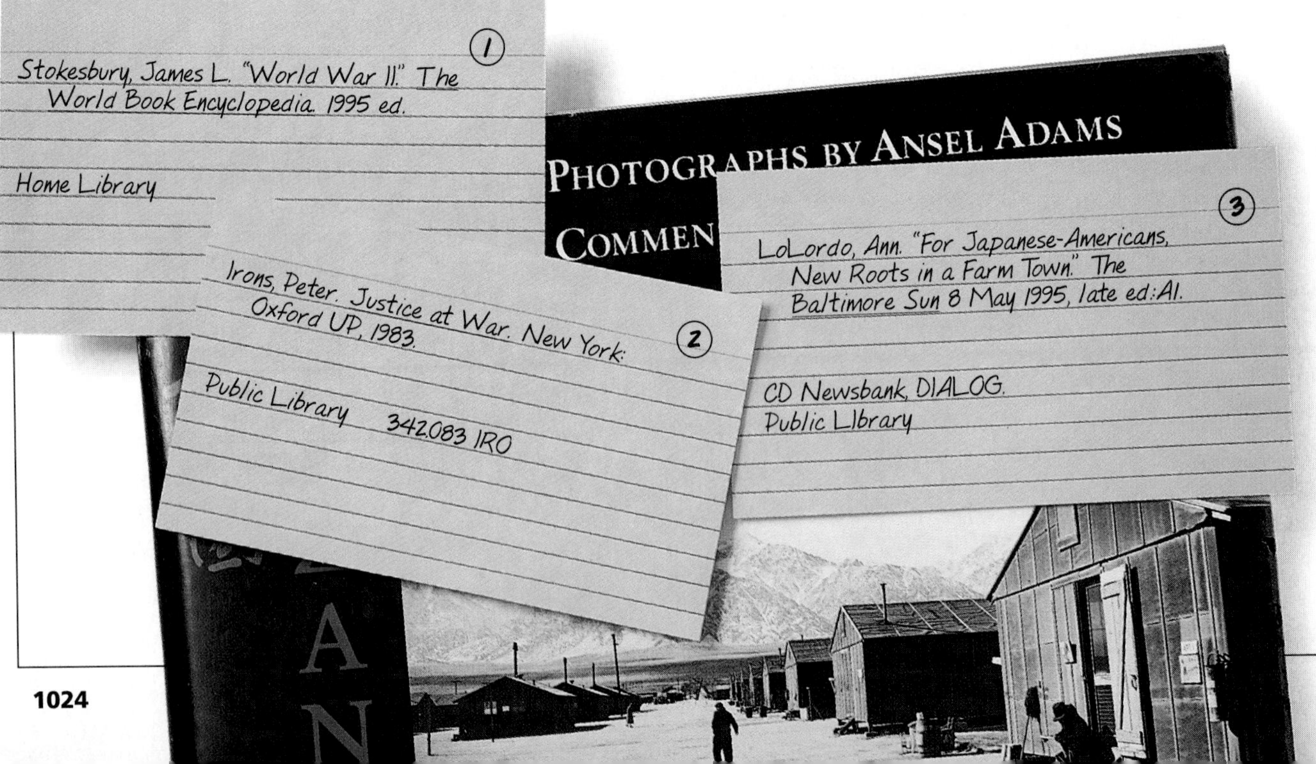

(1)
Stokesbury, James L. "World War II." The World Book Encyclopedia. 1995 ed.
Home Library
PHOTOGRAPHS BY ANSEL ADAMS
(2)
Irons, Peter. Justice at War. New York: Oxford UP, 1983.
Public Library 342.083 IRO
(3)
LoLordo, Ann. "For Japanese-Americans, New Roots in a Farm Town." The Baltimore Sun 8 May 1995, late ed.: A1.
CD Newsbank, DIALOG.
Public Library

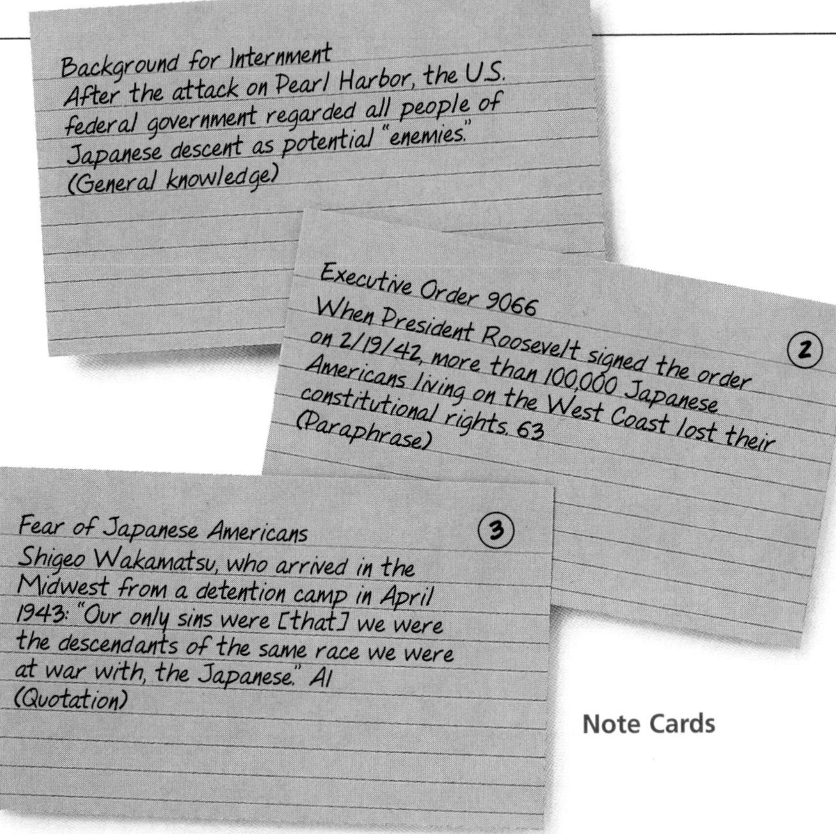

Background for Internment
After the attack on Pearl Harbor, the U.S. federal government regarded all people of Japanese descent as potential "enemies."
(General knowledge)
Executive Order 9066
When President Roosevelt signed the order on 2/19/42, more than 100,000 Japanese Americans living on the West Coast lost their constitutional rights. 63
(Paraphrase)
2
Fear of Japanese Americans
Shigeo Wakamatsu, who arrived in the Midwest from a detention camp in April 1943: "Our only sins were [that] we were the descendants of the same race we were at war with, the Japanese." A1
(Quotation)
3

Note Cards

3 Take Good Notes

Write careful notes as you read your sources. On each card, list the main idea and include only one or two supporting details. Label each note as a quotation, a paraphrase, or general knowledge, as shown in the examples above.

Also include the number of the corresponding source card. This will help you avoid plagiarism—that is, presenting someone else's words as your own. Use these tips for taking good notes:

Use Direct Quotations Direct quotations add interest and authenticity to your report. Be sure you copy the original text word for word. Enclose the material in quotation marks.

Paraphrase Information Rewrite original material in your own words. Make sure you record names, dates, and key facts accurately in the process of rewording information.

Record General Knowledge A fact that appears in at least three sources can be considered general knowledge, but must still be rewritten in your own words.

For more help with note cards, see page 1186 of the Writing Handbook.

SkillBuilder

CRITICAL THINKING

Locating Sources Using Index Terms

The key to a successful search for print resources is knowing what search terms, or index terms, to use. If you don't find enough information under your first index term, try these suggestions:

- Ask the reference librarian if the database you are using has a special list of index terms. Different databases may use different index terms for the same research topics.
- Use alternative spellings or synonyms for the same item (*the 60s, 1960s, the sixties; World War II or Second World War*).
- Try narrowing your search by adding more specific terms (*Japanese Americans, World War II; Japanese Americans, internment camps*).

APPLYING WHAT YOU'VE LEARNED
Look up *superstition, superstitions* in the Magazine Index of INFOTRAC. What information do you find under each term? Try using the tips above in your own research.

THINK & PLAN

Reflecting on Your Topic

1. When paraphrasing sources, did you use your own words to avoid plagiarism?
2. Has your statement of controlling purpose changed? If so, how?

DRAFTING

Creating Your Report

Outline and Rough Draft Now you're ready to pull together your research, note cards, and statement of purpose to write your first draft. Your report should give readers background information about the literature selection and help them appreciate the historical setting of the work.

1 Write a Thesis Statement

At this point, you will need either to turn your statement of purpose into a thesis statement or to create a new thesis statement. The statement explains the main idea that you will develop in your report. Look over the thesis statement that precedes the student writer's outline.

Student's Outline

Report

My Outline

Thesis Statement: Dwight Okita, in his poem "In Response to Executive Order 9066," accurately represents the reactions of many Japanese Americans, who learned in 1942 that they had been declared enemies and would be relocated to detention camps.

I. Background for Executive Order 9066
   A. Japanese attacked Pearl Harbor
   B. All people of Japanese descent labeled enemy
   C. DeWitt and others wanted them isolated
   D. Roosevelt signed order

II. Reactions of Japanese Americans
   A. Shocked by order
   B. Many emphasized how patriotic they were
   C. Complied with order peacefully

Student's Rough Draft

Report

My Rough Draft

In 1942, only a few months after the Japanese attack on Pearl Harbor, Japanese were rounded up as "enemies" of U.S. (Source 1, 497). President Roosevelt signed Executive Order 9066, and more than 100,000 Japanese Americans, many of them U.S. citizens, were removed from their homes and shipped to relocation centers (Source 2, 63). Dwight Okita, in his poem "In Response to Executive Order 9066," accurately represents the reactions of many Japanese Americans when they learned that they had been declared enemies and would be relocated to detention camps.

The title of the poem refers to an executive order created because the government suspected that people of Japanese descent would spy on the U.S. for Japan. General DeWitt, head of the Western Defense Command, pointed out that many of these "enemies" lived in strategic areas (Source 2, 37).

Evacuation orders were posted in Japanese American communities throughout the United States. People were shocked that the government regarded them as enemies. (Put in quotation here.) But nearly all of them obeyed the order, as reflected in the words of the poem's speaker: "Dear Sirs: / Of course I'll come. I've packed my galoshes."

❷ Start Your Draft

Organize Your Data Group note cards with similar headings and put them in an order that seems logical to you. Use the headings to construct an outline, like the one on page 1026. Your thesis statement should be in your first paragraph. When you're ready, begin writing your draft.

Document Your Sources After a quotation or paraphrased information, insert a brief note in parentheses that identifies the source and page number. This parenthetical note will remind you to insert the source name, which will refer readers to the list of Works Cited, at the end of your report. For more on documenting sources, see page 1186 of the Writing Handbook.

❸ Rework and Share

Once you have completed your rough draft, look closely at how you've organized your ideas and credited your sources. To evaluate your draft, ask the following questions.

- Does the opening paragraph clearly state why I am writing this report?
- Have I mentioned the title and author of the literature?
- Have I used a logical form of organization for my report? (The SkillBuilder describes the use of chronological order.)
- What facts, statistics, and other historical evidence do I use to back up my main points?
- What illustrations or pictures would help the reader understand the historical information in my report?

 PEER RESPONSE

Ask peer reviewers to evaluate your research report. You might use these questions as a guide:

- In a few words, what is the subject and purpose of my report?
- How logically have I presented my ideas? Which parts seem out of order or confusing?
- What information do I need to add or delete?

SkillBuilder

 WRITER'S CRAFT

Using Chronological Order
A natural method of organizing historical reports is to use chronological order. The student writer, for example, has used this form to develop his outline. He begins with the period a few months after the attack on Pearl Harbor and lists the chain of events that followed.

You can vary chronological order by inserting statements that clarify the events being described, as the following example shows.

Many white farmers strongly supported the government's decision to relocate Japanese Americans. ***Since the late 1800s, Japanese American farmers had competed with white farmers for California's rich agricultural lands.*** *Executive Order 9066 removed these competitors.*

APPLYING WHAT YOU'VE LEARNED
If you use chronological order, consider whether varying the order or maintaining a strict order of events fits your narrative best.

RETHINK & EVALUATE

Preparing to Revise

1. How accurately have you restated other people's ideas?
2. What type of organization is best for presenting the information in your report?

Finishing Your Report

A Final Check You won't be ready to share your work until you've double-checked the organization of ideas, documentation of sources, and grammar and punctuation.

❶ Revise and Edit

Try the suggestions below as you make final changes to your report.

- Your thesis statement should tell the reader the purpose of your report.
- Make sure all quotations and facts are stated accurately.
- Use the Editing Checklist and the Standards for Evaluation to help you make sure your report is properly documented and free of grammatical and spelling errors.

❷ Prepare a Final Paper

Make a clean copy of your report after you've proofread and edited it. Include a list of Works Cited like the one on the next page. For help preparing your list, see page 1186 of the Writing Handbook.

What is the writer's purpose for this paper?

What facts are you given that explain the title of the poem? What facts do you still need to know?

Student's Final Draft

Pedroza 1

Rocio Pedroza

Ms. Beam

Third Period English

22 April 1997

Dwight Okita's Poem and Executive Order 9066

In 1942, only a few months after the Japanese attack on Pearl Harbor, an event occurred that is unique in American history (Stokesbury 497). With a single order from the White House, more than 100,000 Japanese Americans, many of them U.S. citizens, were removed from their homes and shipped to detention camps (Irons 63). Dwight Okita, in his poem "In Response to Executive Order 9066: ALL AMERICANS OF JAPANESE DESCENT MUST REPORT TO RELOCATION CENTERS," accurately represents the reactions of many Japanese Americans when they learned that they had been declared enemies and would be relocated to detention camps.

The title of the poem refers to an executive order created because the government feared that people of Japanese descent would become spies and saboteurs for Japan. General DeWitt, head of the Western Defense Command, pointed out that many of these "enemies" lived in strategic areas on the West Coast (Irons 37).

Pedroza 5

Government Detention Camps 1942–1945

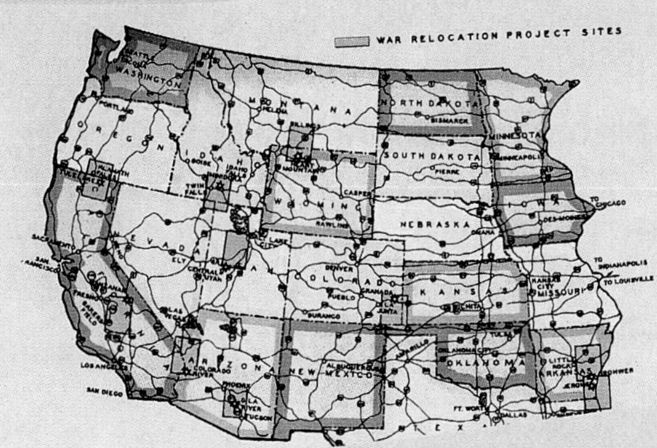

Pedroza 6

Works Cited

Irons, Peter. Justice at War. New York: Oxford UP, 1983.

LoLordo, Ann. "For Japanese-Americans, New Roots in a Farm Town." Baltimore Sun 8 May 1995, late ed.: A1.

Stokesbury, James L. "World War II." The World Book Encyclopedia. 1995 ed.

United States War Office. Final Report: Japanese Evacuation from the West Coast, 1942. Washington: GPO, 1943.

Standards for Evaluation

An effective research report

- begins with a thesis statement that engages the reader's interest
- uses supporting evidence and details from several sources
- gives proper credit for all quotations and paraphrases integrated into the body of the report
- is organized in a logical fashion
- ends with a strong, satisfying conclusion
- includes properly formatted pages and Works Cited list

SkillBuilder

Using Appositive Phrases
Appositive phrases, which are usually set off by commas, are used to define terms or add details about the subject of a sentence. For instance:

General DeWitt supervised the evacuation. He was head of the Western Defense Command.

General DeWitt, head of the Western Defense Command, supervised the evacuation.

Editing Checklist

- Did you correctly punctuate quotations in your report?
- Did you use appositive phrases to define terms or add details about a main point?

REFLECT & ASSESS

Learning from Experience

1. List ways that you could improve your research strategy for your next report.
2. Write a paragraph describing your reactions to the historical events you researched.

PORTFOLIO You might want to include these items in your portfolio with your report.

Reflect & Assess

UNIT SEVEN: CONFLICT AT HOME AND ABROAD

The selections in this unit look at personal experiences related to major historical events ranging from battles overseas to struggles at home. How did this unit affect your understanding of World War II, the Vietnam War, and the culture of the sixties? Explore your ideas by completing one or more of the options in each section.

REFLECTING ON THE UNIT

OPTION 1 **Pictures of War** The selections in Part 1, "Remembering the Wars," deal with the effects of modern warfare on soldiers and civilians. For each selection you read, jot down a few phrases that describe the experiences it presents. Then choose the selection that presents war most vividly to you, and write a paragraph or draw a picture to show how that selection affected you.

OPTION 2 **Then and Now** Part 2, "Power and Protest," offers selections that focus on social causes, attitudes, and lifestyles of the 1960s and thereafter. Decide what impact, if any, these causes, attitudes, and lifestyles have had on your world today. Discuss your ideas with a small group of classmates. Consider whether the impact of the 1960s has been generally positive or negative, and why.

OPTION 3 **Different Kinds of Courage** How courageous are the characters and speakers presented in this unit? For each one that you can form an opinion about, assign a rating from 1 (very courageous) to 5 (not at all courageous) and describe in a few words the kind of courage shown. Then write a few paragraphs about a speaker or character who displays a kind of courage you admire.

REFLECT & ASSESS *Self-Assessment: Make a list of the impressions you had—before you read this unit—about what people felt and thought during World War II, the Vietnam War, and the sixties. Then note whether your reading has confirmed your preconceptions or contradicted them.*

REVIEWING LITERARY CONCEPTS

OPTION 1 **Reflecting on Mood** As you may recall, mood is the feeling or atmosphere that a writer creates for the reader. Think back over the selections in Unit Seven and describe the mood of each in a chart like the one begun here. In the third column, identify a feature of the selection that contributes strongly to the mood, such as setting, figurative language, images, sound, or descriptive details.

Selection	Mood	Feature
"Why Soldiers Won't Talk"	tension	descriptive details about battle's effects on the body

OPTION 2 **Evaluating Theme** Review the selections in this unit to determine the theme, or central idea, of each. Then choose four or five selections and jot down a few phrases to evaluate how the title of each selection connects to its theme. Discuss your opinions with a small group of classmates—different people often discover different themes in the same work.

Self-Assessment: Of the literary concepts explored in this unit, which are more useful in understanding poetry? Which are more useful with prose? Which are useful with both? Use a Venn diagram to classify these literary concepts.

theme | *dialogue*
tone | *repetition*
imagery | *protagonist*
mood | *antagonist*
conflict | *narrator*
rhythm

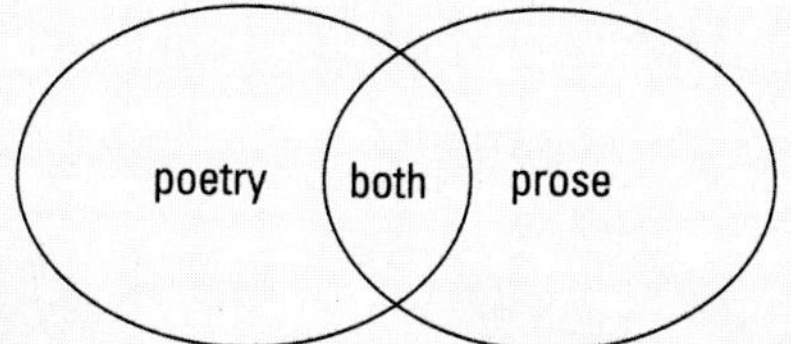

PORTFOLIO BUILDING

- **QuickWrites** Many of the QuickWrites in this unit asked you to write from the point of view of a character in the selection. Review your QuickWrites for this unit and choose one in which adopting a character's point of view helped you understand the selection better. Write a cover note that explains your choice.
- **Writing About Literature** Earlier in this unit you wrote in another author's style. Write a brief note about your experience. How did your appreciation for the author's style change after you attempted to write in it? What are the strengths of the style? What are the differences between your style and the style of the author? Which style do you prefer? Decide whether or not to include your note in your portfolio.
- **Writing from Experience** Earlier in this unit you wrote a historical literature research paper. Reread your paper now. How did your understanding of the selection change as you did your research? What aspects of the selection are clearer than before? About which aspects do you still have questions?
- **Personal Choice** Look back through the writing assignments and the records and evaluations of the activities you completed for this unit. Which one did you think was the most successful? In a cover note, explain what you wanted to accomplish with the writing or the activity and why it succeeded.

Self-Assessment: Look back over the work in your portfolio. In what ways has your writing improved during this year? In what ways do you want to improve your writing further?

SETTING GOALS

Of the conflicts or movements examined in this unit, such as World War II or the feminist movement, which would you like to read more about? In which literary genre would you like to read about this conflict or movement: fiction, nonfiction, poetry, or drama? Consult a librarian to find at least one title to read on your own.

UNIT EIGHT

Issues for Our Time

What unites us is far greater than what divides us as families and friends and Americans and spiritual sojourners on this Earth.

Marian Wright Edelman
Founder of the Children's Defense Fund

Untitled (1985), Keith Haring. Courtesy of the Estate of Keith Haring.

TIME LINE

Issues for Our Time

1977

Steven Jobs and Stephen Wozniak found the Apple Computer Company.

1979

A partial meltdown at the Three Mile Island nuclear power plant in Pennsylvania increases concern over the use of nuclear power; Iranian revolutionaries seize the U.S. embassy in Teheran and hold American hostages for 444 days.

1980

Ronald Reagan is elected president.

Reagan's election began a move toward more conservative policies during the 1980s and 1990s, including the deregulation of businesses and major cuts in taxes and social spending.

1981

MTV begins broadcasting; IBM introduces its first personal computer; Columbia, the first space shuttle to orbit the earth, returns from its maiden flight; Sandra Day O'Connor becomes the first woman on the Supreme Court.

1983

Compact discs become available in the United States.

1984

Scientists announce the identification of the virus that causes AIDS.

1986

After much debate, Congress passes the Immigration Reform and Control Act to reduce the number of illegal immigrants.

The numbers of Asian and Hispanic immigrants increased sharply in the 1970s and 1980s, in part because of a loosening of quotas by the 1965 amendments to the Immigration and Nationality Act and by the Refugee Act of 1980. As a result, calls for restrictions on immigration became widespread during the 1980s. The 1986 act placed new penalties on employers who hired undocumented, or illegal, workers.

1989

The wall dividing Communist East Berlin from West Berlin is abruptly dismantled, hastening the move toward democracy in Eastern Europe and the thawing of the cold war; the oil tanker *Exxon Valdez* hits a reef and leaks more than 8 million gallons of crude oil along the Alaskan coast.

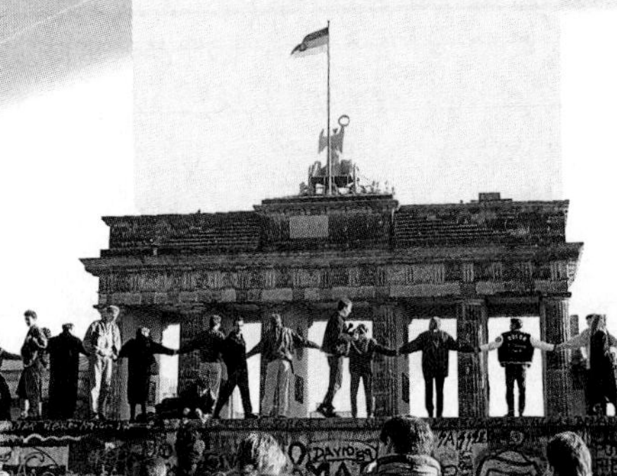

Period *Pieces*

1990

Congress passes the Americans with Disabilities Act, prohibiting discrimination against physically or mentally disabled people in employment, housing, public accommodations, and transportation.

1991

A United Nations coalition, led by U.S. forces, is victorious in the Persian Gulf War after about six weeks of fighting.

1992

Race riots erupt in south central Los Angeles after four white police officers are found not guilty of beating the black motorist Rodney King.

The verdict of not guilty, delivered by an all-white jury, was especially disturbing to African Americans because a videotape of the beating had been broadcast many times on national television. Public anger at the Los Angeles Police Department would explode again three years later, during the sensational double murder trial of the former football star O. J. Simpson. In Simpson's lengthy trial, defense lawyers accused the police of racism, lying, and planting evidence. Simpson was found not guilty by a predominantly black jury.

1993

A bomb blast in an underground garage beneath the World Trade Center in New York City kills 6 people and injures more than 1,000. A year later, 4 Arab defendants are convicted of the bombing.

1994

For the first time, a baseball players' strike causes the cancellation of the World Series.

1995

A bomb destroys the federal building in Oklahoma City, killing 168 people, including 19 children. A national manhunt yields several suspects.

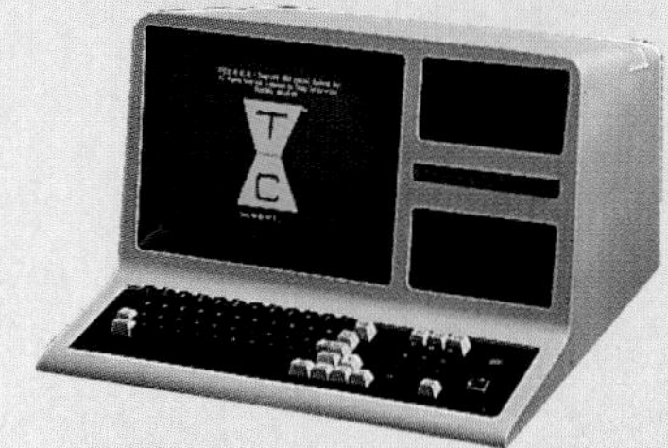

Early computer

Inline skate

Swatch watch

PART 1 INTRODUCTION

Where We Are Today

Closer Together or Farther Apart?

You don't have to wait for a presidential speech to hear views on the state of the Union. As the 20th century ends, concerns are raised in all media, warning of a nation increasingly "polarized," "tribalized," "coming apart at the seams." Commentators decry the "unraveling of the social fabric" and the "breakdown of family values." Are we becoming the Disunited States?

If you compare this period with other historical periods, however, it might seem that the people who live within the nation's boundaries are more united than ever before. Are there any issues today that divide people as deeply (and bloodily) as did independence from Britain, slavery, and secession in years past? Haven't citizenship, civil rights, and economic freedom been extended to certain groups that were discriminated against in other eras? Aren't we more of a single nation now than we were in, say, 1860?

Obviously, it is difficult to say whether Americans today are closer together or farther apart. The literature in this part of Unit Eight examines some of the fault lines along which American society is said to be splitting: family, race and ethnicity, immigration, language, and income.

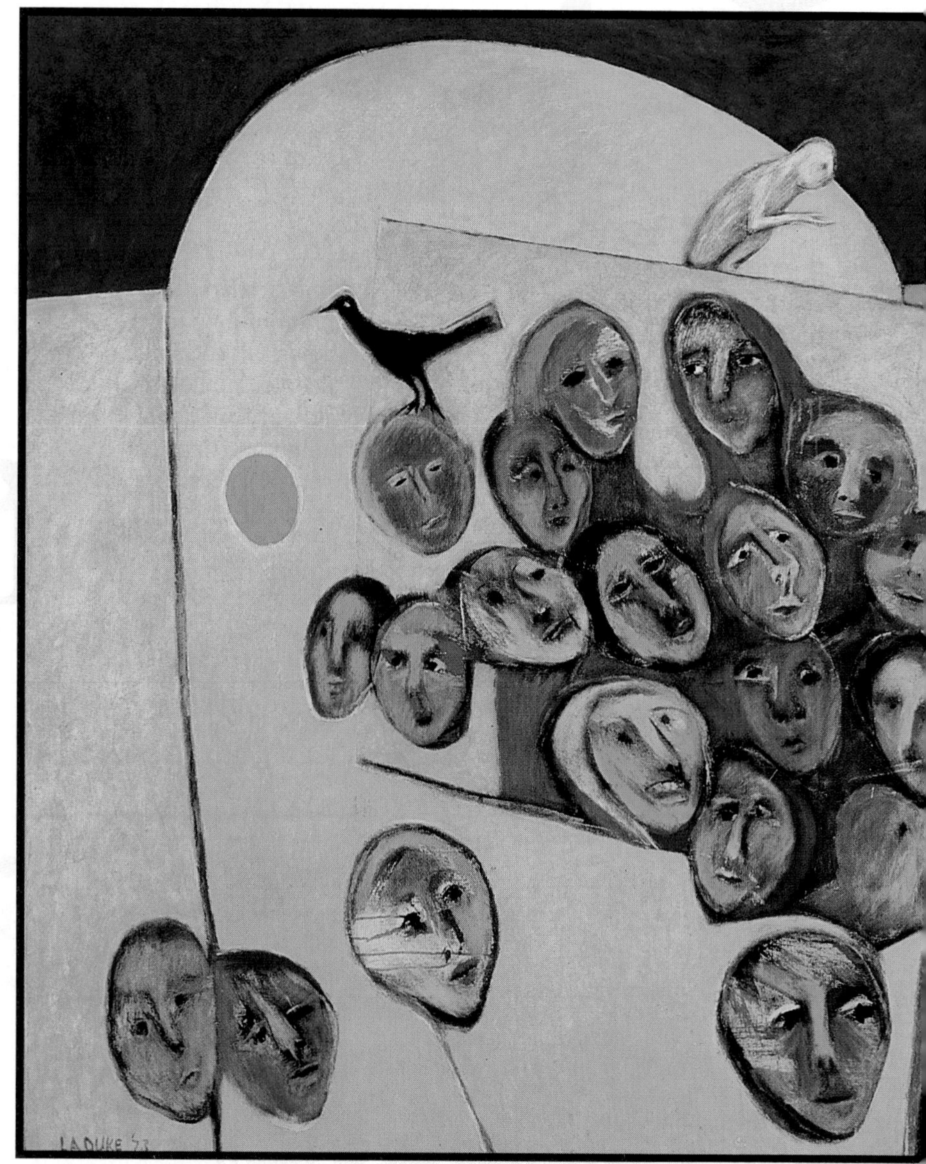

Family Much attention has been given to a perceived weakening of "family values." Commentators point to a rising divorce rate, a growing proportion of out-of-wedlock births, and the increasing necessity for mothers to work outside the home and leave the care of their children to others for part of the day. Worrying about the harmful economic and psychological effects of a father's absence on his children, and how these effects may translate into widespread social ills, some critics wonder whether unhappy couples should again be expected to stay together for the sake of the children, as they were in previous eras. As the father in John Updike's "Separating" prepares to leave his family, he painfully weighs his own desires against his children's needs.

Race and Ethnicity It has become a commonplace that the United States is divided along racial and ethnic lines. Think of the different kinds of people who live here: Native Americans, European Americans, African Americans, Hispanic Americans, Asian Americans—large, sometimes mutually hostile groups divisible into many smaller, sometimes mutually hostile groups whose conflicts erupt in such large-scale incidents as urban riots and such small-scale, daily incidents as kindergarten name-calling. Resentment grows from historical injustices, existing disparities, and remedies for past bias perceived as biased in themselves. No wonder Americans despair

India: Hindu Temple (about 1973), Betty La Duke. Acrylic on canvas, 72″ × 68″, collection of the artist. From *Multicultural Celebrations: The Paintings of Betty La Duke 1972–1992*, by Gloria Orenstein, Pomegranate Publications, 1993.

Voices *from the* TIMES

My dream of America
is like *dá bìn lòuh*
with people of all persuasions
and tastes
sitting down around a common pot
chopsticks and basket scoops here
and there
some cooking squid and others beef
some tofu or watercress
all in one broth
like a stew that really isn't
as each one chooses what he wishes
to eat
only that the pot and fire are shared
along with the good company
and the sweet soup
spooned out at the end of the meal.

Wing Tek Lum
"Chinese Hot Pot"

The language of opposition now appears as a cascading series of manifestos that tell us we cannot live together; we cannot work together; we are not in this together; we are not Americans who have something in common, but racial, ethnic, gender, or sexually identified clans who demand to be "recognized" only or exclusively as "different."

Jean Bethke Elshtain
from *Democracy on Trial*

Please, we can get along here. We can all get along. We've just got to, I mean we're all stuck here for a while. Let's try to work it out. Let's try to beat it.

Rodney King
at a press conference
during the 1992 L.A. riots

Voices *from the* Times

We have allowed materialism to eclipse idealism, and overcompetitiveness to harm families and family values. Millions of people are in fear for the long-term security of their families, and a growing percentage is on the edge of poverty and despair.

Dr. Benjamin Spock
from *A Better World for Our Children*

English-only defies reality. It proposes that there is a single American story in a universal American English that will satisfy the children of the slave master and the slaves, of the conquered and the conquerors, of the immigrant and the exiled and the coerced.

Achy Obejas
Cuban-American writer

America is great not because we speak one language or the other, but because we are united by the fundamental principles that bind our people together: freedom, justice, equal opportunity for all, fairness, democracy.

Baltasar Corrada
former resident commissioner of Puerto Rico

There are no more major civil rights laws to be passed. What we are dealing with now is changing of hearts, changing of perspective and of minds.

Colin Powell
Retired General

of achieving unity. But then, some argue that diversity is what defines America. Where else are so many different people *trying to* live together as a single nation? And even in their outrage and strife, groups are not wanting to tear America apart but to lay claim to it, as in Alan Chong Lau's "the promise," which recalls the past and predicts the future of Asian Americans in this country.

Immigration and Language Immigration is another issue that raises divisive questions for people in the United States. Is there too much immigration, particularly illegal immigration? Are immigrants taking jobs from the native-born or contributing skills and markets to the economy? Should some immigrants be preferred over others? Are federal or local government agencies responsible for meeting immigrants' needs? And what *are* their needs—for example, bilingual education and ballots in native languages, or English instruction? Language is certainly a hot issue in the immigration debate. You will be reading the differing views of former U.S. Senator S. I. Hayakawa, the son of Japanese immigrants, and Carlos Alberto Montaner, a Cuban immigrant, on whether English should be made the official language of the United States. Their writings explore how immigration affects American identity. To some, the national metaphor remains the melting pot, but others would substitute a salad bowl, a mosaic, a tapestry, or a Chinese hot pot (see Voices from the Times).

Income It has been argued that the most dangerous division in the country is that of income. There are more rich, more poor, and fewer in the middle than in recent decades. And for those who are poor, there seems to be less opportunity to escape poverty. Over the years, homelessness has become an increasingly visible problem. It was once startling but is now common to see families with children living on the streets or in shelters. Audrey M. Lee's story "Waiting for Her Train" follows a homeless woman as she struggles to survive and hide her condition from others.

So, are today's Americans closer together or farther apart? Read this sampling of contemporary writings, make connections, debate with classmates, and decide for yourself.

PART 1 *Where We Are Today*

Closer Together or Farther Apart?

PREVIEWING

FICTION

Separating

John Updike

PERSONAL CONNECTION

Nearly half the marriages in the United States end in divorce. Before deciding to divorce, however, many married couples first agree to separate, or stop living together. What do you think are some reasons that married couples separate? How do you think a wife and husband feel once they have decided to separate? If they have children, how do you think the children feel? Gather with other classmates in a small group and discuss these questions, basing your comments on friends' experiences or your own.

LITERARY CONNECTION

You are about to read a story about marital separation by John Updike, one of America's most acclaimed authors. Much of his writing concerns upper-middle-class people caught in what Updike has called "the despair of the daily." These characters lose touch with one another and, in doing so, put a strain on their marriages and their families. "Separating" is one in a series of 17 stories the author wrote about Joan and Richard Maple, which appear in his collection *Too Far To Go* (published in 1979). The Maples stories, written over a period of 23 years, depict the couple's youthful marriage in the 1950s, the birth and growth of four children, their separation after 21 years of marriage, and their eventual divorce. Though the stories depict the breakup of a marriage, they still chronicle lives "in many ways happy," according to Updike. "That a marriage fails is less than ideal; but all things end under heaven. . . . The moral of these stories is that all blessings are mixed."

WRITING CONNECTION

In this story the Maples tell their four children of their decision to separate. In your notebook, write a realistic dialogue in which a parent tells a teenage son or daughter about such a separation. Include the son's or daughter's reaction. As you read the story, compare Updike's dialogue with what you wrote, and evaluate how true to life his story seems.

SEPARATING

John Updike

The day was fair. Brilliant. All that June the weather had mocked the Maples' internal misery with solid sunlight—golden shafts and cascades of green in which their conversations had wormed unseeing, their sad murmuring selves the only stain in Nature. Usually by this time of the year they had acquired tans; but when they met their elder daughter's plane on her return from a year in England they were almost as pale as she, though Judith was too dazzled by the sunny opulent jumble of her native land to notice. They did not spoil her homecoming by telling her immediately. Wait a few days, let her recover from jet lag, had been one of their formulations, in that string of gray dialogues—over coffee, over cocktails, over Cointreau[1]—that had shaped the strategy of their dissolution, while the earth performed its annual stunt of renewal unnoticed beyond their closed windows. Richard had thought to leave at Easter; Joan had insisted they wait until the four children were at last assembled, with all exams passed and ceremonies attended, and the bauble[2] of summer to console them. So he had drudged away, in love, in dread, repairing screens, getting the mowers sharpened, rolling and patching their new tennis court.

The court, clay, had come through its first winter pitted and windswept bare of redcoat. Years ago the Maples had observed how often, among their friends, divorce followed a dramatic home improvement, as if the marriage were making one last effort to live; their own worst crisis had come amid the plaster dust and exposed plumbing of a kitchen renovation. Yet, a summer ago, as canary-yellow bulldozers gaily churned a grassy, daisy-dotted knoll into a muddy plateau, and a crew of pigtailed young men raked and tamped clay into a plane, this transformation did not strike them as ominous, but festive in its

1. **Cointreau** (kwăN-trō'): brand name of an expensive, orange-flavored, syrupy alcoholic beverage.
2. **bauble:** a bright, showy thing.

WORDS TO KNOW

opulent (ŏp'yə-lənt) *adj.* characterized by abundance, extravagance, or wealth
dissolution (dĭs'ə-lo͞o'shən) *n.* a breaking up; disintegration

impudence; their marriage could rend the earth for fun. The next spring, waking each day at dawn to a sliding sensation as if the bed were being tipped, Richard found the barren tennis court—its net and tapes still rolled in the barn—an environment congruous with his mood of purposeful desolation, and the crumbling of handfuls of clay into cracks and holes (dogs had frolicked on the court in a thaw; rivulets had eroded trenches) an activity suitably elemental and interminable. In his sealed heart he hoped the day would never come.

Now it was here. A Friday. Judith was re-acclimated; all four children were assembled, before jobs and camps and visits again scattered them. Joan thought they should be told one by one. Richard was for making an announcement at the table. She said, "I think just making an announcement is a cop-out. They'll start quarrelling and playing to each other instead of focusing. They're each individuals, you know, not just some corporate obstacle to your freedom."

"O.K., O.K. I agree." Joan's plan was exact. That evening, they were giving Judith a belated welcome-home dinner, of lobster and champagne. Then, the party over, they, the two of them, who nineteen years before would push her in a baby carriage along Fifth Avenue to Washington Square,[3] were to walk her out of the house, to the bridge across the salt creek, and tell her, swearing her to secrecy. Then Richard Jr., who was going directly from work to a rock concert in Boston, would be told, either late when he returned on the train or early Saturday morning before he went off to his job; he was seventeen and employed as one of a golf-course maintenance crew. Then the two younger children, John and Margaret, could, as the morning wore on, be informed.

"Mopped up, as it were," Richard said.

"Do you have any better plan? That leaves you the rest of Saturday to answer any questions, pack, and make your wonderful departure."

"No," he said, meaning he had no better plan, and agreed to hers, though to him it showed an edge of false order, a hidden plea for control, like Joan's long chore lists and financial accountings and, in the days when he first knew her, her too-copious lecture notes. Her plan turned one hurdle for him into four—four knife-sharp walls, each with a sheer blind drop on the other side.

All spring he had moved through a world of insides and outsides, of barriers and partitions. He and Joan stood as a thin barrier between the children and the truth. Each moment was a partition, with the past on one side and the future on the other, a future containing this unthinkable *now.* Beyond four knifelike walls a new life for him waited vaguely. His skull cupped a secret, a white face, a face both frightened and soothing, both strange and known, that he wanted to shield from tears, which he felt all about him, solid as the sunlight. So haunted, he had become obsessed with battening down the house against his absence, replacing screens and sash cords, hinges and latches—a Houdini[4] making things snug before his escape.

The lock. He had still to replace a lock on one of the doors of the screened porch. The task, like most such, proved more difficult than he had imagined. The old lock, aluminum frozen by corrosion, had been deliberately rendered obsolete by manufacturers. Three hardware stores had nothing that even approximately matched the mortised hole its removal (surprisingly easy) left. Another hole had to be gouged, with bits too small and saws too big, and the old hole fitted with a block of wood—the chisels dull, the saw rusty, his fingers thick with lack of sleep.

3. **Washington Square:** a fashionable area of Manhattan, in New York City.

4. **Houdini:** Harry Houdini (1874–1926), a famous American magician and escape artist.

WORDS TO KNOW

congruous (kŏng′gro͞o-əs) *adj.* fitting; suitable

elemental (ĕl′ə-mən′tl) *adj.* basic; like a natural force

Frank Wallace (1953), Fairfield Porter. Oil on canvas, 40″ × 30″, Parrish Art Museum, Southampton, New York, gift of the Estate of Fairfield Porter (1980.10.59), photo by Jim Strong.

Each moment was a partition, with the past on one side and the future on the other.

The sun poured down, beyond the porch, on a world of neglect. The bushes already needed pruning, the windward side of the house was shedding flakes of paint, rain would get in when he was gone, insects, rot, death. His family, all those he would lose, filtered through the edges of his awareness as he struggled with screw holes, splinters, opaque instructions, minutiae of metal.

Judith sat on the porch, a princess returned from exile. She regaled them with stories of fuel shortages, of bomb scares in the Underground,[5] of Pakistani workmen loudly lusting after her as she walked past on her way to dance school. Joan came and went, in and out of the house, calmer than she should have been, praising his struggles with the lock as if this were one more and not the last of their long succession of shared chores. The younger of his sons for a few minutes held the rickety screen door while his father clumsily hammered and chiseled, each blow a kind of sob in Richard's ears. His younger daughter, having been at a slumber party, slept on the porch hammock through all the noise—heavy and pink, trusting and forsaken. Time, like the sunlight, continued relentlessly; the sunlight slowly slanted. Today was one of the longest days. The lock clicked, worked. He was through. He had a drink; he drank it on the porch, listening to his daughter. "It was so sweet," she was saying, "during the worst of it, how all the butchers and bakery shops kept open by candlelight. They're all so plucky and cute. From the papers, things sounded so much worse here—people shooting people in gas lines, and everybody freezing."

Richard asked her, "Do you still want to live in England forever?" *Forever:* the concept, now a reality upon him, pressed and scratched at the back of his throat.

"No," Judith confessed, turning her oval face to him, its eyes still childishly far apart, but the lips set as over something succulent and satisfactory. "I was anxious to come home. I'm an American." She was a woman. They had raised her; he and Joan had endured together to raise her, alone of the four. The others had still some raising left in them. Yet it was the thought of telling Judith—the image of her, their first baby, walking between them arm in arm to the bridge—that broke him. The partition between his face and the tears broke. Richard sat down to the celebratory meal with the back of his throat aching; the champagne, the lobster seemed phases of sunshine; he saw them and tasted them through tears. He blinked, swallowed, croakily joked about hay fever. The tears would not stop leaking through; they came not through a hole that could be plugged but through a permeable spot in a membrane, steadily, purely, endlessly, fruitfully. They became, his tears, a shield for himself against these others—their faces, the fact of their assembly, a last time as innocents, at a table where he sat the last time as head. Tears dropped from his nose as he broke the lobster's back; salt flavored his champagne as he sipped it; the raw clench at the back of his throat was delicious. He could not help himself.

His children tried to ignore his tears. Judith, on his right, lit a cigarette, gazed upward in the direction of her too energetic, too sophisticated exhalation; on her other side, John earnestly bent his face to the extraction of the last morsels—legs, tail segments—from the scarlet corpse. Joan, at the opposite end of the table, glanced at him surprised, her reproach displaced by a quick grimace, of forgiveness, or of salute to his superior gift of strategy. Between them, Margaret, no longer called Bean, thirteen and large for her age, gazed from the other side of his pane of tears as if into a shopwindow at something she coveted—at her father, a crystalline heap of splinters and

5. **the Underground:** London's subway system.

WORDS TO KNOW

minutiae (mĭ-nōō'shē-ē') *n.* tiny elements, details, or parts
succulent (sŭk'yə-lənt) *adj.* tasty; delicious
permeable (pûr'mē-ə-bəl) *adj.* able to be passed through

memories. It was not she, however, but John who, in the kitchen, as they cleared the plates and carapaces[6] away, asked Joan the question: *"Why is Daddy crying?"*

Richard heard the question but not the murmured answer. Then he heard Bean cry, "Oh, no-oh!"—the faintly dramatized exclamation of one who had long expected it.

John returned to the table carrying a bowl of salad. He nodded tersely at his father and his lips shaped the conspiratorial words "She told."

"Told what?" Richard asked aloud, insanely.

The boy sat down as if to rebuke his father's distraction with the example of his own good manners. He said quietly, "The separation."

Joan and Margaret returned; the child, in Richard's twisted vision, seemed diminished in size, and relieved, relieved to have had the bogieman at last proved real. He called out to her—the distances at the table had grown immense—"You knew, you always knew," but the clenching at the back of his throat prevented him from making sense of it. From afar he heard Joan talking, levelly, sensibly, reciting what they had prepared: it was a separation for the summer, an experiment. She and Daddy both agreed it would be good for them; they needed space and time to think; they liked each other but did not make each other happy enough, somehow.

Judith, imitating her mother's factual tone, but in her youth off-key, too cool, said, "I think it's silly. You should either live together or get divorced."

Richard's crying, like a wave that has crested and crashed, had become tumultuous; but it was overtopped by another tumult, for John, who had been so reserved, now grew larger and larger at the table. Perhaps his younger sister's being credited with knowing set him off. "Why didn't you *tell* us?" he asked, in a large round voice quite unlike his own. "You should have *told* us you weren't getting along."

Richard was startled into attempting to force words through his tears. "We *do* get along, that's the trouble, so it doesn't show even to us—" *That we do not love each other* was the rest of the sentence; he couldn't finish it.

Joan finished for him, in her style. "And we've always, *especially,* loved our children."

John was not mollified. "What do you care about *us?*" he boomed. "We're just little things you *had.*" His sisters' laughing forced a laugh from him, which he turned hard and parodistic[7]:

6. **carapaces** (kăr′ə-pā′səz): hard outer coverings or shells of animals such as lobsters.

7. **parodistic:** mocking.

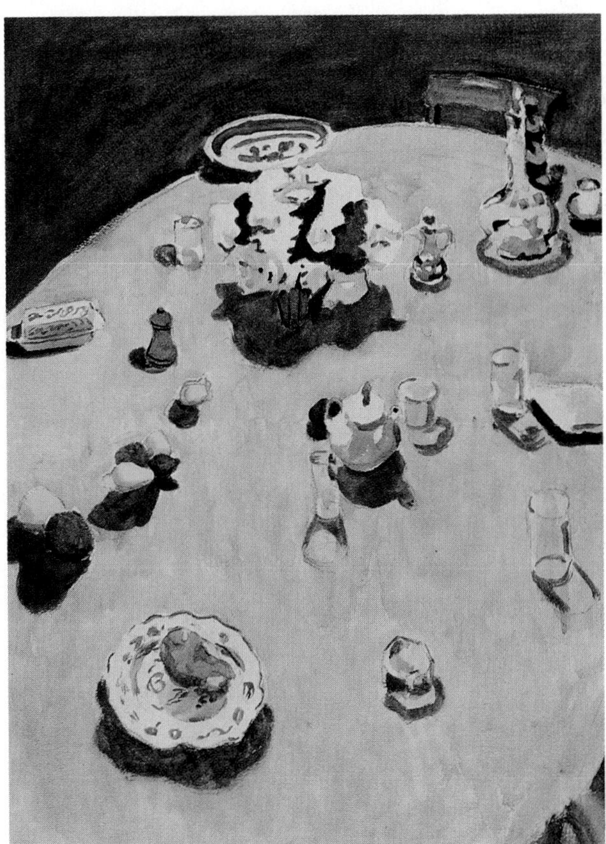

The Table (1970), Fairfield Porter. Collection of Elizabeth Feld.

WORDS TO KNOW

tersely (tûrs′lē) *adv.* briefly
tumultuous (to͝o-mŭl′cho͞o-əs) *adj.* wild and disorderly
mollified (mŏl′ə-fīd′) *adj.* pacified; made calm **mollify** *v.*

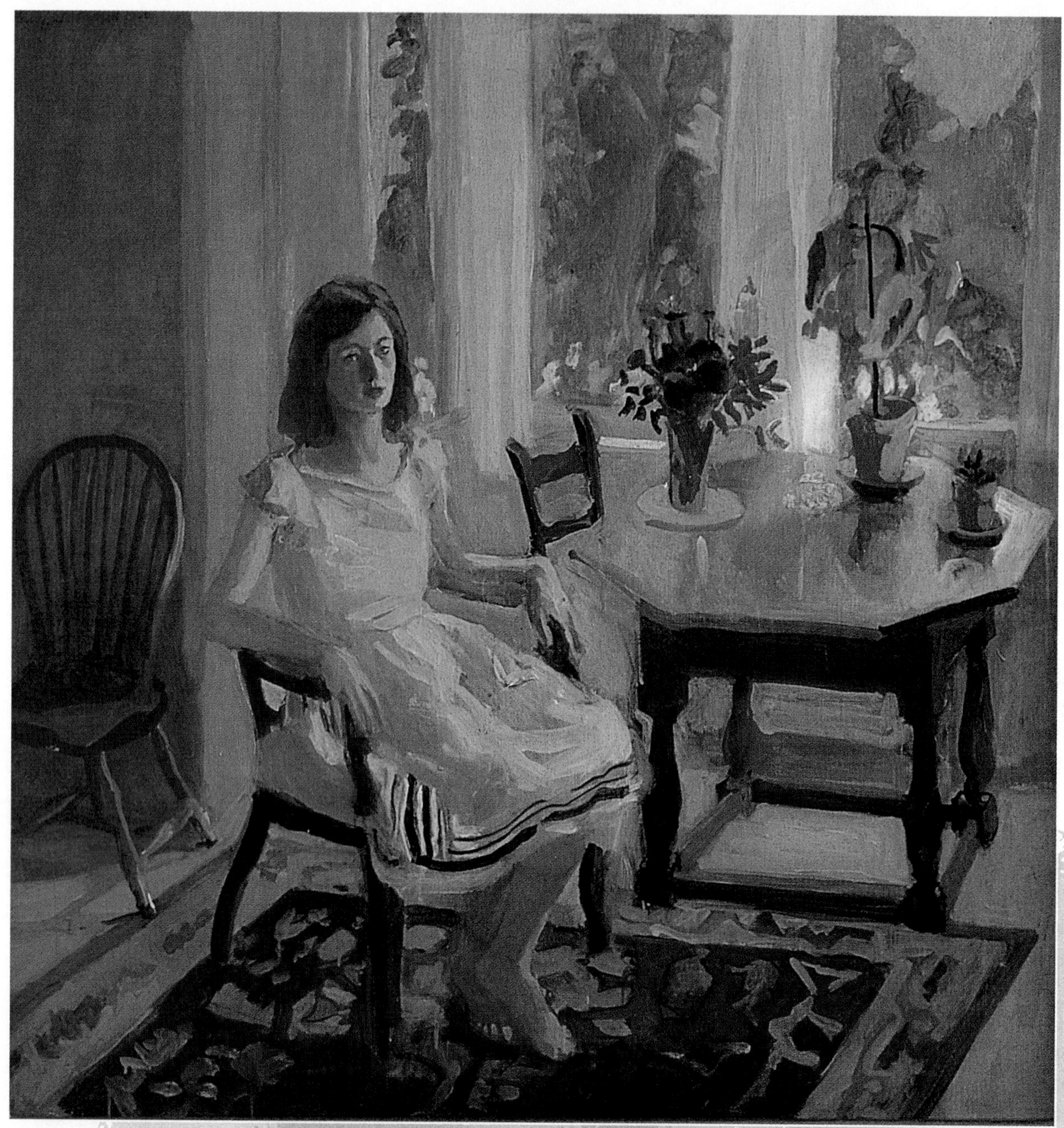

Claire White (1960), Fairfield Porter. Oil on canvas, 45½″ × 45″, collection of Stephen and Sheila Wald, Telluride, Colorado.

Joan came and went, . . .
calmer than she should have been.

"Ha ha *ha*." Richard and Joan realized simultaneously that the child was drunk, on Judith's homecoming champagne. Feeling bound to keep the center of the stage, John took a cigarette from Judith's pack, poked it into his mouth, let it hang from his lower lip, and squinted like a gangster.

"You're not little things we had," Richard called to him. "You're the whole point. But you're grown. Or almost."

The boy was lighting matches. Instead of holding them to his cigarette (for they had never seen him smoke; being "good" had been his way of setting himself apart), he held them to his mother's face, closer and closer, for her to blow out. Then he lit the whole folder—a hiss and then a torch, held against his mother's face. Prismed by tears, the flame filled Richard's vision; he didn't know how it was extinguished. He heard Margaret say, "Oh stop showing off," and saw John, in response, break the cigarette in two and put the halves entirely into his mouth and chew, sticking out his tongue to display the shreds to his sister.

Joan talked to him, reasoning—a fountain of reason, unintelligible. "Talked about it for years . . . our children must help us . . . Daddy and I both want . . ." As the boy listened, he carefully wadded a paper napkin into the leaves of his salad, fashioned a ball of paper and lettuce, and popped it into his mouth, looking around the table for the expected laughter. None came. Judith said, "Be mature," and dismissed a plume of smoke.

Richard got up from this stifling table and led the boy outside. Though the house was in twilight, the outdoors still brimmed with light, the lovely waste light of high summer. Both laughing, he supervised John's spitting out the lettuce and paper and tobacco into the pachysandra.[8] He took him by the hand—a square gritty hand, but for its softness a man's. Yet, it held on. They ran together up into the field, past the tennis court. The raw banking left by the bulldozers was dotted with daisies. Past the court and a flat stretch where they used to play family baseball stood a soft green rise glorious in the sun, each weed and species of grass distinct as illumination on parchment. "I'm sorry, so sorry," Richard cried. "You were the only one who ever tried to help me with all the damn jobs around this place."

Sobbing, safe within his tears and the champagne, John explained, "It's not just the separation, it's the whole crummy year, I *hate* that school, you can't make any friends, the history teacher's a scud."

They sat on the crest of the rise, shaking and warm from their tears but easier in their voices, and Richard tried to focus on the child's sad year—the weekdays long with homework, the weekends spent in his room with model airplanes, while his parents murmured down below, nursing their separation. How selfish, how blind, Richard thought; his eyes felt scoured. He told his son, "We'll think about getting you transferred. Life's too short to be miserable."

They had said what they could, but did not want the moment to heal, and talked on, about the school, about the tennis court, whether it would ever again be as good as it had been that first summer. They walked to inspect it and pressed a few more tapes more firmly down. A little stiltedly, perhaps trying now to make too much of the moment, Richard led the boy to the spot in the field where the view was best, of the metallic blue river, the emerald marsh, the scattered islands velvety with shadow in the low light, the white bits of beach far away. "See," he said. "It goes on being beautiful. It'll be here tomorrow."

"I know," John answered, impatiently. The moment had closed.

Back in the house, the others had opened

8. **pachysandra** (păk′ĭ-săn′drə): small, low-growing, leafy plants used as ground cover.

WORDS TO KNOW

stiltedly (stĭl′tĭd-lē) *adv.* in a stiffly dignified manner

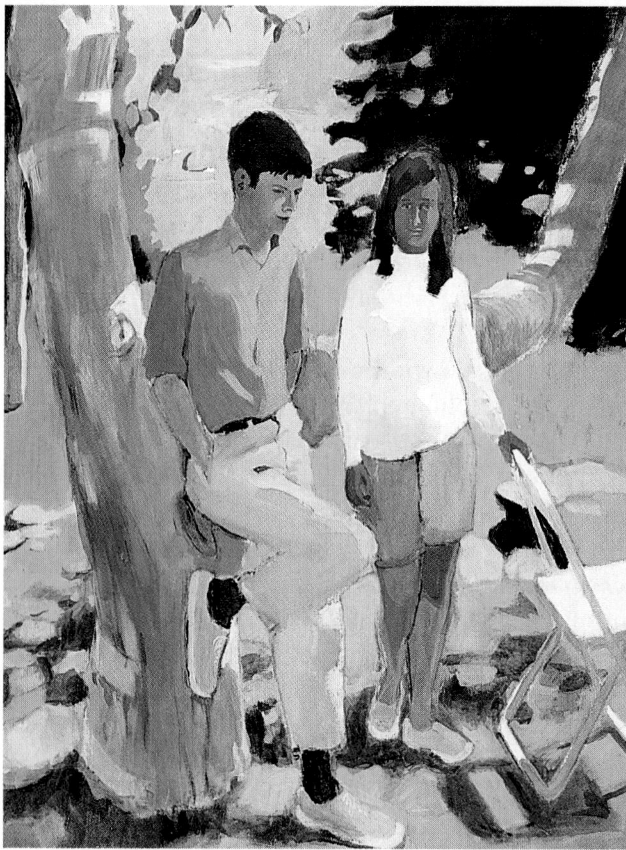

Stephen and Kathy (1965), Fairfield Porter. Oil on canvas. Colby College Museum of Art, Waterville, Maine.

some white wine, the champagne being drunk, and still sat at the table, the three females, gossiping. Where Joan sat had become the head. She turned, showing him a tearless face, and asked, "All right?"

"We're fine," he said, resenting it, though relieved, that the party went on without him.

In bed she explained, "I couldn't cry I guess because I cried so much all spring. It really wasn't fair. It's your idea, and you made it look as though I was kicking you out."

"I'm sorry," he said. "I couldn't stop. I wanted to but couldn't."

"You *didn't* want to. You loved it. You were having your way, making a general announcement."

"I love having it over," he admitted. "God, those kids were great. So brave and funny." John, returned to the house, had settled to a model airplane in his room, and kept shouting down to them, "I'm O.K. No sweat." "And the way," Richard went on, cozy in his relief, "they never questioned the reasons we gave. No thought of a third person. Not even Judith."

"That *was* touching," Joan said.

He gave her a hug. "You were great too. Very reassuring to everybody. Thank you." Guiltily, he realized he did not feel separated.

"You still have Dickie to do," she told him. These words set before him a black mountain in the darkness; its cold breath, its near weight affected his chest. Of the four children, his elder son was most nearly his conscience. Joan did not need to add, "That's one piece of your dirty work I won't do for you."

"I know. I'll do it. You go to sleep."

Within minutes, her breathing slowed, became oblivious and deep. It was quarter to midnight. Dickie's train from the concert would come in at one-fourteen. Richard set the alarm for one. He had slept atrociously for weeks. But whenever he closed his lids some glimpse of the last hours scorched them—Judith exhaling toward the ceiling in a kind of aversion, Bean's mute staring, the sunstruck growth in the field where he and John had rested. The mountain before him moved closer, moved within him; he was huge, momentous. The ache at the back of his throat felt stale. His wife slept as if slain beside him. When, exasperated by his hot lids, his crowded heart, he rose from bed and dressed, she awoke enough to turn over. He told her then, "Joan, if I could undo it all, I would."

"Where would you begin?" she asked. There was no place. Giving him courage, she was always giving him courage. He put on shoes without socks in the dark. The children were breathing in their rooms, the downstairs was hollow. In their confusion they had left lights burning. He turned off all but one, the kitchen overhead. The car started. He had hoped it wouldn't. He met only moonlight on the road; it seemed a diaphanous companion, flickering in the leaves along the roadside, haunting his rearview mirror like a pursuer, melting under his headlights. The center of town, not quite deserted, was eerie at this hour. A young cop in uniform kept company with a gang of T-shirted kids on the steps of the bank. Across from the railroad station, several bars kept open. Customers, mostly young, passed in and out of the warm night, savoring summer's novelty. Voices shouted from cars as they passed; an immense conversation seemed in progress. Richard parked and in his weariness put his head on the passenger seat, out of the commotion and wheeling lights. It was as when, in the movies, an assassin grimly carries his mission through the jostle of a carnival—except the movies cannot show the precipitous, palpable slope you cling to within. You cannot climb back down; you can only fall. The synthetic fabric of the car seat, warmed by his cheek, confided to him an ancient, distant scent of vanilla.

A train whistle caused him to lift his head. It was on time; he had hoped it would be late. The slender drawgates descended. The bell of approach tingled happily. The great metal body, horizontally fluted, rocked to a stop, and sleepy teen-agers disembarked, his son among them. Dickie did not show surprise that this father was meeting him at this terrible hour. He sauntered to the car with two friends, both taller than he. He said "Hi" to his father and took the passenger's seat with an exhausted promptness that expressed gratitude. The friends got in the back, and Richard was grateful; a few more minutes' postponement would be won by driving them home.

He asked, "How was the concert?"

"Groovy," one boy said from the back seat.

"It bit," the other said.

"It was O.K.," Dickie said, moderate by nature, so reasonable that in his childhood the unreason of the world had given him headaches, stomach aches, nausea. When the second friend had been dropped off at his dark house, the boy blurted, "Dad, my eyes are killing me with hay fever! I'm out there cutting that grass all day!"

"Do we still have those drops?"

"They didn't do any good last summer."

"They might this." Richard swung a U-turn on the empty street. The drive home took a few minutes. The mountain was here, in his throat. "Richard," he said, and felt the boy, slumped and rubbing his eyes, go tense at his tone, "I didn't come to meet you just to make your life easier. I came because your mother and I have some news for you, and you're a hard man to get ahold of these days. It's sad news."

"That's O.K." The reassurance came out soft, but quick, as if released from the tip of a spring.

Richard had feared that his tears would return and choke him, but the boy's manliness set an example, and his voice issued forth steady and dry. "It's sad news, but it needn't be tragic news, at least for you. It should have no practical effect on your life, though it's bound to have an emotional effect. You'll work at your job, and go back to school in September. Your mother and I are really proud of what you're making of your life; we don't want that to change at all."

"Yeah," the boy said lightly, on the intake of his breath, holding himself up. They turned the corner; the church they went to loomed like a gutted fort. The home of the woman Richard hoped to marry stood across the green. Her bedroom light burned.

"Your mother and I," he said, "have decided to separate. For the summer. Nothing legal, no divorce yet. We want to see how it feels. For some years now, we haven't been doing enough for each other, making each other as happy as we should be. Have you sensed that?"

"No," the boy said. It was an honest, unemotional answer: true or false in a quiz.

WORDS TO KNOW

diaphanous (dī-ăf'ə-nəs) *adj.* light or fragile in an unearthly way
precipitous (prĭ-sĭp'ĭ-təs) *adj.* steep; almost vertical
palpable (păl'pə-bəl) *adj.* that can be touched or felt

Glad for the factual basis, Richard pursued, even garrulously, the details. His apartment across town, his utter accessibility, the split vacation arrangements, the advantages to the children, the added mobility and variety of the summer. Dickie listened, absorbing. "Do the others know?"

"Yes."

"How did they take it?"

"The girls pretty calmly. John flipped out; he shouted and ate a cigarette and made a salad out of his napkin and told us how much he hated school."

His brother chuckled. "He did?"

"Yeah. The school issue was more upsetting for him than Mom and me. He seemed to feel better for having exploded."

"He did?" The repetition was the first sign that he was stunned.

"Yes. Dickie, I want to tell you something. This last hour, waiting for your train to get in, has been about the worst of my life. I hate this. *Hate* it. My father would have died before doing it to me." He felt immensely lighter, saying this. He had dumped the mountain on the boy. They were home. Moving swiftly as a shadow, Dickie was out of the car, through the bright kitchen. Richard called after him, "Want a glass of milk or anything?"

"No thanks."

"Want us to call the course tomorrow and say you're too sick to work?"

"No, that's all right." The answer was faint, delivered at the door to his room; Richard listened for the slam that went with a tantrum. The door closed normally, gently. The sound was sickening.

Joan had sunk into that first deep trough of sleep and was slow to awake. Richard had to repeat, "I told him."

"What did he say?"

"Nothing much. Could you go say goodnight to him? Please."

She left their room, without putting on a bathrobe. He sluggishly changed back into his pajamas and walked down the hall. Dickie was already in bed, Joan was sitting beside him, and the boy's bedside clock radio was murmuring music. When she stood, an inexplicable light—the moon?—outlined her body through the nightie. Richard sat on the warm place she had indented on the child's narrow mattress. He asked him, "Do you want the radio on like that?"

"It always is."

"Doesn't it keep you awake? It would me."

"No."

"Are you sleepy?"

"Yeah."

"Good. Sure you want to get up and go to work? You've had a big night."

"I want to."

Away at school this winter he had learned for the first time that you can go short of sleep and live. As an infant he had slept with an immobile, sweating intensity that had alarmed his babysitters. In adolescence he had often been the first of the four children to go to bed. Even now, he would go slack in the middle of a television show, his sprawled legs hairy and brown. "O.K. Good boy. Dickie, listen. I love you so much, I never knew how much until now. No matter how this works out, I'll always be with you. Really."

Richard bent to kiss an averted face but his son, sinewy, turned and with wet cheeks embraced him and gave him a kiss, on the lips, passionate as a woman's. In his father's ear he moaned one word, the crucial, intelligent word: "*Why?*"

Why. It was a whistle of wind in a crack, a knife thrust, a window thrown open on emptiness. The white face was gone, the darkness was featureless. Richard had forgotten why. ❖

WORDS TO KNOW

garrulously (găr'ə-ləs-lē) *adv.* talking too much about trifles; talkative

RESPONDING OPTIONS

FROM PERSONAL RESPONSE *TO* CRITICAL ANALYSIS

REFLECT 1. In your notebook, give your reaction to the conversation that Richard and Dickie have in Dickie's bedroom.

RETHINK 2. At the end of the story, did you feel sympathy for Richard? Point to things he says, does, or thinks that caused you to be sympathetic or not.

3. Dickie asks his father, "Why?" and the narrator says, "Richard had forgotten why." What can you gather about why Richard and Joan are separating?

   Consider
   - the explanations they offer their children
   - the "white face" in Richard's mind (pages 1042 and 1050)
   - Richard's remark, "Life's too short to be miserable" (page 1047)

4. Think about Richard's and Joan's different plans for how to tell the children about the separation. What might Joan's plan reveal about her personality? What might Richard's plan reveal about his personality?

RELATE 5. Do you think the behavior of the people in this story is true to life? Explain. Consider the discussion about separation you had for the Personal Connection (page 1040) and the dialogue you wrote for the Writing Connection.

ANOTHER PATHWAY

Cooperative Learning

Imagine that you are making a TV movie of "Separating." With a small group of classmates, select a scene from this story and write stage directions for how the actors should speak their lines. Also write notes about the props, lighting, scenery, costumes, and music you would use to bring this scene to life. Share your ideas with the class.

THE WRITER'S STYLE

To reinforce his themes, Updike often uses **symbols,** things that have concrete meanings in themselves but also represent something beyond their concrete meanings. For instance, at the table Richard cracks the lobster's back, as he has cracked apart his family. The clearing away of the carapaces, or shells, could symbolize the need to clear away the broken shell of the marriage. What symbolism do you find in other objects in the story—for example, the Maples' house and tennis court?

QUICKWRITES

1. Write a **diary entry** from the perspective of a character in the story other than Richard—either Joan or one of the children.
2. Write a brief **character analysis** that examines Richard Maple's behavior and values. Make clear your final judgment of him.
3. Updike wrote three other stories about the Maples after "Separating." What do you think happens to Joan, Richard, and each of their four children in the stories to come? Write up your **predictions.**

PORTFOLIO *Save your writing. You may want to use it later as a springboard to a piece for your portfolio.*

LITERARY CONCEPTS

A stylistic element in this story is the use of **dramatic irony.** Dramatic irony occurs when a reader knows more about a situation than the story's characters know. In "Separating," readers know what the children do not: the parents intend to announce their separation. Why do you think Updike shares this knowledge with his readers from the beginning? What effect did it have on your involvement in the story?

CONCEPT REVIEW: Point of View Although Richard is not the narrator of "Separating," the narration focuses on his point of view. This focus on one character's thoughts, observations, and feelings is called **third-person limited point of view.** How might your response to the story have changed if it had been narrated from the **third-person omniscient point of view,** in which different characters' thoughts and feelings are reported?

WORDS TO KNOW

EXERCISE A For each phrase in the first column, write the letter of the synonymous phrase from the second column.

1. a leaky depot	a. succulent duck
2. a primary need	b. a soothed youth
3. luscious poultry	c. chaotic aquatics
4. stiffly rejected	d. tersely conversing
5. concisely discussing	e. bounteous amounts
6. a mollified minor	f. stiltedly jilted
7. opulent quantities	g. produces minutiae
8. makes dinky pieces	h. chattily flattering
9. tumultuous water sports	i. a permeable terminal
10. garrulously complimenting	j. an elemental essential

EXERCISE B Identify each pair of words as synonyms or antonyms.

1. diaphanous—solid
2. dissolution—union
3. palpable—concrete
4. congruous—appropriate
5. precipitous—flat

JOHN UPDIKE

1932–

In his collection of autobiographical sketches, *Self-Consciousness: Memoirs,* John Updike paints himself as a shy, meek person who loves what is normal and average. Updike attributes his personality in part to a troublesome skin condition called psoriasis, which is characterized by unsightly, scaly skin. He also names psoriasis as one reason he decided to become a writer: "Because of my skin, I counted myself out of any of those jobs—salesman, teacher, financier, movie star—that demand being presentable. What did that leave? Becoming a craftsman of some sort, closeted and unseen—perhaps a cartoonist or a writer, a worker in ink who can hide himself and send out a surrogate presence, a signature that multiplies even while it conceals."

Despite this self-deprecating description of himself, Updike has been fantastically successful, winning numerous awards for his fiction, poetry, and essays. He won a National Book Award for his novel *The Centaur,* a Pulitzer Prize for his novels *Rabbit Is Rich* and *Rabbit at Rest,* and a National Book Critics Circle award for criticism for *Hugging the Shore.* A number of his novels and stories have been adapted as films, television movies, and plays.

Much of Updike's work, like the short story "Separating," explores the tensions in middle-class American families. In an interview, he said: "I like middles. It is in middles that extremes clash, where ambiguity restlessly rules. . . . It seems to me that critics get increasingly querulous and impatient for madder music and stronger wine, when what we need is a greater respect for reality, its secrecy, its music."

OTHER WORKS *The Poorhouse Fair; Rabbit, Run; Pigeon Feathers and Other Stories; Couples*

• *AUTHOR BACKGROUND*

PREVIEWING

POETRY

the promise

Alan Chong Lau

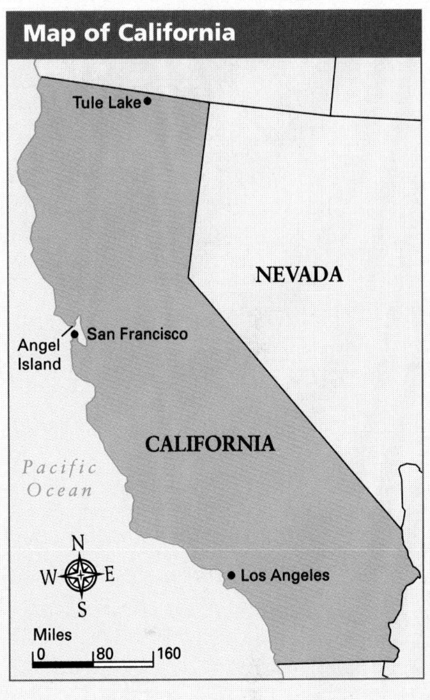

PERSONAL CONNECTION

Imagine visiting a place where an injustice was done to members of your family or ethnic group. Name such a place, if there is one. What feelings might you have at this site, and why? What would you expect to find there now? Respond in your notebook. The speaker in the following poem visits Angel Island and Tule Lake, two sites in California where previous generations of Chinese Americans and Japanese Americans suffered injustices. Read to find out the emotions aroused there—in the past and in the present.

HISTORICAL CONNECTION

In the United States in the mid-1800s, some people viewed the influx of Chinese immigrants as a threat to the employment of white Americans. This anti-Chinese sentiment caused Congress to pass the Chinese Exclusion Act of 1882, which closed U.S. borders to Chinese immigrants except for tourists, merchants, students, and diplomats. When some Chinese entered the country illegally, immigration officials cracked down. All Chinese who arrived on the West Coast between 1910 and 1940 had to go through a detention center on Angel Island, in San Francisco Bay. While they awaited interrogation by officials, would-be immigrants lived in filthy, dilapidated quarters for weeks, months, or even years. Of the 175,000 Chinese people processed at Angel Island, about 10 percent were later deported to China.

As you learned when you read "In Response to Executive Order 9066" (page 929), Japanese Americans living on the West Coast were forcefully relocated to internment camps during World War II. Tule Lake, the camp mentioned in "the promise," was located in northern California in Modoc County. Over the course of the war, 18,789 Japanese Americans were detained at Tule Lake. In recent years, Japanese Americans have made pilgrimages to the sites of these internment camps.

READING CONNECTION

Understanding Form As you read "the promise," keep in mind that the stanzas shift back and forth without warning from past to present, from Angel Island to Tule Lake. Watch for these clues that signal a change of time and scene:

- indentation of stanzas
- transitional words, such as *today,* denoting time
- transitional words, such as *here,* denoting place
- changes in verb tense ("where chinese grandmothers *sat*"; "i *take* a ferry")
- quotation marks signaling another speaker's words

Japanese men rounded up in a 1942 raid.
AP/Wide World Photos.

for sharon lew and the first, second,
third and all generations to come . . .
workers of the soil, all children
of the land

—1—

my grandfather
detained
on an island
of hell named angel

"from your backdoor
how many feet
is the village pond?
in what direction
does your house
lie in relation to it?"
—immigration authority questions

your parents
contained

GUIDE FOR READING

1–4 From these lines you can infer that the speaker is a third-generation Chinese American whose grandfather was detained on Angel Island.

5–11 Immigration officials at Angel Island asked this type of question to try to catch potential Chinese immigrants in falsehoods about their backgrounds; officials would use inconsistent answers as a reason to send the people back to China. Could you answer such a question?

up here in the *original* tules
where it still snows
in april
streaks of white
on engulfing crags of stone

here where man
is a pin
and silence replaces the scream
of anger once righteous enough
to bring tanks grumbling to
the barbed front door

your used barracks
are rented out to new prisoners
migrant workers
who stoop over to pick
the dark mud from their shoes
as geese draw the distance
between peaks

here on an island
of sun bleached rocks
where chinese grandmothers
sat on benches
in the long afternoon
waiting years feet inches
for entrance to gold mountain
the broken glass of windows
lay on the floor
jagged tears eating dust

green thriving bushes
cover walls where inside
poems of despair
ten thousand washed out dreams
are scrawled in bitter blood
as sea gulls cut white patterns
in blue sky

today we rode in chartered buses
to get here
with scant belongings as
your parents once rode in buses

12–18 The speaker is now addressing a Japanese American whose parents were interned at Tule Lake. *Tules* refers to low, swampy land where tules, or bulrushes, grow. What else can you tell about the land from the description?

19–20 What might be the meaning of "man is a pin"?

21–24 When internees at Tule Lake protested their mistreatment by holding work stoppages and mass demonstrations, armed soldiers and tanks were called in to suppress the revolt.

25–31 What does the speaker imply about the migrant workers who now occupy the former barracks at Tule Lake?

38 gold mountain: what the Chinese called California and, by extension, the United States.

39–41 What does this image suggest about the grandmothers' emotions?

44–46 The dormitory walls at Angel Island are covered with poems—some carved, most in ink—written by those detained there. Why do you think the speaker says that the poems are scrawled in blood?

bayonets at every window
like a road sign

a former internee
speaks
"this is the first time
i've been here in . . ."

(eyes scan
tarpaper walls
counting up time spent
a collapsed guardtower
points to the mountains)

"thirty years . . .
it's been . . ."

(the wind cuts us all
to silence

as he no longer
can find words)

today
i take a ferry
across the water
with only a sack lunch
as my grandfather
carried only a bundle wrapped in cloth
tossed in the hold of a ship
like a wet mop
the words on the walls speak
"deprived of my freedom, i stay on this island.

49–54 The speaker and his companion ride chartered buses to visit Tule Lake. Decades earlier, Japanese Americans were taken there by bus against their will, accompanied by soldiers carrying bayonets.

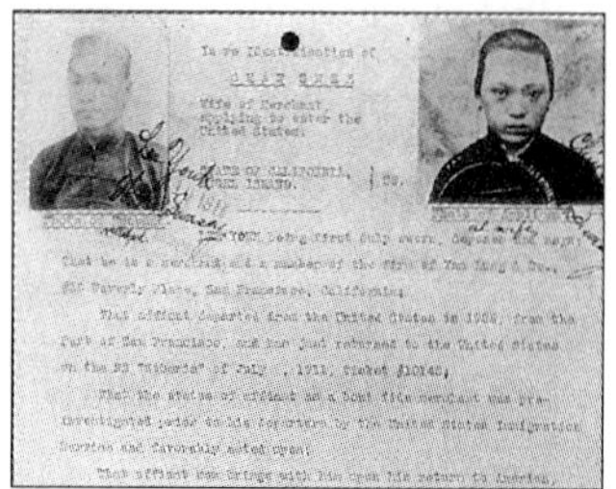

From the Angel Island files: an identification card from 1911.
National Archives, Pacific Sierra Region, San Bruno, California.

66–69 What do you think the visitors' silence means?

70–72 Where is the speaker going on the ferry?

Women and children waiting to be processed in a detention area of Angel Island.
California Historical Society.

the story of my life is bleached—ending up
in prison.
my breast is full of grievances and this poem
is an outlet."

—2—

we come in
all of us with names
not numbers
and

no . . .
we will never
go to tule lake again

and no . . .
i cannot tell you how many feet
the duckpond is from my backdoor

and no . . .
we will never
give up our names

and yes . . .
this land is our land

and yes . . .
we will share it with
people of all tribes

and yes . . .
all your guns
are worthless

and yes . . .
it is the same with your empty words

the earth will eat them
will split them
like pulling off the heads
of rusty nails

78–83 The poems that remained on the walls of the Angel Island immigration facility long after it closed were one of the reasons people prevented the destruction of the facility in 1970.

84–110 What is the speaker implying has changed since the time of the injustices at Angel Island and Tule Lake? To whom is the speaker addressing these remarks?

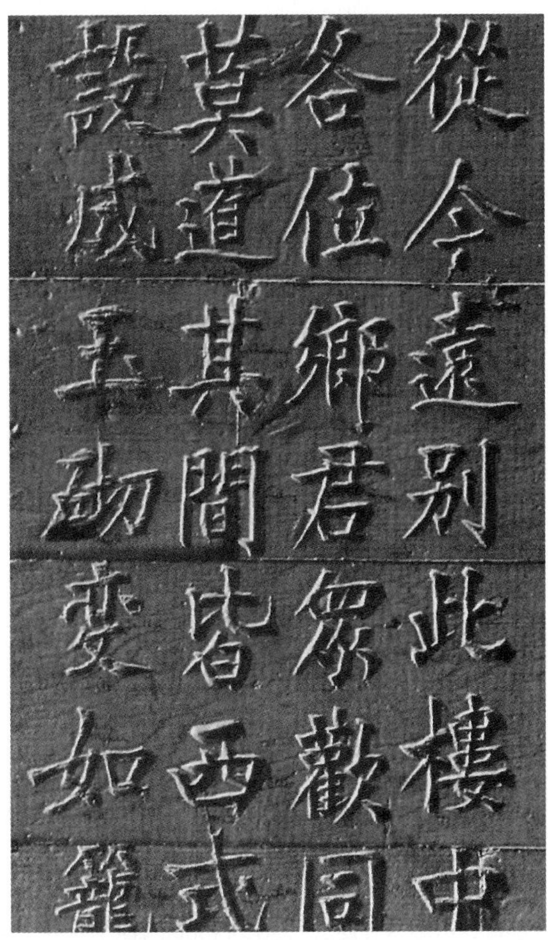

One of many poems written by detainees on the walls of Angel Island. Courtesy of California State Parks. Photo by Mak Takahashi.

RESPONDING OPTIONS

FROM PERSONAL RESPONSE *TO* CRITICAL ANALYSIS

REFLECT **1.** What is your sense of the emotions expressed in this poem? Try to describe them in your notebook.

RETHINK **2.** How do you interpret the last images in the poem?

Consider
- what the "empty words" might be and how "the earth will eat them"
- what you associate with "pulling off the heads / of rusty nails"

3. In your own words, try to summarize the speaker's message in section 2 of the poem. To whom is this message directed?

4. What do you think Angel Island and Tule Lake represent to the speaker?

Consider
- how the two places are similar
- the reaction of the former Tule Lake internee in lines 55–69
- in lines 79–83, the translation of the Chinese poem written at Angel Island
- what the speaker vows in lines 88–93

5. What do you think the title of the poem, "the promise," refers to?

RELATE **6.** Do you think Asian Americans today are considered to be true Americans? What reaction would they get to the claim "this land is our land"? Explain your answer.

ANOTHER PATHWAY

Imagine that Alan Chong Lau has asked you to make a poetry video based on "the promise." Describe, in the correct sequence, the scenes you would need to include. For each scene, answer the following questions: What is the setting? Who are the people in the scene? What details would you focus on?

QUICKWRITES

1. Using details from the poem, write inscriptions for **historical plaques** that the speaker would want placed at Angel Island and Tule Lake. They should summarize what happened at these sites and also suggest how the speaker feels about the places.
2. This part of Unit Eight is titled "Where We Are Today: Closer Together or Farther Apart?" Do you read "the promise" as a poem of togetherness or apartness? Explain your views in a draft of an **interpretive essay.**

PORTFOLIO *Save your writing. You may want to use it later as a springboard to a piece for your portfolio.*

LITERARY LINKS

Compare "the promise" with "Suzie Wong Doesn't Live Here" (page 252), "I, Too" (page 766), and "In Response to Executive Order 9066" (page 929). How similar are the poems in theme and tone? Taken together, what do the poems suggest about the United States?

LITERARY CONCEPTS

Structure refers to the way in which a work of literature is put together. In poetry, structure is the arrangement of words and lines that the poet uses to produce a desired effect. The poem "the promise" has an unusual, collagelike structure. In section 1, the speaker's voice comes first from Angel Island, then abruptly shifts to Tule Lake and back again. The speaker's shifts between past and present are just as abrupt. Interspersed with the speaker's voice are quotations—immigration authority questions, the words of a former Tule Lake internee, a translation of a poem from the walls of Angel Island. A shorter section, with no shifting voice, makes up the last part of the poem. Talk about what holds the different elements together. What links different places? What links different times? What contrasts are made between past and present? How is section 2 related to section 1? Tell what all the parts add up to, in your view.

CONCEPT REVIEW: Imagery This poem contains many images of nature, such as flying geese and seagulls. What do you think the nature imagery contributes to the poem?

CRITIC'S CORNER

To pass the time and to express their feelings, the detainees at Angel Island wrote poems on the dormitory walls. The poem quoted in lines 79–83 is one of 135 that have been preserved and translated. Mr. Ng, a former detainee, recalled: "A lot of people there didn't know how to write poetry. You can't say the poems were great, but they expressed real feelings." Why might people want to preserve such poetry? Discuss your thoughts with a group of classmates.

ACROSS THE CURRICULUM

History *Cooperative Learning* Find out more about the experiences of Chinese immigrants who were detained at Angel Island and Japanese Americans who were interned at Tule Lake and other relocation centers during World War II. Working with other classmates, investigate various aspects of Asian American history related to Lau's poem. In a group presentation, share your findings with the class. You may want to display copies of poems Chinese immigrants wrote on the walls at Angel Island or photographs of the Japanese-American internment camps.

ALAN CHONG LAU

Born in 1948 in Oroville, California, Alan Chong Lau grew up in the town of Paradise in the Sacramento Valley. In the early 1970s he traveled to Japan, where he met his wife, Kazuko. A visual artist as well as a poet, he received a bachelor's degree in art from the University of California at Santa Cruz in 1976. Lau's poem "the promise" appears in his volume of poetry, *Songs for Jadina,* which won an American Book Award from the Before Columbus Foundation. He dedicated this book to his grandmother Jadina and also to "the nameless ones." He said in a 1981 interview: "I wanted to give voices to those who came before, who couldn't tell their stories. I want to tell their story, that they *were* here and *did* exist."

Lau's work has also appeared in the anthologies *The Next World, The Big Aiiieeeee!: An Anthology of Chinese American and Japanese American Literature,* and *Chinese American Poetry: An Anthology.* He wrote *The Buddha Bandits Down Highway 99* with the Asian-American poets Lawson Fusao Inada and Garrett Hongo, and he coedited the anthology *Turning Shadows Into Light: Art and Culture of the Northwest's Early Asian/Pacific Community.* Lau has received several other awards, including a 1983 Creative Artists Fellowship sponsored by the Japan-U.S. Friendship Commission, the National Endowment for the Arts, and the Agency for Cultural Affairs of the Japanese Government.

LASERLINKS
• *HISTORICAL CONNECTION*

PREVIEWING

NONFICTION

The Case for Official English

S. I. Hayakawa (hī′ə-kou′ə)

Why Fear Spanish?

Carlos Alberto Montaner (kär′lôs äl-bĕr′tô môn-tä-nĕr′)

PERSONAL CONNECTION

Although English is the language that is most commonly spoken in the United States, our country has no official national language. Some people believe that Congress should pass a law that makes English the official national language. Do you agree or disagree? Why? Discuss the issue with a small group of your classmates. In your notebook, create a chart like this one to organize your thoughts.

Pros	Cons
promotes national unity	discriminates against immigrants

HISTORICAL CONNECTION

The first selection you will read is an excerpt from a speech delivered by S. I. Hayakawa in 1985. In 1981 Hayakawa, then Republican senator from California, proposed a constitutional amendment that would make English the official national language. He said, "We can speak any language we want at the dinner table, but English is the language of public discourses, of the marketplace and of the voting booth." Although his English Language Amendment did not pass, debate over the issue of "official English" has continued. By 1990, more than a third of the states had passed laws making English their official state language. Supporters of official English believe it is necessary to require a common language to help unify the diverse ethnic groups in the United States. Opponents, on the other hand, feel that official English would discriminate against immigrants and would put an end to bilingual services that help non–English-speaking people do such things as vote, learn, and apply for jobs in their native languages.

Swearing-in ceremony of new U.S. citizens in New York City.

READING CONNECTION

Analyzing Arguments

Throughout your life you will make personal decisions that have important consequences. People will continually try to persuade you to accept their ideas, buy their products, support their political candidates, or vote for their proposals. In order to make the best decisions, you will need to listen to both sides of an argument and weigh different viewpoints. Be ready to challenge statements that don't seem quite true. Draw on your own experience to evaluate the arguments that people present.

One Reader's Response

The suggestions printed below in dark type represent a few of the strategies you can use to evaluate conflicting opinions as you make up your own mind. Following each strategy except the last one, you will find a passage from Hayakawa's speech or Montaner's essay, together with ideas (in the white boxes) that one reader thought about while reading. The last strategy presents thoughts that relate to the issue generally, not to any particular passage.

Look for major ideas and restate them in your own words.

"What is it that has made a society out of the hodgepodge of nationalities, races, and colors represented in the immigrant hordes that people our nation? It is language, of course, that has made communication among all these elements possible. It is with a common language that we have dissolved distrust and fear. It is with language that we have drawn up the understandings and agreements and social contracts that make a society possible."

He's saying that using one language helps make the United States a unified country.

React to what the arguers are saying.

"A language is much more than a way to communicate. By one's own language—and on this Edward Sapir wrote much and well—one masters reality, one takes to oneself and understands all that exists. All: history, interpersonal relations, the most intimate and definitive emotions."

Does he mean that the language you speak makes you see the world differently? How can that be? There are real things—a rose, an apple, a car—that are just there, whatever language you use.

Decide what points matter most to you.

"The ethnic chauvinism of the present Hispanic leadership is an unhealthy trend in present-day America. It threatens a division perhaps more ominous in the long run than the division between blacks and whites."

I think it would be a bad thing if citizens couldn't talk with one another about problems that affect us all.

Think about other information that could help you make a decision.

How would having an official language affect daily life for people?

As you read the two selections, use these strategies to help you develop your own conclusion about whether the United States should have an official language. While reading, jot down restatements, reactions, and questions in your notebook to refer to later.

from

THE CASE FOR OFFICIAL ENGLISH

S. I. Hayakawa

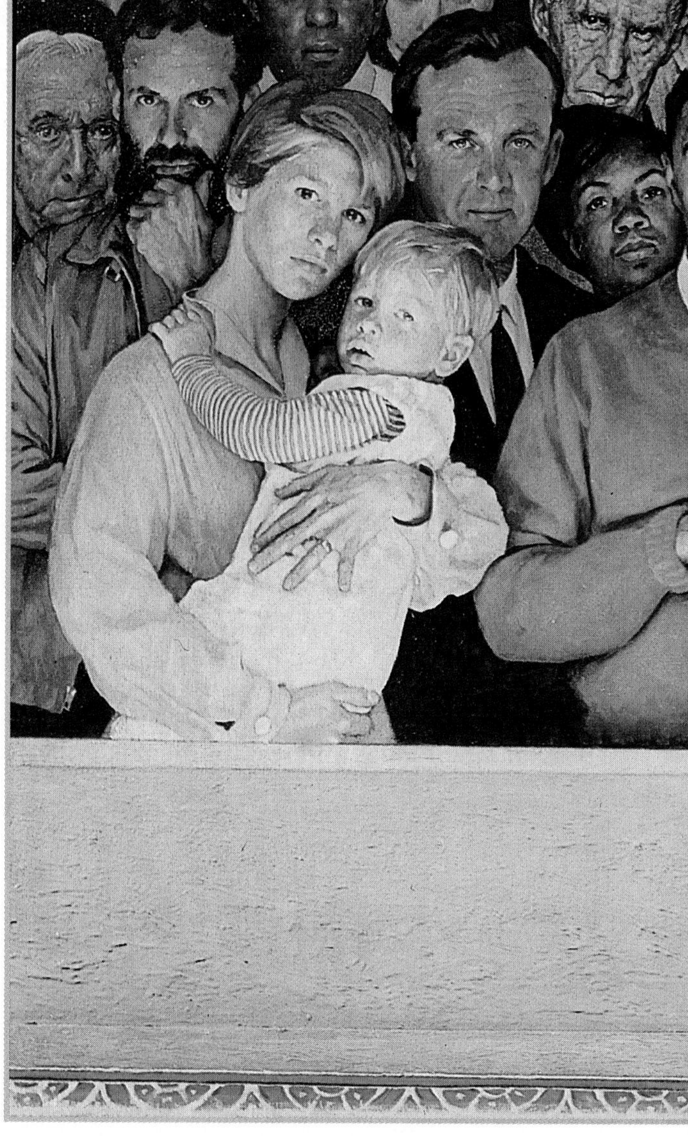

What is it that has made a society out of the hodgepodge of nationalities, races, and colors represented in the immigrant hordes that people our nation? It is language, of course, that has made communication among all these elements possible. It is with a common language that we have dissolved distrust and fear. It is with language that we have drawn up the understandings and agreements and social contracts that make a society possible.

But while language is a necessary cause for our oneness as a society, it is not a sufficient cause. A foreigner cannot, by speaking faultless English, become an Englishman. Paul Theroux, a contemporary novelist and travel writer, has commented on this fact: "Foreigners are always aliens in England. No one becomes English. It's a very tribal society. . . . No one becomes Japanese. . . . No one becomes Nigerian. But Nigerians, Japanese, and English become Americans."

One need not speak faultless American English to become an American. Indeed, one may continue to speak English with an appalling foreign accent. This is true of some of my friends, but they are seen as fully American because of the warmth and enthusiasm with which they enter

A Right to Know (1968), Norman Rockwell. Photo courtesy of The Norman Rockwell Museum at Stockbridge, Massachusetts. Copyright © 1968 the Norman Rockwell Family Trust. Printed by permission of the Norman Rockwell Family Trust.

into the life of the communities in which they live. . . .

In the past several years, strong resistance to the "melting pot" idea has arisen, especially for those who claim to speak for the Hispanic peoples. Instead of a melting pot, they say, the national ideal should be a "salad bowl," in which different elements are thrown together but not "melted," so that the original ingredients retain their distinctive character. In addition to the increasing size of the Spanish-speaking population in our nation, two legislative actions have released this outburst of effort on behalf of the Spanish language and Hispanic culture.

First, there was the so-called "bilingual ballot" mandated in 1975 in an amendment to the Voting Rights Act, which required foreign language ballots when voters of selected language groups reached 5 percent or more in any voting district. The groups chosen to be so favored were Asian Americans (Chinese, Filipino, Japanese, Korean), American Indians, Alaskan Natives, and "peoples of Spanish heritage," that is, Puerto Ricans, Cubans, and Mexican Americans.

Sensitive as Americans have been to racism, especially since the days of the civil rights movement, no one seems to have noticed the profound racism expressed in the amendment that created the bilingual ballot. Brown people, like Mexicans and Puerto Ricans, red people, like American Indians, and yellow people, like the Japanese and Chinese, are assumed not to be smart enough to learn English. No provision is made, however, for non-English-speaking French-Canadians in Maine or Vermont, or for the Hebrew-speaking Hasidic Jews in Brooklyn, who are white and are presumed to be able to learn English without difficulty. Voters in San Francisco encountered ballots in Spanish and Chinese for the first time in the elections of 1980, much to their surprise, since authorizing legislation had been passed by Congress with almost no debate, no roll-call vote, and no public discussion. Naturalized Americans, who had taken the trouble to learn English to become citizens, were especially angry and remain so.

EVEN MALCOLM X, IN HIS FIERY DENUNCIATIONS OF THE RACIAL SITUATION IN AMERICA, WROTE EXCELLENT AND ELOQUENT ENGLISH.

Furthermore, there was the *Lau* decision of the U.S. Supreme Court in response to a suit brought by a Chinese of San Francisco who complained that his children were not being taught English adequately in the public schools they were attending. Justice William O. Douglas, delivering the opinion of the court, wrote: "No specific remedy is urged upon us. Teaching English to the students of Chinese ancestry who do not speak the language is one choice. Giving instructions to this group in Chinese is another. There may be others. Petitioner asks only that the Board of Education be directed to apply its expertise to the problem and rectify the situation." Justice Douglas's decision, concurred in by the entire court, granted the *Lau* petition. Because the *Lau* decision did not specify the method by which English was to be taught, it turned out to be a go-ahead for amazing educational developments, not so much for the Chinese as for Hispanics, who appropriated the decision and took it to apply especially to themselves.

The new U.S. Department of Education, established during the Carter administration, was eager to make its presence known by expanding its bureaucracy and its influence. The department quickly announced a vast program with federal funding for bilingual education, which led to the hiring of Spanish-speaking teachers by the thousands. The department furthermore issued what were known as the Lau Regulations, which required under the threat of withdrawal of federal funds that (1) non-English-speaking pupils be taught English, and that (2) academic subjects be taught in the pupils' own language. The contradiction between these two regulations seems not to have occurred to the educational theorists in the Department of Education. Nor does it seem to trouble, to this day, the huge membership of the National Association for Bilingual Education.[1]

Bilingual education rapidly became a growth industry, requiring more and more teachers. Complaints began to arise from citizens that "bilingual education" was not bilingual at all, since many Spanish-speaking teachers hired for the program were found not to be able to speak English. Despite the ministrations of the Department of Education, or

1. **National Association for Bilingual Education:** At the time Hayakawa spoke, this professional organization had fewer than 2,000 members and an annual budget of less than $250,000, according to its executive director, James J. Lyons.

WORDS TO KNOW

ministration (mĭn'ĭ-strā'shən) *n.* the act of helping or giving aid perhaps because of them, Hispanic students to a shocking degree drop out of school, educated neither in Hispanic nor in American language and culture. "Hispanics are the least educated minority in America, according to a report by the American Council on Education," writes Earl Byrd. "The report says 50 percent of all Hispanic youths in America drop out of high school, and only 7 percent finish college. Twelve percent of black youths and 23 percent of whites finish college. Eighteen percent of all Hispanics in America who are 25 or older are classified as functional illiterates,[2] compared to 10 percent for blacks and 3 percent for whites."

I welcome the Hispanic—and as a Californian, I welcome especially the Mexican—influence on our culture. My wife was wise enough to insist that both our son and daughter learn Spanish as children and to keep reading Spanish as they were growing up. Consequently, my son, a newspaperman, was able to work for six months as an exchange writer for a newspaper in Costa Rica, while a Costa Rican reporter took my son's place in Oregon. My daughter, a graduate of the University of California at Santa Cruz, speaks Spanish, French, and after a year in Monterey Language School, Japanese.

The ethnic chauvinism[3] of the present Hispanic leadership is an unhealthy trend in present-day America. It threatens a division perhaps more ominous in the long run than the division between blacks and whites. Blacks and whites have problems enough with each other, to be sure, but they quarrel with each other in one language. Even Malcolm X, in his fiery denunciations of the racial situation in America, wrote excellent and eloquent English. But the present politically ambitious "Hispanic Caucus"[4] looks forward to a destiny for Spanish-speaking Americans separate from that of Anglo-, Italian-, Polish-, Greek-, Lebanese-, Chinese-, and Afro-Americans, and all the rest of us who rejoice in our ethnic diversity, which gives us our richness as a culture, and the English language, which keeps us in communication with each other to create a unique and vibrant culture. . . . ❖

2. **functional illiterates:** people who cannot read or write well enough to perform anything more than the most basic tasks.

3. **chauvinism** (shō′və-nĭ′zəm): an excessive enthusiasm for one's sex, race, or group, often with contempt for people of the opposite sex, other races, or other groups.

4. **"Hispanic Caucus":** Hispanic members of Congress, who meet to plan and carry out activities related to efforts to increase their political influence.

FROM PERSONAL RESPONSE *TO* CRITICAL ANALYSIS

REFLECT **1.** Which passage in Hayakawa's speech did you react to most strongly? Refer to the notes you made while reading.

RETHINK **2.** How would you restate Hayakawa's arguments in favor of official English? Again, refer to your notes.

3. How persuasive do you find Hayakawa's arguments?

Consider

- what you know that supports the arguments
- what you know that challenges them
- what else you want to know before you take a position

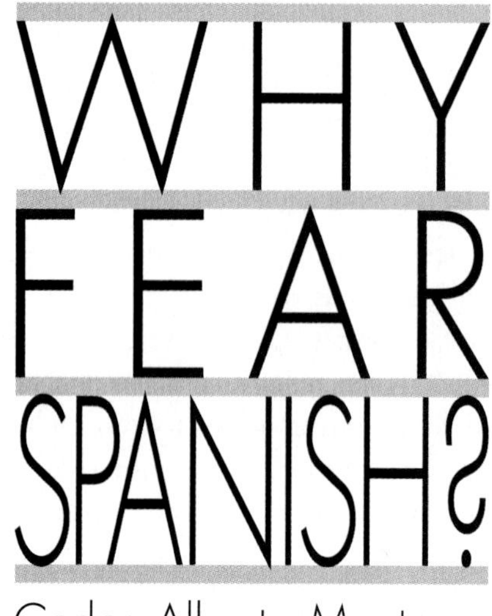

I was walking quietly with my wife on a sidewalk in Miami Beach. We were speaking Spanish, of course, because that is our language. Suddenly, we were accosted by a spry little old lady, wearing a baseball cap and sneakers, who told us: "Talk English. You are in the United States." She continued on her way at once, without stopping to see our reaction. The expression on her face, curiously, was not that of somebody performing a rude action, but of somebody performing a sacred patriotic duty.

And the truth is that the lady in question was not an eccentric madwoman. Thousands, millions of monolingual[1] Americans are mortified that in their country there is a vast minority that constantly speaks a language that they do not understand. It disturbs them to hear Spanish prattle in shops, at work, in restaurants. They are irritated when conversations that they do not understand are held in their presence. Indeed, they are upset to stumble across Spanish-language stations on their radio or television dial, or by the fact that the *Miami Herald* occasionally includes an unsolicited supplement in the language of Castile.[2]

Actually, the old lady's attitude was natural. Miami Beach is, more or less, the United States. And the language of the United States is English. Moreover, one of the key elements in the configuration of a nation is its language. A monolingual American who suddenly finds himself on Miami's Calle Ocho[3] or in San Francisco's Chinatown has the feeling that he is not in his own country. And when one is not in one's own country, one feels endangered. Not faced with any danger in particular, but subject to that diffuse and irrational fear caused by words, expressions, and traits different from our own.

Hostility to a foreign language on our own turf generally does not come from balanced reflection on the advantages or disadvantages of linguistic homogeneity,[4] but from an atavistic reaction that probably has been part of human nature for millions of years, when the differences between the groups that populated the planet might result in the death or destruction of the other. Much more recently, as far as the Greeks were concerned, barbarity flowed from ignorance of Greek. Since then—and, I fear, for all time—foreigners are inevitably considered barbarians.

All right; thus far, I have confined myself to a kindly comprehension of prejudice, but there are other factors that cannot be ignored in approach-

1. **monolingual** (mŏn′ō-lĭng′gwəl): using or knowing only one language.
2. **language of Castile** (kăs-tēl′): Castilian Spanish, the official language of Spain. A different form of Spanish is spoken in Latin America.
3. **Calle Ocho** (kä′yĕ ô′chô) *Spanish:* Eighth Street, which runs through a Spanish-speaking area of Miami.
4. **linguistic homogeneity** (hō′mō-jə-nĕ′ĭ-tē): the state or condition of everyone speaking the same language.

WORDS TO KNOW

accost (ə-kôst′) *v.* to approach and speak to in an aggressive or hostile manner
configuration (kən-fĭg′yə-rā′shən) *n.* the arrangement of parts
atavistic (ăt′ə-vĭs′tĭc) *adj.* reverting to primitive type or behavior

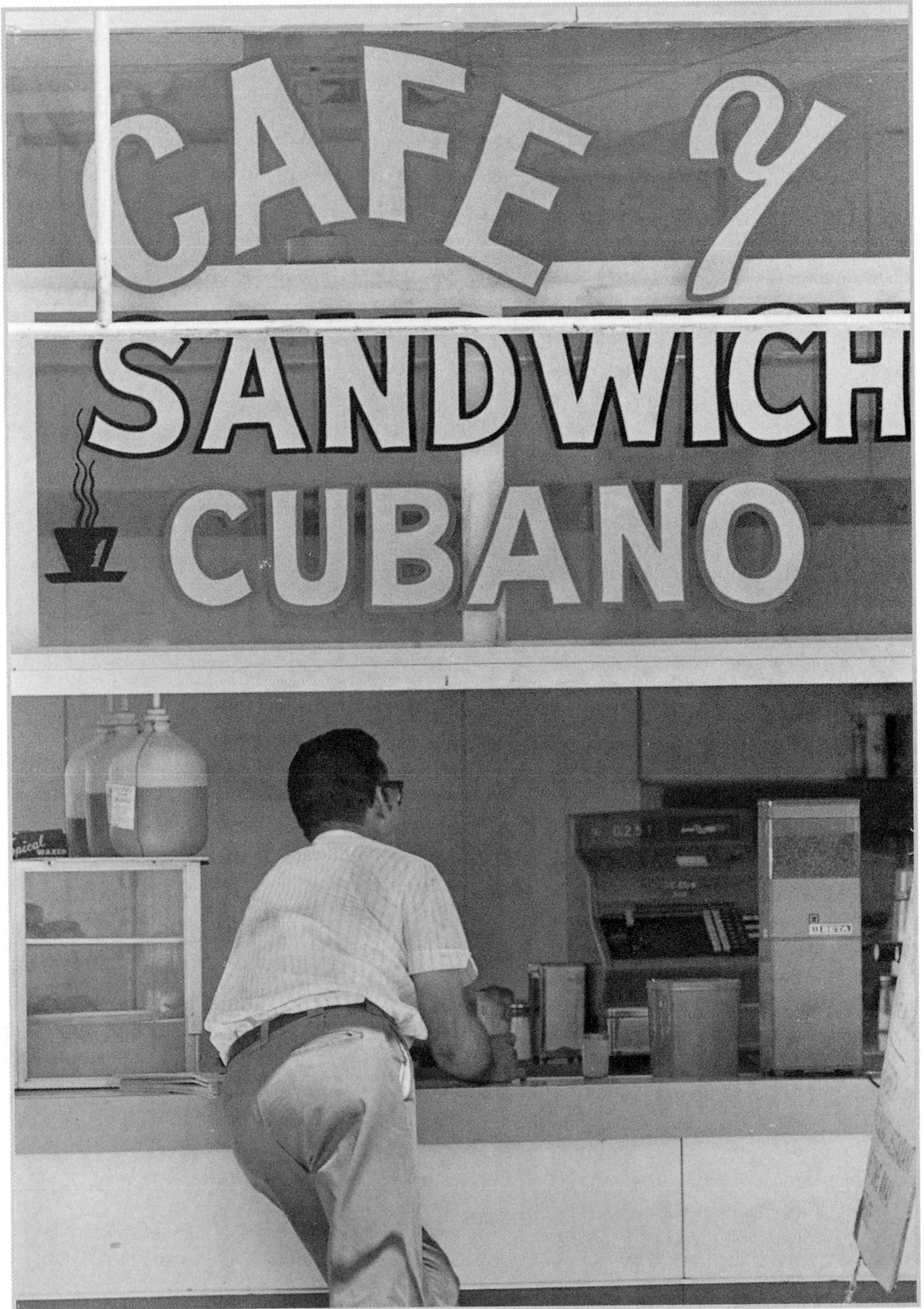

AP/Wide World Photos, Inc.

ing this unhappy problem. A language is much more than a way to communicate. By one's own language—and on this Edward Sapir wrote much and well—one masters reality, one takes to oneself and understands all that exists. All: history, interpersonal relations, the most intimate and definitive emotions. For example, anybody who learns to love in one language will never be able spontaneously to translate his expressions of affection into a language acquired later.

We quarrel, are jealous, love, and hate with certain words, with certain tones, with certain inflections of the voice learned in childhood and adapted to a given set of gestures that also cannot be transported into another language. And this matching of word and message comes solely in the mother tongue. "Language," said the Spanish writer Miguel Unamuno, "is the blood of the spirit." He was right. We cannot do without our own tongue without brutally mutilating our individual consciousness, without being left without blood.

If this is so, is it reasonable to ask millions of human beings to do without this fundamental part of their lives solely so that others are not inconvenienced, or in order to comply with a few debatable rules of urbanity? Is it not more sensible and less painful to explain to monolingual Americans that to live in places where various living tongues converge can have a certain enriching enchantment, because diversity is also an expression of cultural riches?

But, what is more, American society spends thousands of millions of dollars every year in attempting unavailingly to get high school and college students to learn Spanish, because it is assumed that mastery of a second language benefits the country. If this is the rationale, then why ask the bilingual citizens present in the nation to abandon their use of that other language so covetously sought in educational establishments?

Fear of Spanish and the desire that only English be spoken in the United States do not stand up to a calm analysis of reality. The United States is and will continue to be a fundamentally English-speaking nation, but it is a fortunate fact for the country that there are other languages and other marginal cultures capable of enriching the powerful current of the mainstream. This can be perfectly understood by any American, even a monolingual one, if he is capable of savoring a Mexican taco while listening to the Miami Sound Machine's *Conga* or reading a wonderful story by Isaac Bashevis Singer written in Yiddish—very near the spot where we were berated by the irate old lady in baseball cap and sneakers. ❖

INSIGHT

Refugee Ship

Lorna Dee Cervantes

Like wet cornstarch, I slide
past my grandmother's eyes. Bible
at her side, she removes her glasses.
The pudding thickens.

Mama raised me without language.
I'm orphaned from my Spanish name.
The words are foreign, stumbling
on my tongue. I see in the mirror
my reflection: bronzed skin, black hair.

I feel I am a captive
aboard the refugee ship.
The ship that will never dock.
El barco que nunca atraca.[1]

1. ***El barco que nunca atraca*** (ĕl bär′kô kĕ no͞on′kä ä-trä-kä′): This is a translation, in Spanish, of the previous line.

WORDS TO KNOW

urbanity (ûr-băn′ĭ-tē) *n.* courtesy, refinement, or politeness

RESPONDING OPTIONS

FROM PERSONAL RESPONSE *TO* CRITICAL ANALYSIS

REFLECT 1. Which passage in Montaner's essay was most meaningful or provocative to you?

RETHINK 2. How would you summarize Montaner's position on the issue of official English?

RELATE 3. In your view, what do Montaner and Hayakawa agree about, and what do they disagree about?

Consider
- their comments on education
- their comments on American society

4. Ultimately, who is more convincing to you—Montaner or Hayakawa? Why?

5. In your own words, explain the speaker's dilemma in the Insight poem "Refugee Ship." Do you think this speaker would be more likely to agree with Montaner's ideas or Hayakawa's? Support your answer.

6. Go back to the Personal Connection chart (page 1060) you made to organize your thoughts about making English an official language. After reading Montaner's essay, Hayakawa's speech, and Cervantes's poem, has your thinking changed about this issue? Elaborate.

ANOTHER PATHWAY

Cooperative Learning

In a small group, prepare for a class debate about whether English should be made the official language of the United States. Weigh the arguments presented by Hayakawa and Montaner, and add your own ideas. After the debate, decide which side gave the most persuasive arguments and analyze why.

LITERARY CONCEPTS

Persuasion is a type of discourse in which a speaker or a writer tries to convince an audience to adopt an opinion, perform an action, or both. Effective persuasion appeals to both the emotions and the intellect of the reader or listener. Once the audience's emotions, as well as its intellect, are engaged, the writer or speaker has a much better chance of gaining influence. The use of **loaded language,** or strong words and phrases such as *oneness* and *politically ambitious,* can evoke positive and negative emotional reactions in an audience.

In these selections, Hayakawa and Montaner use persuasion to convince readers to accept their points of view about monolingualism and bilingualism. Working with a partner, identify appeals to reason and appeals to emotion in both arguments. Evaluate how these appeals affect the persuasiveness of the works.

QUICKWRITES

1. Draft a **letter** to either Hayakawa, Montaner, or Cervantes asking him or her to clarify his or her ideas. You might, for example, ask Montaner to respond to points that Hayakawa raises or ask Hayakawa to tell where he found the facts he cites in his essay.
2. Should a constitutional amendment be passed making English the official language of the United States? Write an **editorial** to express your opinion and submit it to your school or local newspaper.

PORTFOLIO *Save your writing. You may want to use it later as a springboard to a piece for your portfolio.*

WORDS TO KNOW

Review the Words to Know in the boxes at the bottom of the selection pages. Then write the vocabulary word that best completes each sentence.

1. Rudeness may be common in city life, but that does not make it an example of _____.
2. Good manners demand that we not _____ perfect strangers and bluntly tell them how to behave.
3. Just because certain fears are _____, arising from our early ancestors, does not mean we should act upon these fears.
4. Hayakawa and Montaner would probably agree on the value of diversity in the _____ of our society.
5. However, they could undoubtedly discuss—without resorting to rudeness—even those points on which they disagree, such as whether bilingual education is a _____ or a disservice.

S. I. HAYAKAWA

1906–1992

Born in Vancouver, Canada, Samuel Ichiye Hayakawa was the son of Japanese immigrants. He became a citizen of the United States and earned his Ph.D. in American literature in 1935 from the University of Wisconsin. A noted linguistic scholar, Hayakawa taught college English for more than 30 years. During the late 1960s, he served as president of what was then San Francisco State College.When student riots closed the school, Hayakawa met some demands, rejected others, and reopened the school.

He resigned as president of San Francisco State in 1973 and won election to the U.S. Senate in 1976. While in Washington, he served on several important committees, such as the Senate Foreign Relations Committee, and he proposed a constitutional amendment making English the official national language.

After retiring from the Senate, Hayakawa kept campaigning for official English. His goal, according to Tim W. Ferguson, "was to share its [the English language's] power and beauty more widely, not to exclude." Although English had not been declared the nation's official language by the time of Hayakawa's death in 1992, he was instrumental in bringing this issue into the national spotlight.

OTHER WORKS *Language in Thought and Action*

CARLOS ALBERTO MONTANER

Born in 1943 in Havana, Cuba, Carlos Alberto Montaner was a teenager when Fidel Castro's revolution overthrew the Cuban government in 1959. Arrested in 1960 for protesting Castro's policies, Montaner was sentenced to 20 years in prison. He escaped in 1961 and fled to the United States.

For the next five years Montaner held a variety of jobs and studied Spanish at the University of Miami. Upon graduation he taught Hispanic literature and studied for his doctorate degree. In 1970 he moved to Madrid, Spain, and established a publishing house.

Montaner writes a weekly column called *A quemarropa* (Spanish for "At close range") that appears in newspapers in most of the Spanish-speaking nations of the world. His essays deal with a broad range of subjects, but much of his writing focuses on Cuba and the Castro regime, on human rights concerns, and on Latin American economic development. While criticizing some policies of the United States, Montaner argues that an important reason for the United States position of world leadership is its creative, adaptable people. "These guys—for heaven's sake!—have been creating the world for the last two hundred years." Montaner has become a moderate leader among Cuban exiles.

OTHER WORKS *Secret Report on the Cuban Revolution, 200 Years of Gringos*

LASERLINKS
• *CULTURAL CONNECTION*

Waiting FOR Her Train

AUDREY M. LEE

Christmas at Grand Central Station (1986), David Beynon Pena. Oil on canvas, 25″ × 30″, collection of L. I. Fox. Copyright © David Beynon Pena.

She sits in Thirtieth Street Station watching the newsman over the three-screen television. She is waiting for her train to come in. The station vibrates with arrival and departure of trains. Hers does not arrive. But she has time. Other people are waiting, too. Expectant. Anxious. They have schedules to meet. Destinations. They have purchased tickets—round trip or one-way. She has not purchased her ticket yet. A ticket represents a destination. She has not decided upon her destination. But who is to know . . .

She recognizes the old woman wearing two dresses and two sweaters and carrying the shopping bag full of her possessions. She will not be as obvious as the old lady. There will never be a vagrant[1] look about her. She has locked her possessions in one of the station lockers. Her presence in the station is temporary—just until her train comes in. And for all anyone knows, her baggage is being shipped ahead of her. She is waiting for her train no matter *what* anyone might think.

The railroad workers for the day shift are coming into the station. They are looking at her as usual. They think they know but they don't. Those tolerant looks that express knowing—as if she were a distant relative in their house. A poor distant relative who has had a bad stroke of luck. What of it? She has had a taste of the finer things. She has been to the Art Museum, stood among the Picassos and the Powells—and oh too many paintings to be mentioned. The fact remains that she has been. She knows something about fashion, too. About designing. About labels—labels tell so much about quality. And they lend respectability to clothing. She has no proof that she knows, except the dress she is wearing. Her creditors have reclaimed all the others, along with the shoes. They were right, of course. But they couldn't deny she had discriminating taste.[2]

1. **vagrant** (vā′grənt): like that of a person with no fixed address.
2. **discriminating taste:** a preference for things of higher quality.

Illustration Copyright © Max Ginsburg.

in quiet elegance, the labels of the day's fashion turned in, reassuring against her skin, the quality turned out for everyone to see. That would teach the know-alls. The railroad workers who passed her bench, throwing their tolerant glances. That would prove that she had been waiting for her train after all. That she was going somewhere.

Horn and Hardart opens. She gets up from the bench, brushes the wrinkles that resist her pressure. When she bought the dress it was wrinkle-resistant. She puts on her soiled gloves and respectable walk, feeling the kinks loosen in her knees, giving them a jerk or two when no one is looking. She picks up a newspaper from a bench. Someone is always leaving a newspaper. Then she checks the return coin slots of the telephones. No forgotten dimes. She will not have coffee this morning.

Inside Horn and Hardart, she is reading the specials posted on the menu. Later on breakfast will cost more. She is giving the menu a respectable glance, demonstrating her discriminating taste with proper deliberation. Then with the same deliberating eye, she looks at the long line of people waiting to take advantage of the early morning special breakfasts. A glass of water will do until the line is shorter. That is her reasoning. She tugs decisively at her glove and fills her glass with cool water from the fountain and sits down to a table near the window to read the newspaper. But first she will make the table ready for breakfast. She lays knife, fork and spoon, the napkin. There.

The newspaper. She will choose a supermarket to visit from those advertised. She wonders how

But that is behind her. She must look to the future.

At eight o'clock the Horn and Hardart Restaurant will open. She will go there as usual. And afterwards—well, she would see.

"North Philadelphia. Trenton. Princeton. Newark. New York. Now loading on platform number three."

Not her train. She is waiting for something more exotic. A tropic island with palm trees. There are so many people going places. And so many people returning. She likes this time of morning. Her train would come in the morning. It would pull into the station on velvet springs. And it would purr, not screech. Her man would be waiting with her bags. And she would be clothed many different supermarkets she has shopped in over the past.

Nine o'clock. She is entering the supermarket. She fills her cart with steaks, chops, parsley, fruit. She will eat an orange while she shops. Cheese—she would taste a piece of cheese, too. Not the same brand she had yesterday at the other market. This cheese is sharper. Raisin bread. She will eat a slice or two.

She opens a jar of herring. Herring for breakfast—oh well, one eats what one finds convenient. Besides, fish is a necessary part of the diet, too. The manager is smiling and handing her glove to her.

"Looks like you're having your breakfast . . ."

Kidding her, of course. People are always chewing on something when they go to market. "Yes. You have good herring." The compliment pleases him. "Very good herring," she is saying for emphasis. He is smiling and walking away.

Then she checks the return coin slots of the telephones.

Bananas—bananas are filling. She needs something that will fill her. Meanwhile, she must appear in earnest. She must fill her cart with household articles. A mop handle and mop. That would look impressive jutting from the cart. There—now another bite of banana. Paper napkins from the shelf. Table salt. Black pepper. Paprika . . .

She swallows the last of the banana. Then she puts on her gloves, pushes the cartful of groceries to the front of the store, places it in a respectful position just to one side of the check-out counter, out of the path of shoppers waiting in line for the cashier. And in a respectable voice:

"Cashier—I forgot my purse—I wonder if you would be kind enough to let my cart stay here until I return . . ."

"Certainly, madam."

"I appreciate it. Thanks so much." She burps. Bananas take a while to digest. But she has time.

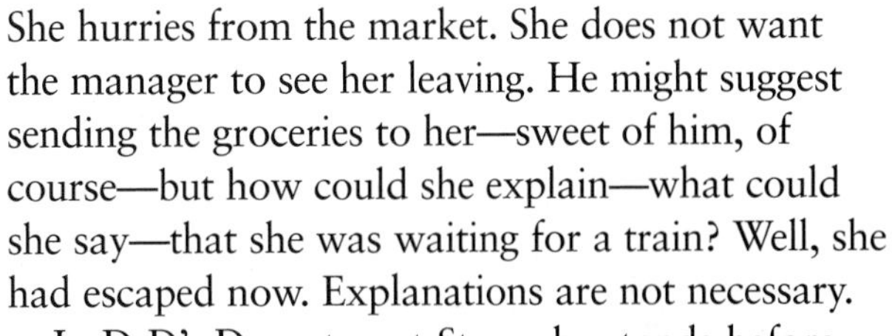

She hurries from the market. She does not want the manager to see her leaving. He might suggest sending the groceries to her—sweet of him, of course—but how could she explain—what could she say—that she was waiting for a train? Well, she had escaped now. Explanations are not necessary.

In D-D's Department Store she stands before the cosmetics counter, trying on a sample lipstick. She doesn't like it well enough to buy it. She tries the expensive face powder which the saleslady mixes for her. A spoonful of white powder. A spoonful of pinkish powder, mint-colored powder. Then blending them with a spatula.

"You look absolutely gorgeous—this is wonderful and it's good for your skin. Put this on and wipe it dry—work that in—truly pink would be equal to your natural—"

"I was looking for something quick and easy. I don't have time to do much in the morning . . ."

"Try this," dipping the spoon into the powder. Wiping the spoon and dipping it into another powder. "This has orange in it. You have to use it sparingly—you need some color—it's a sample portion. Try it out at home—try them both—and see how you like them."

"Thank you very much. Maybe I can come back tomorrow—if I decide I like the way it looks on me. These lights—if I were only at home . . ."

"You'll like it."

One mirror is seldom true. One has to consider the majority of mirrors. She smiles at the woman. Then she walks toward the perfumes. Aura of Emotion—Charles of the Ritz—Desert Flower—Desert Flower is too incongruous[3] a name to be considered by a bench sitter. Still she must try something new. Yesterday it was Heaven Scent. Today—well—it would depend—Chantilly—she felt like

3. **incongruous:** not fitting, suitable, or in agreement; incompatible.

Illustration Copyright © John Collier.

Chantilly—but first . . . She looked at the bottles of perfume and toilet water, picked them up, read their labels. She is a discriminating shopper. All the bottles scrutinized. She picks up the spray bottle of Chantilly. Poof—savors the scent with a sensitive and discriminating nose. That is what she wants. She sprays her ears, wrists, clothing. All very quickly and tastefully. Subtly. She wants to be sure of catching the scent.

"It smells good. May I show you something, madam? We have the talcum, too. It will make a nice set . . ."

She is very discriminating, so she will not answer right away. She has not made up her mind—not really—Chanel No. 5. Intimate.

"Excuse me a minute, madam. I'll wait on this customer—I know you want to take your time—when you decide . . ."

Poof. Chantilly behind her ears once more. Subtly. Discriminatingly. The saleslady is busy. Several customers are waiting. She pulls her gloves securely over her hands, resumes her respectable posture and walks out of the store. The scent does indeed smell good on. Now she will return to the station and wash her gloves. She will lay them on the bench to dry. If only she had a portable hair dryer, she could wash her hair. But portable hair dryers are made for people of means—not for people of predicament.

Back at the station powder room. She washes her gloves, touches her hair, and checks her makeup. The powder goes well with her complexion. And so does the lipstick. She checks her purse, making certain she still has the samples in her purse, touches her hair again, approves. Still she would like to get her hair washed and styled. She will think of a way. But having the new makeup and the perfume makes her feel somewhat refreshed. She will settle down on a bench to watch the pictures, plan the dinner menu, decide upon the evening's entertainment.

And of course, she will watch the evening flow of men and women in and out of the station. But before that, she will check the coin return slots of the telephones. Nothing yet. She will have to wait for her coffee a little longer. The best time to check the slots is just after the rush hour. She might even be able to afford two cups of coffee. And who is there to deny that her train might have arrived by then. ❖

Audrey M. Lee

Like the homeless main character in her story "Waiting for Her Train," Audrey M. Lee has faced difficult circumstances. She has lived alone for most of her life and struggled to support herself by working various jobs: "I have no career. . . . My effort through the years is and has been to survive, with as much dignity as possible." A native of Philadelphia, Lee has worked as a nurse's aide, a clerk and secretary at a publishing company, and a writer.

In creating "Waiting for Her Train," Lee applied scenes she had observed of down-and-out people in train stations and grocery stores to her own experience with financial difficulty and loneliness. The story, which appears in the anthology *What We Must See: Young Black Storytellers* (1971), reflects her deep concern "that there exists an economic and spiritual poverty amid a vast material wealth . . . no human has the right to deny, limit, control the fulfillment of another human because of his race or other origins contrary to his own. Life is too precious and too short to be so denied."

Lee claims she never decided to be a writer, but naturally fell into it due to her "aloneness and a concern for social issues." She is motivated to write by an interest in how people relate to one another. The recipient of a Mary Roberts Rinehart Foundation grant to write short stories, Lee has also written novels and poetry.

OTHER WORKS *The Clarion People, The Workers*

WRITING ABOUT
LITERATURE

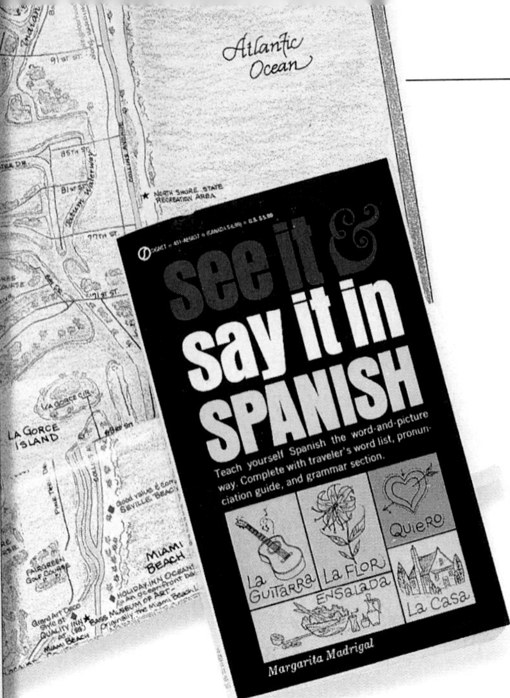

A Natural Reaction

Why do you remember Montaner's essay or Hayakawa's speech? Is it because of their powerful ideas or their use of memorable examples? Essayists, poets, playwrights, and songwriters all know it's the careful use of details that makes ideas unforgettable. On the following pages you will

- see how authors elaborate on their main ideas
- react to the ideas in one of the selections in this unit
- learn how to evaluate the information you receive

The Writer's Style: Elaboration Writers use a variety of details—incidents, quotations, examples, anecdotes, facts, and statistics—to provide convincing, vivid support for their main ideas.

Read the Literature

Notice how the authors of these excerpts use elaboration.

Literature Models

Elaborate with an Incident
Why did Montaner use this incident? How does it support his main idea?

I was walking quietly with my wife on a sidewalk in Miami Beach. We were speaking Spanish, of course, because that is our language. Suddenly, we were accosted by a spry little old lady, wearing a baseball cap and sneakers, who told us: "Talk English. You are in the United States."

Carlos Alberto Montaner, from "Why Fear Spanish?"

Elaborate with a Quotation
How does the quotation back up Hayakawa's initial statement?

But while language is a necessary cause for our oneness as a society, it is not a sufficient cause. A foreigner cannot, by speaking faultless English, become an Englishman. Paul Theroux, a contemporary novelist and travel writer, has commented on this fact: "Foreigners are always aliens in England. No one becomes English. It's a very tribal society. . . . No one becomes Japanese. . . . No one becomes Nigerian. But Nigerians, Japanese, and English become Americans."

S. I. Hayakawa, from "The Case for Official English"

Connect to Life

Newspaper and magazine reporters know the importance of elaboration. They use this technique to make a situation real and relevant to their readers. Notice how the writer of the excerpt below uses facts and statistics.

Newspaper Editorial

The low-income housing tax credit goes to investors, generally corporations, that provide money to non-profit groups for construction or rehabilitation of low-income housing. It helps build 100,000 units of low-income housing a year, or more than 90 percent of all such housing built in the nation.

It is just about the only thing Congress does for urban ghettos, and now Congress wants to change the housing credit's status from permanent to "temporary," a tactic which would probably kill the credit after 1997.

from "Taking aim at the poor"
The Blade, Toledo, Ohio

Elaborate with Facts and Statistics
What is this writer trying to say? Would the editorial be as effective without the statistics?

Try Your Hand: Elaboration

1. **Details, Details** Elaborate on the following statements, using a quotation, statistic, or example.
   - The cafeteria food can stand improvement.
   - Divorce is hard on children.
   - Homelessness is a growing problem.
2. **Problems, Problems** Tell a partner about a problem in your school or neighborhood. Then work together to write a paragraph explaining that problem—using an anecdote, an example, a comparison, or an analogy to make your point.
3. **Elaborate, Elaborate** Look through your notebook and find a paragraph that could benefit from elaboration. Add vivid details to make your entry more memorable.

SkillBuilder

WRITER'S CRAFT

Adding Supporting Details
While the main idea in a piece of writing is very important, it's the details that bring the idea to life and help your readers visualize a problem.

Hayakawa uses legislative details, anecdotes about his family, quotations from experts, and statistics to illustrate the points he is making. Montaner also uses anecdotes and quotations from experts. Notice how Montaner uses a real-life example to help his audience understand and relate to his idea that other languages enrich our culture.

This can be perfectly understood by any American, even a monolingual one, if he is capable of savoring a Mexican taco while listening to the Miami Sound Machine's Conga *or reading a wonderful story by Isaac Bashevis Singer written in Yiddish.*

APPLYING WHAT YOU'VE LEARNED
Go through a local newspaper and highlight and label the types of supporting details used. Which are most common? Which do you think are most effective?

WRITING HANDBOOK

For more information on supporting details, see page 1172 of the Writing Handbook.

Personal Response

How do you feel about divorce? homelessness? bilingual education? The selections in Unit Eight, "Issues for Our Time" present some of the important issues for this decade. It's only natural for you to feel strongly about some and neutral about others. This is your opportunity to take issue with an idea.

GUIDED ASSIGNMENT

Write a Personal Response Your assignment is to respond in some personal way to the literature—reacting to an idea in one of the selections.

tomar, to take
¿va a tomar? are you going to take?
voy a tomar, I'm going to take

¿Va a tomar un taxi?
Sí, voy a tomar un taxi.

¿Va a tomar un tren?
Sí, voy a tomar un tren.

¿Va a tomar un autobús?
Sí, voy a tomar un autobús.

¿Va a tomar un avión?
Sí, voy a tomar un avión.

Vamos a tomar, *we are going to take*
Van a tomar, *they are going to take*

40

Remember that in Spanish you do not say "I'm going to have soup." You say instead, "I'm going to take soup." **(Voy a tomar sopa.)**

¿va a tomar? are you going to take?
pollo, chicken

una ensalada, a salad
chocolate, chocolate (drink)

¿Va a tomar una ensalada?
Sí, voy a tomar una ensalada.

¿Va a tomar café?
Sí, voy a tomar café.

¿Va a tomar sopa?
Sí, voy a tomar sopa.

¿Va a tomar apio?
Sí, voy a tomar apio.

¿Va a tomar pollo?
Sí, voy a tomar pollo.

¿Va a tomar chocolate?
Sí, voy a tomar chocolate.

41

1 Prewrite and Explore

Select an essay, a story, or a poem from this unit that has ideas you feel passionately about or react strongly to.

STATE YOUR POSITION

Read through the selection again. Write down any ideas that you agree with or take issue with. Choose the idea you feel most strongly about. What is your reaction to the idea? State your position on it in one sentence.

CHOOSE A WRITING MODE

What's the best way to respond to this idea? With an article in the local paper? a satirical song? a letter to the author? an essay? a poem? Decide which mode is most appropriate for your response.

LIST YOUR REASONS

List reasons to support your position. You might find reasons in the selection, from your own experience, or from something you've read. Try typing and organizing your notes directly on the computer, as in the example below. Computers make it easy to add, delete, and reorganize ideas.

Student's Prewriting Notes

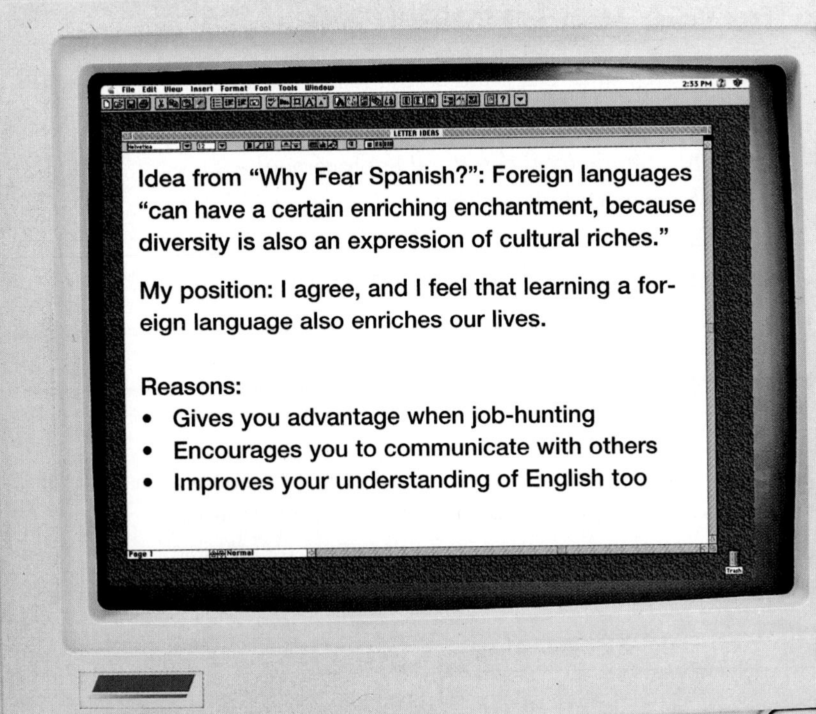

SPANISH
LETTER IDEAS
Idea from "Why Fear Spanish?": Foreign languages "can have a certain enriching enchantment, because diversity is also an expression of cultural riches."
My position: I agree, and I feel that learning a foreign language also enriches our lives.
Reasons:
• Gives you advantage when job-hunting
• Encourages you to communicate with others
• Improves your understanding of English too

2 Write a Draft

Try to get your ideas down as quickly as possible. Don't worry about how they're organized or whether they flow logically. You can always refine your writing later. For now, focus on expressing your personal reactions to one of the author's ideas.

Student's Rough Draft

I have to admit, I'm not crazy about taking foreign languages. Some of those words are so hard to pronounce. And those verbs—who knew that there were so many tenses that needed to be conjugated! I never can remember whether a noun is masculine, feminine, or neuter either.

But I also realize how important it is to know a second language. My dad is always lecturing me on how knowing a foreign language can make the difference between getting hired for a job or being out on the street. He ought to know: he's been passed over for a promotion to foreman more than once, because he doesn't speak Spanish.

Add the example about beauty pageant winners.

3 Draft and Share

Now that you have your ideas out, it's time to refine them. Add elaborative details to make your response more relevant to your reader. Also, see the SkillBuilder at the right for tips on ordering your reasons. Once you've finished your draft, share it with someone else. Get that person's reaction to your personal response.

- Can you restate my position on this issue?
- What is your reaction to my response?
- What details should I add to support my position?

SkillBuilder

Ordering by Importance

When you write your response, it's often difficult to know what to put first—especially if you have several reasons that support your reaction. When deciding which reason to list first, try one of these approaches:

- Start with the most important and end with the least important. Reporters often use this approach, called an inverted pyramid. They want to grab their readers' attention by covering the most important information first.
- Build up from the least important to the most important. Letters, speeches, and pamphlets often use this approach. By saving the most important for last, they build momentum.

Regardless of which order you try, consider using the following as your outline:

Position Statement
- Reason 1
  - evidence
  - evidence
- Reason 2
  - evidence
  - evidence
- Reason 3
  - evidence
  - evidence

APPLYING WHAT YOU'VE LEARNED
As you write your personal response, decide which order of importance is most appropriate, given your writing mode.

4 Revise, Edit, and Send

As you revise your draft, keep your reviewer's suggestions in mind. Review Grammar in Context on the opposite page before you begin editing. How can you use what you've learned in this lesson to respond to ideas in other situations?

Student's Final Response

From Where I Sit
by Andy Grimm

Why Fear Spanish . . . or any other language, for that matter?

For most of us, Spanish, German, and French are subjects to be avoided, endured, or feared. Those unpronounceable words, those impossible-to-conjugate verbs! And who can remember if the word for *pencil* is masculine, feminine, or neuter?

Yet foreign languages should not be feared, but enjoyed. For, as Carlos Alberto Montaner has argued, language adds a richness to our culture, a depth to our lives. On a more personal level, it can also add money to your pocket.

Let's say you're applying for a job—you and 60 other high school students. They all are as smart as you; they've had the same jobs as you. But you're the only one who can speak Spanish/French/German (fill in the blank). Now, who is going to be hired?

What idea is this writer reacting to?

What evidence does this writer supply to support his reasons?

Standards for Evaluation

A personal response
- presents your own reactions to a selection
- uses an appropriate format
- maintains a clear, consistent point of view
- elaborates on your main idea with specific details and examples

Grammar in Context

Active and Passive Voice of Verbs A verb is in the active voice if the subject *performs* the action. If the subject *receives* the action, the verb is in the passive voice. Passive voice uses a form of the verb *be*, plus a past participle. When writing your response, try to use verbs in active voice whenever possible.

Passive voice: A foreign language is taken by only 35 percent of the students in this high school. Rarely is a language taken for four years.

Active voice: Only 35 percent of the students in this high school take a foreign language. Students rarely take a language for four years.

Notice how replacing passive voice with active voice makes the sentence more forceful and less wordy. If your computer has a grammar-check program, use it. Normally such a program will point out sentences that use passive voice.

Try Your Hand: Using Active Voice

On a separate sheet of paper, change the following sentences from passive voice to active voice. You may have to turn the sentence around or add a new subject.

1. Spanish was taken by only 53 students this year.
2. Due to lack of interest, German was dropped from the curriculum last year.
3. Fourth-year Spanish was taken by only three students last semester.
4. A seminar on the foreign-language program is planned by Mr. Rocca for this Friday.
5. Spanish, French, and Russian are offered by the high school.

SkillBuilder

GRAMMAR FROM WRITING

Positioning Adverbs

Where you place an adverb can affect the meaning of a sentence. If you're using passive voice or verb phrases, avoid placing the adverb between the auxiliary and main verb. Notice where Montaner positions his adverb:

I was walking quietly with my wife on a sidewalk in Miami Beach.

Take extra care when using the adverb *only*. If misplaced, it can change the meaning of the sentence. For example, compare these two sentences:

They speak only Spanish at home.
They speak Spanish only at home.

The first sentence implies that Spanish is the only language spoken at home. The second sentence implies that home is the only place where they speak Spanish. As a rule, place *only* just before the word it modifies.

APPLYING WHAT YOU'VE LEARNED

As you write your personal response, experiment with the placement of adverbs. Notice how the position of adverbs affects the meaning of a sentence. Reposition the adverb until you have the meaning you want.

IN MY OPINION . . .

Have you ever been part of an opinion poll? Pollsters are always interested in your reactions to political candidates, new products, television programs, advertising campaigns, and controversial issues.

View Look at the two graphs. In the newsletter, which park district program did most individuals want to cut? On the television news, which program did most individuals want to cut?

Interpret Why was there a difference in figures? Who conducted the surveys? Was there a difference in how the question was asked? Was there a difference in whom was asked? Which program did teenagers want to cut? How about adults?

Discuss Compare notes with other students. Discuss the poll results. What should you keep in mind when reading survey and poll results? Is it possible for pollsters to slant the results, using valid statistics? The SkillBuilder at the right can give you more practice questioning the information you receive.

Teen Talk

the Riverdale Community Youth Center newsletter

Your Opinion: Which Park District Programs Should Be Cut?

Program	Percent
Senior Citizen Center	48%
Day Care Center	30%
Adult Education	12%
Swimming Pool	9%
Youth Center	1%

Last Friday, the Riverdale Town Council voted to cut the park district budget by $200,000. After four hours of discussion, the council was still in deadlock over which program to cut. The council members decided to turn the decision over to the voters. A special commission will survey all registered voters to determine which park district programs to eliminate.

Since none of our Youth Center members are old enough to vote, we decided to conduct our own survey. At Saturday's '50s sock hop, everyone who attended was asked to select one park district pro-gram to cut. Over 150 teens were surveyed.

An overwhelming percentage opted to take the budget cuts out of the Riverdale Senior Citizen Center. The Day Care Center was also targeted

continued page 4

The Youth Center is the only safe place we have to hang out!
—Charmaine

Midnight basketball keeps us off the streets and out of trouble.
—Amb

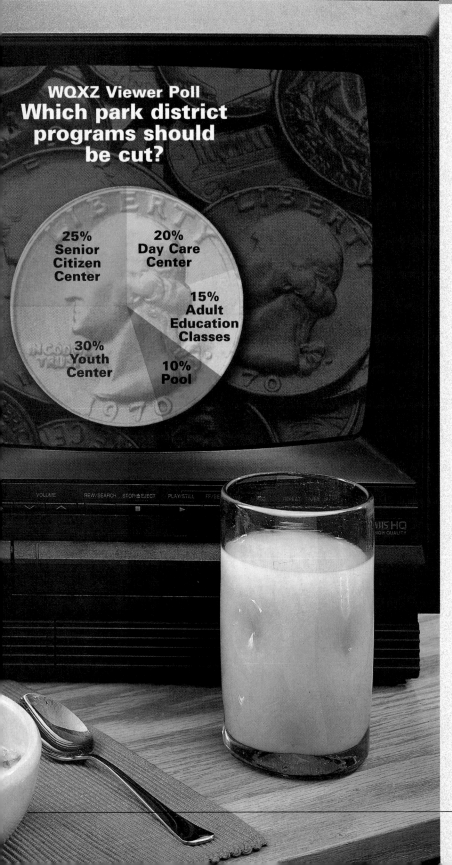

SkillBuilder

 CRITICAL THINKING

Questioning Information
The results of surveys seem pretty straightforward. But pollsters know how to interpret data in several different ways. That's why polls conducted by different groups often reach different conclusions. When you look at survey results, ask yourself questions like these:

- Who prepared the survey? Was it an independent group or a group with an agenda?
- Who was polled? Does the sampling reflect a cross section of all the people involved?
- How large was the sample? Was it large enough to represent opinions accurately?
- Were the questions worded so as to elicit a particular kind of response?

APPLYING WHAT YOU'VE LEARNED
Working in a small group, look at each of the following survey results. What do you need to question?

- Seven out out of ten Americans support laws restricting their freedom of speech.
- Fifty-three percent feel the legal driving age should be raised to 21.
- Two out of every three people surveyed feel the legal voting age should be lowered to 16.
- Ninety-two percent feel the welfare program should be eliminated.

PART 2 INTRODUCTION

Future Directions

Which Way Is Tomorrow?

Picture yourself 30 years in the future, as the parent or relative of a high school student. Predict what the United States will be like as this young person comes of age. What would you hope for him or her? What would you fear? What exciting developments can you forecast?

Contemporary literature reveals much about our hopes and fears for the 21st century. The selections in this part of Unit Eight address questions that perplex Americans now and that will undoubtedly preoccupy the next generation.

What impact will technology have on society? For years we have been hearing dire warnings about how television, computers, and other technologies will affect society as their use widens. For example, among the many accusations against

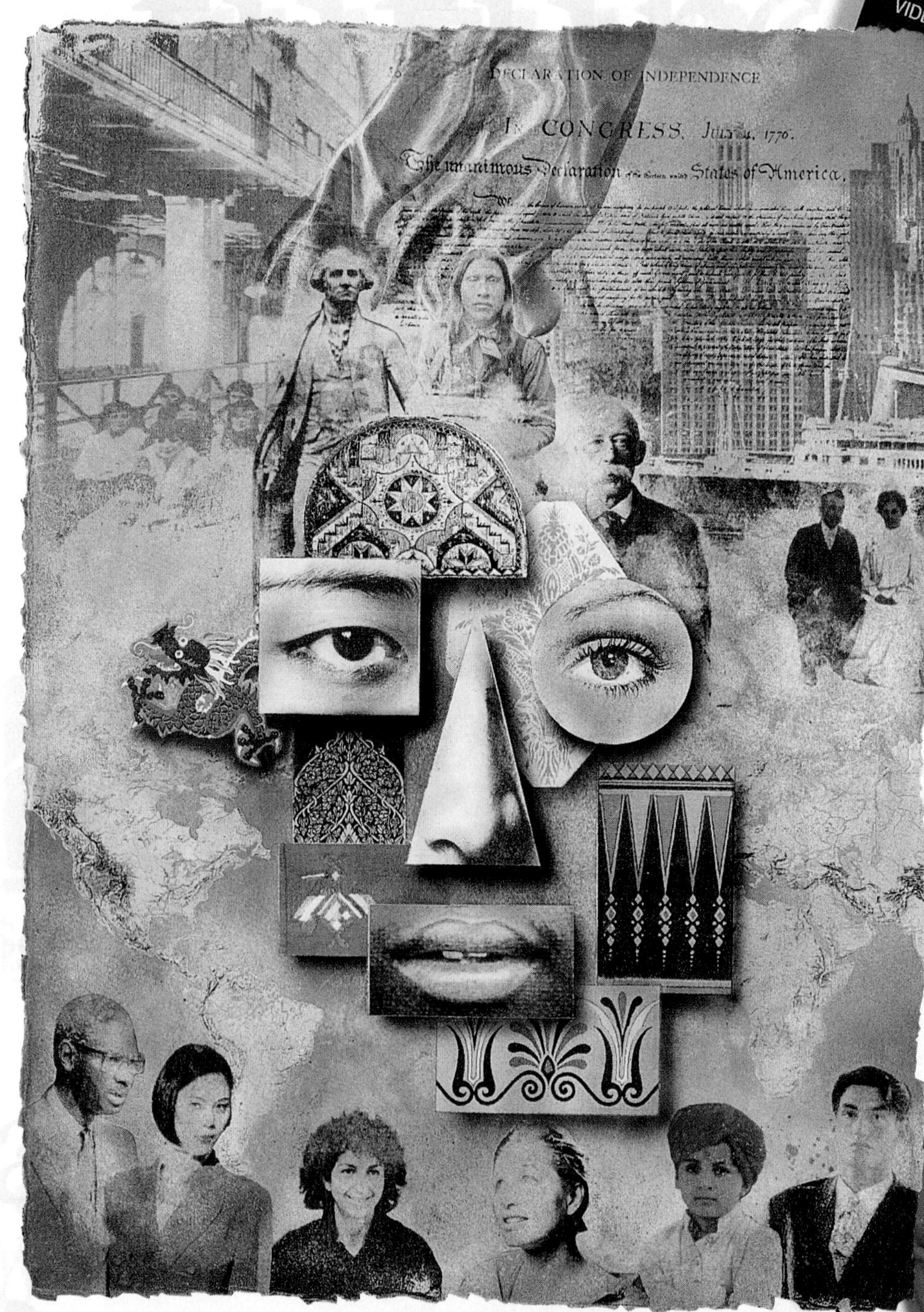

television are that it eats away at our imagination, our analytical ability, and the opportunity for face-to-face conversation. It is said to turn viewers into passive consumers who have unrealistic expectations for their lives. Another frequent claim is that it desensitizes people by exposing them to countless acts of violence. It deforms the political process, many argue, with its instant opinion polls, costly political advertisements, and oversimplification of issues via sound bites.

Of course, television has its defenders, too, as do computers, nuclear technologies, biotechnologies, and other technologies under attack, but antitechnology voices have a long and shrill history, particularly in literature. The main character in Ray Bradbury's science fiction story "The Murderer" smashes his television, his radio, and other machines he encounters daily, believing that they diminish the quality of his life. See if today's world resembles the future world Bradbury predicted in the early 1950s, and judge whether his warning about intrusive technology is worth heeding.

Can we stop the spread of violence? The United States has been called the most violent society in the world. It seems that not a day goes by without reports of sensational crimes—terrorist bombings, gang shoot-outs, mass murders, serial murders, murders of children, murders by children—not to mention the routine beatings, stabbings, and shootings that seem to barely count as news. Periodically, incidents of race-related mass violence occur, such as the 1992 Los Angeles riots following the acquittal of four white police officers charged with beating black motorist Rodney King. In these riots 58 people were killed and about 4,000 were injured.

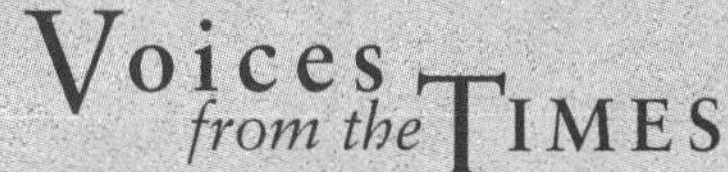

Science Fiction and the Future

Ursula K. Le Guin

We know where the future is. It's in front of us. Right? It lies before us—a great future lies before us—we stride forward confidently into it, every commencement, every election year. And we know where the past is. Behind us, right? So that we have to turn around to see it, and that interrupts our progress ever forward into the future, so we don't really much like to do it.

It seems that the Quechua-speaking peoples of the Andes see all this rather differently. They figure that because the past is what you know, you can see it—it's in front of you, under your nose. This is a mode of perception rather than action, of awareness rather than progress. Since they're quite as logical as we are, they say that the future lies behind—behind your back, over your shoulder. The future is what you *can't* see, unless you turn around and kind of snatch a glimpse. And then sometimes you wish you hadn't, because you've glimpsed what's sneaking up on you from behind. . . . So, as we drag the Andean peoples into our world of progress, pollution, soap operas, and satellites, they are coming backwards—looking over their shoulders to find out where they're going.

I find this an intelligent and appropriate attitude. At least it reminds us that our talk about "going forward into the future" is a metaphor, a piece of mythic thinking taken literally, perhaps even a bluff, based on our macho fear of ever being inactive, receptive, open, quiet, still. Our unquiet clocks make us think that we make time, that we control it. We plug in the timer and make time happen. But in fact the future comes, or is there, whether we rush forward to meet it in supersonic jets with nuclear warheads, or sit on a peak and watch the llamas graze. Morning comes whether you set the alarm or not.

Voices *from the* TIMES

The future is not mere space. This is where I part company with a whole variety of science fiction, the imperialistic kind, as seen in all the Space Wars and Star Wars novels and films and the whole branch of sf that reduces technology to hi-tech. In such fictions, space and the future are synonymous: they are a place we are going to get to, invade, colonize, exploit, and suburbanize.

If we do "get to" space, it's not unlikely that that's how we'll behave there. It is possible that we will "conquer" space. But it is not possible that we will "conquer" the future, because there is no way we can get there. The future is part of the spacetime continuum from which—in the body and in ordinary states of consciousness—we are excluded. We can't even see it. Except for little glimpses over the shoulder.

When we look at what we can't see, what we do see is the stuff inside our heads. Our thoughts and our dreams, the good ones and the bad ones. And it seems to me that when science fiction is really doing its job that's exactly what it's dealing with. Not "the future." It's when we confuse our dreams and ideas with the non-dream world that we're in trouble, when we think the future is a place we own. Then we succumb to wishful thinking and escapism, and our science fiction gets megalomania and thinks that instead of being fiction it's prediction, and the Pentagon and the White House begin to *believe* it, and we get True Believers conquering the future by means of SDI.[1]

As a science-fiction writer I personally prefer to stand still for long periods, like the Quechua, and look at what is, in fact, in front of me: the earth; my fellow beings on it; and the stars.

1. **SDI:** The Strategic Defense Initiative, an antimissile defense system.

Many people fear that such disturbances will recur.

Violence in this country is beginning to be viewed as a monstrous plague; citizens want to know what is causing it, what feeds it, and what can stop it. Writers share the nation's concern. Joyce Carol Oates's story "Hostage" and Garrett Hongo's poem "The Legend" show the ripple effect of sudden, inexplicable acts of violence. Gregory Alan-Williams, a witness to violence during the Los Angeles riots, risked his own life to save a stranger's. His account, excerpted from his book *A Gathering of Heroes,* offers hope to a country that too often sees itself as helpless against violence.

What Is an American? Yes, this question might seem familiar. Crèvecoeur tried to answer it more than 200 years ago, and writers will still be trying to answer it in the 21st century. Americans just won't hold still. Old terms that were used to classify us appear to be losing or changing meaning. For some, *black* and *white* are inadequate designations; there is a movement to create a new "multiracial" category on U.S. census forms for the year 2000. The term *American* itself has expanded in meaning. There is a growing insistence that it apply not only to U.S. citizens but also to those living in all the Americas, particularly in Latin America. With immigration and easy global communication, more and more cultures are being absorbed into U.S. culture, changing the

A family reunion in Austin, Texas

whole in the same way that spices change the flavor of a batter. The Latino influence, for example, is likely to deepen in the future. Latinos are the second-fastest-growing ethnic group in the country, expected to constitute roughly 13 percent of the U.S. population by 2010. Hispanic writers often comment on the nation's unwillingness to see or claim them, an attitude that may be impossible to maintain in the next century. The speaker in "Mexicans Begin Jogging," thoughtlessly assumed to be an illegal alien, is something altogether different and incomprehensible to many: a Mexican American formed in part by baseball and milkshakes. Pat Mora, in "Legal Alien," hints at the pain of being bicultural, considered neither wholly Mexican nor wholly American.

Your question here. The three questions in the previous headings are not the only ones raised by the final selections in this book. As you read these pieces, other questions about the future may leap to mind. Write them down. Talk about them. Tuck them away until you find answers. Who can see tomorrow? No one, but writers have faith that literature, and readers, are part of what will shape it.

PART 2 *Future Directions*

Which Way Is Tomorrow?

PREVIEWING

FICTION

The Murderer

Ray Bradbury

PERSONAL CONNECTION

In this science fiction story, the main character gets fed up with encountering technological conveniences everywhere he goes. Do you sometimes get annoyed at the intrusion of technology into your everyday life? Think about the telephone ringing at dinnertime, with people at the other end of the line selling products or asking for donations. Do you really like hearing Muzak in elevators, a laugh track on a dull TV sitcom, or someone else's portable phone ringing, wristwatch alarm beeping, or radio blaring? What aspects of our omnipresent technology, if any, do you find irritatingly intrusive? Make a list in your notebook. Then discuss your ideas with a small group of classmates.

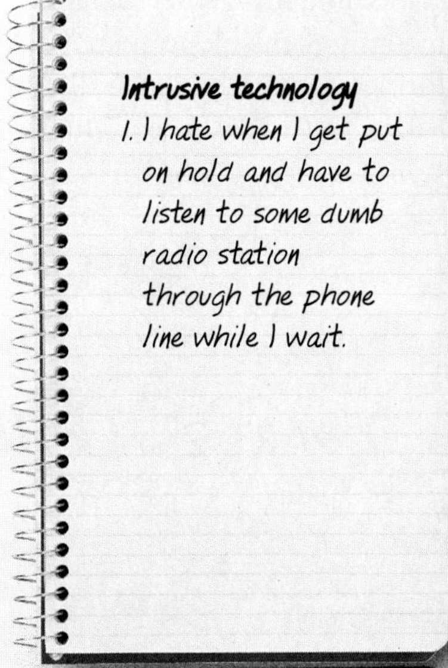

Intrusive technology
1. I hate when I get put on hold and have to listen to some dumb radio station through the phone line while I wait.

LITERARY CONNECTION

Science fiction explores unexpected possibilities of the past or the future, often examining the impact of science and technology on society. Science fiction writers such as Ursula K. Le Guin, Terry Bisson (the author of "They're Made Out of Meat" on page 127), and Ray Bradbury weave together known scientific data and theories as well as imaginary elements to invent stories about what could happen in the future. In the 19th century, inspired by amazing advances in science, writers such as Jules Verne and H. G. Wells began speculating on what the future would bring. Their writings are remarkable today for the accuracy of some of their predictions about the future. Helicopters, space shuttles, and computers, for example, were described in science fiction many years before they were actually developed. As the 20th century brought more technological inventions, the popularity of science fiction increased. Through movies and TV programs such as *Star Trek,* science fiction has continued to attract new audiences.

Illustration for Jules Verne's "A Trip From Earth to the Moon" (1865). Culver Pictures.

WRITING CONNECTION

In your notebook, write about your attitude toward the intrusion of modern technology into your everyday life. Use ideas from the list and the group discussion that you completed for the Personal Connection. Then, as you read "The Murderer," compare your attitude with the attitude of the main character.

Music moved with him in the white halls. He passed an office door: "The Merry Widow Waltz." Another door: *Afternoon of a Faun.* A Third: "Kiss Me Again." He turned into a cross-corridor: "The Sword Dance" buried him in cymbals, drums, pots, pans, knives, forks, thunder, and tin lightning. All washed away as he hurried through an anteroom where a secretary sat nicely stunned by Beethoven's Fifth. He moved himself before her eyes like a hand; she didn't see him.

His wrist radio buzzed.

"Yes?"

"This is Lee, Dad. Don't forget about my allowance."

"Yes, Son, yes. I'm busy."

"Just didn't want you to forget, Dad," said the wrist radio. Tchaikovsky's *Romeo and Juliet* swarmed about the voice and flushed into the long halls.

The psychiatrist moved in the beehive of offices, in the cross-pollination of themes, Stravinsky mating with Bach, Haydn unsuccessfully repulsing Rachmaninoff, Schubert slain by Duke Ellington. He nodded to the humming secretaries and the whistling doctors fresh to their morning work. At his office he checked a few papers with his stenographer, who sang under her breath, then phoned the police captain upstairs. A few minutes later a red light blinked, a voice said from the ceiling:

"Prisoner delivered to Interview Chamber Nine."

He unlocked the chamber door, stepped in, heard the door lock behind him.

"Go away," said the prisoner, smiling.

The psychiatrist was shocked by that smile. A very sunny, pleasant warm thing, a thing that shed bright light upon the room. Dawn among the dark hills. High noon at midnight, that smile. The blue eyes sparkled serenely above that display of self-assured dentistry.

"I'm here to help you," said the psychiatrist, frowning. Something was wrong with the room. He had hesitated the moment he entered. He glanced around. The prisoner laughed. "If you're wondering why it's so quiet in here, I just kicked the radio to death."

Violent, thought the doctor.

The prisoner read this thought, smiled, put out a gentle hand. "No, only to machines that yak-yak-yak."

Bits of the wall radio's tubes and wires lay on the gray carpeting. Ignoring these, feeling that smile upon him like a heat lamp, the psychiatrist sat across from his patient in the unusual silence which was like the gathering of a storm.

"You're Mr. Albert Brock, who calls himself The Murderer?"

Brock nodded pleasantly. "Before we start . . ." He moved quietly and quickly to detach the wrist radio from the doctor's arm. He tucked it in his teeth like a walnut, gritted, heard it crack, handed it back to the appalled psychiatrist as if he had done them both a favor. "That's better."

The psychiatrist stared at the ruined machine. "You're running up quite a damage bill."

"I don't care," smiled the patient. "As the old song goes: 'Don't Care What Happens to Me!' " He hummed it.

The psychiatrist said: "Shall we start?"

"Fine. The first victim, or one of the first, was my telephone. Murder most foul. I shoved it in the kitchen Insinkerator! Stopped the disposal unit in mid-swallow. Poor thing strangled to death. After that I shot the television set!"

The psychiatrist said, "Mmm."

"Fired six shots right through the cathode.[1] Made a beautiful tinkling crash, like a dropped chandelier."

"Nice imagery."

"Thanks, I always dreamt of being a writer."

"Suppose you tell me when you first began to hate the telephone."

"It frightened me as a child. Uncle of mine called it the Ghost Machine. Voices without bodies. Scared the living hell out of me. Later in life I was never comfortable. Seemed to me a phone was an impersonal instrument. If it *felt* like it, it let your personality go through its wires. If it didn't *want* to, it just drained your personality away until what slipped through at the other end was some cold fish of a voice, all steel, copper, plastic, no warmth, no reality. It's easy to say the wrong thing on telephones; the telephone changes your meaning on you. First thing you know, you've made an enemy. Then, of course, the telephone's such a *convenient* thing; it just sits there and *demands* you call someone who doesn't want to be called. Friends were always calling, calling, calling me. Hell, I hadn't any time of my own. When it wasn't the telephone it was the television, the radio, the phonograph. When it wasn't the television or radio or the phonograph it was motion pictures at the corner theater, motion pictures projected, with commercials on low-lying cumulus clouds. It doesn't rain rain any more, it rains soapsuds. When it wasn't High-Fly Cloud advertisements, it was music by Mozzek[2] in every

1. **cathode:** a cathode-ray tube, used in television picture tubes.
2. **Mozzek:** a company that made musical recordings for use as background music in such places as elevators and restaurants.

German poster for Fritz Lang's futuristic film, *Metropolis* (1926). The Granger Collection, New York.

restaurant; music and commercials on the busses I rode to work. When it wasn't music, it was interoffice communications, and my horror chamber of a radio wristwatch on which my friends and my wife phoned every five minutes. What is there about such 'conveniences' that makes them so *temptingly* convenient? The average man thinks, Here I am, time on my hands, and there on my wrist is a wrist telephone, so why not just buzz old Joe up, eh? 'Hello, *hello!*' I love my friends, my wife, humanity, very much, but when one minute my wife calls to say, 'Where are you *now,* dear?' and a friend calls and says, 'Got the best off-color joke to tell you. Seems there was a guy—' And a stranger calls and cries out, 'This is the Find-Fax Poll. What gum are you chewing at this very *instant?*' Well!"

"How did you feel during the week?"

"The fuse lit. On the edge of the cliff. That same afternoon I did what I did at the office."

"Which was?"

"I poured a paper cup of water into the intercommunications system."

The psychiatrist wrote on his pad.

"And the system shorted?"

"Beautifully! The Fourth of July on wheels! My God, stenographers ran around looking *lost!* What an uproar!"

"Felt better temporarily, eh?"

"Fine! Then I got the idea at noon of stomping my wrist radio on the sidewalk. A shrill voice was just yelling out of it at me, 'This is People's Poll Number Nine. What did you eat for lunch?' when I kicked the wrist radio!"

"Felt even *better,* eh?"

"It *grew* on me!" Brock rubbed his hands together. "Why didn't I start a solitary revolution, deliver man from certain 'conveniences'? 'Convenient for who?' I cried. Convenient for friends: 'Hey, Al, thought I'd call you from the locker room out here at Green Hills. Just

"I just rode around feeling of the silence. It's a big bolt

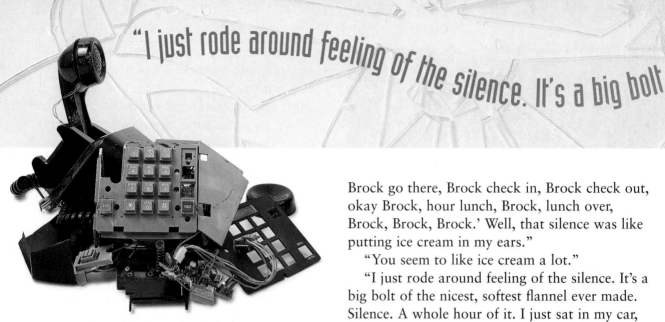

made a sockdolager[3] hole in one! A hole in one, Al! A *beautiful* day. Having a shot of whiskey now. Thought you'd want to know, Al!' Convenient for my office, so when I'm in the field with my radio car there's no moment when I'm not in touch. *In touch! There's* a slimy phrase. Touch, hell. *Gripped!* Pawed, rather. Mauled and massaged and pounded by FM voices. You can't leave your car without checking in: 'Have stopped to visit gas-station men's room.' 'Okay, Brock, step on it!' 'Brock, what *took* you so long?' 'Sorry, sir.' 'Watch it next time, Brock.' '*Yes,* sir!' So, do you know what I did, Doctor? I bought a quart of French chocolate ice cream and spooned it into the car radio transmitter."

"Was there any *special* reason for selecting French chocolate ice cream to spoon into the broadcasting unit?"

Brock thought about it and smiled. "It's my favorite flavor."

"Oh," said the doctor.

"I figured, hell, what's good enough for me is good enough for the radio transmitter."

"What made you think of spooning *ice cream* into the radio?"

"It was a hot day."

The doctor paused.

"And what happened next?"

"Silence happened next. God, it was *beautiful.* That car radio cackling all day, 'Brock go here, Brock go there, Brock check in, Brock check out, okay Brock, hour lunch, Brock, lunch over, Brock, Brock, Brock.' Well, that silence was like putting ice cream in my ears."

"You seem to like ice cream a lot."

"I just rode around feeling of the silence. It's a big bolt of the nicest, softest flannel ever made. Silence. A whole hour of it. I just sat in my car, smiling, feeling of that flannel with my ears. I felt *drunk* with Freedom!"

"Go on."

"Then I got the idea of the portable diathermy machine.[4] I rented one, took it on the bus going home that night. There sat all the tired commuters with their wrist radios, talking to their wives, saying, 'Now I'm at Forty-third, now I'm at Forty-fourth, here I am at Forty-ninth, now turning at Sixty-first.' One husband cursing, 'Well, get *out* of that bar, damn it, and get home and get dinner started, I'm at Seventieth!' And the transit-system radio playing 'Tales from the Vienna Woods,' a canary singing words about a first-rate wheat cereal. Then—I switched on my diathermy! Static! Interference! All wives cut off from husbands grousing about a hard day at the office. All husbands cut off from wives who had just seen their children break a window! The 'Vienna Woods' chopped down, the canary mangled. *Silence!* A terrible, unexpected silence. The bus inhabitants faced with having to converse with each other. Panic! Sheer, animal panic!"

"The police seized you?"

"The bus *had* to stop. After all, the music *was*

3. **sockdolager** (sŏk-dŏl′ə-jər): something outstanding.

4. **diathermy** (dī′ə-thûr′mē) **machine:** a machine that is used for medical purposes and that produces a high-frequency electric current.

of the nicest, softest flannel ever made. Silence. A whole hour of it."

being scrambled, husbands and wives *were* out of touch with reality. Pandemonium, riot, and chaos. Squirrels chattering in cages! A trouble unit arrived, triangulated on me[5] instantly, had me reprimanded, fined, and home, minus my diathermy machine, in jig time."

"Mr. Brock, may I suggest that so far your whole pattern here is not very—practical? If you didn't like transit radios or office radios or car business radios, why didn't you join a fraternity of radio haters, start petitions, get legal and constitutional rulings? After all, this *is* a democracy."

"And I," said Brock, "am that thing best called a minority. I *did* join fraternities, picket, pass petitions, take it to court. Year after year I protested. Everyone laughed. Everyone else *loved* bus radios and commercials. *I* was out of step."

"Then you should have taken it like a good soldier, don't you think? The majority rules."

"But they went too far. If a little music and 'keeping in touch' was charming, they figured a lot would be ten times as charming. I went *wild!* I got home to find my wife hysterical. *Why?* Because she had been completely out of touch with me for half a day. Remember, I did a dance on my wrist radio? Well, that night I laid plans to murder my house."

"Are you *sure* that's how you want me to write it down?"

"That's semantically[6] accurate. Kill it dead. It's one of those talking, singing, humming, weather-reporting, poetry-reading, novel-reciting, jingle-jangling, rockaby-crooning-when-you-go-to-bed houses. A house that screams opera to you in the shower and teaches you Spanish in your sleep. One of those blathering caves where all kinds of electronic Oracles make you feel a trifle larger than a thimble, with stoves that say, 'I'm apricot pie, and I'm *done,*' or 'I'm prime roast beef, so *baste* me!' and other nursery gibberish like that. With beds that rock you to sleep and *shake* you awake. A house that *barely* tolerates humans, I tell you. A front door that barks: 'You've mud on your feet, sir!' And an electronic vacuum hound that snuffles around after you from room to room, inhaling every fingernail or ash you drop. . . ."

"Quietly," suggested the psychiatrist.

"Remember that Gilbert and Sullivan song—'I've Got It on My List, It Never Will Be Missed'? All night I listed grievances. Next morning early I bought a pistol. I *purposely* muddied my feet. I stood at our front door. The front door shrilled, 'Dirty feet, muddy feet! Wipe your feet! Please be *neat!*' I shot the damn thing in its keyhole! I ran to the kitchen, where the stove was just whining, 'Turn me *over!*' In the middle of a mechanical omelet I did the stove to death. Oh, how it sizzled and screamed, 'I'm *shorted!*' Then the telephone rang like a spoiled brat. I shoved it down the Insinkerator. I must state here and now I have *nothing* whatever against the Insinkerator; it was an innocent bystander. I feel sorry for it now, a practical device indeed, which never said a word, purred like a sleepy lion most of the time, and digested our leftovers. I'll have it restored. Then I went in and shot the televisor, that insidious beast, that

5. **triangulated on me:** a reference to triangulation, the process of locating something by means of taking measurements from two fixed points, as can be done with radio signals.

6. **semantically:** in a manner that has to do with the meaning of words.

L'homme au hamac [Man in a hammock] (1913), Albert Gleizes. Oil on canvas, 61⅜" × 51½". Albright-Knox Art Gallery, Buffalo, New York, general purchase fund, 1957.

Medusa,[7] which freezes a billion people to stone every night, staring fixedly, that Siren which called and sang and promised so much and gave, after all, so little, but myself always going back, going back, hoping and waiting until—bang! Like a headless turkey, gobbling, my wife whooped out the front door. The police came. Here I *am!*"

He sat back happily and lit a cigarette.

"And did you realize, in committing these crimes, that the wrist radio, the broadcasting transmitter, the phone, the bus radio, the office intercoms, all were rented or were someone else's property?"

"I would do it all over again, so help me God."

The psychiatrist sat there in the sunshine of that beatific[8] smile.

"You don't want any further help from the

7. **Medusa:** in Greek mythology, a beautiful woman who was punished for loving a god by having her hair turned into snakes; after that, anyone who looked at her turned to stone.

8. **beatific** (bē′ə-tĭf′ĭk): angelic.

Office of Mental Health? You're ready to take the consequences?"

"This is only the beginning," said Mr. Brock. "I'm the vanguard[9] of the small public which is tired of noise and being taken advantage of and pushed around and yelled at, every moment music, every moment in touch with some voice somewhere, do this, do that, quick, quick, now here, now there. You'll *see*. The revolt begins. My name will go down in history!"

"Mmm." The psychiatrist seemed to be thinking.

"It'll take time, of course. It was all so enchanting at first. The very *idea* of these things, the practical uses, was wonderful. They were almost toys, to be played with, but the people got too involved, went too far, and got wrapped up in a pattern of social behavior and couldn't get out, couldn't admit they were *in,* even. So they rationalized their nerves as something else. 'Our modern age,' they said. 'Conditions,' they said. 'High-strung,' they said. But mark my words, the seed has been sown. I got world-wide coverage on TV, radio, films; *there's* an irony for you. That was five days ago. A billion people know about me. Check your financial columns. Any day now. Maybe today. Watch for a sudden spurt, a rise in sales for French chocolate ice cream!"

"I see," said the psychiatrist.

"Can I go back to my nice private cell now, where I can be alone and quiet for six months?"

"Yes," said the psychiatrist quietly.

"Don't worry about me," said Mr. Brock, rising. "I'm just going to sit around for a long time stuffing that nice soft bolt of quiet material in both ears."

"Mmm," said the psychiatrist, going to the door.

"Cheers," said Mr. Brock.

"Yes," said the psychiatrist.

He pressed a code signal on a hidden button, the door opened, he stepped out, the door shut and locked. Alone, he moved in the offices and corridors. The first twenty yards of his walk were accompanied by "Tambourine Chinois." Then it was "Tzigane," Bach's Passacaglia and Fugue in something Minor, "Tiger Rag," "Love Is Like a Cigarette." He took his broken wrist radio from his pocket like a dead praying mantis. He turned in at his office. A bell sounded; a voice came out of the ceiling, "Doctor?"

"Just finished with Brock," said the psychiatrist.

"Diagnosis?"

"Seems completely disoriented, but convivial.[10] Refuses to accept the simplest realities of his environment and work *with* them."

"Prognosis?"[11]

"Indefinite. Left him enjoying a piece of invisible material."

Three phones rang. A duplicate wrist radio in his desk drawer buzzed like a wounded grasshopper. The intercom flashed a pink light and click-clicked. Three phones rang. The drawer buzzed. Music blew in through the open door. The psychiatrist, humming quietly, fitted the new wrist radio to his wrist, flipped the intercom, talked a moment, picked up one telephone, talked, picked up another telephone, talked, picked up the third telephone, talked, touched the wrist-radio button, talked calmly and quietly, his face cool and serene, in the middle of the music and the lights flashing, the phones ringing again, and his hands moving, and his wrist radio buzzing, and the intercoms talking, and voices speaking from the ceiling. And he went on quietly this way through the remainder of a cool, air-conditioned, and long afternoon; telephone, wrist radio, intercom, telephone, wrist radio, intercom, telephone, wrist radio, intercom, telephone, wrist radio, intercom, telephone, wrist radio, intercom, telephone, wrist radio . . . ❖

---

9. **vanguard:** the leader of thought, taste, or opinion in a field.

10. **convivial** (kən-vĭv′ē-əl): merry.

11. **prognosis:** a forecast of the probable course of a disease.

RESPONDING OPTIONS

FROM PERSONAL RESPONSE *TO* CRITICAL ANALYSIS

REFLECT **1.** What did you think of Brock's response to the technology around him? Write down your thoughts in your notebook.

RETHINK **2.** Even though Brock is destroying only machines, why do you think he calls himself The Murderer?

3. Brock predicts that he will ultimately be successful in his quest to deliver society from technological conveniences. Do you agree?

Consider

- the ways people use the machines in the story
- the psychiatrist's comment, "The majority rules."
- Brock's analysis of the way people secretly feel about their machines (page 1095)

4. What do you think Bradbury's purpose was in writing this story?

RELATE **5.** Do you think that technology can someday get out of hand and be too intrusive in our lives, similar to what happens in this story? In explaining your opinion, consider what you wrote for the Previewing activities on page 1088.

ANOTHER PATHWAY

Cooperative Learning

Brock tells the psychiatrist that he joined fraternities, started petitions, took legal action, and picketed to protest the intrusiveness of technological conveniences. With a small group of classmates, prepare a speech either supporting or opposing Brock's campaign. Choose one member of your group to deliver the speech to the class.

LITERARY CONCEPTS

Satire is a literary technique in which a writer ridicules ideas or customs in order to improve society. In "The Murderer," for example, Bradbury satirizes aspects of contemporary society through his creation of a future world inundated with communications technology. Working in a small group, choose three of the following contemporary issues that Bradbury satirizes and find evidence in this story to illustrate Bradbury's attitude toward each of the issues. Then discuss your conclusions with the class.

- the use of advanced technology to communicate
- the need to be in touch
- the availability of silence
- the power of the majority versus the minority
- the use of violent and nonviolent forms of protest

QUICKWRITES

1. Write a TV or radio **news broadcast** about Albert Brock, The Murderer, that could be aired at the time of the story. Predict the public's response to Brock's actions in your broadcast.
2. Do you think that our technological conveniences today are potentially harmful? Draft a **persuasive essay** in which you agree or disagree with Bradbury's vision of the future in this story.

PORTFOLIO *Save your writing. You may want to use it later as a springboard to a piece for your portfolio.*

ALTERNATIVE ACTIVITIES

1. ***Cooperative Learning*** With a small group of classmates, recreate all or part of this story as a **radio play.** Tape-record a dramatic reading, including sound effects and music. Then play the tape for the rest of your class.
2. Imagine you are a cartoonist who shares Brock's views. Draw an **editorial cartoon** based on this story that ridicules society's overuse of technology. Post your cartoon on a classroom bulletin board or submit it to your school newspaper.

CRITIC'S CORNER

Bradbury's reputation as a science fiction writer has long been debated. Some critics think that he is one of the world's greatest science fiction writers, while others argue he is not a science fiction writer at all because he is antiscience and antitechnology. Based on your reading of this story, do you think Bradbury is antiscience and antitechnology? How do you rate him as a science fiction writer?

ACROSS THE CURRICULUM

Technology Although Bradbury wrote this story in the 1950s, the technology he describes is fairly accurate for our time. Research contemporary technological conveniences, such as "talking appliances" and cellular phones, to find today's equivalents of the machines that Bradbury imagined for his story.

RAY BRADBURY

1920–

As a boy growing up in Illinois, Ray Bradbury had a passion for Gothic tales and ghost stories, comics, magic shows, and circuses. He was also haunted by nightmares. When he was about 11, he began writing stories by hand on butcher paper. By the time he was in high school, he had bought a typewriter and started writing reviews, scripts, and science fiction stories. After high school, Bradbury received encouragement from professional science fiction writers, and in the early 1940s he began selling his first stories to popular magazines.

Today Bradbury is considered by some to be one of the foremost fantasy and science fiction writers in the United States. One of his most famous books is *The Martian Chronicles,* originally published in 1950. In this collection of short stories, Bradbury shows how materialistic earth dwellers ruin an older Martian culture, and he addresses such contemporary issues as pollution, racism, censorship, and nuclear war. To Bradbury, scientific knowledge, if improperly used, is more of a potential destroyer of humanity than a savior. He says that, for him, writing science fiction is "a convenient shorthand symbolic way to write of our huge problems. Smog, freeways, cars, atom bombs, most of mankind's trouble these days comes from an abundance of machinery and an undersupply of imagination applied to that machinery. S-f [science fiction] supplies the imagination whereby to judge, suggest alternatives, and provide seedbeds for future improvements."

OTHER WORKS *Fahrenheit 451, The Golden Apples of the Sun, I Sing the Body Electric!, Something Wicked This Way Comes*

LASERLINKS
• *CULTURAL CONNECTION*

PREVIEWING

FICTION

Hostage

Joyce Carol Oates

PERSONAL CONNECTION

In the story you are about to read, the narrator is the victim of a random act of violence. With a group of classmates, talk about recent incidents of violence that you know of, perhaps from newspaper headlines, television news, or local gossip. Then discuss how you think a violent incident emotionally affects those involved—the victim, assailant, and witnesses. How do you think you might react if you were involved in a violent incident?

LITERARY CONNECTION

Joyce Carol Oates frequently writes about ordinary people who are affected by violence. Reviewers have often focused on the violent content of her work, with one saying, "Typical activities in Oates's novels are arson, rape, riot, mental breakdown, murder (plain and fancy, with excursions into patricide, matricide, uxoricide, mass filicide), and suicide." Oates answered her critics in a *New York Times Book Review* essay titled "Why Is Your Writing So Violent?" Responding to the criticism of her violent plots, Oates once replied, "As Flannery O'Connor—another writer frequently attacked for the 'darkness and violence' of her work—has said, No writer is a pessimist; the very act of writing is an optimistic act." By writing about violence in our society, Oates does not intend merely to mirror today's headlines but to "bring about a change of heart."

READING CONNECTION

Linking Characters, Plot, and Theme
As you read "Hostage," use the plentiful details to visualize the narrator, a ninth-grade girl, and her classmate Bruno, the main character in the story. Allow yourself to know these characters and to be drawn into the suspenseful events that befall them. Respond honestly to the violence in the story, but also try to seek meaning in it. Judge for yourself whether Oates creates a distorted or a realistic world, and whether her story can be considered optimistic.

The Metropolitan Post
Honor Student Slain in Gang Crossfire
Daily Tribune
GUNMAN FREES WIFE, CHILDREN AFTER 2-DAY SIEGE
City Times
Shoppers Robbed in Mall Parking Lot

Hostage

Joyce Carol Oates

BY the age of fourteen Bruno Sokolov had the heft and swagger of a near-grown man. His wide shoulders, sturdy neck, dark oily hair wetted and combed sleekly back from his forehead like a rooster's crest, above all his large head and the shrewd squint of his pebble-colored eyes gave him an air unnervingly adult, as if, in junior high school, in the company of children, he was in disguise, yet carelessly in disguise. He wore his older brothers' and even his father's cast-off clothing, rakish combinations that suited him, pin-striped shirts, sweater vests, suspenders, bulky tweed coats and corduroy trousers, cheap leather belts with enormous buckles, even, frequently, for there were always deaths in those big immigrant families, mourning bands around his upper arm that gave him a look both sinister and holy, to which none of our teachers could object. He was smart; he was tough; the natural leader of a neighborhood gang of boys; he carried a switchblade knife, or was believed to do so. He had a strangely scarred forehead—in one version of the story he'd overturned a pan of boiling water on himself as a small child, in another version his mother in a fit of emotion had overturned it on him. He spoke English with a strong accent, musical, yet mocking, as if these sounds were his own invention, these queer eliding vowels and diphthongs,[1] and he had remarkable self-confidence for a boy with his background, the son of Polish-Russian immigrants—out of bravado he ran for, and actually won, our ninth-grade presidency, in a fluke of an election that pitted our teachers' choice, a "good" boy, against a boy whom most of the teachers mistrusted, or feared. Even when Bruno Sokolov spoke intelligently in class there was an overtone of subtle mockery, if not contempt, in his voice. His grades were erratic and he was often absent from school—"family reasons" the usual excuse—and he was famous for intimidating, or harassing, or actually beating up certain of his classmates. His play at football and basketball was that of a steer loosed happily among heifers, and when, as our class president, a black snap-on

1. **eliding vowels and diphthongs:** vowels that are omitted or slurred over and combinations of vowel sounds within single syllables (as in *soil*).

WORDS TO KNOW

rakish (rā′kĭsh) *adj.* dashingly or sportingly stylish; jaunty
subtle (sŭt′l) *adj.* so slight as to be difficult to detect

bow tie around his neck, he addressed the rowdy assemblage from the stage with the aplomb and drawling ease of a radio broadcaster or a politician, shrewd eyes glittering with a sense of his own power, we felt, aroused, laughing at his jokes, a shiver of certitude, rippling among even the dullest of us like a nervous reflex through a school of fish, that we were in the presence of someone distinctive; someone of whom, however we might dislike him, we might be proud.

I didn't know him. I didn't belong to his world. Though my family lived only a block or so from his family in a neighborhood of row houses built in the 1890s and hardly renovated since that time, my grandparents had emigrated from Budapest in the early 1900s and Bruno's parents had come from Lublin, a Polish city near the Russian border, in the early 1930s, and that made a considerable difference. And I was younger than Bruno, younger than most of my classmates—I had been skipped a grade in elementary school, a source of obscure pride and shame to me—so that if he happened to glance toward me, if his squinty amused stare drifted in my direction, there was nothing, it seemed, on which it might snag. I was small, I was brainy, I was invisible. For my part I observed Bruno Sokolov scrupulously, in classes, in the school corridors, making his way down the stairs, pushing ahead in the cafeteria line, actions he seemed to perform without thinking, as if the very size of his body had to be accommodated, his needs and impulses immediately discharged. Even to be teased by Bruno Sokolov was an honor of a kind but it was not an honor casually granted, for the Sokolovs, poor as they were, crowded into their shabby row house with its rear yard lifting to a railway embankment, nonetheless took themselves seriously; they were displaced tradesmen, not Polish peasants.

I didn't belong to his world.

The immigrants' world retained its taxonomical[2] distinctions of class, money, power, "breeding." In America, you were hungry to move up but you had no intention of helping others, outside the family, to move up with you.

The places where imagination takes root . . . There was an oversized winter coat Bruno Sokolov wore in bad weather, Cossack-style, navy blue, with upturned collar, deep pockets, and frayed sleeves, the mere sight of which made me feel confused, light-headed, panicked. There was the back of Bruno's big head, observed slantwise from me in English class, the springy oily dark hair often separating in quills, falling about his ears, and every few weeks a fresh haircut, done at home, crude and brutal, shaved at the neck. There was the sound of his suddenly uplifted voice, ringing and abrasive, often drawling in mockery, the give-and-take, foulmouthed, of young adolescent boys, and my immediate sense of alarm when I heard it, but also my envy: a sharp stabbing envy that cut me like a knife: for of course Bruno Sokolov never spoke my name, even in derision. He gave no sign of knowing it.

The infatuation was hardly love, not even affection, for I often fantasized Bruno Sokolov dying, a violent cinematic death, and took a vengeful pleasure in it; but there was about my feeling for him that sense, common to love, of futility and wild optimism conjoined, a quicken-

2. **taxonomical:** having to do with the science of classification.

WORDS TO KNOW

aplomb (ə-plŏm) *n.* self-confidence
obscure (ŏb-skyŏŏr') *adj.* indistinct; not clearly understood
scrupulously (skrōō'pyə-ləs-lē) *adv.* in an extremely careful and thorough manner; conscientiously
abrasive (ə-brā'sĭv) *adj.* harsh and rough
infatuation (ĭn-făch'ōō-ā'shən) *n.* the state of being completely carried away by foolish or shallow love or affection

ing of the pulse even at the very instant that the quickening, the hope, is checked: *No. Don't.*

Midway in the school year when we were in ninth grade Bruno's father died a strange and much talked-of death and I waited for weeks to tell Bruno how sorry I was that it had happened, approaching him, one day, in the corridor outside our homeroom, with an aggressive sort of shyness, and Bruno stared down at me with a look of blank surprise as if a voice had sounded out of the very air beside him, a voice wrongly intimate and knowing. He was taller than I by more than a head, his height exaggerated by the springy thickness of his hair and the breadth of his shoulders. The shiny-smooth skin of his scar, disappearing under his hair, was serrated and would have been rough to the touch. His eyes were heavy-lidded from lack of sleep or grief and he stared at me for what seemed a long time before saying, with a shrug of his shoulders, "Yeah. Me too." And that was all.

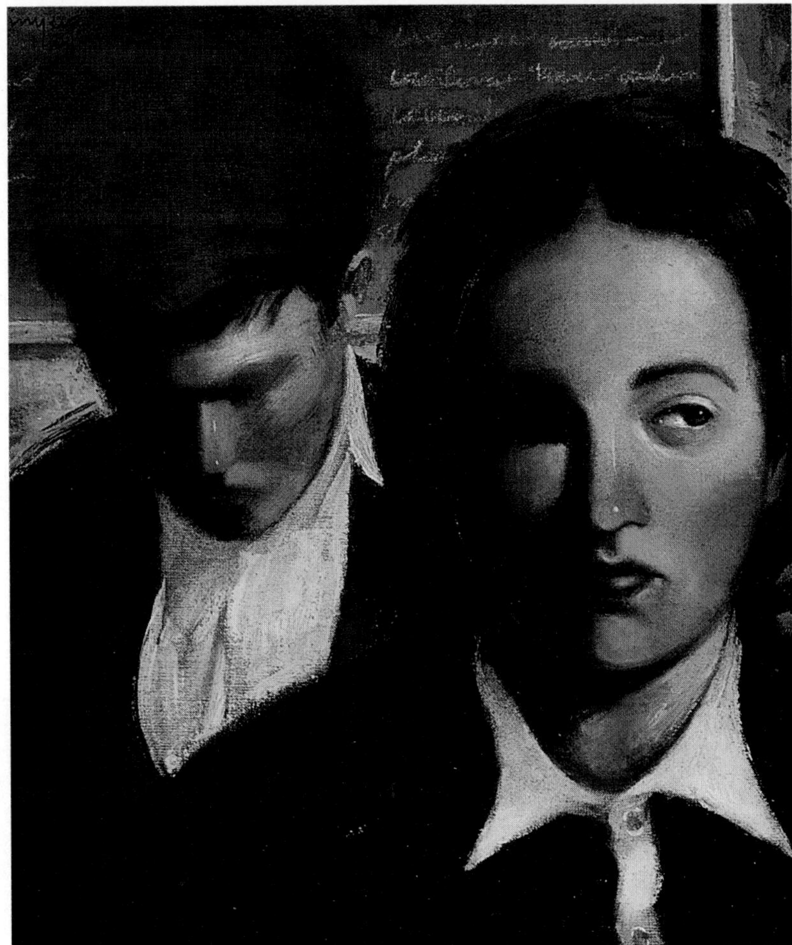

Illustration Copyright © Eric Dinyer.

My heart was beating rapidly, wildly. But that was all.

Even by the standards of our neighborhood Mr. Sokolov had died an unusual death. He was a large fleshy man with deep-set suspicious eyes and bushy but receding hair that gave him a perpetually affronted look; he dressed formally, in dark tight-fitting suits with old-fashioned wide lapels, starched white shirts, dark neckties. He and two brothers owned a small neighborhood grocery with a meat counter, a real butcher's shop as my mother spoke of it, and Mr. Sokolov so dominated the store, took such edgy excitable antagonistic pride in it, that many customers, including my mother, were offended by his manner. In Bruno's father Bruno's coarse sly charm was mere coarseness; he was in the habit of issuing commands, in Polish, to his brothers, in front of customers; the neighborhood belief was that he wasn't quite "right in the head"—and certainly the dislocations of language made for constant misunderstandings, and constant misunderstandings made for what is called, clinically, paranoia, that sense that the world's very tilt is in our disfavor, and that nothing, however accidental-seeming, is accidental. Mr. Sokolov's short temper led him into arguments and even into feuds with neighbors, customers, city authorities, local police; he was tyrannical

WORDS TO KNOW

affronted (ə-frŭn'tĭd) *adj.* intentionally insulted **affront** *v.*
antagonistic (ăn-tăg'ə-nĭs'tĭk) *adj.* openly hostile and aggressive toward another

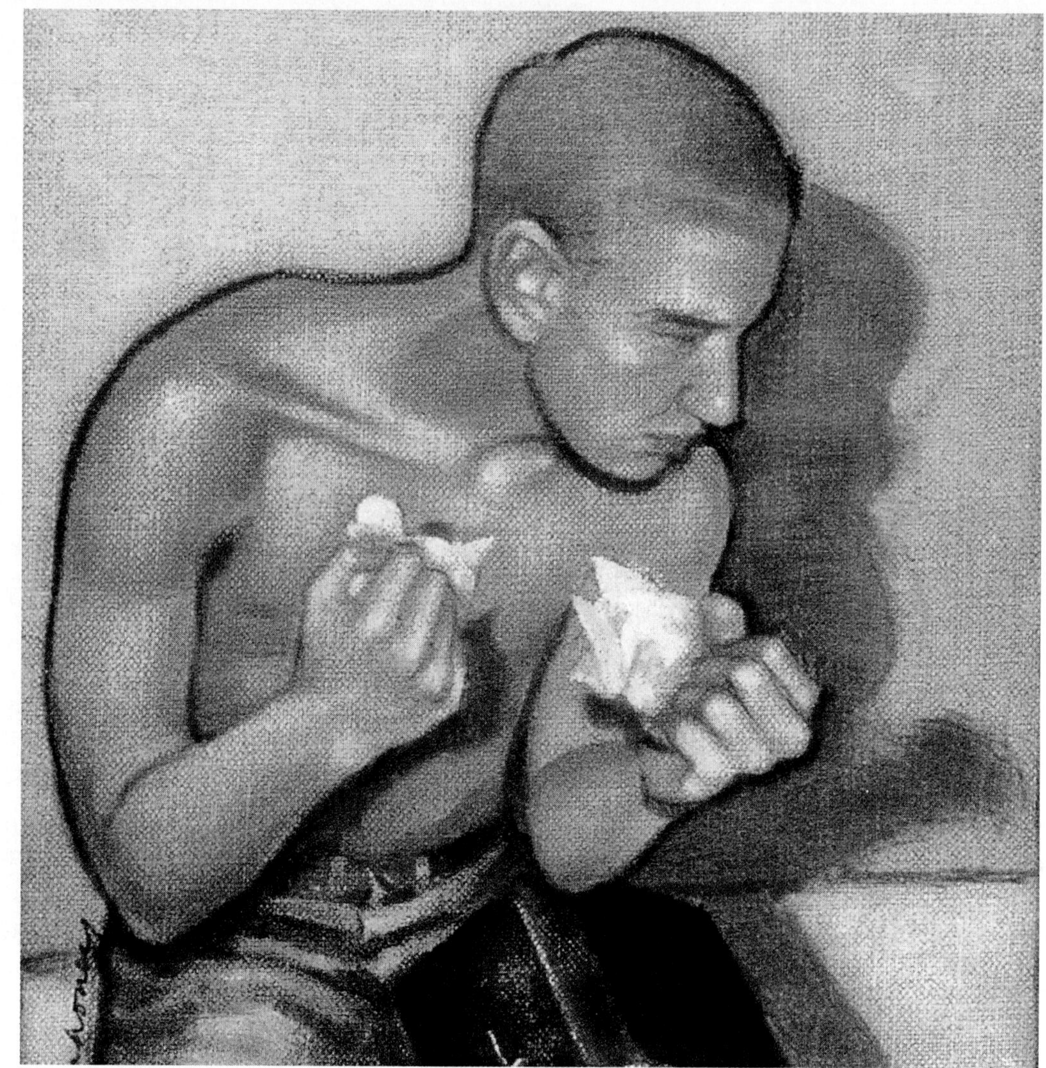

Illustration Copyright © 1987 Katherine Mahoney.

with his family—three sons, two daughters, a wife who spoke virtually no English; he was driven to fits of rage when his store was vandalized, and burglarized, and police failed to arrest the criminals, or even to give the Sokolovs the satisfaction that they were trying to find them. (All this was "Mafia"-related. It was an open secret that the small neighborhood tradesmen were being extorted or were engaged in some elaborate process of attempting to resist extortion.) Mr. Sokolov died, in fact, defending his store: he was hiding at the rear when someone broke in, and he attacked the intruder with a meat cleaver, but was himself shot in the leg, and when the man ran limping and bleeding out into the alley Mr. Sokolov pursued him with the cleaver, limping and bleeding too, and shouting wildly in Polish . . . and somehow Mr. Sokolov and the other man both disappeared. A trail of their commingled blood drops led to an intersection close by, then stopped. Police theorized that a van had been parked there, and that Mr. Sokolov was taken away in it: he was missing for several days, the object of a much-publicized local search, then his body, or rather parts of his body, began to be discovered . . . floating in the canal, carelessly buried at the city dump, tossed into the weedy vacant lot behind St. John the Evangelist Church, to which the Sokolovs belonged. The murderer or murderers were never found and twenty years later, long after Bruno Sokolov himself had died, in Korea, one of his cousins ran for mayor, and narrowly missed winning, on the strength of a passionate campaign against "organized crime" in the city.

On Saturday mornings in all but the worst winter weather I took two city buses downtown to the public library, where, in a windowless ground-floor room set aside for "young adult" readers I searched the shelves for books, especially novels, the search invested with a queer heart-stopping urgency as if the next book I chose, encased in its yellowing plastic cover, *YA* in tall black letters on its spine, might in some way change my life. I was of an age when any change at all seemed promising; I hadn't yet the temperament to conceive of change as fearful. I didn't doubt that *the* book, *the* revelation, awaited me, no matter that the books I actually did read were usually disappointing, too simplistically written and imagined, made up of characters too unswervingly good or bad to be believable. It was the search itself that excited me . . . the look and the feel of the books on their bracketed metal shelves, the smell of the room, a close, warm, stale mixture of floor wax, furniture polish, paper paste, the faint chemical scent of the middle-aged librarian's inky-black dyed hair. Sometimes the very approach to the library—my first glimpse of its Greek Revival portico and columns, its fanning stone steps—aroused me to a sickish apprehension, as if I understood beforehand that whatever I hoped to find there I would not find; or, by the act of finding it, making it my own, I would thereby lose it. The library was further invested with romance since every second or third Saturday I caught sight of Bruno Sokolov there too . . . and one day when I was sitting on the front steps, waiting for the bus, Bruno stooped over me unannounced to ask, in his oddly breezy, brotherly manner, what I'd checked out, and to show me what he had—adult science fiction by Heinlein, Bradbury, Asimov. Did he have a card for upstairs? for adult books? I asked, surprised, and Bruno said, "Sure." Another time he showed me a book with a dark lurid cover, a ghoulish face with red-gleaming eyes, Bram Stoker's *Dracula*—he hadn't checked it out of the library but had simply taken it from a shelf and slipped it inside his coat. Not stealing exactly, Bruno said, because he'd bring it back, probably. "The kind of stuff I like, it's things that make you think, y'know, the weirder the better," he said, smiling and showing big damp yellowed teeth, "—stuff that scares you into thinking, y'know what I mean?" His eyes were heavy-lidded, his lips rather thick, the lower lip in particular; the curious scar high on his forehead gleamed with reflected light. I saw with surprise his thick stubby battered-looking fingers clutching the book, dirt-edged nails, the knuckles nicked and raw, as if he hurt himself casually without knowing what he did, or caring. Or maybe his hands were roughened from work at the grocery. Or from fighting.

I guessed he didn't know my name.

"Yes," I said, looking up at him, "—I know what you mean."

I watched him walk away, my eyes pinching, following his tall figure in its forward-plunging impatient stride until he was out of sight. *Thief,* I thought. *I could turn you in.* It was only the second or third time we'd spoken together and it would be the final time. And I guessed he didn't know my name. Or even know that he didn't know.

It wasn't long afterward, on another Saturday

WORDS TO KNOW

invest (ĭn-vĕst') *v.* to provide with a certain quality
lurid (lŏŏr'ĭd) *adj.* startling and sensational

morning, in late winter, in the library, downstairs, alone, emerging from the women's lavatory—that place of ancient toilets with chain-activated flushes, black-and-white-checked tile encrusted with decades of dirt, incongruously ornate plaster moldings—I heard someone say in a low insinuating voice, "Little girl? Eh? Little girl?—where're you going?" and was crudely awakened from my brooding trance, the usual spellbound state in which I walked about, when I was alone, in those days, dreaming not so much of Bruno Sokolov or one or another boy I knew as of the mysterious stab of emotions they aroused, the angry teasing hope they seemed to embody, and I'd just pushed through the heavy frosted-glass swinging door and saw, there, a few feet away, in the cavernous poorly lit corridor—this was in an alcove, not far from the young adults reading room—one of the hellish sights of my life: a man approaching me, smiling at me, intimate, derisive, accusatory. I had vaguely recalled this man following me down the stairs but I must have told myself, if I'd told myself anything, that he was simply headed for the men's lavatory. "Little girl—c'mon *here*," he said, less patiently. Did he know me? Was I expected to know him? I had seen him around the library and on the street outside, dressed shabbily yet flamboyantly in layers of mismatched clothing, overcoat, sweaters, shirt, filthy woolen scarf wound around his neck, unbuckled overshoes flapping on his feet; he was one of a number of oldish odd-looking and -behaving men who haunted the library, in cold weather especially, spending much of the day in the reference room, where they made a show of reading, or actually did read, the daily newspapers, turning the pages harshly, as if the world's events filled them with contempt. Sometimes they dozed, or muttered to themselves, or drank from pint bottles hidden in much-wrinkled paper bags, or forgot where they were, the precariousness of their welcome, and addressed someone who didn't know them and who quickly edged away. If they caused much disruption one of the librarians, usually a stocky woman with pearl-framed glasses (whom I myself feared for her air of cold authority), ushered them outside, and shut the door behind them. Upon rare occasions police were called but I had never actually seen a policeman arrive.

But here, now, today, for no reason I could guess or would ever be explained to me, one of these men had followed me downstairs to the women's lavatory, speaking excitedly, scolding me, now walking straight at me as if he meant to run me down. He grabbed hold of my arm and wrestled me back against the wall, and the things I was carrying—my little beige leather army surplus purse, an armload of library books—went flying. I saw his coarse-veined face above me, and his white-rimmed rheumy mad eyes, felt his whiskers like wire brush against my skin, and must have screamed, though I don't remember screaming, and he panted, and cursed, and spoke to me with great urgency, now dragging me to the doorway of the men's lavatory, where, I suddenly knew, he would assault me, keep me hostage, kill me—there was no hope for me now. Had I not read of such horrors hinted in the newspaper, or heard of them, whispered, never fully articulated . . .

Yet I might have escaped my assailant, had I squirmed, ducked under his arm, twisted free. He outweighed me by more than one hundred pounds but I might have escaped him and run upstairs screaming for help except that I could not move; all the strength had drained from me. It was as if the mere touch of an adult, an adult's terrible authority, had paralyzed me.

But we were making noise, and the noises echoed in the high-ceilinged space. And then the frosted-glass window of the door to the lavatory shattered and fell in pieces around us. By now

WORDS TO KNOW

incongruously (ĭn-kŏng'gro͞o-əs-lē) *adv.* in a manner that is not fitting, suitable, or in agreement; incompatibly

derisive (dĭ-rī'sĭv) *adj.* mocking or ridiculing; scornful

Illustration Copyright © Greg Spalenka.

the librarian from the young adult room had emerged, and another woman was poking her head around a corner staring at us incredulously, and someone cried out for the madman to leave me alone, and the madman shouted back in a rage, and how many minutes passed in this way, or was it merely seconds, while I crouched unable to move yet trembling violently in a crook of a stranger's arm, breathing in the odors, the stench really, of his desperate being, a sharp smell of alcohol, and dirt-stiffened clothing, and I might have thought of praying, I might have thought of God, but all thoughts were struck from my brain, like shadows in a room blasted by light, and even the thought that I would be held hostage and mutilated and murdered and shamed before all

WORDS TO KNOW **incredulously** (ĭn-krĕj′ə-ləs-lē) *adv.* in a manner showing a lack of belief the world had not the power to make me fight as I might have, and should have fought.

A number of people had gathered, but were shy of approaching us. The librarian with the pearl-framed glasses was trying to reason with my assailant, who, gripping me hard, with a kind of joy, kept saying, "No! No! No you don't—stay away!" His arm was crooked around my head, his elbow pinioning my neck, I half crouched in an awkward position, the side of my face against his coat, the rough material of his coat, and my hair bunched up fallen into my face; I did not think I was crying, for I had not the space or the breath for crying yet my face was wet with tears, my nose ran shamefully as a baby's—and all the while we swayed and lurched and staggered together, as in a comical dance, which, having begun, we could not end, for there was no way of ending, no way of escaping the corner we had backed into. Several times the word *police* was uttered and several times the madman threatened to "kill the little girl" if any police should so much as appear. Shouts and cries burst about us like birds' shrieks echoing in the passageway and then dipping abruptly to silence. My assailant had pulled me into the lavatory, the outer area of sinks and tall narrow mirrors and naked light bulbs, identical to the women's lavatory, it seemed, yet a forbidden space, and I was able to think clearly, for the first time since the madman had grabbed me, *He will have to kill me now to prove he can do it.*

And then the door was pushed open, and Bruno Sokolov appeared, crouched, unhesitating, moving swiftly—he had shoved his way past the witnesses in the corridor, paying no attention to them, drawn by the excitement, the upset, the prospect of a fight, not knowing who I was until he saw me and perhaps not even knowing then, for there wasn't time to think; in describing what happened I am trying to put into words quicksilver actions that took place within seconds, or split seconds: Bruno fierce and direct as on the basketball court when he deliberately ran down another player, pulling the madman off me, yanking him away, the two of them screaming at each other, cursing, like men who know each other well, and there was Bruno of a height with my assailant fending off the man's frenzied windmill blows, the two of them now struggling by the sinks, Bruno punching, stabbing, kicking, a blade flashing in his right hand, and blood splashing on the floor, thick sinewy worms of red splashing on the tiled floor . . . Bruno had taken out his switchblade knife, and Bruno was using it, in wide sweeping furious strokes, cursing the man, saying repeatedly, "Die! Die! Die!" though the man had fallen to his knees shrieking in pain and terror, trying to shield his head with his arms. And there was Bruno in a pea-green army surplus jacket, bareheaded, sweating, crouched above him like a madman himself, his face so doughy-pale and distended in rage I would not have known it, eyes shining with moisture, "Die! *Die!*" with each stroke of the knife . . . but now I ran out of the lavatory and into the corridor, where someone caught me in her arms and walked me hurriedly down the hall to a cubicle of an office, the door shut, locked, a call placed to the emergency room of the closest hospital, the word *assault* uttered, and I saw it was the librarian with the pearl-framed glasses now as solicitous of me as a mother. And I knew I would be safe.

My assailant was a man of fifty-eight, an ex-mental patient now living on a disability pension from the U.S. Navy in a downtown hotel for transients. He did not die from Bruno Sokolov's attack but he was in critical condition for some weeks, semiconscious, and when conscious rarely coherent, unable to explain why he had assaulted me or even to recall that he had done so. Nor did he remember the junior high school boy who'd stabbed him with a wicked eight-inch switchblade knife, wounding him in the chest, belly, groin, arms, and face. His memories, such as they were, were concentrated upon late childhood spent in a rural settlement in western Pennsylvania half a century ago.

Following this much-publicized incident things were never the same again for Bruno Sokolov. As a minor who had, in a sense, behaved heroically, he was not formally charged with any crime (possession of a deadly weapon, for instance, or "aggravated assault") and naturally witnesses testified in his behalf: he had rushed into the lavatory and thrown himself on the madman in order to save me, and then he had fought him, nearly killing him, in self-defense. (So I testified too. So I told everyone. Though I always knew that in the strictest sense it wasn't true.) But a juvenile-court judge placed him on six months' probation, during which time he was obliged to seek psychiatric therapy and to register as an outpatient at a state psychiatric facility, and the shame of that connection so qualified the glamour of Bruno's heroism, and what, literally, he had almost done—*killed a man! stabbed an adult man to death with a switchblade!*—that, in school, he became increasingly withdrawn and sullen, even among his pals, given to unpredictable displays of temper and childish violence, and his grades sharply declined, and he had to resign his class office, and there were intervals when he simply stayed away from school, and the psychiatric therapy was extended for another six months, and there were difficulties in the Sokolov family, and Bruno ran away, tried to enlist in the army, but failed, and came back home, working in the grocery after school and on Saturdays, and through the summer, and in the autumn, in high school; it could never have been the case that this hulking moody overgrown boy might have run for, let alone won, one of the class offices, nor was he on any of the sports teams, hardly a schoolboy any longer but not a man either, bored, ironic, and truculent, out of scale in our classrooms and in our corridors, slamming his locker door shut as if he meant to break it . . . and should a textbook fall from his hand he'd be likely to give it a kick, but not out of clowning high spirits and not inviting you to laugh sharing a joke because there was no joke, only Bruno Sokolov's dangerous eyes shifting like water under wind, and then he'd be gone, no backward glance, hardly more than a tight ticlike grimace to acknowledge the tie, the bond, the secret between us, unspoken, that we were kin almost as blood relatives are kin who have virtually nothing to do with each other publicly and do not in a sense "know" each other at all, a phenomenon common with schoolchildren though perhaps not limited to them. *It's because of me,* I would think, staring after him, *what he is now—my fault.* Though at more sober moments I understood that what Bruno Sokolov had done had nothing to do with me, or no more to do with me than it had with the ex-mental patient he had nearly killed.

By sixteen Bruno Sokolov had quit school, by seventeen he had joined the army, by eighteen he'd been shipped overseas to die within a few months at the Battle of Taegu, Korea. Pvt. First Class Bruno J. Sokolov, his photograph, tough-jawed, squinty-eyed, hopeful, in the evening paper. And the other night I dreamt of him, a boy thirty-four years dead, remembering in the dream what I'd forgotten for years, that none of his friends had ever called him "Bruno" but always "Sokolov" or "Sokki"—"Sockie"—a harsh sibilant magical sound I had yearned to have the right to say, shouting it in the street as others did, and he would have turned, and he would have seen me, and he would have raised his hand in recognition. As if that might have made a difference. ❖

WORDS TO KNOW
sibilant (sĭb'ə-lənt) *adj.* hissing

INSIGHT

The Legend

Garrett Hongo

In Chicago, it is snowing softly
and a man has just done his wash for the week.
He steps into the twilight of early evening,
carrying a wrinkled shopping bag
full of neatly folded clothes,
and, for a moment, enjoys
the feel of warm laundry and crinkled paper,
flannellike against his gloveless hands.
There's a Rembrandt glow on his face,
a triangle of orange in the hollow of his cheek
as a last flash of sunset
blazes the storefronts and lit windows of the street.

He is Asian, Thai or Vietnamese,
and very skinny, dressed as one of the poor
in rumpled suit pants and a plaid mackinaw,
dingy and too large.
He negotiates the slick of ice
on the sidewalk by his car,
opens the Fairlane's back door,
leans to place the laundry in,
and turns, for an instant,
toward the flurry of footsteps
and cries of pedestrians
as a boy—that's all he was—
backs from the corner package store[1]
shooting a pistol, firing it,
once, at the dumbfounded man
who falls forward,
grabbing at his chest.

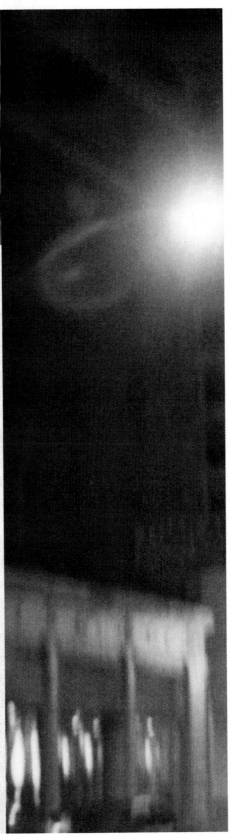

A few sounds escape from his mouth,
a babbling no one understands
as people surround him
bewildered at his speech.
The noises he makes are nothing to them.
The boy has gone, lost
in the light array of foot traffic
dappling the snow with fresh prints.

Tonight, I read about Descartes'[2]
grand courage to doubt everything
except his own miraculous existence
and I feel so distinct
from the wounded man lying on the concrete
I am ashamed.

Let the night sky cover him as he dies.
Let the weaver girl cross the bridge of heaven[3]
and take up his cold hands.

In Memory of Jay Kashiwamura

---

1. **package store:** a liquor store.
2. **René Descartes** (dā-kärt′): a French philosopher, scientist, and mathematician of the 1600s. He believed that the proof of human existence was the ability to think. His most famous statement was "I think, therefore I am."
3. **weaver girl . . . heaven:** In Chinese legend, the weaver girl and her beloved are separated by the "river of Heaven"—the Milky Way. Once a year, magpies spread their wings to form a bridge that allows her to cross the river.

RESPONDING OPTIONS

FROM PERSONAL RESPONSE TO CRITICAL ANALYSIS

REFLECT 1. How did you react to the violence in this story? Write your reaction in your notebook to share in class.

RETHINK 2. How do you explain the narrator's feelings for Bruno at the end of the story?

3. What was your own impression of Bruno, both at the beginning and at the end of the story?

4. Why do you think Bruno stabs the man in the library?

   Consider
   - Bruno's actions and words as he stabs the man
   - the violence Bruno has experienced in his life
   - the narrator's comment that Bruno's act had "no more to do with me than it had with the ex-mental patient he had nearly killed" (page 1107)

5. How do you explain Bruno's behavior after the stabbing?

   Consider
   - how he is perceived by the juvenile-court judge and others
   - your Personal Connection discussion (page 1098) about the emotional effects of violence

6. In your interpretation, who is the "hostage" in this story, and in what sense?

RELATE 7. Compare the depictions of violence in Oates's story and in Garrett Hongo's Insight poem "The Legend." How similar do the writers' views of the world seem to be?

ANOTHER PATHWAY

Cooperative Learning

Gather in groups of five and role-play each of the following characters, telling how the character views Bruno Sokolov and why:

- the narrator
- the madman in the library
- the juvenile-court judge
- one of Bruno's teachers
- Bruno himself

LITERARY CONCEPTS

The ancient Greek philosopher Aristotle defined a **tragic hero** as a character whose basic goodness and superiority are marred by a tragic flaw—a fatal error in judgment that leads to the hero's downfall. Before tragic heroes meet their downfall, they perceive how they have contributed to their own destruction. To what degree do you think Bruno fits this definition of a tragic hero?

QUICKWRITES

1. How do you believe Bruno's life would have turned out if he had not stabbed the man in the library? Write the **profile** of him that might eventually have appeared in the local newspaper. Be prepared to explain your predictions for him.

2. Draft an **expository essay** or sketch out a detailed **diagram** in which you explore the causes and effects of Bruno's actions. Ask a partner to read your work and to make suggestions.

PORTFOLIO *Save your writing. You may want to use it later as a springboard to a piece for your portfolio.*

ALTERNATIVE ACTIVITIES

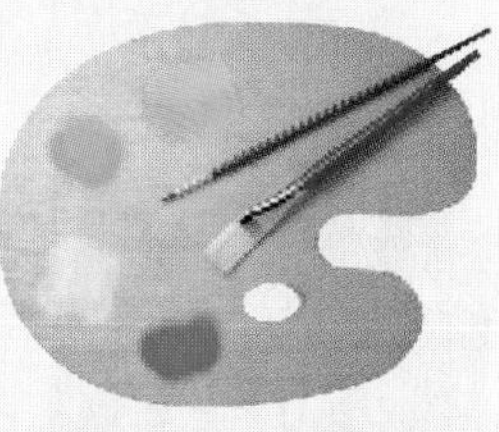

1. Review the many visual details that Oates uses to describe Bruno. Then sketch a **portrait** of him.
2. Was the sentence Bruno received from the juvenile-court judge justified? With a small group of classmates, have a **debate.**

LITERARY LINKS

1. Compare the causes, effects, and perceptions of violence in Oates's story and in Ray Bradbury's "The Murderer" (page 1088). Why are the stories so different in feeling?
2. Oates often has been compared to Flannery O'Connor, author of "The Life You Save May Be Your Own" (page 404). In your view, what do the two writers have in common? How do they differ?

CRITIC'S CORNER

1. One of our student board members, Katie McGuire, made this comment about the story: "At first, the author kept my interest by using a lot of description. . . . However, I think there was *too* much description. If the description was kept minimal, the story would have probably been more interesting." What do *you* think about the amount of description in Oates's story? Why might she have included so much?
2. In an interview, Joyce Carol Oates once argued that "all art is moral, educative, illustrative." To what extent do you think "Hostage" fits this description? What moral issues does it raise? What does it teach or show? Explain.

THE WRITER'S STYLE

Oates's **diction,** or choice of words, is said to be violent, even when it is describing commonplace, trivial events. In her book *The Tragic Vision of Joyce Carol Oates,* the critic Mary Kathryn Grant writes: "By repeatedly describing even the most ordinary of human actions in terms of hostility, brutality, and truculence, Oates creates a totally violent fictive world." How true is this in "Hostage"? Go back through the story and examine the specific words she uses, listing those with violent connotations and noting what they describe.

Violent Words	Describe
"crude and brutal"	Bruno's haircut
"sharp stabbing", "cut me like a knife"	narrator's envy

ACROSS THE CURRICULUM

Mathematics/Sociology In "Hostage," both the narrator and Bruno are touched by violence. Find recent statistics on violent crime in the United States, and use them to answer the following questions and others that interest you: Has violent crime increased in recent years? What proportion of violent crime is committed by teenagers? Has this proportion increased in recent years? You may also want to gather statistics for your own area from a local law-enforcement agency. Display your findings in line, bar, or pie graphs, and discuss with your classmates what these findings suggest about violence in this country.

WORDS TO KNOW

EXERCISE A Review the Words to Know in the boxes at the bottom of the selection pages. Then identify each pair of words as synonyms or antonyms. Afterward, choose a partner and take turns acting out the vocabulary word in each pair.

1. subtle—obvious
2. scrupulously—painstakingly
3. abrasive—soothing
4. rakish—drab
5. incredulously—doubtfully
6. infatuation—crush
7. antagonistic—agreeable
8. invest—supply
9. lurid—boring
10. affronted—offended

EXERCISE B Write the vocabulary word, not used in Exercise A, that best completes each sentence.

1. We often cannot know why people do the things they do; their reasons, motivations, and hopes may be too _____ for anyone else to comprehend.
2. Sometimes the people whose behavior drives others away are those who are, _____, most in need of and eager for friends.
3. Similarly, those who are most _____ may be those who are most afraid of being made fun of themselves.
4. Perhaps Bruno Sokolov was one of these people; perhaps his air of _____ masked deep doubts and insecurities.
5. When he boldly addressed the school assembly or spoke with seeming confidence in class, did he secretly fear _____ sounds of scorn from his listeners?

JOYCE CAROL OATES

1938–

Remarkable both for the quantity and the quality of her work, Joyce Carol Oates has published more than 25 novels, 15 volumes of short stories, and many collections of poems, essays, and plays. She has written an average of two books a year since she published her first collection of short stories, *By the North Gate,* when she was 25 years old. Many of her works, such as the novels *them* and *Wonderland,* hauntingly portray insanity and violence.

Oates was raised in a rural community outside Lockport, New York. Her father was a tool-and-die designer, and her mother was a housewife. Oates attended a one-room school, where her determination and studious habits set her apart from her rowdy classmates. Her mother recalls, "She was always so hard-working, a perfectionist at everything." A brilliant student, Oates graduated Phi Beta Kappa from Syracuse University, where she was valedictorian of her class. In 1961 she earned a master's degree at the University of Wisconsin and married fellow writer Raymond J. Smith.

After winning the National Book Award for *them,* Oates described the aim of her fiction. She said, "I have tried to give a shape to certain obsessions of mid-century Americans—a confusion of love and money, of categories of public and private experience, of . . . an urge to violence as the answer to all problems, an urge to self-annihilation, suicide, the ultimate experience and the ultimate surrender. The use of language is all we have to pit against death and silence."

OTHER WORKS *A Bloodsmoor Romance; Expensive People; The Time Traveler; Where Are You Going, Where Have You Been?; Because It Is Bitter, and Because It Is My Heart*

PREVIEWING

POETRY

Mexicans Begin Jogging
Gary Soto

Legal Alien
Pat Mora

PERSONAL CONNECTION

Both of the poems you are about to read explore what happens when someone is prejudged or is treated differently on the basis of a stereotype. Think of a time when someone judged you without first getting to know you. What was assumed about you, and why? What was your attitude about being prejudged in that way? What difficulties do you think that prejudging might create, for either the person judging or the person being judged? Write your thoughts in your notebook, then discuss them with a small group of classmates.

CULTURAL CONNECTION

These poems present ideas about citizenship and immigration. "Legal alien" is a term applied to an immigrant who has been granted legal permanent residence in the United States, even though he or she is not a U.S. citizen. The speaker in "Mexicans Begin Jogging" is a United States citizen who is mistakenly prejudged to be an "illegal alien"—an immigrant who enters the United States illegally. An estimated 300,000 illegal aliens enter the United States each year. Many of these illegal aliens migrate north to cross the 1,952-mile-long border between the United States and Mexico. The Border Patrol, which was created in 1924, has thus far been unable to control illegal immigration from Mexico. Border Patrol activities include not only efforts to stop entry at the border but also searches to capture illegal immigrants in the United States in order to return them to their home countries.

READING CONNECTION

Recognizing Tone Tone refers to the attitude a writer takes toward the subject he or she is writing about. As you read, notice the tone of "Mexicans Begin Jogging" and "Legal Alien." Watch for clues that indicate each poet's attitude toward being prejudged. Identify images and individual words—nouns, verbs, and adjectives—that convey how each poet feels, and jot them down in your notebook.

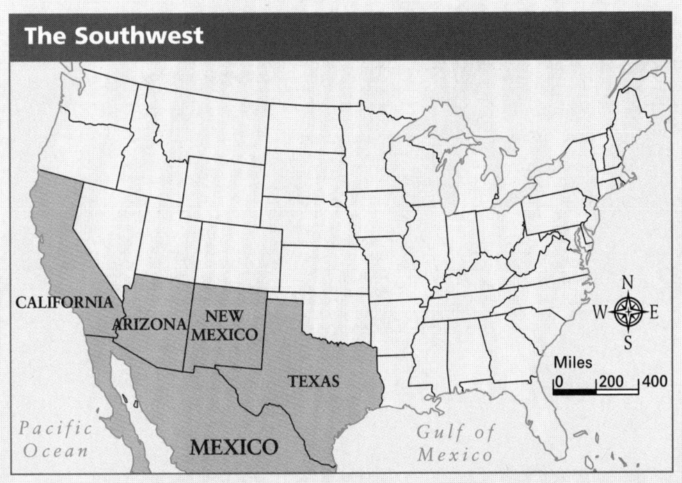

MEXICANS BEGIN JOGGING

GARY SOTO

At the factory I worked
In the fleck of rubber, under the press
Of an oven yellow with flame,
Until the border patrol opened
Their vans and my boss waved for us to run.
"Over the fence, Soto," he shouted,
And I shouted that I was American.
"No time for lies," he said, and pressed
A dollar in my palm, hurrying me
Through the back door.

Since I was on his time, I ran
And became the wag to a short tail of Mexicans—
Ran past the amazed crowds that lined
The street and blurred like photographs, in rain.
I ran from that industrial road to the soft
Houses where people paled at the turn of an autumn sky.
What could I do but yell *vivas*[1]
To baseball, milkshakes, and those sociologists
Who would clock me
As I jog into the next century
On the power of a great, silly grin.

1. *vivas* (vē′väs) *Spanish:* cheers.

Illegal immigrants scaling the wall along the U.S.-Mexican border near Tijuana.
AP/Wide World Photos.

FROM PERSONAL RESPONSE *TO* CRITICAL ANALYSIS

REFLECT

1. If you met the speaker of "Mexicans Begin Jogging," what do you think he would be like? Share your speculations with classmates.

RETHINK

2. Why do you think the speaker runs from the border patrol?
3. How would you describe the speaker's apparent attitude toward being prejudged?
   Consider
   - his indicating in line 7 that he is an American
   - why the speaker cheers for baseball, milkshakes, and sociologists (lines 17–21)
   - the irony of the title of the poem
4. What words and images do you think most effectively convey the tone of this poem?
5. What does the speaker suggest to you about the future direction of the United States in the line "As I jog into the next century"?

Looking through a hole in the border wall.
Copyright © Paul Fusco/Magnum Photos, Inc.

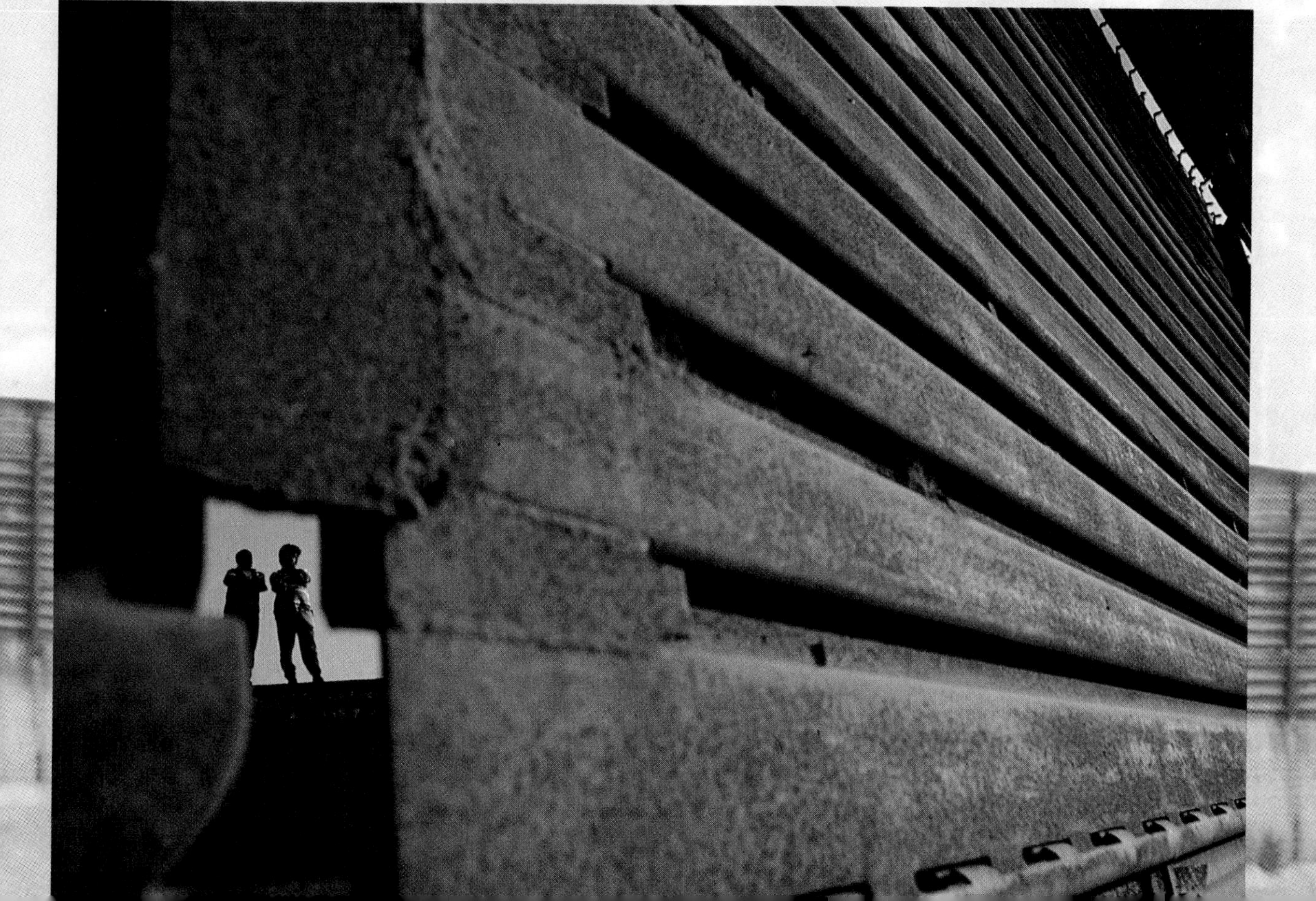

LEGAL ALIEN

PAT MORA

Bi-lingual, Bi-cultural,
able to slip from "How's life?"
to *"Me'stan volviendo loca,"*[1]
able to sit in a paneled office
drafting memos in smooth English,
able to order in fluent Spanish
at a Mexican restaurant,
American but hyphenated,
viewed by Anglos as perhaps exotic,
perhaps inferior, definitely different,
viewed by Mexicans as alien,
(their eyes say, "You may speak
Spanish but you're not like me")
an American to Mexicans
a Mexican to Americans
a handy token
sliding back and forth
between the fringes of both worlds
by smiling
by masking the discomfort
of being pre-judged
Bi-laterally.[2]

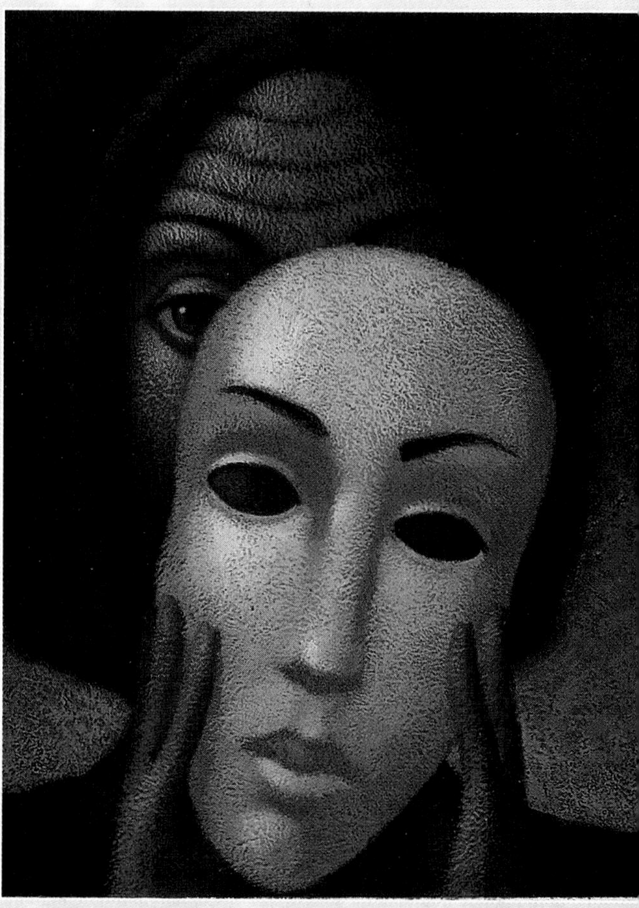

Illustration Copyright © Rob Colvin/Stock Illustration Source.

1. ***"Me'stan volviendo loca"*** (mĕ-stän′ vôl-vē-ĕn′dô lô′kä) *Spanish:* "They're making me crazy."
2. **Bi-laterally:** in a way that is undertaken by two sides equally.

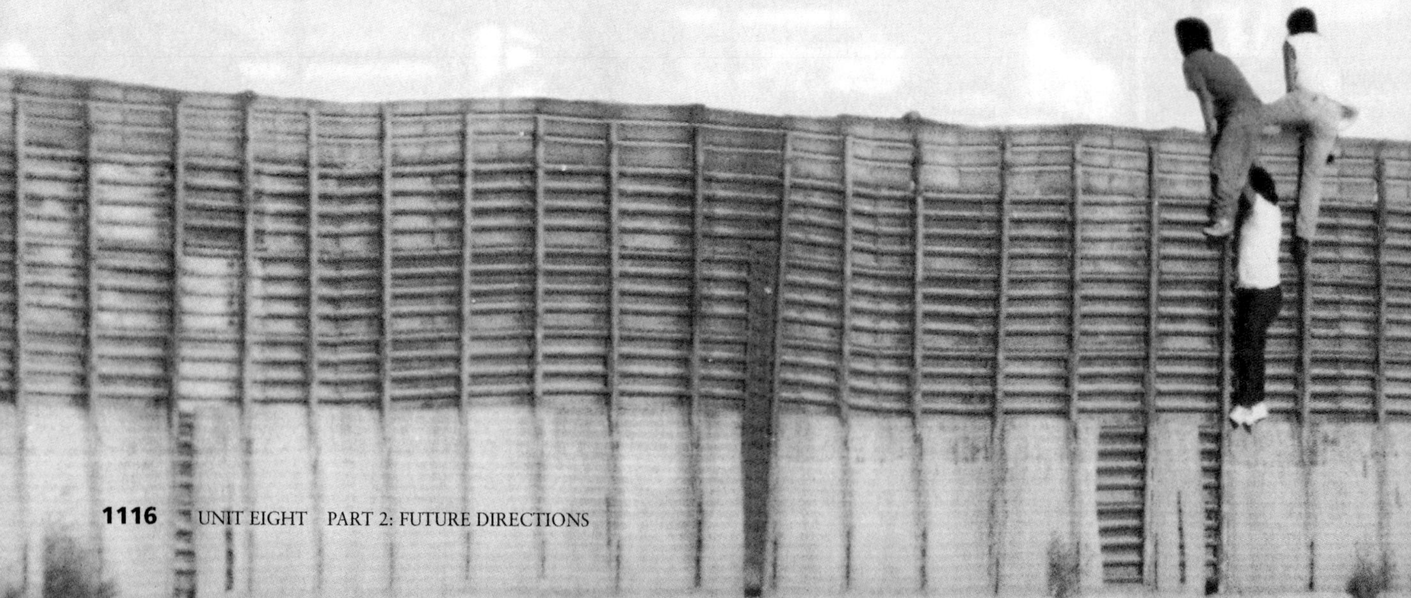

RESPONDING OPTIONS

FROM PERSONAL RESPONSE *TO* CRITICAL ANALYSIS

REFLECT 1. How do you visualize the speaker of "Legal Alien"? Describe the speaker in your notebook.

RETHINK 2. How do you think the speaker feels about being bilingual and bicultural?

Consider
- how she is viewed by Anglos
- how she is viewed by Mexicans

3. Which words and images best communicate the poem's tone to you?

4. What advantages and disadvantages do you see in being bilingual and bicultural? Use details from the poem and ideas from your own experience.

RELATE 5. How would you compare the experiences that "Mexicans Begin Jogging" and "Legal Alien" describe?

6. Recall what you wrote for the Personal Connection (page 1113) about being prejudged. Was your reaction closer to that of the speaker of Soto's poem or Mora's poem? How do you think most people feel about being prejudged?

ANOTHER PATHWAY

Cooperative Learning

With several classmates, plan and perform a dramatization based on one of these poems. For example, you might depict the speaker of "Legal Alien" encountering an Anglo and then a Mexican, or you might act out what happens to the speaker of "Mexicans Begin Jogging" when the Border Patrol arrives.

LITERARY CONCEPTS

The distinguishing name attached to any piece of writing is its **title.** The title of a work of literature may suggest its subject, convey tone, highlight the theme, or pique a reader's interest. What do the titles "Mexicans Begin Jogging" and "Legal Alien" suggest to you about the subject of each of the poems and the poet's attitude toward the subject? What ideas about theme can you take from the titles? Do you think these are good titles for the poems? Share your thoughts with a small group of classmates. Brainstorm some alternative titles that you think capture the essence of each poem.

QUICKWRITES

1. Look back at one of the poems and consider its tone. How might the poem be different if the poet had a different attitude toward the subject? Rewrite three to five **lines** with this attitude.
2. The speakers in these poems are both prejudged because they are Mexican Americans. To express your opinion about being prejudged in general or about your own experience with being prejudged, draft a **guest column** for a student magazine or newspaper.

PORTFOLIO *Save your writing. You may want to use it later as a springboard to a piece for your portfolio.*

ACROSS THE CURRICULUM

Government The title of "Legal Alien" refers to a person who is authorized to live in the United States but is not a citizen of this country. The speaker in "Mexicans Begin Jogging" is a U.S. citizen, though he is perceived not to be. Find out how a person becomes a citizen of the United States. What requirements must someone who was born in another country meet to become a U.S. citizen? How long does the process take? Create a flow chart to illustrate the steps in this process, and share it with the class.

LITERARY LINKS

Cooperative Learning With three classmates, act as S. I. Hayakawa ("The Case for Official English," page 1060), Carlos Alberto Montaner ("Why Fear Spanish?" page 1060), the speaker of "Refugee Ship" (page 1068), and the speaker of "Legal Alien." Stage a discussion the four might have about the issue of bilingualism.

GARY SOTO

1952–

Gary Soto writes poetry that explores his childhood, his adolescence, and his ethnic identity. Growing up in a working-class Mexican-American family in the San Joaquin Valley, Soto worked as a migrant farm worker before entering college. When he encountered Donald Allen's anthology *The New American Poetry,* Soto decided to become a poet. "I discovered this poetry and thought, This is terrific; I'd like to do something like this."

At California State University at Fresno, Soto studied writing with the poet Philip Levine, then earned a master's degree in creative writing from the University of California, Irvine. His first collection of poetry, *The Elements of San Joaquin,* is a bleak portrait of the lives of Mexican Americans. His prose memoirs include *Living up the Street,* which won an American Book Award from the Before Columbus Foundation.

Soto teaches English and Chicano studies at the University of California, Berkeley. He wants his students "to understand how a writer puts things together, to see that it's not simply a mishmash of feelings."

OTHER WORKS *Black Hair, The Tale of Sunlight, Where Sparrows Work Hard, Small Faces*

PAT MORA

1942–

A poet, essayist, and children's book author, Pat Mora was born in the border city of El Paso, Texas. She graduated from Texas Western College and received her master's degree from the University of Texas at El Paso. Mora taught college English for ten years and acted as the host of a radio show, *Voices: The Mexican-American in Perspective.*

The recipient of a poetry award from *New America: Women Artists and Writers of the Southwest,* Mora has also won awards from the Southwest Council of Latin American Studies and the National Association for Chicano Studies. Her work appears in the anthologies *New Worlds of Literature, Hispanics in the United States: An Anthology of Creative Literature,* and *Woman of Her Word: Hispanic Women Write.*

In an interview, Mora identified the sources of her poetic inspiration. "I write, in part, because Hispanic perspectives need to be part of our literary heritage; I want to be part of that validation process. I also write because I am fascinated by the pleasure and power of words."

OTHER WORKS *Borders; Chants; Nepantla: Essays from the Land in the Middle*

LASERLINKS
• *ART GALLERY*

from A Gathering of Heroes

Gregory Alan-Williams

On April 29, 1992, the actor Gregory Alan-Williams was driving down Century Boulevard in South Central Los Angeles, when he heard the news of a jury's acquittal of four white police officers accused of beating the black motorist Rodney King. Later that day, Alan-Williams heard about the riots breaking out in his community. He decided to go to the intersection of Florence and Normandie avenues to try to convince people not to harm one another. After parking his car near the intersection and walking to it, he found himself facing a teeming mob, in which people armed with broken bottles, bricks, and rocks were pelting the cars that passed through the intersection. This excerpt is from Alan-Williams's book recounting his experience during the riots. It begins when a brown Ford Bronco, under attack by the mob, stops in the intersection.

Gregory Alan-Williams carries the beating victim, Takao Hirata, away from Hirata's vehicle. Courtesy of KNBC.

The windshield on the driver's side of the brown Ford Bronco segued almost invisibly from transparent ocean green to frosty white at the brick's impact. New missiles launched from three of the four street corners were already hurtling toward the two-door four-wheeler as it slammed to a stop. The driver quickly leaned right, locking the passenger door, then slammed home the lock nearest him. For a blink of an eye, it appeared that the truck's other glass barriers would hold, but a beat after the new projectiles ricocheted from them, the brittle panes shattered into a thousand hopeless pieces, and collapsed evenly from the window frame. . . .

A dozen or so people sprinted toward the Bronco sitting motionless in the middle of the intersection, ignoring the debris that flew past their heads toward the now nearly windowless vehicle. . . .

Someone behind me shouted as the first blow stunned the driver in his seat. The bottle came through the driver's side window which had been shattered by a metal-rod-wielding "champion"[1] at point-blank range. Like a starter's pistol, the crack of the glass against the driver's skull launched an onslaught of blows from every direction. Someone crawled through the windowless rear hatch and began beating the driver from behind. A tall slender young man ran from the southwest corner, jumped through the missing passenger window, and commenced a one-handed assault with a glass bottle, his legs dangling outside the cab.

From the first blow, the driver had been unable to protect himself. He was battered about like a sad puppet, his movements subject solely to the direction and momentum of his assailants' rage. Within fifteen or twenty seconds, the man lost consciousness, and slumped forward onto the steering wheel. Immediately, he was driven backward to an upright position by several more blows to the head.

As I watched, this brought home vividly something that had happened to me in junior high school in the spring of 1969. I was in the school auditorium; band practice was almost over, and we were waiting for the sound of the buzzer that would signal our release. I twisted apart my shiny black clarinet, swabbed out the saliva and placed the three sections snugly into the soft burgundy velveteen interior of its case. The buzzer went off. All of us began to move up the aisle of the auditorium toward our lockers to gather up our books and then board the buses for home. I was a few feet from the auditorium doors, engaging in some good-natured banter with another student, when some hard object—like a rock—slammed against my mouth: the flesh burst into bleeding pulp against my teeth. The strength of the blow, combined with the downward incline of the aisle, sent me reeling backward into the students behind me. They parted like the Red Sea. I fell over some seats, righted myself and touched two trembling fingers to the pain in my mouth. I could feel the flesh hanging from where my bottom lip had been.

Dazed and bleeding, I staggered back and forth across the aisle, trying to understand what had happened. I was frightened by the feel of my own blood, wet and sticky on my hands. I caught a blurry glimpse of someone standing laughing in the middle of the aisle. I couldn't make out his face, but he was huge. It turned out later that he was a big eighteen-year-old from a high school several miles away. Some kids were standing at the edges of the aisle, others had gathered up ahead and were watching silently from the double doors of the auditorium. A few joined my assailant in laughter. I careened wildly about the auditorium—a pitiful, helpless, hurt child. I didn't know who my assailant was, or why he had struck me. And I had lost my clarinet. I was hoping desperately that someone in this "enlightened landscape" would help me. Help me get away from that huge laughing figure, away from my shame and from those who watched me as I staggered about, bloody and afraid. Eventually a teacher came and helped me to the office.

A few days later, as I sat, stitched and swollen, in the vice principal's office, I came to understand

1. **"champion":** This refers to an earlier remark in which the narrator sarcastically labeled rioters and looters as "champions" of their race and class.

what had happened, for the vice principal said that I had come to his school "walking too tall" and holding my head "a little too high" and many of the students resented it. "So," he said to my mother, "of course, what could you expect?"

Only a short time before I had transferred to this school from a predominantly black school in Des Moines, where I had not seemed to fit in: my "ethnicity" had been questioned, so to speak. I wasn't an athlete, I liked to play the piano, and I "talked funny." I thought I would be happier here. Now I was overwhelmed with despair at the discovery that in this Middle-American educational institution—where I was one of two African-American students—I was not respected as a human being. It was not my ethnicity that was questioned, but my humanity. I carried the scar of the incident for twenty-five years—not only physically, but psychologically, because through it I lost a trusted friend. I realized only recently that I haven't played the clarinet since that day in the auditorium.

Now the vivid memory of that beating and abandonment, some twenty-five years ago, propelled me into the intersection. I remembered too well the feelings I had had, the hurtful words and images—I could not accept this attack, the suffering of this human being. It seemed that he and I had become one, that his suffering and mine, present and past, had fused, and with one loud and silent voice now cried for help within this single irretrievable moment.

My conscience heard our cry, and carried me forward to preserve justice for him and to reclaim justice for myself.

I moved neither slowly nor quickly, not in anger but in extreme sorrow. Sorrow for those who were seeing, but who could not see; sorrow for the ones who saw but who had lost the ability to feel; sorrow for the hated and for those who nurtured hate with their silence. Although the man in the intersection was being robbed of his existence, my sorrow was not for death, but for the prevailing misery of life, and grew from a remembrance of the ache that comes with knowing that one has been exiled from the human heart.

Immediately, he was driven backward to an upright position by several more blows to the head.

"Come on, y'all . . . y'all know this ain't right," I said to several people jockeying for striking positions at the driver's side of the truck. One fellow had his hand on the latch, and was about to open the door. I looked squarely into the eyes of another who had just landed a blow to the driver's face. The bottle he was holding chest high dropped immediately to his side. He took a small step backward, bumping into a short, stout, middle-aged black man, who, with his back and right leg pinned against the vehicle, and his arms outstretched, was trying to hold people back and away from the truck while he pleaded for the driver's life. "Please, please! Don't do this. Please don't hurt him no more!"

The would-be assailant behind me had begun to open the door. With my left hand I gripped the door frame, pushed the door fully open, stepped in between the driver and his attackers, reached inside the cab, and grabbed the unconscious victim under the arms. "Come on man, let's go," I said. I could barely make out, through the blood, that he was of Asian descent. He was heavy and it took a moment to get a solid grip on him. I pulled hard and held my body against his back in order to ease his drop from the truck cab to the street, my face pressed against his blood-soaked hair. Suddenly the light which was coming through the window frame on the passenger side was blotted out by a large figure leaping head first into the cab. Simultaneously, a glass bottle shattered against the Asian man's face, spraying stinging shards across my left cheek.

For a few brief moments, time seemed to slow down tremendously; I felt as if my body and everything around me was moving at half speed. I had been calm as I walked toward the truck. But now, as I felt the tiny particles of glass clinging to my skin, real time resumed, and adrenaline[2] drove me backward and away from the vehicle with my unconscious and bloody stranger firmly in tow. I was praying that my legs would carry us far enough, fast enough, to escape the next blow.

After seeing the man being so easily jostled around the cab of the truck, I was surprised that his unconscious form was so heavy. Because he was so heavy, we were not moving fast enough to outrun the mob. Six or seven feet from the Bronco, a young man ran toward us, bottle in hand, cocking his arm for a hit. I knew what was coming. With all my strength I tried to turn the driver's limp body away from the direction of the attack. Sadly, I was too slow. The beer bottle disintegrated almost silently against the man's already unrecognizable face.

Anger and revulsion leaped into my throat as I watched his assailant scurry away toward the anonymity of the crowd. I cringed at the youngster's cowardice. . . .

For an instant I wanted to hurt him, as he had hurt someone else. I wanted to shake him until he woke from the senseless and bitter nightmare that had terrorized his spirit, and so wickedly altered his reality. I wanted to make him understand that he was the seed of a courageous and compassionate people. And, that although his American ancestors were often hard pressed for life's essentials, and sometimes for life itself, he was infinitely poorer than they. Because unlike those before him, he was now a man without honor. I wished that I could force open his eyes, so that he could look clearly at his victim, and see the truth about himself.

My anger subsided, replaced by a sad awareness that the sick and brutal young man might never perceive the spiritual self-destructiveness of his inhumanity. Perhaps in bitter years to come, as he sought to blame others for his discontent, he would somehow come to comprehend that it is most often our own actions which power the wheels of our fate. If he were very lucky, one day he might be shown, as I had been, that the millstone[3] of dishonor often far exceeds the weight of injustice. For dishonor, self-imposed, grates heavily upon the conscience, and crushes the spirit.

I pulled the still-unconscious man to the sidewalk, laid him on the pavement, and held his head in my hands. He appeared to be coming to, so with urgency, I asked, "Can you walk?"

He shook his head. No.

"Well, you gotta walk or you're gonna die," I told him, lifting him back to his feet.

He was more than wobbly, but managed to hold himself up long enough for me to get one arm around his waist, and his right arm over my shoulder. Unable to see for the blood which ran freely into his eyes, semi-conscious and beaten nearly beyond recognition, miraculously he began to put one foot in front of the other as I guided him down the sidewalk. He held on to me the way a drowning man clings to a life preserver. And then he looked at me in a way that seemed so familiar—I had seen it somewhere before, but couldn't place it. The look came from deep within him, a look that said "thanks," and "congratulations," all at once. Suddenly, I experienced a buoyant and peaceful feeling, a mood so confident and gentle that I knew our communion was a celebration of life. And that, if we survived, from this day forward, we would have that life more abundantly.

"What's your name?" I asked him.

I attributed his unintelligible answer to the

---

2. **adrenaline** (ə-drĕn′ə-lĭn): a hormone secreted in response to stress; it stimulates the heart and increases blood sugar and muscular strength.

3. **millstone:** a large stone used to grind grain, used figuratively here to mean a heavy weight or burden.

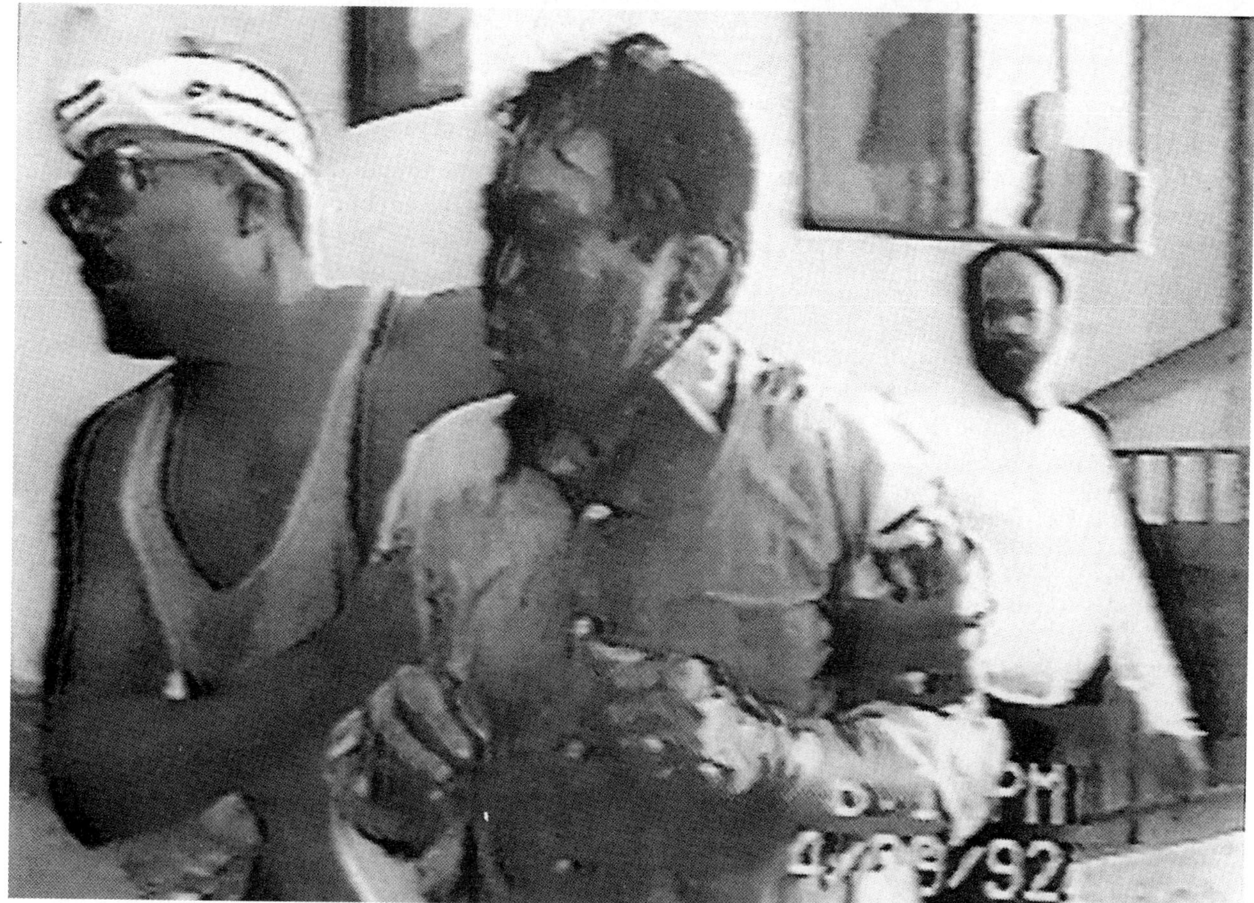

This video footage, taken by a bystander, shows the two men escaping down a side street.
Image by Mark Petty, courtesy of Academy Chicago Publishers.

thickness of a foreign accent and assumed that he was a recent immigrant.

"Welcome to America," I said with a smile. Later I realized that he could not speak because his lips were torn and broken. I also found out later that this American had been born in a government internment camp during the Second World War, and that he had grown up not far from this very street. In response to my mistaken welcome, he raised the one eye which had not swelled shut, and through shattered blood-caked lips, and broken teeth, flashed me a small painful grin.

"Yeah, you Korean . . . , got what you deserved, that's for Latasha Harlins!" a teenage girl screamed as she passed to our right on the sidewalk, referring to the Los Angeles teenager who had been killed by a Korean grocer the previous year. The angry girl's companion stood wide-eyed as we approached, then covered her own gaping, speechless mouth with one hand, closed her eyes, and rushed past us, unable to look upon the face of vengeance.

As we moved down the sidewalk, people parted to let us by. Their expressions varied from shock and horror to broad smiles and indifferent stares. Some burst into tears at the sight of the wounded man. Others, calloused by a brutal existence, glanced in our direction, and continued their curbside conversations. . . .

My friend was getting heavier. I needed to find a safe place for a moment's rest. On our right, in the middle of the block, we turned into a driveway that led to a small apartment building which stood in back of the commercial property that fronted the street. To my left, I noticed another building with rear steps which were not visible from Florence. Relieved, I ducked around the corner of the structure and made a move to set my charge down on the concrete stairs. "Hell no!" a voice from behind me hollered. "Get him the hell out of here!" Across the driveway, a small tan-skinned man struck firmly at the air with the back of his hand, gesturing for us to go away. . . .

I figured we had enough trouble, so I didn't argue. I picked my friend up again and headed back out to the street. The man's female companion began to plead with him on our behalf, but he refused to listen. I sensed, however, that her words had affected him, for as we resumed our journey, we passed directly in front of him and even as he continued to order us off his property, he could no longer look at us. He literally turned his back as he drove us away with his fear. . . .

After several minutes, a great shout went up from the corner: a black-and-white police cruiser had passed, headed toward the intersection, and the bystanders were hailing the officers on our behalf. The squad car backed up, turned, and pulled to a stop in front of us. I smiled when I spoke to them, glad that my mission was nearly accomplished. "This guy's hurt bad, he needs help," I said.

The black officer behind the wheel and his white female partner were silent. They stared at us for twenty or thirty seconds; then, without gesture or word, they drove away. Immediately, adrenaline started losing ground to the fear not so deep inside me. I couldn't believe it. I had kept walking in the certainty that eventually, in the midst of this madness, I would run into a cop or a paramedic. And I had been right, but now they were driving away, and I was so stunned I couldn't even cry out after them. I watched as they made a U-turn at the next intersection and headed back toward us. Again they stopped and looked. The black cop was talking on the radio. The female cop, blond with a Gibson Girl hairstyle,[4] looked at us over the ridge of the seat. The male cop was wearing his "street face," but I could tell that the woman officer was concerned. The look on her face said she wanted to help us, but was somehow prevented from doing so. That look stayed on her face, even as her partner pulled off for the second and final time. . . .

With the departure of the officers, it became clear to all that chaos reigned. . . .

With the departure of the officers, it became clear to all that chaos reigned.

In a reality ruled by madmen, mutes, and cowards, I pulled my friend to his feet and contemplated a new journey. Again he began to turn deliriously, this way and that. "Don't move, damn it, just don't move," I demanded. I held him close like a lover, locking him in an embrace to keep him motionless. We could not turn back. To go north we would have to cross Florence. Continuing east would take us further from the violence but toward what, I could not be sure. The residential road to the south was empty. As far as I could see there were only locked and quiet homes. No crowds, no traffic, just an occasional weary-looking "revolutionary," sidestepping and glancing over his shoulder as he spirited a case of looted liquor toward some hiding place. So south we went, arm over a shoulder, arm around a waist. We had traveled only a short distance when I noticed the blood flowing dark and steady from my friend's left ear.

. . . I wasn't sure what sort of injury the blood indicated, but at that moment I began to fear that his injuries were threatening his life.

I hoped that the light pole would hide my friend from anyone looking south from Florence long enough for me to figure out what to do.

4. **Gibson Girl hairstyle:** a hairstyle created by sweeping the hair up high from the forehead into a bun or roll.

Within seconds a small blue car, full of little brown children, pulled to a stop behind me. A plump brown woman at the wheel leaned past the two children in the front seat and asked, "Do you want me to take him to the hospital?" There was little room left in the car, no way to conceal him except underneath the children. "No, that's okay," I said, "the kids might get hurt."

The woman was still for a moment, then nodded and drove off. As she pulled away, a brown Chevy van rounded the corner from Florence. "Yo man, you want me to take him to the hospital?" asked its lone occupant, a thirtyish black man wearing a black "doo rag" on his head; it hung down to his shoulders.

"Naw . . . that's all right," I said with a frown.

"You sure, partner? He looks like he's hurt pretty bad." The van driver pressed me.

I glanced at the blood still flowing from my semi-conscious friend's ear, then turned back to the driver. "You sure, man? You're gonna take him to the hospital, right?"

The man in the van seemed to appreciate my uncertainty; he became thoughtful for a moment, then replied, "For real, Black. For real."

I lifted my friend to his feet and carried him to the passenger side of the van. The driver leaned over, opened the door, and together we got him securely into the front seat.

"Thanks," I said to the driver, reaching over to shake his hand.

The victim, Takao Hirata, was taken to the Metropolitan Medical Center in downtown Los Angeles. Although severely beaten, he recovered. When Alan-Williams eventually met Hirata and his family in their home, he wept at the sight of the man he had saved, still disfigured but recuperating. Since the day of their first reunion, Hirata and Alan-Williams have become close friends. Recently, Hirata gave Alan-Williams a miniature samurai[5] *helmet, saying, "You are my samurai."*

5. **samurai** (săm′ə-rī′): a member of the Japanese feudal military aristocracy. The samurai code of conduct valued fearlessness, honor, kindness, and loyalty. His supreme duty was to protect his lord, regardless of his own safety.

Gregory Alan-Williams

Gregory Alan-Williams is a writer and an Emmy Award–winning actor best known for his role as Garner Ellerbee in the television series *Baywatch.* He has guest-starred on *Hunter, Fresh Prince of Bel Air,* and *Civil Wars,* and he appeared in the movie *In the Line of Fire.* He helped found the first African-American theater in St. Paul, Minnesota, and he has acted with several major theater troupes. He has also written a play, *The Life and Times of Deacon A. L. Wiley,* which was performed on public television.

Growing up in predominantly white Iowa during the 1960s, Alan-Williams fought racism with anger and hostility, a strategy that he later realized deprived him of friendship and self-love. Now a devotee of Martin Luther King, Jr., he regularly speaks about nonviolence on TV news programs, at schools, and at human rights conferences. The city of Los Angeles honored Alan-Williams for his heroism during the riots. More than a year after the riots, he was called to testify at the trial of the two men charged with beating Takao Hirata, Reginald Denny, and others. Many in the South Central community called him an outsider and a sellout for saving Hirata and testifying against the two young black men. But Alan-Williams defends his actions. For him, violence is not the way to affirm one's humanity in the face of injustice; instead, the solution lies in defining one's own self-worth and in loving one's neighbor.

WRITING FROM EXPERIENCE

WRITING A NARRATIVE

The selections in this unit, "Issues for Our Time," either describe or speculate on current trends in our culture. But imagine if you could move ahead in time. What new trends might emerge? What do you think our society will be like in 20 years? in several centuries? Like Ray Bradbury, you can use science fiction to express your ideas and concerns about where humanity is heading.

GUIDED ASSIGNMENT

Write a Science Fiction Story Write a short story that speculates about some aspect of the future.

Virtual Reality Goggles

1 Look for Story Ideas

Science fiction writers often find their inspiration in the scientific breakthroughs and developments of the present. Isaac Asimov, for instance, based his *I, Robot* series on the emerging science of robotics.

You can use the following suggestions to help you find your own story ideas.

Research Current Trends You can work individually or with one or two others to research current scientific or cultural developments that could serve as the basis for a good story.

Brainstorm with the Class Speculate with your classmates about possible advances in everyday categories: education, transportation, food production, work, sports, or medicine. You might create a web or chart listing your ideas.

Study the Prompts Look over the items pictured on this page and the next, and speculate about story ideas they may inspire. One student decided to use extinction theories and virtual reality as springboards for her science fiction story.

Newspaper Article

Scientists Debate How Dinosaurs Died

Why did dinosaurs die off 65 million years ago? A group of paleontologists met this week to debate extinction theories. Perhaps the least well known is the theory that diseases killed off the massive reptiles. Some scientists speculate that as species migrated, they encountered viruses that they had no resistance to. As a result, the theory says, the reptiles died from a series of viral plagues.

Others say there is more evidence that meteors or comets striking the earth are responsible for mass extinctions. A few astronomers point out that supernova explosions of nearby stars may have destroyed the earth's protective ozone layer and brought about the dinosaurs' demise.

What if in my story the dinosaurs died off from an unexpected cause?

I could do a story about a virtual reality program, set in the future, that gets too real!

Magazine Article

Alternate (Virtual) Reality

Virtual reality is the name of a new technology that creates the illusion of being immersed in an artificial world, or of being present in a remote location in the physical world. To enter virtual reality (VR), a person puts on a head-mounted display (HMD) that looks like a SCUBA mask. A pair of tiny television-tubes, special optics and wide angle lenses, and a device that tracks the position of the user's head are mounted in the HMD so that when it is worn, the normal view of the outside world is completely blocked; in the place of the physical world is substituted a stereographic, three-dimensional computer graphics depiction of a "world model" that exists in a computer. Besides being immersed in the artificial world, the person is able to navigate within that world, and to manipulate it using hands and fingers.

—Howard Rheingold, from *Virtual Reality*

Newspaper Article

Rent-a-Family Fills a Gap

Western industrialization has produced a major change in Japanese family life. Grown children pursuing careers are often too busy to visit their parents or no longer wish to have their elderly parents live with them. That's where Japan Efficiency Headquarters, a business consultant and training company, comes in. The company provides professional actors who serve as substitute "families." Children or elderly parents can hire the actors to visit their real family members. Although this may seem odd, so far the service has been highly successful.

2 Explore Your Ideas

List two or three ideas you have developed for science fiction stories. You can ask "what if" questions that might generate a plot line for each idea. For example, what if the moon could support life? What if all social dates were arranged by lottery?

Thinking on Paper

Your Imagination at Work Many writers find that the more preliminary work they do developing their setting, characters, plot, and conflict, the easier it is to write their story. The guidelines on these pages will help you choose your topic, consider the main story elements, conduct research, and plan your story before you start writing.

Organizational Folder for Story Elements

1 Choose a Story Idea

Select a story idea from your list that really appeals to you. Look over your "what if" responses and the scientific or cultural trend that serves as the basis for the story. Both items should pique your curiosity.

2 Consider Story Elements

A science fiction story, like any other type of story, must have a clear setting, interesting characters, a strong plot, and a good conflict.

Setting Setting tells the reader where and when your story takes place. Will it be on another planet, in a city, inside a machine? Will it be in the near or distant future? The SkillBuilder offers guidelines on how to establish the setting in your science fiction story.

Character Characters are the individuals in your story. Who will your main characters be? Will you use an object, such as a space ship, as one of your main characters? Try writing a brief character sketch for each one.

Plot This is the sequence of events in a story. Will you tell events in chronological order? Or will you move around in time—for example, from present to past and back? You can use a storyboard to help you plan the order of events in your story.

Conflict Conflict is the main problem your characters have to solve. What problems will your characters have to overcome in your story?

You can use color-coded file folders, like the one at left, for articles, pictures, or notes you gather for your story.

3 Research Your Story

You may need to do some background research on the scientific or cultural topic that serves as the basis for your story.

- Brainstorm a list of questions that your research will answer.
- Use databases, books, and popular magazines or newspapers to gather accurate information on your topic. These sources are more readable than technical journals.
- Make sure the concepts you use in the story are believable and accurate. Focus on the key concepts—you don't need to include all you have discovered about the subject.

4 Get the Story Moving

Here are a few strategies to think about before you begin drafting that can keep your story going from start to finish.

Use Dialogue You can use dialogue to reveal character, present information, and move the plot along. For example: "What did you do to my program?" Taleen cried. The computer coughed modestly. "It was only a minor adjustment to your brilliant ideas," it replied. "Well, stop changing my display!" Taleen said.

Show, Don't Tell Let your readers experience your story for themselves. Instead of saying a house is futuristic, for example, you might show how the house cares for its occupants.

Remember the Details In science fiction writing, the details are what make the story believable. Use the information from your research as you work with your characters and plot.

Student's Story Notes

Setting: Cybernetics Institute, New Carlyle, Moon Colony. Story takes place in VR research lab and theater.

Characters: Taleen, a 17-year-old student, is smart, strong willed. Maybe show her parents? Hadrian is a computer, experimental model, always trying to "help" her.

Plot: Virtual reality competition at the Institute—Taleen creates a program that ends up changing the past. Dinosaurs don't all die? Maybe die of different cause.

Conflict: Between main characters; clash of future/past.

SkillBuilder

CRITICAL THINKING

Creating Setting
Setting in science fiction helps the reader visualize your fantasized future. The following questions can help you create vivid settings.

Housing, Tools, Equipment
Describe the room your characters are in. What is the furniture like? What equipment do they use at home or at work? How do things look, feel, smell, or sound?

Transportation How do your characters get from one place to another? Giving this information allows you to describe not only futuristic transportation but also the surrounding city, town, or countryside.

Climate and Landscape Think about your future world. Does it have more than one sun? What is the weather like? What landforms, plants, and animals does it have?

APPLYING WHAT YOU'VE LEARNED
Using one or more of these headings, try freewriting what your imagined future world is like.

THINK & PLAN

Reflecting on Your Topic

1. How can you work information about your topic into your story?
2. What details make your story futuristic? Will readers be able to visualize the world you create?

DRAFTING

Telling Your Story

The Plot Thickens Now you are ready to start turning your ideas into a complete story. These pages offer guidance on how to create the first draft and develop your story as you go along. You may find yourself changing aspects of the conflict, plot, or main characters to make your story more interesting, more dramatic, or more surprising.

1 Writing Your Draft

To help you write your draft, you might pretend you are telling the story to a friend, or imagine one of the characters is telling you the story as you write it down, or visualize the story and record it as it unfolds in your mind's eye. For alternative formats for your story, see the ideas presented in Share Your Work on page 1133.

Student's Discovery Draft

Workspace of Science Fiction

My Discovery Draft

"Dino-Doom" story starts out in the future—maybe around 2097—at the Moon Colony of New Carlyle. Main characters are Hadrian, an interactive computer, and Taleen, a student in a special school, Cybernetics Institute, where virtual reality (VR) research is done. She is smart, strong willed, has copper-colored hair and green eyes, and likes velour clothes.

Taleen and Hadrian are "partners" competing in a virtual reality contest at the Institute. Their category reads "Alternative Reality, Science." In 2040, Dr. G. Yung won the Nobel Prize for proving that the dinosaurs died from a series of viral diseases. Taleen's assignment is to create an alternative explanation for the dinosaurs' mass extinction. She decides to show them being killed off by a giant meteor striking the earth.

Students in her class talk about one scientist's concern that their virtual reality programs are so real they are changing the earth's past. Their teacher says, "That's complete nonsense."

Hadrian keeps "improving" Taleen's ideas—inventing three-legged dinosaurs, adding more meteors, etc. Taleen and Hadrian argue about their ideas. As she presents her program in the competition, she is horrified to find that Hadrian has once again "improved" the display, but it's so spectacular that they win.

Final scene is set back in year 2040. A different team gets the Nobel Prize for proving dinosaurs died as a result of meteors hitting the earth. VR program has changed the past.

Comments on My Discovery Draft

Describe virtual reality room to help reader see the surroundings and equipment.

Maybe use flashback to show her getting her competition assignment.

Should I show other students, teacher to make school more real?

Use dialogue here to reveal character and move plot along—throw in some humor as the two argue!

❷ Review Your Draft

You can ask these questions to help you evaluate the story.

- What technical details do my readers need to know to understand the story?
- What details should be added or dropped from the plot to make it more logical or exciting?
- How can I make my characters more believable? (See the SkillBuilder at the right for tips on presenting characters.)
- What details can I add to make the setting more vivid?
- Should the story be told from first-person or third-person point of view?
- How can I make the ending more satisfying?

❸ Rework and Share

These tips can help you rework the first draft of your story.

Dialogue Make sure every line of dialogue reveals character, advances the story, or provides essential information.

Descriptions Focus on the most important details first (the location of the virtual reality theater) and then add more details (the VR equipment, the seating in the theater). You might try visualizing how a camera begins with one section of a room and moves with the main character to reveal the rest.

Sensory Details The more you can help your readers see, hear, feel, taste, and smell sights and events in your story, the more vivid and real it will seem to them. Look for opportunities in your draft to include sensory details.

Ask peer reviewers to evaluate your story. You might use these questions as a guide.

- How did the story make you feel?
- Was the future I imagined believable? Why or why not?
- How can I explain the scientific or cultural information more clearly?
- What was the most interesting part? the least interesting?
- What made you care about the characters?

SkillBuilder

Presenting Characters
Characters are revealed through their appearance, words, and actions. Try these tips to present believable characters.

Description What details of dress, physical appearance, and personal characteristics make each character unique?

Dialogue What vocabulary, emotional tone, and rhythm does each character use? If one character speaks in short, staccato sentences, try having another character speak in less emotional language for contrast. Try "hearing" each person.

Actions How would each character react to an emergency? to success? to failure? to a challenge? Think about the different ways people you know would act and how their actions define character.

APPLYING WHAT YOU'VE LEARNED
Create a chart that compares and contrasts the description, dialogue, and actions of each character.

RETHINK & EVALUATE

Preparing to Revise

1. What can you do to make your characters more lifelike?
2. How can you show rather than tell an event or a scene?
3. How does the reader know when and where the story takes place?

REVISING AND PUBLISHING

Polishing Your Story

The Final Scene At this stage, you have a chance to look at your story with a fresh eye, consider peer feedback, review your story notes, and make any changes you think are necessary to polish your story.

1 Revise and Edit

Use the hints below, as well as peer comments, the Standards for Evaluation, and the Editing Checklist on the next page to revise and edit your story.

- The reader should be able to easily understand the setting, main characters, and conflict in your story.
- You can use dialogue to convey technical or cultural information to the reader and move the plot along.
- Keep the main conflict fairly simple. The more complex your story, the harder it will be for the reader to follow.
- The ending should be a logical outcome of the events in the story.

List the sensory details the writer used.

How did the writer use dialogue to move the plot along?

Science Fiction Magazine

Oh no! Taleen screamed in her mind. Hadrian had changed the program again! She had not one but *five* meteors to track. Only her lightning-quick reflexes kept the program from crashing.

The judges and audience rode along with the meteors as they entered Earth's atmosphere like streaking columns of fire, then struck the planet's single landmass with devastating force. A series of deafening roars shattered the air, and superheated gases flared out from the impact craters. For hundreds of miles around the explosions, huge reptiles reared their heads, bellowing in fear. Then the air itself caught fire, roasting the dinosaurs where they stood. Plants withered into ash and blew away in the fierce, hot winds. Whole forests became crackling infernos, and rivers boiled and turned to steam in their beds.

When the heat and winds died down, the ruined landscape resembled the surface of the moon. Here and there, the stripped, charred

"Dino-Doom"—cont.

skeleton of a dinosaur protruded from the gray, smoking ash.

For a moment, the judges and audience sat in stunned silence. *I'm dead*, Taleen thought. *Dead.* Then they were on their feet, cheering in a thunderous ovation. She and Hadrian had won the competition.

Stockholm, Sweden Year 2040

Dr. Janet Yusef raised her glass and smiled at the small gathering in the hotel room.

"To the Nobel Prize team who proved that meteorites caused the mass extinction of the dinosaurs!"

One of the scientists spoke up. "Poor Dr. Yung and his disease theory. Imagine, dinosaurs dying of reptilian flu! What an idea!"

The group laughed heartily. Then Dr. Yusef grew thoughtful.

"But what about that three-legged velociraptor we found? It's like something you'd invent with a computer. Very strange."

Everyone agreed it was very strange indeed.

Alternate Realities

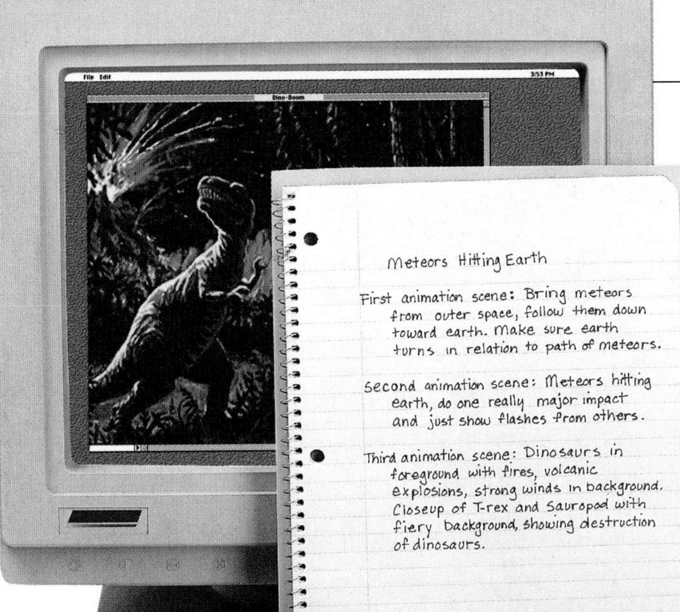

Meteors Hitting Earth
First animation scene: Bring meteors
from outer space, follow them down
toward earth. Make sure earth
turns in relation to path of meteors.
Second animation scene: Meteors hitting
earth, do one really major impact
and just show flashes from others.
Third animation scene: Dinosaurs in
foreground with fires, volcanic
explosions, strong winds in background.
Closeup of T-rex and Sauropod with
fiery background, showing destruction
of dinosaurs.

❷ Share Your Work

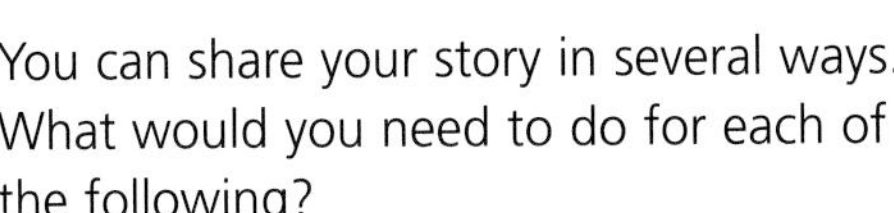

You can share your story in several ways. What would you need to do for each of the following?

- Create a comic book version.
- Turn the story into a script for a video and use special-effects software for the visuals. Ask your teachers or friends to recommend a good software program.
- Make an audiotape recording with sound effects.
- Write the story as a play with staging directions.

Standards for Evaluation

A science fiction short story
- presents a fantasized future based on a current trend
- has a clearly structured plot
- uses sensory details
- has strong, believable characters
- uses realistic dialogue
- has a satisfying ending

SkillBuilder

GRAMMAR FROM WRITING

Using Adjectives

The right adjective can help readers see, smell, taste, feel, and hear sights and events in your story. For example, compare these two sentences.

Here and there, the skeleton of a dinosaur protruded from the ash.

Here and there, the stripped, charred skeleton of a dinosaur protruded from the gray, smoking ash.

However, be sure to choose your adjectives carefully to avoid overwriting your descriptions *(thick, gray, smoking, deadly ash).*

Editing Checklist Use the following tips to revise.

- Have you spelled all technical and scientific words correctly?
- Did you select vivid adjectives to describe events or characters?
- Have you punctuated all dialogue correctly?

REFLECT & ASSESS

Learning from Experience

1. In a brief paragraph, explain how you created the characters and plot in your story.
2. Discuss in class how your story changed as you worked on it.

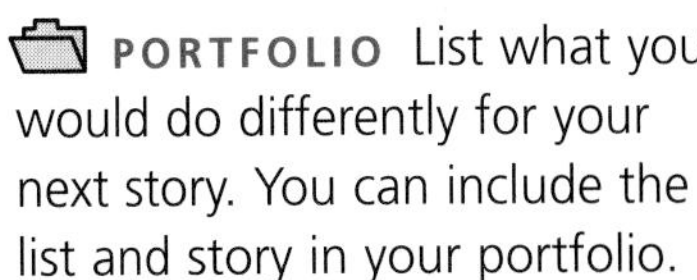

PORTFOLIO List what you would do differently for your next story. You can include the list and story in your portfolio.

REFLECT & ASSESS

UNIT EIGHT: ISSUES FOR OUR TIME

The selections in this unit focus on the present and the future of American society, with particular emphasis on social unity and quality of life. How have your own views about present and future life in the United States been affected by your reading? Choose one or more of the options in each of the following sections to examine what you've learned from the selections in this unit.

REFLECTING ON THE UNIT

OPTION 1 Closer Together or Farther Apart? Examine this unit's selections in relation to the opening quote from Marian Wright Edelman on page 1033. Which characters, writers, or speakers would say that more things unite Americans than divide them? Which would disagree? Gather in a group of four or five, with each member role-playing a different person from the unit. In a discussion of social unity in the United States, each student should classify the country as either united or disunited and should defend that position according to the point of view of the person he or she is playing.

OPTION 2 Looking Ahead Review the selections in this unit and choose four or more writers that most influenced your sense of what social issues will shape the future of the United States. Using the ideas of these writers as support, write a hypothesis of what daily life in the United States will be like 30 years from now. You might include predictions about the applications and influence of technology, the use of English and other languages, and the prevalence of violence.

OPTION 3 Issues for Our Time and the Future Review the selections in this unit, jotting down the social issues or problems that they raise. Choose the three or four issues that are most relevant to your own life and that you think will continue to be so in the future. Then do some freewriting about two of those issues. Explain why you think those issues are important to your life, whether you agree with how writers in this unit presented or interpreted the issues, and whether your opinions about the issues have changed as a result of reading the unit.

REFLECT & ASSESS *Self-Assessment: Now that you have considered how reading the selections in this unit has affected your views about American life and its future, make a two-column chart. In the first column, record the insights you gained about the social issues that influence American social unity and quality of life. In the second column, list the titles of the selections that provided the insights.*

REVIEWING LITERARY CONCEPTS

OPTION 1 Interpreting Symbols You know that symbols are things that have concrete meanings in themselves but also represent something beyond their concrete meanings. Choose five symbols from different selections in this unit, and interpret the symbols by making a chart like the one shown here. Then

Selection	Symbol	Idea or Feeling Represented
from A Gathering of Heroes	samurai helmet	the narrator's courage and honor

write a paragraph explaining which symbol you think most strongly supports a selection's theme.

OPTION 2 **Analyzing the Tragic Hero** You have learned that a tragic hero is a character whose basic superiority is marred by a tragic flaw, or error in judgment, that leads to his or her downfall. Review the selections in this unit. Which characters or actual people would you classify as tragic heroes? Which characters or people have some but not all of the qualities of a tragic hero? Jot down a paragraph explaining your choices.

REFLECT & ASSESS *Self-Assessment: On a sheet of paper, copy the following list of literary terms introduced in this unit. Underline the terms that you feel you understand completely. Put question marks next to any terms that you do not understand fully. Go back through the selections in this unit and consult the Handbook of Literary Terms on page 1142 to review those terms that you put question marks beside.*

dramatic irony	*loaded language*
symbol	*satire*
structure	*tragic hero*
persuasion	*title*

PORTFOLIO BUILDING

- **QuickWrites** Many of the QuickWrites in this unit asked you to express your opinion about a controversial social issue raised in a selection. Choose the response that best expresses an opinion about a social issue that you feel strongly about, and write a cover note explaining your choice. Attach the note to the response and put them in your portfolio.
- **Writing About Literature** Earlier in this unit you wrote a personal response to a selection. Reread your response now and review the reasons you gave for your opinion. In a brief note, describe which reason or example is most important to you.
- **Writing from Experience** Reread the science fiction story you wrote earlier. Imagine that a student magazine wants to publish your story in its next issue. The editor wants to include some background information about your story and about your writing process. In a brief note, tell how you came to write the story, what steps you took to draft it and revise it, and how successful you think your story is.
- **Personal Choice** Think about the activities and writing assignments that you have completed for this unit or the pieces that you have done for yourself. From which did you learn something that you'll apply again elsewhere in your life? Write a note that explains what you learned and how you can apply what you learned, attach it to the piece of writing or your record of the activity, and add both to your portfolio.

REFLECT & ASSESS *Self-Assessment: Now that your portfolio is nearly complete, examine for similarities and patterns the pieces you included. Do they indicate particular writing strengths, favorite topics, or preferred genres? Which piece or pieces are you most proud of?*

SETTING GOALS

Are there any social issues raised in this unit's selections that you would like to learn more about or do more about? Jot down a few thoughts about how you might get involved in a community or political effort to solve those social problems.

Student Resource Bank

Words to Know: Access Guide

A

B

C

D

E

F

Q

R

S

T

U

V

W

Z

Pronunciation Key

Symbol	Examples	Symbol	Examples	Symbol	Examples
ă	at, gas	m	man, seem	v	van, save
ā	ape, day	n	night, mitten	w	web, twice
ä	father, barn	ng	sing, anger	y	yard, lawyer
âr	fair, dare	ŏ	odd, not	z	zoo, reason
b	bell, table	ō	open, road, grow	zh	treasure, garage
ch	chin, lunch	ô	awful, bought, horse	ə	awake, even, pencil, pilot, focus
d	dig, bored	oi	coin, boy	ər	perform, letter
ĕ	egg, ten	o͝o	look, full		
ē	evil, see, meal	o͞o	root, glue, through		**Sounds in Foreign Words**
f	fall, laugh, phrase	ou	out, cow	KH	*German* ich, auch; *Scottish* loch
g	gold, big	p	pig, cap	N	*French* entre, bon, fin
h	hit, inhale	r	rose, star	œ	*French* feu, cœur; *German* schön
hw	white, everywhere	s	sit, face	ü	*French* utile, rue; *German* grün
ĭ	inch, fit	sh	she, mash		
ī	idle, my, tried	t	tap, hopped		
îr	dear, here	th	thing, with		
j	jar, gem, badge	*th*	then, other		
k	keep, cat, luck	ŭ	up, nut		
l	load, rattle	ûr	fur, earn, bird, worm		

Stress Marks

ʹ This mark indicates that the preceding syllable receives the primary stress. For example, in the word *language,* the first syllable is stressed: lăngʹgwĭj.

ʹ This mark is used only in words in which more than one syllable is stressed. It indicates that the preceding syllable is stressed, but somewhat more weakly than the syllable receiving the primary stress. In the word *literature,* for example, the first syllable receives the primary stress, and the last syllable receives a weaker stress: lĭtʹər-ə-cho͝orʹ.

Adapted from *The American Heritage Dictionary of the English Language, Third Edition;* Copyright © 1992 by Houghton Mifflin Company. Used with the permission of Houghton Mifflin Company.

Handbook of Literary Terms

Act An act is a major unit of action in a play, similar to a chapter in a book. Depending on their lengths, plays can have as many as five acts. Lewis Beach's *The Clod* is a one-act play.

See *Scene*.

Allegory An allegory is a work of literature in which people, objects, and events stand for abstract qualities. In an allegory, a bird might represent freedom, for example, or a child might represent innocence. Nathaniel Hawthorne's "Dr. Heidegger's Experiment" can be read as an allegory.

Alliteration Alliteration is the repetition of consonant sounds at the beginnings of words, as in the following line from Edgar Allan Poe's "The Raven": "Doubting, dreaming dreams no mortal ever dared to dream before." Poets use alliteration to impart a musical quality to their poems, to create mood, to reinforce meaning, to emphasize particular words, and to unify lines or stanzas.

Allusion An allusion is an indirect reference to a person, place, event, or literary work with which the author believes the reader will be familiar. For example, Patrick Henry warns colonists not to be "betrayed with a kiss"—a biblical allusion to the Apostle Judas, who betrayed Jesus by kissing him.

Analogy An analogy is a point by point comparison between two things for the purpose of clarifying the less familiar of the two subjects. In "My Dungeon Shook," for example, James Baldwin draws an analogy between his nephew's probable reaction to seeing the stars shining while the sun is out and whites' reaction to blacks moving out of their fixed places.

Anaphora Anaphora is a repetition of a word or words at the beginning of successive lines, clauses, or sentences. Gwendolyn Brooks uses anaphora in lines 2–4 of "Primer for Blacks":

> Blackness
> is a title,
> is a preoccupation,
> is a commitment . . .

See *Repetition.*

Antagonist An antagonist is usually the principal character in opposition to the **protagonist,** or hero of a narrative or drama. The antagonist can also be a force of nature. In Bernard Malamud's "Armistice," for example, the antagonist is Gus Wagner, the meat man, who haggles about the Nazis' war tactics with the protagonist, Morris Lieberman.

See *Character, Protagonist.*

Aphorism An aphorism is a brief statement, usually one sentence long, that expresses a general principle or truth about life. Ralph Waldo Emerson's "Self-Reliance" is sprinkled with such memorable aphorisms as "A foolish consistency is the hobgoblin of little minds."

Assonance Assonance is the repetition of vowel sounds within words. Both poets and prose writers use assonance to impart a musical quality to their works, to create mood, to reinforce meaning, to emphasize particular words, and to unify lines, stanzas, or passages. Note, for example, the assonance in the following lines from "Adolescence—III" by Rita Dove:

> Along the window-sill, the lipstick stubs
> Glittered in their steel shells.

Audience Audience is the person or persons who are intended to read a piece of writing. The intended audience of a work determines its form, style, tone, and the details included. For example, Cabeza de Vaca's audience for *La Relación* was the king of Spain. Hence *La Relación* took the form of a formal report with a patriotic tone that included details of the explorers' hardship and determination. Had the work been addressed to Cabeza de Vaca's wife, it would likely have been less formal and probably would have included details about his personal feelings.

Author's Purpose A writer usually writes for one or more of these purposes: to inform, to entertain, to express himself or herself, or to persuade readers to believe or do something. For example, the purpose of a news report is to inform; the purpose of an editorial is to persuade the readers or audience to do or believe something. Dorothy Parker's story "Here We Are" has the combined purpose of entertaining and imparting insights about human nature and marriage.

Autobiography An autobiography is the story of a person's life written by that person. Generally written from the first-person point of view, autobiographies can vary in style from straightforward chronological accounts to impressionistic narratives. Both *Narrative of the Life of Frederick Douglass, an American Slave* and *Coming of Age in Mississippi* are autobiographies.

Ballad A ballad is a narrative poem that was originally meant to be sung. Traditional ballads are written in four-line stanzas with regular rhythm and rhyme. Ballads often contain dialogue and repetition and suggest more than they actually state. Dudley Randall's "Ballad of Birmingham" is an example of a ballad.

See *Narrative Poem, Rhyme, Rhythm.*

Blank Verse A poem written in blank verse consists of unrhymed lines of iambic pentameter. In other words, each line of blank verse has five pairs of syllables. In most pairs, an unstressed syllable is followed by a stressed syllable. The most versatile of poetic forms, blank verse imitates the natural rhythms of English speech. Robert Frost's poem, "Mending Wall," is written in blank verse.

> I let my neighbor know beyond the hill;
> And on a day we meet to walk the line
> And set the wall between us once again.

See *Meter, Rhythm.*

Character Characters are the people, and sometimes animals or creatures, who take part in the action of a story or novel. Events center on the lives of one or more characters, referred to as **main characters.** The other characters, called **minor characters,** interact with the main characters and help move the story along. In Bernard Malamud's "Armistice," for example, Morris Lieberman and Gus Wagner are main characters, while Leonard, Morris's son, is a minor character.

See *Antagonist, Foil, Protagonist.*

Characterization Characterization refers to the techniques a writer uses to develop characters. There are four basic methods of characterization:

1. A writer may use physical description. In F. Scott Fitzgerald's "Winter Dreams," Judy Jones is described as follows:

   She wore a blue gingham dress, rimmed at throat and shoulders with a white edging that accentuated her tan. . . She was arrestingly beautiful. The color in her cheeks was centered like the color in a picture—it was not a "high" color, but a sort of fluctuating and feverish warmth . . .

2. The character's own actions, words, thoughts, and feelings might be presented. In Fitzgerald's story, after Judy Jones tries to revive the romance between herself and Dexter, she cries and says, "I'm more beautiful than anybody else, . . . why can't I be happy?"

3. The actions, words, thoughts, and feelings of other characters provide another means of developing a character. Mr. Sandwood, in Fitzgerald's story, exclaims about Judy Jones: "My God, she's good-looking!" To which Mr. Hedrick replies: "Good looking! She always looks as if she wanted to be kissed! Turning those big cow-eyes on every calf in town!"

4. The narrator's own direct comments also serve to develop a character. The narrator of "Winter Dreams" says of Judy Jones,

   Whatever Judy wanted, she went after with the full pressure of her charm. There was no divergence of method, no jockeying for position or premeditation of effects—there was very little mental side to any of her affairs. She simply made men conscious to the highest degree of her physical loveliness.

See *Character, Narrator, Point of View.*

Climax In a plot structure, the climax, or **turning point,** is the moment when the reader's interest and emotional intensity reach a peak. The climax usually occurs toward the end of a story and often results in a change in the characters or a solution to the conflict. In Edgar Allan Poe's "The Masque of the Red Death," for example, the climax occurs when the Red Death arrives at the masked ball and is confronted by Prince Prospero. Shortly afterward, Prospero and all of his guests die.

See *Falling Action, Plot, Rising Action.*

Conflict A conflict is a struggle between opposing forces that is the basis of a story's plot. An **external conflict** pits a character against nature, society, or another character. An **internal conflict** is a conflict between opposing forces within a character. In "Coyote and the Buffalo," for example, Coyote's struggle to keep Buffalo Bill from killing him is an external conflict, whereas Coyote's struggle to decide whether to kill and eat the buffalo cow is an internal conflict.

See *Antagonist, Plot.*

Connotation Connotation is the emotional response evoked by a word, in contrast to its **denotation,** which is its literal meaning. *Kitten,* for example, is defined as "a young cat." However, the word also suggests, or connotes, images of softness, warmth, and playfulness.

Consonance Consonance is the repetition of consonant sounds within and at the ends of words, as in the following line from Edgar Allan Poe's poem "The Raven": "Some late visitor entreating entrance at my chamber door."

Corrido A *corrido* is a fast-paced ballad that derives from the Mexican oral tradition. *Corridos* were first sung in Mexico in the mid-19th century and soon spread to the border regions of South Texas. A *corrido* generally involves a cultural conflict. For example, "The Legend of Gregorio Cortez," a prose retelling of a *corrido*, involves the struggle between Mexicans and Anglos in Texas at the beginning of the 20th century.

See *Ballad, Narrative Poem*.

Court Documents Court documents are a written record of what is said in a courtroom during a trial. *The Examination of Sarah Good* contains court documents from the Salem witch trials of 1692.

Cuento A *cuento* is a traditional folk tale that comes from the oral tradition of New Mexico and southern Colorado. First brought to the southwestern part of the United States by Spanish and Mexican settlers, *cuentos* were further influenced by Native American cultures in this area. Early settlers and their descendants told *cuentos* to entertain, reinforce cultural values, and teach traditional customs and beliefs to their children. "The Indian and the Hundred Cows" is an example of a *cuento*.

See *Folk Tale, Oral Literature*.

Cultural Hero A cultural hero is a larger-than-life figure who reflects the values of a people. Rather than being the creation of a single writer, this kind of hero evolves from the telling of folk tales from one generation to the next. The role of the cultural hero is to provide a noble image that will inspire and guide the actions of all who share that culture. Gregorio Cortez, a Mexican–American cultural hero, for example, exhibits family loyalty when he shoots the sheriff who shot Cortez's brother, Román.

Denotation See *Connotation*.

Description Description is writing that helps a reader to picture scenes, events, and characters. Effective description usually relies on imagery, figurative language, and precise diction. The following passage from Willa Cather's "A Wagner Matinee" illustrates the use of vivid descriptive language.

> . . . I saw again the naked house on the prairie, black and grim as a wooden fortress; the black pond where I had learned to swim, its margin pitted with sun-dried cattle tracks; the rain gullied clay banks about the naked house, the four dwarf ash seedlings where the dish-cloths were always hung to dry before the kitchen door.

See *Diction, Figurative Language, Imagery.*

Dialect A dialect is the distinct form of a language as it is spoken in one geographical area or by a particular social or ethnic group. A group's dialect is reflected in its characteristic pronunciations, vocabulary, expressions, and grammatical constructions. When trying to reproduce a given dialect, writers often use unconventional spellings to suggest the way words actually sound. Writers use dialect to establish setting, to provide local color, and to develop characters. In this excerpt from *The Clod,* playwright Lewis Beach reproduces a dialect spoken on the border between the Northern and Southern states during the Civil War:

> Yuh know I ain't got time t' stop an' load when I see the birds. They don't wait fer yuh. Them pigs has got t' be butchered.

Dialogue Dialogue is conversation between two or more characters in all forms of literature. In drama, the story is told almost exclusively through dialogue, which moves the plot forward and reveals character.

See *Drama.*

Diction A writer's or speaker's choice of words is called diction. Diction includes both vocabulary (individual words) and syntax (the order or arrangement of words). Diction can be formal or informal, technical or common, abstract or concrete. In this excerpt from *Stride Toward Freedom*, Martin Luther King Jr.'s diction is very formal, with difficult words and complex sentences:

> When, however, the mass movement repudiates violence while moving resolutely toward its goal, its opponents are revealed as the instigators and practitioners of violence if it occurs.

Drama Drama is literature in which plot and character are developed through dialogue and action; in other words, drama is literature in play form. Dramas are meant to be performed by actors and actresses who appear on stage, before radio microphones, or in front of television or movie cameras.

Unlike other forms of literature, such as fiction or poetry, a work of drama requires the collaboration of many people in order to come to life. In an important sense, a drama in printed form is an incomplete work of art. It is a skeleton that must be fleshed out by a director, actors, set designers, and others who interpret the work and stage a performance.

Most plays are divided into acts, with each act having an emotional peak, or climax, of its own. The acts sometimes are divided into scenes; each scene is limited to a single time and place. Most contemporary plays have two or three acts, although some have only one act. Lewis Beach's *The Clod* and Thornton Wilder's *The Long Christmas Dinner* are examples of one-act plays.

See *Act, Dialogue, Scene, Stage Directions.*

Dramatic Irony See *Irony.*

Epic Poem An epic poem is a long narrative poem on a serious subject presented in an elevated or formal style. An epic traces the adventures of a hero whose actions consist of courageous, even superhuman deeds, which often represent the ideals and values of a group of a nation or race. *I Am Joaquín* is an epic poem.

See *Narrative Poem.*

Epithet An epithet is a brief descriptive phrase that points out traits associated with a particular person or thing. Carl Sandburg's "Chicago" begins with a series of epithets, such as "Hog Butcher for the World."

Essay An essay is a short work of nonfiction that deals with a single subject. Essays are often informal, loosely structured, and highly personal. They can be descriptive, informative, persuasive, narrative, or any combination of these. Henry David Thoreau's *Walden* is an example of an essay.

Exaggeration See *Hyperbole.*

Exposition Exposition is the part of a literary work that provides the background information necessary to understand characters and their actions. Exposition typically occurs at the beginning of a work and introduces the characters, describes the setting, and summarizes significant events that took place before the action begins. The exposition in Dorothy Parker's "Here We Are" introduces the main characters, a young man and woman, who we find out have just married and are on a train on their way to New York City for their honeymoon.

See *Plot.*

Extended Metaphor An extended metaphor is a figure of speech that compares two things at some length and in several ways. Sometimes the comparison is carried throughout a paragraph, a stanza, or an entire selection. Emily Dickinson compares hope to a bird in a famous extended metaphor that begins as follows:

"Hope" is the thing with feathers—
That perches in the soul—
And sings the tune without the words—
And never stops—at all— . . .

External Conflict See *Conflict.*

Fable A fable is a very short folk tale that illustrates a clear, often directly stated, moral. The Pawnee fable "The Lesson of the Birds" teaches the moral of caring for younger generations and providing for their future.

Falling Action In a plot structure, the falling action, or **resolution,** occurs after the climax to reveal the final outcome of events and to tie up any loose ends. In Joyce Carol Oates's "Hostage," the falling action occurs after Bruno attacks the narrator's assailant and nearly kills him. We learn that Bruno is given six months probation and psychiatric care. He withdraws from others, quits school, joins the army, and is shipped to Korea, where he dies in battle.

See *Climax, Plot, Rising Action.*

Fiction Fiction refers to works of prose that contain imaginary elements. Although fiction, like nonfiction, may be based on actual events and real people, it differs from nonfiction in that it is shaped primarily by the writer's imagination. For example, although Garrison Keillor's "Gary Keillor" is based on true autobiographical experiences, it cannot be classified as nonfiction because it is imbued with imaginary events and exaggeration in order to capture the reader's interest. The two major types of fiction are novels and short stories. The four basic elements of a work of fiction are character, setting, plot, and theme.

See *Short Story.*

Figurative Language Figurative language is language that communicates ideas beyond the literal meaning of words. Here is an example from Luis Rodriguez's "Tía Chucha":

Every few years
Tía Chucha would visit the family
in a tornado of song
and open us up
as if we were an overripe avocado.

Figurative language can make descriptions and unfamiliar or difficult ideas easier to understand. The most common types of figurative language, called **figures of speech,** are simile, metaphor, personification, and hyperbole.

See *Hyperbole, Metaphor, Onomatopoeia, Personification, Simile.*

Figures of Speech See *Figurative Language.*

First-Person Point of View See *Point of View.*

Flashback A flashback is a scene that interrupts the action of a narrative to describe events that took place at an earlier time. It provides background helpful in understanding a character's present situation. For example, "A Rose for Emily" opens with Miss Emily's funeral, followed by a flashback that recounts how, when Miss Emily was alive, Colonel Sartoris exempted her from paying taxes.

Foil A foil is a character whose traits contrast with those of another character. For example, a writer might use a minor character as a foil to emphasize the positive traits of the main character. In "The Legend of Gregorio Cortez," the "loud-mouthed, discontented" Román is a foil for his heroic brother, Gregorio Cortez.

See *Character.*

Folk Tale A folk tale is a short, simple story that is handed down, usually by word of mouth, from generation to generation. Folk tales include legends, fairy tales, myths, and fables. Folk tales often teach family obligations or societal values. "Coyote and the Buffalo" is an Okanogan folk tale and "The Indian and the Hundred Cows" is a Hispanic folk tale.

See *Legend, Myth, Fable.*

Foreshadowing Foreshadowing is a writer's use of hints or clues to indicate events that will occur later in a story. Foreshadowing creates suspense and at the same time prepares the reader for what is to come. For example, in Nathaniel Hawthorne's "Dr. Heidegger's Experiment," the former rivalry for the Widow Wycherly foreshadows the rivalry that occurs later in Dr. Heidegger's study.

Form At its simplest, form refers to the physical arrangement of words in a poem—the length and placement of the lines and the grouping of lines into stanzas. The term can also be used to refer to other types of patterning in poetry, anything from rhythm and other sound patterns to the design of a traditional poetic type, such as a sonnet or dramatic monologue. Finally, *form* can be used as a synonym for *genre,* which refers to literary categories, ranging from the broad (short story, novel) to the narrowly defined (sonnet, dramatic monologue).

See *Stanza.*

Free Verse Free verse is poetry that does not have regular patterns of rhyme and meter. The lines in free verse often flow more naturally than do rhymed, metrical lines and thus achieve a rhythm more like everyday human speech. Walt Whitman is generally credited with originating free verse, as in these lines from "I Hear America Singing":

> I hear America singing, the varied carols I hear,
> Those of mechanics, each one singing his as it
> should be blithe and strong,
> The carpenter singing his as he measures his plank
> or beam,
> The mason singing his as he makes ready for work,
> or leaves off work, . . .

See *Meter, Rhyme.*

Gothic Literature Gothic literature is characterized by grotesque characters, bizarre situations, and violent events. Originating in Europe, Gothic literature was a popular form of writing in the United States during the 19th century, especially in the hands of such notables as Edgar Allan Poe and Nathaniel Hawthorne. Interest in Gothic revived in the 20th century among Southern writers such as William Faulkner and Flannery O'Connor.

Haiku Haiku is a highly compressed form of Japanese poetry that creates a brief, clear picture in order to produce an emotional response. that

Haiku relies heavily on imagery, usually drawn from nature, and on the power of suggestion. When written in Japanese, a haiku has three lines of five, seven, and five syllables each. Here is a haiku written in English by the poet W. H. Auden:

> Leaning out over
> The dreadful precipice,
> One contemptuous tree.

Humor Any literature that is intended to induce laughter or amusement in the reader is said to be humorous. Two great American humorists are Mark Twain and James Thurber.

Hyperbole Hyperbole is a figure of speech in which the truth is exaggerated for emphasis or for humorous effect. The expression "I'm so hungry I could eat a horse" is a hyperbole. Américo Paredes's "The Legend of Gregorio Cortez" contains many examples of hyperbole. For example, describing Cortez's abilities as a gunman, the narrator says, "He could put five bullets into a piece of board and not make but one hole, and quicker than you could draw a good deep breath."

Iambic Pentameter See *Meter.*

Imagery The descriptive words and phrases that a writer uses to re-create sensory experiences are called imagery. By appealing to the five senses, imagery helps a reader imagine exactly what the characters and experiences being described are like. The following passage from Washington Irving's "The Devil and Tom Walker" is rich in imagery, which *shows* rather than *tells* the reader that Tom and his wife are miserly:

> They lived in a forlorn-looking house that stood alone and had an air of starvation. A few straggling savin trees, emblems of sterility, grew near it; no smoke ever curled from its chimney . . . A miserable horse, whose ribs were as articulate as the bars of a gridiron, stalked about a field, where a thin carpet of moss . . . tantalized and balked his hunger.

Interior Monologue See *Monologue.*

Internal Conflict See *Conflict.*

Inverted Syntax When a writer reverses the expected order of words, it is called inverted syntax. In the first line of "Upon the Burning of Our House," for example, Anne Bradstreet writes "when rest I took" rather than "when I took rest."

Irony Irony refers to a contrast between appearance and actuality. **Situational irony** is a contrast between what is expected to happen and what actually happens. For example, in "We Aren't Superstitious" Tituba, who confesses to being a witch, is spared while those who deny being witches are hanged. **Dramatic irony** occurs when readers know more about a situation or a character in a story than the characters do. In Flannery O'Connor's "The Life You Save May Be Your Own," for example, readers find out that Mr. Shiftlet is a scoundrel before the other characters do. **Verbal irony** occurs when someone states one thing and means another. The title of Stephen Vincent Benét's "We Aren't Superstitious" is an example of verbal irony, since one of the main ideas in the essay is that we *are* superstitious.

Legend A legend is a story passed down orally from generation to generation and popularly believed to have a historical basis. While some legends may be based on real people or situations, most of the events are either greatly exaggerated or fictitious. Like myths, legends may incorporate supernatural elements and magical deeds. But legends differ from myths in they claim to be stories about real human beings and are often set in a particular time and place. "The Legend of Gregorio Cortez" is an example.

Literary Letter A literary letter is a letter that has been published and read by a wide audience because it was written by a well-known public figure or provides information about the period in which it was written. Abigail Adams's "Letter to John Adams" is an example of a literary letter.

Loaded Language Loaded language consists of words with strong connotations, or emotional associations. Writers and speakers use loaded language most often for persuasive purposes, such as in this example from "Sinners in the Hands of an Angry God":

> The God that holds you over the pit of hell, much as one holds a spider, or some loathsome insect over the fire, abhors you, and is dreadfully provoked.

Local Color Realism Local color realism is a style of writing that truthfully imitates ordinary life and brings a particular region alive by portraying the dialects, dress, mannerisms, customs, character types, and landscapes of that region. Mark Twain frequently uses local color realism in his writing for humorous effect.

Lyric Poem A lyric poem is a short poem in which a single speaker expresses thoughts and feelings in intensely emotional language. In a love lyric, a speaker expresses romantic love. In other lyrics, a speaker may meditate on nature or seek to resolve an emotional crisis. Anne Bradstreet's poem "To My Dear and Loving Husband" is a love lyric.

Main Character See *Character*.

Metaphor A metaphor is a figure of speech that compares two things that have something in common. Unlike similes, metaphors do not use the words *like* or *as,* but make comparisons directly. Abigail Adams's statement "our country is . . . the first and greatest parent" is a metaphor.

Meter Meter is the repetition of a regular rhythmic unit in a line of poetry. Each unit, known as a **foot,** has one stressed syllable (indicated by a ´) and either one or two unstressed syllables (indicated by a ˘). The four basic types of metrical feet are the **iamb,** an unstressed syllable followed by a stressed syllable; the **trochee,** a stressed syllable followed by an unstressed syllable; the **anapest,** two unstressed syllables followed by a stressed syllable; and the **dactyl,** a stressed syllable followed by two unstressed syllables.

Two words are used to describe the meter of a line. The first word describes the type of metrical foot—iambic, trochaic, anapestic, or dactylic—and the second word describes the number of feet in a line: **monometer** (one foot), **dimeter** (two feet), **trimeter** (three feet), **tetrameter** (four feet), **pentameter** (five feet), **hexameter** (six feet), and so forth.

In "To My Dear and Loving Husband," the meter is iambic pentameter, the most common form of meter in English poetry.

> Ĭf év | ĕr mán | wĕre lóved | bў wífe | thĕn thée.

In the following lines from Henry Wadsworth Longfellow's "A Psalm of Life," the meter is trochaic tetrameter:

> Téll mĕ | nót, ĭn | móurnfŭl | númbĕrs,
> Lífe ĭs | bút ăn | émptў | dréam!—

See *Rhythm*.

Minor Character See *Character*.

Modernism Modernism was a literary movement that roughly spanned the time period between the two world wars, 1914–1945. Modernist works are characterized by a high degree of experimentation and spare, elliptical prose. Modernist characters are most often alienated people searching unsuccessfully for meaning and love in their lives. For example, in "The End of Something," Nick Adams feels alienated from his girlfriend and cannot explain why. All he can say is that he feels "as though everything was gone to hell inside" of him. The question of what's bothering Nick isn't answered by the author. Departing from the usual detailed narratorial explanations of his predecessors, Ernest Hemingway gives little direct information about the characters' feelings or thoughts. Instead, the reader has to infer the characters' inner thoughts from their words and actions and from the symbolism in Hemingway's description of the setting.

Monologue In a drama, the speech of a character who is alone on stage, voicing his or her thoughts, is known as a monologue, or a **soliloquy.** In a short story or a poem, the direct presentation of a character's unspoken thoughts is called an **interior monologue.** An interior monologue may jump back and forth between past and present, displaying thoughts, memories, and impressions just as they might occur in a person's mind. "I Stand Here Ironing" is an example of an interior monologue.

Mood Mood is the feeling or atmosphere that a writer creates for the reader. The writer's use of connotation, imagery, figurative language, imagery, sound and rhythm, and descriptive details all contribute to the mood. Note Washington Irving's use of all of these techniques in creating the creepy threatening mood of the following passage:

> The swamp was thickly grown with great gloomy pines and hemlocks, . . . It was full of pits and quagmires, partly covered with weeds and mosses, where the green surface often betrayed the traveler into a gulf of black, smothering mud; . . .

See *Connotation, Diction, Imagery, Figurative Language, Style.*

Myth A myth is a traditional story, passed down through generations, that explains why the world is the way it is. Myths are essentially religious, because they present supernatural events and beings and articulate the values and beliefs of a cultural group. A **creation myth** is a particular kind of myth that explains how the universe, the earth, and life on earth began. "The World on the Turtle's Back" is an Iroquois creation myth.

Narrative A narrative is any type of writing that is primarily concerned with relating an event or a series of events. A narrative can be imaginary, as is a short story or novel, or it can be factual, as is a newspaper account or a work of history. The word *narration* can be used interchangeably with *narrative*, which comes from the Latin word meaning "tell."

See *Fiction, Nonfiction, Novel, Plot, Short Story.*

Narrative Poem A narrative poem is a poem that tells a story using elements of character, setting, and plot to develop a theme. Edgar Allan Poe's "The Raven" is a narrative poem, as is Dudley Randall's "Ballad of Birmingham."

See *Ballad.*

Narrator The narrator of a story is the character or voice that relates the story's events to the reader. For example, the narrator of Joyce Carol Oates's "Hostage" is one of the main characters, a girl in junior high school. The narrator of William Faulkner's "A Rose for

Emily," is an unidentified citizen of Jefferson, Mississippi, Emily Grierson's hometown.

Nonfiction Nonfiction is writing about real people, places, and events. Unlike fiction, nonfiction is largely concerned with factual information, although the writer shapes the information according to his or her purpose and viewpoint. Biography, autobiography, and newspaper articles are examples of nonfiction.

See *Autobiography* and *Essay.*

Novel The novel is an extended work of fiction. Like the short story, a novel is essentially the product of a writer's imagination. The most obvious difference between a novel and a short story is length. Because the novel is considerably longer, a novelist can develop a wider range of characters and a more complex plot.

Onomatopoeia The word *onomatopoeia* literally means "name-making." It is the process of creating or using words that imitate sounds. The *buzz* of the bee, the *honk* of the car horn, the *peep* of the chick are all onomatopoetic, or echoic, words.

Onomatopoeia as a literary technique goes beyond the use of simple echoic words. Writers, particularly poets, choose words whose sounds suggest their denotative and connotative meanings: for example, whisper, kick, gargle, gnash, and clatter.

Open Letter An open letter is addressed to a specific person but published for a wider readership. James Baldwin's "My Dungeon Shook" is an open letter addressed to his nephew but intended for the general public, particularly white Americans.

Oral Literature Oral literature is literature that is passed from one generation to another by performance or word of mouth. Folk tales, fables, myths, chants, and legends are part of the oral tradition of cultures throughout the world.

Paradox A paradox is a statement that seems to contradict itself but may nevertheless suggest an important truth. For example, Henry David Thoreau writes the paradox "I am not as wise as the day I was born." The statement suggests that civilization erases a child's innate wisdom and spiritual awareness.

Parallelism When a speaker or writer expresses ideas of equal worth with the same grammatical form, the technique is called parallelism, or parallel construction. For example, in "I Sit and Look Out," Walt Whitman uses parallel construction by beginning each line or independent clause with the word *I* followed by a verb—*sit, hear, see, mark, observe.*

> I sit and look out upon all the sorrows of the world, and upon all oppression and shame,
>
> I hear secret convulsive sobs from young men at anguish with themselves, remorseful after deeds done,
>
> I see in low life the mother misused by her children, dying, neglected, gaunt, desperate,
>
> I see the wife misused by her husband, I see the treacherous seducer of young women . . .

This parallel construction creates a rolling rhythm, emphasizes the role of the speaker, and conveys that the ideas are all related to the same theme—that the speaker observes "all the sorrows of the world."

Parody Parody is writing that imitates either the style or the subject matter of a literary work for comic effect. In "The Boston Tea Party," Dave Barry parodies serious historical accounts of the Revolutionary era by adding nonsensical elements from modern times.

Personification Personification is a figure of speech in which an object, animal, or idea is given human characteristics. In "Because I could not stop for Death" by Emily Dickinson, death is personified as a kind gentleman.

Persuasive Writing Persuasive writing is intended to convince a reader to adopt a particular opinion or to perform a certain action. The most effective persuasion usually appeals to both the reason and the emotions of an audience. Patrick Henry, Jonathan Edwards, Martin Luther King, Jr., and Malcolm X all use persuasion in their writing.

Plot The plot is the sequence of actions and events in a literary work. Generally, plots are built around a **conflict**—a problem or struggle between two or more opposing forces. Plots usually progress through stages: exposition, rising action, climax, and falling action.

See *Climax, Conflict, Exposition, Falling Action, Rising Action.*

Poetry Poetry is language arranged in lines. Like other forms of literature, poetry attempts to re-create emotions and experiences. Poetry, however, is usually more condensed and suggestive than prose. Because poetry frequently does not include the kind of detail and explanation common to the short story or the novel, poetry tends to leave more to the reader's imagination. Poetry also may require more work on the part of the reader to unlock meaning.

Poems often are divided into stanzas, or paragraph-like groups of lines. The stanzas in a poem may contain the same number of lines or they may vary in length. Some poems have definite patterns of meter and rhyme. Others rely more on the sounds of words and less on fixed rhythms and rhyme schemes. The use of figurative language is also common in poetry.

The form and content of a poem combine to convey meaning. The way that a poem is arranged on the page, the impact of the images, the sounds of the words and phrases, and all the other details that make up a poem work together to help the reader grasp its central idea.

See *Form, Meter, Repetition, Rhyme, Rhythm, Stanza.*

Point of View Point of view refers to the narrative perspective from which events in a story or novel are told. In the **first-person** point of view, the narrator is a character in the work who tells everything in his or her own words and uses the pronouns *I, me, my*. Joyce Carol Oates's "Hostage" is narrated from the first-person point of view.

In the **third-person** point of view, events are related by a voice outside the action, not by one of the characters. A third-person narrator uses pronouns like *he*, *she*, and *they*. In the **third-person omniscient** point of view, the narrator is an all-knowing, objective observer who stands outside the action and reports what different characters are thinking. Flannery O'Connor's "The Life You Save May Be Your Own" is told from the third-person omniscient point of view. In the **third-person limited** point of view, the narrator stands outside the action and focuses on one character's thoughts, observations, and feelings. Richard Wright's "The Man Who Was Almost a Man" is told from the third-person limited point of view, focusing on Dave's thoughts, observations, and feelings.

Props Prop, an abbreviation of *property,* refers to the physical objects that are used in a stage production. In Lewis Beach's *The Clod,* the props include furniture, food, a cook-stove, a towel, guns, a candle, a kettle, and a water pail.

Protagonist The protagonist is the main character or hero in a narrative or drama, usually the one with whom the audience identifies. For example, the young soldier, Rico, is the protagonist of Estela Portillo Trambley's story "Village."

See *Antagonist, Character.*

Protest Poetry Protest poetry is poetry written primarily not to express personal feelings but to persuade readers to support a certain political cause or take a particular action. James Russell Lowell's "Stanzas on Freedom" and Frances Ellen Watkins Harper's "Free Labor" are both protest poems that speak out against slavery.

Psalm A psalm is a sacred song or hymn. Capitalized, the word refers to any of the sacred songs or hymns collected in the Old Testament *Book of Psalms*.

Purpose See *Author's Purpose.*

Quatrain A quatrain is a four-line stanza. The following is a quatrain from Emily Dickinson's poem, "This is my letter to the World":

This is my letter to the World
That never wrote to Me—
The simple News that Nature told—
With tender Majesty

See *Poetry, Stanza.*

Realism In literature, realism has both a general meaning and a special meaning. As a general term, realism refers to any effort to offer an accurate and detailed portrayal of actual life. Thus, critics talk about Shakespeare's realistic portrayals of his characters and praise the medieval poet Chaucer for his realistic descriptions of people from all different social classes.

More specifically, realism also refers to a literary method developed in the nineteenth century. The realists based their writing on careful observations of their contemporary life, often focusing on the middle or lower classes. They attempted to present life objectively and honestly, without the sentimentality or idealism that had characterized earlier literature. Typically, realists developed their settings in great detail in an effort to re-create a specific time and place for the reader. Willa Cather, Kate Chopin, and Mark Twain are all considered realists.

See *Local Color Realism*.

Repetition Repetition is the recurrence of words, phrases, or lines. For example, the first line of "Song of the Sky Loom" is the same as the last line. Sometimes repetition is **incremental:** the structure of a line or stanza is repeated a certain number of times, with a slight variation in wording each time. The sequence "May the warp be . . . / May the weft be . . . / May the border be . . ." is an example of incremental repetition.

See *Anaphora.*

Resolution See *Falling Action.*

Rhetorical Question A rhetorical question is a question to which no answer is expected because the answer is obvious. Rhetorical questions are often used in persuasive writing to emphasize a point or create an emotional effect. For example, Patrick Henry asks this rhetorical question in his "Speech in the Virginia Convention": "Is life so dear, or peace so sweet, as to be purchased at the price of chains and slavery?"

See *Persuasive Writing*.

Rhyme Rhyme is the occurrence of a similar or identical sound at the ends of words, as in *tether* and *together*. **Internal rhyme** occurs within a line, as in the following example from Edgar Allan Poe's "The Raven":

> Ah, distinctly I remember it was in the bleak December;
> And each separate dying ember wrought its ghost upon the floor.
> Eagerly I wished the morrow;—vainly I had sought to borrow
> From my books surcease of sorrow—sorrow for the lost Lenore

End rhyme occurs at the end of a line. The pattern of end rhyme is called the **rhyme scheme** and is charted by assigning a letter, beginning with the letter *a*, to each line. Lines that rhyme are given the same letter. For example, the rhyme scheme of the first stanza of Anne Bradstreet's poem "Upon the Burning of Our House" is *aabbcc*:

> In silent night when rest I took *a*
> For sorrow near I did not look *a*
> I wakened was with thund'ring noise *b*
> And piteous shrieks of dreadful voice. *b*
> That fearful sound of "Fire!" and "Fire!" *c*
> Let no man know is my desire. *c*

The rhyme scheme of Frances Ellen Watkins Harper's "Free Labor" is *abcb:*

> I wear an easy garment, *a*
> O'er it no toiling slave *b*
> Wept tears of hopeless anguish, *c*
> In his passage to the grave. *b*

See *Slant Rhyme.*

Rhyme Scheme See *Rhyme.*

Rhythm Rhythm refers to the pattern or flow of sound created by the arrangement of stressed and unstressed syllables in a line of poetry. Some poems follow a regular pattern, or **meter**, of accented and unaccented syllables. Poets use rhythm to bring out the musical quality of language, to emphasize ideas, to create mood, and to reinforce subject matter.

See *Meter.*

Rising Action In a plot structure, the rising action refers to events that lead to the climax by adding complications or expanding the conflict. Suspense usually builds during the rising action.

See *Climax, Plot, Suspense.*

Romanticism Romanticism was a movement in the arts that flourished in Europe and America throughout much of the 19th century. Romantic writers glorified nature and celebrated individuality. Their treatment of subject was emotional rather than rational, intuitive rather than analytic. Washington Irving and Henry Wadsworth Longfellow were the two most popular American romantic writers.

Sarcasm Sarcasm is a type of **verbal irony** in which seeming praise is actually a bitter expression of disapproval. In "We Aren't Superstitious," for example, Stephen Vincent Benét sarcastically says of the court justices after they convict Sarah Good and Sarah Osborne, "The Justices, no doubt, congratulated themselves on their prompt and intelligent action." Although the comment may seem like praise, its context reveals that Benét scorns, rather than admires, the justices' action.

See *Irony.*

Satire Satire is a literary technique in which ideas or customs are ridiculed for the purpose of improving society. Satire may be gently witty, mildly abrasive, or bitterly critical. Ray Bradbury's "The Murderer" may be said to be a gently witty satire.

Scansion The process of determining meter is known as scansion. To scan a line of poetry means to determine a line's meter.

See *Meter*.

Scene A scene is a subdivision of an act in drama. Each scene usually establishes a different time or place.

See *Act*.

Science Fiction Science fiction is prose writing that presents the possibilities of the past or the future, using known scientific data and theories as well as the creative imagination of the writer. Most science fiction comments on present-day society through the writer's fictional conception of a past or future society. Ray Bradbury's "The Murderer" explores the potential harm of the intrusion of technological conveniences into every aspect of our lives.

Sermon A sermon is a form of religious persuasion in which a speaker exhorts the audience to behave in a more spiritual and moral fashion. "Sinners in the Hands of an Angry God" is a sermon.

Setting The setting of a literary work refers to the time and place in which the action occurs. A story can be set in an imaginary place, such as an enchanted castle, or a real place, such as New York City or Tombstone, Arizona. It can occur in the past, present, or the future. Willa Cather's story "A Wagner Matinee" is set in Boston around the turn of the century.

Short Story A short story is a work of fiction that can be read in one sitting. It usually focuses on one or two major characters and one major conflict.

A short story must be unified; all the elements must work together to produce a total effect. This unity of effect is reinforced through an appropriate title and through the use of symbolism, irony, and other literary devices.

See *Character, Conflict, Fiction, Plot, Setting, Theme*.

Simile A simile is a figure of speech that compares two things that have something in common. A simile states the comparison using *like* or *as,* such as Abigail Adams's statement "power and liberty are like heat and moisture" and Thoreau's statement "we live meanly, like ants."

See *Figurative Language, Metaphor*.

Situational Irony See *Irony*.

Slant Rhyme Slant rhymes are words that do not rhyme exactly. Emily Dickinson uses slant rhymes in the following lines:

"Hope" is the thing with feathers—
That perches in the soul—
And sings the tune without the words—
And never stops—at all—

See *Rhyme*.

Soliloquy See *Monologue*.

Sonnet A sonnet is a 14-line lyric poem that can have any of several possible rhyme schemes. The **Petrarchan sonnet** consists of two parts. The first eight lines, called the octave, usually have the rhyme scheme *abbaabba*. In the last six lines, called the sestet, the rhyme scheme may be *cdecde, cdcdcd*, or another variation. James Weldon Johnson's "My City" is a Petrarchan sonnet. A **Shakespearean sonnet** is divided into three quatrains (groups of four lines) and a couplet (two rhyming lines). Its rhyme scheme is *abab cdcd efef gg.* The couplet usually expresses a response to the important issue developed in the three quatrains. Claude McKay's "If We Must Die" is a Shakespearean sonnet.

See *Quatrain.*

Speaker The speaker of a poem, like the narrator of a story, is the voice that talks to the reader. In some poems, the speaker can be identified with the poet, as in the case of "Tía Chucha," Luis J. Rodriguez's tribute to his aunt. At other times, the speaker is someone or something other than the poet. In Sylvia Plath's poem "Mirror," the speaker is a mirror. In Dwight Okita's "In Response to Executive Order 9066," the speaker is a young girl.

Stage Directions Stage directions are the instructions for the director, performers, and stage crew. Usually set in italics, they are located at the beginning of and throughout a script. Stage directions usually tell the time and place of action and explain how characters move and speak. They also describe scenery, props, lighting, costumes, music, or sound effects.

Stanza A stanza is a group of lines that forms a unit in a poem. A stanza is usually characterized by a common pattern of meter, rhyme, and number of lines. Longfellow's "A Psalm of Life" is written in four-line stanzas. 20th-century poets have experimented more freely with stanza form than did earlier poets, sometimes writing poems that have no stanza breaks at all.

Stereotype A stereotype is an over-simplified image of a person, group, or institution. Sweeping generalizations about "all Southerners" or "every used-car dealer" are stereotypes. Simplified, or stock characters in literature are often called stereotypes. Such characters do not usually demonstrate the complexities of real people. In Washington Irving's "The Devil and Tom Walker," Tom Walker's wife might be seen as a stereotype of a greedy and shrewish wife.

Stream of Consciousness Stream of consciousness is a technique that was developed by modernist writers to present the chronological flow of the seemingly unconnected thoughts, responses, and sensations of a character. In "The Love Song of J. Alfred Prufrock," T. S. Eliot uses this technique to reveal the jumble of thoughts that flow through Prufrock's mind.

Structure The structure of a literary work is the way in which it is put together—the arrangement of its parts. In poetry, structure refers to the arrangement of words and lines to produce a desired effect. A common structural unit in poetry is the stanza, of which there are numerous types. In prose, structure is the arrangement of larger units or parts of a selection. Paragraphs, for example, are a basic unit in prose, as are chapters in novels and acts in plays. The structure of a poem, short story, novel, play, or nonfiction selection usually emphasizes certain important aspects of content.

F. Scott Fitzgerald's "Winter Dreams," for example, is divided into six sections, each section reflecting another stage in Dexter Green's relationship with Judy Jones. Gish Jen's "In the American Society" is divided into two sections. The first section focuses on the father's own society, while the second section focuses on the social part of American society into which the mother wants to fit.

Style Style is the distinctive way in which a work of literature is written. Style refers not so much to what is said but how it is said. Word choice, sentence length, tone, imagery, and use of dialogue all contribute to a writer's style. E. E. Cummings's style, for example, is decidedly unconventional, breaking rules of capitalization, punctuation, diction, and syntax.

Surprise Ending A surprise ending is an unexpected plot twist at the conclusion of a story. Kate Chopin's "The Story of an Hour" ends with a surprise when Mrs. Mallard, who finds out that her husband has not died, has a heart attack and dies herself.

See *Irony*.

Suspense Suspense is the excitement or tension that readers feel as they become involved in a story and eagerly await the outcome. In Ambrose Bierce's "The Occurrence at Owl Creek Bridge," for example, the suspense builds as the reader awaits the outcome of Peyton Farquhar's attempted escape from his hanging at the hands of Union troops.

See *Rising Action*.

Symbol A symbol is a person, place, or object that has a concrete meaning in itself and also stands for something beyond itself, such as an idea or feeling. In "Dr. Heidegger's Experiment," the blooming and fading rose symbolizes the mortality of human life.

Theme Theme is the central idea or ideas the writer wishes to share with the reader. The idea may be a lesson about life or about people and their actions. For example, one theme of "The Masque of the Red Death" could be stated, "No one, not even the wealthiest man, has the power to escape death." Most themes are not obvious and must be inferred by the reader. At times, different readers discover different themes in the same work.

Third-Person Point of View See *Point of View*.

Title The title of a literary work often reflects the meaning of the work. For example, the title of Kurt Vonnegut's "Miss Temptation" refers to the beautiful young actress, Susanna. It also suggests Corporal Fuller's resentful view of Susanna as a temptress who mocks him with her unattainable beauty.

Tone Tone is a writer's attitude toward his or her subject. A writer can communicate tone through diction, choice of details, and direct statements of his or her position. To identify the tone of a work of literature, you might find it helpful to read the work aloud, as if giving a dramatic reading before an audience. The emotions that you convey in reading should give you hints as to the tone of the work.

Unlike mood, which is intended to shape the reader's emotional response to a work, tone reflects the feelings of the writer. For example, Red Jacket's tone is serious and respectful in "Lecture to a Missionary." Dorothy Parker's tone is comically ironic in "Here We Are," while Claude McKay's tone in "If We Must Die" is proud, defiant, and urgent.

See *Connotation, Diction, Mood, Style*.

Tragic Hero The ancient Greek philosopher Aristotle defined a tragic hero as a character whose basic goodness and superiority are marred by a tragic flaw that brings about or contributes to his or her downfall. The flaw may be poor judgment, pride, weakness, or an excess of an admirable quality. The tragic hero recognizes his or her own flaw and its consequences, but only after it is too late to change the course of events. Bruno, the hero of Joyce Carol Oates's "Hostage," might be considered a tragic hero because his excessively violent defense of a young girl leads to his ruin.

Transcendentalism The philosophy of transcendentalism, an American offshoot of German romanticism, was based on a belief that "transcendent forms" of truth exist beyond reason and experience. Ralph Waldo Emerson, the leader of the movement, asserted that every individual is capable of discovering this higher truth on his or her own, through intuition. Henry David Thoreau and Walt Whitman are two well-known transcendentalist writers.

See *Romanticism.*

Trickster Tale A trickster tale is a folk tale about an animal or person who engages in trickery, violence, and magic. Neither all good nor all bad, a trickster may be foolish yet clever, greedy yet helpful, immoral yet moral. "Coyote and the Buffalo" and "Fox and Coyote and Whale" are both trickster tales.

See *Folk Tale.*

Verbal Irony See *Irony.*

Voice The term *voice* refers to a writer's unique use of language that allows a reader to "hear" a human personality in his or her writing. The elements of style that determine a writer's voice include sentence structure, diction, and tone. For example, some writers are noted for their reliance on short, simple sentences, while others make use of long, complicated ones. Certain writers use concrete words, such as *lake* or *cold,* which name things that you can see, hear, feel, taste, or smell. Others prefer abstract terms, such as *memory,* which name things that cannot be perceived with the senses. A writer's tone also leaves its imprint on his or her personal voice.

The term can be applied to the narrator of a selection as well as the writer. For example, in Washington Irving's "The Devil and Tom Walker," the narrator establishes his personality through the diction and tone of his narration. He emerges as a witty, sarcastic character, as shown in his description of Tom's wife and their relationship:

> Tom's wife was a tall termagant, fierce of temper, loud of tongue, and strong of arm. Her voice was often heard in wordy warfare with her husband; and his face sometimes showed signs that their conflicts were not confined to words.

WRITING HANDBOOK

The Writing Process

The writing process consists of four stages: prewriting, drafting, revising and editing, and publishing and reflecting. As the graphic to the right shows, these stages are not steps that you must complete in a set order. Rather, you may return to any one at any time in your writing process, using feedback from your readers along the way.

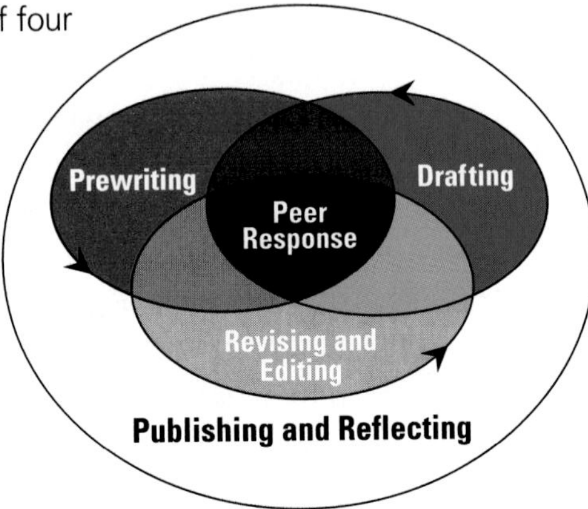

1.1 Prewriting

In the prewriting stage, you explore your ideas and discover what you want to write about.

Finding Ideas for Writing

Ideas for writing can come from just about anywhere: experiences, memories, conversations, dreams, or imaginings. Try one or more of the following techniques to help you find and explore a writing topic.

Personal Techniques
Practice imaging, or trying to remember mainly sensory details about a subject—its look, sound, feel, taste, and smell.
Complete a knowledge inventory to discover what you already know about a subject.
Browse through magazines, newspapers, and on-line bulletin boards for ideas.
Start a clip file of articles that you want to save for future reference. Be sure to label each clip with source information.

Sharing Techniques
With a group, brainstorm a topic by trying to come up with as many ideas as you can without stopping to critique or examine them.
Interview someone who knows a great deal about your topic.

Writing Techniques
After freewriting on a topic, try looping, or choosing your best idea for more freewriting. Repeat the loop at least once. Make a list to help you organize ideas, examine them, or identify areas for further research.

Graphic Techniques
Create a pro-and-con chart to compare the positive and negative aspects of an idea or a course of action. Use a cluster map or tree diagram to explore subordinate ideas that relate to your general topic or central idea.

Determining Your Purpose

At some time during your writing process, you need to consider your purpose, or general reason, for writing. For example, your purpose may be one of the following: to express yourself, to entertain, to explain, to describe, to analyze, or to persuade. To clarify your purpose, ask yourself questions such as these:

- Why did I choose to write about my topic?
- What aspects of the topic mean the most to me?
- What do I want others to think or feel after they read my writing?

Identifying Your Audience

Knowing who will read your writing can help you clarify your purpose, focus your topic, and choose the details and tone that will best communicate your ideas. As you think about your readers, ask yourself questions such as these:

- What does my audience already know about my topic?
- What will they be most interested in?
- What language is most appropriate for this audience?

LINK TO LITERATURE

One purpose for writing is to entertain. For example, the humorist Garrison Keillor draws on an experience from his teenage years in the 1950s to amuse readers. His story "Gary Keillor," on page 335, describes an incident to which almost everyone can relate. It involves being in love, lacking confidence, and wanting to impress others.

1.2 Drafting

In the drafting stage, you put your ideas on paper and allow them to develop and change as you write.

There's no right or wrong way to draft. Sometimes you might be adventuresome and dive right into your writing. At other times, you might draft slowly, planning carefully beforehand. You can combine aspects of these approaches to suit yourself and your writing projects.

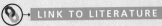

Personal experiences are often the richest source of ideas for writing. Zora Neale Hurston wrote in "How It Feels to Be Colored Me," on page 782, about growing up in a small Florida town where only African Americans lived. Her best-known novel, *Their Eyes Were Watching God*, and her autobiography, *Dust Tracks on a Road*, clearly draw on this background too.

Discovery drafting is a good approach when you've gathered some information on your topic or have a rough idea for writing but are not quite sure how you feel about your subject or what exactly you want to say. You just plunge into your draft and let your ideas lead you where they will. After finishing a discovery draft you may decide to start another draft, do more prewriting, or revise your first draft.

Planned drafting may work better for research reports, critical reviews, and other kinds of formal writing. Try thinking through a writing plan or making an outline before you begin drafting. Then, as you write, you can develop your ideas and fill in the details.

1.3 Using Peer Response

The suggestions and comments your peers or classmates make about your writing are called peer response.

Talking with peers about your writing can help you discover what you want to say or how well you have communicated your ideas. You can ask a peer reader for help at any point in the writing process. For example, your peers can help you develop a topic, narrow your focus, discover confusing passages, or organize your writing.

Questions for Your Peer Readers

You can help your peer readers provide you with the most useful kinds of feedback by following these guidelines:

- Tell readers where you are in the writing process. Are you still trying out ideas, or have you completed a draft?
- Ask questions that will help you get specific information about your writing. Open-ended questions that require more than yes-or-no answers are more likely to give you information you can use as you revise.
- Give your readers plenty of time to respond thoughtfully to your writing.
- Encourage your readers to be honest when they respond to your work. It's OK if you don't agree with them—you always get to decide which changes to make.

The chart on the following page explains different peer-response techniques you might use when you're ready to share your work with others.

Technique	When to Use It	Questions to Ask
Sharing	Use this when you are just exploring ideas or when you want to celebrate the completion of a piece of writing.	Will you please read or listen to my writing without criticizing or making suggestions afterward?
Summarizing	Use this when you want to know if your main idea or goals are clear.	What do you think I'm saying? What's my main idea or message?
Replying	Use this strategy when you want to make your writing richer by adding new ideas.	What are your ideas about my topic? What do you think about what I have said in my piece?
Responding to Specific Features	Use this when you want a quick overview of the strengths and weaknesses of your writing.	Are the ideas supported with enough examples? Did I persuade you? Is the organization clear enough so you could follow the ideas?
Telling	Use this to find out which parts of your writing are affecting readers the way you want and which parts are confusing.	What did you think or feel as you read my words? Would you show me which passage you were reading when you had that response?

Tips for Being a Peer Reader

Follow these guidelines when you respond to someone else's work:

- Respect the writer's feelings.
- Make sure you understand what kind of feedback the writer is looking for, and then respond accordingly.
- Use "I" statements, such as "I like . . . ," "I think . . . ," or "It would help me if. . . ." Remember that your impressions and opinions may not be the same as someone else's.

WRITING TIP

Writers are better able to absorb criticism of their work if they first receive positive feedback. When you act as a peer reader, try to start your review by telling something you like about the piece.

1.4 Revising and Editing

In the revising and editing stage you improve your draft, choose the words that best express your ideas, and proofread for mistakes in spelling, grammar, usage, and punctuation.

The changes you make in your writing during this stage usually fall into three categories: revising for content, revising for structure, and editing to correct mistakes in mechanics. Use the questions and suggestions that follow to help you assess problems in your draft and determine what kinds of changes would improve it.

WRITING TIP

Be sure to consider the needs of your audience as you answer the questions under Revising for Content. For example, before you can determine whether any of your material is unnecessary or irrelevant, you need to identify what your audience already knows.

WRITING TIP

For help identifying and correcting problems that are listed in the Proofreading Checklist, see the Grammar Handbook, pages 1200–1239.

Revising for Content

- Does my writing have a main idea or central focus? Is my thesis clear?
- Have I incorporated adequate detail? Where might I include a telling detail, revealing statistic, or vivid example?
- Is any material unnecessary, irrelevant, or confusing?

Revising for Structure

- Is my writing unified? Do all ideas and supporting details pertain to my main idea or advance my thesis?
- Is my writing clear and coherent? Is the flow of sentences and paragraphs smooth and logical?
- Do I need to add transitional words, phrases, or sentences to make the relationships among ideas clearer?
- Are my sentences well constructed? What sentences might I combine to improve the grace and rhythm of my writing?

Editing to Correct Mistakes in Mechanics

When you are satisfied with your draft, proofread and edit it, correcting any mistakes you might have made in spelling, grammar, usage, and punctuation. You may want to proofread your writing several times, looking for different types of mistakes each time. The following checklist may help you proofread your work.

Proofreading Checklist	
Sentence Structure and Agreement	Are there any run-on sentences or sentence fragments? Do all verbs agree with their subjects? Do all pronouns agree with their antecedents? Are verb tenses correct and consistent?
Forms of Words	Do adverbs and adjectives modify the appropriate words? Are all forms of *be* and other irregular verbs used correctly? Are pronouns used correctly? Are comparative and superlative forms of adjectives correct?
Capitalization, Punctuation, and Spelling	Is any punctuation mark missing or not needed? Are all words spelled correctly? Are all proper nouns and all proper adjectives capitalized?

If you have a printout of your draft or a handwritten copy, mark changes on it by using the proofreading symbols shown in the chart on the next page. The Grammar Handbook, starting on page 1200, includes models for using these symbols.

Proofreading Symbols			
∧	Add letters or words.	/	Make a capital letter lowercase.
⊙	Add a period.	¶	Begin a new paragraph.
≡	Capitalize a letter.	— or ⅁	Delete letters or words.
⊂⊃	Close up space.	∽	Switch the positions of letters, words, or punctuation marks.
∧̦	Add a comma.		

1.5 Publishing and Reflecting

After you've completed a writing project, consider sharing it with a wider audience—even when you've produced it for a class assignment. Reflecting on your writing process is another good way to bring closure to a writing project.

Creative Publishing Ideas

Following are some ideas for publishing and sharing your writing.

- Post your writing on an electronic bulletin board or send it to others via e-mail.
- Create a multimedia presentation and share it with classmates.
- Publish your writing in a school newspaper or literary magazine.
- Present your work orally in a report, a speech, a reading, or a dramatic performance.
- Submit your writing to a local newspaper or a magazine that publishes student writing.
- Form a writing exchange group with other students.

WRITING TIP

You might work with other students to publish an anthology of class writing. Then exchange your anthology with another class or another school. Reading the work of other student writers will help you get ideas for new writing projects and for ways to improve your work.

Reflecting on Your Writing

Think about your writing process and consider whether you'd like to add your writing to your portfolio. You might attach to your work a note in which you answer questions like these:

- What did I learn about myself and my subject through this writing project?
- Which parts of the writing process did I most and least enjoy?
- As I wrote, what was my biggest problem? How did I solve it?
- What did I learn that I can use the next time I write?

Building Blocks of Good Writing

2.1 Introductions

A good introduction catches your reader's interest and often presents the main idea of your writing. To introduce your writing effectively, try one of the following methods.

Make a Surprising Statement

Beginning with a startling or an interesting fact can capture your reader's curiosity about the subject, as in the example below.

> The Great Pyramid at Giza in Egypt covers about 13 acres of land and consists of more than two million blocks of limestone that workers cut and shaped by hand. Its size alone indicates the value of this monument to ancient Egyptian culture.

Provide a Description

A vivid description sets a mood and brings a scene to life for your reader. The following introduces a narrative about a day at an Indiana waterfall.

> The dark, sheltering walls of the gorge curved and flowed. You'd expect echoes, but somehow stone and moss and gray-green lichens absorbed all sound, even the rush of water over the rock projection.

Pose a Question

Beginning with a question can make your reader want to read on to find out the answer. The following introduction asks a question to get the reader interested in the history of the English language.

A lively description is a good means for introducing the characters or the setting of a narrative. In the selection "Gary Keillor," on page 335, the author's opening description helps readers visualize him at age 16: "I stood six feet two inches tall and weighed a hundred and forty pounds. I was intense and had the metabolism of a wolverine. I ate two or three lunches a day and three full dinners at night."

The English word *caravan* comes from the Persian language; the word *beauty* comes from the French. How did English come to be a mix of such different languages?

LINK TO LITERATURE

Opening with a question involves the reader from the outset in the thought process of the author. The excerpt from "The Case for Official English," on page 1060, begins with a strong question: "What is it that has made a society out of the hodgepodge of nationalities, races, and colors represented in the immigrant hordes that people our nation?" The reader's interest is immediately captured.

Relate an Anecdote

Beginning with a brief anecdote, or story, can hook readers and help you make a point in a dramatic way. The following anecdote begins a discussion on a student's understanding of the teaching profession.

In my sophomore year, I ended up in my mother's biology class. On the first day, I hesitantly raised my hand and asked, "Mrs. Littleton?" It was strange not to call her "Mom." From that moment on I started seeing all of my teachers from a different perspective.

Address the Reader Directly

Speaking directly to readers in your introduction establishes a friendly, informal tone and involves them in your topic.

Wandering around old cemeteries may seem like a morbid activity. You'd be surprised, however, to discover that many interesting witticisms appear on tombstones and sometimes reveal the personalities of the people the stones memorialize.

Begin with a Thesis Statement

A thesis statement expressing a paper's main idea may be woven into both the beginning and the end of nonfiction writing. The following is a thesis statement that introduces an analysis of a short story.

The narrator of Faulkner's "A Rose for Emily" shows the title character's independence and her determination to have her own way, but the narrator also presents clues that foreshadow the disturbing truth that lies beneath Emily's gentility.

2.2 Paragraphs

A paragraph is made up of sentences that work together to develop an idea or accomplish a purpose. Whether or not it contains a topic sentence stating the main idea, a good paragraph must have both unity and coherence.

Unity

A paragraph has unity when all the sentences support and develop one stated or implied idea. Use the following techniques to create unity in your paragraphs.

The same techniques that create unity in paragraphs can be used to create unity in an entire paper. Be sure that all of your paragraphs support the thesis statement or the implied main idea of your paper. If a paragraph includes information irrelevant to the main idea, you should delete it or revise it to establish a clear connection.

Write a Topic Sentence A topic sentence states the main idea of the paragraph; all the other sentences in the paragraph provide supporting details. A topic sentence is often the first sentence in a paragraph, as shown in the model below. However, it may also appear later in the paragraph or at the end, to summarize or reinforce the main idea.

> *Constructing a skyscraper presents engineers with complex and unusual problems to solve.* They must calculate the depth at which they should build the foundations, which help to support the weight of the structure. After estimating the force of high winds likely to affect the building, they must design a structure that can sway slightly but remain structurally sound. Finally, they must ensure the construction process does not harm adjacent structures.

Relate All Sentences to an Implied Main Idea A paragraph can be unified without a topic sentence as long as every sentence supports the implied, or unstated, main idea. In the example below, all the sentences work together to create a unified impression of a student's anxiety about taking a test.

> Every year during fire safety week, we expect to have at least one fire drill. Last year I spent the whole week hoping it would happen during my fourth-hour history exam on Friday. As third hour progressed, I concentrated less on geometry proofs and more on trying to guess when the principal would set off the alarm. I thought, "Please, Ms. Varecjka, save me."

Coherence

A paragraph is coherent when all its sentences are related to one another and flow logically from one to the next. The following techniques will help you achieve coherence in paragraphs.

- Present your ideas in the most logical order.
- Use pronouns, synonyms, and repeated words to connect ideas.
- Use transitional devices to show the relationships among ideas.

In the example below, the italicized words show how the writer used some of these techniques to create a unified paragraph.

> Medical engineers are experimenting with new methods for treating damaged or diseased body tissue. *For example, they* are taking healthy cells of a specific type of *tissue* and attaching *them* to a biodegradable plastic form that imitates the structure of *that tissue. The cells* on *the form* reproduce, creating new tissue. Over time, *the form* degrades, leaving only *the living structure, which* can then be implanted. Eventually, *engineers* hope to use *this method* to create entire organs and other body parts.

WRITING TIP

You can use the techniques at the left to create coherence in an entire paper. Be sure that paragraphs flow logically from one to the next.

2.3 Transitions

Transitions are words and phrases that show the connections between details, such as relationships in time and space, order of importance, causes and effects, and similarities or differences.

Time or Sequence

Some transitions help to clarify the sequence of events over time. When you are telling a story or describing a process, you can connect ideas with such transitional words as *first, second, always, then, next, later, soon, before, finally, after, earlier, afterward,* and *tomorrow.*

> In the 1980s officials in Portland, Oregon, shifted funds allocated for a city freeway to public-transit development. *After* a light-rail system was completed, air pollution lessened, and *soon* businesses along the train lines boomed. *Finally,* a waterfront park replaced the former freeway site alongside the river that divides downtown Portland.

LINK TO LITERATURE

Notice the use of transitions on pages 172 and 173 of "We Aren't Superstitious." The author Stephen Vincent Benét uses transitions such as *soon, meanwhile,* and *the next day* to clarify the order of events leading up to the Salem witch trials.

Spatial Relationships

Transitional words and phrases such as *in front of, behind, next to, along, nearest, lowest, above, below, underneath, on the left,* and *in the middle* can help readers visualize a scene.

> In honor of Mr. Silberstein's retirement, we hung photos of the plays he directed over the last 31 years *around* the entire theater lobby. *Under* each photo, we posted cards sent by his former students and colleagues.

Degree

Transitions such as *mainly, strongest, weakest, first, second, most important, least important, worst,* and *best* may be used to rank ideas or to show degree of importance, as in the model below.

> The team projects in history class were a nice change from the usual tests and quizzes, but *more important,* working together helped us to understand the subject thoroughly.

Compare and Contrast

Words and phrases such as *similarly, likewise, also, like, as, neither . . . nor,* and *either . . . or* show similarity between details. *However, by contrast, yet, but, unlike, instead, whereas,* and *while* show difference. Note the use of both types of transitions in the model below.

> Artificial sweeteners and sugar *both* sweeten food, *but* artificial sweeteners have few, if any, calories. Sugar, *however,* can act as a natural preservative in foods, *whereas* most artificial sweeteners have a more limited shelf life.

Cause and Effect

When you are writing about a cause-and-effect relationship, use transitional words and phrases such as *since, because, thus, therefore, so, due to, for this reason,* and *as a result* to help clarify that relationship and to make your writing coherent.

WRITING TIP

Note how cause-and-effect transitions clarify causal relationships in the selection from Henry David Thoreau's *Walden,* on page 297. For example, to explain his reason for moving to Walden Pond, he states, "I went to the woods because I wished to live deliberately."

In grade school, I read all of Laura Ingalls Wilder's *Little House* books. I enjoyed them *because* they described places I have lived in or visited. *Consequently*, I still seek out books by other Midwestern writers, such as William Least Heat-Moon and Jon Hassler.

2.4 Elaboration

Elaboration is the process of developing a writing idea by providing specific supporting details that are appropriate for the purpose and form of your writing.

Facts and Statistics

A fact is a statement that can be verified, while a statistic is a fact stated in numbers. As in the model below, any facts or statistics you use should strongly support the main idea.

Although best known for his midnight ride, Paul Revere actively contributed to the patriot cause throughout the war. He cast bronze cannon, manufactured gunpowder, and printed the first Continental paper currency.

WRITING TIP

Facts and statistics can be used to explain more than one idea, depending on how you interpret the information for the reader. Be certain that you clearly and logically establish how the facts you have chosen support your writing.

Sensory Details

Details that show how something looks, sounds, smells, tastes, or feels can enliven a description. Which senses does the writer appeal to in the following paragraph?

The hot, yeasty air of the bakery steamed up the windows and the eyeglasses of the customers who sought its warmth. The bakers, working in shorts and T-shirts, welcomed the cold gusts of wind when the customers rushed inside.

Incidents

One way to illustrate a point is to relate an incident or tell a story, as in the example on the following page.

Using mnemonic devices can help you remember things that may not otherwise be easy to recall. When I needed to memorize the periodic table for my chemistry class, I created a song that had words beginning with the same letters as the abbreviations for the chemical compounds. Of course, I had to sing it to myself during the exam.

LINK TO LITERATURE

In "Lecture to a Missionary," on page 229, Red Jacket provides examples of how white people deceived Native Americans. These examples support his argument that Native Americans should not necessarily believe what white people tell them about religion.

Examples

An example can help make an abstract or a complex idea concrete for the reader.

Mr. Rediger's students respected him for his integrity. For example, when he did not know the answer to a student's question, he would simply say he didn't know and would come back to class the next day with the answer.

Quotations

Choose quotations that clearly support your points and be sure that you copy each quotation word for word. Always remember to credit the source.

In Robert Frost's "Mending Wall," the speaker suggests that the physical wall he and his neighbor build only symbolizes the wall created in their minds. He says that they cast a spell to keep the stones in place "until our backs are turned!" Whether or not the wall remains standing is not as important as their memory of creating a division.

2.5 Description

A good description contains carefully chosen details that create a unified impression for the reader.

Description is an important part of most writing genres—essays, stories, biography, and poetry, for example. Effective description can help readers to recognize the significance of an issue, to visualize a scene, or to understand a character.

Use a Variety of Details

If you include plenty of sensory details, the reader can better imagine the scene you are describing. In the example below, the sensory details help capture the feeling of a motorcycle ride.

> The placid cornfields of deep summer blurred on either side of me. Wind enveloped us; the wheels hummed on the pavement. John's brown leather jacket smelled safe, warm, strong. On the straightaway we seemed to sit quietly, but leaning into curves we knew we were flying, skimming just an inch or two off the ground.

LINK TO LITERATURE

Notice the description of Tom T. Shiftlet throughout "The Life You Save May Be Your Own," on page 404. Notice how Flannery O'Connor uses details of Shiftlet's appearance and behavior to show that this character isn't always saying what he thinks or feels.

Show, Don't Tell

Simply telling your readers about an event or an idea in a general way does not give them a clear impression. Showing your readers the specific details, however, helps them develop a better sense of your subject. The following example just tells what the writer enjoys.

> I enjoy ice-skating on the pond behind our house.

The sentences below use descriptive details to show what he enjoys.

> Ice-skating on the pond behind our house is a Saturday morning ritual for me. I get up early and trudge along the undisturbed white path, carrying a shovel and my skates. After lacing up my skates, I methodically clear away the fresh snow. Then I warm myself up by racing around the perimeter of the pond. My favorite part of the ritual, however, is lazily tracing circular patterns across the ice that will disappear under yet another blanket of white before I return the next Saturday.

Use Figurative Language

Figurative language is descriptive writing that evokes associations beyond the literal meaning of words. The following types of figurative language can make your descriptions clear and fresh.

WRITING TIP

Be careful not to mix metaphors, or use two or more comparisons that create a confusing image. *He stormed in, as threatening as a thunder cloud, but melted at the sight of the frisky little puppy.*

WRITING TIP

Clarify your descriptive writing by choosing precise words. For example, replace general nouns (*bird*) with more specific nouns (*red-winged blackbird*).

- A **simile** is a figure of speech comparing two essentially unlike things, signaling the comparison with a word such as *like* or *as.*
- A **metaphor** is a figure of speech describing something by speaking of it as if it were something else, without using a word such as *like* or *as* to signal the comparison.

In the example below, the comparison describes a pianist's skill by using a metaphor.

> His fingers flew across the keyboard, fluttering in a blur, and then landed lightly.

Organize Your Details

Organize descriptions carefully to create a clear image for your reader. Descriptive details may be organized chronologically, spatially, by order of importance, or by order of impression.

> He wanted to fall asleep, but a branch kept tapping against his window, and the fan overhead whirred louder than usual. When these noises didn't bother him anymore, he was certain he could hear a faucet dripping in the kitchen.

2.6 Conclusions

A conclusion should leave readers with a strong final impression. Try any of the following approaches for concluding your writing.

Restate Your Thesis

A good way to conclude an essay is by restating your thesis, or main idea, in different words. The conclusion below restates the thesis introduced in an example on page 1167.

> The narrator of "A Rose for Emily" provides clues to the lengths to which this apparently refined woman would go in order to repay affronts to her dignity and pride. In the final scene, however, the narrator still surprises the reader with the disturbing extent of Emily's strong will.

Ask a Question

Try asking a question that sums up what you have said and gives readers something new to think about. The question below concludes an appeal to increase the number of job-training programs.

> Since the burden of supporting those who cannot compete in the job market falls on the employed, shouldn't we increase job-training opportunities for the unemployed?

Make a Recommendation

When you are persuading your audience to take a position on an issue, you can conclude by recommending a specific course of action.

> Although the director of the 1995 movie *The Scarlet Letter* sets out to retell Hawthorne's novel on-screen, in my opinion, it does not do justice to the text. If you want to experience this classic story, read the book.

LINK TO LITERATURE

If your goal is to explore two sides of an issue, as in an argument analysis, your conclusion might summarize the two sides and recommend that readers make up their own minds on the issue.

Make a Prediction

Readers are concerned about matters that may affect them and therefore are moved by a conclusion that predicts the future.

> Participating in the mock job interviews sponsored by the chamber of commerce will give you a head start on your summer job search and in future job interviews after graduation.

Summarize Your Information

A summary restates the writer's main ideas, reinforcing the thesis of a piece of writing. The model below concludes by summarizing the major points in an essay on a proposed program for city parks.

> The new park program will make the city more attractive, provide safer recreational facilities, and offer part-time summer jobs for students.

3 Narrative Writing

Narrative writing tells a story. If you write a story from your imagination, it is called a fictional narrative. A true story about actual events is called a nonfictional narrative.

Writing Standards

Good narrative writing

- includes descriptive details and dialogue to develop the characters, setting, and plot
- has a clear beginning, middle, and end
- has a logical organization with clues and transitions to help the reader understand the order of events
- maintains a consistent tone and point of view
- uses language that is appropriate for the audience
- demonstrates the significance of events or ideas

Key Techniques of Narrative Writing

Describe the Setting

The setting is the time and place of a narrative. In the example below, the details set the scene for the action of the narrative.

Example
The flickering candlelight casts long shadows on the walls. Lying on his deathbed, the old man thinks back on his life as a Founding Father.

Clearly Organize the Events

Choose the important events and explain them in an order that is easy to understand. In a fictional narrative, this series of events is the story's plot.

Example
- the old man lies on his deathbed
- he thinks about the Declaration of Independence and his friends Thomas Jefferson and John Adams
- he thinks about how different Jefferson and Adams were
- just before losing consciousness, the old man realizes that differences can strengthen the nation

Depict Characters Vividly

Use vivid details to show your readers what your characters look like, what they say, and what they think.

Example
He had known and respected both presidents. Jefferson was as lavish in his spending as he was in his thinking. Adams, no less a great thinker, had simpler tastes.

Organizing Narrative Writing

One way to organize a piece of narrative writing is to arrange the order of events by starting *in medias res,* or in the middle of things, as shown in Option 1.

Option 1

Flashback	Example
• Begin with the conflict	The old man wonders whether people remember the struggles and efforts that led up to the signing of the Declaration of Independence.
• Present the events leading up to the conflict	On his deathbed, the old man reminisces about the signing of the Declaration of Independence and his friendship with Thomas Jefferson and John Adams in his younger days.
• Present the resolution, or outcome of the conflict	Just before he loses consciousness, the old man realizes that a people's willingness to accept leaders with different personalities and styles helps make a country great.

WRITING TIP

Historical Fiction A nonfictional narrative based on real or imagined historical events is called historical fiction. In the example at the left, a fictional character reminisces about two real-life presidents, John Adams and Thomas Jefferson.

It is also possible in narrative writing to arrange the events in chronological order, as shown in Option 2. When the telling of a fictional narrative focuses on a central conflict, the story's plot may follow the model shown in Option 3.

Option 2

Focus on Events

- Introduce characters and setting
- Show event 1
- Show event 2
- End, perhaps showing the significance of the events

Option 3

Focus on Conflict

- Describe the main characters and setting
- Present the conflict
- Relate the events that make the conflict complex and cause the characters to change
- Present the resolution, or outcome of the conflict

WRITING TIP

Dialogue Dialogue is an effective way of depicting characters in a narrative. As you write dialogue, choose words that express your characters' personalities and show how they feel about one another.

Explanatory Writing

LINK TO LITERATURE

Explanatory writing provides many opportunities to explore issues in literature. The examples on the following pages use explanatory writing techniques to examine features in Willa Cather's "A Wagner Matinee," on page 541.

Explanatory writing informs and explains. For example, you can use it to evaluate the effects of a new law, to compare two movie reviews, or to analyze a piece of literature.

Types of Explanatory Writing

Compare and Contrast

Compare-and-contrast writing explores the similarities and differences between two or more subjects.

Example
Music assumes a different role in Aunt Georgiana's life when she leaves Boston for a homestead in Nebraska.

Cause and Effect

Cause-and-effect writing explains why something happened, why certain conditions exist, or what resulted from an action or a condition.

Example
Life on a Nebraska homestead has altered Aunt Georgiana both physically and emotionally.

Analysis

Analysis explains how something works, how it is defined, or what its parts are.

Example
By taking the reader back in time, the narrator of "A Wagner Matinee" reveals the process of his aunt rediscovering her passion for music while they listen to an orchestra's performance of opera music.

Problem-Solution

Problem-solution writing states a problem, analyzes the problem, and then proposes a solution to it.

Example
Like the character of Aunt Georgiana who misses a part of her past that she values, I want to recapture some of the culture of South Korea, where I lived until I was adopted at age five.

4.1 Compare and Contrast

Compare-and-contrast writing explores the similarities and differences between two or more subjects.

Organizing Compare-and-Contrast Writing

Compare-and-contrast writing can be organized in different ways. The examples below demonstrate feature-by-feature organization and subject-by-subject organization.

Option 1

Feature by Feature	Example
Feature 1	Aunt Georgiana has taught music in both Boston and Nebraska.
• Subject A	In Boston she was a music teacher by profession.
• Subject B	In Nebraska she teaches music to her nephew as she sews for the farmhands.
Feature 2	Aunt Georgiana had more opportunities to hear music in Boston than she does in Nebraska.
• Subject A	In Boston she attended opera and symphony performances.
• Subject B	In Nebraska the only music she hears is at Methodist church services.

Option 2

Subject by Subject	Example
Subject A	In Boston, Aunt Georgiana's life was built around her passion for music.
• Feature 1	She was a music teacher by profession.
• Feature 2	She attended opera and symphony performances.
Subject B	In Nebraska the work on the homestead forces her to repress her passion for music.
• Feature 1	
• Feature 2	

Writing Standards

Good compare-and-contrast writing

- clearly identifies the subjects that are being compared and contrasted
- includes specific, relevant details
- follows a clear plan of organization dealing with the same features of both subjects under discussion
- uses language and details appropriate to the audience
- uses transitional words and phrases to clarify similarities and differences

WRITING TIP

Remember your purpose for comparing the items you are writing about and support your purpose with expressive language and specific details.

Writing Standards

Good cause-and-effect writing

- clearly states the cause-and-effect relationship being examined
- shows clear connections between causes and effects
- presents causes and effects in a logical order and uses transitions effectively
- uses facts, examples, and other details to illustrate each cause and effect
- uses language and details appropriate to the audience

WRITING TIP

Possible topics for cause-and-effect writing are important historical events that had an impact on society. For example, what caused the stock market crash in 1929? What were the results? You can explore current events and their potential outcomes as well.

4.2 Cause and Effect

Cause-and-effect writing explains why something happened, why certain conditions exist, or what resulted from an action or a condition.

Organizing Cause-and-Effect Writing

Your organization will depend on your topic and purpose for writing. If your focus is on explaining the effects of an event, such as the passage of a law, you might first state the cause and then explain the effects (Option 1). If you want to explain the causes of an event such as the closing of a factory, you might first state the effect and then examine its causes (Option 2). Sometimes you'll want to describe a chain of cause-and-effect relationships (Option 3) to explore a topic such as the disappearance of tropical rain forests or the development of home computers.

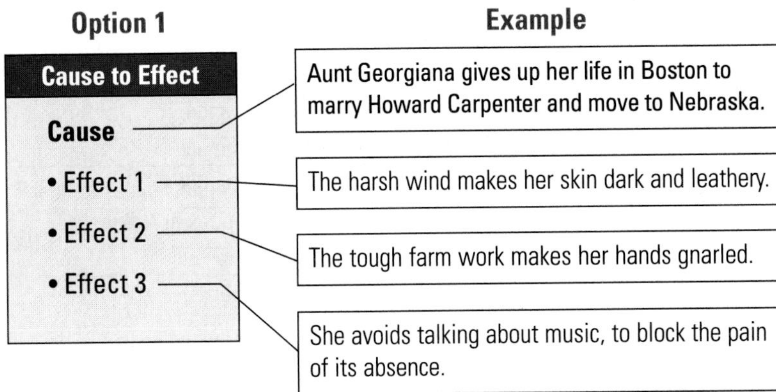

Option 1
Example
Cause to Effect
Cause
• Effect 1
• Effect 2
• Effect 3
Aunt Georgiana gives up her life in Boston to marry Howard Carpenter and move to Nebraska.
The harsh wind makes her skin dark and leathery.
The tough farm work makes her hands gnarled.
She avoids talking about music, to block the pain of its absence.

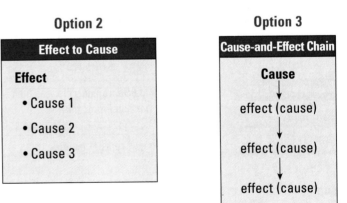

Option 2

Effect to Cause

Effect
- Cause 1
- Cause 2
- Cause 3

Option 3

Cause-and-Effect Chain

Cause
↓
effect (cause)
↓
effect (cause)
↓
effect (cause)

Remember: You cannot assume that a cause-and-effect relationship exists simply because one event follows another. Be sure your facts indicate that the effect could not have happened without the cause.

4.3 Problem-Solution

Problem-solution writing clearly states a problem, analyzes the problem, and proposes a solution to the problem.

Organizing Problem-Solution Writing

Your organization will depend on the goal of your problem-solution piece, your intended audience, and the specific problem you choose to address. The organizational methods outlined below are effective for different kinds of problem-solution writing.

Option 1

Simple Problem-Solution	Example
Description of problem and why it needs to be solved	Like the character of Aunt Georgiana, I want to get back in touch with my past. I want to recapture some of the culture of South Korea, where I lived until I was adopted at age five.
Recommended solution	I should take courses about Korean culture and learn to speak Korean again.
Explanation of solution	Taking courses would help me understand the history and culture that I feel is a part of who I am.
Conclusion	Filling in the gaps from my childhood will help me to develop confidence about who I am.

Option 2

Deciding Between Solutions	Example
Description of problem	I want to recapture some of the culture of South Korea, where I lived until I was adopted at age five.
Solution A	I could take courses about Korean culture and learn to speak Korean again.
• Pros	Taking courses would help me understand the history and culture of Korea.
• Cons	Taking classes will provide information but will not recapture the memories for me.
Solution B	I could save money and plan a trip to Korea to tour the country and to visit the orphanage I lived in.
• Pros	
• Cons	
Recommendation	

Writing Standards

Good problem-solution writing

- identifies the problem and helps the reader understand the issues involved
- analyzes the causes and effects of the problem
- integrates quotes, facts, and statistics into the text
- explores potential solutions to the problem and recommends the best one(s)
- uses language, tone, and details appropriate to the audience

WRITING TIP

Ask a classmate to read and respond to your problem-solution writing. Here are some questions for your peer reader to respond to: Is my language clear? Is the writing organized in a way that is easy to follow? Do the proposed solutions seem logical?

4.4 Analysis

In an analysis you try to help your readers understand a subject by explaining how it works, how it is defined, or what its parts are.

The details you include will depend upon the kind of analysis you're writing.

- A **process analysis** should provide background information—such as definitions of terms and a list of needed equipment—and then explain each important step or stage in the process. For example, you might explain the steps to program a VCR or the stages in a plant's growth cycle.
- A **definition** should include the most important characteristics of the subject. To define a quality, such as honesty, you might include the characteristic of telling the truth.
- A **parts analysis** should describe each of the parts, groups, or types that make up the subject. For example, you might analyze the human brain by looking at its parts, analyze a new law by looking at how different groups are affected by it, or analyze jazz music by describing the different styles of jazz.

Writing Standards

A good analysis

- hooks the reader's attention with a strong introduction
- clearly states the subject and its individual parts
- uses a specific organizing structure to provide a logical flow of information
- shows connections among facts and ideas through subordinate clauses and transitional words and phrases
- uses language and details appropriate for the audience

Organizing Your Analysis

Organize your details in a logical order appropriate for the kind of analysis you're writing. A process analysis is usually organized chronologically, with steps or stages in the order they occur.

Option 1: Process Analysis	Example
Introduce topic	By taking the reader back in time, the narrator of "A Wagner Matinee" reveals the process of his aunt's rediscovering her passion for music.
Background information	The aunt's return to Boston reintroduces her to a past she has almost forgotten.
Explain steps: • Step 1	The narrator tells of his aunt's musical training and concertgoing when she was a young woman.
• Step 2	He recalls her giving him music lessons and singing to him when he was ill.
• Step 3	He describes how the concert music breaks through the years of deprivation on the farm.

WRITING TIP

Introductions You may want to begin your analysis with a vivid description of the subject to capture the reader's attention. For example, to introduce the process analysis at the right, you might quote the narrator's description of the aunt at the end of the symphonic performance.

You can organize the details in a definition or parts analysis in order of importance or impression.

Option 2

Definition	Example
Introduce term	The similes in "A Wagner Matinee" create clear images and contribute to the story's theme.
General definition	A simile describes one thing by comparing it to a different thing that shares a similar quality. A simile uses *like* or *as*.
Give example	One effective simile in "A Wagner Matinee" is the narrator's comparison of the bare stage to the winter cornfields of Nebraska.
Explain qualities	
• Quality 1	In this simile, the image of the winter cornfield is easily visualized and suggests how abandoned the stage is.
• Quality 2	This simile also reinforces the theme by connecting barrenness and loss with the cornfields the aunt must return to.

WRITING TIP

Conclusions An effective way to conclude an analysis is to return to your thesis and restate it in different words.

The following parts analysis explains the parts of an opera, such as the ones mentioned in "A Wagner Matinee."

Option 3

Parts Analysis	Example
Introduce subject	Operas, such as those mentioned in "A Wagner Matinee," have distinct parts that serve different purposes.
Explain parts	
• Part 1	The overture is the instrumental music introducing the opera.
• Part 2	A leitmotif is a brief instrumental passage that introduces ideas, places, or characters whenever they appear.
• Part 3	A recitative is a simple, typically speechlike song that is the dialogue between characters.
• Part 4	An aria is a sung monologue that reveals a character's thoughts or feelings.

5

Persuasive Writing

Persuasive writing allows you to use the power of language to inform and influence others.

Writing Standards

Good persuasive writing

- clearly states the issue and the writer's position
- gives opinions and supports them with facts or reasons
- has a reasonable and respectful tone
- takes into account and answers opposing views
- uses sound logic and effective language
- concludes by summing up reasons or calling for action

Key Techniques of Persuasive Writing

State Your Opinion

Taking a stand on an issue and clearly stating your opinion are essential to every piece of persuasive writing you do.

Example
Our school should offer academic credit for student internships as part of the junior and senior curriculum.

Know Your Audience

Knowing who will read your writing will help you decide what information you need to share and what tone you should use to communicate your message. In the example below, the writer has chosen a formal tone that is appropriate for a proposal to school officials.

Example
Internships that apply coursework show the relevance of academic subjects to everyday life, teach students to apply what they have learned, and help to prepare them for the future.

Support Your Opinion

Using reasons, examples, facts, statistics, and anecdotes to support your opinion will show your audience why you feel the way you do.

Example
Interviews are an important part of a job search. Students with internship experience will have already gone through the interview process and will be comfortable and confident in later interviews.

Organizing Persuasive Writing

In persuasive writing, you need to gather information to support your opinions. Here are some ways you can organize that material to convince your audience.

Option 1

Reasons for Your Opinion	Example
Your opinion	Our school should offer academic credit for student internships as part of the junior and senior curriculum.
• Reason 1	Internships provide valuable work experience and reinforce what students are learning in the classroom.
• Reason 2	Students may discover new areas of interest.
• Reason 3	Students who succeed in a work environment while in school show initiative—creating a positive impression on future employers.

Depending on the purpose and form of your writing, you may want to show the weaknesses of other opinions as you explain the strengths of your own. Two options for persuasive writing that include opposing viewpoints are shown below.

Option 2

Why Your Opinion Is Stronger

Your opinion
- your reasons

Other opinion
- evidence refuting reasons for other opinion and showing strengths of your opinion

Option 3

Why Another Opinion Is Weaker

Other opinion
- reasons

Your opinion
- reasons supporting your opinion and pointing out the weaknesses of the other side

Remember: Persuasive writing can take many forms, including literary analyses, speeches, newspaper editorials, and advertisements. Choose your form according to the audience you want to reach.

WRITING TIP

Introductions Capture your readers' attention in the introduction to your piece. Try opening with a quote, a statistic, or an anecdote that shows the importance of your topic.

WRITING TIP

Conclusion Writing persuasively means convincing the reader to feel the way you do about something. Your conclusion in a persuasive essay might summarize your opinion, make a final appeal, or urge the reader to take action.

6 Research Report Writing

A research report explores a topic in depth, incorporating information from a variety of sources.

Writing Standards

Good research report writing

- clearly states the purpose of the report in a thesis statement
- uses evidence and details from a variety of sources to support the thesis
- contains only accurate and relevant information
- documents sources correctly
- develops the topic logically and includes appropriate transitions
- includes a properly formatted Works Cited list

Key Techniques of Research Report Writing

Clarify Your Thesis

A thesis statement is one or two sentences clearly stating the main idea that you will develop in your report. A thesis may also indicate the organizational pattern you will follow and reflect your tone and point of view.

Example

Although Arthur Miller used dramatic license to rework the Salem witch hunts into a compelling play, *The Crucible* does accurately recount many of the events documented in trial records, sermons, and firsthand narratives from the time of the accusations.

Support Your Ideas

You should support your ideas with relevant evidence—facts, anecdotes, and statistics—from reliable sources. In the example below, the writer supports a claim about the historical events and the plot of the play.

Example

In the play, Abigail claims that the girls' conjuring of spirits was only for sport. Robert A. Martin suggests that the girls who began the hysteria, such as Abigail Williams, had experimented in witchcraft as a sport or a break from the oppressive environment of the Puritan community (95).

Document Your Sources

You need to document, or credit, the sources you use in your writing. In the example below, the writer uses a quotation as a supporting detail and documents the source.

Example

Like his dramatic counterpart, the real Reverend Samuel Parris preached sermons that contributed to the witchcraft hysteria by making his parishioners suspicious of one another. In his sermon on March 27, 1692, he stated, "Let none then build their hopes of Salvation meerly upon this, that they are Church-members. This you & I may be, & yet Devils for all that" (Cooper and Minkema 197).

Evaluating Sources

To help you determine whether your sources are reliable and contain useful and accurate information, use the following checklist.

Checklist for Evaluating Your Sources	
Authoritative	Someone who has written several books or articles on your subject or whose work has been published in a well-respected newspaper or journal may be considered an authority.
Up-to-date	Check the publication dates to see if the source contains the most current research on your subject.
Respected	In general, tabloid newspapers and popular-interest magazines are not reliable sources. If you have questions about whether you are using a respected source, ask your librarian.

WRITING TIP

For additional help, see the research report about Japanese Americans during World War II on pages 1022–1029 or see McDougal Littell's *Writing Research Papers.*

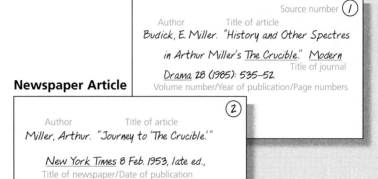

Making Source Cards

For each source you find, record the bibliographic information on a separate index card. You will need this information to give credit to the sources you use in your paper. The samples at the right show how to make source cards for journal articles, newspaper articles, and books. You will use the source number on each card to identify the notes you take during your research.

Journal Article

Newspaper Article

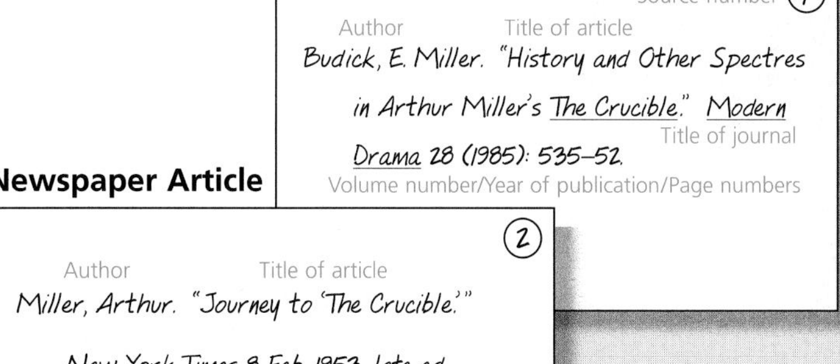

Source number 1
Author
Title of article
Budick, E. Miller. "History and Other Spectres
in Arthur Miller's The Crucible." Modern
Title of journal
Drama 28 (1985): 535–52.
Volume number/Year of publication/Page numbers
2
Author
Title of article
Miller, Arthur. "Journey to 'The Crucible.'"
New York Times 8 Feb. 1953, late ed.,
Title of newspaper/Date of publication
sec. 2: 3.
Section number/Page number

Book

3
Author
Title
Boyer, Paul, and Stephen Nissenbaum. Salem
Possessed: The Social Origins of
Date of publication
Witchcraft. Cambridge: Harvard UP, 1974.
City of publication/Publisher
Location of source
Library call number
Public Library
301.21 B791s

Taking Notes

As you read your sources, record on note cards information that is relevant to the purpose of your research. You will probably use all three of the following note-taking methods.

- **Paraphrase,** or restate in your own words, the main ideas and supporting details from a passage.
- **Summarize,** or rephrase the original material in fewer words, trying to capture the key ideas.
- **Quote,** or copy the original text word for word, if you think the author's own words best clarify a particular point. Use quotation marks to signal the beginning and the end of the quotation.

Paraphrase

Main idea
Number of Accusations
Source number (3)

By October of 1692, hundreds of persons had been accused of witchcraft—so many that the court could not keep accurate records. About 150 of the accused were imprisoned and 19 were executed. 30–31
Page numbers

Type of note
(Paraphrase)

Organizing Your Research Report

Making an outline can help guide the drafting process. Begin by reading over your note cards and sorting them into groups. The main-idea headings may help you find connections among the notes. Then arrange the groups of related note cards so that the ideas flow logically from one group to the next.

Note the format for a topic outline shown below. Remember that in a topic outline, items of the same degree of importance should be parallel in form. For instance, if A is a noun, then B and C should also be nouns. Subtopics need not be parallel with main topics.

History and Fiction in The Crucible

Introduction—the play accurately reflects aspects of the historical record

I. Historical evidence of the causes of the witch hunts

A. Puritan beliefs in witchcraft

B. Reasons for accusations in Salem

1. Rivalries in the community

2. Samuel Parris's sermons

II. Historical accuracy of the play

Documenting Your Sources

When you quote, paraphrase, or summarize information from one of your sources, you need to credit that source, using parenthetical documentation.

Guidelines for Parenthetical Documentation	
Work by One Author	Put the author's last name and the page reference in parentheses: **(Budick 537)**. If you mention the author's name in the sentence, put only the page reference in parentheses: **(537)**.
Work by Two or Three Authors	Put the authors' last names and the page reference in parentheses: **(Boyer and Nissenbaum 180)**.
Work by More than Three Authors	Give the first author's last name followed by *et al.*, and the page reference: **(Elliott et al. 37)**.
Work with No Author Given	Give the title or a shortened version and the page reference: **("Puritanism" 810)**.
One of Two or More Works by Same Author	Give the author's last name, the title or a shortened version, and the page reference: **(Miller, "Journey" 3)**.

WRITING TIP

Plagiarism Presenting someone else's writing or ideas as your own is plagiarism. To avoid plagiarism, you need to credit sources as noted at the right. However, if a piece of information is common knowledge—information available in several sources—you do not need to credit a source. To see an example of parenthetical documentation, see the essay on page 1028.

Following MLA Manuscript Guidelines

The final copy of your report should follow the Modern Language Association guidelines for manuscript preparation.

- The heading in the upper left-hand corner of the first page should include your name, your teacher's name, the course name, and the date, each on a separate line.
- Below the heading, center the title on the page.
- Number all the pages consecutively in the upper right-hand corner, one-half inch from the top. Also, include your last name before the page number.
- Double-space the entire paper.
- Except for the margins above the page numbers, leave one-inch margins on all sides of every page.

The Works Cited list at the end of your report is an alphabetized list of the sources you have used and documented. The additional line or lines of each entry are indented one-half inch.

WRITING TIP

When your report includes a quotation that is longer than four lines, set it off from the rest of the text by indenting the entire quotation one inch from the left margin. In this case, you should not use quotation marks.

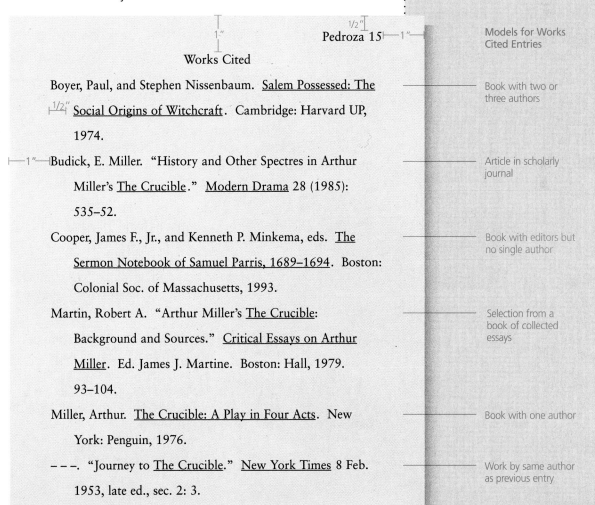

Models for Works Cited Entries

1/2″ 1″ Pedroza 15 1″

Works Cited

Boyer, Paul, and Stephen Nissenbaum. Salem Possessed: The Social Origins of Witchcraft. Cambridge: Harvard UP, 1974. — Book with two or three authors

Budick, E. Miller. "History and Other Spectres in Arthur Miller's The Crucible." Modern Drama 28 (1985): 535–52. — Article in scholarly journal

Cooper, James F., Jr., and Kenneth P. Minkema, eds. The Sermon Notebook of Samuel Parris, 1689–1694. Boston: Colonial Soc. of Massachusetts, 1993. — Book with editors but no single author

Martin, Robert A. "Arthur Miller's The Crucible: Background and Sources." Critical Essays on Arthur Miller. Ed. James J. Martine. Boston: Hall, 1979. 93–104. — Selection from a book of collected essays

Miller, Arthur. The Crucible: A Play in Four Acts. New York: Penguin, 1976. — Book with one author

---. "Journey to The Crucible." New York Times 8 Feb. 1953, late ed., sec. 2: 3. — Work by same author as previous entry

Getting Information Electronically

Electronic resources provide you with a convenient and efficient way to gather information.

1.1 On-line Resources

When you use your computer to communicate with another computer or with another person using a computer, you are working "on-line." On-line resources include commercial information services and information available on the Internet.

Commercial Information Services

You can subscribe to various services that offer information such as the following:

- up-to-date news, weather, and sports reports
- access to encyclopedias, magazines, newspapers, dictionaries, almanacs, and databases (collections of information)
- electronic mail (e-mail) to and from other users
- forums, or ongoing electronic conversations among users interested in a particular topic

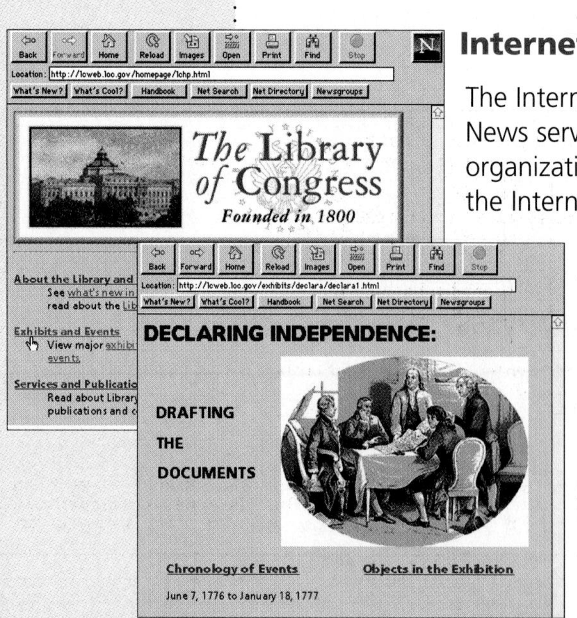

Internet

The Internet is a vast network of computers. News services, libraries, universities, researchers, organizations, and government agencies use the Internet to communicate and to distribute information. The Internet includes two key features:

- **World Wide Web,** which provides you with information on particular subjects and links you to related topics and resources (such as the linked Web pages shown at the left)
- **Electronic mail** (e-mail), which allows you to communicate with other e-mail users worldwide

1.2 CD-ROM

A CD-ROM (compact disc–read-only memory) stores data that may include text, sound, photographs, and video.

Almost any kind of information can be found on CD-ROMs, which you can use at the library or purchase, including

- encyclopedias, almanacs, and indexes
- other reference books on a variety of subjects
- news reports from newspapers, magazines, television, or radio
- museum art collections
- back issues of magazines
- literature collections

WHAT YOU'LL NEED

- To access on-line resources, you need a computer with a modem linked to a telephone line. Your school computer lab or resource center may be linked to the Internet or to a commercial information service.
- To use CD-ROMs, you need a computer system with a CD-ROM player.

1.3 Library Computer Services

Many libraries offer computerized catalogs and a variety of other electronic resources.

Computerized Catalogs

You may search for a book in a library by typing the title, author, subject, or key words into a computer terminal. When you find the book you're looking for, the screen will display the bibliographic information and the current availability of the book. When a particular work is not available, you may be able to search the catalogs of other libraries.

Other Electronic Resources

In addition to computerized catalogs, many libraries offer electronic versions of books or other reference materials. They may also have a variety of indexes on CD-ROM, which allow you to search for magazine or newspaper articles on any topic you choose. When you have found an article on the topic you want, the screen will display the kind of information shown at the right.

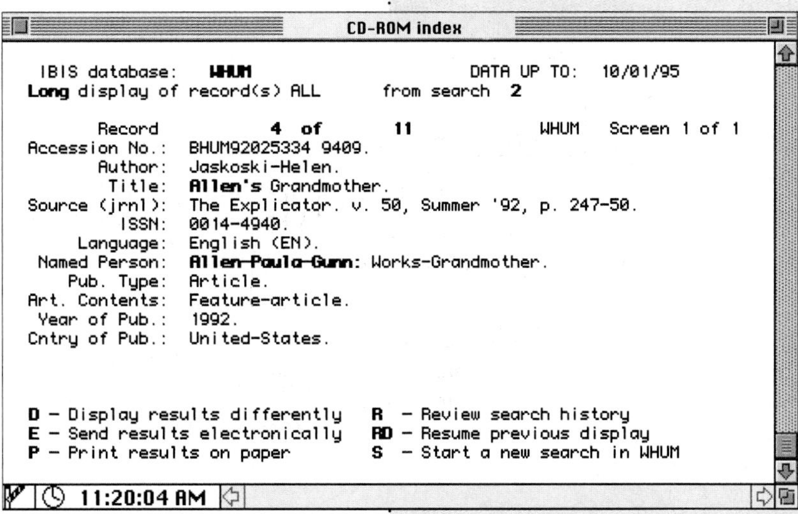

Word Processing

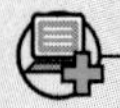

WHAT YOU'LL NEED

- Computer
- Word-processing program
- Printer

Word-processing programs allow you to draft, revise, edit, and format your writing and to produce neat, professional-looking papers. They also allow you to share your writing with others.

2.1 Revising and Editing

Improving the quality of your writing becomes easier when you use a word-processing program to revise and edit.

Revising a Document

Most word-processing programs allow you to make the following kinds of changes:

- add or delete words
- move text from one location in your document to another
- undo a change you have made in the text
- save a document with a new name, allowing you to keep old drafts for reference
- view more than one document at a time, so you can copy text from one document and add it to another

Editing a Document

Many word-processing programs have the following features to help you catch errors and polish your writing:

- The **spell checker** automatically finds misspelled words and suggests possible corrections.
- The **grammar checker** spots possible grammatical errors and suggests ways you might correct them.
- The **thesaurus** suggests synonyms for a word you want to replace.
- The **dictionary** will give you the definitions of words so you can be sure you have used words correctly.
- The **search and replace** feature searches your whole document and corrects every occurrence of something you want to change, such as a misspelled name.

WRITING TIP

Spell checkers and grammar checkers offer suggestions for corrections, but you must carefully assess these suggestions before picking the right one. Making such an assessment involves looking at the suggested change in the context of your writing.

2.2 Formatting Your Work

Format is the layout and appearance of your writing on the page. You may choose your formatting options before or after you write.

Formatting Type

You may want to make changes in the typeface, type size, and type style of the words in your document. For each of these, your word-processing program will most likely have several options to choose from. These options allow you to

- change the typeface to create a different look for the words in your document
- change the type size of the entire document or of just the headings of sections in the paper
- change the type style when necessary; for example, use italics or underline for the titles of books and magazines

Typeface	Size	Style
Geneva	7-point Times	*Italic*
Times	10-point Times	**Bold**
Chicago	12-point Times	Underline
Courier	14-point Times	

Formatting Pages

Not only can you change the way individual words look; you can also change the way they are arranged on the page. Some of the formatting decisions you make will depend on how you plan to use a printout of a draft or on the guidelines of an assignment.

- Set the line spacing, or the amount of space you need between lines of text. Double spacing is commonly used for final drafts.

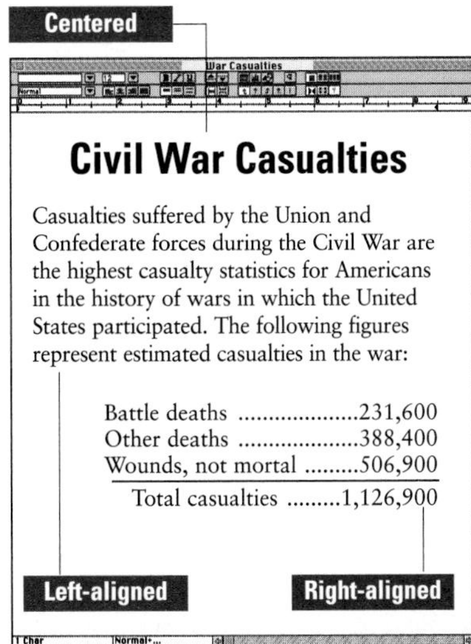

Centered
War Casualties
Civil War Casualties
Casualties suffered by the Union and Confederate forces during the Civil War are the highest casualty statistics for Americans in the history of wars in which the United States participated. The following figures represent estimated casualties in the war:
Battle deaths 231,600
Other deaths 388,400
Wounds, not mortal 506,900
Total casualties 1,126,900
Left-aligned
Right-aligned

- Set the margins, or the amount of white space around the edges of your text. A one-inch margin on all sides is commonly used for final drafts.
- Create a header for the top of the page or a footer for the bottom if you want to include such information as your name, the date, or the page number on every page.
- Determine the alignment of your text. The screen at the left shows your options.

WRITING TIP

Keep your format simple. Your goal is to create not only an attractive document but also one that is easy to read. Your readers will have difficulty if you change the type formatting frequently.

TECHNOLOGY TIP

Some word-processing programs or other software packages provide preset templates, or patterns, for writing outlines, memos, letters, newsletters, or invitations. If you use one of these templates, you will not need to adjust the formatting.

2.3 Working Collaboratively

Computers allow you to share your writing electronically. Send a copy of your work to someone via e-mail or put it in someone's drop box if your computer is linked to other computers on a network. Then use the feedback of your peers to help you improve the quality of your writing.

TECHNOLOGY TIP

Some word-processing programs, such as the Writing Coach software referred to in this book, allow you to leave notes for your peer readers in the side column or in a separate text box. If you wish, leave those areas blank so your readers can write comments or questions.

Peer Editing on a Computer

The writer and the reader can both benefit from the convenience of peer editing "on screen," or at the computer.

- Be sure to save your current draft and then make a copy of it for each of your peer readers.
- You might have each peer reader use a different typeface or type style for making comments, as shown in the example below.
- Ask each of your readers to include his or her initials in the file name.
- If your computer allows you to open more than one file at a time, open each reviewer's file and refer to the files as you revise your draft.

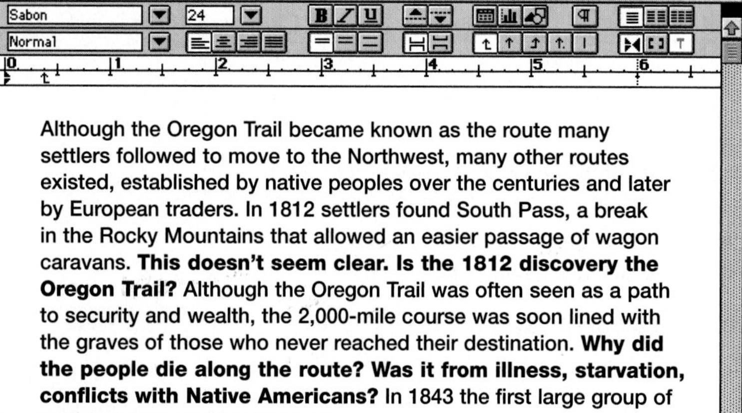

Although the Oregon Trail became known as the route many settlers followed to move to the Northwest, many other routes existed, established by native peoples over the centuries and later by European traders. In 1812 settlers found South Pass, a break in the Rocky Mountains that allowed an easier passage of wagon caravans. **This doesn't seem clear. Is the 1812 discovery the Oregon Trail?** Although the Oregon Trail was often seen as a path to security and wealth, the 2,000-mile course was soon lined with the graves of those who never reached their destination. **Why did the people die along the route? Was it from illness, starvation, conflicts with Native Americans?** In 1843 the first large group of settlers traveled along the trail.

Peer Editing on a Printout

Some peer readers prefer to respond to a draft on paper rather than on the computer.

- Double-space or triple-space your document so that your peer editor can make suggestions between the lines.
- Leave extra-wide margins to give your readers room to note their reactions and questions as they read.
- Print out your draft and photocopy it if you want to share it with more than one reader.

Using Visuals

3

Tables, graphs, diagrams, and pictures often communicate information more effectively than words alone do. Many computer programs allow you to create visuals to use with your written text.

3.1 When to Use Visuals

Use visuals in your work to illustrate complex concepts and processes or to make a page look more interesting.

Although you should not expect a visual to do all the work of written text, combining words and pictures or graphics can increase the understanding and enjoyment of your writing. Many computer programs allow you to create and insert graphs, tables, time lines, diagrams, and flow charts into your document. An art program allows you to create border designs for a title page or to draw an unusual character or setting for narrative or descriptive writing. You may also be able to add clip art, or premade pictures, to your document. Clip art can be used to illustrate an idea or concept in your writing or to make your writing more appealing for young readers.

WHAT YOU'LL NEED

- A graphics program to create visuals
- Access to clip-art files from a CD-ROM, a computer disk, or an on-line service

3.2 Kinds of Visuals

The visuals you choose will depend on the type of information you want to present to your readers.

TECHNOLOGY TIP

A spreadsheet program provides you with a preset table for your statistics and performs any necessary calculations.

Tables

Tables allow you to arrange facts or numbers into rows and columns so that your reader can compare information more easily. In many word-processing programs, you can create a table by choosing the number of vertical columns and horizontal rows you need and then entering information in each box, as the illustration shows.

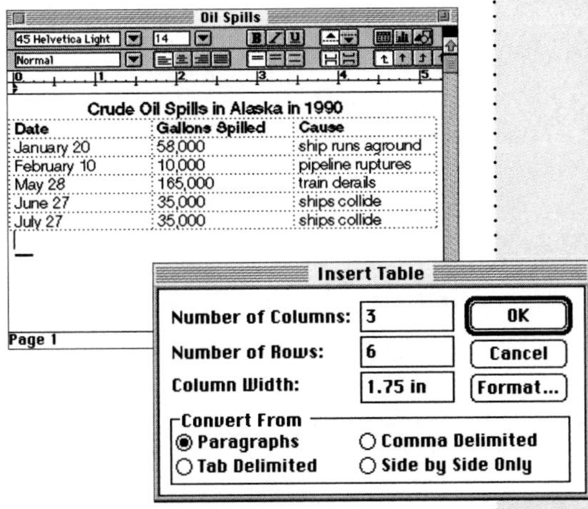

Crude Oil Spills in Alaska in 1990

Date	Gallons Spilled	Cause
January 20	58,000	ship runs aground
February 10	10,000	pipeline ruptures
May 28	165,000	train derails
June 27	35,000	ships collide
July 27	35,000	ships collide

WRITING TIP

Be sure that you have effectively integrated your written texts and visuals. The body of your text should refer to the information in your visuals and explain the relevance of the information. Also, captions, headings, and labels in your visuals should clearly identify each component.

Graphs and Charts

You can sometimes use a graph or chart to help communicate complex information in a clear visual image. For example, you could use a line graph like the one at the right to show how a trend changes over time, a bar graph to compare statistics from different years, or a pie chart to compare percentages. You might want to explore displaying data in more than one visual format before deciding which will work best for you.

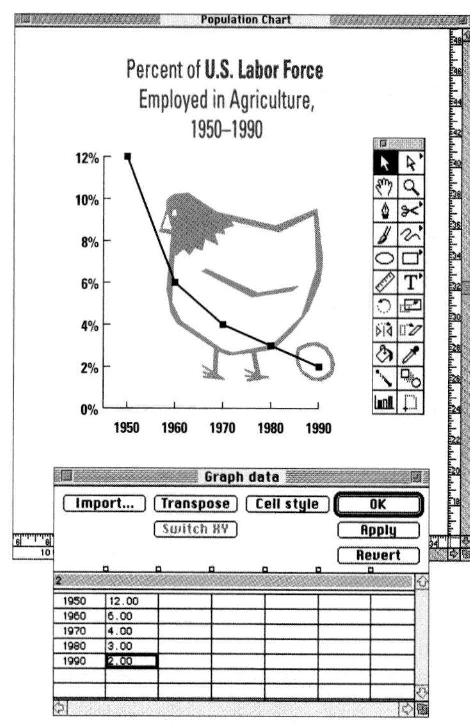

Other Visuals

Art and design programs allow you to create visuals for your writing. Many programs include the following features:

- drawing tools that allow you to draw, color, and shade pictures, such as one shown below
- clip art that you can copy or change with drawing tools
- page borders that you can use to decorate title pages, invitations, or brochures
- text options that allow you to combine words with your illustrations
- tools for making geometric shapes in flow charts, time lines, and diagrams that show a process or sequence of events

Prism Illustration

Splitting Light

Prism

Spectrum of colors

White light

Paint Style

Creating a Multimedia Presentation

4

A multimedia presentation is a combination of text, sound, and visuals such as photographs, videos, and animation. Your audience reads, hears, and sees your presentation at a computer, following different "paths" you create to lead the user through the information you have gathered.

4.1 Features of Multimedia Programs

To start planning your multimedia presentation, you need to know what options are available to you. You can combine sound, photos, videos, and animation to enhance any text you write about your topic.

WHAT YOU'LL NEED

- Individual programs to create and edit the text, graphics, sound, and videos you will use
- A multimedia authoring program that allows you to combine these elements and create links between the screens

Sound

Including sound in your presentation can help your audience understand information in your written text. For example, the user may be able to listen and learn from

- the pronunciation of an unfamiliar or foreign word
- a speech
- a recorded news interview
- a musical selection
- a dramatic reading of a work of literature

Photos and Videos

Photographs and live-action videos can make your subject come alive for the user. Here are some examples:

- videotaped news coverage of a historical event
- videos of music, dance, or theater performances
- charts and diagrams
- photos of an artist's work
- photos or video of a geographical setting that is important to the written text

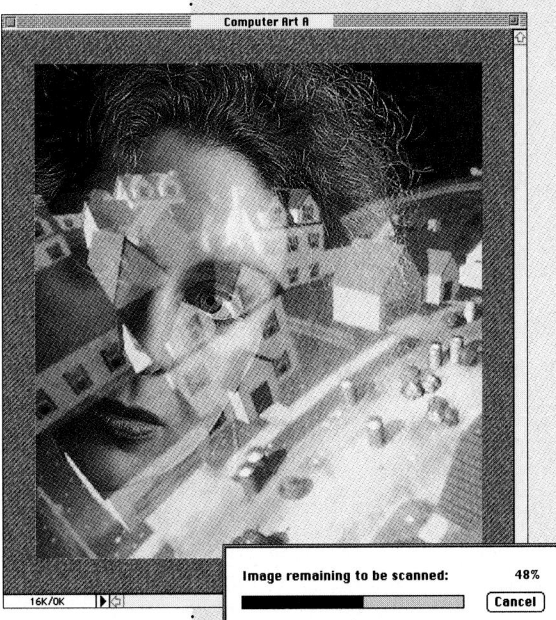

TECHNOLOGY TIP

You can download photos, sound, and video from Internet sources onto your computer. This process allows you to add elements to your multimedia presentation that would usually require complex editing equipment.

Animation

Many graphics programs allow you to add animation, or movement, to the visuals in your presentation. Animated figures add to the user's enjoyment and understanding of what you present. You can use animation to illustrate

- what happens in a story
- the steps in a process
- changes in a chart, graph, or diagram
- how your user can explore information in your presentation

4.2 Planning Your Presentation

To create a multimedia presentation, first choose your topic and decide what you want to include. Then plan how you want your user to move through your presentation.

Imagine that you are creating a multimedia presentation about Donna Cox, an artist who is exploring the use of computer art from an interesting perspective. You know you want to include the following items:

- text introduction to computer art
- information about the artist
- self-portrait of the artist
- videotaped interview with the artist
- text analysis of her work
- your own self-portrait, using computer art
- taped analysis of your work

TECHNOLOGY TIP

You can now find CD-ROMs with videos of things like wildlife, weather, street scenes, and events, and other CD-ROMs with recordings of famous speeches, musical selections, and dramatic readings.

You can choose one of the following ways to organize your presentation:

- step by step with only one path, or order, in which the user can see and hear the information
- a branching path that allows users to make some choices about what they will see and hear, and in what order

A flow chart can help you figure out the path a user can take through your presentation. Each box in the flow chart on the following page represents something about the artist for the user to read, see, or hear. The arrows on the flow chart show a branching path the user can follow.

Whenever boxes branch in more than one direction, it means that the user can choose which item to see or hear first.

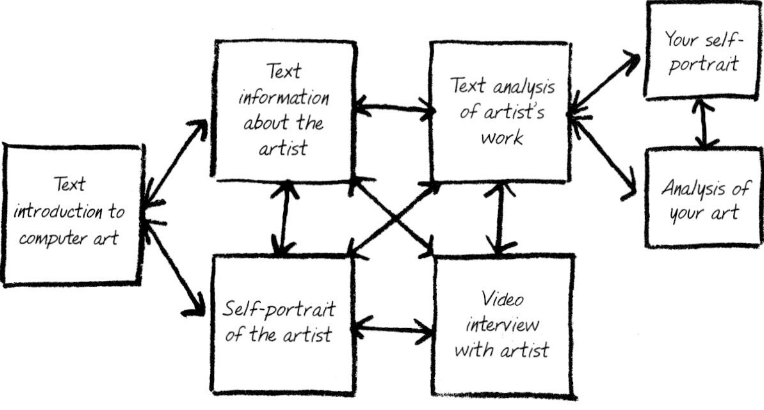

4.3 Guiding Your User

Your user will need directions to follow the path you have planned for your multimedia presentation.

Most multimedia authoring programs allow you to create screens that include text or audio directions that guide the user from one part of your presentation to the next. In the example below, the user can choose between several paths, and directions on the screen explain how to make the choice.

If you need help creating your multimedia presentation, ask your school's technology adviser. You may also be able to get help from your classmates or your software manual.

The user clicks on a button to select any of these options.

Navigational buttons can take the user back and forth, one screen at a time.

This screen shows the artist's self-portrait.

WRITING TIP

You usually need permission from the person or organization that owns the copyright on materials if you want to copy them. You do not need permission, however, if you are not making money from your presentation, if you use it only for educational purposes, and if you use only a small percentage of the original material.

GRAMMAR HANDBOOK

Writing Complete Sentences

1.1 Sentence Fragments

A sentence fragment is a group of words that does not express a complete thought. A sentence fragment may be missing a subject, a predicate, or both.

Completing an Incomplete Thought

You can correct a sentence fragment by adding the missing subject, predicate, or both to complete the thought.

> The author of "Thoughts on the African-American Novel" says that the novel fills a literary need. ^African Americans ~~d~~Don't hear their own tales or history orally anymore. Even African-American music ^is not completely their own anymore.

When a fragment is a subordinate clause, you can join the fragment to an existing sentence and change the punctuation, or you can rewrite the clause so that it can stand alone.

> When African Americans shared their traditional literature with one another^, ~~T~~they responded to presentations orally.

Correcting Punctuation

When a fragment is a phrase, you may be able to connect it to a complete sentence. Simply change the punctuation.

> In this day and age, ~~T~~the novel offers another means for expressing the African-American cultural experience.

APPLY WHAT YOU'VE LEARNED

Rewrite this paragraph, correcting the items that are sentence fragments.

[1]Many African-American novelists have expressed their experience through their art. [2]Some of Maya Angelou's autobiographical works, *I Know Why the Caged Bird Sings, Gather Together in My Name,* and *Heart of a Woman.* [3]Seem like novels. [4]Other writers' novels read like autobiographies. [5]For example, James Baldwin's works, such as *Another Country* and *Go Tell It on the Mountain.* [6]Ralph Ellison's *Invisible Man,* which spoke for at least one generation. [7]Is considered one of the classics of black experience. [8]Richard Wright, another writer who found racial discrimination here intolerable. [9]Moved to Paris. [10]Where he spent most of his adult years. [11]Of his highly acclaimed works. [12]*Native Son* is best known.

1.2 Run-On Sentences

A run-on sentence consists of two or more sentences incorrectly written as one. It is unclear where one idea ends and the next begins.

Forming Separate Sentences

One way to correct a run-on sentence is to form two separate sentences. Use a period or other end punctuation after the first complete thought, and capitalize the first letter of the next sentence.

"High Horse's Courting" describes a Native American form of "dating," from the perspective of a lovesick young man he agonizes over how to win the woman he loves.

Sometimes a writer mistakenly uses a comma instead of a period to separate two complete thoughts. You can correct this kind of mistake, called a comma splice, by changing the comma to a period and capitalizing the first letter of the second sentence.

The simple story seems believable, anyone who has been in love can sympathize with the young man's desperation.

REVISING TIP

To correct run-on sentences, read them to yourself, noticing where you naturally pause between ideas. The pause usually indicates where you should place end punctuation.

Joining Sentences

If the ideas expressed in a run-on sentence are closely related, you may wish to join them to form a compound sentence. One way to do this is to use a comma and a coordinating conjunction to join the main clauses.

> The brave tries pleading, gift giving, force, and deception *but* the father responds to none of these approaches.

Use a semicolon alone, or with a conjunctive adverb, to join main clauses having closely related ideas.

Some commonly used conjunctive adverbs are *however, therefore, nevertheless,* and *besides.*

> The story expresses the anguish of a young man who aches to marry the love of his life; *however,* it is also amusing. Each attempt to convince the girl's father to give him the girl fails; *besides,* his attempts to run off with her meet with disaster.

APPLY WHAT YOU'VE LEARNED

Rewrite this paragraph, correcting the run-on sentences.

[1]In "High Horse's Courting" the young man tries to follow the traditional custom for wooing a bride this involves presenting the girl's father with a "bride price." [2]Ancient Native American courtship and marriage customs varied, in some groups a couple had only to live together to be considered married. [3]The Hopi and some Northwest Pacific Coast groups required elaborate, time-consuming rituals these might take many months. [4]Before a Hopi girl could become a bride, she had to move into her mother-in-law's house, the groom's family sewed her wedding dress. [5]She cooked and cleaned for the family this showed what a good wife she would make. [6]The choice of a husband or wife sometimes fell to the couple often it was the responsibility of the parents. [7]Many customs of the Pacific Northwest Indians involved gift exchanges, gifts might be given before and during the ceremony, as well as for years after the wedding.

Making Subjects and Verbs Agree

2

2.1 Simple and Compound Subjects

A verb must agree in number with its subject. The word *number* refers to whether a word is singular or plural. When a word refers to one thing, it is singular. When it refers to more than one thing, it is plural.

Agreement with Simple Subjects

Use a singular verb with a singular subject.

When the subject is a singular noun, use the singular form of the verb. The present-tense third-person singular form of a regular verb usually ends in *-s* or *-es*.

In "Life for My Child Is Simple" the speaker rejoice^s that her son trust^s the world enough to dare.

Use a plural verb with a plural subject.

The joys of a child ~~is~~ *are* simple; tipping over a house of building blocks can make a youngster happy.

Agreement with Compound Subjects

Use a plural verb with a compound subject whose parts are joined by *and,* regardless of the number of each part.

The speaker and her child wishes for "joy of undeep and unabiding things."

REVISING TIP

To find the subject of a sentence, first find the verb. Then ask *who* or *what* the verb refers to. Say the subject and the verb together to see whether they agree.

When the parts of a compound subject are joined by *or* or *nor,* make the verb agree in number with the part that is closer to it.

> We guess that either the speaker or those near her sees risk all around, so the son's fearlessness warms her heart.

APPLY WHAT YOU'VE LEARNED

Correct verb errors in this paragraph.

[1]Sometimes people's conversation or their writing are like whistling in the dark. [2]In "Life for My Child Is Simple" neither the child's acts nor his reaching out are like that. [3]Neither danger nor daring inspire his risk taking. [4]Gwendolyn Brooks and many other good writers draws from their own experience. [5]Brooks's early life in Topeka and her later upbringing in Chicago provides background for her writing. [6]Brooks's poems and novels exposes the life of African Americans in northern urban ghettos. [7]A woman or a child are often the featured subject. [8]In 1949 Brooks's second collection were awarded the Pulitzer Prize. [9]Although her earlier books had found success through prestigious mainstream publishers, since 1967 her work have been published by an African-American firm. [10]This choice reveal her political conviction that African-American enterprise cannot grow without the support of its own community. [11]Brooks are the first African-American woman ever to serve as poetry consultant to the Library of Congress.

2.2 Pronoun Subjects

When a pronoun is used as a subject, the verb must agree with it in number.

Agreement with Personal Pronouns

When the subject is a singular personal pronoun, use a singular verb. When the subject is plural, use a plural verb.

Singular pronouns are *I, you, he, she,* and *it.* Plural pronouns are *we, you,* and *they.*

> The poems "Richard Cory" and "We Wear the Mask" have similar themes. They concerns people that society does not truly know.

When *he, she,* or *it* is the part of a compound subject that is closer to the verb and the parts are joined by *or* or *nor,* use a singular verb. When a pronoun is part of a compound subject whose parts are joined by *and,* use a plural verb.

> Although Richard Cory is envied, neither the smiling "we" in Paul Laurence Dunbar's poem nor he ~~are~~ is what people think. Cory and they dissembles.

Agreement with Indefinite Pronouns

When the subject is a singular indefinite pronoun, use the singular form of the verb.

The following are singular indefinite pronouns: *another, either, nobody, anybody, everybody, no one, anyone, everyone, someone, one, anything, everything, each,* and *neither*.

> Everyone assume s that Richard Cory was "everything to make us wish that we were in his place," but nobody know s the anguish he is feeling.

When the subject is a plural indefinite pronoun, use the plural form of the verb.

The following are plural indefinite pronouns: *both, few, many,* and *several*.

> Few knows the inner workings of another human being. Many considers the surface an accurate reflection of what lies inside. However, several probably endures pain or sorrow.

REVISING TIP

In many sentences an indefinite pronoun is followed by a prepositional phrase that can help you determine whether the subject is singular or plural. Remember, however, that the object of the preposition is not the subject of the sentence.

The indefinite pronouns *some, all, any, none,* and *most* can be either singular or plural. When the pronoun refers to one thing, use a singular verb. When the pronoun refers to several things, use a plural verb.

Some pretends to be happy in order to spare others' feelings. Most of the pretense spring from a need to protect oneself or to be found acceptable in society.

APPLY WHAT YOU'VE LEARNED

In each sentence write the correct form of the verb.

1 Edwin Arlington Robinson and Paul Laurence Dunbar (speak, speaks) of showing a false face to the world. 2 Others (write, writes) of similar subterfuge. 3 Henry David Thoreau believed that most of us (lead, leads) "lives of quiet desperation." 4 Edna St. Vincent Millay wrote, "Many a man (is, are) making friends with death . . . for lack of love alone." 5 In *A Passage to India* no one (know, knows) that the man without a collar stud is not slovenly but gracious. 6 He (has, have) given away one of his own studs to help someone else out. 7 In the poetry of Emily Dickinson, she (refer, refers) often to the burden of appearing acceptable. 8 Other writers and she (communicate, communicates) through their writing, a "letter to the World." 9 In *Invisible Man* Ralph Ellison describes the experience of an African American; neither his character nor he (is, are) truly "seen" by society. 10 Much of our literature (discuss, discusses) our failures of perception.

2.3 Common Agreement Problems

Several other situations can cause problems in subject-verb agreement.

Interrupting Words and Phrases

Be sure the verb agrees with its subject when words or phrases come between them.

The subject of a verb is never found in a prepositional phrase or an appositive, which may follow the subject and come before the verb. Other phrases can also separate a subject and its verb.

In "This is my letter to the World" Emily Dickinson, a poet whose popularity has remained fairly constant, show^s herself to be more than just a nature poet.

When phrases—such as those beginning with *including, as well as, along with, such as,* and *in addition to*—separate subjects and verbs, be sure that the verbs agree with the subjects.

The poem "Success is counted sweetest," as well as many similar poems, speak^s of life's frequent trials. The images, such as that of a soldier dying just as he hears the trumpet announcing victory, ~~is~~ ^are frequently disturbing.

Inverted Sentences

When the simple subject comes after the verb, be sure the verb agrees with the subject in number.

A sentence in which the subject follows the verb is called an inverted sentence. Questions are usually in inverted form, as are sentences beginning with *Here* and *There.* (*What is hope? There stands the tree.*)

Full of obstacles ~~are~~ ^is the life depicted in "'Hope' is the thing with feathers." How do^es the poet retain her faith in the face of these obstacles? There ~~is~~ ^are times when hope prevails despite all.

REVISING TIP

The forms of *do, be,* and *have* can be main verbs or helping verbs. They can also be part of contractions with *not* (*doesn't—don't, isn't—aren't, hasn't—haven't*). In every case, the verb should agree in number with its subject.

REVISING TIP

To check subject-verb agreement in inverted sentences, place the subject before the verb. For example, change *Here is a poem* to *A poem is here.*

 REVISING TIP

To find the subject, look carefully at words that come before the verb. Remember that the subject may not be the noun or pronoun closest to the verb.

Singular Nouns with Plural Forms

Be sure to use a singular verb when the subject is a noun that is singular in meaning but appears to be plural.

Words such as *barracks, news,* and *headquarters* appear to be plural because they end in *-s*. However, these words are often singular in meaning. Words ending in *-ics* that refer to sciences or branches of study (*logistics, ethics, hermeneutics, physics*) are also singular.

> In "Because I Could Not Stop for Death" Dickinson's series of images convey^s aspects of her own funeral. The "carriage" is a hearse; the "house," her tomb.

Collective Nouns

Use a singular verb when the subject is a collective noun—such as *team, flock,* or *jury*—that refers to a group acting as a unit. Use a plural verb when the collective noun refers to members of the group acting individually.

> Why do^es the group of children playing in the schoolyard ignore the hearse as it passes? Their play may suggest a lack of concern or simply the idea that life goes on.

Nouns of Time, Weight, Measure, Number

Use a singular verb with a subject that identifies a period of time, a weight, a measure, or a number.

> Thirty years ~~are~~ ^is not long to have been writing poetry, considering the 2,000 poems Dickinson wrote.

Titles

Use a singular verb when the subject is the title of a work of art, literature, or music, even though the title may contain plural words.

> *Poems of Emily Dickinson* include^s many poems that dwell on the theme of death.

Predicate Nominatives

Use a verb that agrees with the subject, not with the predicate nominative, when the subject is different in number from the predicate nominative.

> My friend ~~are~~ ^is a Dickinson scholar and professor. Her colleagues and she form~~s~~ a Dickinson admiration society.

REVISING TIP

The fact that a title is set off by quotation marks, italics, or underscoring helps to remind you that it is singular and takes a singular verb.

APPLY WHAT YOU'VE LEARNED

Write the correct form of each verb.

1 Emily Dickinson's huge body of poems (is, are) published in single-volume and three-volume editions. **2** Thomas H. Johnson's single-volume collection (contain, contains) all of her poems. **3** His three-volume edition also (include, includes) her own variants and those of friends, relatives, and editors. **4** *Poems of Emily Dickinson,* as well as Dickinson's *Letters,* (provide, provides) scholars with considerable information. **5** A whole university faculty (has, have) been able to consider her complete works with authority. **6** The field of Dickinson scholarship (was, were) difficult before the poet's works were edited and republished in 1955. **7** This basis for study (reveal, reveals) much that she might not have wanted scrutinized. **8** Dickinson, a recluse in her later years, (was, were) determined to guard her privacy. **9** More than 2,000 poems, as well as her letters, (tell, tells) us a great deal. **10** There (is, are) still much that we do not know, however. **11** To whom (was, were) her love poems written? **12** Why (do, does) her simple life and poetry fascinate us so?

Using Nouns and Pronouns

3.1 Plural and Possessive Nouns

Nouns refer to people, places, things, and ideas. A noun is plural when it refers to more than one person, place, thing, or idea. A possessive noun shows who or what owns something.

Plural Nouns

Follow these guidelines to form noun plurals.

- For most nouns, add *-s* (*letter—letters, battle—battles*).
- For nouns ending in *s, sh, ch, x,* or *z,* add *-es* (*process—processes, marsh—marshes*).
- For nouns ending in a consonant and *y,* change the *y* to *i* and add *-es* (*dandy—dandies, fairy—fairies*).
- For most nouns that end in a consonant and *o,* add *-es* (*potato—potatoes, hero—heroes*).
- For many nouns that end in *f* or *fe,* change the *f* to *v* and add *-s* or *-es* (*life—lives, leaf—leaves*).

Some nouns have the same spelling in both the singular and the plural: *elk, trout, antelope*. Some noun plurals have irregular forms that don't follow any rule: *mice, oxen*.

REVISING TIP

The dictionary usually lists the plural form of a noun if it is formed irregularly or if it might be formed in more than one way. For example, the plural of *ellipsis* is *ellipses.* Dictionary listings are especially helpful for nouns that end in *o, f,* and *fe*.

> Abigail Adams wrote many letteres to her husband that reveal her as one of those ~~wifes~~ wives rare at the time; "Letter to John Adams" expresses her independent mind.

Possessive Nouns

Follow these guidelines to form possessive nouns.

- Add an apostrophe and *-s* to form the possessive of a singular noun or a plural noun that does not end in *-s* (*niece—niece's, friend—friend's, women—women's*).
- Add only an apostrophe to plural nouns that end in *-s* (*uncles—uncles', enemies—enemies'*).

The letter was written two months after the British troops' departure from Boston. The people's cause had triumphed.

APPLY WHAT YOU'VE LEARNED

Correct the errors in plurals and possessives.

1 Letters from Abigail Adams refer to peoples decision to leave Boston. **2** Some colonist's evacuation coincided with that of the British. **3** Colonists who left considered themselves patriotes. **4** Americans, however, saw them as traitor's. **5** The emigrants who remained loyal to the crown called themselves United Empire Loyalistes. **6** About 40,000 of these peoples settled in southeastern Canada. **7** In this way, they escaped the resentment of American's and received free land grants. **8** These English settler's soon made up a majority of the population in what had been French-speaking Nova Scotia and Quebec. **9** The mens' and womens' voices in government led to the establishment of New Brunswick. **10** Canadian's who trace their ancestors back to the United Empire Loyalists are as proud of their heritage as are the Daughter's of the American Revolution.

3.2 Pronoun Forms

There are first-person, second-person, and third-person personal pronouns. A personal pronoun has three forms: the subject form, the object form, and the possessive form.

Subject Pronouns

Use the subject form of a pronoun when it is the subject of a sentence or the subject of a clause. *I, you, he, she, it, we,* and *they* are subject pronouns.

Problems usually arise when a noun and a pronoun—or two pronouns—are used in a compound subject or compound object. To see whether you are using the correct form, read the sentence with just one pronoun.

"The Boston Tea Party" offers a new slant on American history. You and ~~me~~ I may enjoy reconsidering a familiar and serious story in a lighthearted way.

LINK TO LITERATURE

Notice how Dave Barry uses pronouns to avoid repetition of nouns and to create an informal effect throughout "The Boston Tea Party," on page 211.

REVISING TIP

To check the form of a predicate pronoun, see whether the sentence still makes sense when the subject and the predicate pronoun are reversed. (*It was she. She was it.*)

Use the subject form of a pronoun when it is a predicate pronoun following a linking verb.

You often hear the object form used for a predicate pronoun in casual conversation. (*It is me.*) However, the subject form is preferred for more formal writing.

> As for the Boston patriots, if the humorist Dave Barry had been ~~them~~ they, the Boston Tea Party might have been more lively. Another advocate of adding lemon and sweetener to the tea would be ~~me~~ I.

Object Pronouns

Use the object form of a pronoun when it is the object of a verb, a verbal, or a preposition. *Me, you, him, her, it, us,* and *them* are object pronouns.

> The article talks about U.S. Postal Service employees. If Franklin were in charge of ~~they~~ them, the job would give both the employees and ~~he~~ him something better to do than plan tea parties and conduct dangerous electrical experiments.

Possessive Pronouns

Never use an apostrophe with a possessive pronoun. *My, mine, your, yours, his, her, hers, its, our, ours, their,* and *theirs* are possessive pronouns.

> Our country has had it's share of satirists. Their knowledge of history is usually better than mine or your's.

APPLY WHAT YOU'VE LEARNED

Write the following sentences, correcting pronoun errors.

[1]In "The Boston Tea Party" Dave Barry tells you and I a story we have all heard before. [2]Other authors have written satires about the American Revolution, including the musical play *1776;* an approach like their's adds a light touch to a heavy subject. [3]Similar satires include a recording by Stan Freberg on the same subject; my family and me really enjoy it's approach. [4]The record may be as enjoyable to you as it is to my friends and I. [5]*A Funny Thing Happened on the Way to the Forum* is another humorous musical stage play and movie that is based on history and still amuses critics and I. [6]If you were me, would you be on the lookout for other satires of history?

3.3 Pronoun Antecedents

An antecedent is the noun or pronoun to which a personal pronoun refers. The antecedent usually precedes the pronoun.

Pronoun and Antecedent Agreement

A pronoun must agree with its antecedent in number, person, and gender.

Use a singular pronoun to refer to a singular antecedent; use a plural pronoun to refer to a plural antecedent.

Do not allow interrupters to determine the number of the personal pronoun.

> In *The Autobiography of Mark Twain* the author describes a touring mesmerizer's act that was performed over a period of two weeks. Young Twain participated in ~~them~~ it.

LINK TO LITERATURE

Notice how Mark Twain's pronouns agree with their antecedents throughout the excerpt from *The Autobiography of Mark Twain* on page 530. Readers have no trouble distinguishing between the feelings of the young man and the hypnotist in the passage.

If the antecedent is a noun that could refer to either a male or a female, use *he or she* (*him or her, his or her*), or reword the sentence to avoid the singular pronoun.

> Each volunteer who appears on stage seems easily hypnotized. Like Twain, ~~they~~ he or she wants to believe that the show is amazing, mystifying—and legitimate.

REVISING TIP

You could also revise the example at the left this way: ***The volunteers who appear on stage seem*** *easily hypnotized. Like Twain, they want to believe that the show is amazing, mystifying—and legitimate.*

REVISING TIP

To avoid vague pronoun reference, do not use *this* or *that* alone to start a clause. Instead, include a word stating the thing or idea to which *this* or *that* refers—*this alternative, this concept, that theory*.

Be sure that the antecedent of a pronoun is clear.

In most cases do not use a pronoun to refer to an entire idea or clause. Writing is much clearer if the exact reference is specified.

> The others were easily hypnotized. ~~It~~ Their success made young Mark Twain bitterly jealous.

Unclear Antecedents

Make sure that each personal pronoun has a clear reference.

Clarify unidentified references.

The words *it, they, this, which,* and *that* can create problems because they may appear without antecedents.

> ~~In~~ This excerpt from *The Autobiography of Mark Twain*~~, it~~ suggests that people are gullible.

Clarify ambiguous references.

Ambiguous means "having two or more possible meanings." A pronoun reference is ambiguous if the pronoun may refer to more than one word.

> Both Twain and the hypnotist engaged ~~his~~ the audience.

Compound Antecedents Joined by *Or* or *Nor*

When two or more singular antecedents are joined by *or* or *nor,* use a singular pronoun. When two or more plural antecedents are joined by *or* or *nor,* use a plural pronoun.

> Either Twain or the hypnotist might have revealed ~~their~~ his deception.

When one singular and one plural antecedent are joined by *or* or *nor,* use the noun or pronoun nearer the verb to determine whether the pronoun should be singular or plural.

Neither young Twain nor the members of the audience left disappointed; ~~he~~ they saw a great performance.

Indefinite Pronouns as Antecedents

When a singular indefinite pronoun is the antecedent, use *he or she* (*him or her, his or her*), or rewrite the sentence.

Everyone got ~~their~~ his or her 25 cents' worth.

REVISING TIP

Avoid the indefinite use of *you* and *they*.

~~They~~ People say that whether ~~you are~~ one is a spectator or a performer, ~~you are~~ everyone is part of the show.

APPLY WHAT YOU'VE LEARNED

Correct the pronouns to clarify antecedents.

[1]In *The Autobiography of Mark Twain* it says that hypnotism was used for entertainment. [2]In the 1770s Franz Mesmer believed that when the forces of "animal magnetism" were released, it could result in healing. [3]Sigmund Freud employed relaxation techniques that they called hypnosis. [4]Everyone once thought hypnosis was a trancelike state; we now realize it is merely a relaxed one. [5]A patient can be induced to relax by suggesting that they do so. [6]Mark Twain might have been unconvinced by Mesmer because he could not be hypnotized. [7]However, neither Mesmer nor Freud used their studies to dupe people. [8]Either hypnotism's therapeutic benefits or entertainment value might have their validity questioned.

3.4 Pronoun Usage

The form that a pronoun takes is always determined by its function within its own clause or sentence.

Who and *Whom*

Use *who* or *whoever* as the subject of a clause or a sentence.

In "Here We Are" it is the bride who~~m~~ sees veiled insults in the groom's most inoffensive observations.

REVISING TIP

In the example at the left, *who* is the subject of the clause *who sees veiled insults in the groom's most inoffensive observations.*

REVISING TIP

Sometimes changing the order of the words in a sentence enables one to see the error easily. *Whom* is the object of the preposition *with*. (*You sympathize with whom?*)

Use *whom* as the direct or indirect object of a verb or verbal and as the object of a preposition.

People often use *who* for *whom* when speaking informally. However, in written English the pronouns should be used correctly.

> Who^m do you most sympathize with—the groom, who wants the honeymoon to begin happily, or the bride, who interprets his words negatively?

In trying to determine the correct pronoun form, ignore interrupters that come between the subject and the verb.

In the example that follows, *who* should replace *whom* because the pronoun is the subject of the sentence.

> Whom of the two do you think is creating the conflict?

Pronouns in Contractions

Do not confuse these contractions—*it's, they're, who's,* and *you're*—with possessive pronouns that sound the same—*its, their, whose,* and *your*.

> Dorothy Parker's humor is frequently bitter, and it's sharpness is evident in this piece. When the bride and groom argue, their dialogue makes clear ~~whose~~ who's the overly sensitive one.

Pronouns with Nouns

Determine the correct form of the pronoun in phrases such as *we students* and *us pupils* by imagining what the sentence would look like if the pronoun appeared without the noun that follows the pronoun.

~~Us~~ We readers laugh at the newly married couple's polite conversation. Does poking fun at them disturb you or me?

Pronouns in Comparisons

Be sure you use the correct form of a pronoun in a comparison.

Than or *as* often begins an elliptical clause, one in which some words have been left out. To decide which form of the pronoun to use, fill in the missing words.

Like Oscar Wilde, Parker is better remembered for her quotations than for her writing. Few exhibited sharper wit or fashioned more clever insults than ~~her.~~ she [did].

Avoiding Shifts in Person

Be sure that a pronoun agrees with its antecedent in person.

One, everyone, and *everybody* are in the third person. They should be referred to by the third-person pronouns.

Everyone can laugh at the famous review line "Miss Hepburn ran the whole gamut of emotions from A to B," but ~~you~~ he or she may not realize that Parker is the person who wrote it.

APPLY WHAT YOU'VE LEARNED

Correct the errors in pronoun usage.

[1]Dorothy Parker, whom, as you know, wrote "Here We Are," was a member of the Algonquin Round Table. [2]Us readers know that these writers met casually between 1919 and 1943 at the Algonquin Hotel in New York. [3]Everyone thinks of dry wit and sophistication when we think of the group. [4]George S. Kaufman may have been the most caustic of the members, but Parker was probably more clever than him. [5]Their both no funnier than Parker's close friend Robert Benchley, who you may have seen in old movies. [6]It's him with who Parker had a partnership for a short while. [7]People would assign he and she writing projects together or separately. [8]What fun it would have been for we readers to join such a group for lunch at the Algonquin Hotel.

4 Using Modifiers Effectively

4.1 Adjective or Adverb?

Use an adjective to modify a noun or a pronoun. Use an adverb to modify a verb, an adjective, or another adverb.

> In "A Blizzard Under Blue Sky" the narrator is a strong character who treats her unexpected^ly severe~~ly~~ depression by intelligent^ly shifting her focus to physical survival.

REVISING TIP

Always determine first which word is being modified. For example, in the example at the right, *depression* is a noun, so its modifier must be an adjective, *severe*. *Severe* is an adjective, so its modifier must be the adverb *unexpectedly.*

Use an adjective after a linking verb to describe the subject.

In addition to forms of the verb *be,* the following are linking verbs: *become, seem, appear, look, sound, feel, taste, grow,* and *smell*.

> The narrator seems calm~~ly~~ after her time in the mountains; her judgment appears sound~~ly~~.

APPLY WHAT YOU'VE LEARNED

Select the correct modifiers in the following sentences.

1. "A Blizzard Under Blue Sky" is set among (dazzling, dazzlingly) mountains in Utah.
2. Utah's highest peaks cluster north and east of (busy, busily) Salt Lake Valley.
3. The narrator is (desperate, desperately) to escape the (polluted, pollutedly) air in the (high, highly) populated valley.
4. (Considerable, Considerably) manufacturing and industry exist in the valley.
5. People work (steady, steadily) on mining, construction, and computing equipment.
6. They (diligent, diligently) run food processing plants that are (profitable, profitably).
7. The narrator (probable, probably) drove north or east to her winter camp.
8. North of the valley, three Idaho forests—the Sawtooth, Caribou, and Cache—create a (safe, safely) haven for city dwellers.
9. East of the valley, in Utah, two more forests—the Wasatch and the Ashley—offer a (peaceful, peacefully) refuge.

4.2 Comparisons and Negatives

Comparative and Superlative Modifiers

Use the comparative form of an adjective or adverb to compare two things or actions. Use the superlative form to compare more than two things or actions.

Form the comparative by adding *-er* to short modifiers or by using the word *more* with longer modifiers. Form the superlative by adding *-est* or by adding the word *most.*

In "Dr. Heidegger's Experiment" several old people face the ~~most~~ greatest temptation of their lives. Can people ever really use their youth ~~intelligentlier~~ more intelligently if they are given a second chance?

Illogical Comparisons

Avoid comparisons that don't make sense because of missing words or illogical construction.

Dr. Heidegger's decision was more sensible than that of the old people. His choice was easier than theirs, though—he chose not to drink the magical water.

REVISING TIP

Without the added words, the comparisons in the example at the left are hard to understand. In the first sentence, the reader wonders why two unlike things—a decision and a group of people—are being compared. The second sentence has no subject, which makes it confusing.

Double Negatives

To avoid double negatives in comparisons, use only one negative word in a clause.

Besides *not* and *no*, the following are negative words: *never, nobody, none, no one, nothing, nowhere, hardly,* and *scarcely*.

The old people ~~didn't hardly learn anything~~ learned nothing from their self-defeating pasts.

APPLY WHAT YOU'VE LEARNED

Rewrite these sentences, correcting mistakes in modifiers.

1. Aged characters in "Dr. Heidegger's Experiment" reclaimed youth by drinking the more magical of all waters.
2. People have often sought youth and healing at the most remotest hot springs and natural mineral baths.
3. They thought they couldn't scarcely go on without this wonderfulest liquid.
4. However, one of these springs had the more bitter water of any other spring.
5. Yet water is one of the most powerfulest health-promoting substances.
6. There is more water than there is any substance in our bodies.
7. Water is importanter than any other substance in biochemical processes.
8. Minerals in body water permit metabolic reactions to occur most efficient.
9. Nothing doesn't contribute to poor muscle tone and fatigue as much as insufficient body water.
10. Lack of fresh drinking water leads to death quicklier than lack of food.

4.3 Misplaced or Dangling Modifiers

A misplaced modifier is separated from the word it modifies. It may appear to modify the wrong word and can confuse the reader. A dangling modifier seems unrelated to any word in the sentence. Misplaced and dangling modifiers are usually phrases or clauses.

Misplaced Modifier

Place a modifier near the word it modifies.

In "America and I" the shifts ^ distract me from the author's apparent purpose (in voice).

REVISING TIP

Misplaced modifiers cause confusion. Without the change shown in the example at the right, the reader wonders what a "purpose in voice" is.

Dangling Modifier

Be sure a modifier describes a particular word in the sentence.

~~Hidden within~~ *Struggling with* the clumsy diction of an immigrant, she tries to show sophistication and elegance of mind.

APPLY WHAT YOU'VE LEARNED

Correct the mistakes in the placement of modifiers in these sentences.

1. The narrator in "America and I" tells a story of prejudice, a Russian Jew.
2. In the 1100s other Christian Europeans increased their harassment of Jews along with the Crusaders.
3. England and France expelled Jews in the 1200s and 1300s, but other countries took in many of the refugees, such as Poland and Russia.
4. Russia had not yet achieved nationhood, floundering amid devastation and invasion.
5. The Russians still graciously received refugees, invaded by the Mongols.
6. Plagued by the Black Death, persecution continued in Germany.
7. German Jews often settled in Poland, Lithuania, and Russia, having emigrated.
8. In 1346 the Polish king protected Jews in many ways legally.

4.4 Special Problems with Modifiers

The following terms are frequently misused in spoken English. Be careful to use them correctly in written English.

Bad and *Badly*

Always use *bad* as an adjective, whether before a noun or after a linking verb. *Badly* should generally be used to modify an action verb.

Two instances of foreshadowing occur in "The Clod," in which soldiers treat Mary, a farmer's wife, very bad^ly.

This, That, These, Those, and *Them*

Whether used as adjectives or pronouns, *this* and *these* refer to people and things that are nearby, and *that* and *those* refer to people and things that are farther away.

Them is a pronoun; it never modifies a noun. *Those* may be a pronoun or an adjective.

Mary's husband has a loaded gun handy for killing birds. Mary hates the gun but kills ~~them~~ those soldiers with it.

REVISING TIP

Avoid the use of *here* with *this* and *these*; also, do not use *there* with *that* and *those*.

Those ~~there~~ soldiers spoke differently from Mary and Thaddeus. They seemed to think they were better than these ~~here~~ farm people.

Few, Fewer, Fewest and *Little, Less, Least*

***Few, fewer,* and *fewest* refer to numbers of things that can be counted. *Little, less,* and *least* refer to amounts or quantities.**

> One of the soldiers keeps telling Mary that their mission is one of life or death, and that her needs are of ~~few~~ little importance.

Misplacement of *Only*

For clarity, *only* should be positioned before the word or words it modifies.

The misplacement of *only* can alter, and sometimes confuse, the meaning of a sentence. Notice in the example below the difference in meaning when *only* is moved.

> If the soldiers had treated Mary only courteously, they would have saved their own lives and accomplished their mission as well.

APPLY WHAT YOU'VE LEARNED

Rewrite these sentences, correcting errors in modifiers.

1. The plot of "The Clod" shows how less hours of sleep affects the farm wife.
2. Mary needed rest very bad.
3. She and old Thaddeus only live at the country home near the battlefront.
4. She felt fury at the demands and the insults handed out by them soldiers.
5. These men kept her from getting the little hours of sleep available to her before her next day's chores.
6. For most people, too few sleep can cause listlessness, fatigue, irritability, and an inability to concentrate.
7. Other conditions and behaviors emerge as well, including those: hallucinations, paranoia, and occasional aggressiveness.
8. The average person needs at fewest six hours of sleep each night.
9. Mary's relative clumsiness and her lack of interest in serving these soldiers reflect behavior typical of sleep-deprived people.
10. Would Mary have been so tired and irritated if her husband only had taken a share of the workload?
11. He claimed that "the Lord seed fit t' lay me up" bad and "ailin'" and that he could hunt only birds and kill hogs.

Using Verbs Correctly

5

5.1 Verb Tenses and Forms

Verb tense shows the time of an action or a condition. Writers sometimes cause confusion when they use different verb tenses in describing actions that occur at the same time.

Consistent Use of Tenses

When two or more actions occur at the same time or in sequence, use the same verb tense to describe the actions.

"The Long Christmas Dinner" portrays 90 years of the Bayards' holiday meals. Today, people ~~reacted~~ react to family gatherings in much the same way as the Bayards.

A shift in tense is necessary when two events occur at different times or out of sequence. The tenses of the verbs should clearly indicate that one action precedes the other.

I ~~felt~~ feel that this play ~~will~~ would be interesting to watch but hard to analyze unless a person ~~will~~ read it.

Tense	Verb Form
Present	work/works
Past	worked
Future	will/shall work
Present perfect	have/has worked
Past perfect	had worked
Future perfect	will/shall have worked

REVISING TIP

In telling a story, be careful not to shift tenses so often that the reader finds the sequence of events unclear.

REVISING TIP

The past tense and past participle of regular verbs have the same spelling. Both forms end in *-d* or *-ed*. However, you usually double the final consonant before adding *-ed* when a short-vowel sound precedes the consonant (*slip—slipped, knit—knitted, rot—rotted, pat—patted, stub—stubbed*).

Past Tense and Past Participle

The simple past form of a verb can always stand alone. The past participle of the following irregular verbs should always be used with a helping verb.

Present Tense	Past Tense	Past Participle
bring	brought	(have, had) brought
catch	caught	(have, had) caught
eat	ate	(have, had) eaten
flee	fled	(have, had) fled
fling	flung	(have, had) flung
get	got	(have, had) got, gotten
lead	led	(have, had) led
lend	lent	(have, had) lent
lose	lost	(have, had) lost
rise	rose	(have, had) risen
see	saw	(have, had) seen
show	showed	(have, had) shown
sit	sat	(have, had) sat
sting	stung	(have, had) stung
swing	swung	(have, had) swung
am	was	(have, had) been

had
The family ^ eaten so many dinners together that the audience really feels distressed when characters rise to go through death's door.

APPLY WHAT YOU'VE LEARNED

Choose the correct verb from each pair in parentheses.

1. "The Long Christmas Dinner" shows how generations echo one another: the members of each generation (speak, spoke) almost the same words.
2. Physics has (showed, shown) that sound reflected by a large surface creates an echo.
3. Imitation of another often (shows, showed) admiration for that person.
4. From birth, a child (imitates, imitated) his or her parents or guardians.
5. Only as he or she (got, gets) a separate sense of self can a child decide that doing as the parents do makes sense.
6. Even so, unless a child (sees, saw) a reason to behave differently, he or she is likely to behave as the parents or guardian did.
7. One who has (went, gone) lives on in the unconscious actions of others.

5.2 Commonly Confused Verbs

The following verb pairs are often confused.

Affect and *Effect*

Affect **means "to influence."** ***Effect*** **means "to cause."**

In "I Stand Here Ironing" a mother worries that poverty has ~~effected~~ affected her daughter Emily. However, Emily is strong enough to ~~affect~~ effect needed changes in her own life.

Lie and *Lay, Sit* and *Set*

Lie **means "to rest in a flat position" or "to be in a certain place";** ***lay*** **means "to put or place."** ***Sit*** **means "to be in a seated position";** ***set*** **means "to put or place."**

As Emily was growing up, she often ~~set~~ sat near her mother, seeking assurance that she had been beautiful, her baby pictures ~~laying~~ lying there to remind them.

REVISING TIP

If you're uncertain about which verb to use, check to see whether the verb has an object. The verbs *lie* and *sit* never have objects—and they both refer to position. The verbs *lay* and *set* both have objects—and they have the same meaning.

Rise and *Raise*

Rise **means "to move upward."** ***Raise*** **means "to move something upward."**

In refusing to ~~raise~~ rise from bed to answer Emily, her mother failed to make her daughter feel safe.

Learn and *Teach*

Learn **means "to gain knowledge or skill."** ***Teach*** **means "to help someone learn."**

Emily ~~learned~~ taught her mother what a child needs.

REVISING TIP

When no movement is implied, *bring* may be used to mean "produce a result."

Bring and *Take*

***Bring* refers to movement toward or with the speaker. *Take* refers to movement away from the speaker.**

When returning from the orphanage, Emily ~~took~~ brought with her a fear of closeness. She later ~~brought~~ took that fear out of her life and replaced it with strength.

Here are the principal parts of these troublesome verb pairs.

Present Tense	Past Tense	Past Participle
affect effect	affected effected	(have, had) affected (have, had) effected
lie lay	lay laid	(have, had) lain (have, had) laid
sit set	sat set	(have, had) sat (have, had) set
rise raise	rose raised	(have, had) risen (have, had) raised
learn teach	learned taught	(have, had) learned (have, had) taught
bring take	brought took	(have, had) brought (have, had) taken

APPLY WHAT YOU'VE LEARNED

Correct any verbs that are used incorrectly.

1. Emily in "I Stand Here Ironing" had emotional scars from her childhood that effected her later years.
2. As she was growing up, she seemed to take no intelligence or fluency to her speech.
3. As the story begins, Emily's mother has a message from a counselor who wants to rise Emily's spirits somehow.
4. Emily has learned herself to seem witty, confident, and strong most of the time.
5. The author of Emily's story is Tillie Olsen, a woman who herself had to raise above many difficulties in order to write.
6. For many years Olsen had to sit aside her dreams while she cared for her family and worked outside the home.
7. She had to lie aside her writing, which she had begun to do seriously by age 20.
8. Olsen affected change by stressing that everyone has a chance to make an artistic contribution, regardless of race or gender.

Correcting Capitalization

6

6.1 Proper Nouns and Adjectives

A common noun is the name of a class of persons, places, things, or ideas. A proper noun is the name of a particular person, place, thing, or idea. A proper adjective is an adjective formed from a proper noun. Capitalize all proper nouns and proper adjectives.

Names and Titles

Capitalize the name of a person and the initials that stand for the name of a person.

> In "Gary Keillor" garrison e. keillor recounts his high school escapades with dede petersen and elaine eggert.

Capitalize a title used before a name or an abbreviation for the title. In general, do not capitalize either a title that follows a name or a title that stands alone.

> Gary's teacher, miss rasmussen, played the class a recording of sir john gielgud reading poetry.

Capitalize a title indicating a family relationship when it is used before or as someone's name (*Aunt Vera, Grandpa*) but not when used simply to identify a person (*Marco's uncle*).

> Gary's uncle earl and aunt myrna let him hang around at their house. He constantly did chores for his Aunt.

LINK TO LITERATURE

In "Gary Keillor," on page 335, notice how Garrison Keillor refers to specific places, people, and things. These precise names help you visualize scenes.

REVISING TIP

Prefixes and suffixes such as *ex-* and *-elect* are not capitalized when used with a title. (*The article, published in December 1968, mentions President-**elect** Nixon.*)

Languages, Nationalities, Religious Terms

Capitalize languages and nationalities, as well as religious names and terms. Do not capitalize the words *god* and *goddess* when they refer to mythological deities.

Capitalize languages and nationalities, such as *Norwegian, Bengali, Hebrew, Japanese, French,* and *Turkish*. Capitalize religious names and terms, such as *God, Buddha,* the *Bible,* and the *Koran*.

REVISING TIP

Do not capitalize pronouns that refer to a deity. (*God's in his heaven.*)

Being an entertainer was Gary's dream, but he reminded himself that he was a christian and believed that showing off was not proper.

School Subjects

Capitalize the name of a specific school course (*Astronomy 201, Ancient History*). Do not capitalize a general reference to a school subject (*physical education, computer science*).

Bewildered by Plane Geometry, Gary might have felt a bit better about history 3 or Creative Writing 1.

Organizations, Institutions

Capitalize the important words in the official names of organizations and institutions (*Congress, Kendall College*).

Do not capitalize words that represent kinds of organizations or institutions (*school, church, university*) or words that refer to a specific organization when they are not part of its official name (*at the university*).

REVISING TIP

Do not capitalize minor words in a proper noun that is made up of several words. (*School of the Performing Arts*)

A student at new tryon high school, he looked forward to attending a University in a year or two.

Geographical Names, Events, Time Periods

Capitalize geographical names—as well as the names of events, historical periods and documents, holidays, months, and days—but not the names of seasons or directions.

Names	Examples
Continents	Australia, North America, Africa
Bodies of water	Caribbean Sea, Delaware Bay, Hudson River
Political units	the United States, Wisconsin, the Bronx
Areas of a country	the Midwest, New England
Public areas	Central Park, Yosemite National Park
Roads and structures	Wall Street, the Taj Mahal
Events	French and Indian Wars, the Russian Revolution
Documents	Treaty of Westminster, the Constitution
Periods of history	the Dark Ages, the Enlightenment
Holidays	Fourth of July, Veterans Day
Months and days	October, Wednesday
Seasons	autumn, summer
Directions	south, northeast

Gary had finagled a trip to colorado with his cousins during the summer, but now it was an ugly Spring in the midwest. He hung around with the west river road crowd, who helped him rehearse for monday's show.

REVISING TIP

Do not capitalize a reference that does not use the full name of a place, an event, or a period. (*We visited Yosemite but stayed at the* ***park*** *for only two days.*)

APPLY WHAT YOU'VE LEARNED

Rewrite the following sentences, correcting errors in capitalization.

1. "Gary Keillor" takes place in the Spring of 1959.
2. That was the year my Mother was born, my uncle Bill joined the navy, and my grandfather started to teach philosophy 101 at farnsworth college.
3. What else was going on in the united states that Spring and that year?
4. Dwight d. eisenhower was President then; he had been a General in world war II.
5. I wonder whether barbie dolls had been invented yet, or g.i. joe dolls.
6. Did you know that in 1959 Bill mauldin won the pulitzer prize for his cartoons a second time?
7. Fishing made big news; Edward b. Elliott landed a 97-pound blue catfish on the banks of the missouri river in south dakota.
8. More students were enrolling in General Science and mathematics Classes.
9. In international news, a czechoslovakian chemist won the nobel prize.
10. The first international congress of oceanography was held in New York.

6.2 Titles of Created Works

The titles of published material follow certain capitalization rules.

Books, Plays, Magazines, Newspapers, Films

Capitalize the first word, last word, and all other important words in the title of a book, play, periodical, newspaper, or film. Underline or italicize the title to set it off.

Within a title, do not capitalize articles, conjunctions, and prepositions of fewer than five letters unless they appear at the beginning or the end of the title.

Emerson's essay "Self-Reliance" can be found in his 1841 book entitled essays, first series.

Poems, Stories, Articles

Capitalize the first word, last word, and all other important words in the title of a poem, a short story or an article. Enclose the title in quotation marks.

Other works of his include lectures such as the conduct of life, a book entitled nature, and poems such as uriel and bacchus.

APPLY WHAT YOU'VE LEARNED

Rewrite the sentences, correcting the punctuation and capitalization of titles.

1. In the excerpt from self-reliance, Ralph Waldo Emerson presents part of his personal philosophy.
2. Emerson and other members of his transcendentalist movement published a journal called the dial.
3. Emerson's full-length books include representative men and English traits.
4. Emerson's best essay, according to many literary critics, is entitled Experience.
5. Another transcendentalist was Henry David Thoreau, author of the book walden and the essay civil disobedience.
6. Thoreau wrote two essays attacking slavery: slavery in Massachusetts and A plea for Captain John Brown.

Correcting Punctuation

7

7.1 Punctuating Compound Sentences

Punctuation helps organize sentences that have more than one clause.

Commas in Compound Sentences

Use a comma before the conjunction that joins the clauses of a compound sentence.

Do not use a comma before the conjunction that joins a compound subject or a compound predicate.

"In the American Society" by Gish Jen presents an interesting character study of a Chinese immigrant family, and it contrasts financial success with social adaptation.

Semicolons in Compound Sentences

Use a semicolon between the clauses of a compound sentence when no conjunction is used. Use a semicolon before a conjunctive adverb that joins the clauses of a compound sentence.

Conjunctive adverbs include *therefore, however, consequently, nevertheless,* and *besides.* You should place a comma after a conjunctive adverb in a compound sentence.

Mona and Callie, the daughters, have little trouble adapting to American ways; their father, on the other hand, adheres to his traditional values.

REVISING TIP

Even when clauses are connected by a coordinating conjunction, you should use a semicolon between them if one or both clauses contain a comma. (*In the story "In the American Society" the mother accuses her daughters of copying American ways; but she herself is interested in espadrilles, wallpaper, and the country club.*)

APPLY WHAT YOU'VE LEARNED

Rewrite this paragraph, correcting problems with commas or semicolons.

[1]Almost everyone in the United States is an immigrant or a descendant of immigrants during the first great immigrant waves people came from Europe. [2]Irish and German immigration increased in the1840s and German immigration continued through the 1880s. [3]Poles and Eastern European immigrants came to the United States mainly between 1880 and 1920 they were fleeing poverty and, in some instances, religious persecution. [4]Many Chinese immigrants had come to the West Coast in the mid-19th century and these hard workers helped to build the railroads and staff the mining camps. [5]A "gentleman's agreement" was made with Japan in 1907 and it stopped the immigration of Japanese laborers into the United States. [6]In the latter half of the 20th century, large numbers of Mexicans and Cubans entered the United States therefore many large cities now have large Hispanic populations. [7]Among the most recent additions to this country's census rolls are Cambodians, Laotians, and Vietnamese here they found a refuge from Communist-dominated governments.

7.2 Setting Off Elements in a Sentence

Most elements that are not essential to a sentence are set off by commas or by other punctuation marks to highlight the main idea of the sentence. A nonessential element merely adds information to an already complete sentence. An essential element is necessary to convey the accurate meaning of the sentence; without it, the meaning is unclear.

Commas

You should often use a comma to separate an introductory word or phrase from the rest of the sentence.

An introductory prepositional phrase usually need not be set off with a comma. However, you should use a comma for two or more prepositional phrases or for a phrase that includes a verb or a verbal.

In *Blue Highways* by William Least Heat-Moon ^ the author describes an encounter with a modern member of the Hopi tribe. Immediately ^ the good feeling between the two men becomes apparent.

LINK TO LITERATURE

In "Blue Highways" William Least Heat-Moon adds to the variety and interest of his sentences by introducing elements that are set off with commas. Notice especially the use of commas in the description of Hopi beliefs on page 113.

In a complex sentence, set off an introductory subordinate clause with a comma.

> As the two men speak, the reader learns of the aspirations of the young Hopi.

Use commas to set off a word or group of words that interrupt the flow of a sentence. When a subordinate clause interrupts the main clause, set off the subordinate clause with commas only if it is not essential.

> The young medical student, although pursuing a scientific career, has not abandoned the religion of his ancestors. He tries to explain, as best he can, what his beliefs involve.

REVISING TIP

To tell whether a subordinate clause is essential or nonessential, say the sentence without the clause. If the basic meaning changes, the clause is essential and should not be set off with commas.

The words shown in the chart below are commonly used to begin a subordinate clause. When such words appear with introductory or interrupting clauses, they usually signal the need for one or more commas.

Words Often Used to Introduce Subordinate Clauses				
Subordinating Conjunctions	after although as as if as long as as much as as though	because before even if even though if in order that provided	since so that than though till unless until	whatever when whenever where wherever while
Relative Pronouns	which	who	whom	whose

Parentheses

Use parentheses to set off material that is only incidentally connected to the main idea of a sentence.

The Navajo people given large land grants by the government outnumber and surround the Hopis.

Dashes

Use dashes to set off a word, or a group of words, that abruptly interrupts the flow of a sentence.

Kendrick Fritz his father took the name during World War II tries to overcome prejudice against Native Americans.

Colons

Use a colon to introduce a list of items or a long quotation. Never use a colon after a preposition or after a verb when the items listed are essential to the clause.

Native Americans face many problems poverty, few employment opportunities, medical needs, and prejudice.

Use a colon between two sentences when the second explains or summarizes the first.

Kendrick Fritz and his family try to meet the medical needs of their people his mother and sister are employed at the hospital where he hopes to practice medicine himself.

REVISING TIP

Try saying the sentence without the interrupter; if the basic meaning doesn't change, you should use punctuation (commas, dashes, or parentheses) to set off the interrupter.

REVISING TIP

A colon often follows a word or phrase such as *these* or *the following items*. (*Heat-Moon relied on these: a good map, his van, and his spirit of openness to what is new.*)

For Clarity

Use commas to prevent misreading or misunderstanding.

With a kachina doll around, the room of Kendrick Fritz reminded him of his people's traditions.

REVISING TIP

Sometimes when a comma is missing, parts of a sentence can be grouped in more than one way by a reader. A comma separates the parts so they can be read in only one way.

APPLY WHAT YOU'VE LEARNED

Rewrite these sentences. Add commas, parentheses, dashes, and colons where necessary.

[1]In *Blue Highways* by William Least Heat-Moon the author describes a meeting with a medical student who is a Hopi. [2]When Hopi children are very young both boys and girls are initiated into the kachina cult. [3]Kachinas are spirit people some are spirits of the dead who live among the Hopi for six months. [4]Kachina dolls given to children particularly to little girls are representations of these spirits. [5]These dolls represent a prayer for a number of things rain, good crops, fertility, and other blessings. [6]The dolls they are called *tihus* are hung from the walls of houses. [7]Flat, slablike dolls which are called *puchtihu* are hung on the cradles of tiny babies to protect them from harm. [8]After boys are initiated into the kachina rites they may stay in the kiva it's an underground ceremonial room. [9]Normally girls and women are not admitted to the kiva except to whitewash the walls or bring food during ceremonies. [10]The oldest evidence of a kachina doll it dates back to the 12th or 13th century was found near Phoenix, Arizona.

7.3 Elements in a Series

Use commas to separate three or more elements in a series and to separate multiple adjectives preceding a noun.

Subjects, Verbs, Objects, and Other Elements

Use a comma after every item except the last in a series of three or more items.

The three or more items can be nouns, verbs, adjectives, adverbs, phrases, independent clauses, or other parts of a sentence.

In "The Case for Official English" S. I. Hayakawa maintains that language makes a single society from a variety of nationalities, races, and colors.

REVISING TIP

Note in the example that a comma followed by a conjunction precedes the last element in the series. That comma is always used.

Two or More Adjectives

When more than one adjective precedes a noun, in most cases use a comma after each adjective except the last one.

If you can't reverse the order of adjectives without changing the meaning or if you can't use the word *and* between them, do not separate them with a comma.

> Ethnic diversity combined with the English language can, according to Senator Hayakawa, create a unique,vibrant culture.

APPLY WHAT YOU'VE LEARNED

Rewrite the paragraph, correcting the comma errors.

1 Scholars classify languages into a number of large distinct families. 2 The Indo-European family includes such different languages as English German French Polish Russian Greek and Gaelic. 3 Many words in these languages take endings that show gender number person and tense. 4 Language scholars believe that language developed slowly from primitive sounds like grunts barks and hoots. 5 Language is constantly changing often through the addition of words for new advanced inventions.

7.4 Dates, Addresses, and Letters

Punctuation in addresses, dates, and letters makes information easy to understand.

Dates

Use a comma after the day and the year to set off the date from the rest of the sentence.

> In *Narrative of the Life of Frederick Douglass* we learn that on January 1,1833,Douglass went to live with Mr. Covey.

REVISING TIP

In dates that include only the month and the year, do not use a comma after the month. (*Frederick Douglass's encounter with cruelty in* ***August 1833*** *resulted in his escape from slavery.*)

Addresses

In an address with more than one part, use a comma after each part to set it off from the rest of the sentence.

> Douglass was born in Tuckahoe, Maryland, not far from Baltimore.

Parts of a Letter

Use a comma after the greeting and after the closing of a letter.

> Dear Aunt Felicia,
>
> Thank you for the book about Frederick Douglass. I really enjoyed it.
>
> Your nephew,
>
> Sam

REVISING TIP

In an address that includes the ZIP code, do not use a comma between the state abbreviation and the ZIP code.

APPLY WHAT YOU'VE LEARNED

Rewrite the following sentences, correcting the comma errors.

1. In *Narrative of the Life of Frederick Douglass* the writer tells of his life long before January 1 1863 when President Lincoln freed the slaves in the Confederate states.
2. Slavery held an important role in the Southern economy; this importance is evident in an ad dated August 23 1852 in which a reward was offered for a runaway slave.
3. Frederick Douglass, Harriet Tubman, and William Lloyd Garrison were among those who opposed the institution of slavery; on January 1 1831 Garrison published the first issue of *The Liberator,* an abolitionist newspaper.
4. John Brown, a fanatical abolitionist, in October 1859 marched to Harper's Ferry Virginia and attacked the U.S. arsenal there.
5. Dear Sheila

   I am writing a report on the abolitionist movement in U.S. history. Can you suggest any sources?

   Your friend
   Ed

7.5 Quotations

Quotation marks tell readers who said what. Incorrectly placed or missing quotation marks lead to misunderstanding.

Direct Quotation from a Source

Use quotation marks at the beginning and the end of a direct quotation from source material and to set off the title of a short work. Do not use quotation marks to set off an indirect quotation.

"Don't leave this house until that animal is dead," says Lily's mother in "The Consolation of Nature." The class was discussing this and other short stories.

Introducing a Quotation

Introduce a short direct quotation with a comma. Use a colon for a long quotation. Capitalize the first word in a direct quotation but not in an indirect one.

John said, "I liked that short story."

Kerry replied, "Yes, I think it's amazing that a writer can turn a simple incident into an interesting story."

End Punctuation

Place periods inside quotation marks. Place question marks and exclamation points inside quotation marks if they belong to the quotation; place them outside if they do not belong to the quotation. Place semicolons outside quotation marks.

"Do you know of any other short stories like that?" asked Aileen.

John replied, "There's always O. Henry"; and Kerry added, "What a great talent he had!"

REVISING TIP

Use a colon to introduce a long quotation. (*Lincoln's Gettysburg Address states: "Four score and seven years ago, our fathers . . ."*)

REVISING TIP

If quoted words are from a written source and are not complete sentences, begin the quote with a lowercase letter. (*Valerie Martin says that moonflowers are "like pools of milk among the dark leaves that covered the fence."*)

Use a comma to end a quotation that is a complete sentence followed by explanatory words.

"I prefer Flannery O'Connor's stories myself," added Clare.

Divided Quotations

Capitalize the first word of the second part of a direct quotation if it begins a new sentence.

"You can't ignore Poe's stories," says John. "he always makes me shiver."

Do not capitalize the first word of the second part of a divided quotation if it does not begin a new sentence.

"Let's make a catalog," suggested Kerry, "Listing the titles and authors of short stories we'd recommend to friends."

REVISING TIP

Should the first word of the second part of a divided quotation be capitalized? Imagine the quotation without the explanatory words. If a capital letter would not be used, then do not use one in the divided quotation.

APPLY WHAT YOU'VE LEARNED

Rewrite the sentences, inserting quotation marks and correcting punctuation errors.

1Ray began the first meeting of our short story club by announcing formally the meeting will please come to order. **2**"Let's decide how we'll proceed" he added. **3**"I think," said Brenda, "That we should choose a different author each week." **4**"I agree," said Kelly. "which author shall we discuss first"? **5**Several students suggested "that it would be fun to start with someone familiar like O. Henry." **6**"What a drag"! exclaimed John. "Who doesn't know all his stories by heart"? **7**"Well, that's the idea" chimed in Ray. "we can get everyone involved in a discussion right away, even those who haven't had time to read something new." **8**After some further questions, the group agreed to review The Gift of the Magi and The Fourth Ingredient before their next meeting.

8 Grammar Glossary

This glossary contains various terms you need to understand when you use the Grammar Handbook. Used as a reference source, this glossary will help you explore grammar concepts and the ways they relate to one another.

Abbreviation An abbreviation is a shortened form of a word or word group; it is often made up of initials. (*ACLU, lb., pt.*)

Active voice. *See* **Voice.**

Adjective An adjective modifies, or describes, a noun or a pronoun. (*strong* odor, I feel *awkward.*)

A ***predicate adjective*** follows a linking verb and describes the subject. (The child looked *anxious.*)

A ***proper adjective*** is formed from a proper noun. (*European* style, *Swedish* meatballs)

The ***comparative*** form of an adjective compares two items. (*more athletic, sparser*)

The ***superlative*** form of an adjective compares more than two things. (*most delicious, tiniest*)

What Adjectives Tell	Examples
How many	*many* pages *some* liquid
What kind	*long* speech *slight* change
Which one(s)	*this* statement *those* desserts

Adjective phrase. *See* **Phrase.**

Adverb An adverb modifies a verb, an adjective, or another adverb. (Alan writes *well.*)

The ***comparative*** form of an adverb compares two actions. (*more slowly, closer*)

The ***superlative*** form of an adverb compares more than two actions. (*most seriously, soonest*)

What Adverbs Tell	Examples
How	sing *loudly* run *quickly*
When	will come *soon* arrived *later*
Where	went *away* fell *down*
To what extent	*very* sick *really* unusual

Adverb, conjunctive. *See* **Conjunctive adverb.**

Adverb phrase. *See* **Phrase.**

Agreement Sentence parts that correspond with one another are said to be in agreement.

In ***pronoun-antecedent agreement,*** a pronoun and the word it refers to are the same in number, gender, and person. (Anita found *her* earrings. The *girls* found *their* coats.)

In ***subject-verb agreement,*** the subject and verb in a sentence are the same in number. (*I know* Bob. *He has* a dog.)

Ambiguous reference An ambiguous reference occurs when a pronoun may refer to more than one word. (Simone told Kay that *she* was scheduled to bring refreshments.)

Antecedent An antecedent is the noun or pronoun to which a pronoun refers. (*I* helped *my* sister. *Anthony* left *his* house at 8 A.M.)

Appositive An appositive is a noun or phrase that explains one or more words in a sentence. (Zoe, *a dancer*, is in the school play.)

An ***essential appositive*** is needed to make the sense of a sentence complete. (My brother *Ralph* goes to college.)

A ***nonessential appositive*** is one that adds information to a sentence but is not necessary to its sense. (Jerry Lewis, *an American comedian,* is considered a comedic genius in France.)

Article Articles are the special adjectives *a, an,* and *the.* (*the* air, *a* frog)

The ***definite article*** (the word *the*) refers to a particular thing. (*the* swamp)

An ***indefinite article*** indicates that a noun is not unique but is one of many of its kind. (*a* box, *an* apple)

Auxiliary verb. *See* **Verb.**

Clause A clause is a group of words that contains a verb and its subject. (*Clowns tumble*)

An ***adjective clause*** is a subordinate clause that modifies a noun or pronoun. (Our family owned the boat *that the storm destroyed.*)

An ***adverb clause*** is a subordinate clause used as an adverb to modify a verb, an adjective, or an adverb. (Don't open the gifts *until the guests arrive.*)

A ***noun clause*** is a subordinate clause that is used as a noun. (*What her friend said* troubled Maureen.)

An ***elliptical clause*** is a clause from which a word or words have been omitted. (Ann knows more about history *than I.*)

A ***main (independent) clause*** can stand by itself as a sentence. (*the students arrived*)

A ***subordinate (dependent) clause*** does not express a complete thought and cannot stand by itself. (*if you solve the problem*)

Clause	Example
Main (independent)	The shutters creaked noisily
Subordinate (dependent)	as the storm raged.

Collective noun. *See* **Noun.**

Comma splice A comma splice is an error caused when two sentences are separated with a comma instead of a correct end mark. (*The canoe capsized, the boaters swam to safety.*)

Common noun. *See* **Noun.**

Comparative. *See* **Adjective; Adverb.**

Complement A complement is a word or group of words that completes the meaning of the verb. (Jo made the *announcement.*) *See also* **Direct object; Indirect object.**

An ***objective complement*** is a word or a group of words that follows a direct object and renames or describes that object. (My mother considered the bake sale a *success.*)

A ***subject complement*** follows a linking verb and renames or describes the subject. (The day looked *dreary.*) *See* **Noun, predicate; Adjective, predicate.**

Complete predicate The complete predicate of a sentence consists of the main verb plus any words that modify or complete the verb's meaning. (Pets *respond to praise.*)

Complete subject In a sentence the complete subject consists of the simple subject plus any words that modify or describe the simple subject. (*The new store in the mall* carries hockey equipment.)

Sentence Part	Example
Complete subject	The mayor of the town
Complete predicate	asked for volunteer drivers.

Compound sentence part A sentence element that consists of two or more subjects, predicates, objects, or other parts is compound. (*Sue* and *Cal* jog. Lupe *reads* and *writes.* Kwok trains *Labradors* and *poodles.*)

Conjunction A conjunction is a word or words that links other words or groups of words.

A ***coordinating conjunction*** connects related words, groups of words, or sentences. (*and, but, or*)

A ***correlative conjunction*** is one of a pair of conjunctions that work together to connect sentence parts. (*either . . . or, neither . . . nor, not only . . . but also, whether . . . or, both . . . and*)

A ***subordinating conjunction*** introduces a subordinate clause. (*after, although, as, as if, as long as, as though, because, before, if, in order that, provided, since, so that, than, though, till, unless, until, whatever, when, whenever, where, wherever, while*)

Conjunctive adverb A conjunctive adverb joins the clauses of a compound sentence. (*however, therefore, besides*)

Contraction A contraction is formed by joining two words and substituting an apostrophe for a letter or letters left out of one of the words. (*we'll, couldn't*)

Coordinating conjunction. *See* **Conjunction.**

Correlative conjunction. *See* **Conjunction.**

Dangling modifier A dangling modifier is one that does not clearly modify any word in the sentence. (*Dashing across the room,* the notebook dropped from my hand.)

Demonstrative pronoun. *See* **Pronoun.**

Dependent clause. *See* **Clause.**

Direct object A direct object receives the action of a verb. Direct objects follow transitive verbs. (Carrie recorded the *minutes.*)

Direct quotation. *See* **Quotation.**

Divided quotation. *See* **Quotation.**

Double negative A double negative is an incorrect use of two negative words when only one is needed. (*Nobody doesn't* want to help me.)

End mark An end mark is one of several punctuation marks that can end a sentence. See the chart on page 1244.

Fragment. *See* **Sentence fragment.**

Future tense. *See* **Verb tense.**

Gender The gender of a personal pronoun indicates whether the person or thing referred to is male, female, or neuter. (Amanda is a girl who knows what *she* wants.)

Gerund A gerund is a verbal that ends in *-ing* and functions as a noun. (*Skydiving* is a hazardous hobby.)

Helping verb. *See* **Verb, auxiliary.**

Illogical comparison An illogical comparison is a comparison that does not make sense because words are missing or illogical. (Martin enjoys boxing *more than any sport.*)

Indefinite pronoun. *See* **Pronoun.**

Indefinite reference Indefinite reference occurs when a pronoun refers to an idea that is vaguely expressed. (Marie visited Italy, and she loved *them.*)

Independent clause. *See* **Clause.**

Indirect object An indirect object tells to whom or for whom (sometimes to what or for what) something is done. (Al gave *Ray* a book.)

Indirect question An indirect question tells what someone asked without using the person's exact words. (*I asked Joe where he lived.*)

Indirect quotation. *See* **Quotation.**

Infinitive An infinitive is a verbal beginning with *to* that functions as a noun, an adjective, or an adverb. (I want *to go.*)

Intensive pronoun. *See* **Pronoun.**

Interjection An interjection is a word or phrase used to express strong feeling. (*Aha! No way!*)

Interrogative pronoun. *See* **Pronoun.**

Intransitive verb. *See* **Verb.**

Inverted sentence An inverted sentence is one in which the subject comes after the verb. (*Here comes the parade. Where are the study questions for the history exam?*)

Irregular verb. *See* **Verb.**

Linking verb. *See* **Verb.**

Main clause. *See* **Clause.**

Main verb. *See* **Verb.**

Modifier A modifier makes another word more precise; modifiers most often are adjectives or adverbs; they may also be phrases, verbals, or clauses that function as adjectives or adverbs. (*large* vase, smiled *broadly,* child *in a crib*)

An ***essential modifier*** is one that is necessary to the meaning of a sentence. (Anybody *who lives in the area* should come to the meeting. No one *from the company* can enter the contest.)

A ***nonessential modifier*** is one that merely adds more information to a sentence that is clear without the addition. (The new student, *clutching his schedule,* looked for his next class.)

Noun A noun names a person, a place, a thing, or an idea. (*Joan, room, desk, loyalty*)

An ***abstract noun*** names an idea, a quality, or a feeling. (*hope*)

A ***collective noun*** names a group of things. (*band*)

A ***common noun*** is a general name of a person, a place, a thing, or an idea. (*clerk, hospital, kite, integrity*)

A ***compound noun*** contains two or more words. (*drive shaft, chalkboard, soldier-statesman*)

A ***noun of direct address*** is the name of a person being directly spoken to. (*Alice,* do you plan to visit the hospital? Come home, *Lou,* because we miss you.)

A ***possessive noun*** shows who or what owns something. (*Arturo's* car, *Ruth's* pet)

A ***predicate noun*** follows a linking verb and renames the subject. (Anita is my *friend.*)

A ***proper noun*** names a particular person, place, or thing. (*Joan Lunden, Columbia College, Ballet Russe*)

Number A word is **singular** in number if it refers to just one person, place, thing, idea, or action and **plural** in number if it refers to more than one person, place, thing, idea, or action. (The words *he, bird,* and *sings* are singular in number. The words *they, birds,* and *sing* are plural.)

Object of a preposition The object of a preposition is the noun or pronoun that follows a preposition. (John took his friend with *him.* They stopped along the *way.*)

Object of a verb The object of a verb receives the action of a verb. (My brother joined the *army.*)

Participle A participle is often used as part of a verb phrase. (had *started*) It can also be used as a verbal that functions as an adjective. (the *crumbling* walls, the flag *flying* outside the school)

The ***present participle*** is formed by adding *-ing* to the present tense of a verb. (*Stopping* for a rest, we noticed the fall colors.)

The ***past participle*** of a regular verb is formed by adding *-d* or *-ed* to the present tense. The past participle of irregular verbs does not follow this pattern. (The *tattered* book lay there. *Painted* emblems decorated the walls. A meal *eaten* with friends tastes delicious.)

Passive voice *See* **Voice.**

Past tense. *See* **Verb tense.**

Perfect tenses. *See* **Verb tense.**

Person The person of pronouns is a means of classifying them.

A ***first-person*** pronoun refers to the person speaking. (*I* stutter.)

A ***second-person*** pronoun refers to the person spoken to. (*You* forgot.)

A ***third-person*** pronoun refers to some other person(s) or thing(s) being spoken of. (*She* called.)

Personal pronoun. *See* **Pronoun.**

Phrase A phrase is a group of related words that does not contain a verb and its subject. (*before the storm, answering the telephone*)

An ***adjective phrase*** modifies a noun or a pronoun. (Few *of the fans* stayed until the end of the game.)

An ***adverb phrase*** modifies a verb, an adjective, or an adverb. (Susan sat *near the door.*)

An ***appositive phrase*** explains one or more words in a sentence. (The attorney, *a specialist in his field,* was often asked for advice.)

A ***gerund phrase*** consists of a gerund and its modifiers and complements. (*Swimming in the ocean* frightened her.)

An ***infinitive phrase*** consists of an infinitive, its modifiers, and its complements. (May liked *to attend musical theater.*)

A ***participial phrase*** consists of a participle and its modifiers and complements. (*Holding my pass,* I boarded the bus.)

A ***prepositional phrase*** consists of a preposition, its object, and the object's modifiers. (The first unit *in the parade* stopped *at the grandstand.*)

A ***verb phrase*** consists of a main verb and one or more auxiliary verbs. (*can be stopped*)

Possessive A noun or pronoun that is possessive shows ownership. (*Joan's* assignment, *its* tail)

Possessive noun. *See* **Noun.**

Possessive pronoun. *See* **Pronoun.**

Predicate The predicate of a sentence tells what the subject is or does. (The couple *hired a reliable babysitter*. Clare *feels tired today.*) *See* **Complete predicate.**

Predicate adjective. *See* **Adjective.**

Predicate nominative A predicate nominative is a noun or pronoun that follows a linking verb and renames or explains the subject. (Nancy is a *volunteer.* The skipper was *he.*)

Predicate pronoun. *See* **Pronoun.**

Preposition A preposition is a word that relates its object to another part of the sentence or to the sentence as a whole. (I received a gift *from* my aunt.)

Prepositional phrase. *See* **Phrase.**

Present tense. *See* **Verb tense.**

Progressive form. *See* **Verb.**

Pronoun A pronoun replaces a noun or another pronoun. (Alana said that *she* felt sick.) Some pronouns allow a writer to avoid repeating a noun. Other pronouns let a writer refer to an unknown or unidentified person or thing.

A ***demonstrative pronoun*** singles out one or more persons or things. (*That* is my favorite beverage.)

An ***indefinite pronoun*** refers to an unidentified person or thing. (*Anyone* might have entered the building. Is *everyone* aware of the problem?)

An ***intensive pronoun*** emphasizes a noun or pronoun. (The coach *himself* made the call.)

An ***interrogative pronoun*** asks a question. (*Who* has the answer?)

A ***personal pronoun*** refers to the first, second, or third person. (*I* came. *You* saw. *He* conquered.)

A ***possessive pronoun*** shows ownership. (*My* dog won a blue ribbon. How is *your* sister?)

A ***predicate pronoun*** follows a linking verb and renames the subject. (The best player is *he.*)

A ***reflexive pronoun*** reflects an action back on the subject of the sentence. (Gabby blamed *herself.*)

A ***relative pronoun*** relates a subordinate clause to the word it modifies. (The instructor *who* taught our class gave interesting lessons.)

Pronoun-antecedent agreement. *See* **Agreement.**

Pronoun forms

The ***subject form of a pronoun*** is used when the pronoun is the subject of a sentence or follows a linking verb as a predicate pronoun. (*He* helped Ed. The winner was *I*.)

The ***object form of a pronoun*** is used when the pronoun is the direct or indirect object of a verb or a verbal or the object of a preposition. (Vi read *her* a story. Ed will work with *them.* John mailed the letter after sealing *it*.)

Proper adjective. *See* **Adjective.**

Proper noun. *See* **Noun.**

Punctuation Punctuation clarifies the structure of sentences. See the punctuation chart below.

Quotation A quotation consists of words from another speaker or writer.

A ***direct quotation*** is the exact words of a speaker or writer. (Mark said, *"Too many students want to work on the yearbook."*)

A ***divided quotation*** is a quotation separated by words that identify the speaker. (*"Too many students,"* said Mark, *"want to work on the yearbook."*)

An ***indirect quotation*** repeats what a person said without using the exact words. (*Mark said that too many students want to work on the yearbook.*)

Reflexive pronoun. *See* **Pronoun.**

Regular verb. *See* **Verb.**

Relative pronoun. *See* **Pronoun.**

Run-on sentence A run-on sentence consists of two or more sentences written incorrectly as one. (*I was late for work the boss almost fired me.*)

Sentence A sentence expresses a complete thought. The chart at the top of the next page shows the four kinds of sentences.

A ***complex sentence*** contains one main clause and one or more subordinate clauses. (*The train started before I got off. If it rains, cancel the car wash.*)

A ***compound sentence*** is made up of two or more simple sentences combined with a comma and a conjunction or with a semicolon. (*The club held its meeting, but three members were absent.*)

A ***simple sentence*** consists of only one main clause. (*The whole team attended the meeting. Bill and Art were late.*)

Punctuation	Uses	Examples
Apostrophe (')	Shows possession Forms a contraction	Kim's homework students' essays He'll help. They're playing.
Colon (:)	Introduces a list or long quotation Divides some compound sentences	these authors: Twain, Stevenson, and Joyce We made a promise: we would meet every year.
Comma (,)	Separates ideas Separates modifiers Separates items in series	The alarm went off, and I jumped out of bed. We read the lively, funny stories. They bought fruit, vegetables, and yogurt.
Exclamation point (!)	Ends an exclamatory sentence	I knew you could do it!
Hyphen (-)	Joins words in some compound nouns	sergeant-at-arms, great-grandmother
Period (.)	Ends a declarative sentence Indicates most abbreviations	They spent the day at the museum. qt. vol. Ave. Jr. Sept.
Question mark (?)	Ends an interrogative sentence	Where is my hat?
Semicolon (;)	Divides some compound sentences Separates items in series that contain commas	Rose arrived early; she brought refreshments. The bag contained bread, fresh from the bakery; cheese, soft and spreadable; and a pound of butter.

Kind of Sentence	Example
Declarative (statement)	He shut the door.
Exclamatory (strong feeling)	She's hurt!
Imperative (request, command)	Open the door.
Interrogative (question)	Who's coming?

Sentence fragment A sentence fragment is a group of words that is only part of a sentence. (*After they left. Standing at attention.*)

Simple predicate The simple predicate is the verb in the predicate. (Sam *operates* the newsstand.)

Simple subject The simple subject is the key noun or pronoun in the subject. (Plastic *bottles* are recycled.)

Split infinitive A split infinitive occurs when a modifier is placed between the word *to* and the verb in an infinitive. (*to quickly respond*)

Subject The subject is the part of a sentence that tells whom or what the sentence is about. (*Nina* returned.) *See* **Complete subject; Simple subject.**

Subject-verb agreement. *See* **Agreement.**

Subordinate clause. *See* **Clause.**

Superlative. *See* **Adjective; Adverb.**

Transitive verb. *See* **Verb.**

Unidentified reference An unidentified reference can occur when the word *it, they, this, which,* or *that* is used. (In the novel *it* tells about a group of boys living together without adults.)

Verb A verb expresses an action, a condition, or a state of being.

An ***action verb*** tells what the subject does, has done, or will do. The action may be physical or mental. (Sergei *struggled.*)

An ***auxiliary verb*** is added to a main verb to express tense, add emphasis, or otherwise affect the meaning of the verb. Together the auxiliary and main verb make up a verb phrase. (*do* try, *has* closed, *will* enjoy)

A ***linking verb*** expresses a state of being or connects the subject with a word or words that describe the subject. (The ice *feels* cold.) Linking verbs include *appear, be* (*am, are, is, was, were, been, being*), *become, feel, grow, look, remain, seem, smell, sound,* and *taste.*

A ***main verb*** describes action or state of being; it may have one or more auxiliaries. (may be *seen*)

The ***progressive form*** of a verb shows continuing action. (Cats *were meowing.*)

The past tense and past participle of a ***regular verb*** are formed by adding *-d* or *-ed.* (*collect, collected*) An ***irregular verb*** does not follow this pattern. (*drink, drank, drunk; buy, bought, bought*)

The action of a ***transitive verb*** is directed toward someone or something, called the object of a verb. (Ralph *takes* lessons.) An ***intransitive verb*** has no object. (Guy *listened* to my advice.)

Verb phrase. *See* **Phrase.**

Verb tense Verb tense shows the time of an action or the time of a state of being.

The ***present tense*** places an action or condition in the present. (Stu *prefers* a quiet room.)

The ***past tense*** places an action or condition in the past. (We *left.*)

The ***future tense*** places an action or condition in the future. (They *will study.*)

A ***simple tense*** refers to any one of the present, past, or future tenses.

The ***present perfect tense*** describes actions in an indefinite past time or an action that began in the past and continues in the present. (*has taught, have tried*)

The ***past perfect tense*** describes one action that happened before another action in the past. (*had obtained*)

The ***future perfect tense*** describes an event that will be finished before another future action begins. (*will have noticed*)

Verbal A verbal is formed from a verb and acts as a noun, an adjective, or an adverb.

Verbal	Example
Gerund (used as a noun)	*Skating* well takes practice.
Infinitive (used as a noun, an adjective, or an adverb)	They offered *to find* me a job.
Participle (used as an adjective)	The letter, *begun* earlier, was finally finished.

Voice The voice of a verb depends on whether the subject performs or receives the action of the verb.

In the ***active voice*** the subject of the sentence performs the action. (Monica *ran* outside.)

In the ***passive voice*** the subject of the sentence receives the action of the verb. (The keys *were given* to the teachers.)

Index of Fine Art

Index of Skills

Literary Terms

Reading and Critical Thinking Skills

Grammar, Usage, and Mechanics

Writing Skills, Modes, and Formats

Vocabulary Skills

Research and Study Skills

Speaking, Listening, and Viewing

Index of Titles and Authors

Page numbers that appear in italics refer to biographical information.

Acknowledgments *(continued)*

Beacon Press: "Deer Woman," from *Grandmother of the Light* by Paula Gunn Allen; Copyright © 1991 by Paula Gunn Allen. Reprinted by permission of Beacon Press.

International Marine Publishing Company: Excerpt from *The Log of Christopher Columbus* by Robert Fuson; Copyright © 1987 by Robert H. Fuson, all rights reserved. Original English language edition published by International Marine Publishing Co., Camden, Maine, USA.

Simon J. Ortiz: "My Father's Song," from *Going for the Rain* by Simon J. Ortiz. Reprinted by permission of the author.

Simon & Schuster: Excerpts from *Adventures in the Unknown Interior of America* by Cabeza de Vaca, edited by Cyclone Covey; Copyright © 1961 by Macmillan Publishing Company. Reprinted with the permission of Simon & Schuster.

Alfred A. Knopf, Inc.: Excerpts from *Of Plymouth Plantation 1620–1647* by William Bradford, edited by Samuel Eliot Morison; Copyright 1952 by Samuel Eliot Morison, renewed 1980 by Emily M. Beck. By permission of Alfred A. Knopf, Inc.

American History/Cowles Magazine: "Women and Children First" by Alicia Crane Williams, from *American History,* November/December 1993. Reprinted courtesy of Cowles Magazines, publisher of *American History.*

Little, Brown and Company: Excerpt from *Blue Highways* by William Least Heat-Moon; Copyright © 1982 by William Least Heat-Moon. By permission of Little, Brown and Company.

Random House, Inc.: "My Sojourn in the Lands of My Ancestors," from *All God's Children Need Traveling Shoes* by Maya Angelou; Copyright © 1986 by Maya Angelou. Reprinted by permission of Random House, Inc.

Susan Ann Protter, Agent for Terry Bisson: "They're Made out of Meat" by Terry Bisson, originally published in *Omni Magazine*, April 1991; Copyright © 1991 by Terry Bisson. Reprinted by permission of the author's agent. All rights reserved.

Unit Two

Brandt & Brandt Literary Agents, Inc.: "We Aren't Superstitious" by Stephen Vincent Benét; Copyright 1937 by Esquire, Inc., Copyright renewed © 1965 by Thomas C. Benét, Rachel Benét Lewis, Stephanie B. Mahin. Reprinted by permission of Brandt & Brandt Literary Agents, Inc.

Dell Books: "Miss Temptation," from *Welcome to the Monkey House* by Kurt Vonnegut, Jr.; Copyright © 1961 by Kurt Vonnegut, Jr. By permission of Delacorte Press/Seymour Lawrence, a division of Bantam Doubleday Dell Publishing Group, Inc.

Random House, Inc.: Excerpt from "The Boston Tea Party," from *Dave Barry Slept Here* by Dave Barry; Copyright © 1989 by Dave Barry. Reprinted by permission of Random House, Inc.

University of Oklahoma Press: "Lecture to a Missionary" by Red Jacket, from *American Indian Literature: An Anthology*, revised edition, edited by Alan R. Velie; Copyright © 1979, 1991 by the University of Oklahoma Press.

Joan Daves Agency: Excerpt from *Stride Toward Freedom* by Martin Luther King, Jr.; Copyright © 1958 by Martin Luther King, Jr., renewed 1986 by Coretta Scott King. Reprinted by arrangement with The Heirs to the Estate of Martin Luther King, Jr.

Pathfinder Press: Excerpt from "Necessary to Protect Ourselves," from *Malcolm X: The Last Speeches*; Copyright © 1989 by Betty Shabazz, Bruce Perry, Pathfinder Press. Reprinted by permission of Pathfinder Press.

Rodolfo Gonzales: Excerpts in both Spanish and English from *I Am Joaquín* by Rodolfo Gonzales. By permission of the author.

Diane Mei Lin Mark: "Suzie Wong Doesn't Live Here" by Diane Mei Lin Mark. By permission of the author.

Unit Three

Augsburg Fortress Publishers: Excerpt from *Hippies in Our Midst* by D. L. Earisman; Copyright © 1968 by Fortress Press. Used by permission of Augsburg Fortress Publishers.

New Directions Publishing Company: "Danse Russe" from *Collected Poems 1909–1939 vol. 1* by William Carlos Williams; Copyright 1938 by New Directions Publishing Corp.

Liveright Publishing Corporation: "anyone lived in a pretty how town," from *Complete Poems, 1904–1962* by E. E. Cummings, edited by George J. Firmage; Copyright © 1940, 1968, 1991 by the Trustees for the E. E. Cummings Trust. By permission of Liveright Publishing Corp.

Curbstone Press: "Tía Chucha," from *The Concrete River* by Luis J. Rodriguez (Curbstone Press, 1991). Reprinted with permission of Curbstone Press. Distributed by Consortium.

Firebrand Books: "Ending Poem," from *Getting Home Alive* by Aurora Levins Morales and Rosario Morales; Copyright © 1986 by Aurora Levins Morales and Rosario Morales. By permission of Firebrand Books, Ithaca, N.Y.

Ellen Levine Literary Agency, Inc.: "Gary Keillor," from *The Book of Guys* by Garrison Keillor; Copyright © 1993 by Garrison Keillor. Reprinted by permission of Garrison Keillor.

Stephen King: Excerpt from *Danse Macabre* by Stephen King. Copyright © Stephen King. All rights reserved. Reprinted with permission.

Random House, Inc.: "A Rose for Emily," from *Collected Stories of William Faulkner* by William Faulkner; Copyright © 1930 and renewed 1958 by William Faulkner. Reprinted by permission of Random House, Inc.

Harcourt Brace & Company: "The Life You Save May Be Your Own," from *A Good Man Is Hard to Find* by Flannery O'Connor; Copyright 1953 by Flannery O'Connor, renewed © 1981 by Regina O'Connor. By permission of Harcourt Brace & Company.

Houghton Mifflin Company: "The Consolation of Nature," from *The Consolation of Nature and Other Stories* by Valerie Martin; Copyright © 1988 by Valerie Martin. Reprinted by permission of Houghton Mifflin Company. All rights reserved.

Unit Four

Samuel French, Inc.: *The Clod* by Lewis Beach. Copyright 1914 by Lewis Beach, Copyright 1921 by Brentano's, Copyright 1942 (in renewal) by Lewis Beach, Copyright 1949 (in renewal) by Robert H. Cook.

CAUTION: Professionals and amateurs are hereby warned that *The Clod* being fully protected under the Copyright laws of the United States of America, the British Commonwealth countries, including Canada, and the other countries of the Copyright Union, is subject to a royalty. All rights, including professional, amateur, motion picture, recitation, public reading, radio, television and cable broadcasting, and the rights of translation into foreign languages, are strictly reserved. Any inquiry regarding the availability of performance rights or the purchase of individual copies of the authorized acting edition, must be directed to Samuel French Inc., 45 West 25 Street, NY, NY 10010 with other locations in Hollywood and Toronto, Canada.

Doubleday: From *Coming of Age in Mississippi* by Anne Moody; Copyright © 1968 by Anne Moody. Used by permission of Doubleday, a division of Bantam Doubleday Dell Publishing Group, Inc.

Liveright Publishing Corporation: "Frederick Douglass," from *Angle of Ascent: New and Selected Poems* by Robert Hayden; Copyright © 1975, 1972, 1970, 1966 by Robert Hayden. By permission of Liveright Publishing Corporation.

Dudley Randall: "Ballad of Birmingham" by Dudley Randall. Reprinted by permission of the author.

Museum of New Mexico Press: "The Indian and the Hundred Cows," from *Cuentos: Tales from the Hispanic Southwest* by José Griego y Maestas and Rudolfo Anaya; Copyright © 1980 in English and Spanish. By permission of the Museum of New Mexico Press.

University of Nebraska Press: "High Horse's Courting," from *Black Elk Speaks* by Black Elk and John G. Neihardt; Copyright © 1932, 1959, 1972 by John G. Neihardt, Copyright © 1961 by the John G. Neihardt Trust. By permission of the University of Nebraska Press.

HarperCollins Publishers, Inc.: Chapter 11 from *The Autobiography of Mark Twain,* edited by Charles Neider; Copyright © 1917, 1940, 1958, 1959 by The Mark Twain Company, Copyright 1924, 1945, 1952 by Clara Clemens Samossoud, Copyright © 1959 by Charles Neider. Reprinted by permission of HarperCollins Publishers, Inc.

University of Texas Press: "The Legend of Gregorio Cortez," from *With His Pistol in His Hand: A Border Ballad and Its Hero* by Americo Paredes; Copyright © 1958, renewed 1986. Reprinted by permission of the author and the University of Texas Press.

W. W. Norton & Company, Inc.: "A Blizzard Under Blue Sky," from *Cowboys Are My Weakness* by Pam Houston; Copyright © 1992 by Pam Houston. By permission of W. W. Norton & Company, Inc.

Unit Five

The Feminist Press: Excerpt from *Complaints and Disorders: The Sexual Politics of Sickness* by Barbara Ehrenreich and Deirdre English. Published by The Feminist Press at the City University of New York. All rights reserved.

Kitchen Table Press: "Seventeen Syllables," from *Seventeen Syllables and Other Stories* by Hisaye Yamamoto; Copyright © 1988 by Hisaye Yamamoto and Kitchen Table: Women of Color Press. Used by permission of the author and of Kitchen Table: Women of Color Press, P.O. Box 908, Latham, NY 12110 on all reprinted materials.

Dell Books: "I Stand Here Ironing," from *Tell Me a Riddle* by Tillie Olsen; Copyright © 1956, 1957, 1960, 1961 by Tillie Olsen. Used by permission of Delacorte Press/Seymour Lawrence, a division of Bantam Doubleday Dell Publishing Group, Inc.

Susan Bergholz Literary Services: "Ironing Their Clothes," from *Homecoming* by Julia Alvarez; Copyright © 1986 by Julia Alvarez. Published by E. P. Dutton, a division of Penguin U.S.A. in 1995 and by Plume, an imprint of New American Library in 1996. Originally published by Grove Press in 1986.

Rita Dove: "Adolescence III," from *The Yellow House on the Corner* by Rita

Dove; Copyright © 1980 by Rita Dove. Reprinted by permission of the author.

Harcourt Brace & Company: "Chicago," from *Chicago Poems* by Carl Sandburg; Copyright 1916 by Holt, Rinehart and Winston, Inc., renewed 1944 by Carl Sandburg. Reprinted by permission of Harcourt Brace & Company.

Hilary Masters: "Lucinda Matlock," from *Spoon River Anthology* by Edgar Lee Masters, originally published by The Macmillan Company. By permission of Ellen C. Masters.

Scribner: "Winter Dreams," from *All the Sad Young Men* by F. Scott Fitzgerald; Copyright 1922 by Metropolitan Publications, Inc., Copyright renewed 1950 by Frances Scott Fitzgerald Lanahan. Reprinted with the permission of Scribner, an imprint of Simon & Schuster, Inc.

Persea Books: "America and I," from *The Open Cage* by Anzia Yezierska; Copyright © 1979 by Louise Levitas Henriksen. Reprinted by permission of Persea Books.

American Heritage: Excerpts from "A Nation of Immigrants" by Bernard A. Weisberger, from *American Heritage*, February/March 1994 issue; Copyright © 1994 by Forbes, Inc. Reprinted by permission of American Heritage Magazine, a division of Forbes, Inc.

Maxine Groffsky, Agent for Gish Jen: "In the American Society" by Gish Jen; Copyright © 1986 by Gish Jen. First published in *The Southern Review,* Summer 1986. Reprinted by permission of the author.

Northeastern University Press: "Defining the Grateful Gesture," from *Valentino's Hair* by Yvonne Sapia; Copyright © 1987 by Yvonne Sapia. Reprinted with permission of Northeastern University Press.

Lucy Honig: "English as a Second Language" by Lucy Honig, first published in *Witness,* vol. IV, no. 1, 1990; Copyright © Lucy Honig. Reprinted by permission of the author.

Unit Six

Farrar, Straus & Giroux, Inc.: Excerpt from "When the Negro Was in Vogue," from *The Big Sea* by Langston Hughes; Copyright © 1940 by Langston Hughes, Copyright renewed © 1968 by Arna Bontemps and George Houston Bass. Reprinted by permission of Hill and Wang, a division of Farrar, Straus & Giroux, Inc.

Alfred A. Knopf, Inc.: "I, Too" and "The Weary Blues," from *Selected Poems* by Langston Hughes; Copyright 1926 by Alfred A. Knopf, Inc., Copyright renewed 1945 by Langston Hughes. Reprinted by permission of Alfred A. Knopf, Inc.

Harcourt Brace & Company: "My City," from *The Book of American Negro Poetry* by James Weldon Johnson; Copyright 1931 by Harcourt Brace & Company, renewed 1959 by Grace Nail Johnson. Reprinted by permission of the publisher.

GRM Associates, Inc., Agents for the Estate of Ida M. Cullen: "Any Human to Another," from *The Medea and Some Poems* by Countee Cullen; Copyright 1935 by Harper & Brothers; Copyright renewed © 1963 by Ida M. Cullen.

The Archives of Claude McKay: "If We Must Die," from *Selected Poems of Claude McKay* by Claude McKay; Copyright © 1957 by Harcourt Brace. Used by permission of The Archives of Claude McKay, Carl Cowl, Administrator.

Harold Ober Associates, Inc.: "A Black Man Talks of Reaping," from *Personals* by Arna Bontemps; Copyright © 1963 by Arna Bontemps. By permission of Harold Ober Associates, Inc.

Estate of Zora Neale Hurston: "How It Feels to Be Colored Me" by Zora Neale Hurston, from *I Love Myself When I Am Laughing: A Zora Neale Hurston Reader,* edited by Alice Walker. By permission of the Estate of Zora Neale Hurston.

University of Illinois Press: Excerpts from "Zora Neale Hurston—A Cautionary Tale and a Partisan View" by Alice Walker, foreword to *Zora Neale Hurston: A Literary Biography* by Robert E. Hemenway. Copyright © 1977 by the Board of Trustees of the University of Illinois. Used with the permission of Alice Walker and the University of Illinois Press.

James Baldwin Estate: "My Dungeon Shook" was originally published in the *Progressive;* © 1962 by James Baldwin, Copyright renewed. Collected in *The Fire Next Time*, published by Vintage Books. Reprinted with the permission of the James Baldwin Estate.

Gwendolyn Brooks: "Primer for Blacks," from *Primer for Blacks* and "Life for My Child is Simple," from *Blacks* by Gwendolyn Brooks; Copyright © 1991. Publisher, Third World Press, Chicago. By permission of Gwendolyn Brooks.

Doubleday: "Thoughts on the African-American Novel" by Toni Morrison; Copyright © 1983 by Toni Morrison, from *Black Women Writers (1950–1980)* by Mari Evans. By permission of Doubleday, a division of Bantam Doubleday Dell Publishing Group, Inc.

Liveright Publishing Corporation: First four lines from "Karintha," from *Cane* by Jean Toomer; Copyright 1923 by Boni & Liveright, renewed © 1951 by Jean Toomer. By permission of Liveright Publishing Corporation.

Scribner: "The End of Something," from *In Our Time* by Ernest Hemingway; Copyright 1925 Charles Scribner's Sons, Copyright renewed 1953 by Ernest Hemingway. Reprinted with the permission of Scribner, an imprint of Simon & Schuster, Inc.

Viking Penguin: "Here We Are" by Dorothy Parker; Copyright 1931, renewed 1959 by Dorothy Parker, from *The Portable Dorothy Parker,* introduction by Brendan Gill. Used by permission of Viking Penguin, a division of Penguin Books USA, Inc.

Faber and Faber Limited: "The Love Song of J. Alfred Prufrock," from *Collected Poems 1909–1962* by T. S. Eliot. By permission of Faber and Faber Ltd. for Canadian rights. American rights are in public domain.

John Hawkins & Associates, Inc.: "The Man Who Was Almost a Man," from *Eight Men* by Richard Wright; Copyright © 1961 by Richard Wright. Reprinted by permission of John Hawkins & Associates, Inc.

HarperCollins Publishers, Inc.: *The Long Christmas Dinner*, from *The Long Christmas Dinner and Other Plays in One Act* by Thornton Wilder; Copyright 1931 by Yale University Press and Coward-McCann, Inc. Copyright © 1959 by Thornton Wilder. Reprinted by permission of HarperCollins Publishers, Inc.

Henry Holt and Company, Inc.: "Mending Wall," "Acquainted with the Night," and "Out, Out—," from *The Poetry of Robert Frost,* edited by Edward Connery Lathem; Copyright 1956 by Robert Frost, Copyright 1928, 1969 by Henry Holt and Co., Inc. Reprinted by permission of Henry Holt and Co., Inc.

HarperCollins Publishers, Inc., and Faber and Faber Limited: "Mirror," from *Crossing the Water* by Sylvia Plath; Copyright © 1963 by Ted Hughes. Originally appeared in *The New Yorker*. Reprinted by permission of HarperCollins Publishers, Inc., and Faber and Faber Ltd.

Houghton Mifflin Company: "Self in 1958," from *Live or Die* by Anne Sexton; Copyright © 1966 by Anne Sexton. Reprinted by permission of Houghton Mifflin Company. All rights reserved.

HarperCollins Publishers, Inc.: "Homework," from *One Way or Another* by Peter Cameron; Copyright © 1986 by Peter Cameron. Reprinted by permission of HarperCollins Publishers, Inc.

Unit Seven

Pantheon Books: Excerpts from *The Good War* by Studs Terkel; Copyright © 1984 by Studs Terkel. Reprinted by permission of Pantheon Books, a division of Random House, Inc.

Russell & Volkening, Inc.: "Armistice," from *The People and Uncollected Stories* by Bernard Malamud; Copyright © 1989 by Ann Malamud. Reprinted by the permission of Russell & Volkening as agents for the author.

Farrar, Straus & Giroux, Inc.: "The Death of the Ball Turret Gunner," from *The Complete Poems* by Randall Jarrell; Copyright © 1969 by Mrs. Randall Jarrell.

Viking Penguin: "Symptoms" ("Why Soldiers Don't Talk"), from *Once There Was a War* by John Steinbeck; Copyright 1943, 1958 by John Steinbeck. Renewed © 1971 by Elaine Steinbeck, John Steinbeck IV, and Thomas Steinbeck. Used by permission of Viking Penguin, a division of Penguin Books USA, Inc.

Farrar, Straus & Giroux, Inc.: Excerpt from "Letter from Paradise, 21°19′N., 157°52′W.," from *Slouching Towards Bethlehem* by Joan Didion; Copyright © 1966, 1968 by Joan Didion. Reprinted by permission of Farrar, Straus & Giroux, Inc.

Dwight Okita: "In Response to Executive Order 9066," from *Crossing with the Light* by Dwight Okita (Tía Chucha Press, Chicago); Copyright © 1992. Used by permission of the author.

Estela P. Trambley: "Village" by Estela Portillo; Copyright © 1989 by Estela Portillo. By permission of the author, Estela Portillo Trambley.

Bernard Edelman: "Letter to Red" by George Olsen, from *Dear America: Letters Home from Vietnam*, edited by Bernard Edelman for the New York Vietnam Veterans Memorial Commission.

University Press of New England: "Camouflaging the Chimera," from *Dien Cai Dau* by Yusef Komunyakaa; Copyright © 1988 by Yusef Komunyakaa, published by Wesleyan University Press. By permission of University Press of New England.

Leona P. Schecter Literary Agency: "Deciding," from *Shallow Graves* by Wendy Wilder Larsen and Tran Thi Nga. By permission of Leona P. Schecter Literary Agency.

Houghton Mifflin Company: "Ambush," from *The Things They Carried* by Tim O'Brien; Copyright © 1990 by Tim O'Brien. Reprinted by permission of Houghton Mifflin Co./Seymour Lawrence. All rights reserved.

Special Rider Music: One verse from "The Times They Are A-Changin'" by Bob Dylan, from *Bob Dylan Song Book;* © 1963, 1964 by Warner Brothers, © renewed 1991 by Special Rider Music.

International Creative Management: *Wandering* by Lanford Wilson; Copyright © 1967 by Lanford Wilson, Copyright renewed. Reprinted by permission of International Creative Management, Inc.

New Directions Publishing Corp.: "At the Justice Department, November 15, 1969," from *Poems 1968–1972* by Denise Levertov; Copyright © 1969 by Denise Levertov. Reprinted by permission of New Directions Publishing Corp.

William Morrow & Company, Inc.: "Revolutionary Dreams," from *The Women and the Men* by Nikki Giovanni; Copyright © 1970, 1974, 1975 by Nikki Giovanni. By permission of William Morrow & Company, Inc.

Henry Holt and Company, Inc.: "Sisterhood," from *Outrageous Acts and Everyday Rebellions* by Gloria Steinem; Copyright © 1983 by Gloria Steinem, Copyright © 1984 by East Toledo Productions, Inc. Reprinted by permission of Henry Holt and Co., Inc.

Ms. Magazine: Excerpts from "Mother's Choice" by Anna Quindlen, from *Ms.*

Magazine, February 1988; Copyright © 1988 by Anna Quindlen. Reprinted by permission of Ms. Magazine.

Russell & Volkening, Inc.: "Teenage Wasteland" by Anne Tyler, from *Seventeen Magazine*, November 1983; Copyright © 1983 by Anne Tyler. Reprinted by permission of Russell & Volkening as agents for the author.

Writers House: "El Patrón" by Nash Candelaria, from *Cuentos Chicanos,* edited by Rudolfo A. Anaya and Antonio Márquez; Copyright © 1984 by Nash Candelaria. By permission of Writers House as agent for Nash Candelaria.

Diane Burns: "Sure You Can Ask Me a Personal Question" by Diane Burns, from *Songs from This Earth on Turtle's Back,* edited by Joseph Bruchac. By permission of Diane Burns.

Unit Eight

Wing Tek Lum: "Chinese Hot Pot" by Wing Tek Lum, from *Chinese American Poetry,* edited by L. Ling-chi Wang and Henry Yiheng Zhao. By permission of Wing Tek Lum.

Washington Institute Press: Excerpt from "The Case for Official English," from *One Nation—Indivisible? The English Language Amendment* by S. I. Hayakawa; Copyright © 1985 by Washington Institute for Values in Public Policy. By permission of Washington Institute Press.

Carlos A. Montaner: "Why Fear Spanish?" by Carlos A. Montaner, from *Miami Herald*, April 25, 1988. By permission of the author.

Arte Publico Press: "Refugee Ship" by Lorna Dee Cervantes, from *A Decade of Hispanic Literature: An Anniversary Anthology* (Houston: Arte Publico Press—University of Houston, 1982). Reprinted by permission of Arte Publico Press.

Alfred A. Knopf, Inc.: "Separating," from *Problems and Other Stories* by John Updike; Copyright © 1975 by John Updike. Reprinted by permission of Alfred A. Knopf, Inc.

Alan Lau: "the promise" by Alan Lau, from *Chinese American Poetry,* edited by L. Ling-chi Wang and Henry Yiheng Zhao. By permission of Alan Lau, author of *Songs for Jandina* (Greenfield Review Press).

Audrey Lee: "Waiting for Her Train," by Audrey Lee; Copyright © 1971 by Audrey Lee. By permission of the author.

Grove/Atlantic, Inc.: "Science Fiction and the Future," from *Dancing at the Edge of the World* by Ursula K. Le Guin; Copyright © 1985 by Ursula K. Le Guin. Used by permission of Grove/Atlantic, Inc.

Don Congdon Associates, Inc.: "The Murderer" by Ray Bradbury, from *Argosy* magazine; copyright © 1953, renewed 1981 by Ray Bradbury. Reprinted by permission of Don Congdon Associates, Inc.

John Hawkins & Associates, Inc.: "Hostage," from *Heat, and Other Stories* by Joyce Carol Oates, published by Plume; Copyright © 1991 The Ontario Review, Inc. Reprinted by permission of John Hawkins & Associates, Inc.

Alfred A. Knopf, Inc.: "The Legend," from *The River of Heaven* by Garrett Hongo; Copyright © 1988 by Garrett Hongo. Reprinted by permission of Alfred A. Knopf, Inc.

Chronicle Books: "Mexicans Begin Jogging" by Gary Soto, from *Gary Soto: New & Selected Poems*; Copyright © 1995; published by Chronicle Books.

Arte Publico Press: "Legal Alien," from *Chants* by Pat Mora is reprinted with permission from the publisher, Arte Publico Press—University of Houston. Copyright © 1985 by Pat Mora.

Academy Chicago Publishers: Excerpts from *A Gathering of Heroes* by Gregory Alan-Williams. Reprinted by arrangement with Academy Chicago Publishers.

Art Credits

Author photographs and portraits

52 Photo by Lee H. Marmon. **67** *bottom* Photo by Marlene Foster-Ortiz. **87** *bottom,* **107** *bottom,* **242** *right* The Granger Collection, New York. **100, 222** *top* Culver Pictures. **116, 193** *bottom* AP/Wide World Photos. **126** UPI/Bettmann. **129** *bottom* Larry Laszlo, Comedia. **167, 215, 228** *bottom,* **242** *left,* **275** Stock Montage. **183** The Bettmann Archive. **222** *bottom* National Gallery of Art, Washington, D.C. **233** *bottom* Courtesy of the Bureau of American Ethnology, Smithsonian Institution, Washington, D.C. **290, 343** FPG International. **296** *bottom* The New-York Historical Society. **311** National Portrait Gallery, Smithsonian Institution, Washington, D.C./Art Resource, New York. **321** *bottom* Museum of The City of New York. **327** *bottom left,* **391** *bottom,* **555** National Archives. **327** *bottom right* By permission of the Houghton Library, Harvard University. **334** Copyright © 1986 Linda Haas. **368, 457, 463** *left* From the collections of the Library of Congress. **403** The Granger Collection, New York. **416, 653** AP/Wide World Photos. **476, 604** Culver Pictures. **501** *bottom* Copyright © Layle Silbert. **529** Smithsonian Institution, Washington, D.C. **574** *right* Arte Publico Press. **579** Photo by Steve Griffin. **622, 674** *left* Stock Montage. **627** Missouri Historical Society, St. Louis, MO. **641** Karen Huie. **655** Fred Viebahn. **674** *right* Illinois State Historical Library, Springfield, Ill. **679** *left* Moorland-Spingarn Research Center; *right* The Bettmann Archive. **702, 834** *bottom,* **865** National Archives. **732** *bottom* Photo by Jerry Bauer. **771** *bottom,* **776** *right* National Portrait Gallery, Smithsonian Institution, Washington, D.C./Art Resource, New York. **776** *left,* **781** *right* Fisk University. **781** *bottom left,* **790** Yale Collection of American Literature, Beinecke Rare Book and Manuscript Library, Estate of Carl van Vechten, Joseph Solomon, Executor. **798, 826, 844, 852** *bottom,* **881** *bottom* The Granger Collection, New York. **804** Howard Simmons. **807** Copyright © Layle Silbert. **888, 921, 928** *left,* **936** *left,* **978, 995, 1008** *right,* **1052, 1112** AP/Wide World Photos. **893** Copyright © Elena Seibert. **928** *right* Copyright © 1995 Elliott Erwitt/Magnum Photos. **948** *right* Achilles Studio. **955** *bottom left* Carolyn Wright. **959** Photo by Jerry Bauer. **983** *bottom* Copyright © Nancy Crampton. **1070** UPI/Bettmann. **1097** Jay Kay Klein. **1118** *right* Arte Publico Press. **1125** Everett Collection.

Commissioned Art and Photography

2 *top,* **4–5, 76–77, 118–120, 123, 136, 193, 194, 198, 199, 254, 256–257, 261, 355, 378, 381, 382, 384, 387, 388, 393, 428–429, 432–435, 440** *barbed wire,* **459, 475, 480, 485, 488, 494, 496, 504–505, 508–509, 513, 543** *inset,* **557, 572, 586–587, 656–658, 702** *top,* **748** *bottom,* **754, 761, 792–794, 804** *top,* **808, 810–813, 838–841, 864, 867, 870–871, 873, 874, 877, 879, 883, 885** *foreground,* **886, 894–895, 898, 907, 960–968, 1022–1029, 1035, 1076–1083, 1092, 1093, 1094** *background,* **1097** *top,* **1098, 1119** *background,* **1121, 1124, 1126–1133** Sharon Hoogstraten.

18 *bottom* John Sandford.

19 Rebecca McClellan.

68–74, 130–135, 137, 196–197, 255, 260, 344–348, 350 *top right, center right,* **351** *center right, bottom left,* **430, 431, 502–503, 506–507, 582–583, 660–661, 748** *top,* **749–752, 809, 896–897, 900** *bottom,* **901** Allan Landau.

278–281, 284, 287 Marlene Kay Goodman.

417 *top left,* **423, 426** Vincent McIndoe.

453 *inset,* **543, 544, 548** Judith DuFour Love.

492-493 Robert Tanenbaum.

Time Lines

16–17 *corn, Pocahontas, smallpox victims* The Granger Collection, New York; *cliff dwellings* Copyright © 1993 North Wind Pictures; *foot warmer* Copyright © Winterthur Museum; *compass* Copyright © Robert Frerck/Odyssey/Chicago.
142–143 *Sir Isaac Newton* (18th century), unknown artist. Trinity College, Cambridge, Great Britain/Art Resource, New York. Photo Copyright © Erich Lessing; *war* Copyright © 1993 North Wind Pictures; *statue* Copyright © Philip Jon Bailey; *teapot* (about 1799) by Paul Revere, silver, 7¼″, courtesy of the Museum of Fine Arts, Boston, gift of James Longley; *wig* The Bettmann Archive; *watch* (two images) Copyright © Christie's Images.
266–267 *compass* Smithsonian Institution, Washington, D.C.; *The Trail of Tears* (1942), Robert Lindneux. The Granger Collection, New York; *The Liberator, suffragette stamp* The Granger Collection, New York; *telegraph, cotton gin* Smithsonian Institution, Washington, D.C.; *Levi's jeans* Courtesy of The Bancroft Library; *clock* (two images), private collection, Art Resource, New York.
440–441 *book, poster, money* The Granger Collection, New York; *buffalo* Copyright © Paul Horsted; *locomotive* Copyright © Chuck Place Photography; *clock* (two images) Bridgeman/Art Resource, New York.
592–593 *statue, car, poster, washing machine* The Granger Collection, New York; *airplane* The Bettmann Archive; *watch* (two images), from *Pocket Watches* by Leonardo Leonardi and Gabriele Ribolini. Copyright © 1994, published by Chronicle Books.
760–761 *Nude Descending a Staircase, No. 2* (1912), Marcel Duchamp, oil on canvas, 58″ × 35″, Philadelphia Museum of Art, Louise and Walter Arensberg Collection (50-134-59); *Louis Armstrong, airplane, woman* The Bettmann Archive; *wristwatch* (two images), private collection.
906–907 *mushroom cloud, television* AP/Wide World Photos; *Betty Friedan* Copyright © 1971 Michael Ginsburg/Magnum Photos; *John F. Kennedy* Copyright © 1960 Bob Henriques/Magnum Photos; *Cesar Chavez* Copyright © AP/Wide World Photos; *Richard Nixon, Twiggy* Copyright © Archive Photos; *watch* (two images), private collection.
1034–1035 *Three Mile Island, Berlin Wall, Oklahoma City federal building* AP/Wide World Photos; *computer* Cameramann International, Ltd.; *wristwatch* (two images), private collection.

The editors have made every effort to trace the ownership of all copyrighted art and photography found in this book and to make full acknowledgment for their use. Omissions brought to our attention will be corrected in a subsequent edition.

Miscellaneous Art Credits

xii Van Bergen Overmantel (1732–1733), attributed to John Heaten. Oil on wood (fireboard), 15¼″ × 7′ 3½″, New York State Historical Association, Cooperstown, New York. Copyright © New York State Historical Association. **xv** *Il ridotto* [The foyer] (about 1757–1760), Pietro Longhi. Oil on canvas, 62.5 cm 51 cm, Fondazione Scientifica Querini Stampaglia, Venice, Italy, Erich Lessing/Art Resource, New York. **xxv** *Three Folk Musicians* (1967), Romare Bearden. Collage on canvas on board, 50″ × 60″. Courtesy of the Estate of Romare Bearden.

xxx–1 Copyright © Peter Poulides/Tony Stone Images. **2** *bottom left* Pottery by Lucy Leuppe McKelvey, Navajo. Courtesy, McGees Beyond Native Tradition Gallery, Holbrook, Arizona. Photo Copyright © 1988 Jerry Jacka. All rights reserved; *bottom right* Copyright © M. Northrup/Photonica. **3** *top* Copyright © 1994 Stephen Simpson/FPG International; *bottom left* Copyright © 1993 Ron Chapple/FPG International; *bottom right* Copyright © James Schwabel/Panoramic Images. **18** *top left* Photograph by John Oldenkamp and Cynthia Sabransky, from the David T. Vernon Collection, Colter Bay Indian Arts Museum at Grand Teton National Park, Wyoming. **20** *top* AP/Wide World Photos; *bottom* Copyright © 1993 Allen Russell/Profiles West. **22** The Granger Collection, New York. **26, 27** Detail of *Creation Legend*, Tom (Two Arrows) Dorsey. Philbrook Museum of Art, Tulsa, Oklahoma (46.24). **30** *bottom* Illustration by David Cunningham. **32** *inset* Copyright © School of American Research Press. Photo by Deborah Flynn. **37** Copyright © Daniel J. Cox/Liaison International. **55** *deer* Copyright © Kathi Lamm/Tony Stone Images; *woman* Copyright © Gary Nolton/Tony Stone Images. **74–75** Copyright © Syndey Byrd. **78** Newberry Library, Chicago. **80** *El Marquez Don Francisco Pisarro de Truxillo* (17th century), unknown artist. The Granger Collection, New York. **90** *foreground* Wood River Gallery, Mill Valley, California; *background* Copyright © D. Bowen/WestLight. **107** Head of a Benin king. Werner Forman Archive, courtesy of Entwistle Gallery, London/Art Resource, New York. **111–113** From *Blue Highways* by William Least Heat-Moon. Copyright © 1982 by William Least Heat-Moon. By permission of Little, Brown and Company. **127** Copyright © 1996 Dave Archer/The Image Bank, Chicago. **129** Copyright © 1996 Chris Alan Wilton/The Image Bank, Chicago. **130** *inset* Copyright © Matthew McVay/Tony Stone Images. **131** *inset* Muskogee *Daily Phoenix*. **132** *inset* Copyright © Jerry Jacka, courtesy *Native Peoples* magazine, Phoenix, Arizona. **133** *inset* Copyright © W. & D. McIntyre/Photo Researchers. **150, 161, 165** Copyright © David Fitzgerald/Tony Stone Images. **155** Culver Pictures. **168** Copyright © Archive Photos. **177** Detail of *Levant for E.W.R.* (1954), Theodoros Stamos. Oil on canvas, 80″ × 70″, Albright-Knox Art Gallery, Buffalo, New York, gift of Seymour H. Knox, 1958. **184** Detail of *Summertime* (1943), Edward Hopper. Oil on canvas, $29\frac{1}{8}$″ × 44″, Delaware Art Museum, Gift of Dora Sexton Brown, 1962 (62-68). **189** Detail of *Portrait of Orleans* (1950), Edward Hopper. The Fine Arts Museums of San Francisco, fractional gift of Jerrold and June Kingsley, (1991.32). **196** Reprinted with permission from *Variety*®. **200–201** Copyright © 1963 Bob Adelman/Magnum Photos, Inc. **202** *bottom left, Portrait of Thomas Jefferson* (1805), Gilbert Stuart. Gift of the Regents of the Smithsonian Institution, the Thomas Jefferson Memorial Foundation, and the Enid and Crosby Kemper Foundation. National Portrait Gallery, Smithsonian Institution, Washington, D.C./Art Resource, New York. Used by permission of Art Resource, New York, and the Thomas Jefferson Memorial Foundation. **203** *top, Abigail Adams* (1829), Jarvis F. Hanks. Courtesy, Charles Ames, Esq.; *bottom* The Granger Collection, New York. **206, 218, 220, 221** The Granger Collection, New York. **261** *inset* Copyright © Ron Chapple/FPG International. **272** Archive Photos. **273** Copyright © D. Bowen/WestLight. **298** *inset* Copyright © John Shaw. **302** Copyright © Art Wolfe/Tony Stone Images. **303** Copyright © Jake Wyman/Photonica. **307** Copyright © John Shaw. **310** AP/Wide World Photos. **313** Detail of *Cliff Dwellers* (1913), George Bellows. Oil on canvas. $40\frac{3}{16}$″ × $42\frac{1}{6}$″, Los Angeles County Museum of Art, Los Angeles County Fund. Copyright © 1995 Museum Associates, Los Angeles County Museum of Art, all rights reserved. **317** *baby* Copyright © 1995 Brian McWeeney/Photonica; *grass*

Copyright © James Berkly/Tony Stone. **321** *top* Copyright © Tomek Sikora/The Image Bank. **350** *U.S. flag* Photo Copyright © Ed Pritchard/Tony Stone Images; *arrows* Copyright © Philip and Karen Smith/Tony Stone Images; *red cross* Courtesy American Red Cross; *Olympic flag* Photo Copyright © Mark Green/Tony Stone Images. **351** *stop sign* Copyright © Ken Biggs/Tony Stone Images; *dove* Copyright © Sue Streeter/Tony Stone Images; *Statue of Liberty* Copyright © Rohan/Tony Stone Images; *skull* Copyright © David Woodfall/Tony Stone Images; *fist* Copyright © Stuart McClymont/Tony Stone Images. **352** Copyright © Van Phillips/Leo de Wys Inc. **353** Copyright © Penny Tweedie/Tony Stone Images. **364–365** Copyright © 1986 Alberto Baudo/The Stock Market. **375** The Granger Collection, New York. **377** Detail of *La danse à la campagne* [The country dance] (1883), Pierre Auguste Renoir. Private collection. **391** Copyright © 1988 George Obremski/The Image Bank. **392** *left* Courtesy of Yoknapatawpha Press, Oxford, Mississippi; *right* Copyright © 1989 G. Beechler/The Image Bank. **417** *right* Detail of *Putting up Her Hair* (1983), Malcolm T. Liepke, Courtesy of Eleanor Ettinger Gallery, New York. **428** *inset* Courtesy Stephanie Vogt. **429** *top right* Courtesy Sue Baugh; *center* illustration by Beata Szpura. **430** *top* Courtesy Kristin Perantoni; *bottom* Courtesy Hayun Cho. **442** *bottom, Battle of Franklin, Tennessee, 30 November 1864* (1891), Kurz and Allison. Lithograph, The Granger Collection, New York. **443** *bottom* Courtesy of the U.S. Postal Service. **444** *left* Courtesy of the U.S. Postal Service; *center* Courtesy of Chicago Historical Society. **445** *left,* **455, 459** *right* The Granger Collection, New York. **447** The Bettmann Archive. **454** National Archives of Canada (C-28186). **456** Detail of *Head of a Negro* (1777–1778), John Singleton Copley. Paint on canvas, 53.3 cm × 41.3 cm, The Detroit Institute of Arts, Founders Society Purchase, Gibbs-Williams Fund. **460–461** Collection of The New-York Historical Society. **474** *man* Chicago Historical Society; *woman* Meserve Collection, Library of Congress. **477** Meserve Collection, Library of Congress. **479** Smithsonian Institution, Washington, D.C. **486** Used with special permission from Berea College and the Doris Ulmann Foundation. **489** *Cavalry Soldier* (1863), Winslow Homer. Black chalk on brown paper, 14¼″ × 7 15/16″, Cooper-Hewitt, National Design Museum, gift of Charles Savage Homer, Smithsonian Institution/Art Resource, New York. Photo by Ken Pelka. **508** *center, Mighty Marvel Western #19* and all titles and characters included thereupon: ™ and © 1996 Marvel Characters, Inc. Used with permission. **510** *center* Collection of The New-York Historical Society. **511** *top* Library of Congress; *bottom* South Dakota State Historical Society. **518** Detail of *Castle Mission*, John Runne. Copyright © John Runne, Evergreen Art Company, Evergreen, Colorado. **541** The Granger Collection, New York. **577–579** Copyright © Sherman Hine/Masterfile. **592, 594** *below*, **595** The Granger Collection, New York. **580** *top* Copyright © W. Cody/WestLight. **581** *left* Reuters/Bettmann; *right* James Woodcock/*Billings Gazette*. **587** *inset* Copyright © David Young-Wolff/Tony Stone Images. **596** *left* Courtesy of Chicago Historical Society; *right* The Granger Collection, New York. **605** The Bettmann Archive. **619** Culver Pictures. **623** *right* H. Armstrong Roberts. **660–661** *top* Detail of "Returning Sails at Gyotoku" from the series *Eight Views of the Edo Suburbs* (about 1837–1838, Edo period), Ichiryusai Hiroshige, Japanese, 1796–1858. Woodblock print, 23.5 × 36 cm. The Art Institute of Chicago, Clarence Buckingham Collection (1943.708). Photo Copyright © 1993 The Art Institute of Chicago, all rights reserved. **662–663** Photo by Dorothea Lange, courtesy of the Library of Congress. **664** *family,* **664–665** *statue* The Granger Collection, New York. **665** *top* The Bettmann Archive. **666** The Granger Collection, New York. **704** Photo by Lewis W. Hine. Courtesy of George Eastman House, Rochester, New York. **708** The Granger Collection, New York. **732**

Copyright © N. McFarland/Superstock. **748** Courtesy of The Estate of Keith Haring. **749** *left* Photo by Lois Greenfield, courtesy Hubbard Street Dance Chicago; *right, West Side Story* Copyright © 1961 United Artists Pictures, Inc. All rights reserved. Movie poster courtesy of MGM/UA. **750** *left* From *The Kingfisher Children's Encyclopedia*, Copyright © 1992 Grisewood & Dempsey Ltd. Reprinted with the permission of Larousse Kingfisher Chambers Inc., New York; *right* Photograph of performance artist John Kelly by Paula Court. **754** *inset* Copyright © Bernd Fuchs/Westlight. **762** *bottom left* UPI/Bettmann; *top right* Copyright © 1969 James Vander Zee. All rights reserved. **762–763** *bottom* UPI/Bettmann. **764** AP/Wide World Photos. **766** Culver Pictures. **787** *Mules and Men* by Zora Neale Hurston. Copyright © 1935 Zora Neale Hurston. Cover design by Suzanne Noli. Cover illustration copyright © David Diaz. Reproduced by permission of HarperCollins. All rights reserved. **800** Copyright © 1992 Ron Rovtar/FPG International. **805** *left* Cover of *Beloved* by Toni Morrison, Copyright © 1988 by New American Library, used with permission of Dutton Signet, a division of Penguin Books U.S.A.; *top right* Cover of *Song of Solomon* by Toni Morrison, Copyright © 1978 by New American Library, used with permission of Dutton Signet, a division of Penguin Books U.S.A.; *bottom right* Cover of *The Bluest Eye* by Toni Morrison, Copyright © 1989 Plume, used with permission of Dutton Signet, a division of Penguin Books U.S.A. Cover illustration by Thomas Blackshear. **808** *inset,* **810** *inset* Michael Ochs Archives/Venice, California. **814** *top right* Courtesy Kristin Perantoni; *center left, center, center right* Archive Photos/Lambert Studios; *bottom left* Superstock; *bottom center* Copyright © 1995 Gary Buss/FPG International; *bottom right* Courtesy Martin Farrell. **815** *top left* Courtesy Janette McKenna; *top right* Archive Photos; *center left* Courtesy Mike Rawnsley; *center right* Archive Photos/Lambert Studios; *bottom left* Superstock; *bottom right* Copyright © 1995 David Sacks/FPG International. **816** *bottom,* **816–817** *background* Copyright © Imperial War Museum. **817** *bottom right* The Bettmann Archive. **818** *left* National Archives. **822** Copyright © 1993 Thayer Syme/FPG International, New York. **827** *top* Copyright © Skjold/PhotoEdit; *bottom* Copyright © 1994 Anthony Beaverson/Lifestock. **832** Copyright © D. J. McKay. **834** *top* Copyright © Mary Kate Denny/PhotoEdit. **852** *top* The Granger Collection, New York. **854–855** Courtesy of *Life* Magazine. Copyright © Margaret Bourke-White Estate. **856** Courtesy of Sears, Roebuck and Co. **866** Copyright © 1989 Gabe Palmer/Mugshots/The Stock Market. **882** Copyright © 1991 Photoworld/FPG International. **885** *background* Copyright © 1995 FPG International. **895** *shells* From the collection of Lee and Jan Kremer; *cat* Courtesy of Anna Pietraszek; *car* Copyright © Ray F. Hillstrom. **896** Copyright © AAA. Reproduced by permission. **898** *foreground* Shell from the collection of Lee and Jan Kremer; *background* Copyright © 1994 Bill Losh/FPG International. **900** *inset* Copyright © 1994 Dennis Frates. **908** *bottom center* National Archives. **909** *top* Copyright © 1944 Robert Capa/Magnum Photos. **910** Copyright © Donald J. Weber. **920** *top* UPI/Bettmann; *bottom* Photo by George Skrigin. **925** Copyright © 1968 Donald McCullin/Magnum Photos. **933** *left* Evacuation day, May 8, 1942, Dorothea Lange. War Relocation Authority; *top right* AP/Wide World Photos; *bottom right* UPI/Bettmann Newsphotos. **934** *top left* UPI/Bettmann; *top right* Pledge of Allegiance at Rafael Weill Elementary School a few weeks prior to evacuation, 1942. Dorothea Lange, War Relocation Authority; *center right* One of the many boundary signs posted around the Tule Lake Center, 1943. Charles Mace, War Relocation Authority; *bottom* Manzanar Relocation Center, 1942. Dorothea Lange, War Relocation Authority. **948** Detail of *Marble Mountain Patrol* (1966), Sherman

Loudermilk. Watercolor, courtesy of U.S. Marine Corps Museum Art Collection. **955** *top left* UPI/Bettmann. **958** *Caucasian man* Copyright © Howard Grey/Tony Stone Images; *Vietnamese man* Copyright © 1969 Marc Riboud/Magnum Photos Inc.; *rainforest* Copyright © Art Wolfe/Tony Stone Images. **966** *bottom* Courtesy Nancy Drew Inc., Niles, Michigan. **967** *top* Copyright © 1994 James Yochum. **968** AP/Wide World Photos. **969** Photo by John Paul Filo for *Life* Magazine. Copyright © Time, Inc. **970** *top* Courtesy *The Cleveland Plain Dealer; bottom* AP/Wide World Photos. **971, 991** Photo by John Olson for *Life* Magazine. Copyright © Time Inc. **979** Photo by Bernie Boston. **1008** *left* Copyright © Kevin Horan/Tony Stone Images. **1022** Photo by Clem Albers, courtesy National Archives. **1024** *Manzanar* Copyright © 1988 by John Armor and Peter Wright. Reprinted with permission of Times Books, a division of Random House, Inc. Cover photograph by Ansel Adams, courtesy the Library of Congress. **1033** *top* Detail of *Untitled* (1985), Keith Haring. Courtesy of the Estate of Keith Haring. **1037** Copyright © Martin Chaffer/Tony Stone Images. **1038** Copyright © 1996 Carl Fischer Photography, Inc. All rights reserved. **1040** Copyright © Bruce Ayres/Tony Stone Images. **1060** AP/Wide World Photos. **1076** *See It and Say It in Spanish* Copyright © 1961 by Margarita Madrigal. Reprinted by permission of Regents Publishing Co., a division of Simon & Schuster Inc.; *inset* Copyright © Peter Pearson/Tony Stone Images. **1080** Reprinted with permission of *The Miami Herald*; **1082** *insets* Copyright © David Young-Wolff/Tony Stone Images. **1084** Illustration by J. W. Stewart. **1086** Copyright © Robert E. Daemmrich/Tony Stone Images. **1097** *bottom* Illustration by Jules Verne. Culver Pictures. **1108–1109, 1109** Photo by Amy Ahlstrom. **1127** American Photo Library, Tokyo, Japan. **1128** *top, center insets* Copyright © Mark Farina/Stock Illustration Source; *bottom inset* Copyright © Wayne Geehan/Stock Illustration Source. **1176** The Bettmann Archive. **1178** Copyright © Ron Thomas/FPG International. **1184** Copyright © Robert E. Daemmrich/Tony Stone Images. **1186** Photofest. **1190** Netscape, Netscape Navigator, and the Netscape Communications Corporation Logo are trademarks of Netscape Communications Corporation; *insets* Courtesy Library of Congress. **1193–1195** Screen shots reprinted with permission from Microsoft Corporation. **1196** Used with express permission. Adobe and Adobe Illustrator are trademarks of Adobe Systems Incorporated. **1197** Photo by Bill Wiegand.

Teacher Review Panels *(continued)*

Eileen Jones, English Department Chairperson, Spanish River High School, Palm Beach County School District

Jan McClure, Winter Park High School Orange County School District

Wanza Murray, English Department Chairperson (retired), Vero Beach Senior High School, Indian River City School District

Shirley Nichols, Language Arts Curriculum Specialist Supervisor, Marion County School District

Debbie Nostro, Ocoee Middle School, Orange County School District

Barbara Quinaz, Assistant Principal, Horace Mann Middle School, Dade County School District

OHIO

Joseph Bako, English Department Chairperson, Carl Shuler Middle School,

Cleveland City School District

Deb Delisle, Language Arts Department Chairperson, Ballard Brady Middle School, Orange School District

Ellen Geisler, English/Language Arts Department Chairperson, Mentor Senior High School, Mentor School District

Dr. Mary Gove, English Department Chairperson, Shaw High School, East Cleveland School District

Loraine Hammack, Executive Teacher of the English Department, Beachwood High School, Beachwood City School District

Sue Nelson, Shaw High School, East Cleveland School District

Mary Jane Reed, English Department Chairperson, Solon High School, Solon City School District

Nancy Strauch, English Department Chairperson, Nordonia High School, Nordonia Hills City School Dictrict

Ruth Vukovich, Hubbard High School, Hubbard Exempted Village School District

TEXAS

Anita Arnold, English Department Chairperson, Thomas Jefferson High School, San Antonio Independent School District

Gilbert Barraza, J.M. Hanks High School, Ysleta School District

Sandi Capps, Dwight D. Eisenhower High School, Alding Independent School District

Judy Chapman, English Department Chairperson, Lawrence D. Bell High School, Hurst-Euless-Bedford School District

Pat Fox, Grapevine High School, Grapevine-Colley School District

LaVerne Johnson, McAllen Memorial High School, McAllen Independent School District

Donna Matsumura, W.H. Adamson High School, Dallas Independent School District

Ruby Mayes, Waltrip High School, Houston Independent School District

Mary McFarland, Amarillo High School, Amarillo Independent School District

Adrienne Thrasher, A.N. McCallum High School, Austin Independent School District

CALIFORNIA

Steve Bass, 8th Grade Team Leader, Meadowbrook Middle School, Ponway Unified School District

Cynthia Brickey, 8th Grade Academic Block Teacher, Kastner Intermediate School, Clovis Unified School District

Karen Buxton, English Department Chairperson, Winston Churchill Middle School, San Juan School District

Bonnie Garrett, Davis Middle School, Compton School District

Sally Jackson, Madrona Middle School, Torrance Unified School District

Sharon Kerson, Los Angeles Center for Enriched Studies, Los Angeles Unified School District

Gail Kidd, Center Middle School, Azusa School District

Corey Lay, ESL Department Chairperson, Chester Nimitz Middle School, Los Angeles Unified School District

Myra LeBendig, Forshay Learning Center, Los Angeles Unified School District

Dan Manske, Elmhurst Middle School, Oakland Unified School District

Joe Olague, Language Arts Department Chairperson, Alder Middle School, Fontana School District

Pat Salo, 6th Grade Village Leader, Hidden Valley Middle School, Escondido Elementary School District

Manuscript Reviewers *(continued)*

Beverly Ann Barge, Wasilla High School, Wasilla, Alaska

Sharon Batson, Westbury High School, Houston, Texas

Louann Bohman, Wilbur Cross High School, New Haven, Connecticut

Rose Mary Bolden, J. F. Kimball High School, Dallas, Texas

Angela Boyd, Andrews High School, Andrews, Texas

Judith H. Briant, Armwood High School, Seffner, Florida

Hugh Delle Broadway, McCullough High School, The Woodlands, Texas

Stephan P. Clarke, Spencerport High School, Spencerport, New York

Dr. Shawn Eric DeNight, Miami Edison Senior High School, Miami, Florida

JoAnna R. Exacoustas, La Serna High School, Whittier, California

Linda Ferguson, English Department Head, Tyee High School, Seattle, Washington

Ellen Geisler, Mentor Senior High School, Mentor, Ohio

Ricardo Godoy, English Department Chairman, Moody High School, Corpus Christi, Texas

Robert Henderson, West Muskingum High School, Zanesville, Ohio

Martha Watt Hosenfeld, English Department Chairperson, Churchville-Chili High School, Churchville, New York

Janice M. Johnson, Assistant Principal, Union High School, Grand Rapids, Michigan

Eileen S. Jones, English Department Chair, Spanish River Community High School, Boca Raton, Florida

Paula S. L'Homme, West Orange High School, Winter Garden, Florida

Bonnie J. Mansell, Downey Adult School, Downey, California

Ruth McClain, Paint Valley High School, Bainbridge, Ohio

Rebecca Miller, Taft High School, San Antonio, Texas

Deborah Lynn Moeller, Western High School, Fort Lauderdale High School

Bobbi Darrell Montgomery, Batavia High School, Batavia, Ohio

Wanza Murray, Vero Beach High School, Vero Beach, Florida

Marjorie M. Nolan, Language Arts Department Head, William M. Raines Sr. High School, Jacksonville, Florida

Julia Pferdehirt, free-lance writer, former Special Education teacher, Middleton, Wisconsin

Pauline Sahakian, English Department Chairperson, San Marcos High School, San Marcos, Texas

Jacqueline Y. Schmidt, Department Chairperson and Coordinator of English, San Marcos High School, San Marcos, Texas

John Sferro, Butler High School, Vandalia, Ohio

Faye S. Spangler, Versailles High School, Versailles, Ohio

Milinda Schwab, Judson High School, Converse, Texas

Rita Stecich, Evergreen Park Community High School, Evergreen Park, Illinois

GayleAnn Turnage, Abeline High School, Abeline, Texas

Ruth Vukovich, Hubbard High School, Hubbard, Ohio

Charlotte Washington, Westwood Middle School, Grand Rapids, Michigan

Tom Watson, Westbridge Academy, Grand Rapids, Michigan